— THIRD CANADIAN EDITION —

MARKETING

THIRD CANADIAN EDITION

MARKETING

DHRUV GREWAL, Ph.D.
Babson College

MICHAEL LEVY, Ph.D.
Babson College

SHIRLEY LICHTI, B.A., M.A.
Wilfrid Laurier University

AJAX PERSAUD, Ph.D.
University of Ottawa

McGraw-Hill
Ryerson

MARKETING
THIRD CANADIAN EDITION

The Internet addresses listed in the text were accurate at the time of publication. The inclusion of a Web site does not indicate an endorsement by the authors or McGraw-Hill Ryerson, and McGraw-Hill Ryerson does not guarantee the accuracy of the information presented at these sites.

ISBN-13: 978-1-25-903065-9
ISBN-10: 1-25-903065-2

3 4 5 6 7 8 9 10 WEB 1 9 8 7 6 5

Printed and bound in Canada.

Care has been taken to trace ownership of copyright material contained in this text; however, the publisher will welcome any information that enables them to rectify any reference or credit for subsequent editions.

Director of Product Management: *Rhondda McNabb*
Senior Product Manager: *Karen Fozard*
Executive Marketing Manager: *Joy Armitage Taylor*
Product Developer: *Amy Rydzanicz*
Senior Product Team Associate: *Marina Seguin*
Supervising Editor: *Jessica Barnoski*
Photo/Permissions Editor: *Tracy Leonard*
Copy Editor: *Karen Rolfe*
Plant Production Coordinator: *Sheryl MacAdam*
Manufacturing Production Coordinator: *Lena Keating*
Cover Design: *ArtPlus Limited*
Cover Image: *Leigh Prather/Alamy*
Interior Design: *ArtPlus Limited*
Page Layout: *ArtPlus Limited*
Printer: *Webcom*

Library and Archives Canada Cataloguing in Publication

Grewal, Dhruv, author
    Marketing / Dhruv Grewal (Babson College), Michael Levy (Babson College), Shirley Lichti (Wilfrid Laurier University), Ajax Persaud (University of Ottawa). —Third Canadian edition.

Revision of: Marketing / Dhruv Grewal ... [et al.].—2nd Canadian ed. —Toronto : McGraw-Hill Ryerson, ©2012. Includes bibliographical references and index. ISBN 978-1-25-903065-9 (bound)

    1. Marketing—Textbooks. I. Levy, Michael, 1950-, author II. Lichti, Shirley, author III. Persaud, Ajax, 1959-, author IV. Title.

HF5415.G75 2015   658.8   C2014-906462-4

dedication

To our families for their never-ending support.

To my wife Diana and my children, Lauren and Alex.
—Dhruv Grewal

To my wife Marcia and daughter Eva.
—Michael Levy

In memory of my marketing mentor, Dr. Gordon McDougall.
With thanks to my ever so patient husband, John, and my son, Stephen.
—Shirley Lichti

Authors Michael Levy (left) and Dhruv Grewal (right).

Dhruv Grewal, Ph.D. (Virginia Tech), is the Toyota Chair in Commerce and Electronic Business and a Professor of Marketing at Babson College. He was awarded the 2010 AMS Cutco/Vector Distinguished Educator Award, the 2010 Lifetime Achievement Award in Retailing (AMA Retailing SIG), and in 2005 the Lifetime Achievement in Behavioral Pricing Award (Fordham University, November 2005). He is a Distinguished Fellow of the Academy of Marketing Science. He was ranked first in the marketing field in terms of publications in the top-six marketing journals during the 1991–1998 period and again for the 2000–2007 period. He has served as VP Research and Conferences, American Marketing Association Academic Council (1999–2001), and as VP Development for the Academy of Marketing Science (2000–2002). He was co-editor of *Journal of Retailing* from 2001 to 2007. He co-chaired the 1993 Academy of Marketing Science Conference, the 1998 Winter American Marketing Association Conference, the 2001 American Marketing Association Doctoral Consortium, and the American Marketing Association 2006 Summer Educators Conference.

He has published more than 95 articles in journals such as the *Journal of Retailing, Journal of Marketing, Journal of Consumer Research, Journal of Marketing Research,* and *Journal of the Academy of Marketing Science,* as well as other journals. He currently serves on numerous editorial review boards, such as the *Journal of Retailing, Journal of Marketing, Journal of the Academy of Marketing Science, Journal of Interactive Marketing, Journal of Business Research,* and *Journal of Public Policy & Marketing.*

He has won a number of awards for his teaching: 2005 Sherwin-Williams Distinguished Teaching Award, Society for Marketing Advances, 2003 American Marketing Association, Award for Innovative Excellence in Marketing Education, 1999 Academy of Marketing Science Great Teachers in Marketing Award, Executive MBA Teaching Excellence Award (1998), School of Business Teaching Excellence Awards (1993, 1999), and Virginia Tech Certificate of Recognition for Outstanding Teaching (1989).

He has taught executive seminars/courses and/or worked on research projects with numerous firms, such as IRI, TJX, RadioShack, Telcordia, Khimetriks, Profit-Logic, Monsanto, McKinsey, Ericsson, Council of Insurance Agents & Brokers (CIAB), Met-Life, AT&T, Motorola, Nextel, FP&L, Lucent, Sabre, Goodyear Tire & Rubber Company, Sherwin Williams, Esso International, Asahi, and numerous law firms. He has taught seminars in the United States, Europe, and Asia.

Michael Levy, Ph.D. (Ohio State University), is the Charles Clarke Reynolds Professor of Marketing and Director of the Retail Supply Chain Institute at Babson College. He received his Ph.D. in business administration from The Ohio State University and his undergraduate and M.S. degrees in business administration from the University of Colorado at Boulder. He taught at Southern Methodist University before joining the faculty as professor and chair of the marketing department at the University of Miami.

Professor Levy received the 2009 Lifetime Achievement Award from the American Marketing Association Retailing Special Interest Group. He was rated one of the Best Researchers in Marketing in a survey published in *Marketing Educator* in Summer 1997. He has developed a strong stream of research in retailing, business logistics, financial retailing strategy, pricing, and sales management. He has published more than 50 articles in leading marketing and logistics journals, including the *Journal of Retailing, Journal of Marketing, Journal of the Academy of Marketing Science,* and *Journal of Marketing Research.* He currently serves on the editorial review board of the *Journal of Retailing, International Journal of Logistics Management, International Journal of Logistics and Materials Management,* and *European Business Review.* He is co-author of *Retailing Management,* eighth edition (2012), the bestselling college-level retailing text in the world. Professor Levy was co-editor of the *Journal of Retailing* from 2001 to 2007. He co-chaired the 1993 Academy of Marketing Science conference and the 2006 Summer American Marketing Association conference.

Professor Levy has worked in retailing and related disciplines throughout his professional life. Prior to his academic career, he worked for several retailers and a housewares distributor in Colorado. He has performed research projects with many retailers and retail technology firms, including Accenture, Federated Department Stores, Khimetrics (SAP), Mervyn's, Neiman Marcus, ProfitLogic (Oracle), Zale Corporation, and numerous law firms.

Shirley Lichti, B.A., M.A., has taught in the School of Business and Economics (SBE) at Wilfrid Laurier University since 1993 as a part-time and full-time instructor. She has taught a range of undergraduate and graduate courses, including Introductory Marketing; Building and Managing Products, Services, and Brands; Integrated Marketing Communications; and Consumer Behaviour. Shirley has an extensive background in marketing, advertising, promotion, and training, which was developed during a 14-year career with IBM. She has worked in Canada, the Caribbean, and Japan.

A dedicated educator, Shirley was recognized with the 2002 SBE Outstanding Teacher Award. She was honoured to be included as one of Laurier's "Most Popular Professors" in the *MacLean's Guide to Canadian Universities* in 2003, 2004, 2005, and 2006. In 2007, Shirley was recognized by the Ontario Ministry of Training, Colleges and Universities with The LIFT Award for Teaching Excellence.

She also runs Marketing Magic, a Waterloo-based marketing communication consulting and training company. She has been a featured keynote speaker at conferences and has developed and delivered marketing seminars and workshops for many organizations. Her clients include small companies, ranging from the Stratford Festival to Fortune 500 companies such as Manulife Financial, Scotiabank, and Lexus Canada.

For more than 10 years, Shirley wrote a regular marketing column for *The Record*. She has been an active board member and volunteer in many organizations, including Communitech, the Business Success for Women Conference, K-W Business Women's Association, and the Sexual Assault Support Centre of Waterloo Region.

Ajax Persaud, Ph.D., is an Associate Professor of Marketing and the founding Director of the Master of Science in Management program at the Telfer School of Management, University of Ottawa. Professor Persaud has more than 15 years of post-secondary teaching experience at colleges and universities in Canada and overseas. He has taught several undergraduate and graduate courses, including Marketing, Electronic Marketing, Digital Marketing Technologies, High-Tech Marketing, Marketing Strategy, New Product Development, Entrepreneurial Finance, R&D Management, Technology and Innovation Management, Economics, and Quantitative Methods. He has received several awards and nominations for teaching and research excellence. In 2005, he was awarded the University of Ottawa Excellence in Education Prize for excellence in teaching and research.

Professor Persaud has published material in journals, conference papers, and four books, including *E-Business Innovations: Cases and Readings* and *Managing Innovations Through Corporate Global R&D*. His research has been published in leading journals, such as *Journal of Product Innovation Management, IEEE Transactions on Engineering Management, Journal of Technology Transfer,* and the *Canadian Journal of Administrative Sciences.* He has also served as academic reviewer for many journals, including *Journal of Product Innovation Management, IEEE Transactions on Engineering Management, and Journal of Asia Pacific Marketing.*

As well, he has delivered many executive seminars and workshops and has consulted for many organizations in Guyana, Canada, and Europe. He is an active community volunteer, contributing both his time and his money, for many worthy causes and charities, focusing on education and disadvantaged children and youths.

brief contents

table of contents

SECTION TWO   Understanding the Marketplace   108

SECTION THREE   Targeting the Marketplace   166

SECTION FOUR Value Creation 240

9 Product, Branding, and Packaging Decisions 275

10 Services: The Intangible Product 305

SECTION FIVE   Transacting Value   334

SECTION SIX — Value Delivery: Designing the Distribution Channel and Supply Chain   370

SECTION SEVEN   Value Communication   430

15 Advertising, Sales Promotions, and Personal Selling   469

SECTION EIGHT Marketing in the Global Environment 530

THE FUNCTION OF MARKETING IS MULTI-FACETED, BUT ITS FUNDAMENTAL PURPOSE IS TO CREATE VALUE. CONSIDER THESE EXAMPLES:

Why do people buy lululemon yoga pants for well over $100 when they could buy another pair at Walmart for under $20? The answer lies in marketing brand value: lululemon has created a cache for its branded clothing with grassroots advertising and innovative fabrics and styles. When trendsetters start to wear these brands, others follow.

Similarly, why would anyone pay for bottled water when they could get it for free from a tap? Companies such as Aberfoyle Springs, Clearly Canadian, Canadian Springs, and Montclair have created bottled water products that offer customers the convenience of an easy-to-carry format. But after years of explosive growth, the industry is facing challenges. Environmental concerns have led to unprecedented criticism related to the sea of plastic bottles hitting landfill and recycling sites. Many municipalities have banned bottled water outright.

Regardless of your age, your gender, or the city in which you live, you already know something about marketing. You have been an involved consumer in the marketing process since childhood when, for example, you accompanied your mother or father to the grocery store and asked to buy a particular brand of cereal because you saw a friend eating it or heard about it on television. The prize inside the box of cereal was of value to you as a child; the nutritional information offered on the box panel was of value to your mother or father. Once you begin to explore the many ways in which companies and brands create value for their customers through marketing, you will also begin to appreciate the complex set of decisions and activities that are necessary to provide you with the products and services you use every day.

changes to the third canadian edition

The prevalence and power of the Internet has created a marketplace of more informed and savvy customers than ever before. Those who teach the marketers of the future need to account for the consumer's ability to assess the marketplace at their fingertips and discern good value from poor value. ***Marketing***, Third Canadian Edition, is all about the core concepts and tools that help marketers create value for customers. Throughout this book you will find many examples that define how companies create value for customers through branding, packaging, pricing, retailing, service, and advertising. We introduce the concept of value in Chapter 1 and carry it through the entire text.

SECTION ONE — Assessing the Marketplace

The first section of the text contains three chapters and the central theme of the section is "Assessing the Marketplace." Following an introduction to marketing in Chapter 1, Chapter 2 focuses on how a firm develops a marketing plan. A central theme of the chapter is how firms can effectively create, capture, deliver, and communicate value to their customers. Finally, Chapter 3, Analyzing the Marketing Environment, focuses on how marketers can systematically uncover and evaluate opportunities.

Changes to Section One include:

- New Chapter Vignettes in Chapters 1 and 2, and a revised Chapter Vignette for Chapter 3.
- New Social & Mobile Marketing boxes in all three chapters.
- New Sustainable Marketing box in Chapter 3.
- New Entrepreneurial Marketing boxes in all chapters.

- Revised coverage on marketing orientations in Chapter 1 to make it easier for students to appreciate the different ways marketing is practiced. Also, added a short discussion and an example showing how the four Ps need to be integrated and coordinated into a seamless whole rather than treated as individual components of the marketing mix.
- More emphasis on the role of social media in marketing and the importance of sustainable marketing in Chapter 1.
- A continued focus on ethics with new Ethical Dilemma boxes in Chapters 1 and 3.
- The marketing strategies section was revised to make it simpler to follow.
- The inclusion of an appendix that walks students through the process and components of Writing a Marketing Plan.
- A discussion of the recession in the economic factors section in Chapter 3.

SECTION TWO — Understanding the Marketplace

The second section of the book deals with "Understanding the Marketplace" and is composed of two chapters. Chapter 4, Consumer Behaviour, focuses on all aspects of understanding why consumers purchase products and services. The consumer decision process is highlighted. Chapter 5, Business-to-Business Marketing, focuses on all aspects pertaining to why and how business-to-business buying takes place.

Changes to Section Two include:

- New Chapter Vignette in Chapter 4.
- New Social & Mobile Marketing boxes in Chapters 4 and 5.

- New Entrepreneurial Marketing boxes in Chapters 4 and 5.
- New Chapter Case Study in Chapter 5.
- New examples of strategies and tactics marketers use at each stage of the consumer process in Chapter 4.
- A discussion in Chapter 4 about how marketers can mitigate the various risks associated with the consumer buying decision.
- A new section in Chapter 5 about the challenges in reaching and serving B2B customers.

SECTION THREE Targeting the Marketplace

The third section of the book deals with "Targeting the Marketplace." Chapter 6 focuses on segmentation, targeting, and positioning. In this chapter, we focus on how firms segment the marketplace, pick a target market, and then position their good/service in line with their customers' needs and wants. Chapter 7, Marketing Research, identifies the various tools and techniques that marketers use to uncover these needs and ensure that they create goods and services that provide value to their target markets.

Changes to Section Three include:

- A new Chapter Vignette for Chapter 7.
- New Social & Mobile Marketing boxes in Chapters 6 and 7.

- A new Ethical Dilemma box in Chapter 7.
- A new Sustainable Marketing box in Chapter 6.
- Revised Chapter Case Studies.
- A new Real Marketer profile in Chapter 7.
- Added an expanded discussion in Chapter 7 explaining how marketers use research, including examples of the types of objectives set and how the research might be conducted.
- The addition of an appendix, Using Secondary Data to Assess Customer Lifetime Value (CLV), to demonstrate the expected financial contribution from a customer to a company's overall profitability over the course of the relationship.

SECTION FOUR Value Creation

Marketing, Third Canadian Edition, devotes three chapters to **Value Creation**. The first two, Chapter 8, Developing New Products, and Chapter 9, Product, Branding, and Packaging Decisions, cover the development and management of products and brands. While many of the concepts involved in developing and managing services are similar to those of physical brands, Chapter 10, Services: The Intangible Product, addresses the unique challenges of the marketing of services.

Changes to Section Four include:

- New Chapter Vignettes in Chapters 8, 9 and 10.
- New Social & Mobile Marketing boxes in all three chapters.

- New Ethical Dilemma boxes in Chapters 9 and 10.
- New Entrepreneurial Marketing boxes in Chapters 8 and 9.
- A new Real Marketer profile in Chapter 10.
- New Chapter Case Studies in Chapters 8 and 10, and a revised Chapter Case Study in Chapter 9.
- A discussion of metrics in Chapter 10 in a section titled "Evaluating Service Quality by Using Well-Established Marketing Metrics."

SECTION FIVE Transacting Value

Pricing is the activity within a firm responsible for **Transacting Value** by bringing in money and affecting revenues. Chapter 11 examines the importance of setting the right price, the relationship between price and quantity sold, break-even analysis, the impact of price wars, and how the Internet has changed the way people shop.

Changes to Section Five include:

- A new Chapter Vignette.
- The following new boxed features: Social & Mobile Marketing, Sustainable Marketing, Ethical Dilemma.

- A revised Chapter Case Study.
- An expanded discussion of competition that now includes four levels: oligopolistic competition, monopolistic competition, pure competition, and monopoly.
- An updated discussion of daily deal companies, such as Groupon and WagJag, that reflects how companies are offering pricing deals to groups of consumers.

SECTION SIX   Value Delivery: Designing the Marketing Channel and Supply Chain

One important reason why Walmart has become the world's largest retailer is its **Value Delivery** system. It times the delivery of merchandise so the merchandise gets to stores just in time to meet customer demand. To achieve this, it has initiated many innovative programs with its vendors and developed sophisticated transportation and warehousing systems. *Marketing*, Third Canadian Edition, devotes two chapters to value delivery. Chapter 12 takes a look at marketing channels, distribution strategy, and supply chain, while Chapter 13 concentrates on retailing.

Changes to Section Six include:

- A new Chapter Vignette in Chapter 12, and a revised Chapter Vignette in Chapter 13.
- The following new boxed features: Social & Mobile Marketing and Entrepreneurial Marketing.
- A new Real Marketer Profile for Chapter 12.
- The discussion on retailing in Chapter 13 has been revised to show students how retail partners are chosen, identifying the types of retailers a company may want to use, creating a retail strategy, and exploring a multichannel strategy. This last section in multichannel retailing contains significantly new content.

SECTION SEVEN   Value Communications

Today's methods of **Value Communication** are complex because of new technologies that add email, blogs, the Internet, and social media to the advertising mix that once utilized only radio and television to relay messages to consumers. *Marketing*, Third Canadian Edition, devotes two chapters to value communication. Chapter 14 introduces the breadth of integrated marketing communications. Chapter 15 is devoted to advertising, sales promotions, and personal selling. Chapter 16 is an all new addition to the textbook focusing on Social and Mobile Marketing.

Changes to Section Seven include:

- New Chapter Vignettes for Chapters 15 and 16.
- New Social & Mobile Marketing boxes in all three chapters.

- Reorganization of Chapter 14 to present the Steps in Planning an IMC Campaign first, followed by the IMC Tools available for use in campaigns.
- A new Entrepreneurial Marketing box in Chapter 16.
- Revised in-depth coverage of direct marketing in Chapter 14.
- Expanded information in Chapter 14, under "Digital Media" heading, to focus more on online ads, social media, and mobile apps.
- New section on implementing a Google AdWords campaign in Chapter 14.
- New Real Marketer profile in Chapter 15.

SECTION EIGHT   Marketing in the Global Environment

Most firms are involved in **Global Marketing** at some level. In less than 10 years, lululemon has been transformed into a global company and a great Canadian success story in the athletic and sportswear industry. But even small entrepreneurial firms are also involved because they get their materials, products, or services from firms located in other countries. Chapter 17 is devoted exclusively to this topic. Chapter 18 focuses on Ethics and Socially Responsible Marketing and has been moved from Connect to the hard copy edition of the textbook. The chapter provides rich illustrations of corporate responsibility and introduces an ethical decision-making framework that is useful for

assessing potential ethically troubling situations that are posed throughout the rest of the book. It can be used to set the tone for ethical material throughout the textbook as desired.

Changes to Section Eight include:

- New Chapter Vignettes.
- New Chapter Case Studies.
- The following new boxed features: Ethical Dilemma, Social & Mobile Marketing, and Entrepreneurial Marketing.
- A new Sustainable Marketing box for Chapter 18.

In addition to our emphasis on value in *Marketing*, Third Canadian Edition, you will also find integrated and highlighted coverage of ethics, entrepreneurship, services, social and mobile marketing, sustainability, and globalization within the framework of the marketing discipline:

Chapters 1 to 18 each contain an **Ethical Dilemma box** with a compelling ethical discussion and end-of-chapter discussion questions that force students to consider and evaluate each situation. The Third Canadian Edition contains thirteen new Ethical Dilemmas.

Ethical Dilemma 10.1 — Fake Reviews[51]

Yelp, TripAdvisor, and Amazon have all made user ratings and reviews a familiar—and even essential—part of the online toolbox for shoppers and other consumers. From the consumer's perspective, what better preparation could there be for a major purchase than to see what other, objective customers have to say about the product or service under consideration?

For retailers and service professionals, online reviews offer a huge benefit too. For some companies, especially small service providers that cannot afford much market-

post reviews—and promised that if those reviews were positive, the customer would receive a complete refund. Within weeks, nearly all of the company's 355 online reviews gave the VIP Deals leather case four or five stars. But Amazon guidelines prohibit compensation for customer reviews, and the VIP Deals page soon disappeared.

A leather case for your iPad is one thing. Accurate, truthful information takes on paramount importance for a service like plastic surgery. But Lifestyle Lift seemed to disregard customers' expectations that they could

Entrepreneurship. An entrepreneurial spirit pervades most marketing innovations and is necessary to keep firms growing and healthy. *Marketing*, Third Canadian Edition, nurtures that entrepreneurial spirit by providing examples of young entrepreneurial firms and successful entrepreneurs such as lululemon, Cora's Restaurants, Bullfrog Power, AWAKE Chocolate, and more.

Entrepreneurial Marketing 3.1 — Turning Trash into Cash[75]

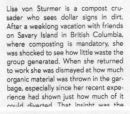

Lisa von Sturmer is a compost crusader who sees dollar signs in dirt. After a weeklong vacation with friends on Savary Island in British Columbia, where composting is mandatory, she was shocked to see how little waste the group generated. When she returned to work she was dismayed at how much organic material was thrown in the garbage, especially since her recent experience had shown just how much of it could diverted. That insight was the

business grow to $212,000 in the second year, leaving enough profits to pay von Sturmer a salary of $55,000. In spite of having no business background, von Sturmer has won numerous awards including the 2010 Small Business BC's Best Business Concept award,[76] and 2012 Canadian Youth Business Foundation's National Best Green Business award.[77] By the third year, the company had contracts with 82 offices in Vancouver, Richmond

And each chapter contains an **Entrepreneurial Marketing box** that depicts recognizable and interesting young entrepreneurial firms. There are 12 new Entrepreneurial Marketing boxes in the Third Canadian Edition. Special focus is given to successful entrepreneurs who have pitched their business ideas on CBC's *Dragons' Den*.

To complement the Entrepreneurial Marketing and other inset boxes, there are 14 videos from CBC's *Dragons' Den* available on Connect which correspond with specific boxes and examples in the text such as how AWAKE Chocolate worked with David Chilton to secure distribution for their new products. The *Dragons' Den* logo signifies which examples have a video.

Social & Mobile Marketing boxes further explore the explosive growth of tools such as Facebook, YouTube, and Twitter, which help marketers communicate with their target markets and promote products or services to them.

For example, Chapter 14 discusses how Visa uses Twitter to launch its #Smallenfreuden campaign to convince consumers to use their credit cards for smaller purchases.

Social and Mobile Marketing 14.1 — Do You #smallenfreuden?

When orange billboards popped up in Toronto asking "DO YOU #smallenfreuden?," consumers were confused. No identifying information was included—no tagline, no logo, no hints as to what company was behind the teaser campaign. And what the heck did *smallenfreuden* mean?

One week later, Visa Canada stepped forward claiming the #smallenfreuden campaign stood for the joy of small; in this case, making small purchases using your Visa card. Because smallenfreuden was an unusual word, the creative team at Visa's ad agency, BBDO, felt it made sense to introduce consumers to the term

aired during playoff games. Social media saw heavy use throughout the campaign with promoted trends and promoted tweets on Twitter. Consumers could win a trip to NHL final games through "The Visa Ultimate NHL Experience Contest" which was run on Facebook.

The objectives of the campaign were to spark intrigue, create awareness, and drive engagement. It certainly created a buzz, generating more than 20,00 social media mentions for @VisaCA (five times higher than the usual daily average), and 50 million views on Twitter.[70] A YouTube video attracted 400,000 views.[71] Twitter Canada chose #smallenfreuden as one of

Sustainable Marketing boxes encourage students to consider the environmental concerns that marketers face in bringing new products and services to the market. Many companies have faced increased scrutiny and criticism over the use of plastic packaging and recycling issues. The boxes will help students see how smart marketers are embracing sustainability for the good of their companies as well as for consumers.

Sustainable Marketing 12.1 | **Driving the Bottom Line**

If you like Frito-Lay SunChips, you may remember its 100 percent compostable bag. Made primarily of the plant-based material polylactic acid, the bag will completely break down in 14 weeks. It was all part of Frito-Lay Canada's "Leave No Trace" sustainability vision. The company set clear goals to use less water, electricity, and fuel and to reduce waste for everything it makes, moves, and sells.[33] At Frito-Lay, financial achievement is gauged by social and environmental performance.

With one of the largest private delivery fleets in Canada, Frito-Lay is keenly aware of the profound effect efficient vehicles can have on its carbon footprint. It has

the majority of routes from its distribution centres in Brampton, Ottawa, Surrey, and Laval. The electricity the vehicles used was offset by renewable energy credits, and even the batteries could be recycled at the end of their lives. Due to the impact of cold Canadian winters on overall battery life, the trucks have since been relocated to the United States, where the fleet is enjoying a dramatic expansion.

The company's sustainability initiatives go far beyond fleet management. Frito-Lay Canada's efforts have resulted in saving 5.4 billion litres of water since 1999. It has been able to divert over 95 percent of manufacturing

For example, in Chapter 12 we discuss Frito Lay Canada initiatives such as reducing water and electrical consumption, optimizing delivery routes and switching to zero-emission electric vehicles.

Real Marketer Profile boxes appear in eight chapters. They focus on the transition students make from attending post-secondary education to applying their marketing skills in the "real" world. While some of the profiles feature relatively new graduates who are still with their first employer, others show the career paths that grads and seasoned veterans have taken within a company or in a new role at a different organization.

REAL MARKETER PROFILE | David Chilton

Armed with a degree in economics and an award for achieving the highest mark in the country on the Canadian Securities Course, David Chilton started his career as a stockbroker. Working with clients led him to the realization that while there were a lot of books about personal finances, there weren't many that made the topic easy to understand. He soon changed that, publishing *The Wealthy Barber*, when he was only 27 years old. The book introduced Canadians to Roy, a barber who imparted sound financial advice while

Podleski sisters in Granet Publishing to produce two more best-selling cookbooks: *Crazy Plates* and *Eat, Shrink & Be Merry!*

Chilton also worked with the sisters to bring a frozen entrée, Crazy Plates, to Loblaws grocery stores. While normally very difficult to secure distribution, Chilton said that "having a great brand and sales of over 1.3 million cookbooks"[41] helped open doors. However, initial sales of the frozen food line did not meet expectations. While consumers loved the concept, the packaging and large size didn't

For example, in Chapter 12 we discuss David Chilton's phenomenal success story from new grad, to stockbroker, to author, to publisher, to one of the dragons on CBC's *Dragons' Den*.

REINFORCING LEARNING

Learning Objectives

Listed at the beginning of each chapter, **Learning Objectives** show students the main concepts discussed inside. These Learning Objectives are then presented in the margins throughout the chapter when they are introduced. At the end of each chapter, the Learning Objectives are revisited and reviewed, reinforcing for students the key sections in the chapter and allowing them to follow their own progress to know where they need help.

LEARNING OBJECTIVES

After studying this chapter you should be able to

LO1 Define a marketing strategy

LO2 Describe the elements of a marketing plan

LO3 Analyze a marketing situation using a SWOT analysis

LO4 Explain how a firm chooses what consumer group(s) to pursue with its marketing efforts

LO5 Outline the implementation of the marketing mix as a means to increase customer value

LO6 Describe how firms grow their businesses

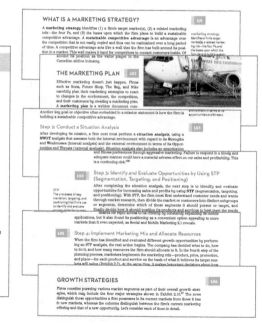

Chapter Vignette

Each chapter begins with a Chapter Vignette that helps to introduce and illustrate some of the main content that follows. These vignettes have been carefully selected to pique student interest and are designed to provide real-world examples of how the theory has been applied by a variety of companies. There are 12 new Chapter Vignettes in the Third Canadian Edition.

Overview of Marketing

It's nearing the end of the spring semester, and it's a hot day. Leaving the sweltering classroom to go study, you and your friends decide to grab a drink. Someone suggests iced coffee. There are several options on campus. Now the negotiations begin: Tim Hortons Iced Capp or a Starbucks Mocha Frappuccino? Someone wants a soy-based beverage instead of a milk-based drink. Another friend insists it's time for everyone to check out the new McCafé for an Iced Latte. Although McDonalds does not have a location on campus, your friend argues that the McCafé latte is cheaper and has fewer calories. Each of these drinks represents a cool treat, and various companies provide multiple options. So what's the difference among them, and what makes customers loyal to one choice over another?

Let's think about the options available for any caffeine indulgence: hot, cold, or frozen; dark, medium or light roast; and plain, flavoured, or blended drinks. You can also choose from reduced-fat, soy, organic, or fair-trade, or add whipped cream, cinnamon, or chocolate sprinkles. In the grocery store, while brands such as Nabob, Maxwell House and Nescafe dominate the coffee aisle, you can also find products from Tim Hortons and Starbucks on the shelves. McDonalds recently started to sell bagged coffee in its Canadian restaurants so the company may be eyeing the grocery channel in the future, as well.

To build and maintain a loyal customer base, each company must distinguish itself from its competitors by offering products, services, and a strong brand that appeal to customers. Ranked number one in the Reputation Institute's survey of Canada's top brands in 2013 and offering over 3400 restaurants, Tim Hortons is a brand many consumers gravitate toward.[1] Having convenient locations and a variety of product offerings has helped it win 42 percent of the quick-service restaurant traffic in Canada.[2] The company has differentiated itself through its community involvement as a sponsor of Timbit minor sports. Its Children's Foundation highlights some of the company's corporate social responsibility initiatives. For example, storeowners hold annual Camp Days, donating coffee sales and collecting public donations to help send children from economically disadvantaged families to camp. The Tim Hortons Coffee Partnership has been working for almost a decade to improve the lives of coffee growers in South America. The company publicly reports on sustainability and responsibility efforts, is committed to building more LEED Certified restaurants[3] and, as part of a new pilot project, allows owners of electric vehicles to charge their cars at no cost.[4]

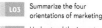

LEARNING OBJECTIVES

After studying this chapter you should be able to

LO1 Define the role of marketing and explain its core concepts

LO2 Describe how marketers create value for a product or service

LO3 Summarize the four orientations of marketing

LO4 Understand the importance of marketing both within and outside the firm

Unique End-of-Chapter Applications and Exercises

- **Marketing Applications.** Student-tested at Wilfrid Laurier University and the University of Ottawa, these Marketing Application questions encourage students to become more critical in their thinking of how marketing theory relates to practice. At least one of the Marketing Applications in each chapter poses an ethical dilemma based on material covered in the chapter.

- **Net Savvy.** Each chapter contains two exercises that drive students to the Internet to apply material covered in the text. For example, in Chapter 15, we direct students to the Concerned Children's Advertisers website (www.cca-kids.ca), one of the major self-regulatory bodies for children's advertising. We ask students to choose a PSA and discuss how these ads are used to deliver CCA's message.

- **End-of-Chapter Cases.** Each chapter ends with a two- or three-page case covering a current marketing idea, concept, or company.

CONNECT

McGraw-Hill Connect™ is a web-based assignment and assessment platform that gives students the means to better connect with their coursework, with their instructors, and with the important concepts that they will need to know for success now and in the future.

With Connect, instructors can deliver assignments, quizzes, and tests online. Questions are presented in an auto-gradable format and tied to the text's learning objectives. Instructors can edit existing questions and author entirely new problems. They can also track individual student performance–by question, by assignment, or in relation to the class overall—with detailed grade reports, and integrate grade reports easily with Learning Management Systems (LMS) such as WebCT and Blackboard. And much more.

The Connect Instructor Library provides all the critical resources instructors will need to build their courses, including a Test Bank, Instructor's Manual, and ready-made PowerPoint presentations:

- The **Test Bank** includes more than 2000 multiple-choice, true/false, and short essay questions. Each question is categorized according to learning objective, level of Bloom's taxonomy, and correct answer.

- The computerized test bank is also available through EZ Test Online—a flexible and easy-to-use electronic testing program—that allows instructors to create tests from book-specific items. EZ Test accommodates a wide range of question types and allows instructors to add their own questions. Test items are also available in Word format (rich text format). For secure online testing, exams created in EZ Test can be exported to WebCT and Blackboard. EZ Test Online is supported at www.mhhe.com/eztest, where users can download a Quick Start Guide, access FAQs, or log a ticket for help with specific issues.

- The **Instructor's Manual** contains learning objectives, key terms with definitions, a detailed lecture outline, suggested Internet resources, and in-class activities.

- **PowerPoint slides** include key lecture points and images from the text. As an aid for instructors who wish to create their own presentations, an **Image Bank** containing all visual elements from the text is also available.

- **Videos** of 18 segments in a variety of lengths will provide flexibility for your class. Firms featured in the videos include AWAKE Chocolate, Steeped Tea, Ten Tree Apparel, Cole+Parker, and many more successful entrepreneurs who pitched their businesses on CBC's *Dragons' Den* series.

By choosing Connect, instructors are providing their students with a powerful tool for improving academic performance and truly mastering course material. Connect allows students to practise important skills at their own pace and on their own schedule. Importantly, students' assessment results and instructors' feedback are all saved online–so students can continually review their progress and plot their course to success.

Connect also provides 24/7 online access to an eBook—an online edition of the text—to aid them in successfully completing their work, wherever and whenever they choose.

CONNECT FOR STUDENTS

Connect provides students with a powerful tool for improving academic performance and truly mastering course material, plus 24/7 online access to an interactive and searchable eBook. Connect allows students to practise important skills at their own pace and on their own schedule.

LEARNSMART

LEARNSMART

No two students are alike. Why should their learning paths be? LearnSmart uses revolutionary adaptive technology to build a learning experience unique to each student's individual needs. It starts by identifying the topics a student knows and does not know. As the student progresses, LearnSmart adapts and adjusts the content based on his or her individual strengths, weaknesses and confidence, ensuring that every minute spent studying with LearnSmart is the most efficient and productive study time possible.

SMARTBOOK

SMARTBOOK

As the first and only adaptive reading experience, SmartBook is changing the way students read and learn. SmartBook creates a personalized reading experience by highlighting the most important concepts a student needs to learn at that moment in time. As a student engages with SmartBook, the reading experience continuously adapts by highlighting content based on what each student knows and doesn't know. This ensures that he or she is focused on the content needed to close specific knowledge gaps, while it simultaneously promotes long-term learning.

INSIGHT

connectINSIGHT

New to the third Canadian edition of Grewal! Visualized data tailored to your needs as an instructor make it possible to quickly confirm early signals of success, or identify early warning signs regarding student performance or concept mastery—even while on the go.

SUPERIOR LEARNING SOLUTIONS AND SUPPORT

The McGraw-Hill Ryerson team is ready to help you assess and integrate any of our products, technology, and services into your course for optimal teaching and learning performance. Whether it's helping your students improve their grades, or putting your entire course online, the McGraw-Hill Ryerson team is here to help you do it. Contact your Learning Solutions Consultant today to learn how to maximize all of McGraw-Hill Ryerson's resources!

For more information on the latest technology and Learning Solutions offered by McGraw-Hill Ryerson and its partners, please visit us online: www.mheducation.ca/he/solutions.

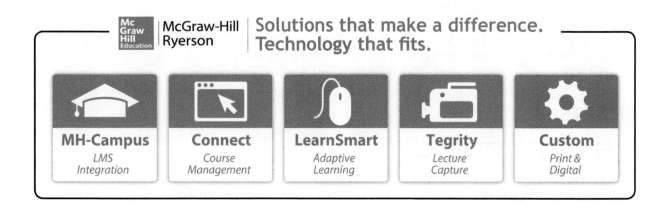

acknowledgements

I could not have completed this text without the help of others. In particular, I would like to thank Stacey Biggar, who diligently worked with me throughout the project as an invaluable research assistant and sounding board. My thanks go as well to the many Wilfrid Laurier University students and professors who took the time to provide feedback on the chapter content, cases, and exercises.

Additionally, I would like to thank Sahar Khan, Mark Rosenzweig, and Stephen Hayes, who worked as research assistants on this book.

A special thanks to the many talented staff and freelance members at McGraw-Hill Ryerson—Karen Fozard, Amy Rydzanicz, Alison Derry, Tracy Leonard, Jessica Barnoski, Karen Rolfe, and Joy Armitage Taylor. You made my job so much easier. It was a pleasure working with you.

I gratefully acknowledge feedback and constructive criticism from marketing colleagues across Canada.

Tom Arhontoudis	George Brown College
Stephen Grant	University of New Brunswick
Warveni Jap	Thompson Rivers University
Ingrid Kajzer	Mitchell Royal Roads University
Eric Li	University of British Columbia
James Liu	Assiniboine College
Rosemary Peros	University of Waterloo
Michael Rod	Carleton University
Robert Saks	Concordia University
Margery Taylor	George Brown College
Duane Weaver	Vancouver Island University
David Williams	University of Saskatchewan

Shirley Lichti

CHAPTER **1**

Overview of Marketing

It's nearing the end of the spring semester, and it's a hot day. Leaving the sweltering classroom to go study, you and your friends decide to grab a drink. Someone suggests iced coffee. There are several options on campus. Now the negotiations begin: Tim Hortons Iced Capp or a Starbucks Mocha Frappuccino? Someone wants a soy-based beverage instead of a milk-based drink. Another friend insists it's time for everyone to check out the new McCafé for an Iced Latte. Although McDonalds does not have a location on campus, your friend argues that the McCafé latte is cheaper and has fewer calories. Each of these drinks represents a cool treat, and various companies provide multiple options. So what's the difference among them, and what makes customers loyal to one choice over another?

Let's think about the options available for any caffeine indulgence: hot, cold, or frozen; dark, medium or light roast; and plain, flavoured, or blended drinks. You can also choose from reduced-fat, soy, organic, or fair-trade, or add whipped cream, cinnamon, or chocolate sprinkles. In the grocery store, while brands such as Nabob, Maxwell House and Nescafe dominate the coffee aisle, you can also find products from Tim Hortons and Starbucks on the shelves. McDonalds recently started to sell bagged coffee in its Canadian restaurants so the company may be eyeing the grocery channel in the future, as well.

To build and maintain a loyal customer base, each company must distinguish itself from its competitors by offering products, services, and a strong brand that appeal to customers. Ranked number one in the Reputation Institute's survey of Canada's top brands in 2013 and offering over 3400 restaurants, Tim Hortons is a brand many consumers gravitate toward.[1] Having convenient locations and a variety of product offerings has helped it win 42 percent of the quick-service restaurant traffic in Canada.[2] The company has differentiated itself through its community involvement as a sponsor of Timbit minor sports. Its Children's Foundation highlights some of the company's corporate social responsibility initiatives. For example, storeowners hold annual Camp Days, donating coffee sales and collecting public donations to help send children from economically disadvantaged families to camp. The Tim Hortons Coffee Partnership has been working for almost a decade to improve the lives of coffee growers in South America. The company publicly reports on sustainability and responsibility efforts, is committed to building more LEED Certified restaurants[3] and, as part of a new pilot project, allows owners of electric vehicles to charge their cars at no cost.[4]

LEARNING OBJECTIVES

After studying this chapter you should be able to

LO1 Define the role of marketing and explain its core concepts

LO2 Describe how marketers create value for a product or service

LO3 Summarize the four orientations of marketing

LO4 Understand the importance of marketing both within and outside the firm

To ensure consumers keep coming back, Tim Hortons runs promotions such as Roll Up the Rim, which has been running annually for over 25 years, or its new Chill to Win Iced Capp contest. It connects with consumers on social media through Facebook, Twitter, and Pinterest and has rolled out TimmyMe, a mobile app designed to simplify orders for office workers when it's their turn to go for a "Timmy Run." The company even rolled out its own TV channel, TimsTV, streaming news, weather, and sports content as well as programming to highlight its community activities such as free skating or swimming dates and Camp Day.[5]

As this example demonstrates, companies constantly protect their brand in the market. Businesses must grow and change their product offerings and corporate citizenry to keep pace with customer needs and tastes. Its emphasis on freshness and variety helps Tim Hortons succeed in providing good value to its customers. ▌

WHAT IS MARKETING?

Unlike other subjects you may have studied, marketing is already very familiar to you. You start your day by agreeing to do the dishes in exchange for a freshly made cup of coffee. Then you fill up your car with gas. You attend a class that you have chosen and paid for. After class, you pick up lunch (and maybe an iced coffee!), which you consume while checking Facebook messages on your iPad. Then you get your hair cut and check out a movie. On your bus ride home you listen to new songs on iTunes and maybe even buy some. In each case, you have acted as the buyer and made a decision about whether you should part with your time and/or money to receive a particular service or type of merchandise. If, after you return home from the movie, you decide to auction your old smartphone on eBay, you have become a seller. In each of these transactions, you were engaged in marketing because you were exchanging something of value that satisfies a need.

This chapter will look at the definition of marketing and at how marketing is used to create value in products or in services. We will see how the interrelated marketing mix—or four Ps—create, transact, communicate, and deliver value. We will look at where marketing happens and how it has evolved over the years into today's concept of value-based marketing. Lastly, we will discuss why marketing is an important function for any successful firm.

The Canadian Marketing Association states that "**Marketing** is a set of business practices designed to plan for and present an organization's products or services in ways that build effective customer relationships."[6] What does this definition really mean? Good marketing is not a random activity; it requires thoughtful planning with an emphasis on the ethical implications of any of those decisions on consumers and society in general. Firms develop a **marketing plan** (see Chapter 2) that specifies their marketing activities for a specific period of time. The marketing plan is broken down into various components—how the product or service will be conceived or designed, how much it should cost, where and how it will be promoted, and how it will get to the consumer. In any exchange, the buyer and the seller should be satisfied with the value they obtained from a transaction. In our earlier example, you should be satisfied or even delighted with

marketing
A set of business practices designed to plan for and present an organization's products or services in ways that build effective customer relationships.

marketing plan
A written document composed of an analysis of the current marketing situation, opportunities and threats for the firm, marketing objectives and strategy specified in terms of the four Ps, action programs, and projected or pro forma income (and other financial) statements.

EXHIBIT 1.1　Core Aspects of Marketing

the song you downloaded, and Apple should be satisfied with the amount of money it received from you. The core aspects of marketing are shown in Exhibit 1.1. Let's see how they look in practice.

Marketing Is About Satisfying Customer Needs and Wants

Understanding and satisfying consumer needs and wants is fundamental to marketing success. A **need** is when a person feels deprived of the basic necessities of life, such as food, clothing, shelter, or safety. A **want** is the particular way in which the person chooses to fulfill his or her need, which is shaped by a person's knowledge, culture, and personality. For example, when we are hungry, we need something to eat. Some people want a submarine sandwich to satisfy that hunger, whereas others want a salad and some soup instead. The topic of understanding customer needs is described in detail in Chapter 4, which deals with consumer behaviour.

To understand customer needs and wants, the company must first identify the customers or **market** for its product or service. In the broadest terms, the market refers to the world of trade. More narrowly, however, the market can be segmented or divided into groups of people who are pertinent to an organization for particular reasons. For example, the marketplace for soft drinks may include most people in the world, but as Pepsi and Coke battle each other worldwide, they divide the global population into a host of categories: men versus women, calorie-conscious or not, people who prefer carbonated versus noncarbonated drinks, and multiple categories of flavour preferences, among others.[7] If you manufacture a beverage with zero calories, you want to know for which market segments your product is most relevant, then make sure that you build a marketing strategy that targets those groups. Certain diet- and health-conscious customers may prefer Diet Coke or Diet Pepsi; others may opt for bottled water products like Dasani or Aquafina.

Although marketers would prefer to sell their products and services to everyone, it is not practical to do so. Because marketing costs money, good marketers carefully seek out potential customers who have both an interest in the product and an ability to buy it. For example, most people need some form of transportation, and many people

LO1

need
Basic necessities, such as food, clothing, shelter, and safety.

want
The particular way in which a person chooses to satisfy a need, which is shaped by a person's knowledge, culture, and personality.

market
Refers to the groups of people who need or want a company's products or services and have the ability and willingness to buy them.

nothing refreshes like a
diet pepsi.

Coke and Pepsi are constantly battling to be number one.

target market
The customer segment or group to whom the firm is interested in selling its products and services.

exchange
The trade of things of value between the buyer and the seller so that each is better off as a result.

Purchasing a Rihanna song from the iTunes store entails an exchange. The customer gets the song and Apple gets money and information.

probably would like to own the new hybrid from Lexus. Starting at more than $110,000, the Lexus LS 600h L is one of the most sophisticated hybrid cars on the market. But Lexus is not actually interested in everyone who wants an LS 600h L, because not everyone can afford to spend that much on a car. Instead, Lexus defines its viable **target market** as those consumers who want and can afford such a product.[8] Although not all companies focus on such a specific and wealthy target, all marketers are interested in finding the buyers who are most likely to be interested in their offerings.

The process of how companies segment the market for their products and services and then choose which segment to target and how best to reach that segment is described in Chapter 6. The process of identifying customer segments the company wants to target with its products and services requires market research. The types of market research that help marketers make good decisions about various aspects of the marketing mix are discussed in Chapter 7.

Marketing Entails an Exchange

Marketing is about an **exchange**—the trade of things of value between the buyer and the seller so that each is better off as a result. As depicted in Exhibit 1.2, sellers provide goods or services, then communicate and facilitate the delivery of their offering to consumers. Buyers complete the exchange by giving money and information to the seller. Suppose you learn about a new Rihanna album by hearing one of her songs on XM Satellite radio, The same day, a friend tweets on Twitter that she loves the new album, and so you visit the Rihanna Facebook fan page, which offers several recommendations. From there, you visit iTunes where you can purchase the song you heard, multiple songs, or the entire album. You begin with the song you heard, which you love even more after hearing it several times. So you go back to iTunes and take advantage of its offer to complete the album by downloading the rest of the songs to your iTunes library. Your billing information is already in the company's system, saving you from having to enter your credit card number or other information. Furthermore, iTunes creates a record of your purchase, which it uses, together with your other purchase trends, to create personalized recommendations of other albums or songs that you might like. This example shows how Apple uses the valuable information you provide to facilitate future exchanges and solidify its relationship with you.

EXHIBIT 1.2 Exchange: The Underpinning of Seller—Buyer Relationships

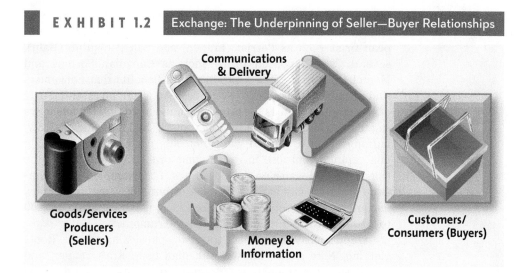

Communications & Delivery

Goods/Services Producers (Sellers)

Money & Information

Customers/ Consumers (Buyers)

Marketing Requires Marketing Mix Decisions

Marketing traditionally has been divided into a set of four interrelated decisions known as the **marketing mix**, or **four Ps**: product, price, place, and promotion, as shown in Exhibit 1.3.[9] Together, the four Ps compose the marketing mix, which is the controllable set of activities that the firm uses to respond to the wants of its target markets. But what does each of these elements in the marketing mix entail?

L02

marketing mix (four Ps) Product, price, place, and promotion—the controllable set of activities that a firm uses to respond to the wants of its target markets.

Product: Creating Value
The fundamental purpose of marketing is to create value by developing a variety of offerings, including goods, services, and ideas, to satisfy customer needs. Take, for example, water. Not too long ago, consumers perceived this

EXHIBIT 1.3 Marketing Mix Decisions

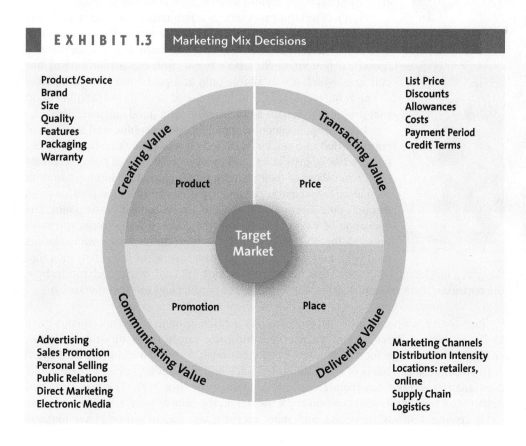

Product/Service
Brand
Size
Quality
Features
Packaging
Warranty

Creating Value — **Product**

Transacting Value — **Price**

List Price
Discounts
Allowances
Costs
Payment Period
Credit Terms

Target Market

Communicating Value — **Promotion**

Delivering Value — **Place**

Advertising
Sales Promotion
Personal Selling
Public Relations
Direct Marketing
Electronic Media

Marketing Channels
Distribution Intensity
Locations: retailers, online
Supply Chain
Logistics

goods
Items that can be physically touched.

services
Intangible customer benefits that are produced by people or machines and cannot be separated from the producer.

Montclair has created a product with benefits that consumers find valuable.

Rafael Nadal adds value to the Nike brand.

ideas
Thoughts, opinions, philosophies, and intellectual concepts.

price
The overall sacrifice a consumer is willing to make—money, time, energy—to acquire a specific product or service.

basic commodity as simply water. It came out of a faucet and was consumed for drinking and washing. But taking a cue from European firms such as Perrier (France) and San Pellegrino (Italy), several Canadian-based firms, such as Canadian Springs and Montclair, have created a product with benefits that consumers find valuable. In addition to easy access to water, an essential part of this created value is the product's brand image, which lets users say to the world, "I'm healthy," "I'm smart," and "I'm chic."[10] Growing opposition to bottled water not only makes it seem socially unacceptable, but also has seen some organizations banning the sale of bottled water on their premises. For example, the University of Ottawa has banned the sale of bottled water on campus, declaring itself a bottled water–free zone; it has set aside $75,000 to install new water fountains across the campus.[11]

Goods are items that you can physically touch. Roots clothing, Nike shoes, Molson Canadian beer, Kraft Dinner, and countless other products are examples of goods. As we describe in Chapter 2, Nike primarily makes shoes but also adds value to its products. For example, it offers custom designs under its Nike ID brand that increase their fashionable appeal and enlists popular celebrities such as Rafael Nadal to add their names to the designs.

Unlike goods, **services** are intangible customer benefits that are produced by people or machines and cannot be separated from the producer. Air travel, banking, insurance, beauty treatments, and entertainment all are services. If you attend a hockey or football game, you are consuming a service. Getting money from your bank by using an ATM or teller is another example of using a service. In this case, cash machines usually add value to your banking experience by being conveniently located, fast, and easy to use.

Many offerings represent a combination of goods and services. When you go to Hakim Optical, for example, you can have your eyes examined (service) and purchase new contact lenses (good). If you enjoy Rihanna's music, you can attend one of her concerts, which are available only at a particular time and place. At the concert, you can purchase one of her CDs—a tangible good that provides you with a combination of a good and a service.

Ideas include thoughts, opinions, philosophies, and intellectual concepts that also can be marketed. Groups promoting bicycle safety go to schools, give talks, and sponsor bike helmet poster contests for the members of their primary target market: children. Then their secondary target market segment, parents and siblings, gets involved through their interactions with the young contest participants. The exchange of value occurs when the children listen to the sponsor's presentation and wear their helmets while bicycling, which means they have adopted, or become "purchasers," of the safety idea that the group marketed. In Chapters 8, 9, and 10 of this book, you will learn much more about the decisions, theories, applications, and strategies of product and services marketing.

Price: Transacting Value   Everything has a price, though it doesn't always have to be monetary. **Price**, therefore, is everything the buyer gives up—money, time, energy—in exchange for the product. Marketers must determine the price of a product carefully on the basis of the potential buyer's belief about its value. For example, Air Canada can take you from Toronto to Vancouver or New York. The price you pay depends on how far in advance you book the ticket, the time of year, whether you want to fly economy or business class, and, more recently, whether or not you have luggage to check in. Passengers are charged a fee if they have more than one piece of check-in luggage. If you value the convenience of buying your ticket at the last minute for a ski trip between Christmas and New Year's Day and you want to fly business class, you can expect to pay four or five times as much as you would for the cheapest available ticket. That is, you have traded a lower price for convenience. For marketers, the key to determining prices is figuring out how much customers are willing to pay so that they are satisfied with the purchase and the seller achieves a reasonable profit. In Chapter 11, you will learn much more about pricing concepts, decisions, and strategies.

Place: Delivering Value

The third P, place, describes all the activities necessary to get the product from the manufacturer or producer to the right customer when that customer wants it. Place deals specifically with retailing and marketing channel management. Marketing channel management, also known as supply chain management, is the set of approaches and techniques that firms employ to efficiently and effectively integrate their suppliers, manufacturers, warehouses, stores, and other firms involved in the transaction (e.g., transportation companies) into a seamless value chain in which merchandise is produced and distributed in the right quantities, to the right locations, and at the right time, while minimizing systemwide costs and satisfying the service levels required by the customers.

In the frozen desserts domain, for example, marketing channel considerations have pushed a growing number of businesses to adopt multiple convenient locations and self-service delivery systems. Rather than requiring a large, free-standing store, TCBY or Yogurty's have set up smaller kiosk-type storefronts. In these more conveniently located places (which also require fewer staff and therefore reduce costs for the company), consumers can choose exactly what they want on their desserts. Many marketing students initially overlook the importance of distribution management because a lot of distribution activities occur behind the scenes. But without a strong and efficient distribution system, merchandise isn't available when or where customers want it. They are disappointed, and sales and profits suffer. Place or distribution activities and decisions are discussed in detail in Chapter 12.

Promotion: Communicating Value

Even the best products and services will go unsold if marketers cannot communicate their value to customers. Promotion is communication by a marketer that informs, persuades, and reminds potential buyers about a product or service to influence their opinions or elicit a response. Promotion generally can enhance a product or service's value, as happened for Parasuco jeans. The company's

Parasuco is known for its provocative advertising, which appears on billboards and uses celebrities to market its denim lines.

provocative advertising has helped create an image that says more than "Use this product and you will look good." Rather, the promotion sells youth, style, and sex appeal. Social and Mobile Marketing 1.1 considers how Facebook communicates its value by encouraging networks of users and businesses beyond its site.

The four Ps work together. Although marketers deliver value through each of the four Ps individually, they can deliver greater value to consumers by treating the 4Ps as a whole rather than as separate components. That is, the product or service offered must satisfy the target customers' specific needs and wants, be priced appropriately, be available at locations where customers want it, and be promoted in a manner and through media that are consistent with the target consumers. For instance, luxury or high-fashion items from retailers such as Coach, Louis Vuitton, and Swarovski are well made, priced at a premium, available at exclusive locations, and promoted only in certain media where the advertisements emphasize style, fashion, sex appeal, and so on.

Marketing Can Be Performed by Both Individuals and Organizations

B2C (business-to-consumer)
The process in which businesses sell to consumers.

B2B (business-to-business)
The process of selling merchandise or services from one business to another.

C2C (consumer-to-consumer)
The process in which consumers sell to other consumers.

Imagine how complicated the world would be if you had to buy everything you consumed directly from producers or manufacturers. You would have to go from farm to farm buying your food and then from manufacturer to manufacturer to purchase the table, plates, and utensils you need to eat that food. Fortunately, marketing intermediaries, such as retailers, accumulate merchandise from producers in large amounts and then sell it to you in smaller amounts. The process in which businesses sell to consumers is known as **B2C (business-to-consumer)** marketing, whereas the process of selling merchandise or services from one business to another is called **B2B (business-to-business)** marketing. Some companies, such as GE (General Electric), are engaged in both B2B and B2C marketing at the same time. However, with the advent of various auction sites, such as eBay and Kijiji, and payment sites, such as PayPal, consumers have started marketing their products and services to other consumers, which requires a third category in which consumers sell to other consumers, or **C2C (consumer-to-consumer)** marketing. Individuals can also undertake activities to market themselves. When you apply for a job, for instance, the research you do about the firm, the resumé and cover

Social and Mobile Marketing 1.1

Facebook Networks the Web[12]

Facebook would love it if you checked your account daily (or even hourly). It has 1.26 billion users,[13] more than half of whom log in daily and spend an average of 55 minutes per day on the site. Canada has the most active Facebook users in the world, with 74 percent checking in daily.[14] Facebook has expanded the network in which it operates by making it easier for users to share information outside Facebook.

Social plug-ins are those "Like" buttons you see on a website that encourage a social experience outside Facebook. Social plug-ins make it easier for the user to share content from other websites with friends with a single click; if users "Like" the content, whether an article, a restaurant, or a band, this preference gets shared automatically on their Facebook newsfeed. Friends in turn can link easily to the liked site, creating benefits for both the external company and Facebook—and users. Companies thus place "Like" buttons on their web pages to drive more traffic to Facebook, and then enjoy more return traffic from Facebook to their own web pages.

Around 2.5 million websites contain "Like" buttons, and 10,000 more get added every day. And users like the "Like" button too. Only 13 percent of users ever write reviews on websites, but a much higher percentage of people are willing to click "Like." It is easy, and it gives Facebook users a simple way to communicate with friends and possibly extend their social influence.

Businesses can use Facebook users' information to target potential customers. For example, Yelp can use your preferences to give you personalized information on restaurants or music venues, because Yelp can access songs that you "like" on Pandora, and also the restaurants that you "like" on Yelp.com. Even IMBD, the comprehensive site for movie lovers, is getting in on the game, gathering Facebook users' favourite movies and television shows. By getting to know all those 1 billion users, Facebook offers incredibly relevant and increasingly useful information to advertisers—which is why its annual advertising revenues of more than $1 billion continue to grow.

letter you submit with your application, and the way you dress for an interview and conduct yourself during it are all forms of marketing activities. Accountants, lawyers, financial planners, physicians, and other professional service providers also market their services.

Regardless of whether organizations or individuals are engaged in B2B, B2C, or C2C marketing, one thing seems to be clear: **social media** is quickly becoming an integral part of their marketing and communications strategies. Social media is widely used in federal elections in Canada, as politicians try to win the hearts and minds of Canadians. Even more dramatically, social media played a major role in the crises observed in several Mideast countries. Social media was used to organize protesters and to report news of events in these countries to the rest of the world as the events unfolded in real time.

social media
The use of digital tools to easily and quickly create and share content to foster dialogue, social relationships, and personal identities.

Marketing Impacts Many Stakeholders

Most people think of marketing as a way for firms to make profits, but marketing works equally well in the nonprofit sector. Think about what influenced your selection of your college or university, other than family, friends, and convenience. It's likely that your college or university has a sophisticated marketing program to attract and retain students. Hospitals, theatres, charities, museums, religious institutions, politicians, and even governments rely on marketing to communicate their message to their constituents. As Sustainable Marketing 1.1 shows, some marketers are greening their marketing practices to communicate that they are socially responsible in their business practices.

Marketing is often designed to benefit an entire industry, which can help many firms simultaneously. The dairy industry has used a very successful, award-winning campaign with its slogan "Got Milk?" aimed at different target segments. This campaign has not only created high levels of awareness about the benefits of drinking milk, but also increased milk consumption in various target segments,[15] possibly through the use of celebrities such as Demi Lovato and athletes such as soccer superstar David Beckham. Although

The dairy industry's "Got Milk?" ad campaign created high levels of awareness about the benefits of drinking milk and has increased milk consumption by using celebrities such as David Beckham and singer/songwriter/actress Demi Lovato.

Sustainable Marketing 1.1

Green Your Marketing Practices

The idea of sustainable development, or sustainability, is popular these days among groups representing various segments of society such as the media, environmentalists, nonprofit organizations, politicians, business executives, and even consumers. But what exactly does sustainability mean, how widespread is the adoption of sustainable development practices and policies among businesses, and what are the benefits of sustainability?

You might be surprised to learn that sustainability seems to mean different things to different people. For instance, a global survey of 1,749 business executives by McKinsey & Company reported that 55 percent say that sustainability is about managing environmental issues such as greenhouse-gas emissions, energy efficiency, waste management, green-product development, and water conservation. Further, 48 percent say it is about governance issues such as complying with regulations, maintaining ethical practices, and meeting accepted industry standards; and 41 percent say it includes the management of social issues such as working conditions and labour standards.[16] In a nutshell, it seems that organizations that practise sustainability must strive to conduct their business in such a way as to minimize harm to the environment, follow good governance practices, and comply with social standards.

Indeed, a truly comprehensive and proactive approach to sustainability requires that businesses develop practices and policies around all three perspectives: environmental, governance, and social. This means that sustainability practices and policies must be embedded in all facets of the organization, from human resource management to manufacturing, marketing, production, planning, investments, and corporate strategy. Also, sustainability must involve all employees, from the CEO to the employee on the shop floor. Implementing a comprehensive sustainability program is quite expensive and so many businesses tend to do the bare minimum or implement low-cost programs. In fact, according to the McKinsey Global Survey, 36 percent of executives believe that the main benefit of sustainability is that it improves corporate and brand reputation, while less than 20 percent believe that it improves operational efficiency, lowers costs, presents growth opportunities (new markets and products), or strengthens competitive position.

As consumers have become more aware of the environmental impact of products or services they use, many companies use green marketing claims as evidence of their commitment to sustainable development. This rapid rise in claims has left some consumers wondering if they are being "greenwashed." Their skepticism may be warranted as there are no laws in Canada specifically governing green claims.[17] Throughout this book, we will present various examples of sustainable marketing efforts undertaken by Canadian companies.

---

hugely successful, the campaign has run its course and shifted to a new tagline, "Milk Life" focusing on milk as a source of protein. The new campaign continues to benefit the entire dairy industry, not just one brand.

Now that we've examined what marketing is and how it creates value, let's consider how it fits into the world of commerce, as well as into society in general.

LO3   The Four Orientations of Marketing

Marketing didn't get to its current prominence among individuals, corporations, and society at large overnight. Over the last 100 years, marketing has evolved from an activity designed simply to produce and sell products to an integral business function aimed at creating value for consumers and the company's shareholders. As we have examined marketing practices over the years, we have observed four different marketing orientations or philosophies: product orientation, sales orientation, market orientation, and value-based orientation. (see Exhibit 1.4)

Product Orientation Product-oriented companies focus on developing and distributing innovative products with little concern about whether the products best satisfy customers' needs. This philosophy is best illustrated by a famous quote made around the turn of the 20th century by Henry Ford, the founder of Ford Motor Company, who remarked, "Customers can have any colour they want so long as it's black." Manufacturers believed that a good product would sell itself, and retail stores typically were considered places to hold the merchandise until a consumer wanted it. Companies with a product orientation

EXHIBIT 1.4 | Marketing Evolution: Product, Sales, Market, and Value

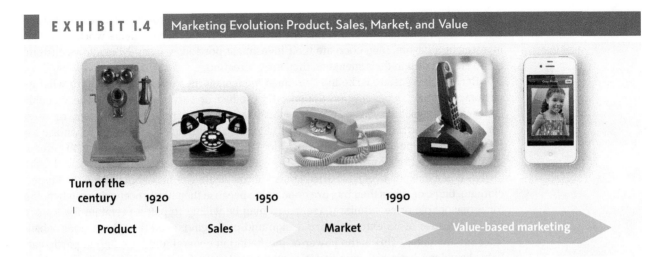

| Turn of the century | 1920 | 1950 | 1990 |
| Product | Sales | Market | Value-based marketing |

generally start out by thinking about the product they want to build; they try selling the product after it is developed rather than starting with an understanding of the customers' needs and then developing a product to satisfy those needs.

Sales Orientation Companies that have a sales orientation basically view marketing as a selling function where companies try to sell as many of their products as possible rather than focus on making products consumers really want. These firms typically depend on heavy doses of personal selling and advertising to attract new customers. Companies with a selling orientation tend to focus on making a sale or on each transaction rather than building long-term customer relationships. They generally believe that if consumers try their products, they will like them. The focus of these companies tends to be driven by the products or services they have to offer more so than on consumer needs and wants. Profits come from sales volume rather than from repeat business from satisfied customers.

Market Orientation Market-oriented companies start out by focusing on what consumers want and need before they design, make, or attempt to sell their products and services. They believe that customers have choice and make purchase decisions based on several factors, including quality, convenience, and price. Basically, the "customer is king," and the market is a buyer's market since consumers wield tremendous power. In this orientation, marketers' role is to understand and respond to the needs of consumers and to do everything possible to satisfy them. There is a focus on making marketing an integrated process throughout the entire company rather just in one department. Satisfied customers become long-term loyal customers, contributing to bottom-line profitability.

Value-based Orientation Most successful firms today are market oriented.[18] That means they have gone beyond a product or sales orientation and attempt to discover and satisfy their customers' needs and wants. Some marketing firms recognized that there was more to good marketing. To compete successfully, they would have to focus on the triple bottom line: people (consumer needs and wants), profits (long-term profitable relationships with customers and suppliers), and planet (do all this in a way that is socially and environmentally responsible.) Value-based companies provide their customers with greater value than their competitors.

Value reflects the relationship of benefits to costs, or what you *get* for what you *give*.[19] In a marketing context, customers seek a fair return in goods and/or services for their hard-earned money and scarce time. They want products or services that meet their specific needs or wants and that are offered at a price that they believe is good value. A creative

value
Reflects the relationship of benefits to costs, or what the consumer *gets* for what he or she *gives*.

way to provide value to customers is to engage in *value cocreation*.[20] In this case, customers can act as collaborators to create the product or service. When clients work with their investment advisors, they cocreate their investment portfolios; when Nike allows customers to custom design their sneakers, they are cocreating.

Every value-based marketing firm must implement its strategy according to what its customers value. Depending on the specific product or service for sale, these valuable benefits could include speed, convenience, size, accuracy, price, cost-savings, or user-friendliness. Sometimes providing greater value means providing a lot of merchandise for relatively little money, such as Subway's foot-long subs for $5 or a diamond for 40 percent off the suggested retail price at Costco. But value is in the eye of the beholder and doesn't always come inexpensively. Satisfied Louis Vuitton customers probably believe the Vuitton clothing, bags, or shoes they buy are good value because they have received many benefits for a reasonable price. Similarly, teenagers may be willing to pay a premium for Apple's iPhone because of its extraordinary design and packaging, even though cheaper substitutes are available. This is the power of marketing in general and branding in particular. Value-based marketing is examined in greater detail in the following section.

HOW DO FIRMS BECOME MORE VALUE DRIVEN?

Firms become value driven by focusing on four activities. First, they share information about their customers and competitors across their own organization and with other firms that might be involved in getting the product or service to the marketplace, such as manufacturers and transportation companies. Second, they strive to balance their customers' benefits and costs. Third, they concentrate on building relationships with customers. Fourth, they need to take advantage of new technologies and connect with their customers using social and mobile media.

Fashion designers for Zara, the Spain-based fashion retailer, collect purchase information and research customer trends to determine what their customers will want to wear in the next few weeks. They share this information with other departments to forecast sales and co-ordinate deliveries.

Sharing Information

In a value-based, market-oriented firm, marketers share information about customers and competitors that has been collected through customer relationship management, and integrate it across the firm's various departments. The fashion designers for Zara, the Spain-based fashion retailer, for instance, collect purchase information and research customer trends to determine what their customers will want to wear in the next few weeks; simultaneously, the logisticians—those persons in charge of getting the merchandise to the stores—use the same purchase history to forecast sales and allocate appropriate merchandise to individual stores. Sharing and coordinating such information represents a critical success factor for any firm. Imagine what might happen if Zara's advertising department were to plan a special promotion but not share its sales projections with those people in charge of creating the merchandise or getting it to stores.

Balancing Benefits with Costs

Value-oriented marketers constantly measure the benefits that customers perceive against the cost of their offering. In this task, they use available customer data to find opportunities in which they can better satisfy their customers' needs and in turn develop long-term loyalties. Such a value-based orientation has helped Canadian Tire and Walmart outperform other department stores, and WestJet Airlines and Southwest Airlines outperform mainstream carriers.

Until recently, it sometimes cost more to fly within Europe than to fly from the United States to Europe. But low-frills, low-cost carriers such as Ryanair and easyJet,[21] modelled on Southwest Airlines and JetBlue Airways, now offer customers what they want: cheap intra-Europe airfares. Like their American counterparts, Ryanair and easyJet offer no food service and generally fly to and from out-of-the-way airports, such as Stansted, which is about 55 kilometres northeast of London. But many customers find value despite such minor inconveniences. Consider, for example, the London to Salzburg, Austria, route for $65 or the London to Sweden flight for $70. Values such as these are also what have given low-cost carriers in the United States approximately 25 percent of the market share. They are so popular that conventional airlines have started their own low-frills/low-cost airlines: Singapore Airlines provides Tiger Airways and Australia's Qantas offers Jetstar.

To provide a great value, U.K.–based easyJet offers no food service and generally flies to and from out-of-the-way airports.

Building Relationships with Customers

During the past decade or so, marketers have begun to develop a **relational orientation** as they have realized the need to think about customers in terms of relationships rather than transactions.[22] To build relationships, firms focus on the lifetime value of the relationship, not how much money is made during each transaction. Apple ensures its new innovations are compatible with existing products to ensure consumers maintain a long-term relationship with the company across all their electronic needs.

This relationship approach uses a process known as **customer relationship management (CRM)**, a business philosophy and set of strategies, programs, and systems that focus on identifying and building loyalty among the firm's most valued customers.[23] Firms that employ CRM systematically collect information about their customers' needs and then use that information to target their best customers with the products, services, and special promotions that appear most important to them.

Connecting with Customers Using Social and Mobile Media

Marketers are steadily embracing new technologies, such as social and mobile media, to allow them to connect better with their customers and thereby serve their needs more effectively. Businesses take social and mobile media seriously, including these advanced tools in the development of their marketing strategies. Approximately three-quarters of North American companies now use social media tools for marketing purposes, and 46 percent of Internet users worldwide interact with social media on a daily basis.[24] The explosive growth of mobile phones in India and China means that more than 77 percent of the world's population subscribes to mobile services.[25]

Yet even with this astounding penetration, only 16 percent of the world's population uses Facebook. North America and United Kingdom may be approaching saturation, but there is still huge growth potential for social networks. Before users can sign up for Facebook though, they need access to high-speed Internet.[26] Other countries continue to experience higher Facebook growth rates as they gain greater Internet access and as Facebook becomes available in more languages (around 70 currently). Brazil and Russia have only about 40 percent Internet penetration, and only 33 percent of Chinese people and less than 7 percent of consumers in India have access to the Internet. Furthermore, on a worldwide basis:[27]

- Facebook has more than 1.26 billion users.
- The average Facebook user spends more than 55 minutes per day there.

relational orientation
A method of building a relationship with customers based on the philosophy that buyers and sellers should develop a long-term relationship.

customer relationship management (CRM)
A business philosophy and set of strategies, programs, and systems that focus on identifying and building loyalty among the firm's most valued customers.

Marketers connect with customers by using social and mobile media.

- The average user has 130 Facebook friends.
- 20 million Facebook users "Like" fan pages per day.
- 60 million status updates occur each day on Facebook.
- Approximately 250 million photos get uploaded to Facebook every day.
- Twitter has 646 million users, who generate an average of 58 million tweets every day.
- Twitter handles more than 2.1 billion daily search queries.
- LinkedIn has more than 277 million professional users.
- Approximately 3 million companies have LinkedIn pages.
- Over 3 billion videos are streamed every day on YouTube.
- Every minute, 100 hours' worth of video gets uploaded to YouTube.
- Foursquare, the mobile social network, hosts more than 45 million users, with 25,000 new users joining every day.
- Foursquare averages 5 billion check-ins daily; the average user checks in three to four times.
- Internet users worldwide spend more hours per week with social media than with any other online pursuit.

Beyond social media sites, online travel agencies such as Expedia, Travelocity, and Priceline have become the first place that users go to book travel arrangements: 46 percent of online hotel bookings take place through one of these portals.[28] Customers who book hotels using travel agencies become loyal to the agency that gives them the lowest prices, rather than to any particular hotel brand. So hotels are using social media and mobile applications to lure customers back to their specific brands by engaging in conversations with them and allowing fans of the page to book their hotel reservations through Facebook. Some hotel chains have mobile applications that allow customers to make changes to their reservations, shift check-in and check-out times, and add amenities or services to their stays. The hotels know a lot about their customers, because they collect information about their previous visits, including the type of room they stayed in, their preferences (from pillows to drinks consumed from the minibar), and the type of room service they prefer.

Several restaurant chains are exploiting location-based social media applications, such as Foursquare, Urbanspoon, Foodspotting, and Facebook Places. These customers tend to be more loyal and can help spread the word to others about the restaurant.[29] Using location-based applications on mobile phones, restaurants connect with their customers immediately; customers using these apps visit restaurants nearly twice as often as those who don't. The result is that users are driving the way brands and stores are interacting with social media.

LO4 WHY IS MARKETING IMPORTANT?

Marketing was once only an afterthought to production. Early marketing philosophy went something like this: "We've made it; now how do we get rid of it?" Today, marketing has evolved into a major business function that crosses all areas of a firm or organization, as illustrated in Exhibit 1.5. Marketing advises production about how much of the company's product to make and then tells logistics when to ship it. It creates mutually valuable relationships between the company and the firms from which it buys. It identifies those elements that local customers value and makes it possible for the firm to expand globally. Marketing has had a significant impact on consumers as well. Without marketing, it would be difficult for any of us to learn about new products and services. Understanding marketing can even help you find a job after you graduate.

EXHIBIT 1.5 Importance of Marketing

Expands Global Presence

Can Be Entrepreneurial

Pervasive Across Organization

Importance of Marketing

Enriches Society

Makes Life Easier

Pervasive Across Supply Chain

Marketing Expands Firms' Global Presence

A generation ago, Coca-Cola was available in many nations, but Levi's and most other American and Canadian brands were not. But today most jeans, including those by Levi Strauss & Co. and Parasuco, are made in places other than Canada and the United States and are available nearly everywhere. Thanks to MTV and other global entertainment venues, cheap foreign travel, and the Internet, you share many of your consumption behaviours with college and university students in countries all over the globe. The best fashions, music, and even food trends disseminate rapidly around the world.

Take a look at your next shopping bag. Whether it contains groceries or apparel, you will

Levi Strauss & Co. helps retailers manage their inventory so they don't run out of stock.

Starbucks has adjusted its menu to meet customer wants in the Japanese market more effectively.

find goods from many countries: produce from Mexico, jeans from Italy, T-shirts from China. Global manufacturers and retailers continue to make inroads into the Canadian market. Companies such as Honda, Sony, and Heineken sell as well in Canada as they do in their home countries. Sweden's fashion retailer H&M operates in 38 countries, including Canada.[30] Its upscale competitor, Spain's Zara, operates in more than 80 countries, including Canada.[31] Starbucks even adjusted its menu to meet customer wants in the Japanese market more effectively. How does marketing contribute to a company's successful global expansion? Understanding customers is critical. Without the knowledge that can be gained by analyzing new customers' needs and wants on a segment-by-segment, region-by-region basis—one of marketing's main tasks—it would be difficult for a firm to expand globally.

Marketing Is Pervasive Across Marketing Channel Members

Firms typically do not work in isolation. Manufacturers buy raw materials and components from suppliers, which they sell to retailers or other businesses after they have turned the materials into their products (see Exhibit 1.6). Every time materials or products are bought or sold, they are transported to a different location, which sometimes requires that they be stored in a warehouse operated by yet another organization. The group of firms and set of techniques and approaches firms use to make and deliver a given set of goods and services is commonly referred to as a **supply chain**. Excellent supply chains effectively and efficiently integrate their supply chain partners—suppliers, manufacturers, warehouses, stores, and transportation intermediaries—to produce and distribute goods in the right quantities, to the right locations, and at the right time. Supply chain management is discussed in detail in Chapter 12; but, for now, let's consider the value of the supply chain in marketing.

Consider Loblaw, Canada's largest food distributor, and its relationships with its manufacturers and trading partners. A few years ago, Loblaw's supply chain system suffered from several inefficiencies that drove up its costs substantially.[32] For example, inaccurate demand forecasts led trading partners to stock huge inventory to meet unpredictable demand. Inefficient use of customer data meant that stock replenishment was made by estimation rather than true customer data. Disconnected supply

supply chain
The group of firms and set of techniques and approaches firms use to make and deliver a given set of goods and services.

EXHIBIT 1.6   Supply Chain

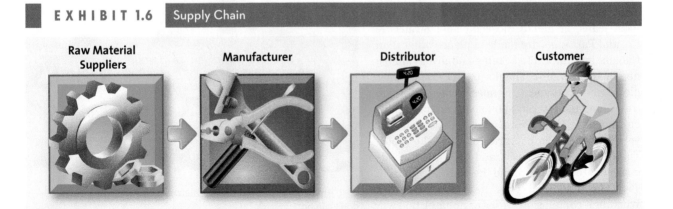

Raw Material Suppliers → Manufacturer → Distributor → Customer

chain systems, limited collaboration, reduced information sharing, and supply variability led to poor quality information on which to base sales forecasts, production plans, and replenishment schemes. The company has since made many changes to improve the efficiency of its supply chain. Loblaw's participation in a radio frequency identification (RFID) pilot project for the grocery industry conducted by the Canadian RFID Centre has helped it improve its operations. Preliminary results seem to indicate that Loblaw has improved its inventory management and use of promotions.

Marketing Enriches Society

Should marketing focus on factors other than financial profitability, such as good corporate citizenry? Many of Canada's best-known corporations seem to think so, because they encourage their employees to participate in activities that benefit their communities and invest heavily in socially responsible actions and charities. For example, HP Canada donated equipment packages to two First Nations communities as part of a pilot project to increase the literacy and technology skills of local youths. More than 700 at-risk youths in these communities will now have access to leading-edge technology. According to the president of the RCMP Foundation, HP's gift will aid its efforts to divert youths toward positive activities and away from the negative choices of drinking alcohol, doing drugs, participating in violence, and dropping out of school.[33] Canadian companies recognize that a strong social orientation is in both their and their customers' best interest. It shows the consumer that the firm can be trusted with their business. Also, investors view firms that operate with high levels of corporate responsibility and ethics as safe investments. Similarly, firms have come to realize that good corporate citizenship through socially responsible actions should be a priority because it will help their bottom line in the long run.[34] In a world in which consumers constantly hear about negative examples of ethics, the need for companies to live up to their ethical promises becomes even more important. Ethical Dilemma 1.1 outlines the challenges companies face when they attempt to go green.

Ron Joyce cofounded the Tim Hortons donut chain and was the first franchisee.

Marketing Can Be Entrepreneurial

Whereas marketing plays a major role in the success of large corporations, it also is at the centre of the successes of numerous new ventures initiated by entrepreneurs, or people who organize, operate, and assume the risk of a business venture.[35] Key to the success of many such entrepreneurs is that they launch ventures that aim to satisfy unfilled needs. Some examples of successful ventures (and their founders) that understood their customers and added value include:

● Tim Hortons (Ron Joyce)
● lululemon (Chip Wilson)

Ron Joyce is best known for partnering with hockey legend Tim Horton to cofound the Canadian coffee chain Tim Hortons. Joyce met Horton while walking the beat as an officer with the Hamilton Police Force. The first shop opened in 1964 and served only coffee and doughnuts.[36] From humble beginnings, that first store in Hamilton became the launch pad for future growth. As the first franchisee, Joyce quickly set up three locations. By 1974, the chain had grown to 40 stores. When Tim Horton was killed in a car accident, Joyce bought his shares. He has won numerous awards and honorary degrees, and in 1999 was

When you think of lululemon, you probably think of Chip (Dennis) Wilson, who founded the athletic apparel retailer.

Ethical Dilemma 1.1   **Going Green**

The Ben & Jerry's ice cream brand was built on more than fabulous flavours. With every double scoop of Chunky Monkey, owners Ben Cohen and Jerry Greenfield invited customers to help make the world better. They donated 7.5 percent of profits to charity, paid employees a living wage and good benefits, and bought their Brazil nuts from a co-operative of indigenous Amazon farmers.[37] Combining a delicious ice cream with this socially responsible focus on the "triple bottom line" of profits, people, and planet appealed to consumers and investors alike.

It also drew suitors. In 2000, the corporate giant Unilever purchased Ben & Jerry's at a price that Cohen and Greenfield could not refuse. Doing so would have deprived their shareholders of a fair profit. Facing questions about whether the ice cream company's social responsibility mission would survive, Unilever took steps to preserve some of the promises and features of the original brand. Although it was forced to drop the "all-natural" label from packaging and began using processed ingredients, like partially hydrogenated soybean oil, it has attempted to shift its procurement practices to fair-trade sources. Charitable donations from its foundation total $1.8 million annually. These activities continue because the corporation views them as good business practices.

Procter & Gamble (P&G) has staked its claim and commitment to environmental sustainability and social responsibility by retooling its business practices. While some companies use the Green Seal® stamp to certify that their manufacturing processes meet environmental standards, P&G's Professional Green Guarantee is a company-specific promise that all its products, packaging, and operations are environmentally and humanly safe.[38] In a recent sustainability overview, P&G stated that its goal was "to touch and improve lives, now and for generations to come."[39] It has enlisted both suppliers and social responsibility experts in pursuit of those goals. Its first annual Supplier Environmental Scorecard rated the 310 suppliers that agreed to participate, according to their emissions and resource consumption.[40] Thus far, P&G's self-set goals appear within reach: it has reduced its nonrenewable energy consumption by 16 percent, cut landfill-bound waste by 57 percent, decreased carbon emissions by 12 percent, and lowered water consumption by 22 percent.

These firms recognize the benefit of becoming more ethically and socially responsible, and their activities resonate with their customers. Why don't all firms make enriching society a core value and major activity?

inducted into the Canadian Business Hall of Fame and named Entrepreneur of the Year for Ontario and Canada.[41]

Another extraordinary entrepreneur and marketer is Chip (Dennis) Wilson. A self-made billionaire, Wilson got his start in the surf, skate, and snowboard industry. After trying his first yoga class, his discontent with the cotton clothing available provided him with the opportunity to indulge his passion in athletic fabrics. He opened his first lululemon store in Kitslano, British Columbia, in 2000 and took the company public in 2007.[42] Today the company has a market capitalization of almost $11.4 billion[43] and has stores or showrooms in Canada, the United States, the United Kingdom, Australia, China, Germany, Holland, New Zealand, and Singapore.[44]

Great and distinguished entrepreneurs have a vision of how certain combinations of products and services can satisfy unfilled needs. They find and understand a marketing opportunity (i.e., the unfilled need), conduct a thorough examination of the marketplace, and develop and communicate the value of their products and services to potential consumers.

Entrepreneurial Marketing 1.1

Welcome to the *Dragons' Den*

Although large companies such as Tim Hortons and lululemon often dominate media stories, a CIBC study indicates that over half a million people launched new businesses in 2012.[45] So it's not surprising that many Canadians regularly watch CBC's popular reality show, *Dragons' Den*. While the concept originated in Japan, versions of the show are broadcast all over the world.

Dragons' Den has been on the air in Canada since 2006. Each new season features aspiring entrepreneurs looking to secure funding for their business concepts. Not all succeed. Entrepreneurs in their own right, the Dragons need to be ruthless when investing their money. Companies that get a nod from Dragons benefit from both a cash and knowledge infusion.

The most recent Dragons include successful entrepreneurs Jim Treliving of Boston Pizza International, Arlene Dickinson of Venture Communications, restaurant magnate and celebrity chef Vikram Vij (Vij's, Rangoli, My Shanti), Michael Wekerle from merchant bank Difference Capital, and David Chilton of The Wealthy Barber fame. While each Dragon is newsworthy as a result of successful business ventures, the show's popularity has made each one a household name. The show has not only attracted millions of viewers, but also propelled many of the small businesses featured to higher levels.

Throughout this textbook we will feature *Dragons' Den* stories to illustrate a variety of marketing concepts and to highlight the importance of entrepreneurial pursuits in Canada today. And since not all companies win the hearts of the Dragons, we will also include a discussion of some of those stories.

LEARNING OBJECTIVES REVIEW

LO1 Define the role of marketing and explain its core concepts

In definition form, "marketing is a set of business practices designed to plan for and present an organization's products or services in ways that build effective customer relationships." Marketing strives to *create value* in many ways. If marketers are to succeed, their customers must believe that the firm's products and services are valuable; that is, the products and services are worth more to the customers than they cost.

Marketers also enhance the value of products and services through various forms of *communication*, such as advertising and personal selling. Through communications, marketers educate and inform customers about the benefits of their products and services and thereby increase their perceived value.

Marketers facilitate the *delivery of value* by ensuring the right products and services are available when, where, and in the quantities their customers want. Better marketers are not concerned about just one transaction with their customers; they recognize the value of loyal customers and strive to develop *long-term relationships* with them.

LO2 Describe how marketers create value for a product or service

Value represents the relationship of benefits to costs. Firms can improve their value by increasing benefits, reducing costs, or both. The best firms integrate a value orientation into everything they do. If a move doesn't increase benefits or reduce costs, it probably shouldn't occur.

Firms become value driven by finding out as much as they can about their customers and those customers' needs and wants. They share this information with their partners, both up and down the supply chain, so the entire chain collectively can focus on the customer. The key to true value-based marketing is the ability to design products and services that achieve the right balance between benefits and costs—not too little, not too much.

Value-based marketers aren't necessarily worried about how much money they will make on the next sale. Instead, they are concerned with developing a lasting relationship with their customers so those customers return again and again.

LO3 Summarize the four orientations of marketing

Firms that are *product oriented* tend to believe that a good product will sell itself. Manufacturers are concerned with product innovation, not with satisfying the needs of individual consumers, and keep producing with the assumption that people will buy it. Marketing with this orientation is simply about informing the customer that a product exists, whether it is used at all.

In the case of a *sales orientation*, firms rely on a sales team to sell. Production is maximized and then heavy doses of personal selling and advertising help distribute and sell the product. The role of marketing is focused only on the sale of products.

If a firm is *market oriented*, it celebrates the customer. Here the customer can decide what is best for him or her, based on the attributes of a product or service. Rather than simply produce and sell, manufacturers with this orientation seek to learn customer needs and wants, and design products to fit the customers. Marketing plays an important role to communicate the different attributes, or value, created by each product.

Most successful firms today have transcended other views and instead support a *value-based orientation*. In addition to discovering needs and wants, it is critical to deliver more value to customers than competitors. Value reflects the relationship of benefits to costs, or what you get for what you give. Marketing plays an integral role not only in creating and delivering that valuable product, but also in communicating the value, especially in relation to other products available, and transacting the value through to customers.

L04 **Understand the importance of marketing both within and outside the firm**

Successful firms integrate marketing throughout their organizations so that marketing activities coordinate with other functional areas, such as product design, production, logistics, and human resources, enabling them to get the right product to the right customers at the right time. Marketing helps facilitate the smooth flow of goods through the supply chain, all the way from raw materials to the consumer. From a personal perspective, the marketing function facilitates your buying process, and can support your career goals.

Marketing also can be important for society through its embrace of solid, ethical business practices. Firms "do the right thing" when they sponsor charitable events, seek to reduce environmental impacts, and avoid unethical practices. Such efforts endear the firm to customers. Finally, marketing is a cornerstone of entrepreneurialism. Many great companies been founded by outstanding marketers, and an entrepreneurial spirit pervades the marketing decisions of firms of all sizes.

KEY TERMS

- B2B (business-to-business)
- B2C (business-to-consumer)
- C2C (consumer-to-consumer)
- customer relationship management (CRM)
- exchange
- goods
- ideas

- market
- marketing
- marketing mix (four Ps)
- marketing plan
- need
- price
- relational orientation

- services
- social media
- supply chain
- target market
- value
- value cocreation
- want

CONCEPT REVIEW

1. What is marketing and why is it important?

2. Is the marketing mix (the four Ps) enough to guarantee successful marketing? Explain.

3. Explain how a strike at one of a company's supplier firms or a new technology would influence the company's marketing efforts.

4. Discuss the main elements of value-based marketing. List four ways in which marketing helps to create value.

5. Explain the relationship between customer value and customer satisfaction.

6. Generally, all companies are in business to generate profits and increase shareholder value. Yet, the Canadian Marketing Association's definition of marketing does not explicitly mention profits or shareholder value. Why do you think these are not included in the definition? Should they be included?

7. Today, many marketers are not interested in selling their products and services to everyone who wants them; instead, they want to sell them only to selected target markets. What do you think the main reasons are for targeting specific market segments?

8. Give reasons that you think understanding customer needs and wants is fundamental to marketing success. How can marketers go about understanding customer needs and wants?

9. Which marketing orientation would most likely help a company build strong customer relationships that are profitable? Why?

10. Explain how customer value is created or increased when the company's marketing department works closely with other departments within the firm as well as with the firm's suppliers and customers.

MARKETING APPLICATIONS

1. When apparel manufacturers develop their marketing strategies, do they concentrate on satisfying their customers' needs or wants? What about a utility company? A cellphone company?

2. Choose a product that you use every day. Describe its four Ps.

3. One of your friends was recently watching TV and saw an advertisement that she liked. She said, "Wow, that was great marketing!" Was the ad in fact marketing? Why?

4. Mercedes-Benz manufactures the Smart Car, which sells for around $16,000, and the SL 65 AMG 2-door Roadster for over $100,000. Is Mercedes providing the target markets for these cars with a good value? Explain why.

5. Assume you have been hired by the marketing department of a major consumer products manufacturer such as Colgate-Palmolive. You are having lunch with some new colleagues in the finance, manufacturing, and logistics departments. They are arguing that the company could save millions of dollars if it just got rid of the marketing department. Develop an argument that would persuade them otherwise.

6. Why do marketers find it important to embrace societal needs and ethical business practices? Provide an example of a societal need or ethical business practice being addressed by a specific marketer.

7. Visit the website of Rogers Communications (www.rogers.com) and compare the four Ps marketing mix for the BlackBerry Q10 and the Apple iPhone 5. What factors might explain the differences you observe?

8. For many consumers, the difference between Dasani water made by Coca-Cola (www.dasani.com) and Aquafina water made by Pepsi (www.aquafina.com) is hardly noticeable. However, both companies and their loyal customers would argue that there are many differences between these two brands of water. What is your view? Explain how customer perceptions and emotions may influence the way they value a company's product.

9. As described in this chapter, customer relationship management is a very important aspect of value-based marketing. Pick any one of Canada's major retailers, e.g., The Bay (www.hbc.com), Loblaw (www.loblaws.ca), or Shoppers Drug Mart (www.shoppersdrugmart.ca), and explain how it goes about building strong customer relationships with its customers.

10. When first introduced, BlackBerry's PlayBook was seen as a competitor to Apple's iPad. Visit Apple's website (www.apple.com) and the BlackBerry website (www.blackberry.com) to learn more about these two products. What do you think the main value proposition is for each product? Why do you think the iPad has come out as the winner?

NET SAVVY

1. Happy Planet (www.happyplanet.com), a Vancouver-based organic juice producer, is an emerging player in the organic beverage market. It supplies all of Canada and some of the United States with organic juice. Visit its website and describe how the company delivers value above and beyond that provided by traditional grocery retailers. Describe the ways in which the company communicates this value through its website.

2. Montréal Biodôme (http://www2.ville.montreal.qc.ca/biodome) has developed an excellent reputation in international scientific and cultural circles for the diversity of its collection. Visit its website and describe the ways in which it creates value for patrons. What else could Montréal Biodôme do to offer even more value to its patrons?

CHAPTER CASE STUDY

LULULEMON: REVOLUTIONIZING THE GLOBAL ATHLETICS AND SPORTS APPAREL INDUSTRY[46]

In 1998, Chip Wilson, the creative mind behind the lululemon athletica brand, started his yoga-inspired athletic apparel manufacturing and retailing business in Kitsilano, a trendy Vancouver neighbourhood. His original goal was to have one store in Kitsilano, and never grow beyond that. But within a few years, lululemon was transformed into a global brand and a great Canadian success story in the athletic and sportswear industry.

lululemon has experienced exponential growth since its creation in 1998. By the end of 2013, it had expanded around the world to 254 stores, all of which are company owned. The company has stores in Canada, the United States, Australia, and New Zealand.[47] In addition, seven stores are branded ivivva athletica, which specialize in dance-inspired apparel for female youths.

lululemon's revenue also grew exponentially, from $40.7 million in 2004 to $1.6 billion in 2014.[48] The company's earnings are reported in U.S. dollars, therefore, a strong Canadian dollar works in the firm's favour for its U.S. sales. The company's workforce increased by more than 287 percent between 2007 and 2013, from around 1,650 employees in January 2007 to 6,383 employees in January 2013.[49]

lululemon retail stores are primarily at street locations, in lifestyle centres, and in malls next to premium retailers such as Banana Republic, Lacoste, Cartier, Gucci, and Whole Foods Market. Its top selling store in West Edmonton Mall in Edmonton, Alberta, generates about $26 million in sales. At $8,125 per square foot each year, its sales outstrip other retailers such as Apple and Tiffany.[50] In addition to company-owned stores, lululemon also sells directly to consumers through its e-commerce website, which was launched in 2009, and through wholesalers: premium yoga studios, health clubs, and fitness centres. Sales through its e-commerce website accounted for 16 percent of revenues in 2012. The e-commerce site is designed to enhance the company's brand image and make its products accessible in more markets beyond physical stores. lululemon's premium wholesalers offer an alternative distribution channel for some core customers. Strategically, the wholesale channel was never meant to be a big contributor to overall sales (actual contribution is about 2 percent annually) but, like the company's e-commerce site, this channel was designed to build brand awareness, especially in new markets, including those outside of North America.

The market for athletic apparel is highly competitive. Competitors include established companies that are expanding their production and marketing of performance products, as well as frequent new entrants to the market. lululemon competes directly with wholesalers and retailers of athletic apparel such as Nike, Adidas, Reebok, Under Armour, and even Walmart. It also competes with retailers that focus specifically on women's athletic apparel, including lucy activewear, The Gap's Athleta collection, and bebe's Sport collection.

The athletic apparel industry mainly competes on the basis of brand image and recognition, product quality, innovation, style, distribution, and price. From its very beginning, lululemon's approach to sports clothing was different from the industry standard. When global brands in the 1990s focused primarily on men and made only minor changes to the men's lines to create women's clothing, lululemon developed sport clothing specifically for women. Similarly, when sports clothing was designed primarily for comfort and functionality, lululemon offered customers not only comfortable and functional clothing, but also fashionable clothing made of breathable fabric. lululemon offered products that capitalized on the growing trends of female participation in sports, specifically yoga, and the demand for clothing made from sustainable materials. lululemon successfully competed on the basis of its premium brand image, its focus on women, and its technical product innovation. Its vertical retail distribution strategy also differentiates it from competitors and enables the company to more effectively control its brand image.

So far, lululemon has successfully stolen market share from established global companies that have dominated the market for years. It has become a major force within the industry even though its line of sportswear goods and accessories are not cheap relative to the competition. If you want a pair of lululemon pants, prepare to fork over about $100 and another $50 for a top. By any metric, lululemon's success on the international stage within such a short period of time is phenomenal, especially since many excellent Canadian companies have failed in the United States and other global markets.

lululemon's marketing activities are designed to create brand awareness primarily through word of mouth from customers and community ambassadors: yoga instructors, personal trainers, or up-and-coming athletes from the local community endorse its products. These ambassadors wear lululemon merchandise and their photographs are usually displayed in stores so customers can see them. The company also uses these professionals to gain insights and feedback on designs and other aspects of its products. Rarely, if ever, does lululemon follow the lead of competing brands, such as Nike or Adidas, and use expensive celebrity endorsements. lululemon does however use hard-hitting, even controversial, promotional events, such as when it opened its Kingston, Ontario, store, where it offered free clothing to the first 30 customers who entered the store naked or topless.[51] It also relies on local and national media for free publicity of its events, merchandise, and company story.

In addition to its unique marketing campaigns, lululemon takes great care in choosing where to establish its stores and whom to partner with. Its understanding of the culture of new markets and the manner in which it enters those markets and connects with customers are also important elements of its strategy. lululemon "eyes global markets but seeks local advice"[52] that is, it works closely with its customers—yogis and athletes in local communities—for continuous research and product feedback. These customers help lululemon set the standard in technical fabrics and functional designs. It has cultivated strong relationships with the local communities where it operates. For example, it encourages interactions with local communities at its regular meetings with local designers. It has developed a strong local organization by partnering with local companies. For example, originally most of its Australian stores were franchised, although the company has increased its equity interest in its Australian joint venture partner, New Harbour Yoga Pty, from 13 percent to 80.3 percent. The increased ownership is widely viewed as providing the foundation for lululemon's expansion in the Australian market and to test its ability to support strategic international expansion over the longer term.

In terms of its sourcing strategy, lululemon does not own or operate manufacturing facilities, nor does it contract directly with third-party vendors for fabrics and finished goods. The fabric used in its products is sourced by its manufacturers from a limited number of preapproved suppliers. The company works with a group of approximately 50 manufacturers, 5 of which produced approximately 60 percent of its products. No single manufacturer produced more than 25 percent of the products. Approximately 54 percent of its products are produced in Southeast Asia, 34 percent in China, 3 percent in North America, and the remaining 9 percent in Israel, Peru, Egypt, and others. North American manufacturers provide the company with the speed-to-market necessary to respond quickly to changing trends and increased demand. Distribution of finished products in North America is done centrally from distribution facilities in Vancouver, British Columbia, and Sumner, Washington. Merchandise is typically shipped to stores through third-party delivery services multiple times per week, providing a steady flow of new inventory.

Customers are individuals who work, play, and share lululemon's vision of creating healthier, happier, and more fun lives!

Despite its excellent growth record and strong brand image, things have not always gone smoothly for lululemon. For example, in 2007, *The New York Times* reported that the alleged beneficial health claims by lululemon regarding the therapeutic benefits of its VitaSea line were untrue based on independent tests. The firm's customers were angry, and some even threatened lawsuits against the company for making false claims. lululemon responded with independent laboratory testing that substantiated its claims; however, later, the Competition Bureau of Canada required the firm to remove all related claims from its products. Then, in 2008, lululemon closed its operations in Japan because of weakness in that market. In 2009, it faced two high-profile classaction lawsuits from employees in the United States. Three former hourly company employees alleged that lululemon violated various California Labor Code sections by requiring employees to wear lululemon clothing during working hours without reimbursing them for the cost of the clothing and by paying certain bonus payments in the form of lululemon gift cards redeemable only for lululemon merchandise. In another case, a former hourly company employee filed a class action lawsuit and alleged that lululemon violated various California Labor Code sections by failing to pay employees for certain rest and meal breaks and "off the clock" work. lululemon settled both cases.

Looking ahead, challenges faced by lululemon's CEO Laurent Potdevin and the company's management team include decisions about how many stores and showrooms to open, the balance between online and retail selling, and the best strategy for growth abroad. With a long-term goal of expanding the firm's global footprint, senior executives must decide whether to grow by opening company-owned stores or franchises, or by acquiring or partnering with foreign firms through joint ventures. Senior executives know that partnering with companies with significant experience and proven success in the target country is to their advantage. However, they also realize that they may have to give up some control if they pursue the partnership route. In terms of revenue growth, lululemon's senior executives believe that the first priority remains growing existing stores, the second priority is e-commerce, and the third priority is new store openings, especially outside North America.

Questions

1. What factors do you think are responsible for the phenomenal success of lululemon? Are the reasons for its success sustainable over the next decade?

2. Why do you think that the fallout from *The New York Times* story regarding lululemon's misleading claims was short lived?

3. As stated at the end of the case, management is faced with two major decisions regarding the future of lululemon. One decision pertains to the mode of entry into new global markets (i.e., establishing company-owned stores or joint ventures). The second decision concerns where to focus its efforts for revenue growth (i.e., first at existing stores, then at e-commerce, and then at new stores). Discuss the advantages and disadvantages of the various options. What course of action would you recommend?

CHAPTER **2**

NOT WITHOUT A FIGHT

Developing Marketing Strategies and a Marketing Plan

In athletic competitions, the goal is clear: Win! For companies that design, produce, and sell athletic equipment to help runners, players, and competitors achieve their best performance, the idea of victory is similar. However, the competition that takes place between companies aiming to appeal to their valuable customers—whoever they are—is a little more complicated than who crosses a finish line first.

When it comes to Nike and adidas, for example, the competitive contest spans a wealth of product lines, target markets, and marketing approaches. Thus, the firms must carefully and precisely determine the marketing strategies and plans that they use to appeal to customers and ensure their survival and success.

Created by runners in Oregon, Nike began in the early 1970s as an American company, focused mainly on the American market.[1] Its first running shoes featured a then-innovative design with a waffle-patterned sole. The customers were mainly elite runners, determined to find the lightest shoe they could. But as Forrest Gump recounted, running also was gaining popularity among casual athletes, and just like Forrest, many members of this community wore Nikes.

By 1984, the company had gone public and found Michael Jordan. The entire market—and the very concept of sponsorship—changed forever. The Air Jordan line of basketball shoes turned Nike into a massive success, with broad appeal to sports fans of virtually all ages. Nike continues to affiliate with high-profile, elite basketball players, including 48 NBA All-Stars, such as Dwayne Wade, Kobe Bryant, and LeBron James.[2]

Basketball shoes may be the most well known site for the brand's famous swoosh logo, but Nike also has branched into other related sectors. For example, it owns Cole-Haan, which makes dress and casual street shoes.[3] It produces other components of athletic uniforms for both professionals (e.g., team jerseys) and casual buyers (e.g., tracksuits, gym bags). It also purchased Umbro, another sports brand that has appealed mainly to soccer enthusiasts in the past.

This purchase of Umbro suggests that Nike is taking on its main competitor, adidas, directly in a market that previously had been dominated by adidas. As a

adidas spokesperson and NBA star Dwight Howard at an adidas Crazy Light Challenge event in Tokyo, Japan.

European company, started in Germany in the early 20th century, adidas began by designing mainly soccer (or in Europe, football) shoes, as well as some track and field footwear.

Today it has spread into other sports, though its focus on international sponsorships of the Olympic Games and the World Cup continues to reflect its origins. It also seems determined to challenge Nike's dominance on the basketball court. With young stars such as Derrick Rose and Dwight Howard as spokespeople, adidas has initiated an advertising offensive, mocking Nike's shoes as heavier, less technologically advanced, and bland.[4] It also purchased a third competitor in the market, Reebok, in 2005, in a clear effort to gain U.S. market share.

Although their primary markets continue to differ, Nike and adidas are involved in a turf war in more and more segments. Faced with the resulting challenges, they have struggled to enhance their reputations for innovation, while also keeping their costs low. For example, Nike introduced its iPod-focused partnership with Apple. With the Nike+ sensor inserted in their shoes, runners can program their iPods to play a collection of songs that matches their distance or time goals.[5] The sensor also keeps track of their speed and distance, and Nike saves the data and provides platforms for social interactions among runners in the same area. Not to be outdone, adidas has moved to introduce the micro-A smart shoe, whose sensors determine the athlete's performance, together with the environmental conditions, then adjust the cushioning and airflow in the shoe to match the conditions.

To produce these high-tech versions of their footwear, both companies outsource production to countries other than their home base.[6] Nike suffered a major public relations scandal in the 1990s when activists uncovered human rights abuses in some Nike factories. Since then, the company has worked actively to improve its reputation, led the way in mandating regulations for overseas factories, and donated heavily to philanthropic causes. Although its move to international production is more recent, adidas regards its presence in less developed areas as an inroad to consumers in these markets; its sponsorship of the Beijing Olympics also represented its strong push for dominance in China.

Nike maintains a strong lead in this race: It commands approximately 33 percent of the worldwide market, whereas adidas owns only 22 percent.[7] A count in recent Olympic track and field trials showed that Nike was sponsoring nearly 60 percent of the U.S. athletes present, while adidas shoes appeared on less than 13 percent of these elite feet.[8] But this competition is less a 100 metre dash than a marathon. When it comes to their race for market share, Nike and adidas have miles to go, and a strong competitor is always in their sights. ▮

In this chapter, we start by discussing marketing strategy, which outlines the specific actions a firm intends to implement to appeal to potential customers. Then we discuss how to create a marketing plan, which provides a blueprint for implementing the strategy. The chapter concludes with a discussion of strategies firms use to grow. Appendix 2A explains how to write a marketing plan and provides an annotated example.

WHAT IS A MARKETING STRATEGY?

LO1

A **marketing strategy** identifies (1) a firm's target market(s), (2) a related marketing mix—the four Ps, and (3) the bases upon which the firm plans to build a sustainable competitive advantage. A **sustainable competitive advantage** is an advantage over the competition that is not easily copied and thus can be maintained over a long period of time. A competitive advantage acts like a wall that the firm has built around its position in a market. This wall makes it hard for competitors to contact customers inside. Of course, if the marketer has built a wall around an attractive target market, competitors will attempt to break down this wall. As discussed in Entrepreneurial Marketing 2.1, having a sustainable competitive advantage is equally important to investors.

For Nike, its thickest wall is its strong brand, based on years of technological breakthroughs. This has created a strong customer base of loyal patrons who know the Nike swoosh well and consider the brand as a first option when they need running, basketball, or even just casual athletic shoes. Over time, all advantages can be eroded by competitive forces but, by building high, thick walls, firms can sustain their advantage, minimize competitive pressure, and boost profits for a longer time. Thus, establishing a sustainable competitive advantage is key to long-term financial performance.[9]

Likewise, Starbucks and Tim Hortons have built walls that appeal to different target markets. And so they implement their marketing mixes—the four Ps—in different ways, with very different marketing strategies. Although both stores' customers seek a good cup of coffee and a tasty pastry, Starbucks attempts to reach customers who want a coffee-drinking experience that includes a warm, social atmosphere and personable baristas to make their esoteric drinks. And people are willing to pay relatively high prices for this. Tim Hortons customers, on the other hand, aren't particularly interested in having an experience. They just want a good-tasting cup of coffee at a fair price, and to get in and out of the store quickly.

There are four overarching strategies that focus on aspects of the marketing mix to create and deliver value and to develop sustainable competitive advantages, as we depict in Exhibit 2.1:[10]

- **Customer excellence**: Focuses on retaining loyal customers and excellent customer service.
- **Operational excellence**: Achieved through efficient operations and excellent supply chain and human resource management.
- **Product excellence**: Having products with high perceived value and effective branding and positioning.
- **Locational excellence**: Having a good physical location and Internet presence.

Customer Excellence

Customer excellence is achieved when a firm develops value-based strategies for retaining loyal customers and provides outstanding customer service.

Retaining Loyal Customers   Sometimes, the methods a firm uses to maintain a sustainable competitive advantage help attract and maintain loyal customers. For instance, having a strong brand, unique merchandise, and superior customer service all help solidify a loyal customer base. But in addition, having loyal customers is, in and of itself, an important method of sustaining an advantage over competitors.

marketing strategy
Identifies a firm's target market(s), a related marketing mix—the four Ps, and the bases upon which the firm plans to build a sustainable competitive advantage.

sustainable competitive advantage
Something the firm can persistently do better than its competitors that is not easily copied and thus can be maintained over a long period of time.

customer excellence
Involves a focus on retaining loyal customers and excellent customer service.

operational excellence
Involves a focus on efficient operations and excellent supply chain management.

product excellence
Involves a focus on achieving high-quality products and effective branding and positioning.

locational excellence
Involves a focus on a good physical location and Internet presence.

Entrepreneurial Marketing 2.1   Beauty Experience in a Box

Jennifer Ruparell's marketing strategy revolves around the concept of a "beauty experience in a box."[11] Her online company, BeautyGram, is based in Calgary and offers consumers a beautifully packaged alternative to sending flowers or a standard gift basket. Trained as an aesthetician, Jennifer was a beauty junkie who took inspiration from her customers, who told her they wished they got gifts they were more excited about.[12]

And so she created a company to provide women with decadent beauty products that would stimulate the senses. Customers can choose from six different themed beauty grams including ones for best friend, bride, and baby. There is also an option to design your own BeautyGram to pamper women with items such as cosmetics, jewellery, clothing, and chocolates. Prices range from $30 to $250. If you live in the Calgary area, your gift will be delivered to the lucky recipient in a bright pink BeautyGram smart car. The company also ships within Canada and the United States.

Jennifer developed her marketing plan and launched the company in the fall of 2011. Although she spent little money on marketing, she realized sales of just over $50,000 in her first year. On track to triple that revenue in her second year, she was ready to pitch her concept on CBC's *Dragons' Den*, hoping to secure an investment of $100,000 for a 30 percent share of her company.

BeautyGrams are carefully packaged in bright pink boxes and delivered in smart cars in the Calgary area.

With profit margins of between 30–50 percent and a solid base of repeat customers, she felt she was on track to quickly grow sales and negotiate even better margins with her suppliers.

The Dragons were harder to convince than her customers. Kevin O'Leary argued that it was an interesting idea but that there was a lot of competition for gift baskets and that it would be very difficult to keep competition from copying her concept. Arlene Dickinson noted that BeautyGrams sent to offices would not likely be delivered to the recipient in person but rather to a receptionist and so the unique delivery aspect would be lost.

While some of the Dragons liked the concept, David Chilton pointed out that she would need to do a half a million dollars in sales to break even and that her valuation was already fairly rich based on her funding request. In the end, Jennifer Ruparell was not successful in convincing any of the Dragons to invest in BeautyGram. However, that has not deterred her from sticking to her marketing plan strategy. Since appearing on the show, sales have tripled and she has expanded beyond the local Calgary area to ship all across Canada. Economies of scale in purchasing have reaped benefits and her profit margins have increased 10 percent.[13] Although the business tends to be very seasonal, Ruparell has not seen copycat competitors.

Loyalty is more than simply preferring to purchase from one firm instead of another;[14] it means that customers are reluctant to patronize competitive firms. Loyal customers buy Nike apparel for all their sporting and casual needs, even if adidas goes on sale or opens a new store right around the corner from their home.

More and more firms realize the value of achieving customer excellence through focusing their strategy on retaining their loyal customers. Nike doesn't think in terms of selling a single pair of fashionable shoes for $100; instead, it focuses on satisfying the customer who buys track shoes for herself, Cole-Haan dress shoes for her spouse, soccer shoes for her daughter, and basketball shoes for her son. Conservatively, she might buy five pairs of shoes every year for 20 years. She is not a $100 customer; combining all purchases for her family over the years, she is at least a $10,000 shoe customer—and that doesn't even count the shorts, shirts, and socks she adds on to her purchases. Viewing customers with a lifetime value perspective, rather than on a transaction-by-transaction basis, is key to modern customer retention programs.[15] We will examine how the lifetime value of a customer is calculated in Appendix 7A.

Marketers use several methods to build customer loyalty. With its long history in the sport, adidas is clearly positioned as a provider of soccer cleats, far more so than Nike.

EXHIBIT 2.1 Macro Strategies for Developing Customer Value

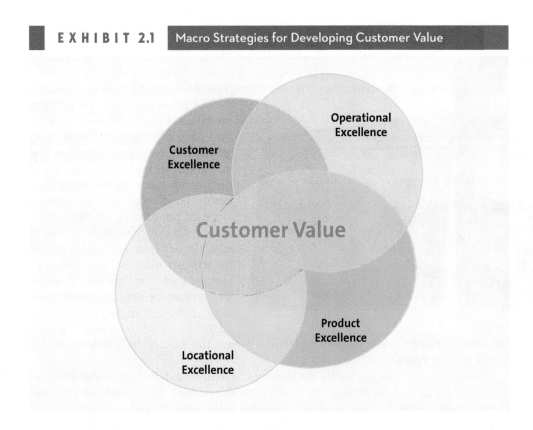

That positioning helps explain why Nike might have bought Umbro. But Nike also left the Umbro brand name alone, so that it could continue to appeal to players of one of the fastest-growing sports in the world.

Another method of achieving customer loyalty is to create an emotional attachment through loyalty programs.[16] Loyalty programs, which constitute part of an overall customer relationship management (CRM) program, prevail in many industries, from airlines to hotels to movie theatres to retail stores. Three-quarters of Canadians and Americans belong to at least one loyalty program.[17] Although the benefits to consumers of loyalty programs are limited since only a small percentage of customers save enough points to claim their rewards, loyalty programs are a boon to marketers. With such programs, companies can combine membership data with customer purchase data to develop a deeper understanding of the customer. Companies often use this data to tailor their offerings to better meet the needs of their loyal customers. For instance, by analyzing their databases, financial institutions, such as Bank of Montreal, develop profiles of customers who have defected in the past and use that information to identify customers who may defect in the future. Once it identifies these customers, the firm can implement special retention programs to keep them.

Customer Service Marketers may also build sustainable competitive advantage by offering excellent customer service,[18] though consistently offering excellent service can prove difficult. Customer service is provided by employees, and invariably, humans are less consistent than machines. On every visit, for example, Starbucks must attempt to ensure that every single barista greets customers in a friendly way and makes drinks consistently. Firms that offer good customer service must instill its importance in their employees over a long period of time so that it becomes part of the organizational culture. Although it may take considerable time and effort to build a reputation for customer service, once a marketer has earned a good service reputation, it can sustain this advantage for a long time because a competitor is hard pressed to develop a comparable reputation.

Operational Excellence

Firms achieve *operational excellence*, the second way to achieve a sustainable competitive advantage, through their efficient operations, excellent supply chain management, and strong relationships with their suppliers.

All marketers strive for efficient operations to get their customers the merchandise they want, when they want it, in the required quantities, and at a lower delivered cost than that of their competitors. By so doing, they ensure good value to their customers, earn profitability for themselves, and satisfy their customers' needs. In addition, efficient operations enable firms to provide their consumers with lower-priced merchandise. Even if their prices are not lower than those of the competition, they may use the additional margin they earn to attract customers away from competitors by offering even better service, merchandise assortments, or visual presentations.

Netflix customers can receive videos instantly using their tablet, TV, or computer.

Firms achieve efficiencies by developing sophisticated distribution and information systems as well as strong relationships with vendors. Like customer relationships, vendor relations must be developed over the long term and generally cannot be easily undermined by a competitor.[19] Furthermore, firms with strong relationships may gain exclusive rights to

- sell merchandise in a particular region
- obtain special terms of purchase that are not available to competitors
- receive popular merchandise that may be in short supply

The supply chain for Netflix represented a remarkable innovation when the company first started: With its high-tech distribution centres, it got movies to most of its subscribers overnight. Its current streaming services expand its offering even further, allowing subscribers to access various movies and television shows immediately through gaming devices (e.g., Wii), tablets (e.g., iPad), Internet-enabled televisions, or computers. Its supply chain continues to evolve and become increasingly efficient. The case study at the end of this chapter provides additional information about the methods Netflix has used to become a dominant player in media streaming and in the entertainment industry—as well as some of the challenges it has faced recently.

Product Excellence

Product excellence, the third way to achieve a sustainable competitive advantage, occurs by having products with high perceived value and effective branding and positioning. Some firms have difficulty developing a competitive advantage through their merchandise and service offerings, especially if competitors can deliver similar products or services easily. However, others have been able to maintain their sustainable competitive advantage by investing in their brand itself; positioning their product or service by using a clear, distinctive brand image; and constantly reinforcing that image through their merchandise, service, and promotion. For instance, *The Globe and Mail* and Interbrand's top Canadian brands—RBC Financial Group, Shoppers Drug Mart, Bell, Tim Hortons, Molson, Rona, and Loblaw—are all leaders in their respective industries, at least in part because they have strong brands and a clear position in the marketplace.[20]

One of the world's leading consumer electronics brands, Apple overtook the mobile music market and displaced established market leaders, such as Sony, with its iPod and iTunes combination. Although critics claimed that there was nothing revolutionary about the iPod technology, the fact still remains that Apple not only redesigned the mobile music device to make it an accessory that consumers felt proud to carry and display, but also revolutionized how music is purchased and consumed with its iTunes store. The iPhone and iPad are two other hugely successful products that have further consolidated Apple's brand image as a world-class innovative technology company with an enviable reputation for building high-quality, well-designed, and fashionable products. How did Apple come from behind to dislodge established market leaders and create such buzz around its technology? According to various reports, Apple's former CEO Steve Jobs saw Apple as a marketing company first. Understanding customer needs and satisfying those needs is what it does best. Technology comes second.

Locational Excellence

Location is particularly important for retailers and service providers. Many say the three most important things in retailing are location, location, location. Most people will not walk or drive very far when looking to buy a cup of coffee. A competitive advantage based on location is sustainable because it is not easily duplicated.

Tim Hortons and Starbucks have developed a strong competitive advantage with their location selection. They have such a high density of stores in some markets that it makes it very difficult for a competitor to enter a market and find good locations. Of course, when McDonald's entered the fancy coffee drink battle, it did not need to worry too much about finding new locations; its stores already appeared nearly everywhere!

Multiple Sources of Advantage

In most cases, however, a single strategy, such as low prices or excellent service, is not sufficient to build a sustainable competitive advantage. Firms require multiple approaches to build a wall around their position that stands as high as possible. For example, WestJet has achieved success by providing customers with good value that meets their expectations, offering good customer service, maintaining good customer relations, and offering great prices. The company has consistently positioned itself as a carrier that provides good service at a good value—customers get to their destination on time for a reasonable price. At the same time, its customers don't have extraordinary expectations and don't expect food service, seat assignments, or flights out of certain airports.[21] By fulfilling all of these strategies, WestJet has developed a huge cadre of loyal customers and has built a very high wall around its position as the value player in the Canadian airline industry.

THE MARKETING PLAN LO2

Effective marketing doesn't just happen. Firms such as Rona, Future Shop, The Bay, and Nike carefully plan their marketing strategies to react to changes in the environment, the competition, and their customers by creating a marketing plan. A marketing plan is a written document composed of an analysis of the current marketing situation, opportunities and threats for the firm, marketing

WestJet Airlines provides good service at a good price—a good value—and they have fun doing it!

planning phase
Where marketing executives and other top managers define the mission and objectives of the business, and evaluate the situation by assessing how various players, both inside and outside the organization, affect the firm's potential for success.

implementation phase
Where marketing managers identify and evaluate different opportunities by engaging in a process known as segmentation, targeting, and positioning. They then develop and implement the marketing mix by using the four Ps

control phase
The part of the strategic marketing planning process when managers evaluate the performance of the marketing strategy and take any necessary corrective actions.

objectives and strategy specified in terms of the four Ps, action programs, and projected or pro forma income (and other financial) statements.[22] The three major phases of the marketing plan are planning, implementation, and control.[23]

Although most people do not have a written plan that outlines what they are planning to accomplish in the next year, and how they expect to do it, firms do need such a document. It is important that everyone involved in implementing the plan knows what the overall objectives for the firm are and how they will be met. Other stakeholders, such as investors and potential investors, also want to know what the firm plans to do. A written marketing plan also provides a reference point for evaluating whether or not the firm met its objectives.

A marketing plan entails five steps, depicted in Exhibit 2.2. In Step 1 of the **planning phase**, marketing executives, in conjunction with other top managers, define the mission and objectives of the business. For the second step, they evaluate the situation by assessing how various players, both inside and outside the organization, affect the firm's potential for success (Step 2). In the **implementation phase**, marketing managers identify and evaluate different opportunities by engaging in a process known as segmentation, targeting, and positioning (STP) (Step 3). They then are responsible for implementing the marketing mix by using the four Ps (Step 4). Finally, the **control phase** entails evaluating the performance of the marketing strategy by using marketing metrics and taking any necessary corrective actions (Step 5).

As indicated in Exhibit 2.2, it is not always necessary to go through the entire process for every evaluation (Step 5). For instance, a firm could evaluate its performance in Step 5, and then go directly to Step 2 to conduct a situation analysis without redefining its overall mission.

EXHIBIT 2.2   Developing a Marketing Plan

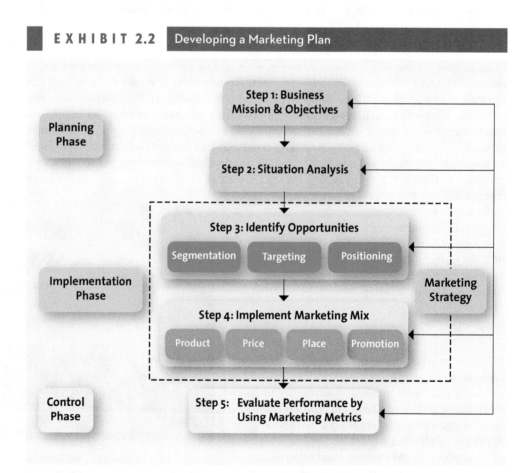

We will first discuss each step involved in developing a marketing plan. Then we consider ways of analyzing a marketing situation, as well as identifying and evaluating marketing opportunities. We also examine some specific strategies marketers use to grow a business. Finally, we consider how the implementation of the marketing mix increases customer value. A sample marketing plan outline and a marketing plan are provided in Appendix 2A, following this chapter.

Step 1: Define the Business Mission and Objectives

The **mission statement**, a broad description of a firm's objectives and the scope of activities it plans to undertake,[24] attempts to answer two main questions: What type of business are we? and What do we need to do to accomplish our goals and objectives? These fundamental business issues must be answered at the highest corporate levels before marketing executives can get involved. Most firms want to maximize shareholders' wealth by increasing the value of the firm's stock and paying dividends.[25] However, owners of small, privately held firms frequently have other objectives, such as achieving a specific level of income and avoiding risks, while not-for-profit organizations set nonmonetary objectives. (See Exhibit 2.3 for several mission statement examples.)

Nonprofit organizations, such as the Heart and Stroke Foundation, specify nonmonetary objectives such as improving the health of Canadians through research, health promotion, and advocacy. Tim Horton's mission is very focused: delivering superior quality products and services to customers and being the quality leader in what it does.[26] Nike's and adidas's mission statements are sufficiently broad to encompass the diversity and global nature of their businesses. For all these organizations, marketing holds the primary responsibility of enhancing the value of the company's products for its customers and other constituents, whether or not the company pursues profit. Another key goal or objective often embedded in a mission statement is how the firm is building a sustainable competitive advantage.

Step 2: Conduct a Situation Analysis

After developing its mission, a firm next must perform a **situation analysis**, using a **SWOT** analysis that assesses both the internal environment with regard to its **S**trengths and **W**eaknesses (internal analysis) and the external environment in terms of its **O**pportunities and **T**hreats (external analysis). Situation analysis also includes an examination

mission statement
A broad description of a firm's objectives and the scope of activities it plans to undertake; attempts to answer two main questions: What type of business is it? and What does it need to do to accomplish its goals and objectives?

situation analysis (SWOT)
The second step in a marketing plan; uses a SWOT analysis that assesses both the internal environment with regard to its **s**trengths and **w**eaknesses and the external environment in terms of its **o**pportunities and **t**hreats.

LO3

E X H I B I T   2.3   Mission Statements

Nike's mission is "to bring inspiration and innovation to every athlete* in the world." (With its asterisk, it defines an athlete by quoting one of its founders: "If you have a body, you are an athlete.")

adidas's mission states that "The adidas group strives to be the global leader in the sporting goods industry with brands built on a passion for sport and a sporting lifestyle."

The Heart and Stroke Foundation mission is to improve the health of Canadians by preventing and reducing disability and death from heart disease and stroke through research, health promotion, and advocacy.

Tim Hortons states "Our guiding mission is to deliver superior quality products and services for our customers and communities through leadership, innovation and partnerships. Our vision is to be the quality leader in everything we do."

Sources: "Nike's Mission Statement," http://help-en-us.nike.com/app/answers/detail/a_id/113/p/3897, "adidas Group Annual Report," http://careers.adidas-group.com/mission-and-values.aspx, "About Us," www.heartandstrokefoundation.ca; "Company Facts," www.timhortons.com/ca/en/about/2908.html.

of market trends, customer analysis, and competitive analysis. Additionally, the firms should assess the opportunities and uncertainties of the marketplace due to changes in **C**ultural, **D**emographic, **S**ocial, **T**echnological, **E**conomic, and **P**olitical forces (CDSTEP), factors that are discussed in Chapter 3.

A SWOT analysis is designed to help the firm determine areas in which it is strong and can compete effectively and areas where it is weak and vulnerable to competitive attacks. It also enables the firm to understand where it has sustainable competitive advantage or unique advantages that cannot be easily copied by competitors and how it can leverage those advantages in response to new opportunities arising from changes in its external environment. By understanding its competitive strengths and weaknesses, the firm will be better positioned to address weaknesses and deal with threats arising from its external business environment. A SWOT analysis requires the firm to undertake a critical assessment of its resources, capabilities, organization, strategies, and performance in relation to competitors. Similarly, the firm must conduct a careful analysis of changes in the environment and understand how they affect its business, whether they represent threats or opportunities. Strengths and weaknesses are within the control of the firm, and it can take actions to alleviate weaknesses and consolidate its strengths. Opportunities and threats are outside the control of the firm; therefore, the firm can decide only how it wants to respond.

Exhibit 2.4 lists several general elements that are usually examined when conducting a SWOT analysis. The relevance of specific elements will depend on the nature of the firm. This list is for illustration purposes and is by no means exhaustive.

Consider how Nike might conduct a SWOT analysis as outlined in Exhibit 2.5. We focus on Nike here, but we also recognize that its marketing managers might find it helpful to perform parallel analyses for competitors, such as adidas. Because a company's strengths (Exhibit 2.5, upper left) refer to the positive internal attributes of the firm, in this example we might include Nike's great brand recognition and the visibility of the celebrities who wear its products. Furthermore, its introduction of the Nike+ iPod

---

EXHIBIT 2.4 | Examples of Elements Considered in a SWOT Analysis

Environment	Evaluation	
	Positive	**Negative**
Internal	**Strengths** • Superior resources and capabilities • Superior management, marketing, technical talent • Strong brand • Superior product offerings • Extensive marketing reach • Wide distribution networks (national/global) • Strong financial resources • Excellent geographic location • Proprietary technologies/Intellectual property • Strong base of loyal customers	**Weaknesses** • Little or no brand recognition • Lack of financial resources • Lack of other resources and capabilities • Lack of marketing, management, and technical talent • Limited market reach or distribution network • No propriety technology • Poor location • Limited customer base or loyalty • Lack of credibility
External	**Opportunities** • CDSTEP changes that offer opportunities for the firm to serve new markets with existing products and/or pursue completely new market opportunities • Existing firms exit the market because of financial or other difficulties (i.e., reduced competition) • Acquiring another firm and gaining market access, new customers, new technology and expertise, and financial resources	**Threats** • Political or regulatory changes (e.g., new laws affecting business or products) • New entrants into the industry or market • New technology that could render existing technology or business practices obsolete • Natural or human-made disasters • Recession or economic downturn that affects consumers' purchasing power and confidence • Changes in sociocultural or demographic trends

continued the innovative tradition that has marked Nike since it first came up with waffle-soled running shoes. Its name recognition makes consumers more likely to try out these innovations when they appear on the market—especially when they see their favourite athlete wearing similar apparel on the court or in the field.

Yet every firm has its weaknesses, and Nike is no exception. Weaknesses (Exhibit 2.5, upper right) are negative attributes of the firm. Nike relies heavily—perhaps even too heavily—on its athletic shoe lines, especially for running and basketball. The NBA lockout for the 2012 season put undue stress on its sales in this segment. Not only would players and teams stop buying, but as the old saying goes, "Out of sight, out of mind." If the players are not on the court, their fans aren't thinking about them, and then sales will suffer.[27] In response to the popular emergence of other options, such as "toning" and "barefoot" models, Nike has largely suggested they are fads that will not last, stressing instead its traditional athletic shoe models.[28]

Nike's strengths include its innovative product tradition. It introduced the Nike+ iPod sensor that, when inserted into shoes, gives the runner instant feedback about running time, distance, pace, and calories burned.

Opportunities (Exhibit 2.5, lower left) pertain to positive aspects of the external environment. Among Nike's opportunities, it appears determined to pursue dominance in other, sometime niche, sports markets. For the Olympic Games, it introduced footwear for less familiar sports, including fencing, wrestling, and equestrian events.[29] This goal also aligns with another notable opportunity for Nike, that is, growth in global markets. It sells products in 170 countries worldwide, through independent distributors, Nike stores, the website, and licences.[30] It aims to expand further, and it has devoted significant resources to improving its prominence among European football players and fans.[31]

Finally, threats (Exhibit 2.5, lower right) represent the negative aspects of the company's external environment. For example, its widespread market dominance makes Nike the primary target for all its competitors,[32] from adidas to New Balance to Li Ning, China's largest shoe maker. All of these firms want to take market share from Nike, which means the

EXHIBIT 2.5		Examples of Elements in a SWOT Analysis		
	Environment	**Evaluation**		
		Positive		**Negative**
Nike	Internal	**Strengths** • Strong brand • Strong celebrity endorsers • Innovative products		**Weakness** • Overreliance on footwear
	External	**Opportunity** • Emerging countries • Other fashion segments		**Threats** • Cheaper imports • Imitation products • Retail becoming price competitive
adidas	Internal	**Strengths** • Strong brand • Portfolio of brands • Strong global presence		**Weakness** • Management of numerous brands
	External	**Opportunity** • Emerging countries		**Threats** • Cheaper imports • Imitation products • Recessionary forces

company must constantly be a little bit on the defensive. Furthermore, a perpetual threat for any apparel company is staying fashionable, as Nike itself acknowledges: "We must … respond to trends and shifts in consumer preferences by adjusting the mix of existing product offerings, developing new products, styles and categories, and influencing sports and fitness preferences through aggressive marketing. Failure to respond in a timely and adequate manner could have a material adverse effect on our sales and profitability. This is a continuing risk."[33]

Step 3: Identify and Evaluate Opportunities by Using STP (Segmentation, Targeting, and Positioning)

L04

STP
The processes of segmentation, targeting, and positioning that firms use to identify and evaluate opportunities for increasing sales and profits.

market segment
A group of consumers who respond similarly to a firm's marketing efforts.

market segmentation
The process of dividing the market into distinct groups of customers—where each individual group has similar needs, wants, or characteristics—who therefore might appreciate products or services geared especially for them in similar ways.

After completing the situation analysis, the next step is to identify and evaluate opportunities for increasing sales and profits by using **STP** (segmentation, targeting, and positioning). With STP, the firm must first understand customer needs and wants through market research, then divide the market or customers into distinct subgroups or segments, determine which of those segments it should pursue or target, and finally decide how it should position its products and services to best meet the needs of those chosen targets. The criteria to evaluate target segments are discussed in detail in Chapter 6.

Segmentation   Many types of customers appear in any market, and most firms cannot satisfy everyone's needs. For instance, among Internet users, some users do research online, some shop, some look for entertainment, and many do all three. Each of these groups might be a **market segment** consisting of consumers who respond similarly to a firm's marketing efforts. The process of dividing the market into distinct groups of customers where each individual group has similar needs, wants, or characteristics—who therefore might appreciate products or services geared especially for them in similar ways—is called **market segmentation**. Let's look at Hertz, the car rental company. The example in Exhibit 2.6 reveals that one of the Hertz segments is the Fun Collection, which includes the Corvette ZHZ and Chevrolet Camaro, targeting single people and couples wanting to have a bit of fun. Its Prestige Collection, featuring the Cadillac Escalade and Infiniti QX56, targets business customers and families who prefer a luxurious ride. With its Green collection of cars such as the Toyota Prius and Ford Fusion, Hertz appeals to environmentally conscious customers, and with its SUV/Minivan collection, it brings in families. It also offers commercial vans for service customers.[34] Note that Hertz uses a variety of demographic factors—gender, age, income, interests—to identify customers who might want the Fun, Prestige, Green, and SUV/Minivan collections. But it also applies psychographic or behavioural factors, such as a preference for style or a need to move possessions across town, to identify likely consumers of the Fun Collection and its commercial vans. Firms may

EXHIBIT 2.6   Hertz Market Segmentation

	Segment 1	Segment 2	Segment 3	Segment 4	Segment 5
Segments	Single people and couples who want to have a bit of fun	Business customers and families who prefer a luxurious ride	Environmentally conscious customers	Families	Commercial customers
	Fun Collection	Prestige Collection	Green Collection	SUV/minivan & crossover	Commercial Van/ Truck
Cars Offered	Corvette ZHZ	Infiniti QX56	Toyota Prius	Toyota Rav 4	Ford Cargo Van
	Chevrolet Camaro	Cadillac Escalade	Ford Fusion	Ford Explorer	

Hertz targets several markets. Its "Fun Collection" (left) appeals to fun-loving singles and couples while its "Prestige Collection" (right) appeals to business customers and families who prefer a luxurious ride.

also segment consumers based on benefits sought or geographic factors, which will be discussed in Chapter 6.

Going back to our Nike example, we can see that it segments customers based on gender and how the products are used. Nike focuses on the following segments: men's training, women's training, running, basketball, football (soccer), action sports, sportswear, and golf.

Targeting   After a firm has identified the various market segments it might pursue, it evaluates each segment's attractiveness and decides which to pursue by using a process known as **target marketing** or **targeting**. For example, Hertz realizes that its primary appeal for the SUV/Minivan collection centres on young families, so the bulk of its marketing efforts for this business is directed toward that group. Similarly, potato chip manufacturers have divided the market into many submarkets or segments. Frito-Lay Canada, for instance, makes cheesy Doritos (R) tortilla chips for the teen segment and created Lay's (R) wasabi and curry potato chips for Asian-Canadians.[35]

Positioning   Finally, when the firm decides which segments to pursue, it must determine how it wants to be positioned within those segments. **Market positioning** involves the process of defining the marketing mix variables so that target customers have a clear, distinct, desirable understanding of what the product does or represents in comparison with competing products. Hertz positions itself as a quality car (and truck) rental company that is the first choice for each of its target segments. In its marketing communications, it stresses that customers will get peace of mind when they rent from Hertz, the market leader in the car rental business, and be able to enjoy their journey (e.g., leisure consumers) and reduce travel time (e.g., business consumers).

target marketing/ targeting
The process of evaluating the attractiveness of various segments and then deciding which to pursue as a market.

market positioning
Involves the process of defining the marketing mix variables so that target customers have a clear, distinct, desirable understanding of what the product does or represents in comparison with competing products.

PepsiCo Canada targets several markets with many different types of chips and carbonated beverages.

To segment the coffee drinker market, Starbucks uses a variety of methods, including geography (e.g., college campuses versus shopping/ business districts) and benefits (e.g., drinkers of caffeinated versus decaffeinated products). After determining which of those segments represent effective targets, Starbucks positions itself as a firm that develops a variety of products that match the wants and needs of the different market segments—espresso drinks, coffees, teas, bottled drinks, pastries, and cooler foods.

After identifying its target segments, a firm must evaluate each of its strategic opportunities. A method of examining which segments to pursue is described in the Growth Strategies section later in the chapter. Firms are typically most successful when they focus on opportunities that build on their strengths relative to those of their competition. In Step 4 of the marketing plan, the firm implements its marketing mix and allocates resources to different products and services.

For example, Pizza Hut decided to jump on changing consumer desires for rapid access to its offering by constantly expanding its mobile applications, but it also found its positioning as a convenient option appealing to more markets than it even expected, as Social and Mobile Marketing 2.1 reveals.

L05   Step 4: Implement Marketing Mix and Allocate Resources

When the firm has identified and evaluated different growth opportunities by performing an STP analysis, the real action begins. The company has decided what to do, how to do it, and how many resources the firm should allocate to it. In the fourth step of the planning process, marketers implement the marketing mix—product, price, promotion, and place—for each product and service on the basis of what it believes its target markets will value (Exhibit 2.7). At the same time, it makes important decisions about how it will allocate its scarce resources to its various products and services. Each element of the four Ps must be fully integrated to achieve a coherent strategy.

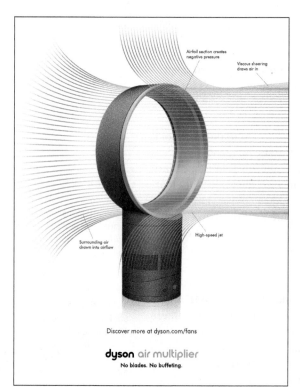

Discover more at dyson.com/fans

dyson air multiplier
No blades. No buffeting.

Dyson creates value with its innovative products.

Product and Value Creation Products, which include services, constitute the first of the four Ps. Because the key to the success of any marketing program is the creation of value, firms attempt to develop products and services that customers perceive as valuable enough to buy. Dyson fans and fan heaters draw in and redirect surrounding air without potentially dangerous or fast spinning blades or visible heating elements. Although more expensive than conventional fans and space heaters, these sculpturally beautiful appliances are perceived by consumers to be a valuable alternative to products that haven't significantly changed since the early 1900s. You'll learn more about product and branding decisions in Chapters 8 and 9.

Price and Value for Money The second element of the marketing mix is price. As part of the exchange process, a firm provides a product or a service, or some combination thereof, and in return it receives money. Value-based marketing requires that firms charge a price that customers perceive as giving them good value for the products and services they receive. It is important for a firm to have a clear focus in terms of what products to sell, where to

Social and Mobile Marketing 2.1

Truly Mobile Pizza[36]

The pizza delivery business has always been mobile in one sense, but Pizza Hut is making sure that it spreads into mobile commerce as well. This first-mover introduced its mobile website in 2007, an iPhone application in 2009, and apps for the iPad, Android, and Windows Mobile 7 in 2010.

The decision to go mobile was based on a few insights that Pizza Hut gleaned from its market research. In particular, if it did not offer mobile access quickly, its competitors might be first to do so in the competitive pizza delivery market. The Pizza Hut app lets customers order food through a user-friendly experience, but it also makes sure to identify the closest store locations for delivery or pickup service.

Without much information about who the consumers who would use the app were, Pizza Hut anticipated more orders from college-aged men, who do not like to cook and want their food on demand, but also are not willing to stop a video game to take the time to order food through more traditional channels. The assumption seemed reasonable—but it also was dead wrong. Further market research, based on the introduction of the app, has shown that there are just as many pizza connoisseurs with iPhones who are older than 55 as there are 13- to 24-year-olds ordering.

Pizza Hut's mobile app makes ordering pizza a piece of cake.

buy them, and what methods to use in selling them. Pricing is the only activity that actually brings in money by generating revenues. If a price is set too high, it will not generate much volume. If a price is set too low, it may result in lower-than-necessary margins and profits. Therefore, marketers should base price on the value that the customer perceives. Dyson fans retail for $150 or more while conventional fans retail for around $25. Customers thus can decide just what they want from their fan and choose the one at the price they prefer. Pricing decisions and strategies are discussed in detail in Chapter 11.

Place and Value Delivery   For the third P, place, the firm must be able to make the product or service

EXHIBIT 2.7   Developing the Marketing Mix

Customers purchase Lee Valley woodworking and gardening tools by catalogue, by phone, online, or in store.

The Salvation Army is one of a few not-for-profit organizations that leverages the Internet effectively.

readily accessible when and where the customer wants it. Consider Lee Valley Tools, a small Ottawa-based company and one of the world's leading mail-order and retail suppliers of innovative woodworking and gardening tools. The company was founded more than 30 years ago as a catalogue mail-order supplier of woodworking and gardening tools by entrepreneur Leonard Lee. Over the years, Lee has opened 11 stores across Canada and launched a fully functional e-commerce website, leevalley.com. To make its products and services accessible to all of its customers, Lee Valley has integrated its stores and catalogue operations with its online presence and used place to create value in its delivery process. Through its website, Lee Valley is able to reach a wider market segment more efficiently and cost-effectively. Thus, Lee Valley turned the integration of its different channels into a seamless customer experience, a key value driver for the company.[37] Chapters 12 and 13 deal with in-depth place, or distribution, decisions. Although many companies have developed sophisticated website and online marketing strategies to deliver place value for their customers, the same cannot be said for nonprofit organizations.

Promotion and Value Communication   The fourth P of the marketing mix is promotion. Marketers communicate the value of their offering, or the value proposition, to their customers through a variety of media, including TV, radio, magazines, buses, trains, blimps, sales promotion, publicity, the sales force, and the Internet. It is now possible for firms in out-of-the-way locations to expand their market area to the whole world. For example, Canadians living in places such as Africa, Australia, and New Zealand can order their favourite authentic Canadian products that they cannot find in these countries through the Ottawa-based Country Grocer website, www.thecountrygrocer.com.[38] Similarly, Cupcakes by Heather and Lori, located in the Lower Mainland of Vancouver, British Columbia—sells millions of cupcakes each week to customers across Canada and the United States.[39] Daily deal websites such as Groupon or LivingSocial offer another way to get the word out. Many smaller companies find that these sites give them greater name recognition than they ever could have achieved on their own. Retailers add value to their offerings through their efficient and effective communications strategies, which will be discussed in more detail in Chapters 14, 15, and 16.

Marketers must consider the most efficient and effective methods to communicate with their customers. This goes back to understanding customers, the value created, and the message being communicated. An increasing number of companies are using the Internet and their own websites to advertise and communicate with their customers and build closer relationships. For example, apart from enabling customers to order tools through its website, Lee Valley uses it to tell customers of upcoming training seminars that are held in its physical stores. These seminars teach customers about the use and care of the tools and demonstrate new, innovative tools being developed. The website also contains a variety of technical articles on woodworking and gardening that help customers learn more and enjoy their favourite activities. The regular e-newsletter, which customers sign up for, provides technical information, trade-show dates, company news, special event dates, and other topics of interest to woodworkers and gardeners. Customers can even send letters about their experiences with specific tools, which are posted publicly on the company's website. Lee Valley is building loyal customer relationships one customer at a time.

Research has shown that this type of campaign is much more effective than either mail or TV advertising. Nevertheless, marketers must balance the effectiveness of their value communication activities with their costs. In addition to the Internet, many Canadian companies spend a large portion of their marketing budgets on sales promotions because Canadian consumers are increasingly becoming more value conscious. In fact, spending on sales promotion has exceeded spending on advertising in Canada.[40] Sponsorship of charitable and community-based events is gaining in popularity in Canada as companies try to demonstrate social responsibility. Corporate sponsorships of charitable events have always been viewed with suspicion from some segments of society, while others have embraced it as a beneficial activity. Ethical Dilemma 2.1 examines the financial relationships between corporations and charities that raise questions concerning the credibility of charities and the motivations of corporate donors.

In addition to developing the four Ps and allocating resources, marketing managers must develop schedules: timelines for each activity and the personnel responsible for the respective activity to avoid bottlenecks and ensure smooth and timely implementation of the marketing mix activities. Also, marketers must design the organization that will be responsible for putting the plan into action. This organization is usually represented in the form of an organizational chart. In most established companies, the marketing organization already exists and marketing managers must simply assign responsibilities to various employees within the marketing department. The marketing organization is usually responsible for the day-to-day operational decisions involved in executing the plan.

Step 5: Evaluate Performance by Using Marketing Metrics

The final step in the planning process includes evaluating the results of the strategy and implementation program by using marketing metrics. A metric is a measuring system that quantifies a trend, dynamic, or characteristic. Metrics are used to explain why

Ethical Dilemma 2.1 — **Corporate "Do"nations or "Don't"nations for Charities[41]**

Many Canadians rely on the services offered by charities and many charities rely on corporate donations to fund these services. Charities are admired for the services they offer, the programs they deliver, the resources they provide, and the goodwill that they build within the community. Most charities advocate a specific cause, such as cancer research or women's rights. They seek to promote awareness and generate solutions for the betterment of their constituents. Charities are heavily reliant on the work of volunteers and the donations of individuals to achieve their missions. While Canadians are generous donors, with an average of 85 percent of Canadians contributing to charities,[42] corporations are still the primary source of funding for charities. This issue raises questions about the partnerships formed between charities and corporations. Complications arise when charities partner with corporations that sell products or represent ideas that conflict with the charity's message or purpose. Nearly every charitable organization faces this challenge.

Consider the Heart and Stroke Foundation, whose mandate is to eliminate cardiovascular disease and promote healthy living. One of its leading donors is the Boston Pizza Foundation. Critics say that two slices of the restaurant's pepperoni pizza contain 400 calories and 900 milligrams of sodium—hardly a step in the right direction to fight cardiovascular disease! Also consider the Canadian Cancer Society, which is adamant about the need for protection against harmful environmental carcinogens. Despite this, its top donors include companies that have been highly criticized by environmentalists for releasing carcinogens and polluting the environment. These companies include Suncor Energy, Syncrude Canada, and Husky Energy.

With such a dependence on corporate donations, is it possible for charitable organizations to stay true to their missions and motivate positive change without being compromised in the process? Should charities continue to accept donations from corporations they are struggling against?

things happened and to project the future. They make it possible to compare results across regions, business units, product lines, and time periods. The firm can determine why it achieved or did not achieve its performance goals with the help of these metrics. Understanding the causes of the performance, regardless of whether that performance exceeded, met, or fell below the firm's goals, enables firms to make appropriate adjustments.

Typically, managers begin by reviewing the implementation programs, and their analysis may indicate that the strategy (or even the mission statement) needs to be reconsidered. Problems can arise both when firms successfully implement poor strategies and when they poorly implement good strategies.

Who Is Accountable for Performance?

At each level of an organization, the business unit and its manager should be held accountable only for the revenues, expenses, and profits that they can control. Expenses that affect several levels of the organization, such as the labour and capital expenses associated with operating a corporate headquarters, shouldn't be arbitrarily assigned to lower levels. In the case of a store, for example, it may be appropriate to evaluate performance objectives based on sales, sales associate productivity, and energy costs. If the corporate office lowers prices to get rid of merchandise and therefore profits suffer, then it's not fair to assess a store manager's performance based on the resulting decline in store profit.

Performance evaluations are used to pinpoint problem areas. Reasons that performance may be above or below planned levels must be examined. Perhaps the managers involved in setting the objectives aren't very good at making estimates. If so, they may need to be trained in forecasting.

Actual performance may be different than the plan predicts because of circumstances beyond the manager's control. For example, there may have been a recession. Assuming the recession wasn't predicted, or was more severe or lasted longer than anticipated, there are several relevant questions: How quickly were plans adjusted? How rapidly and appropriately were pricing and promotional policies modified? In short, did the manager react to salvage an adverse situation, or did those reactions worsen the situation?

Performance Objectives and Metrics

Many factors contribute to a firm's overall performance, which make it hard to find a single metric to evaluate performance. One approach is to compare a firm's performance over time or to competing firms, using common financial metrics such as sales and profits. Another method of assessing performance is to view the firm's products or services as a portfolio. Depending on the firm's relative performance, the profits from some products or services are used to fuel growth for others.

Financial Performance Metrics

Some commonly used metrics to assess performance include revenues, or sales, and profits. For instance, sales are a global measure of a firm's activity level. However, a manager could easily increase sales by lowering prices, but the profit realized on that merchandise (gross margin) would suffer as a result. Clearly, an attempt to maximize one metric may lower another. Managers must therefore understand how their actions affect multiple performance metrics. It's usually unwise to use only one metric because it rarely tells the whole story.

In addition to assessing the absolute level of sales and profits, a firm may wish to measure the relative level of sales and profits. For example, a relative metric of sales or profits is its increase or decrease over the prior year. Additionally, a firm may compare its growth in sales or profits relative to other benchmark companies (e.g., Pizza Pizza may compare itself to Pizza Hut).

The metrics used to evaluate a firm vary depending on (1) the level of the organization at which the decision is made and (2) the resources the manager controls. For example, while the top executives of a firm have control over all of the firm's resources and resulting expenses, a regional sales manager has control over only the sales and expenses generated by his or her salespeople.

Let's look at Nike's sales revenue and profits (after taxes) and compare them with those of adidas (Exhibit 2.8).

A corporate consciousness of the importance of social responsibility grows, firms are starting to report corporate social responsibility metrics in major areas, such as their impact on the environment, their ability to diversify their workforce, their energy conservation initiatives, and their policies on protecting the human rights of their employees and the employees of their suppliers.

Social Responsibility Performance Metrics As Canadian companies become more convinced of the importance of social responsibility, we will likely see an increasing number of companies report corporate social responsibility metrics, such as their impact on the environment, their ability to diversify their workforce, their energy conservation initiatives, and their policies on protecting the human rights of their employees and the employees of their suppliers. Sustainable Marketing 2.1 presents an example that illustrates the importance of having such performance metrics.

Strategic Planning Is Not Sequential

The planning process in Exhibit 2.2 suggests that managers follow a set sequence when they make strategic decisions. Namely, after they've defined the business mission, they perform the situation analysis; identify opportunities; evaluate alternatives; set objectives; allocate resources; develop the implementation plan; and, finally, evaluate their performance and make adjustments. But actual planning processes can move back and forth among these steps. For example, a situation analysis may uncover a logical alternative, even though this alternative might not be included in the mission statement, which would mean that the mission statement would need to be revised. Or, the development of the implementation plan might reveal that insufficient resources have been allocated to a particular product for it to achieve its objective. In that case, the firm would need to either change the objective or increase the resources; alternatively, the marketer might consider not investing in the product at all.

Now that we have gone through the steps of the strategic marketing planning process, let's look at some strategies that have been responsible for making many marketing firms successful. First we look at portfolio analysis, and then some product-market growth strategies.

Portfolio Analysis In portfolio analysis, for example, management evaluates the firm's various products and businesses—its "portfolio"—and allocates resources according to which products are expected to be the most profitable for the firm in

▉ **EXHIBIT 2.8**	Performance Metrics: Nike vs. adidas		
		2012	**2013**	**% Change**
Nike	Net Sales	$24.1B	$25.3B	9.5%
	Net Profit	$ 2.2B	$ 2.5B	9%
	Net Profit/Net Sales	9%	10%	
Adidas	Net Sales	€2B	€1.9B	–5%
	Net Profit	€.5B	€.1B	–80%
	Net Profit/Net Sales	2.5%	.5%	

Sustainable Marketing 2.1

Birks: A Diamond in the Rough?[43]

When striving to achieve sustainability, small changes can make a huge difference. Birks & Mayors, founder of Birks, realizes the impact that small changes can have on its economic, environmental, and social performance. In an industry where sustainability is very challenging because of the nature of the supply chain, Birks is attempting to distinguish itself through corporate social responsibility and by turning sustainability into its new gold standard. Birks' commitment to the Kimberley Process means it does not sell conflict diamonds (also known as blood diamonds) mined in war zones. Most of the gold it purchases comes from organizations that adhere to ecologically and socially responsible mining practices. Birks is reinforcing its commitment to the environment by introducing recyclable shopping bags. It also encourages employees to suggest ways that the company can improve its sustainable performance. These are some of the steps that Birks is taking to fulfill its mandate of being as sustainable as possible by addressing the controllable aspects of its operations.

Birks' sustainability efforts can drive success and create a competitive advantage. However, its efforts will have little impact unless it takes steps to make stakeholders aware of the positive changes it is implementing. Before it can inform stakeholders about positive improvements, Birks needs to have a method of measuring the results of the changes. This need highlights the importance of performance metrics. Adequate analytical metrics enable

Birks is turning sustainability into a new gold standard.

organizations to capture crucial qualitative and quantitative information that allows for tracking the success of sustainability strategies. Such tracking will allow Birks to consistently meet its established environmental and social standards and provide greater transparency and credibility for stakeholders. Once analytical metrics are used to enlighten stakeholders, Birks can leverage its sustainability initiatives as a point of differentiation. Clear and compelling communication to stakeholders about how the changes are making a huge difference in the jewellery industry will likely allow Birks continued financial stability within a sustainable enterprise.

---

strategic business unit (SBU)

A division of the company that can be managed somewhat independently from other divisions since it markets a specific set of products to a clearly defined group of customers.

product line

A group of products that consumers may use together or perceive as similar in some way.

the future. Portfolio analysis is typically performed at the **strategic business unit (SBU)** or **product line** level of the firm, though managers can also use it to analyze brands or even individual items. An SBU is a division of the company that can be managed somewhat independently from other divisions since it markets a specific set of products to a clearly defined group of customers. For example, Loblaw Companies Limited consists of its general merchandise, drugstores, President's Choice brand, and financial products and services operations.[44] Each of these is an SBU. A product line, in contrast, is a group of products that consumers may use together or perceive as similar in some way. There are several product lines within Loblaw's PC Financial services SBU: PC banking, PC MasterCard, mortgages, and insurance.

Loblaw Companies Limited

Loblaws	valu-mart	Joe Fresh	Maxi
Real Canadian Superstore	Fortinos	bloorstreet market	Extra Foods
Zehrs Markets	Provigo	SaveEasy	Joe Fresh
No Frills	Dominion	Wholesale Club	PC Financial

The table above shows some of the business lines of Loblaw Companies Limited.

BOSTON CONSULTING GROUP'S PORTFOLIO ANALYSIS

One of the most popular portfolio analysis methods, developed by the Boston Consulting Group (BCG), requires that firms classify all their products into a two-by-two matrix, as depicted in Exhibit 2.9.[45] The circles represent brands, and their sizes are in direct proportion to the brands' annual sales—that is, larger circles correspond to higher levels of sales and smaller circles indicate lower levels of sales. The horizontal axis represents the relative market share. In general, market share is the percentage of a market accounted for by a specific entity,[46] and it is used to establish the product's strength in a particular market. It is usually discussed in units, revenue, or sales. A special type of market share metric, relative market share, is used in this application because it provides managers with a product's relative strength, compared to that of the largest firm in the industry.[47] The vertical axis is the market growth rate, or the annual rate of growth of the specific market in which the product competes. Market growth rate thus measures how attractive a particular market is. Each quadrant has been named on the basis of the amount of resources it generates for and requires from the firm.

Stars. Stars (upper left quadrant) occur in high-growth markets and are high–market share products. That is, stars often require a heavy resource investment in things such as promotions and new production facilities to fuel their rapid growth. As their market growth slows, stars will migrate from heavy users of resources to heavy generators of resources and become cash cows.

Cash cows. Cash cows (lower left quadrant) are in low-growth markets but are high–market share products. Because these products have already received heavy investments to develop their high market share, they have excess resources that can be spun off to those products that need it. For example, in Exhibit 2.9, Brand C can use its excess resources to fund products in the question mark quadrant.

relative market share
A measure of the product's strength in a particular market, defined as the sales of the focal product divided by the sales achieved by the largest firm in the industry.

market growth rate
The annual rate of growth of the specific market in which the product competes.

EXHIBIT 2.9   Boston Consulting Group Product Portfolio Analysis

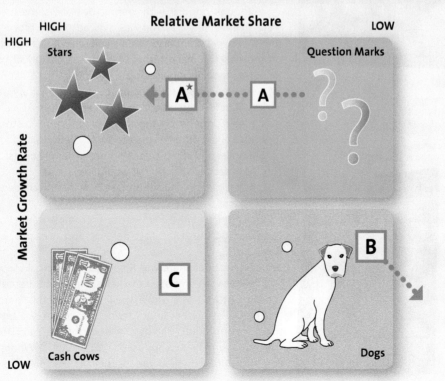

Question marks. Question marks (upper right quadrant) appear in high-growth markets but have relatively low market shares; thus, they are often the most managerially intensive products in that they require significant resources to maintain and potentially increase their market share. Managers must decide whether to infuse question marks with resources generated by the cash cows, so that they can become stars, or withdraw resources and eventually phase out the products. Brand A, for instance, is currently a question mark, but by infusing it with resources, the firm hopes to turn it into a star.

Dogs. Dogs (lower right quadrant) are in low-growth markets and have relatively low market shares. Although they may generate enough resources to sustain themselves, dogs are not destined for stardom and should be phased out unless they are needed to complement or boost the sales of another product or for competitive purposes. In this case, the company has decided to stop making Brand B.

Now let's look at Apple and some of its products. The four that we will focus our attention on are:

- iPhone
- iPod
- iMac Desktop
- iPad

Let's consider each of these products and place them into the BCG matrix based on these data. While Android sales have caused sales to slow, the iPhone is still a star with a high growth rate (36.4 percent). By the end of 2012, Apple sold 47.8 million units in its fourth quarter alone, making its relative market share 75 percent.[48] In the fourth quarter of 2013, it sold 51 million units.[49]

In which Boston Consulting Group quadrant do these products fit?

Apple's iPod is a different story. With a staggering absolute market share consistently above 70 percent, its relative market share is also 100 percent, and with more than 300 million iPods sold in a little over 10 years, it is definitely an important product for Apple.[50] Unfortunately, the MP3 market is contracting (the market shrank by 22 percent from 2011 to 2012). Combine the lack of growth with a large relative market share, and it is likely that the iPod is a cash cow for Apple.[51]

Although popular with graphic designers, the growth rate of the Mac Desktop has slowed to a pitiful 1 percent.[52] Given that it also has a small relative market share in the desktop market, the iMac can be tentatively classified as a dog. Should Apple get rid of the iMac? For at least two reasons, this is probably a bad idea. First, it risks alienating graphic designers and other Apple loyalists who depend on the iMac. Since these customers may also enjoy other Apple products, their dissatisfaction might adversely affect sales of these other products. Second, discontinuing the iMac would leave a gaping hole in its portfolio, and would therefore hurt its brand image as a computer company.

Then we have the iPad with an incredible sales growth rate from 2011 to 2012 of 61.6 percent, and sales of approximately 19.5 million units as of early 2013.[53, 54] In 2011, its absolute market share was 59 percent, making it the market leader with a relative market share of 100 percent.[55] Looking at 2012 as a whole, the iPad captured 57 percent of the tablet market (more than 1 out of every 2 tablets sold was an iPad). But by the end of 2012 its absolute market share had dropped to 51 percent.[56] Where on the BCG matrix would you classify the iPad? Would you argue that a 51 percent absolute market share places it in the star category, or would you be more conservative and put it as a question mark, citing the steady erosion of absolute market share? Will Apple be able to continue to grow and maintain its market share leader position by releasing a new version of the iPad?

Although quite useful for conceptualizing the resource allocation task, the BCG approach, and others like it, are often difficult to implement in practice. In particular, it is difficult to accurately measure both relative market share and industry growth. Furthermore, other measures could easily serve as substitutes to represent a product's competitive position and the market's relative attractiveness. Another issue for marketers is the potential self-fulfilling prophecy of placing a product into a quadrant. That is, suppose a product is classified as a dog although it has the potential of being a question mark. The firm might reduce support for the product and lose sales to the point that it abandons the product, which might have become profitable if provided with sufficient resources.

Because of these limitations, many firms have tempered their use of matrix approaches to achieve a more balanced approach to allocating their resources. Instead of assigning allocation decisions to the top levels of the organization, many firms start at lower management levels and employ checks and balances to force managers at each level of the organizational hierarchy to negotiate with those above and below them to reach their final decisions.

GROWTH STRATEGIES

L06

Firms consider pursuing various market segments as part of their overall growth strategies, which may include the four major strategies shown in Exhibit 2.10.[57] The rows distinguish those opportunities a firm possesses in its current markets from those it has in new markets, whereas the columns distinguish between the firm's current marketing offering and that of a new opportunity. Let's consider each of them in detail.

EXHIBIT 2.10 Market/Product and Services Strategies

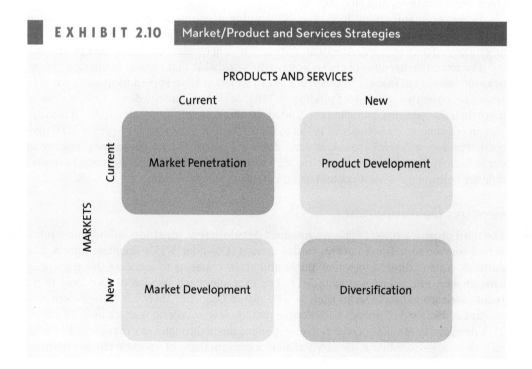

Market Penetration

A **market penetration strategy** employs the existing marketing mix and focuses the firm's efforts on existing customers. Such a growth strategy might be achieved by encouraging current customers to patronize the firm more often or buy more merchandise on each visit or by attracting new consumers from within the firm's existing target market. A market penetration strategy generally requires greater marketing efforts, such as increased advertising, additional sales and promotions, or intensified distribution efforts in geographic areas in which the product or service is already sold.

To penetrate its target market, TV network MTV found that it needed new ways to engage its viewers. The young audience to which MTV traditionally appeals consists of text-messaging, video-gaming multitaskers who no longer accept plain video programming on their televisions. The network is working hard to develop additional strategies and outlets to retain viewers, as well as to encourage them to spend more time interacting with its content. MTV discovered that interactions with the audience through alternative channels increase ratings for its shows. In addition to producing and airing reality shows such as *America's Best Dance Crew* and *Jersey Shore*, MTV has partnered with video game producer Yoostar to offer "Yoostar on MTV" for Xbox 360. The game provides a massive library of constantly updated shows, music videos, and recordings of live events. Using the green-screen technology contained in the game, fans of these shows can insert themselves into scenes in which they've already seen their more famous teen peers. Of course, the game also allows them to upload their completed performance to Facebook, Twitter, or a Yoostar-dedicated website.[58] On MTV's website, dedicated forums, blogs, and activities for each show also encourage viewers to connect with characters in their shows. Viewers can not only talk about the characters as if they were friends, but also buy the products they wear and download the music played during the show.[59]

Market Development

A **market development strategy** employs the existing marketing offering to reach new market segments, whether domestic or international or segments not currently served by the firm. International expansion is generally riskier than domestic expansion because firms must deal with differences in government regulations, cultural traditions, supply chain considerations, and language.

However, many firms, including MTV, enjoy a competitive advantage in global markets—such as Mexico, Latin America, Europe, China, and Japan—because, especially among young people, North American culture is widely emulated for consumer products.

For example, because of rising prosperity worldwide and rapidly increasing access to cable television, fashion trends from North America have spread to young people in emerging countries. Since its founding in 1981, MTV has expanded, with niche sites in more than 20 countries, including the United Kingdom, Japan, Brazil, and India. It is available in 562 million households in 161 countries and 33 languages.[60] The global MTV generation prefers soft drinks to tea, athletic shoes to sandals, French fries to rice, and credit cards to cash. To achieve such growth, MTV leveraged its existing media content but also delivers culturally relevant content using local DJs and show formats.

Product Development

The third growth strategy option, a **product development strategy**, offers a new product or service to a firm's current target market. Consider MTV's dynamic lineup: The network constantly develops new pilots and show concepts to increase the amount of time viewers can spend watching MTV. For example, each version of *The Real World* reality series, and newer series such as *Generation Cryo* and *Faking It* all represent new programs designed to attract and retain existing viewers. Along with its new TV series, MTV develops new online products to engage consumers through more than 25 niche blogs, as well as a website that it uses to dominate a greater share of viewers' minds and time.

These various MTV-branded niche sites pertain to social, political, and environmental issues that appeal to different segments in its target market. The sites further encourage viewers to get involved in real-world issues (not *The Real World* issues) through mobile technologies. By visiting the sites, MTV promises that consumers can share mobile content, educate themselves, and take action on important issues.[61]

Diversification

A **diversification strategy**, the last of the growth strategies from Exhibit 2.10, introduces a new product or service to a market segment that is currently not served. Diversification opportunities may be either related or unrelated. In a related diversification opportunity, the current target market and/or marketing mix shares something in common with the new opportunity. In other words, the firm might be able to purchase from existing vendors, use the same distribution and/or management information system, or advertise in the same newspapers to target markets that are similar to its

diversification strategy
A growth strategy whereby a firm introduces a new product or service to a market segment that it does not currently serve.

REAL MARKETER PROFILE   Kelli Wood

After graduating from Wilfrid Laurier University's Bachelor of Business Administration program with a specialization in Marketing, I decided to pursue my passion for sports by applying to work at Maple Leaf Sports and Entertainment (MLSE) in Toronto. MLSE proudly owns the Toronto Maple Leafs and the Toronto Raptors and is one of the most reputable sports and entertainment companies in the world. In 2006, in partnership with the City of Toronto, MLSE purchased the rights to launch a Major League Soccer (MLS) team in the Toronto market. Luckily for me, a marketing position for Toronto FC was posted just weeks after I graduated.

I had to find a creative way to apply for the job, as I knew that competition would be fierce because so many people want to follow their passion to work in sports, and very few marketers get the chance to build a brand from scratch. I figured that the best way to get a marketing job was to demonstrate how I could uniquely market and position the most important brand that I could ever manage: myself.

My creative approach to my resumé and interview process not only helped me get interviewed first over several hundred other candidates, but also got me the job of my dreams. I stayed at Toronto FC for almost five seasons, quarterbacking all marketing initiatives for the club, and being a part of the brand launch, the 2008 MLS All-Star Game, the International Friendly between Toronto FC and Real Madrid, and the 2010 MLS Cup. Our tiny team earned top honours across our industry, breaking countless

records for ticket sales, sponsorship, and creative work, and were awarded one of the most prestigious industry awards in 2009 by being named *Strategy Magazine*'s Brand of the Year.

In March 2011, I left MLSE to join Sid Lee, a Montreal-based advertising agency. Working agency side on the account team for an international creative powerhouse is a big leap from being on the client side of a niche, local brand. I was assigned to help lead the rebranding efforts for a massive international client and helped multiple creative campaigns morph into 16 different languages and have presence across 5 continents using a variety of media. I've always had a passion for creativity, and the position gave me the opportunity to be closer to the work, and gain experience in speaking to different segments and product categories. During my time there, Sid Lee was named Agency of the Year by *Marketing Magazine* in 2011, for the third year consecutive year.

As a self-taught illustrator, I also launched a small illustration company, Little Big Words. In the summer of 2012, a long-dreamed-of opportunity knocked. I had submitted my portfolio to the prestigious One of a Kind Show in Toronto, was selected as a featured artisan, and awarded a scholarship by Etsy for my portfolio of work. As a result, I left Sid Lee and have been working to turn a bunch of coffee-table scribbles into a business with a heartbeat ever since. Little Big Words has become a boutique illustration company that's in love with designing imaginative paper products, with an eye on launching to the North American wholesale market at the National Stationery Show in New York for 2014.

current consumers. MTV has pursued related diversification by introducing TV series that focus on more positive social messages, instead of on wealth, celebrities, and excessive youth culture (e.g., *The Hills, My Super Sweet 16*). In series such as *I Used to Be Fat* and *Made*, recognizable and seemingly similar teens still appeal to viewers and provide a healthy dose of drama. However, the plotlines of these shows focus on how people overcome adversity or struggle with everyday challenges to attain some level of happiness.[62]

In contrast, in an unrelated diversification, the new business lacks any common elements with the present business. Unrelated diversifications do not capitalize on either core strengths associated with markets or with products. Thus, they would be viewed as very risky. In the technology innovation company 3M, however, we find an excellent and successful example of unrelated diversification strategies: What began as a sandpaper products company now markets its products in six major business segments, from consumer office supplies to orthodontic technologies.[63]

While all four growth strategies present unique challenges for marketers, a market penetration strategy is the easiest to implement since it focuses on promoting existing products to existing customers. In this case, marketers know both their products and markets. With market development or product development, marketers have experience with one element and must learn the other element. Diversification requires marketers to go outside both their current products and markets, and the risks of making mistakes are substantially greater with this strategy. The particular growth strategy a company chooses depends on its goals and capabilities, among other things. Also, marketers tend to pursue multiple growth strategies simultaneously.

downsizing
Exiting markets, reducing product portfolios, or closing certain businesses or store or plant locations.

Marketers may also develop strategies for **downsizing** their business operations by either exiting markets or reducing their product portfolios. They may exit markets or abandon products for many reasons; for example, because they have entered new markets where they have little or no experience; diversified into markets or products that do not quite fit with current products, markets, or capabilities; developed products that offer very little value for customers; or encountered declining demand for some products.

LEARNING OBJECTIVES REVIEW

LO1   Define a marketing strategy

A marketing strategy identifies (1) a firm's target markets(s), (2) a related marketing mix (four Ps), and (3) the bases on which the firm plans to build a sustainable competitive advantage. Firms use four macro strategies to build their sustainable competitive advantage. Customer excellence focuses on retaining loyal customers and excellent customer service. Operational excellence is achieved through efficient operations and excellent supply chain and human resource management. Product excellence entails having products with high perceived value and effective branding and positioning. Finally, locational excellence entails having a good physical location and Internet presence.

LO2   Describe the elements of a marketing plan

A marketing plan is composed of an analysis of the current marketing situation, its objectives, the strategy for the four Ps, and appropriate financial statements. A marketing plan represents the output of a three-phase process: planning, implementation, and control. The planning phase requires that managers first define the firm's mission and vision, which helps to answer the questions "What business are we in now?" and "What do we intend to be in the future?" In the planning phase, managers conduct a situation analysis to evaluate how various players, both inside and outside the organization, affect the firm's potential for success. In the second phase, implementation, the firm identifies and evaluates different opportunities through a process known as segmentation, targeting, and positioning, and develops the marketing mix, the four Ps. Specifically, managers focus on implementing the marketing mix, allocating resources, designing the marketing organization, and developing schedules and action plans. Finally, in the control phase, the firm evaluates its performance to determine what worked, what didn't, and how performance can be improved in the future.

L03 Analyze a marketing situation using a SWOT analysis

SWOT stands for strengths, weaknesses, opportunities, and threats. A SWOT analysis occurs during the second step in the strategic planning process, the situation analysis. By analyzing what the firm is good at (its strengths), where it could improve (its weaknesses), where in the marketplace it might excel (its opportunities), and what is happening in the marketplace that could harm the firm (its threats), managers can assess their firm's situation accurately and plan its strategy accordingly.

L04 Explain how a firm chooses what consumer group(s) to pursue with its marketing efforts

Once a firm identifies different marketing opportunities, it must determine which are the best to pursue. To accomplish this task, marketers go through a segmentation, targeting, and positioning (STP) process. Firms segment various markets by dividing the total market into those groups of customers with different needs, wants, or characteristics who therefore might appreciate products or services geared especially toward them. After identifying the different segments, the firm goes after, or targets, certain groups on the basis of the firm's perceived ability to satisfy the needs of those groups better and more profitably than competitors. To complete the STP process, firms position their products or services according to the marketing mix variables so that target customers have a clear, distinctive, and desirable understanding of what the product or service does or represents relative to competing products or services.

L05 Outline the implementation of the marketing mix as a means to increase customer value

The marketing mix consists of the four Ps—product, price, promotion, and place—and each P contributes to customer value. To provide value, the firm must offer a mix of products and services at prices its target markets will view as indicating good value. Thus, firms make trade-offs between the first two Ps, product and price, to give customers the best value. The third P, promotion, informs customers and helps them form a positive image about the firm and its products and services. The last P, place, adds value by getting the appropriate products and services to customers when they want them and in the quantities they need.

L06 Describe how firms grow their businesses

Firms use four basic growth strategies: market penetration, market development, product development, and diversification. A market penetration strategy directs the firm's efforts toward existing customers and uses the present marketing mix. In other words, it attempts to get current customers to buy more. In a market development strategy, the firm uses its current marketing mix to appeal to new market segments, as might occur in international expansion. A product development growth strategy involves offering a new product or service to the firm's current target market. Finally, a diversification strategy takes place when a firm introduces a new product or service to a new customer segment. Sometimes a diversification strategy relates to the firm's current business, such as when a women's clothing manufacturer starts making and selling men's clothes, but a more risky strategy is when a firm diversifies into a completely unrelated business.

KEY TERMS

- control phase
- customer excellence
- diversification strategy
- downsizing
- implementation phase
- locational excellence
- market development strategy
- market growth rate
- market penetration strategy
- market positioning
- market segment
- market segmentation
- marketing strategy
- mission statement
- operational excellence
- planning phase
- product development strategy
- product excellence
- product line
- relative market share
- situation analysis (SWOT)
- STP
- strategic business unit (SBU)
- sustainable competitive advantage
- target marketing/targeting

CONCEPT REVIEW

1. Briefly describe the activities involved at each of the three phases of the marketing planning process: (1) planning, (2) implementation, and (3) control.

2. What is meant by a mission or vision statement? What purpose does a mission statement serve and how does it influence marketing planning?

3. What does SWOT mean? List two benefits of SWOT analyses. What do you think the differences are between a SWOT analysis for the entire firm and a SWOT analysis for a product?

4. What type of information is required to conduct a SWOT analysis and where do marketers typically look for this information?

5. Why are segmentation, targeting, and positioning (STP) crucial for identifying and evaluating market opportunities? How does STP influence the development of the marketing mix—the four Ps?

6. Describe the four growth strategies that firms typically pursue. Use a fast-food restaurant or a grocery chain in Canada (e.g., Loblaw, Safeway, or Food Basics) to illustrate each of the four growth strategies.

7. Of the four growth strategies described in the chapter, which is the most risky? Which is the easiest to implement? Why?

8. Identify and describe the four strategies that firms could use to grow their business. What other strategies could companies use to compete in the market?

9. What are the four components of the BCG Matrix? When would "stars" be preferred over "cash cows"?

10. Explain why in the BCG Matrix all products start out as questions marks and either end up as stars, cash cows, or dogs.

MARKETING APPLICATIONS

1. How has WestJet created a sustainable competitive advantage?

2. Perform a SWOT analysis for your college or university.

3. Describe the primary target markets for the Toronto Blue Jays, Victoria's Secret, and Gatorade. How do these three firms position their products and services so that they appeal to their respective target markets?

4. Pick your favourite product, service provider, or retailer. How do marketers add value to it through the implementation of the four Ps?

5. Choose three retailers. You believe the first builds customer value through product excellence, the second through operational excellence, and the third through customer excellence. Justify your answer.

6. Visit the website of your bank and try to identify how it uses STP to develop various types of bank accounts (products) and charge different fees (price) for different types of accounts.

7. Select a company with which you are familiar or search online to find a company that has pursued a diversification strategy as one of its growth strategies. How successful was the company's diversification strategy? What factors do you think account for its success or failure?

8. Imagine that you have just developed and launched a new sports bike for cycling enthusiasts and your business has become an instant success. You would like to capitalize on this success and fame to grow your business. Explain how you would go about expanding your business over the next three years.

9. Using the sports bike scenario from the previous question, describe what kinds of analysis you might conduct before deciding which growth strategies to implement.

10. You and a few of your classmates are planning to open a new spa facility near the campus of your university. Explain how you would segment the market for your services, which segment you would target, and how you would position your spa to the chosen target market.

TOOLKIT

SWOT ANALYSIS

Assume you are a marketing analyst for a major company and are trying to conduct a situation analysis by using SWOT analysis. Use the toolkit provided on Connect and complete the SWOT grids for each company by using the appropriate items.

NET SAVVY

1. Petro-Canada is considered a progressive company in terms of its values and the mission statement that drives its business. Visit its website (www.petro-canada.ca) and review the portion that discusses the company, its mission, and its values. Discuss aspects of its mission and values that might be considered progressive. Do you believe its progressive attitude creates a special position in the market that contributes to a sustainable competitive advantage?

2. More and more firms seem to be entering the dating service industry. Visit eHarmony (www.eharmony.com) and tour its website to find the types of activities and methods such companies use to help match compatible couples. Analyze the environment that might affect Internet dating services by using a SWOT analysis.

CHAPTER CASE STUDY

THE NETFLIX ROLLERCOASTER[64]

Founded in 1997, Netflix revolutionized the movie rental industry, attracting 36 million subscribers in over 40 countries today. With no brick-and-mortar stores, the marketing strategy relied on taking customer orders online and mailing the movies to their homes. Reed Hastings, the CEO of Netflix, came up with the idea after being charged late fees for keeping a rental movie past its due date. His concept offered convenience and no late fees; users could keep the movies as long as they wanted. The company quickly grew, reaching 1 million subscribers by 2002. Customers could choose from several flat-rate monthly subscription options and keep up to eight movies out at a time. Videos were returned using a prepaid and preaddressed envelope. Netflix then automatically mailed the next video on the customer's video queue. Customers could change and update their queues as often as they wanted.

The growing number of customers and profits made Netflix's management and stockholders quite happy. Observers praised it as a top company, a great investment, and a stellar example of how innovation could drive profits and growth.

Netflix was innovative, yet careful analysis of the situation suggested some serious threats. First, several competitors had entered the market to compete directly with Netflix. In the United States, Blockbuster, which enjoyed great name recognition, added mail delivery services to its existing brick-and-mortar stores. Redbox came onto the scene, allowing patrons to borrow first-run, popular movies from conveniently located boxes for just $1 per day. Second, the U.S. Postal Service noted the need to shut down hundreds of local branches and possibly halt Saturday service. This threat was significant since Netflix relied heavily on the mail to help it get movies to customers quickly. Third, some cable companies and satellite operators were doing more with pay-per-view options. Not limited to special events or boxing matches, this model was being applied to movies immediately after their video release.

In response, Netflix started down a new path: Customers could view unlimited streaming of movies and TV shows for the same monthly fee they were paying for receiving discs in the mail. The new offering was a nearly instant hit, picked up and enjoyed by most of its subscribers. This response encouraged Netflix to expand the option. In addition to streaming through their computers, users could use platforms that would deliver its titles to the Nintendo Wii, Xbox 360, PlayStation 3, and TiVo. Hardware options from Panasonic, Insignia, and Seagate soon joined, though even these were outshone when Netflix also introduced an iPad application.

While the company responded to these threats, it made a series of strategic missteps. Netflix realized it was leaving money on the table by providing both mail and streaming service for the same price it had previously been charging for just the mail service. It was offering more value and reasoned that it could charge a higher price.

It launched a streaming-only plan for $7.99 per month in November 2010. At the same time, it increased the cost of each of its DVD plans by $1 each. If customers wanted both, they could sign up for the streaming plan and add DVDs for $2. Netflix anticipated that most users would drop the mail service, because so many consumers seemed heading toward streaming. But they discovered that subscribers wanted both. The selection of titles for the mail service was significantly greater than that available through streaming, so customers still found value in it.

In July 2011, Netflix announced a disastrous new pricing plan. For unlimited streaming, customers paid $7.99 per month. For one-disc-at-a-time (the most basic mail plan), customers would pay $7.99 per month. If they wanted both, they paid $15.98. Customers were furious. For many of them, the new plan represented a 60 percent price hike. About 1 million customers dropped the service. The negative press about the company, especially in social media, was intense. On Netflix's own blog, more than 12,000 comments were posted in response to the announcement, and readers would be hard pressed to find one with a positive tone. But investors considered the price move a smart one, and Netflix's stock prices rose.

Two months later Hastings tried to spin the DVD rental business off under a new name, "Qwikster" and use Netflix for the streaming business. Now, in addition to paying more, customers would need to visit two separate Internet sites to manage their movies, rather than just handling streaming and mail services on Netflix.com. It took less than a month for Hastings to back down and reverse the split. Both services would stay with Netflix, though the price increase would remain in place. But the damage had been done. More customers left and Netflix's stock price plummeted.

Canadians, of course, were not impacted as this drama unfolded in the United States. That's because when Netflix launched its service in Canada in September 2010, only streaming was offered. Introductory offers allowed Canadians to get one month free and then pay $7.99 a month thereafter. While many customers signed up, some were disappointed to learn that the large selection of movies and TV shows their American friends could choose from was not available in Canada due to licensing issues. Although there are 10,625 unique titles available in the United States, the Canadian library offers only 2,647. With over 2.5 million Canadian subscribers, it's not surprising that Netflix followed this first foray into international waters by expanding further: Latin America and the Caribbean in 2011, the United Kingdom and Ireland in early 2012, and Finland, Denmark, Sweden, and Norway in late 2012.

Competition, particularly in the United States, has further intensified. Netflix faces multichannel video programming distributors such as HBO GO and Showtime Anywhere in the States and SkyGo and BBC iPlayer in the United Kingdom. Cable companies Time Warner and Comcast provide on-demand content. Additionally, direct broadcast satellite providers (DIRECTV, Echostar) and telecommunications providers (AT&T, Verizon) are hot on Netflix's heels. More recently, Amazon.com, iTunes, Walmart, and Best Buy have all introduced online movie viewing. That competition has been slower to materialize in Canada.

While Netflix believes that international expansion will provide a significant source of growth in the future, for the time being, having to grow a member base from scratch takes time. The marketing and licensing costs involved in establishing new markets has resulted in bottom-line losses and the company expects significant losses for the near future. As the company pursues a strategy of market development, the ups and downs of international expansion must feel a little like being on a roller coaster.

Questions

1. Explain Netflix's marketing strategy. Can it sustain its competitive advantage? Why or why not?

2. Perform a SWOT analysis for Netflix. What are its biggest threats? Which opportunities should it pursue?

3. What is the best way for Netflix to grow its business? Justify your answer.

Appendix 2A

Writing a Marketing Plan

Have a plan. Follow the plan, and you'll be surprised how successful you can be. Most people don't have a plan. That's why it's easy to beat most folks.

—Paul "Bear" Bryant, football coach, University of Alabama

WHY WRITE A MARKETING PLAN?[1]

As a student, you likely plan out much in your life—where to meet for dinner, how much time to spend studying for exams, which courses to take next semester, how to get home for winter break, and so on. Plans enable us to figure out where we want to go and how we might get there.

For a firm, the goal is not much different. Any company that wants to succeed (which means any firm whatsoever) needs to plan for a variety of contingencies, and marketing represents one of the most significant. A marketing plan—which we defined in Chapter 2 as a written document composed of an analysis of the current marketing situation, opportunities and threats for the firm, marketing objectives and strategy specified in terms of the four Ps, action programs, and projected or pro forma income (and other financial) statements—enables marketing personnel and the firm as a whole to understand their own actions, the market in which they operate, their future direction, and the means to obtain support for new initiatives.[2]

Because these elements—internal activities, external environments, goals, and forms of support—differ for every firm, the marketing plan is different for each firm as well. However, several guidelines apply to marketing plans in general; this appendix summarizes those points and offers an annotated example.

MARKETING PLAN VERSUS BUSINESS PLAN

Of course, firms consider more than marketing when they make plans and therefore commonly develop business plans as well. Yet, as this book highlights, marketing constitutes such an important element of business that business plans and marketing plans coincide in many ways.[3] Both marketing and business plans generally encompass the following:

1. Executive summary
2. Company overview
3. Objectives/goals, usually according to strategic plan and focus
4. Situation analysis
5. STP analysis (market/product/customer analysis)
6. Marketing strategy
7. Financial projections
8. Implementation plan
9. Evaluation and control metrics

However, a business plan also includes details about R&D and operations, and both documents may feature details about other key topics, depending on the focus of the company and the plan.

STRUCTURE OF A MARKETING PLAN

This section briefly describes each of the elements of a marketing plan.[4]

Executive Summary

The executive summary essentially tells the reader why he or she is reading this marketing plan—what changes require consideration, what new products need discussion, and so forth—and suggests possible actions to take in response to the information the plan contains.

Company Overview

In this section, the plan provides a brief description of the company, including perhaps its mission statement, background, and competitive advantages.

Objectives/Goals

This section offers more specifics about why readers are reading the marketing plan. What does the company want to achieve, both overall and with this particular marketing plan?

Situation Analysis

Recall from Chapter 2 that a situation analysis generally relies on SWOT considerations; therefore, this section describes the strengths, weaknesses, opportunities, and threats facing the company.

STP Analysis

The analysis proceeds by assessing the market in which the company functions, the products it currently offers or plans to offer in the future, and the characteristics of current or potential customers.

Marketing Strategy

The marketing strategy may be very specific, especially if the plan pertains to, for example, a stable product in a familiar market, or it may be somewhat open to varied possibilities, such as when the firm plans to enter a new market with an innovative product.

Financial Projections

On the basis of the knowledge already obtained, the marketing plan should provide possible developments and returns on the marketing investments outlined in the marketing strategy.

Implementation Plan

This portion of the marketing plan includes the timing of promotional activities, when monitoring will take place, and how expansions likely will proceed.

Evaluation and Control Metrics

The firm must have a means of assessing the marketing plan's recommendations; the marketing plan therefore must indicate the methods for undertaking this assessment, whether quantitatively or qualitatively.

Appendix

The final section(s) offers additional information that might be of benefit, such as a list of key personnel, data limitations that may influence the findings, and suggestions of the plan, relevant legislation, and so forth.

INFORMATION SOURCES[5]

When writing a marketing plan, you likely can turn to a variety of your firm's in-house information sources, including annual reports, previous marketing plans, published mission statements, and so on. In addition, various sources offer suggestions and examples that may provide you with direction and ideas. Exhibits 7.5 and 7.6 also list many sources that you may find very helpful.

- Knowthis.com—"a knowledge source for marketing" (www.knowthis.com/principles-of-marketing-tutorials/how-to-write-a-marketing-plan)
- Encyclopedia of American Industries—introduces industry structure; arranged by SIC and NAICS codes
- Standard & Poor's NetAdvantage—surveys of more than 50 different industries, with financial data about companies in each industry
- Investext Plus—brokerage house reports
- IBISWorld—market research on thousands of industries; classified by NAICS code
- Statistics Canada surveys on virtually all aspects of business, the economy, social statistics, and population data—a vast variety of statistics on a range of topics
- Statistics Canada Census—detailed statistical data gathered every 10 years on all aspects of the Canadian population
- LifeStyle Market Analyst—lifestyle information about geographic areas, lifestyle interest groups, and age and income groups
- Mediamark Reporter—information about demographics, lifestyles, product and brand usage, and advertising media preferences
- Arbitron/Scarborough—local market consumer information for various media in 75 local markets for consumer retail shopping behaviour, product consumption, media usage, lifestyle behaviour, and demographics
- Simmons Study of Media and Markets—products and consumer characteristics; various media audiences and their characteristics
- Rand McNally Commercial Atlas and Marketing Guide—maps and tables showing demographic, industrial, transportation, railroad, airline, and hospital data

- Annual & 10-K reports from Thomson ONE Banker, Edgar, and LexisNexis—business descriptions, product listings, distribution channels, possible impact of regulations and lawsuits, and discussions of strategic issues
- MarketResearch.com Academic—market research reports on a variety of consumer products
- Mintel Reports Database—market research reports focusing on consumer products, lifestyles, retailing, and international travel industry

LINGUISTIC AND VISUAL SUGGESTIONS

Again, recall that all marketing plans differ, because all firms differ. However, just as rules exist that dictate what makes for good writing, some rules or guidelines apply to all well-written marketing plans

- Maintain a professional attitude in the writing and presentation.
- Keep descriptions and summaries concise. Get to the point.
- Use standard, edited English.
- Proofread the entire plan multiple times to catch grammatical, spelling, or other such errors that could dampen the professionalism of the writing.
- Adopt a businesslike tone; avoid flowery or jargon-filled writing.
- Employ direct, rather than passive, and present, rather than past, tense whenever possible (e.g., "We plan to achieve 30 percent growth in two years" rather than "The plan was that 30 percent growth would be achieved by the firm within two years").
- Be positive.
- Yet avoid meaningless superlatives (e.g., "Our goal is tremendous growth").
- Be specific; use quantitative information whenever possible.
- Insert graphics to convey important concepts succinctly, including photos, graphs, illustrations, and charts.
- However, avoid using so many visual elements that they clutter the plan.
- Lay out the plan clearly and logically.
- Organize sections logically, using multiple levels of headings, distinguished clearly by font differences (e.g., bold for first-level heads, italics for second-level heads).
- Consider the use of bullet points or numbered lists to emphasize important points.
- Exploit modern technology (e.g., graphics software, page-layout software, laser printers) to ensure the plan looks professional.
- Adopt an appropriate font to make the text easy to read and visually appealing— avoid using anything smaller than 10-point font at a minimum.
- Avoid unusual or decorative fonts; stick with a common serif type to make the text easy to read.
- Consider binding the report with a clear cover and an attractive title page.
- Generally aim for a plan that consists of 15–30 pages.

PeopleAhead MARKETING PLAN ILLUSTRATION[6]

PeopleAhead Marketing Plan: Condensed

1. Executive Summary

PeopleAhead focuses on career advancement done right. Instead of making job search a one-time event, PeopleAhead provides a platform for people to find, advance, and develop their careers by sharing career goals, discussing professional development plans, and socializing with other professionals.

PeopleAhead culminates the career advancement experience with its proprietary TrueMatch® technology, which identifies synergies between the companies hiring talent (employers) and PeopleAhead members (job candidates) who wish to be hired. By anonymously presenting only prequalified career opportunities to members, who confirm their interest and recommend others, PeopleAhead transforms the ineffective online hiring process into a highly efficient career-matching system. PeopleAhead was founded by Carlos Larracilla and Tom Chevalier to improve people's lives by helping them achieve their career aspirations. The vision for PeopleAhead was conceived of in January 2006, with a notion that personality alignment is critical to matching the right people with the right career opportunities. Since then, the idea has grown and morphed into a company that matches the right person with the right career opportunity by aligning personality, competencies, experience, and interests.

Tom and Carlos combine human resources, system development, and sales experience to deliver a groundbreaking, TrueMatch®-branded talent matching network that makes it easier for people to achieve their career aspirations and improves the way companies identify individuals who will be able to contribute to their long-term success. The organizational chart of PeopleAhead is available in Appendix A.

Instead of using separate "Executive Summary" and "Company Overview" sections, this marketing plan begins with a general overview that includes both aspects and answers the key questions: "What type of business are we?" and "What do we need to do to accomplish our objectives?" (see Chapter 2).

As this plan does, a marketing plan should start with a positive, upbeat assessment of what the company does and what it hopes to continue doing.

Note the personalization of the company founders, which may help readers feel connected to the company.

2. Strategic Objectives

2.1. Mission

PeopleAhead's mission is to help individuals with career advancement and improve the human capital in companies. The site will act as a networking platform for professionals and career matching as opposed to job and resumé-posting searches.

2.2. Goals

- Use brand-matching technology: TrueMatch®
- Build critical mass of users.
- Drive traffic to the website through marketing blitzes.
- Utilize word-of-mouth advertising from satisfied users.

2.3. Business Summary

- *Business Customers:* This group provides PeopleAhead's revenues. Customers purchase contact information about the Top Ten PROfiles gleaned from the individual member base that have been sorted and ranked by the TrueMatch® technology. PeopleAhead will focus on small and medium businesses (see Market Segmentation section), because these entities are underserved by large competitors in the online recruitment market, and because research shows that this demographic has a less efficient recruitment process that would benefit most readily from PeopleAhead's services. Within this segment, customers include HR managers who are responsible for the sourcing of candidates, functional area managers who require new talent for their team, and executives whose business objectives rely on human capital and efficiency of operations.

- *Individual Members:* This group does not pay for services but is the main source of data points for PeopleAhead's TrueMatch® system. PeopleAhead will focus on building a base of individual members who range from recent graduates to individuals with 5–7 years of continuous employment. Ideal members are those who are currently employed or will be graduating within nine months and are "poised" to make a career change. These individuals can utilize the services to the fullest extent and are valuable candidates for business customers.

2.4. Competitive Advantage

- *TrueMatch® offers a branded technology,* marketed to both business customers and individual candidates for its "black box" value proposition, which establishes PeopleAhead as the category leader for recruitment-matching software. This technology provides a point of differentiation from competitors, which may have technically similar matching software but constantly need to reinforce their marketing messages with explanations of their value proposition.

- *For individual candidates,* PeopleAhead will be the favoured career advancement platform online, where individuals enthusiastically create a history and have connections (invited friends, co-workers, and mentors) in place that will make PeopleAhead a staple among their favourite websites. PeopleAhead delivers TrueMatch® career opportunities, professional development plans that let people establish a professional record, and valuable career advancement tools, including automatic position feedback, "recommend-a-friend," and team-based career networking.

- *For business customers,* PeopleAhead makes online sourcing and qualification of candidates quick and efficient by prequalifying potential candidates, seeking recommendations for hard-to-find individuals, and delivering only the Top 10 most highly

The paragraph provides a general outline of the firm's objectives; the bulleted list offers more specific goals, and the subsequent sections go into more detail about the various factors that may influence these objectives.

By referring to another section, the plan makes clear where it is heading and enables readers to cross-reference the information.

The plan acknowledges both a general, potential target market and the ideal targets.

As Chapter 2 suggests, the plan notes PeopleAhead's sustainable competitive advantage as part of its overall mission statement.

qualified candidates who have preconfirmed interest in the available position. PeopleAhead will be the most effective candidate-company matching platform available in the market, delivering prequalified, preconfirmed candidates.

In discussing both the external market and the internal advantages of PeopleAhead, the plan carefully distinguishes between individual job candidates and businesses, thus differentiating the focus and objectives according to this segmentation.

3. Situation Analysis—Online Recruitment

Online recruitment is the system whereby companies use the Web to locate and qualify prospective candidates for available positions. The methods employed by online recruitment service providers to serve this market range from resumé aggregation to assessment test application to linking strategies. However, the common underlying objective is to locate candidates who would not be found by traditional recruitment methods and use computing power to qualify candidates quickly and with more accuracy than would be possible manually.

3.1. Industry Analysis

Large online recruitment websites make this a tedious process by requiring companies to search through many resumés manually to find the "right" candidate. Other sites solicit recommendations for positions. However, resumés are often "enhanced," such that almost all candidates appear qualified, and information found in the resumé or provided through a recommendation is simply insufficient to make an educated hiring decision. Companies need more information and intelligent tools that make this screening process more accurate.

3.1.1. Market Size

The market size for both member segments in 2005 was as follows:

Figures provide a visually attractive break in the text and summarize a lot of information in an easy-to-read format.

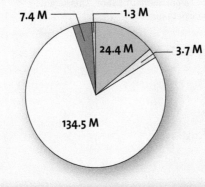

Individual Members Segments

7.4 M — 1.3 M
24.4 M — 3.7 M
134.5 M

■ Senior college students   ☐ Current employees
■ Other college students   ■ Unemployed
☐ Graduate program students

Company Members Segments

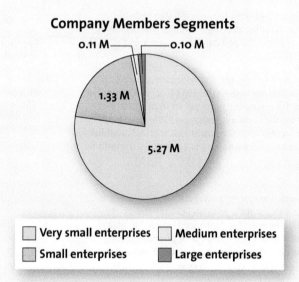

0.11 M ———   ——— 0.10 M

1.33 M

5.27 M

☐ Very small enterprises ☐ Medium enterprises
☐ Small enterprises ■ Large enterprises

The most critical issue in examining market size is the relationship between the number of companies and the number of workers employed, because sales are based on the number of positions (profiles purchased), not the number of companies that use the service.

The following figure shows the number of people employed by each enterprise market segment as of January 2006, according to the U.S. Department of Labor. This segment information will be useful in defining PeopleAhead's target market.

Employment by Enterprise Type

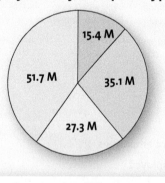

15.4 M

51.7 M

35.1 M

27.3 M

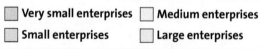

☐ Very small enterprises ☐ Medium enterprises
☐ Small enterprises ☐ Large enterprises

3.1.2. Market Growth

PeopleAhead will operate in the online recruitment market. The growth of this industry is subject to two primary constraints: U.S. economic health and online recruitment advertisement adoption rates. Understanding these constraints will help to identify PeopleAhead's opportunity. General indicators suggest the U.S. economy (GDP) will grow at an average annual rate of 4 percent for the next decade.[7] Online recruitment advertising is expected to grow by 35 percent per year to reach $7.6 billion by 2010.[8] Not only is the market expanding, but it is exhibiting rapid adoption by new entities, as the following graph shows.[9]

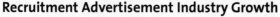

Another visually attractive graph summarizes complicated information easily. The use of high-quality colour can add a professional feel to a marketing plan.

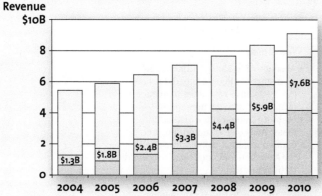

Recruitment Advertisement Industry Growth

3.1.3. Market Needs

- **The right person for the right position:** The right employee for one company or position is not the same for all others. Companies must locate intelligent individuals with relevant experience, and prefer people who are aligned with the position requirements in terms of personality, competencies, and fit with the company culture.

- **Prescreening qualification tools:** Increasing the number of candidates through online recruitment can be advantageous, but it can also be a hindrance. When sourcing candidates, recruiters need tools that help them qualify applicants.

- **Time savings:** Companies need to complete the online sourcing and qualification of candidates quickly. Leaving positions unfilled can cause critical performance gaps to emerge within the company.

3.1.4. Market Trends

The methods by which online recruitment service providers deliver candidates has been undergoing a migration from resumé aggregation and search services such as Monster and CareerBuilder to new Web 2.0 methodologies that include passive recruitment, "meta tagging," and social networking.

The underlying objective of these Web 2.0 services is to allow individuals to remain on a few trusted websites while enabling companies to access those individuals for financial purposes. In parallel, the focus is moving from aggregation of unique visitors toward engaging existing users more intensively. Internet users are growing familiar with sites that encourage socializing, collaborating, and distributing private information online to help to improve network benefits, and need to be engaged to maintain contact.

3.2. SWOT Analysis

	Segment 1	Segment 2
Internal	**Strengths** • Industry best practices: The networking model used by PeopleAhead draws on the industry accepted "best practices" contact protocols drawn from multiple industries, including online feedback, recruitment, and social networking and offline professional networking. TrueMatch® software aligns business objectives with appropriate candidates. • Team expertise: The combined talents of the founders include human resources, system development, sales, and marketing. • Web development expertise: PeopleAhead has partnered with an award-winning European software development provider. This company provides quality usually reserved for high-budget projects, at terms that are favourable for a start-up company.	**Weaknesses** • Absence of industry "influentials": As a start-up, PeopleAhead does not currently have resources to attract influential industry managers. • Inability to guarantee critical mass: As is true of many Internet companies, the business must solve the "chicken and egg" puzzle to build critical mass. • Verifying efficiency of matching capabilities: In theory, the system has an absolute guarantee of effectiveness; computations make decisions rather than humans. However, the matching capabilities must be verified as accurate to gain widespread acceptance. • Broad target market: Because PeopleAhead is targeting a wide range of businesses, the product being developed has not been "customized" ideally for each segment.
External	**Opportunities** • Service gap: Recruiters are not pleased with current online recruitment vendors. • Industry gap: Job turnover is every 3.5 years per person. • Demand for productive candidates. • Online recruitment advertising: Growing by 35% per year, to reach $7.6 billion by 2010.[10]	**Threats** • Convergence: existing competitors may form strategic alliances and establish powerful positions before PeopleAhead can establish itself. • Inability to protect model: Very little intellectual property created by online websites is protected by law. Although PeopleAhead will pursue aggressive IP protection strategies, the model could be copied or mimicked by competitors. *(continued)*

Before engaging in a firm-specific SWOT analysis (see Chapter 2), this marketing plan assesses the external market environment further and thus establishes a basis for the subsequent SWOT analysis.

Note that the analysis uses outside sources to support its claims.

External   Opportunities

- Fragmented business models: Online recruitment is fragmented by recruitment methodology: active (people who need jobs), passive (people who are not looking but would move if enticed), poised (people unsatisfied with jobs they have), and network (finding people of interest based on who or what they know).

Threats

- Inadequate differentiation: Inability to explain our differentiation would relegate PeopleAhead to (unfair) comparisons with competitors. Without differentiation, PeopleAhead will not be able to create scale through network effects.

3.3. Competition

Most online recruitment websites compete in the active recruitment market, including Monster, CareerBuilder, and Yahoo/HotJobs. The pervasive segment includes job seekers who actively look for jobs, post their resumés, and search for jobs on company websites. Most active recruiters offer free services to users and charge companies on a fee basis. Companies can post jobs and search for candidate resumés in the database (average fee for local searches is $500 and nationwide is $1000). In this first-generation online recruitment business model, competitors face the challenge to make the process more user-friendly and reduce the effort required to make these sites deliver results.

- **Monster:** Monster.com is the sixteenth most visited website in the United States, with more than 43 million professionals in its viewer base. Monster earns revenue from job postings, access to its resumé database, and advertisements on websites of partner companies.

- **Careerbuilder:** Careerbuilder.com has experienced 75 percent growth for the past five years. This job post/resumé search company uses its media ownership to attract "passive" candidates from partner websites. It achieves growth through affiliate partnerships that host job searches on affiliated web pages, such as Google, MSN, AOL, USA Today, Earthlink, BellSouth, and CNN. Job posting is the primary activity, sold together with or separately from resumé searches.

- **Passive Recruitment:** The second generation of online recruitment locates candidates who are not necessarily looking for jobs but who could be convinced to move to a new position if the right opportunity was presented. The most recognized competitors in this category include Jobster, LinkedIn, and H3 (Appendix B).

3.4. Company Analysis

PeopleAhead's mission is simple: improve people's lives through career advancement. PeopleAhead recognizes that career advancement means many things to many people and provides a fresh perspective on career networking that is flexible yet powerful:

- **Users are not alone:** Finding a job is not easy. Why search solo? PeopleAhead unites groups of friends, co-workers, and mentors to create natural, team-based career discovery.

- **Job posting is not natural:** People spend countless hours searching job listings and posting resumés, only to be overlooked because their writing style or resumé format does not match an overburdened recruiter's preference. Good people make great companies, not resumés. PeopleAhead's TrueMatch® technology matches the right people with the right position. No posting, no applying—just good, quality matches.

If PeopleAhead chooses to adopt a competitor-based pricing strategy (see Chapter 11), detailed information about how other recruitment firms work will be mandatory.

Information about competitors' revenues, customers, growth, and so forth often is available publicly through a variety of sources.

For information that may not belong in the main text, an appendix offers an effective means to provide detail without distracting readers.

This section offers the "product" component of the market/product/customer analysis. Because People-Ahead's product is mostly a service (see Chapter 10), it focuses on some intangible features of its offering.

- Professionals being professionals: There is a place online for social networking, pet networking, and music networking. So why is there no outlet for career networking online—the activity that consumes the majority of our professional lives? PeopleAhead is a place where professionals share their experiences, achievements, and objectives with other professionals that care and can be found by employers who value their professionalism.

3.5. Customer Analysis

PeopleAhead's R&D efforts show that the impetus to improve recruitment effectivity is pervasive and that unmet needs revolve around a few core issues: the ability to find qualified talent, establishing a fit between the candidate and the company culture, verifying the candidate's career progression, and working quickly and cost-effectively. The following customer characteristics represent ideal attributes that align with PeopleAhead's service offering. This information might be used in conjunction with the Marketing Strategy.

3.5.1. Business Customer

- **Industry:** Because companies that value human capital are more likely to take a chance on a startup that promotes professional development, the broadly defined professional services industry, including insurance, banking, and consulting, is the primary focus.

- **Functional area:** PeopleAhead's system identifies "people" people, so positions that require human interaction are more aligned with system capabilities than those with stringent skill requirements, sets such as programming or accounting.

- **Size:** Large businesses (>1000 employees) have high-volume requirements and demand vendors with proven track records; small businesses (<25 employees) hire fewer people and may not justify acquisition costs. PeopleAhead aligns best with medium-sized customers.

- **Hiring need:** PeopleAhead serves two types of searches very well: those with too many applicants and those with too few applicants. By drawing applicants that most systems overlook and delivering only the most qualified applicants, the system assures the right candidate is identified quickly.

3.5.2. Individual Member

- **Background:** People who value professional development and are familiar with computer networking technologies; most are likely college educated, motivated by career success, and aware of their professional competencies/deficiencies.

- **Situation:** Members should have a professional development plan to share with others who can help them achieve their objectives—likely people who are inquisitive about their professional future and not content with their current situation. The common industry terminology for this group of people is "poised candidates."

- **Outlook:** Proactive people who research, plan, self-educate, and talk about their career. Probably the clearest example of proactivity is a student who devotes time, effort, and financial resources toward career advancement.

The last—and some would say most important—piece of the analysis puzzle: customers.

Although the introduction to this appendix and the plan's organization suggest that analyses of competitors, products, and customers are separate, as this plan shows, a firm usually cannot address one without considering the other. Here, in the Business Customer section, the plan notes what PeopleAhead's competitors fail to do and therefore why it offers a more valuable service.

Understanding a target customer is not just about numbers. PeopleAhead tries to consider what customers think and feel when searching for jobs too.

4. Marketing Strategy

4.1. Market Segmentation

4.1.1. Business Customers

- Small enterprises. Businesses with 10–99 employees. Companies with fewer than 10 employees are categorized as "Very Small Enterprises" and will not be a primary target market.
- Medium enterprises. Businesses with 100–1000 employees.

4.1.2. Individual Members

- Senior college students. Students in the process of searching for a first career.
- Graduate program students. Mid-career candidates searching for new career opportunities, such as internships, part-time during enrollment, or full-time after graduation.
- Current employees. Persons who are currently employed but are poised to locate better career opportunities.
- Unemployed. Persons searching for a job not included in previous segments.

4.2. Target Market

PeopleAhead plans to focus resources on small to medium enterprises (SMEs) in the New England Metro market, including Boston, Providence, Hartford, Stamford, Norwalk, Worcester, and Springfield. Online recruitment companies compete for national recruitment spending, but most job seekers are locally based, so market penetration is possible by covering a single geographical location. By maintaining this focus, PeopleAhead will be better equipped to build a critical mass of users that represent the job-seeking population and thus improve both users' and customers' experience, customer service, and the use of financial resources.

4.3. User Positioning

To the proactive professional, PeopleAhead is career advancement done right—providing a platform to discover, plan, and advance careers by uniting friends, co-workers, and mentors with companies searching for the right talent.

5. Marketing Mix

5.1. Products/Services Offered

The first planned offering is group profiling; users self-associate with groups to share development plans. Access to groupings is permission based and similar to social networking. Members will be able to share professional experiences with people they know. Group profiling may prompt "voyeur" networking, such that members join to view the profiles of the people they know.

   PeopleAhead will then open group profiling to business customers, who will be granted access to groups of members to target people they want to hire.

   The next added feature will be user feedback on professional development plans. PeopleAhead will track data from successful member profile matches to provide feedback for members who have not been matched successfully.

The plan continues with the same segmentation throughout. Here the plan discusses targeting and what makes each segment attractive.

By already identifying key markets in the previous section, the plan provides a foundation for a more specific targeting statement in this section.

The final step in the STP process: positioning for the segmented, targeted market.

PeopleAhead's mission

Given its own section in this plan, a discussion of the marketing mix constitutes a key element of the strategic planning process (see Chapter 2).

According to well-known marketing concepts, the marketing mix consists of the four Ps: product (service here), price, place (distribution here), and promotion.

The product (service) offering must establish the value for consumers: Why should they expend effort or resources to obtain the offering?

5.2. Price

In addition to a basic pricing schedule, PeopleAhead will offer bulk pricing and contract pricing to business customers to satisfy unique customer needs. The pricing model is expected to remain constant, but customer feed-back will be analyzed to ensure alignment with their requirements.

Continuing the new customer acquisition plan, PeopleAhead will encourage new trials by offering promotional pricing to new customers.

5.3. Distribution

- PeopleAhead Challenge: The PeopleAhead Challenge will act as a primary user acquisition strategy. Selection will be focused on successful target segments demanded by customers.

- Direct Sales: Direct customer contact is the preferred method of communication during the first six months. Telesales is the anticipated eventual sales model, due to reduced costs and quicker customer sales cycle, but it limits intimacy between the customer and PeopleAhead. During the initial stages, intimacy and excellent customer service are more highly desired than reduced cost, and direct sales achieves that objective.

- Industry Events: Attendance at HR industry and recruitment events will supplement direct sales efforts.

- Challenge Groups: Word-of-mouth distribution by PeopleAhead members.

5.4. Promotion

- Public Profiling: When the product is ready, with proper precautions for protecting competitive advantages, PeopleAhead can increase its Web presence. Strategies include contributing articles to recruitment publishers, writing op/ed pieces, public profiling of the founders on websites such as LinkedIn, Ziggs, and ZoomInfo, and blogging.

- Blogger Community Testimonials: Influential users of blogs will be invited to try the system and be granted "exclusive" access to the inner workings of the site. A subsequent linking blitz will put opinion pieces in front of recruiters, job seekers, and the investment community.

- Strategic Alliances: PeopleAhead offers a product that complements the services offered by many large organizations. Partner opportunities exist with

  a. universities, colleges, academic institutions

  b. professional associations, clubs, industry affiliation groups

  c. online associations, groups, blogs

  d. professional services firms, outplacement firms, and executive search firms

Strategic alliances serve multiple purposes: They can help PeopleAhead increase public exposure, increase the user base, expand product offerings, and increase revenue opportunities. These benefits will be considered and partnerships proposed prior to the official launch. For strategic purposes, PeopleAhead prefers to focus on product development in the near term (three months) and then reassess potential alliances after system efficacy has been proven.

Making the product (service) available where and when consumers want it may seem somewhat easier for PeopleAhead because of the vast development of the Internet; however, the firm still needs to consider how it can ensure people know where and how to access its offering.

The plan offers a specific time frame, which recognizes the potential need to make changes in the future, as the market dictates.

Peopleahead.com

delivers:

↗ Target marketing for hard-to-fill positions

↗ Qualified & pre-confirmed candidates

↗ Intelligent candidate ranking tools

↗ Results

6. Financials

Startup costs consist primarily of website design and development, legal representation (business formation, contract negotiation, and intellectual property protection), and general overhead. PeopleAhead projects start-up expenditures of $70,000 during inception, of which $30,000 has been funded by the founding team.

After the website launches, the cost structure will consist of sales agent salaries, general and administrative operating costs, and marketing. In the first year, marketing expenses are projected to be $6250 per month. Monthly overhead likely will reach $24,750 and remain constant.

The marketing plan needs to identify not only costs, but also potential revenues to cover those costs.

Certain assumptions or marketing research form the basis for its estimation of start-up costs.

This section contains a lot of numbers in a small space; the graphs and tables help to depict those numbers clearly and visually.

A. Projected Income Statement

Pro Forma Income Statement

	Year 1	Year 2	Year 3	Year 4	Year 5
Sales	$56,453	$2,683,665	$8,170,655	$16,312,843	$30,921,013
Gross Margin	$54,194	$2,316,318	$7,383,829	$14,780,329	$28,244,172
Gross Margin %	96.00%	86.31%	90.37%	90.61%	91.34%
Net Profit	($156,906)	$717,403	$3,356,768	$7,035,155	$14,180,041

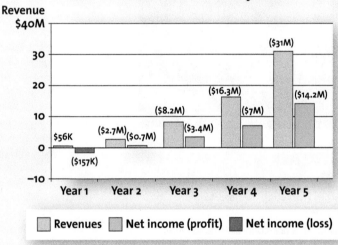

Revenue and Net Income Projections

7. Implementation Plan

The launch of PeopleAhead will use a phased approach, beginning with building brand awareness. Brand awareness should be developed through the founders' visible presence at professional events, online searches, membership in professional associations, networking, and strategic alliances. This visibility will help to gain investment capital.

7.1. Objective—Growth

- During the first six months of commercial availability, the primary objective is to expand both the user and customer base to maintain a 100:1 user to customer ratio.
  - **Business Customers:** Sign 24 regular customers and 72 occasional customers. Execute 117 position matches.
  - **Individual Members:** Convert 10,000 people to PeopleAhead members.

7.2. Marketing Objectives—Growth

- **PeopleAhead Challenge:** Pursue groups that were effective during Beta trial and represent a cohesive set of profiles. Expand and refine the Challenge to reflect lessons learned.
- **Increase member networking activity:** Increase user numbers through networking initiated by existing members. Improve user experience to promote networking.
- **Increase profile completeness:** Increase user engagement with platform.
- **Generate traffic.**
- **Public relations campaign (PR):** Increase awareness of PeopleAhead brand through concentrated PR efforts directed at the target market of customers and users.

> This plan divides the objectives into three categories: overall objective, marketing, and financial. Although this is a marketing plan, it must also include other aspects that influence marketing, such as financial status.

7.3. Financial Objectives

- **Efficient marketing expenditures:** 9,000 target users (10,000 year-end total −1000 during beta) × $5.00 target acquisition cost = $45,000 budget.

- **Revenue:** $482.50 per position × 117 positions = $56,452.50 revenue.

> By offering quantitative, direct goals, PeopleAhead ensures that it can measure its progress toward those goals.

7.4. Key Success Factors

- **Economical marketing to relevant constituents:** PeopleAhead needs to establish communication (distribution) channels that pinpoint relevant constituents in a manner consistent with mission values. Limited by resources, chosen channels must aggregate many relevant eyes with free, minimal, or deferred costs involved.

- **Crafting of brand identity:** The contrast between PeopleAhead and competitors lies not only in product differentiation, but also in the company's mission statement and delivery. One-time job search is available from thousands of online recruitment sources. Social networking has been covered from diverse angles, attracting many different audiences. The challenge is to associate www.PeopleAhead.com and TrueMatch® technology with "career advancement done right." The goal is to become the only company that a person thinks of for long-term career discovery, advancement, and development.

- **Efficient value delivery:** The base of customers (both individual and business) needs to receive the proposed value in a timely manner, with consideration given to quality versus quantity of results, alignment with existing objectives, and overall experience with the PeopleAhead brand.

- **Critical mass of business customers and individual users:** The matching process requires that both customers and users exist in the system from the outset of commercialization. This need brings to the forefront the "chicken and egg" scenario; establishing either customers or users requires the other constituent to exist already. The exact number that constitutes "critical mass" ranges from 100 users per position to 10 users per position, depending on compatibility between each constituency.

- **System effectivity:** The ability of PeopleAhead's TrueMatch® software to provide relevant candidate recommendations is critical. The effectiveness of the software depends on the algorithms that match users with positions and the networking protocol that initiates recommendations between users and the people they know. Proposing an inappropriate match could jeopardize the credibility of the system.

- **Intellectual property (IP) strategy:** PeopleAhead is engaged in two primary segments of online enterprise: online recruitment and social networking. Existing competitors have made many efforts to protect their methodologies through U.S. patents. However, precedent has not been established for the legal assertions made by these companies. As a result, PeopleAhead will assume an offensive IP strategy, consisting of diligent IP infringement review, patent application where appropriate, and aggressive trade secret protection of best practices.

- **Financial support:** The founders' investment is sufficient to form the business core and take delivery of PeopleAhead's website and software. Financial support will be required to fund operations, execute the IP strategy, and secure customers and users to meet financial targets. Without funding, PeopleAhead will not be able to proceed beyond the product development stage.

- **Sales process:** PeopleAhead's business model requires the acquisition of both business customers who have available positions and users who will be matched with those positions. These two constituents may be reached through different sales processes without overlap.

8. Evaluation and Control

PeopleAhead will evaluate user profiles to identify sets of profiles that are valuable to new business customers, which will aid in the selection of subsequent target market customers.

8.1. Business Customer

The evaluation section retains the segmentation scheme established previously between business customers and individual members.

Face-to-face meetings, phone conversations, and email survey contacts with people from a range of industries, company sizes, and functional areas provide a means to (1) build relationships with prospective customers, (2) understand customer needs, and (3) ensure alignment between PeopleAhead's product and customers' recruitment preferences. A summary of the key findings is listed here:

- **Employee fit:** Will the applicant fit our corporate culture? Will the applicant fit with the team we're considering? Will the applicants' competencies fit with the position requirements?
- **Pay for performance:** Objections to recruitment services focus not on price (though it is a consideration) but rather on lack of performance.
- **Unqualified applicants:** Many people who want a job apply, whether they are qualified or not. Recruiters then must scan resumés and weed out unqualified applicants instead of getting to know the qualified applicants.
- **Hard costs vs. soft costs:** Most companies track the recruitment costs of hiring providers, but few measure the time costs of hiring, opportunity costs of hiring the wrong employee, or productivity costs of leaving a position unfilled. Recruitment performance must be easy to measure. Value selling is difficult in human resources departments.
- **Valuable recommendations:** Most recruiters use online recruitment as a necessary but ineffective means of candidate sourcing, secondary to recommendations. Recommendations include the recommender's judgment of the candidate's fit with the available position.

8.2. Individual Members

Periodic surveys of various prospective users of online recruitment services indicate (1) current services, (2) methods that work well, and (3) biggest problems with online recruitment providers. The following is a qualitative summary of the key findings:

- **Willingness to try:** Careers are important to people; they are averse to spending time uploading resumé information to online recruitment websites only because of the lack of perceived value. They will spend time when the career opportunities are perceived as valuable.
- **Frustration:** Job seekers are frustrated with available online recruitment providers. Networking is the favoured method for career advancement.
- **Lack of differentiation:** Regardless of the qualifications a job seeker possesses, it is difficult to make them evident in a traditional resumé.

- **Motivation shift over time:** Early professionals are motivated by financial rewards. Mid-career professionals recommend people because it helps the people they know. Late-career professionals hope to improve their own job search opportunities.

Appendix A. Organizational Chart of PeopleAhead —————————————————

Appendix B. Competition: Passive Recruiters

Additional useful information that might clutter the plan should appear in an appendix. The appendices are not included in this illustration.

CHAPTER **3**

Analyzing the Marketing Environment

As we learned in Chapter 2, it is important for firms to continuously monitor their internal and external environments to identify new opportunities or threats to their business. Such analyses help firms identify areas where they are vulnerable to competition and areas where they are dominant. Firms then develop strategies or action plans to attack the competition or defend their market position. Let's see how Canadian Tire, an icon of Canadian retailing, has used knowledge of its environment to maintain its position for almost 100 years.

Canadian Tire's legacy started with a single Hamilton Tire and Garage Limited store just west of Toronto, which was purchased by brothers John and Alfred Billes in 1922. They renamed the company Canadian Tire Corporation in 1927 and grew it into a powerhouse. Today, Canadian Tire has six business units: Canadian Tire Retail (CTR), Canadian Tire Financial Services, Canadian Tire Petroleum, PartSource, Mark's (formerly Mark's Work Wearhouse) and FGL Sports. CTR has a network of more than 491 retail stores that offer everything from automotive parts and services to sports, leisure, and home equipment and products. CT Petroleum is one of the largest independent retailers of gasoline, with a network of 300 agent-operated gas bars, 295 convenience stores, 82 car washes, 13 pit stops, and 89 propane stations. CT Financial Services, through its Options MasterCard, has more than 5 million credit card customers. PartSource, an automotive parts specialty chain that sells to professional automotive installers and "do-it-yourselfers," consists of 86 stores. Mark's consists of 385 stores, of which 37 are franchises. Mark's has 39 percent market share in the industrial clothes market.[1] FGL Sports has 421 stores, of which 184 are franchises. Canadian Tire, through its various businesses, employs more than 85,000 people and earned revenues of C$11.8 billion, with profits of C$564 million, in 2013.

Canadian Tire is one of the most trusted brands in Canada. In 2013, it was named Retailer of the Year, one of the Best Brands in Canada, and one of Canada's Most Successful Companies; it also earned a spot on Canada's Top Ten Most Reputable Brands for the ninth year in a row. It has a unique assortment of products and services, a modern store network, and global sourcing capabilities. It is also the market leader in 17 of the top 20 selling categories, such as backyard, exercise, and household consumables.[2] The company does an excellent job of leveraging its trusted Canadian Tire brand across its multiple businesses.[3]

LEARNING OBJECTIVES

After studying this chapter you should be able to

LO1 Outline how the factors in a firm's microenvironment influence its marketing strategy

LO2 Identify the factors in a firm's macroenvironment and explain how they influence the overall marketing strategy

LO3 Identify important social and natural trends that impact marketing decisions

Because of Canadian Tire's level of success over the years, one wonders about its secret for success and whether it has always been smooth sailing for the company.

Canadian Tire has received lumps, bumps, and bruises on several occasions. For example, in 1982, Canadian Tire debuted in the United States, but the venture failed miserably, and by 1985 the company was forced to withdraw.[4] In 1992, the company decided to take another stab at the U.S. market under the name Auto Source. It again failed and bailed out in 1995, after three years and huge losses.[5] Despite these and other challenges, Canadian Tire has emerged as a successful and well-managed business. Its success has been attributed to many things, including its vision, good strategic planning, and excellent execution of its marketing strategies. However, one important element that cannot be discounted is its ability to understand and manage its microenvironment and macroenvironment.

For example, when global giants Walmart, Home Depot, and Lowes entered the already crowded Canadian market, many industry analysts feared that their deep pockets and aggressive business strategies would spell the end of Canadian Tire. However, as we have seen over the last decade, Canadian Tire has not only held its own against these global behemoths, but also steadily grown. The company implemented a wide range of strategies aimed at improving cost efficiencies and productivity, enhancing customer service, bolstering its brands, growing its businesses, strengthening its loyalty program, and renewing its store concepts. For example, it continuously changed its store formats in response to changing demographic and social trends. In 2003, it launched its 20/20 store format,[6] which featured an updated layout, new and expanded product assortments, a customer care centre, new store signage, and a redesigned exterior store facade. Recently, the company rolled out its latest store formats, dubbed Smart stores and Small Market stores.[7] Smart stores have a racetrack floor plan that offers more space for high-growth categories and helps customers find products more easily through better signage and logical product adjacencies. Small Market stores include a Mark's store and a gas bar. The company has responded to advancing technology by integrating its website into its physical store operations and upgrading its information technology and communication infrastructure. It has adopted a wide range of environmental technologies aimed at reducing its carbon footprint. It grew through the acquisition of Mark's Work Wearhouse, pursuing a broader target market that includes children and young women. Its expansion continued in 2011 with the purchase of FGL Sports, which includes store banners such as Sport Chek, Atmosphere, National Sports, Hockey Experts, and Nevada Bob's Golf among others.

Like other retailing businesses, Canadian Tire cannot escape the challenges of the economy and other external factors that affect its businesses, but it must find a way to minimize the impact. In past years, unseasonably warm winters have sometimes resulted in poor sales of winter products. However, improvements in employment in resource-based Alberta and British Columbia have led to increased sales of industrial wear at Mark's. The Financial Services division had to set aside a greater amount for loan losses because of higher bankruptcies among its customers. However, lower interest costs helped to improve the financial situation. Government-mandated increases in the hourly minimum wage increased labour costs.[8] And in 2013, Target entered Canada, further intensifying the competitive retail environment.

What do you think Canadian Tire's sustainable competitive advantages are? What factors in the macroenvironment seemed to impact Canadian Tire's business strategy? ▌

A MARKETING ENVIRONMENT ANALYSIS FRAMEWORK

As the chapter vignette suggests, marketers who understand and manage the changes in their marketing environments are able to adapt their product and service offerings to meet new challenges and opportunities. Canadian Tire, for example, introduced three new store formats between 2003 and 2008, based on its understanding of the marketplace. Many marketers get their ideas for new products or services from monitoring and studying the marketing environment, as demonstrated in the case of Kobo and eBooks at the end of this chapter. Analyzing the marketing environment also helps marketers assess their continued strengths and the value of their products and services, and any weaknesses resulting from changes in the marketing environment.

Companies analyze their marketing environment using a framework. At the heart of the analysis is, as always, the consumer. Consumers may be influenced directly by the firm's microenvironment, including the immediate actions of the focal company, the company's competition, and the corporate partners that work with the firm to make and supply products and services to consumers. The firm, and therefore consumers indirectly, is influenced by the macroenvironment, which includes influences such as culture and demographics, as well as social, technological, economic, and political/legal factors. We'll discuss each of these components in detail in this chapter and suggest how they interrelate. Exhibit 3.1 also illustrates these ideas.

EXHIBIT 3.1 — Understanding the Marketing Environment

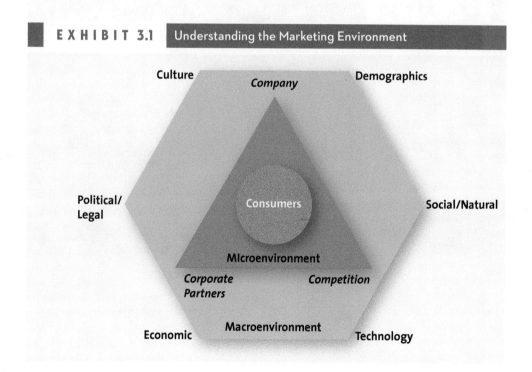

One of the goals of value-based marketing is to provide greater value to consumers than competitors offer. This provision requires that the marketing firm looks at the entire business process from a consumer's point of view.[9] Consumers' needs and wants, as well as their ability to purchase, are affected by a host of factors that change and evolve over time. Firms use a variety of tools to keep track of their competitors' activities and communicate with their corporate partners. Furthermore, they monitor their macroenvironment to determine how such factors influence consumers and how they should respond to them. Sometimes, firms can even anticipate trends. For example, pharmaceutical companies have done an excellent job of monitoring market trends and consumers, and responding to consumers' needs. Based on observing and monitoring the aging baby boomer generation of consumers, they have made and marketed drugs to lower cholesterol, improve sexual performance, slow aging, and stem hair loss.

LO1 MICROENVIRONMENTAL FACTORS

Exhibit 3.2 illustrates the factors affecting consumers' microenvironment: the company (i.e., its capabilities), its competition, and its corporate partners.

Company Capabilities

In the firm's microenvironment, the first factor that affects the consumer is the firm itself. Successful marketing firms focus their efforts on satisfying customer needs that match their core competencies. The primary strength of Apple, for instance, originally rested in the design, manufacture, distribution, and promotion of Macintosh computers. But Apple has successfully leveraged its core competency in the digital audio player arena with its iPod, iPhone, and iPad. It recognized a trend among consumers for sleek but functional portable devices, which can become one of their personal accessories. Marketers can use an analysis of the external environment, like the SWOT analysis described in Chapter 2, to categorize an opportunity as either attractive or unattractive and, if it appears attractive, to assess it relative to the firm's existing competencies.

EXHIBIT 3.2 Understanding the Microenvironment

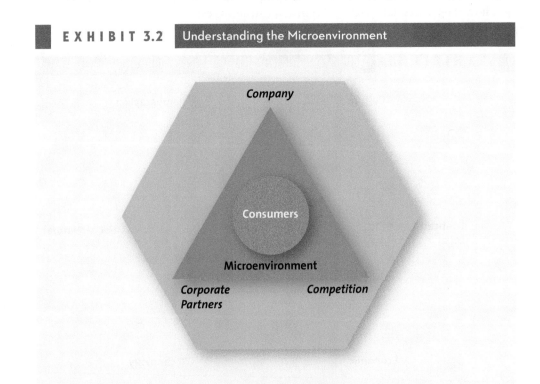

Gillette and Schick introduced similar razors almost simultaneously.

Competition

Competition also significantly affects consumers in the microenvironment. Greater competition may mean more choices for consumers, which influences their buying decisions. It is critical that marketers understand their firm's competitors, including their strengths, weaknesses, and likely reactions to the marketing activities their own firm undertakes. When Colgate introduced Colgate Total toothpaste, promising total protection of your teeth, P&G responded with Crest Pro-Health, which promises to protect all areas where dentists check most.[10] No one would want to get caught in the war between the two razor giants, Gillette Co. and Energizer USA, which makes Schick razors, as each manufacturer works to add ever more blades to its disposable razors.[11] Gillette accused Schick of engaging in false and misleading advertising when ads claimed that its Hydro razor would hydrate skin. Schick's parent company countered with the complaint that Gillette's Fusion ProGlide Razor ads attempt to deceive when they assert that the blades are "Gillette's thinnest blades ever." All these efforts represent the companies' recognition of what their closest competitor is doing, as well as their attempts to halt tactics they consider damaging. But at the same time, each razor company touts its benefits over its competitors, because the ultimate goal, of course, is to appeal to consumers.

Firms use **competitive intelligence (CI)** to collect and synthesize information about their position with respect to their rivals. In this way, CI enables companies to anticipate changes in the marketplace rather than merely react to them.[12] In Canada, an Ipsos Reid study conducted on behalf of the Marketing Research and Intelligence Association reports that while overall awareness of various business intelligence components ranges from medium to high among CI decision makers and business executives, existing CI activities are fairly limited in practice, and require more resources and attention in the future. The study found that less than half of decision makers say that their company is involved in various CI initiatives.[13]

The strategies to gather CI can range from simply sending a retail employee to a competitive store to check merchandise, prices, and foot traffic to more involved methods, such as

- reviewing public materials, including websites, press releases, industry journals, annual reports, subscription databases, permit applications, patent applications, and trade shows

- interviewing customers, suppliers, partners, or former employees

- analyzing a rival's marketing tactics, distribution practices, pricing, and hiring needs

These more sophisticated CI strategies are implicitly obvious in the modern smartphone market. Even though the first cellphone was invented in 1973, it wasn't until the

competitive intelligence (CI) Used by firms to collect and synthesize information about their position with respect to their rivals; enables companies to anticipate changes in the marketplace rather than merely react to them.

Who copied whom? Apple and Samsung engaged in a patent infringement lawsuit.

mid-90s that the introduction of features like text messaging and PDA functions catalyzed an industry metamorphosis that continues to this day. Amidst the frenzy of continuously evolving technologies, and increasing market competition to serve ever-changing consumer preferences, Apple Inc. has established itself as a front-runner in the smartphone industry. With the introduction of its first generation iPhone, one of the first phones to use a multi-touch interface, Apple secured itself a strong position in the market and in the hearts and minds of consumers. As of March 2014, Apple has sold more than 500 million iPhones.[14] Even so, after facing very strong competition from Samsung's Galaxy line of products, which first appeared on the market in 2009, Apple has been dethroned. And so began a battle for the title of the "King of Smartphones" and global market share. This has entailed the release of subsequent versions of the Galaxy and the iPhone 5, creative marketing campaigns with Samsung branding the Galaxy as the "anti-iPhone," and costly promotional strategies to ensure consumer loyalty and retention. It also resulted in a very high profile lawsuit against Samsung for patent infringement. In situations such as this, it becomes critical for firms to keep close tabs on each other's activities by using CI techniques. If Samsung hadn't paid attention to the market's response to Apple's innovation in design and interface technology, it may never have introduced the Galaxy.

Although CI is widely regarded as a necessary function in today's world, certain uses of this information have come under ethical and legal scrutiny. Take, for example, Apple's case against Samsung. In April 2011, Apple launched a lawsuit against Samsung, claiming deliberate patent infringement on four design patents. These alleged patent infringements in question pertained to features such as the tap-to-zoom, pinch-to-zoom, and bounce-back scrolling.[15] Apple supported these allegations by illustrating the evolution of the design of Samsung phones prior to and after the release of the iPhone in 2007. Apple also presented evidence citing that prior to the launch of the Galaxy Tab, Google and other third parties had warned Samsung that the product too closely resembled the iPad. Google reportedly even asked Samsung to revise the product for a more "distinguishable design." In light of these allegations, Samsung countersued Apple for the alleged infringement of five of its patents. To support this stance, Samsung cited that in 2006 prior to the conception of the iPhone, an article dwelling on the design of Samsung devices was circulated to Apple executives. Immediately following the review of this article, Apple's designers were instructed to conceive a "Samsung-like" design for an Apple phone.[16] In the end, the jury ruled in favour of Apple, finding that Samsung had in fact deliberately violated a series of Apple patents whereas Apple did not violate any of Samsung's patents. Samsung was then instructed to pay Apple $1 billion in damages.[17] While some believe that this decision could potentially limit market competition and consumer choice, others argue that it forces companies to innovate rather than imitate. This lawsuit is just one in a series of many dealing with patent infringement in the smartphone industry. One year later, the U.S. International Trade Commission ruled that some iPhone products did in fact violate a Samsung patent and overturned the case.[18]

Another misuse of CI can be seen in Air Canada's case against WestJet. A lawsuit occurred based on allegations that WestJet management used the password of a former Air Canada employee to access a website maintained by Air Canada to download confidential information. WestJet countersued by alleging Air Canada used private investigators to search through recycling material at the home of a WestJet executive.

WestJet later accepted full responsibility for its misconduct, which was unethical and unacceptable. Even worse, this practice was undertaken with the knowledge of the highest management levels of WestJet and was not halted until discovered by Air Canada. WestJet apologized to its competitor and Air Canada top executive Robert Milton. WestJet has also paid $5 million to Air Canada for its investigation and litigation costs, and made a $10 million donation to children's charities in the names of both airlines.[19]

Corporate Partners

Few firms operate in isolation. For example, automobile manufacturers collaborate with suppliers of sheet metal, tire manufacturers, component part makers, unions, transport companies, and dealerships to produce and market their automobiles successfully. Even firms such as Dell, which makes its own computers and sells them to customers, must purchase components, consulting services, advertising, and transportation from others. Parties that work with the focal firm are its corporate partners. Consider an example that demonstrates the role these partners play and how they work with the firm to create a single, efficient manufacturing system. Unlike most outdoor clothing manufacturers that use synthetic nonrenewable materials, Nau makes outdoor and ski clothing from renewable sources such as corn and recycled plastic bottles. The company was founded by a team of entrepreneurs who left companies such as Nike and Patagonia. To develop rugged and beautiful clothing from sustainable materials, these founders turned to manufacturing partners around the world to develop new fabrics, such as PLA (polylactic acid), a fast-wicking biopolymer made from corn. To complement the new fabrics, the company uses only organic cotton and wool from "happy sheep," provided by partners in the ranching industry that embrace animal-friendly practices. Thus, Nau not only represents the cutting edge of sustainability and green business, but also clearly demonstrates how "going green" can prompt companies to work more closely with their partners to innovate.[20]

Nau works with its corporate partners to a socially responsible strategy.

L02

MACROENVIRONMENTAL FACTORS

In addition to understanding the company itself, its competition, and its corporate partners, marketers must also understand the **macroenvironmental factors** that operate in the external environment, namely, the culture, demographics, social/natural trends, technological advances, economic situation, and political/legal environment, or CDSTEP, as shown in Exhibit 3.3.

Culture

Culture   We broadly define **culture** as the shared meanings, beliefs, morals, values, and customs of a group of people.[21] Transmitted by words, literature, and institutions, culture is passed down from generation to generation and learned over time. You participate in many cultures. For example, based on your family's cultural heritage, perhaps your mealtime traditions include eating rugelach, a traditional Jewish pastry, or sharing corned beef and cabbage to celebrate your Irish ancestry on St. Patrick's Day. Your school or workplace also shares its own common culture. In a broader sense, you also participate in the cultural aspects of the town and country in which you live. The challenge for marketers is to have products or services identifiable by and relevant to a particular group of people. Our various cultures influence what, why, how, where, and when we buy. Two dimensions of culture that marketers must take into account as they develop their marketing strategies are the culture of the country and that of a region within a country.

Country Culture   The visible nuances of a **country's culture**, such as artifacts, behaviour, dress, symbols, physical settings, ceremonies, language differences, colours and tastes, and food preferences, are easy to spot. But the subtle aspects of culture generally are trickier to identify and navigate. BMW's Mini and other global automobile manufacturers have successfully bridged the cultural gap by producing advertising that appeals to the same target market across countries. The pictures and copy are the same. The only thing that changes is the language.

macroenvironmental factors
Aspects of the external environment—culture, demographics, social trends, technological advances, economic situation, and political/legal environment (CDSTEP)—that affect companies.

culture
The shared meanings, beliefs, morals, values, and customs of a group of people.

country's culture
Easy-to-spot visible nuances that are particular to a country, such as dress, symbols, ceremonies, language, colours, and food preferences, and more subtle aspects, which are trickier to identify.

EXHIBIT 3.3   The Macroenvironment

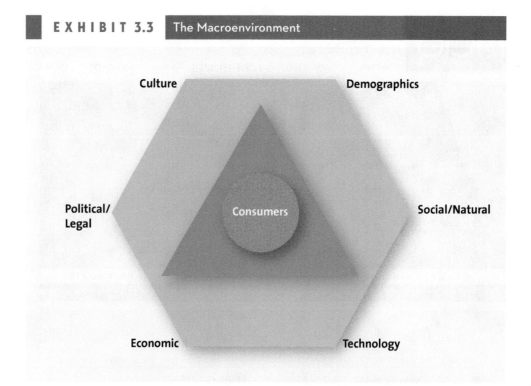

Some firms, such as BMW's Mini, have successfully bridged the cultural gap by producing advertising that appeals to the same target market across countries.

Regional Subcultures   The region in which people live in a particular country affects the way they react to different cultural rituals, or even how they refer to a particular product category. A resident of Quebec is 25 percent less likely to buy a hot prepared meal or reheatable meal than a resident of Ontario. This difference is attributed to Quebec women's desire to cook as a way to be more involved in their family's lives. As well, Quebec consumers are less price sensitive when grocery shopping than residents of Ontario. In Quebec, the most popular stores are IGA and Metro, as compared with No Frills and Food Basics in Ontario.[22] These kinds of differences can be the insight that helps a marketer make a strong connection with a consumer, rather than communicating the same way to all Canadians.

Another example of a regional subcultural difference is how we refer to our beverages. For instance, 37 percent of Canadians refer to carbonated beverages as *soda*, whereas another 40 percent call it *pop*, and an additional 17 percent call any such beverage a "Coke," even when the drink is a Pepsi. Eat lunch in British Columbia, and you'll have the best luck ordering a pop, but if you head to Quebec for dinner, you'd better order a *soft drink*. Imagine the difficulty these firms have in developing promotional materials that transcend regional boundaries.[23]

Demographics

Demographics indicate the characteristics of human populations and segments, especially those used to identify consumer markets. Typical demographics such as age—which includes generational cohorts—gender, income, race, and ethnicity are readily available from market research firms such as Nielsen, Ipsos Reid, Leger Marketing, and Statistics Canada. For instance, Nielsen collects information about TV viewership and sells it to networks and potential advertisers. The networks then use this information to set their advertising fees, whereas advertisers use it to choose the best shows on which to advertise. For a show popular among the desirable 18- to 35-year-old viewing segment, a network can charge the highest fees. But advertisers also might want to know whether a show is more popular with women than men or with urban or rural viewers. Demographics thus provide an easily understood "snapshot" of the typical consumer in a specific target market.

demographics
Characteristics of human populations and segments, especially those used to identify consumer markets, such as age, gender, income, race, ethnicity, and education.

Marketers position their products and services differently depending on which generational cohort they are targeting.

generational cohort
A group of people of the same generation who typically have similar purchase behaviours because they have shared experiences and are in the same stage of life.

tweens
Generational cohort of people who are not quite teenagers but are not young children either (ages 9 to 12); they're in beTWEEN.

Watch out for tweens. They are fast, multitasking, technology savvy, and easily bored.

In the next few sections, we examine how firms use such demographics to assess their customers' needs and position themselves to deliver better value for those customers.

Generational Cohorts A group of people of the same generation, **generational cohorts**, have similar purchase behaviours because they have shared experiences and are in the same stage of life. For instance, baby boomers, made up of people born between 1946 and 1965, and Generation Xers, people born between 1966 and 1971, both gravitate toward products and services that foster a casual lifestyle; however, they tend to do so for different reasons.[24] The aging baby boomers, who grew up with jeans and khakis and brought casual dressing into the business arena, are often trying to maintain their youth. Gen Xers, in contrast, typically wear jeans and khakis because they are less impressed with the symbols of conspicuous consumption that their parents seem to have embraced. Although there are many ways to cut the generational pie, we discuss five major groups: tweens, Generation Y, Generation X, baby boomers, and seniors.

Tweens.   Tweens—not quite teenagers but not young children either—sit in beTWEEN. The importance of **tweens** to marketers stems from their immense buying power, estimated at $2.9 billion annually in Canada and $200 billion annually in the United States.[25] Canadian tweens also influence another $20 billion annually in family purchases. Marketers feel the tween effect in many areas, but particularly in the cellphone market. Tween users make great use of advanced features such as web surfing, photo capabilities, and texting. Although smartphones, such as the BlackBerry and iPhone, historically targeted older users, companies today recognize the massive market for the features of these products among the tween segment.

In Canada, tweens spend their money mainly on food and drinks, electronics (gaming consoles and games, digital music players, cellphones, and computers) and clothing. They learn about new products mainly from TV shows and friends. Although they enjoy the attention they get from marketers, they are not an easy group to market to. Three in four Canadian tweens make shopping decisions jointly with their parents.[26] Tweens are also known as speeders, because they do everything at lightning speed.[27] Since tweens are the first generation born after the emergence of the Internet, technology has no novelty for them. They have grown up as "digital natives." They communicate with friends via instant messenger while talking on a cellphone and flipping through TV channels simultaneously. As a result, marketers are inventing increasingly innovative ways to reach tweens through the Internet. Marketers must be careful with this cohort though; once they get bored, tweens are gone, off doing something else. So firms need to engage them quickly and with sincerity. Many companies, such as McCain Foods with its frozen pizza and Sony with its PlayStation, have developed innovative media campaigns to market to this group.

And what do tweens like? In the food industry, they lean toward products such as Yoplait's Yop. For toys and clothing, they have made Build-A-Bear Workshop, Claire's, and West 49 immensely popular. However, because they have little of their own money, tweens tend to be value conscious, which makes them key targets for retailers such as Ardene, Hollister, American Eagle Outfitters, and Old Navy. Because tweens still go shopping with their parents, they are developing an affinity for the same brands, prompting retailers to develop special product lines to accommodate their demands. But at some point, such accommodation may cross the line into exploitation as Ethical Dilemma 3.1 suggests.

By the time a child is three years old, he or she can recognize an average of 100 brand logos.[28] Marketers can make use of this information to ensure that their logos and advertising communication are prominent on packaging, as well as on the toys themselves, to ensure that children demand their brand from gift-giving parents.

The influence does not stop with toys, though. More and more companies are placing advertisements in schools and on buses.[29] And even though Facebook and similar sites officially require users to be at least 13 years of age, reports suggest that nearly 8 million Facebook visitors actually are younger than 12.[30] Although initially, most social media sites adopted this age restriction so that they could avoid meeting regulations associated with youthful users, it appears they are switching tactics in response to this widespread usage among young digital natives.

For Facebook and similar sites, inviting children to join offers two main advantages. First, it encourages their brand loyalty to the site itself. If a child creates a

Is expanding demographic target markets to ever-younger children a boon for marketers? Or is it a danger to children?

Facebook profile at the age of 10, she is unlikely to take it down by the time she is 15 or 18 or even 26 years old. Second, by making the concept of sharing information more familiar to users from a very young age, Facebook helps encourage the type of behaviours it needs from consumers for it to survive. If digital natives have few expectations of privacy but instead share all their preferences online, advertisers enjoy greater access to their ideas and thoughts.

Brands can then use this information to market their own products to children. The makers of sugary drinks have done so extensively. Despite concerns about childhood obesity and the ethics of marketing nutritionally void foods to children, no laws prevent brands from hosting Facebook pages or creating a Twitter account to appeal to children.

Of course, access also potentially extends to sexual predators and others who might harm children. Some findings suggest that at least 1 million children are harassed or bullied through Facebook each year.[31]

Generation Y. Generation Y, also called **millennials** or the "echo boom" generation, represent just over 9 million Canadians, or about 27 percent of the population.[32] This group also varies the most in age, ranging from people in their 20s to people in their 40s who have started their own families.[33] Generation Y grew up in a more media-intensive and brand-conscious era than their parents. Thus, they are more skeptical about what they hear in the media, which makes marketing to this group even more challenging. If Gen Y members believe the sell is "too hard," they won't buy. Regardless of where they live, they watch an hour less TV than an average household, use the Internet at work for personal reasons, and expect a healthy option at fast-food restaurants.[34] Gen Yers are Internet and technology savvy and love digital electronics such as cellphones, digital music players, digital cameras, and video games. Members of Gen Y often look the same across countries. MTV and CNN are available in most developed countries and so these consumers have similar lifestyles, as well as music and entertainment tastes. Even their "uniforms" of jeans, running shoes, and T-shirts are similar.

In the next few years, many Gen Yers will be starting families and will be prime targets for homes and durable household products such as appliances, furniture, and gardening equipment and tools. In addition, now that Gen Y is established in the workplace, it is becoming apparent that its members have different expectations and requirements than those of other cohorts. Gen Y puts a strong emphasis

Generation Y/ millennials
Generational cohort of people born between 1972 and 1992; the biggest cohort since the original postwar baby boom.

Multitasking is no big deal for Gen Y.

on balancing work and life; these young adults want a good job, but they also want to live in a location that supports their lifestyle.

Generation X
Generational cohort of people born between 1966 and 1971.

Generation X.   The next group, **Generation X**, includes people born between 1966 and 1971. This group represents more than 2.8 million Canadians, or about 8 percent of the Canadian population.[35] Unlike their baby boomer parents, Gen X is the first generation of latchkey kids (those who grew up in homes in which both parents worked), and 50 percent of them have divorced parents. These young adults, having grown up in times of economic recession, are more likely than previous generations to be unemployed, carry higher debt loads, travel the world, and move far away from their parents; they are also more likely to live longer with their parents, compared with baby boomers, who, at their age, couldn't wait to move away from home.[36]

Gen Xers possesses considerable spending power because they tend to wait to get married and buy houses later in life. However, they are unlikely to enjoy greater prosperity than their parents. They're much less interested in shopping than their parents and are far more cynical, which tends to make them astute consumers. They demand convenience and tend to be less likely to believe advertising claims or what salespeople tell them. Marketing to Gen X is difficult, but word-of-mouth advertising from people they know and trust can give marketers the credibility needed to market to this cohort. Because of their experience as children of working parents who had little time to shop, Gen X were shopping savvy at an early age and knew how to make shopping decisions by the time they were teenagers. As a result, they grew more knowledgeable about products and more risk averse than other generational cohorts. Finally, Gen X is much less interested in status products than older generations, not because they can't afford luxury brands but because they just don't see the point. Many companies such as Harley-Davidson and the Starwood Hotels and Resorts chain have developed products targeted specifically to Gen X.

baby boomers
Generational cohort of people born after World War II until 1965.

Baby Boomers.   After World War II, the birth rate in Canada rose sharply, resulting in a group known as the **baby boomers**, who were born between 1946 and 1965. They are the largest cohort of Canadians, representing 30 percent of the population. Although the baby boomer generation spans 18 years, experts agree that its members share several traits that set them apart from those born before World War II. First, they are individualistic. Second,

No matter how old they get, baby boomers will always love rock 'n' roll.

leisure time is a high priority for them. Third, they believe that they will always be able to take care of themselves, partly driven by their feeling of economic security, even though they are a little careless about the way they spend their money. Fourth, they have an obsession with maintaining their youth. Fifth and finally, they will always love rock 'n' roll.

The oldest baby boomers have reached age 65 and many have already retired. The baby boomers' quest for youth, in both attitude and appearance, provides a massive market for anti-aging products, cosmetics, pharmaceuticals, and biotechnology. It is estimated that this pursuit of youth will push the market for anti-aging products in the United States from $80 billion to more than $114 billion by 2015.[37] Salon services used to be a purely feminine domain, but with boomers rapidly aging, providers are recognizing the potential of positioning themselves as being in the rejuvenation business. In ways that previous generations would have considered unthinkable, men have begun pampering themselves with salon services such as manicures, facials, and pedicures. Indeed, many boomers, including older baby boomers, are driving sports cars and going on adventure-based vacations.

Food companies have also targeted baby boomers with healthier options for cereals, frozen entrees, and snacks that have low fat, and no cholesterol or sugar. General Mills has added extra calcium to Yoplait Original yogurt in an attempt to help women increase their daily calcium requirements, reduced the sodium in products like Cheerios and Progresso soups, and created a new version of Total cereal containing omega-3 fatty acids, which are good for heart health.

Retailers also recognize the immense buying power of the aging baby boomers, so they cater directly to them with larger fonts in signage, staff available to read the small print on product packaging, and seating options in stores. They note that their older customers, even those with moderate incomes, are more focused on quality than price and retailers make decisions on what merchandise to carry accordingly.

Seniors. **Seniors** are over the age of 65 and make up Canada's fastest-growing group.[38] Between 2006 and 2011, the number of seniors in Canada grew from 4.3 million to nearly 5 million. (As noted previously, the oldest baby boomers have now reached their "senior" years.) Their share of the population increased to 15.8 percent. Fifty-six percent of seniors are women. According to Statistics Canada, by 2016 the number of seniors is expected to outnumber the number of children in Canada.[39] But just because they are a large and growing segment, are they necessarily an important market segment for marketers to pursue? They're more likely to complain, need special attention, and take time browsing before making a purchase compared with younger groups. However, they generally have time to shop and money to spend.

seniors
North America's fastest-growing generational cohort; people aged 65 and older.

What do they spend their money on? Travel, second homes, luxury cars, electronic equipment, investments, home furnishings, and clothing are frequent purchases. Specifically, seniors tend to like "made in Canada" items and recognizable brand names (but generally not designer labels), value, quality, and classic styles. They're typically loyal and willing to spend but are extremely quality conscious and demand hassle-free shopping, particularly in terms of convenient locations. Because most mature customers don't need the basics, they prefer to buy a few high-quality items rather than a larger number of low-quality items.[40]

Income The median income of Canadian families in 2010 was approximately $72,240.[41] Canadians may be classified into distinct groups based on their income and other factors such as background, education, and occupation: upper class, middle class, working class (or low-income earners), and underclass (at or below poverty). *Upper-class* consumers are very affluent, and their spending patterns are not influenced by economic conditions. They have high discretionary incomes and tend to purchase luxury items. The top 10 percent of Canadians have family income in excess of $80,000. They are more likely to be highly educated and work in managerial and executive roles. About 48 percent of Canadian households are in the upper class.[42]

The Fuel Cell Car and Experiment Kit appeals to an affluent consumer at specialty retailer Hammacher Schlemmer.

Middle-class families earn between $30,000 and $70,000, with the majority tending toward the higher end of this scale. They can afford a good life most of the time. They tend to be careful about their spending and are often value conscious. Approximately 38 percent of Canadian households fall in the middle class. *Working-class*, or low-income families, earn between $20,000 and $30,000, barely sufficient income to cover their basic needs. According to a report by Statistics Canada, the richest 20 percent of Canadians spend 5 or 6 times more in every shopping category than the poorest 20 percent of Canadians.[43] Family income distribution in Canada varies by province, education level, gender, and profession. This broad range in incomes creates marketing opportunities at both the high and low ends of the market.

Although some marketers choose to target only affluent population segments, others have had great success delivering value to middle- and low-income earners. Consider, for example, the toys presented by the specialty retailer Hammacher Schlemmer versus the mass appeal of Walmart's toy sections. Toy buyers at Walmart are looking for inexpensive products; those at Hammacher Schlemmer go to great lengths to find unusual toys such as the Fuel Cell Car and Experiment Kit pictured.[44]

Another aspect of the income demographic relates to the concept of value. Why are customers searching for this value more today than in recent decades? During the first three decades after World War II, most families experienced real income growth but, after 1980, that growth began to idle. Family incomes have stayed slightly ahead of inflation (the general rate of price increases), but their health care costs, property taxes, and tuition bills have risen much faster than inflation.

Education Studies show that higher levels of education lead to better jobs and higher incomes.[45] Moreover, average annual earnings are higher for those with degrees than for those without. For example, in 2008, the median earnings for Canadians with a bachelor's degree were $44,100, a master's degree $60,000, and a doctorate $65,000. Those with a college diploma earned on average $38,000, and those with less than a high school education earned considerably less at $30,900.[46] The median income for immigrants with a university degree was $36,451, and without a university degree $27,698.[47]

For some products, marketers can combine education level with other data such as occupation and income to obtain quite accurate predictions of purchase behaviour. For instance, a full-time college or university student with a part-time job may have relatively little personal income but will spend his or her disposable dollars differently than would a high school graduate who works in a factory and earns a similar income. College and university students tend to be engaged in playing sports and going to nightclubs, whereas the high school graduate more likely watches sports and goes to bars. Marketers are therefore quite cognizant of the interaction among education, income, and occupation.

Gender Years ago, gender roles appeared clear, but those male/female roles have been blurred. This shift in attitude and behaviour affects the way many firms design and promote their products and services. For example, more firms are careful about gender neutrality in positioning their products and, furthermore, attempt to transcend gender boundaries whenever they can.

From cars to copiers, sweaters to sweeteners, women make the majority of purchasing decisions and then influence most of the remainder. For instance, despite the traditional view that hardware stores appeal mostly to men, women shoppers are so important

Since women are such an important segment of their customers, Rona, the giant home-improvement chain, has designed its stores with women in mind.

to Rona, the home improvement chain, that the stores have been designed with women in mind.[48] Furthermore, women now head more than 20 percent of Canadian households.[49] Clearly, the working women's segment is a large, complex, and lucrative market.

But that doesn't mean marketers have forgotten about men. The days of commercials that show Mom alone with the kids are over. To reflect changing family roles, commercials for most children's gear now include Dad interacting with the kids and being involved in purchase decisions. Although the gap is narrowing, men still earn more money than women. In 2008, women earned an average of 71.3 percent of what men earned—that is, women earned $44,700, while men earned $62,600. The difference is much lower for women aged 25 to 29 entering the workforce; these women earned 15 percent less than men, or 85 cents for each dollar earned by men.[50]

Ethnicity Statistics Canada data shows that the ethnic composition of Canada has changed over the last two decades and will continue to change in the next decade. Current research shows that 1 out of every 5 Canadians was not born here, accounting for nearly 70 percent of Canada's population growth. If this trend continues, Canada's population growth will be attributed almost exclusively to immigration by 2030.[51] The two fastest-growing groups are the Chinese (from Hong Kong, mainland China, and Taiwan) and South Asians (from India, Pakistan, Sri Lanka, and Bangladesh). It is estimated that ethnic groups or visible minorities will make up about 8.5 million or 23 percent of Canada's population by 2017 because of immigration and increasing birth rates among various ethnic groups.[52] Many new immigrants choose to settle in Montreal, Toronto, or Vancouver; however, areas such as Calgary, Edmonton, Winnipeg, and London are growing in popularity. These groups of South Asians and Chinese are typically young, educated, and wealthy. Currently, more than a quarter of all visible minorities in Canada are under 14 years; thus, they are likely to have considerable influence over the economy in the future. South Asians are the largest ethnic group in Ontario.[53] Aboriginal people represent another key to Canada's diverse ethnicities, representing 4.3 percent of the total population. Unlike immigrant groups who live primarily in Canada's most urban areas, Aboriginal people live mostly in the territories, Western provinces, and Ontario. This population has been growing at a fast pace; from 2006 to 2011, it grew by 20.1 percent.[54]

Women are no longer the only family member doing the grocery shopping.

Sobeys' FreshCo stores were designed with the needs of ethnic consumers in mind.

In 2005 the average income earned in this group was $35,501.[55] Will a growing population present new opportunities for businesses to market to Aboriginal people?

What does this ethnic demographic shift mean for marketers? Simply put, the growing number of ethnic groups or visible minorities represents both a challenge and a marketing opportunity. The challenge is for marketers to understand the culture, value, and spending patterns of the various groups and determine the best way to communicate and serve them. The creative director of Fat Free Communications, a Toronto ad agency, argues that most bank advertising employs "very superficial ways of acknowledging the (ethnic) community, which a lot of people in the community actually find irritating." Chris Bhang, a vice-president at Allard Johnson Communications, admonishes marketers to "be colloquial, be creative but be relevant."[56]

In terms of marketing opportunity, it is estimated that ethnic groups spend more than $42 billion on retail goods and services, and the average Chinese household spends $63,500 per year, compared with the Canadian average of $58,500. In general, ethnic Canadians spend more than their white counterparts on big-ticket items such as cars, clothing, and home furnishings. Many also have an affinity for brand-name products because they equate them with quality.[57]

Recognizing this huge opportunity and believing that much of its future growth will come from ethnic markets, Canadian grocery heavyweight Sobeys has developed a new store concept, FreshCo, specifically targeted to the unique needs of the ethnic consumer. The company started in Ontario by converting some existing Price Chopper stores in particularly diverse Brampton and Mississauga markets to the new FreshCo model. Since then it has launched over 75 stores across Ontario.[58] The concept is a value-driven store with low prices like No Frills or Food Basics but with a focus on fresh produce, halal meats, and freshly baked breads (unlike most discount banners) to meet the demands of ethnic clientele. As well, the layout of the store is different. After the store's layout guides consumers through the fresh produce, bakery, and meat departments, as in a typical retail grocery store, the natural flow of the store takes shoppers through the extended international foods aisle, which highlights Asian, West Indian, Middle Eastern, and Eastern European food products, before the customers reach the centre grocery aisles.[59] Sobeys has also committed to adapting the FreshCo store assortments to match the demographics of the surrounding neighbourhood, including teaming up with local suppliers.[60] The success of FreshCo will depend, in part, on the success that Sobeys marketers have in getting grocery shoppers to move away from smaller ethnic grocery stores and other ethnic-targeted stores—such as T&T Supermarket, which was acquired by Loblaw in 2009—that are the typical grocery choice for ethnic consumers.

It's no doubt that other grocery stores will respond to remain competitive. Some of the tactics retailers are taking to accommodate the ethnic consumer include adapting signs and flyers to feature different languages; choosing ethnic-targeted media to advertise; celebrating important ethnic holidays such as Chinese New Year, Ramadan, Eid, and Hanukkah with events, promotions, and seasonal products; and offering ethnic merchandise for sale and ensuring it is merchandised correctly.[61]

Technological Advances

technological advances
Technological changes that have contributed to the improvement of the value of both products and services in the past few decades.

Technological advances have accelerated greatly during the past few decades, improving the value of both products and services. Consumers have constant access to the Internet everywhere they go via WiFi, and 3G and 4G services. Smartphones using the Apple, BlackBerry, and Android operating systems allow for greater computing, data storage, and communication. Tablet computers have extended mobile computing even further by offering a larger mobile interface in environments that traditionally limited access. Flat-screen and high-definition televisions, as well as video on demand, have changed the way we view TV, and their impact is expected only to increase in the next few years.

These examples of advanced technology make consumers increasingly dependent on the help they can provide, especially in terms of making decisions and communicating with others. Netflix suggests which movies we should watch, Pandora outlines the music we should listen to, and Amazon tells us what we should read. Nearfield communication technology takes payments, coupons, and loyalty card data from customers as they walk by the scanner. The next wave of mobile applications is likely to involve wireless payments, such that customers' phones also serve as "m-wallets."

Firms use the technology called RFID (radio frequency identification device) to track an item from the moment it was manufactured, through the distribution system, to the retail store, and into the hands of the final consumer. Because they are able to determine exactly how much of each product is at a given point in the supply chain, retailers can also communicate with their suppliers and collaboratively plan to meet their inventory needs.

As Social and Mobile Marketing 3.1 shows, mobile devices enhance the customer's experience by making it easier to interact with the manufacturer or retailer or other customers, and they add a new channel of access, which makes customers more loyal and more likely to spend more with a particular retailer. Walgreens' applications allow customers to order prescriptions or review their prescription history, check the in-store inventories, and print photos. Steve Madden, the footwear retailer, attracts more than 10 percent of its web traffic from mobile devices—which earns it more than $1 million in mobile sales annually. Furthermore, these shoppers spend an average of seven minutes on Steve Madden's mobile site.[62] Whereas customers view an average of seven web pages during online visits, they browse only four or five pages in a mobile setting.

 ## Social and Mobile Marketing 3.1 | Foursquare's Promise and Facebook's Response

The location-based mobile platform Foursquare not only awards badges to frequent customers to reflect their status in certain locations, but also helps people find the locations their friends are frequenting and gives them helpful tips about local bars, restaurants, parks, museums, grocery stores, and movie theatres—such as where to park or what not to order. For the 250,000 companies that appear on the platform,[63] Foursquare also provides an effective means to attract, appeal to, and retain loyal customers.

A Foursquare user who checks in to a local restaurant, for example, accumulates points and rewards, in the form of badges. These badges earn the user discounts and coupons on future visits to the restaurant, as long as he or she keeps checking in at the site. The more a user visits, the more incentives she or he receives. To up the ante even more, customers can earn additional points for bringing along a friend on their next visit and getting that friend to check in at the same time. The social aspects of Foursquare go still further: Users often leave reviews of the venues they visit and then plan ahead to determine the places they will go next, according to what other similar users have said about a location.

For the companies, these uses provide remarkable insights into target markets.[64] They know who is visiting, when, how often, and with whom. Finally, because the concept is based on rewarding frequent visitors, companies know they are devoting their best efforts to their best, most loyal customers.

By gathering the vast information from all its users, both consumers and sellers, Foursquare can issue on-target recommendations of other places to go. Did you visit a coffee shop on Elm Street? Foursquare thinks you might find the tea house on Oak Lane interesting as well. If another fellow fan of the local pizza joint also tends to check in at the movie theatre down the street, Foursquare can suggest you might like it too.

But Foursquare isn't the only game in town. Facebook also allows users to check in at locations and has the advantage of a much larger social network—more than 1.26 billion users,[65] compared with Foursquare's 45 million or so.[66] Facebook fans can tag friends who are with them, to show how many people are showing up at a particular location. This tool means Facebook can learn about its users and the places they or their friends like to go to. Marketers then can use this information to learn more about their customers, including the places they prefer and how those preferences align with their other interests—as communicated by their Facebook profile.

Mobile applications are not just about shopping with a phone. People access the web more often through smartphones than through laptops and desktops combined. But mobile experiences cannot be identical to web experiences, because the interface is different, and thus the way users employ the sites differ. In particular, the smaller screen on mobile devices means that less information must convey the same brand image.

Different technology adoption levels also matter to marketers when communicating a new product or using a new media type. As noted so far and as described throughout this book in the Social and Mobile Marketing boxes, not only are marketers trying to make social media an integral part of their marketing strategy, but also consumers are also using social media to share information and their experiences and frustrations with products, services, and marketers. The relative ease with which consumers can use social media has dramatically increased the power of consumers to affect a firm's marketing strategy. Some firms have embraced social media as a way to get excellent feedback from consumers, which is then used to design new or redesign existing products, services, and marketing campaigns and strategies. Moreover, even traditional media such as TV networks are encouraging consumers to share their experiences, gripes, and frustrations through their websites; these consumer accounts are then aired. For example, the CBC show *The National* has a Go Public link on its website, which encourages consumers to share their stories; one story is reported on every night that the show airs.[67] One story concerned Sears' Kenmore stoves, which consumers said would turn on by themselves, posing a very dangerous and unsafe situation. And, because they were dissatisfied with the response from Sears, the consumers went public with their story. Needless to say, this story generated a lot of negative publicity for Sears.

Economic Situation

economic situation
Economic changes that affect the way consumers buy merchandise and spend money; see *inflation, foreign currency fluctuations, interest rates,* and *recession.*

inflation
Refers to the persistent increase in the prices of goods and services.

foreign currency fluctuations
Changes in the value of a country's currency relative to the currency of another country; can influence consumer spending.

Marketers monitor the general **economic situation**, both in their home country and abroad, because it affects the way consumers buy merchandise and spend money. Some major factors that influence the state of an economy include the rate of inflation, foreign currency exchange rates, interest rates, and recession.

Inflation refers to the persistent increase in the prices of goods and services.[68] Increasing prices cause the purchasing power of the dollar to decline; in other words, a dollar buys less than it used to.

In a similar fashion, **foreign currency fluctuations** can influence consumer spending. For instance, on January 21, 2007, C$1.00 was worth US$0.6179, the lowest exchange rate ever between these two currencies. In less than four months, the value of the Canadian dollar relative to the U.S. dollar increased to $0.9071[69]—a 32 percent increase—and by September the Canadian dollar increased to $1.10. After hovering at parity for two years, the Canadian dollar dropped to $0.90 and continues to fluctuate. Rapid increases in the exchange rate between the currencies of Canada and the United States, our largest trading partner, have both negative and positive consequences for Canadian marketers, depending on whether they are exporters or importers and whether they report their earnings in Canadian or U.S. dollars. The exchange rate changes also have serious implications for consumers. As the value of the Canadian dollar increases compared with the U.S. dollar, merchandise made in Canada and exported to the United States becomes more costly to Americans, and Canadian exporting companies suddenly lose a good chunk of their cost advantage. However, imports of products made in the United States cost less for both Canadian importers and consumers.

Another perhaps unexpected result of the strength of the Canadian dollar compared with the U.S. dollar is that imports of raw material from the United States are cheaper. During such inflationary times, "made in America" claims become more important, which means that Canadian manufacturers and U.S. retailers that specialize in Canadian merchandise must decide whether they should attempt to maintain their profit margins or accept a lower price to keep their customer base. It is not always easy for marketers to respond quickly to rapid increases; however, marketers who monitor the economic environment have the advantage, as they will be able to adjust their strategies if they foresee the increase.

Interest rates represent the cost of borrowing money. For example, when customers borrow money from a bank, they agree to pay back the loan, plus the interest that accrues. The interest, in effect, is the cost to the customers or the fee the bank charges those customers for borrowing the money. Likewise, if a customer opens a savings account at a bank, he or she will earn interest on the amount saved, which means the interest becomes the fee the consumer gets for "loaning" the money to the bank. If the interest rate goes up, consumers have an incentive to save more, because they earn more for loaning the bank their money; when interest rates go down, however, consumers generally borrow more.

For instance, when the Bank of Canada cut its overnight lending rate, the rate at which it lends to banks, by 4.25 percent to 0.25 percent in April 2009, record numbers of Canadians took advantage of the historic low interest rates and took out mortgages. The 0.25 percent interest rate broke the previous record low of 1.12 percent, which was set in 1958, 50 years earlier. The cut was considered absolutely necessary to deal with the worsening global economic and financial crisis. Although the overnight lending rate has been at 1 percent since October 2010,[70] cheap credit has led to a situation in Canada where the average Canadian income-to-debt ratio is 150—that is, for every $1 earned, Canadians owe $1.50. If this situation continues, it could exert negative consequences on the economy and ultimately on consumers and marketers.[71]

Finally, **recession** is a period of economic downturn when the economic growth of the country is negative for at least two consecutive quarters. We last experienced this in 2008–2009. In a recession, the stock market declines sharply, unemployment increases, business and consumer confidence falls, and spending by both businesses and consumers is severely reduced.

In recessionary times, consumers alter their spending patterns by postponing big-ticket or discretionary items and look for the best deals for items they need. Marketers must adjust their marketing strategies accordingly. Most marketers try to cut costs, lower prices to keep their existing customers and to attract new customers, and may even introduce slightly lower quality goods or reduce the level of services offered in order to manage costs. In a recession, some industries do well and others struggle. Marketers must be vigilant in monitoring the environment and understanding the impact economic downturn has on their business.

How do these four important economic factors—inflation, foreign currency fluctuations, interest rates, and recession—affect a firm's ability to market goods and services? Shifts in the four economic factors make marketing easier for some and harder for others. For instance, when inflation increases, consumers probably don't buy less food, but they may shift their expenditures from expensive steaks to less-expensive hamburgers. Grocery stores and inexpensive restaurants win, but expensive restaurants lose. Consumers also buy less discretionary merchandise. For instance, the sale of expensive jewellery, fancy cars, and extravagant vacations will decrease but, curiously, the sale of low-cost luxuries, such as personal care products and home entertainment, tends to increase. It appears that, instead of rewarding themselves with a new Lexus or a health spa vacation, consumers buy a few cosmetics and stream a movie. As noted above, lower interest rates encourage more consumers to borrow to finance purchases, especially of big-ticket or discretionary items such as cars, houses, furniture, and home entertainment systems. Not surprisingly, the building industry and housing market did extremely well in the period leading up to the recent recession. As consumers switched from more- to less-expensive goods and services and demanding greater value, marketers who were able to adjust their offering did much better than those that did not change their value offering.

interest rates
Represent the cost of borrowing money.

recession
A period of economic downturn when the economic growth of the country is negative for at least two consecutive quarters.

Tourists from many other countries flock to the United States to shop because the value of the dollar is low compared with their own currency.

Political/Legal Environment

The **political/legal environment** comprises political parties, government organizations, and legislation and laws that promote or inhibit trade and marketing activities. Organizations must fully understand and comply with any legislation regarding fair competition, consumer protection, or industry-specific regulation. Since the turn of the century, the government has enacted laws that promote both fair trade and competition by prohibiting the formation of monopolies or alliances that would damage a competitive marketplace, fostering fair pricing practices for all suppliers and consumers, and promoting free trade agreements among foreign nations.

Legislation also has been enacted to protect consumers in a variety of ways. First, regulations require manufacturers to abstain from false or misleading advertising practices that might mislead consumers, such as claims that a medication can cure a disease when in fact it causes other health risks. Second, manufacturers are required to identify and remove any harmful or hazardous materials (e.g., asbestos) that might place a consumer at risk. Third, organizations must adhere to fair and reasonable business practices when they communicate with consumers. For example, Montreal, Maine, and Atlantic Railway (MMA) seems to have ignored its own safety procedures regarding the use of hand brakes, which resulted in the fourth deadliest rail accident in Canadian history, killing 42 people and devastating the town of Lac Megontic's core.

Last but not least, the government enacts laws focused on specific industries and on consumers. These laws may be geared toward increasing competition, such as the deregulation of the telephone and energy industries. Or they may be in response to current events or to achieve specific objectives, such as when the governments of Ontario and British Columbia introduced the harmonized sales tax (HST) to improve the competitiveness of Canadian businesses, or when the federal government introduced the one-year home renovation tax credit to encourage consumers to spend during the recession. Similarly, the government has developed laws to regulate consumer behaviour, such as banning smoking in some areas, mandating child car seats, and requiring drivers to use only hands-free cellphones.

Generally, government regulations may have a negative or positive impact on marketers. On the positive side, certain laws create an opportunity for marketers to sell more of their products, as was the case with Bluetooth devices or car seats. Also, regulation may help to create a level playing field for competition and set standards for marketers to follow. In other cases, regulation tends to increase the cost of compliance; compliance usually requires more paperwork, time, effort, and money, and may cause delays when government approval is needed. Some of the most significant legislation affecting marketing interests appears in Exhibits 3.4 and 3.5.

L03 Social and Natural Trends

Social and natural trends shape consumer values in Canada and the United States, and around the world. These trends tend to change over time in their popularity and importance, and savvy marketers work hard to identify emerging trends to understand whether they present an opportunity or pose a threat to their business. Here, we discuss a few current social and natural trends of key importance today. This list is by no means exhaustive but includes greener consumers, marketing to children, privacy concerns, the time-poor society, and health and wellness concerns.

Greener Consumers[72] **Green marketing** involves a strategic effort by firms to supply customers with environmentally friendly merchandise. Although this "green" trend is not new, it is growing. Many consumers, concerned about everything from the purity of air and water to the safety of beef and salmon, believe that each person can make a difference in the environment. A study found that more than 90 percent of Canadians feel that individuals can take action to reduce air pollution. More than half of Canadian households now recycle their soft-drink bottles, cardboard boxes, and newspapers. In many cities across Canada, the use of pesticides on lawns is banned and

EXHIBIT 3.4	Major Federal Legislation to Protect Competition and Consumers

Access to Information Act	Interest Act
Bankruptcy Act	Investment Canada Act
Bills of Exchange Act	Lobbyist Registration Act
Broadcasting Act	Official Languages Act
Canada Agricultural Product Standards Act	Patent Act
Canada Corporations Act	Personal Information Protection and Electronic Documents Act (PIPEDA)
Canada Dairy Products Act	Privacy Act
Canada Human Rights Act	Small Loans Act
Canada Small Business Financing Act	Standards Council of Canada Act
Competition Act	Textile Labelling Act
Consumer Packaging and Labelling Act	Trade-Marks Act
Copyright Act	True Labelling Act
Criminal Code	Weight and Measures Act
Electricity and Gas Inspection Act	Winding-up Act
Food and Drugs Act	
Income Tax Act	

EXHIBIT 3.5	Marketing Practices Covered by the Competition Act

Law	Description
Price	
Price fixing	Sellers conspire to set the price of a product, usually higher than it would be in a free market
Price discrimination	Charging different prices to different (competing) buyers for goods of the same quality and of the same quantity
Predatory pricing	Pricing that is intended to drive competitors out of the market or keep competitors from entering the market—usually low prices
Resale price maintenance	Manufacturers or channel members try to influence the price at which the product is sold to subsequent purchasers
Bid rigging	Sellers collude to set prices in response to bids or quotations for products
External	
Misleading advertising	All types of advertising about a product or service that are false or misleading
Bait-and-switch	Sellers try to attract customers to their stores by offering a low price on a product (bait); but, once the customers are in the store, sellers try to persuade them to buy a higher-priced item (switch)
Referral selling	Incentives offered to consumers to provide the names of other potential consumers
Distribution (Place)	
Refusal to deal	A seller refuses to sell products or services to legitimate buyers
Exclusive dealing	A seller refuses to sell to other channel members unless that member agrees to buy exclusively from that particular seller
Pyramid selling	Schemes where salespersons are paid to recruit other salespeople, and each new salesperson pays for the right to recruit other salespeople, with some of that money going to earlier recruiters. Participants are often asked to buy a specific quantity of goods or are knowingly sold unreasonable quantities of goods and are not allowed to return the goods on commercially reasonable terms.

many consumers are trying alternative, environmentally friendly lawn care treatment. Also, a growing number of cities across Canada are introducing the "green bin" program that encourages consumers to recycle their food and yard waste to make compost for gardening. Initial results suggest that this program is hugely successful everywhere it has been introduced. Composting has also spawned business opportunities as seen in Entrepreneurial Marketing 3.1. The trend for green marketing is likely to persist as we still have a long way to go. According to a Conference Board of Canada report, Canadians produce more garbage than any other country in the developed world and use almost double the amount of freshwater of other countries.[73]

For companies selling environmentally friendly products, the green marketing trend represents a great opportunity. Firms that sell products considered harmful to the environment may find this trend a threat to their business and must innovate to stay in business. Companies also need to rise above suspicions of "greenwashing." To show it is a responsible retailer, Rona has adopted a strict scientific method that monitors a product over all stages of its lifecycle: acquisition of materials, manufacturing, packaging and transportation, and finally, use and end of life.[74] The Sustainable Marketing boxes

Entrepreneurial Marketing 3.1

Turning Trash into Cash[75]

Lisa von Sturmer is a compost crusader who sees dollar signs in dirt. After a weeklong vacation with friends on Savary Island in British Columbia, where composting is mandatory, she was shocked to see how little waste the group generated. When she returned to work she was dismayed at how much organic material was thrown in the garbage, especially since her recent experience had shown just how much of it could diverted. That insight was the impetus to launch Growing City, a service to pick up food scraps from offices in the Vancouver area.

According to von Sturmer, 67 percent of Canadian waste today comes from the office and industrial sector. And that's a growing problem. In 2015 organic materials will be banned from landfill sites in Vancouver. Other municipalities and provinces across Canada will also implement bans in the coming years. And that is putting pressure on companies to change the

Lisa von Sturmer turns trash into cash with her Growing City office compost bins.

way they deal with organic waste. The solution? Growing City will place stainless steel compost bins in your office kitchens. Employees simply put their food scraps in the bins and Growing City staff does the rest: picks them up, empties and cleans them, and takes the organic material away to an industrial composting facility in Delta, BC.

Growing City was founded in late 2010. In only two years it diverted 130 tonnes of waste from landfills. Plus, the company made money doing it: $100,000 in sales the first year. Referrals and word-of-mouth helped the

business grow to $212,000 in the second year, leaving enough profits to pay von Sturmer a salary of $55,000. In spite of having no business background, von Sturmer has won numerous awards including the 2010 Small Business BC's Best Business Concept award,[76] and 2012 Canadian Youth Business Foundation's National Best Green Business award.[77] By the third year, the company had contracts with 82 offices in Vancouver, Richmond, and Burnaby and was expanding to Surrey. It has also been subcontracted to handle organics for other companies, including one of Canada's largest recycling companies.

Having started Growing City with a $15,000 loan from the Canadian Business Foundation, von Sturmer needed money to grow. When she pitched on CBC's *Dragons' Den*, she asked for an investment of $100,000 for a 25 percent share of her company, telling the Dragons that she'd had requests for franchises and needed their help to do this. Her compelling presentation led three Dragons to express interest. In the end, she took an offer from Jim Treliving who could provide both a cash infusion and help with franchising.

In 2013, the Vancouver market produced 270 tonnes of organic waste. By 2015 it will have to deal with 540 tonnes, representing almost $200 million in revenue and putting Growing City on track to turn more trash into cash.

throughout this book provide many more examples of how individual Canadians and businesses are taking actions to reduce the harmful effects of their consumption and production decisions.

The demand for green-oriented products has been a boon to the firms that supply them. For instance, marketers encourage consumers to replace their older versions of washing machines and dishwashers with water- and energy-saving models and to invest in phosphate-free laundry powder and mercury-free, rechargeable batteries. Canada's love affair with recycling also has created markets for recycled build-

Spawned by environmental concerns and rising gas prices, consumers are demanding more fuel-efficient hybrid cars.

ing products, packaging, paper goods, and even sweaters and sneakers. Similarly, this raised energy consciousness has spurred the growth of more-efficient appliances, lighting, and heating and cooling systems in homes and offices. Health-conscious consumers continue to fuel the markets for organic foods, natural cleaning and personal care products, air- and water-filtration devices, bottled water, and organic fertilizers. By offering environmental responsibility, these green products add an extra ounce of value that other products don't have, as illustrated in Sustainable Marketing 3.1.

 Sustainable Marketing 3.1 **Bullfrog Power Leaps onto the Green Scene[78]**

Canadians are becoming increasingly conscious about how their purchase and consumption decisions impact the environment. In an effort to offset the harmful environmental effects of the products they consume, many Canadians are reducing their carbon footprint by subscribing to a wide variety of environmentally friendly initiatives. They believe that each person can make a difference, and they are taking whatever action they can to reduce negative environmental effects.

Tom Heintzman, president of Bullfrog Power, recognizes this growing social trend. He is capitalizing on the green trend by providing Canadian consumers with an energy alternative, helping them reduce their carbon footprint. Heintzman believes that it is important for Canadians to consider clean energy, especially since the Kyoto Protocol expired in 2012 and its goals were not achieved. As a result of this lack of progress, Heintzman believes it's important for individuals to lead. By making clean energy choices available, he believes that individuals can exert their unique power to change the world.

Heintzman's company, Bullfrog Power, is based in Toronto and provides 100 percent green electricity. The company opened in Ontario in September 2005 and has since successfully expanded its operations and services to British Columbia, Alberta, Nova Scotia, New

Brunswick, and Prince Edward Island. Bullfrog Power addresses climate change and environmental issues that are growing social trends. The company uses electricity that comes from wind and hydro facilities instead of more-polluting sources such as coal, oil, nuclear, and natural gas. Bullfrog Power ensures that the amount of electricity used by its consumers is matched by the amount of renewable electricity that the company's wind turbines and low-impact water generators channel into the local grid. This option means that residents do not need to purchase any additional equipment or wiring to switch to a greener energy alternative, which appeals to consumers because it is simple for them to take action to create a greener environment.

The change toward a greener environment is being embraced, despite the fact that green energy can be more costly. Bullfrog Power is a relatively expensive product. It is targeted toward a specific demographic that has a high level of income and a high level of education and is therefore more aware of environmental issues. These individuals are willing to pay more for products that align with their values. By understanding important social trends and targeting specific demographics, Bullfrog Power is reshaping the electricity landscape and leading the switch to greener energy.

Marketing to Children[79]   In the past 20 years, child obesity has doubled in Canada, leading to skyrocketing rates of high blood pressure, high cholesterol, early signs of heart disease, and Type 2 diabetes among children. In response, the Center for Science and the Public Interest (CSPI) has proposed *Guidelines for Responsible Food Marketing to Children,* which outlines a variety of changes to advertising directed at children. The CSPI notes that children are highly impressionable, and most food advertising to these young consumers touts high-calorie, low-nutrition products, associated in advertising with various toys, cartoons, and celebrities. The new guidelines require advertisers to market food in reasonably proportioned sizes. The advertised food items also must provide basic nutrients, have less than 30 percent of their total calories from fat, and include no added sweeteners. The advertising also cannot be aired during children's programming, and companies cannot link unhealthy foods with cartoon and celebrity figures. For example, Burger King no longer uses SpongeBob SquarePants to promote burgers and fries. Other organizations such as the Chronic Disease Prevention Alliance of Canada (CDPAC) and health and citizens' groups are also working to ensure proper advertising to children.[80]

Privacy Concerns   More and more consumers worldwide sense a loss of privacy. At the same time that the Internet has created an erupting volcano of accessibility to consumer information, improvements in computer storage facilities and the manipulation of information have led to more and better credit-check services. In addition, consumers are constantly reminded that their identity may not be their own, as in the humorous series of Citibank commercials that depict unsuspecting credit card users who have had their identities stolen. In one, a sweet-looking older woman describes her new pickup truck in a deep, masculine voiceover. Although these commercials promote a new credit card with identity theft protection, most consumers have no such protection. In April 2011, Epsilon, a Dallas, Texas–based marketing firm that controls the email databases of more than 2,500 business clients and sends more than 40 billion marketing messages to consumers per year on behalf of its clients, reported that hackers had breached its system. Epsilon's list of clients includes some of the biggest U.S. corporations with global reach: AIR MILES, Best Buy, Marriott, Hilton Hotels, JPMorgan Chase, Citigroup, Capital One Financial, Walgreens, Kroeger, U.S. Bancorp, and several others. Investigators regard this data breach as one of the biggest in U.S. history.[81] In December 2013, Target stores suffered a data breach affecting 40 million debit and credit cards.[82] Although the breach impacted Americans primarily, it is hardly surprising that more than three-quarters of Canadians are concerned about the security and privacy of the information they provide over the Internet.[83]

Time-poor consumers multitask to cope with their lack of leisure time.

The Time-Poor Society   Reaching a target market has always been a major challenge, but it is made even more complicated by several trends that increase the difficulty of grabbing those markets' attention. First, in the majority of families, both parents work, and the kids are busier than ever. For example, on average, Canadians worked 8.9 hours during a typical workday, but 25 percent said they devote more than 10 hours a day to their work. That means Canadians have less time for leisure and to spend with family. Canadian workers spend about 200 hours less with family per year than they did two decades ago.[84]

Second, consumers today have hundreds of shows and programs available to them through TV, radio, PDAs, DVDs, smartphones, personal computers, and the Internet. With many shows and programs available on the Internet, consumers can choose when, where, and what shows they want to watch or listen to at their convenience. By fast-forwarding thorough the commercials, they can catch an entire one-hour show in approximately 47 minutes, which means they miss all the messages marketers are attempting to send them.

Third, many consumers attempt to cope with their lack of leisure time by multitasking: watching TV or listening to music while talking on the telephone or doing homework. Their divided attention means they simply cannot focus as well on the advertisements that appear in those media.

Self-checkout lanes speed the shopping process, but do they improve customer service?

Marketers are thus faced with the challenge of finding more creative ways to get their marketing messages out to consumers under these ever-changing media consumption trends. Some marketers have responded to the challenge of getting consumers' attention by, for example, moving some of their advertising expenditures from traditional venues such as TV and print media to instant messaging, Internet-based reviews and ads, social media ads, movie screens, fortune cookies, baggage claim conveyor belts, billboards, and ads in airports and on taxis, buses, and mass transport vehicles.[85] Retailers are doing their part by making their products available to customers whenever and wherever they want. For instance, retailers such as Sears Canada and The Bay are becoming full-fledged multichannel retailers that offer stores, catalogues, and Internet shopping options. Others, such as Metro, Shoppers Drug Mart, and Walmart, have extended their hours of operation so that their customers can shop during hours that they aren't working. In addition, automated processes such as self-checkout lanes and electronic kiosks speed the shopping process and provide customers with product and ordering information.

To find and develop methods to make life easier for many diverse consumers in a time-poor society, marketers often rely on technology, another macroenvironmental factor we discussed earlier in this section.

Health and Wellness Concerns

Health concerns, especially those pertaining to children, are prevalent, critical, and widespread. In Canada, 60.1 percent of adult men and 44.2 percent of adult women are categorized as obese or overweight.[86] In the past 20 years, child obesity has doubled and teenage obesity tripled in North America, leading to skyrocketing rates of high blood pressure, high cholesterol, early signs of heart disease, and Type 2 diabetes among children.

As the same time, consumers' interest in improving their health has opened up several new markets and niches focused on healthy living. For example, consumer spending on yoga classes, mats, and clothing has increased consistently, leading to an 87 percent increase in yoga product spending in the last five years.[87] Yoga studios actually combine multiple modern trends: As the economy sours, people face increasing stress, which they hope to reduce through yoga. In addition, yoga studios are relatively inexpensive to open and operate, so entrepreneurs and consumers appreciate the value for the money they offer. And of course, North Americans are always on the lookout for exercise methods that can help them shed pounds and match media images of athletic prowess.

LEARNING OBJECTIVES REVIEW

 Outline how the factors in a firm's microenvironment influence its marketing strategy

The three factors in a firm's microenvironment are its capabilities, corporate partners, and competition. Everything a firm does should utilize its strengths and revolve around the customer; without the customer, nothing gets sold. Firms must discover their customers' wants and needs and then be able to provide a valuable product or service that will satisfy those needs. If there were only one firm and many customers, a marketer's life would be a piece of cake. But because this setup rarely occurs, firms must monitor their competitors to discover how they might be appealing to their customers. Without competitive intelligence, a firm's customers might soon belong to its competitors. Though life would certainly be easier without competitors, it would be difficult, if not impossible, without corporate partners. Good marketing firms work closely with their suppliers, marketing research firms, consultants, and transportation firms to coordinate the extensive process of discovering what customers want and getting it to them when and where they want it. Each of these activities—identifying corporate strengths, discovering customer needs, and working with corporate partners—is central to the firm's marketing strategy and helps add value to firms' products and services.

LO2 **Identify the factors in a firm's macroenvironment and explain how they influence its overall marketing strategy**

The factors in the firm's external environment are culture, demographics, social and natural trends, technological advances, economic situation, and political/legal environment (CDSTEP). A clear understanding of these factors enables marketers to understand whether they pose threats or present new opportunities.

What are the chances that a fast-food hamburger restaurant would be successful in a predominantly Hindu neighbourhood? Not very good. Marketers must be sensitive to such cultural issues to be successful, and then they must also consider competitors as well as customer demographics—age, gender, income, race, ethnicity, and education—to identify specific customer groups. In any society, major social and natural trends influence the way people live. Understanding these trends can help marketers serve their customers better. At no other time in history has technology moved so rapidly and had such a pervasive influence on the way we live. Not only do marketers help to develop technologies for practical, everyday uses, but technological advances also help marketers provide consumers with more products and services more quickly and efficiently. The general state of the economy influences how people spend their disposable income. When the economy is healthy, marketing success comes relatively easily. But when the economy gets bumpy, only well-honed marketing skill can yield long-term successes. Naturally, all firms must abide by the law, but many legal issues also affect marketing directly. These laws can be broken into those that pertain to competitive practices, such as antitrust legislation, and those designed to protect consumers from unfair or dangerous practices, such as warning labels on cigarette packages.

LO3 **Identify important social and natural trends that impact marketing decisions**

In any society, major social and natural trends influence the way people live. Social trends have a tremendous impact on what consumers purchase and consume. Understanding these trends—such as price sensitivity, health and wellness, green marketing, privacy issues, and the time-poor society—can help marketers serve their customers better by offering them products and services that closely match their needs and wants.

KEY TERMS

- baby boomers
- competitive intelligence (CI)
- country culture
- culture
- demographics
- economic situation
- foreign currency fluctuations

- Generation X
- Generation Y/millennials
- generational cohort
- green marketing
- inflation
- interest rates
- macroenvironmental factors

- political/legal environment
- recession
- seniors
- technological advances
- tweens

CONCEPT REVIEW

1. List the three elements a firm must assess before looking externally (i.e., microenvironmental factors).

2. List and describe the elements of a firm's macroenvironment. Select a Canadian company that you think has done a great job at managing the macroenvironmental factors and discuss what it has done.

3. List five ways in which baby boomers, Generation X, and Generation Y are different.

4. If a store permanently offers extended shopping hours, what macroenvironmental factor(s) is it appealing to?

5. List some of the important social and natural trends affecting the Canadian market.

6. Besides language, explain why using the same advertisement for Ontario and for Quebec wouldn't be equally successful.

7. Why should marketers care about engaging tweens quickly and sincerely?

8. How do changes in the value of the Canadian dollar vis-à-vis the U.S. dollar affect Canadian companies that sell to American consumers?

9. Why is understanding cultures and subcultures so important in marketing?

10. The Chinese and South Asian consumer segment is rapidly growing in Canada. What opportunities and challenges does this trend pose for food and grocery retailers? What strategies could they use to market effectively to this segment of consumers?

MARKETING APPLICATIONS

1. Assume you are going to open a new store. Describe it. Who are your competitors? What would you do to monitor your competitors' actions?

2. In which generational cohort do you belong? What about your parents? How would you approach buying a car differently than your parents? What about buying an outfit to wear to a party? How can firms use their knowledge of generational cohorts to market their products and services better?

3. How can firms use customer demographics such as income, education, and ethnicity to market to their customers better?

4. Identify some of the changes in the gender landscape. Describe how they might affect the marketing practices of (a) men's apparel retailers (b) do-it-yourself home improvement retailers, and (c) upscale salon services.

5. Identify some recent technological innovations in the marketplace and describe how they have affected consumers' everyday activities.

6. Do you feel that firms are invading or could invade your privacy? Why or why not?

7. Why should Canadian companies selling goods in the United States care about the value of the U.S. dollar?

8. Time-poor consumers have adopted various approaches to "buy" themselves more time, such as (a) voluntarily simplifying their complex lives (b) using new technologies for greater empowerment and control (c) using their time productively when travelling or commuting, and (d) multitasking. Identify and describe some products and services that consumers use to implement each of these strategies.

9. Identify a company that you believe does a particularly good job of marketing to different cultural groups. Justify your answer.

10. You have recently been hired by a major department store in its marketing department. Your boss informs you that you will supervise a field research study. You arrive at your assigned store and find that the study consists of shadowing customers. The store has set up a "private" shopping event for store credit card holders. All who attend must swipe their cards to receive the special discount coupon book. The shadow shoppers (who the store manager hired) are given hand-held devices loaded with a specific customer's information and past purchase behaviour. Thus, each shadow shopper knows the name, address, income, family size, and spending patterns for the customer she or he is observing. You begin to feel uncomfortable about this study since the consumers have no idea they are being tracked, nor do they know the level of confidential information about them that a stranger can access. You are also concerned that the shadow customers are not regular employees or employees of an established marketing research provider. What, if anything, would or should you do about your concerns?

NET SAVVY

1. Seventh Generation is the leading brand of nontoxic, environmentally safe household products in Canada (products are sold at Home Depot). Visit Seventh Generation's website (http://www.seventhgeneration.com) and review the philosophy behind the business. Next, review the site to identify the products that the company offers. Briefly summarize some of the consumer trends you note, and describe the ways in which the company's products address the wants and needs of its customers.

2. Visit the Cool Hunter (http://www.thecoolhunter.net) and identify examples that would provide marketers with insights regarding social trends.

CHAPTER CASE STUDY

WILL E-BOOKS REPLACE PRINT BOOKS?[88]

E-books have been with us for more than a decade now, but they have largely remained a niche market.[89] Early e-book readers (or e-readers), such as the Rocket eBook in 1998 and the Sony LIBRIé in 2004, failed to gain widespread consumer acceptance. However, in recent years, there has been an increase in the demand for e-books and e-readers. Many industry analysts view this resurgence in demand as the tipping point for e-books to move from a niche market to a mainstream market. Despite the numerous opportunities facing the industry, it still must overcome many challenges to achieve its full potential. Nevertheless, the e-book landscape is increasingly crowded as new competitors enter the market. One entrant is Kobo, a small e-book service provider that got its start in Canada. Kobo entered the market with a vastly different approach that it hopes will forever change the way people buy and read books. Its goal is to enable e-book consumers to be able to read any book, anytime, anywhere, and on any device of their choice through its open software application. This is in stark contradiction to the industry norm of using a closed system. For example, only the Kindle e-reader can plug into Amazon's e-book store and download titles. Can Kobo really change industry practices and emerge as the global market leader for e-books? Will e-books replace print books and spell the death of the chain bookstore? What will it take for this to happen?

E-books: The Concept and Benefits

Generally, *e-books* refers to digital content such as books, newspapers, and magazines that are offered in a format that can be read by various technology devices, including laptops, smartphones, tablets, and dedicated e-book readers such as Amazon's Kindle, Barnes & Noble's Nook, and the Kobo e-reader. Some common e-book formats are PDF, ePub, and PubIt. Most e-books are text-based, with virtually no interactivity or multimedia elements. Since e-books can be read from a variety of devices, consumers do not necessarily have to purchase an e-reader. However, e-readers seem to provide a better reading experience and offer more features than other devices. Except for Kobo's open, cross-platform e-reader application system, most applications currently in the market are closed or proprietary systems. This restriction means that consumers who buy Amazon's Kindle can purchase and download e-books from Amazon's store, but those with other e-readers, such as Barnes & Noble's Nook or a Sony e-reader, cannot load titles from Amazon as they can be read only on the Kindle. These types of closed systems limit consumer choices, stifle competition and innovation, and hamper the development of the industry. The Kobo software application, ePub, is an open system designed to give consumers access to content regardless of the readers they choose.

How and why do consumers purchase e-books? E-books can be bought as downloads from the websites of e-book service providers or their retailers. Consumers with dedicated e-readers could purchase books directly from their e-book provider via WiFi, 3G, or a computer or device that is connected to the Internet, depending on the capability of their e-readers. Consumers with e-readers that do not have WiFi or 3G capability must first download the e-book on another Internet-connected device and then transfer the e-book to their e-reader via USB or Bluetooth.

E-books are appealing for many reasons and each consumer will have his or her own motivation for choosing e-books. Environmentally conscious consumers may choose e-books because they save on paper, ink, printing, and all the harmful effects the printing industry has on the environment. Consumers who prefer to read on a screen will find e-books appealing since they can adjust the typeface, type size, and backlight on their devices to make reading easier. Consumers who like to read and do not want to carry around several books will find the e-reader a convenient alternative since they can store multiple books in one small device. Consumers who want to purchase any title, anytime, anyplace will also find e-readers, especially those with WiFi or 3G capability, very appealing. For price-conscious consumers, e-books are often cheaper than books, but they may have to incur additional cost to buy an e-reader. For publishers, e-books are faster and cheaper to produce and distribute than print books. They are also much easier to update or correct. Thus, e-book providers could offer customers a better price and still earn a good margin. For authors and content providers who own copyrights to their works, e-books offer a cheaper and faster way for their works to be published.

The Opportunities and Challenges

The resurgence in demand for e-books can be traced back to three broader social trends. First, a growing number of publishers and content providers are increasing the amount of content they make available via e-books. Second, it is a growing trend for people to carry PDAs and spend a considerable amount of time reading on a small, mobile screen. People who grew up with the Internet and cellphones are particularly likely to do this. Consequently, making the transition to an e-reader should be relatively easy for them. Third, the trend among people of all ages to communicate, interact, collaborate, and socialize through mobile devices and mobile media could make the acceptance of e-books and e-readers more plausible. In fact, less than four years after Amazon launched the Kindle, its e-book sales surpassed sales of hard-copy books, with 105 e-books sold for every 100 print books.[90]

Despite the benefits of e-books, the industry must overcome challenges before e-books become a widespread phenomenon. In the past, a major stumbling block was the cost and quality of e-book readers. Industry analysts argued that current e-reader prices ranging from $139 to $299 were far too expensive to make using them an economical choice for the mass market. Also, early e-readers lacked many basic features needed to create a functional and enjoyable reading experience. Today e-readers such as the Kobo Mini can be purchased for as little as $79. While today's e-readers have improved, e-books are still primarily text-based and offer very little multimedia, interactive, and "smart" features that could enrich the reading experience. For instance, an e-book on weight loss could potentially enable readers to interact with it by entering, for example, their weight, age, sex, and other relevant information, and immediately suggest a diet and exercise plan based on the information provided. Essentially, the technology must keep pace with the needs of consumers for convenience, affordability, and functionality. Complicating matters is the fact that every e-book service provider has its own proprietary e-book application, which fragments the market and undermines its long-term vibrancy.

Kobo, the Canadian Player

What role can Kobo play to change the game? Kobo was launched in December 2009, with backing from Indigo Books and Music, Borders, REDgroup Retail, and Cheung Kong Holdings. Indigo Books and Music controlled about 60 percent of the company until it sold its shares to Japanese firm Rakuten in 2012. In March and June 2010, Kobo entered the United Kingdom and the United States, respectively. It also established distribution channels in the European Union, Australia, New Zealand, Hong Kong, and other territories. Additionally, Kobo established partnerships with publishers, manufacturers, and retailers around the world in order to source content, distribute its e-reader device and application, and get its application preloaded on various technologies, such as smartphones, tablets, and laptops. Kobo has more than 3 million e-books, magazines and newspapers, covering a wide range of genres and bestsellers from around the world. It has readers in more than 190 countries and has access to 100 million consumers through its distribution partners.

The Kobo application is available for free download at the App Store, BlackBerry App World, Palm App Catalog, Android Marketplace, or http://www.kobobooks.com. Kobo features thousands of free e-books, so users can try e-reading for free. Kobo's e-reader application allows users to read e-books in both standard ePUB and PDF formats. The e-reader application supports a range of hardware options with various screen types, including eInk and LCD screens.

When first introduced, it did not have 3G or WiFi connectivity, a colour screen, or audio play-back features like the Kindle or the Nook, as these elements would drive up the price. The e-books had to be purchased through Kobo's website, using a computer or a smartphone, and then transferred to the Kobo e-reader via Bluetooth or USB. That has all changed with new models now available.

Basically, the Kobo e-reader device and software application aims to make electronic reading more enjoyable, affordable, and accessible. Experts say that its most crucial feature is that it operates on an open platform. When you buy a Kobo e-book, it can be downloaded on your Kobo device or, if you prefer, your desktop, laptop, smartphone, or Sony e-reader. According to Kobo, consumers who buy a Kobo e-reader can switch to another device at any time and transfer the books they have already bought to the new device. This means that the library a consumer creates with Kobo is easily portable to another device.

The smallest of Kobo's e-readers, the Mini, is priced at $79 (the lowest e-reader price in the market). It is capable of holding up to 1,000 e-books. Amazon has added new options to its popular Kindle line ranging in price from US$119 to $399, with the smallest model capable of holding up to 1,100 e-books. Almost all e-readers have the capability of storing more e-books by using external memory. A comparison of the Kobo e-Reader with other leading devices is presented in the table below.

Brand	iPad Mini	Google Nexus 10	Kindle Fire HD	Kindle Paperwhite	Nook HD	Nook Simple Touch with Glow Light	Kobo Aura HD	Kobo Glo Wireless
Price	$410	$409	$199	$119	$199	$119	$169	$129
Screen Size	7.9"	10"	7"	6"	7"	6"	6.9"	6"
Resolution	1024 × 768	2560 × 1600	1280 × 800	1024 × 768	1440 × 900	1024 × 768	1440 × 1080	1024 × 758
Wireless	✓	✓	✓	✓	✓	✓	✓	✓
Touch Screen	✓	✓	✓	✓	✓	✓	✓	✓
Colour	✓	✓	✓	X	✓	X	X	X

For a more detailed comparison of these and other models on more dimensions, visit http://ebook-reader-review.toptenreviews.com.

The following quotations give a flavour of the media perceptions of some of Kobo's devices.

Kobo Aura HD: It's a big improvement on the Kobo ink and looks incredibly crisp and makes reading that much more pleasurable. —**Tech Radar**

Kobo Mini: Priced at US$79.99, it's considerably cheaper than its bigger specced brothers, as well as rivals such as the Kindle Fire, the Nook Simple Touch and even the cheapest Amazon e-reader, the Kindle. —**Tech Radar**

The Future

Not every publisher in the book industry has been willing to concede the future of reading to technology companies. Penguin Books, for example, was slow to accept the ePub format embraced by Kobo and others, wanting to embed audio, video, and streaming into its digital content. The ePub format, which is the standard for e-books at present, is designed to support traditional narrative text but not this cool stuff. Although sales had been fast growing, research from IDC indicates that e-reader shipments have declined since 2011. Much of this decline is due to competition from new, low-priced tablets. As the price gap narrows, many consumers are opting for multipurpose tablets over dedicated e-readers. According to Deloitte Canada, another new challenge for e-reader manufacturers is that consumers tend to stick with their first purchase, resulting in virtually no upgrade cycle.

Yet, in spite of these worrying trends, Kobo saw its e-reader customers grow by 2.5 million in the first quarter of 2013. It now has 14.5 million users, with 15 percent of those coming from the United States. The new Aura HD model represents more than 25 percent of e-readers sold. And while the jury may still be out on e-readers, PricewaterhouseCoopers projects that e-book sales will surpass print books by 2017. If its predictions are correct, that should create a rosy future for e-book companies.

Questions

1. Briefly explain what the competitive advantages of Kobo's e-book system are. Are these advantages sustainable over time?

2. What factors in Kobo's microenvironment do you think are responsible for Kobo's success?

3. Identify and describe the macroenvironmental factors that could influence the success of Kobo's business in the future.

For more information on the resources available from McGraw-Hill Ryerson, go to www.mheducation.ca/he/solutions.

CHAPTER 4

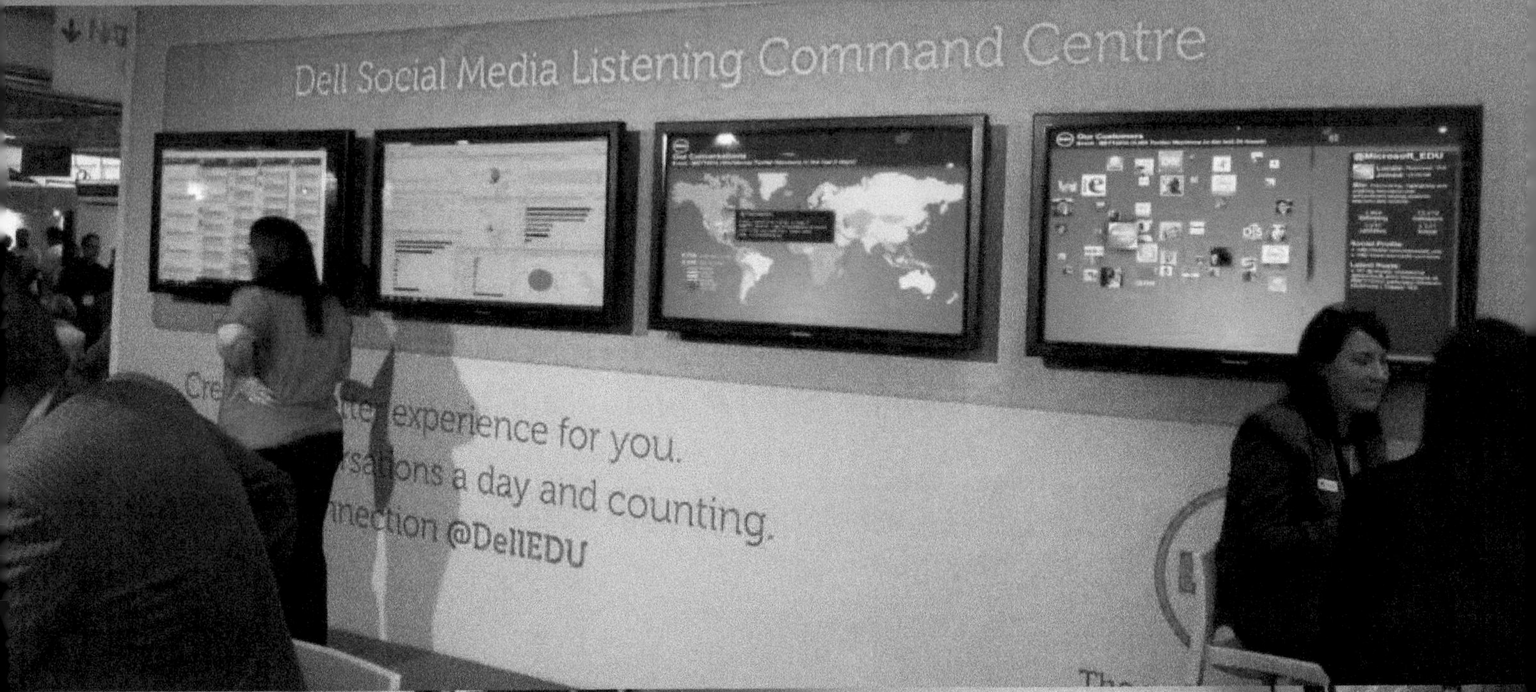

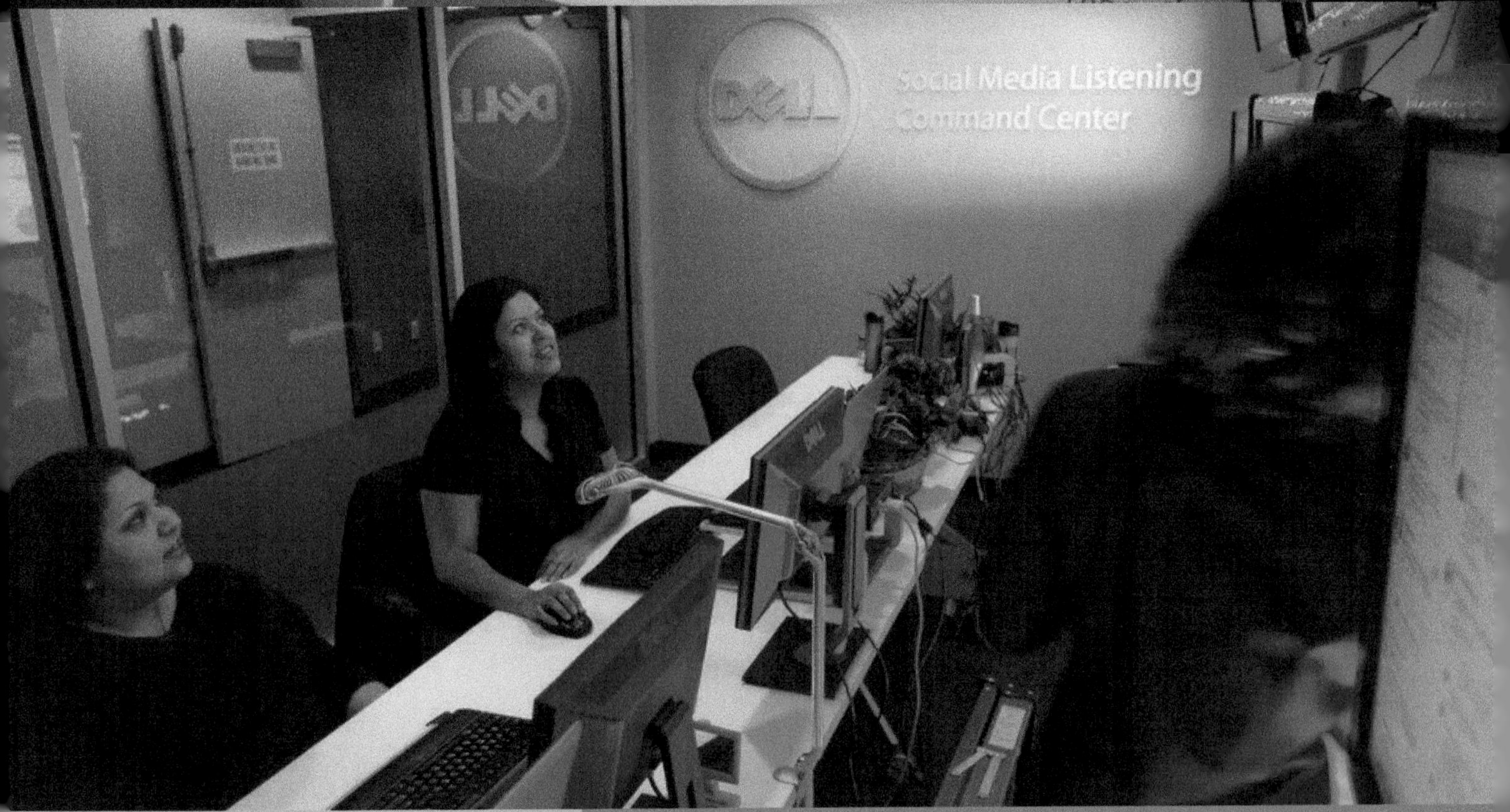

SECTION TWO
UNDERSTANDING THE MARKETPLACE

Consumer Behaviour

Social media has revolutionized how companies communicate with, listen to, and learn about their customers. The volume of information generated can be a powerful tool for improving all business operations, including product design, technical support, and customer service. Few companies have mastered this transformational potential better than Dell, one of the world's largest providers of fast-evolving breakthrough IT solutions for home and business. It understands that the consumer should be at the heart of all marketing decisions and strategies. Today, Dell is viewed as one of the top social media brands worldwide.[1]

The company has always valued consumer input, according to founder and CEO Michael Dell: "One of Dell's founding principles was really about listening and learning from our customers, and being able to take that feedback to improve."[2] Now social media channels like Facebook and Twitter have vastly accelerated that learning curve.[3] Dell still offers traditional online support forums, which post questions and answers for different user groups and by topic. A link to Dell's mobile phone app also helps users stay connected on the road. These tools help consumers both when they are evaluating new hardware as well as after they have purchased it.

Dell's multiple, highly developed social media channels differ qualitatively as well. They give the company and its customers the immediacy of instant chat and conversations. Through Facebook, LinkedIn, Twitter, and Google+, as well as Dell's flagship blog Direct2Dell.com and a host of other blogs, it has vastly diversified its marketing channels to target each different audience. In addition to customer support, the new media provide company and product news and food for thought to its customers about digital business and digital life. In turn, they enable the company to monitor and learn from fast-shifting user conversations.[4]

How does a company draw meaning about its products from the thousands of Facebook, Twitter, and other social media interactions that occur daily? Listening and analysis—or social media monitoring—is key, enabling companies to identify customer needs and trends. For example, with its social media monitoring partner Radian6, Dell conducts a form of market research called "sentiment analysis" to gather, categorize, and interpret vast volumes of online customer discussions. The Radian6 coupling of text analysis and high-volume digital content

LEARNING OBJECTIVES

After studying this chapter you should be able to

LO1 Describe the steps in the consumer buying decision process

LO2 Identify what determines how much time consumers will spend searching for information before buying a product or service

LO3 Summarize how psychological, social, and situational factors influence consumers' buying behaviour

LO4 Explain how involvement influences the consumer buying decision process

gathering technologies means Dell can monitor approximately 25,000 conversations a day.[5]

Dell gathers and monitors these online chats and posts, and engages in other discussions from its new Social Media Listening Command Center. The staff includes 70 trained employees who follow and respond to social media conversations in 11 languages. All tweets, Facebook posts, and other comments that warrant a Dell response are answered within 24 hours.[6]

And Dell is not just listening online. At its annual consumer advisory meetings, key bloggers and other digital opinion leaders sit around a table with Dell leadership and staff in open-ended discussions about company products, services, and processes. One blogger last year described herself and other Dell users as "an army of resources" that Dell should continue to "mobilize."[7] And that's clearly Dell's strategic intent. In its aggressive integration of social media, Dell has made the customer a critical partner in the design and evolution of its products and services.

All of us purchase goods and services; therefore, we are all consumers at one time or another. But we are also complex and irrational creatures who cannot always explain our own actions, making the job of marketing managers even more difficult because without a deep understanding of consumers' behaviour, marketing managers will not be able to properly satisfy the needs and wants of their customers.

To understand consumer behaviour, we must ask why people buy products or services, or even specific brands. Using principles and theories from sociology and psychology, marketers have been able to decipher many consumer actions and develop basic strategies for dealing with their behaviour. Generally, people buy one product or service instead of another because they perceive it to be the better value for them; that is, the ratio of benefits to costs is higher for that product or service than for any other.[8] However, "benefits" can be subtle and far from rationally conceived, as we shall see. Consider the tens of thousands of Canadians who purchased Apple's iPhone 5s on the very first day it was released in Canada. In making the decision to abandon or replace their feature phone with the iPhone, they must have asked themselves:

- What is the additional overall value I am getting for the price I am paying for the iPhone 5s?

- What will friends, family, and coworkers think about my latest gadget? ▮

We begin this chapter by exploring the process that consumers go through when buying products and services. Then we discuss the psychological, social, and situational factors that influence this consumer decision process. We end the chapter with a discussion of how the level of consumer involvement influences the buying decision process. Throughout the chapter, we illustrate what firms can do to influence consumers to purchase their products and services.

THE CONSUMER DECISION PROCESS

L01

The consumer decision process model represents the steps that consumers go through before, during, and after making purchases. Because marketers often find it difficult to determine how consumers make purchasing decisions, it is useful for us to break down the process into a series of steps and to examine each step individually,[9] as in Exhibit 4.1.

Step 1: Need Recognition

The consumer decision process begins when consumers recognize they have an unsatisfied need and want to go from their needy state to a different, desired state. The greater the discrepancy between these two states, the greater the **need recognition** will be. For example, your stomach tells you that you are hungry, and you would rather not have that particular feeling. If you are only a little hungry, you may ignore the feeling and decide to eat later. But if your stomach is growling and you cannot concentrate, the need—the difference between your actual (hungry) state and your desired (not hungry) state—is greater, and you'll want to eat immediately to get to your desired state. Consumer needs like these can be classified as functional, psychological, or both.[10]

need recognition
The beginning of the consumer decision process; occurs when consumers recognize they have an unsatisfied need and want to go from their needy state to a different, desired state.

Functional Needs **Functional needs** pertain to the performance of a product or service. For years, materials such as GORE-TEX, Polartec, and Thinsulate have been viewed as functionally superior to others that might be used in rugged, high-performance outerwear. Knowing that consumers seek out these materials, high-end outdoor manufacturers, such as North Face, prominently display the material content on each piece of clothing and equipment they offer.

functional needs
Pertain to the performance of a product or service.

Psychological Needs **Psychological needs** pertain to the personal gratification consumers associate with a product and/or service. Shoes, for instance, provide a functional need: to keep feet clean and protect them from the elements. So why would anyone pay $500 to $1,500 for shoes that may do neither? Because that consumer is seeking a way to satisfy psychological needs. Christian Louboutin's shoes, with their signature red soles, may be the hottest shoes on the market.[11] Sarah Jessica Parker was spotted in a pair on the set of the *Sex and the City* movie, a pair showed up in an episode of *Dirty Sexy Money*, and BMW featured the shoes in a commercial. Penelope Cruz, Catherine Deneuve, Lady Gaga, Ashley Olsen, Beyoncé, and Angelina Jolie have also been photographed wearing Louboutin shoes. As a result of all this media attention, there

psychological needs
Pertain to the personal gratification consumers associate with a product or service.

EXHIBIT 4.1 The Consumer Decision Process

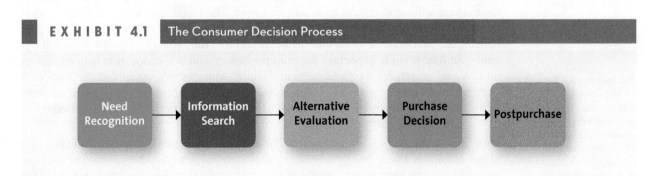

Do Christian Louboutin's shoes satisfy functional or psychological needs?

Does this motorcycle satisfy functional or psychological needs?

is a strong demand for Louboutin shoes by women who just love exciting (and expensive) shoes. Not surprisingly, when designers at Yves Saint Laurent made a red suede shoe with a red sole, Louboutin immediately responded by filing a lawsuit against Yves Saint Laurent.[12]

Both these examples highlight that the vast majority of products and services are likely to satisfy both functional and psychological needs, albeit in different degrees. Whereas the functional characteristics of GORE-TEX are its main selling point, it also maintains a fashionable appeal for mountain climber wannabes. In contrast, Christian Louboutin shoes satisfy psychological needs that overshadow the functional needs they serve. You can get a $15 haircut at First Choice Haircutters or spend $80 or more to get basically the same thing at an upscale salon. Are the two haircuts objectively different? The answer might vary depending on which you believe represents a good haircut and good value. One person might value getting a really good deal; another might enjoy the extra attention and amenities associated with a fancy salon.

A key to successful marketing is determining the correct balance of functional and psychological needs that best appeals to the firm's target markets. Harley-Davidson, for instance, produces motorcycles that do much more than get their riders to the mall and back. Harleys are a way of life for motorcycle enthusiasts who want to ride and have fun. Even though other manufacturers, such as Yamaha, Honda, Suzuki, and Kawasaki, offer functional, dependable, and fast motorcycles, they cannot compete with the Harley mystique.

So, what can marketers do at the need recognition stage to influence consumer purchase decisions? Marketers use numerous tactics to either remind customers of a need or create new needs. Researching and understanding what products and services customers need or want and why, are the first steps in developing appropriate tactics. Common tactics marketers employ include using reminder advertising for their products, creating awareness about a new product and its capabilities, showing how a product could enhance consumers' image, and even altering the physical layout of a store or where products are placed in stores. For example, placing products near checkout lanes or placing products that customers buy together (e.g., eggs and bread) near each other means when customers come to buy one item (eggs), they are reminded of the other item (bread).

L02   Step 2: Information Search

The second step, after a consumer recognizes a need, is to search for information about the various options that exist to satisfy that need. The length and intensity of the search are based on several factors, including the degree of perceived risk associated with purchasing the product or service and the importance of the product to the consumer. If the way your hair is cut is important to your appearance and self-image, you may engage in an involved search for the right salon and stylist. Alternatively, an athlete looking for a buzz cut might go to the closest, most convenient, and cheapest barber shop. Regardless of the required search level, there are two key types of information: internal and external.

internal search for information
Occurs when the buyer examines his or her own memory and knowledge about the product or service, gathered through past experiences.

Internal Search for Information   In an **internal search for information**, the buyer examines his or her own memory and knowledge about the product or service, gathered through past experiences. For example, every time Katie wants to eat salad for lunch, she and her friends go to Cultures. But if she's craving dessert, she heads straight to Just Desserts. In making these choices, she relies on her memory of past experiences when she has eaten at these restaurants.

External Search for Information In an **external search for information**, the buyer seeks information outside his or her personal knowledge base to help make the buying decision. Consumers might fill in their personal knowledge gaps by talking with friends, family, or a salesperson. They can also scour commercial media for unsponsored and (it is hoped) unbiased information, such as that available through *Consumer Reports*, or peruse sponsored media such as magazines, TV, or radio. With the explosive growth of smartphones with web-browsing capability and of social media, consumers turn to the Internet for information in real time simply because they have their phones with them all the time. For example, while flipping through a magazine, Katie might see a pair of jeans worn by a favourite celebrity, and then search for more information using her smartphone. In the process, she may read feedback posted on a blog from satisfied customers who have purchased these jeans. These reviews could influence her decision, prompting her to visit the company's website, check the sizing, and order the jeans. And she can do all this without leaving the comfort of her home.

external search for information
Occurs when the buyer seeks information outside his or her personal knowledge base to help make the buying decision.

Factors Affecting Consumers' Search Processes It is important for marketers to understand the many factors that affect consumers' search processes. Among them are the following:

- *The perceived benefits versus perceived costs of search.* Is it worth the time and effort to search for information about a product or service? For instance, most families spend a lot of time researching the automobile market before they make a purchase because cars are a relatively expensive and important purchase with significant safety implications, whereas families likely spend little time researching which inexpensive plastic toy car to buy for the youngest member of the family.

- *The locus of control.* People who have an **internal locus of control** believe they have some control over the outcomes of their actions, in which case they generally engage in more search activities. With an **external locus of control**, consumers believe that fate or other external factors control all outcomes. In that case, they believe it doesn't matter how much information they gather; if they make a wise decision, it isn't to their credit, and if they make a poor one, it isn't their fault. For example, if Brad believes he can get a better deal when buying his first car, he will conduct an extensive search for information and try to use the information when negotiating his purchase. However, if Brad feels that regardless of what information he has, he can do little to influence the outcome of the deal, he will not engage in an extensive search.

internal locus of control
Refers to when consumers believe they have some control over the outcomes of their actions, in which case they generally engage in more search activities.

external locus of control
Refers to when consumers believe that fate or other external factors control all outcomes.

- *Actual or perceived risk.* Five types of risk associated with purchase decisions can delay or discourage a purchase: performance, financial, social, physiological, and psychological. The higher the risk, the more likely the consumer is to engage in an extended search.

  Performance risk involves the perceived danger inherent in a poorly performing product or service. An example of performance risk might be the possibility that Brad's sports car does not start or breaks down on the day he is supposed to take his girlfriend out for a drive to show off his new car.

  Financial risk is risk associated with a monetary outlay and includes the initial cost of the purchase, as well as the costs of using the item or service. Car manufacturers, for instance, recognize that extended warranties help alleviate financial risk because consumers fear extensive postpurchase repair costs. For example, Brad bought two additional years of warranty over the manufacturer's standard "3-year, 60,000 kilometre" coverage for his sports car to reduce his financial risk within the first five years of buying the car.

performance risk
Involves the perceived danger inherent in a poorly performing product or service.

financial risk
Risk associated with a monetary outlay; includes the initial cost of the purchase, as well as the costs of using the item or service.

social risk
Involves the fears that consumers suffer when they worry others might not regard their purchases positively.

physiological risk
Risk associated with the fear of an actual harm should the product not perform properly.

psychological risk
Associated with the way people will feel if the product or service does not convey the right image.

evaluative criteria
Consist of a set of salient, or important, attributes about a particular product that are used to compare alternative products.

Social risk involves the fears that consumers suffer when they worry others might not regard their purchases positively. When buying a dress, consumers like Katie, Brad's girlfriend, consider what her friends would think. Alternatively, since a job interview is so important, Katie might make a conscious effort to assert a distinctive identity or make a statement by buying a unique, more stylish, and possibly more expensive dress than her friends would typically buy.

Physiological risk could also be called safety risk. Whereas performance risk involves what might happen if a product does not perform as expected, physiological (or safety) risk refers to the fear of actual harm should the product not perform properly. Although physiological risk is typically not an issue with apparel, it can be an important issue when buying other products, such as a car. External agencies and government bodies publish safety ratings for cars to help assuage this risk. Consumers compare the safety records of their various choices because they recognize the real danger to their well-being if the automobile they purchase fails to perform a basic task, such as stopping when the driver steps on the brakes. An example of this is the safety recalls by Honda, Toyota, and Nissan that recalled over 200,000 cars in Canada due to issues with faulty airbags that sent pieces of plastic flying when the inflator burst.

Finally, **psychological risks** are those risks associated with the way people will feel if the product or service does not convey the right image. For example, Brad looked up reviews of the various sports cars and asked his friends their opinions because he wanted people to perceive his choice as a really good one.

Knowing that consumers go through various levels of information search, marketers must try to understand the sources customers use to search for information and the importance of each source. With this knowledge, marketers could implement various tactics, including providing information about their products or even educating customers about their product in general or a product category as a way to build trust and credibility (e.g., teaching consumers about digital cameras or photography while promoting their own brand of camera). Additionally, marketers must ensure they communicate tactics aimed at reducing risks to customers. For example, marketers can provide guarantees through which defective products can be returned for a full refund or replaced at the company's expense, or that allow consumers to return products if they are not completely satisfied with them. Marketers also sometimes reduce the perception of risk by showing consumers that others have purchased the product and are proud owners or users.

Step 3: Alternative Evaluation

Once consumers have recognized a problem and explored the possible options, they must sift through the choices available and evaluate the alternatives. Alternative evaluation often occurs while consumers are engaged in the process of information search. For example, a vegetarian consumer might learn about a new brand of yogurt that he or she can immediately rule out as a viable alternative because it contains unsuitable animal by-products. Consumers forgo alternative evaluations altogether when buying habitual (convenience) products; you'll rarely catch a loyal skim milk drinker buying a carton of full fat milk.

When consumers begin to evaluate different alternatives, they often base their evaluations on a set of important attributes or evaluative criteria. **Evaluative criteria** consist of a set of salient, or important, attributes about a particular product that are used to compare alternative products. For example, a consumer

What evaluative criteria would you consider when choosing a hair salon?

looking to buy a new HDTV might take into consideration things such as features, selling price, looks, and popularity of the different brands. At times, however, it becomes difficult to evaluate different brands or stores because there are so many choices, especially when those choices involve technical criteria, as in the HDTV market.

To simplify the potentially complicated decision process, consumers use shortcuts such as determinant attributes and consumer decision rules. **Determinant attributes** are product or service features that are *important* to the buyer and on which competing brands or stores are perceived to *differ*.[13] Because many important and desirable attributes are equal among the various choices, consumers look for something special—a determinant attribute—to differentiate one brand or store from another and on which to base their choice. Determinant attributes may appear perfectly rational, such as health and nutrition claims offered by certain foods and beverages, or they may be more subtle and psychologically based, such as the red soles on a pair of Christian Louboutin heels. Ethical Dilemma 4.1 highlights the use of determinant attributes describing food and beverages marketed as natural or organic when in fact they are not.

What evaluative criteria would you consider when choosing one of these shampoo brands?

determinant attributes Product or service features that are important to the buyer and on which competing brands or stores are perceived to differ.

Ethical Dilemma 4.1

Wearing the "Healthy" Label: Natural and Organic Foods

With competition for shelf space always at a premium, today's supermarket aisles are more crowded than ever. Much of the new competition comes from natural and organic foods, which comprised more than 4 percent of the $673 billion U.S. food industry in 2010.[14]

For a consumer facing a dizzying array of choices, these natural foods offer a unique appeal: They promise to improve personal and planetary health. Organic and natural food companies claim that their foods are safer and more nutritious because they are produced with only natural ingredients.

Consumers generally believe that these claims mean the food contains no artificial or highly processed ingredients.[15] Yet Snapple's "natural" bottled iced tea contains high-fructose corn syrup, a highly processed, and recently controversial, form of sugar. For example, most organic strawberry farmers use seeds and plants from nurseries that are not organic, including growers producing fruit for Driscoll Strawberry Associates, the largest berry distributor in the world.[16] The farmers argue that once their plants bear fruit, they halt their use of chemical pesticides and herbicides, so the berries

How healthy is Snapple?

themselves are still organic. These companies thus might be contradicting consumer expectations, but they are not actually violating U.S. federal requirements.

For the consumer, the organic and natural food experience is also about perception. Some shoppers may believe these foods deliver healthful benefits, but studies also reveal that simply identifying a grocery item as a "health food" may affect their eating experience. Students given snacks labelled "health bars" reported feeling hungry afterward and craving foods they enjoyed more. In another study, respondents widely perceived "that 'healthy' isn't going to meet enjoyment goals," which likely reflects consumers' assumption that "healthy foods won't taste good."[17] Cornell University researchers asked mall visitors to taste products such as cookies, chips, and yogurt. One option was labelled "organic" while the other was called "regular." Although the items were actually identical, when asked to report on their perceptions, consumers told researchers the "organic" products were tastier. The consumers also believed that these products were lower in fat, lower in calories, higher in fibre, and more nutritious than the "regular" products.[18]

consumer decision rules
The set of criteria consumers use consciously or subconsciously to quickly and efficiently select from among several alternatives.

compensatory decision rule
Is at work when the consumer is evaluating alternatives and trades off one characteristic against another, such that good characteristics compensate for bad ones.

Consumer decision rules are the set of criteria that consumers use consciously or subconsciously to quickly and efficiently select from among several alternatives. These rules take several different forms: compensatory, noncompensatory, or decision heuristics.

Compensatory A **compensatory decision rule** assumes that the consumer, when evaluating alternatives, trades off one characteristic against another, such that good characteristics compensate for bad characteristics.[19] For instance, when Brad was looking to buy a new car he considered several factors, such as mileage, style, price, and accessories. Even if the car is priced a little higher than Brad was planning to spend, the superb mileage offsets, or *compensates* for, the higher price.

Although Brad probably would not go through the formal process of making the purchasing decision based on the model described in Exhibit 4.2, it illustrates how a compensatory model would work. Brad assigns weights to each factor depending on their importance to him. These weights must add up to 1.0. So, for instance, mileage is the most important with a weight of 0.4, and style is least important with a weight of 0.1. Then Brad assigns weights to how well each of the cars might perform, with 1 being very poor, and 10 being very good. For instance, he thinks Toyota has the best mileage, so he assigns it a 10. Brad multiplies each performance rating by its importance rating to get an overall score for each car. The rating for Toyota in this example is the highest of the three cars ($[0.4 \times 10] + [0.1 \times 8] + [0.3 \times 6] + [0.2 \times 8] = 8.2$).

noncompensatory decision rule
Is at work when consumers choose a product or service on the basis of a subset of its characteristics, regardless of the values of its other attributes.

Noncompensatory Sometimes, however, consumers use a **noncompensatory decision rule**, in which they choose a product or service on the basis of a subset of its characteristics, regardless of the values of its other attributes.[20] Thus, Brad might find a car with a lot of accessories and great mileage that costs considerably more than he is willing to spend but rejects the car simply on the basis of price. Because the Nissan offers a better price (he rated the price of a Toyota as 6 and a Nissan as 10 on the 10-point scale), he decides that the strength of the good points of the Toyota does not compensate for its biggest weakness—a high ticket price. Thus, based on compensatory decision rules, Brad should choose the Toyota car; but, using a noncompensatory decision rule, the price of the cars, Brad chose the Nissan.

Once consumers have considered the possible alternatives and weighed the pros and cons, they can move toward a purchase decision. Social and Mobile Marketing 4.1 illustrates how social networks help consumers choose among alternatives.

decision heuristics
Mental shortcuts that help consumers narrow down choices; examples include price, brand, and product presentation.

Decision Heuristics Not everyone uses compensatory or noncompensatory decision rules. Some people use **decision heuristics**, which are mental shortcuts that help them narrow down their choices. Some examples of these heuristics follow:

- *Price.* Consumers can choose the more expensive option, thinking they are getting better quality along with the higher price ("You get what you pay for"), or they might buy the product priced in the middle of the alternatives, neither the most

EXHIBIT 4.2 Compensatory Versus Noncompensatory Choices for Buying a Car

	Mileage	Style	Price	Accessories	Overall Score
Importance Weight	0.4	0.1	0.3	0.2	
Toyota	10	8	6	8	8.2
Honda	8	9	8	3	7.1
Nissan	6	8	10	5	7.2

Evaluations are based on a 1 (very poor) to 10 (very good) scale.
Based on the noncompensatory decision rule (based on price), Nissan is the best candidate for purchase.

Social and Mobile Marketing 4.1

Shopping Online with Friends[21]

At one time, you needed to convince friends to get in the car and go shopping with you to get their opinion on an item you were considering for purchase. Thanks to the Internet though, social shopping has become far easier and more user friendly, because consumers can bring along friends without anyone ever leaving their home. Applications, such as a technology called ShopTogether owned by Buy.com, allow for collaborations among friends on a retailer's site.

E-retailers with ShopTogether let customers bring their friends to the e-retailer so they can shop together. According to the company that produces ShopTogether, retailers using this technology find that shoppers place 25 percent more items in their carts, spend 400 percent more time on the site, and increase their order value by 50 percent. Other estimates indicate retailers also achieve a 15 percent increase in online sales and much higher conversion rates—that is, the number of browsing customers who become actual purchasing customers.

On the MAC beauty products website for example, customers can scan, browse independently, or see what friends are viewing, as well as show friends some items, chat with those friends, and then save their favourite items in a list. An instant messaging program allows up to four people to join in, each of whom can easily add products to the chat conversation to show others what they prefer. Other retailers using the ShopTogether technology include GNC, Mattel, and Charlotte Russe.

The U.S. teen apparel e-retailer Wet Seal uses Sesh.com, a sophisticated technology that shoppers can use to discuss products in a chat window. Friends also can write notes to others in the various sections and use a "pen" to draw on the site. One person controls the navigation at a time, guiding the others through the site as they discuss the products together.

Facebook's Stucck application even allows users to go beyond retailers' websites and post side-by-side comparisons of multiple product options they're "stuck" between in their decision. Then their social media contacts can vote on which option the consumer should choose. The application, of course, makes it easy for consumers to click quickly to a site to buy the favoured choice.

Friends can discuss products in Wet Seal's chat window.

---

expensive nor the cheapest, thinking that it is a good compromise between the two extremes.[22]

- *Brand.* Always buying brand-name goods allows some consumers to feel safe with their choices. Purchasing a national brand, even if it is more expensive, gives many consumers the sense that they are buying a higher quality item.[23] For example, many consumers buy more expensive Tylenol or Advil pain relief tablets over Shoppers Drug Mart's Life-brand pain tablets because they believe the former are higher quality products, despite identical ingredients in the generic brand.

- *Product presentation.* Many times, the manner in which a product is presented can influence the decision process. For example, two similar homes that are comparably priced will be perceived quite differently if one is presented in a perfectly clean and uncluttered condition, with fresh flowers and the smell of chocolate chip cookies wafting through it, whereas the other appears messy, has too much furniture for the rooms, and emits an unappealing smell. Consumers want to see that some effort has been put into the selling process, and just the way the product is presented can make or break a sale.[24]

Generally, the extent of alternative evaluation depends on several factors, such as the types of products or services (specialty, shopping, or convenience), the importance of the purchase, the perceived risks, and the expressive value of the purchase (i.e., to what extent the customers feel the product reflects an aspect of their personality).

The distinctive style of these lululemon yoga pants is a determinant attribute that distinguishes the product from other brands.

Shopping products tend to involve greater evaluation than convenience products. The purchase of highly expressive products that carry greater risks and that are more important to consumers involve more evaluation than the purchase of products that are less expressive or that have lower perceived risks.

Marketers can assist consumers in their evaluation process not only by educating them about the company's products, but also by providing detailed comparison information on price, technical specifications, unique features and benefits, and so on. Marketers may even provide free samples or trials of their products, which may enable consumers to compare the actual products.

Step 4: Purchase Decision

After evaluating the alternatives, customers are ready to buy. However, they don't always patronize the store or purchase the brand or item on which they had originally decided. It may not be available at the retail store or there may be some other stumbling block. Retailers therefore turn to the conversion rate to measure how well they have converted purchase intentions into purchases. One method of measuring the conversion rate is the number of real or virtual abandoned carts in the retailer's store or website.

Retailers use various tactics to increase the chances that customers will convert their positive evaluations into purchases. They can reduce the number of abandoned carts by making it easier to purchase merchandise. Most importantly, they should have plenty of stock on hand of the merchandise that customers want. Retailers can also reduce the actual wait time to buy merchandise by opening more checkout lanes and placing them conveniently inside the store. To reduce perceived wait times, they might install digital displays to entertain customers waiting in line.[25]

To encourage customers to make purchase decisions, Zappos.com and Overstock.com create urgency by alerting customers when an item in their shopping cart is almost sold out. Other online retailers, such as Gilt, offer items for a specified 36-hour period or until they run out, and Neiman Marcus runs two-hour, online-only sales. Many retailers send reminder emails to visitors about items in carts they have abandoned.[26]

ritual consumption
Refers to a pattern of behaviours tied to life events that affect what and how people consume.

After consumers purchase the product or service, they usually consume it, or "put it to the test." A special type of consumption is called **ritual consumption**, which refers to a pattern of behaviours tied to life events that affect what and how we consume. These behaviours tend to have symbolic meanings and vary greatly by culture. They might take the form of everyday rituals, such as Brad going to Tim Hortons for his daily morning coffee or you brushing your teeth, or they can be reserved for special occasions, such as rites of passage or holiday rituals. Many firms try to tie their products and services to ritual consumption; just imagine, where would Hallmark be without holidays?

Situational factors can help facilitate purchases: having the merchandise in stock, offering multiple payment options (e.g., cash, cheque, credit card, debit card, interest-free loans, no down payment), having many checkout lanes open and placing the checkouts conveniently in the store, installing digital displays to entertain customers waiting in line,[27] and offering tactics such as delivery, price-match guarantee, a warranty, or a simple return policy. Additional factors that affect whether the purchase decision is made immediately or later, such as store atmospherics, shopping situation, and temporal states, are discussed later in this chapter.

Step 5: Postpurchase

The final step of the consumer decision process is postpurchase behaviour. Marketers are particularly interested in postpurchase behaviour because it entails actual, rather than potential, customers. Marketers hope to create satisfied customers who

EXHIBIT 4.3   Postpurchase Outcomes

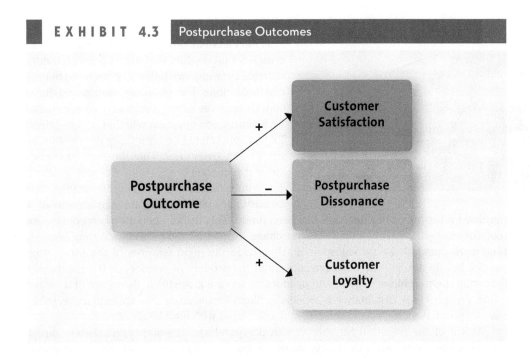

become loyal, purchase again, and spread positive word-of-mouth. However, dissatisfied customers are not likely to patronize the store again and will spread negative word-of-mouth.

There are three possible postpurchase outcomes, as illustrated in Exhibit 4.3: customer satisfaction, postpurchase cognitive dissonance (buyer's remorse), and customer loyalty (or disloyalty).

Customer Satisfaction   Setting unrealistically high consumer expectations of the product through advertising, personal selling, or other types of promotion may lead to higher initial sales, but eventually it will result in dissatisfaction when the product fails to achieve these high performance expectations. This failure can lead to dissatisfied customers and the potential for negative word-of-mouth. For example, Starbucks recognized that it should worry when its market research suggested that it was not meeting customer expectations in terms of speed of service. With higher-than-average coffee cup prices, customers expect fast and precise service.[28]

Many retailers don't "put their best foot forward"; no matter how good their merchandise and service may be, if their store is not clean and appealing, customers are not likely to enter.

Marketers can take the following steps to ensure postpurchase satisfaction:

- Build realistic expectations—not too high and not too low—and deliver on those expectations.

- Demonstrate correct product use; improper usage can cause dissatisfaction.

- Stand behind the product or service by providing money-back guarantees and warranties.

- Encourage customer feedback, which cuts down on negative word-of-mouth and helps marketers adjust their offerings.

- Periodically make contact with customers and thank them for their support. This contact reminds customers the marketer cares about their business and wants them to be satisfied. It also provides an opportunity to correct any problems. Customers appreciate human contact, though it is more expensive for marketers than email or postal mail contacts.

Consumers often feel dissonance when purchasing products or services.

postpurchase dissonance
An internal conflict that arises from an inconsistency between two beliefs, or between beliefs and behaviour; buyer's remorse.

Postpurchase Cognitive Dissonance

Postpurchase dissonance (or buyer's remorse) is an internal conflict that arises from an inconsistency between two beliefs, or between beliefs and behaviour. For example, you might have buyer's remorse after purchasing an expensive TV because you question whether a high-priced TV has appreciably better quality than a similar-size TV at a lower price. Thus, postpurchase cognitive dissonance is a feeling of regret, guilt, or grave uneasiness, which generally occurs when a consumer questions the appropriateness of a purchase after his or her decision has been made. This usually occurs when consumers feel, for example, that they made the purchase without all the information they needed, they were persuaded by a salesperson, they liked the good features of the product or service but do not like the negative aspects of the product or service, or if immediately following the purchase they see the product or service advertised elsewhere at a better value. Postpurchase dissonance is especially likely for products that are expensive, infrequently purchased, highly expressive, and associated with high levels of risk.

Aware of the negativity involved with postpurchase dissonance, marketers direct efforts at consumers after they have made the purchase to address the issue. For example, after Brad bought a Honda Civic, Honda Canada sent him a letter thanking him for his purchase and positively reinforcing the message that he made a wise decision by mentioning the high quality of the product's design and production. Included with the letter was a customer satisfaction survey (CSI) that asks about Brad's satisfaction with the dealership, salesperson, and other aspects of his purchase experience. Brad also received additional information about Honda services available to Honda Civic owners. To reduce the dissonance, Brad can take several actions:

- Pay attention to positive information about the Honda Civic, such as looking up reviews by owners and car buffs on the Internet.
- Get positive feedback from friends about his new sports car.
- Seek negative information about sports cars he did not buy. Reading these reviews makes him feel more comfortable with his purchase decision.

Customer Loyalty

Customer loyalty develops over time with multiple repeat purchases of the product or brand from the same marketer. In the postpurchase stage of the decision-making process, marketers attempt to build and nurture a loyal relationship with their customers from the very first purchase and with each subsequent purchase. They want customers to be satisfied with their purchase every time and buy from the same company again. Loyal customers will buy only certain brands and shop at certain stores, and they do not consider other brands or firms in their decision. As we explained in Chapter 2, such customers are therefore very valuable to firms, and marketers have designed customer relationship management (CRM) programs specifically to retain them.

Undesirable Consumer Behaviour

Although firms want satisfied, loyal customers, sometimes they fail to attain them. Passive consumers are those who don't repeat purchase or fail to recommend the product to others. More serious and potentially damaging, however, is negative consumer behaviour, such as negative word-of-mouth and rumours.

negative word-of-mouth
Occurs when consumers spread negative information about a product, service, or store to others.

Negative word-of-mouth occurs when consumers spread negative information about a product, service, or store to others. When customers' expectations are met or even exceeded, they often don't tell anyone about it. But when consumers believe that they have been treated unfairly in some way, they usually want to complain, often to many people. The Internet has provided an effective method of spreading negative

Whirlpool posts both good and bad comments on Twitter. It believes that posting negative comments opens up discussions and emphasizes the proactive measures the company is taking to remedy service or product failures.

word-of-mouth to millions of people instantaneously through personal blogs, Twitter, and corporate websites. To lessen the impact of negative word-of-mouth, firms provide customer service representatives—whether online, on the phone, or in stores—to handle and respond to complaints.

Some companies allow customers to post comments and complaints on their social media sites. For example, Whirlpool set up Facebook pages for its appliance brands, Maytag, KitchenAid, and Whirlpool. Customers can share their thoughts on these sites without fear of their negative feedback being deleted. Whirlpool believes it should "keep the bad" to open up discussions and emphasize the proactive measures the company is taking to remedy service or product failures. If a customer believes that positive action will be taken as a result of the complaint, he or she is less likely to complain to family and friends or through the Internet. (A detailed example of word-of-mouth appears in Chapter 10.)

FACTORS INFLUENCING CONSUMER BUYING DECISIONS

L03

The consumer decision process can be influenced by several factors, as illustrated in Exhibit 4.4. First are psychological factors, which are influences internal to the customer, such as motives, attitudes, perceptions, learning, and lifestyles. Second, social factors, such as family, reference groups, and culture, also influence the decision process. Third, situational factors, such as the specific purchase situation, a particular shopping situation, and temporal states (the time of day), affect the decision process.

Every decision people make as consumers will take them through some form of the consumer decision process. But, like life itself, this process does not exist in a vacuum.

Psychological Factors

Although marketers themselves can influence purchase decisions, a host of psychological factors affects the way people receive marketers' messages. Among them are motives, attitudes, perceptions, learning, and lifestyles. In this section, we examine how such psychological factors can influence the consumer decision process.

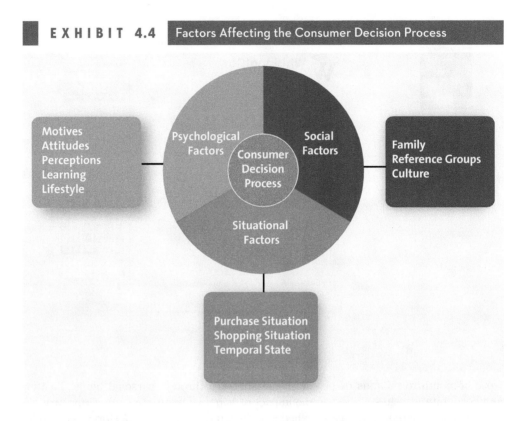

EXHIBIT 4.4   Factors Affecting the Consumer Decision Process

Motives   In Chapter 1, we argued that marketing is all about satisfying customer needs and wants. When a need, such as thirst, or a want, such as a Diet Coke, is not satisfied, it motivates us, or drives us, to get satisfaction. So, a **motive** is a need or want that is strong enough to cause the person to seek satisfaction.

People have several types of motives. One of the best-known paradigms for explaining these motive types was developed by Abraham Maslow more than 30 years ago.[29] Maslow categorized five groups of needs, namely, physiological (e.g., food, water, shelter), safety (e.g., secure employment, health), love (e.g., friendship, family), esteem (e.g., confidence, respect), and self-actualization (people engage in personal growth activities and attempt to meet their intellectual, aesthetic, creative, and other such needs). The pyramid in Exhibit 4.5 demonstrates the theoretical progression of those needs.

Physiological needs deal with the basic biological necessities of life: food, drink, rest, and shelter. Although for most people in developed countries these basic needs are generally met, there are those in both developed and less-developed countries who are less fortunate. However, everyone remains concerned with meeting these basic needs. Marketers seize every opportunity to convert these needs into wants by reminding us to eat at Taco Bell, drink milk, sleep on a Simmons Beautyrest mattress, and stay at a Marriott.

Safety needs pertain to protection and physical well-being. The marketplace is full of products and services that are designed to make you safer, such as airbags in cars and burglar alarms in homes, or healthier, such as vitamins and organic meats and vegetables.

Love (social) needs relate to our interactions with others. Haircuts and makeup make you look more attractive, and deodorants prevent odour. Greeting cards help you express your feelings toward others.

Esteem needs allow people to satisfy their inner desires. Yoga, meditation, health clubs, and many books appeal to people's desires to grow or maintain a happy, satisfied outlook on life.

motive
A need or want that is strong enough to cause the person to seek satisfaction.

physiological needs
Relate to the basic biological necessities of life: food, drink, rest, and shelter.

safety needs
Pertain to protection and physical well-being.

love (social) needs
Relate to our interactions with others.

esteem needs
Allow people to satisfy their inner desires.

EXHIBIT 4.5   Maslow's Hierarchy of Needs

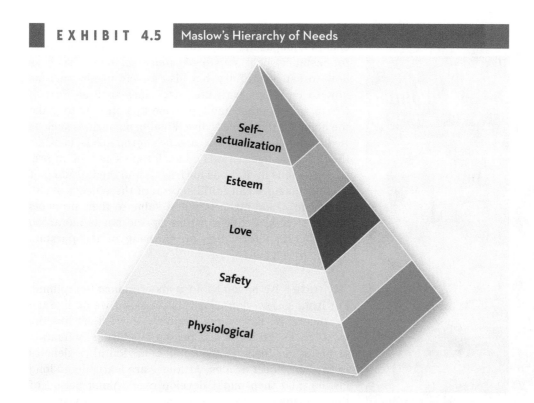

- Self-actualization
- Esteem
- Love
- Safety
- Physiological

Finally, **self-actualization** occurs when you feel completely satisfied with your life and how you live. You don't care what others think. You drive a Prius because it suits the person you are, not because some celebrity endorses it or because you want others to think better of you.

self-actualization
Occurs when you feel completely satisfied with your life and how you live.

Taco Bell satisfies physiological needs.

Yoga satisfies self-esteem needs by helping people satisfy their inner desires.

Which hierarchy of needs do these magazines fulfill?

Which of these needs applies when a consumer purchases a magazine? Magazines such as *Weight Watchers*, for instance, help satisfy *physiological* needs, such as how to eat healthfully, but also *esteem* needs, such as how to be happy with life. Magazines such as *Family Circle*, on the other hand, provide tips on how to make the home a *safer* place to live. Finally, magazines such as *Weddings* help satisfy *love and belonging* needs, because they provide instructions on such topics as how to prepare gracious invitations for friends and family. Many of these magazines can fulfill several of these needs simultaneously. Good marketers add value to their products or services by nudging people up the needs hierarchy and offering information on as many of the pyramid needs as they can.

Attitude   We have attitudes about almost everything. For instance, we don't like this class, but we do like the instructor. We like where we live, but we don't like the weather. An **attitude** is a person's enduring evaluation of his or her feelings about and behavioural tendencies toward an object or idea. Attitudes are learned and long lasting, and they might develop over a long period of time, though they can also abruptly change. For instance, you might like your instructor for much of the semester—until she returns your first exam. One thing we all have in common is that our attitudes have the ability to influence our decisions and actions.

An attitude consists of three components. The **cognitive component** reflects what we *believe* to be true, the **affective component** involves what we *feel* about the issue at hand—our like or dislike of something—and the **behavioural component** comprises the *action(s)* we take based on what we know and feel. For example, Ed and Tracy Lee see an ad for a Volvo that shows a family of five driving down the road, the kids strapped into their car seats and mom and dad talking in the front. An announcer lists the features included with each model, as well as government safety ratings that indicate Volvo is the safest brand on the road in its class. On the basis of this advertisement, Ed and Tracy believe that the government statistics must be true and that the car is therefore safe (cognitive component). Watching the happy family looking comfortable while driving this safe car allows Ed and Tracy to feel that they would like to have this car for their family (affective). Thus encouraged, they go to the Volvo dealership closest to them to make a purchase (behavioural).

Ideally, agreement exists among these components. When there is incongruence among the three however, cognitive dissonance might occur. Suppose, for instance, that though Ed and Tracy believe the Volvo is safe and they like the car, they buy another brand because it is cheaper. It is likely that they will experience the discomfort of buyers' remorse, or cognitive dissonance.

Although attitudes are pervasive and usually slow to change, the important fact from a marketer's point of view is that they can be influenced and perhaps changed through persuasive communications and personal experience. Marketing communication—through salespeople, advertisements, free samples, or other such methods—can attempt to change what people believe to be true about a product or service (cognitive) or how they feel toward it (affective). If the marketer is successful, the cognitive and affective components work in concert to affect behaviour. Continuing

attitude
A person's enduring evaluation of his or her feelings about and behavioural tendencies toward an object or idea; consists of three components: cognitive, affective, and behavioural.

cognitive component
A component of attitude that reflects what a person believes to be true.

affective component
A component of attitude that reflects what a person feels about the issue at hand—his or her like or dislike of something.

behavioural component
A component of attitude that comprises the actions a person takes with regard to the issue at hand.

with our example, suppose that prior to viewing the ad, Ed and Tracy thought that a Toyota Camry was the safest car on the road, but they liked the looks of the Volvo. The ad positively influenced the cognitive component of their attitude toward Volvo, making it consistent with the affective component.

Perception Another psychological factor, **perception**, is the process by which we select, organize, and interpret information to form a meaningful picture of the world. Perception influences our acquisition and consumption of goods and services through our tendency to assign meaning to things such as colour, symbols, taste, and packaging. Culture, tradition, and our overall upbringing determine our perceptual view of the world. For instance, Tracy has always wanted a Volvo because her best friend in university had one, and they had a great time driving across the country together one summer. However, based on his past experiences, Ed has a different perception. Ed thinks Volvos are slow, stodgy, unfashionable, and meant to be driven by little old ladies with grey hair—though they

People buy Volvos because they believe they are safe (cognitive component of an attitude), because they like them (affective), and because they have many convenient dealerships to visit (behavioural).

are safe! Volvo has worked hard in recent years to overcome this long-standing, negative perceptual bias that Ed and many others hold by creating faster cars with more stylish designs and by using promotion to reposition the brand to portray a more positive image.

perception
The process by which people select, organize, and interpret information to form a meaningful picture of the world.

In trying to influence perceptions, marketers must understand and focus on the four components of perception: *selective exposure, selective attention, selective comprehension*, and *selective retention*. People who look at the news and sports channels only, but not the comedy or women's TV network channels, are engaged in selective exposure because they are excluding other programs or channels. Similarly, consumers who listen to only messages that are consistent with their beliefs, and not others, are practising selective attention. For instance, although someone may look at the sports channel, he or she may watch hockey, soccer, or baseball but not boxing or wrestling because these may be too violent for his or her taste. Selective comprehension occurs when consumers interpret a marketing message in a way that is different from what the marketer intends. For example, a Dolce & Gabbana ad was intended to be edgy and sexual but consumers felt that it reinforced stereotypes about rape and degraded women. Knowing this, marketers can target their communications in those media that maximize exposure to their target market and create messages that are consistent with their beliefs and attitudes so that they will pay attention to the messages and interpret them in the intended way. Finally, selective retention describes the situation where consumers do not remember all the information they see, read, or hear. Marketers can provide the information in various other forms such as print, online, and other displays to reinforce their message.

Learning **Learning** refers to a change in a person's thought process or behaviour that arises from experience and takes place throughout the consumer decision process. For instance, after Brad recognized that he wanted a sports car, he started looking for ads and searching for reviews and articles on the Internet. He learned from each new piece of information, so that his thoughts about sports cars were different from what they were before he had read anything. In addition, Brad liked the salesperson at the dealership who served him. Brad learned from this experience, and it became part of his memory to be used in the future, possibly so he would recommend the dealership or salesperson to his friends.

learning
Refers to a change in a person's thought process or behaviour that arises from experience and takes place throughout the consumer decision process.

Entrepreneurial Marketing 4.1

Socks that Start Businesses

Many of us have heard the saying "sharing is caring." Today's entrepreneurs are taking this concept to a completely new level unimaginable just a few years ago. The concept of One for One has developed into an emerging business trend with companies like Tom's Shoes donating one pair of shoes for each pair sold. Diana and Jeff House wanted to take this concept farther, giving it a life of its own, one that would take it into the future and make it sustainable. They founded Cole + Parker, named for jazz greats John Coltrane and Charlie Parker,[30] with a One for Many business model.

Based in London, Ontario, Cole + Parker sells socks: bold, colourful, creative, premium-quality socks. Working with a world-class designer, Diana and Jeff came up with socks that make a statement, let you stand out in a crowd, and, well, jazz up your life. The socks sell for $24 a pair. Cole + Parker's tagline is Socks that Start Businesses because 1 percent of all sales revenue is used to help entrepreneurs in developing countries.

To implement the One for Many concept, the couple works with nonprofit partner Kiva, the largest microfinance organization in the world. Kiva has a proven track record, having facilitated more than $550 million in loans, with a 99 percent repayment rate.[31] Entrepreneurs receive loans and the opportunity to start businesses. Every dollar of sock revenue generated goes directly to entrepreneurs as Kiva does not charge any administrative fees.

Consider why people would pay $24 for socks. While the socks have that cool factor, people who buy them like the fact that their purchases help others. To illustrate, let's revisit some of the factors that affect consumer buying decisions. Psychological factors such as motives, attitudes, and lifestyle likely play a role. Purchasers may be motivated by esteem or self-actualization needs as shown in Exhibit 4.5 (Maslow's Hierarchy of Needs). Their attitude may be shaped by an affective component that makes them feel good about the socks, which prompts the behavioural component, resulting in taking action to buy the socks. Lifestyle can also play a part because the socks are fun and trendy. For consumers who are looking for a way to differentiate themselves, buying Cole + Parker socks lets them express their personality.

To raise money and visibility for their fledgling company, Diana and Jeff pitched their idea on CBC's *Dragons' Den*. At that time, they had been in business for only two weeks. Still, they had generated $32,000 worth of socks selling online only. They found a champion in David Chilton. Since then, distribution has expanded dramatically. The socks are now sold in over 100 retail outlets in Canada and the United States. Diana says their goal is to have 1,000 retailers, primarily smaller, privately owned, upscale men's stores[32] whose clients are looking for a little socks appeal.

Learning affects both attitudes and perceptions. Throughout the buying process, Brad's attitudes shifted. The cognitive component changed for him when he learned that the dealership offers various additional services at low costs to Honda Civic owners. Once he started getting the additional services (e.g., free car washes, special rates for car detailing), he realized how much he liked the service, which indicates the affective component, and he then subscribed to it—the behavioural component. Each time Brad was exposed to information about the service, he learned something different that affected his perception of the dealership. Before he tried it, Brad hadn't realized how friendly and helpful the people at the dealership were; thus, his perception of the dealership service changed through learning.

Lifestyle **Lifestyle** refers to the way consumers spend their time and money to live. For many consumers, the question of whether the product or service fits with their actual lifestyle, which may be fairly sedentary, or their perceived lifestyle, which might be outdoorsy, is an important one. Some of the many consumers sporting North Face jackets certainly need the high-tech, cold-weather gear because they are planning their next hike up Mount Robson and want to be sure they have sufficient protection against the elements. Others, however, simply like the image that the jacket conveys—the image that they might be leaving for their own mountain-climbing expedition any day now—even if the closest they have come to this trip has been shovelling their driveway. Similarly, people buy the Hummer luxury four-wheel-drive SUV so that they can get over almost any off-road obstacle, but they also like the leather seats with lumbar support, six-speaker audio system preloaded with XM satellite radio, remote key-less entry system, and the fact that they can whiz over speed bumps at the local grocery store.

A person's perceptions and ability to learn are affected by their social experiences, which we discuss next. Furthermore, Sustainable Marketing 4.1 shows how consumers' changing attitudes and lifestyles are influencing the types of foods they buy and consume.

lifestyle
Refers to the way consumers spend their time and money.

Social Factors

Exhibit 4.4 illustrates that the consumer decision process is also influenced by the external, social environment, which consists of the customer's family, reference groups, and culture.[33]

Family Many purchase decisions are made about products or services that the entire family will consume or use. Thus, firms must consider how families make purchase decisions and understand how various family members might influence these decisions.

When families make purchase decisions, they often consider the needs of all the family members. In choosing a restaurant, for example, all the family members may participate in the decision making. In other situations, however, different members of the family may take on different roles. For example, Brad recalled that when he was a kid, his dad and two older brothers were the ones who looked through car magazines and *Consumer Reports* to search for information about a new car. But once the family arrived at the dealership, his dad, not his brothers, decided which model and colour to buy, and his mom negotiated the final deal.

Despite that example, children and adolescents play an increasingly important role in family buying decisions. For instance, the tween segment alone in Canada is estimated to spend $2.9 billion per year on personal items such as snacks, soft drinks, electronics, and apparel. Tweens in Canada also indirectly influence family purchases in excess of $20 billion on big-ticket items such as recreation, vacations, technology, and the family car.[34]

Influencing a group that holds this much spending power is vitally important. Traditional food retailers are already caught in a squeeze between Walmart, which lures low-end customers, and specialty retailers, such as Whole Foods, which target the high end. Knowing how children influence food-buying decisions is a strategic opportunity for traditional supermarkets and their suppliers to exploit. Getting this group to prefer one store, chain, or product over another can make a difference in the bottom line, as well as in the chances for survival in a difficult marketplace.[35]

Family members often influence buying decisions.

Sustainable Marketing 4.1

Consumers Warm Up to Organic Foods

Organic agriculture, previously seen as a niche market, is registering rapid growth, with Canadian sales nearly tripling from 2006 to 2012. This flourishing market for organic food was valued at about $3.7 billion in 2012,[36] and the growth of demand for organic food is expected to continue. This increased demand has been attributed to various food scares, including concerns about the use of pesticides and food additives, and the increased use of genetically modified organisms in food production.[37] The organic industry integrates all aspects of a pesticide-free, fertilizer-free production process by using specific standards and is subject to a rigorous certification system.

What Is Organic Food?

There is often confusion about the true definition of organic among consumers. When comparing organic food to conventional food products, consumers of organic food generally describe it as "pesticide free" and "hormone free," with "no chemicals," "no pollutants," "no antibiotics," and "no genetically modified organisms"; thus, it is considered "natural." They also describe organic products as more nutritious, tasty, better looking, fresher, and without a uniform shape.

The Organic Food Consumer Profile

Although consumers of organic food differ in terms of their sociodemographic profile, we can say that they are mainly women, who buy in larger quantities and more frequently than men. Although age is not an important factor, younger consumers show a higher willingness to buy organic because of their greater environmental concerns, but cannot always afford to. Families often introduce organic foods with the arrival of a baby, which leads to substantial changes in food consumption habits. In 2001, a total of 71 percent of Canadians had at least tried organic foods. By 2013, 58 percent of all Canadians bought organic products on a weekly basis. Furthermore 98 percent of Canadians expect to maintain their spending on organic fruit and vegetables over the next year.[38]

Consumers' Motivations to Buy Organic Food

In Canada, consumers identify health, the environment, and supporting local farmers as being the principal values

that explain their organic food consumption.[39] Interestingly, consumers express that a socially responsible behaviour motivates them to support the local economy. More generally, in several different European countries, studies highlighted the following consumers' life values: values centred on the human being, on the environment, and on animals' well-being. Overall, organics are perceived as less associated with health risks than their conventional counterparts. For Canadians, health motivation is more an avoidance motivation (e.g., to avoid ingesting chemicals) than an approach motivation (e.g., to acquire nutritional benefits). Consumers' desire to maximize their personal health and well-being is another important motivation. The main reasons preventing consumers from buying organic foods are their high price, their lack of wide availability, their unsatisfactory quality, consumer satisfaction with current purchases, consumers' lack of familiarity with organic foods, consumer mistrust of organic labels, limited choice, and lack of perceived value.

Trust in Organic Food

Consumers rely on several indicators in order to trust the products. Therefore, marketers can use different tactics to encourage consumers not only to trust the brand and the label, but also to trust partners, such as producers. For now, when it comes to consumption of organic products, brand does not yet appear to be the main source of trust. Labelling and certification issues prevail, as consumers are either unfamiliar with or confused by labels or do not know to what degree they can trust certification labels. Generally, consumers want to learn more about the source of organic products and the production practices they are produced under.

Consumers' trust of points of sale seems to be an important factor in deciding where they buy organic foods. Supermarkets are increasingly successful but must deal with a lack of trust, especially for regular consumers of organic food, whereas specialty shops are associated with personal relationships, knowledge, and trust. Consumer knowledge and awareness are also important in the organic foods market since they affect people's perception and attitudes, and, ultimately, buying decisions.

---

reference group

One or more persons an individual uses as a basis for comparison regarding beliefs, feelings, and behaviours.

Reference Groups A **reference group** is one or more persons an individual uses as a basis for comparison regarding beliefs, feelings, and behaviours. A consumer might have various reference groups, including family, friends, coworkers, or famous people the consumer would like to emulate. These reference groups affect buying decisions by (1) offering information (2) providing rewards for specific purchasing behaviours, and (3) enhancing a consumer's self-image.

Reference groups provide information to consumers directly through conversation or indirectly through observation. For example, when Emily, a second-year business student at the University of British Columbia saw that almost all her colleagues had a smartphone (iPhone, BlackBerry, or Android), she quickly decided it was time for her to purchase a smartphone in order to fit in with her peers.

Some reference groups also influence behaviours by rewarding behaviour that meets with their approval or chastising those who engage in behaviour that doesn't. For example, smokers are often criticized by their friends and made to smoke outside or in restricted areas.

Consumers can identify and affiliate with reference groups to create, enhance, or maintain their self-image. Customers who want to be seen as "earthy" might buy Birkenstock sandals, whereas those wanting to be seen as "high fashion" might buy Christian Louboutin shoes, as we discussed earlier in this chapter.

A survey of Canadian and American teenagers showed that Hollister, American Eagle, West Coast Brands, and Abercrombie & Fitch are the most popular brands among this group.[40] Some stores, such as Abercrombie & Fitch, play on these forms of influence and hire sales associates they hope will serve as a reference group for customers who shop there. These hip, attractive, and somewhat aloof employees are required to wear the latest store apparel—thereby serving as living mannequins for customers to emulate.

Culture We defined culture in Chapter 3 as the shared meanings, beliefs, morals, values, and customs of a group of people. Your cultural group might be as small as your reference group at school or as large as the country in which you live or the religion in which you participate. For instance, the culture at Brad's university evokes a "high-achiever" attitude. This reputation influences, to some extent, the way he spends his leisure time, the types of people he hangs out with, and the kinds of products he buys. Culture is one of the most pervasive factors influencing consumer behaviour. Therefore, marketers must work hard to understand how it is different not only in Canada but also in those countries to which they plan to market their products. Marketing strategies that may work in Canada or North America may not work well in Japan or India because consumers in those countries are culturally different, as discussed in Chapter 17. Additionally, even within Canada, there are cultural differences between various subgroups or subcultures. A subculture is a group of people whose beliefs and values are different from the rest of the larger society in which they live. Examples of subcultures in Canada include French-Canadian subculture, Chinese-Canadian subculture, South-Asian subculture, and Acadian subculture. Research has shown that Chinese- and Asian-Canadians prefer to do business with marketers who truly understand their culture and needs rather than those who have very superficial ways of acknowledging their community, which a lot of people in the community find irritating.[41]

Marketers are working hard to understand how culture affects consumer behaviour in Canada. For example, Clorox commissioned research to zero in on South Asians and Chinese, the country's two largest ethnic groups. The research showed them tastes and preferences in a variety of categories. The findings led the company to launch a limited edition Year of the Dragon red Brita water filter to celebrate Chinese New Year. It quickly became one of Clorox's fastest selling products, growing sales by 25 percent in January and February that year.[42] The following year, Lego launched a specially designed Creator set to celebrate the Year of the Snake. Grocers have responded to Canada's changing cultural makeup by carrying a much wider

Marketers work to understand consumer culture and respond with unique products, such as the Year of the Snake creator set from Lego.

selection of ethnic foods on store shelves. These days it's hard to find a grocery store that doesn't carry fresh sushi. The Sobeys store in Thornhill employs multiple rabbis to oversee kosher food section to ensure that meat preparation follows strict Jewish dietary rules and that baked goods are milk-free. Its Brampton store carries a large selection of East Indian foods and halal meat is available for Muslim families in the Malton store.

Situational Factors

situational factors
Factors affecting the consumer decision process; those that are specific to the purchase and shopping situation and temporal state that may override, or at least influence, psychological and social issues.

Psychological and social factors typically influence the consumer decision process the same way each time. For example, your motivation to quench your thirst usually drives you to drink a Pepsi, and your reference group at the workplace coerces you to wear appropriate attire. But sometimes, **situational factors**, or factors specific to the situation, override, or at least influence, psychological and social issues. These situational factors are related to the purchase and shopping situation, as well as to the temporal state, as illustrated in Exhibit 4.4.

Purchase Situation
Customers may be predisposed to purchase certain products or services because of some underlying psychological trait or social factor, but these factors may change in certain purchase situations. For instance, Priya Persaud, a Vancouverite, considers herself a thrifty, cautious shopper—someone who likes to get a good deal. But her best friend is getting married, and she wants to buy the couple a silver tray. If the tray were for herself, she would probably go to Stokes, Home Sense, or possibly even Walmart. But since it is for her best friend, she went to Birks. Why? To purchase something fitting for the special occasion of a wedding.

Shopping Situation
Consumers might be ready to purchase a product or service but for a variety of reasons be completely derailed once they arrive in the store. Marketers use several techniques to influence consumers at this choice stage of the decision process. Consider the following techniques:

Abercrombie & Fitch stores blast loud dance music through powerful speakers and pump the company's signature cologne, Fierce, into the air.

- *Store atmosphere.* Some retailers and service providers have developed unique images that are based at least in part on their internal environment, also known as their atmospherics.[43] Research has shown that, if used in concert with other aspects of a retailer's strategy, music, scent, lighting, and even colour can positively influence the decision process.[44] For example, Abercrombie & Fitch aggressively positions itself as a lifestyle brand called "Casual Luxury." Its stores are plastered with photos of physically attractive young models, blasted with loud dance music through powerful speakers, and pumped full of the company's signature cologne, Fierce. The stores are also staffed with attractive models, young salespeople who embody the Abercrombie & Fitch lifestyle: attractive, athletic, popular, enthusiastic, and outgoing.[45] Restaurants, such as Rainforest Cafe, have developed internal environments that are not only pleasant, but also consistent with their food and service.

- *Salespeople.* Well-trained sales personnel can influence the sale at the point of purchase by pointing out the advantages of one item over another and by encouraging multiple purchases. The salesperson at Birks, for instance, explained to Priya why one platter was better than the next and suggested some serving pieces to go with it.

- *Crowding.* Customers can feel crowded because there are too many people, too much merchandise, or lines that are too long. If there are too many people in a store, some people become distracted and may even leave.[46] Others have difficulty purchasing if the merchandise is packed too closely together. This issue is a particular problem for shoppers with mobility disabilities.

- *In-store demonstrations.* The taste and smell of new food items may attract people to try something they normally wouldn't. Similarly, some fashion retailers offer "trunk shows," during which their vendors show their whole line on a certain day. During these well-advertised events, customers are often enticed to purchase that day because they get special assistance from the salespeople and can order merchandise that the retailer otherwise does not carry.

In-store demonstrations entice people to buy.

- *Promotions.* Retailers employ various promotional vehicles to influence customers once they have arrived in the store. For instance, an unadvertised price promotion can alter a person's preconceived buying plan. Multi-item discounts, such as "buy one, get one free" sales, are popular means to get people to buy more than they normally would. Because many people regard clipping coupons from the newspaper as too much trouble, some stores make coupons available in the store. Another form of promotion is offering a "free" gift with the purchase of a good or service. This type of promotion is particularly popular with cosmetics.

- *Packaging.* It is difficult to make a product stand out in the crowd when it competes for shelf space with several other brands. This problem is particularly difficult for consumer packaged goods, such as groceries and health and beauty products. Marketers therefore spend millions of dollars designing and updating their packages to be more appealing and eye catching than their competitors'.

Temporal State Our state of mind at any particular time can alter our preconceived notions of what we are going to purchase. For instance, some people are "morning people," whereas others function better at night. In turn, a purchase situation may have different appeal levels depending on the time of day and the type of person the consumer is. Mood swings can also alter consumer behaviour. Suppose Priya received a parking ticket just prior to shopping at Birks. It is likely that she would be less receptive to the salesperson's influence than if she came into the store in a good mood. Her bad mood may even cause her to have a less positive postpurchase feeling about the store. Unfortunately, such temporal factors are usually beyond the control of even the most creative marketer.

As we've seen, people's lives are lived in different contexts and consumer decisions are made in unique contexts. Marketers who understand this fact are better positioned to serve their target consumers. All the factors that affect the consumer decision process that we have discussed—psychological factors, social factors, and situational factors—are all impacted by the level of consumer involvement, the subject of the next section.

INVOLVEMENT AND CONSUMER BUYING DECISIONS **LO4**

Consumers engage in two types of buying process/decisions depending on their level of involvement: extended problem solving for high-priced, risky, infrequent, or highly expressive purchases; and limited problem solving, which includes impulse buying and habitual purchases/decision making. **Involvement** is the consumer's degree of interest or concern in the product or service.[47] Consumers may have different levels of involvement for the

involvement
The consumer's degree of interest or concern in the product or service.

same type of product. One consumer behaviour theory, the elaboration likelihood model, illustrated in Exhibit 4.6, proposes that high- and low-involvement consumers process different aspects of a marketing message or advertisement.

If both types of consumers viewed ads for hybrids produced by Toyota and Ford, the high-involvement consumer (e.g., Katie who is researching hybrids) will scrutinize all the information provided (e.g., gas savings, eco-friendly) and process the key elements of the message deeply. As a consequence, Katie, an involved consumer, is likely to either end up judging the ad to be truthful and forming a favourable impression of the product or alternatively viewing the message as superficial and developing negative product impressions (i.e., her research suggests the product is not as good as it is being portrayed).

In contrast, a low-involvement consumer will likely process the same advertisement in a less thorough manner. Such a consumer might pay less attention to the key elements of the message (e.g., gas savings, eco-friendly) and focus on heuristic elements such as brand name (Toyota), price, and the presence of a celebrity endorser. The impressions of the low-involvement consumer are likely to be more superficial.

Extended Problem Solving

As we noted at the beginning of this chapter, the buying process begins when consumers recognize that they have an unsatisfied need. Katie recognized her need to have access to transportation when she went away to college. She sought information by asking for advice from her friends, by reading consumer reports, and by researching online. Once she decided that a car and not a bike or the bus was her best option, she visited several car dealerships to test drive the models she was interested in and to find out which dealer offered the best price. Finally, after considerable time and effort spent analyzing her alternatives, Katie purchased a Toyota Prius. This process is an example of **extended problem solving**, which is common when the customer perceives that the purchase decision entails a great deal of risk. The potential risks associated with Katie's decision to buy her car include financial (Did I pay too much?), physiological (Will it keep me safe in an accident?), social (Will my friends think I look cool?), performance (Will the car perform as expected?), and psychological (Will the car convey the right image of me?) risks. To reduce her perceived risk, Katie spent a lot of effort searching for information about cars before she actually made her purchase.

extended problem solving
A purchase decision process during which the consumer devotes considerable time and effort to analyzing alternatives; often occurs when the consumer perceives that the purchase decision entails a great deal of risk.

EXHIBIT 4.6 Elaboration Likelihood Model

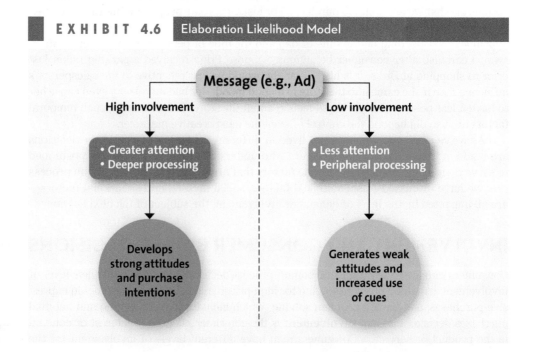

What type of buying decisions does each of these products represent?

Limited Problem Solving

Limited problem solving occurs during a purchase decision that calls for, at most, a moderate amount of effort and time. Customers engage in this type of buying process when they have had some prior experience with the product or service and the perceived risk is moderate. Limited problem solving usually relies on past experience more than on external information. For some people even a car purchase could require limited effort.

A common type of limited problem solving is **impulse buying**, a buying decision made by customers on the spot when they see the merchandise.[48] When Katie went to the grocery store to do her weekly shopping, she saw a display case of popcorn and Dr Pepper near the checkout counter. Knowing that some of her friends were coming to her place to watch a movie later, she stocked up. The popcorn and pop were an impulse purchase. Katie didn't go through the entire decision process; instead, she recognized her need and jumped directly to the purchase stage without spending any time searching for additional information or evaluating alternatives. The grocery store facilitated this impulse purchase by providing easily accessible cues (i.e., by offering the popcorn and soft drinks in a prominent display, at an accessible location in the store, and at a reasonable price).

Some purchases require even less thought. **Habitual decision making** describes a purchase decision process in which consumers engage with little conscious effort. On her way home from the grocery store, for example, Katie drove past a Tim Hortons and swung into the drive-through for a maple pecan Danish and an Iced Capp. She did not ponder the potential benefits of going to Second Cup or Starbucks; rather, she simply reacted to the cue provided by the sign and engaged in habitual decision making. Marketers strive to attract and maintain habitual purchasers by creating strong brands and store loyalty (see Chapter 9) because these customers don't even consider alternative brands or stores. Marketers who are trying to get consumers to switch to their brands often use marketing tactics that require greater involvement in the

limited problem solving
Occurs during a purchase decision that calls for, at most, a moderate amount of effort and time.

impulse buying
A buying decision made by customers on the spot when they see the merchandise.

habitual decision making
A purchase decision process in which consumers engage with little conscious effort.

purchase decisions. For instance, toothpaste is a habitual or routine purchase; however, in attempts to lure customers away from each other's products, both Crest and Colgate have developed toothpaste with a variety of ingredients and benefits designed to get customers to stop and think that all toothpastes are not created equal and that toothpaste is just not toothpaste—it offers various health benefits. The same thing can be said of bread and a host of other consumer packaged goods.

LEARNING OBJECTIVES REVIEW

LO1 Describe the steps in the consumer buying decision process

The consumer buying process consists of five main steps: First, during need recognition, consumers simply realize they have an unsatisfied need or want that they hope to address. Sometimes the needs are simple: I need food because I am hungry. Often, however, they become more complex: I want to buy my girlfriend an engagement ring. Second, they begin to search for information to determine how to satisfy that need. Generally, the more important the purchase, the more time and effort the consumer will spend on the search process. Firms facilitate this search by providing promotional materials and personal selling. Third, during the alternative evaluation stage, they assess the various options available to them to determine which is the best for their purposes. Fourth, the purchase stage involves obtaining and using the product. Fifth and finally, consumers enter the postpurchase stage, during which they determine whether they are satisfied or dissatisfied with their choice, or if they experience postpurchase dissonance. Every marketer wants satisfied customers, but when instead they are confronted with dissatisfied customers who are in some way unsure about their purchase, marketers must proactively turn the situation around. If they don't, the customer may be gone for good.

LO2 Identify what determines how much time consumers will spend searching for information before buying a product or service

A variety of factors affect consumers' searches for information about a potential purchase. First, they consider the time and effort associated with searching versus the benefits derived from the search. Second, people who have an internal locus of control—those who believe they have control over the outcomes of their actions—are more likely to spend time searching for information than those with an external locus of control. Third, consumers who perceive a high performance, financial, social, physiological, or psychological risk associated with the purchase will spend relatively more time searching for information than those who do not.

LO3 Summarize how psychological, social, and situational factors influence consumers' buying behaviour

First and foremost, firms must design their products and services to meet their customers' wants and needs, but understanding certain aspects of consumer behaviour can help as well. For instance, it is important to understand people's motives (i.e., what drives them to buy), their attitudes (i.e., how they feel about a product or service), and their perceptions (i.e., how information about that product or service fits into their worldview). Knowledge about these psychological characteristics helps firms design and provide products and services that their customers want and need.

In addition, people don't live in a vacuum. Consumers are influenced by their family, their reference groups, and their culture. Understanding these social groups and people's roles within them provides important insights into consumers' buying behaviour. Finally, although consumers already carry a host of psychological and social factors along with them on a shopping expedition, certain other factors can influence a purchase at the point of sale. For instance, customers might change their buying behaviour because the purchase situation is different than the one they are used to. Also, things can happen to customers, both positive and negative, once they are in a store that might alter their preconceived notion of what they plan to purchase. Finally, people can be just plain finicky, and being in an unusually good or extremely bad mood can also alter a purchase decision. The more firms understand these psychological, social, and situational factors, the more likely they will be to influence purchase decisions.

LO4 Explain how involvement influences the consumer buying decision process

More involved consumers, who are more interested or invested in the product or service they are considering, tend to engage in extended problem solving. They gather lots of information, scrutinize it carefully, and then make their decisions with caution, to minimize any risk they may confront. In contrast, less involved consumers often engage in limited problem solving, undertake impulse purchases, or rely on habit to make their purchase decisions. Some purchasing decisions require limited problem solving because the perceived risk of the purchase is low or the consumer has previous experience purchasing the product or service. Impulse and habitual purchases fall in this category.

KEY TERMS

- affective component
- attitude
- behavioural component
- cognitive component
- compensatory decision rule
- consumer decision rules
- decision heuristics
- determinant attributes
- esteem needs
- evaluative criteria
- extended problem solving
- external locus of control
- external search for information
- financial risk

- functional needs
- habitual decision making
- impulse buying
- internal locus of control
- internal search for information
- involvement
- learning
- lifestyle
- limited problem solving
- love (social) needs
- motive
- need recognition
- negative word-of-mouth
- noncompensatory decision rule

- perception
- performance risk
- physiological needs
- physiological risk
- postpurchase dissonance
- psychological needs
- psychological risk
- reference group
- ritual consumption
- safety needs
- self-actualization
- situational factors
- social risk
- specialty goods/services

CONCEPT REVIEW

1. Give three reasons it is important for marketers to understand the factors that influence consumers' purchasing decisions.

2. List the five steps of the consumer buying decision process. What should be the primary focus of marketing strategy at the alternative evaluation stage? The purchase stage?

3. What are the primary factors that affect consumers' search processes? What marketing strategies can marketers employ to ensure that customers get the information they need in order to make their shopping decisions?

4. Briefly explain how the extent of problem solving influences consumers' buying behaviour and describe four strategies marketers could use to facilitate consumer purchasing in each case. Give examples of products you would classify as high-involvement purchases.

5. Identify and briefly explain the five psychological factors that influence consumer buying decisions.

6. What marketing tactics could be used to break through customers' selective perception (i.e., selective exposure, selective attention, selective comprehension, and selective retention)?

7. How can marketers use Maslow's hierarchy-of-needs model to develop successful marketing programs for their target market?

8. Briefly explain how social and situational considerations influence customer buying decisions.

9. Perceived risks are a key determinant of consumer buying decisions. Explain what is meant by perceived risks and identify tactics marketers could use to mitigate these risks.

10. Culture is one of the most important but least understood influences on consumer buying decisions. Explain how marketers can ensure that their marketing efforts are suited to their culturally diverse target market. What are the challenges involved in developing such efforts?

MARKETING APPLICATIONS

1. Does buying Kashi cereal satisfy a consumer's functional or psychological need? How might this information help a Kashi brand manager better promote the product?

2. When consumers buy a new notebook, what sort (internal versus external) of information search would they conduct? If you were a marketing manager for Sony, how would you use this information?

3. Explain the factors that affect the amount of time and effort that a consumer might take when choosing an oral

surgeon to get his or her wisdom teeth removed. How would your answer change if the consumer were looking for a dentist to get a cleaning? How should the office manager for a dental practice use this information?

4. When evaluating different alternatives for a Saturday night outing at a fine restaurant, explain how a consumer would use decision heuristics to narrow down the choice of restaurants. Give examples of heuristics such as price, brand, and presentation in your answer.

5. What can retailers do to make sure that they have satisfied customers after the sale is complete?

6. Tazo blends exotic green teas, spearmint, and rare herbs to create a tea called Zen. Using Maslow's hierarchy of needs, explain which need(s) are being fulfilled by this tea.

7. Identify and describe the three social factors that influence the consumer decision process. Provide an example of how each of these might influence the purchase of the necessary products and services for a family vacation.

8. Nike has developed a new shoe for long-distance runners that is designed to minimize wear and tear on the joints and tendons. Develop a theme for an advertising strategy that ensures all three components of attitude are positively covered.

9. What can a marketer do to positively influence a situation in which a consumer is ready to buy but has not yet done so?

10. You were recently hired by a retail and catalogue company that promotes itself as a Canadian firm selling only Canadian-made goods. The products featured in advertising and in the catalogues tell the stories of the firms that produced the goods in Canada. The sales response to the firm's Made in Canada position has been incredible and growth has been impressive. One day while speaking to a vendor, you learn a shipment of merchandise will be delayed since the product is coming from overseas and is late. A few days later you hear a similar story. As it turns out, the firm just barely earns the Made in Canada label. Although technically the products meet the standard to be classified as Canadian-made, you worry that the firm is not being truthful to its customers. You decide to write a letter to the vice-president of marketing detailing your concerns. What would you put in the letter?

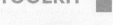

TOOLKIT

CONSUMER BEHAVIOUR

Jill is trying to decide, once and for all, which soft-drink company is her favourite. She has created a chart to help her decide. She has rated Coca-Cola, Pepsi-Cola, and Jones Soda in terms of price, taste, variety, and packaging. She has also assessed how important each of these four attributes is in terms of her evaluations. Use the toolkit provided on Connect to determine which cola Jill will choose by using a compensatory model. Which cola would she choose if she used a noncompensatory model? If you were Jill, which model would you use, the compensatory or the noncompensatory? Why?

NET SAVVY

1. Visit the Harley-Davidson website (http://www.harley-davidson.com) and review the information provided about its Harley Owners Group (HOG). Describe the efforts the company makes to maintain customer loyalty through its programs. What are the benefits to HOG members? Discuss how these measures might be effective in creating value for members.

2. Customers use a variety of methods to provide feedback to companies about their experiences. Planetfeed-back.com was developed as one such venue. Visit its website (http://www.planetfeedback.com) and identify the types of feedback that customers can provide. Look over the feedback about Ford, and summarize some of the most recent comments. What is the ratio of positive to negative comments about Ford during the last year or so? Describe the effect these comments might have on customer perceptions of Ford.

CHAPTER CASE STUDY

WEIGHT WATCHERS VERSUS JENNY CRAIG[49]

Want to lose weight? For about the 24 percent of adult Canadians who are considered obese, the answer is probably yes.[50] For weight-loss companies, that's the right answer.

The weight-loss industry in Canada and the United States, worth more than $60 billion in 2010, is growing steadily because lifestyles and food choices are working against the desire to lose weight. Most Canadians spend their days sitting in front of a computer and their evenings sitting in front of a TV; about 68 percent of Canadians live sedentary lives. No wonder that 56 percent, or more than 1.2 million, Canadian youths aged 15 to 19 years old are either overweight or obese. The corresponding number for adults is 51 percent, or more than 14.2 million Canadians.[51] Restaurant meals, prepared foods, and high-fat/high-sugar snacks have replaced home-cooked meals, whole grains, and fresh produce. These habits are fattening profits for the weight-loss industry as well as expanding belt sizes. By the time you factor in diet pills, specially packaged weight-loss meals and snacks, diet programs, and a whole range of products and services promising bodies fit for bathing suits, you've got a market projected to be worth more than $586.3 billion annually in the United States and Canada.[52] Three recognized diet aid behemoths, Weight Watchers, Jenny Craig, and Slim-Fast, share a substantial piece of the pie. These companies stress flexibility to fit a wide range of lifestyles, and showcase their success stories. But each approaches dieting differently in its quest for new members.

The Big Three

Founded in 1963, Weight Watchers International now boasts groups in more than 30 countries worldwide. The program encourages members to track their daily food intake, exercise, hunger levels, and emotions related to eating. Dieters record meals and snacks in a paper or electronic journal. All foods are assigned point values, calculated based on calories, fat, and fibre, and members have a daily point allotment based on individual weight and lifestyle. Although members can follow the Weight Watchers regimen without support, the company notes that the most successful members are those who weigh in at weekly group sessions and attend meetings. During these half-hour meetings, a group leader discusses a particular topic, such as holiday eating, measuring and weighing foods for portion control, or eating out. Members are given an opportunity to swap ideas and recipes that have worked for them, admit their mistakes and request support, and be acknowledged for successes. Weight Watcher members can prepare their own food, dine out, or purchase Weight Watcher–prepared or –endorsed dinners, snacks, and desserts at most grocery stores. To further support dieters in making healthy food choices, Weight Watchers recently changed its point system, increasing the number of points for fat content and reducing them for fibre.

Recently rated the top weight-loss program by *Consumer Reports on Health*, Jenny Craig promises a unique and comprehensive plan for food, body, and mind.[53] Members eat meals and snacks prepared and packaged by Jenny Craig, supplemented by fresh fruits and vegetables. Jenny Craig's offerings provide portion control and accommodate busy schedules by reducing meal prep time. Members meet weekly on a one-on-one basis with a personal counsellor and are encouraged to develop an exercise program. Like Weight Watchers, Jenny Craig offers customized programs for men and teenagers and for those who prefer to lose weight on their own rather than travel to a centre. Jenny Craig bested Weight Watchers and other diet programs in the *Consumer Reports on Health* ranking because of members' success in weight loss, the duration of time they remained committed to the program, and the nutritional value of the foods.[54]

Slim-Fast, which ranked second in the *Consumer Reports on Health* ratings, offers dieters a combination of three small and healthy snacks, two meal-replacement shakes, and one 500-calorie meal daily.[55] By eating six small meals daily, dieters maintain steady glucose levels, and the plan ensures adequate intakes of carbohydrates, protein, and fibre.[56]

To entice men to use its program, Jenny Craig uses Jason Alexander, the actor who played George Costanza on the TV series *Seinfeld*, as a spokesperson (pictured with another Jenny Craig spokesperson, Valerie Bertinelli, teenage TV star from the late 70s of *One Day at a Time* and *Touched by an Angel*.)

Other diet programs abound but, while many people lose weight on these regimens, the loss tends to be temporary because the diets are based on unsustainable eating patterns, such as eliminating major food groups. Additionally, the big diet companies offer social reinforcement and flexibility, which appears to help people remain committed to their weight-loss programs.

Defining the Difference

Perhaps the most significant difference between Jenny Craig, Slim-Fast, and Weight Watchers is the amount of effort required. Jenny Craig dieters don't have to think about what they eat; everything is prepared for them. Dieters on the Weight Watchers plan must learn how to make the right choices from among the foods that surround them in their daily lives. Slim-Fast combines both ease and education, but it provides fewer choices for controlled meals than Jenny Craig does. Each program competes heavily for members, particularly in the early months of the year, when Canadians return to the scales after indulging over the holidays.

The diet giants are locked in another battle as well, this one targeted at men.[57] Although a completely different program isn't needed—both sexes need to cut calories and increase exercise—marketing specifically to men has the power to bring in new members. While the Weight Watchers' programs are identical for men and women, the men's website is tailored to male interests and concerns, focusing more on working out and less on the eating plan. The men's site also mentions the link between obesity and erectile dysfunction, implying that a man's sex life might improve if he loses weight.

Jenny Craig's men's program is also very similar to its women's program but is tweaked to accommodate differences in food cravings and issues with portion control. Men on this program, Jenny Craig promises, can still have a beer and fries once in a while. To further entice men to their program, Jenny Craig uses Jason Alexander, who played George Costanza on the TV series *Seinfeld*, as its spokesperson.

The Slim-Fast program tends to appeal to men because they like to lose weight on their own rather than participating in group meetings.[58] The company has used male celebrities, including a former New York mayor, to sell its products.

Technology Support for Dieters

Dieters have a variety of electronic devices to help track food consumption and exercise. Using any Internet-ready device, Weight Watcher members can check point values for foods, including meals at popular restaurants, and add snacks or meals to their daily journal. Similar services and applications for fitness training are available via cellphone applications. Using a camera-equipped cellphone, for example, dieters can photograph a meal and send the picture to a registered dietitian, who replies with recommendations for modifying portions or food choices. Theoretically, this approach is more honest than keeping a food diary since dieters may be tempted not to record full amounts. These services require additional fees though.

Questions

1. Trace how you might go through the steps in the consumer decision process if you were thinking of going on a diet and using either of these diet programs.

2. How have Weight Watchers, Slim-Fast, and Jenny Craig created value?

3. Identify the determinant attributes that set the Weight Watchers', Slim-Fast, and Jenny Craig's programs apart from each other. Use those attributes to develop a compensatory purchasing model like the one found in Exhibit 4.2.

4. How can Weight Watchers, Slim-Fast, and Jenny Craig increase the probability of customer satisfaction?

5. Which factors examined in the chapter do you think would have the most impact on consumers' propensity to go on a diet and choose either of these diet programs?

For more information on the resources available from McGraw-Hill Ryerson, go to www.mheducation.ca/he/solutions.

CHAPTER **5**

Business-to-Business Marketing

Most of us know that RBC Royal Bank is Canada's largest commercial bank; however, not many people know that RBC buys more than $5 billion worth of goods and services each year from its approved vendors in a variety of B2B transactions.[1] So, what kinds of goods and services are purchased, and how does a company become an approved vendor? These purchases include a wide range of items from toilet paper to office supplies to advertising and a host of other products and services that are used for the bank's operations. In addition, RBC buys goods and services in support of its sponsorship events and community causes. For example, RBC purchased millions of dollars worth of goods as a partner of the Olympic and Paralympic Winter Games and the Olympic and Paralympic Torch Relays. It added a new category listing for Vancouver 2010 to its Supplier Information Form (described below) that allowed potential vendors the opportunity to highlight their interest in providing a product or service during the Games.

To be considered a potential vendor, a business must first register with RBC by completing and submitting a Supplier Information Form. This form requires potential vendors to provide information that helps RBC gain a better understanding of the companies that want to supply their goods and services. This information is entered into RBC's Potential Supplier Database, where it is kept for two years. RBC's procurement group, which is responsible for all purchases of goods and services for all RBC's business units, uses this database as the primary source of vendor information to assess the market for new sourcing opportunities. RBC contacts vendors in whose products and services it is interested.

In addition to registering on RBC's website by using the Supplier Information Form, potential vendors must meet other requirements if they want to be one of the many small, medium, and large businesses supplying RBC. First, vendors must offer high-quality goods and services with top-notch customer service and have e-procurement capability because RBC wants to efficiently and cost-effectively buy goods and services. Second, vendors must meet certain environmental and social criteria. RBC's supplier management policy requires that RBC gather information on key areas of supplier operations, including, but not limited to, environmental management systems, health and safety management systems, NGO relationships and evidence of any activism

LEARNING OBJECTIVES

After studying this chapter you should be able to

LO1 Describe the nature and composition of B2B markets

LO2 Explain the key differences between B2B buying and B2C buying

LO3 Explain the ways B2B firms classify and segment their markets

LO4 Describe the B2B buying process

LO5 Identify the roles within the buying centre

LO6 Detail different buying situations

campaigns, impacts on indigenous communities, and labour standards. The review process ensures that RBC gathers the appropriate environmental and social information regarding suppliers' operations and the products and service they offer to make informed procurement decisions.

RBC's centralized, structured, and technology-driven buying process is designed to improve the efficiency of the buying process and help ensure that RBC gets good value for the billions of dollars it spends annually. What do you think are some of the strengths and drawbacks of RBC's centralized buying process? █

business-to-business (B2B) marketing
The process of buying and selling goods or services to be used in the production of other goods and services, for consumption by the buying organization, or for resale by wholesalers and retailers.

Business-to-business (B2B) marketing refers to the process of buying and selling goods or services to be used in the production of other goods and services, for consumption by the buying organization, or for resale by wholesalers and retailers. Therefore, B2B marketing involves manufacturers, wholesalers, retailers, and service firms that market goods and services to other businesses but not to the ultimate consumer. The distinction between a B2B and a B2C transaction is not the product or service itself; rather, it is the ultimate purchaser and *user of* that product or service. Had your jeans been sold to an industrial supply firm, which then sold them to a custodial firm whose employees would wear them on the job, the transaction would still be a B2B transaction because the jeans are being purchased and used by a business rather than by an individual household consumer.

In this chapter, we will look at the different types of B2B markets and examine the B2B buying process with an eye toward how it differs from the B2C buying process, which we discussed in Chapter 4. Several factors influence the B2B buying process, and we discuss these as well. Finally, the chapter concludes with a discussion about the role of the Internet and its influence on the way B2B marketing is conducted.

LO1 B2B MARKETS

Just like organizations that sell directly to final consumers in B2C transactions, B2B firms focus their efforts on serving specific types of customer markets to create value for those customers.[2] For instance, RBC maintains a dedicated group of account executives to service its small business and commercial banking clients. As the largest Canadian commercial bank, RBC manages assets of more than $620 billion, and its online capabilities generate a tremendous amount of traffic and span many different service requirements, including cash management, foreign exchange, international trade, borrowing and credit, online banking, and investment advice.

As in RBC's case, many firms find it more productive to focus their efforts on key industries or market segments rather than on ultimate consumers. Cossette Communication Group and BBDO Canada, two of Canada's largest advertising agencies, provide advertising, public relations, and other marketing communications services to large and small business clients across Canada. Similarly, Canada's Magna International designs, develops, and manufactures automotive systems, assemblies, modules, and components primarily for sale to original equipment manufacturers (OEMs) of cars and light trucks in North America, Europe, Asia, South America, and Africa.[3]

In the chapter vignette, we saw how various manufacturers and resellers market their products to RBC by registering as a vendor on RBC's e-procurement system. Basically, manufacturers, resellers, institutions, and governments are all involved in B2B transactions (see Exhibit 5.1). In the next sections, we describe each of these B2B organizations.

EXHIBIT 5.1 B2B Markets

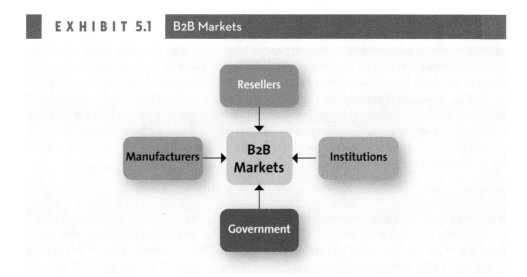

Manufacturers or Producers

Manufacturers buy raw materials, components, and parts that allow them to manufacture their own goods. For example, the German-based Volkswagen Group, the largest auto manufacturer in Europe, owns and distributes the Audi, Bentley, Bugatti, Lamborghini, Seat, Skoda, Scania VW, and VW Commercial Vehicles brands.[4] Whereas purchasing agents formerly spent 70 percent of their time searching for, analyzing, validating, and forwarding information about parts and components, today they can use VWSupplyGroup.com to communicate with suppliers for all transactions, from procurement to logistics.

The system is used by 45,600 suppliers, who were engaged in transactions worth 2.13 billion euros (or nearly C$3 billion).[5] Purchasing agents receive product descriptions directly from suppliers online, which means search processes that used to take two hours now require about nine minutes. Users of the system receive alerts of potential parts shortages before they occur and thus can focus on efficiencies instead of redundant paperwork.

IBM provided the consulting services necessary to design the Volkswagen Group's system. IBM, which was once a major manufacturer of computers and related products,

German-based Volkswagen Group communicates directly with suppliers to acquire parts and components for its cars like this Bentley.

now generates over 90 percent of its profits from its software, consulting, and financing businesses—all of which are considered services. Like Volkswagen Group, it requires a host of B2B products and services to support these businesses. For instance, the airlines that IBM consultants and service providers rely on to shuttle them around the globe also utilize a mix of products like airplanes and fuel, as well as consulting, legal, and other services.

Today, many B2B companies are demanding, as a condition for doing business, that suppliers demonstrate social responsibility by putting in place policies and practices to reduce their carbon footprint. Sustainable Marketing 5.1 explains how a small company saves money while improving its corporate image as a socially responsible organization by implementing eco-friendly printing technology.

Resellers

resellers
Marketing intermediaries that resell manufactured products without significantly altering their form.

Resellers are marketing intermediaries that resell manufactured products without significantly altering their form. For instance, wholesalers and distributors buy jeans from 7 For All Mankind and sell them to retailers (a B2B transaction), and retailers in turn resell those same jeans to the ultimate consumer (a B2C transaction). Wholesalers, distributors, and retailers are all resellers. The Retail Council of Canada estimates that in 2013 there were more than 215,000 retail establishments in Canada, which employed 2 million Canadians and generated sales of $436 billion. With over 2 million Canadians working in the retail industry, it is the country's largest employer.[6] Similarly, the wholesale sector consisted of 120,000 firms, employed 743,259 Canadians, and generated sales of $564 billion in 2011.[7] The role of wholesalers, retailers, and other intermediaries involved in the distribution of goods is discussed in greater detail in Chapters 12 and 13.

Institutions, such as hospitals, educational organizations, prisons, religious organizations, and other nonprofit organizations, also purchase all kinds of goods and services for the people they serve. For instance, there are 161,000 nonprofit organizations in Canada, employing about 2 million people and generating revenues in excess of $110 billion annually.[8] Public institutions engage in B2B relationships to fulfill their needs for capital construction, equipment, supplies, food, and janitorial services. A public school board with a $40 million annual budget for textbooks has

Sustainable Marketing 5.1   Eco-friendly Printing Produces Cost-Savings[9]

Thistle Printing Limited is a small business based in Toronto, Ontario. The 79-year-old company prints posters, newsletters, business cards, catalogues, and books for other businesses. Although it is a small firm, Thistle Printing is aiming to stand out from competitors by implementing a series of sustainable eco-changes. The printing industry is not known for being particularly environmentally friendly because of its paper consumption and hazardous waste creation. However, Thistle Printing is trying to differentiate itself as an eco-friendly organization by capturing, cleaning, and reusing chemicals from its printing process.

Thistle Printing views sustainability as a process, not an endpoint, and, as a result, it is introducing a series of changes that will alleviate its impact on the environment. It hired a green consulting firm, EcoSafe, to conduct a three-month pollution prevention assessment. As a result of the findings from this assessment, Thistle Printing has installed a solvent recycler and a closed-loop fountain recirculation system, which will reduce the amount of harmful chemicals emitted in its printing process. These changes were costly, but Thistle Printing realized that implementing sustainable changes will cut costs in the long run and positively impact its bottom line. Implementing the new eco-friendly changes initially cost Thistle Printing approximately $39,000, but the changes will save more than $30,400 per year.

In addition to the monetary benefits, making sustainable environmental changes will appeal to customers who are increasingly embracing the green culture. The sustainable changes that Thistle Printing has made are not going unnoticed. The company has won eco-awards from the Toronto Region Sustainability Program and the industry magazine PrintAction.

Thistle Printing plans to continue its commitment to sustainability.

Entrepreneurial Marketing 5.1 | Mapping Your Way[10]

Most students can relate to the frustration of finding their way around campus. Visitors to hospitals, malls, and even casinos, face similar navigational issues. While a GPS might help you find your way to a street address, it won't help once you are inside. Users want wayfinding solutions; however, it is the organizations that ultimately need to be sold. The decision makers are the colleges, universities or hospitals. That's a lengthy and expensive process, especially when "You are Here" stationary signage provides organizations with a basic solution. MappedIn, a Waterloo-based company aims to change that with its high-tech approach.

Cofounder Hongwei Lui says MappedIn is a wayfinding, analytics and marketing platform. Through touchscreen kiosks and mobile apps, MappedIn lets institutions provide up-to-date information about their venue to visitors and customers, communicate information in real-time about deals and promotions, and gather metrics about how people navigate through their buildings. Back-end management tools give the organizations valuable feedback, reduce existing overhead, help generate new revenue, and improve bottom-line profitability.

At hospitals, MappedIn kiosks can make the visit more enjoyable and more productive. Interactive kiosks let visitors direct themselves to where they want or need to be instead of having to stop frequently and ask staff members for help. The mobile app lets users access navigation even more easily. When patients are late or miss appointments because they get lost in the building, it costs hospitals money. Kiosks can also be used to recognize and honour donors. By actively recognizing these people, it provides an opportunity to incent visitors to donate and generate inquiries from potential advertisers or sponsors.

Students at Conestoga College in Kitchener, Ontario, can use a kiosk and/or an app to map their way on campus.

No matter how good your solution is, selling to institutions takes a long time. Most organizations have buying committees and use a Request for Proposal to begin the process. Looking for investors to help fund and grow the business, Hongwei Lui and Desmond Choi pitched MappedIn on CBC's *Dragons' Den*. They focused on a shopping mall application during their pitch although they also provide solutions for universities, colleges, hospital foundations, casinos and convention centres. All of the Dragons were impressed with the company's potential, showing that MappedIn has mapped out a way to make money.

significant buying power, enabling it to take advantage of bulk discounts that would not be available to individual schools. Colleges, universities and hospitals all need solutions to help students and visitors find their way around their premises as seen in Entrepreneurial Marketing 5.1.

Government

In most countries, the central government tends to be one of the largest purchasers of goods and services. For example, the Canadian federal government spends about $240 billion annually on procuring goods and services. If you add in the amounts spent by provincial and municipal governments, as well as the academic, social, and health sectors, this amount increases to more than $550 billion annually. The bulk of the federal government's buying of goods and services is done centrally by Public Works and Government Services Canada on behalf of more than 85 departments, agencies, Crown corporations, and Special Operating Agencies.[11] Information about government buying can be obtained from Business Access Canada or from MERX.[12] MERX is the most complete source of Canadian public tenders, private tenders, U.S. tenders, and private-sector construction news available in Canada. MERX makes it possible

MERX is the most complete source of public tenders, private tenders, U.S. tenders, and private-sector construction news available in Canada

for businesses of any size to have easy and affordable access to billions of dollars in contracting opportunities with the Government of Canada, participating provincial and municipal governments, the U.S. Government, state and local governments, and the private sector.[13]

Key Challenges of Reaching B2B Clients

For marketers to be effective and successful at B2B marketing, they must master three key challenges for each business customer they want to serve. The first challenge is to identify the right persons or decision makers within the organizations who can authorize or influence purchases. Second, marketers must understand the buying process of each potential client. The third challenge is to identify the factors that influence the buying process of potential clients. B2B markets differ in varying degrees on these three dimensions; hence, marketers must invest the time and resources to understand these challenges. For example, institutional buyers, such as nursing homes and universities, tend to have relatively small budgets and therefore seek the best value when buying products and services for their organizations. That is, if two suppliers are offering roughly similar products, they may opt for the supplier with the lower price. Governments, on the other hand, make much larger purchases, but their buying processes must not only satisfy strict policy guidelines and directives set by the government, but also meet international trade rules set by the World Trade Organization (WTO) or the North American Free Trade Agreement (NAFTA). Additionally, government purchases are subject to public scrutiny and can be subjected to legal challenges or be cancelled or modified. Governments consider a wide range of factors in their purchases and may not always purchase from the vendor with the lowest price. Institutional organizations are not under such public scrutiny and rarely disclose their purchase decisions and practices, although they may try to make their buying processes transparent. Finally, private-sector companies, such as manufacturers, producers, and resellers rarely, if ever, disclose their buying criteria or buying process. They are likely to engage in reciprocal buying, a situation where two companies agree to buy each other's products as appropriate.

To address the complexity of B2B markets, many companies have salespeople or a sales team dedicated to specific clients. For instance, many companies wishing to sell to the government (e.g., IBM, Microsoft) have business–government relations experts or departments.

Let us now explore in a little more detail some of the unique characteristics of B2B markets that distinguish them from B2C markets. Exhibit 5.2 lists the key characteristics of B2B and B2C buying behaviour.

LO2   Differences Between B2B and B2C Markets

derived demand
The linkage between consumers' demand for a company's output and its purchase of necessary inputs to manufacture or assemble that particular output.

Market Characteristics   In B2C markets, consumers buy goods to satisfy their own individual or household needs and are heavily influenced by price, personal tastes, brand reputation, or personal recommendations of friends and family. In B2B markets, demand for goods and services is often derived from B2C sales in the same supply chain. More specifically, **derived demand** is the linkage between consumers' demand for a company's output and its purchase of necessary inputs to manufacture or assemble

EXHIBIT 5.2	Characteristics of B2B Buying as Compared with B2C Buying

Market Characteristics
- Demand for business products is derived, fluctuates more, and more frequently
- Fewer customers, more geographically concentrated, and orders are larger
- Demand is more inelastic

Product Characteristics
- Products are technical in nature and purchased based on specifications
- Mainly raw and semifinished goods are purchased
- Heavy emphasis is placed on delivery time, technical assistance, after-sale service, and financing assistance

Buying Process Characteristics
- Buying decision is more complex
- Buying may involve competitive bidding, negotiated pricing, and complex financial arrangements
- Buying involves qualified, professional buyers who follow a more formalized buying process
- Buying criteria and objective are specified, as are procedures for evaluating and selecting vendors and products
- Multiple people with varied interests participate in purchase decisions
- Reciprocal arrangements exist, and negotiations between buyers and sellers are common
- Buyers and sellers usually work closely to build close long-term relationships
- Online buying over the Internet is common

Marketing Mix Characteristics
- Direct selling is the primary form of selling and physical distribution is often essential
- Advertising is technical in nature, and promotions emphasize personal selling
- Price is often negotiated, inelastic, frequently affected by trade and quantity discounts. Price usually includes a service or maintenance component

that particular output. For instance, the demand for raw denim used to make 7 For All Mankind jeans is derived from the sale of the jeans to consumers. Thus, demand for raw material and semifinished goods purchased by business firms tend to fluctuate more, and more frequently. In addition, demand in many business markets is inelastic—that is, the total demand for goods is not affected much by price changes in the short run. For instance, a small increase in the price for raw denim will not cause a huge drop in the demand for denim in the apparel industry in the short run. Another characteristic of B2B markets is that the number of business buyers is substantially fewer than in B2C markets, and the business buyers are more concentrated in big cities, towns, and industrial areas. Also, the sizes of the orders are substantially larger than consumer purchases. For example, Bombardier announced that SkyWest signed an order valued at US$9.36 billion for 100 175-E2 airplanes, with options for 100 more, at the 2013 Paris Air Show.[14]

Product Characteristics In B2B markets, the products ordered are primarily raw materials and semifinished goods that are processed or assembled into finished goods for the ultimate consumers. For example, Dell orders all the computer components from different suppliers and then assembles the computers before shipping to the final consumer. In certain B2B markets (e.g., aerospace, medical, pharmaceutical, shipping, defence), the products are very technical and sophisticated in nature and must conform to technical standards specified by the buyer. Thus, the raw materials, components, and semifinished goods undergo rigorous testing before shipping. Also, orders must be delivered on the dates agreed to by both buyers and sellers. Technical services and financing assistance are important aspects of B2B buying behaviour. Companies such as Bombardier often provide vendor financing—a practice where a company provides its customer with a loan that is used to buy goods from the company.[15] In B2C markets, consumers buy finished goods for their own personal consumption.

Buying Process Characteristics   Generally, for routine purchases or small-dollar-value purchases, only one or a few individuals within a department or the company may be responsible for the buying decision. However, for purchases of highly technical or complex products involving thousands or millions of dollars, the buying effort is much more structured, formalized, and professional. More people are usually involved in complex buying decisions. They are usually technically trained and qualified professionals, and they represent different interests (e.g., managerial, technical, and departmental) within the organization. The group of people involved in the buying decision is often referred to as the buying centre, which is described in detail below. Most companies have formal policies and procedures to guide buying decisions that must be closely followed by the people involved in the buying decisions. Examples of such procedures include rules governing competitive bidding, negotiated pricing, complex financial arrangements, buying criteria, and objectives, as well as procedures for evaluating competitive bids.

Another major difference between B2B and B2C buying lies in the nature of the relationship between the firm and its suppliers. Generally, the buying decision is based on negotiations, which for complex purchases could be quite extended. The negotiated contract normally covers a range of concerns, including price, delivery, warranty, technical specifications, and claim policies. In B2B markets, buyers and sellers strive to develop close relationships with each other and so will often provide help or advice to ensure a win-win situation for both parties. For example, Shepherd Thermoforming and Packaging, a leading Canadian manufacturer of plastic products ranging from your hot tub to your chocolate tray, Tylenol package, smoke detector cover, and other plastic accoutrement in your homes and cars, noted that its B2B customers often chose to come in and work with its engineering staff to create the desired look and product functionality that they needed.[16]

In addition, some firms may engage in reciprocal buying arrangements—a practice where two firms agree to buy each other's products and services. Clearly, reciprocal buying has both negative and positive consequences for both the buying and selling firms involved, as well as for other suppliers. Two such consequences are that it excludes other vendors from participating in the buying process and may limit the firms to each other's products, which may not be the best thing.

Marketing Mix Characteristics   Another major difference between the typical B2B and B2C transaction is the role of the salesperson. On the one hand, while salespeople are an important component of the communications mix for B2C transactions such as sales of real estate, insurance, jewellery, consumer electronics, and high-end apparel, most fast-moving consumer goods (FMCG) found in grocery and discount stores are not sold with the aid of salespeople. On the other hand, in most B2B sales, the salesperson is an integral component of the transaction. Pharmaceutical manufacturers rely primarily on sales representatives to promote their drugs to doctors. Also, many manufacturers provide trade and quantity discounts to resellers for carrying their products.

LO3

B2B Classification System and Segmentation

North American Industry Classification System (NAICS) codes A classification scheme that categorizes all firms into a hierarchical set of six-digit codes.

Statistics Canada collects data about business activity in Canada through its classification scheme, which categorizes all firms into a hierarchical set of six-digit **North American Industry Classification System (NAICS) codes**.[17] The NAICS was developed jointly by Canada, the United States, and Mexico to provide comparable statistics about business activity in all of North America. The NAICS codes replaced the Standard Industrial Classification (SIC) system that had been in use since the 1930s. The NAICS groups economic activity into 20 sectors and 928 Canadian industries. The NAICS six-digit numerical system works as shown in Exhibit 5.3. The first two digits represent the sector in the economy (e.g., 51 is the information sector); the third digit represents

EXHIBIT 5.3	Telecommunications NAICS Codes
NAICS Code	**Level**
51	Information
515	Broadcasting except Internet
5151	Radio and Television Broadcasting
51511	Radio Broadcasting
515111	Radio Networks

Source: http://www.ic.gc.ca/cis-sic/cis-sic.nsf/IDE/cis-sic51defe.html (accessed July 6, 2010).

The NAICS classification system could help a high-tech telecommunications components manufacturer identify groups of customers to pursue.

the subsector (e.g., 515 is "Broadcasting except Internet"); the fourth digit represents the industry group; the fifth digit represents a specific subgroup within the industry; and the full six digits refer to the country-level or national industry. The NAICS system is revised periodically to add new industries or to consolidate or delete others.

The NAICS classification system can be quite useful to B2B marketers for segmenting and targeting markets. Suppose, for instance, that a high-tech telecommunications components manufacturer has developed a new product that will significantly speed data transmission. Which of the types of firms listed under NAICS classification 515111 (radio networks) would be the most worthwhile to pursue as customers? To answer this question, the components manufacturer would first do research, probably by having company sales representatives conduct interviews, to determine which types of firms would find the new component most useful for their products. Then, using the NAICS data collected by Statistics Canada or the U.S. Census Bureau, the manufacturer could assess the number, size, and geographical dispersion of firms within each type, which might indicate both the product's potential and the types of firms that constitute the target market.

In addition to NAICS, marketers may segment B2B markets in several other ways, including geographic location (e.g., by country, provinces, region, cities), firm size (e.g., by the number of employees in the firm or by sales volume), account size (by small, medium, and large accounts or purchase size), and types of products purchased.

THE B2B BUYING PROCESS

LO4

The B2B buying process (Exhibit 5.4) parallels the B2C process, though it differs in many ways. Both start with need recognition, but the information search and alternative evaluation stages are more formal and structured in the B2B process. Typically, B2B buyers specify their needs in writing and ask potential suppliers to submit formal proposals, whereas B2C buying decisions are usually made by individuals or families and sometimes are unplanned or impulsive. For an individual to buy a tablet computer, all that is required is a trip to the store or a few minutes online and perhaps some preliminary research about iPads versus competitors. For a school board to buy 1,000 tablet computers, however, it must complete requisition forms, accept bids from manufacturers, and obtain approval for the expenditure. The final decision rests with a committee, as is the case for most B2B buying decisions, which often demand a great deal of consideration. Finally, in B2C buying situations, customers evaluate their purchase decision and sometimes experience postpurchase dissonance. However, formal performance evaluations of the vendor and the products sold generally do not occur, as they do in the B2B setting. Let's examine all six

EXHIBIT 5.4   B2B Buying Process

Need Recognition → Product Specification → RFP Process → Proposal Analysis and Supplier Selection → Order Specification (Purchase) → Vendor Performance Assessment Using Metrics

stages in the context of a school board buying tablets for elementary school students as a resource.

Stage 1: Need Recognition

In the first stage of the B2B buying process, the buying organization recognizes, through either internal or external sources, that it has an unfilled need. The Sault Ste. Marie, Ontario, school board wants to introduce computer tablets into its elementary school resource programs to help build literacy and matching skills for students. A group of educators has reviewed pedagogical literature that describes how these devices can help students learn better, because they can directly interact with the materials rather than only hearing information or seeing it on a whiteboard. Using this information, they have convinced the school board to provide sufficient funding. They are ready to purchase 1,000 tablets.

Stage 2: Product Specification

After recognizing the need and considering alternative solutions, including laptop and desktop computers, the school board wrote a list of potential specifications that vendors might use to develop their proposals. The board's specifications include screen size, battery life, processor speed, how the device connects to the Internet, and delivery date. In addition, the board has requested that a bundle of educational apps be preloaded on the tablets, that all other apps be removed, and that each tablet come equipped with a screen protector, power cord, cover, stand, keyboard, and headphones. The school board has also requested a three-year service contract that includes replacement within 24 hours for any tablets that are returned to the vendor for servicing.

request for proposals (RFP)
A process through which buying organizations invite alternative suppliers to bid on supplying their required components.

Stage 3: RFP Process

The **request for proposals (RFP)** is a common process through which buying organizations invite alternative suppliers to bid on supplying their required components. The purchasing company may simply post its RFP needs on its website, work through various B2B web portals, or contact potential suppliers directly. Firms may narrow the process to a few suppliers, often those with which they have existing relationships.

The first step in the B2B decision process is to recognize that the schools need to purchase 1000 tablets.

In a recent case, the Royal Ontario Museum in Toronto issued a complicated RFP with an unprecedented request for caterers who responded to pay an annual fee of $10,000 for up to 10 years to earn points in the assessment process. While the fee might secure a place on the preferred vendor list, it is not a guarantee of winning any catering business.[18] As discussed in Entrepreneurial Marketing 5.2, responding to RFPs can be time consuming and costly.

Because the school board likely does not have a preferred vendor, it issues an RFP and invites various

Entrepreneurial Marketing 5.2 — Tilting Pixels on the Web[19]

Matt Inglot had to get his father to register his first company, Lizard Soft, because, at the time, Inglot was still in high school. The company offered web hosting and custom software applications, and was Inglot's first taste of entrepreneurship. The experience made him realize that his future held possibilities other than getting a degree and going to work for a company like Microsoft. Inglot's next venture, Tilted Pixel, was formed out of necessity in 2005 when the startup company he worked for went bankrupt. As a second-year university student pursuing a double degree in business and computer science, Inglot had bills to pay and so he started developing websites. He bought a friend dinner and a beer in exchange for designing his logo, which is still in use today at the Waterloo-based company. Soon he was working on his first client's website, at a price of only $300 because Inglot had no idea how much to charge.

Inglot knew from the start that he wanted to build a scalable web development company, so after two years, he rented office space and hired employees. Business growth necessitated two important changes: adjusting his approach to further education and developing a business plan. Inglot switched to part-time studies, making Tilted Pixel his full-time endeavour. He developed a business strategy to generate higher revenues in order to cover his increased overhead. New procedures and a proposal template for quotations were created. His sales process became more formalized. He also raised prices to reflect the added-value services of the company's consultative approach, which helped clients achieve success online.

Tilted Pixel's customer mix changed too. Although Inglot was still targeting mostly small to medium-sized businesses, now he focused on those with at least $1 million in revenues, an amount that ensured the companies had a marketing budget. The company found a niche in the local food segment. A website it designed for FoodLink (http://www.foodlink.ca) featured an online map to help consumers learn about and find local food. This work helped land more business. Tilted Pixel beat out 97 other competitors in a request for proposal (RFP) to develop a website for a Toronto-based food company. Since most new business comes by referral and through networking, Tilted Pixel rarely responds to RFPs unless there is a high chance of success. One RFP the company received had 23 pages of bidding requirements before it got to a description of the website specifications. Inglot said the cost to respond could never be recouped if he won the business.

Today the company has five employees and a proprietary web development platform. It plans to expand into major cities in Canada after Inglot graduates. He aims to shake up the industry and a few pixels, saying, "What Second Cup did for coffee, and what McDonald's did for fast food, Tilted Pixel will do for web development."

tablet suppliers, technology companies, and other interested parties to bid on the contract. Smaller companies may lack the ability to attract broad attention to their requests, so they might turn to a web portal, an Internet site whose purpose is to be a major starting point for users when they connect to the web. Although there are general portals such as Yahoo or MSN, B2B partners connect to specialized or niche portals to participate in online information exchanges and transactions. These exchanges help streamline procurement or distribution processes. Portals can provide tremendous cost savings because they eliminate periodic negotiations and routine paperwork, and they offer the means to form a supply chain that can respond quickly to the buyer's needs.

Stage 4: Proposal Analysis and Supplier Selection

The buying organization, in conjunction with its critical decision makers, evaluates all the proposals it receives in response to its RFP. At this stage, the school board reviews all proposals it receives with the school board, representatives from the teachers' union, and perhaps interested parents. Many firms narrow the process to a few suppliers, often those with which they have existing relationships, and discuss key terms of the sale, such as price, quality, delivery, and financing. Some firms have a policy that requires them to negotiate with several suppliers, particularly if the product or service represents a critical component or aspect of the business. This policy keeps suppliers on their toes; they know that the buying firm can always shift a greater portion of its business to an alternative supplier if it offers better terms.

The school board evaluates proposals on the basis of the amount of experience the vendor has with tablet computers and similar technology products, because it wants to make sure that its investment is reliable in the short term and flexible enough to accommodate new apps or updates. In addition, the board wants to be sure the technology will remain relevant in the longer term and not become obsolete. The vendor's ability to meet its specifications also is important, because if a battery needs to recharge in the middle of the school day, for example, a student may not have access to the device and may fall behind classmates. The vendor's financial position also provides an important indication of whether the vendor will be able to stay in business.

Stage 5: Order Specification (Purchase)

In the fifth stage, the firm places its order with its preferred supplier (or suppliers). The order will include a detailed description of the goods, prices, delivery dates, and, in some cases, penalties if the order is not filled on time. The supplier then will send an acknowledgment that it has received the order and fill it by the specified date. In the case of the school's tablets, the terms are clearly laid out regarding when and how the vendor is expected to perform any preventive maintenance, who the contact person is for any problems with delivery or the tablets themselves, and under what circumstances the vendor will be expected to provide a replacement for a malfunctioning tablet. Issues like maintenance and replacement are important to the school, because it cannot afford to keep an inventory of extra tablets on hand.

Stage 6: Vendor Performance Assessment Using Metrics

Just as in the consumer buying process, firms analyze their vendors' performance so they can make decisions about their future purchases. The difference is that, in a B2B setting, this analysis is typically more formal and objective. Let's consider how the school board might evaluate the tablet vendor's performance, as in Exhibit 5.5, using the following metrics: delivery (based on promised delivery date), quality, customer service, and issue resolution.

1. The buying team develops a list of issues that it believes are important to consider in the vendor evaluation.

2. To determine the importance of each issue (column 1), the buying team assigns an importance score to each (column 2). The more important the issue, the higher its score, but the importance scores must add up to 1. In this case, the buying team believes that customer service and quality are most important, whereas the issue resolution and delivery are comparatively less important.

3. In the third column, the buying team assigns numbers that reflect its judgments about how well the vendor performs. Using a five-point scale, where 1 equals "poor

EXHIBIT 5.5 Evaluating a Vendor's Performance

(1) Key Issues	(2) Importance Score	(3) Vendors Performance	(4) Importance × Performance (2) × (3)
Customer Service	.40	5	2.0
Issue Resolution	.20	4	0.8
Delivery	.10	5	0.5
Quality	.30	3	0.9
Total	1.0		4.2

performance" and 5 equals "excellent performance," the school district decides that the tablet vendor performs quite well on all issues except product quality.

4. To calculate an overall performance score in the fourth column, the team combines the importance of each issue and the vendor's performance scores by multiplying them. Because the tablet vendor performed well on the most important issues, when we add the importance/performance scores in column 4, we find that the overall evaluation is pretty good—4.2 on a five-point scale.

Although most B2B organizations utilize the buying process described above as a way to ensure they get the best value for their money, some organizations simply operate based on a sole source or on longer-term business relationships, as in the case of Value Village, which is described in Ethical Dilemma 5.1.

THE BUYING CENTRE

L05

The six-stage B2B buying process may be influenced by three factors within the purchasing organization: the buying centre, the buying organization's philosophy or corporate culture, and the buying situation. In most large organizations, several people typically are responsible for the buying decisions. These **buying centre** participants can range from employees who have a formal role in purchasing decisions (e.g., the purchasing or procurement department), to members of the design team that is specifying the particular equipment or raw material needed, to employees who will be using a new machine that is being ordered. All these employees are likely to play different roles in the buying process, which vendors must understand and adapt to in their marketing and sales efforts.

buying centre
The group of people typically responsible for the buying decisions in large organizations.

Ethical Dilemma 5.1 — Value Village Cozies Up to Charities

We have all received phone calls from charitable organizations, such as the Cerebral Palsy Association of Canada or the Canadian Diabetes Association, asking for donations of cash or household items and clothing. Most of us are more than willing to donate to these causes, believing that our donations are going to the needy. But have you ever stopped to wonder where your gently used clothing and household items are actually going?

Many of us assume that these charities distribute them to families in need. But did you know that nonprofit organizations such as the Cerebral Palsy Association of Canada and the Canadian Diabetes Association actually sell the items they receive to Value Village, a privately owned, U.S., for-profit corporation? Charities claim that the money received from Value Village is used to fund their programs and help them fulfill their mission since they receive little financial support from government sources.

Unlike the Salvation Army or the Women In Need Society (WINS), Value Village is not a nonprofit thrift store; it is a multimillion-dollar corporation. Value Village has a distinct business model. It has formed alliances with local nonprofit organizations and purchases donated items from them by weight at a preset bulk rate, which is never made public. Critics, however, have indicated that the rates are extremely low and the charities have very little negotiating power.

Not surprisingly, claims are mounting that Value Village is exploiting people's goodwill to make a profit. Critics point out that Value Village is benefiting from the good name of nonprofit organizations because people believe that they are donating to a charity and not to a profit-seeking entity. Additionally, other nonprofit thrift organizations, such as the Salvation Army, are also seeking donations to help generate funds to run their programs. So is it fair that Value Village may be benefiting from the guise of falling into the same category as other thrift stores?

Value Village points out that it has never attempted to position itself as anything but a for-profit organization. It defends its unique business model, which involves partnering with local charities in a B2B setting. It is proud of its contribution to the community: providing support to local charities while offering quality affordable goods to its customers. Value Village is also proud of its efforts to embrace the green culture by recycling unwanted goods and keeping them out of landfills.

Is Value Village being a good corporate citizen with its unique business model? Or is it a profit-seeking corporation that is unfairly taking away much needed donations from nonprofit organizations? Are charities that sell donated items to Value Village engaging in unethical business practices by not publicly informing donors of their business model?

Many people are involved in making B2B purchasing decisions.

initiator
The buying centre participant who first suggests buying the particular product or service.

influencer
The buying centre participant whose views influence other members of the buying centre in making the final decision.

decider
The buying centre participant who ultimately determines any part of or the entire buying decision—whether to buy, what to buy, how to buy, or where to buy.

buyer
The buying centre participant who handles the paperwork of the actual purchase.

user
The person who consumes or uses the product or service purchased by the buying centre.

gatekeeper
The buying centre participant who controls information or access to decision makers and influencers.

We can categorize six different buying roles within a typical buying centre (see Exhibit 5.6.) One or more people may take on a certain role, or one person may take on more than one of the following roles: "(1) **initiator**, the person who first suggests buying the particular product or service; (2) **influencer**, the person whose views influence other members of the buying centre in making the final decision; (3) **decider**, the person who ultimately determines any part of or the entire buying decision—whether to buy, what to buy, how to buy, or where to buy; (4) **buyer**, the person who handles the paperwork of the actual purchase; (5) **user**, the person(s) who consumes or uses the product or service; and (6) **gatekeeper**, the person(s) who controls information or access, or both, to decision makers and influencers."[20]

To illustrate how a buying centre operates, consider purchases made by a hospital. Where do hospitals obtain their X-ray machines, syringes, bedpans, or as discussed previously in Entrepreneurial Marketing 5.1, wayfinding solutions? Why are some medical procedures covered in whole or in part by insurance, whereas others are not? Why might your doctor recommend one type of allergy medication instead of another?

The Initiator—Your Doctor When you seek treatment from your physician, he or she *initiates* the buying process by determining the products and services that will best address and treat your illness or injury. For example, say that you fell backward off your snowboard and, in trying to catch yourself, shattered your elbow. You require surgery to mend the affected area, which includes the insertion of several screws to hold the bones in place. Your doctor promptly notifies the hospital to schedule a time for the procedure and specifies the brand of screws she wants on hand for your surgery.

EXHIBIT 5.6 The Buying Centre Roles

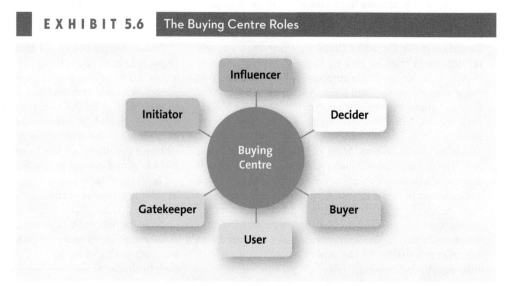

The Influencer—The Medical Device Supplier, the Pharmacy For years, your doctor has been using ElbowMed screws, a slightly higher-priced screw. Her first introduction to ElbowMed screws came from the company's sales representative, who visited her office to demonstrate how ElbowMed's screws were far superior to those of its competition. Your doctor recognized ElbowMed as good value. Armed with empirical data and case studies, ElbowMed's sales rep effectively *influenced* your doctor's decision to use that screw.

The Decider—The Hospital Even though your doctor requested ElbowMed screws, the hospital ultimately is responsible for *deciding* whether to buy ElbowMed screws. The hospital supplies the operating room, instrumentation, and surgical supplies, and therefore, the hospital administrators must weigh a variety of factors to determine not only whether the ElbowMed screw is best for patients, but also whether using ElbowMed screws involves a cost that is justified.

The Buyer—The Hospital's Materials Manager The actual *buyer* of the screw will likely be the hospital's materials manager, who is charged with buying and maintaining inventory for the hospital in the most cost-effective manner. Whereas ElbowMed screws are specific to your type of procedure, other items, such as gauze and sutures, may be purchased through a group purchasing organization (GPO), which obtains better prices through volume buying.

The User—The Patient Ultimately though, the buying process for this procedure will be greatly affected by the *user*, namely, you and your broken elbow. If you are uncomfortable with the procedure or have read about alternative procedures that you prefer, you may decide that ElbowMed screws are not the best treatment.

The Gatekeeper—The Purchasing Department The hospital's purchasing department may believe that ElbowMed screws are too expensive and that other screws deliver equally effective results. Therefore, it might ask the hospital to reconsider the purchase of the screws.

In the end, the final purchase decision must take into consideration every single buying centre participant.

Organizational Culture

A firm's **organizational culture** reflects the set of values, traditions, and customs that guides its managers' and employees' behaviour. The firm's culture often comprises a set of unspoken guidelines that employees share with one another through various work situations. For example, Walmart buyers are not allowed to accept even the smallest gift from a vendor, not even a cup of coffee. This rule highlights the company's overall corporate culture: It is a low-cost operator whose buyers must base their decisions only on the products' and vendors' merits.

Organizational culture can have a profound influence on purchasing decisions, and corporate buying centre cultures might be divided into four general types: autocratic, democratic, consultative, and consensus, as illustrated in Exhibit 5.7. Knowing which buying centre culture is prevalent in a given organization helps the seller decide how to approach that particular client, how and to whom to deliver pertinent information, and to whom to make the sales presentations.

In an **autocratic buying centre**, though there may be multiple participants, one person makes the decision alone, whereas the majority rules in a **democratic buying centre**. A **consultative buying centre** uses one person to make a decision, but he or she solicits input from others before doing so. Finally, in a **consensus buying centre**, all members of the team must reach a collective agreement that they can support a particular purchase.[21]

organizational culture
Reflects the set of values, traditions, and customs that guides a firm's employees' behaviour.

autocratic buying centre
A buying centre in which one person makes the decision alone, though there may be multiple participants.

democratic buying centre
A buying centre in which the majority rules in making decisions.

consultative buying centre
A buying centre in which one person makes the decision, but he or she solicits input from others before doing so.

consensus buying centre
A buying centre in which all members of the team must reach a collective agreement that they can support a particular purchase.

EXHIBIT 5.7 Organizational Buying Culture

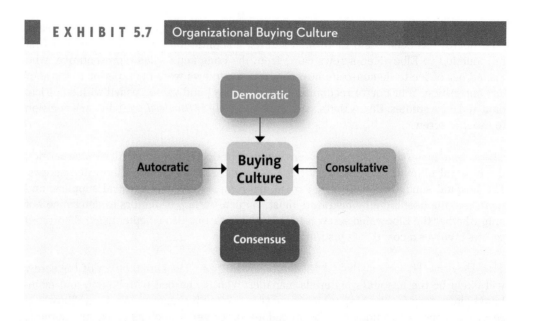

Cultures act like living, breathing entities that change and grow, just as organizations do. Even within some companies, culture may vary by geography, division, or functional department. Whether you are a member of the buying centre or a supplier trying to sell to it, it is extremely important to understand its culture and the roles of the key players in the buying process. Not knowing the roles of the key players in that case could waste a lot of time—both yours and the buying centre's—and could even alienate the real decision maker.

Building B2B Relationships

In B2B contexts, there are a vast variety of ways to enhance relationships, and these methods seem to be advancing and evolving by the minute. For example, blogs and social media can build awareness, provide search engine results, educate potential and existing clients about products or services, and warm up a seemingly cold corporate culture.[22] An expert who offers advice and knowledge about products increases brand awareness, and a blog is a great medium for this information. Web analytics, such as traffic on the website and the number of comments, can offer tangible evaluations, but a better measure is how often the blog gets mentioned elsewhere, the media attention it receives, and the interaction, involvement, intimacy, and influence that it promotes.

The LinkedIn social network is mainly used for professional networking in the B2B marketplace (see Social and Mobile Marketing 5.1). Twitter, the microblogging site, is also valuable for B2B marketers, because they can communicate with other businesses as often as they want. Companies such as HootSuite and TweetDeck make it easier for companies using Twitter to manage their followers, update their posts, track analytics, and even schedule Tweets, just as they would to manage a traditional marketing campaign.[23]

The majority of B2B marketers use white papers for their marketing efforts, and 71 percent of B2B buyers regularly read them prior to making a purchase.[24] When executives confront an unfulfilled business need, they normally turn to white papers. Their B2B partner may have a technologically advanced solution, but buyers have to understand the solution before they can consider a purchase. A good white paper provides information about the industry and its challenges in an educational context, rather than a promotional sense, to avoid seeming like simply propaganda. That is, the goal of white papers is to provide valuable information that a businessperson can easily understand and that will help the company address its problems with new solutions.

Social and Mobile Marketing 5.1   **Making the Most of LinkedIn**

Business-to-business (B2B) marketing may seem relatively impersonal, but even in formalized, standardized buying situations, personal relationships count. Social media, with a bit of a tweak, play a key role in this setting, just as well as in consumer contexts. Perhaps the best example is LinkedIn, the social media site for business professionals. Launched in 2003, the site has been attracting about 1 million members weekly. In the spring of 2014, its worldwide membership surpassed 277 million registered members. The site is available in 19 languages and 200 countries, helping B2B interactions overcome geographical boundaries.[25]

In particular, LinkedIn can boast that executives from all the Fortune 500 companies have memberships on its site. Accordingly, its promise for networking, whether individually or for the company, is virtually unsurpassed. Such networking entails several key groups:[26]

- *Customers and prospective customers.* LinkedIn allows a firm or its representatives to introduce themselves to possible buyers, using a credible and easily accessible format.

- *Investors.* The LinkedIn page offers tangible evidence of the firm's existence and its promise, which is critical information for outsiders who might be willing to invest in its development.

- *Suppliers.* By starting their own group on LinkedIn, B2B buyers might better identify which suppliers in the market are best matched with their needs and most interested in providing the resources they need.

- *Employees and prospective employees.* LinkedIn is a great source for finding employees who are diligent, professional, interested, and qualified. Furthermore,

LinkedIn is perhaps the best social media site for networking with business professionals.

if a firm retains its links to former employees, it can gain a good source of referrals—assuming those employees left on good terms.

- *Analysts.* The job of an analyst is to find detailed information about a company and then recommend it, or not, to the market. LinkedIn gives firms a means to provide that information in a credible but still firm-controlled context.

The site also provides sophisticated analytics for keeping track of all these networking opportunities. Users can see who visited their pages, which descriptions they viewed, and even compare their LinkedIn performance against competitors' pages.[27]

BUYING SITUATIONS   L06

The type of buying situation also affects the B2B decision process. Most B2B buying situations can be categorized into three types: new buys, modified rebuys, and straight rebuys (see Exhibit 5.8). To illustrate the nuances between these three buying situations, we portray how Dell develops relationships with some of its business customers after first targeting them.

Dell has been very successful in the B2B market, primarily because it is flexible, maintains a customer focus, and provides complete product solutions at value prices. Dell uses strong sales relationships and database marketing to understand what its customers want and how to fulfill those wants. First, Dell advertises heavily to educational and government institutions during the second and third quarters of the year, which coincides with the start of their buying cycle. Second, Dell's salespeople understand the financial and resource constraints that these groups face, so it offers complete packages of software, hardware, and IT services and provides installers who not only set up the equipment, but also remove old hardware. Third, Dell works closely with its buyers to obtain feedback and solicit help from its product development teams so that production is geared toward customer needs. Fourth, Dell divides its accounts into three categories:

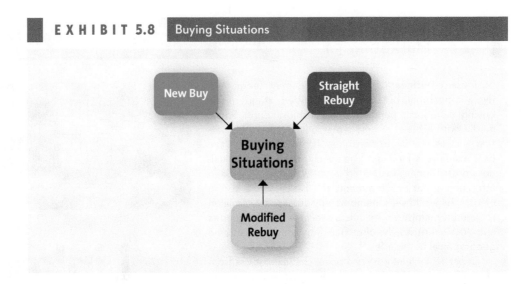

EXHIBIT 5.8 Buying Situations

new buy

In a B2B setting, a purchase of a good or service for the first time; the buying decision is likely to be quite involved because the buyer or the buying organization does not have any experience with the item.

modified rebuy

Refers to when the buyer has purchased a similar product in the past but has decided to change some specifications, such as the desired price, quality level, customer service level, and options.

straight rebuy

Refers to when the buyer or buying organization simply buys additional units of products that had previously been purchased.

acquisition, development, and retention. Working with key decision makers, the company maintains consistent contact with each account and maximizes every dollar it allocates toward technology spending.[28]

In a **new buy** situation, a customer purchases a good or service for the first time,[29] which means the buying decision is likely to be quite involved because the buyer or the buying organization does not have any experience with the item. In the B2B context, the buying centre is likely to proceed through all six steps in the buying process and involve many people in the buying decision. Typical new buys might range from capital equipment to components that the firm previously made itself but now has decided to purchase instead. For example, the University of Ottawa bought its first video-conferencing equipment and facility to enhance its distance-education capability. Prior to this, the school relied mainly on its audiographics network, which carried the voices of professors, students, and teaching aides over two telephone lines, one for voice and one for the graphics portion of the course over the Internet.

In a **modified rebuy**, the buyer has purchased a similar product in the past but has decided to change some specifications, such as the desired price, quality level, customer service level, and options. Current vendors are likely to have an advantage in acquiring the sale in a modified rebuy situation, as long as the reason for the modification is not dissatisfaction with the vendor or its products. For example, a few years ago, many universities across Canada replaced the huge CRT monitors in their students' labs with flat-screen LCD monitors.

A **straight rebuy** occurs when the buyer or buying organization simply buys additional units of products that had previously been purchased. A tremendous amount of B2B purchases are likely to fall in the straight rebuy category. For example, a couple of years after the purchase of its first video-conferencing equipment, the University of Ottawa was satisfied with its initial purchase and bought some more. Currently, the university has five video-conferencing rooms that can seat between 18 and 88 students.

These varied types of buying situations call for very different marketing and selling strategies. The most complex and difficult is the new buy because it requires the buying organization to make changes in its current practices and purchases. As a result, several members of the buying centre will likely become involved, and the level of their involvement will be more intense than in the case of modified and straight rebuys. In new buying situations, buying centre members also typically spend more time at each stage of the B2B buying process, similar to the extended decision-making process that consumers use in the B2C process. In comparison, in modified rebuys, the buyers spend less time at each stage of the B2B buying process, similar to limited decision making in the B2C process (see Chapter 4).

REAL MARKETER PROFILE: Ryan Burgio and Sourov De

Sourov De: My first job out of school was with Unilever Canada as an assistant brand manager (ABM). I graduated from Wilfrid Laurier University with an Honours Bachelor of Business Administration and learned about the job through the Laurier Career Centre's email notifications about companies looking to hire marketing and business grads. I saw the job posting and applied with a résumé by email. I knew the job posting would be competitive, and I really wanted Unilever's HR manager to notice my application. The email address of the HR manager was written in the job posting, and the email address included the HR manager's name. So I thought, what the heck, I'll call Unilever's main line, ask for the HR manager by name, and politely ask her if she received my email and resume. I had nothing to lose, and I thought that a personal call would be a great way to get noticed. Talking to the HR manager was a lot easier than I thought; I got through to her right away, and I ended up joking around with her about how my last name is abnormally short. I think she liked my personality and initiative.

While at Unilever, I was the ABM of a $9 million marketing campaign to nationally relaunch Suave Hair Care. After working at Unilever, I left the corporate marketing world to pursue an entrepreneurial career. I helped manage the launch of the *Eat, Shrink and Be Merry!* cookbook brand into the U.S. market. After the launch, my business partner Ryan Burgio and I launched Stryve Group, a marketing firm that specializes in social media marketing. I made the career move from corporate brand management to entrepreneurship because I find the work I do now more personally meaningful. I enjoy the challenge of thinking innovatively and building a venture from the ground up.

Starting a marketing firm at the age of 26 has been the most interesting and exciting project I've worked on. Building our company has been an incredible exercise in marketing. Every day we work on refining what our company's value proposition is, who our ideal clients are, and how to get our marketing message out to those clients in the most effective way.

I love marketing because it's a mixture of psychology, science, art, business strategy, and competition. Ultimately, I think we are all trying to sell or market our ideas or ourselves, whether or not we're in the "business of marketing." Marketing is a passion of mine because I see its application in the world around me in almost everything people do on a daily basis.

Ryan Burgio: I was incredibly lucky to gain employment through my experience with the co-op program at Wilfrid Laurier University (Honours Economics and Business Administration). During my second work term, I was employed by Daggerwing Group, a management and marketing consulting firm that works with senior executives to improve business results from marketing, sales, and customer management activities. I was offered a full-time position after completion of my work term.

Daggerwing Group provided a dynamic work environment that allowed me to work on a variety of interesting and challenging client projects. As a senior associate, I consulted with clients on areas such as marketing analytics, campaign execution, organizational structure, business development, and customer relationship management.

My time at Daggerwing Group was very satisfying; however, my passion for entrepreneurship soon overcame me. I became involved in the launch of Janet and Greta Podleski's bestselling cookbook *Eat, Shrink and Be Merry!* into the U.S. market. That experience and my time at Daggerwing Group gave me an incredible understanding of marketing, so I decided to parlay that knowledge into the launch of Stryve Group, a marketing firm that specializes in social media marketing. My business partner Sourov De and I have built Stryve Group since it launched in 2008 and have loved every minute of it.

I have never encountered anything more exciting or interesting than building my own business step-by-step, day-by-day, challenge-by-challenge. It's been an amazing experience throughout. At Stryve Group, we've had the opportunity to work on a variety of projects, but my favourite has been working with a retail chain in the United States on the launch of a new concept of retail outlets. The opportunity to see our marketing work drive business results has been incredible.

Why did I pursue entrepreneurship? I think the following quote characterizes my feelings: "An entrepreneur equals a quixotic mix of smarts plus stubbornness that eventually makes you unemployable by anybody but yourself."[30]

I love marketing because it is the ultimate blend of business and creativity, of right-brain and left-brain capabilities. One moment I can be using statistical analysis to measure the effectiveness of a campaign, and the next I'm analyzing colour palettes for a website design. No other aspect of business allows you the opportunity to do both.

In straight rebuys, however, the buyer is often the only member of the buying centre involved in the process. Similar to a consumer's habitual purchase, straight rebuys often enable the buyer to recognize the firm's need and go directly to the fifth step in the B2B buying process, skipping the product specification, RFP process, and proposal analysis and supplier selection steps.

In various ways, B2B marketing both differs from and mirrors the consumer behavior (B2C) process we detailed in Chapter 4. The differences in the six stages of the buying process make sense in view of the many unique factors that come into play. The constitution of the buying centre (initiator, influencer, decider, buyer, user, and gatekeeper), the culture of the purchasing firm (autocratic, democratic, consultative, or consensus), and the context of the buying situation (new buy, modified rebuy, straight rebuy) all influence the B2B buying process in various ways, which means that sellers must be constantly aware of these factors if they want to be successful in their sales attempts. Finally, just as it has done seemingly everywhere we look, the Internet has radically changed some elements of the B2B world, increasing the frequency of both private electronic exchanges and auctions.

LEARNING OBJECTIVES REVIEW

  Describe the nature and composition of B2B markets

The B2B market comprises four groups of organizations: manufacturers/producers, resellers, governments, and institutions. Manufacturers such as HP and Dell spend huge amounts to buy raw materials and parts for the computers, printers, and other products they produce. Similarly, producers such as farmers spend a great deal of money to buy fertilizers, seeds, and other agricultural products for their crops. Resellers are mainly wholesalers, distributors, and retailers who distribute the goods of manufacturers. In Canada, wholesale and retail trades are among the largest sectors of the economy. The government sector—federal, provincial, and municipal—in Canada and in most other countries is the largest buyer in a country. Institutions such as nonprofit organizations, universities, and prisons also spend millions of dollars buying finished products for their organizations and clients. The B2B market is substantially larger than the B2C market in terms of both volume and value of their purchases.

LO2 **Explain the key differences between B2B buying and B2C buying**

B2B markets are different from B2C markets in terms of (1) the characteristics of market demand; (2) the types, value, and volume of products bought; (3) the nature of the buying process, which is more formalized and professional, and involves more people; and (4) the nature of the marketing mix—personal and online selling is more prevalent and prices are negotiated and inelastic in the short run. At first glance, the B2B buying process looks similar to the consumer process described in Chapter 4. It starts with need recognition and ends with an evaluation of the product's or service's performance. But it is really quite different, primarily because of its formality. For instance, in the second stage, product specification, the buying group spells out very specific requirements for the products or services it wants to purchase. Then, in the RFP process of the third stage, the buying firm announces its need for a product or service and solicits formal proposals. In the fourth stage, buyers analyze the various proposals and select a supplier. Unlike the consumer process, the fifth stage, in which the B2B firm places the order, is very formal and spells out every detail of the sales contract.

  Explain the ways B2B firms classify and segment their markets

The basic principles behind market segmentation remain the same for both B2B and consumer markets. Specifically, B2B firms want to divide the market into groups of customers with different needs, wants, or characteristics and that therefore might appreciate products or services geared especially toward them. On a broad level, B2B firms divide the market into four types: manufacturers or producers, resellers, institutions, and government. Each of these types is described in more detail in the summary for Learning Objective 1. To assist in their market segmentation, B2B businesses can use the NAICS, developed by Canada, the United States, and Mexico, to identify potential customers by type and then develop marketing strategies to reach them. Businesses may also segment B2B markets by account size and types of products purchased.

LO4 **Describe the B2B buying process**

Similar to the B2C buying process, the B2B process consists of several stages: need recognition, product specification, the RFP process, proposal analysis and supplier selection, order specification (purchase), and vendor performance assessment using metrics. The B2B process tends to be more formalized and structured than the B2C buying process. Also, suppliers and customers tend to be more involved in the B2B buying process, which is dependent to a large extent on the close relationships between the company and its suppliers and customers.

LO5 **Identify the roles within the buying centre**

The initiator first suggests the purchase. The influencer affects important people's perceptions and final decisions. The decider ultimately determines at least some of the buying decision—whether, what, how, or where to buy. The buyer handles the details of the actual purchase. The user consumes or employs the product or service. The gatekeeper controls information and access to decision makers and influencers.

In B2B situations, it is likely that several people, organized into a buying centre, will be involved in making the purchase decision. The vendor must understand the relationships among the participants of the buying centre to be effective. A firm's organizational culture can also influence the decision process. For instance, if a firm is trying to sell to a young, high-tech computer component manufacturer, it might be advised to send salespeople who are fluent in technology-speak and can easily relate to the customer. Firm culture consists of unspoken guidelines that employees share through various work situations. They generally can be classified as autocratic, such that one person makes most decisions; democratic, where the majority rules; consultative, in which one person makes decisions based on the input of others; or consensus, which requires all members of the team to reach collective agreement.

LO6 **Detail different buying situations**

The buying process depends to a great extent on the situation. If a firm is purchasing a product or service for the first time (i.e., new buy), the process is much more involved than if it is engaging in a straight rebuy of the same item again. A modified rebuy falls somewhere in the middle, such that the buyer wants essentially the same thing but with slightly different terms or features.

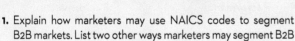

KEY TERMS

- autocratic buying centre
- business-to-business (B2B) marketing,
- buyer
- buying centre
- consensus buying centre
- consultative buying centre
- decider
- democratic buying centre
- derived demand
- gatekeeper
- influencer
- initiator
- modified rebuy
- new buy
- North American Industry Classification System (NAICS) codes
- organizational culture
- request for proposals (RFP)
- resellers
- straight rebuy
- user

CONCEPT REVIEW

1. Explain how marketers may use NAICS codes to segment B2B markets. List two other ways marketers may segment B2B markets. Support your answer with appropriate examples.

2. List and discuss the unique characteristics of B2B markets relative to B2C markets.

3. What are the major differences between the consumer buying process discussed in Chapter 4 and the B2B buying process discussed in this chapter?

4. Explain why all B2B purchases may not go through all the stages of the B2B buying decision process and why some may go through the process in a more systematic and rigorous manner. Give examples of buying situations to support your answer.

5. What are the key bases for distinguishing between new buys, modified buys, and straight rebuys? Support your answer with three clear examples.

6. List five specific ways in which the Internet has enhanced B2B buying and decision making.

7. Explain the concept of the buying centre. What factors may influence the behaviour of the buying centre? What is the role of gatekeepers in buying centres, and how do they influence the buying decision?

8. Explain how understanding the role, structure, and behaviour of a buying centre may help a marketer sell to B2B buyers.

9. This book claims that the six-step B2B buying process is similar to the five-step B2C buying process. How would you go about mapping the B2B process to fit the B2C process?

10. How does understanding the organizational culture and buying centre's culture of a potential B2B customer help a salesperson who is targeting that organization?

MARKETING APPLICATIONS

1. Provide an example of each of the four key types of B2B organizations.

2. Mazda is trying to assess the performance of two manufacturers that could supply music systems for its vehicles. Using the information below, determine which manufacturer Mazda should use (see table below).

3. Imagine you have written this book and are going to attempt to sell it to your school. Identify the six members of the buying centre. What role would each play in the decision process? Rank them in terms of how much influence they would have on the decision, with 1 being most influential and 6 being least influential. Will this ranking be different in other situations?

4. Provide an example of the three types of buying situations that the bookstore at your school might face when buying textbooks.

5. Describe the organizational culture at your school or job. How is it different from the one at the last school you attended or the last job you had?

6. Nike manufactures shoes and sportswear. How has the Internet changed the way this company communicates with its suppliers and retail customers?

7. You have just started to work in the purchasing office of a major oil processing firm. The purchasing manager has asked you to assist in writing an RFP for a major purchase. The manager gives you a sheet detailing the specifications for the RFP. While reading the specifications you realize that they have been written to be extremely favourable to one bidder. How should you handle this situation?

8. You have recently been hired by Cognos as a salesperson for its suite of business intelligence applications, Pick one prospective company you plan to sell to and explain how you would go about identifying the persons in the different roles in the buying centre for the chosen company. How would you try to target the needs of the different members in the buying centre?

9. Cognos has developed a new business intelligence application that it would like to sell to some of its existing customers. You are part of the sales team. How would your approach to selling to an existing customer be different from selling to a new customer?

10. You are the owner of a mid-sized company (about 450 employees) that has a call centre that specializes in providing 24-hour technical support for individual computer owners. One day a sales rep from Dell, HP, or Lenovo approaches you with a business proposal that goes something like this: If you buy all of your computer supplies from us, we will make you our exclusive call centre operator for all of Ontario and Quebec. Assume that all the conditions of the offer made to you are favourable. Will you accept the offer? Do you think that accepting such an offer is ethical?

Performance Evaluation of Brands			
Issues	**Importance Weights**	**Manufacturer A's Performance**	**Manufacturer B's Performance**
Sound	0.4	5	3
Cost	0.3	2	4
Delivery time	0.1	2	2
Brand cache	0.2	5	1
Total	**1**		4.2

Notes: Performance is rated on a 5-point scale, where 1 is "Poor" and 5 is "Excellent."

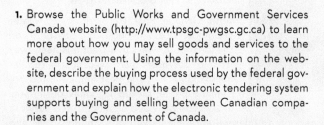

TOOLKIT

B2B VENDOR ANALYSIS

Help David evaluate two software vendors. He has created a chart to help him decide which one to pick. He has rated the two vendors on brand strength, timeliness of deliveries, product quality, and ease of ordering. His firm is generally most interested in quality and then in timeliness. Reputation is somewhat important. The ease of ordering is least important. Use the toolkit provided on Connect to specify the importance weights and help David pick the best software vendor.

NET SAVVY

1. Browse the Public Works and Government Services Canada website (http://www.tpsgc-pwgsc.gc.ca) to learn more about how you may sell goods and services to the federal government. Using the information on the website, describe the buying process used by the federal government and explain how the electronic tendering system supports buying and selling between Canadian companies and the Government of Canada.

2. Mark's Work Wearhouse, a Canadian company that currently operates mainly in the B2C market, has hired you as its government–business relations officer with the primary task of helping the company move into the B2B marketplace, selling its merchandise primarily to government departments. Explain how you would go about getting Mark's ready to do business with the Canadian government. Hint: You will find helpful information on the following websites: Public Works and Government Services Canada (http://www.tpsgc-pwgsc.gc.ca), Business Access Canada (https://buyandsell.gc.ca), and Industry Canada (http://www.ic.gc.ca).

CHAPTER CASE STUDY

UPS: FROM SHIPPING TO SUPPLY CHAIN[31]

Overview

In 1907, an enterprising teenager borrowed $100 to start a business running errands, delivering packages, carrying notes or bags, and even ferrying food from restaurants to customers. Messengers travelled on foot or, when the trip was longer, by bicycle. More than a century later, that young man's business has morphed into United Parcel Service (UPS), a $45.3 billion company that serves 220 countries and territories, employs more than 400,000 people,[32] and includes UPS Air Cargo, UPS Mail Innovations, Mail Boxes Etc., Inc., and UPS Freight, as well as a supply-chain financing company, global management consulting firm, and logistics and supply chain solutions services.[33] The company started its Canadian operations in Toronto in 1975 with a single car. Today UPS Canada has over 850 store locations, drop boxes, and authorized shipping outlets and a delivery fleet of 3,049 vehicles.[34]

Over the past century, as technology and demands have changed, the company has upgraded its delivery methods by adding trucks, ocean and train delivery, and even its own jet cargo fleet. Although its fleet of trucks might not be quite as environmentally friendly as bicycles, UPS carefully manages its delivery dispatches in an attempt to minimize both fuel use and emissions. It is incorporating electric vehicles into its delivery fleet, saving 477,000 litres of diesel fuel every year,[35] and moving from fossil fuel–burning vehicles to biodiesel blends.[36] In the air, the company adopts a "continuous descent approach" for its carriers, which reportedly reduces pollutants by as much as 34 percent compared with traditional, step-like airplane descents.[37]

UPS also has expanded into international markets and developed systems to help track the more than 15.1 million packages that pass through its corporate hands each day. This expertise prompted UPS's most recent transition: from a global package and information delivery company to a facilitator of global commerce, capable of providing supply chain solutions to customers.

UPS uses environmentally friendly hybrid electric vehicles for some of its fleet.

Through acquisitions and restructuring, the company has added logistics and distribution, consulting, mail, e-commerce, financial services, and international trade management to its portfolio of client services. UPS believes that these new services help customers focus on their own core competencies while protecting UPS from competitors. Building a business line based on information technology rather than fuel use also helps improve the company's environmental profile and build a profit stream protected from rising fuel costs.[38]

Competitive Challenges

Both Canada Post (through its Purolator courier service) and FedEx are constantly on the lookout for ways to attract business away from UPS. Threatened by drops in regular mail volume, Canada Post implemented on-demand parcel pickup for small businesses in 2011 and provided enhanced web services to online retailers in 2012. It also negotiated bilateral agreements with the United States and China to accommodate the 40 percent of parcels that arrive in Canada from international origins.[39] Similar to UPS, FedEx has expanded its service offerings, but its expansion has focused on copying services (FedEx Kinko's), along with virtually real-time tracking of ground, freight, and express shipments. FedEx is UPS's largest global competitor, with $42.7 billion in revenue and more than 300,000 employees.[40]

Adding Value for Business Customers

The expansion of its business offerings enables UPS to handle a vast array of its client company's operations, including storage, assembly, and repair of merchandise. It even provides customer service functions that demand minimal client involvement. For example, for the French pet food company Royal Canin, UPS employees mix, pack, and ship all sold dog and cat food. In addition to cutting the product delivery time, this model eliminates Royal Canin's need for a U.S. warehouse.

For Toshiba, UPS not only transports broken computers but also fixes and ships them back to their original owners, usually within 24 hours! This approach relieves Toshiba of the need to run repair facilities when its core competency is computer production and design. It also gets a repaired machine back to customers more quickly. And when there is a problem, UPS offers perhaps the most valuable service for both Toshiba and its customers, that is, a scapegoat. As the former CEO of UPS Michael Eskew noted, "Customers wanted one throat to choke when the pressure was on to deliver. We offered them UPS's throat."[41]

These supportive relationships entail not just profits but also an element of UPS's approach to environmental and social sustainability. The company has worked over the past decade to use more environmentally responsible packaging, reduce water use, support community disaster relief programs, provide charitable contributions, and contribute to employee development, as well as undertake initiatives to reduce carbon emissions. As part of these efforts, the company is working with business customers and other stakeholders to improve accountability for resource use. These relationships ensure that all business partners are focused on balancing environmental concerns and profits, and providing value to the communities and individuals who help make them successful.

Spreading the Word

UPS's sustainability efforts are far reaching. Recognizing that different audiences interpret sustainability in different ways, UPS has worked with nonprofit groups and nongovernmental organizations to better understand stakeholder expectations. As a result of these conversations, UPS is developing new sustainability programs that will provide direction for competitors and other transportation companies, and seeking ways to participate in public policy issues that enhance the environmental and social responsibility of businesses.

Furthermore, advertisements directed to its targeted demographic go beyond the conventional methods of television and print media. For example, a recent campaign introduced the free "UPS Mobile" app that works on BlackBerry and Android platforms. The app lets businesses easily manage shipments on the go, tracking packages, searching UPS locations and even printing shipping labels.[42] Targeting BlackBerry users helped focus messaging on the right audience, because they tend to be businesspeople.

Questions

1. Describe how you would expect firms to interact with UPS. Use the steps in the B2B buying process discussed in the chapter to facilitate your discussion.

2. Manufacturers, resellers, government, and auctioneers on eBay all have alternative delivery options. Describe some ways that UPS provides greater value to these various types of customers than its competitors can. (You may want to review its website at http://www.UPS.com.)

CHAPTER **6**

Segmentation, Targeting, and Positioning

Coca-Cola creates many different products to help it meet the needs of its consumers. Today, the Coca-Cola Company is one of the largest consumer packaged-goods companies in the world but when it first introduced Coca-Cola in 1886, sales averaged a modest nine drinks per day.[1] Its growth, driven largely by a remarkably disciplined approach to marketing, has led to Coke products being sold in more than 200 countries at an astounding rate of 1.8 billion servings per day.[2] Yet Coca-Cola continually faces the unique challenge of a mature cola market, which means growth rates overall are low, and to increase sales it must either take customers away from other beverage companies or encourage existing customers to drink more cola—neither of which is an easy task.

Part of the company's solution pertains to its approach to new product development.[3] For example, Coke creates unique products for various specific market segments. Because those unique products appeal to specific groups, Coke can increase its sales without cannibalizing the sales of its other products. Have you ever stopped drinking soft drinks in an attempt to limit the amount of caffeine you drink? Coke wants you to know that it feels your pain and therefore offers Caffeine-Free Coca-Cola and Diet Coke. Still like your caffeine but want to minimize the amount you drink right before bedtime? Why not purchase a case of each, saving your regular Coke for when you need a midday pick-me-up and your Caffeine-Free Coke for your after-dinner thirst? By introducing decaffeinated versions of its traditional drinks, Coca-Cola could increase the number it sells each day without cannibalizing sales because the consumers targeted by these products had already been avoiding Coca-Cola to reduce their caffeine intake.

Through its efforts to identify and target such specific market segments, Coca-Cola has grown its stable of consumer brands to more than 400 products.[4] Consider the plight of Diet Coke. "Real men" didn't want to drink a diet product which they stigmatized as a "girly" drink that only women consumed. But Coca-Cola had a plan: the high-profile launch of Coke Zero avoided the dreaded word diet[5] and specifically targeted men through its packaging, promotions, and image. By targeting men between the ages of 18 to 34 years who wanted to drink a low-calorie cola but would not purchase Diet Coke, the company increased its sales of Coke-branded products by one-third.[6]

A successful new product introduction needs to combine an innovative product with a marketing campaign that communicates the value of that new product to the targeted segment. Thus, for the Coke Zero launch, Coca-Cola designed a campaign supported by advertisements on TV and radio, in print, on outdoor billboards, and online, as well as through widespread sampling programs and opportunities. Little mention was made of the lack of calories or dietetic element of the new offering; instead, the advertising was focused on the similarity of the taste between Coke and Coke Zero and used dark, bold colours. The marketing campaign even included a fantasy football game, "Fantasy Football Fever," available on the Coke Zero website, that was regularly featured in ESPN fantasy-sports podcasts.

By using gender to segment the diet cola market, Coca-Cola was able to customize the advertising for Coke Zero to appeal to men, whereas Diet Coke ads concentrated on women. Coke Zero became one of the most successful launches in the company's long history.[7]

Some people like fruit-based drinks, while others like highly caffeinated energy drinks. Some people want a diet product; others care primarily about how well the product hydrates after a workout. Still other people demand affordable beverages, whereas some prefer the drinks to be organic. More likely though, a group of people desires a drink that is dark in colour, cola-flavoured, and caffeinated. Another group demands a drink that is light in colour, citrus-flavoured, and low calorie. Each of these product attributes potentially appeals to a different group of people, or market segment. ∎

In Chapter 1, we learned that marketing is about satisfying consumers' wants and needs. A company could make one type of beverage and hope that every customer would buy it, but that's the kind of mistake that causes companies to go out of business. Beverage manufacturers could analyze the market to determine the different types of drinks people want and then make several varieties that cater to the wants of specific groups. It is not enough just to make the product, however. Drink manufacturers, such as Coca-Cola, must position their products in the minds of their target market so those consumers understand why a particular drink meets their needs better than competitive brands do. Chapter 3 noted how companies analyze their markets and the environment around them to determine the different kinds of products and services people want. This process requires a plan, as we discussed in Chapter 2. As you recall, the third step of this plan is identifying and evaluating opportunities by performing a segmentation, targeting and positioning analysis. This chapter now expands on that very analysis.

In the chapter vignette, Coca-Cola identified the various groups, or market segments, of cola drinkers who would respond similarly to the firm's marketing efforts. Those who like caffeine-free regular cola are one market segment; people who prefer diet cola constitute a different segment. After evaluating the attractiveness of different market segments, Coca-Cola decided to concentrate its new product line on one group of consumers—its target market—because it believes it could satisfy this group's needs better than its competitors could.

Once the target market was identified, Coca-Cola had to convince members of the targeted group that when it comes to soft drinks, their choice should be Coke Zero. It achieved this task by defining the marketing mix variables so that the target customers had a clear, distinctive, desirable understanding of what the product or services do or represent, relative to competing products. To achieve its market positioning, Coca-Cola designed a lifestyle advertising campaign that has positioned Coke Zero as the only diet drink with the taste of regular Coca-Cola. The idea is to get customers to recall Coke Zero at the need recognition stage of the consumer buying process described in Chapter 4. The company has also made sure that the drink is available almost anywhere its customers would want to buy it.

THE SEGMENTATION-TARGETING-POSITIONING PROCESS

In this chapter, we discuss how a firm conducts a market segmentation or STP analysis. We start by discussing market segmentation, or how a segmentation strategy fits into a firm's overall strategy and objectives and which segments are worth pursuing. Then we consider how to choose a target market or markets by evaluating each segment's attractiveness and, on the basis of this evaluation, choosing which segment or segments to pursue. Finally, we describe how a firm develops its positioning strategy. The segmentation, targeting, and positioning process is shown in Exhibit 6.1.

Step 1: Establish Overall Strategy or Objectives

As discussed in Chapter 2, the first step in the planning process is to articulate the mission and the objectives of the company's marketing strategy clearly. The segmentation strategy must then be consistent with and derived from the firm's mission and objectives, as well as its current situation—its strengths, weaknesses, opportunities, and threats (SWOT). Coca-Cola's objective, for instance, is to increase sales in a mature industry. The company recognized its strengths were its globally recognized brand name and its ability to place new products on retailers' shelves. Its primary weakness was that it didn't have a product line for the emerging market segments. Identifying this potentially large and profitable market segment before many of its mainstream competitors offered a great opportunity, though following through on that opportunity could lead to a significant threat: competitive retaliation. Coca-Cola's decision to pursue a target market of health-conscious men is clearly consistent with its overall strategy and objectives.

Now let's take a look at the methods, or bases, that can be used to segment the market.

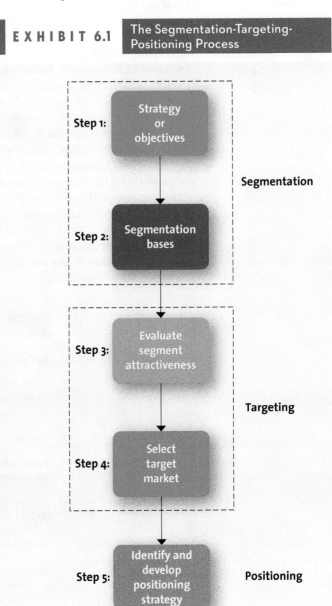

EXHIBIT 6.1 The Segmentation-Targeting-Positioning Process

Step 1: Strategy or objectives

Step 2: Segmentation bases

— Segmentation

Step 3: Evaluate segment attractiveness

Step 4: Select target market

— Targeting

Step 5: Identify and develop positioning strategy

— Positioning

Step 2: Segmentation Bases

The second step in the segmentation process is to use a formal approach to segment the market. This step develops descriptions of the different segments, and their needs, wants, and characteristics, which helps firms better understand the profile of the customers in each segment. With this information, they can distinguish the customer similarities within a segment and dissimilarities across segments. Soft-drink marketers, for instance, have broken up the carbonated-beverage landscape into caffeinated or decaffeinated, regular (with sugar) or diet, and cola versus something else. This segmentation method is based on the benefits that consumers derive from the products.

Marketers use various segmentation bases, including geographic, demographic, psychographic, and behavioural, or a combination of these segmentation approaches (see Exhibit 6.2).

geographic segmentation
The grouping of consumers on the basis of where they live.

Geographic Segmentation   **Geographic segmentation** organizes customers into groups on the basis of where they live. Thus, a market could be grouped by country (Canada, Germany, China), by region (Atlantic Canada, Western Canada), by areas within a region (province, city, neighbourhoods, area codes), or by climate and topography (warm, cold and snowy, mountainous). Not surprisingly, geographic segmentation is most useful for companies whose products satisfy needs that vary by region. As discussed in Sustainable Marketing 6.1, population and the number of companies in a geographic area can also be used to define target markets.

Firms can provide the same basic goods or services to all segments even if they market globally or nationally; but better marketers make adjustments to meet the needs of smaller geographic groups. For instance, a national grocery store chain, such as Sobeys or Loblaws, runs similar stores with similar assortments in various locations across Canada. Within those similar stores though, a significant percentage of the assortment of goods will vary by region, city, or even neighbourhood, depending on the different needs of the customers who surround each location.

Consider a new superstore in Surrey, British Columbia, designed to cater specifically to the surrounding South East Asian (Punjabi) neighbourhood. In the produce section, piles of shiny, green pasilla chiles sit beside paddle-shaped cactus leaves and bumpy, brown yucca roots. At the meat counter, a customer greets a clerk in Punjabi and asks him to marinate some meat.

EXHIBIT 6.2	**Bases for Segmenting Markets**
Segmentation Base	**Sample Segments**
Geographic	Continent (North America, Asia, Europe, Africa), country, region (West Coast, Prairies, Central, Maritimes), province, city, urban, suburban, rural, climate
Demographic	Age, gender, income, education, occupation, race, marital status, family size, family life cycle, religion, ethnic background (white, black, Asian, Indian, German, Irish, Arab), generational cohort (baby boomer, Generation X, Generation Y), home ownership
Psychographic	Lifestyle (innovators, thinkers, achievers, experiencers, believers, strivers, makers, survivors), personality/self-concept (conservative, liberal, adventuresome, outgoing, health- and fitness-conscious), social class (upper class, middle class, working class)
Behavioural	Benefits sought (convenience, economy, prestige, quality, speed, service, environmental impact), usage (heavy, moderate, light, nonuser, ex-user, potential user, first-time user), loyalty (not loyal, somewhat loyal, completely loyal)

 Sustainable Marketing 6.1

Thinking Out of the Box[8]

You've probably opened many boxes and found them packed with Styrofoam "peanuts." Commonly used to protect products being shipped and fill up the empty space in boxes, the peanuts are lightweight, work well and are relatively inexpensive. It's what happens to them after they've done their job that creates a problem. According to the Packaging Association of Canada, it costs an estimated $12 billion annually to collect, recover, and dispose of discarded packaging material in North America.[9]

Scott MacRae travelled to Finland in 2011 in search of a better solution. He found a machine that transforms enormous rolls of 100 percent recycled Kraft paper into twisted peanut-like shapes. The end result is cheaper and more environmentally friendly than traditional styrofoam, plastic, or cornstarch fillers. Plus, the "papernuts" interlock, ensuring that the contents of the box won't migrate during shipping. MacRae secured a Canada-wide license from the Finnish engineer who came up with the technology to sell the papernuts and the equipment that manufactures it.

Together with business partner Joanne Secord, he launched PaperNuts in St. Catharines, Ontario. The challenge was to identify the target market. Originally their plan was to make the product, bag it, and sell it to companies for use in their shipping departments. Later on they hoped to rent machines as a Factory-in-a-Box, allowing companies to produce unlimited papernuts on site. PaperNuts estimated they could make $1 million in the first year by selling paper to companies. After appearing on CBC's *Dragons' Den* to pitch their idea, they got calls from all over the world and learned that many companies wanted to own, not rent the machines. Other companies requested licences to resell the equipment.

The PaperNuts Factory-in-a-Box produces environmentally friendly packing material that is easily recycled.

Thinking out of the box, MacRae and Second changed their plan, and secured the global rights to PaperNuts. They embarked on a geographical approach to segmenting the market. Other factors used to define their target market included the industry, population (number of companies in a geographic area), and the number of exports (countries that ship high volumes such as China and Korea.) Exclusive licences have already been set up with distributors to resell the equipment in geographic territories covering the Ottawa area and the province of Alberta. More opportunities are being explored across Ontario as well as in Russia. Under the new arrangement, companies can buy rolls of paper from PaperNuts or source it themselves. MacRae and Secord earn a royalty on every papernut produced and the satisfaction of knowing that their solution can be easily recycled.

As you will read in the chapter case study, M&M Meat Shops used geographic segmentation to launch stores in the urban core of large cities, moving away from its traditional suburban-outlet-only strategy.

Demographic Segmentation **Demographic segmentation** groups consumers according to easily measured, objective characteristics such as age, gender, income, education, race, occupation, religion, marital status, family size, family life cycle, and home ownership. These variables represent the most common means to define segments because they are easy to identify. For example, car makers often consider market segments defined by their income levels. Kellogg's uses age to define segments for its line of breakfast cereals. Froot Loops and Rice Krispies are for kids, while Special K and All-Bran are for adults. In addition, demographically segmented markets are easy to reach. For instance, if McCain's or Pizza Hut wants to advertise their newest pizza to kids, they can easily determine that the best time for TV ads would be during cartoons shown on Saturday morning or after school on weekdays. By considering the viewer profiles of various TV shows, McCain's and Pizza Hut can find those that fit their target market's demographic profile.

demographic segmentation
The grouping of consumers according to easily measured, objective characteristics such as age, gender, income, and education.

As discussed in Chapter 3, generational cohorts are often used by marketers. Millennials are often targeted by marketers. For example, Tourism Australia launched a campaign to attract Canadians under 30 years old to consider the country's working holiday visa program.[10] Retailers such as The Gap offer different products in their stores (Gap Kids, baby Gap, Gap) based on the age of the target market. The company also addresses consumers in the same age group whose income levels vary by offering a variety of store options such as The Gap, Old Navy, and Banana Republic. Another demographic variable, gender, plays a very important role in how firms market products and services. For instance, realizing that there were many water enhancers, such as Crystal Light, for women but nothing for men, Kraft introduced Mio for a new target market of millennial males.[11] TV viewing habits vary significantly between men and women. Men tend to channel surf—switching quickly from channel to channel—and watch prime-time shows more often if they are action oriented and have physically attractive cast members. Women, in contrast, tend to view shows to which they can personally relate through the situational plot or characters and shows recommended by friends.[12] A brand such as Gillette, which sells razors for both men and women, will consider the gender appeal of various shows when it buys advertising time on TV. Also, as discussed in Chapter 3, the growth of ethnic Canadians from mainland China, Hong Kong, Taiwan, Philippines, and South East Asia (India, Pakistan, Sri Lanka) has led companies to develop marketing mixes and strategies targeted to these groups.

However, demographics may not be useful for defining the target segments for other companies. For example, demographics are poor predictors of the users of activewear, such as jogging suits and athletic shoes. At one time, firms such as Nike assumed that activewear would be purchased exclusively by young, active people, but the health and fitness trend has led people of all ages to buy such merchandise. Furthermore, relatively inactive consumers of all ages, incomes, and education find activewear more comfortable than traditional street clothes. Because it is relatively easy to gather information, demographic variables are often used for segmenting markets. Depending on the nature of the product and market, however, marketers may find it more advantageous to combine demographic segmentation with other segmentation bases, described below, to derive a richer understanding of their potential customers. The Nike example shows that stereotyping could lead to poor STP strategies rather than a deep understanding of market segments.

Proctor & Gamble uses an important demographic factor, gender, to sell different types of razors to men (Fusion ad on the left) and women (Venus ad on the right).

Psychographic Segmentation Of the various methods for segmenting, or breaking down the market, **psychographics** is the one that delves into how consumers describe themselves. Usually marketers determine (through demographics, buying patterns, or usage) into which segment an individual consumer falls. But psychographics allows people to describe themselves by using those characteristics that help them choose how they occupy their time (behaviour) and what underlying psychological reasons determine those choices.[13] For example, a person might have a strong need for inclusion or belonging, which motivates him or her to seek out activities that involve others, which then influences the products he or she buys to fit in with the group. If a consumer becomes attached to a group that enjoys literary discussions, he or she is motivated to buy the latest books and spend

Marketers such as Benetton want their ads to appeal to one's self-concept. "I'm like them, so I should buy their products."

time in stores such as Indigo. Such self-segmentation by the consumer could be very valuable knowledge for bookstore managers trying to find new ways of attracting customers. Determining psychographics involves knowing and understanding three components: self-values, self-concept, and lifestyles.

Self-values are life goals, not just the goals one wants to accomplish in a day. In this context, they refer to overriding desires that drive how a person lives his or her life. Examples of self-value goals might include self-respect, self-fulfillment, or a sense of belonging. This motivation causes people to develop self-images of how they want to be and then determine a way of life that will help them arrive at these ultimate goals. From a marketing point of view, self-values help determine the benefits the target market may be looking for from a product. Lexus uses the tagline "Relentless Pursuit of Perfection" and BMW uses "'Designed for Driving Pleasure" to target these values. In this sense, the underlying, fundamental, personal need that pushes a person to seek out certain products or brands stems from his or her desire to fulfill a self-value, or goal.

How does that underlying goal affect the individual? It does so through **self-concept**, or the image people have of themselves.[14] A person who has a goal to belong may see, or want to see, himself or herself as a fun-loving, gregarious type whom people wish to be around. Marketers can make use of this image through communications that show their products being used by groups of laughing people who are having a good time. The connection emerges between the group fun and the product being shown and connotes a certain lifestyle. TV commercials for dating services such as eHarmony use this technique to sell their services. L'Oréal uses the tagline, "Because I'm Worth It," for its hair colour products.

Lifestyles, the third component of people's psychographic makeup, are the ways we live.[15] If values provide an end goal and self-concept is the way one sees oneself in the context of that goal, lifestyles are how we live our lives to achieve goals. Someone with a strong sense of belonging who sees himself as a "people person" will probably live in a well-populated area that allows for many activities. He likely will join clubs or partake in activities that attract like-minded people. Marketers thus have a built-in target group with similar interests and buying desires. lululemon quickly built a global empire of sportswear clothing and accessories based not on demographics but on the philosophy of a healthy, balanced, fun-filled lifestyle.

One of the most storied lifestyles in North American legend is the Harley way of life. The open road, wind in your hair, rebelling against conventions—the image nearly always depicted by men like Dennis Hopper in Easy Rider. But the notions of freedom, rebellion, and standing out from a crowd vastly appeal to all sorts of people. In response, Harley-Davidson has shifted its STP methods to define four main target markets: core (white men older than 35 years), young adults (both genders, 18–34 years), women (white

psychographics
This segmentation base delves into how consumers describe themselves; allows people to describe themselves by using those characteristics that help them choose how they occupy their time (behaviour) and what underlying psychological reasons determine those choices.

self-values
Goals for life, not just the goals one wants to accomplish in a day; a component of psychographics that refers to overriding desires that drive how a person lives his or her life.

self-concept
The image a person has of himself or herself; a component of psychographics.

lifestyles
Lifestyles are how we live our lives to achieve goals.

Using lifestyle segmentation, Harley-Davidson has four main target markets, including white women older than 35 years.

VALS™
A psychographical tool developed by Strategic Business Insights, classifies consumers into eight segments: Innovators, Thinkers, Believers, Achievers, Strivers, Experiencers, Makers, or Survivors.

and older than 35 years), and diverse (men and women, African American and Hispanic, older than 35 years).[16]

The most widely used psychographic system is the **VALS™**, owned and operated by Strategic Business Insights (SBI).[17] On the basis of their answers to the VALS™ questionnaire (http://www.strategicbusinessinsights.com/vals/presurvey.shtml), consumers are classified into the eight segments in the two dimensions shown in Exhibit 6.3. On the vertical dimension, segments are described by their resources, including their income, education, health, energy level, and degree of innovativeness. The upper segments have more resources and are more innovative than those on the bottom.

The horizontal dimension shows the segment's primary motivation. Consumers buy many products and services because of their primary motivations—that is, how they see themselves in the world and how that self-image governs their activities. The three universal primary motives are ideals, achievement, and self-expression. People who are primarily motivated by ideals are guided by knowledge and principles, whereas those who are motivated by achievement look for products and services that demonstrate success to their peers. Exhibit 6.4 provides a description of the VALS™ types.

EXHIBIT 6.3   VALS™ Framework

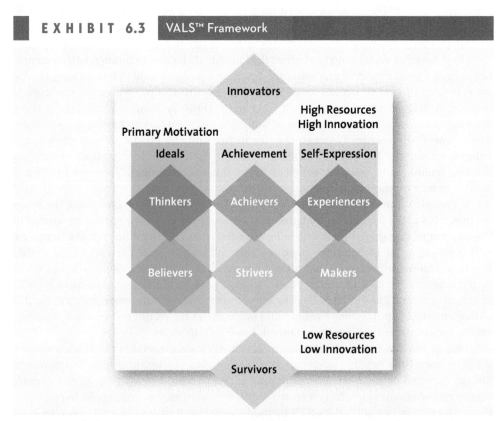

Source: Reprinted with permission of Strategic Business Insights (SBI): www.strategicbusinessinsights.com/VALS.

Using the VALS Questionnaire, in a survey "thinkers" (left) can be identified and contrasted with "makers" (right). "Thinkers" are motivated by ideals, whereas "makers" are prompted to buy based on their need for self-expression in a physical, hands-on way.

VALS™ enables firms to identify target segments and their underlying motivations. It shows correlations between psychology and lifestyle choices. For instance, a Japanese auto manufacturer repositioned its product line to better understand consumer perceptions of its product mix. The insights which resulted from the VALS™ analysis led to an advertising campaign that increased sales by 60 percent in six months.[18] In another case, VALS was used to help a medical centre identify those customers most interested in and able to afford cosmetic surgery. By identifying the underlying motivations of its target customers, the centre's ad agency developed a campaign that was so successful it had to be pulled early to avoid overbooking its scheduling capabilities.

EXHIBIT 6.4	Description of VALS™ Categories		
Innovators	**Thinkers**	**Believers**	**Achievers**
• Successful, sophisticated, take-charge people • High self-esteem • Change leaders • Established and emerging business leaders • Very active consumers • Purchases reflect cultivated taste for finer things	• Mature, satisfied, comfortable • Value responsibility • Well-educated, knowledge seekers • Respect for authority • Conservative, practical consumers • Like durability and clear value	• Conservative conventionalists • Concrete beliefs around family, religion, community • Deep-rooted moral codes • Established routines • Predictable, loyal consumers • Choose familiar products and established brands	• Goal-oriented lifestyles • Deep commitment to career and family • Respect for authority • Value stability, self-discovery • Active consumers • Favour prestige products that demonstrate their success, time-saving products
Strivers	**Experiencers**	**Makers**	**Survivors**
• Trendy and fun-loving • Money defines success • Favour stylish products • Active yet impulsive consumers • Shopping is a social activity and a display of status • Spend as much as they can	• Seek variety and excitement • Active in sports and social activities • Enthusiastic, impulsive consumers • Spend high proportion of income on fashion and entertainment • Want to look good and have cool stuff	• Practical people with constructive skills • Value self-sufficiency • Traditional views of family and work • Suspicious of new ideas • Unimpressed by material possessions • Prefer value over luxury	• Believe the world is changing too quickly • Comfortable with familiarity • Concerned with safety and security • Always focused on meeting needs not fulfilling wants • Cautious consumers • Loyal to favourite brands • Love a good deal

Source: The VALS™ Types. http://www.strategicbusinessinsights.com/vals/ustypes.shtml (accessed August 12, 2014).

Firms are finding that psychographics are a very good complement to demographics to produce an in-depth profile and predict consumer behaviour. For instance, first-year college students and some day labourers may share similar demographics such as their age, education, and income, but they spend their income quite differently because of their very different mindsets. Likewise, Harpreet and Javinder are both 30 years old, married and college graduates. From a demographic standpoint they are the same, yet Harpreet is risk averse while Javinder is a risk taker. Harpreet is socially conscious. Javinder is focused on himself. Lumping these two men in the same target market does not make sense because they think and act very differently.

There are limitations to using psychographic segmentation however. Psychographics are not as objective as demographics, and it is harder to identify potential customers. With demographics, for example, a firm such as Nike can easily identify its customers as men or women and then direct its marketing strategies to each group differently. The problem is that not all men are alike, as we saw with Harpreet and Javinder. Women are not all alike either! Since it can be difficult to identify and target "thinkers" versus "makers," psychographic segmentation is often used in conjunction with other segmentation methods.[19]

Behavioural Segmentation

behavioural segmentation
Groups consumers based on the benefits they derive from products or services, their usage rate, their loyalty, and the occasion.

Behavioural segmentation groups consumers on the basis of the benefits they derive from products or services, their usage rates of products or services, their loyalty and the occasion for which the product or service is used. Some universities consider interest in sustainability initiatives as a way to segment and target both students and their parents. Because marketing is about satisfying consumers' needs and wants, dividing the market into segments whose needs and wants are best satisfied by the product benefits can be very powerful. It is also relatively easy to portray a product's or service's benefits in the firm's communication strategies: their usage rates of products or services, their user status, and their loyalty. Some companies track consumer behaviour and use it for better customer experiences or interactions with the firm. For example, Amazon makes recommendations to customers while they are browsing its site by matching their profiles to those of other customers.

occasion segmentation
Groups consumers based on when they purchase or consume a product or service.

Behavioural segmentation based on when a product or service is purchased or consumed is called **occasion segmentation**. Moores Clothing for Men uses this type of segmentation to develop its merchandise selection and its promotions. Sometimes men need a suit for their everyday work, but other suits are expressly for special occasions, like a prom or a wedding. Snack food companies like Frito-Lay also make and promote snacks for various occasions—individual servings of potato chips for a snack on the run, but 16-ounce bags for parties.

benefit segmentation
Groups consumers based on the benefits they derive from products or services.

As mentioned previously, **benefit segmentation** looks at the benefits customers derive from products or services. Because marketing is all about satisfying needs and wants, dividing the market into segments according to which consumers' needs and wants your offerings can best satisfy makes a lot of sense. Social and Mobile Marketing 6.1 describes how Heinz is using social media to convey the specific benefits of its new balsamic vinegar ketchup.

An excellent illustration of benefit segmentation can be found in RBC Royal Bank's approach. Although it considers that its customers may fall into as many as market segments, its primary categorization centres on the benefits that customers seek from a bank. RBC divides personal (i.e., nonbusiness) customers into five primary benefit groups: Youth, Nexus, Borrowers/Builders, Wealth Accumulators, and Wealth Preservers.[20] As the names of these segments suggest, RBC approaches them according to the benefits they want their banks to provide, such as the accumulation or the preservation of their wealth.

Hollywood is a constant and effective practitioner of benefit segmentation. Although all movies may seem to provide the same service—entertainment for a few hours—film producers know that people visit the theatre or stream films to get a variety of benefits and so they market them accordingly. Need a laugh? Try the latest comedy. Want to cry

Social and Mobile Marketing 6.1

Trials of a Bottle of Ketchup[21]

When you sell a product whose recipe hardly ever changes, it can be hard to create much excitement or buzz. But the rarity of changes also means that virtually any move you make provokes commentary. When Heinz Ketchup changed its label in 2009, replacing the picture of a gherkin that had been there since the 1890s with a ripe tomato, there were some complaints. But the brand also enjoyed a bit more press than was usual, which helped it emphasize a key selling point: that all its ketchup was made from tomatoes the company had grown from seed.

The change in that case was related to packaging, not the contents of the bottle. To build buzz about an entirely new flavour—Heinz Tomato Ketchup Blended with Balsamic Vinegar—Heinz realized it needed an entirely new approach. As consumer goods firms have learned from several examples of failed flavour changes (e.g., New Coke), it's never a good idea to eliminate old favourites. Rather, Heinz left traditional bottles on shelves and offered a limited release of the balsamic version to its faithful fan base. To define those customers, it went beyond simple purchase counts or segmentation based on any demographic considerations. It prioritized people who followed the Heinz Ketchup Facebook page.

For those who had already indicated their loyalty, Heinz granted the right to order a $2.49 bottle of the limited-edition ketchup (with a $2 shipping fee), compared with $1.89 for the regular flavour. If consumers purchased a bottle online through Facebook, they received 25 cents off and a free sample of the new Heinz Dip 'N Squeeze Ketchup package. Heinz Ketchup Blended with Balsamic Vinegar was available for purchase on Facebook from November 14 through December, when it also became available at select retailers (including Walmart, Safeway, and other regional stores). The "limited edition" offering would be available in stores through March, then offered permanently depending on the demand.

At least, that was the plan. On November 14, the Facebook launch of Heinz Ketchup Blended with Balsamic Vinegar was disrupted by unforeseen technical difficulties. Heinz received an overwhelming response from consumers placing orders for the balsamic ketchup via Facebook, which led to the technical difficulties. The plan was to resume the offering within 24 hours. The online buzz began, but not quite in the way Heinz had hoped.

Consumers complained directly on the page. Heinz responded to fans on the Facebook page, notifying them of the technical difficulties. Everyone who contacted Heinz on the Heinz Ketchup Facebook wall on November 14 and 15 received a free bottle with their order plus free shipping. On a social network even a few hours' delay seems like an eternity.

The Heinz Ketchup Facebook page received 86,000 new likes during the balsamic ketchup promotion period. Clearly these potential customers do not fit into the other segmentation schemes. They have self-selected into a segment based on a perceived *benefit*.

Heinz extensively used Facebook to introduce its new Ketchup Blended with Balsamic Vinegar.

and then feel warm and fuzzy? Take in a romance. By the time you leave the theatre, you will feel heartwarmingly happy because the lead characters are sure to have overcome their differences to find love.

Firms have long known that it pays to retain loyal customers. Loyal customers are those who feel so strongly that the firm can meet their relevant needs best that any competitors are virtually excluded from their consideration—that is, these customers buy almost exclusively from the firm.[22] These loyal customers are the most profitable in the long term.[23] In light of the high cost of finding new customers and the

loyalty segmentation
Strategy of investing in retention and loyalty initiatives to retain the firm's most profitable customers.

profitability of loyal customers, today's companies are using **loyalty segmentation** and investing in retention and loyalty initiatives to retain their most profitable customers. Canadians are crazy about loyalty cards, with nearly 9 in 10 adults (87 percent) actively participating in at least one loyalty program, whether it's retail or air travel. Loyalty card participation cuts across all demographics, for instance, 96 percent of affluent consumers actively participate in a loyalty program, 78 percent of young adults (18 to 25 years old), 90 percent of seniors (60 years or older), and 95 percent of women (25 to 49) do as well. In the United States, only 39.5 percent of the general population actively participates in a loyalty program.[24] Yet even before Target opened its first stores in Canada in 2103, it offered consumers its REDcard, a loyalty program that gives a 5 percent discount on purchases made with the store's credit or debit card. In response, Loblaw rolled out a digital loyalty program that lets it target and reward customers with offers tied to their specific needs.

Airlines definitely believe that all customers aren't created equal. At Air Canada, the customers who have flown the most miles with the company, the "Super Elite," receive a distinctive card, personalized Air Canada Super Elite luggage tags, special access to Aeroplan Reward seats, priority reservation waitlist, preferred seat selection, Air Canada concierge service, priority airport check-in, extra checked-baggage allowance, priority boarding, guaranteed reservations for full-fare tickets, and priority baggage handling, among other benefits.[25] None of these special services are available to the occasional flyer.

Usage rate (heavy users, regular users, light users, occasional users) can also be used as a segmentation variable. For example, fast-food restaurants often use promotional coupons to target occasional visitors to their restaurant or to entice people who have never visited their restaurants to come in and try their food and services.

Using Multiple Segmentation Methods   Although all segmentation methods are useful, each has its unique advantages and disadvantages. For example, segmenting by demographics and geography is easy because information about who the customers are and where they are located is readily available, but these characteristics don't help marketers determine their customer needs. Because "birds of a feather flock together," companies use a combination of geographic, demographic, and lifestyle characteristics, called geodemographic segmentation, to classify consumers.[26] Consumers in the same neighbourhoods tend to buy the same types of cars, appliances, and apparel; shop at the same types of retailers, and behave similarly to media and promotions. One tool used by Canada Post for **geodemographic segmentation** in Canada is PSYTE cluster profiles. The PSYTE system groups all neighbourhoods in Canada into 60 different lifestyles clusters with specific locations. The information in Exhibit 6.5 describes three **PSYTE clusters**.[27] PRIZM CE, a tool developed by Environics Research, groups Canadians into one of 66 lifestyle types—with names such as Cosmopolitan Elite, Electric Avenues, Les Chics, and Lunch at Tim's—and is also widely used in Canada. The system provides a Canadian segmentation model that has linked geodemographics to psychographics, incorporating "Social Values" data from Environics Research with demographics and product preferences to explain consumer behaviour.[28]

Geodemographic segmentation can be particularly useful for retailers because customers typically patronize stores close to their neighbourhood. Thus, retailers can use geodemographic segmentation to tailor each store's assortment to the preferences of the local community. If a toy chain discovers that one of its stores is surrounded by "Big Sky Families," it can adjust its offerings to include less expensive merchandise. This kind of segmentation is also useful for finding new locations; retailers identify their "best" locations and determine what type of people live in the area surrounding those stores, according to the geodemographic clusters. They can then find other potential locations where similar segments reside. Geodemographic systems, such as PSYTE and PRIZM CE, can also help marketers track and compare sales performance among various clusters in different locations.

geodemographic segmentation
The grouping of consumers on the basis of a combination of geographic, demographic, and lifestyle characteristics.

PSYTE clusters
The grouping of all neighbourhoods in Canada into 60 different lifestyles clusters.

EXHIBIT 6.5 PSYTE Cluster

Cluster Name	Urban Lower Middle (U4): Urban Bohemia	Suburban Affluent (S1): Suburban Affluence	Suburban Affluent (S1): Asian Heights
Description	From body piercing to tattoos, Urban Bohemia includes a diverse population by design. A neighbourhood with a youthful skew, this cluster occupies itself in a variety of artistic, retail, and generally creative employment. Men and women employed in cultural, artistic, and entertainment-related jobs abound. Household maintainers under age 25, many with college degrees, are also found in this cluster.	This cluster with a flair for fine living represents both old and new wealth. Because wealth accumulates throughout life stages, this cluster exhibits an older skew with many empty nests. Suburban Affluence indexes high on managerial and technical employment and are married with children.	Asian ancestries combined with hard work and growing wealth create and mould these upscale neighbourhoods. Asian Heights represents the affirmation of dreams cultivated through generations of immigrants and often through hardship. These families boost local economies as well as family prospects. Asian Heights indexes high on Chinese, Korean, and Japanese immigration as well as households of six or more persons.
Average Household Income	$46,000	$166,000	$96,000

Source: Used by permission of Pitney Bowes Software.

Knowing what benefits customers are seeking or how the product or service fits a particular lifestyle is important for designing an overall marketing strategy, but such segmentation schemes present a problem for marketers attempting to identify specifically which customers are seeking these benefits. Thus, firms often employ a combination of segmentation methods, using demographics and geography, as discussed above, to identify and target marketing communications to their customers, and then using benefits or lifestyles to design the product or service and the substance of the marketing message. See Real World Segmentation Example for an example of how multiple segmentation methods can combine to develop a richer segmentation strategy for financial markets.

Step 3: Evaluate Segment Attractiveness   LO2

The third step in the segmentation process involves evaluating the attractiveness of the various segments. To undertake this evaluation, marketers first must determine whether the segment is worth pursuing by using several descriptive criteria: Is the segment identifiable, reachable, responsive, and substantial and profitable? (See Exhibit 6.6.)

The financial services consulting firm LIMRA targets four identifiable segments based on demographics and lifestyle data to best meet the needs of middle-income households getting ready to retire.

REAL-WORLD SEGMENTATION EXAMPLE

Segmenting the Financial Services Market by Using Demographics and Lifestyles[29, 30, 31, 32]

LIMRA, a financial services research and consulting organization, that operates in Canada and the United States, surveyed its consumers to determine their personal financial objectives and the type of lifestyle they wanted when they retired. The survey yielded four identifiable segments for middle-income households, as described in the chart below.

Steve Hall is a financial consultant who is prospecting for new customers. What can he do with combined demographic and lifestyle LIMRA data? The demographic data can identify the type of people in a segment, how firms might reach these people through the media or other selling vehicles, and how profitable the segments may be. For instance, Steve has found a group of "Worker Bees" who are self-employed, over 40, and have relatively high incomes. The lifestyle data then can be used to help design products and promotional messages that are relevant to this group. For instance, Steve historically would study a customer's portfolio and his or her attitude toward taking financial risks before preparing a retirement package for that customer. But knowing the type of lifestyles to which these "Worker Bees" aspire when they retire enables the sales agent to better match customers' lifestyles and the financial planning process. Since the "Worker Bees" are very entrepreneurial and love to work, Steve designs a sales presentation that stresses how much money they need to save over the coming years to maintain their relatively modest lifestyle and enable them to continue to work as long as they wish or are physically able.

Demographic and Retirement Lifestyle Segmentation for the Financial Services Market[33]

		Pragmatic Planners	Worker Bees	Grand Thinkers	Status Quo
DEMOGRAPHIC CHARACTERISTICS		✓ Single ✓ No dependent children ✓ Educated ✓ Moderate income ✓ Have discretionary income ✓ Under 45 years old	✓ Couples ✓ Less formal education ✓ High income ✓ High investable assets ✓ Over 40 ✓ Self-employed	✓ Couples ✓ Broad education levels ✓ Moderate incomes ✓ Broad age ranges	✓ Couples ✓ With dependent children ✓ Less formal education ✓ Broad income range ✓ Over 40
PERCENTAGE OF MIDDLE-MARKET HOUSEHOLDS		30 percent	15 percent	34 percent	21 percent
RETIREMENT LIFESTYLE GOALS		✓ Save to buy home ✓ Eliminate or reduce debt ✓ Save for retirement ✓ Maintain modest but comfortable standard of living ✓ Spend time with family ✓ Enjoy leisure activities	✓ Start or expand business ✓ Save for retirement ✓ Maintain modest but comfortable living standard ✓ Start or run business ✓ Keep working in a capacity similar to today's	✓ Save to buy home ✓ Protect family in case of death ✓ Eliminate or reduce debt ✓ Save for retirement ✓ Maintain modest but comfortable standard of living ✓ Spend time with family ✓ Enjoy leisure activities	✓ Protect family in case of death ✓ Protect family in case of disability ✓ Eliminate or reduce debt ✓ Save for retirement ✓ Maintain modest but comfortable standard of living ✓ Spend time with family

E X H I B I T   6.6　Evaluation of Segment Attractiveness

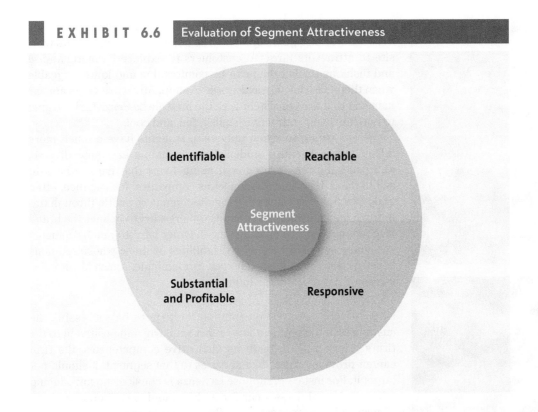

Identifiable　Firms must determine who is within their market to be able to design products or services to meet their needs. It is equally important to ensure that the segments are distinct from one another because too much overlap between segments means that distinct marketing strategies aren't necessary to meet segment members' needs.

The Gap has identified several distinct segments to pursue. Recognizing that many of its core customers had families, The Gap opened GapKids and babyGap. Its research also indicated an opportunity to compete with Victoria's Secret in the women's intimate apparel market, so it opened GapBody. Finally, though The Gap is largely successful with middle-of-the-road customers, it was too expensive for some customers and not fashion-forward enough for others. Its Old Navy and Banana Republic stores appeal better to these markets.

La Senza must ensure any new segment it considers is identifiable, reachable, responsive, substantial, and profitable.

Reachable　The best product or service cannot have any impact if that market cannot be reached (or accessed) through persuasive communications and product distribution. Consumers must know the product or service exists, understand what it can do for them, and recognize how to buy it.

La Senza is one of Canada's leading specialty retailers of women's lingerie and apparel. It is composed of La Senza Lingerie, La Senza Girl, La Senza Express, La Senza International, La Senza Spirit, and lasenza.com, and it sells through stores and the Internet. La Senza Girl does not sell through the Internet but has

The Gap has identified several distinct segments to pursue. Two of its brands: Gap (top) and Gap Kids (bottom) appeal to different target markets.

a straightforward plan for reaching its target customers: girls between 7 and 14 years of age.[34] The company simply uses its website to attract its targeted customers to explore its merchandise and fashions so that they can be comfortable and knowledgeable when they visit the physical stores to shop. Advertisements appear in media that are consistent with the lifestyle La Senza Girl is trying to portray: lively, attractive, stylish, fun, and cool.

Firms trying to reach university students have a much more difficult time because students' media habits are quite diverse, and generally they are cynical about firms that try too hard to sell to them. High-end fashion jeans companies, for instance, often underpromote their lines or promote them very subtly through traditional media because if their customers start to believe the brand is too mainstream, they won't buy it. Other hard-to-reach segments are composed of people with disabilities or those whose religious beliefs restrict their media choices. For example, Amish Mennonites eschew TV, radio, and the Internet.

Responsive   For a segmentation strategy to be successful, the customers in the segment must react similarly and positively to the firm's offering. If, through its distinctive competencies, the firm cannot provide products or services to that segment, it should not target it. For instance, suppose La Senza is considering introducing a line of formal dress wear for its large and very lucrative 18- to 35-year-old customer segment. People in this market are currently purchasing formal dress wear at stores such as The Bay, Holt Renfrew, and Les Ailes de la Mode (Wings of Fashion). In contrast, La Senza has built a reputation for carrying a full range of intimate, stylish, and sexy day-wear and sleepwear bras, panties, camisoles, pyjamas, and nightshirts and competes best in this apparel line. Although the formal dress wear segment meets all the other criteria for a successful segment, La Senza should not pursue it because the market probably will not be responsive to it.

Substantial and Profitable   Once the firm has identified its potential target markets, it needs to measure their size and growth potential. If a market is too small or its buying power insignificant, it won't generate sufficient profits or be able to support the marketing mix activities. Although The Gap had identified potential new target markets to pursue, it was imperative for the company to determine whether the market for women's intimate apparel was small or large. If it was relatively small, the company would fit the products into its regular stores. If it was large, the products would require their own space. The Gap experimented cautiously with the new concept by first placing a section of intimate apparel in some of its stores. Over time, Gap managers realized the potential of the concept and began to roll out GapBody stores.

Marketers must also focus their assessments on the potential profitability of each segment, both current and future. Some key factors to keep in mind in this analysis include market growth (current size and expected growth rate), market competitiveness (number of competitors, entry barriers, product substitutes), and market access (ease of developing or accessing distribution channels and brand familiarity). Some straightforward calculations can help illustrate the profitability of a segment:[35]

Segment profitability = (Segment size × Segment adoption percentage × Purchase behaviour × Profit margin percentage) – Fixed costs

Which segment will be more profitable to Mark's, its traditional market for rugged work clothes (left), or the fashion-forward segment (right)?

where

Segment size = Number of people in the segment

Segment adoption percentage = Percentage of customers in the segment who are likely to adopt the product/service

Purchase behaviour = Purchase price × Number of times the customer would buy the product or service during a given time period

Profit margin percentage = (Selling price – Variable costs) ÷ Selling price

Fixed costs = Advertising expenditure, rent, utilities, insurance, administration, salaries

To illustrate how a business might determine a segment's profitability, consider Camillo's startup lawn service. He is trying to determine whether to target homeowners or businesses in a small prairie town. Exhibit 6.7 estimates the profitability of the two segments. The homeowner segment is much larger than the business segment, but there are already several lawn services with established customers. There is much less competition in the business segment. So, the segment adoption rate for the homeowner segment is only 1 percent, compared with 20 percent for the business segment. Camillo can charge a much higher price to businesses, and they utilize lawn services more frequently. The profit margin for the business segment is higher as well because Camillo can use large equipment to cut the grass and therefore save on variable labour costs. However, the fixed costs for purchasing and maintaining the large equipment are much higher for the

EXHIBIT 6.7	Profitability of Two Market Segments for Camillo's Lawn Service	
	Homeowners	**Businesses**
Segment size	75,000	1,000
Segment adoption percentage	1%	20%
Purchase behaviour Purchase price Frequency of purchase	$100 12 times	$500 20 times
Profit margin percentage	60%	80%
Fixed costs	$400,000	$1,000,000
Segment profit	$140,000	$600,000

business segment. Furthermore, he needs to spend more money obtaining and maintaining the business customers, whereas he would use less expensive door-to-door flyers to reach household customers. On the basis of these informed predictions, Camillo decides the business segment is more profitable for his lawn service.

Using this formula, several segments could appear to be equally profitable. In some cases, it is more accurate to evaluate the profitability of a segment over the lifetime of one of its typical customers—that is, through customer lifetime value (CLV), the total value of purchases of the customer over a lifetime of patronage. For example, Ken Danns has been a loyal Costco customer for the last five years, spending about $300 per week at Costco. He plans to continue patronizing Costco for at least another five years. To Costco, Ken Danns is not a $300 customer but a $156,000 customer if he patronizes Costco for 10 years ($300 × 52 weeks × 10 years). To address the issue of CLV, marketers consider factors such as how long the customer will remain loyal to the firm, the defection rate (percentage of customers who switch on a yearly basis), the costs of replacing lost customers (advertising, promotion), whether customers will buy more or more-expensive merchandise in the future, and other such factors.[36] See Appendix 7A for more details on determining the lifetime value of customers.

Now that we've evaluated each segment's attractiveness (Step 3), we can select the target markets to pursue (Step 4).

Step 4: Select Target Market

The fourth step in the STP process is selecting a target market. The key factor likely to affect this decision is the marketer's ability to pursue such an opportunity or target segment. Thus, as we mentioned in Chapter 2, a firm is likely to assess both the attractiveness of the opportunity (opportunities and threats based on the SWOT analysis—i.e., profitability of the segment) and its own competencies (strengths and weaknesses based on SWOT analysis) very carefully.

Determining how to select target markets is not always straightforward. Exhibit 6.8 illustrates several targeting strategies, which are now discussed in more detail.

Undifferentiated Targeting Strategy, or Mass Marketing

undifferentiated targeting strategy (mass marketing)
A marketing strategy a firm can use if the product or service is perceived to provide the same benefits to everyone, with no need to develop separate strategies for different groups.

When everyone might be considered a potential user of its product, a firm uses an **undifferentiated targeting strategy (mass marketing)** (see Exhibit 6.8). If the product or service is perceived to provide the same benefits to everyone, there simply is no need to develop separate strategies for different groups. Although not a common strategy in today's complex marketplace, an undifferentiated strategy can be effective for very basic items, such as salt, sugar, or greetings cards. However, even those firms that offer salt, sugar, or greeting cards now are trying to differentiate their products, as is the case with Hallmark.

An undifferentiated strategy also is common among smaller firms that offer products or services that consumers perceive to be indistinguishable, such as a neighbourhood bakery. But again, more marketing-savvy entrepreneurs typically try to differentiate themselves in the marketplace. The corner bakery thus becomes "Kettleman's Bagel" or "The Great Canadian Bagel." By making their commodity-like products appear special, these companies add value for the customer and differentiate themselves from their competition.

What about gasoline? Everyone with a car needs it. Yet gasoline companies have vigorously moved from an undifferentiated strategy to a differentiated one by segmenting their market into low-, medium-, and high-octane gasoline users. Esso even uses its Speedpass to differentiate its quick service to consumers: with just a swipe at the pump with Speedpass, you are ready to pump gas—no need to swipe cards, enter personal information, or sign receipts. Plus customers earn Esso Extra points or Aeroplan Miles on every eligible purchase made at Esso. Points can be redeemed for gas, car washes, snacks, and travel rewards.

EXHIBIT 6.8 | Targeting Strategies

Mass or Undifferentiated

Differentiated

Concentrated

Micromarketing One-to-One

Differentiated Targeting Strategy   Firms using a **differentiated targeting strategy** target several market segments with a different offering for each (see Exhibit 6.8). La Senza, for instance, employs three store formats—La Senza, La Senza Girl, and La Senza Express—to appeal to three different segments respectively: (1) confident, fashion-forward 18- to 35-year-old women; (2) younger girls; and (3) women looking for the ultimate destination for bras and panties for everyday and trend-forward styles.[37] In a similar fashion, Adidas Group appeals to various segments through its various companies, including Adidas Reebok (athletic shoes), Rockport (comfortable walking shoes), and TaylorMade-Adidas Golf lines of clothing and footwear.

Firms embrace differentiated segmentation because it helps them obtain a bigger share of the market and increase the market for their products overall. The more retail formats La Senza develops to reach different market segments, the more apparel and accessories it can and will sell. Offering several different lingerie lines enables La Senza to appeal to more customer segments than if it had just one line. Furthermore, providing products or services that appeal to multiple segments helps diversify the business, thereby lowering the company's overall risk. For example, if a line directed toward one segment is performing poorly, the impact on the firm's profitability can be offset by revenue from another line that is doing well.

But a differentiated strategy can be expensive. Consider La Senza's investment in accessories alone. The firm must develop, manufacture, transport, store, and promote the accessories separately for each of its store concepts.

differentiated targeting strategy
A strategy through which a firm targets several market segments with a different offering for each.

Abercrombie & Fitch targets the 18- to 22-year-old market with a hip, edgy image.

concentrated (or niche) targeting strategy
A marketing strategy of selecting a single, primary target market and focusing all energies on providing a product to fit that market's needs.

Concentrated (Niche) Targeting Strategy When an organization selects a single, primary target market and focuses all its energies on providing a product to fit that market's needs, it is using a **concentrated (or niche) targeting strategy** (see Exhibit 6.8). Entrepreneurial startup ventures often benefit from using a concentrated strategy, which allows them to employ their limited resources more efficiently. The story of Cora's restaurants in Entrepreneurial Marketing 6.1 is an example of a niche strategy since it focuses on serving breakfast and brunch only; restaurants are open only until 3 p.m. Gennum Corporation of Burlington, Ontario, is another example of a niche strategy; it is the world's leading innovator in micro-circuitry for hearing aids—a niche market.

For example, if you've ever shopped at Abercrombie & Fitch (A&F), chances are you're younger than 30 years of age. Since its inception, A&F has pursued a calculated concentrated targeting strategy by deliberately targeting the young and good-looking crowd with a hip, edgy strategy. Thus, when older or "unhip" consumers don't find it appealing, that doesn't bother the company one bit. Its whole brand experience is designed to create an impression of exclusivity for its 18- to 22-year-old customers.[38] For instance, rather than display items in brightly lit windows, as most clothing retailers do, it carefully shutters off the outside of its stores so that customers have to enter to see the merchandise. Once inside, they confront not a brightly lit interior that helps customers find what they're looking for but rather a dark, loud environment with an almost overwhelming scent of heavy cologne. The stores are carefully designed to make shopping an emotional experience for core customers; but, for the parents of these customers, that experience is usually unpleasant. But then, they're not part of the target market A&F is trying to attract.[39]

Micromarketing[40] Take a look at your collection of belts. Have you ever had a belt made to match your exact specifications? When a firm tailors a product or service to suit an individual customer's wants or needs, it is undertaking an extreme form of segmentation called **micromarketing (one-to-one) marketing** (see Exhibit 6.8). Small producers and service providers generally can tailor their offering to individual customers more easily, whereas it is far more difficult for larger companies to achieve this degree of segmentation. Nonetheless, companies such as Dell and Lands' End have capitalized on Internet technologies to offer "custom-made" computers, dress shirts, chinos, and jeans. Firms, such as Build-a-Bear Workshop, that interact on a one-to-one basis with many people to create custom-made products or services are engaged in **mass customization**, providing one-to-one marketing to the masses. Sport Chek offers several options to consumers who want custom products. A Reebok "build-your-own" sneaker kiosk lets consumers create their own designs, which are shipped to them four to six weeks later. Sports fans can create a custom Toronto Maple Leaf, Toronto Blue Jay, or Team Canada jersey that includes the name and number of their favourite player.[41]

The Internet helps companies cater to very small segments, sometimes as small as one customer at a time, relatively efficiently and inexpensively (e.g., mortgage and insurance sites provide personalized quotes). An Internet-based company can offer one-to-one service more inexpensively than can other venues, such as retail stores or

micromarketing (one-to-one) marketing
An extreme form of segmentation that tailors a product or service to suit an individual customer's wants or needs.

mass customization
The practice of interacting on a one-to-one basis with many people to create custom-made products or services; providing one-to-one marketing to the masses.

Entrepreneurial Marketing 6.1 | Chez Cora: The Business of Breakfast

When Cora Tsouflidou became a single mother to three teenage children, she bought a small eatery, worked hard, tripled its value, and sold it. From there she worked her way up from a hostess to the general manager in a well-known Montreal restaurant, mastering her foodservice industry knowledge along the way.[42]

These skills served her well when she bought a defunct 29-seat snack bar in Montreal's Ville St-Laurent in 1987 and launched the first Chez Cora restaurant. Plates garnished with a variety of artistically presented fresh fruits made Cora's dishes both unique and popular. Her homey, healthy food was a hit, which led to franchising the first Chez Cora in Quebec, followed by franchising Cora's Breakfast and Lunch across the rest of the country. Today, there are more than 120 Cora's restaurants in nine provinces, all of which have traditional family-style breakfast and lunch menus featuring new dishes created and tested by Cora herself.

When deciding to open a new franchise, the company starts with a demographic analysis to determine whether

Cora's serves up healthy fare featuring a variety of colourful fruits with each meal.

there are enough people in an area to feed a Cora's restaurant.[43] Psychographics and behavioural segmentation are also important to identify and attract customers who are interested in healthy lifestyles and want the benefit of nutritious meals.

A unique strategy attracts franchisees based on their desired lifestyle. Restaurants serve only breakfast and lunch and thus are open between 6 a.m. and 3 p.m., an approach born out of necessity from Cora's early days as a single mom. These hours are considerably shorter than most restaurant operations and thus appeal to franchisees, allowing them to spend more time with their families.

It's not surprising that Cora's image is used in advertising campaigns. She looks like a mom who really cares about family, which resonates with both customers and franchisees. Behind that colourful image is a self-made business woman who has won the Governor General's Award and the Ernst & Young Entrepreneur of the Year Award.[44] Cora's unique business plan has made Cora's one of the fastest-growing restaurant chains in Canada.

telephone-based businesses. For example, frequent fliers of Air Canada can check prices and choose special services online at a fraction of the cost that the company would incur for a phone consultation with a ticket agent.

The Internet also simplifies customer identification. Cookies, or small text files a website stores in a visitor's browser, provide a unique identification of each potential customer who visits and details how the customer has searched the site. Marketers also can ask visitors to fill out an online registration form. Using such information, the company can make a variety of recommendations to customers. Amazon.ca is renowned for the algorithms it uses to provide recommendations for related products to customers as they browse the site, which match customer profiles to those of other customers. The marketing strategy is customized in real time, using known and accurate data about the customer. Customers can even do the work themselves, both to create items for themselves and to find the perfect gifts for others.[45] Mars' M&Ms site (http://www.mymms.com) lets customers customize their own M&M's with personalized greetings, including messages for birthday parties, sporting events, graduations, and weddings—even wedding proposals!

The degree to which firms should segment their markets—from no segmentation to one segment to multiple segments to one-to-one segments—depends on the balance the firm wants to achieve between the added perceived customer value that segmentation can offer and its cost.

Sometimes firms' target market selection also can raise serious ethical concerns. Ethical Dilemma 6.1 examines the issue of marketing high-end designer clothing to teens.

http://www.mymms.com allows customers to customize their candy.

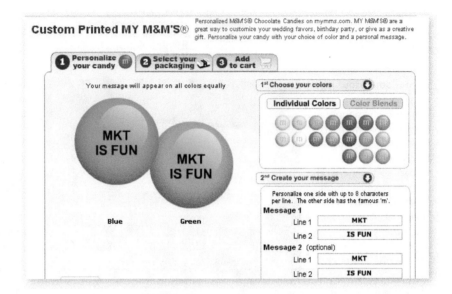

Ethical Dilemma 6.1   Designer Labels Target Teens

What happens when marketing to a segment works too well? Take, for example, designer labels targeting teens 13 to 17 years of age. In 2007, designer labels accounted for 15.4 percent of teen clothing purchases; just three years earlier, these labels earned only 9.6 percent. Yet among adults older than 18 years of age, the 7 percent market share designer labels maintain has remained constant.[46] So what can explain these trends?

High-end designers are taking advantage of teens' desire for fashion and bragging rights to sell apparel to younger consumers by targeting them intensively with advertising and product placements. Luxury brands targeting kids include Dolce & Gabbana and Armani, which have created their own separate teen lines, as well as Michael Kors, Coach, Dooney & Bourke, and Dior, which target young consumers with accessories. Even retailers are cashing in on the trend; department stores such as Nordstrom have added Burberry and Prada products to their children's departments. As a result, tweens are showing up to school with their $225 Dooney & Bourke gym bags in tow.[47]

The effects of intense advertising to kids also appear in the form of more sophisticated brand opinions among younger and younger consumers. Four years ago, 15 percent of teens claimed to love Armani;

Should fashion companies target teens?

today that level has reached 27 percent. In schools across the country, the effects of increased advertising to kids have also resulted in massive increases in "fashion bullying"—that is, when students are targeted because they do not wear the "right" clothing or designers. More than one-third of all middle school students say that they have been bullied because of what they wear. Although this form of bullying certainly is not new, guidance counsellors say that fashion bullying has reached a new level of intensity as more designers launch collections targeted at kids.

Fashion companies face an ethical dilemma: How much should they target teens? Clearly, these companies hope to gain lifetime aficionados by reaching out to consumers at a young age, with the goal of turning them into loyal repeat customers. However, some advertising appears to be encouraging fashion bullying. Furthermore, luxury purchases such as designer handbags and totes are specifically created to be exclusive. When teens buy luxury goods at more than twice the rate of the general population, it suggests that parents are funding a fashion habit that they may not engage in themselves and that may not be sustainable for those children when they grow up and have to pay their own way. Should the designers care? What do you think?

Step 5: Identify and Develop Positioning Strategy

LO4

The last step in developing a market segmentation strategy is **positioning**. Positioning is the mental picture or perception—the thoughts, feelings, and impressions—that people have about a company, its products and brands relative to competing products, brands, or companies. This mental picture is formed from multiple sources such as friends, family, relatives, and reference groups; published articles in magazines and newspapers; reports and stories from radio, TV, and the Internet; as well as the customer's own experience. Regardless of whether companies want them to or not, consumers form their own ideas and feelings about a product or brand, and it is those very ideas and emotions that drive them toward or away from a brand or company. The positioning strategy can help communicate the firm's or the product's value proposition, which communicates the customer benefits to be received from a product or service and thereby provides reasons for wanting to purchase it. Positioning is one of the most important but difficult and least understood aspects of marketing strategy development. Why?

positioning
The mental picture that people have about a company and its products or services relative to competitors.

It is not easy to shape consumers' perceptions in the way marketers may want. It is also difficult because while marketers must keep their positioning fresh to keep abreast with the ever-changing marketplace, consumers' perceptions are enduring and do not change easily. Positioning is very risky for marketers because if it is not done correctly, the brand may not succeed in the marketplace. Effective positioning requires that marketers not only shape their customers' thinking and feelings, but also evolve these feelings as they reposition their products and brands to keep up with the dynamic marketplace. For example, Old Spice successfully repositioned itself from "your father's after-shave" to a fresh new product sought by younger consumers. It is now a leading brand offering soap, body wash, body spray, shave, gel, deodorant, and antiperspirant products.

Market positioning involves a process of defining the marketing mix variables so that target customers have a clear, distinctive, desirable understanding of what the product does or represents in comparison with competing products. Effective positioning is about letting consumers know what the company's unique value proposition is and for whom it is intended. Clarity of this message is crucial for successful positioning. For example, Abercrombie & Fitch offers casual luxury to young, sexy, athletic- and cheerleading-type university students and does not make clothing for people who are overweight. Its advertising messages, models, store design, and merchandise all reinforce this message.

A firm's positioning strategies must focus on the value a product or service offers the target consumer, or how it is better than competitors' products and services. When positioning against competitors, the objective is to play up how the brand being marketed provides the desired benefits better than those of competitors. Positioning strategies are realized by communicating particular messages (i.e., the **positioning statement**) in persuasive communications through different media.

positioning statement
Expresses how a company wants to be perceived by consumers.

In Exhibit 6.9, we illustrate some elements of a positioning statement as follows:

1. target market
2. offering name or brand
3. product/service category or concept
4. unique point of difference/benefits

Let's focus on a couple of well-known products, Gatorade and 7-Up, and their potential value propositions (brackets added to separate the components):

- **Gatorade:**[48] For [athletes around the world] [Gatorade] is the [sports drink] that [represents the heart and soul of athleticism. Unlike water, it gives the fuel for working muscles, fluid for hydration, and electrolytes to help replace what is lost in sweat before, during, and after activity to get the most out of your body].

- **7-Up:**[49] For [noncola consumers] [7-Up] is a [noncaffeinated soft drink] that [is light, refreshing, lemon-lime flavoured. Unlike colas, it has a crisp, bubbly, and clean taste].

■ **EXHIBIT 6.9** Positioning Statement Elements	Gatorade	7-Up
Target Market	For atheletes around the world	For noncola consumers
Offering name or brand	Gatorade	7-Up
Product/service category or concept:	is the sports drink	is a noncaffeinated soft drink
Unique point of difference/ benefits	representing the heart and soul of athleticism. Unlike water, it gives the fuel for working muscles, fluid for hydration, and electrolytes to help replace what is lost in sweat before, during, and after activity to get the most out of your body.	that is light, refreshing, lemon-lime flavoured. Unlike colas it has a crisp, bubbly, and clean taste.

Positioning Methods

Usually, firms position their products and services based on different methods such as value, product attributes, benefits and symbolism, and competition. Let's explore each of these in a bit more detail.

Value   Value is a popular positioning method because the relationship of price to quality is among the most important considerations for consumers when they make a purchase decision. Remember that value does not necessarily mean low priced. For example, in the kids' toy market, Mega Bloks uses a low-price, value-based strategy, whereas its competitor, Lego, relies on a high-price positioning strategy. Watchmaker Patek Philippe uses the advertising tagline, "You never actually own a Patek Philippe. You merely take care of it for the next generation," to encourage buyers to consider its arm candy an investment.[50] Other brands that rely on a similar idea of luxury value include Hermes, Chanel, and Mercedes-Benz.

Some companies claim that they are offering the same value for much less money. This type of positioning is common among wireless service providers (e.g., Rogers, Bell, TELUS), cable/satellite TV and radio providers (Sirius, Rogers), electronics retailers (Future Shop), and department stores (Target). Companies such as Internet Superstore, Buy.com, and TigerDirect emphasize that consumers are getting the best computer deals anywhere and at much lower prices. Finally, companies may use value positioning to let consumers know that while they are getting much less, they are also paying much less. WestJet, dollar stores (e.g., Buck or Two, Dollar Store), and countless retailers targeting cost-conscious consumers commonly use this strategy.

Product Attributes   Another common positioning strategy focuses on those attributes that are most important to the target market. Car company Volvo traditionally positioned itself for the safety-conscious driver but now wants to stretch its safety image to one focused on driving performance and excitement. The company expects the positioning adjustment to be difficult but achievable, because so many of Volvo's boxier vehicles remain on the road today, which reinforces its more conservative image. Volvo's goal is not to abandon the safety perception associated with the brand but rather to expand its image to compete with other top luxury brands.[51] Positioning strategies that are based on product attributes tend to focus on product leadership, emphasizing dimensions such as innovation, quality, performance, design, and reliability. 3M and HP focus on their innovations while Rockport focuses on comfort and a wide selection of shoes for all occasions. Cora's, a product-attributes success story, is able to compete in the highly

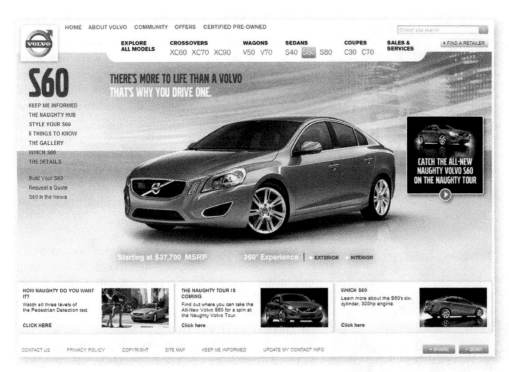

Can Volvo reposition its cars to be more exciting with higher performance without losing its traditional position that appeals to safety-conscious drivers?

competitive restaurant market by attracting a target market that wants a healthy and homey breakfast (see Entrepreneurial Marketing 6.1.)

Benefits and Symbolism

This type of positioning emphasizes the benefits of the brand as well as the psychological meaning of the brand to consumers. For example, Lolë is about technical but versatile clothing in a casual, modern style, and strikes a balance between active life and social life, nature and urban lifestyle, well-being and energy. La Senza Express is the ultimate destination dedicated to bras and panties, and Abercrombie & Fitch is about casual luxury.[52] The meanings created by these brands are often the reasons consumers buy them rather than lesser-known brands that sometimes offer similar benefits or quality. For established companies, a well-known symbol can also be used as a positioning tool, especially to appeal to loyal customers. What comes to mind when you think of Colonel Sanders, the Jolly Green Giant, the Gerber Baby, or Tony the Tiger? Or consider the Nike swoosh or the Ralph Lauren polo player. These symbols are so strong and well known that they create a position for the brand that distinguishes it from its competition.

Competition

Firms can choose to position their products or services *head-to-head* against a specific competitor or an entire product/service classification on similar attributes within the target market. Using head-to-head positioning, Avis positioned itself alongside Hertz with its message "Avis is only no. 2 in rental cars. So why go with us? We try harder (When you're not the biggest, you have to.)."[53] Head-to-head positioning can lead to price wars such as the "cola wars" and "cellphone wars," which are good for consumers but bad for businesses. Marketers must be careful that they don't position their product too closely to their competition because they risk confusing customers or facing legal challenges. If, for instance, their package or logo looks too much like a competitor's, they might be opening themselves up to a trademark infringement lawsuit. Numerous store brands have been challenged for having packaging confusingly similar to that of national brands. McDonald's, for example, sues anyone who uses the *Mc* prefix. It sued Quality Inns International when it named its no-frills chain McSleep Inns.[54] However, courts have allowed parody jeans for full-figured women to be sold under the Lardashe label, despite the objections of Jordache jeans.

Goodrich positions its tires as the ones without the blimp to set them apart from Goodyear.

perceptual map
Displays, in two or more dimensions, the position of products or brands in the consumer's mind.

ideal point
The position at which a particular market segment's ideal product would lie on a perceptual map.

Firms can also choose a *differentiation* strategy by going after a less competitive, smaller market niche.[55] For instance, Goodrich tires were promoted as "The Other Guys," or the ones without the blimp, to set them apart from Goodyear tires. McDonalds, which is historically known as the world's number-one beef burger joint has responded to industry critics and health-conscious consumers by improving the "health of its menu" with more healthy choices such as salads and chicken sandwiches. In doing so, it tried to avoid competition with archrivals Wendy's and Burger King while minimizing the impact of cannibalization of its existing menu items.

Market Leadership Instead of positioning head-to-head, companies, especially market leaders, may emphasize their leadership position within their industry. Canadian companies such as the RBC Royal Bank, Loblaw, and Canadian Tire, and global companies such as Amazon, Intel, HP, Google, and eBay play up their status as market leaders in their respective industry. Each of these companies is the leader in their industry and so consumers often perceive them as setting the standards of their industry.

Positioning by Using Perceptual Mapping

Now that we've identified the various methods firms use to position their products and services, let's look at the steps they go through to establish that position. When developing a positioning strategy, firms go through six important steps. Before you read about these steps though, take a look at Exhibit 6.10 (Charts A-D), a hypothetical perceptual map of the soft-drink industry. A **perceptual map** displays, in two or more dimensions, the position of products or brands in the consumer's mind. We have chosen two dimensions for illustrative purposes: sweet versus light taste (vertical) and less natural versus healthy (horizontal). Although this industry is quite complex, we have simplified the diagram to include only a few players in the market. The position of each brand is denoted by a small circle, and the numbered circles denote a consumer's **ideal point**—where a particular market segment's ideal product would lie on the map. The larger the numbered circle, the larger the market size.

To derive a perceptual map such as this, marketers follow steps.

1. *Determine consumers' perceptions and evaluations of the firm's product or service in relation to competitors.* Marketers determine their brand's position by asking consumers a series of questions about their and competitors' products. For instance, they might ask how the consumer uses the existing product or services, what items the consumer regards as alternative sources to satisfy his or her needs, what the person likes or dislikes about the brand in relation to competitors, and what might make that person choose one brand over another. Exhibit 6.10A depicts the six products using two dimensions (light taste–sweet taste; and less natural–healthy).

2. *Identify the market's ideal points and size.* On a perceptual map, marketers can represent the size of current and potential markets. For example, Exhibit 6.10B uses different sized ovals that correspond to the market size. Ideal point 1 represents the largest market, so if the firm does not already have a product

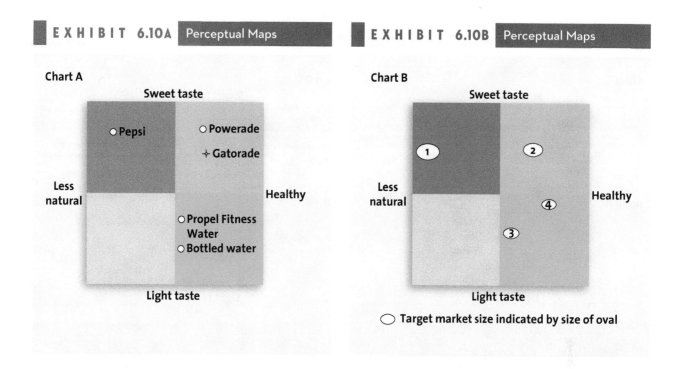

EXHIBIT 6.10A Perceptual Maps

Chart A

EXHIBIT 6.10B Perceptual Maps

Chart B

○ Target market size indicated by size of oval

positioned close to this point, it should consider an introduction. Point 3 is the smallest market, so there are relatively few customers who want a healthy, light-tasting drink. This is not to suggest that this market should be ignored; however, the company might want to consider a niche, rather than mass, market strategy for this group of consumers.

3. *Identify competitors' positions.* When the firm understands how its customers view its brand relative to competitors', it must study how those same competitors position themselves. For instance, Powerade positions itself closely to Gatorade, which means they appear next to each other on the perceptual map and appeal to target market 2. (See Exhibit 6.10C.) They are also often found next to each other on store shelves, are similarly priced, and are viewed by customers as sports drinks. Gatorade knows that its sports drink is perceived to be more like Powerade than like its own Propel Fitness Water (located near target market 3), or Coke (target market 1).

4. *Determine consumer preferences.* The firm knows what the consumer thinks of the products or services in the marketplace and their positions relative to one another. Now it must find out what the consumer really wants—that is, determine the "ideal" product or service that appeals to each market. For example, a huge market exists for traditional Gatorade, and that market is shared by Powerade. Gatorade also recognizes a market, depicted as the ideal product for segment 4 on the perceptual map, of consumers who would prefer a less sweet, less calorie-laden drink that offers the same rejuvenating properties as Gatorade. Currently, no product is adequately serving market 4.

5. *Select the position.* Continuing with the Gatorade example, the company has three choices to appeal to the "less sweet sports drink" target market 4. It could develop a new product to meet the needs of market 4. (See Exhibit 6.10D.) Alternatively, it could adjust or reposition its marketing approach—its product and promotion—to sell original Gatorade to market 4. Finally, it could ignore what target market 4 really wants and hope that consumers will be attracted to the original Gatorade because it is closer to their ideal product than anything else on the market.

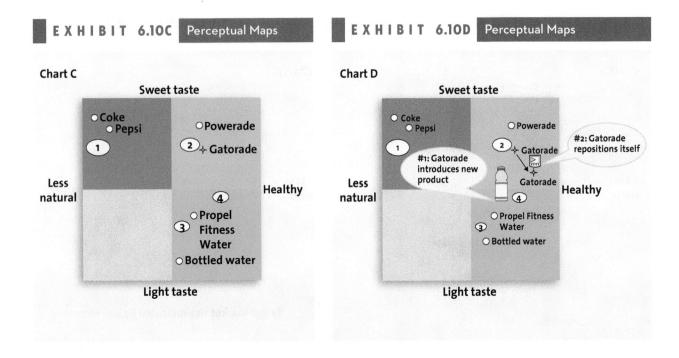

EXHIBIT 6.10C Perceptual Maps

EXHIBIT 6.10D Perceptual Maps

6. *Monitor the positioning strategy.* Markets are not stagnant. Consumers' tastes shift, and competitors react to those shifts. Attempting to maintain the same position year after year can spell disaster for any company. Thus, firms must always view the first three steps of the positioning process as ongoing, with adjustments made in step 4 as necessary.

Repositioning

Sometimes firms try to change their positioning. In its earliest days, Skechers was mostly a lifestyle brand, with hip styles and vibrant designs that appealed to young trendsetters and hipsters, both men and women. When it realized that older consumers wanted hip lifestyle shoes too, it introduced its Shape-Up line and repositioned its image accordingly. Electronics retailer The Source wanted to convince consumers that it was more than just a place to buy batteries or accessories. It shifted its positioning to "On the Go" to promote stores as a destination for top tier electronic products.[56] Tiffany & Co. has long been known for luxury jewellery that is most often purchased by wealthy individuals. In the 1990s, the company, following a trend of

Gatorade with football player Jason Taylor (left) and Powerade with soccer player David Beckham (right) are positioned to compete for target market 3 in Exhibit 6.10.

"affordable luxury," tried to reposition by expanding its product assortment to appeal more to the middle class. Tiffany introduced a silver charm bracelet priced at $110 that became very popular with teenagers and resulted in explosive sales growth for the company. Although it was a financial success, at least in the short term, the image of inexpensive silver jewellery alienated older, more affluent customers who now viewed Tiffany as a common brand. In response, the company increased prices on its silver products by 30 percent in an attempt to reclaim its position as a luxury jeweller.

Good marketers constantly reevaluate their brand's position to determine when to reposition it. Companies should reposition their brands to keep up with changes in the marketplace or to put a fresh spin on their stale and stodgy brand. Many companies that operate on the idea "if it ain't broke, then don't fix it" often find out too late that their brand needs a serious makeover. The result is that their positioning is so badly damaged that it takes years and huge budgets to rebuild. Proactive companies change or tinker with their positioning to keep up with market dynamics. For example, for most of General Electric Company's history, its positioning was based on product—"We Bring Good Things to Life"—which served GE very well. More recently, GE replaced that positioning with one that focuses on its rich history of innovation: "Imagination at Work."

Brand repositioning refers to a strategy in which marketers change a brand's focus to target new markets or realign the brand's core emphasis with changing market preferences.[57] Although repositioning can improve the brand's fit with its target segment or boost the vitality of old brands, it is not without costs and risks. Firms often need to spend tremendous amounts of money to make tangible changes to the product and packages, as well as intangible changes to the brand's image through various forms of promotion. These costs may not be recovered if the repositioned brand and messages are not credible to the consumer or if the firm has mistaken a fad for a long-term market trend.

brand repositioning (rebranding)
A strategy in which marketers change a brand's focus to target new markets or realign the brand's core emphasis with changing market preferences.

Yet even when they enjoy the benefits of their well-known name and reputations, brands may find it necessary to reposition, even if that means challenging hundreds of years of tradition. For example, Procter & Gamble's (P&G) Ivory soap brand first appeared in 1879, promoted with an image of purity in white, subdued packaging. The new Ivory comes in brightly coloured packages, with cyan, purple, and green splashed across the wrappers and bottles. This new approach nevertheless links to and builds on the brand's well-established position. In humorous televised ads running in select cities with strong markets for the brand, P&G mocks how complicated the use of soap has become today. Unusual soaps made to look like waffles with syrup and sugar contrast against the pure bars that Ivory continues to offer. Yet the repackaging and new advertising push definitely reflect a repositioning. The Ivory brand has long appealed to both men and women, but P&G aims to improve its annual sales of less than $100 million by making a devoted push to appeal to young moms, in addition to keeping core customers.[58]

Repositioning can change the quality image of the brand, as noted earlier in the Tiffany example.

P&G's new ad campaign is positioned to appeal to young moms, in addition to keeping its core customers.

However, WestJet successfully repositioned itself from a no-frills low-cost leader to a considerably higher quality airline by adding luxuries such as leather seats and seat-back LCD TV screens. Repositioning can breathe life into old brands. Although repositioning can improve the brand's fit with its target segment or boost the vitality of old brands, it is not without costs and risks. Firms often need to spend tremendous amounts of money to make tangible changes to the product and packages, as well as intangible changes to the brand's image through advertising. These costs may not be recovered if the repositioned brand and messages are not credible to the consumer or if the firm has mistaken a fad for a long-term market trend.

LEARNING OBJECTIVES REVIEW

 LO1   **Describe the bases marketers use to segment a market**

There is really no one "best" method to segment a market. Firms choose from various segmentation bases depending on the type of product/service they offer and their goals for the segmentation strategy. For instance, if the firm wants to identify its customers easily, geographic or demographic segmentation likely will work best. But if the firm is trying to dig deeper into why customers might buy its offering, then life-style, benefits, or loyalty segmentation work best. Geodemographic segmentation provides a nice blend of geographic, demographic, and psychographic approaches. Typically, a combination of several segmentation methods is most effective.

LO2   **Identify the criteria for determining the attractiveness of a segment and whether it is worth pursuing (targeting)**

Marketers use several criteria to assess a segment's attractiveness. First, the customer should be *identifiable*—companies must know what types of people are in the market so they can direct their efforts appropriately. Second, the market must be *reachable*—the firm must be able to reach the segment through effective communications and distribution. Third, the firm must be *responsive* to the needs of customers in a segment. It must be able to deliver a product or service that the segment will embrace. Finally, the market must be *substantial* enough to be worth pursuing. If relatively few people appear in a segment, it is probably not cost-effective to direct special marketing mix efforts toward them. Additionally, the segment must be *profitable*, both in the near term and over the lifetime of the customer.

LO3   **Explain the differences among targeting strategies: undifferentiated, differentiated, concentrated, or micromarketing**

Firms use a targeting strategy after they have identified the segments. An *undifferentiated strategy* is really no segmentation at all and works for only products or services that most consumers consider to be commodities. The difference between a *differentiated* and a *concentrated strategy* is that the differentiated approach targets multiple segments, whereas the concentrated targets only one. Larger firms with multiple product/service offerings generally use a differentiated strategy; smaller firms or those with a limited product/service offering often use a concentrated strategy. Firms that employ a *micromarketing* or *one-to-one marketing strategy* tailor their product/service offering to each customer—that is, it is custom-made. In the past, micromarketing was reserved primarily for artisans, tailors, or other craftspeople who would make items exactly as the customer wanted. Recently, however, larger manufacturers and retailers have begun experimenting with custom-made merchandise as well. Service providers, in contrast, are largely familiar with customizing their offering. Hair salons could not flourish if every customer got the same cut.

 LO4   **Define positioning and describe how firms do it**

Positioning is the "P" in the STP (segmentation, targeting, and positioning) process. It refers to how customers think about a product, service, or brand in the market relative to competitors' offerings. Firms position their products and services according to several criteria. Some focus on their offering's *value*—customers get a lot for what the product or service costs. Others determine the most *important product attributes* for customers and position their offering on the basis of those attributes. *Benefits* and *symbols* can also be used for positioning, though few products or services are associated with symbols that are compelling enough to drive people to buy. Companies may also use their dominant position in their market—*market leadership*—to position their products or services. Finally, *competition* is one of the most common positioning methods and relies on the favourable comparison of the firm's offering with the products or services marketed by competitors (head-to-head). Companies may also choose to compete by differentiating their value proposition.

KEY TERMS

- behavioural segmentation
- benefit segmentation
- brand repositioning (rebranding)
- concentrated (or niche) targeting strategy
- demographic segmentation
- differentiated targeting strategy
- geodemographic segmentation
- geographic segmentation

- ideal point
- lifestyles
- loyalty segmentation
- mass customization
- micromarketing (one-to-one marketing)
- occasion segmentation
- perceptual map
- positioning statement

- positioning
- psychographics
- PSYTE clusters
- self-concept
- self-values
- undifferentiated targeting strategy (mass marketing)
- VALS™

CONCEPT REVIEW

1. How do segmentation, targeting, and positioning add value to a company's value proposition?

2. Outline the steps in the STP process. What are some of the key decisions marketers have to make at each step?

3. List the bases that can be used to segment a market for a product or service. Which of these bases is considered to be the most difficult to use and which is the easiest? Why?

4. Describe the segmentation bases you think Coca-Cola used to develop its target segment. What kinds of products do you think this segment was buying before Coca-Cola introduced its Coke Zero brand? Thinking back to the consumer buying decision process, what kind of strategies do you think were necessary to get this segment to switch to Coke Zero?

5. List the four types of targeting strategies companies can use to serve selected market segments. What are the main points to consider before selecting one or more of these strategies? What are the advantages and disadvantages of each strategy, and how can competitors influence the strategy a company chooses?

6. Explain the difference between positioning and a positioning statement. Why do you think marketers find market positioning one of the most difficult aspects of the STP process? How can marketers try to influence the positioning of their products or services in the marketplace?

7. List four types of strategies companies could use to position their products or services in the marketplace. When Home Depot says, "You Can Do It, We Can Help," for what type of positioning is it striving?

8. What is a perceptual map? How is it used in developing positioning strategies or identifying market opportunities?

9. Why should marketers consider repositioning their brand? Explain what is meant by repositioning and the major challenges and risks inherent in repositioning.

10. An online news article suggests that Sony is thinking of repositioning its PlayStation 4 game console as a computer. Do you think that Sony can do this successfully? Give reasons. Do you think consumers will ever see the PlayStation as a computer? Why or why not?

MARKETING APPLICATIONS

1. What segmentation methods would you suggest for a small entrepreneur starting her own business selling gourmet chocolates? Justify why you would recommend those methods.

2. You have been asked to identify various segments in the market and then a potential targeting strategy. Describe the segments for a pet supply store. Justify the best targeting strategy to use.

3. Various methods are used to target markets. Identify the typical customer for each of the four methods discussed in the text.

4. How and why would a retailer use micromarketing?

5. You have been asked to evaluate the attractiveness of several potential market segments. What criteria should you use to evaluate those segments? Why are these appropriate criteria?

6. A small-business owner is trying to evaluate the profitability of different segments. What are the key factors he or she must consider? For how long should the business owner conduct the evaluation?

7. Think about the various soft drink brands that you know (e.g., Coke, Pepsi, 7-Up, Gatorade, Powerade). How do those brands position themselves in the market?

8. Put yourself in the position of an entrepreneur who is developing a new product to introduce into the market. Briefly describe the product. Then, develop the segmentation, targeting, and positioning strategy for marketing the new product. Be sure to discuss (a) the overall strategy (b) characteristics of the target market (c) why that target market is attractive, and (d) the positioning strategy. Provide justifications for your decisions.

9. Think of a specific company or organization that uses various types of promotional material to market its offerings. (The Internet, magazine ads, newspaper ads, catalogues, newspaper inserts, direct mail pieces, and flyers might all be sources of promotional materials.) Locate two or three promotional pieces for the company and use them as a basis to analyze the segment(s) being targeted. Describe the basic segmentation strategy reflected in these materials, and describe characteristics of the target market according to the materials. Be sure to include a copy of all the materials used in the analysis.

10. You have been hired recently by a large bank in its credit card marketing division. The bank has relationships with a large number of colleges and universities and prints a wide variety of credit cards featuring college and university logos, images, and the like. You have been asked to oversee the implementation of a new program targeting first-year students at the schools with which the bank has a relationship. The bank has already purchased the names and home addresses of the incoming students. You have been told that no credit checks will be required for these cards as long as the student is older than 18 years of age. The bank plans a first-day-of-school marketing blitz that includes free hats, T-shirts, and book promotions, as well as free pizza, if the students simply fill out an application. Do you think it is a good idea to offer this program to these new students?

TOOLKIT

MARKET POSITION MAP ANALYSIS

Assume you are a brand manager for a major manufacturer. You have identified a number of market segments and are trying to understand how its products are positioned relative to other manufacturers'. Use the toolkit provided on Connect to conduct a market position analysis.

NET SAVVY

1. Go to the L'Oréal Canada website (http://www.loreal paris.ca) and try to describe the segmentation approach it uses to group customers. Apply the vocabulary presented in this chapter to describe its segmentation strategy. Then click on "Haircare," and look for "Re-Nutrition." Who do you think is the target market for this product? How would you describe L'Oréal's product positioning in Canada?

2. Suppose you want to open a specialty coffee and treats shop near your university campus. You think collecting some demographic data will be a helpful starting point. Your first hunch is to use StatsCan but, from prior experience, you realize this will be difficult and time consuming. Help is on the way. Go to SRC's FreeDemographics website (http://www.freedemographics.com) and register to use this free service. Use this site to generate a report on the demographics of the area where you want to locate your coffee shop. How helpful is this site?

CHAPTER CASE STUDY

M&M MEAT SHOPS: USING DEMOGRAPHICS TO DRIVE DECISIONS[59]

Known as the store with hundreds of meal ideas but only one aisle, M&M Meat Shops is Canada's largest retail chain of specialty frozen foods, with more than 450 locations coast to coast. The demand for ready-to-heat food is increasing as home-cooked meals become more difficult in time-strapped households, an important demographic for the company.

The first store opened in October 1980, based on a consumer insight by founders Mark Nowak and Mac Voisin that it was not possible to buy restaurant-quality steaks in retail outlets. Neither Nowak, a lawyer, nor Voisin, an engineer, had much marketing experience. However, when the company started offering franchises, they recognized the need to have a segmentation methodology to help them assess potential new locations.

M&M Meat Shops uses demographics as well as a segmentation system, MOSAIC, to gain insights into their trade areas and their customers, and to help refine M&M Meat Shops' understanding of who has the best lifestyle fit for the company.

Demographic data helps the company understand whether a trade area has potential. It is demographics that highlight whether an area is, for example, experiencing growth or decline in population, whether the area is home to more apartment dwellers than home owners, as well as what the dominant language is. Segmentation systems pick up where univariate demographics leave off and help define neighbourhoods more thoroughly. Two neighbours with similar incomes, religious backgrounds, and housing can have very different lifestyles and buying habits, and it's vitally important for a marketer to be able to identify these differences.

Although its head office personnel have worked with PSYTE Canada Advantage (described earlier in this chapter), today M&M Meat Shops uses a sophisticated segmentation, MOSAIC, that classifies its customer data into one of 150 different lifestyle clusters. The MOSAIC system incorporates thousands of variables from as many areas as possible (e.g., occupation dwellings, ethnicity, mobility, house value, household income, language), which provides M&M Meat Shops with a more precise look at its trade areas and helps define its customer base.

In Ontario, one of the top clusters for M&M Meat Shops is known as "Wine with Dinner." This group is university-educated, athletic, and lives in single, detached homes with larger-than-average families. They have an average household income of $70,000 and spend a lot of money on home decor and gardening.

Using information produced through segmentation analysis efforts, M&M Meat Shops selects which target markets to pursue. Its target customer is typically a woman (age 35 and older) with a very active family life that includes two or more children. These consumers are time starved and need convenient food options. Having identified the best target markets, the company turns its efforts to finding more consumers who fit the profile and reaching them with relevant campaigns.

As the country becomes much more multicultural, ongoing analysis is conducted to understand the changing Canadian population. According to Census data, the face of Canada continues to change at a fairly rapid pace. Many of the new residents who call Canada home are new immigrants. By 2031 it is expected that more than 80 percent of Canada's population growth will

The M&M Max Card allows the company to track 94 percent of all sales transactions, gathering valuable information about consumer shopping habits.

M&M Uptown stores are designed to fit the urban lifestyle, with extended hours of operation and an edgier décor.

M&M Meat Shops uses census data combined with its MAX card loyalty program to better serve growing ethnic markets. For example, butter chicken was featured in sales flyers during Diwali celebrations.

come from immigration.[60] These new Canadians are a potentially huge market for retailers. Armed with such insights, M&M Meat Shops started to research the complexities of ethnic marketing and offer new food items such as Butter Chicken, Won Ton Soup, and Asian Style Ginger Sauce.

Although M&M Meat Shops is predominantly a suburban chain, it has launched a new urban concept called M&M Meat Shops Uptown. The first locations were in downtown Toronto and feature edgier decor than the suburban outlets. This new concept is designed to fit the urban lifestyle, with extended hours of operation as well as the inclusion of specialty products, such as indoor grills and computer kiosks, to help customers create their own menus and download recipes.[61]

Other expansion plans for M&M Meat Shops included a foray into the United States. Determining where to open the first U.S. stores was a massive undertaking. One step in this research was to compare the company's top Canadian MOSAIC clusters to U.S. MOSAIC clusters to check for similarities in lifestyle. (The Canadian and U.S. clusters are totally different.) Because these lifestyle systems are a combination of demographic and psychographic information, they help identify areas in the United States that have very similar lifestyles to M&M Meat Shops' strongest Canadian markets.

Ohio was identified as a good fit; however, the entry into the U.S. market under the MyMenu brand was ill timed, coinciding with the recession of late 2008 and throughout 2009. The company quickly changed direction. Instead of sticking with its original strategy of opening suburban stores in strip malls, it went to a store-within-a-store format. Three outlets were opened in Toledo, Maumee, and Columbus in the Andersons Store. In business since 1952, this U.S. retailer offers general merchandise, home improvement, and outdoor lawn-care products, specialty foods, and wine. While the original strategy was to expand, the company has since closed all of its U.S. locations.

Knowing it pays to retain loyal customers, the company's MAX program rewards its most loyal customers. The program also provides the company with valuable consumer insights. M&M Meat Shops says that 94 percent of all sales transactions are tracked through the program and that 93 percent of customers, or 5.7 million Canadians, have a MAX card. Data collected from the card, such as postal codes, are used to understand how far customers travel to outlets—useful information when determining locations of new stores. It also helps more narrowly focus advertising efforts to reach the core customer profile.

Segmentation data and loyalty program data are provided to franchisees to help them to increase market penetration in their trade areas and even to determine what mix of products to stock. M&M's approach adds value to franchisees, helping them to first attract and then keep their best customers.

Questions

1. Describe the type of segmentation strategy M&M Meat Shops uses to serve its suburban markets. Provide support for your answer.

2. Why would a different strategy be needed for its Uptown urban store locations?

3. Why do companies such as M&M Meat Shops need to use a combination of segmentation approaches when identifying potential target markets?

4. What are some key demographic differences M&M Meat Shops should consider for future expansion in the U.S. market?

5. Besides adapting its advertising to reflect different cultural holidays, what are some other ways M&M Meat Shops could reach out to Canada's growing ethnic population?

For more information on the resources available from McGraw-Hill Ryerson, go to www.mheducation.ca/he/solutions.

CHAPTER 7

Marketing Research

When used in games and movies, virtual reality allows people to participate in scenarios they might never encounter in daily life. Special 3D glasses and realistically rendered images create the sensation of "being there"—whether "there" is in the midst of a military operation, climbing Mt. Everest, or playing a challenging game of tennis. When applied to marketing research, this same technology provides manufacturers with valuable information about how consumers are likely to respond to new products and product displays. Used properly, virtual shopping tools provide more accurate information about customer behaviours than traditional research methods and are more efficient than field testing.[1]

Virtual store testing is not especially new. Companies such as Procter & Gamble (P&G) have been using these tools to conduct market research for more than a decade.[2] But as the technology has evolved, P&G's reliance on it to create, test, and improve package designs, shelf displays, and store layouts has increased.[3] Today, more than three-quarters of global manufacturers' business initiatives rely on virtual solution tools.

For P&G, virtual reality centres on life-sized, 3D images of new products as they might appear on a retailer's shelves, which helps create a fully interactive world. As consumers peruse the shelves, sophisticated software analyzes their reactions, providing insight into common responses to packaging and messaging. Product development teams use this information to make improvements early in the design process, which in turn increases the speed to market, reduces the number of costly physical prototypes, and maximizes the chances of success when the product actually goes live.

The technology also allows P&G to create virtual store environments for analyzing product placement strategies. Marketing researchers supply retailers with information and customer feedback from these tests to help them improve customer satisfaction and build sales. The approach can be used for a single product, such as a new type of fabric refresher aimed at sports enthusiasts. Or it can be used to research an entire line of new products in a private environment, which enables an innovating firm to protect its strategic marketing decisions from snooping competitors.[4]

Today's refinements in virtual reality for marketing research are making the software easier to use for both business decision makers and communicators. The technology has also evolved to provide remarkably realistic

LEARNING OBJECTIVES

After studying this chapter you should be able to

LO1 Identify the five steps in the marketing research process

LO2 Describe the various secondary data sources

LO3 Describe primary data collection techniques and summarize the differences between secondary data and primary data

LO4 Outline ethical issues firms encounter when conducting marketing research

graphics and interactivity, which improve insights into consumer responses.[5] Such advanced forms of market research are helping firms like Procter & Gamble understand how to serve its customers and business partners better. And better service means better profits. ∎

marketing research
A set of techniques and principles for systematically collecting, recording, analyzing, and interpreting data that can aid decision makers involved in marketing goods, services, or ideas.

As the P&G example shows, **marketing research** is a key prerequisite to successful decision making; it consists of a set of techniques and principles for systematically collecting, recording, analyzing, and interpreting data that can aid decision makers involved in marketing goods, services, or ideas.[6] When marketing managers attempt to develop their strategies, marketing research can provide valuable information that will help them make segmentation, positioning, product, place, price, and promotion decisions. Marketing research is also key to understanding topics such as consumer and B2B buying behaviour (Chapters 3 and 4); global marketing and cultural differences (Chapter 17); new product development, branding, and customer service (Chapters 8 to 10); and for assessing the effectiveness of pricing, promotions, and product and service delivery strategies (Chapters 11 to 15).

This chapter begins by discussing the five steps in the marketing research process. Then, we evaluate the various types of data used in marketing research and data collection methods. We will also examine the circumstances under which it is ethical to collect and use customer information in marketing research.

Firms invest millions of dollars in marketing research every year. Canada's market research industry is valued at just under a half-billion dollars. Some of the major players in Canada's multimillion dollar market research and polling industry include Angus Reid, COMPAS, Harris/Decima, EKOS Research Associates, Ipsos Reid, Leger Marketing, Pollara, and the Strategic Counsel. In addition, there are foreign-owned firms with offices in Canada, such as Nielsen Canada and Forrester Research. Why do marketers find this research valuable? First, it helps reduce some of the uncertainty under which they currently operate. Successful managers know when research might help their decision making and then take appropriate steps to acquire the information they need. Second, marketing research provides a crucial link between firms and their environments, which enables firms to be customer oriented because they build their strategies by using customer input and continual feedback. Third, by constantly monitoring their competitors, firms can anticipate and respond quickly to competitive moves. Fourth, ongoing marketing research can identify emerging opportunities and new and improved ways of satisfying consumer needs and wants from changes in the external environment.

Politicians and nonprofit organizations do research to understand their constituencies.

If you think market research is applicable only to corporate or retailing ventures, think again. Nonprofit organizations and governments also use research to serve their constituencies better. Political parties have been slicing and dicing the voting public for decades to determine relevant messages for different demographics. Politicians desperately want to understand who makes up the voting public to determine how to reach them. They want to know not only your political views, but also your media habits, such as what magazines you subscribe to, so they can target you more effectively.[7] To do so, they rely on the five-step marketing research process we describe in this chapter. We also discuss some of the ethical implications of collecting and using information. In Appendix 7A, we detail the concept of customer lifetime value (CLV), a popular metric to determine a customer's value to a firm.

THE MARKETING RESEARCH PROCESS

LO1

Managers consider several factors before embarking on a marketing research project. First, will the research be useful? Will it provide insights beyond what the managers already know and reduce uncertainty associated with the project? Second, is top management committed to the project and willing to abide by the results of the research? Related to both of these questions is the value of the research. Marketing research can be very expensive, and if the results won't be useful or management does not abide by the findings, it represents a waste of money. Third, should the marketing research project be small or large? A project might involve a simple analysis of data that the firm already has, or it could be an in-depth assessment that costs hundreds of thousands of dollars and takes months to complete.

The marketing research process itself consists of five steps, as shown in Exhibit 7.1. Although the stages of the marketing research process are shown as a step-by-step progression, of course, research doesn't always happen this way. Sometimes, researchers go back and forth from one step to another as the need arises. For example, marketers may establish a specific research objective, which they follow with data collection and preliminary analysis. If they uncover new information during the data collection step or if the findings of the analysis spotlight new research needs, they might redefine their objectives and begin again from a new starting point. A major automobile manufacturer once set out to identify consumer responses to its new company logo, only to discover in preliminary focus groups that some of the respondents thought the company had gone out of business! Clearly, those researchers had to regroup and set out in a different direction with an entirely different objective.

Before embarking on a research project, it is important to plan the entire project in advance. When setting up a questionnaire, marketers should consider the data collection process and anticipate the types of analyses that might produce meaningful results for decision makers. For example, open-ended questions on a questionnaire can slow down the coding process and make it difficult to run some sophisticated statistical analyses. If the decision makers want a sophisticated analysis fast, a questionnaire filled with open-ended questions may not be the best choice. By planning the entire research process well in advance of starting the project, researchers can avoid unnecessary alterations to the research plan as they move through the process. Now let's examine each step of the research process in more detail.

Step 1: Define the Research Problem and Objectives

Because research is both expensive and time consuming, it is important to establish in advance exactly what problem needs to be solved. Correctly defining the problem is one

EXHIBIT 7.1 The Marketing Research Process

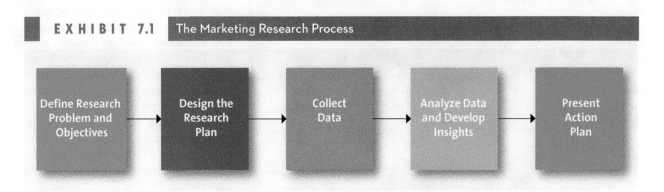

Define Research Problem and Objectives → Design the Research Plan → Collect Data → Analyze Data and Develop Insights → Present Action Plan

of the most important elements of the marketing research process. To underscore the importance of this first step, some marketing researchers claim that this aspect is the most difficult of the marketing research process. Why? If you define the problem incorrectly, you will more than likely end up with the wrong solution even though the rest of the process is done perfectly. On the contrary, if you define the problem correctly but fail to carry out the rest of the process correctly, you may end up with results that may be useless or even misleading. Once the research problem is defined, marketers must specify the research objectives or questions to be answered. Marketing research efforts and resources can be wasted if the research objectives are poorly defined.[8] Poor design arises from three major sources: basing research on irrelevant research questions, focusing on research questions that marketing research cannot answer, or addressing research questions to which the answers are already known.

Consider the following scenario: McDonald's wants a better understanding of its customers' experience. It also needs to understand how customers view the experience at Wendy's, a main competitor. Finally, McDonald's hopes to gain some insight into how it should set a price for and market its latest combo meal of a hamburger, fries, and drink. Any one of these questions could initiate a research project. The complexity of the project that the company eventually undertakes depends on how much time and resources it has available, as well as the amount of in-depth knowledge it needs. Research objectives are driven by business issues that companies want to examine and can use a wide variety of testing methods and inputs as shown in Exhibit 7.2.

When conducting research, it's also important to separate the symptoms of a problem from the actual problem. For example, Pria, the owner of a small clothing store in downtown Ottawa that caters to girls between the ages of 10 and 16, thought that the declining sales she was observing in her store were due to inadequate or poor advertising. She increased her advertising and promotions to boost sales and regain her lost customers. Unfortunately, this effort provided only temporary benefits, and the declining sales continued after the promotions ended. After hiring a marketing researcher, Pria realized that the declining sales were just a symptom of the real problem: outdated merchandise. She learned that the current target market of 10- to 16-year-olds is quite different from their predecessors, the girls who were this age when Pria first opened her store.

Step 2: Design the Research Plan

After researchers have defined the problem to be addressed, the second step is to design the market research plan. In this step, researchers identify the type of data needed and determine the type of research necessary to collect it. Recall that the objectives of the project drive the type of data needed, as outlined in Step 1. Let's look at how this second step works using the McDonald's customer experience. McDonald's needs to ask its customers about their McDonald's experience. However, because people don't always tell the whole truth in surveys, the company also may want to observe customers to see how they actually enter the stores, interact with employees, and consume the product.

The project's design might begin with available data, such as information that shows people with children often come into the restaurants at lunchtime and order Happy Meals. Then McDonald's market researchers can start to ask customers specific questions about their McDonald's experience.

McDonald's assesses its customers' market experience by examining available data, and then asks customers about their experience with products like Happy Meals.

EXHIBIT 7.2	Research Objectives		
Business Issue	**Research Objectives**	**Testing Method**	**Inputs Needed**
Evaluate new launch idea	Gain consumer feedback on new product ideas. Can also be used to evaluate changes to an existing product.	Concept testing	Product concepts including image and description, group of qualified consumers
Evaluate new flavour of cereal against other flavours	Measure consumer purchase intent for new launch with actual live product in a central, controlled environment.	Central location test (CLT)	Product concepts including image and description, control product samples, new product samples, group of qualified consumers
Test new flavour of cookies or a new formulation of laundry detergent	Measure consumer purchase intent for new launch with actual live product in their typical daily life.	Home usage test (HUT)	Product concepts including image and description, actual product samples, group of qualified consumers
Measure the effect of a major product change, like branding or significant downsizing	Quantitatively measure product appeal before and after the change. May also include qualitative feedback on specific areas.	Restager research	Product concepts for current and new product, including image and description, group of qualified consumers
Predict success of new packaging design	Measure consumer purchase intent for and appeal of packaging redesign.	Packaging testing	Product packaging including current and new designs, group of qualified consumers
Assess consumer attitudes and behaviours on a particular category such as snack foods	Understand consumer opinions and self-reported behaviours on a category of products: what they choose and avoid, why, when, where, and how it is consumed.	Usage and attitude study	Formal questionnaire, group of qualified consumers
Map out how a consumer shops the dairy aisle in a grocery store	Collect real-time observations of an individual in your specific target market performing a specific task.	Live consumer immersion	Discussion guide, moderator, consumer (one at a time)
Evaluate new idea for communications campaign	Gain qualitative feedback on a small number of topics; for example, determine preference between Campaign A and B. A moderator will guide the discussion but the participants are free to give any feedback they'd like.	Focus group	Discussion guide, advertising samples, moderator, focus group participants (4–10 at a time)

Step 3: Collect Data

Data collection begins only after the research design process. Based on the design of the project, data can be collected from secondary or primary data sources. Secondary data are pieces of information that have been collected prior to the start of the focal research project. **Secondary data** include both external and internal data sources. **Primary data**, in contrast, are those data collected to address specific research needs. Some common primary data collection methods include focus groups, in-depth interviews, and surveys. More discussion on secondary and primary data follows later in the chapter.

For our hypothetical fast-food scenario, McDonald's may decide to get relevant secondary data from external providers such as National Purchase Diary Panel and Nielsen. The data might include the prices of different ingredients, sales figures, growth or decline in the category, and advertising and promotional spending. McDonald's is likely to gather pertinent data about sales from its franchisees. However, it also wants competitor data,

secondary data
Pieces of information that have been collected prior to the start of the focal project.

primary data
Data collected to address the specific research needs/questions currently under investigation. Some primary data collection methods include focus groups, in-depth interviews, and surveys.

overall food consumption data, and other information about the quick service restaurant category, which it likely obtains from appropriate syndicated data providers. Based on the data, it might decide to follow up with some primary data using a survey.

No company can ask every customer their opinions or observe every customer, so researchers must choose a group of customers who represent the customers of interest, or a sample, and then generalize their opinions to describe all customers with the same characteristics. They may choose the sample participants at random to represent the entire customer market. Or they may choose to select the sample on the basis of some characteristic, such as whether they have children, so they can research the experience associated with buying a Happy Meal.

Marketing researchers use various methods of asking questions to measure the issues they are tackling. Different types of scales are used to measure certain concepts such as attitudes, perceived quality, perceived value, loyalty, and convenience. In our hypothetical McDonald's scenario, assume the research team has developed a questionnaire (see Exhibit 7.3), using a few different types of questions. Section A measures the customer's experience in McDonald's, Section B measures the customer's experience in Wendy's, Section C measures the customer's habits at McDonald's, and Section D measures customer demographics.[9]

Furthermore, suppose the research team administered the survey to 1000 customers. The results of the first question, "McDonald's food tastes good," were as follows:

1	2	3	4	5
Strongly Disagree	**Disagree**	**Neither Agree nor Disagree**	**Agree**	**Stongly Agree**
N = 50	N = 50	N = 100	N = 300	N = 500

Their responses are indicated by "N = ." Marketers could report several metrics. But two common metrics would be that 80 percent [(300 + 500)/1,000] of respondents had high satisfaction since they responded to "Agree" or "Strongly Agree." It could also be reported that satisfaction was high because the mean was 4.15 [(50 × 1 + 50 × 2 + 100 × 3 + 300 × 4 + 500 × 5)/1,000] on the 5-point scale.

Step 4: Analyze Data and Develop Insights

The next step in the marketing research process—analyzing and interpreting the data—should be both thorough and methodical. To generate meaningful information, researchers analyze and make use of the collected data. In this context, **data** can be defined as raw numbers or other factual information that, on their own, have limited value to marketers. However, when the data are interpreted, they become **information**, which results from organizing, analyzing, and interpreting the data, and putting it into a form that is useful to marketing decision makers. For example, a checkout scanner in the grocery store collects sales data about individual consumer purchases. Not until those data are categorized and examined do they provide information about which products and services were purchased together or how an in-store promotional activity translated into sales.

For example, a cologne firm learns from secondary data sources that its product is priced lower than its competition, it spends more money on traditional advertising in fashion magazines, and it is slowly losing market share to a new upstart competitor. Putting these disparate data points together provides information that indicates the need to find out what is so good about the competitor's new cologne. The firm commissions a series of focus groups, which is useful in developing a survey of users of its cologne and of its competitor. The survey provides conclusive information that the firm uses to change its strategy. In particular, it found that its product's scent was a

data
Raw numbers or other factual information of limited value.

information
Data that has been organized, analyzed, interpreted, and converted into a useful form for decision makers.

EXHIBIT 7.3   A Hypothetical Fast-Food Survey

Please take a few minutes to tell us about your experience at McDonald's and Wendy's. For each question, please respond by checking the box that applies or writing your response in the space provided.

Please Evaluate Your Experience at McDonald's

A. McDonald's

	Strongly Disagree 1	Disagree 2	Neither Agree or Disagree 3	Agree 4	Stongly Agree 5
McDonald's food tastes good	☐	☐	☐	☑	☐
McDonald's is clean	☐	☐	☐	☑	☐
McDonald's has low prices	☐	☐	☐	☑	☐

B. Wendy's

	Strongly Disagree 1	Disagree 2	Neither Agree or Disagree 3	Agree 4	Stongly Agree 5
Wendy's food tastes good	☐	☐	☐	☑	☐
Wendy's is clean	☐	☐	☐	☑	☐
Wendy's has low prices	☐	☐	☐	☑	☐

C. McDonald's

	Never	1–2 times	3–4 times	More than 5 times
In the last month, how many times have you been to McDonald's?	☐	☐	☐	☑

On average, how much do you spend each visit at McDonald's? $ _____

What is your favourite item at McDonald's?   _____

D. Please Tell Us About Yourself

	under 16	17–24	25–35	36+
What is your age?	☐	☐	☐	☐

	Male	Female		
What is your gender?	☐	☐		

little too strong and wasn't as appealing to its younger target market. It also discovered that peers have a tremendous influence on scent preferences. So the company decided to tone down the scent and reapportion its promotional budget to include more innovative social media initiatives through Twitter, Facebook, and YouTube. Data analysis might be as simple as calculating the average purchases of different customer segments or as complex as forecasting sales by market segment by using elaborate statistical techniques.

For the McDonald's example, we can summarize the results of the survey (from Exhibit 7.3) in Exhibit 7.4. Both McDonald's and Wendy's scored the same on the

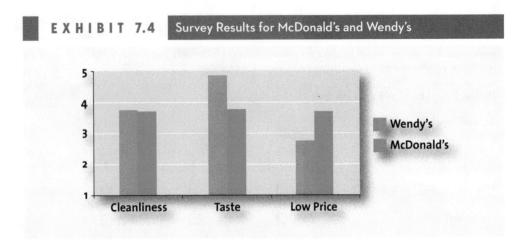

EXHIBIT 7.4 Survey Results for McDonald's and Wendy's

cleanliness of the restaurant, but McDonald's had lower prices, while Wendy's food tasted better. McDonald's may want to improve the taste of its food to better compete with Wendy's.

The purpose of converting data to information is to describe, explain, predict, and/or evaluate a particular situation and then use it to develop insights. For example, Pria, the downtown Ottawa-based retailer of tween clothing, learned that her core customers live in various suburbs around downtown. This piece of data takes on new meaning when she learns that none of these customers were drawn to her store by a clever and expensive direct mail campaign. By analyzing data she collected through a survey, she discovered that her core customers are working professionals who are drawn to the store when they walk by it on their way to and from work, not people from the upscale apartments in the downtown region whom she targeted with her direct mail advertisements.

Data analysis might be as simple as calculating the average purchases of different customer segments or as complex as forecasting sales by market segment by using elaborate statistical techniques. Coinstar, a worldwide leader in self-service coin counting, has begun analyzing marketing research in increasingly sophisticated ways. The company operates machines in more than 10,000 supermarkets in Canada, the United States, and the United Kingdom. Consumers use the machines, which can count up to 600 coins per minute, to process large volumes of change that they exchange for a voucher good for cash or groceries. Since it was founded in 1991, the company has tried to identify new and profitable locations on an ongoing basis as demand for its services continues to grow. When the company was small, coming up with "best guesses"

Coinstar, a worldwide leader of self-service coin-counting machines, uses sophisticated regression models to identify and rank potential locations for its machines.

of prime locations based on intuition worked out well, but Coinstar researchers recently developed regression models to identify and rank potential locations for its "green machines." This approach greatly improved Coinstar's ability to find prospective locations and forecast those areas that had the best potential for growth and profitability. The company can now capitalize on the estimated $7.7 billion in coins sitting in people's homes, waiting to be converted to paper money or grocery purchases.[10]

It is important for market researchers to analyze and interpret the data in an objective manner. They should not try to hide or sugar-coat findings that are different from what they had hoped for. Misinterpreting the findings or manipulating the statistics to suit the researcher's hunch or prediction could lead to the wrong decision, which could have serious consequences for marketers. The temptation to lie with statistics is something market researchers must always be aware of and try to avoid.

Step 5: Present Action Plan

In the final phase of the marketing research process, the analyst prepares the results and presents them to decision makers, who undertake appropriate marketing actions and strategies. A typical marketing research presentation includes an executive summary, the body of the report (which discusses the research objectives, methodology used, and detailed findings), the conclusions, the limitations, and appropriate supplemental tables, figures, and appendices. To be effective, written reports must be short, interesting, methodical, precise, lucid, and free of errors.[11] Furthermore, the reports should use a style appropriate to the audience, be devoid of technical jargon, and include recommendations that managers can actually implement.

Let's go back to the hypothetical McDonald's scenario. According to the research findings, the company is doing fine in terms of cleanliness (as are its competitors), it is perceived to have lower prices, and the taste of its food could be improved. Based on the analysis and insights gained, McDonald's could hire chefs to improve its menu and food offerings. It would also want to highlight these additional offerings in its advertisements and promotions by pointing out how they were created by chefs. McDonald's should also consider performing additional pricing research to determine whether its lower prices are positively impacting sales and profits, or whether it should price more competitively with Wendy's. Now let's take a closer look at sources of secondary and primary data.

SECONDARY DATA

LO2

A marketing research project often begins with a review of the relevant secondary data. Secondary data might come from free or very inexpensive external sources such as census data, information from trade associations, books, journal articles, and reports published in magazines and newspapers. Although readily accessible, these inexpensive sources may not be specific or timely enough to solve the marketer's research needs and objectives. Firms also can purchase more specific or applicable secondary data from specialized research firms. Finally, secondary sources can be accessed through internal sources, including the company's sales invoices, customer lists, and other reports generated by the company itself.

In political settings, such secondary data can be critical for candidates running for office. Major political parties develop proprietary databases that contain vast information about voters, broken down by demographic and geographic information. Before a local politician, canvasser, or poll taker even knocks on doors in a neighbourhood, he or she likely knows which houses are inhabited by retirees, who has a subscription to *The Globe and Mail*, and for whom the residents said they voted in the last election. All these traits can give hints about the voters' likely concerns, which a good politician can address immediately upon knocking on the door. Such research also can dictate tactics for designing broader campaign materials, or zero in on very specific issues.

Internal Secondary Data One of the most valuable resources firms have at their disposal is their rich cache of customer information and purchase history. However, it can be difficult to make sense of the millions or even billions of pieces of individual data, which are stored in large computer files called data warehouses. For this reason, firms find it necessary to use data-mining techniques to extract valuable information from their databases.

Data mining uses a variety of statistical analysis tools to uncover previously unknown patterns in the data or relationships among variables. Some retailers try to customize their product and service offerings to match the needs of their customers.

data mining
The use of statistical analysis tools to search for patterns in data or relationships among variables.

Marketers use data-mining techniques to determine what items people buy at the same time so they can be promoted and displayed together.

For instance, the U.K. grocer Tesco uses its loyalty card to collect massive amounts of information about its individual customers. Every time a loyalty card member buys something, the card is scanned, and the store captures key purchase data, specific to that member. But these specific data are basically useless until Tesco mines and analyzes them to identify three income groups: upscale, middle income, and less affluent. With this mined information, Tesco has been able to create appealing private-label product offerings for each group, according to their preferences, and began targeting promotions to each customer according to his or her income classification. Since 2000, Tesco's market share has grown by more than 20 percent.[12]

If you watch content on Netflix, your viewing habits become valuable data that are added to a global database and mined for insights. The algorithm at the core of the Netflix software records every action subscribers take, allowing the company to analyze what content you watch, at what time of day, and how much you watch at a given time. Correlations can then be established, for example, between actors and movies, movie genres, or actors themselves, and used to make recommendations to subscribers. The software also identifies what scenes in an episode or movie are watched the most, and if scenes get skipped, which can then be compared to user reviews and ratings. Although collecting data from one person would not prove very helpful, a wealth of data can be mined from 36 million subscribers.

Data mining can also enable a home improvement retailer such as Lowe's to learn that 25 percent of the time its customers buy a garden hose, they also purchase a sprinkler. With such information, the retailer may decide to put the garden hoses next to the sprinklers in the store. Outside the retail realm, an investment firm might use statistical techniques to group clients according to their income, age, type of securities purchased, and prior investment experience. This categorization identifies different segments to which the firm can offer valuable packages that meet their specific needs. The firm also can tailor separate marketing programs to each of these segments. Data mining thus can be useful for a broad range of situations and organizations. By analyzing the enormous amount of information that it possesses about its customers, companies have developed statistical models that help identify when a customer is dissatisfied with his or her service. Once the company identifies an unhappy customer, it can follow up and proactively address that customer's issues. By mining customer data and information, the company also reduced its churn levels. Churn is the number of participants who discontinue use of a service, divided by the average number of total participants.

Overall, firms hope to use data mining to generate customer-based analytics that they can apply to their strategic decision making, and thereby make good customers better, and make better customers their best. Firms can also use secondary data to assess the profitability of their customers by determining the customer lifetime value (CLV). We offer more details about calculating CLV in Appendix 7A.

External Secondary Data   Some sources of external secondary data can be accessed quickly and at relatively low cost. For example, Statistics Canada data on retail trade provides data about sales of different types of retail establishments either free or inexpensively. These patterns may be the only accurate sources available to a new small business that wants to determine the size of its potential market. For such a firm, gathering accurate and comprehensive data on its own would be quite difficult. Researchers must ensure that the secondary data they use, especially from external sources, are current and relevant, and can shed light on the research problem or objectives. More examples of external secondary data are listed in Exhibits 7.5 and 7.6.

Sometimes, however, secondary data are not adequate to meet researchers' needs. Because the data initially were acquired for some purpose other than the research question at hand, they may not be completely relevant. For instance, Statistics Canada's Census is a great source for demographic data about a particular market area, and it can be easily accessed at a low cost. However, the data are collected only every 10 years, so they quickly become outdated. For example, if a firm were interested in opening a retail flooring store in 2018, it would have to rely on Statistics Canada Census data

---

EXHIBIT 7.5 Sample List of Sources for Secondary Data[13]

Guides, Indexes, and Directories
Business Periodicals Index
Canadian Almanac and Directory
Canadian News Index
Canadian Periodical Index
Canadian Small Business Index and
   Directory
Canadian Trade Index
Directory of Canadian Associations
Fraser's Canadian Trade Directory
Predicasts F&S Index
Scott's Directories
Standard Periodical Directory

Periodicals and Newspapers
Advertising Age
Adweek
American Demographics
Business Horizons
Canadian Business
Canadian Consumer
Canadian Grocer
Forbes
Fortune
Harvard Business Review
Journal of Advertising
Journal of Marketing Management
Journal of Personal Selling and Sales
Management
Journal of Small Business Management
Marketing Magazine
Marketing & Media Decisions
Marketing News
Canadian Grocer
Sales and Marketing Management
The Globe and Mail
Financial Post
Financial Post Magazine
The Wall Street Journal

Databases
CANSIM (Statistics Canada)
CompuServe
Dialog
Dow Jones
Factiva
FPinfomart
Infoglobe
LexisNexis
SEDAR
SymphonyIRI Group

Statistics Canada and Other Government Publications
Annual Retail Trade
Canadian Economic Observer
Canada Yearbook
Family Expenditure Guide
Market Research Handbook
Statistics Canada Catalogue
Western Economic Diversification Canada
Ontario Ministry for Economic Development
   and Trade
Department of Foreign Affairs and Trade
U.S. Census
Stat-USA

Trade Sources
Aberdeen Research
Nielsen
Conference Board of Canada
Dun & Bradstreet Canada
Financial Post Publishing
Find/SVP
Gale Research
Interactive Advertising Bureau
Jupiter Research
Forrester Research
MacLean Hunter Research Bureau
MapInfo Canada
Predicasts International

Online Sources
Websites of competitors
White papers from industry associations
Search engines
Industry publication websites
Competitive annual reports
Business and strategy sites
   (e.g., http://www.canadianbusiness.com)
News alerts and online news searches
   (e.g., Google Alerts)
Finance sites for publicly traded companies
   (e.g., Yahoo! Finance)
Wikipedia (Always validate data from here!)
The Free Library
   (http://www.thefreelibrary.com)

EXHIBIT 7.6	**Syndicated Data Providers in Canada and the United States and Their Services**
Bureau of Broadcasting Measurement (http://bbm.ca)	Provides broadcast measurement and consumer behaviour data, as well as intelligence to broadcasters, advertisers, and agencies on audience behaviours during and after broadcasts.
GfK Mediamark Research Inc. (http://www.gfkmri.com)	Supplies multimedia audience research pertaining to media and marketing planning for advertised brands.
GfK NOP (http://www.gfknop.com)	The mKids US research study tracks mobile telephone ownership and usage, brand affinities, and entertainment habits of American youth between 12 and 19 years of age.
Ipsos Canada, Harris/Decima, Leger Marketing, Angus Reid, SES Research, EKOS Research Associates, The Strategic Counsel, Pollara, and COMPAS	Provides polling services and marketing research on all aspects of marketing, including loyalty, branding, media analysis, pricing, position, image enhancement, customer satisfaction, focus groups, online panels, and surveys across many industries.
J.D. Power and Associates (http://www.jdpower.com)	Widely known for its automotive ratings, the company produces quality and customer satisfaction research for a variety of industries.
National Purchase Diary Group (http://www.npd.com)	Tracking services provide information about product movement and consumer behaviour in a variety of industries.
Nielsen (http://www.nielsen.com)	With its market measurement services, the company tracks the sales of consumer packaged goods, gathered at the point of sale in retail stores of all types and sizes.
Print Measurement Bureau (http://www.pmb.ca)	Provides single-source data on print readership, nonprint media exposure, product usage, and lifestyles of Canadians. It uses an annual sample of 24,000 to measure the readership of more than 115 publications and consumer usage of more than 2,500 products and brands.
Research and Markets (http://www.researchandmarkets.com)	Promotes itself as a "one-stop shop" for market research and data from most leading publishers, consultants, and analysts.
Roper Centre for Public Opinion Research (http://www.ropercenter.uconn.edu)	The General Social Survey is one of the United States longest-running surveys of social, cultural, and political indicators.
Simmons Market Research Bureau (http://www.smrb.com)	Reports on the products American consumers buy, the brands they prefer, and their lifestyles, attitudes, and media preferences.
Yankelovich (http://www.yankelovich.com)	The MONITOR tracks the consumer attitudes, values, and lifestyles shaping the American marketplace.

collected in 2011, which would be seven years old. If it hoped to locate in an area where housing starts are projected to grow rapidly in the next three to four years, these data would not include any of these new housing developments and thus would not provide much in the way of insights.

Although the secondary data described above is either free or inexpensive and can be quickly accessed, they may not always be adequate to answer the research objective. Under these circumstances, marketers may find it useful to purchase external secondary data called **syndicated data**, which are data available for a fee from commercial research firms such as SymphonyIRI Group, National Purchase Diary Panel, Nielsen, and Leger Marketing. Exhibit 7.6 contains information about various firms that provide syndicated data. For our hypothetical cologne example, the pertinent data available from these sources might include the prices of various colognes, sales figures, growth or decline in the category, and advertising and promotional spending. Consumer packaged-goods firms that sell to wholesalers often lack the means to gather pertinent data directly from the retailers that sell their products to consumers, which

syndicated data
Data available for a fee from commercial research firms such as Symphony IRI Group, National Diary Panel, Nielsen, and Leger Marketing.

makes syndicated data a valuable resource for them. Some syndicated data providers also offer information about shifting brand preferences and product usage in households, which they gather from consumer panels.

Scanner data are obtained from scanner readings of UPC codes at checkout counters and used in quantitative research. Whenever you go into your local grocery store, your purchases are rung up by using scanner systems. The data from these purchases are likely to be acquired by leading marketing research firms, such as SymphonyIRI Group or Nielsen. They use this information to help leading consumer packaged-goods firms (e.g., Kellogg's, Pepsi, and Kraft) assess what is happening in the marketplace. For example, a firm can determine what would happen to sales if it reduced its price by 10 percent in a given month. Did sales increase, decrease, or stay the same?

Panel data are information collected from a group of consumers (the panel) over time. The data collected from the panelists often include records of what they have purchased (i.e., secondary data), as well as their responses to survey questions that the client gives to the panel to ask the panelists (i.e., primary data). Secondary panel data thus might show that when Diet Pepsi is offered at a deep discount, 80 percent of usual Diet Coke consumers switch to Diet Pepsi. Primary panel data could give insights into what they think of each option.

Leger Marketing, one of the largest Canadian-owned independent marketing research and polling firms, has an online panel of 350,000 people that represents various consumer segments of the Canadian population. This impressive panel makes it possible for Leger Marketing to complete surveys among the general public and more-specific consumer segments. It is therefore hardly surprising that Leger Marketing can offer marketers a 48-hour service—a solution for businesses and decision makers who wish to receive reliable information quickly from a large representative sample of consumers regarding their marketing campaigns, products, and brands. Leger Marketing offers its clients strategic advice in a wide array of areas, including media and advertising analysis, marketing planning, market research, product launch, segmentation analysis, positioning, customer satisfaction and loyalty strategies, pricing and packaging strategies, mystery shoppers,

scanner data
A type of quantitative research that uses data obtained from scanner readings of UPC codes at checkout counters.

panel data
A type of quantitative research that involves collecting information from a group of consumers (the panel) over time; data collected may be from a survey or a record of purchases.

Syndicated external secondary data are scanner readings of UPC codes at checkout counters (left) and from panel data collected from consumers that electronically record their purchases (right).

and image assessment. It also offers website analytics, which marketers can use to evaluate and improve the performance of their websites.[14]

Overall though, both panel and scanner data provide firms with a comprehensive picture of what consumers are buying or not buying. The key difference between scanner research and panel research is how the data get aggregated. Scanner research typically focuses on weekly consumption of a particular product at a given unit of analysis (e.g., individual store, chain, region); panel research focuses on the total weekly consumption by a particular person or household. We discuss how marketing researchers use panel data to answer specific research questions further in the primary data section.

Remember, when it comes to secondary data, marketers must pay careful attention to how the secondary data were collected. Despite the great deal of data available on the Internet and elsewhere, easy access does not ensure that the data are trustworthy. Without knowing the research design, for instance, information pertaining to the purpose of the research, sample size, respondents, response rate, questions asked, and so on, researchers could make wrong or misleading inferences or conclusions. The Internet is a huge repository of all sorts of information about consumers, including shopping behaviours, attitudes, perceptions, and even emotions. Marketers are increasingly relying on technologies to mine this data to help them learn more about customers so they can serve them better. In Appendix 7A, we explain how secondary data can be used to assess customer lifetime value (CLV), a popular marketing metric to determine a customer's value to a firm.

L03   PRIMARY DATA COLLECTION TECHNIQUES

In many cases, the information researchers need is available only through primary data, or data collected to address the specific research needs/questions currently under investigation. Marketers collect primary data by using a variety of means, such as observing consumer behaviour, conducting focus groups, or surveying customers by using the mail, telephone, in-person interviews, or the Internet. Primary data collection can help eliminate some of the problems inherent to secondary data. Depending on the nature of the research problem, the primary data collection can use a qualitative or a quantitative approach.

A major advantage of primary research is that it can be tailored to fit the research questions; however, it also has its own set of disadvantages. For one thing, it is usually more costly to collect primary than secondary data, and the collection typically takes longer. Furthermore, marketers often require extensive training and experience to design and collect primary data that are unbiased, valid, and reliable. For a summary of the advantages and disadvantages of each type of research, see Exhibit 7.7. Biased data results when, for example, the sample does not represent the entire population, researchers inject their own biases by the way they ask questions or try to get respondents to answer in specific ways, or the respondents may be the wrong people or provide answers they think researchers want to hear.

qualitative research
Attempts to begin to understand the phenomenon of interest; also provides initial information when the problem lacks any clear definition.

Exploratory in nature, **qualitative research** attempts to begin to understand the phenomenon of interest; it also provides initial information that helps the researcher more clearly formulate the research problem or objectives. Qualitative research is more informal than quantitative research methods and includes observation, following social media sites, in-depth interviews, focus groups, and projective techniques (see Exhibit 7.8). Sustainable Marketing 7.1 shows how researchers are using qualitative research methods to develop a better understanding of how organizations can build sustainability into their organizational culture.

Data collection through primary research requires that the researcher makes several important decisions. These decisions include which methods to use (see Exhibit 7.8 for a list of methods), what types of sampling plan are best in light of the research objective,

E X H I B I T   7.7 | Advantages and Disadvantages of Secondary and Primary Data

Type	Examples	Advantages	Disadvantages
Secondary Research	• Census data • Sales invoices • Internet information • Books • Journal articles • Syndicated data	• Saves time in collecting data because they are readily available • Reduces data collection costs	• Information may not be precisely relevant to information needs • Information may not be as timely as needed • Sources may not be original; therefore, usefulness is an issue • Methodologies for collecting data may not be relevant or may contain bias in the subject matter
Primary Research	• Observed consumer behaviour • Focus groups • In-depth interviews • Surveys • Experiments	• Is specific to the immediate data needs and topic at hand • Offers behavioural insights generally not available from secondary research	• Information is usually more costly to collect • Data typically takes longer to collect • It often requires more sophisticated training and experience to design and collect unbiased, valid, and reliable data

what types of research instruments (e.g., questionnaire, observation) to use, how the research instrument should be designed (described below), and how best to contact potential respondents (telephone, online, in-person, or by mail). Improper execution of any of these important aspects of primary data collection could seriously reduce the reliability and validity of the research study.

Simply put, **reliability** is the extent to which you will get the same result if the study is repeated under identical situations.[15] For example, on a Saturday in August you randomly stop shoppers in a mall and ask them to fill out a short questionnaire about why they shop at that particular mall. Let's say your data analysis shows that the reason they shop at that mall is because they get very good deals. Now, if you were to repeat the study in the same mall, using the same questionnaire, on another Saturday, and randomly ask shoppers to fill out the questionnaire, you should find the same result: people shop at the mall because they get good deals. If you found otherwise, then the reliability of your study is called into question. Validity is the extent to which the study actually measures what it is supposed to measure.[16] For example, suppose you want to measure consumers' trust in online retailers by using a questionnaire. **Validity** seeks to determine whether the questions you asked on the questionnaire actually measure online trust or if they measure some other construct. It is important to note that a market research study must be both reliable and valid for it to be useful.

One very important aspect of market research that can affect the reliability and validity of a study is the sampling plan. Often it is too difficult, impractical, or costly to study the entire group of consumers, so marketers usually select a **sample**, a segment

reliability
The extent to which the same result is achieved when a study is repeated under identical situations.

validity
The extent to which a study measures what it is supposed to measure.

sample
A segment or subset of the population that adequately represents the entire population of interest.

E X H I B I T   7.8 | Qualitative Versus Quantitative Data Collection

Sustainable Marketing 7.1 — Embedding Sustainability in the Organizational Culture[17]

Going green, eco-awareness, corporate social responsibility, and the triple bottom line (people, planet, and profit) are all terms that organizations are using to redefine their organizational strategies. Many companies are striving to incorporate sustainability practices into their corporate cultures. They realize that to stay competitive they need to embrace sustainability strategies that will create long-term value for stakeholders. However, with little information available on how to implement sustainability practices, organizations are apprehensive about how to make sustainability a part of their corporate culture.

Research is being jointly conducted by the Network for Business Sustainability, which operates out of Ivey School of Business, and Canadian Business for Social Responsibility, which is a nonprofit business organization. The objective of the research is to provide organizations with a framework for incorporating sustainability into their corporate culture. The project is designed so that information and data can be collected from a few organizations that are successfully implementing sustainability initiatives. These organizations include LoyaltyOne, which is using eco-friendly Smart cars as company transportation when employees need to travel

for business, and InterfaceFLOR, which is part of a Canada-wide effort to divert used carpeting from landfills. The data being collected is linked to factors that contribute to the success of a sustainability strategy. Success is largely attributed to commitment from both employees and management. Interviews and panel discussions are conducted to gauge levels of commitment. Questions used to demonstrate the level of organizational commitment may include the following: What types of initiatives are being undertaken? How much of our resources are being devoted to these initiatives?

After the data is collected, it will be compiled, analyzed, and interpreted into useful and meaningful information. This information will be presented in a report about best sustainable practices. The report will provide a reference point for many organizations that are striving to make corporate sustainability a part of their cultures.

Because a systematic research process was used to define the objectives, design the study, collect relevant data, and interpret results, many organizations are being provided with reliable information that could enable them to successfully develop and implement their own sustainability strategies and cultures.

---

or subset of the population that adequately represents the entire population of interest. For example, if you are interested in studying the loyalty of Canadian teenage boys to brand-name clothing, then your population is all Canadian teenage boys and your sample is the small subset of boys selected for your study. How you select the sample is also very important. Three important questions that must be answered are (1) who should be surveyed, (2) how big should the sample be, and (3) what types of sampling procedure to use; for example, simple random sampling, convenience sampling, stratified sampling, or cluster sampling. Each of these sampling procedures has its advantages and disadvantages, and the decision as to which one to use will depend on the research objectives of the study. Although there is a formula in statistics to calculate required sample size, as a rule of thumb, sample sizes should be large enough to ensure the reliability of the study. Generally, larger samples tend to yield more reliable results up to a certain point.

quantitative research
Provides the information needed to confirm preliminary insights, which managers can use to pursue appropriate courses of action.

If the firm is ready to move beyond preliminary insights gained from qualitative research, it is likely ready to engage in **quantitative research**, which provides the information needed to confirm those insights and that managers can use to pursue appropriate courses of action. For marketing researchers, quantitative research offers a means to confirm implicit hunches through surveys, formal studies such as specific experiments, scanner and panel data, or some combination of these (see Exhibit 7.8, right side). Quantitative research also enables researchers to test their prediction or **hypothesis**, which is a statement or proposition predicting a particular relationship among multiple variables. The following is an example of a hypothesis: customer satisfaction leads to or is positively related to customer loyalty.

hypothesis
A statement or proposition predicting a particular relationship among multiple variables that can be tested through research.

We now examine each of these primary data collection techniques, starting with the qualitative and ending with the quantitative. Exhibit 7.9 highlights some of the differences between these methods. Many research projects use qualitative research as the first phase of the research process and then follow it up with quantitative research.

EXHIBIT 7.9	Advantages and Disadvantages of Secondary and Primary Data	
Research Project Components	**Qualitative Research**	**Quantitative Research**
Research purpose	General: to generate preliminary insights about people, relationships, feelings, perceptions, a situation, or even the discovery of new ideas	Specific: to verify insights and aid in selecting a course of action
Data needs	Fuzzy	Clear
Data sources	Ill defined	Well defined
Data collection form	Open-ended, rough	Usually structured
Sample	Relatively small, often not randomly drawn; subjectively selected to maximize generalization of insights	Relatively large and randomly drawn; objectively selected to permit generalization of findings
Data collection	Often flexible; no set procedure	Generally rigid; well laid out procedure
Data analysis	Typically nonquantitative—mainly interpretive and subjective based on content analysis	Formal; typically quantitative—descriptive or predictive based on statistical analysis
Inferences/Recommendations	More tentative than final	More final than tentative
Researcher skills	Need strong interpersonal communication, observational, interpretation of text or visual data skills	Need strong statistical analysis and interpretation of numbers skills

Sources: A. Parasuraman, D. Grewal, and R. Krishnan, *Marketing Research*, 2nd ed. Copyright © 2007 by Houghton Mifflin Company; J. Hair Jr., R. Bush, and D. Ortinau, *Marketing Research in the Digital Information Environment*, 4th ed. McGraw-Hill Irwin, 2009. Adapted with permission.

Qualitative Research Methods

Observation The *observation* research method entails examining purchase and consumption behaviours through personal means or the use of technology, such as video camera or other tracking devices. For example, researchers might observe customers while they shop or when they go about their daily lives, during which processes they use a variety of products. Observation can last for a very brief period of time (e.g., two hours watching teenagers shop for clothing in the mall), or it may take days or weeks (e.g., researchers live with families to observe their use of products). When consumers are unable to articulate their experiences, observation research becomes particularly useful. How else could researchers determine which educational toys babies choose to play with or confirm purchase details that consumers might not be able to recall accurately?

Ethnography is an observational method that studies people in their daily lives and activities in their homes, work, and communities. It is often used to determine how consumers might use a product. This type of research yields insights and intimate details that respondents may not be able to articulate or otherwise share. It is increasingly being used by companies (e.g., Unilever, P&G, Miller Brewing Co.). Ethnographic studies require highly trained researchers. They often use video cameras, audio recording devices, and diaries to keep detailed records of their observations. Analysis of ethnographic data requires very experienced and knowledgeable market researchers to make sense of hours of video tapes, audio tapes, or a volume of notes from the researcher's diary.

Observation may be the best method, and sometimes the only way, to determine how consumers might use a product, and therefore be useful for designing and marketing

observation
A qualitative research method that entails examining purchase and consumption behaviours through personal or video camera scrutiny.

ethnography
An observational method that studies people in their daily lives and activities in their homes, work, and communities.

By watching women in rural China wash their hair, Procter & Gamble learned that even their poorest customers wanted beautiful hair, but it has to be packaged affordably.

it. By watching women wash their hair in a rural town in China, Procter & Gamble recognized the fallacy of its assumption that the poorest consumers were only interested in functionality of a product—how to get hair clean. One woman struggled to find ways to wash her long hair effectively, even in the face of severe water shortages, rather than cut off what she considered the source of her beauty. Based on their research, P&G has added value by selling Rejoice shampoo inexpensively ($1.50) to a market that was using alternative options such as laundry detergent. Other observations pushed P&G to develop a more skin-sensitive laundry detergent after noting how many people in developing markets wash their clothes by hand.[18]

These insights might be helpful, both for the company that gathers them and for consumers who ultimately benefit from better products. But Ethical Dilemma 7.1 also raises a key question: Should people be informed that they are being watched?

Social Media   Social media sites are a booming source of data for marketers. Marketers have realized that social media can provide valuable information that could aid their marketing research and strategy endeavours. In particular, contributors to social media sites rarely are shy about providing their opinions about the firm's own products or its competitors' offerings. If companies can monitor, gather, and mine these vast social media data, they can learn a lot about their customers' likes, dislikes, and preferences. They then might cross-reference such social media commentary with consumers' past purchases to derive a better sense of what they want. Customers also appear keen to submit their opinions about their friends' purchases, interests, polls, and blogs.

Blogs in particular represent valuable sources of marketing research insights. Marketers are paying attention to online reviews about everything from restaurants to running shoes to recycling.[19] On the Videogum blog, the bylined writers invite constant commentary from a community of readers, who go by the collective nickname "Monsters." Their reviews are tongue-in-cheek and a little mischievous, but they also offer justifications and reasons for why the movie *Drive* was one of the best of the year, and then why its star Ryan Gosling also qualifies as one of the 10 best actors.[20] The Truth About Cars blog is known for its unflinchingly objective reviews of various makes and models, as well as discussions about the industry as a whole, marketing tactics, and global competition, among other topics.[21]

Part of what makes blogs so valuable is also what makes them challenging for firms. Bloggers are usually, but not always, unaffiliated with the companies that produce the items they review, which means they have no reason to hold back from negative commentary. When ConAgra tried a hidden camera experiment with a group of food bloggers, it suffered significant backlash throughout the blogosphere. It invited the writers to a dinner, supposedly with a gourmet chef, then fed them a frozen lasagna meal to gauge their responses. Not only did the victims of the prank find it less than funny, they also blasted ConAgra for exposing them, without their permission, to the preservatives and processed ingredients contained in the frozen dinners.[22]

Another creative use of social media for market research involves building online communities for companies. When it considered the launch of its South Beach

Ethical Dilemma 7.1 Watching Consumers

How does sitting in a mall or standing in a store checking out the people in the corner add up to bona fide market research? Well, for Paco Underhill and his company Envirosell, that's just another day on the job.

Envirosell's wide-ranging projects encompass firms in a broad variety of industries. According to its mission statement, Envirosell focuses "on how people, products and spaces interrelate. Our research environments, once rooted in bricks and mortar retail, now span to cover spaces as huge and chaotic as train stations and airports. We've worked in libraries, doctor offices, model homes, showrooms, and every kind of food service imaginable. Our clients are merchants, consumer goods manufacturers, banks, trade associations, not for profits, government agencies and the full spectrum of design, advertising and marketing agencies."[23]

Envirosell observed consumers in 12 Staples stores, videotaping their movements through the stores for eight hours each research day, as a means to better understand how consumers actually shopped around the various departments to gather products, view signs, and interact with sales associates. Researchers also conducted interviews with shoppers. On the basis of the results of these studies, Staples rolled out a new store format that focuses on solving customer problems by combining service with self-service rather than just selling individual items. Staples' sales associates can now provide a higher level of service in those areas that demand it, and the new store format gives customers the tools to be self-sufficient if they choose to browse on their own.

Using observational research, marketing research can identify information that would not be accessible to them through more traditional marketing research means—a respondent to a simple questionnaire or people involved

in an interview probably would not be able to provide insightful information about the patterns they follow when walking through a store or a mall. But the method also extends into people's homes. For example, the Swiss firm Givaudan conducted observational research with Chinese consumers to determine how they cook and consume chicken. The research team followed a volunteer, Mrs. Wu, as she shopped in the local market for the exact chicken she wanted butchered to take home. The team then entered her home, observed as she cooked it (until she shooed them out of the kitchen so she could arrange the final dish), and sat with the family as they ate. The researchers noted each ingredient Mrs. Wu used, the exact methods she applied to create the meal, and even how the family disposed of the bones. (For your information, in China, it is considered perfectly acceptable to spit out bones onto the tablecloth.)

As a summary of their report notes, their research confirmed that "consuming chicken in China involves an array of sensory experiences—visual, olfactory, gustatory and tactile—so profoundly different from Western experience that an understanding of chicken flavour cannot be understood without referencing Chinese culture as its source."[24] In most cases, researchers obtain consent from the consumers they are watching and videotaping; in other cases though, they do not. The ethical dilemma for marketing researchers centres around whether to use observational techniques in which the subjects are not informed that they are being studied, like viewing customers in a mall or a retail store. Observing uninformed consumers very well may lead to important insights that would not otherwise be discovered. But do the results justify the methodology?

By videotaping customers' movements in a store, marketers can better understand how consumers actually shopped around the various departments to gather products, view signs, and interact with sales associates.

product line, Kraft hired Communispace to create a virtual community of target consumers: 150 women who wanted to lose weight and 150 "health and wellness" opinion leaders. The participants openly shared their frustrations and difficulties managing their weight, because the community environment prompted them to sense that everyone else on the site struggled with similar issues and concerns. By monitoring the community, Kraft learned that it would need to educate consumers about the South Beach Diet and would need to offer products that could address cravings throughout the day, not just at mealtimes. Six months after the line's introduction, Kraft had earned profits of $100 million.[25]

Noting these various opportunities and market research sources online, many companies—including Ford Motor Co., PepsiCo, Coca-Cola, and WestJet Airlines—have added "heads of social media" to their management teams. These managers take responsibility for scanning the web for blogs, postings, tweets, or Facebook posts in which customers mention their experience with a brand. By staying abreast of this continuous stream of information, companies can gather the most up-to-date news about their company, products, and services, as well as their competitors'. These social media searches allow companies to learn about customers' perceptions and resolve customer complaints they may never have heard about through other channels.[26] Social media has its pros and cons, as seen in Exhibit 7.10, and is best used in combination with other research techniques.

The data gathered through the searches also undergo careful analyses: Are customer sentiments generally positive, negative, or neutral? What sort of intensity or interest levels do they imply? How many customers are talking about the firm's products, and how many focus instead on competitors'? This data analysis is understandably challenging, considering the amount of data available online. However, monitoring consumer sentiments has grown easier with the development of social media monitoring platforms.

Radian6 is steadily becoming one of the most sought-after firms for monitoring customers using sentiment mining. Using social media sites like Facebook, Twitter, and online blogs, Radian6 and other firms collect consumer comments about companies and their products. The data are then analyzed to distill customer attitudes toward and preferences for products and advertising campaigns. Scouring millions of sites by combining automated online search tools with text analysis techniques, sentiment mining yields qualitative data that provide new insight into what consumers really think. Companies plugged into this real-time information can become more nimble, allowing for quick changes in a product roll-out or a new advertising campaign. Some companies take it a step further, by joining the online conversation with customers, a process

EXHIBIT 7.10	Pros and Cons of Using Social Media in Research[27]		
Pros	**Result**	**Cons**	**Result**
Large accessible sample	Greater objectivity	Not a statistically representative sample	Could skew findings
People of all ages use social media	Wider sample, greater representation	Feedback may not be well thought out	Not useful to research problem
Large amount of information posted on social media sites	Easier to find data related to your brand	Anonymity	Could encourage extreme opinions and comments
Very current feedback	High relevance	No depth of information about consumer	Cannot distinguish differences among consumers
Consumers freely offer opinions and insights	No interviewer bias	Conversations are observed only	No opportunity to probe for more detail
Can search for and filter data	More timely	No consent to study data	Potential ethical issues

called *social engagement.*[28] As seen in Social and Mobile Marketing 7.1, Starbucks actively seeks out ideas idea from consumers.

In-Depth Interviews   In an **in-depth interview**, trained researchers ask questions, listen to and record the answers, and then pose additional questions to clarify or expand on a particular issue. For instance, in addition to simply watching teenagers shop for apparel, interviewers might stop them one at a time in the mall to ask them a few questions, such as "We noticed that you went into and came out of Abercrombie & Fitch very quickly, and without buying anything. Why was that?" If the subject responds that no one had bothered to wait on her, the interviewer might ask a follow-up question, such as "Oh? Has that happened to you before?" or "Do you expect sales assistance in that store?" The results often provide insights that help managers better understand the nature of their industry, as well as important trends and consumer preferences, which can be invaluable for developing marketing strategies.

In-depth interviews have quite a few benefits. They can provide an historical context for the phenomenon of interest, particularly when they include industry experts or experienced consumers. They also can communicate how people really feel about a product or service at the individual level, a level that rarely emerges from other

in-depth interview
A research technique in which trained researchers ask questions, listen to and record the answers, and then pose additional questions to clarify or expand on a particular issue.

Social and Mobile Marketing 7.1

Your Ideas in Action at Starbucks

Consumers use the Internet and social media as a part of their daily lives to share information, discuss interests, and air grievances. Starbucks recognized that its loyal consumers wanted to share ideas for new products and a website (MyStarbucksIdea.com) was launched and supported by a Twitter page (@MyStarbucksIdea) to make it easy for them to do so. Since its customers know better than anyone how and what they want the company to serve them, Starbucks is encouraging customers to submit their ideas, revolutionary or otherwise.

This example of corporate democracy in action allows anyone who signs up for an account to make suggestions. Almost 45,000 Twitter followers[29] and others can discuss and vote on the ideas in an online forum while Starbucks watches to see which ideas are the most popular. All "Ideas in Action" have icons beside them to note whether they are under review, reviewed, in the works, or launched.

Involving consumers in this way is a gold mine for Starbucks because it provides a way to invite customers into the research lab, so to speak. Integrating customer views into a company's new product development process can provide an untapped source of new ideas, refinements to existing products, and access to a knowledgeable

Customer feedback led to a "splash stick" to prevent drinks from spilling.

test market—all at little or no cost. In its first five years, consumers cast over 2 million votes and submitted more than 150,000 ideas, resulting in 277 innovations that the company has implemented.[30]

One example of a new product introduction that resulted from consumer feedback was the addition of soy-based beverages to cater to lactose-intolerant customers. Although the website is a great place for Starbucks to get feedback on new products customers want, ideas are not restricted to that category. Feedback is also welcome in other categories, including "experience ideas" (ordering, payment, pickup, atmosphere, locations) and "involvement ideas" (building communities, social responsibility.)

Some of the posted ideas include[31]

- Create a splash stick to prevent spills from drink lid.

- Don't throw out used Starbucks cards. Instead give people a 25 cent credit for reloading them.

- Add ice cubes made from coffee to iced coffee drinks so the beverage doesn't become diluted.

- Offer gluten-free food.

- Showcase local art in stores to provide a new experience for customers and shine a light on local artists.

A consumer is being interviewed.

focus group

A research technique in which a small group of persons (usually 8 to 12) comes together for an in-depth discussion about a particular topic, with the conversation guided by a trained moderator using an unstructured method of inquiry.

methods that use group discussions. Finally, marketers can use the results of in-depth interviews to develop surveys. In-depth interviews, however, are relatively expensive and time consuming. One interview may cost $200 or more, depending on its length and the characteristics of the people used in the sample. For instance, if the sample requires medical doctors, the costs of getting interviews will be higher than intercepting teenagers at a mall.

Focus Group Interviews   In a **focus group**, a small group of persons (usually 8 to 12) comes together for an in-depth discussion about a particular topic. Using an unstructured method of inquiry, a trained moderator guides the conversation on the basis of a predetermined general outline of the topics of interest. Researchers usually record the interactions on videotape or audiotape so they can carefully comb through the interviews later to catch any patterns of verbal or nonverbal responses.

In particular, focus groups gather qualitative data about initial reactions to a new or existing product or service, opinions about different competitive offerings, or reactions to marketing stimuli, like a new ad campaign or point-of-purchase display materials.

To obtain new information to help it continue its innovative success derived from its introduction of low-sodium choices, Campbell's Soup conducted extensive focus groups with female shoppers who indicated they would buy ready-to-eat soups. The groups clearly revealed the women's top priorities: a nutritious soup that contained the ingredients they would use if they made soup. They wanted, for example, white-meat chicken, fresh vegetables, and sea salt. In addition, focus group participants were equally clear about what they did not want, like high fructose corn syrup, MSG, and other ingredients whose names they could not even pronounce.[32] The resulting Select Harvest product line showcases the 100 percent natural, flavourful, and healthful ingredients, including vegetables and whole grains. The packaging also reflects the focus groups' preferences, using a simple, clean design that highlights the short list of ingredients. In its first year on the market, the line generated $202 million in sales.[33]

The growth of online technology, as well as computer and video capabilities, has provided tremendous benefits for focus group research, which now often takes place online. For example, eFocusGroups offers a secure site as a platform for companies to listen in on focus groups and even interact with consumers, without anyone having to travel. The client company not only saves costs but also gains access to a broader range of potential customers who live in various neighbourhoods, provinces, or even countries. Because eFocusGroups automatically records all the online interactions, the company also has a detailed, verbatim transcript of consumers' comments and responses.[34] However, these online focus groups rarely include video feeds, so companies lose some important information that can be gleaned from body language.

Virtual focus groups have started to make inroads into the market researchers' toolkit. Lego, for instance, invited more than 10,000 kids to participate in a virtual focus group to get ideas for new products.[35] The participants

Campbell's Soup learned from focus groups that women want a nutritious soup that contains ingredients they would use if they made it from scratch. This information helped them develop their Select Harvest line.

saw short lists of proposed toys and clicked on the ones they liked. They ranked their choices and even suggested new ideas. These ideas were fed, in turn, to other potential customers and were rated against the ideas from Lego's own toy creators. The new suggestions, in turn, got creative juices flowing among still other potential customers. The resulting product, the Star Wars Imperial Star Destroyer, was different from anything else in Lego's 73-year history—it was Lego's largest and most expensive set ever, at 3,100 parts and with a $300 price tag. Its first production run sold out in less than five weeks.

Lego's Star Wars Imperial Star Destroyer, at 3,100 parts and with a $300 price tag, was designed with the help of virtual focus groups.

Projective Technique

A **projective technique** is a type of qualitative research in which subjects are provided a scenario and asked to express their thoughts and feelings about it. For example, consumers may be shown a cartoon that has a consumer looking at a shelf display in a supermarket with a text box above the consumer. The respondent would write in his or her thoughts on the issue in the text box. Thus, the cartoon allows respondents to visualize the situation and project their thoughts or feelings by filling out the text box.

projective technique
A type of qualitative research in which subjects are provided a scenario and asked to express their thoughts and feelings about it.

One question that must be going through your mind at this stage is which of these primary qualitative data collection techniques are used most frequently. Generally, focus groups and in-depth interviews are used more frequently than personal observations, especially ethnography. Deciding which technique to use depends on several important considerations, such as the objective of the research, the cost to undertake the research, the time required to undertake the research, how soon the results are needed, and whether the marketer has the research expertise in-house or has to hire a market research firm to do the research, especially with methods such as ethnography and projective techniques. Normally, marketers have to make a trade-off between these considerations to get the results in a timely and cost-effective manner. Often a company may use several methods together to get actionable results.

Quantitative Research Methods

Quantitative research is intended to verify insights and to aid decision makers in selecting a specific course of action.[36] Quantitative research can be descriptive in nature, such as when it profiles a typical user or nonuser of a particular brand according to a survey. It can also be experimental, such as when a soft-drink producer conducts a taste test to determine which formulation of a green, high-caffeine drink is preferred by customers. Quantitative research can also be collected from the merchandise that is scanned at a store, or from a group of customers, known as a panel, who record all of their purchases. In this section, we will discuss the following quantitative research techniques: survey, panel, and experimental.

Survey Research

Arguably a survey is the most popular type of quantitative, primary data collection method used in marketing research. It is widely used to study consumers' attitudes, preferences, behaviours, and knowledge about products and brands. It is generally more cost-effective than other methods for reaching a large sample of consumers. Hockey Canada and Bauer Hockey wanted to understand why more children were not playing hockey. Surveys of 875 families in Ontario and Nova Scotia revealed some interesting findings: the game was viewed as not fun, too time consuming, not affordable, and having safety concerns.[37] Pilot programs to "Grow the Game" have since been launched to change attitudes and attract new players.

Survey questionnaires usually yield quantitative data that can be easily analyzed by using sophisticated statistical methods to examine the relationships among variables. However, it suffers from a few shortcomings. Consumers may be unable to answer some of the questions on the questionnaire, may not be able recall the information, or may even interpret the questions differently than the researchers intended. Some may even try to answer the questions according to what they think the researchers want. Another big problem, especially in the data analysis phase, is when respondents answer some but not all the questions on the questionnaire. Incomplete data makes the analysis and interpretation of the data more complicated and tricky.

A **survey** is a systematic means of collecting information from people that generally uses a **questionnaire**. A questionnaire is a form that features a set of questions designed to gather information from respondents and thereby accomplish the researchers' objectives. Survey questionnaires can take different forms: phone, mail, or fax, delivered via the Internet, or even conducted in person, for example, mall intercepts. Individual questions on a questionnaire can be either unstructured or structured. **Unstructured questions** are open-ended and allow respondents to answer in their own words. An unstructured question like "What are the most important characteristics for choosing a brand of shampoo?" yields an unstructured response. However, the same question could be posed to respondents in a structured format by providing a fixed set of response categories, such as price, fragrance, ability to clean, and dandruff control, and then asking respondents to rate the importance of each. **Structured questions** thus are closed-ended questions for which a discrete set of response alternatives, or specific answers, is provided for respondents to evaluate (see Exhibit 7.11).

Developing a questionnaire is part art and part science. The questions must be carefully designed to address the specific set of research questions. Moreover, for a questionnaire to produce meaningful results, its questions cannot be misleading in any fashion (e.g., open to multiple interpretations), and they must address only one issue at a time. Furthermore, they must be worded in vocabulary that will be familiar and comfortable to those being surveyed. More specifically, the questions should be sequenced appropriately: general questions first, more specific questions next, and demographic questions at the end. Finally, the layout and appearance of the questionnaire must be professional and easy to follow, with appropriate instructions in suitable places. For some tips on what *not* to do when designing a questionnaire, see Exhibit 7.12.

Similar to focus groups, marketing surveys can be conducted either online or offline, but online marketing surveys offer researchers the chance to develop a database quickly

survey
A systematic means of collecting information from people using a questionnaire.

questionnaire
A form that features a set of questions designed to gather information from respondents and thereby accomplish the researchers' objectives; questions can be either unstructured or structured.

unstructured questions
Open-ended questions that allow respondents to answer in their own words.

structured questions
Closed-ended questions for which a discrete set of response alternatives, or specific answers, is provided for respondents to evaluate.

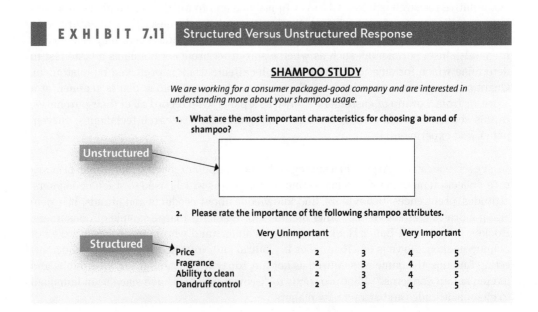

EXHIBIT 7.11   Structured Versus Unstructured Response

SHAMPOO STUDY

We are working for a consumer packaged-good company and are interested in understanding more about your shampoo usage.

1. **What are the most important characteristics for choosing a brand of shampoo?**

Unstructured

2. Please rate the importance of the following shampoo attributes.

	Very Unimportant			Very Important	
Price	1	2	3	4	5
Fragrance	1	2	3	4	5
Ability to clean	1	2	3	4	5
Dandruff control	1	2	3	4	5

Structured

EXHIBIT 7.12	**What Not to Do When Designing a Questionnaire[38]**	
Issue	**Good Question**	**Bad Question**
Avoid questions the respondent cannot easily or accurately answer.	When was the last time you went to the grocery store?	How much money did you spend on groceries last month?
Avoid sensitive questions unless they are absolutely necessary.	Do you take vitamins?	Do you dye your hair?
Avoid double-barrelled questions, which refer to more than one issue with only one set of responses.	1. Do you think Justin Trudeau would make a good prime minister? 2. Do you think Elizabeth May would make a good prime minister?	Do you think that Elizabeth May or Justin Trudeau would make a good prime minister?
Avoid leading questions, which steer respondents to a particular response, irrespective of their true beliefs.	Please rate how safe you believe a Volvo is on a scale of 1 to 10, with 1 being not safe and 10 being very safe.	Volvo is the safest car on the road, right?
Avoid one-sided questions that present only one side of the issue.	To what extent do you feel fast food contributes to adult obesity? 1: Does not contribute, 5: Main cause	Fast food is responsible for adult obesity: Agree/Disagree
Avoid questions with implicit assumptions, which presume the same point of reference for all respondents.	Should children be allowed to drink Coca-Cola in school?	Since caffeine is a stimulant, should children be allowed to drink Coca-Cola in school?
Avoid complex questions and those that may seem unfamiliar to respondents.	What brand of wristwatch do you typically wear?	Do you believe that mechanical watches are better than quartz watches?

with many responses, whereas offline marketing surveys provide a more direct approach that includes interactions with the target market.

Web surveys have steadily grown as a percentage of all quantitative surveys. Many online survey tools let researchers quickly design a survey, launch it, download the data, and analyze the data even as the survey is progressing, as well as at the end of the data collection. SurveyMonkey and Qualtrics are two popular online survey tools with vastly different capabilities, services, and pricing models. Online surveys have a lot to offer marketers with tight deadlines and small budgets.[39] Response rates are relatively high. Typical response rates run from 1 to 2 percent for mail and 10 to 15 percent for phone surveys. For online surveys, in contrast, the response rate can reach 30 to 35 percent, or even higher in B2B research. It is inexpensive. An average 20-minute phone interview can cost $30 to $40, compared with $7 to $10 for an online interview. Costs likely will continue to fall more as users become more familiar with the online survey process. Results are processed and received quickly. Reports and summaries can be developed in real time and delivered directly to managers in simple, easy-to-digest reports, complete with colour, graphics, and charts. Traditional phone or mail surveys require laborious data collection, tabulation, summary, and distribution before anyone can grasp their results. The Internet can also be used to collect data other than that available from quantitative surveys. If consumers give a firm permission to market to them, the firm can collect data about their usage of its website and other Internet applications. In addition, open-ended questionnaires can be used to collect more in-depth qualitative data.

Online marketing surveys enable researchers to develop a database quickly with many responses at a relatively low cost.

Panel Research As previously discussed, panel research can be either secondary or primary. In this section, we consider the use of a panel to collect primary data. Shaw Media wanted to collect insights for three of its channels: Global Television, HGTV, and Food Network Canada. To do this it needed to understand attitudes and purchase intention toward brands featured in the programming and advertising. Online panels of 5,000 people for each channel[40] now help collect feedback used to enhance Shaw's offerings. Walmart's Asda subsidiary in the United Kingdom uses an 18,000-customer panel it calls "Pulse of the Nation" to help it determine which products to carry. Asda sends emails to each participant with product images and descriptions of potential new products. The customers' responses indicate whether they think the product should be carried in the stores. As a thank-you for participating, those customers who respond are automatically entered in a draw for free prizes.[41]

experimental research
A type of quantitative research that systematically manipulates one or more variables to determine which variable has a causal effect on another variable.

Experimental Research **Experimental research** is a type of quantitative research that systematically manipulates one or more variables to determine which variable(s) have a causal effect on another variable. In the hypothetical McDonald's example, the research team was trying to determine the most profitable price for a new combo item (a hamburger, fries, and a drink). Assume that the fixed cost of developing the item is $300,000, and the variable cost, which is primarily composed of the cost of the food itself, is $2.00. McDonald's puts the item on the menu at four different prices in four different markets (see Exhibit 7.13). In general, the more expensive the item, the less it will sell. But, by running this experiment, the restaurant chain determines the most profitable item is the second least expensive item ($5.00). These findings suggest some people may have believed the most expensive item ($7.00) was too expensive, so they refused to buy it. The least expensive item ($4.00) sold fairly well, but McDonald's did not make as much money on each item sold. In this experiment, the changes in price likely caused the changes in quantities sold and therefore affected the restaurant's profitability.

Using an experiment, McDonald's would "test" the price of new menu items to determine which is the most profitable.

	1	**2**	**3**	**4**	**5**
Market	**Unit Price**	**Market Demand at Price (in Units)**	**Total Revenue (Col. 1 × Col. 2)**	**Total Cost of Units Sold ($300,000 Fixed Cost; $2.00/ unit Variable Cost)**	**Total Profits (Col. 3 – Col. 4)**
1	$4	200,000	$800,000	$700,000	$100,000
2	5	150,000	750,000	600,000	150,000
3	6	100,000	600,000	500,000	100,000
4	7	50,000	350,000	400,000	(50,000)

EXHIBIT 7.13 Hypothetical Pricing Experiment for McDonald's

Now that we have discussed the various secondary and primary data collection methods, we can see that both primary data and secondary data have certain inherent advantages and disadvantages. Regardless of how marketers collect data, research can be an expensive process for entrepreneurs working on a shoestring budget. Entrepreneurial Marketing 7.1 suggests a host of avenues entrepreneurs might pursue.

EMERGING TECHNOLOGY AND THE ETHICS OF USING CUSTOMER INFORMATION

LO4

As we will note in Chapter 18, upholding strong business ethics requires more than a token nod to ethics in the mission statement. A strong ethical orientation must be an integral part of a firm's marketing strategy and decision making. In Chapter 18, we will discuss how marketers have a duty to understand and address the concerns of the various stakeholders in the firm.

As technology continues to advance rapidly, especially in terms of a firm's ability to link data sets and build enormous databases that contain information on millions of customers, marketing researchers must be careful to not abuse their ability to access these data, which can be very sensitive. Unauthorized sharing of customer data with third parties or for purposes other than legitimate company business is a serious breach of customer trust. Also, marketers must take every step possible to protect customer data from security breaches from hackers and other unauthorized individuals. In the event of a security breach, the company must quickly notify its affected customers and state clearly what steps it is taking to protect their data and privacy.

More and more, consumers want to be assured that they have control over the information that has been collected about them through various means, such as a website or product registration or rebate form. Consumers' anxiety has become so intense that the Canadian government has implemented various regulations, such as the Privacy Act, that govern the collection, use, disclosure, and retention of personal information by federal government institutions, and the Personal Information Protection and Electronic Documents Act (PIPEDA), which governs the collection, use, disclosure, and retention of personal information by certain parts of the private sector.[42] When conducting marketing research, researchers must assure respondents that the information they provide will be treated as confidential and used solely for the purpose of research. Without such assurances, consumers will be reluctant to either provide honest responses to marketing research inquiries or even agree to participate in the first place.

It is extremely important to adhere to ethical practices when conducting marketing research. The Canadian Marketing Association, for example, provides three

Entrepreneurial Marketing 7.1

Marketing Research on a Shoestring Budget

Imagine your company needs some research conducted but has a relatively small budget. Fortunately, marketing research does not have to have a high price tag, though it always takes drive and knowledge. Here are some ways to uncover the information you and your company might need without breaking the bank.

Objective: What is it that you need to know?

- *Network.* Use the directory on your cellphone to call friends and professional colleagues. In most cases, researchers probably already know people in the industry who will be able to share their knowledge. They can help marketers determine what their objectives should be in upcoming research projects.

Customer Analysis: Who are your customers, and what do they want?

- *Customers.* Talk with current and prospective customers. Ask them the right questions, and they will provide the necessary answers. This approach is remarkably cheap because it entails only the researcher's labour, though it will require a large time commitment. Marketers need to take care how they ask the questions; people tend to provide answers that they think the questioner wants to hear or that seem socially acceptable.

- *Online.* Use a search engine such as Google by typing in some appropriate keywords.

- *Statistics Canada.* Statistics Canada is an important source of information. At http://www.statcan.gc.ca, industry, demographic, and economic reports are accessible for free. Although not known for its ease of use, the website offers a wealth of information.

Competitive Analysis: What are your competitors doing?

Secondary Sources: Many are listed in Exhibit 7.5 in this chapter.

- *Websites.* Visit competitors' websites, if they have them. Learn about their products and services, pricing, management teams, and philosophies. Read their press releases. You can even infer what parts of the businesses are thriving by reading their career pages.

- *SEC Filings.* If competitors are public companies in the United States, they are required to file 10K forms annually with the Securities Exchange Commission (SEC). Search for SEC filings by using http://finance.yahoo.com or http://money.msn.com, both of which provide sales and expense numbers,

in addition to other important information in the footnotes. In Canada, most public companies file securities documents and information on SEDAR (http://www.sedar.com).

- *University Libraries Electronic Databases.* Most Canadian universities subscribe to several electronic business databases that provide information on Canadian companies. These databases are usually accessible remotely by students, staff, and alumnus at no cost to users. A sample of these databases includes Canadian Business Resource, Canadian Business & Current Affairs, Factiva, *Financial Post* databases, MarketResearch.com, Mergent Online, Mergent WebReports, ProQuest Asian Business and Reference, and ProQuest European Business. Many of these databases provide company profiles, financial data, contact information, and short stories or case studies on company successes, failures, and innovations.

- *Go there.* If competitors are smaller mom-and-pop stores, visit them. Hang out in front of the store armed with a pad and paper and count the number of people who walk in. Then calculate the percentage of people who walk out having purchased something. Use logic and judgment. Have the customers purchased items that appear to have high profit margins? Find out where and what competitors are advertising.

Focus Groups, Surveys, and Analyst Reports: What detailed information can you gather?

- *Be specific.* Determine precisely what information is required; it is very costly to pay for research that does not assist in a decision or provide strategic direction.

- *Surveys.* Determine what form will provide the most value. Phone surveys cost about $40 per interview, mailings average from $5,000 to $15,000 for 200 responses, and email and Internet-based surveys are usually much cheaper.

- *Focus groups.* Although focus groups can be more expensive, there are ways to cut corners. Develop the questions in-house, and don't outsource the moderator or facility. It is important, however, to find the right participants.

- *Analyst reports.* Prewritten reports, covering a broad price range and a wide variety of questions, are available for purchase from the hundreds of companies that write and sell reports. Two of the best known are http://www.forrester.com and http://www.hoovers.com.

guidelines for conducting marketing research: (1) it prohibits selling or fundraising under the guise of conducting research, (2) it supports maintaining research integrity by avoiding misrepresentation or the omission of pertinent research data, and (3) it encourages the fair treatment of clients and suppliers. Numerous codes of conduct written by various marketing research societies all reinforce the duty of researchers to respect the rights of the subjects in the course of their research. The bottom line: Marketing research should be used only to produce unbiased, factual information.

Laws have yet to catch up with advances in other areas, including social media, neuromarketing, and facial recognition software. As we noted previously in this chapter, social media have grown into an important resource for marketing researchers because consumers are so willing and likely to share their attitudes and opinions there. In this case, protecting consumers' privacy is mainly up to the consumer.

In contrast, consumers have little control over facial recognition software that allows companies to detect demographic information based on their appearances. For example, digital billboards embedded with such software can identify passersby and then display ads targeted to them, based on their age, gender, and attention level.[43] The resulting communication is precisely targeted, which should make the advertisement more interesting to the consumer walking by—though it also could lead to embarrassing encounters. Imagine, for example, a teenager with skin problems having a billboard loudly broadcast an acne product ad as he walks by!

REAL MARKETER PROFILE   Tim Penner (former President, P&G Canada)

When I think about consumer research, I'm reminded of a presentation I heard at P&G over 30 years ago, when I was just starting my career. The presenter showed a video of a consumer named "Ina," who was going through her household chores, doing the laundry and cleaning her house. Ina did some things that seemed a bit silly. She didn't follow the usage instructions very closely and she had a number of quirky habits. I remember my peers and I chuckling as we watched the video of Ina's cleaning regimen.

The presenter later informed us that Ina was an actress, but everything she did in her cleaning regimen had come from in-depth research of what real consumers do. He showed us the video to impress upon us a very important message, and we should remember the message by remembering Ina. INA stands for "I'm Not Average." One of the most important things that marketers need to learn is that they need to suppress their personal experiences and their personal habits, because those experiences are not average. Instead of relying on their personal experiences, marketers need to listen very carefully to what real consumers say and do. The insights that a marketer discovers by watching and listening to real consumers can lead to

innovative new products and marketing campaigns that really connect with real consumers.

One of the areas where this message proved to be particularly relevant was in-store. As a marketer, I would often look at packaging or in-store materials in a conference room and think the work was quite brilliant. But when I researched these in-store materials with consumers, by putting them in a simulated store environment and asking consumers to shop the section, I often learned that consumers hadn't even noticed the in-store materials that I thought were so clever. Even a video screen in the aisle would often go completely unseen by consumers intent on finding a brand. You see, when consumers shop, they are bombarded by so many messages and symbols that their brain has to select a few things to look for. Their brain deselects a lot of extraneous information. The clever words on the label and the images on in-store signage can go completely unnoticed. Once again, it's not the opinion of the marketer that matters. It is only by exposing real consumers to the work, in a representative situation, that you can really understand the merits of an idea.

Never forget Ina!

On Facebook, facial detection software applied to photographs eliminates the need for users to continue to tag the same people multiple times. It also stores all users' biometric data. Biometric data include one or more physical traits such as facial characteristics, iris scans, or fingerprints. Facebookers can turn off the facial detection function, but their biometric data is still collected. In Germany, with its strict privacy laws, regulators have demanded that Facebook stop collecting any biometric data.

Going even deeper than using biometric data, neuromarketing claims the ability to read consumers' minds, using wireless electroencephalogram (EEG) scanners that measure the involuntary brainwaves that occur when they view a product, advertisement, or brand images. Such insights would be invaluable for marketers to discover what truly appeals to consumers. For example, do people love the iPad because of its functionality, or is the true source of its appeal the curves of the tablet, which appeal to a primal preference in humans?[44] But as anyone who has ever seen a science fiction movie can imagine, the potential for abuses of such tools are immense. And a key question remains: Do any consumers want marketers reading their brain waves and marketing goods and services to them in a manner that bypasses their conscious thoughts?

LEARNING OBJECTIVES REVIEW

Identify the five steps in the marketing research process

There are five steps in the marketing research process. The first step is to define the research problem and objectives, which sounds so simple that managers often gloss over it. But this step is crucial to the success of any research project because, quite simply, the research must answer those questions that are important for making decisions. In the second step, designing the research plan, researchers identify the type of data that are needed, whether primary or secondary, on the basis of the objectives of the project from Step 1, and then determine the type of research that enables them to collect those data. The third step involves deciding on the data collection process and collecting the data. Depending on the research objectives and the findings from the secondary data search, researchers will choose either qualitative or quantitative research. Qualitative research usually involves observation, in-depth interviews, or projective techniques, whereas if the project calls for conclusive research, the researchers may perform a survey or an experiment, or use panel data. The fourth step is to analyze and interpret the data, and the fifth and final step is to present an action plan. Although these steps appear to progress in a linear fashion, researchers often work backward through the process as they learn at each step.

LO2 Describe the various secondary data sources

Secondary data are pieces of information that have been collected from other sources, such as the Census, internal company sources, the Internet, books, articles, trade associations,

or syndicated data services. Research projects typically start with secondary research, which provides a background for what information is already known and what research has been done previously. External secondary data are pieces of information that have been collected from other sources, such as Statistics Canada, the Internet, books, articles, magazines, newspapers, trade associations, scanner data, panel data, or syndicated data services. Internal secondary data are derived from internal company records such as sales, customer lists, and other company reports.

LO3 Describe primary data collection techniques and summarize the differences between secondary data and primary data

Primary data are collected to address specific research needs. Techniques used for primary qualitative research include observation, social media, in-depth interviews, focus groups and projective techniques. Quantitative research is used to verify the insights gained from exploratory qualitative research and to aid in choosing a course of action. Techniques used for primary quantitative research include surveys (both offline and online), panel data, and experiments. With both types of research, the specific methods managers choose depends foremost on the marketing research objectives, which must be balanced by other considerations such as costs, timeliness, and usefulness of the results.

Compared with primary research, secondary research is quicker, easier, and generally less expensive. The ability to use secondary data also requires less methodological expertise. However, because secondary research is collected for reasons other than those pertaining to the specific problem at hand, the information may be dated, biased, or simply not specific enough to answer the research questions. Primary research, in contrast, can be designed to answer very specific questions, but it also tends to be more expensive and time consuming.

 L04 **Outline ethical issues firms encounter when conducting marketing research**

Marketing researchers have obligations to their subjects and to society to behave in an ethical manner. Marketing researchers should gain permission to collect information on consumers, and it should be for the sole purpose of conducting marketing research endeavours. Information should not be collected under the guise of marketing research when the intent is to sell products or to fundraise. In addition, marketers must take responsibility for protecting any information they collect.

KEY TERMS

- data
- data mining
- ethnography
- experimental research
- focus group
- hypothesis
- in-depth interview
- information
- marketing research

- observation
- panel data
- primary data
- projective technique
- quantitative research
- qualitative research
- questionnaire
- reliability
- sample

- scanner data
- secondary data
- structured questions
- survey
- syndicated data
- unstructured questions
- validity

CONCEPT REVIEW

1. Is marketing research really necessary? Defend your answer.

2. Briefly describe the steps in the marketing research process. Explain why it is important to clearly define the research problem and objectives from the very outset of the process.

3. What is the difference between secondary and primary data? What are some of the advantages of each type of data? When should each type of data be used?

4. In data collection methods, researchers may choose between qualitative research methods or quantitative research methods, or use both methods. What considerations guide their choice of data collection methods?

5. Today, information and communications technologies (ICT), including the Internet, are changing not only the way marketing is practised, but also how market research is conducted. In response, many companies are using a wide variety of observational methods (e.g., GPS, RFID, video cameras, audio devices, ethnography) to gather customer data. Discuss the ethical issues underlying the increasing use of observational research methods that use technology.

6. Marketing research is designed to help marketers make better decisions on various aspects of their businesses. The quality of research findings is as good as the quality of the data on which they are based. What are some things marketers could do to ensure that they obtain the best quality data?

7. Explain the main advantages and disadvantages of using the Internet for marketing research versus conventional offline methods.

8. Identify and explain the ways in which the design of a market research study could reduce the reliability and validity of the study. Can a market research study that has high reliability lack validity? Can a study that has high validity lack reliability? Explain your answers.

9. What do you think are some of the differences between qualitative data collection methods, which are mainly exploratory, and quantitative research methods, which are more conclusive in nature? Which type of method should a researcher prefer and why?

10. Explain some of the problems and challenges market researchers face in the data analysis and interpretation stage of the marketing research process. Should they report these problems when presenting their action plan? Why or why not?

MARKETING APPLICATIONS

1. A large department store collects data about what its customers buy and stores these data in a data warehouse. If you were the store's buyer for children's clothing, what would you want to know from the data warehouse that would help you be a more successful buyer?

2. Identify a nonprofit organization that might use marketing research, and describe one example of a meaningful research project that it might conduct. Discuss how this project would be useful to the organization.

3. Marketing researchers do not always go through the steps in the marketing research process in sequential order. Provide an example of a research project that might not follow this sequence.

4. A new men's clothing store is trying to determine whether there is a significant market for its type of merchandise in a specific location where it is considering putting a store. Would it be most likely to use primary or secondary data, or a combination of the two, to answer this question?

5. A high-tech firm has just developed a new technology to correct bad vision without surgery or contact lenses. The company needs to estimate the demand for such a service. Would it use primary or secondary data, or a combination of the two?

6. A bank manager notices that by the time customers get to the teller, they seem irritated and impatient. She wants to investigate the problem further, so she hires you to design a research project to figure out what is bothering the customers. The bank wants two studies: (a) several focus groups of its customers and (b) an online survey of 500 customers. Which study is qualitative and which is quantitative?

7. PomWonderful has developed a coffee-flavoured pomegranate beverage, and it wants to determine whether it should begin to market it throughout Canada. The company used two separate studies to help develop the advertising campaign:

   - a focus group to identify the appropriate advertising message for the new beverage
   - a survey to assess the effectiveness of the advertising campaign for the new PomWonderful beverage

   Which study was qualitative and which was quantitative?

8. What other studies would you recommend that PomWonderful undertake?

9. Suppose your university wants to modify its course scheduling procedures to better serve students. What are some secondary sources of information that might be used to conduct research into this topic? Describe how these sources might be used. Describe a method you could use to gather primary research data about the topic. Would you recommend a specific order in obtaining each of these types of data? Explain your answer.

10. Tony is planning to launch a new shampoo and is trying to decide what features and price would interest consumers. He sends a request for proposal to four marketing research vendors, and three respond, as described in the table below. Which vendor should Tony use? Explain your rationale for picking this vendor over the others.

Vendor A	Vendor B	Vendor C
The vendor that Tony has used in the past, it estimates it can get the job done for $200,000 in two months. The vendor plans to do a telephone-based survey analysis and use secondary data.	Tony's key competitor has used this vendor, which claims that it can get the job done for $150,000 in one month. This vendor plans to do a telephone-based survey analysis and use secondary data. During a discussion pertaining to its price and time estimates, the vendor indicates it will draw on insights it has learned from a recent report prepared for one of Tony's competitors.	This well-known vendor has recently started to focus on consumer packaged-goods clients. It quotes a price of $180,000 and a time of one month. The vendor plans to conduct an Internet-based survey analysis and use secondary data.

NET SAVVY

1. Go to the website of either Harris/Decima (http://www.decima.com) or Ipsos Canada (http://www.ipsos.ca), which administer public opinion polls. Search the site for results from any recent survey that is available for free. Print out the results. Identify the objective(s) of the survey. Discuss one of the major findings, and provide an interpretation of the data.

2. Select two online survey tools (e.g., SurveyMonkey, Qualtrics, Zoomerang, Survey Solutions) and compare and contrast them in terms of their features, capabilities, ease of use, support service, pricing models, clientele, and any other characteristics you think would be useful for a market researcher to know.

CHAPTER CASE STUDY

MOBILE SURVEYS PROVIDE REAL-TIME CUSTOMER INSIGHTS[45]

Shoeless Joe's Sports Grill is an award-winning restaurant and bar located primarily in Ontario cities, such as Ajax, Whitby, Oshawa, Pickering, Peterborough, and Cornwall, and in the Greater Toronto Area. It offers customers a casual dining and bar experience, where they can relax and enjoy a meal and drinks while watching on huge TV screens their favourite sports or games: the Stanley Cup finals, the Super Bowl, World Cup Soccer, or a great UFC matchup. Shoeless Joe's offers patrons exceptional food, service, and entertainment in an atmosphere that appeals to today's discriminating diners.[46] Shoeless Joe's goal is to set the industry standard among sports-themed restaurants and bars for service, environment, quality, and profits.

The thriving restaurant, established in 1985, was named after the legendary baseball star Joe "Shoeless" Jackson. Initially, Shoeless Joe's was not as successful as its namesake. When Fred Lopreiato and his nephew Nick purchased Shoeless Joe's in 1987, it was a struggling Toronto-based restaurant with no theme; it was certainly not a well-known brand. However, Fred and Nick had a game plan; they had always imagined the enormous potential of a sports-themed restaurant. The pair converted the restaurant into a more casual venue with an inviting, informal atmosphere, catering to customers—sports fans, families, and individuals—between the ages of 25 and 49.

The reinvented Shoeless Joe's turned out to be a winner, with a 50 percent increase in profits after the first year and another 35 percent increase the following year.[47] The restaurant continued to be extremely successful, so much so that Fred and Nick opened a second location in 1991. As the adage goes, success breeds success, and this was precisely the case with Shoeless Joe's. Fred and Nick had to decide whether to open more company-owned restaurants or franchise their business. They opted for franchising since they felt that it was the most effective way to grow their business. Thus, in 1997 the first Shoeless Joe's franchise was launched in Toronto. Since then Shoeless Joe's has opened over 35 franchises across Ontario. Fred and Nick plan to open 8 to 10 new franchises every year: an ambitious expansion strategy for such a small company, particularly in these tough economic times.

Although Fred and Nick remain excited about the growth potential for their business and intend to pursue an aggressive expansion strategy, they are not willing to compromise on two fundamental principles, even if it means delaying their expansion. The two principles that have always guided their successful expansion are finding the right franchisees and finding the most suitable locations. Finding the right franchisee is an intense, personal process involving in-depth interviews and analysis with potential franchisees to determine the right fit. Finding the right location is a more complex task requiring the consideration of many important variables, most of which are usually outside the control of the company. These variables include neighbourhood demographic factors, physical surroundings, accessibility, real estate, and market trends, among many others. To assist it in making the right location choice, Shoeless Joe's leverages technology to help it gather and analyze key information that will provide useful insights easily and quickly. To help it execute its aggressive expansion strategy, Shoeless Joe's used Pitney Bowes Business Insight's (PBBI) location intelligence solutions and consulting service.

Pitney Bowes is a leading global provider of expertise and technology tools that help companies find the best business solution in the most cost-effective way. Shoeless Joe's was the first company in Canada to implement PBBI's FACES (Faster, Accurate, Current, Economical Surveys) tool to gain access to real-time customer data.[48] FACES is a new mobile consumer survey system that gauges consumer perceptions and opinions on customer service or any other business dimension. It is a unique and professional survey system that uses current technology to collect consumer data at the point of experience. FACES catalogues data in a secure database, conducts sophisticated analysis, and delivers actionable insight, all in real time.

Shoeless Joe's used in-depth interviews to find franchises and mobile surveys to collect consumer perceptions and opinions.

With this unique system, consumers may feel more inclined to participate in a survey because it is fast, easy, interactive, and less intrusive than the traditional paper-and-pen method of collecting information. The FACES survey enables Shoeless Joe's to create customized surveys to assist it in collecting consumer data. This system is extremely useful and efficient because, unlike conventional survey tools, Shoeless Joe's can make adjustments to the survey questions to keep target customers' profiles up to date and accessible. This creates a more streamlined process and helps Shoeless Joe's gain a better understanding of target customers by creating in-depth customer profiles.

In its initial project, Shoeless Joe's created a survey with 10 questions and deployed it in 4 of its 38 locations.[49] Survey questions included asking customers about where they were from, where they were headed next, their spending patterns, the frequency of their visits to the restaurant, their level of satisfaction, the competition, and so on.

On busy nights, two staff members are responsible for conducting the survey, going from table to table by using an electronic mobile device, such as a PDA or a smartphone, to collect survey information from patrons. The FACES system allows Shoeless Joe's to quickly download the survey data and perform analysis that gives a snapshot of the results. Having real-time customer information collected by staff members is extremely valuable for Shoeless Joe's decision-making process, helping the company to better understand its competition and to evaluate potential areas for expansion. The information provided also equips Shoeless Joe's with the insights it needs to make decisions regarding real estate, marketing, merchandising, and branding.

Questions

1. What do you consider to be the strengths and limitations of the FACES tool that Shoeless Joe's is using to capture information to make location decisions based on customers' insights?

2. What are the methodological drawbacks of the way in which Shoeless Joe's employees go about collecting survey responses from customers?

3. How do the drawbacks identified in the previous question affect the validity and reliability of the data collected? Discuss.

4. Would you recommend that Shoeless Joe's also use other methods to collect the data it needs? What are the advantages of the methods you would recommend over the method it currently uses?

Appendix 7A

Using Secondary Data to Assess Customer Lifetime Value (CLV)

This appendix examines how secondary data from customer transactions can help determine the value of a customer over time. Specifically, **customer lifetime value (CLV)** refers to the expected financial contribution from a particular customer to the firm's profits over the course of their relationship.[1]

To estimate CLV, firms use past behaviours to forecast future purchases, the gross margin from these purchases, and the costs associated with servicing the customers. Some costs associated with maintaining customer relationships include communicating with customers through advertising, personal selling, or other promotional vehicles to acquire their business initially and then retain it over time.

Measures of CLV typically apply to a group or segment of customers and use available secondary data. A basic formula for CLV,[2] with the assumption that revenues and profits arrive at the start of the year, is as follows:

$$CLV = \frac{\sum_{t=1}^{T}[\text{profit at } t \times \text{retention rate}^{t-1}]}{(1+i)^{t-1}} - \text{acquisition costs}$$

To implement this CLV formula, we must answer the following questions:

1. How many years (t) can we expect to do business with a customer? The total number of years is denoted by T.

2. What can we expect the annual profits to be from an individual customer or an average customer? These profits are based on sales minus the costs of merchandise and the costs of serving and retaining the customer.

3. What is the retention rate, that is, the average percentage of customers who continue to purchase from the firm from one time period to another? A 90 percent retention rate means that if we have 100 customers in the first year, we will have 90 of those at the beginning of the second year.

4. What is the discount rate (i)? The discount rate is based on the idea that a dollar is worth less in the future than it is today, so the company can use it to adjust future profits and determine a customer's value today for the customer's purchases in the future. For example, if the discount rate is 10 percent, $100 in profits at the beginning of year 2 are worth only $90.91 (100/(1 + 0.1)) at the beginning of year 1.

customer lifetime value (CLV)
The expected financial contribution from a particular customer to the firm's profits over the course of their relationship.

Consider Gregory Missoni, a fairly new client of Very Clean Cleaners who switched from his other dry cleaner because Very Clean sent him $100 worth of coupons in a direct mailing.

Greg just picked up his $200 shirt from Very Clean and found that the dry cleaner had broken a brown button and replaced it with a white button. When he complained, the clerk acted as if it were no big deal. Greg explained to the clerk that it was a very expensive shirt that deserved more careful handling and then asked to speak with the manager. At this point, how important is it that the manager makes sure Greg is satisfied, so that he will continue to bring his dry cleaning to Very Clean Cleaners? To answer this question, the manager uses the following information:

- It cost Very Clean $100 to acquire Greg as a customer. Thus, the acquisition cost is $100.
- Very Clean expects Greg to remain a client for 5 years (time horizon T = 5 years).
- Very Clean expects to make a $1,000 profit each year from Greg's dry cleaning.
- On average, 10 percent of customers defect to another cleaner each year. Therefore, the expected retention rate is 90 percent.
- The discount rate is 10 percent per year (i in this illustration). For simplicity, Very Clean assumes all profits are accrued at the beginning of the year.

Applying the formula, such that CLV equals the profits from years 1 to 5, less the acquisition costs, we obtain the following:

$$\text{CLV} = \underbrace{\frac{\$1,000 \times (0.90)^0}{(1 + 0.1)^0}}_{\textbf{Year 1}} + \underbrace{\frac{\$1,000 \times (0.90)^1}{(1 + 0.1)^1}}_{\textbf{Year 2}} + \underbrace{\frac{\$1,000 \times (0.90)^2}{(1 + 0.1)^2}}_{\textbf{Year 3}}$$

$$\underbrace{\frac{\$1,000 \times (0.90)^3}{(1 + 0.1)^3}}_{\textbf{Year 4}} + \underbrace{\frac{\$1,000 \times (0.90)^4}{(1 + 0.1)^4}}_{\textbf{Year 5}} - \$100$$

Or

$$\text{CLV} = \$1,000 + \$818.2 + \$669.4 + \$547.7 + \$448.1 - \$100 = \$3,383.40$$

Let's see how the formula works. The expected profit from Greg is $1,000 per year. Very Clean assumes profits accrue at the beginning of the year, so the profits for the first year equal $1,000; they are not affected by the retention rate or the discount rate.

However, the retention and discount rates have effects on the profits for the subsequent time periods. In the second year, the retention rate, which Very Clean determined was 90 percent (i.e., 90 percent of customers continue to do business with it) modifies profits, such that expected profits in the second year equal $1,000 × 90% = $900. Moreover, the discount rate is applied such that the profits received in the second year are worth less than if they had been received in the first year. Therefore, the $900 received at the beginning of the second year must be divided by 1.1, which is equivalent to $818.20.

Using similar calculations for the third year, the expected profits adjusted for retention are $1,000 × 0.9 × 0.9 = $810. The discount rate then reduces the profit to $810 ÷ 1.12 = $669.40 in today's dollars. (Note that the discount rate is squared because it refers to two years in the future.) After calculating the adjusted and discounted profits for the fourth and fifth years in similar fashion, we realize the sum of estimated discounted profits for five years is \$3,483.40. However, we still must subtract the \$100 spent to acquire Greg, which provides a CLV of \$3,383.40.

According to this analysis, it would be a good idea for the manager to take a long-term perspective when evaluating how to respond to Greg's complaint about his button. Greg cannot be viewed as a \$2.50 customer, as he would be if Very Clean determined his value based on the cost of laundering his shirt, nor should he be viewed as a \$200 customer, based on the cost of the shirt. He actually is worth a lot more than that.

$$\text{CLV} = \text{profits} \times \left[1 + \frac{\text{retention rate}}{(\$1 + \text{discount rate} + \text{retention rate})} \right] - \text{acquisition costs}$$

$$= \$1{,}000 \left[1 + \frac{0.9}{(1 + 0.1 - 0.9)} \right] - \$100$$

$$= \$1{,}000 \times (1 + 4.5) - \$100$$

$$= \$5{,}500 - \$100 = \$5{,}400$$

For illustrative purposes, we have simplified the CLV calculations in this example. We assumed that the average profits remain constant at \$1,000. But firms usually expect profits to grow over time, or else grow, level off, and then perhaps decline. Retention costs, such as special promotions used to keep Greg coming back, also do not appear in our illustration, though such additional costs would reduce annual profits and CLV. Finally, we assume a five-year time horizon; the CLV obviously would differ for longer or shorter periods. For an infinite time horizon, with first period payments upfront, the formula becomes fairly simple:[3]

This illustration thus explains how firms can use secondary data to calculate CLV; it further demonstrates the importance of knowing a customer's lifetime value when executing marketing tactics and strategies. Several CLV problems can be accessed on Connect.

CHAPTER 8

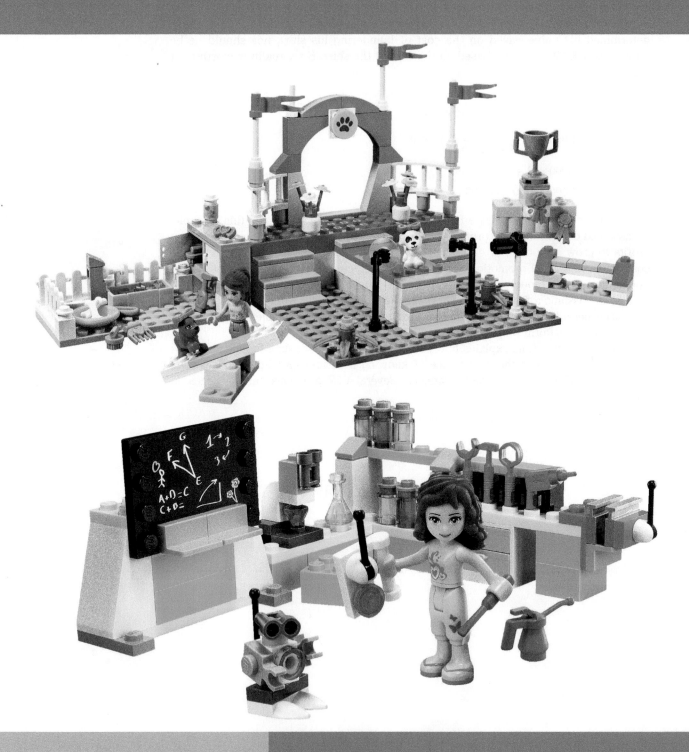

Developing New Products

When LEGO first arrived in North America in the early 1960s, the company had devised a set of principles for the design of the moulded stud-and-tube bricks:[1]

- unlimited play potential
- for girls and for boys
- fun for every age
- year-round play
- healthy, quiet play
- long hours of play
- development, imagination, creativity
- the more LEGO, the greater the value
- extra sets available
- quality in every detail

Over time, the Danish firm grew to become one of the top toy manufacturers in the world, introducing new sets and variations on its basic theme, including an extensive line of Star Wars models (as well as lines related to other popular movie franchises), basic robot technology, and superhero-themed collections. Perhaps unintentionally, it appeared that LEGO had come to violate one of its basic principles, in that its toys appealed widely to boys but not specifically to girls.

Faced with declining profits in early 2000, LEGO had determined that the popularity of video and automated games meant it needed to refocus on these areas. It developed LEGO-branded video games to match its Star Wars line of building sets. It pushed its website and interactive opportunities. The "My Lego Network" social media site encouraged children to build their own web pages, personalized with pictures of their LEGO creations, music, and sticker compositions.[2]

But these changes caused some members of the LEGO team to worry about the effects on its long-standing traditions. Perhaps the predesigned sets were hindering creativity, rather than encouraging it. Maybe telling kids to go online was not really healthy for long-lasting play. And perhaps product lines focused on pirates, science fiction, and robots were not appealing enough to girls and the ways they like to play.

In market research involving in-depth observations of children playing—on their own and as they wished, without any direction or guidance from outside—LEGO gained some notable insights.[3] For example, rather than appealing to children by simplifying its toys, LEGO had made its sets too easy to construct, without room for careful thought or creativity. The observational research showed that children wanted a sense of mastery and accomplishment, not just instant gratification. In addition, its research with girls revealed that they were not uninterested in building. They just wanted to tell stories to go along with their construction—an effort that was undermined by the preset stories in LEGO video games. As a LEGO vice president summarized, "We heard very clear requests from moms and girls for more details and interior building, a brighter colour palette, a more realistic figure, role-play opportunities and a story line that they would find interesting."[4]

Enter LEGO Friends, mini-doll figures whose names, back stories, and adventures are up to girls to develop and include in their own narratives.[5] The friends—Mia, Emma, Stephanie, Olivia, and Andrea—live in tree houses, drive convertibles, run a beauty parlour and a bakery, and play with their dogs. The colour schemes for all the sets are heavy in pink and purple. Furthermore, the doll figures are slimmer and curvier than the traditional, blocky LEGO figures.

For some parents, these new products that appeal to a new segment of consumers are problematic: The LEGO Friends do not require children to complete the assembly to begin playing, which seemingly could diminish girls' sense of accomplishment. Others suggest that the offerings of beauty parlour and café sets reinforce gender stereotypes, without allowing room for female firefighters or politicians—or space explorers or pirates, for that matter. If the new sets are expressly for girls, does that imply that the old sets were really only for boys?[6]

LEGO insists that it has always tried to appeal to girls through its wide variety of products. And though the final tallies are not in yet on this brand-new product, LEGO's legacy suggests it may be on to something big. By focusing on sets, instead of just free-form blocks, LEGO tripled its profits. Three LEGO sets sell every second worldwide.[7] Today, by appealing to girls with an entirely new product, perhaps it can increase that rate to four or five per second. ▮

---

product
Anything that is of value to a consumer and can be offered through a marketing exchange.

Few three-letter words are more exciting than "new." It brings forth an image of freshness, adventure, and excitement. Yet "new" also is a complex term when it comes to market offerings, because it might mean adding something new to an existing product, introducing a flavour never offered before, or relying on different packaging that provides added value. But the most exhilarating type of new product is something never seen before. Thousands of patent applications pursue this elusive prize: a successful and truly innovative new product.

Imagine living 200 years ago. You cook your meals on a stove fuelled by coal or wood. As a student, you do your homework by hand, illuminated only by candlelight. You get to school on foot, by horseback, or in a horse-drawn carriage, if you're really fortunate. Your classroom is small and basic, and you have very few classmates. The professor simply lectures and writes on a chalkboard.

Today you finish your homework on a laptop with word-processing software that appears to have a mind of its own and corrects your spelling automatically. Your climate-controlled room has ample electric lighting. While you work on your laptop, you can also talk with a friend by using the hands-free headset of your phone. On your way to school, in your car, you pick up fast food from a convenient drive-through window while browsing or listening to your personal selection of songs playing through your car speakers, connected to your iPod. Your friend calls to discuss a slight change to an assignment, so you pull over to grab your BlackBerry, make the necessary changes, and email the assignment from your smartphone to your professor. When you arrive at university, you sit in a 200-person classroom where you plug in your laptop, take notes on it and use it to digitally record the lecture. The professor adds notes on the day's PowerPoint presentations by using her tablet computer. You have already downloaded the PowerPoint presentations and add similar notes through your own laptop. After class, to complete your planning for a last-minute party, you send out a Facebook invitation to your friends and ask for responses to get a head count. Then you text your roommate, telling her to get food and drinks for the right number of people, which she orders through an online grocer that will deliver later in the day.

Our lives are defined by the many new products and services developed through scientific and technological advances and by the added features included in products we have always used.

This chapter deals with the first P in the marketing mix: product, specifically new products. As a key element of a firm's marketing mix (four Ps) strategies, product strategies are central to the creation of value for the consumer. A product is anything that is of value to a consumer and can be offered through a marketing exchange. In addition to goods, such as toothpaste, or services, such as a haircut, products might also be places (e.g., Whistler, British Columbia), ideas (e.g., "stop smoking"), organizations (e.g., Canadian Blood Services), people (e.g., Taylor Swift), or communities (e.g., Facebook.com) that create value for consumers in their respective competitive marketing arenas.

Product branding and packaging will be examined in the next chapter. Now we explore how companies add value to firms' product and service offerings through innovation. We also look at the process firms go through to develop new products and services. We conclude the chapter with an examination of how new products and services are adopted by the market and how firms change their marketing mix as the product or service moves through its life cycle.

WHY DO FIRMS CREATE NEW PRODUCTS?

L01

New market offerings provide value to both firms and customers. But the degree to which they do so depends on how new they really are. When we say a "new product," we don't necessarily mean that the product has never existed before—kids have played with LEGO for a long time, but LEGO Friends are new for them. Completely new-to-the-market products represent fewer than 10 percent of all new product introductions each year. (Refer to Sustainable Marketing 8.1 for an example of a "new product" that improves on an existing concept.) It is more useful to think of the degree of newness of a product on a continuum from "new-to-the-world"—as WiFi was a few years ago—to "slightly repositioned," such as the repositioning of Kraft's Capri Sun brand of ready-to-drink beverages, which was repackaged in a bigger pouch to appeal more to teens. Regardless of where on the continuum a new product fits, firms have to innovate.

LEGO Friends live in tree houses and are designed to appeal to girls.

Sustainable Marketing 8.1

Making Your Next Move Green

Moving is stressful! Before you can even start packing you have to go to local stores to snag free boxes. If they don't have enough, you have to buy some. Having to buy, build, and dispose of all those boxes is a needless hassle and expense. And, worst of all, those cardboard boxes may contain dirt, bacteria, and other things you really don't want all over your stuff.

Now there's a better, more sustainable solution. Founded in 2008 in Vancouver by Doug Burgoyne, Frogbox will rent you reusable plastic boxes, an eco-friendly alternative to traditional cardboard moving boxes. Burgyone estimates that Greater Vancouver uses about 450,000 cardboard moving boxes every month and Seattle uses about 1 million.[8]

Unlike cardboard boxes, the Frogbox solution has a low impact on the environment, as its boxes can be reused hundreds of times. The boxes are 2.4 cubic feet (70 litres). To put this in perspective, approximately 25 boxes would be needed to move the contents of a one-bedroom apartment.

Frogbox will rent you as many boxes as you need for a week or longer, and it can deliver them and pick them up when you've finished with your move. The boxes stack neatly inside each other and don't require any assembly, eliminating the need to spend hours building and taping cardboard boxes.

The Frogbox name is fitting because both the company and frogs have a connection to the sustainable environment. And Frogbox donates 1 percent of gross revenues to frog habitation restoration.[9] But its sustainability efforts are hopping in other areas too. For example, the company uses solar energy to power its website and waste-generated biodiesel to fuel its fleet vehicles.

The company has big goals. Currently, it has locations in Vancouver, Seattle, and Toronto but wants to expand into the top 30 cities in North America in the next five years. Frogbox aims to redefine how people move, making it easier on you, easier on your wallet, and, best of all, easier on the planet.

Frogbox offers an eco-friendly alternative to traditional cardboard moving boxes.

---

innovation

The process by which ideas are transformed into new products and services that will help firms grow.

Innovation is the process by which ideas are transformed into new products and services that will help firms grow. Without innovation and its resulting new products and services, firms would have only two choices: continue to market current products to current customers or take the same product to another market with similar customers.

Although innovation strategies may not work in the short run—some estimates indicate that only about 3 percent of new products actually succeed—overriding long-term reasons compel firms to introduce new products and services. Firms innovate for a number of reasons, as we discuss next.

Changing Customer Needs

When they add new products to their offerings, firms can create and deliver value more effectively by satisfying the changing needs of their current and new customers or simply by keeping customers from getting bored with the current product or service offering. For example, Unilever's Dove Beauty Bar product line successfully extended the brand into hair, face, and skin-care lines, all under the Dove umbrella. Today, Dove loyalists can enjoy not only bar soap, but also anti-perspirants and deodorants, moisturizing lotions, cleansers, toners, shampoo, conditioner, and much more.[10] Sometimes, companies can identify problems and develop products that customers never knew they needed. For example, a car wash offers a basic wash; a wash and polish; or a wash, polish, and undercarriage wash. Customers may never have thought about washing the undercarriage of their car prior to their exposure to the new service offering. In other cases, the firms take a well-known offering and innovate to make it more interesting, as Dyson has done for the vacuum cleaner. According to the company's mythology, James Dyson caught sight of a local sawmill that used a cyclone to collect sawdust from the air, and then decided to apply the concept to a vacuum cleaner so he could create a vacuum that won't lose suction. The experience he had developing and protecting his innovative technology also formed the company's present innovation process, which relies heavily on secrecy, protection of ideas, and risk taking.

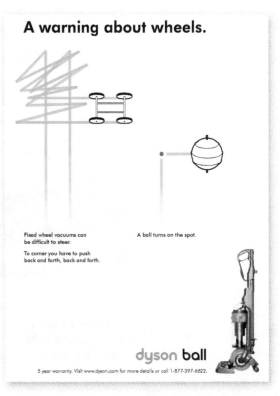

Dyson added value by taking a well-known product, the vacuum cleaner, and redesigning it so that it won't lose suction.

Market Saturation

The longer a product exists in the marketplace, the more likely it is that the market will become saturated. Without new products or services, the value of the firm will ultimately decline. Imagine, for example, if car companies simply expected that people would keep their cars until they stopped running.[11] If that were the case, there would be no need to come up with new and innovative models; companies could just stick with the models that sell well. But few consumers actually keep the same car that long. Even those who want to stay with the same make and model often want something new, just to add some variety to their lives. So car companies revamp their models every year, whether by including new features, such as GPS or a more powerful engine, or by redesigning the entire look of the vehicle. The firms sustain their growth by getting consumers excited by the new looks and new features, prompting many car buyers to exchange their old vehicle years before its functional life is over.

Saturated markets can also offer opportunities for a company that is willing to adopt a new process or mentality. At one point in time, mass marketers would not even consider entering a market that they believed would not earn at least $50 million. But General Mills is looking to niche markets for its future growth. Whereas only 1 percent of the North American population suffers from celiac disease—a condition that damages the digestive system when sufferers ingest gluten—a much higher percentage of consumers say they want to reduce or eliminate gluten, a wheat protein, from their diet. As awareness increases, those percentages are growing, such that the North American market could be worth more than $6.3 billion. General Mills has created more than 300 gluten-free products, including both variations on its regular offerings, like Chex cereals, and brand new concepts, such as gluten-free desserts and pancake mixes.[12]

Managing Risk Through Diversity

Through innovation, firms often create a broader portfolio of products, which helps them diversify their risk and enhance firm value better than a single product can.[13] If some products in a portfolio are doing poorly, others may be doing well. As we saw in the chapter vignette, tapping innovative ideas allows companies to create new products to add to their existing portfolio. Firms with multiple products are better able to withstand external shocks, including changes in consumer preferences or intensive competitive activity. For this reason, firms such as 3M demand that a specific

The Kellogg's Special K line's risk is lessened by offering many variations of its basic cereal product.

percentage of their sales each year must come from new products introduced within the previous few years. And, in the cereal aisle, Kellogg's offers many variations of its long-standing basic Special K product, including cereal bars and protein shakes. This diversification enables the company to achieve better results than it would with just one kind of Special K cereal.

Fashion Cycles

To generate sales, apparel fashion designers produce entirely new product selections a few times a year.

In industries that rely on fashion trends and experience short product life cycles—including apparel, arts, books, and software—most sales come from new products. For example, a motion picture generates most of its theatre, DVD, and cable TV revenues within a year of its release. If the same selection of books were always available for sale, with no new titles, there would be no reason to buy more. Consumers of computer software and video games demand new products because once they have "beaten" the game, they want to be challenged by another game or experience the most recent version, as the remarkable sales of successive versions of the Madden NFL game exemplify.[14] In the case of apparel, fashion designers produce entirely new product selections a few times per year.

Video games like Madden NFL are "fashionable" because consumers demand new versions. Once they have "beaten" the game, they want to be challenged with a new experience.

Improving Business Relationships

New products do not always target end consumers; sometimes they function to improve relationships with suppliers. For example, Kraft, the maker of Capri Sun, found that its lemonade flavour was selling poorly. Through a little market research, it realized that the reason was the placement of the packages in pallets. Because it was placed at the bottom of the stack in pallets, lemonade was the last flavour retailers would sell. By changing and innovating its pallet, Kraft offered chimney stacks for each flavour, enabling the retail stockers to reach whichever flavour they needed easily. Sales of Capri Sun's lemonade improved by 162 percent.[15]

Innovation and Value

New product introductions, especially new-to-the-world products that create new markets, can add tremendous value to firms. These new products, services, or processes are called **pioneers**, breakthroughs or "disruptive" because they establish a completely new market or radically change both the rules of competition and consumer preferences in a market.[16] Generally, disruptive products require a higher level of learning from consumers and offer many more benefits than predecessor products. For example, consumers had to spend a lot of time learning about the Internet to adopt it but, now that they have mastered this, its benefits have changed the way they work, play, and interact with people. On the other hand, WiFi does not require a lot of learning yet offers consumers tremendous flexibility and freedom in the way they work, communicate, and interact—anytime and anywhere once there is a WiFi hot spot or if they subscribe to mobile wireless. The Apple iPod is a pioneer product. It not only changed the way people listen to music, but also created an entirely new industry devoted to accessories, such as cases, ear buds, docking stations, and speakers. Although Apple offers many of these accessories itself, other companies have jumped on the bandwagon, ensuring that you can strap your iPod to your arm while on the move or insert it into the base of a desk lamp equipped with speakers to get music and light from your desk. And don't forget: The iPod also launched perhaps the most notable other recent pioneer, the iPhone, along with the innovative iTunes service, the iPod Touch, and even the iPad.[17]

pioneers
New product introductions that establish a completely new market or radically change both the rules of competition and consumer preferences in a market; also called breakthroughs.

Pioneers have the advantage of being **first movers**; as the first to create the market or product category, they become readily recognizable to consumers and thus establish a commanding and early market share lead. As an example, for decades consumers bought and used the Sony Walkman for mobile music, which required them to buy and carry tapes or CDs. Apple's iPod eliminated the need for CDs with its iTunes service—a radically new service associated with a digital mobile device. Freedom and convenience—the ability to carry more than 10,000 songs plus photos and videos and to share these with friends—have dramatically changed the concept of mobile music players as first introduced by Sony. Studies also have found that market pioneers can command a greater market share over a longer time period than later entrants can.[18]

first movers
Product pioneers that are the first to create a market or product category, making them readily recognizable to consumers and thus establishing a commanding and early market share lead.

This finding does not imply, however, that all pioneers succeed.[19] In many cases, imitators capitalize on the weaknesses of pioneers and subsequently gain advantage in the market. Because pioneering products and brands face the uphill task of establishing the market alone, they pave the way for followers, which can spend less marketing effort creating demand for the product category and instead focus directly on creating demand for their specific brand. Also, because the pioneer is the first product in the market, it often has a less sophisticated design and may be priced relatively higher, leaving room for better and lower-priced competitive products.

Not all new products succeed in the marketplace. The majority of new products are failures. As many as 95 percent of all consumer goods fail, and products across all markets and industries suffer failure rates of 50 to 80 percent.[20] Why? There are many reasons, but the following are most common: (1) they offer consumers too few benefits compared with existing products; (2) they are too complex or require substantial learning and effort before consumers can use them, and (3) bad timing—that is, they are introduced at a time when consumers are not ready for such new products or services. Firms may also overextend their abilities or competencies by venturing into products or services that are inconsistent with their brand image and/or value proposition. We discuss some infamous product failures in Exhibit 8.1.

Even if they succeed, new-to-the-world products are not adopted by everyone at the same time. Rather, they diffuse or spread through a population in a process known as diffusion or adoption of innovation.

LO2 ADOPTION OF INNOVATION

diffusion of innovation
The process by which the use of an innovation, whether a product or a service, spreads throughout a market group over time and over various categories of adopters.

The process by which the use of an innovation—whether a product or a service—spreads throughout a market group, over time and over various categories of adopters, is referred to as **diffusion of innovation**[21] or adoption of innovation. The theory surrounding diffusion or adoption of innovation helps marketers understand the rate at which consumers are likely to adopt a new product or service. It also gives them a means to identify potential markets for their new products or services and predict their potential sales, even before they introduce the innovations.

As the consumer adoption cycle in Exhibit 8.2 shows, the number of users of an innovative product or service spreads through the population over time and generally follows a bell-shaped curve. A few people buy the product or service at first, then increasingly more buy, and finally fewer people buy as the degree of the diffusion slows. For example, it took close to 20 years to get about 90 percent of Canadians to use ATMs (automated teller machines) but within five years more than 60 percent of Canadians adopted the

EXHIBIT 8.1	Illustrative Product Failures

Product	Concept	Why It Failed
New Coke	In response to growing market pressure, Coca-Cola launched a reformulated version of its classic cola in 1985 that was so hated it was pulled from shelves three months later.	Coke underestimated the consumer's affinity to the original formulation and their unwillingness to change.
Sony Betamax	In 1975, Sony bet big on the Betamax, one the first ever mass-produced home video recording systems.	Unfortunately, the next year JVC launched the VHS player, ensuing a format-war similar to the Blu-Ray and HD-DVD format wars of 2006.
Harley Davidson Perfume	After being successful with lighters and T-shirts bearing the Harley logo, Harley Davidson branched out into its own line of perfumes "associated" with the motorcycle lifestyle.	Although lighters and T-shirts may resonate with the Harley image, customers were not as attracted to smelling like a motorcycle.
Bic Underwear	Bic is well-known for its disposable products: pens, lighters, and razors. Capitalizing on their ability to cross product categories, Bic began producing underwear.	The concept of buying underwear from a company well known for disposable pens was confusing and off-putting to consumers.
Frito Lay Lemonade	To Frito Lay, lemonade seemed like a reasonable enough brand extension. After all, the high salt content of corn chips often leads consumers to search out something to quench their thirst.	Associating a salty snack with a supposed "thirst quencher" did not go over well.
Colgate Kitchen Entrees	Colgate launched a line of frozen dinners. Apparently the idea was that consumers would enjoy eating a Colgate meal and then using Colgate on their toothbrush afterward.	The association of toothpaste with a chicken stirfry was something customers did not find appetizing.

Source: DailyFinance.com, Top 25 Biggest Product Flops of All Time. http://www.dailyfinance.com/photos/top-25-biggest-product-flops-of-all-time/3662621.

EXHIBIT 8.2   Consumer Adoption Cycle

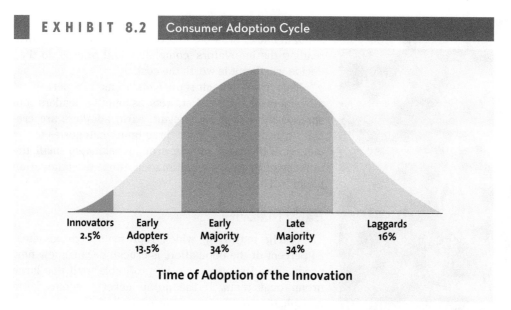

Time of Adoption of the Innovation

| Innovators 2.5% | Early Adopters 13.5% | Early Majority 34% | Late Majority 34% | Laggards 16% |

Source: Adapted from Everett M. Rodgers, Diffusion of Innovation (New York: The Free Press, 1983).

Internet. Comparing the iPod and Sony Walkman, Merrill Lynch analyst Steve Milunovich observes that after only 2.5 years, iPod shipments were approximately 1 million units ahead of the Walkman's pace after being on the market for the same period of time in the 1980s when the Walkman was first released.[22] Apple's iPad reached 1 million units in its first 28 days—less than half the 74 days it took for the iPhone to reach the same milestone.[23]

Purchasers can be divided into five groups according to how soon they buy the product after it has been introduced.

Innovators

Innovators are those buyers who want to be the first on the block to have the new product or service. These buyers enjoy taking risks, are regarded as highly knowledgeable, and are not price sensitive. You probably know someone who is an innovator—or perhaps you are one for a particular product or service category. For example, the person who stood in line for days to be sure to get a ticket for the very first showing of the latest superhero movie is an innovator in that context. Firms that invest in the latest technology, either to use in their products or services or to make the firm more efficient, also are considered innovators. Typically, innovators keep themselves very well informed about the product category by subscribing to trade and specialty magazines, talking to other "experts," searching the Internet, and attending product-related forums, seminars, and special events. Typically, innovators represent only about 2.5 percent of the total market for any new product or service.

However, these innovators are crucial to the success of any new product or service because they help the product gain market acceptance. Through talking and spreading positive word-of-mouth about the new product, they prove instrumental in bringing in the next adopter category, known as early adopters.

Early Adopters

The second subgroup that begins to use a product or service innovation is the **early adopters**. They generally don't like to take as much risk as innovators but instead wait and purchase the product after careful review. Early adopters tend to enjoy novelty and often are regarded as the opinion leaders for particular product categories. Thus, this market waits for the first reviews of the latest movie before purchasing a ticket, though

innovators
Those buyers who want to be the first to have the new product or service.

early adopters
The second group of consumers in the diffusion of innovation model, after innovators, to use a product or service innovation; generally don't like to take as much risk as innovators.

When you go see a movie like *The Avengers*, are you an early adopter, early majority, late majority, or laggard?

they likely still go a week or two after it opens. They don't stand in line to grab the first Samsung Galaxy; only after reading the innovators' complaints and praises do they decide whether it is worth the cost.

This group, which represents about 13.5 percent of all buyers in the market, acts as opinion leaders and spreads the word. As a result, early adopters are crucial for bringing the other three buyer categories to the market. If the early adopter group is relatively small, the number of people who ultimately adopt the innovation likely will also be small.

Early Majority

The **early majority**, which represents approximately 34 percent of the population, is crucial because few new products and services can be profitable until this large group buys them. If the group never becomes large enough, the product or service typically fails.

The early majority group differs in many ways from buyers in the first two stages. Its members don't like to take as much risk and therefore tend to wait until "the bugs" are worked out of a particular product or service. If we continue our application to movies, this group probably streams the latest Marvel movie when it first becomes available for streaming. Thus, they experience little risk, because all the reviews are in, and their costs are lower because they're streaming the movie instead of going to the theatre. When early majority customers enter the market, the number of competitors in the marketplace usually also has reached its peak, so these buyers have many different price and quality choices.

Late Majority

early majority
A group of consumers in the diffusion of innovation model that represents approximately 34 percent of the population; members don't like to take much risk and therefore tend to wait until bugs are worked out.

At 34 percent of the market, the **late majority** is the last group of buyers to enter a new product market; when they do, the product has achieved its full market potential. Perhaps these movie watchers wait until the latest movie has been available online for months or when it finally comes to cable television. Either way, they watch the movie long after the other consumers interested in it have already seen it. By the time the late majority enters the market, sales tend to level off or may be in decline.

Laggards

late majority
The last group of buyers to enter a new product market.

Laggards make up roughly 16 percent of the market. These consumers like to avoid change and rely on traditional products until they are no longer available.[24] In some cases, laggards may never adopt a certain product or service. When the final *Iron Man* movie eventually shows up on regular TV networks, they are likely to go ahead and watch it. Other examples of laggards are households that still use rotary phones versus touchtone models or listen to music on audiocassettes because they do not own an MP3 player. Very few companies actively pursue these customers.

laggards
Consumers who like to avoid change and rely on traditional products until they are no longer available.

Using the Adoption Cycle

Using the diffusion of innovation theory or adoption cycle, firms can predict which types of customers will buy their new product or service immediately after its introduction, as well as later as the product gets more and more accepted by the market. With this knowledge, the firm can develop effective promotion, pricing, and other marketing strategies to push acceptance among each customer group.

When Amazon first introduced its Kindle e-book reader for around $400, it sold out in less than five hours.[25] The Kindle 2 arrived at an initial price of $359. Within six months, Amazon announced a price below $300, to acknowledge the inroads made by competitors such as Barnes & Noble, Sony, and Apple.[26] Then as the market continued to grow—to approximately 20 million buyers—and Apple's iPad shifted expectations, Amazon plunged ahead with its "iPad killer," the Kindle Fire, priced at just under $200. The plan seems to have been successful; although Amazon does not publish sales numbers, estimates indicate that it sold approximately 6 million Kindle Fire devices within just a few months of its introduction.[27]

However, because different products are adopted at different rates, marketers must understand what the diffusion curve for the new product looks like, as well as the characteristics of the target customers in each stage of the diffusion. For example, the marketing decisions for e-readers are notably different from the parallel decisions for electronic books. When the e-readers first emerged on the market, the price of e-books was a fraction of the price of hardcover versions—a policy that made sense to consumers. But as e-readers have grown increasingly popular and widespread, the price of e-books has become comparable to, and in some cases higher than, the price of the hardcover versions.[28] The speed with which products are adopted depends on several product characteristics, illustrated in Exhibit 8.3. In the next sections, we'll look at how Apple has responded to Amazon's Kindle and the e-reader and tablet market as a whole with its iPad.

Relative Advantage If a product is perceived to be better than substitutes, then the diffusion will be relatively quick. Instead of offering just an e-reader, Apple developed a multipurpose "tablet" device (the iPad). When launched, the iPad had several relative advantages, including a touch screen, a vibrant and large colour screen, access to various games and apps, and the ability to watch videos and listen to music.[29]

Compatibility Most business professionals and executives have to make decisions in a timely fashion and be able to communicate their decisions in a timely manner also;

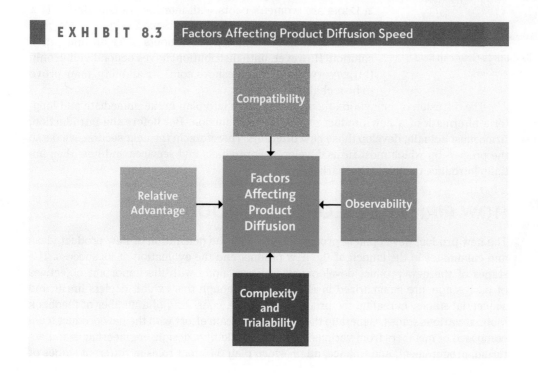

EXHIBIT 8.3 Factors Affecting Product Diffusion Speed

What made BlackBerry successful? It has a strong relative advantage to other smartphones. It is compatible with people's current behaviour. Products are easily observable by others. It is not complex and is easy to try.

Boots designed by Elizabeth LeGear can hold credit cards, a cellphone, and keys.

they need real-time information to do this. The BlackBerry is compatible with this mode of operation, and so its popularity is hardly surprising. Similarly, the ritual of "having a coffee" is well ingrained in many cultures, including Canadian culture. "Having a coffee" is consistent with people's past behaviour, their needs, and their values. Since people are accustomed to drinking coffee, it has been relatively easy for Starbucks to acquire customers in Canada. The diffusion has been much slower in countries such as China and Japan, where tea has been the traditional drink.

Observability
When products are easily observed, their benefits or uses are easily communicated to others, which enhances the diffusion process. Consumers seeing their friends using the iPad, seeing the devices on television or on YouTube, or reading about them in the deluge of media coverage surrounding each iPad release may be convinced to purchase one as well. In contrast, since people may not want to talk about their Botox treatments to reduce wrinkles, the use of this product is less easily observed by others and therefore diffused more slowly.

Complexity and Trialability
Products that are relatively less complex are also relatively easy to try. These products will generally diffuse more quickly than those that are not. Most customers who may be interested in purchasing a new tablet know that they can go to any Apple store and immediately try it there in the store. The options for trying a Kindle are a little more complex. Due to the lack of Amazon stores, consumers may not be aware that they can get one at The Source or Staples. But even the consumers who go to one of these stores often run into an availability problem—whereas Apple stores may have dozens of iPads for customers to try, electronics stores typically have just a few floor models. Purse 'n Boots are women's boots with interior pockets that hold a cellphone, credit cards, change, and keys. Designed in Calgary by Elizabeth LeGear, the patented boots offer an innovative solution. However, until distribution moves beyond online only (http://www.elizabethanneshoes.com), trialability may prove to be a challenge.

The diffusion of innovation theory thus comes into play in the immediate and long-term aftermath of a new product or service introduction. But before the introduction, firms must actually develop those new offerings. Therefore, in the next section, we detail the process by which most firms develop new products and services and how they initially introduce them into the market.

L03 HOW FIRMS DEVELOP NEW PRODUCTS

The new product development process begins with the generation of new product ideas and culminates in the launch of the new product and the evaluation of its success. The stages of the new product development process, along with the important objectives of each stage, are summarized in Exhibit 8.4. Although this exhibit depicts linear and sequential stages, in reality, the process is iterative, consisting of a number of feedback loops at various stages. Generally the process is a team effort with the new product team composed of members from various functions: marketing, design, engineering, manufacturing, procurement, and finance, all of which play different roles at different stages of

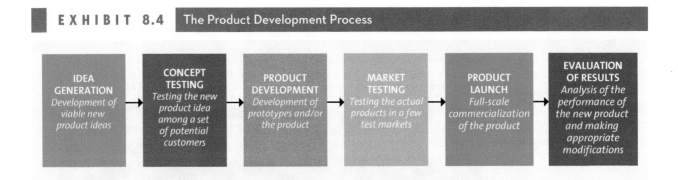

EXHIBIT 8.4 The Product Development Process

IDEA GENERATION
Development of viable new product ideas

CONCEPT TESTING
Testing the new product idea among a set of potential customers

PRODUCT DEVELOPMENT
Development of prototypes and/or the product

MARKET TESTING
Testing the actual products in a few test markets

PRODUCT LAUNCH
Full-scale commercialization of the product

EVALUATION OF RESULTS
Analysis of the performance of the new product and making appropriate modifications

the process. Marketing plays a crucial role in the new product development process by communicating customer needs and wants and marketplace preferences and attitudes to the research and development (R&D) and engineering group.

Bear in mind that it's not always necessary to take a new product through each stage in the process. Substantially new products will likely follow the process fairly closely, while products imitating a successful product from a competitor, having a low development cost, or involving incremental changes (such as line extensions) may skip one or more steps. For example, P&G launched its Folgers brand of decaffeinated crystal coffee without market testing. Although skipping stages in the new product development process is very risky, companies often do it to reduce costs or launch new products quickly.

Idea Generation

To generate ideas for new products, a firm can use its own internal R&D efforts, collaborate with other firms and institutions, license technology from research-intensive firms, brainstorm, research competitors' products and services, and/or conduct consumer research. Sometimes new product ideas come from employees, customers, suppliers, and partners or are generated by attending trade shows and conferences. Companies also generate ideas by using reverse engineering or, in more extreme cases, even by digging through a competitor's garbage. See Exhibit 8.5 for an example of how employee ideas resulted in a new product. Firms that want to be pioneers rely more extensively on R&D efforts, whereas those that tend to adopt a follower strategy are more likely to scan the market for ideas. Let's look at each of these idea sources.

Internal Research and Development Many firms have their own R&D departments, in which scientists work to solve complex problems and develop new ideas.[30] Historically, firms such as IBM in the computer industry, Black and Decker in the consumer goods industry, 3M in the industrial goods industry, and Merck and Pfizer in the pharmaceuticals industry have relied on R&D efforts for their new products. In other industries, such as software, music, and motion pictures, product development efforts also tend to come from internal ideas and investments. 3M is known for innovation and has product offerings spanning an incredible range of categories from health care to highway safety, from office and pet care products to fly fishing equipment and solar film. Because the company is committed to providing useful, new products to customers, 3M reinvests a significant percentage of its revenues in research.[31] It allows its researchers to spend time pursuing their own interests so when industrial architects asked 3M for some ideas for lighting their studios, it put one of its creative designers on the project. The result, the nine-foot Hoop Light, won 3M design awards at interior design international competitions.[32]

The product development costs for firms are quite high, but the resulting new product or service has a good chance of being a technological or market breakthrough. Firms expect such products to generate enough revenue and profits to make the costs of R&D

Post-it® Notes were not a planned product. Spencer Silver was working at the 3M research laboratories in 1970 trying to find a strong adhesive. He developed a new adhesive, but it was even weaker than what 3M already manufactured. It stuck to objects but could easily be lifted off.

No one knew what to do with the adhesive but Silver didn't discard it. Then one Sunday, four years later, another 3M scientist named Arthur Fry was singing in the church's choir. He used markers to keep his place in the hymnal, but they kept falling out of the book. Remembering Silver's adhesive, Fry used some to coat his markers. Success! With the weak adhesive, the markers stayed in place, yet lifted off the pages without damaging them. 3M began distributing Post-it® Notes nationwide in 1980—10 years after Silver developed the super weak adhesive. Today, they are one of the most popular office products available.

Source: Adapted from Post-it® Note History, http://www.ideafinder.com/history/inventions/postit.htm (accessed April 24, 2014).

worthwhile; however, R&D investments generally are considered continuous investments, so firms may lose money on a few new products. In the long run though, these firms are betting that a few extremely successful new products, often known as blockbusters, can generate enough revenues and profits to cover the losses from other introductions that might not fare so well.

Some global firms also are taking an approach called "reverse innovation." They turn to subsidiaries in less developed markets for new product ideas. From its Shanghai research centre, Coca-Cola developed Minute Maid Pulpy, a new juice drink that the corporation has moved into 19 countries and is now worth more than $1 billion. Levi's Denizen brand got its start in India and China, where the company worked on ideas for producing more affordable jeans. In the U.S. market, Denizen jeans sell for about half the cost of a pair of regular Levi's.[33]

Licensing   For many new scientific and technological products, firms buy the rights to use the technology or ideas from other research-intensive firms through a licensing agreement. This approach saves the high costs of in-house R&D, but it means that the firm is banking on a solution that already exists but has not been marketed. For example, many pharmaceutical firms license products developed by biotechnology firms such as Amgen, Biogen, and Genentech. Because most biotechnology firms are smaller, tend to be very research focused, and lack the resources and expertise to market their own innovations, they are content to obtain some development financing and royalties on sales of their product from the pharmaceutical firms.[34] As discussed in Entrepreneurial Marketing 8.1, sometimes licensing offers an ideal solution to companies seeking to get their designs to market faster.

Entrepreneurial Marketing 8.1 — Rise and Shine[35]

Tired of commuting an hour and a half each way to and from college, Lee Renshaw often stayed on campus or at his girlfriend's house overnight. He soon got used to living out of a duffel bag. Although his travel problem was solved, new ones were created. Packing his clothes in a duffel bag left him looking wrinkled and he was unable to easily find things. After many late nights experimenting, he came up with a concept for a duffel bag that hangs and comes with built-in portable shelves, keeping clothes organized and ready to wear. The bag even had a hamper in the bottom to hold clothes for laundering.

With a background in industrial design, Lee recognized that there had been very little innovation in the luggage industry since wheels were added to make bags roll. Armed with this knowledge, he got a design patent on the way his shelves attached inside the bag and pulled out for use. He enlisted his brother Sean and formed Rise and Hang Travel Gear. It took two years of development, and another 18 months to get the bag to market. They ordered 2,000 bags and sold 100 at $70 each. The early sales helped prove the concept. But to get department stores interested in carrying his product, Lee would need an entire line of luggage.

Marketing became a big challenge. The ideal solution was to find a licensee to make and sell the bags. Lee pitched his idea on CBC's *Dragons' Den* and got overwhelming approval. The brothers accepted a deal with David Chilton and Arlene Dickinson, however, ended up not taking it. A lot of time and due diligence passes after taping the show, with no guarantee it will ever make it to air. And so Lee and Sean kept exploring options and managed to secure distribution via the Shopping Channel. They hired a public relations firm in Florida that got them on the *Today Show* with Kathy Lee Gifford and Hoda Kotb. The resulting exposure crashed their website and got their bag featured in *Men's Health*.

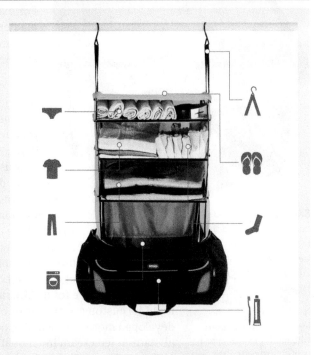

The Rise and Hang Weekender bag features shelving for easy packing and retrieval of clothes.

It also attracted a licensee. A deal was struck, giving the brothers sign-off on all new designs and a royalty on each bag sold. The licensee looks after manufacturing and sales. Their website collects demographic data that helps the brothers brainstorm new design ideas. There are now plans for a whole line of luggage including a low-end, midline, carry-on, and higher-end model with wheels. The midline model is branded with the Elle name. Licenses to sell the line on QVC and the Home Shopping Network will help the bag rise and shine even further.

Brainstorming Firms often engage in brainstorming sessions during which a group works together to generate ideas. One of the key characteristics of a brainstorming session is that no idea can be immediately accepted or rejected. The moderator of the session may channel participants' attention to specific product features and attributes, performance expectations, or packaging. Only at the end of the session do the members vote on the best ideas or combinations of ideas. Those ideas that receive the most votes are carried forward to the next stage of the product development process.

Competitors' Products A new product entry by a competitor may trigger a market opportunity for a firm, which can use reverse engineering to understand the competitor's product and then bring an improved version to market. **Reverse engineering** involves taking apart a competitor's product, analyzing it, and creating an improved product that does not infringe on the competitor's patents, if any exist. This copycat approach to new product development is widespread and practised by even the most

reverse engineering Involves taking apart a competitor's product, analyzing it, and creating an improved product that does not infringe on the competitor's patents, if any exist.

Staples observed how customers opened their mail in the kitchen and so developed the Mailmate shredder to look like a kitchen appliance.

lead users
Innovative product users who modify existing products according to their own ideas to suit their specific needs.

These innovative consumers are called lead users because they modify existing products according to their own ideas to suit their specific needs.

research-intensive firms. Copycat consumer goods show up in grocery and drugstore products, as well as in technologically more complex products such as automobiles and computers. For example, China Unicom Ltd., the state-controlled telecommunications giant ranked as China's second-biggest mobile operator, launched RedBerry, a new product aimed squarely at BlackBerry.[36]

Customer Input Listening to the customer is essential for successful idea generation.[37]Prior studies have found that as much as 85 percent of all new business-to-business (B2B) product ideas come from customers.[38] Because customers for B2B products are relatively few in number, firms can follow their use of products closely and survey them often for suggestions and ideas to improve those products. The firm's design and development team then works on these suggestions, sometimes in consultation with the customer. This joint effort between the selling firm and the customer significantly increases the probability that the customer eventually will buy the new product.

Customer input in B2C markets comes from a variety of sources. In some cases, consumers may not expressly demand a new product, though their behaviour demonstrates their desire for it. After analyzing its sales data, Walmart realized that the majority of its customers always or often buy store brands rather than national brands. So it developed more varied and appealing versions of its Great Value store brand, including all-natural ice cream in innovative flavours like cake batter and mocha mud.[39] Staples observed how people use products in their homes and noticed that people opened their mail in the kitchen but waited to shred it until they got to their office. Using this information, Staples designed the Mailmate, a stainless steel shredder that looks like a kitchen appliance so it blends in with the kitchen decor and customers can shred their mail instantly after opening it.[40]

Companies also realize that their customers are on the web—writing customer reviews on retailers' websites and talking about their experiences on Yelp.com or Twitter. By monitoring feedback through these online communities, companies can get better ideas about new products or necessary changes to existing ones. Many companies also proactively develop their own online communities to focus the conversations around topics in which they are interested.

A particularly successful customer input approach is to analyze **lead users**, those innovative product users who modify existing products according to their own ideas to suit their specific needs.[41] These lead users have customized the firm's products; other customers might wish to do so as well. Studying lead users helps the firm understand general market trends that might be just on the horizon. Manufacturers and retailers of fashion products often spot new trends by noticing how trendsetters have altered their clothing and shoes. For instance, designers of high-fashion jeans distress their products in different ways depending on signals they pick up "on the street." One season, jeans appear with whiskers; the next, holes; the next, paint spots.

At the end of the idea-generation stage, the firm should have several ideas that it can take forward to the next stage: concept testing.

Concept Testing

Ideas with potential are developed further into **concepts**, which in this context refers to brief written descriptions of the product; its technology, working principles, and forms; and what customer needs it would satisfy.[42] A concept might also include visual images of what the product would look like.

Concept testing refers to the process in which a concept statement is presented to potential buyers representative of the target market or users to obtain their reactions. These reactions enable the developer to estimate the sales value of the product or service concept, possibly make changes to enhance its sales value, and determine whether the idea is worth further development.[43] If the concept fails to meet customers' expectations, it is doubtful it would succeed if it were to be produced and marketed. Because concept testing occurs very early in the new product introduction process, even before a real product has been made, it helps the firm avoid the costs of unnecessary product development.

The concept for an electric scooter might be written as follows:

> The product is a lightweight electric scooter that can be easily folded and taken with you inside a building or on public transportation. The scooter weighs 25 pounds [11 kg]. It travels at speeds of up to 15 miles [24 km] per hour and can go about 12 miles [19 km] on a single charge. The scooter can be recharged in about two hours from a standard electric outlet. The scooter is easy to ride and has simple controls—just an accelerator button and a brake. It sells for $299.[44]

Concept testing progresses along the research techniques described in Chapter 7. The firm likely starts with qualitative research, such as in-depth interviews or focus groups, to test the concept, after which it can undertake quantitative research through Internet or mall-intercept surveys. Video clips on the Internet might show a virtual prototype and the way the product or service works so that potential customers can evaluate it.[45] In a mall-intercept survey, an interviewer would provide a description of the concept to the respondent and then ask several questions to obtain his or her feedback.

The most important question pertains to the respondent's purchase intentions if the product or service were to be made available. Marketers also should ask whether the product would satisfy a need that other products currently are not meeting. Depending on the type of product or service, researchers might also ask about the expected frequency of purchase, how much customers would buy, whether they would buy it for themselves or as a gift, when they would buy, and whether the price information (if provided) indicates a good value. In addition, marketers usually collect some demographic information so they can analyze which consumer segments are likely to be most interested in the product.

Some concepts never make it past this stage, particularly if respondents seem uninterested. Those that do receive high evaluations from potential consumers, however, move on to the next step, product development.

Product Development

Product development or product design entails a process of balancing various engineering, manufacturing, marketing, and economic considerations to develop a product's form and features or a service's features. An engineering team develops a product prototype that is based on research findings from the previous concept testing step, as well as their own knowledge about materials and technology. A **prototype** is the first physical form or service description of a new product, still in rough or tentative form that has the same properties as a new product but is produced through different manufacturing processes, sometimes even crafted individually.[46]

Product prototypes are usually tested through alpha and beta testing. In **alpha testing**, the firm attempts to determine whether the product will perform according to its

concepts
Brief written descriptions of a product or service; its technology, working principles, and forms; and what customer needs it would satisfy.

concept testing
The process in which a concept statement that describes a product or a service is presented to potential buyers or users to obtain their reactions.

product development
Entails a process of balancing various engineering, manufacturing, marketing, and economic considerations to develop a product.

prototype
The first physical form or service description of a new product, still in rough or tentative form, that has the same properties as a new product but is produced through different manufacturing processes, sometimes even crafted individually.

alpha testing
An attempt by the firm to determine whether a product will perform according to its design and whether it satisfies the need for which it was intended; occurs in the firm's R&D department.

Ben & Jerry's uses alpha testing with its own employees to make sure its products have the right taste and feel.

design and whether it satisfies the need for which it was intended.[47] Rather than using potential consumers, alpha tests occur in the firm's R&D department. For instance, Ben & Jerry's alpha tests all its proposed new ice cream flavours on its own employees at its corporate headquarters in Vermont.

As discussed in Ethical Dilemma 8.1, many people, consumer groups, and governmental agencies are concerned when alpha testing involves tests on animals, particularly when it comes to pharmaceuticals and cosmetics.

In contrast, **beta testing** uses potential consumers, who examine the product prototype in a "real use" setting to determine its functionality, performance, potential problems, and other issues specific to its use. The firm might develop several prototype products that it gives to users, and then survey those users to determine whether the prod-

beta testing
Having potential consumers examine a product prototype in a real-use setting to determine its functionality, performance, potential problems, and other issues specific to its use.

uct worked as intended and to identify any issues that need resolution.

Household products manufacturer Kimberly-Clark uses virtual testing in the beta-testing phase of its product development process. The consumer goods company uses a virtual store aisle that mimics a real-life shopping experience by creating a realistic picture of the interior of the store. A retina-tracking device records the movement of a test customer who "shops" the virtual aisle of a store and chooses certain products to investigate further in the virtual simulation. Thus, consumer companies can demonstrate the likely success, or failure, of a product without actually having to produce it for a market and, potentially, expose its secrets to competitors.[48]

Market Testing

The firm has developed its new product or service and tested the prototypes. Now it must test the market for the new product with a trial batch of products although, as mentioned earlier, companies sometimes skip this step because of competitive, timing, or cost pressures. These tests can take two forms: premarket testing or test marketing.

premarket test
Conducted before a product or service is brought to market to determine how many customers will try and then continue to use it.

Premarket Tests
Firms conduct **premarket tests** before they actually bring a product or service to market to determine how many customers will try and then continue to use the product or service according to a small group of potential consumers. One popular proprietary premarket test version is called Nielsen BASES. During the test, potential customers are exposed to the marketing mix variables, such as the advertising, and then surveyed and given a sample of the product to try.[49] After some period of time, during which the potential customers try the product, they are surveyed about whether they would buy/use the product again. This second survey indicates an estimation of the probability of a consumer's repeat purchase. From these data, the firm generates a sales estimate for the new product that enables it to decide whether to introduce the product, abandon it, redesign it before introduction, or revise the marketing plan. An early evaluation of this sort—that is, before the product is introduced to the whole market—saves marketers the costs of a nationwide launch if the product fails.

Sometimes firms simulate a product or service introduction,[50] in which case potential customers view the advertising of various currently available products or services along with advertising for the new product or service. They receive money to buy the product or service from a simulated environment, such as a mock web page or store, and respond to a survey after they make their purchases. This test thus can determine the effectiveness of a firm's advertising as well as the expected trial rates for the new product.

Should Firms Test on Animals?

Product testing on animals has been a primary issue for animal right activists for years.[51] As public opposition to animal testing increases, so do many companies' declarations that they "do not test products on animals." However, such statements can be misleading because even though the whole product may not have been tested on animals, the individual ingredients may have been. To help clarify any confusion, companies can apply to the Coalition for Consumer Information on Cosmetics (CCIC), a national group formed by eight animal welfare group members, and be certified as "cruelty free." They can then purchase the trademarked Leaping Bunny Logo from CCIC for use on their labels.

One of the founding principles of The Body Shop, and one that has resonated well with its customers, is that its products are free of animal testing. While the website for The Body Shop states that it has never tested or commissioned testing of its ingredients or products on animals, many of the ingredients in its products were in fact tested on animals by other companies. This discrepancy caused confusion and resulted in the company changing the labels on its products from "not tested on animals" to "against animal testing" because it is impossible to avoid ingredients ever tested on animals.[52] Another major cosmetics manufacturer, P&G, has eliminated animal testing on more than 80 percent of its products. It uses a combination of vitro testing, computer modelling, and historical data to determine the safety of new products and ingredients. These methods are more expensive than more traditional methods, but P&G claims that the results are better. If performed correctly, new chemicals can either be dropped from consideration or pushed forward in as little as three days compared with the six months previously required for animal testing.

However, animal welfare groups continue to push P&G and other firms to stop the use of animal testing altogether. People for the Ethical Treatment of Animals (PETA) publicly cites companies it accuses of engaging in animal testing and other activities considered to be inhumane, and praises those that do not. PETA's efforts have caused firms like Hugo Boss, H&M, and Liz Claiborne to stop buying their wool from Australia because some Australian sheep farmers shear their sheep's wool in inhumane ways. The European Union has passed a ban

Activists of the People for the Ethical Treatment of Animals (PETA) participate in a protest against animal slaughter near a mall where Hermes—the French luxury goods company—has a store in Jakarta, Indonesia. PETA demanded Hermes stop selling exotic animal skin products.

on animal testing altogether. As of 2009, any cosmetic tested on animals, even in other parts of the world, cannot be sold in the European Union. However, the cosmetic industry is worried that this ban will not only affect their companies' sales, but also their customers' ability to find the products they want. The E.U. cosmetics industry successfully lobbied for an extension on certain areas of toxicity testing to provide more time to find alternatives. The cosmetic industry believes it will be difficult to find alternative testing methods in time. If it cannot, then it will have fewer ingredients to make the products consumers want.

The issues involved in animal testing for cosmetics are complex. At the broadest level, should firms be allowed to develop products that customers want, even if there is some potential harm to the environment or to those animals that share the environment with humans? More specifically, should firms be allowed to test products on animals, even when those products are not specifically designed to improve the health and well-being of their human users? After all, these products may make their users more attractive, but they will not save their lives. Does the testing that is performed endanger the lives or health of the animals?

Test Marketing A method of determining the success potential of a new product, test marketing introduces the offering to a limited geographical area (usually a few cities) prior to a national launch. A **test marketing** effort uses all the elements of the marketing mix. It includes promotions such as advertising and coupons, just as if the product were being introduced nationally, and the product appears in targeted retail outlets, with appropriate pricing. On the basis of the results of the test marketing, the firm can estimate demand for the entire market. McDonald's tested its McCafé

test marketing
Introduces a new product or service to a limited geographical area (usually a few cities) prior to a national launch.

concept—cappuccinos, lattes, European-style pastries—in 70 Atlantic Canada locations to determine whether it should roll them out across the country.[53]

Test marketing costs more and takes longer than premarket tests, which may provide an advantage to competitors that could get a similar or better product to market first. For this reason, some firms might launch new products without extensive consumer testing and rely instead on intuition, instincts, and guts.[54] However, test marketing offers a key advantage: The firm can study actual consumer behaviour, which is more reliable than a simulated test. Labatt chose Calgary and Edmonton as the test markets for its Brazilian Brahma beer. As a test market, Calgary offers an attractive demographic in terms of income levels, lifestyle, and a relatively youthful population.

Other cities are used for test markets for a variety of reasons. London, Ontario, is often chosen because its population is reflective of a "typical" Canadian city. That might be why Tim Hortons tested a dark roast coffee in London as well as in Columbus, Ohio.[55] Winnipeg is a good location to test shampoos and skin lotions for dry skin because of its long, cold winters. Recognizing that health food is no longer a niche segment, Loblaw tested a small, health-focused retail store concept in Toronto called Nutshell Live Life Well. The pilot store on King Street in Toronto was designed to attract the urban shoppers who flock to upscale grocers such as Whole Foods. The store sold a variety of prepared, fresh, and packaged foods, as well as health and beauty products, vitamins and supplements, and prescription drugs from an in-store pharmacy.[56] Loblaw cancelled the pilot after making a bid to buy Shoppers Drug Mart. In the restaurant industry, "fast-casual" chains have experienced the fastest growth. As a result, KFC is testing a new concept with a location called "KFCeleven." The name is a nod to the 11 herbs and spices used by Colonel Sanders in the original recipe. The new venue features boneless pieces of chicken, fresh salads, flatbread sandwiches, rice bowls, garlic mashed potatoes, and waffle fries aimed at winning back consumers in their 20s and 30s who moved to chains perceived as offering better food for only marginally higher prices.[57]

Many firms use BehaviorScan to improve the probability of success during the test marketing phase of a new product introduction. BehaviorScan utilizes consumer panel data collected passively at the point of sale in stores and through home scanning to measure individual household first-time trial and repeat purchases. New products are placed in stores within one week of introduction, rather than the typical 8- to 12-week period. Since more sales data are collected in a shorter period of time than conventional test-marketing methods, first-year sales can be estimated after just 16 to 24 weeks in the test market.[58] Once the market demand is estimated, the product is released nationally.

However, sometimes test marketing can result in tipping your hand to competitors, who carefully monitor sales and preemptively launch their own products. For instance, Kellogg's tracked sales of Toast'ems during test marketing by General Foods. Noting they were becoming popular, they quickly went national with Pop-Tarts before the test was finished. General Foods invented freeze-dried coffee and was in the midst of test marketing its Maxim brand when Nestlé launched Taster's Choice, which went on to become the leading brand.[59]

Product Launch

If the market testing returns with positive results, the firm is ready to introduce the product to the entire market. This is the most critical step in the new product introduction and requires tremendous financial resources and extensive co-ordination of all aspects of the marketing mix. If the new product launch is a failure, it may be difficult for the product—and perhaps the firm—to recover. In the food and beverage industry, where new product failure rates are as high as 78 percent, Kraft minimizes its risk through a new product development process that includes consumer research. Some products show great promise after launch though, as Exhibit 8.6 describes.

| EXHIBIT 8.6 | Best New Products[60] |

Below is sampling of winners as voted by Canadians in the Product of the Year Awards.

Product	Company	Category
Pepperidge Farms Cracker Chips	Campbell Company of Canada	Dry Snacks
iogo Greko	Aliments Ultimata Foods	Greek Yogurt
Maple Leaf Bacon Portions	Maple Leaf Foods	Fresh Packaged Meats

Source: http://productoftheyear.ca/winners/winning-products/winning-products-2013/ (accessed July 18, 2013).

So what does a product launch involve? First, the firm confirms its target market(s) and decides how the product will be positioned. This is done using research it has gathered on consumer perceptions and tests it has conducted, as well as any competitive considerations. Then the firm finalizes the remaining marketing mix variables for the new product, including the marketing budget for the first year.[61]

Promotion The test results help the firm determine an appropriate integrated marketing communications strategy.[62] For products that are somewhat complex or conceptually new, marketers may need to provide for more consumer education about the product's benefits than they would for simpler and more familiar products. The quantum dot technology that is being developed to improve the LCD screens on televisions, computers, and mobile phones is not something that most consumers understand. But marketers can encourage their adoption by highlighting the clearly evident appeal of energy efficiency, longer battery life, and more vibrant colour offered by the innovative technology.[63] In addition, technical support staff, like Apple's Geniuses, often must be trained to answer customer questions that may arise immediately after the launch of a new technical innovation.

Place The firm must have an adequate quantity of products available for shipment and to keep in stock at relevant stores. The product offering should also be as complete as possible. For example, a firm launching a new printer should ensure it has an adequate supply of the related cartridges or toners. Interested consumers can purchase an iPhone from any Bell, Rogers, or TELUS wireless product location. This accessibility not only provides the new product in a convenient location, but also allows the opportunity for tailored customer service and subscription to appropriate service plans.

Price The firm needs to ensure that it gets the price right. It is sometimes easier to start with a higher price and offer promotions (e.g., coupons, rebates) and then over time to lower the price than it is to introduce the new product at a low price and then try to raise it. The BlackBerry Q10 is a premium telecommunications product commanding a fitting price of $699.95 without a service contract. However, carriers entice new buyers by bundling a reduced price for the Q10 if a service plan is included. The price can drop by hundreds of dollars, or even to zero with a long-term contract.[64]

Timing The timing of the launch may be important, depending on the product.[65] Hollywood studios typically release movies targeted toward general audiences (i.e., those rated G or PG) during the summer when children are out of school. New automobile models traditionally are released for sale during September, and fashion products are launched just before the season of the year for which they are intended.

Evaluation of Results

After the product has been launched, marketers must undertake a critical postlaunch review to determine whether the product and its launch were a success or a failure and what additional resources or changes to the marketing mix are needed, if any. Some products never make it out of the introduction stage and are almost laughable in retrospect. Bic underwear?[66] Harley Davidson perfume? Bottled water for pets? Firms measure the success of a new product by three interrelated factors: (1) its satisfaction of technical requirements, such as performance; (2) customer acceptance; and (3) its satisfaction of the firm's financial requirements, such as sales and profits.[67] If the product is not performing sufficiently well, poor customer acceptance will result, which in turn leads to poor financial performance. McDonald's introduced salads in 2003 to compete against Wendy's. However, McDonald's CEO Donald Thompson recently stated that salads are a failed strategy, representing only 1 to 2 percent of total sales.[68] The new product development process, when followed rationally and sequentially, helps avoid such domino-type failures. Coca-Cola learned from past mistakes when launching Coke Freestyle as seen in Social & Mobile Marketing 8.1. The product life cycle, discussed in the next section, helps marketers manage their products' marketing mix during and after its introduction.

Social and Mobile Marketing 8.1

Freestyle's "Fountain of You" Works for Everyone[69]

Coca-Cola may never totally outlive its failed New Coke product introduction, but its latest innovation, the Freestyle machine, seems like a good step in that direction. With this introduction, Coke has set out to reinvent the fountain experience and give customers more choice. The result has been a product success for all stakeholders.

For consumers, the Freestyle vending machines provide access to more than 100 Coke soft drink brands, offering endless options and combinations of caffeine, flavour, and calories. As an example, there are 90 different caffeine-free options on every machine!

For supply chain partners, such as restaurants and convenience stores, the Freestyle machines offer high-tech capabilities. Computer software connects every machine to a global supply chain, which enables immediate replenishment and the virtual elimination of out-of-stock situations. It also gives the partners a new revenue stream.

For Coca-Cola, the machines help create loyalty, allowing endless personalization and making each consumer feel special. Moreover, Freestyle software tracks exactly what was ordered on each machine. It knows what machines to refill and provides valuable research insights since it learns

The Coca-Cola Freestyle vending machine lets customers mix their own combination of flavours and share it with friends on Facebook.

which products customers prefer in which markets. One research insight shows that Caffeine Free Diet Coke is popular after 3 p.m., so this option could be added to traditional machines with heavy afternoon traffic.[70] Advertising can be targeted more precisely, based on completely accurate preference information provided by consumers.

Coca-Cola is harnessing the power of this valuable marketing machine through social and mobile media, too. The Freestyle Facebook fan page allows consumers to start conversations, sharing their favourite mixes and comparing them with those of their friends. On Twitter the @ccfreestyle profile tweets out new locations where fans can find the machine and keeps them engaged by asking them to vote on questions such as whether Minute Maid with Raspberry is better than Fanta with Raspberry. An app has been developed for iOS and Android devices that serves as a location finder and memory game.[71]

The "Fountain of You" campaign has helped accelerate awareness, buzz, and consumer excitement for Freestyle, resulting in strong purchase intent and trial. Consumers post photos of the machine to social media platforms and become brand ambassadors through their comments.

THE PRODUCT LIFE CYCLE

The **product life cycle** (PLC) defines the stages that new products move through as they enter, get established in, and ultimately leave the marketplace and thereby offers marketers a starting point for their strategy planning. Exhibit 8.7A illustrates a typical product life cycle, including the industry sales and profits over time. In their life cycles, products pass through four stages: introduction, growth, maturity, and decline. When innovators start buying the product, the product enters the **introduction stage** of its life cycle. In the **growth stage**, the product gains acceptance, demand and sales increase, and competitors emerge in the product category. In the **maturity stage**, industry sales reach their peak, so firms try to rejuvenate their products by adding new features or repositioning them. If these efforts succeed, the product achieves new life.[72] If not, it goes into the **decline stage** and eventually exits the market.

Not every product follows the same life cycle curve. Many products, such as home appliances, stay in the maturity period for a very long time. Manufacturers may add features to dishwashing machines, but the mature product category remains essentially the same. It seems unlikely to enter the decline stage unless some innovative, superior solution comes along to replace it.

The product life cycle also offers a useful tool for managers to analyze the types of strategies that may be required over the life of their products. Even the strategic emphasis of a firm and its marketing mix (four Ps) strategies can be adapted from insights about the characteristics of each stage of the cycle, as we summarize in Exhibit 8.7B.

Let's look at each of these stages in depth.

Introduction Stage

The introduction stage for a new, innovative product or service usually starts with a single firm, and innovators are the ones to try the new offering. Some new-to-the-world products and services that defined their own product category and industry include the telephone (invented by Alexander Graham Bell in 1876), the transistor semiconductor

product life cycle
Defines the stages that new products move through as they enter, get established in, and ultimately leave the marketplace and thereby offers marketers a starting point for their strategy planning.

introduction stage
Stage of the product life cycle when innovators start buying the product.

growth stage
Stage of the product life cycle when the product gains acceptance, demand and sales increase, and competitors emerge in the product category.

maturity stage
Stage of the product life cycle when industry sales reach their peak, so firms try to rejuvenate their products by adding new features or repositioning them.

decline stage
Stage of the product life cycle when sales decline and the product eventually exits the market.

EXHIBIT 8.7A Product Life Cycle

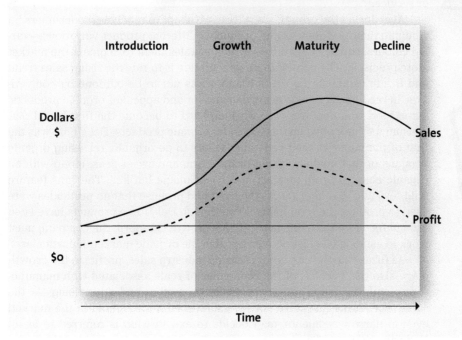

EXHIBIT 8.7B Characteristics of Different Stages of the Product Life Cycle

	Introduction	Growth	Maturity	Decline
Sales	Low	Rising	Peak	Declining
Profits	Negative or low	Rapidly rising	Peak to declining	Declining
Typical consumers	Innovators	Early adopters and early majority	Late majority	Laggards
Competitors (number of firms and products)	One or few	Few but increasing	High number of competitors and competitive products	Low number of competitors and products

These new-to-the-world products defined their own product category and industry. The telephone (top) was invented in 1876, and the Sony Walkman (bottom) came out in 1979.

(Bell Laboratories in 1947), the Walkman portable cassette player (Sony in 1979), the Internet browser (Netscape in 1994), iTunes (Apple in 2001), BlackBerry (RIM in 2003), Blu-ray (Sony in 2006) and iPad (Apple in 2010). Sensing the viability and commercialization possibilities of this market-creating new product, other firms soon enter the market with similar or improved products at lower prices. The same pattern holds for less innovative products such as apparel, some music, or even a new soft-drink flavour. The introduction stage is characterized by initial losses to the firm because of its high startup costs and low levels of sales revenue as the product begins to take off. If the product is successful, firms may start seeing profits toward the end of this stage.

Growth Stage

The growth stage of the product life cycle is marked by a growing number of product adopters, rapid growth in industry sales, and increases in both the number of competitors and the number of available product versions.[73] The market becomes more segmented and consumer preferences more varied, which increases the potential for new markets or new uses of the product or service.[74]

Also during the growth stage, firms attempt to reach new consumers by studying their preferences and producing different product variations—varied colours, styles, or features—which enables them to segment the market more precisely. The goal of this segmentation is to ride the rising sales trend and firmly establish the firm's brand, so as not to be outdone by competitors. In recognizing the growing demand for and appeal of organic products, many food manufacturers are working hard to become the first brand that consumers think of when they consider organic products. Del Monte was the first of the major canned vegetable sellers to go organic, releasing organic versions of its tomatoes, green beans, corn, and sweet peas, along with an organic chicken broth product under its College Inn line. The cans feature bold "organic" banners across the front and promise that no pesticides were used to produce the food items. Even though Del Monte products have been around for more than 100 years, in this growth category, the company must work to establish its distinctive appeal in the organic market in particular.[75]

As firms ride the crest of increasing industry sales, profits in the growth stage also rise because of the economies of scale associated with manufacturing and marketing costs, especially promotion and advertising. At the same time, firms that have not yet established a stronghold in the market, even in narrow segments, may decide to exit in what is referred to as an "industry shakeout."

Maturity Stage

The maturity stage of the product life cycle is characterized by the adoption of the product by the late majority and intense competition for market share among firms. Marketing costs (e.g., promotion, distribution) increase as these firms vigorously defend their market share against competitors. At the same time, they face intense competition on price as the average price of the product falls substantially compared with the shifts during the previous two stages of the life cycle. Lower prices and increased marketing costs begin to erode the profit margins for many firms. In the later phases of the maturity stage, the market has become quite saturated, and practically all potential customers for the product have already adopted the product. Such saturated markets are prevalent in developed countries; in Canada, most consumer packaged goods found in grocery and discount stores are already in the maturity stage.

Firms may pursue several strategies during this stage to increase their customer base and/or defend their market share, such as entering into new markets and market segments and developing new products or promotions. See Exhibit 8.8 for additional strategies for extending the maturity stage of the product life cycle.

Entry into New Markets or Market Segments   Because the market is saturated at this point, firms may attempt to enter new geographical markets, including international markets (as we will discuss in Chapter 17), that may be less saturated. For example, Whirlpool has started manufacturing washing machines for Brazil, China, and India that it prices lower than those it sells in North America to attract the large consumer base of lower-income consumers in these countries.[76] In many developing economies, the large and growing proportion of middle-class households is just beginning to buy the home, kitchen, and entertainment appliances that have been fairly standard in Canadian households for several decades. In India alone, the roughly 487 million middle-class consumers will spend $420 billion on a variety of consumer products in the next four years.[77]

EXHIBIT 8.8   Strategies for Extending the Product Life Cycle

Strategy	Example
Develop new uses for products	• Baking soda is now promoted for deodorizing refrigerators, as an environmentally friendly cleaning product, and much more.
Modify the product: • Change quality • Boost performance • Alter appearance	• Add graphite to tennis racquets and golf clubs • Enhance computer chip speed • Modify packaging; change colours, or introduce a new scent
Increase frequency of use	• Dentyne gum is promoted as a way to help clean your teeth when you can't brush after a meal.
Increase the number of users	• Tums have always contained calcium, but when this fact was promoted, people concerned about bone density began to purchase the product.
Find new users	• Club Med introduced vacations geared to baby boomers, seniors, golfers, and those looking for cruises after some of their original target market of swinging singles got married and had children.
Reposition product	• Suntan lotion has evolved to become sunscreen protection. • Vitamin D is sold as a cancer deterrent.
Tweak marketing strategy	• Greeting cards are sold in supermarkets. • Upscale cosmetics are sold in drug stores.

To generate sales in a mature world, Dial Corporation has developed a laundry sheet that includes detergent, fabric softener, and antistatic agents to appeal to a new market segment that wants a premium product while saving money, without cannibalizing its core customer groups.

However, even in mature markets, firms may be able to find new market segments. Laundry may be a mundane chore that most people dislike, but it is also a huge marketing opportunity. New product development tends to focus on the detergent delivery methods. So in North America, where laundry tablets have never been very popular (consumers prefer to pour their liquid detergent and thus control the amount they add to the wash basket), Dial has developed a laundry sheet, similar to the dryer sheets used as fabric softeners. This 3-in-1 product includes laundry detergent, fabric softener, and antistatic agents.[78] It is less expensive than purchasing premium brand versions of the three items. Dial hopes to appeal to a new market segment that wants a premium product and to save money, without cannibalizing its core customer groups.

New market opportunities also may emerge through simple product design changes, such as in the market for "wipes." Just a few years ago, baby wipes accounted for most of the sales of personal wipes, but P&G's Oil of Olay Facial Cleansing Cloths and Unilever's Ponds Age-Defying wipes have recently gained significant market share.[79] In the household sector, products such as P&G's Swiffer, the electrostatic wipe for mopping floors, have expanded the market greatly. Clorox has added premoistened Armor All wipes to its do-it-yourself car cleaning line[80] and the Clorox® ToiletWand™ for consumers who don't enjoy unsightly and unsanitary toilet brushes hanging around in their bathrooms.[81] Although the household cleaning and cosmetic markets are both well established and mature, marketers working in these product categories saw trends early and moved to create new products that offer value for consumers.

Development of New Products Despite market saturation, firms continually introduce new products with improved features or find new uses for existing products because they need constant innovation and product proliferation to defend market share during intense competition. Firms such as 3M, P&G, and HP, for instance, continuously introduce new products. Innovations by such firms ensure that they are able to retain or grow their respective market shares. KFC took its expertise with an existing product line consisting of different types of fried chicken and developed Kentucky Grilled Chicken, a relatively innovative product for a mature market. And Hallmark initiated the "Life is a Special Occasion" campaign to suggest that every day is a good day to send a greeting, increasing the reasons and times when people are likely to buy cards.

Decline Stage

Firms with products in the decline stage either position themselves for a niche segment of diehard consumers or those with special needs, or they completely exit the market. The few laggards who have not yet tried the product or service enter the market at this stage. Take vinyl long-playing records (LPs) for example. In an age of CDs and Internet-downloaded music in MP3 and other formats, it may seem surprising that vinyl records are still made and sold. Although the sales of vinyl LPs have been declining in the

Just a few years ago, baby wipes accounted for most of the sales of personal wipes. Firms have seen the opportunity to enter new markets, so products have proliferated.

past 15 years, about 2 million are sold in the United States each year. In Canada, vinyl sales declined from $913,000 in 2000 to $608,000 three years later compared with CD sales that same year of $686,976,000.[82] Still, diehard music lovers prefer the unique sound of a vinyl record to the digital sound of CDs and music in other formats. Because the grooves in vinyl records create sound waves that are similar to those of a live performance, and therefore provide a more authentic sound, night-club DJs, discerning music listeners, and collectors prefer them. Even some younger listeners have been buying vinyl records, influenced perhaps by their parents' collections, the sound, or simply the uniqueness of an LP. In Edmonton, independent and high-profile bands alike are competing for limited record-pressing resources, a sign that vinyl is in vogue again.[83] The nostalgia factor associated with the old albums has given new life to the older medium.

In spite of some die-hard music lovers who prefer vinyl, long-playing records have experienced years of falling sales and are in the decline stage.

Aiding this continued demand is the fact that there are simply too many albums of music from the predigital era that are available only on vinyl. It may take many years, maybe even decades, for all the music from earlier generations to be digitized. Many collectors are attracted to old albums for their history, as evidenced by the sale of a one-of-a-kind Velvet Underground recording for US$25,200.[84]

The Shape of the Product Life Cycle Curve

In theory, the product life cycle curve is assumed to be bell-shaped with regard to sales and profits. In reality, however, each product or service has its own individual shape; some move more rapidly through their product life cycles than others, depending on how different the product or service is from products currently in the market and how valuable it is to the consumer. New products and services that consumers accept very quickly have higher consumer adoption rates very early in their product life cycles and move faster across the various stages.

For example, DVD players and DVDs moved much faster than VCRs across the life cycle curve and have already reached the maturity stage, likely because consumers who already owned VCRs were accustomed to recording TV shows and playing prerecorded movies and programs. It also was easy to switch VCR customers to DVD technology because DVDs were more durable and had better resolution than video-tapes. Finally, prices for DVDs and DVD players dropped more quickly and drastically than did VCR prices, which made the new technology a better value.

Lastly, as shown in Exhibit 8.9, the type of product affects variations in the shape of the product life cycle curve. When first introduced, microwaves were considered high-learning products and spent much longer in the introduction stage than subsequent low-learning products such as microwave popcorn. Fads move through the stages very quickly while fashion products tend to be cyclical in nature. For example, wide ties for men and suit lapels may be out of style today but may well become fashionable again in the future.

Strategies Based on Product Life Cycle: Some Caveats

Although the product life cycle concept provides a starting point for managers to think about the strategy they want to implement during each stage of the life cycle of a product, this tool must be used with care. The most challenging part of applying the product life cycle concept is that managers do not know exactly what shape each product's life cycle will take, so there is no way to know precisely what stage a product is in. If, for example, a product experiences several seasons of declining sales, a manager may decide that it has moved from the growth stage to the decline stage and stop promoting the product.

EXHIBIT 8.9　Variations on the Product Life Cycle Curve

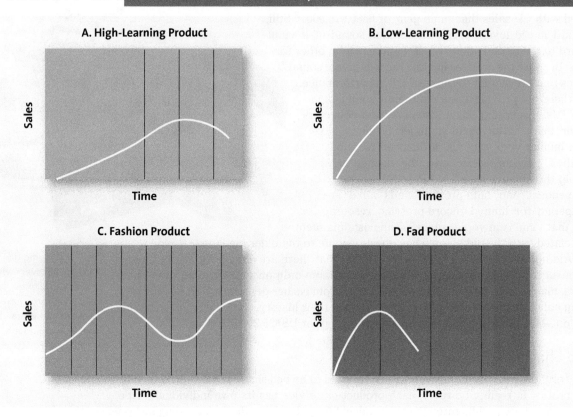

As a result, of course, sales decline further. The manager then believes he or she made the right decision because the product continues to follow a predetermined life cycle. But what if the original sales decline was due to a poor strategy or increased competition—issues that could have been addressed with positive marketing support? In this case, the product life cycle decision became a self-fulfilling prophecy, and a growth product was doomed to an unnecessary decline.[85]

LEARNING OBJECTIVES REVIEW

 Identify the reasons firms create new products

Firms need to innovate to respond to changing customer needs, prevent decline in sales, avoid market saturation, diversify their risk, and respond to short product life cycles. This is especially true in industries such as fashion, apparel, arts, books, and software markets, where most sales come from new products. New products and services keep current customers coming back for more and induce new customers into the market. Risky, new-to-the-world products have tremendous potential because they are the first in the market to offer something that has never before been available.

 Describe the diffusion of innovation theory and how managers can use it to make product line decisions

The diffusion of innovation theory helps firms predict which types of customers will buy their products or services immediately upon introduction, and as they gain more acceptance in the market. Innovators are those buyers who want to be the first to have the new product or service. Early adopters do not take as much risk as innovators but instead wait and purchase the product after careful review. The members of the early majority really don't like to take risk and therefore tend to wait until "the bugs" have been worked out of a particular product or service. The late majority are buyers who purchase the product after it has achieved its full market potential. Finally, laggards like to avoid change and rely on traditional products until they are no longer available. Laggards may never adopt a certain product or service.

 L03 **List the stages involved in developing new products and services**

When firms develop new products, they go through several steps. First, they generate ideas for the product or service by using several alternative techniques, such as internal research and development, licensing, brainstorming, tracking competitors' products or services, or working with customers. Second, firms test their concepts by either describing the idea of the new product or service to potential customers or showing them images of what the product would look like. Third, the design process entails determining what the product or service will actually include and provide; fourth,

firms test-market their designs. Fifth, if everything goes well in the test market, the product is launched. Sixth, firms must evaluate the new product or service to determine its success.

L04 **Describe the product life cycle and summarize how it is used to make product line decisions**

The product life cycle helps firms make marketing mix decisions on the basis of the product's stage in its life cycle. In the introduction stage, companies attempt to gain a strong foothold in the market quickly by appealing to innovators. During the growth stage, the objective is to establish the brand firmly. When the product reaches the maturity stage, firms compete intensely for market share, and many potential customers already own the product or use the service. Eventually, most products enter the decline phase, during which firms withdraw marketing support and eventually phase out the product. Knowing where a product or service is in its life cycle helps managers determine its specific strategy at any given point in time.

KEY TERMS

- alpha testing
- beta testing
- concept testing
- concepts
- decline stage
- diffusion of innovation
- early adopters
- early majority
- first movers

- growth stage
- innovation
- innovators
- introduction stage
- laggards
- late majority
- lead users
- maturity stage
- pioneers

- premarket test
- product
- product development (product design)
- product life cycle
- prototype
- reverse engineering
- test marketing

CONCEPT REVIEW

1. Explain how new product or service innovations add value to the firm.

2. Sketch and describe the diffusion of innovation curve. How can marketers use the information provided by this curve to make marketing strategies and decisions?

3. Identify and discuss the factors that influence the adoption of new products.

4. List the steps in the new product development process. Describe some of the sources companies use to generate ideas for new products at the beginning of this process.

5. Why might a company need to exercise caution during the test marketing stage of the new development process?

6. What other factors besides the product itself does a company need to finalize during the product launch stage?

7. Do all products go through each and every stage of this process? Explain your answer.

8. What is the product life cycle (PLC)? Describe the characteristics of each stage of the PLC in terms of sales, profits, typical consumers, competition, and four Ps strategies.

9. Describe some of the strategies companies can use to extend the life of a mature product.

10. Explain why the product life cycle is not a fail-proof tool in managing products.

MARKETING APPLICATIONS

1. Some people think that a product should be considered "new" only if it is completely new to the market and has never existed before. Describe or give examples of other types of new products.

2. Panasonic's new 3D HD personal camcorder allows users to record live events in three dimensions, instead of two. How quickly do you think this product will diffuse among the Canadian population? Describe the types of people whom you expect will be in each of the diffusion of innovation stages.

3. Are there any advantages for companies that are the first to introduce products that create new markets? Justify your answer. If you see advantages, explain why some new products fail.

4. Identify and describe the ways that companies generate new product ideas. Which of these ways involve the customer? How can firms assess the value of the ideas that customers generate?

5. Describe an example of a new product or service that is targeted at the student market. Using the concept testing discussion in this chapter, describe how you would conduct a concept test for this product or service.

6. How does the Internet help companies gain customer input on their existing and new products?

7. Nature's Path is about to introduce a type of granola and is in the market testing phase of the new product development process. Describe two ways that Nature's Path might conduct initial market testing prior to launching this new product.

8. What shampoo do you use? What stage of the product life cycle is it in? Is the shampoo manufacturer's marketing strategy—its four Ps—consistent with the product's stage in its life cycle? Explain.

9. In what stage of the product life cycle is the PlayStation 4 video game console? Is Sony's marketing strategy—its four Ps—consistent with the product's stage in its life cycle? How is it different from that of the shampoo in the previous question? Explain.

10. You have recently been hired by a cosmetics company for its product development group. The firm's brand is a top-selling, high-end line of cosmetics. The head of the development team has just presented research that shows that tween girls, aged 9 to 12, are very interested in cosmetics and have money to spend on them. The decision is made to create a line of tween cosmetics based on the existing adult line. As the product moves through development you begin to notice that the team seems to lean toward a very edgy and sexual theme for the line, including naming the various lines "Envy," "Desire," "Prowl," and "Fatal Attraction." You begin to wonder if this concept is too much for girls in the targeted age group. Explain your thoughts.

NET SAVVY

1. Go to the *Canadian Living* Best New Products Awards website (http://www.canadianliving.com/life/best_new_product_awards) and search for an interesting new product. Is this an innovative, new-to-the-world product? Discuss the extent to which the new product has the properties that would be important for new product design and development.

2. The automotive industry is constantly adding new and different products to cars and trucks. Conduct an Internet or library database search for innovative new automotive technologies. Choose products that fit each stage of the product life cycle, and justify your choices.

APPLE FURTHER TRANSFORMS THE USER EXPERIENCE WITH THE IPAD

Skeptics yawned a bit when Apple rolled out its iPad 2. Reviewers acknowledged that Apple's updated tablet did have two cameras and a gyroscope. But the prelaunch prediction was that the new version was basically the same as the iPad, only thinner, lighter, and twice as fast. Then people began using it, and they discovered once again that Apple had further transformed the digital experience.

What the iPad 2 Offers

A tablet is meant to be held, not set on your lap or atop a desk. Apple's new iPad—15 percent lighter, just .34 inches thick, with rounded edges, and speedier than ever—is a pleasure to hold. The Motorola Xoom, considered the best Android competitor, felt massive by comparison. And despite the iPad 2's lighter, slimmer dimensions, its battery still held a charge for 10 hours. Like competing tablets, Apple's new iPad featured a camera on the back to record high-definition video, along with a low-resolution front camera for video phone calls. The more expensive models offered online capability. With a simple $40 adapter, the iPad 2 could be connected to a high-definition television too, making it a great platform for viewing slideshows, presentations, or movies.[86]

But one of the simplest innovations was the one reviewers hailed as "magic." Apple's new SmartCover, a rigid, hinged sheet of polyurethane (or for $70, leather), could be used to prop up the iPad, so the user could watch movies or freely use the on-screen keyboard with both hands. Opening and closing the cover turned the iPad on or off almost instantaneously. Given modern consumers' expectations that digital devices will keep getting faster, that time-saver was bound to please.[87]

These descriptions involve the physical aspects. Apple also transformed the overall user experience. With the new speed and ease of iPad 2, Apple had finally made using a digital tablet more like reading a book. No buttons to press, and no menus to scroll through. Ratcheting up its competition with other e-readers, Apple had delivered "the swiftness of print." Users could just open the iPad 2 and start reading. Email, the news, a novel for their subway ride—everything was instantly available. In terms of Apple's other advantages in the tablet market, users could immediately turn to the 65,000 apps already available for the iPad, not to mention the 290,000 iPhone applications that could also be used on the iPad.[88]

A stable price tag was perhaps its biggest competitive edge. The starting price for the iPad 2 was the same as that for the original iPad: $499, and much less than Samsung's Galaxy Tab or Motorola's Xoom, two tough Android competitors.[89] Within nine months of the iPad 2 launch, Apple had sold 15 million devices, generating $9.5 billion in revenue.

Apple's financial efficiency remains tough to duplicate. Enormous cash reserves, estimated at $60 billion, enable the company to form strategic partnerships with component manufacturers and secure volume discounts. It avoids licensing fees for some high-cost items by having them designed in-house by a company it owns. Revenue from its successful App Store helps subsidize the price of the iPad. And Apple's global network of retail stores eliminates markups by third-party sellers, like Best Buy.[90]

What's Happening in the Market

The digital tablet market has exploded. International Data Corporation (IDC) says the market grew to over 230 million units worldwide, surpassing the sales of portable PCs in 2013 and is forecast to hit over 400 million units by 2017.[91] Critics had once questioned whether consumers really would spring for yet one more digital device, but the numbers have proved those skeptics wrong.

User habits also are changing. The digital tablet offers a popular online shopping venue, especially for affluent consumers. Retailers such as Macy's, Abercrombie & Fitch, and The Gap report that their customers who browse their Internet sites with a digital tablet are more likely to complete the purchase than are online shoppers who use computers or smartphones. In addition, those consumers using the new digital tablets to shop tend to buy high-end, high-priced items, typically spending 10 to 20 percent more than other online shoppers.[92] Market research confirms these findings by developing a matching profile of tablet owners: They tend to be wealthier, so the new online format helps retailers tap into a higher-spending market niche.

Consequently, advertisers have shifted their behaviour. Shopping networks and individual retailers now feature videos, slideshows, and "how-to" demonstrations in their catalogues, as they seek to exploit the digital capabilities of the new tablets.

What Others Are Doing and How Apple Will Respond

In almost no time, Apple's iPad 2 faced nearly 100 competitors, vying for a place in the tablet market.[93] Some offered customers a benefit or two that could not be found on the iPad 2, such as the Flash capability provided by the Androids for viewing videos and animation on the Web. Others offer the ability to dictate text, using a program that sends the information into any box that accepts typing. Another popular option is a navigation application that displays turn-by-turn travel directions on GPS-generated maps.[94]

Amazon jumped into the market too with its Kindle Fire, an updated e-reader with digital tablet capabilities, priced at only $199. With competition mounting, observers predicted that Apple would make key changes in its next iPad release. Dedicated forums have been full of discussion about the possible inclusion of Siri, Apple's sophisticated vocal interface, on the iPad 3 (a feature available on the iPhone4 and iPhone5).[95]

But Apple's biggest move amid these prerelease rumours has been its announcement that it has added digital textbooks to its next iPad—something that Amazon's Kindle and the Nook from Barnes & Noble already offer. Apple's entry into the digital textbook market is fuelled by its partnerships with a number of textbook publishers. Apple offers these publishing partners three key capabilities: its iBooks2, an e-book reading application for the iPad; iBooks Author, an e-book authoring tool for the iPad; and iTunes U, an expanded online commerce platform for digital textbooks. The first slated release would include a trio of high school textbooks: biology, algebra 1, and environmental science.[96]

Proponents suggest that digital textbooks offer students a wealth of benefits, including interactive connections with the information, access to constantly updated study material, lighter backpacks, and lower prices than paper-bound textbooks. But some opponents doubt that the promised savings on individual texts will ever fully materialize, because the major cost for traditional publishing has always been taken up by research and writing, not printing and production.[97] Considering that the textbook industry is undergoing a digital transformation, Apple's collaboration with two of the largest textbook publishers in North America could represent a major coup.

The iFuture

Although the iPad was initially met with skepticism on the part of some analysts, Apple dominated the market with almost 90 percent market share among tablets in its first year.[98] While market share for the iPad has eroded over time, it continues to dominate. The iPad 4th Generation and the iPad Mini sold 3 million units the first weekend. The iPad remains one of the premium tablets on the market with an entry price of $459 for the 16GB Mini.[99]

As CEO, Jobs had a reputation in the marketplace for his creative genius and for personally seeing new products successfully from the initial idea to the product launch. He had been credited with an uncanny ability to spot the next revolutionary innovation that would change the landscape of the marketplace. That's a tough reputation to maintain. And yet, only four months after the introduction of the iPad, Apple surpassed Microsoft as the largest technology company in the world based on market capitalization.[100] Jobs reinvented Apple as a provider of must-have tech gadgets.

With the death of Steve Jobs on October 5, 2011, many people have speculated how Apple will fare in the future. Some argue that with Apple's stock falling to its lowest point in a year, coupled with no new product categories, Apple may have lost its magic touch. With increasing competition from BlackBerry, Google, Samsung, and Microsoft, Apple no longer is viewed as invincible. Combined with recent blunders, such as the Genius bar ads at the London Olympics and the critically panned launch of the Maps app, it is clear Apple is not immune to making mistakes.[101] On the other hand, Apple is still selling products at an astonishing rate. The iPhone 5 sold over 47 million phones in the last three months of 2012, and the iPad still holds a 52 percent market share. So is Apple losing its momentum in the market? Only time will tell.[102]

Questions

1. At what stage in the product life cycle is the iPad?

2. How well has Apple responded to the changing competitive landscape for digital tablets, particularly the emergence of the Androids?

3. Which iPad 4 features create the most value for users?

4. How will the iPad stack up against the e-textbook options on other digital tablets?

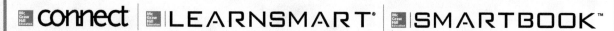

For more information on the resources available from McGraw-Hill Ryerson, go to www.mheducation.ca/he/solutions.

CHAPTER 9

Product, Branding, and Packaging Decisions

Look around. You see them everywhere: in remote communities, in heavily populated business districts, on university campuses, even on Justin Trudeau's family holiday card. From humble roots as a product designed to protect people who worked in extreme cold conditions, Canada Goose parkas have now also become a fashion statement for the urban chic. Fusing function with fashion while staying true to its heritage, Canada Goose offers the highest quality outerwear in the world.

The brand has undergone a lot of change since 1957 when Sam Tick started Metro Sportswear Ltd in Toronto, making clothing and outerwear for automotive and industrial companies. In 1970, the company moved into down-filled manufacturing and began producing a wide range of down-filled jackets for private-label brands such as Eddie Bauer, L.L.Bean, and others. The company went on to make its own down-filled parkas, known at first as Snow Goose[1] and then as Canada Goose—all made entirely in Canada.

In 1997, Tick's grandson, Dani Reiss, joined the company to earn money to travel. He stayed on after listening to consumers tell him how much they loved the made-in-Canada coats. Using goose and duck down and trimmed with coyote fur, the coats are designed with the company's mission in mind: to free people from the cold, no matter where they live, and empower them to experience more from life. The coats have become so popular that a holographic badge has been added to prevent counterfeiting.

Consumers seek products with authentic stories and love the mythology of Canada, the Arctic, wide-open spaces, and the polar bear.[2] Reiss says that "made-in-Canada" is a brand differentiator. Visit the Canada Goose website and you'll see stories of Yukon Quest dogsledders, world-class mountaineers, and adventure athletes who swear by the brand. In the early days, Reiss spread word of mouth by giving jackets to bouncers who stood outside in the cold for long periods. Canada Goose has also been used in the film industry, outfitting film crews on movie sets where it is cold. The parkas have been featured in movies such as *Man of Steel*, *World War Z*, and *National Treasure*.[3] A partnership with Fairmont Hotels has outfitted all doormen and bellmen with a Canada Goose jacket, making the brand very visible.

LEARNING OBJECTIVES

After studying this chapter you should be able to

LO1 Describe the components of a product

LO2 Identify the types of consumer products

LO3 Explain the difference between a product mix's breadth and a product line's depth

LO4 Identify the advantages that brands provide firms and consumers

LO5 Summarize the components of brand equity

LO6 Describe the types of branding strategies used by firms

LO7 State how a product's packaging and label contribute to a firm's overall strategy

Today, social media also helps spread the word. Consumers love to share their own stories on platforms like Facebook and Twitter, helping to make Canada Goose a Canadian success story. In the past decade, sales have grown more than 4,000 percent with no signs of slowing. Sales projections this year are nearing $150 million, representing 40 percent annual growth.[4] Canada Goose has not only created a valued product, but also built strong brand equity, high customer awareness, and intense loyalty. ▌

This chapter is the second that deals with the first P in the marketing mix: product. In the last chapter, you learned that developing new products is key to a firm's marketing mix and central to the creation of value for consumers. Continuing our discussion, we now explore how companies add value to their offerings by developing an assortment of products and product lines and by creating strong brands.

This chapter begins with a discussion of the complexity and types of products. Next we examine how firms adjust their product lines to meet and respond to changing market conditions. Then we turn our attention to branding: Why are brands valuable to the firm, and what are the different branding strategies firms use? We also never want to underestimate the value of a product's packaging and labelling in product strategies and promotion. Packaging and labelling must send out a strong message from the shelf: Buy me! The final section of this chapter examines packaging and labelling issues.

COMPLEXITY OF PRODUCTS AND TYPES OF PRODUCTS

L01

Complexity of Products

core customer value
The basic problem-solving benefits that consumers are seeking.

There is more to a product than its physical characteristics or its basic service function. Marketers involved with the development, design, and sale of products think of them in an interrelated fashion as depicted in Exhibit 9.1. At the centre is the **core customer value**, which defines the basic problem-solving benefits that consumers are seeking. When Canada Goose makes coats, when Mars manufactures M&M's, and when Trek designs its bicycles, this is their core question: What are customers looking for? Do people buy Canada Goose jackets for extreme cold weather defence or because they want to make a fashion statement? With Mars, is it a sweet, great-tasting snack, or is it an energy boost? With Trek, is the bike being used for basic green transportation (a cruiser), or is it for speed and excitement (a road, hybrid, or mountain bike)?

Marketers convert core customer value into an *actual product*. Attributes such as the brand name, features/design, quality level, and packaging are considered, though the importance of these attributes varies depending on the product. The Trek Madone 6 Series features a carbon frame that is light, stiff, and comfortable; an advanced shifting system; and other high-tech features. Not only is it beautiful to look at, but customers also can choose from three different fits: pro, performance, and touring. Canada Goose coats are made with goose down, coyote fur and premium materials to offer superior warmth.

associated services (or augmented product)
The nonphysical attributes of the product, including product warranties, financing, product support, and after-sale service.

The **associated services** in Exhibit 9.1, also referred to as the **augmented product**, include the nonphysical aspects of the product, such as product warranties, financing,

EXHIBIT 9.1 Product Complexity

product support, and after-sale service. For example, Canada Goose coats come with a lifetime warranty for defects in materials or workmanship. The amount of associated services varies depending on the product. The associated services for a package of M&M's may include only a customer complaint line, which means they are relatively less important than the associated services for a Trek bicycle. The frame of the Madone 6 Series bicycle is guaranteed for the lifetime of the original owner. Trek sells its bikes only to shops that have the expertise to properly service them. Every possible consumer question is answered on Trek's comprehensive website. Trek even has a financing program that allows customers to purchase a new bike on credit.

When developing or changing a product, marketers start with the core customer value to determine what their potential customers are seeking. Then they make the actual physical product and add associated services to round out the offering.

Types of Products

Marketers consider the types of products they are designing and selling because that impacts how they promote, price, and distribute their products. There are two primary categories of products and services based on who is buying them: consumers or businesses (Chapter 5 discusses products for businesses).

Consumer products are products and services used by people for their personal use. Marketers further classify these products by the way they are used and purchased.

consumer products
Products and services used by people for their personal use.

Specialty Products/Services
Specialty products/services are products or services toward which customers show such a strong preference that they will expend considerable effort to search for the best suppliers. Road bike enthusiasts, like those interested in the Trek Madone 6 Series, will devote lots of time and effort to selecting just the right bike. Other examples might include luxury cars, legal or medical professionals, or designer apparel. For now, Canada Goose can be considered a specialty product. The extensive process used to approve authorized retailers helps maintain a premium image.[5]

L02

Shopping Products/Services
Shopping products/services are products or services, such as furniture, apparel, fragrances, appliances, and travel alternatives, for

Pop and bread are generally considered convenience goods (left). Shoes and T-shirts are shopping goods (middle). Products made by designers such as Polo Ralph Lauren are specialty goods (right).

which consumers will spend a fair amount of time comparing alternatives. When people need new sneakers, for instance, they will go from store to store shopping—trying shoes on, comparing alternatives, and chatting with salespeople. Canada Goose jackets may become a shopping product as more authorized retailers are added.

Convenience Products/Services Convenience products/services are those products or services for which the consumer is not willing to spend any effort to evaluate prior to purchase. They are frequently purchased commodity items, usually purchased with very little thought, such as common beverages, bread, or soap.

Unsought Products/Services Unsought products/services are products consumers either do not normally think of buying (e.g. funeral services, fire extinguishers) or do not know about. Because of their very nature, these products require lots of marketing effort and various forms of promotion. When new-to-the-world products, such as GPS systems, are first introduced, they often represent unsought products. Do you have cold hands and don't know what to do about it? You must not have heard yet of HeatMax HotHands Hand Warmers, air-activated packets that provide warmth for up to 10 hours.

Specialty goods/services are products or services toward which the customer shows a strong preference and for which he or she will expend considerable effort to search for the best suppliers. Because Brad wants the best sports car for his money, he searches carefully on the Internet for reviews and talks to friends who own sports cars before he starts shopping. Similarly, environmentally minded consumers, who would consider purchasing only a Prius or another hybrid car would devote lots of time and effort to selecting just the right one.

Shopping goods/services are products or services, such as apparel, fragrances, and appliances, for which consumers will spend a fair amount of time comparing alternatives. When Brad decides to buy a new pair of running shoes for himself, he will go from store to store shopping—trying on shoes, comparing alternatives, and chatting with salespeople.

Convenience goods/services are those products or services for which the consumer is not willing to spend any effort to evaluate prior to purchase. They are commodity items that are frequently purchased, usually with very little thought. Items such as pop, bread, and soap typically fall into this category.

specialty goods/services
Products or services toward which the customer shows a strong preference and for which he or she will expend considerable effort to search for the best suppliers.

shopping goods/services
Products or services, such as apparel, fragrances, and appliances, for which consumers will spend time comparing alternatives.

convenience goods/ services
Products or services for which the consumer is not willing to spend any effort to evaluate prior to purchase.

L03   PRODUCT MIX AND PRODUCT LINE DECISIONS

product mix
The complete set of all products offered by a firm.

product lines
Groups of associated items, such as those that consumers use together or think of as part of a group of similar products.

product category
An assortment of items that the customer sees as reasonable substitutes for one another.

The complete set of all products offered by a firm is called its **product mix**. Colgate-Palmolive's product mix is shown in Exhibit 9.2. The product mix typically consists of various **product lines**, which are groups of associated items, such as items that consumers use together or think of as part of a group of similar products. Colgate-Palmolive's product lines include oral care, personal care, household care, fabric care, and pet nutrition. While the main focus for Canada Goose is jackets, its product lines also include snow pants, hats, and gloves.

Within each product line, there are often multiple product categories. A **product category** is an assortment of items that the customer sees as reasonable substitutes for one another. For example, in the oral care product line, Colgate-Palmolive offers several categories with a variety of offerings to choose from in each: toothpaste, whitening products, toothbrushes, kid's oral-care products, floss, and oral first aid. Each category within a product line may use the same or different

EXHIBIT 9.2 | Colgate-Palmolive Product Mix

Product Lines
Product line breadth

	Oral Care	Personal Care	Household Care	Fabric Care	Pet Nutrition
Product Categories ↕ *Product line depth*	Toothpaste (Colgate Total) Toothbrush (Colgate Plus) Kids' products (Colgate Barbie Bubble Fruit toothpaste) Whitening products (Colgate Simply White) Floss (Colgate Total Dental Floss) Oral first aid (Colgate Orabase)	Deodorants (Speed Stick) Bar soap (Irish Spring) Body wash (Soft Soap) Hand wash (Soft Soap) Men's toiletries (Skin Bracer Aftershave)	Dishwashing liquid (Palmolive) Automatic dishwashing liquid (Palmolive) Household cleaners (Ajax) Dish wipes (Palmolive)	Laundry detergents (Fab) Fabric softener (Fleecy)	Hill's Pet Nutrition, Inc.—subsidiary Dog food (Science Diet) Cat food (Science Diet)

Source: http://www.colgate.com.

brands, which are the names, terms, designs, symbols, or any other features that identify one seller's good or service as distinct from those of other sellers.[6] For instance, Colgate-Palmolive offers several brands of toothbrushes (e.g., 360°, Motion Whitening, Massager, Navigator).

The product mix reflects the breadth and depth of a company's product lines. A firm's **product mix breadth** (sometimes also referred to as variety) represents the number of product lines offered by the firm; Colgate-Palmolive has five, as indicated by the five columns in Exhibit 9.2. **Product line depth**, in contrast, is the number of products within a product line. Within Colgate-Palmolive's oral-care line, for example, it offers toothpaste, toothbrushes, kids' products, and so forth. Its pet nutrition product line, however, comprises fewer offerings and therefore has less depth. In our Canada Goose example, Arctic program jackets, parkas, vests, mountaineer jackets, bomber jackets, hoodies, trench coats, and technical shells show product line depth for jackets.

Within each product category are a number of individual items called **stock keeping units (SKUs)**, which are the smallest unit available for inventory control. For instance, within the toothpaste category, Colgate-Palmolive offers 49 Colgate SKUs that represent various sizes, flavours, and configurations of Colgate Herbal White, Colgate Total, and Colgate Fresh Confidence.[7] Each individual product is a unique SKU. The 100 millilitre size of Colgate Total Clean Mint is one SKU, while the 100-millilitre package of Colgate Total Whitening Paste is a second SKU. The same size package of Colgate Total Advanced Fresh Gel represents a third SKU. The category depth is the number of SKUs within a category. Each SKU has its own unique product code (UPC) code as well.

However, adding unlimited numbers of new products can have adverse consequences. Too much variety in the product mix is often too costly to maintain, and too many brands may weaken the firm's brand reputation.[8] In the past several years, for example, Revlon undertook a significant restructuring. It introduced a new line, Vital Radiance, aimed at women over the age of 45 years. But this line cut into the sales of its other brands and harmed its reputation among younger consumers, so Revlon eliminated the Vital Radiance line, to refocus on those products and markets that were doing well.[9]

So why do firms change their product mix's breadth or depth?

brands
The names, terms, designs, symbols, or any other features that identify one seller's good or service as distinct from those of other sellers.

product mix breadth
The number of product lines, or variety, offered by the firm.

product line depth
The number of products within a product line.

stock keeping units (SKUs)
Individual items within each product category; the smallest unit available for inventory control.

Starbucks increased its product mix breadth by adding Natural Fusions flavoured coffee. It was a natural extension when the company learned that more than 60 percent of its consumers enjoyed flavoured coffees.

Change Product Mix Breadth

Exhibit 9.3 offers a hypothetical example of a company with four product lines in its product mix. Firms may change their product mix breadth by either adding to or deleting entire product lines.

Increase Breadth   Firms often add new product lines to capture new or evolving markets, increase sales, and compete in new venues (e.g., addition of Product Line D in Exhibit 9.3) With the introduction of VIA Ready Brew, Starbucks changed the way people thought about instant coffee. The new line is expected to produce more than a billion dollars in sales.[10] And when the company learned that more than 60 percent of its consumers enjoyed flavoured coffee, it introduced Natural Fusions, a line of premium coffee available for sale in grocery stores in vanilla, cinnamon, and caramel flavours. As part of Starbucks' business strategy, it was a natural way to grow its consumer products business.[11]

Decrease Breadth   Sometimes it is necessary to delete entire product lines to address changing market conditions or meet internal strategic priorities (e.g., deletion of Product Line C in Exhibit 9.3). A few years ago, SC Johnson sold off many products in its skin care line, including its successful Aveeno brand, to Johnson & Johnson.[12] The firm no longer competes in the skin care business but it remains a strong competitor in its original product lines, such as home cleaning (Pledge, Windex), air care (Glade), and home storage (Saran, Ziploc).[13]

EXHIBIT 9.3   Changes to a Product Mix

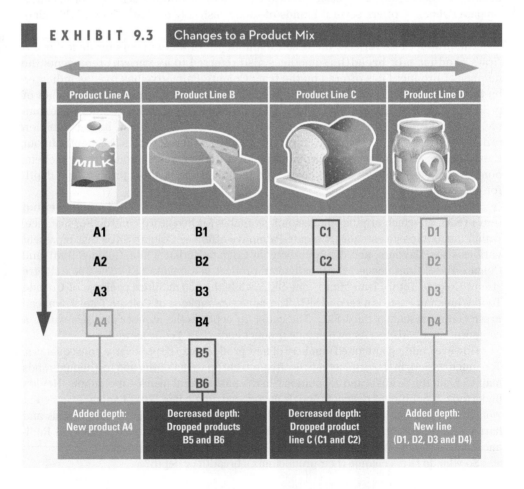

Change Product Line Depth

As with product line breadth, firms occasionally either add to or delete from their product line depth (see Exhibit 9.3).

Increase Depth   Firms may add new products within a line to address changing consumer preferences or preempt competitors while boosting sales (e.g., addition of A4 in Exhibit 9.3). Levi Strauss & Co. introduced its Signature line of low-cost jeans to be sold through Walmart. Jeans in the Signature line are priced at only $21 to $23 a pair, almost half the price of the popular Levi's 505 and 501 brands (the "red tab" line) sold through department stores.[14] The firm's decision was an attempt to get a much-needed sales boost in the face of tough competition from the likes of Diesel and Parasuco and to reach new target markets by selling through other retailers. A firm may also add new products to its product line to serve new target segments. Social and Mobile Marketing 9.1 provides an example of Axe expanding its fragrance product line to create a version for women.

Decrease Depth   From time to time, it is necessary to delete product categories to realign resources (e.g., deletion of B5 and B6 in Exhibit 9.3). The decision to delete products is never taken lightly. Generally, substantial investments have been made to develop

Social and Mobile Marketing 9.1 | Axe Brands' "Anarchy" Fragrance and Graphic Novel

Axe body spray already owned 75 percent of the men's fragrance market, so when its owner, Unilever, wanted to grow the brand, it needed to expand its product depth. A new scent, Axe Anarchy, was offered in both male and female versions, to exploit the promise of irresistible sexuality that has proven so successful so far.

In a decade's worth of controversial Axe commercials, average guys drew very attractive women to them, simply by spraying themselves with the scent. The Anarchy message is even more edgy. As the name suggests, the product promises the notion of sexual energy that goes slightly out of control. An early commercial depicts a chaotic series of events, including a car pile-up, in which a man and a woman remain oblivious to the havoc but gravitate toward each other until they are just inches apart. "Unleash the chaos," the screen recommends, as the video cuts to shots of the two actors spraying themselves. "New Axe Anarchy for him and for her."[15]

Noting its youthful target market, Unilever also wanted to ensure that the advertising medium for Anarchy fit the brand extension, so the company unleashed an interactive digital campaign in the form of an online graphic novel. The serialized, comic book fantasy about the chaotic exploits of the "Anarchy Girls" would evolve in real time, in response to viewer input. The author and X-Men creator Scott Lobdell was hired to create the narrative, in collaboration with any of the 2.3 million fans who registered on YouTube, Facebook, Twitter, and Axe's other social channels to help shape the story.[16]

The marketing subtext was clear: Break the narrative and also break through sexually, which seemed to offer a potent message for young women. But some observers remain unconvinced that Axe's bold, crowd-sourced digital venture will help the brand make the crossover into the women's body spray market. Could graphic novels, with their traditionally young male audience, really connect with young women?[17] Would Axe's explosive brand expansion strategy actually alienate the very audience that built its body spray brand, that is, average-guy male teens trying to attract a special girl? Would advertising to girls make Axe lose credibility among boys?

To promote the Axe Anarchy fragrance to young men and women, Unilever created a comic book fantasy about "Anarchy Girls," available in real time on YouTube and other social media.

the brand and manufacture the products. Consumer goods firms, such as P&G and Unilever, make pruning decisions regularly to eliminate unprofitable items and refocus their marketing efforts on more profitable items. For example, when executives at consumer goods giant Unilever noted flat sales and declining profits, they recognized they were carrying a lot of excess baggage. The company took decisive action to divest itself of 400 core brands, such as Ragu pasta sauces and Sunlight laundry detergent, reducing its portfolio from 1,600 brands. This move made Unilever more competitive with rivals such as P&G and freed up resources for future acquisitions, such as Ben & Jerry's.[18]

Change Number of SKUs

A very common and ongoing activity for many firms is the addition or deletion of SKUs in existing categories to stimulate sales or react to consumer demand. Fashion manufacturers and their retailers, for instance, change their SKUs every season. Generally, these changes are minor, such as a different colour or fabric. Sometimes though, the change is more drastic, such as when jeans manufacturers lower the waistline or flare the legs of their products.

Product Line Decisions for Services

Many of the strategies used to make product line decisions for physical products can also be applied to services. For instance, a service provider such as a bank typically offers different product lines for its business and retail (consumer) accounts; those product lines are further divided into categories based on the needs of different target markets.

On the retail side, banks offer savings and chequing accounts to individual consumers. The different types of accounts thus are equivalent to SKUs. The RBC Royal Bank is Canada's largest bank, as measured by assets, and serves more than 14 million personal, business, public sector, and institutional clients through offices in North America and 34 countries around the world.[19] It offers a variety of chequing account products to meet the needs of its different target markets. For example, the RBC VIP account has high monthly fees and offers an all-inclusive package covering multiple accounts, unlimited transactions, and a free premium Visa card. Students can take advantage of an RBC No Limit Banking for Students account with unlimited debits, a no-fee credit card, and moderate monthly fees. For customers who use fewer than 15 transactions per month, the RBC Day to Day Banking account offers very low monthly fees.[20]

BRANDING

A company lives or dies based on brand awareness. Consumers can't buy products that they don't know exist. Branding provides a way for a firm to differentiate its product offerings from those of its competitors and can be used to represent the name of a firm and its entire product mix (General Motors), one product line (Chevrolet), or a single item (Corvette). Both Snapple and Tropicana make and sell fruit drinks; yet a consumer may choose one over the other because of the associations that the brands evoke. Brand names, logos, symbols, characters, slogans, jingles, and even distinctive packages constitute the various brand elements firms use,[21] which they usually choose to be easy for consumers to recognize and remember. For example, most consumers are aware of the Nike Swoosh logo and would recognize it even if the word *Nike* did not appear on the product or in an advertisement. Exhibit 9.4 summarizes these brand elements.

When customers see an ad for Coca-Cola, they immediately make associations with familiar attributes, such as taste, to help them make quick decisions.

Have a Coke and a smile

EXHIBIT 9.4   What Makes a Brand?

Brand Element	Description
Brand name	The spoken component of branding, it can either describe the product or service/product characteristics and/or be composed of words invented or derived from colloquial or contemporary language. Examples include Comfort Inn (suggests product characteristics), Apple (no association with the product), or Accenture (invented term).
URLs (uniform resource locators) or domain names	The location of pages on the Internet, which often substitutes for the firm's name, such as Yahoo! and Amazon.
Logos and symbols	Logos are visual branding elements that stand for corporate names or trademarks. Symbols are logos without words. Examples include the Nike Swoosh and the Mercedes star.
Characters	Brand symbols that could be human, animal, or animated. Examples include the Pillsbury Doughboy and the Jolly Green Giant.
Slogans	Short phrases used to describe the brand or persuade consumers about some characteristics of the brand. Examples include State Farm's "Like A Good Neighbour" and Tim Hortons "Always Fresh."
Jingles	Audio messages about the brand that are composed of words or distinctive music. Examples are Intel's four-note sound signature that accompanies the "Intel Inside" slogan.

Source: Adapted from Kevin Lane Keller, *Strategic Brand Management,* 2nd ed. (Upper Saddle River, NJ: Prentice Hall, 2003).

Value of Branding

LO4

Brands add value to merchandise and services beyond physical and functional characteristics or the pure act of performing the service.[22] Let's examine some ways in which brands add value for both customers and the firm (see Exhibit 9.5).

Brands Facilitate Purchasing   Brands are often easily recognized by consumers and, because they signify a certain quality level and contain familiar attributes, brands help consumers make quick decisions.[23] Imagine how much time it would take to buy groceries if the brands on the shelves were unfamiliar! The cola market is a particularly strong example of this benefit. Some people think cola is cola, such that one brand is not too different from another. But branding has made it easy for Pepsi drinkers to find the familiar logo on the store shelf and more likely that they simply buy one of Pepsi's other products, should they decide to switch to a diet soda or a flavoured version. From promotions, past purchases, or information from friends and family, they recognize the offering before they even read any text on the label, and they likely possess a perception of the brand's level of quality, how it tastes, whether it is a good value, and, most importantly, whether they like it and want to buy it.

Brands Establish Loyalty   Over time and with continued use, consumers learn to trust certain brands. They know, for instance, that Band-Aid® bandages always perform in the exact same way. Many customers

EXHIBIT 9.5   Value of Branding

The fact that consumers are familiar with lululemon as a brand helps the company reduce marketing costs.

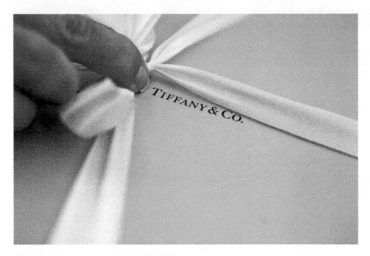

Tiffany & Co. works hard to protect its brand, including its famous blue box.

become loyal to certain brands and wouldn't consider switching brands. In some cases, they may feel a strong affinity to certain brands. For instance, Coca-Cola drinkers don't drink Pepsi, and wouldn't touch a Dr Pepper. Other consumers are loyal to Canada Goose and feel as though they are part of a club.[24] As a result of this loyalty, these companies can maintain great depth in their product lines since their customers will buy other brands within their product mix.

Brands Protect from Competition and Price Competition Strong brands are somewhat protected from competition and price competition. Because such brands are more established in the market and have a more loyal customer base, neither competitive pressures on price nor retail-level competition is as threatening to the firm. Lacoste is known for its golf shirts. Although many similar brands are available and some retailers offer their own brands, Lacoste is perceived to be of superior quality, and garners a certain status among its users, and, therefore, can command a premium price. Likewise, consumers willingly pay a premium for Canada Goose jackets, which are recognized as a best-of-breed-brand.

Brands Reduce Marketing Costs Firms with well-known brands can spend relatively less on marketing costs than firms with little-known brands because the brand sells itself. People have become familiar with lululemon's white, stylized "A" logo, so its advertisements don't need to explain what the company is or what it does. People just know. The popularity of Canada Goose, spread by word-of-mouth and supported by partnerships and sponsorships, reduces the need to invest in a lot of print advertising.[25]

Brands Are Assets Brands are also assets that can be legally protected through trademarks and copyrights and thus constitute a unique ownership for the firm. Firms sometimes have to fight to keep their brands "pure." Rolex and Canada Goose are ever watchful to ensure that the value of their brands is not diluted with counterfeit merchandise or sales through unauthorized dealers. Likewise, Tiffany & Co.'s iconic blue box is instantly recognizable and associated with high-quality items.

brand equity
The set of assets and liabilities linked to a brand that add to or subtract from the value provided by the product or service.

Brands Impact Market Value Having well-known brands can have a direct impact on the company's bottom line. The value of a brand can be calculated by assessing the earning potential of the brand over the next 12 months;[26] see examples of Canada's most valuable brands in Exhibit 9.6.

L05   ## Brand Equity

To understand branding, we look at three areas: brand equity, brand ownership, and brand names, as illustrated in Exhibit 9.7. The value of a brand translates into **brand equity**, or the set of assets and liabilities linked to a brand that add to or subtract from the value

EXHIBIT 9.6 Canada's 10 Most Valuable Brands[27]

Rank	Brand	Sector	2013 Brand Value (C$ Million)
1	Royal Bank of Canada	Financial Services	11,060
2	TD Bank	Financial Services	10,855
3	Scotiabank	Financial Services	7,717
4	Bank of Montreal	Financial Services	7,114
5	Bell	Telecom	7,081
6	CIBC	Financial Services	5,028
7	Rogers	Telecom	4,787
8	Telus	Telecom	4,290
9	Enbridge	Energy	4,093
10	Bombardier	Transportation	4,090

Source: Brand Finance Canada.

EXHIBIT 9.7 Brand Overview

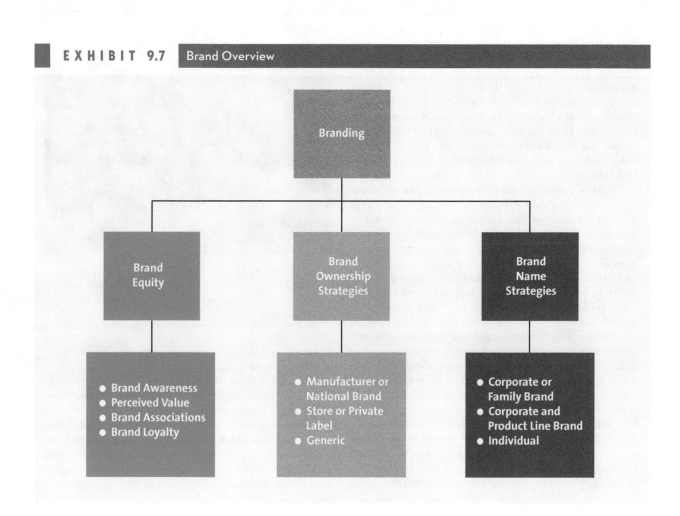

provided by the product or service.[28] Brand health must be actively managed to maintain a positive image. A recall of lululemon yoga pants, for example, could hurt brand equity in the absence of corrective action. Apple ranks number one on the best global brands list with a value of $98.3 billion; Coca Cola is third with $79.2 billion. McDonald's is seventh, with a value of just over $40 billion.[29] Like the physical possessions of a firm, brands are assets the firm can build, manage, and harness over time to increase its revenue, profitability, and overall value. Firms spend millions of dollars on promotion, advertising, and other marketing efforts throughout a brand's life cycle. Sometimes this spending comes close to crossing ethical lines as described in Ethical Dilemma 9.1. However, marketing expenditures allocated carefully can result in greater brand recognition, awareness, and consumer loyalty for the brand, enhancing overall brand equity.

How do we know how "good" a brand is, or how much equity it has? Experts look at four aspects of a brand to determine its equity: brand awareness, perceived value, brand associations, and brand loyalty.

Brand Awareness   **Brand awareness** measures how many consumers in a market are familiar with the brand and what it stands for, and have an opinion about that brand. The more aware or familiar customers are with a brand, the easier their decision-making process will be. Familiarity matters most for products that are bought without much thought, such as soap or chewing gum. However, brand awareness is also important for

brand awareness
Measures how many consumers in a market are familiar with the brand and what it stands for; created through repeated exposures of the various brand elements (brand name, logo, symbol, character, packaging, or slogan) in the firm's communications to consumers.

Ethical Dilemma 9.1   "Video Girl" Barbie Brings Girls to Foursquare

Barbie, the dress-up toy that taught generations of girls what nurses and airline stewardesses look like, has now become a Video Girl with implications for the online generation. As Mattel's gushing, hot-pink YouTube video explains, the new Barbie Video Girl doll "is kind of amazing."[30] She has a tiny video camera in her necklace, an LCD screen on her back, and editing software tucked inside. The new Barbie can record up to 25 minutes of video that "you can download to your computer with a pink USB cable."

And the Video Girl doesn't stop there. She's a "celebrity" Foursquare user that can stay in touch with fans through the location-based social networking website by uploading clues for the Barbie Video Scavenger Hunt.[31] It's the perfect game for Foursquare, which encourages smartphone users to gather and share information while browsing in restaurants and shops. Now girls who aspire to be like Barbie Video Girls can check in as well and perhaps win the scavenger hunt. But is that what parents want?

Mattel's initiative blurs the line between play and advertising, though such confusion is nothing new in an industry that uses children's television shows and movies as marketing vehicles.[32] Spurred by the success of *Transformers: Revenge of the Fallen* and *Hot Wheels: Battle Force 5*, toy companies are investing heavily in content. Hasbro launched a cable channel, The Hub, to target 6- to 12-year-old viewers.[33] Mattel requires new toy designers to focus on offerings that can be branded simultaneously through a television show, feature film, or game.[34] In 2010, Disney announced that its movie

At New York City's Barbie Fashion Night Out (FNO), a fan scans a QR code of a Barbie wearing Alexis Bittar jewellery. Barbie invited FNO-goers to shop her closet via a city-wide scavenger hunt.

financing would be prioritized according to toy merchandising potentials.[35]

Groups such as the Coalition for a Commercial-Free Childhood object to this conflation of play and purchasing, especially as the industry reaches into children's lives with everywhere, anytime digital and mobile formats. There are calls to protect children from unauthorized use of cookies and other online tracking mechanisms. But even such limits would do nothing to stop Virtual Girl Barbie from moving playtime online.

These brands have such predominance in their product market that the brand name is used as the generic product category.

infrequently purchased items or items the consumer has never purchased before. If the consumer recognizes the brand, it probably has attributes that make it valuable.[36] For those who have never purchased a Toyota, for instance, just being aware of the brand can help facilitate a purchase. Certain brands gain such predominance in a particular product market over time that they become synonymous with the product itself; that is, the brand name starts being used as the generic product category. Examples include Kleenex tissue, Clorox bleach, Xerox copiers, Band-Aid bandages, and Rollerblade inline skates. Companies must be vigilant in protecting their brand names, because if they are used so generically, over time, the brand itself can lose its trademark status. Thermos, trampoline, linoleum, and yo-yo are all examples of brands that lost their trademark status. Aspirin has become a generic brand in the United States; however, it remains a registered trademark in Canada.[37]

Marketers create brand awareness through repeated exposures of the various brand elements (brand name, logo, symbol, character, packaging, or slogan) in the firm's communications to consumers. Such communication media include advertising and promotions, personal selling, sponsorship and event marketing, publicity, public relations, and social media (see Chapters 14, 15 and 16).[38] Because consumer awareness is one of the most important steps in creating a strong brand, firms are willing to spend tremendous amounts of money advertising the brand, including more than $3.8 million for just one 30-second spot on TV during the Super Bowl.

Perceived Value Brand awareness alone does not ensure a strong brand. Consumers could be aware of a brand but have a negative opinion of its value or the firm's reputation. **Perceived value** is the relationship between a product or service's benefits and its cost. Customers usually determine the offering's value in relationship to that of its close competitors. If they feel an inexpensive brand is about the same quality as a premium brand, the perceived value of the cheaper choice is high. Many private-label brands are less expensive than brands developed by manufacturers. These brands, commonly found in supermarkets or drugstores, have seen a rise in popularity in recent years because of their high perceived value.

perceived value
The relationship between a product or service's benefits and its cost.

Retailers such as Target and Giant Tiger specialize in providing great value. Certainly, merchandise at these stores is not always of the highest possible quality, and the apparel is not the most fashion-forward. But customers don't necessarily want to buy a wastebasket that will last for 50 years and be suitable for display in a living room, nor do they need to show up at school looking like they came from a fashion-show runway. Instead, they want products to do what they were designed to do and

First Choice Haircutters, a national haircutting chain, provides its customers with great value because the haircut is better than good and the price is more than reasonable.

Dove rewarded consumers for their loyalty with double Optimum points at Shoppers Drug Mart.

brand associations
The mental links that consumers make between a brand and its key product attributes; can involve a logo, slogan, or famous personality.

brand personality
Refers to a set of human characteristics associated with a brand, which has symbolic or self-expressive meanings for consumers.

brand loyalty
Occurs when a consumer buys the same brand's product or service repeatedly over time rather than buying from multiple suppliers within the same category.

be available at a reasonable price. First Choice Haircutters, a national haircutting chain, provides "Affordable, Professional Haircare"—usually at one-half to one-third salon prices. Its customers perceive the chain to be a great value because the haircut is better than good and the price is more than reasonable.

Brand Associations **Brand associations** reflect the mental links that consumers make between a brand and its key product attributes, such as a logo, slogan, or famous personality. These brand associations often result from a firm's advertising and promotion efforts. Toyota's hybrid car, the Prius, is known for being economical, stylish, and good for the environment. Associations with specific attributes help create differentiation between the brand and its competitors; for example, Volvo stresses that its cars are made with consumer safety in mind. Firms also attempt to create specific associations for their brands with positive consumer emotions, such as fun, friendship, good feelings, family gatherings, and parties. State Farm Insurance uses the slogan "like a good neighbour, State Farm is there." Hallmark Cards associates its brand with helping people show they care about quality: "When you care enough to send the very best."

Firms sometimes even develop a personality for their brands, as if the brand were human. **Brand personality** refers to a set of human characteristics associated with a brand[39] that has symbolic or self-expressive meanings for consumers.[40] Brand personality elements include male, female, young, old, fun loving, and conservative, as well as qualities such as fresh, smooth, round, clean, or floral.[41] McDonald's has created a fun-loving, youth-oriented brand personality with its golden arches, brightly lit and coloured restaurants, exciting and youthful packaging and advertising, and spokesperson and mascot Ronald McDonald, the clown.

Brand Loyalty **Brand loyalty** occurs when a consumer buys the same brand's product or service repeatedly over time rather than buying from multiple suppliers within the same category.[42] Therefore, brand-loyal customers are an important source of value for firms. First, such consumers are often less sensitive to price. In return, firms sometimes reward loyal consumers with loyalty or customer relationship management (CRM) programs, such as points that customers can redeem for extra discounts or free services, advance notice of sale items, and invitations to special events sponsored by the company. Second, the marketing costs of reaching loyal consumers are much lower because the firm does not have to spend money on advertising and promotion campaigns to attract these customers. Loyal consumers simply do not need persuasion or an extra push to buy the firm's brands. Third, loyal customers tend to praise the virtues of their favourite products, retailers, or services. This positive word-of-mouth reaches potential customers and reinforces the perceived value at no cost to the firm. Fourth, a high level of brand loyalty insulates the firm from competition because, as we noted in Chapter 2, brand-loyal customers do not switch to competitors' brands, even when provided with a variety of incentives.

As noted previously, firms can manage brand loyalty through CRM programs. They create associations and clubs to provide a community feeling among loyal customers,[43] such as Harley-Davidson's Harley Owners Group (HOG), which the company formed in 1983 so Harley owners could meet with other owners in their communities. More than 1,000 HOG chapters worldwide host a total of almost 1 million members. Airlines, hotels, long-distance telephone providers, credit card companies, and retailers have developed frequent buyer/user programs to reward their loyal customers.

BRANDING STRATEGIES

Firms institute a variety of brand-related strategies to create and manage key brand assets, such as the decision to own the brands, establishing a branding policy, extending the brand name to other products and markets, co-operatively using the brand name with that of another firm, and licensing the brand to other firms.

Brand Ownership

Brands can be owned by any firm in the supply chain, whether manufacturers, wholesalers, or retailers. There are three basic brand ownership strategies: manufacturer brands, private-label or store brands, and generic brands (see Exhibit 9.8). **Manufacturer brands** are owned and managed by the manufacturer, and include Nike, Mountain Dew, KitchenAid, and Marriott. The majority of the brands marketed in Canada are manufacturer brands. Manufacturing firms spend millions of dollars each year to promote their brands. For example, P&G spends about $100 million in media expenditures annually to promote its Tide brand of liquid and powdered detergents.[44] By owning their brands, manufacturers retain more control over their marketing strategy, are able to choose the appropriate market segments and positioning for the brand, and can build the brand and thereby create their own brand equity.

> **manufacturer brands**
> Brands owned and managed by the manufacturer.

Brands that are owned and managed by retailers, in contrast, are called **private-label brands (store brands)**. Some manufacturers prefer to make only private-label merchandise because the costs of national branding and marketing are prohibitive, whereas other firms manufacture both their own brand and merchandise for other brands or retailers. For instance, Whirlpool sells appliances under its own name and also makes them for Sears under the Kenmore brand. President's Choice, a private label developed and marketed by Canada's largest food distributor, Loblaw, is extremely successful in Canada and parts of the United States.[45] President's Choice is positioned as a premium, high-quality private label with moderate prices.[46] Private-label brands are particularly common in supermarkets, discount stores, and drugstores. Their popularity among consumers depends on several factors, including consumer preferences for a lower-cost brand and the trust consumers

> **private-label brands (store brands)**
> Brands developed and marketed by a retailer and available only from that retailer.

EXHIBIT 9.8   Brand Ownership Strategies

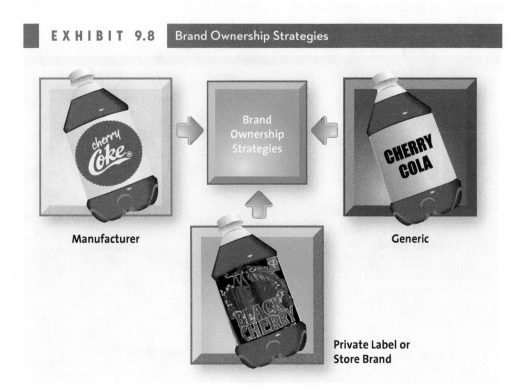

Manufacturer

Brand Ownership Strategies

Generic

Private Label or Store Brand

imagination at work

All of General Electric's brands carry the GE brand name, so they all benefit from the brand awareness associated with the corporate name.

generic
A product sold without a brand name, typically in commodities markets.

corporate brand
The use of a firm's own corporate name to brand all of its product lines and products.

have in the store and its brand. Such private-label brands, especially those marketed by large chains such as Walmart and Costco, are fast gaining in popularity and consumer loyalty. President's Choice Decadent Chocolate Chip Cookies is Canada's best-selling brand of cookies.[47] Private-label brands have also gained popularity in apparel and other categories found in department and specialty stores. The Bay, for instance, provides several store brands, including Beaumark, Mantles, Truly, and Togo.

Generic products are those sold without brand names, typically in commodities markets. For instance, shoppers can purchase unbranded salt, grains, produce, meat, or nuts in grocery stores. Hardware stores often sell unbranded screws, nuts, and lumber. However, even in these markets, the popularity and acceptance of generic products has declined. Consumers question the quality and origin of the products, and retailers have found better profit potential and the ability to build brand equity with manufacturer and store brands. For example, many fruits and vegetables sold through supermarket chains now carry either the manufacturer's brand name (e.g., Dole bananas) or the store's.

Naming Brands and Product Lines

Although there is no simple way to decide how to name a brand or a product line, the more the products vary in their usage or performance, the more likely it is that the firm should use individual brands. For example, General Motors utilizes several different individual brands (Cadillac, Chevrolet, GMC), each catering to very different target markets and meeting different needs. Hyundai, on the other hand, utilizes only one brand since usage and level of performance are relatively homogeneous. Firms use several very different strategies to name their brands and product lines (see Exhibit 9.9).

Corporate Brands
A firm can use its own corporate name to brand all its product lines and products, such as the General Electric Company, which brands its appliances prominently with the GE brand name. Similarly, all products sold through The Gap stores (Gap, GapKids, babyGap, GapMaternity, GapBody) bear only The Gap brand name. When all products are sold under one **corporate brand**, the individual brands benefit from the overall brand awareness associated with the firm's name.

EXHIBIT 9.9   Brand Name Strategies

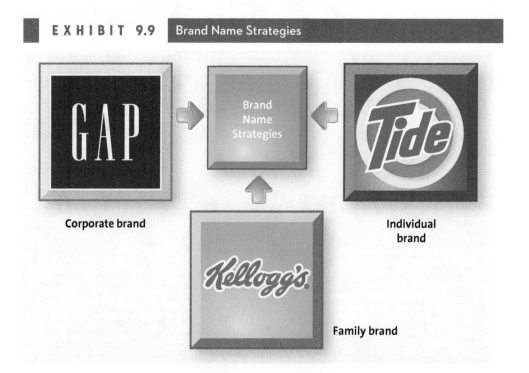

Family Brands

A firm also could use its corporate name to brand similar product lines and products. For example, Kellogg's incorporates its company name into the brand name for its cereal brands (e.g., Kellogg's Corn Flakes, Kellogg's Froot Loops, Kellogg's Rice Krispies) helping to maintain its powerhouse status on grocery store shelves. When all products in a line are sold under one **family brand**, individual brands benefit from the overall awareness associated with the family name.

Individual Brands

A firm can use **individual brand** names for each of its products. For example, in its house and home products line, P&G markets various detergent products (Tide, Gain, Cheer, Downy, Febreze), paper products (Bounty, Charmin), household cleaners (Mr. Clean, Swiffer), and dishwashing products (Cascade, Dawn, Joy). Furthermore, it markets brands in various other product lines, such as personal and beauty products (Olay, Old Spice, Secret, CoverGirl), health and wellness products (Pepto-Bismol, Oral-B, Puffs), baby products (Pampers, Huggies), and pet nutrition and care products (Iams).[48] Similarly, Loblaw operates across Canada under the following brands: Atlantic Superstore, Dominion, Extra Foods, Fortinos, Loblaws, Maxi, No Frills, Provigo, Your Independent Grocer, and Zehrs. Sobeys operates under the following retail banners: Sobeys, IGA Extra, IGA, Foodland, and Price Chopper. Individual brands allow a company to compete within one category, for example, laundry detergent, offering a variety of products to different target markets. And if one brand experiences problems, other products with unique brand names are protected from any negative association with the failed brand.

Choosing a Name

What's in a name? When it comes to naming new products, companies should consider the following desirable qualities: (1) The brand name should be descriptive and suggestive of benefits and qualities associated with the product. For example, the name *Sunkist* evokes images of oranges ripening on the trees kissed by the sun. (2) The brand name should be easy to pronounce, recognize, and remember, such as Tide, Crest, or Kodak. (3) The company should be able to register the brand name as a trademark and legally protect it. (4) For companies looking to global markets, the brand name should be easy to translate into other languages. Starbucks invited Canadians to submit names for a new Blonde Roast coffee. The winning name was True North Blend, reflecting the stunning geography, vast landscape, and spirit of Canada.

Did you know that Research In Motion (now BlackBerry) bounced around the idea of PocketLink as a name for what later became BlackBerry? While PocketLink was descriptive, the company wanted something catchier. The company got help from Lexicon Branding, which briefly considered strawberry—the keyboard looked like seeds on a strawberry to them—but discarded it as being too slow a word. BlackBerry rolled off the

---

Kellogg's uses a family branding strategy in which several product lines are sold under one name.

family brand
The use of a combination of the company brand name and individual brand name to distinguish a firm's products.

individual brand
The use of individual brand names for each of a firm's products.

When asked to submit names for a new Starbucks Blonde Roast coffee, Canadians came up with True North.

tongue much faster, used alliteration, was composed of two short five-letter words, and had an image of being playful and friendly.[49]

Sometimes a change of name is in order. Vancouver's Backwoods Brewery had been selling its beer to restaurants and bars for nearly a decade when it decided to rebrand as Dead Frog. Competing against whacky wine names such as Fat Bastard and Cat's Pee on a Gooseberry Bush, beer marketing had been pretty conservative. The company wanted a memorable but irreverent name that would appeal to a younger audience.[50] And chances are that a band called Rainbow Butt Monkeys never would have become a hit sensation. While it may have been memorable, band members received a better reception after they changed their name to Finger Eleven.

Brand Extension

brand extension
The use of the same brand name for new products being introduced to the same or new markets.

brand dilution
Occurs when a brand extension adversely affects consumer perceptions about the attributes the core brand is believed to hold.

A **brand extension** refers to the use of the same brand name for new products being introduced to the same or new markets.[51] The dental hygiene market, for instance, is full of brand extensions; Colgate, Crest, and Butler all sell toothpaste, toothbrushes, and other dental hygiene products. Roots has extended its brand from athletic clothing to leather bags, yoga wear and accessories, and even a line of baby clothes. Brand extensions are also common in global expansions. For example, Coca-Cola, Nike, Starbucks, and Levi's are sold the world over under the same name.

There are several advantages to using the same brand name for new products. First, because the brand name is already well established, such as the Canada Goose example discussed in the chapter vignette, the firm can spend less in developing consumer brand awareness and brand associations for the new product.[52] Gillette's Braun brand started selling kitchen appliances (coffeemakers, toasters, food processors, blenders, juicers), and then extended into various other product categories, including shaving (dry razors, beard care), beauty care (cordless hair stylers), oral care (power toothbrushes), and steam irons.[53]

Second, if the brand is known for its high quality, that perception will carry over to the new product. Consumers who had not used the Neutrogena brand before trying the brand extension, Neutrogena Wave power cleanser, might be encouraged to try Neutrogena's core product line of cleansers and moisturizing lotions, especially if their experience with the Wave has been positive.[54]

Third, when brand extensions are used for complementary products, a synergy exists between the two products that can increase overall sales. For example, Frito Lay markets both chips and dips under its Frito-Lay and Doritos brand names.[55] When people buy the chips, they tend to buy the dips as well.

Not all brand extensions are successful, however. Some can dilute brand equity.[56] **Brand dilution** occurs when the brand extension adversely affects consumer perceptions about the attributes the core brand is believed to hold.[57] For example, Cadbury's association with fine chocolates and candy was weakened when the company extended its brand name to mainstream food products such as mashed potatoes and

Crest uses a brand extension strategy since it uses the same brand name for many related products.

Brand extensions are often used for complementary products such as chips and dips.

soups.[58] While Life Savers soft drinks did well in prelaunch taste tests, they didn't do well in subsequent sales.

To prevent the potentially negative consequences of brand extensions, firms must consider the following caveats:

Life Savers unsuccessfully attempted a brand extension strategy with its line of soft drinks.

- Marketers should carefully evaluate the fit between the product class of the core brand and that of the extension.[59] If the fit between the product categories is high, consumers will consider the extension credible, and the brand association will be stronger for the extension. When Starbucks introduced VIA, its line of instant coffee, it made sense to consumers.

- Firms should carefully evaluate consumer perceptions of the attributes of the core brand and seek out similar attributes for the extension because brand-specific associations are very important for extensions.[60] For example, if HP printers were associated with reliability, performance, and value, consumers would expect the same brand-specific attributes in other products that carried the HP brand name.

- Firms should refrain from extending the brand name to too many products and product categories to avoid diluting the brand and damaging brand equity. While Donald Trump has been quite successful lending his name to real estate properties and TV shows, he was unsuccessful in extending his name to branding steaks.

- Firms should consider whether the brand extension will be distanced from the core brand, especially if the firm wants to use some but not all of the existing brand associations. Marriott has budget, mid-tier, and luxury hotels. Its luxury hotels, including the Ritz-Carlton, Edition, and Renaissance, do not use the name Marriott at all.[61]

Cobranding

Cobranding is the practice of marketing two or more brands together, on the same package or promotion. Primarily because of credit card companies, such as Visa and MasterCard, the practice has greatly increased in the past decade. Airlines were among the first to cobrand with credit card companies (such as the CIBC Aeroplan Visa Card); but, recently, firms in other industries, such as banking, retail, and restaurants, have begun forming similar alliances, resulting in cards such as BMO Mosaic MasterCard, TD Gold Visa, and President's Choice MasterCard, to name a few.

cobranding
The practice of marketing two or more brands together, on the same package or promotion.

Cobranding enhances consumers' perceptions of product quality[62] by signalling otherwise unobservable product quality through links between the firm's brand and a well-known quality brand. For example, Yum Brands frequently combines two or more of its restaurant chains, including A&W, KFC, Long John Silver's, Pizza Hut, and Taco Bell, into one store space.[63] This cobranding strategy is designed to appeal to diverse market segments and extend the hours in which each restaurant attracts customers. Loblaw partnered with Mattel in a cobranding agreement for its affordable fashion line, Joe Fresh, to create a limited-edition collection of Barbie-branded sleepwear and underwear.[64] Tim Hortons found that its customers responded enthusiastically to its efforts to cobrand with Cold Stone Creamery ice cream in the United States. It tested then launched the concept in its Canadian stores.[65] Recently it discontinued the brand in Canada.

However, there are some risks to cobranding, especially when customers for each of the brands are vastly different. For example, the Burger King and Häagen-Dazs cobranding strategy failed because the customer profiles for each brand were too different.[66] Cobranding may also fail when there are financial disputes or conflicts of interest.[67]

Brand Licensing

Brand licensing is a contractual arrangement between firms, whereby one firm allows another to use its brand name, logo, symbols, and/or characters in exchange for a negotiated fee.[68] Brand licensing is common for toys, apparel, accessories, and entertainment products, such as video games. The firm that provides the right to use its brand (licensor) obtains revenues through royalty payments from the firm that has obtained the right to use the brand (licensee). These royalty payments sometimes take the form of an upfront, lump-sum licensing fee or may be based on the dollar value of sales of the licensed merchandise.

Several aspects of a brand can be licensed. Popular apparel designers, such as Ralph Lauren, Calvin Klein, and Eddie Bauer, and luxury goods manufacturers often license the right to use their brand name on a variety of products. The Porsche name is used by Grundig radios and also appears on watches, luggage sets, and tennis racquets. The computer world has even capitalized on the Porsche brand name with the game *Need for Speed: Porsche Unleashed*. Canadian Tire has built on the growing popularity of NASCAR racing to become the official automotive retailer of NASCAR in Canada.[69] One very popular form of licensing is the use of characters created in books and other media. Such entertainment licensing has generated tremendous revenues for movie studios such as Disney, Lucas Films (think of the *Star Wars* memorabilia), and New Line (licensor of *Lord of the Rings* toys and collectibles), as well as for comic book publishers such as Marvel Entertainment (*Spider-Man*). A long-standing staple of licensing has been major league sports teams that play in the NBA, NFL, or NHL.

Licensing is an effective form of attracting visibility for the brand and thereby building brand equity while also generating additional revenue. There are, however, some risks associated with it. For the licensor, the major risk is the dilution of its brand equity through overexposure of the brand, especially if the brand name and characters are used inappropriately.[70]

LO7 PACKAGING

Packaging is an important brand element with more tangible or physical benefits than the other brand elements because packages come in different types and offer a variety of benefits to consumers, manufacturers, and retailers. Packaging attracts the consumer's attention, enables products to stand out from their competitors, and offers a promotional tool (e.g., "NEW" and "IMPROVED" promises on labels.) It also allows the same product to appeal to different markets with different sizes, such that convenience stores stock little packages that travellers can buy at the last minute, whereas Costco sells extra-large versions of products. As discussed in Entrepreneurial Marketing 9.1, packaging plays a key role in launching a new product.

But packaging also serves to protect products. Wrappers and exterior cartons protect eggs from being broken and help prevent tampering with products such as toothpaste. Packaging provides the UPC label used by retail scanners as well as contents, directions, and other additional product information. The package can also be an important marketing tool for the manufacturer if it is used to convey the brand's positioning. Cosmetics giant Estée Lauder considers packaging to be primarily about brand image, so its packages portray a modern, sophisticated look that is immediately recognizable.[71] Packaging is considered by many marketers to be the last frontier in advertising because of its role in promoting products to consumers on the floor of the store at the point of purchase. Packaging may also affect consumers' emotions and drive impulse buying. The shapes of fragrance, perfume, and deodorant bottles and containers are good examples of marketers extending the use of packaging beyond a distribution function to encourage purchase and differentiation. Many children also pressure their parents to buy products, like breakfast cereal, more because of the

Entrepreneurial Marketing 9.1   **Three Farmers[72]**

Camelina sativa? Perhaps the biggest hurdle in launching Three Farmers after getting novel foods approval from Health Canada, was educating consumers about the ancient grain used to produce camelina oil. Sisters Nathasha and Elysia Vanenkurk explained on CBC's *Dragons' Den* that camelina originated in Northern Europe and had historically been used as cooking oil until it fell out of favour in the 16th century. A nutritionally dense seed, camelina is rich in Omega 3 and 6, which can be difficult to incorporate in your diet if you don't like fish. It can be used at high temperatures (up to 475°F) and won't break down. Plus it has an 18-month shelf life without refrigeration, highly unusual for omega oils.

Although the grain had never been grown in Saskatchewan, it was drought resistant and cold tolerant, making it a perfect crop. The sisters joined their father and two neighbouring farmers to form Three Farmers, to grow camelina and produce cold-pressed oil. Each sister brings unique skills to the partnership: Natasha, a business grad from the University of Saskatchewan and Elysia, a Red Seal chef who had worked with celebrity chef Susur Lee.

The oil market is extremely competitive. It's incredibly difficult to convince someone who has been using olive oil for years to switch to something new. To do this meant offering a unique, high quality product with a great brand story and attractive packaging. Chef Elysia says camelina oil has a great taste profile—light flavour, earthy fragrance and slightly nutty taste. That unique edge helped the sisters convince retailers that their product wasn't just cooking oil.

Packaging played a key role. Elysia says they chose tinted glass bottles because they look classier than tins and protect the cold-pressed oil which is very sensitive to light. Round bottles provide production efficiencies when wrapping labels around them. The sisters wanted a heritage authentic story to match the product and

Three Farmers Camelina Oil is a unique and versatile product that is healthy and tastes great.

even the website is designed with that in mind, featuring stories about the three farmers who grow the camelina. Consumer feedback has been useful, too, and led to a change from a twist cap to a spout like a wine bottle to pour better.

The brand is packaged in two sizes and has already had line extensions with new flavours (roasted garlic and chili infused, and roasted onion and basil). It sells at independent stores across Canada for about $15 for a 500 ml bottle. Consumers love the brand's story, a Canadian product from a family business based on sustainable practices. Each bottle offers traceability back to the farmer who grew the camelina and even to the field in which it was grown simply by scanning the QR code on the package or entering the code on the web. Such transparency is unique, says Elysia. Very few products offer traceability, something she feels is an important trend in the food industry.

packaging than for the product. In these instances, packaging acts as a point of differentiation and makes consumers feel proud to own the brand.

Some packaging changes are designed to make the product more ecological, such as PepsiCo's response to concerns about the waste associated with bottled water. To reduce the amount of plastic it uses, PepsiCo has decreased the weight of its water bottles by 20 percent, which means less plastic in landfills.

Sometimes packaging changes can backfire though, such as when Tropicana changed its packaging to feature a picture of a glass of juice, rather than the familiar straw in an orange. Customers balked, and said the new image was reminiscent of a generic bargain brand. The company poorly misjudged its customers' loyalty to its existing brand position, as exemplified by its packaging. Frito Lay's efforts to launch compostable SunChips packaging resulted in many consumers complaining that the bags were too noisy.

Coca-Cola's Fridge Packs boosted sales. Consumers were able to store 12 cans in their refrigerators conveniently, making it easy to grab a cold drink whenever they wanted one.

Many consumers experience "wrap rage"—a great frustration with packaging that makes it seemingly impossible to get at the actual products. So companies are moving away from traditional clamshells, which are the curved plastic package around many electronics goods, because they are so difficult to open. Costco has replaced the clam-shells with packaging made of coated paperboard; it still requires scissors to be opened but is flat and therefore can be opened easily.

Retailers' priorities for packaging, however, differ. They want convenience in terms of displaying and selling the product. For customers, Coca-Cola's Fridge Pack of 12 cans offers a compact shape and convenience when carrying it home and storing it in their refrigerators; for retailers, the packaging offers the means to easily stack the packages on their shelves.

In addition, items may often be packed into larger cartons, pallets, or containers to facilitate shipment and storage from the manufacturer to the retailer. These shipping packages benefit the manufacturer and the retailer in that they protect the shipment during transit; aid in loading, unloading, and storage; and allow cost efficiencies because of the larger order and shipment sizes.

Because packaging is critical to the firm's brand positioning and shelf appeal, many innovations in design and materials have occurred in the past few decades. Some examples include[73]

● **Stand-up, reclosable zipper pouches.** Capri Sun's stand-up pouch juice drink took the lead; now a variety of products and pouch types are available, including pouches with reclosable zippers. You can even buy tuna in a stand-up pouch and cheese in reclosable zipper pouches.

● **Aluminum beverage cans.** First introduced in 1965, cans dominated the beverage market by 1985. Even some water and energy drink brands now are available in aluminum cans.

● **Aseptic packaging.** Tetra Pak and IP provided designs and machinery that increased the shelf life of beverages without refrigeration. They are used primarily by juice marketers but also by some soup companies.

● **Child-resistant/senior-friendly packages.** Products that are harmful to children under the age of five years, such as drugs and medicines, solvents, chemicals, and pesticides, are packaged with child-resistant tops. Seniors appreciate packages that are light, easy to handle, easy to read, and easy to open. Responding to consumer feedback, McNeil Consumer Healthcare in Canada developed the E-Z Open cap, a non-child-resistant closure specifically targeted to customers with arthritis.[74]

Innovative packages can enhance a product's positioning and shelf appeal. Consider reclosable packages, child-resistant/senior-friendly packages, ring-pull aluminum cans, aseptic drink bottles, and twist-off tops.

● **Green and biodegradable packaging.** Today's environmentally conscious consumers are demanding less packaging and want to be able to easily recycle it. See Sustainable Marketing 9.1 to read about Coca-Cola's new, fully recyclable PlantBottle. Vancouver-based Earthcycle Packaging launched compostable palm fibre–based packaging for items such as takeout food and produce. Palm fibre takes about 90 days to decompose and is being used by Loblaw and Walmart.[75] And P&G converted all of its liquid laundry brands (e.g., Tide, Gain, Cheer) to a concentrated formula in containers half the previous size. Retailers appreciated the storage and shelf-space savings of the smaller packages.[76]

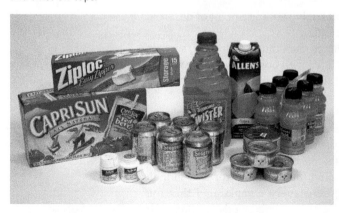

LABELLING

Labels on products and packages provide information the consumer needs for his or her purchase decision and consumption of the product. In that they identify the product and brand, labels are also an important element of branding and can be used for promotion. The information required on them must comply with general and industry-specific laws and regulations, including the constituents or ingredients contained in the product, where the product was made, directions for use, and/or safety precautions.

Many labelling requirements stem from various laws, including the Competition Act, the Consumer Packaging and Labelling Act and Regulations, the Food and Drugs Act, and the Hazardous Materials Act. Several federal agencies, industry groups, and consumer watchdogs carefully monitor product labels. The Food and Drugs Act regulates the information on food, drugs, and cosmetics package labels. Quaker Canada had to wait for Health Canada approval before it could state on its labels that oat fibre helps reduce cholesterol. The Consumer Packaging and Labelling Act covers food products and ensures that the claims made by the manufacturer are true and that labels accurately reflect ingredients and quantities. All this has to be done in both of Canada's official languages, French and English.

Manufacturers' claims on labels also can be subject to criticisms by various consumer groups. In the United Kingdom, the consumer watchdog group ITC ruled that Danone's Shape yogurt was not "virtually fat free," as its label claimed. The Dairy Industry Federation guidelines state that only products containing less than 0.3 grams

 Sustainable Marketing 9.1 | **Message in a Bottle**

Most consumers are accustomed to seeing ads from Coca-Cola telling them about the great product inside the bottle. Recently, the company has been sending a message about the bottle itself. A sustainable packaging goal to reduce its environmental footprint led the company to the introduction of the PlantBottle. Coca-Cola's commitment to responsible citizenship includes conservation of natural resources and protection of the soil, water, and climate required to sustain life on Earth.[77] Like bottles used in the past, PlantBottle is fully recyclable. Unlike previous petroleum-based PET plastic bottles, this new bottle has a lower reliance on nonrenewable resources and reduces carbon emissions, with 30 percent of materials coming from sugar cane and molasses.

The bottle was introduced in Canada for the Vancouver Olympics and contains a little green symbol to help consumers recognize the change to more environmentally friendly packaging. The plan has been to carefully and specifically launch in green-conscious cities; for example, the bottle was introduced in Copenhagen, Denmark,

Coca-Cola's fully recyclable Plant Bottle has won awards for packaging innovation.

just in time for the conference on climate change.[78] Coca-Cola now uses the PlantBottle for its single-serve Odwalla juice line-in Canada and plans to use it in place of all its PET bottles by 2020. More than 2.5 million bottles have been distributed globally, eliminating 30,000 metric tons of CO_2.[79]

Coca-Cola's sustainability efforts go well beyond the PlantBottle. It works with a number of organizations, including the Bill and Melinda Gates Foundation, to help implement sustainable farming practices in various parts of the world. It also works with WWF (World Wildlife Fund/World Wide Fund for Nature) on the Better Sugar Initiative to promote improvements in the key environmental and social impacts of sugarcane production and primary processing.[80]

PlantBottle has already been recognized as a unique new technology. It won a gold award at the DuPont Awards for Packaging Innovation for its demonstrated breakthrough packaging innovation.[81] In the first full year of using the PlantBottle product, Coca-Cola hopes to produce up to 2 billion bottles.[82] Now that's a message in a bottle.

The packaging and label for BioBest Maximmunité highlight the fact that the product contains probiotic cultures.

of fat per every 100 grams could be called "virtually fat free," but Danone's Shape yogurt contained three times that amount.[83]

A product label is much more than just a sticker on the package; it is a communication tool. Many of the elements on the label are required by laws and regulations (i.e., ingredients, fat content, sodium content, serving size, calories), but other elements of the label remain within the control of the manufacturer. How manufacturers use labels to communicate the benefits of their products to consumers varies by the product. For example, the label for BioBest Maximmunité highlights the fact that the drink contains probiotic cultures. Many other products highlight other specific ingredients, vitamin content, or nutrient content. This focus signals to consumers that the product offers these benefits. Although often overlooked, the importance of the label as a communication tool should not be underestimated.

REAL MARKETER PROFILE | Stacey Biggar

I studied Business Administration, specializing in Brand Communications. After completing my degree, my passion for cooking fuelled me to study Culinary Arts for the following year, with a plan to combine both business and food as a career.

I found my first job online searching for jobs like I'd experienced on co-op, and tailored my cover letter and resumé to each posting that sounded interesting. My first job was in the marketing department at Parmalat Canada with brands such as Black Diamond cheese and Astro yogurt.

Some days involved managing agency partners to design coupons and websites; other days were dedicated to writing business proposals for new product launches, or attending commercial shoots for new TV ads. Outside the office, I've attended focus group research sessions, promotional activations, and in-store demonstrations of new products to consumers.

The most exciting projects were working on new product launches! Some were simple line extensions of existing products, like new flavours of yogurt, but the really challenging ones involved bringing completely new products or categories to market, like BioBest yogurt with plant sterols. These new launches required leadership right from business case to live product. It was one of the first food products in Canada ever to contain plant sterols, proven to lower cholesterol. The focus on launching quickly meant efficiency was essential, demanding smart decisions, fast. The need for speed to market also challenged me to work closely with our cross-functional team and agency partners to reduce timelines to less than one-third of what they typically would be.

We were able to launch in less than four months after receiving approval for using plant sterols in Canada!

Then I made a change to work for Unilever Canada, focusing on long-term planning, communication strategy, and innovations for Becel margarine. This position was a contrast to typical brand management roles as it was completely separate from the day-to-day business management and focused on strategy and research. After gaining strong experience through both roles, I recently made a change to become brand manager on the cookies business at Mondelez Canada, where I am responsible for some beloved Canadian cookie brands like Peek Freans and Dad's oatmeal cookies. I have been lucky that my career has allowed me to combine my skills in marketing with my passion for food to work on leading food brands.

The most exciting part about brand management is that every day is different. Daily activities could range from brainstorming new innovations to balancing budgets, planning research projects, having conversations with sales about how to increase distribution for your products, explaining strategy to creative agencies, or giving final feedback on a new TV commercial. The variety of the role keeps things very engaging and challenges you to develop a very broad base of business and interpersonal skills. It's also fulfilling to see your products on grocery store shelves or watch TV and see your communication strategy in action. It's a great feeling to know you are helping to make consumers' lives better by offering new products that address true consumer needs, from the yogurt cooler to the cookie aisle!

LEARNING OBJECTIVES REVIEW

LO1 **Describe the components of a product**

The product itself is important but so are its associated services, such as support or financing. Other elements combine to produce the core customer value of a product: the brand name, quality level, packaging, and additional features.

LO2 **Identify the types of consumer products**

These products tend to be classified into four groups: specialty, shopping, convenience, and unsought products. Each classification involves a different purchase situation and consumer goal.

LO3 **Explain the difference between a product mix's breadth and a product line's depth**

Breadth, or variety, entails the number of product lines that a company offers. Depth involves the number of categories in one specific product line. Firms grow their product lines by adding either new product categories or new SKUs within a product category. The decision to add products should be made carefully. Excessive product line expansions can confuse consumers and dilute the appeal of the brand's core products. Sometimes products or product lines become unprofitable, the firm's priorities change, or consumer preferences shift. When this happens, firms must prune their product lines by deleting items or possibly even entire product categories.

LO4 **Identify the advantages that brands provide firms and consumers**

Brands facilitate the consumer search process. Some customers are loyal to certain brands, which essentially protects those brands from competition. In addition, brands are valuable in a legal sense, in that trademarks and copyrights protect firms from counterfeiters and knock-off artists. Firms with well-known brands can spend relatively less on marketing because the brand and its associations help

sell the product. Finally, brands have real market value as a company asset.

LO5 **Summarize the components of brand equity**

Brand equity summarizes the value that a brand adds, or subtracts, from the offering's value. It comprises brand awareness, or how many consumers in the market are familiar with the brand; brand associations, which are the links consumers make between the brand and its image; and brand loyalty, which occurs when a consumer will buy only that brand's offer. Brand equity also encompasses the concept of perceived value, which is a subjective measure that consumers develop to assess the costs of obtaining the brand.

LO6 **Describe the types of branding strategies used by firms**

Firms use a variety of strategies to manage their brands. First, they must decide whether to offer national, private-label, or generic brands. Second, they have a choice of using an overall corporate brand or a collection of product line or individual brands. Third, to reach new markets or extend their current market, they can extend their current brands to new products. Fourth, firms can cobrand with another brand to create sales and profit synergies for both. Fifth, firms with strong brands have the opportunity to license their brands to other firms.

LO7 **State how a product's packaging and label contribute to a firm's overall strategy**

Like brands, packaging and labels help sell the product and facilitate its use. The package holds the product, and its label provides product information. The package also provides additional consumer information on its label and facilitates transportation and storage for both retailers and their customers. Labels have become increasingly important to consumers because they supply important safety, nutritional, and product usage information.

KEY TERMS

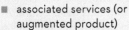

- associated services (or augmented product)
- brands
- brand associations
- brand awareness
- brand dilution
- brand equity
- brand extension
- brand licensing
- brand loyalty

- brand personality
- cobranding
- consumer products
- convenience goods/services
- core customer value
- corporate brand
- family brand
- generic
- individual brand
- manufacturer brands

- perceived value
- private-label brands (store brands)
- product category
- product mix
- product mix breadth
- product line depth
- product lines
- shopping goods/services
- specialty goods/services
- stock keeping units (SKUs)

CONCEPT REVIEW

1. Explain the differences between product mix breadth and product line depth. Why is understanding this difference important?

2. Explain why branding is important to marketers. What value do customers derive from purchasing and using brand name products?

3. What is brand equity? Describe the strategies marketers could employ to increase the value of their brand equity.

4. Differentiate between a manufacturer's brand, generic brand, and store brand. Should retailers carry all three types of brands? Why?

5. Describe the desirable qualities companies should consider when choosing product names.

6. What are the advantages of using the same brand name and extending it to new products?

7. Explain how brand licensing differs from cobranding.

8. What is cobranding? When does it make sense for a company to use a cobranding strategy?

9. Explain how marketers increase the value of their product offering through packaging. Discuss the ethical issues surrounding product packaging and labelling. How might some of these issues be resolved?

10. Explain how labelling could be used as a marketing weapon rather than just providing legally required information.

MARKETING APPLICATIONS

1. Prepared foods at Whole Foods Market, the world's largest retailer of organic foods, are very profitable. To make them even more profitable, suggest two strategies that would alter the product mix breadth and depth.

2. Visit a grocery store and look for Colgate Total toothpaste on the shelves. How many different SKUs (including all sizes and flavour variations) are sold at the store? What are the advantages and disadvantages of having so many different variations?

3. Suppose you have just been hired by a jewellery manufacturer as a marketing consultant. The manufacturer has been making private-label jewellery for 75 years but is thinking about developing its own brand of jewellery. Discuss the advantages and disadvantages of such a strategy.

4. Identify a specific brand that has developed a high level of brand equity. What specific aspects of that brand establish its brand equity?

5. Are you loyal to any brands? If so, pick one and explain why you believe you are loyal, beyond that you simply like the brand. If not, pick a brand that you like and explain how you would feel and act differently toward the brand if you were loyal to it.

6. Ford Motor Company owns several brands: Ford, Lincoln, Mercury, Mazda, and Aston Martin. Within each brand are many models, each of which has a unique identifying name. Wouldn't it be easier to just identify them all as Fords? Justify your answer.

7. Unlike Ford Motor Company, BMW has only one brand and gives each car it makes a number instead of a name, for example, the BMW Series 3, Series 5, or Series 7. What are the advantages to BMW of this approach?

8. Identify a specific company that has recently introduced a new brand extension to the marketplace. Discuss whether you believe the brand extension example you provided will benefit or harm the firm.

9. Do you think all food sold in a grocery store should have an ingredient and nutrition label? Consider the perspectives of consumers, the manufacturer, and the store.

10. You are hired by a small bakery interested in distributing its product through supermarkets. The market for the bakery's products has been steadily growing and it is time to expand distribution now that the bakery has expanded its production capacity. You have an appointment with the manager of a local grocery chain. The manager is familiar with the bakery's products and is excited about the possibility of having them in the store. He has asked you to come up with a plan to package your products in a way that makes them attractive to shoppers, keeps baked goods fresh, and uses the least amount of packaging possible to satisfy even the most stringent environmentalist. You've never had to deal with this issue before. At the bakery, goods are packed in paper bags after being selected from protective glass displays. Come up with a package that works for the retailer and is affordable for the bakery.

NET SAVVY

1. Visit the P&G website (http://www.pg.ca). Identify and briefly describe its different *product lines*. Now identify one of its *product categories*, and discuss the *depth* of that particular category.

2. Interbrand Corporation is a leading brand consultancy firm headquartered in New York that conducts research on the monetary value of different brands. Visit the company's website (http://www.interbrand.com) and access the most recent "Best Global Brands" survey. Identify the top five brands, their brand values, and their countries of origin. Describe changes in the rankings of these firms from the previous year. Why do you think the rankings changed? Identify the brands with the greatest increase and the greatest decrease in terms of percentage change in brand value from the previous year.

CHAPTER CASE STUDY

BAND-AID® BRAND PRODUCTS: BUILDING ON THE VALUE OF THE BRAND[84, 85]

Part of global giant Johnson & Johnson's Consumer Products Company, Band-Aid is widely known as a leader in the wound-care market. With its dominant share of the market, the brand is widely recognized and respected by consumers and health care professionals alike. Known as an innovator of wound-care products, the company continues to introduce new products that exploit creative technologies, one of which led *Good Housekeeping* magazine to name Band-Aid Brand Liquid Bandage a "Good Buy" award winner. From its early beginnings to today, the company has excelled at providing value to its customers and demonstrated that people across the world can trust the brand.

The Brand Begins

Necessity is the mother of invention, and in the case of Band-Aid, the saying applies. Back in 1920, when Earl Dickson came home from his cotton-buying job at Johnson & Johnson, he would always find a hot meal that his wife Josephine had prepared for him. He also found visible burns and cuts on Josephine from her kitchen labours, which prompted Earl to piece together gauze squares and adhesive tape to cover her wounds. Soon, Earl decided to prepare ready-made bandages in this fashion, with pieces of gauze at intervals along the tape so that Josephine could cut the premade strip and tend to her wounds throughout the day. When the product was first launched in the market, the bandages were made by hand, were not sterile, and had annual sales of just $3,000.

The Company Today

Today, Band-Aid products are machine-made and completely sterile. A visit to the company's website (http://www.bandaid.com) reveals the distance Band-Aid has come from the early tape and gauze product, as well as the modern demand for over-the-counter first-aid products in a variety of categories.

In keeping with its long history of product innovations, the company continues to invest in new product development and marketing (Exhibit 9.10). Band-Aids come in a host of styles, including those with popular characters for kids; uniquely shaped bandages for various parts of the body; antibiotic Band-Aids to help fight

Band-Aids come in a variety of sizes and styles.

germs; waterproof products with aloe to treat burns; scar-healing strips; bandages in clear plastic, stretchy cloth, and round and square shapes; and treated and untreated pads. Moreover, the Band-Aid franchise has expanded to include various ointments, gauze, tapes, and kits for a plethora of first-aid needs. For example, One-Step Cleansing + Infection Protection Foam antiseptic cleans and heals wounds without the need for antibiotic ointment; Calamine Spray dries rashes from poison ivy; Bug-Bite Relief Patches relieve itching and prevent scratching; and FIRST AID TO GO!® Mini First-Aid Kits include essential travel-sized products.

But new product introductions by Band-Aid don't come cheap. For example, $17 million of the $28 million marketing budget was allocated to just three new product extensions. Advanced Healing Blister Block, a round, waterproof cushioning strip to heal and prevent foot blisters, received $7 million in marketing support to tout its ability to promote fast, natural healing. Finger Care Tough Strips obtained a marketing budget of $5 million and was rolled out as an extension of regular finger-care products. Finally, Extra Large Tough Strips were also supported with $5 million for marketing.[86] Previous years' launches were similarly supported, including Liquid Bandages ($7 million), Water Block Bandages ($8 million), and Hurt-Free Antiseptic Wash ($5 million).

The company moved into the digital realm when it introduced the "Magic Vision" iOS app. The app used augmented reality that let children scan special Band-Aids to see digital animations with Sesame Street characters. Although the actual product is used for scrapes, cuts and minor "boo boos," bandages often serve a placebo effect, making children feel better simply having one applied. How sticky, absorbent or healing the bandages are don't represent the core reason children love them. The Muppet Band-Aids made children feel better by "entertaining the hurt away."[87] The company is in an enviable position. People around the world see the value of Band-Aid products to heal, prevent, and repair minor nicks, cuts, scrapes, wounds, and bruises. Continued product innovations and line expansions likely will help the company continue to be the most recognized name in tape, bandages, and gauze.

EXHIBIT 9.10	Examples of Band-Aid Product Innovations

Year	Product Innovation
1920	Band-Aid brand adhesive bandages—7.5-cm wide and 46-cm long—introduced to the market
1924	First machine-made, sterile bandages
1940	Packaging adds red strings to open bandage packages
1951	Plastic strips
1956	Decorated bandages
1958	Sheer vinyl bandages
1994	Sport-strip bandages
1997	Antibiotic adhesive bandages with ointment on the pad
2000	Advanced healing strips for wound care
2001	Liquid bandage that promotes fast healing
2003	Scar-healing technology that fades red and raised scars
2007	Plus Antibiotic bandages to reduce infection and scars
2009	Anti-Blister Stick to reduce rubbing on skin and prevent blisters
2012	Flexible Fabric bandages use QuiltVent Technology to let wounds breathe

Source: http://www.bandaid.com.

Questions

1. Visit the company's website (http://www.bandaid.com) and identify and describe the different product lines that it markets. How would you describe its product line breadth?

2. Review the different product categories in each of the company's product lines. Which has the greatest breadth? Which has the least?

3. Look at the new products that the company offers. Identify which are extensions of the Band-Aid brand name and which are not. Discuss the extent to which the brand extensions might dilute brand equity.

4. Review the company's products designed for children. To what extent do these use manufacturer (national) branding? Private-label (store) branding? Licensed branding? Justify your answers. What added values do these products offer compared with regular Band-Aid protection products?

For more information on the resources available from McGraw-Hill Ryerson, go to www.mheducation.ca/he/solutions.

CHAPTER 10

Services: The Intangible Product

"Who has time to be without the car for a whole day?" When Heather Murphy and Craig Howes ran custom window franchises, having their vehicles serviced was a big frustration. It took too much time to have the tires changed and cost them $6,000 a day in lost revenue. The most expensive part of changing tires was vehicle downtime. And so they launched GoTire, Canada's first mobile tire service business.[1] Offering an entire shop in a van, their motto is "We bring the shop to you."

The intangible nature of services means consumers can't always see what they are getting before they buy it. Murphy and Howes developed their business with a view to franchising and knew they would have to focus on tangibility. One way GoTire achieves this is with professional-looking trucks emblazoned with the company logo. The trucks not only add tangibility to the service, but also serve as mobile billboards. An investment in a high quality video before their *Dragons' Den* appearance impressed the Dragons and has since been repurposed to attract franchisees. Videos are created of all new franchisees so prospective customers can see who will be delivering the service, making customers more comfortable trying the service.

Another challenge for GoTire is the seasonal nature of tire changes. It's busy in the spring and fall but what happens in the shoulder season? You can't hold services in inventory like you can with products. To spread demand throughout the year, franchises offer mobile windshield service and auto detailing. Other optional services, such as emergency unlock, battery sales, battery service, and headlight restoration help increase demand. A "Tire Hotel" is used to house tires in the off-season. It's a great feature for people who live in apartments or don't want to use space in their garage. Murphy says it's also a customer retention system because once someone leaves their tires with you, you know the person will be coming back. GoTire contacts all customers who use the Tire Hotel to book tire changes in advance of the first snowfall, to further even out demand.

Guarantees are used to de-risk the service and deal with inseparability. While all tire manufacturers offer warranties, Murphy says they aren't always very good. GoTire offers low-cost insurance that provides a tire repair guarantee. A warranty is offered on windshield repairs. If the windshield breaks within six months of being repaired, customers can apply the cost of the repair to a new windshield.

Extensive training helps overcome inconsistency and ensures franchisees are ready to launch their business. Training lasts for three weeks and addresses technical skills, product knowledge, sales and marketing, as well as how to set up an office and warehouse. Each franchisee receives social media training on Facebook and Twitter and learns GoTire's proprietary Customer Relationship Management (CRM) system. Because brand consistency is key, franchisees receive a brand standards guide complete with templates for brochures, invoices, and promotional materials.

Addressing the unique characteristics of services paid dividends. GoTire broke even in its first year, has over 30 franchises coast to coast, and is Canada's fastest-growing mobile tire franchise.[2] ∎

service
Any intangible offering that cannot be physically possessed.

customer service
Specifically refers to human or mechanical activities firms undertake to help satisfy their customers' needs and wants.

Whereas a **service** is any intangible offering that involves a deed, performance, or effort that cannot be physically possessed,[3] **customer service** specifically refers to human or mechanical activities that firms undertake to help satisfy their customers' needs and wants. By providing good customer service, firms add value to their products or services.

In this chapter, we examine the unique characteristics of services that differentiate them from products. Then we discuss how companies can provide great service and use elements in the Gaps model to help them meet customer expectations. Lastly, we look at how companies can recover from inevitable service failures.

Exhibit 10.1 illustrates the continuum from a pure service to a pure product. Some firms lie somewhere in the middle and include some service and some product or sell products with an "embedded" service element (e.g., restaurants). As we noted in Chapter 2, even firms engaged primarily in selling a product, such as apparel stores, typically view service as a method to maintain a sustainable competitive advantage. This chapter takes an inclusive view of services as anything from pure service businesses to a business that uses service as a differentiating tool to help it sell physical products.

EXHIBIT 10.1   The Service–Product Continuum

| Doctor | Hotel | Dry Cleaners | Restaurant | Apparel Specialty Store | Grocery Store |

Service Dominant ⟵⟶ **Product Dominant**

Specialized services like personal training are thriving.

Economies of developed countries such as Canada have become increasingly dependent on services. For example, the service sector makes up more than 70 percent of Canada's economy, the lion's share of jobs, and is growing far faster than goods-producing industries. This dependence and the growth of service-oriented economies in developed countries have emerged for several reasons.

First, it is generally less expensive for firms to manufacture their products in less-developed countries. Even if the goods are finished in Canada, some of their components likely were produced elsewhere. In turn, the proportion of service production to goods production in Canada, and other similar economies, has steadily increased over time.

Second, household maintenance activities, which many people performed by themselves in the past, have become quite specialized. Food preparation, lawn maintenance, house cleaning, laundry and dry cleaning, hair care, and automobile maintenance all are often performed by specialists in the modern economy.

Third, people place a high value on convenience and leisure. Most households have little time for the household maintenance tasks mentioned earlier, and many are willing to pay others to do their chores. People are demanding more specialized services—everything from plumbers to personal trainers, from massage therapists to tax specialists, from lawyers to travel and leisure specialists. As the Canadian population ages, the need for health care professionals—not only doctors and nurses, but also assisted-living facilities and nursing homes—also increases.

SERVICES MARKETING DIFFERS FROM PRODUCT MARKETING

L01

The marketing of services differs from product marketing because of four fundamental differences unique to services: they are intangible, inseparable, variable, and perishable.[4] To help remember these differences, think of them as the four Is of services in that they are Intangible, Inseparable from their providers, Inconsistent (variable), and cannot be held in Inventory (perishable). (See Exhibit 10.2.) These differences make marketing services considerably more challenging than marketing products. This section examines these four differences and discusses how they affect marketing strategies.

■ **E X H I B I T   10.2**   Core Differences between Services and Goods

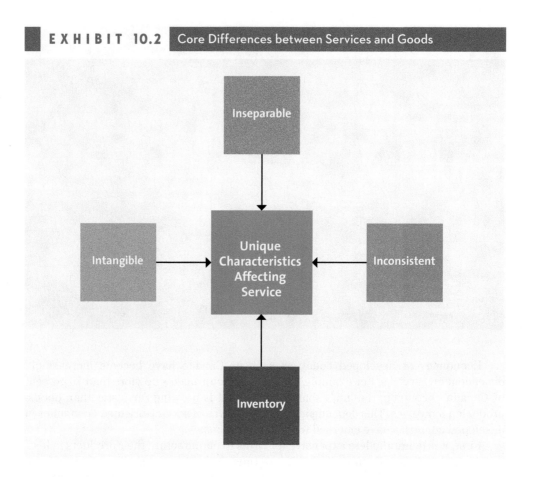

Intangible

As the title of this chapter implies, the most fundamental difference between products and services is that services are **intangible**; they cannot be touched, tasted, or seen like a pure product can. When you get a physical examination, you see and hear the doctor, but the service itself is intangible. This intangibility can prove highly challenging to marketers. For instance, it makes it difficult to convey the benefits of services. Try describing whether the experience of visiting your dentist was good or bad and why. Health care service providers (e.g., physicians, dentists) offer cues to help their customers experience and perceive their service more positively, such as a waiting room stocked with TV sets, computer games, and toys for children; upscale beverages; and comfortable chairs to create an atmosphere that appeals to the target market.

Similarly, Starbucks has always enhanced its service offering by providing a comfortable and cozy atmosphere for drinking coffee, working, reading, or chatting with friends. It adds tangibility to its service by creating a warm and inviting environment and offering free WiFi to customers nationwide. RBC Royal Bank offers clients *my*Finance-Tracker, an online financial management tool that tracks expenses, categorizes transactions, and provides advanced budgeting capabilities for personal banking and credit card accounts.[5] The tool improves RBC's service offering and adds tangibility to the banking experience by helping clients save time and money.

Furthermore, a service is also difficult to promote because it can't be shown directly to potential customers. Marketers must therefore creatively employ symbols and images to promote and sell services, as Walt Disney World does in using its advertising to evoke images of happy families and nostalgic memories of Mickey Mouse and previous visits to the theme park. Likewise, Cirque du Soleil, considered Canada's top cultural export, adds tangibility to its performances with mesmerizingly

intangible
A characteristic of a service; it cannot be touched, tasted, or seen like a pure product can.

staged acrobatics, which are backed by a live orchestra playing an original score. The entire circus experience is carefully co-ordinated to create memorable impressions—the Porta Potties on its big-top sites even have running water.[6] Fans can also buy a wide variety of Cirque du Soleil–branded merchandise (e.g., music, videos, books, clothing, and accessories) to extend their positive memories of the performances. In another example, professional medical services provide appropriate images of personnel doing their jobs in white coats surrounded by high-tech equipment. Dentists provide patients with tangible evidence of their visits in the form of free toothbrushes. Educational institutions promote the quality of their services by touting their famous faculty and alumni, as well as their accreditations. They also often use images of happy students sitting spellbound in front of a fascinating professor or going on to lucrative careers of their own.

At Starbucks, customers can have a drink, pick up iTunes Pick of the Week cards, and surf the Internet by using the stores' free WiFi access.

Because of the intangibility of services, the images marketers use reinforce the benefit or value that a service provides. Professional service providers, such as doctors, lawyers, accountants, and consultants, depend heavily on consumers' perceptions of their integrity and trustworthiness. Yet the promotional campaigns some of these professionals use have been criticized by their peers and consumer welfare groups. Tension is created when service providers such as personal injury lawyers use aggressive marketing tactics to attract clients to their service but still attempt to maintain a perception of integrity and trustworthiness, or when invasion of privacy becomes an issue.

Inseparable Production and Consumption

Unlike a pair of jeans that may have been made months before their purchase, services are produced and consumed at the same time—that is, service and consumption are **inseparable**. Because service production can't be separated from consumption, astute service marketers provide opportunities for their customers to get directly involved in the service. Health care providers have found, for instance, that the more control they allow their patients in determining their course of treatment, the more satisfied those patients are.[7]

inseparable
A characteristic of a service: it is produced and consumed at the same time—that is, service and consumption are inseparable.

Because the service is inseparable from its consumption, customers rarely have the opportunity to try the service before they purchase it. And after the service has been performed, it can't be returned. Imagine telling your dentist that you want a "test" cavity filled before he or she starts drilling a real one or asking to try out a new look before your stylist lops several inches off your hair. Because the purchase risk in these scenarios can be relatively high, services sometimes provide extended warranties and 100 percent satisfaction guarantees, such as First Choice Haircutters, which promotes "Affordable, Professional Haircare. Guaranteed." Many hotels (e.g., Comfort Inn, Comfort Suites, Quality Inn, Sleep Inn, Clarion) post claims advising guests, "If you are not satisfied with your accommodations or our service, please advise the front desk of a problem right away and give them an opportunity to correct the situation. If the hotel staff is unable to satisfy you, they will give you up to one night's free stay."[8]

Inconsistent

The more humans that are needed to provide a service, the more likely that the service's quality will be **inconsistent** or variable. A hair stylist may give bad haircuts in the morning because he or she went out the night before; yet, that stylist may still offer a better service than the undertrained stylist working at the next station. A restaurant, which offers a mixture of services and products, generally can control its food quality but not the variability in food preparation or delivery. If a consumer has a problem with a

inconsistent
A characteristic of a service: its quality may vary because it is provided by humans.

Enterprise Rent-A-Car reduces its service inconsistency through training and standardization. You get the same great service everywhere you go.

Nerds on Site matches clients with a "Primary Nerd" to ensure personalized service.

product, it can be replaced, remade, destroyed, or, if it is already in the supply chain, recalled. In many cases, the problem can even be fixed before the product gets into consumers' hands. But an inferior service can't be recalled; by the time the firm recognizes a problem, the damage has been done.

Some marketers of services strive to reduce service inconsistency through training and standardization. Enterprise Rent-A-Car, for instance, has worked to standardize its service delivery across North America and, to that end, provides extensive training to its associates. Go to any Enterprise outlet at any airport and chances are you will be greeted in the same personalized way. The airport shuttle drivers will load and unload your bags. When you get off the shuttle, you will be greeted by name, and your car will be ready to go in minutes. This smooth and pleasant service transaction is the result of the company's very specific service standards and excellent training program.

Marketers also can use the inconsistent nature of services to their advantage. A micromarketing segmentation strategy can customize a service to meet customers' needs exactly (see Chapter 6). Technology services company Nerds On Site will come to your home or office and take care of any repair or service your PC might need: setting up a network, cleaning your hard drive, or designing or hosting your website. Each customer's needs are different, so Nerds On Site employs a cadre of consultants who possess a variety of skills. Clients are matched with their very own "Primary Nerd" on the basis of their needs, which allows for a fully personalized service offering.

Such micromarketing can be expensive to deliver though, particularly for a firm that offers multiple services. Consumers also may get confused or even irritated if they must pay for each little service. Imagine a hotel that charged separately for each bed, towel, bar of soap, minute of TV use, and lap in the swimming pool. Instead, service providers usually bundle their services into one package and charge a single price. For example, Club Med resorts offer all-inclusive amenity packages for one price, which includes, for example, a flight from Montreal to Club Med Punta Cana, Dominican Republic, and then accommodations, meals, snacks, bar service, and sports and entertainment activities once you arrive for about $1,800 for seven nights—include a friend for $1,300 more![9]

In an alternative approach, some service providers tackle the inconsistency issue by replacing people with machines. For simple transactions such as getting cash, using an ATM is usually quicker and more convenient—and less variable—than waiting in line for a bank teller. Self-checkout machines are multiplying in grocery and discount stores at blistering speed. Even libraries are installing self-checkout machines for books. Canadians are accustomed to serving themselves and quickly adopt new technology. An Ipsos Reid/NCR study showed that 56 percent of Canadians are more likely to shop at stores with self-service than those without.[10]

Self-checkouts can be successful and increase customer loyalty, because they appeal to shoppers who want to move quickly and believe they can zip through checkouts faster by using the machines. Although expensive, the machines reduce labour costs; one cashier can oversee the operation of four to eight self-checkouts. And the machines don't have to be trained—nor do they ever come to work late or with a bad attitude, thereby reducing service inconsistency.

Building on the popularity of self-serve technology, an app-based taxi service, Hailo, has been launched in Toronto. Consumers with an iPhone or Android smartphone can

Consumers can electronically order a cab and pay for it with the Hailo app-based taxi service.

use its GPS technology to find the closest available Hailo taxi. They receive the cab's number, location, and driver's name instantly and another message when the cab arrives. Customers who use the service need not worry about being short of cash since transactions are handled with an on-file credit card. Receipts are emailed to passengers at the end of each trip.[11] In less than a year, over 50,000 consumers downloaded the app and 1,400 Toronto cab drivers[12] signed up for Hailo. The company plans to extend the service to other Canadian cities.

Many retailers have installed Internet-enabled kiosks. In addition to offering customers the opportunity to order merchandise not available in the store, kiosks can provide routine customer service, freeing employees to deal with more demanding customer requests and problems and reducing service variability. For example, customers can use kiosks to locate merchandise in the store and determine whether specific products, brands, and sizes are available. Kiosks can also be used to automate existing store services, such as gift registry management, rain cheques, film dropoff, credit applications, and preordering service for bakeries and delicatessens.

The technological delivery of services sometimes causes additional problems. Customers may not embrace the idea of replacing a human with a machine for business interactions or have problems using the technology. In addition, the technology may not perform adequately, such as self-checkout scanners that fail to scan all merchandise or ATMs that run out of money or are out of order. In late 2013, an Ipsos survey showed that self-checkouts in grocery stores result in customer dissatisfaction and queuing problems. Nor have the anticipated reductions in staff been realized.[13] As a result, some grocery stores are reconsidering plans to add more machines.

Do self-checkout machines increase or reduce consumers' perception of service?

The Internet has reduced service inconsistency in several areas. Customers can purchase travel items (e.g., airline tickets, hotel rooms, rental cars), concert and movie tickets, insurance, mortgages, and merchandise directly via the Internet or by cellphone. Cineplex launched mobile applications for BlackBerry, iPhone, and Android smartphones to allow customers to buy movie tickets faster. The apps not only reduce inconsistency for movie goers, but also reduce costs for theatres. And if the customer wants more information than is available online, websites provide ways to contact customer service personnel by email or telephone. According to comScore MobiLens data, the app is ranked the seventh most popular mobile brand in Canada.[14]

Beyond online benefits, the Internet has also reduced service inconsistency. At the William Lutsky YMCA in Edmonton, members can use FitLinxx, a computerized system, to track their workout performance. New users establish goals, workouts, and schedules, and receive detailed workout programs (e.g., at least 14 abdominal muscle workouts pop up when users select "abs"). FitLinxx learns users' programs, coaches them individually throughout workouts, and tracks progress over time. The system not only has health benefits for users, who always get a consistent workout but also has boosted customer retention, and users typically exercise more often than average.[15]

Inventory

inventory
A characteristic of a service; it is perishable and cannot be stored for future use.

Services are perishable because they cannot be held in **inventory** or stored for use in the future. You can't stockpile a yoga class like you could a six-pack of beer, for instance. The perishability of services provides both challenges and opportunities to marketers in terms of the critical task of matching demand and supply. As long as the demand for and the supply of the service match closely, there is no problem; but, unfortunately, this perfect matching rarely occurs. A ski area, for instance, can be open as long as there is snow, even at night, but demand peaks on weekends and holidays, so ski areas often offer less expensive tickets during off-peak periods to stimulate demand. Airlines, cruise ships, movie theatres, and restaurants confront similar challenges and attack them in similar ways. Airlines offer promotional pricing to encourage people to book flights during the off-season, and movie theatres routinely discount matinee showings when demand is typically lower. Looking to increase facility usage and reach new audiences, Cineplex Galaxy started broadcasting NHL games live in Canadian cities. For some hockey fans, it's the next best thing to being there, and at a ticket price of $10.95, fans pay only a fraction of the cost of watching, for example, the Toronto Maple Leafs at the Air Canada Centre, which costs between $23 and $381 a ticket.[16] Cineplex followed with livestreaming of concerts such as the Tragically Hip, Metropolitan Opera performances, WWE events and other shows.

Balancing the ups and downs of demand and capacity is challenging. As noted earlier, unlike products, services can't be stockpiled in inventory. For services companies, excess demand results in having to turn customers away in peak periods, while excess capacity may mean less desirable expense to revenue ratios. For example, dental hygienists, rent, and other expenses still need to be paid even if customers forget their appointments, so dental offices maximize capacity by making advance reminder calls to patients or by charging cancellation fees to clients who do not show up for their appointments without adequate notice. Hotel reservation systems offer guaranteed late arrivals, ensuring that

Since services are perishable, service providers such as ski areas offer less expensive tickets at night to stimulate demand.

Guy Drouin is banking on the fact that regardless of how the economy is doing, people still want to have fun. And he hopes they'll do it at Calypso Park, Canada's largest themed water park. Drouin has been preoccupied with theme parks ever since 1963, when his father started charging a fee to tobogganers who wanted to sled down his Quebec City hill. When Drouin took over the business in 1971, he modernized things, added

Water features such as Pirate's Aquaplay make Calypso Park an exciting adventure.

cross-country ski trails and skating tracks, and hosted the park's first off-season event, a motorcycle competition.[17] Over the next 10 years, he continued to expand Valcartier Vacation Village's winter activities, and in 1980 he introduced water features.

At the time, there were very few water parks. Since then, they've taken off; there are more than 1,000 in North America, according to the World Waterpark Association. Approximately 80 million people visited water parks in Canada, the United States, and Mexico during the summer of 2008, with attendance growing by 3 to 5 percent annually over the last five years.[18]

And so it was a logical next step for Drouin to expand his business by building Calypso Park, a new park that opened in 2010. Located in Limoges, Ontario, the park features 35 waterslides and a wide variety of other activities, including two international-calibre beach volleyball courts. Although Limoges is a small town, the 40 hectare water park is only 20 minutes from Ottawa and 75 minutes from Montreal. The location in the Ottawa-Gatineau region was carefully chosen based

on consumer demographics. According to Statistics Canada, the average family income was $75,200, compared to the national average of $68,800.[19] Best of all, there was no real competition within a 100 kilometre radius.

Being at the mercy of the weather makes managing the ups and downs of capacity and demand at Calypso Park challenging. People still go to amusement parks when it rains; but, they go to a water park only when it's sunny. Only open in the summer, bad weather can spell disaster for Calypso, a challenge its Quebec cousin, Valcartier Vacation Village, has avoided by being open year-round. It's a water park in the summer and an outdoor enthusiast's playground in the winter.

To help counter weather concerns, Drouin maintains Calypso's water temperature at 27 degrees Celsius, toasty enough to keep park attendance high even if the air temperature is cool.[20] Another perk for park visitors is "Money at my fingertip," a point of sale payment system that uses biometric technology to give guests access to their money for food, beverages, or other merchandise.[21] The convenience of being able to make purchases without having to carry money, especially when you're wearing a swimsuit, helps deal with service inconsistency and adds to the overall park experience. Attention to details such as these should ensure that the warm Caribbean atmosphere of Calypso Park makes a big splash with customers.

revenue is not forfeited by holding rooms until very late in the day. Dealing with the ups and downs of weather can also pose a challenge to some businesses, as discussed in Entrepreneurial Marketing 10.1.

PROVIDING GREAT SERVICE: THE GAPS MODEL

LO2

Certainly, providing great service is not easy, and it requires a diligent effort to analyze service processes step by step in order to improve them. We now examine what is known as the Gaps model, which is designed to highlight those areas where customers believe they are getting less or poorer services than they expect (the gaps) and how these gaps can be closed.

Customers have certain expectations about how a service should be delivered. When the delivery of that service fails to meet those expectations, a **service gap** results. The Gaps model (Exhibit 10.3) is designed to encourage the systematic examination of all aspects of the service delivery process and prescribe the steps needed to develop an optimal service strategy.[22]

service gap
Results when a service fails to meet the expectations that customers have about how it should be delivered.

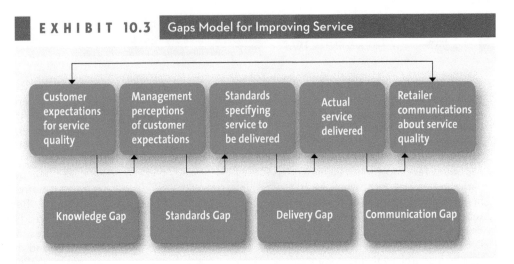

EXHIBIT 10.3   Gaps Model for Improving Service

Customer expectations for service quality	Management perceptions of customer expectations	Standards specifying service to be delivered	Actual service delivered	Retailer communications about service quality

Knowledge Gap	Standards Gap	Delivery Gap	Communication Gap

Source: Michael Levy and Barton Weitz, *Retailing Management*, 6th ed. (Burr Ridge, IL: McGraw-Hill, 2007). Adapted from Valerie Zeithaml, A. Parasuraman, and Leonard Berry, *Delivering Quality Customer Service* (New York: The Free Press, 1990) and Valerie Zeithaml, Leonard Berry, and A. Parasuraman, "Communication and Control Processes in the Delivery of Service Quality," *Journal of Marketing* 52, no. 2 (April 1988), pp. 35–48.

knowledge gap
Reflects the difference between customers' expectations and the firm's perception of those expectations.

standards gap
Pertains to the difference between the firm's perceptions of customers' expectations and the service standards it sets.

delivery gap
The difference between the firm's service standards and the actual service it provides to customers.

communication gap
Refers to the difference between the actual service provided to customers and the service that the firm's promotion program promises.

What service gaps did Marcia experience while on vacation at the Paradise Motel in Muskoka?

As Exhibit 10.3 shows, there are four service gaps:

1. The **knowledge gap** reflects the difference between customers' expectations and the firm's perception of those customer expectations. Firms can close this gap by matching customer expectations with actual service through research.

2. The **standards gap** pertains to the difference between the firm's perceptions of customers' expectations and the service standards it sets. Firms can narrow this gap by setting appropriate service standards and measuring service performance.

3. The **delivery gap** is the difference between the firm's service standards and the actual service it provides to customers. This gap can be closed by getting employees to meet or exceed service standards.

4. The **communication gap** refers to the difference between the actual service provided to customers and the service that the firm's promotion program promises. Generally firms can close this gap if they are more realistic about the services they can provide and manage customer expectations effectively.

As we discuss the four gaps, we will apply them to the experience that Marcia Kessler had with a motel in Muskoka, Ontario. She saw an ad for a weekend package that quoted a very reasonable daily rate and listed the amenities available at Paradise Motel: free babysitting services, a piano bar with a nightly singer, a free continental breakfast, a heated swimming pool, and newly decorated rooms. When she booked the room, Marcia discovered that the price advertised was not available during the weekend, and a three-day minimum stay was required. After checking in with a very unpleasant person at the front desk, Marcia and her husband found that their room appeared circa 1950 and had not been cleaned. When she complained, all she got was attitude from the assistant manager. Resigned to the fact that

they were slated to spend the weekend, she decided to go for a swim. Unfortunately, the water was "heated" by Georgian Bay and hovered around 10 degrees. No one was using the babysitting services because there were few young children at the resort. It turns out the piano bar singer was the second cousin of the owner, and he couldn't carry a tune, let alone play the piano very well. The continental breakfast must have come all the way from another continent, because everything was stale and tasteless. Marcia couldn't wait to get home.

The Knowledge Gap: Knowing What Customers Want

An important early step in providing good service is knowing what the customer wants. While the motel offered babysitting services, most of its customers did not have kids, had not brought them on their trip, or simply did not want to use the service. However, all guests want their rooms cleaned prior to check-in.

To reduce the knowledge gap, firms must understand the customers' expectations, which can be accomplished through customer research and by increasing the interaction and communication between managers and employees.

Understanding Customer Expectations
Customers' expectations are based on their knowledge and experiences.[23] Marcia's expectations were that her room would be ready and clean when she got there, the swimming pool would be heated, the singer would be able to sing, and the breakfast would be fresh.

Expectations vary according to the type of service. Marcia's expectations might have been higher, for instance, if she were staying at a Fairmont rather than the Paradise Motel. At Fairmont, she might expect employees to know her by name, be aware of her dietary preferences, and have placed fresh fruit of her choice and fresh-cut flowers in her room before she arrived.

People's expectations also vary depending on the situation. Marcia may be satisfied with both the preceding hotel properties, depending on the circumstances. If she were travelling on business, the Paradise Motel might be fine, but if she were celebrating her tenth wedding anniversary, she probably would prefer the Fairmont. Regardless of these choices, however, the service provider needs to know and understand the expectations of the customers in its target market.

Evaluating Service Quality by Using Well-Established Marketing Metrics
To meet or exceed customers' expectations, marketers must determine what those expectations are. Yet because of their intangibility, the **service quality**, or customers' perceptions of how well a service meets or exceeds their expectations, often is difficult for customers to evaluate.[24]

> **service quality**
> Customers' perceptions of how well a service meets or exceeds their expectations.

Customers generally use five distinct service dimensions to determine overall service quality: reliability, responsiveness, assurance, empathy, and tangibles (Exhibit 10.4).

If you were to apply the five service dimensions to your own decision-making process when you selected a university—which provides the service of education—you might find results like those in Exhibit 10.5.

If your expectations include an individualized experience at a state-of-the-art institution, perhaps University B is a better alternative for you. But if you are relying heavily on academic performance and career placement from your university experience, then University A might be a better choice. If a strong culture and tradition are important to you, University A offers this type of environment. What were your expectations, and how did your university choices fall within these service dimensions?

Marketing research (see Chapter 7) provides a means to better understand consumers' service expectations and their perceptions of service quality. This research can be extensive and expensive, or it can be integrated into a firm's everyday interactions with customers. Today, most service firms have developed voice-of-customer programs and employ ongoing marketing research to assess how well they are meeting their customers' expectations.

EXHIBIT 10.4 | Building Blocks of Service Quality

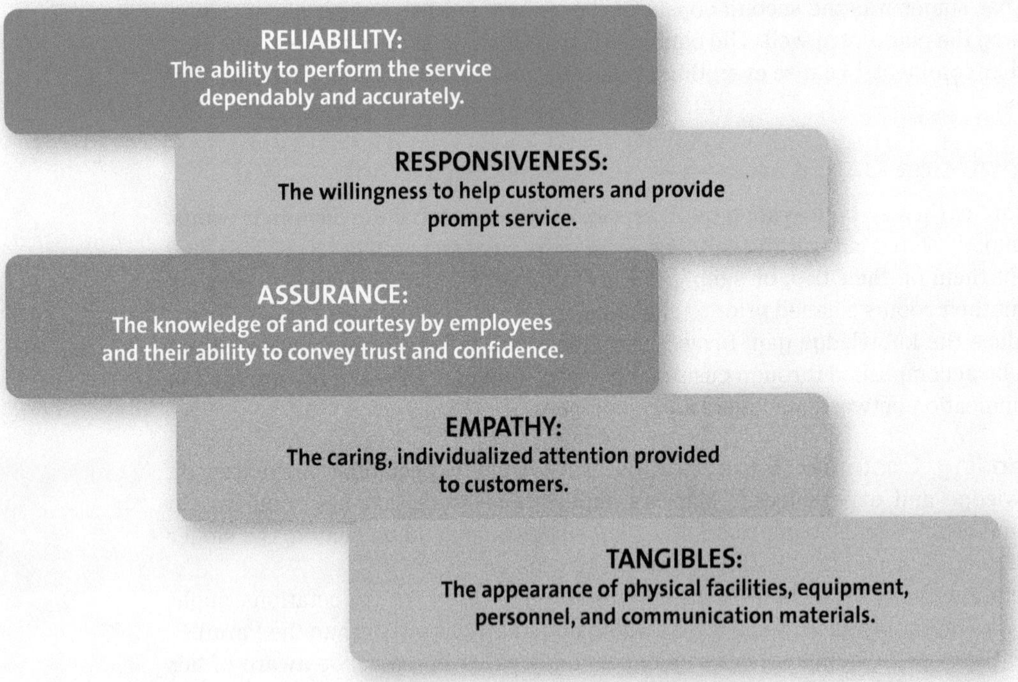

RELIABILITY:
The ability to perform the service dependably and accurately.

RESPONSIVENESS:
The willingness to help customers and provide prompt service.

ASSURANCE:
The knowledge of and courtesy by employees and their ability to convey trust and confidence.

EMPATHY:
The caring, individualized attention provided to customers.

TANGIBLES:
The appearance of physical facilities, equipment, personnel, and communication materials.

voice-of-customer (VOC) program
An ongoing marketing research system that collects customer insights and intelligence to influence and drive business decisions.

A systematic **voice-of-customer (VOC) program** collects customer insights and intelligence to influence and drive business decisions. For instance, Dell launched IdeaStorm.com, an online forum that allows people to submit ideas for improving its products and services. The community votes on the best ideas and if they make sense, the company will act on them. When IdeaStorm.com contributors wanted Linux pre-installed on their PCs and notebooks, Dell surveyed 100,000 customers to get more insights and ended up implementing the idea. Three months after launching

EXHIBIT 10.5 | Collegiate Service Dimensions

	University A	**University B**
Reliability	Offers sound curriculum with extensive placement services and internships.	Curriculum covers all the basics but important courses are not always available. Career placement is haphazard at best.
Responsiveness	Slow to respond to application. Very structured visitation policy. Rather inflexible with regard to personal inquiries or additional meetings.	Quick response during application process. Open visitation policy. Offers variety of campus resources to help with decision making.
Assurance	Staff seems very confident in reputation and services.	Informal staff who convey enthusiasm for institution.
Empathy	Seems to process student body as a whole rather than according to individual needs or concerns.	Very interested in providing a unique experience for each student.
Tangibles	Very traditional campus with old-world look and feel. Facilities are manicured. Dorm rooms are large, but bathrooms are a little old.	New campus with modern architecture. Campus is less manicured. Dorm rooms are spacious with newer bathrooms.

IdeaStorm.com more than 3,500 ideas had been posted.[25] Aeroplan uses online surveys and conducts in-person "kitchen table" meetings with selected members, asking them everything from what their redemption experience is like to what new services and improvements they'd like to see.[26] Feedback from FedEx's VOC program, involving in-person meetings with business customers, resulted in the development of its intra-Canada deferred (two-day) service.[27]

Sustainable Marketing 10.1 provides a glimpse into how the voice-of-customer insights can be applied to employees in the green building industry.

An important marketing metric to evaluate how well firms perform on the five service quality dimensions (Exhibit 10.4), the concept of the **zone of tolerance** refers to the area between customers' expectations regarding their desired service and the minimum level of acceptable service—that is, the difference between what the customer really wants and what he or she will accept before going elsewhere.[28] To define the zone of tolerance, firms ask a series of questions about each service quality dimension that relate to

- the desired and expected level of service for each dimension, from low to high
- customers' perceptions of how well the focal service performs and how well a competitive service performs, from low to high
- the importance of each service quality dimension.

Exhibit 10.6 illustrates the results of such an analysis for Lou's Local Diner, a family-owned restaurant. The rankings on the left are based on a 9-point scale, on which 1 is low and 9 is high. The length of each box illustrates the zone of tolerance for each service quality dimension. For instance, according to the length of the reliability box, customers expect a fairly high level of reliability (top of the box) and will also accept only a fairly high level of reliability (bottom of the box). On the other end of the scale, customers expect a high level of assurance (top of the box) but will accept a fairly low level (bottom of the box). This difference is to be expected, because the customers also were asked to assign an importance score to the five service quality dimensions so that the total equals 100 percent (see bottom of Exhibit 10.6). Looking at the average importance score, we

zone of tolerance
The area between customers' expectations regarding their desired service and the minimum level of acceptable service—that is, the difference between what the customer really wants and what he or she will accept before going elsewhere.

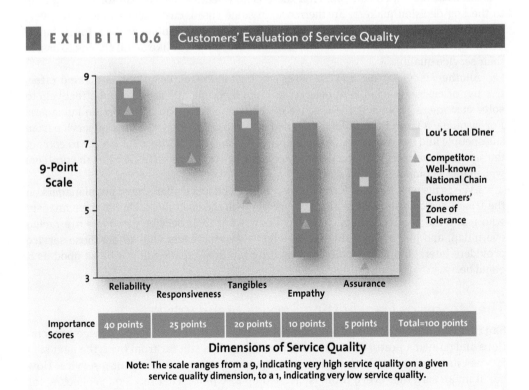

EXHIBIT 10.6 | Customers' Evaluation of Service Quality

Note: The scale ranges from a 9, indicating very high service quality on a given service quality dimension, to a 1, indicating very low service quality.

Lou's Local Diner always rates higher than its primary competitor, a well-known national chain, on each service quality dimension.

conclude that reliability is relatively important to these customers, but assurance is not. So customers have a fairly narrow zone of tolerance for service dimensions that are fairly important to them and a wider range of tolerance for those service dimensions that are less important. Also note that Lou's Local Diner always rates higher than its primary competitor, Well-Known National Chain, on each dimension.

Further note that Well-Known National Chain scores below the zone of tolerance on the tangibles dimension, meaning that customers are not willing to accept the way the restaurant looks and smells. Lou's Local Diner, in contrast, performs above the zone of tolerance on the responsiveness dimension—maybe even too well. Lou's may wish to conduct further research to verify which responsiveness aspects it is performing so well, and then consider toning those aspects down. For example, being responsive to customers' desires to have a diner that serves breakfast 24 hours a day can be expensive and may not add any further value to Lou's Local Diner, because customers would accept more limited times.

A very straightforward and inexpensive method of collecting consumers' perceptions of service quality is to gather them at the time of the sale. Service providers can ask customers how they liked the service—though customers often are hesitant to provide negative feedback directly to the person who provided the service—or distribute a simple questionnaire. Starbucks customers can rate their experience by visiting the web survey at the bottom of their receipts. Using this method, a customer does not have to make the complaint directly to the barista who may have caused the problem, but Starbucks still gets almost instantaneous feedback. The company must take care not to lose much of this information, which can happen if there is no effective mechanism for filtering it up to the key decision makers. Furthermore, in some cases, customers cannot effectively evaluate the service until several days or weeks later. Automobile dealers, for instance, often call their customers a week after they perform a service like an oil change to assess their service quality.

Another excellent method for assessing customers' expectations is making effective use of customer-complaint behaviour. Even if complaints are handled effectively to solve customers' problems, the essence of the complaint is too often lost on managers. For instance, a large PC retailer responded to complaints about the lack of service from salespeople and issues with products by providing an email address for people to contact the service department. Contacting the company proved to be difficult when the problem was that the computer wasn't working.[29]

Even firms with the best formal research mechanisms in place must put managers on the front lines occasionally to interact directly with the customers. Unless the managers who make the service quality decisions know what their service providers are facing every day, and unless they can talk directly to the customers with whom those service providers interact, any customer service program they create will not be as good as it could be.

LO3 The Standards Gap: Setting Service Standards

Say the Paradise Motel in Muskoka set out to determine its customers' service expectations and gained a pretty good idea of them. Its work is still far from over; the next step is to set its service standards and develop systems to ensure high-quality service. How can it make sure that every room is cleaned by 2:00 p.m.? That the food is checked for

Sustainable Marketing 10.1 | Walking the Green Building Talk

When you are Canada's largest consulting firm exclusively dedicated to green buildings and communities, you need to do more than just provide great service. You need to walk the talk. Enermodal Engineering, the foremost LEED (Leadership in Energy and Environmental Design) consulting firm, designed its new headquarters, A Grander View, on the banks of the Grand River in Kitchener, Ontario, to the highest LEED Platinum certifications. Unlike other companies that may have difficulty showing their services directly to potential customers, Enermodal can point to its own building, which is Canada's most energy-efficient office, using 82 percent less energy than a conventional office.

Established in 1980 by University of Waterloo engineering graduate Stephen Carpenter, Enermodal has offices in Kitchener, Toronto, Edmonton, Calgary, Winnipeg, Halifax, and Vancouver. It has certified more than 45 percent of all LEED Canada buildings and is currently working on sustainability projects worth over $5 billion.[30] The company's projects vary from public schools, hospitals, and a sportsplex, to a Museum of Human Rights and 23 new buildings on Toronto's scenic waterfront. It also worked with Fifth Town Artisan Cheese, a socially and environmentally responsible producer of handmade cheese in Picton, Ontario, to build an award-winning state-of-the-art green factory and retail outlet. One of its notable features is a subterranean cheese-aging cave that reduces the energy required to maintain a steady cool temperature year-round.[31]

In 2009, Enermodal became one of the first companies in the Region of Waterloo to become a Gold pledging partner with Sustainable Waterloo's Regional Carbon Initiative. Sustainable Waterloo is a nonprofit organization helping corporations reduce their environmental impact. Carpenter has committed Enermodal to a reduction target of 100 percent in 10 years.[32] Carbon neutrality encompasses everything from building energy use and business travel to employee commuting. Policies to reduce energy use by computers include programming them to go into "idle" mode after five minutes without use and into "sleep" mode after 30 minutes, saving 7 to 15 percent of the computer's operating energy with no loss in performance. Vacancy sensors turn off lights when rooms are not in use and the use of ultra-low plumbing fixtures and a rainwater cistern reduce indoor water use by 80 percent.[33] Business travel is minimized through the use of a video conferencing system. And when business trips are unavoidable, Enermodal employees can use a high-efficiency carshare vehicle at the office instead of their own potentially more gas-intensive vehicle.

Service companies need to collect and understand voice-of-customer insights. Enermodal applies this to employees in their roles as internal customers and helps them lead more sustainable lives as well. For example, catered lunches have a local and/or organic purchasing policy for all company events; company bikes are available for employee use, along with bike repair kits; incentives of up to $3,000 are offered for the purchase of a high-efficiency vehicle; 60 percent of public transit costs are reimbursed; staff are offered free low-flow shower heads, compost bins, and rain barrels; and employee garden plots are available at A Grander View.[34] Employees are so passionate about the environment that some of them travelled to work by canoe during the Canada-wide Commuter Challenge.

Senior management recognizes that environmental sustainability is key to attracting and keeping top talent as well.[35] Enermodal has been named one of the fastest growing firms in North America, with annual growth of 35 percent over the past three years. It's also been recognized as one of Canada's 50 greenest employers,[36] demonstrating to customers and employees that the company walks the green building talk.

Some Enermodal employees travelled to work by canoe during the annual Canada-wide Commuter Challenge.

freshness and quality every day? The firm needs to set high service standards, enforce these standards, and train employees on how to perform their tasks to these standards. Managers must lead by example and demonstrate high service standards, which will permeate throughout the organization.

Service providers, like this housekeeper at a hotel, generally want to do a good job, but they need to be trained to know exactly what a good job entails.

Achieving Service Goals Through Training

To deliver consistently high-quality service, firms must set specific, measurable goals based on customers' expectations; to help ensure that quality, the employees should be involved in the goal setting. For instance, although the most efficient process at Paradise Motel would be to start cleaning rooms at 8:00 a.m. and finish by 5:00 p.m., many guests want to sleep late and new arrivals want to get into their room as soon as they arrive. A customer-oriented standard would mandate that the rooms get cleaned between 10:00 a.m. and 2:00 p.m.

Service providers generally want to do a good job, as long as they know what is expected of them. Motel employees should be shown, for instance, exactly how managers expect them to clean a room and what specific tasks they are responsible for performing.

While front-line service employees can be taught specific tasks related to their jobs, it is simply not enough to tell employees to "be nice" or "do what customers want." A quality goal should be specific: "Greet every customer you encounter with 'Good morning/afternoon/evening, Sir or Miss.' Try to greet customers by name."

In extreme cases, such training becomes even more crucial. From long ticket lines to cancelled flights to lost baggage, customer service incidents are on the rise in the airline industry. Faced with mounting complaints, airlines are responding with better employee training geared toward identifying and defusing potentially explosive situations. For example, Delta Airlines has implemented a "Customer First" training program for its ground operations, customer service agents, flight attendants, and pilots that mandates specific performance measures and standardized practices throughout Delta's service areas. Policies for service during delays, such as providing snacks on board or trucking food out to waiting planes and offering status updates every 15 minutes, have given employees the tools and guidelines they need to better service their customers.[37]

Commitment to Service Quality

Service providers take their cues from management. If managers strive for excellent service, treat their customers well, and demand the same attitudes from everyone in the organization, it is likely employees will do the same. Take, for example, WestJet CEO, Gregg Saretsky. Named one of Canada's most respected CEOs in the tenth annual Canada's Most Respected Corporations Survey, executives such as Saretsky are perfectly happy to clean cabins and lend a hand on flights when they are passengers. WestJet's legendary reputation for customer service has resulted in revenues of nearly $3.7 billion and years of record-breaking net earnings.[38] This commitment to service quality has been modelled by company executives from the start. When WestJet launched in 1996, executive vice-president Don Bell spent a lot of time in the airline's call centre fielding questions and booking flights for customers.[39]

Employees who understand that operating on time is a critical component to service quality and guest experience work hard to improve on-time performance. In 2013, 73.8 percent of flights arrived within 15 minutes of their scheduled time.[40] Sales agents also strive to provide the highest standard of customer service. Their efforts were recognized when the Sales Super Centre was named the Best Call Centre in the country in an airline survey conducted by *Canadian Business Magazine's* consumer reports department. An employee profit-sharing plan provides rewards beyond public recognition. The vast majority of employees belong to the WestJet Employee Share Purchase Plan, making them owners of the company and giving them all the more reason to ensure high levels of service quality. This has resulted in WestJet being named as one of Canada's Best Employers and in its induction into Canada's Most Admired Corporate Cultures Hall of Fame.

The Delivery Gap: Delivering Service Quality

The delivery gap is where "the rubber meets the road," where the customer directly interacts with the service provider. Even if there are no other gaps, a delivery gap always results in a service failure. Marcia experienced several delivery gaps at the Paradise Motel: the unclean room, the assistant manager's attitude, the unheated swimming pool, the poor piano bar singer, and the stale food.

Delivery gaps can be reduced when employees are empowered to act in the customers' and the firm's best interests and are supported in their efforts so they can do their jobs effectively.[41] Technology can also be employed to reduce delivery gaps (see Exhibit 10.7).

Empowering Service Providers In this context, **empowerment** means allowing employees to make decisions about how service is provided to customers. When front-line employees are authorized to make decisions to help their customers, service quality generally improves.[42] Best Buy, for instance, has re-engineered its organizational structure to empower employees to be more involved in the day-to-day running of the business and to make adjustments as necessary. The new employee-centric culture has helped Best Buy significantly lower its employee turnover rate. Happy employees make for happy customers.[43]

However, empowering service providers can be difficult and costly. In cases in which the service is very repetitive and routine, such as at a fast-food restaurant, it might be more efficient and easier for service providers to follow a few simple rules. For instance, if a customer doesn't like his hamburger, ask him what he would like instead or offer him a refund. If an exceptional circumstance that does not fit the rules arises, then a manager should handle the issue.

Empowerment becomes more important when price points edge higher and services are more individualized. The Keg Steakhouse & Bar hires the best staff and empowers them through superlative training programs. Staff members are professional—their friendliness, warmth, personality, and enthusiasm are all part of The Keg dining experience. It is because of this that The Keg has been consistently recognized as one of the 50 Best Employers in Canada.[44]

Providing Support and Incentives A service provider's job can often be difficult, especially when customers are unpleasant or less than reasonable. The old cliché "Service with a smile" remains the best approach. To ensure that service is delivered properly, management needs to support the service provider.

empowerment
In the context of service delivery, means allowing employees to make decisions about how service is provided to customers.

EXHIBIT 10.7 Methods to Reduce Delivery Gaps

Empower Employees — Reduce Delivery Gaps — Use Technology
Provide Support & Incentives

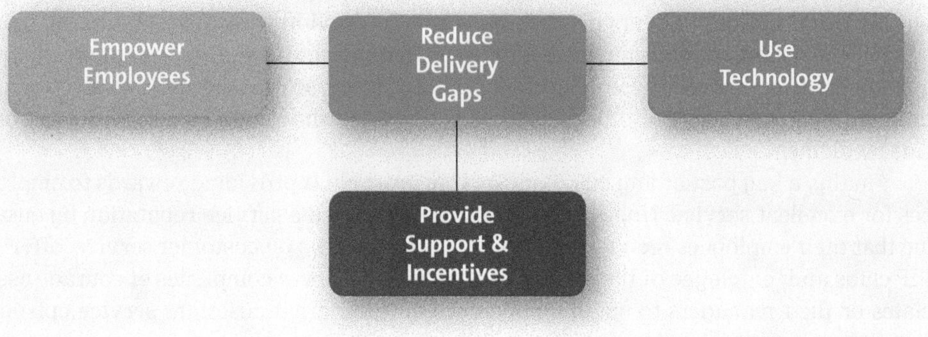

The Keg is successful, in part, because it empowers its employees to satisfy customers.

First, managers and coworkers should provide emotional support to service providers by demonstrating a concern for their well-being and by standing behind their decisions. Because it can be very disconcerting when a waiter is abused by a customer who believes her food was improperly prepared, for instance, restaurant managers must be supportive and understanding and work to help employees get through their often emotional reaction to the berating they might experience.[45] When the waiter is empowered to rectify the situation by giving the customer new food and a free dessert, the manager also must stand behind the waiter's decision, not punish her for giving away too much, and thereby provide the needed support.

Second, service providers require instrumental support—the systems and equipment to deliver the service properly. Many retailers provide state-of-the-art instrumental support for their service providers. In-store kiosks help sales associates provide more detailed and complete product information and enable them to make sales of merchandise that is either not carried in the store or is temporarily out of stock.

Third, the support that managers provide must be consistent and coherent throughout the organization. Patients expect physicians to provide great patient care by using state-of-the-art procedures and medications; yet many doctors must squeeze more people into their office hours. These conflicting goals can be so frustrating and emotionally draining on physicians and other health care providers that some have found work outside medicine.

Finally, a key part of any customer service program is providing rewards to employees for excellent service. Numerous firms have developed a service reputation by ensuring that their employees recognize the value the firm places on customer service, offering VIP clubs and "employee of the month" service awards. Some companies encourage associates or their managers to stand up and recount their great customer service episodes from the past week.[46]

Using Technology   Technology has become an increasingly important method for facilitating the delivery of services. Since the mid-1990s, with the widespread usage of the Internet, firms have invested heavily in technologies that have enabled customers to buy more quickly, more easily, and with more information than in the past. Electronic kiosks, for instance, have found their way into many service venues. Ticketing kiosks at airports allow customers to get boarding passes and seat assignments, often in less than a minute. As previously noted, electronic kiosks and other technologies can reduce the inconsistency of providing a service. Kiosks and self-checkout machines can also help close the delivery gap.

Web-enabled services have also changed the way firms do business. The need for convenience has driven some fitness companies and personal trainers to offer online classes and services. In Bolton, Ontario, Lee-Anne Simpson teaches a variety of classes via Skype through her company Revive Fitness Training and Wellness Centre. And in Steinbach, Manitoba, Tami Tyson holds live online bootcamps that have been a hit with new mothers who can't get away from the house for conventional gym workouts.[47]

Using technology to facilitate service delivery can provide many benefits, such as access to a wider variety of services, a greater degree of control by the customer over the services, and the ability to obtain information. Management also benefits from the increased efficiency in service processes through reduced servicing costs and, in some cases, can develop a competitive advantage over less service-oriented competitors.[48]

Technological advances that help close the delivery gap are expanding. Salons and cosmetics counters use kiosks to show customers how they would look with different beauty products and various hair colours. Stores enable customers to scan price tags and then have a kiosk recommend complementary items. Touchscreen terminals at tables at Chuck E. Cheese let customers order food and play games.[49] The technological delivery of services can cause problems, though. Some customers have problems using the technology. Supermarket self-checkout devices are too challenging for some customers. In other cases, the technology may not perform adequately, such as ATMs that run out of money or are out of order.

The Communication Gap: Communicating the Service Promise

Poor communication between marketers and their customers can result in a mismatch between an ad campaign's or a salesperson's promises and the service the firm can actually offer. Although firms have difficulty controlling service quality because it can vary from day to day and from provider to provider, they have nearly constant control over how they communicate their service package to their customers. This control involves a significant responsibility, as Ethical and Societal Dilemma 10.1 notes.

If a firm promises more than it can deliver, customers' expectations won't be met. An advertisement may lure a customer into a service situation once but, if the service doesn't deliver on the promise, the customer may never return. Dissatisfied customers also are likely to tell others about the underperforming service, using word-of-mouth or, increasingly, the Internet, which has become an important channel for dissatisfied customers to vent their frustrations.

The communication gap can be reduced by managing customer expectations. Suppose you need an operation, and the surgeon explains, "You'll be out of the hospital in five days and back to your normal routine in a month." You have the surgery and feel well enough to leave the hospital three days later. Two weeks after that, you're playing tennis again. Clearly, you will tend to think your surgeon is a genius. However, regardless of the operation's success, if you had to stay in the hospital for 10 days and it took you two months to recover, you would undoubtedly be upset.

Promising only what you can deliver, or possibly even a little less, is an important way to control the communication gap.[50] For instance, when FedEx first issued its next-day delivery guarantee—"Absolutely, Positively There by 10:30 a.m."—it achieved a

Yelp, TripAdvisor, and Amazon have all made user ratings and reviews a familiar—and even essential—part of the online toolbox for shoppers and other consumers. From the consumer's perspective, what better preparation could there be for a major purchase than to see what other, objective customers have to say about the product or service under consideration?

For retailers and service professionals, online reviews offer a huge benefit too. For some companies, especially small service providers that cannot afford much marketing, online reviews function as a low-cost form of advertising. A business seeking to meet or exceed customer expectations receives valuable, candid feedback from customers, which it can use to measure how well it is meeting customer expectations. Some firms even use this feedback in their formal voice-of-customer programs to improve company operations.

But who benefits from fake consumer reviews? Seemingly the company might, assuming it does not get caught. But federal regulators are taking action to ensure that such deceptive advertising does not pay, and recent events suggest that companies that fake their reviews often get caught.

VIP Deals, an online retailer that sells leather cases for digital tablets on Amazon, invited its customers to post reviews—and promised that if those reviews were positive, the customer would receive a complete refund. Within weeks, nearly all of the company's 355 online reviews gave the VIP Deals leather case four or five stars. But Amazon guidelines prohibit compensation for customer reviews, and the VIP Deals page soon disappeared.

A leather case for your iPad is one thing. Accurate, truthful information takes on paramount importance for a service like plastic surgery. But Lifestyle Lift seemed to disregard customers' expectations that they could receive truthful information. When unhappy customers started posting too many negative comments on its website, the company launched a cover-up, rather than investigating the complaints to help its physicians and staff address the problems. On bogus websites, fictitious posters gave high praise to the company, while also asserting that previously posted complaints had been phony.

Crowd-sourced online opinions of consumers have become a major source of information about products and services (recall our discussion of crowd-sourcing in Chapter 9). When that information is authentic, it serves consumers and companies both. But when companies manipulate online reviews, it seems as if all of society is harmed. What—if anything—should be done about it?

competitive advantage until others matched its promise. Now FedEx often gives next-day service when the customer has paid only for second-day service. If the package arrives on the second day, it meets expectations. If it arrives a day early, it exceeds them. Social and Mobile Marketing 10.1 highlights how technology can be used to listen to and communicate with customers.

A relatively easy way to manage customer expectations considers both the time the expectation is created and the time the service is provided. Expectations typically are created through promotions, whether in advertising or personal selling. For instance, if a salesperson promises a client that work can be performed in one day, and it actually takes a week, the client will be disappointed. However, if the salesperson co-ordinates the work with those responsible for the service delivery, the client's expectations likely will be met.

Customer expectations can also be managed when the service is delivered. Recorded messages can tell customers who have telephoned a company how many minutes they will have to wait before the next operator is available. Sellers automatically inform online customers of any items that are out of stock. Whether online or in a store, retailers can warn their customers to shop early during a sale because supplies of the sale item are limited. People are generally reasonable when they are warned that some aspect of the service may be below their expectations. They just don't like surprises!

LO4   SERVICE RECOVERY

Despite a firm's best efforts, sometimes service providers fail to meet customer expectations. When this happens, the best course of action is to attempt to make amends with the customer and learn from the experience. Of course, it is best to avoid a service failure

Social and Mobile Marketing 10.1

Educating Customers Using HubSpot[52]

Today's marketers reach customers via a new set of inbound marketing tools that includes blogging, tweeting, websites, search engine optimization, and analytics. However, effectively using these disconnected strategies requires time and technical savvy. To simplify matters, HubSpot helps its clients post content on websites, Twitter, and other social media platforms, and tracks the results with its proprietary software.

Canadian Mountain Holidays Heli-Skiing & Summer Adventures (CMH) provides helicopter transport, lodging, and guides for ski, snowboard, and hiking vacations. The adventure company had tried out a number of web-based tactics but found their approaches cumbersome and inefficient. Furthermore, without data capture, they had no ability to analyze the effectiveness of their efforts. However, after using HubSpot's analytics to help them co-ordinate and disseminate their social media messages and then analyze the results for three years, CMH documented a 387 percent increase in traffic from social marketing and a 772 percent increase in leads.

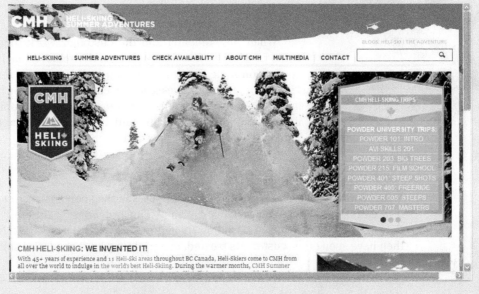

Looking for an amazing vacation? Try out CMH.

altogether, but when it does occur, the firm has a unique opportunity to demonstrate its customer commitment.[53] Effective service recovery efforts can significantly increase customer satisfaction, purchase intentions, and positive word–of-mouth, though customers' postrecovery satisfaction levels usually fall lower than their satisfaction level prior to the service failure.[54]

Remember the Paradise Motel in Muskoka? It could have made amends with Marcia Kessler after its service failures if it had taken some relatively simple, immediate steps: the assistant manager could have apologized for his bad behaviour and quickly upgraded her to a suite and/or given her a free night's lodging for a future stay. The motel could also have given her a free lunch or dinner to make up for the bad breakfast. None of these actions would have cost the motel much money. Had it used the customer lifetime value approach we described in Chapter 6, the motel would have realized that by not taking action, it lost Marcia as a customer forever. Over the next few years, she could have been responsible for several thousand dollars in sales. Instead, Marcia is likely to spread negative word-of-mouth about the motel to her friends and family, and through social media like Yelp.com because of its failure to recover. Quite simply, effective service recovery entails (1) listening to the customer, (2) providing a fair solution, and (3) resolving the problem quickly.[55]

When a service failure occurs, such as receiving a poor meal at a restaurant, goodwill can be recovered by giving the customer a free dessert.

Listening to the Customer

Firms often don't find out about service failures until a customer complains. Whether the firm has a formal complaint department or the complaint is offered directly to the service provider, the customer must have the opportunity to air the complaint completely, and the firm must listen carefully to what he or she is saying.

Customers can become very emotional about a service failure, whether the failure is serious (a botched surgical operation) or minor (the wrong change at a restaurant). In many cases, the customer may just want to be heard, and the service provider should give the customer all the time he or she needs to "get it out." The very process of describing a perceived wrong to a sympathetic listener is therapeutic in and of itself. Service providers therefore should welcome the opportunity to be that sympathetic ear, listen carefully, and appear anxious to rectify the situation to ensure it doesn't happen again.[56]

When the company and the customer work together, the outcome is often better than either could achieve on their own. This cocreation logic applies especially well to service recovery. A service failure is a negative experience, but when customers participate in its resolution, it results in a more positive outcome than simply listening to their complaint and providing a preapproved set of potential solutions that may satisfy them.

Finding a Fair Solution

Most people realize that mistakes happen. But when they happen, customers want to be treated fairly, whether that means distributive or procedural fairness.[57] Their perception of what *fair* means is based on their previous experience with other firms, how they have seen other customers treated, material they have read, and stories recounted by their friends.

distributive fairness
Pertains to a customer's perception of the benefits he or she received compared with the costs (inconvenience or loss) that resulted from a service failure.

Distributive Fairness   **Distributive fairness** pertains to a customer's perception of the benefits he or she received compared with the costs (inconvenience or loss). Customers want to be compensated a fair amount for a perceived loss that resulted from a service failure. If, for instance, a person arrives at the airport gate and finds her flight is overbooked, she may believe that taking the next flight that day and receiving a travel voucher is adequate compensation for the inconvenience. But if no flights are available until the next day, the traveller may require additional compensation, such as overnight accommodations, meals, and a round-trip ticket to be used at a later date.[58]

When handling returns or other services issues, it is important to use procedures that are perceived to be fair by the customers.

The key to distributive fairness, of course, is listening carefully to the customer. One customer, travelling on vacation, may be satisfied with a travel voucher, whereas another may need to get to the destination on time because of a business appointment. Regardless of how the problem is solved, customers typically want tangible restitution—in this case, to get to their destination—not just an apology. If providing a tangible restitution isn't possible, the next best thing is to assure the customer that steps are being taken to prevent the failure from recurring.

Procedural Fairness With regard to complaints, **procedural fairness** refers to the perceived fairness of the process used to resolve them. Customers want efficient complaint procedures over whose outcomes they have some influence. Furthermore, customers tend to believe they have been treated fairly if the service providers follow specific

procedural fairness
Refers to the customer's perception of the fairness of the process used to resolve complaints about service.

REAL MARKETER PROFILE   Marc-Olivier Vachon

The idea behind Kangaride struck like lightning: why not enable people to share something they don't often think of as a resource, like seats in their car? Long-distance ridesharing on an occasional basis (for example, between Toronto and Montreal or Edmonton and Calgary) is a concept with a clear selling proposition: passengers travel for less and drivers get help paying for gas. From the eager perspective of a budding entrepreneur in Montreal, this seemed like one of those ideas that would spread like wildfire. Marketing the idea would be a piece of cake, right? However, gaining traction proved to be quite the challenge. Ridesharing sounds good on paper, [but] we really didn't know how many people would actually use it, no matter how brilliantly we built our service and website. Two major hurdles needed to be overcome.

Hurdle 1: Perception about safety and reliability

When we asked people about ridesharing, we almost invariably heard concerns about safety or reliability: "I can't see myself travelling with people I don't even know!" And "How can I be sure my driver/passenger is going to show up?" Both are concerns I had when hitchhiking around the country, and later when trying to hook up with passengers through classified ads' websites.

This is why we built both the service and our communication strategy around these simple words: We care. First and foremost, Kangaride needed to be a team of dedicated individuals providing a very high level of professional monitoring while maintaining constant communication with customers.

In the very beginning, it seemed a little crazy to validate all of our drivers' licences. It seemed even crazier to build a customer service centre that would take calls 7 days a week, 365 days a year. These things represented a sizeable investment for a start-up with no proof of concept, but not doing them was not an option. Our marketing strategy depended on it. And contrary to most services you will find on the web, we clearly advertised our phone number on every page. Why? Because we actually wanted people to give us a call! If we were to make ridesharing an option as safe and reliable as a bus service, collaboration with our customers was paramount.

Hurdle 2: This is no splash

Your idea may be excellent, even revolutionary, but not all people will share your visionary outlook on the world.

In other words, it probably won't make the big splash you have in mind. When launching Kangaride, we were a little disappointed with the pace at which the idea was adopted. Still caught in the preconceived notion that success would translate in supersonic adoption, we tried to make a splash in the public eye (marketing, press relations, stunts), but to no avail. Our participation on CBC's *Dragons' Den* was probably our very last attempt and brought to light something that we had all taken for granted: the most powerful form of marketing is customer service. Period.

When our pitch aired on CBC, coast to coast, a thousand new people subscribed to Kangaride in the next few days. This represents the average number of people who join the service on a weekly basis without any publicity on our part. And the secret behind that is no secret at all. World-class execution and truly caring about your customers is what gets people talking about you. The word-of-mouth we created was far from instantaneous, but it had grown appreciably over time—very slowly at first, but very steadily, one phone call at a time, one reliable ride at a time, just like a trickling brook turns into a quiet but very powerful river.

This is the ultimate form of marketing. It's what we do best and, for us, is the easiest thing in the world. Kangaride does not get its 15 minutes of fame every week on TV, but from a consistent focus on customer service. Between making a splash or feeding a river, we choose the river. Every day.

company guidelines, though rigid adherence to rules can have damaging effects. For example, requiring a manager's approval for every return, no matter how small, can take several minutes and therefore can irritate everyone in the checkout line.

Consider the local convenience store that sells cigarettes. The store owner has implemented a policy that everyone under 19 years of age who attempts to purchase them must show valid identification. If the store clerks comply, the customers see and accept it as part of the purchasing protocol and perceive it as fair for everyone.

Resolving Problems Quickly

The longer it takes to resolve a service failure, the more irritated the customer will become and the more people he or she is likely to tell about the problem. To resolve service failures quickly, firms need clear policies, adequate training for their employees, and empowered employees. Extended health care insurance companies, for instance, have made a concerted effort in recent years to avoid service failures that occur because customers' insurance claims have not been handled quickly or to the customers' satisfaction.

Companies should welcome complaints, make it easy for customers to provide feedback, and listen carefully to what customers have to say. Although customers may be complaining, they are nevertheless exhibiting a degree of loyalty and a genuine desire to get their problem fixed. Of customers who do complain, 56 to 70 percent will do business with the company again if the complaint is resolved. That goes up to 96 percent if the complaint is resolved quickly!

It may seem overly simple, but to recover effectively from service failures, firms must not only listen to the customers' complaints but also act on them. It is the implementation of this simple rule that offers firms such challenges.

LEARNING OBJECTIVES REVIEW

 LO1   **Describe how marketing a service differs from marketing a product by applying the principles of intangibility, inseparability, inconsistency, and inventory**

First and foremost, services are intangible—they can't be seen or touched—which makes it difficult to describe a service's benefits or promote it to others. Service providers attempt to reduce the impact of the service's intangibility by enhancing its delivery with more tangible attributes, such as a nice atmosphere or price benefits. Second, services are produced and consumed at the same time. Third, services are more inconsistent than products, though service providers attempt to reduce this variability through standardization, training, service bundling, and technology. Fourth, because services can't be stockpiled, marketers provide incentives to stagger demand over time.

 LO2   **Outline the four gaps in the Gaps Model used to understand and manage customer expectations**

A knowledge gap occurs when marketers don't understand what their customers want. They may not be providing customers enough or the right service, in which case customers will be disappointed. To understand customer expectations, marketers analyze service quality through comprehensive studies and by interacting with customers. The standards gap is the difference between the firm's perceptions of customers' expectations and the service standards it sets. The delivery gap is the difference between the firm's service standards and the actual service it provides to customers. The communication gap refers to the difference between the actual service provided to customers and the service that the firm's promotion program promises.

Describe strategies that firms can use to help employees provide better service

First, appropriate service standards and measurements of service performance help close the standards gap. Firms need to demonstrate a strong commitment to service by setting high standards and enforcing these standards, and lead through example. Next they should provide training to employees regarding how to do their job and interact with customers to address the delivery gap. Then, they can empower service providers to solve service issues and problems and provide employees with both emotional support and the tools they need to do a good job. The service program should be consistent throughout the organization. Service providers need incentives that encourage them to do a good job. Lastly, firms close the communications gap by managing customer expectations and promising only what they can deliver.

 Identify three service recovery strategies

In the best-case scenario, the service does not fail in the first place. But failures are inevitable. When they do happen, the firm must make amends to the customer by (1) listening and involving the customer in the service recovery, (2) finding a fair solution to the problem that compensates the customer for the failure and follows procedures that the customer believes are fair, and (3) resolving the problem quickly.

KEY TERMS

- communication gap
- customer service
- delivery gap
- distributive fairness
- empowerment
- inconsistent

- inseparable
- intangible
- inventory
- knowledge gap
- procedural fairness
- service

- service gap
- service quality
- standards gap
- voice-of-customer (VOC) program
- zone of tolerance

CONCEPT REVIEW

1. Describe the four dimensions in which services marketing is different from product marketing.

2. Why is intangibility described as the most fundamental difference between products and services?

3. Discuss the actions companies can implement to minimize the potential negative impact of service inconsistency on the delivery of customer service.

4. How can companies deal with the perishability of their services?

5. Identify the components of the Gaps model. Describe each component and explain the strategies companies can implement to reduce the gaps in service delivery.

6. Describe the five dimensions of service quality that consumers often use to judge the quality of a service experience.

7. Explain how the use of technology can help companies deliver higher quality service.

8. Discuss why underpromising and overdelivering is an important way to control the communication gap.

9. What is meant by service recovery? How can companies use service recovery to ensure that a service failure does not lead to a lost customer?

10. Explain the differences between distributive and procedural fairness in the context of service recovery.

MARKETING APPLICATIONS

1. Those companies from which you purchase products and services are not pure sellers of services, nor are they pure sellers of products. What services does a department store provide? What goods does a dentist provide?

2. You have been sitting in the waiting room of your doctor's office for an hour. With the knowledge that products are different than services, develop a list of the things the office manager could do to improve the overall service delivery. Consider how the office might overcome problems of intangibility, inseparability, inconsistency, and inventory issues associated with services.

3. You have conducted a zone of tolerance analysis for a local dry cleaner. You find that the length of the reliability and responsiveness boxes are much greater than those of the other three service quality dimensions. You also find that the dry cleaner is positioned above the zone box on reliability but below the box on responsiveness. What should you tell the manager of the dry cleaner to do?

4. Assume you were hired by the local grocery store to help assess its service quality. How would you go about undertaking this project?

5. What should a restaurant server do who is faced with an irate customer who has received undercooked food after a long wait? How can the server avoid a service failure by being empowered? What should the server do?

6. Describe a specific situation in which a service provider could have avoided a service failure if he or she had been empowered by an employer to do so. What should the service provider have done?

7. What types of support and incentives could your university provide advisers to help make them more attentive to students' needs?

8. What technologies do you use that help facilitate your transactions with a specific retailer or service provider?

Would you rather use the technology or engage in a face-to-face relationship with a person? How, if at all, would your parents' answer be different to these two questions?

9. A local health club is running a promotional campaign that promises you can lose an inch a month off your waist if you join the club and follow its program. How might this claim cause a communication gap? What should the club do to avoid a service failure?

10. You are hired by a career consulting firm that promises to market new graduates to high-paying employers. The firm provides potential clients with an impressive client list. It charges the clients a fee, and then a separate finder's fee if the client gets a position. The firm aggressively markets its services and has a large client base. You learn that the firm simply takes any submitted résumés and posts them to a variety of online job search engines. The firm never actually contacts any firms on its clients' behalf. The CEO, himself a recent university grad, tells you that the firm never promises that the firm will contact potential employees themselves, only that the firm has access to employers and will distribute clients' résumés. What do you think of the career consulting firm's practices?

TOOLKIT

SERVICES ZONE OF TOLERANCE

Use the toolkit provided on Connect to assess the zone of tolerance for several service providers.

NET SAVVY

1. What services does WestJet offer (http://www.westjet.com)? Compare its services to those offered by Air Canada (http://www.aircanada.ca) by using the five service quality dimensions (tangibility, responsiveness, reliability, assurance, and empathy).

2. Evaluate the ease with which you can make hotel reservations when using Fairmont's (http://www.fairmont.com) online reservation system. Check out the hotel's privacy policy. Are you comfortable with its use of cookies to identify visitors when they return to the site?

CHAPTER CASE STUDY

ZIPCAR: DELIVERING ONLY AS MUCH DRIVING AS YOU WANT

Canadians have enjoyed a long love affair with their cars. The growth of the auto industry led to the expectation that your car would be waiting for you at the curb every morning. But that expectation is now changing for many city dwellers, frustrated by the soaring costs and parking pressures that confront modern drivers. For them, Zipcar, the world's leading car-sharing company,[59] offers the pleasure of driving without the hassles of ownership.

The Cambridge, Massachusetts–based company rents self-service vehicles by the hour or day to urban residents who prefer to pay for only the minimal amount of driving they absolutely need. Car sharing eliminates issues related to parking shortages; overnight parking restrictions; or soaring gas, insurance, and tax bills. That promise resonates well with consumer expectations on many fronts, especially among Zipcar's primary urban customers, suburbanites who just work in the city, and the large segments of college or university students who also enjoy the service. Zipcar access provides a convenient solution to students, faculty, and staff who live on or near campus and helps college or university administrators reduce demand for the limited parking available.[60]

Still, Zipcar CEO Scott Griffith realizes that the company's biggest growth obstacle is consumers' inability to envision life without a car.[61] To push an attitude shift, Zipcar makes the car-sharing experience as easy as possible, with just four simple steps:

1. Join the network.

2. Reserve your car online or from your smartphone.

3. Unlock the car with your Zipcard.

4. Drive away.

Today the car-sharing network has more than 673,000 members and 8,900 vehicles in 16 major metropolitan areas and on 250 campuses throughout the United States, Canada, and Britain.[62] With so many locations, the company could bring convenient car sharing to a far larger market; it estimates that 10 million residents, business commuters, and college or university students now live or work just a short walk away from an available Zipcar.[63]

Zipcars are for people who don't need a car all the time, like urbanites and university students.

Zipcar is banking on more than shifting attitudes. Emerging trends due to the economic downturn and changing buying habits have helped spur growth. On average, automobiles consume 19 percent of household incomes,[64] yet many cars stand idle for 90 percent of each day. Drivers seeking a less expensive and less wasteful alternative might save up to 70 percent on their transportation costs. There is a one-time fee of $30 for an individual to join Zipcar with hourly rates of $9.25 or $79 per day.[65] The average member spends $428 a year.[66]

Zipcar's service model fits in with the emergence of on-demand, pay-per-use options, such as Netflix for movies, iTunes for music, and e-readers for books. Moreover, the popularity of mobile shopping and the growing expectation that they can order anything, anywhere, anytime from their smartphones have made urban young adults and college students two of Zipcar's most fervent member groups. For these "Zipsters," ordering up a set of wheels on the go is far more appealing than being saddled with car payments.

A strong urban public transportation system also helps make car sharing more attractive. That's why Zipcar started off in high-density urban areas such as Boston, New York, Toronto, and Vancouver, with their great public transportation systems already in place. Wherever subways and buses work, car sharing can extend the transit system's reach. By locating cars near transit route endpoints, travellers gain an easy extension on subway or bus schedules to their final destinations. Zipcar even offers members an overnight option, for grabbing a car in the evening and returning it the next morning.

Finally, the logic of car sharing works well in settings marked by increased urbanization. According to the United Nations, cities will contain 59 percent of the world's population by 2030.[67] Many of these areas already face congestion, space demands, and environmental threats from crowding too many gas-driven vehicles into a small, population-dense space. Griffith estimates that for every car Zipcar puts on the road, 15–20 personal cars are taken off.[68] Thus some cities work with the company to identify and secure parking spaces close to subway stops and rail stations. Zipcar also provides fleet management services to local, municipal, and federal agencies.

Car sharing could translate into a $10 billion market globally.[69] Cities in Europe and Asia are well primed for car sharing, by virtue of their strong rail systems, heavy reliance on public transit, and widespread adoption of mobile and wireless technologies. A deal with Spain's largest car-sharing company, Avancar, was a first venture in Zipcar's global expansion.[70]

Such growth requires strong logistics, and Zipcar is backed by a corps of fleet managers and vehicle co-ordinators who track, schedule, and oversee vehicle maintenance; proprietary hardware and software technology that helps it communicate with drivers and track vehicles; and a large fleet that includes hybrid vehicles for fuel efficiency, as well as minivans to appeal to families who want to take a trip to the beach.[71] Zipcar estimates that it processes 2.6 million reservations per year, and its reservation system has almost never failed.[72]

These behind-the-scenes moves aim to make Zipcar's service simple, convenient, and reliable. But failures are inevitable, as one customer's experience showed. The customer went to pick up his designated vehicle at the time and place reserved for him, but he discovered no car there. The Zipcar representative told him that it might be out, being serviced or cleaned, or it could have been delayed by another driver running late. But such excuses did little to alleviate the frustration of being stuck with no transportation.

Learning of his predicament, Zipcar tried but was unable to find another car in close proximity. Therefore, it quickly authorized the customer to take a taxi and promised to reimburse him up to $100. Although the "free ride" did not altogether mitigate the stress and inconvenience of the service failure, Zipcar's response showed him that the company was committed to doing right by him, even if that meant sending business to a competitor, the taxi company.

The considerable dimensions of a global car-sharing market are already emerging. Zipcar's experience and first-mover status in the market positions it well to compete. But the race to dominate is sure to intensify, especially as traditional car rental companies with great name recognition, such as Hertz and Enterprise, move into the marketplace.[73] Perhaps it is no surprise that Avis purchased Zipcar in early 2013.[74] It didn't take long for the company to make the cars available at Pearson International Airport in Toronto.[75] How well Zipcar performs in the future depends mostly on its ability to meet its own standards for customer service—simplicity, convenience, and reliability—consistently and effectively.

Questions

1. Using the building blocks (five dimensions) of service quality (see Exhibit 10.4), evaluate Zipcar.

2. Compare Zipcar's service quality performance with that of the most recent car rental service (e.g., Hertz, Enterprise) that you have used.

3. How well has Zipcar handled service failure situations? What could it do to improve recovery efforts?

For more information on the resources available from McGraw-Hill Ryerson, go to www.mheducation.ca/he/solutions.

CHAPTER **11**

GROUPON
Q What are you looking for?   📍 Vancouver, BC   🛒 CART   JEREMEY ⌄

All Deals   Goods   Getaways   Reserve   Freebies   Gift Shop

Marlena Salon & Day Spa - Vancouver, BC

One or Three 60-Minute Spa Mani-Pedis with Lavender Foot Scrubs

FROM

$35

BUY! ▸

VALUE	DISCOUNT	YOU SAVE
$105	67%	$70

🎁 GIVE AS A GIFT

🕐 Limited time remaining!

LIMITED QUANTITY AVAILABLE
👥 **Over 1,000 bought**

      f Like 245

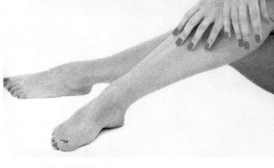

❤ Pampered   ❤ Well-Groomed

In a Nutshell

Nail techs trim and shape nails, tend to cuticles, and remove dead skin with a lavender foot scrub

The Fine Print

Expires 180 days after purchase. Limit 1 per person, may buy 1 additional as a gift. Valid only for option purchased. Appointment required. 48hr cancellation notice required. New clients only. Vouchers are non-transferable. Not valid with other offers. Merchant is solely responsible to purchasers for the care and quality of the advertised goods and services.

Give back this
#GivingTuesday with
Groupon Grassroots

LEARN MORE

Customers Also Viewed

C$25 for
C$49.99 at
25Dates.com
On Location

$219 for $415
at Great Wolf
Lodge Grand
Mound
Centralia, WA

C$16.99 for
C$44 at
Clarisonic-
Compatible
Brush-Head 2-
Pack
Online Deal

Pricing Concepts and Strategies: Establishing Value

Pricing is a key part of the value proposition for any purchase. While value reflects the relationship between benefits and costs, deeply discounted products or services cause retailers to lose money. However, if these promotions accomplish other strategic goals, such as bringing in new customers, they can be tremendously valuable. Success depends on reaching a wide audience of interested consumers with a deal that can't be ignored. Finding the model that delivers this one-two punch is the genius behind Groupon.com.

Every day, Groupon alerts its users to several "featured deals." The discounts are organized according to the major cities that Groupon serves, offered to site users who live in or near those markets. A woman living in North Vancouver, for example, receives offers for discounts to nail salons nearby. Economically, the deals are attractive: $10 worth of pizza for $5, a 40 percent discount on "The Wizard of Oz" tickets at Ed Mirvish Theatre[1] in Toronto, or nearly half off interactive cooking classes that culminate with a four-course gourmet meal.[2] They often revolve around social events, like classes or dining out, and encourage access to goods or services that customers may find appealing but have been unwilling to try, whether because they appear frivolous (e.g., spa services) or because of cost (e.g., hot air balloon rides).

The owner of the pizza chain offering 50–percent off coupons had 9,000 responses. A Chicago Art Institute promotion that offered a 64 percent discount on membership added 5,000 new members, an impressive addition to the 85,000 members the museum had accumulated in the previous century. Business owners, Groupon warns, need to be ready for this kind of interest. Some small businesses cap their offers to avoid overwhelming staff or frustrating customers who may have to wait months for an appointment.

Groupon itself faces an avalanche of interest from site users and businesses. An uncertain economy increases its appeal among users, which has triggered growth rates of up to 25 percent in just one month. Groupon has sold more than 400 million deals to its 200 million subscribers,[3] most of whom are young professionals in their 20s and 30s, a highly desirable target market.

Businesses see Groupon as a cost-effective way to bring in new customers; 120 were lined up for promotions in Chicago, where Groupon launched in 2008. Since then, Groupon has expanded operations to 48 countries and over 500 markets worldwide.[4] Today, merchants are able to offer ongoing deals, not just time-limited ones to drive traffic to their stores. In March 2014, 75 percent of the merchants working with Groupon took advantage of its e-commerce marketplace to run recurring deals.[5] At the time of Groupon's initial public offering, the company had fewer than 1,000 active deals globally. By March 2014, it had more than 200,000 from over 650,000 merchants.

At a time when retailers are investing their marketing dollars with great care, Groupon's payment structure encourages businesses to sign on. If the promotion is successful, Groupon takes a share of the profits. If it's unsuccessful, neither Groupon nor the company makes money. Businesses offering the deals are happy because 82 percent of customers say they are likely to return again, and 77 percent of customers spend more money than offered through the deal.[6]

Still, the future of the daily deal is unknown. Consumers suffering from deal fatigue are tired of having their inboxes filled with irrelevant offers. Some analysts believe that Groupon and other daily deal sites will be absorbed by larger online entities, and that companies like Amazon, Google, and Facebook will have a daily deal as part of their marketing strategy. Few daily deals are expected to survive as independent businesses. ∎

LO1 THE IMPORTANCE OF PRICING

Coming up with the "right" price is never easy, as the opening example shows. How might this new option for finding deals cause shifts overall—both in what consumers are willing to pay and in what manufacturers can charge? What kinds of effects might Groupon have on future sales of products and services that customers first find on this deal site? What other members of the market might such price changes affect? To answer such questions, we examine various pricing concepts and strategies in this chapter.

A lot rides on marketers setting the right price, so it's important to understand the role price plays in the marketing mix. We start by explaining what "price" is as a marketing concept, why it is important, how marketers set pricing objectives, and how various factors influence price setting. Then, we extend this foundation by focusing on specific pricing strategies as well as the psychological aspects of pricing. Lastly, we describe various B2B and consumer pricing tactics and some important legal and ethical issues associated with pricing.

Imagine that a consumer realizes that to save money on a particular item, she will have to drive an additional 20 kilometres. She may judge that her time and travel costs are not worth the savings, so even though the price tag is higher at a nearby store, she judges the overall cost of buying the product there to be lower. To include aspects of price such as this, we define price as the overall sacrifice a consumer is willing to make to acquire a specific product or service. This sacrifice usually includes the money that must be paid to the seller to acquire the item but it also may involve other sacrifices, whether nonmonetary, such as the value of the time necessary to acquire the product or service, or monetary, such as travel costs, taxes, and shipping costs, all of which the buyer must give up to take possession of the product.[7]

Consumers judge the benefits a product delivers against the sacrifice necessary to obtain it, and then make a purchase decision based on this overall judgment of value. Thus, a great but overpriced product can be judged as low in value and may not sell as well as an inferior but well-priced item. In turn, we cannot define price without referring to the product or service associated with it. The key to successful pricing is to match the product or service with the consumer's value perceptions.

That key raises a related question: If firms can price their products or services too high, can they price them too low as well? Quite simply, yes. A price set too low may signal low quality, poor performance, or other negative attributes about the product or service. Consumers don't necessarily want a low price all the time or for all products. Rather, they want high value, which may come with a relatively high or low price, depending on the bundle of benefits the product or service delivers.

Price is the only element of the marketing mix that generates revenue. Every other element in the marketing mix may be perfect but, with the wrong price, sales simply will not occur. Research has consistently shown that consumers usually rank price as one of the most important factors in their purchase decisions.[8]

Price is the most challenging of the four Ps to manage, partly because it is often the least understood. Historically, managers have treated price as an afterthought to their marketing strategy, setting prices according to what competitors were charging or, worse yet, by adding up their costs and tacking on a desired profit to set the sales price. Prices rarely changed except in response to radical shifts in market conditions. Even today, pricing decisions often fail to reflect our current understanding of the role of price in the marketing mix.

Moreover, managers have held an overly simplistic view of the role of price, considering it simply the amount of money a consumer must part with to acquire a product or service. We now know that price is not only a sacrifice but also an information cue as well. That is, consumers use the price of a product or service to judge its quality,[9] particularly when they are less knowledgeable about the product category. For example, most college and university students know little about fine wine, so if a student found herself in the Vintages section of the liquor store and had to make a decision about which bottle to purchase, she might judge the quality of the various options according to their prices and assume that a higher price means higher quality.

In summary, marketers should view pricing decisions as a strategic opportunity to create value rather than as an afterthought to the rest of the marketing mix. Price communicates more than how much a product or service costs; it can signal quality, or lack thereof. Let's now turn to the five basic components of pricing strategies.

When shopping for wine, most of us infer that a higher price means higher quality.

LO2   THE FIVE CS OF PRICING

Successful pricing strategies are built through the five critical components: company objectives, customers, costs, competition, and channel members (see Exhibit 11.1). We examine these components in some detail because each makes a significant contribution to formulating good pricing decisions.[10] To start, the first step is to develop the company's pricing objectives.

Company Objectives

By now, you know that different firms embrace different goals. Walmart, for example, wants to be seen as a value-based company and so uses **everyday low pricing** (EDLP), whereas Holt Renfrew's high prices reflect its high-fashion image.

Each firm embraces an objective that fits with where management thinks the firm needs to go to be successful, in whatever way they define success. These specific objectives usually reflect how the firm intends to grow. Do managers want it to grow by increasing profits, increasing sales, decreasing competition, or building customer satisfaction?

Company objectives are not as simple as they might first appear; they often can be expressed in slightly different forms that mean very different things. Exhibit 11.2 introduces some common company objectives and examples of their implications for pricing strategies. These objectives are not always mutually exclusive, because a firm may embrace two or more noncompeting objectives.

profit orientation
A company objective that can be implemented by focusing on target profit pricing, maximizing profits, or target return pricing.

target profit pricing
A pricing strategy implemented by firms when they have a particular profit goal as their overriding concern; uses price to stimulate a certain level of sales at a certain profit per unit.

maximizing profits strategy
A mathematical model that captures all the factors required to explain and predict sales and profits, which should be able to identify the price at which its profits are maximized.

Profit Orientation   Even though all company objectives may ultimately be oriented toward making a profit, firms implement a **profit orientation** by focusing on target profit pricing, maximizing profits, or target return pricing.

- Firms usually implement **target profit pricing** when they have a particular profit goal as their overriding concern. To meet this targeted profit objective, firms use price to stimulate a certain level of sales at a certain profit per unit.

- The **maximizing profits strategy** relies primarily on economic theory. If a firm can accurately specify a mathematical model that captures all the factors required to explain and predict sales and profits, it should be able to identify the price at which its profits are maximized. Gathering the data on all these relevant factors and coming up with an accurate mathematical model is an extremely difficult undertaking.

EXHIBIT 11.1   Five Cs of Pricing

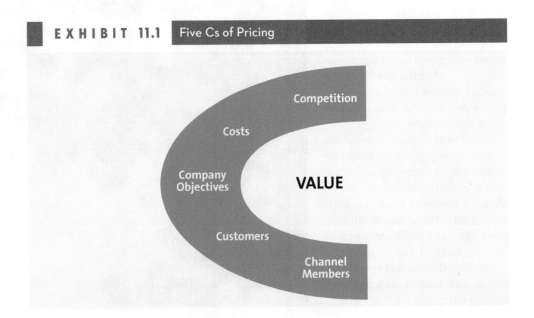

EXHIBIT 11.2	Company Objectives and Pricing Strategy Implications
Company Objective	**Examples of Pricing Strategy Implications**
Profit oriented	Institute a companywide policy that all products must provide for at least an 18 percent profit margin to reach a particular profit goal for the firm.
Sales oriented	Set prices very low to generate new sales and take sales away from competitors, even if profits suffer.
Competitor oriented	Set prices very low to discourage more competitors from entering the market. Set prices higher than competitor to signal higher quality or market leadership. Match competitor prices to show similar value.
Customer oriented	Target a market segment of consumers who highly value a particular product benefit and set prices relatively high (referred to as premium pricing).

● Other firms, less concerned with the absolute level of profits and more interested in the rate at which their profits are generated relative to their investments, typically use **target return pricing** and other pricing strategies designed to produce a specific return on their investment.

Sales Orientation Firms using a **sales orientation** to set prices believe that increasing sales will help the firm more than increasing profits. For example, a new health club might focus on unit sales or market share and therefore be willing to set a lower membership fee and accept less profit at first. In contrast, a high-end jewellery store, such as Tiffany & Co. might focus on dollar sales and maintain higher prices. This store relies on its prestige image, as well as the image of its suppliers, to generate sales. Even though it sells fewer units, it can still generate high dollar sales levels.

Some firms may be more concerned about their overall market share than about dollar sales per se because they believe that market share better reflects their success relative to the market conditions than do sales alone. A firm may set low prices to discourage new firms from entering the market, encourage current firms to leave the market, take market share away from competitors—all to gain overall market share. For example, though Apple has sold more than 10 billion songs since the introduction of its iTunes service, it wants to keep increasing its market share, especially as competitors make inroads. So, instead of the previous fixed priced structure of 99 cents per song, Apple offers three price tiers (69 cents, 99 cents, and $1.29) based on popularity and recency of the songs. The most popular songs cost the most, but by charging less for others, Apple aims to increase its sales per customer.[11]

Adopting a market share objective does not always imply setting low prices. Rarely is the lowest-price offering the dominant brand in a given market. Heinz ketchup, Philadelphia cream cheese, Crest toothpaste, and Nike athletic shoes have all dominated their markets, yet all are premium-priced brands. Thus, companies can gain market share simply by offering a high-quality product at a fair price, as long as they generate high-value

target return pricing
A pricing strategy implemented by firms less concerned with the absolute level of profits and more interested in the rate at which their profits are generated relative to their investments; designed to produce a specific return on investment, usually expressed as a percentage of sales.

sales orientation
A company objective based on the belief that increasing sales will help the firm more than will increasing profits.

Tiffany & Co. keeps its prices high even during a recession to protect its prestigious image, symbolized by its famous blue box.

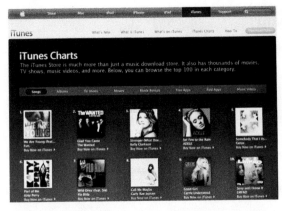

Apple offers three price tiers based on popularity and recency of songs.

competitor orientation
A company objective based on the premise that the firm should measure itself primarily against its competition.

competitive parity
A firm's strategy of setting prices that are similar to those of major competitors.

customer orientation
Pricing orientation that explicitly invokes the concept of customer value and setting prices to match consumer expectations.

demand curve
Shows how many units of a product or service consumers will demand during a specific period at different prices.

perceptions among consumers. Although the concept of value is not overtly expressed in sales-oriented strategies, it is at least implicit because for sales to increase, consumers must see greater value.

Competitor Orientation

When firms undertake a **competitor orientation**, they strategize according to the premise that they should measure themselves primarily against their competition. Some firms focus on **competitive parity**, which means they set prices that are similar to those of their major competitors. Value is only implicitly considered in competitor-oriented strategies, in the sense that competitors may be using value as part of their pricing strategies, so copying their strategy might provide value.

Customer Orientation

A **customer orientation** explicitly invokes the concept of value. Sometimes a firm may attempt to increase value by focusing on customer satisfaction and setting prices to match consumer expectations. Or a firm can use a "no-haggle" price structure to make the purchase process simpler and easier for consumers, thereby lowering the overall price and ultimately increasing value. Some car companies have embraced the "no-haggle" price policy to do just that.

Firms also may offer very high-priced, "state-of-the-art" products or services in full anticipation of limited sales. These offerings are designed to enhance the company's reputation and image and thereby increase the company's value in the minds of consumers. For example, Paradigm, a Canadian speaker manufacturer in Mississauga, Ontario, produces what many audiophiles consider a high-value product, offering speakers priced as low as $320 per pair. However, Paradigm also offers a high-end pair of speakers for $8,500. Although few people will spend $8,500 on a pair of speakers, this "statement" speaker communicates what the company is capable of and can increase the image of the firm and the rest of its products—even that $320 pair of speakers. For an unprecedented 22 years in a row, Paradigm has been rated number one best price/value by *Inside Track*.[12] Setting prices with a close eye to how consumers develop their perceptions of value can often be the most effective pricing strategy, especially if it is supported by consistent advertising and distribution strategies.

After a company has a good grasp on its overall objectives, it must implement pricing strategies that enable it to achieve those objectives. As the second step in this process, the firm should look toward consumer demand to lay the foundation for its pricing strategy.

Can you tell the difference between the $8,500 and the $320 Paradigm speaker?

Customers

The second C of the five Cs of pricing is the most important because it is about understanding consumers' reactions to different prices. Consumers want value and, as you may recall, price is half of the value equation.

To determine how firms account for consumers' preferences when they develop pricing strategies, we must first lay a foundation of traditional economic theory that helps explain how prices are related to demand (consumers' desire for products) and how managers can incorporate this knowledge into their pricing strategies.

Demand Curves and Pricing

A **demand curve** shows how many units of a product or service consumers will demand during a specific period of time at different prices. Although we call them "curves," demand curves can be either straight or curved, as Exhibit 11.3 shows. Of course, any static demand curve assumes that everything else remains unchanged. For example, marketers creating a demand

EXHIBIT 11.3   Demand Curves for Teeth Whitening Kits

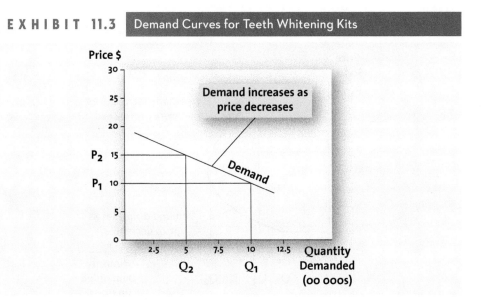

curve must assume that the firm will not increase its expenditures on advertising and that the economy will not change in any significant way.

Exhibit 11.3 illustrates the common downward-sloping demand curve in which, as price increases, demand for the product or service decreases. In this case, consumers will buy more teeth whitening kits as the price decreases. We can expect to uncover a demand curve similar to this one for many, if not most, products and services.

The horizontal axis measures the quantity demanded for the kits in units and plots it against the various price possibilities indicated on the vertical axis. Each point on the demand curve then represents the quantity demanded at a specific price. So, in this instance, if the price of a kit is $10 per unit ($P_1$), the demand is 1,000,000 units (Q_1), but if the price were set at $15 ($P_2$), the demand would be only 500,000 units (Q_2). The firm will sell far more kits at $10 each than at $15 each. Why? Because of the greater value this price point offers.

Knowing the demand curve for a product or service enables a firm to examine different prices in terms of the resulting demand and relative to its overall objective. In our preceding example, the music retailer will generate a total of $10,000,000 in sales at the $10 price ($10 × 1,000,000 units) and $7,500,000 in sales at the $15 price ($15 × 500,000 units). In this case, given only the two choices of $10 or $15, the $10 price is preferable as long as the firm wants to maximize its sales in terms of dollars and units. But what about a firm that is more interested in profit? To calculate profit, it must consider its costs, which we cover in the next section.

Interestingly enough, not all products or services follow the downward-sloping demand curve for all levels of price depicted in Exhibit 11.3. Consider **prestige products or services**, which consumers purchase for their status rather than their functionality. The higher the price, the greater the status associated with it and the greater the exclusivity, because fewer people can afford to purchase it. Most important, in this case, a higher price also leads to a greater quantity sold—up to a certain point. When customers value the increase in prestige more than the price differential between the prestige product and other products, the prestige product attains the greater value overall.

Exhibit 11.4 illustrates a demand curve for a hypothetical prestige service, such as a Caribbean cruise. As the graph indicates, when the price increases from $1,000 ($P_1$) to $5,000 ($P_2$), the quantity demanded actually increases from 200,000 (Q_1) to 500,000 (Q_2) units. However, when the price increases to $8,000 ($P_3$), the demand then decreases to 300,000 (Q_3) units, after peaking at about 500,000.

Although the firm likely will earn more profit selling 300,000 cruises at $8,000 each than 500,000 cruises at $5,000 each, we do not know for sure until we consider costs.

prestige products or services
Those that consumers purchase for status rather than functionality.

EXHIBIT 11.4 Prestige Product Demand Curve

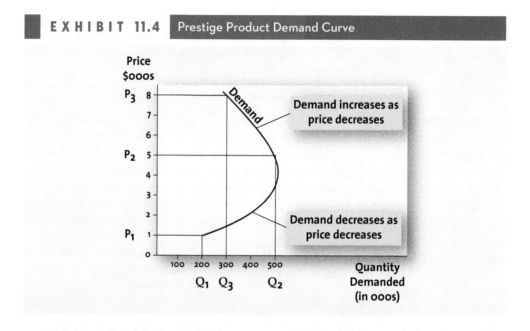

However, we do know that more consumers are willing to book the cruise as the price increases initially from $1,000 to $5,000 and that most consumers will choose an alternative vacation as the price increases further from $5,000 to $8,000.

Price Elasticity of Demand   Although we now know something about how consumers react to different price levels, we still need to determine how consumers respond to actual changes in price. Consumers are generally less sensitive to price increases for necessary items, such as milk, because they have to purchase these items even if the price climbs. When the price of milk goes up, demand does not fall significantly. However, if the price of steak rises beyond a certain point, people will buy less because there are many substitutes. Marketers need to know how consumers will respond to a price increase (or decrease) for a specific product or brand so they can determine whether it makes sense for them to raise or lower prices.

Price elasticity of demand measures how changes in a price affect the quantity of the product demanded. We can calculate it with the following formula:

price elasticity of demand

Measures how changes in a price affect the quantity of the product demanded; specifically, the ratio of the percentage change in quantity demanded to the percentage change in price.

$$\text{Price elasticity of demand} = \frac{\%\ \text{change in quantity demanded}}{\%\ \text{change in price}}$$

Consumers are less sensitive to the price of milk (left) than to steak (right). When the price of milk goes up, demand does not fall significantly because people still need to buy milk. However, if the price of steak rises beyond a certain point, people will buy less because they can turn to the many substitutes for steak.

In general, the market for a product or service is price sensitive (or **elastic**) when the price elasticity is less than –1: that is, when a 1 percent decrease in price produces more than a 1 percent increase in the quantity sold. In an elastic scenario, relatively small changes in price will generate fairly large changes in the quantity demanded, so if a firm is trying to increase its sales, it can do so by lowering prices.

The market for a product is generally viewed as price insensitive (or **inelastic**) when its price elasticity is greater than –1: that is, when a 1 percent decrease in price results in less than a 1 percent increase in quantity sold. Generally, if a firm must raise prices, it is helpful to do so with inelastic products or services because in such a market, fewer customers will stop buying or reduce their purchases—customers just don't notice or care about the lower price.

Consumers are generally more sensitive to price increases than to price decreases.[13] Also, the price elasticity of demand usually changes at different points in the demand curve unless the curve is actually a straight line, as in Exhibit 11.3. For instance, a prestige product or service, such as our Caribbean cruise example in Exhibit 11.4, enjoys a highly inelastic demand curve up to a certain point, so price increases do not affect sales significantly. But when the price reaches that certain point, consumers start turning to other alternatives because the value of the cruise has finally been reduced by the extremely high price.

The Canadian economy has experienced the full force of this elasticity phenomenon during the past few years, as the U.S. dollar has lost ground to other major world currencies. In January 2002, the exchange rate was C$0.62 for a U.S. dollar. By 2011, the Canadian currency had appreciated significantly. The exchange rate hovered near parity before falling to $0.90 in 2014. An American family planning a two-week vacation in 2002 would have found that a US$5,000 budget stretched nicely to more than C$8,000. Today the same family would have less to spend because of currency fluctuations. Not surprisingly, a Consumer Confidence Survey by the U.S. Conference Board indicates that U.S. tourism intentions have softened,[14] as Canada is no longer perceived as such a good bargain.

Factors Influencing Price Elasticity of Demand

We have illustrated how price elasticity of demand varies across different products and at different points along a demand curve, as well as how it can change over time. What causes these differences in the price elasticity of demand? We discuss a few of the more important factors next.

Income Effect. Generally, as people's income increases, their spending behaviour changes: They tend to shift their demand from lower-priced products to higher-priced alternatives. That is, consumers may buy steak instead of ground beef and splurge on

elastic
Refers to a market for a product or service that is price sensitive; that is, relatively small changes in price will generate fairly large changes in the quantity demanded.

inelastic
Refers to a market for a product or service that is price insensitive; that is, relatively small changes in price will not generate large changes in the quantity demanded.

Travelling to Canada on vacation is much more expensive for Americans today than it was a decade ago because of currency fluctuations.

If there are many close substitutes for a product, customers will be sensitive to small price changes, and the product will be highly price elastic. If, for instance, Skippy raises its price, many customers will switch to another brand.

income effect
Refers to the change in the quantity of a product demanded by consumers because of a change in their income.

substitution effect
Refers to consumers' ability to substitute other products for the focal brand, thus increasing the price elasticity of demand for the focal brand.

cross-price elasticity
The percentage change in demand for Product A that occurs in response to a percentage change in price of Product B.

complementary products
Products whose demand curves are positively related, such that they rise or fall together; a percentage increase in demand for one results in a percentage increase in demand for the other.

substitute products
Products for which changes in demand are negatively related—that is, a percentage increase in the quantity demanded for Product A results in a percentage decrease in the quantity demanded for Product B.

a movie a week instead of one per month. In turn, when the economy is good and consumers' incomes are rising overall, the price elasticity of steak or movies may actually drop, even though the price remains constant. Conversely, when incomes drop, consumers turn to less expensive alternatives or purchase less. This **income effect** refers to the change in the quantity of a product demanded by consumers because of a change in their income.

Substitution Effect. The **substitution effect** refers to consumers' ability to substitute other products for the focal brand. The greater the availability of substitute products, the higher the price elasticity of demand for any given product will be. For example, there are many close substitutes for the various brands of peanut butter. If Skippy raises its prices, many consumers will turn to Jif, President's Choice, or another brand because they can easily find lower-priced substitutes. Extremely brand-loyal consumers, however, are willing to pay a higher price because in their minds, Skippy still offers better value than the competing brands.

Keep in mind that marketing plays a critical role in making consumers brand loyal, making the price elasticity of demand for some brands very low. For example, Polo Ralph Lauren sells millions of its classic polo shirts at $65, while shirts of equal quality but without the polo player logo sell for much less. Getting consumers to believe that a particular brand is unique or extraordinary in some way makes other brands seem less substitutable.

Price Elasticity. **Cross-price elasticity** is the percentage change in the quantity of Product A demanded compared with the percentage change in price in Product B. For example, when the price of Blu-ray players dropped rapidly, the demand for Blu-ray discs also increased rapidly. Products such as Blu-ray discs and Blu-ray players are **complementary products**, which are products whose demands are positively related, such that they rise or fall together. In other words, a percentage increase in the quantity demanded for Product A results in a percentage increase in the quantity demanded for Product B.[15] However, when the price for Blu-ray players dropped, the demand for DVD players went down, so Blu-ray players and DVD players are **substitute products** because changes in their demand are negatively related. Today, shopping bots like TheFind.com and Bizrate.com have made it much easier for people to shop for substitutable products like consumer electronics, which has affected the price elasticity of demand.

Clearly, knowing how prices affect sales is important, but it cannot give us the whole picture. To know how profitable a pricing strategy will be, we must also consider the third C, costs.

Costs

To make effective pricing decisions, firms must understand their cost structures so they can determine the degree to which their products or services will be profitable at different prices. In general, prices should *not* be based on costs because consumers make purchase decisions based on their perceived value; they care little about the firm's costs to produce and sell a product or deliver a service. Consumers use just the price they must pay and the benefits they may receive to judge value; they will not pay a higher price for an inferior product simply because the firm cannot be as cost-efficient as its competitors.

If, for instance, a CD were available at both Chapters and Walmart, most consumers would buy it at Walmart, where it likely will be priced lower. But many consumers see additional benefits to shopping at Chapters because it also offers a good selection of books, they can find their choice more easily, or they enjoy buying a CD while sipping a latte they have purchased from the same place. If consumers did not value these benefits, Chapters would not survive.

Although companies incur many different types of costs as a natural part of doing business, there are two primary cost categories: variable and fixed.

Variable Costs

Variable costs are those costs, primarily labour and materials, which vary with production volume. As a firm produces more or less of a good or service, the total variable costs increase or decrease at the same time. Because each unit of the product produced incurs the same cost, marketers generally express variable costs on a per-unit basis. Continuing with our CD example, the variable costs include the labour needed to burn each CD; the costs of the blank CDs, jewel cases, and labels; and royalties paid to the artist. Each of these costs is incurred each time the producer makes a new CD.

In the service industry, variable costs are far more complex. A hotel, for instance, incurs certain variable costs each time it rents a room, including the costs associated with the labour and supplies necessary to clean and restock the room. Note that the hotel does not incur these costs if the room is not booked. Suppose that a particular hotel calculates its total variable costs to be $20 per room; each time it rents a room, it incurs $20 in variable costs. If the hotel rents out 100 rooms on a given night, the total variable cost is $2,000 ($20/room × 100 rooms).

Variable costs tend to change depending on the quantity produced. If a record producer creates five CDs, it must pay a set amount for each one. If it makes 500, though, it can probably get the discs at a lower price by buying in bulk. Though not always the case, variable costs per unit may go up or down (for all units) with significant changes in volume.

variable costs
Those costs, primarily labour and materials, that vary with production volume.

Fixed Costs

Fixed costs are those costs that remain essentially at the same level, regardless of any changes in the volume of production. Typically, these costs include items such as rent, utilities, insurance, administrative salaries (for executives and higher-level managers), and the depreciation of the physical plant and equipment. Across reasonable fluctuations in production volume, these costs remain stable; whether the producer makes 5 or 500 CDs, the rent it pays for the building in which it burns the CDs remains unchanged.

fixed costs
Those costs that remain essentially at the same level, regardless of any changes in the volume of production.

Total Cost

Finally, the **total cost** is simply the sum of the variable and fixed costs. For example, in one year, our hypothetical hotel incurred $100,000 in fixed costs. We also know that because the hotel booked 10,000 room nights, its total variable cost is $200,000 (10,000 room nights × $20/room). Thus, its total cost is $300,000.

Next, we illustrate how to use these costs in simple analyses that can inform managerial decision making about setting prices.

total cost
The sum of the variable and fixed costs.

Break-Even Analysis and Decision Making

A useful technique that enables managers to examine the relationships among cost, price, revenue, and profit over different levels of production and sales is called the break-even analysis. Central to this analysis is the determination of the **break-even point**, or the point at which the number of units sold generates just enough revenue to equal the total costs. At this point, profits are zero.

How do we determine the break-even point? Although profit, which represents the difference between the total cost and the total revenue (total revenue or sales = selling price of each unit sold × number of units sold) can indicate how much money the firm is making or losing at a single period of time, it cannot tell managers how many units a firm must produce and sell before it stops losing money and at least breaks even.

Exhibit 11.5 presents the various cost and revenue information we have discussed in a graphic format.

break-even point
The point at which the number of units sold generates just enough revenue to equal the total costs; at this point, profits are zero.

Please visit Connect for online tutorials and exercises on break-even analysis and other financial concepts.

EXHIBIT 11.5 Break-Even Analysis

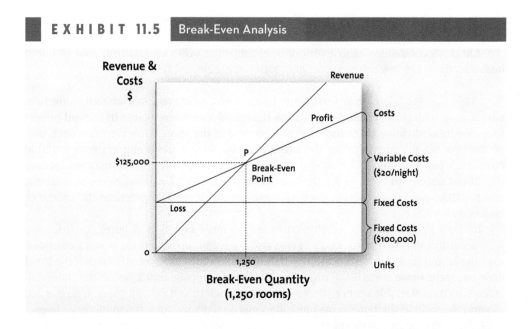

Break-Even Quantity
(1,250 rooms)

Let's use the hotel example to illustrate the break-even analysis. Recall that the fixed costs are $100,000 and the variable costs are $20/room rented. If the rooms rent for $100 per night, how many rooms must the hotel rent over the course of a year to break even? If we study the graph, we find the break-even point at 1,250, which means that the hotel must rent 1,250 rooms before its revenues equal its costs. If it rents fewer rooms, it loses money; if it rents more, it makes a profit. To determine the break-even point in units mathematically, we must consider fixed costs and the **contribution per unit**, which is the price less the variable cost per unit. We use the following formula to calculate the break-even point in units:

contribution per unit
Equals the price less the variable cost per unit; variable used to determine the break-even point in units.

$$\text{Break-even points (units)} = \frac{\text{Fixed costs}}{\text{Contribution per unit}}$$

In this case,

$$\text{Break-even points (units)} = \frac{\$100,000}{100 - 20 = \$80} = 1,250 \text{ room nights}$$

When the hotel has crossed that break-even point of 1,250 rooms, it will then start earning profit at the same rate of the contribution per unit. So if the hotel rents 2,500 rooms—1,250 rooms more than the break-even point—its profit will be $100,000 (1,250 rooms × $80 contribution per unit).

Although a break-even analysis cannot actually help managers set prices, it does help them assess their pricing strategies because it clarifies the conditions in which different prices may make a product or service profitable. It becomes an even more powerful tool when performed on a range of possible prices for comparative purposes. For example, the hotel management could analyze various prices, not just $100, to determine how many hotel rooms it would have to rent at what price to make a $200,000 profit.

Naturally, however, a break-even analysis has limitations. First, it is unlikely that a hotel has one specific price that it charges for each and every room, so the price it would use in its break-even analysis probably represents an average price that attempts to account for these variances. Second, prices often get reduced as quantity increases because the costs decrease, so firms must perform several break-even analyses at different quantities.

Third, a break-even analysis cannot indicate for sure how many rooms will be rented or, in the case of products, how many units will sell at a given price. It tells the firm only what its costs, revenues, and profitability will be given a set price and

an assumed quantity. To determine how many units the firm actually will sell, it must bring in the demand estimates we discussed previously.

In a hotel, the cost of the physical structure is fixed—it is incurred even if no rooms are rented. The costs to clean towels and sheets are variable—the more rooms that are rented, the more the costs.

Competition

Because the fourth C, competition, has a profound impact on pricing strategies,[16] we use this section to focus on its effect, as well as on how competitors react to certain pricing strategies. There are four levels of competition—monopoly, oligopolistic, monopolistic, and pure—and each has its own set of pricing challenges and opportunities (see Exhibit 11.6).

In a **monopoly**, only one firm provides the product or service in a particular industry, and as such results in less price competition. For example, in the utilities industry, there is only one provider of power in each region of the country—Hydro One in most of Ontario and SaskPower in Saskatchewan. Power companies operate more efficiently when there is one service provider, so the government regulates the pricing of utility monopolies to prevent them from raising prices uncontrollably. Monopolies have had a long history in the United States, starting with Standard Oil, which the government broke up in 1911. A monopoly that restricts competition by controlling an industry can be deemed illegal and broken apart by the government.

monopoly
Occurs when only one firm provides the product or service in a particular industry.

When a market is characterized by **oligopolistic competition**, only a few firms dominate. Firms typically change their prices in reaction to competition to avoid upsetting an otherwise stable competitive environment. Often-cited examples of oligopolistic markets include the banking industry, the retail gasoline industry, and commercial airline travel.

oligopolistic competition
Occurs when only a few firms dominate a market.

Sometimes reactions to prices in oligopolistic markets can result in a **price war**, which occurs when two or more firms compete primarily by lowering their prices. Price wars often appear in the airline industry when a low-cost provider enters a market in which established carriers already exist. But what motivates firms to enter price wars?[17] In the airline example, the new entrants might want to gain market share, whereas the established airlines drop their prices to preserve their market share. Other reasons include avoiding the appearance of being insensitive to consumers and simply overreacting to a price decrease offered by competitors. In many cases, companies do not need to respond to price cuts with price cuts of their own[18] because consumers do not buy solely on the basis of price. Better service, higher quality, and brand loyalty might be used as competitive strategies instead.

price war
Occurs when two or more firms compete primarily by lowering their prices.

EXHIBIT 11.6 Four Levels of Competition: Can you match each photo to its respective type of competition?

Less Price Competition | More Price Competition

Monopoly
One firm controls the market

Oligopoly
A handful of firms control the market

Fewer Firms

Monopolistic Competition
Many firms selling differentiated products at different prices

Pure Competition
Many firms selling commodities for the same prices

Many Firms

monopolistic competition
Occurs when many firms sell closely related but not homogeneous products; these products may be viewed as substitutes but are not perfect substitutes.

pure competition
Occurs when different companies sell commodity products that consumers perceive as substitutable; price usually is set according to the laws of supply and demand.

Monopolistic competition occurs when many firms are competing for customers in a given market but their products are differentiated. When so many firms compete, product differentiation rather than a strict pricing competition tends to appeal to consumers. This form of competition is the most common. Hundreds of firms make wristwatches, and the market is highly differentiated. For example, Timex is known for durability, Swatch for style, Armani for fashion, and Rolex for prestige.

With **pure competition**, consumers perceive a large number of sellers of standardized products or commodities as substitutable, such as grains, spices, gold, or minerals. In such markets, price usually is set according to the laws of supply and demand. For example, wheat is wheat, so it does not matter to a commercial bakery whose wheat it buys. However, the secret to pricing success in a pure competition market is not necessarily to offer the lowest price because doing so might create a price war and erode profits. Instead, some firms have brilliantly decommoditized their products. For example, coffee beans used to be regarded as all the same, and then Juan Valdez and the Colombian Coffee Growers Federation made their "100% Colombian Coffee" special, ensuring that coffee drinkers now know the difference between those beans and everything else.

When a commodity can be differentiated somehow, even if simply by a sticker or logo, there is an opportunity for consumers to identify it as distinct from the rest, and in this case, firms can at least partially extricate their product from a pure-competitive market.

Channel Members

Channel members—manufacturers, wholesalers, and retailers—can have different perspectives when it comes to pricing strategies. Consider a manufacturer that is focused on increasing the image and reputation of its brand but working with a retailer that is primarily concerned with increasing its sales. The manufacturer may desire to keep prices higher to convey a better image, whereas the retailer wants lower prices and will accept lower profits to move the product, regardless of consumers' impressions of the brand. Unless channel members carefully communicate their pricing goals and select channel partners that agree with them, conflict will surely arise.

Channels can be very difficult to manage, and distribution outside normal channels does occur. A **grey market**, for example, employs irregular but not necessarily illegal methods; generally, it legally circumvents authorized channels of distribution to sell goods at prices lower than those intended by the manufacturer.[19]

TV sets and other consumer electronics are commonly sold in the grey market.

Many manufacturers of consumer electronics therefore require retailers to sign an agreement that demands certain activities (and prohibits others) before they may become authorized dealers. But if a retailer has too many high-definition TVs in stock, it may sell them at just above its own cost to an unauthorized discount dealer. This move places the merchandise on the street at prices far below what authorized dealers can charge, and in the long term, it may tarnish the image of the manufacturer if the discount dealer fails to provide sufficient return policies, support, service, and so forth.

To discourage this type of grey market distribution, some manufacturers, such as Fujitsu, have resorted to large disclaimers on their websites, packaging, and other communications to warn consumers that the manufacturer's product warranty becomes null and void unless the item has been purchased from an authorized dealer.[20]

grey market
Employs irregular but not necessarily illegal methods; generally, it legally circumvents authorized channels of distribution to sell goods at prices lower than those intended by the manufacturer.

OTHER INFLUENCES ON PRICING

Thus far, we have focused mainly on product- and firm-specific factors—the five Cs—that influence pricing. Now we turn to broader factors that have a more sweeping effect on pricing in general: the Internet and economic factors.

The Internet

The shift among consumers to acquiring more and more products, services, and information online has made them more price sensitive and opened new categories of products to those who could not access them previously. Gourmet foods, books, music, movies, electronics, and even contact lenses are just a few of the product categories that present a significant online presence. Because they have gained access to rare cheeses, breads, meats, spices, and confections, consumers are demanding more from their local grocery stores in terms of selection and variety and have become more sensitive about prices. Furthermore, consumers' ability to buy electronics at highly discounted prices online has pushed bricks-and-mortar stores to attempt to focus consumers' attention on prepurchase advice and expertise, consulting services, and after-sales service—and away from price.

The growth of online auction sites, such as eBay and Kijiji, enables consumers to find the best prices for any product, new or used, quickly, which again increases their price sensitivity and reduces the costs associated with finding lower-price alternatives.[21] Consumers know more about not only prices, but also the firms, their products, their competitors, and the markets in which they compete. A study by the Internet Innovation Alliance found that in 2012 households with Internet access saved US$8,870 by comparison shopping, searching for discounts and coupons, plus time and gas savings by not visiting brick-and-mortar stores.[22]

New mobile apps that enable consumers to find the best prices for any product quickly, which again increases their price sensitivity and reduces the costs associated with finding lower-price alternatives.[23] **Showrooming** is when customers visit a store to touch, feel, and even discuss a product's features with a sales associate, and then purchase it online from another retailer at a lower price. It is particularly popular with customers purchasing electronics.

showrooming
Occurs when consumers visit a physical store to get information about a product but then buy online from another retailer that offers a lower price.

Stores like H&M have introduced disposable chic to Canadians.

As discussed in the opening vignette, another trend affecting pricing has been the growth of online daily coupon promotions from companies such as Groupon or WagJag. In Toronto, The Butchers promoted $175 of organic meat for $55 through Dealfind. It sold 11,500 coupons in three days, worth $632,500, and set a North American record for the largest promotion by an independent store in a single city.[24] Although The Butchers had been in business for more than 10 years, the online coupon promotion resulted in huge growth in its customer base.

Economic Factors

Two interrelated trends that have merged to impact pricing decisions are the increase in consumers' disposable income and status consciousness. Some consumers appear willing to spend money for products that can convey status in some way. Products once considered only for the very rich, such as Rolex watches and Mercedes-Benz cars, are now owned by more working professionals. Although such prestige products are still aimed at the elite, more and more consumers are making the financial leap to attain them.

At the same time, however, a countervailing trend finds customers attempting to shop cheap with 74 percent of shoppers surveyed saying they are more sensitive to price in 2013 over the previous year.[25] The popularity of everyday low price retailers, such as Walmart and Giant Tiger, among customers who can afford to shop at department and specialty stores, illustrates that it is cool to save a buck. Retailers such as H&M and Loblaws, with its Joe Fresh line of clothing, have introduced disposable chic and cross-shopping into Canadians' shopping habits. In this context, **cross-shopping** is the pattern of buying both premium and low-priced merchandise or patronizing both expensive, status-oriented retailers and price-oriented retailers. These stores offer fashionable merchandise at great values—values so good that if items last for only a few wearings, it doesn't matter to the customers. The net impact of these contradictory trends on prices has been that some prestige items have become more expensive, whereas many other items have become cheaper.

cross-shopping
The pattern of buying both premium and low-priced merchandise or patronizing both expensive, status-oriented retailers and price-oriented retailers.

Finally, the economic environment at local, regional, national, and global levels influences pricing. Starting at the top, the growth of the global economy has changed the nature of competition around the world. Many firms maintain a presence in multiple countries: products are designed in one country, the parts are manufactured in another, the final product assembled in a third, and after-sales service is handled by a call centre in a fourth. By thinking globally, firms can seek out the most cost-efficient methods of providing goods and services to their customers.

On a more local level, the economy still can influence pricing. Competition, disposable income, and unemployment all may signal the need for different pricing strategies. For instance, rural areas are often subjected to higher prices because it costs more to get products there and because competition is lower. Similarly, retailers often charge higher prices in areas populated by people who have more disposable income and enjoy low unemployment rates.

LO3   PRICING METHODS AND STRATEGIES

Coming up with the "right" price is never easy. If the BlackBerry Z10 had been priced at a low point initially, how might it have affected future sales? Firms embrace different objectives, face different market conditions, and operate in different manners; thus, they employ unique pricing strategies that seem best for the particular set of circumstances in which they find themselves. Even a single firm needs different strategies across its products and services and over time as market conditions change. The choice of a pricing strategy is specific to the product/service and target market. Although firms tend to rely on similar strategies when they can, each product or service requires its own specific strategy because no two are ever exactly the same in terms of the marketing mix. Cost-based, competitor-based, and value-based strategies are discussed in this section.

Cost-based Methods

As their name implies, **cost-based pricing methods** determine the final price to charge by starting with the cost. Cost-based methods do not recognize the role that consumers or competitors' prices play in the marketplace. Although relatively simple compared with other methods used to set prices, cost-based pricing requires that all costs can be identified and calculated on a per-unit basis. Moreover, the process assumes that these costs will not vary much for different levels of production. If they do, the price might need to be raised or lowered according to the production level. Thus, with cost-based pricing, prices are usually set on the basis of estimates of average costs.

cost-based pricing method
Determines the final price to charge by starting with the cost, without recognizing the role that consumers or competitors' prices play in the marketplace.

Competitor-based Methods

Most firms know that consumers compare the prices of their products with the different product/price combinations competitors offer. Thus, using a **competitor-based pricing method**, they may set their prices to reflect the way they want consumers to interpret their own prices relative to the competitors' offerings. For example, setting a price very close to a competitor's price signals to consumers that the product is similar, whereas setting the price much higher signals greater features, better quality, or some other valued benefit.

competitor-based pricing method
An approach that attempts to reflect how the firm wants consumers to interpret its products relative to the competitors' offerings.

Value-based Methods

Value-based pricing methods include approaches to setting prices that focus on the overall value of the product offering as perceived by the consumer. Consumers determine value by comparing the benefits they expect the product to deliver with the sacrifice they will need to make to acquire the product. Of course, different consumers perceive value differently. When Vancouver band Wintermitts went on tour, it offered CDs for sale at $10. In an attempt to encourage fans to access the band's music digitally, download cards were priced at $5. To band members' surprise, they sold out of CDs and sold only half as many download cards as expected.[26] As noted in Sustainable Marketing 11.1, Walmart is known for low prices and is now aiming to be seen as a sustainability leader as well. So how does a manager use value-based pricing methods? We consider two key approaches.

value-based pricing method
Focuses on the overall value of the product offering as perceived by consumers, who determine value by comparing the benefits they expect the product to deliver with the sacrifice they will need to make to acquire the product.

Improvement Value Method
With this method, the manager must estimate the improvement value of a new product or service. This **improvement value** represents an estimate of how much more (or less) consumers are willing to pay for a product relative to other comparable products. For example, suppose a major telecommunications company has developed a new cellphone. Using any of a host of research methods, such as consumer surveys, the manager could get customers to assess the new product relative to an existing product and provide an estimate of how much better it is, or its improvement value. Cinemas understand that movie-goers will pay more for improved viewing experiences: about $3 more for 3D and a $7 premium for IMAX. Premium tickets account for 36 percent of box office sales for Cineplex.[27]

improvement value
Represents an estimate of how much more (or less) consumers are willing to pay for a product relative to other comparable products.

Cost of Ownership Method
Another value-based method for setting prices determines the total cost of owning the product over its useful life. Using the **cost of ownership method**, consumers may be willing to pay more for a particular product because, over its entire lifetime, it will eventually cost less to own than a cheaper alternative.[28]

cost of ownership method
A value-based method for setting prices that determines the total cost of owning the product over its useful life.

Sustainable Marketing 11.1

It Isn't Easy to Sell to Walmart[29]

Walmart is known for its low prices and for driving its vendors nearly to tears to get them. Now it is pressuring its vendors to supply it with environmentally friendly merchandise with labels to prove it. In the future, merchandise sold at Walmart will have the environmental equivalent of nutrition labels, providing information on the product's carbon footprint, the amount of water and air pollution used to produce it, and other environmental issues. To measure how a vendor's products are doing, it has developed a sustainability index that simultaneously takes several issues into consideration. From this index it developed scorecards to help its buyers further evaluate products.

Walmart required its top 200 factories to become 20 percent more energy efficient by 2012—a feat that many experts believed impossible, even with Walmart's help. Initial results proved promising. For example, Jiangsu Redbud Dyeing Technology in China cut coal consumption by one-tenth and is attempting to cut its toxic emissions to zero. Waste was reduced by 80 percent by the end of 2012 as part of its Zero Waste initiative.[30]

Walmart hasn't always been touted as a good corporate citizen. In the 1990s, it came to light that workers at some factories producing clothing for Walmart were subjected to inhumane conditions. More recently, two governmental organizations accused Walmart of buying from 15 factories that engage in abuse and labour violations, including child labour, 19-hour shifts, and below-subsistence wages.[31]

Some wonder why Walmart is attempting to position itself as the retail industry's sustainability leader. Certainly, initiatives that show that it is a good corporate citizen enhance its image. But it expects it to be good for business as well. Its customers, especially those born after 1980, are increasingly concerned about how the products they use impact the environment and the people who produce them. Also, Walmart believes that many of these initiatives will help streamline supply chain processes and therefore provide additional financial benefits to its suppliers and customers.

Consider, for example, that an energy-efficient fluorescent light bulb costs $3 and is expected to last 6,000 hours. Alternatively, a conventional light bulb costs $1 but its average life is only 1,500 hours. Even though the fluorescent bulb is expected to last four times longer than a conventional bulb, it costs only three times as much. Using the cost of ownership method, and considering the cost per hour, the fluorescent bulb manufacturer could charge $4 for each bulb to give it an equivalent cost to a conventional bulb. However, given its research indicated that many consumers would be reluctant to spend $4 for a bulb, the manufacturer chose to charge only $3, thereby offering customers greater value.

Although value-based pricing strategies can be quite effective, they also necessitate a great deal of consumer research to be implemented successfully. Sellers must know how consumers in different market segments will attach value to the benefits delivered by their products. They also must account for changes in consumer attitudes because the way customers perceive value today may not be the way they perceive it tomorrow.

Is the improvement value on the BlackBerry Q10 sufficiently greater than competitive products so that a higher price can be charged for it?

NEW PRODUCT PRICING STRATEGIES

Developing pricing strategies for new products is one of the most challenging tasks a manager can undertake. When the new product is just another "me-too" product, similar to what already appears on the market, this job is somewhat easier because the product's approximate value has already been established. But when the product is truly innovative, or what we call "new to the world," determining consumers' perceptions of its value and pricing it accordingly becomes far more difficult. Let's turn our attention to two distinct pricing strategies for new products: skimming and penetration.

Price Skimming

In many markets, and particularly for new and innovative products or services, innovators and early adopters (see Chapter 8) are willing to pay a higher price to obtain the new product or service. This strategy, known as **price skimming**, appeals to these segments of consumers who are willing to pay the premium price to have the innovation first. This tactic is particularly common in technology markets, where sellers know that *Call of Duty* fans will wait in line for hours, desperate to be the first to own the newest version. These innovators are willing to pay top dollar to get the new product and its exciting enhancements. After this high-price market segment becomes saturated and sales begin to slow down, companies generally lower the price to capture (or skim) the next most price-sensitive market segment, which is willing to pay a somewhat lower price. This process can continue until the demand for the product has been satisfied, even at the lowest price points. Luxury products are often an exception. For example, Louis Vuitton does not lower the price of its bags, but rather, keeps prices high to support its prestige image.

Price skimming is often used for high demand video games like Call of Duty because fans will pay a higher price to be one of the first to own the newest version.

For price skimming to work, the product or service must be perceived as breaking new ground in some way, offering consumers new benefits currently unavailable in alternative products. Firms use skimming strategies for a variety of reasons. Some may start by pricing relatively high to signal high quality to the market. Others may decide to price high at first to limit demand, which gives them time to build their production capacities. Similarly, some firms employ a skimming strategy to try to quickly earn back some of the high R&D investments they made for the new product. Finally, firms employ skimming strategies to test consumers' price sensitivity. A firm that prices too high can always lower the price; but, if the price is initially set too low, it is almost impossible to raise it without significant consumer resistance.

For a skimming pricing strategy to be successful, competitors cannot be able to enter the market easily; otherwise, price competition will likely force lower prices and undermine the whole strategy. Competitors might be prevented from entering the market through patent protections, their inability to copy the innovation (because it is complex to manufacture, its raw materials are hard to get, or the product relies on proprietary technology), or the high costs of entry.

Skimming strategies also face a significant potential drawback in the relatively high unit costs often associated with producing small volumes of products. Therefore, firms must consider the trade-off between earning a higher price and suffering higher production costs. Price skimming also can cause discontent for consumers. Those who pay a higher price to purchase the latest iPhone early may feel cheated if the prices drop quickly.

Market Penetration Pricing

Instead of setting the price high, firms using **market penetration pricing** set the initial price low for the introduction of the new product or service. Their objective is to build sales, market share, and profits quickly. The low market penetration price encourages consumers to purchase the product immediately. With price skimming, profits are generated through margin, whereas with penetration pricing, profits flow through volume. Although it is not always the case, many firms expect the unit cost to drop significantly as the accumulated volume sold increases, an effect known as the **experience curve effect**. With this effect, as sales continue to grow, the costs continue to drop, allowing even further reductions in the price.

In addition to offering the potential to build sales, market share, and profits, penetration pricing discourages competitors from entering the market because the

price skimming
A strategy of selling a new product or service at a high price that innovators and early adopters are willing to pay to obtain it; after the high-price market segment becomes saturated and sales begin to slow down, the firm generally lowers the price to capture (or skim) the next most price-sensitive segment.

market penetration pricing
A pricing strategy of setting the initial price low for the introduction of the new product or service, with the objective of building sales, market share, and profits quickly.

experience curve effect
Refers to the drop in unit cost as the accumulated volume sold increases; as sales continue to grow, the costs continue to drop, allowing even further reductions in the price.

profit margin is relatively low. Furthermore, if the costs to produce the product drop because of the accumulated volume, competitors that enter the market later will face higher unit costs, at least until their volume catches up with the early entrant.

A penetration strategy also has its drawbacks. First, the firm must have the capacity to satisfy a rapid rise in demand—or at least be able to add that capacity quickly. Second, low price does not signal high quality. Of course, a price below their expectations decreases the risk for consumers to purchase the product and test its quality for themselves. Third, firms should avoid a penetration pricing strategy if some segments of the market are willing to pay more for the product; otherwise, the firm is just "leaving money on the table."

PSYCHOLOGICAL FACTORS AFFECTING VALUE-BASED PRICING STRATEGIES

Understanding the psychology underlying the way consumers arrive at their perceptions, make judgments, and finally invoke a choice is critical to effective pricing strategies, so marketers must examine some of the more important psychological processes that influence consumers' reactions to and use of price. When consumers are exposed to a price, they assign meaning to it by placing it into a category, such as "expensive," "a deal," "cheap," "overpriced," or even "fair."

In this section, we examine some of the factors that influence this psychological process of adding meaning to, or evaluating, price.[32] Look at how one woman with an incredible vision launched a new product based on a unique concept in Entrepreneurial Marketing 11.1.

reference price
The price against which buyers compare the actual selling price of the product and that facilitates their evaluation process.

In this ad, Sears provides a reference price of $24.99, in small print, to reflect the regular price of Lee jeans.

Consumers' Use of Reference Prices

A **reference price** is the price against which buyers compare the actual selling price of the product and that facilitates their evaluation process. The seller labels the reference price as the "regular price" or an "original price." When consumers view the "sale price" and compare it with the provided external reference price, their perceptions of the value of the deal will likely increase.[33] In the advertisement shown to the right, Sears has provided an external reference price, in smaller print and labelled "Reg.," to indicate that $24.99 is the regular price of Lee jeans. In addition, the advertisement highlights the current "sale" price of $21.99. Thus, the external reference price suggests to consumers that they are getting a good deal and will save money. However, as Ethical Dilemma 11.1 notes, sometimes the veracity of such a reference price is open to challenge.

Consumers may also rely on reference prices stored in their memory—perhaps the last price they paid or what they expect to pay.[34] For instance, a consumer seated in a restaurant viewing the price of a large pepperoni pizza as $12 may recall that the price she usually pays for a large pepperoni pizza at another restaurant is only $10 and may judge the menu price as high.

Entrepreneurial Marketing 11.1

Sweet Smell of Success

Most entrepreneurs start their businesses in hopes of making a profit. While this goal was part of Barbara Stegemann's plan, she had another driving motivation: changing the face of the Afghan heroin industry. Her Halifax company, The 7 Virtues Communications Group, has helped large companies and government organizations adapt to their changing environments. Now she's promoting sustainable business development in war-torn Afghanistan by encouraging a group of male and female farmers to abandon their poppy fields to grow orange blossoms for use as fragrance oil.

A feasibility study conducted in 2004 showed that Afghans were well positioned to tap into the US$18.4 billion international flavour and fragrance market.[35] The study determined that essential oils were high in value and low in volume; in other words, like the opium produced from poppies, small quantities are worth a lot of money. Stegemann was inspired by her friendship with Captain Trevor Greene, who served in Afghanistan. In spite of sustaining serious injuries during his stay, he was ready to return to the country. "Perfume not Poppies" became her philosophy as she set out to capture some of the $600 million Canadians spend annually on perfume.[36]

Stegemann met with officials from the Canadian International Development Agency, the Afghan embassy in Ottawa, and the Canada Afghanistan Business Council. These connections led to an extraordinary

Psychological pricing and a "Perfume not Poppies" philosophy is helping to sell 7 Virtues perfume.

partnership with an Afghan company, Gulestan, owned by Abdullah Arsala, that produces essential oils.[37] The first cup of orange blossom oil cost Stegemann $2,000, enough to produce 1,000 bottles of perfume. The new product was introduced on March 8, 2010,[38] International Women's Day, a fitting day since most of the orange blossoms farmers are women. The next year Stegemann promised to buy their entire crop, which would allow her to produce 8,000 to 12,000 bottles.

Psychological pricing is often used in the fragrance industry, as consumers seek must-have products. Priced at $70 for 50 millilitres, 7 Virtues is not inexpensive; yet, price hasn't been a deterrent. In fact, the story behind 7 Virtues helped the perfume to fly off shelves. In spite of the relatively high price point, on launch day, nearly one-third of Stegemann's stock sold.[39]

One year after the launch, Stegemann successfully pitched on CBC's *Dragons' Den*. Since then, two new product lines have been added. One fragrance based on organic vetiver from Haiti,[40] was inspired by farmers who had been devastated by earthquakes in 2010. A Middle East Peace fragrance, "Make Perfume Not War," was launched on the International Day of Peace in September 2012.[41] Stegemann was recognized as the Top Game Changer by the Dragons and viewers for making a positive impact on the world.[42]

Odd Prices

Have you ever wondered why prices rarely end in round amounts, like $3.00 or $23.00? In various product categories, **odd prices**, or those that end in odd numbers, usually 9, are very common, such as $3.99, $11.99, and $7.77. Most marketers believe that odd pricing got its start as a way to prevent sales clerks from just pocketing money. Because the price was odd, the clerk would have to open the cash register for change, which required that the sale be rung up on the register.

Some sellers believe that consumers mentally truncate the actual price, making the perceived price appear lower than it really is. For example, if the price is $21.99, consumers may focus more on the $21 than on the 99 cents, which may cause them to perceive the price as significantly lower than $22.00, even

odd prices
Prices that end in odd numbers, usually 9, such as $3.99.

Odd prices signal to consumers that the price is low.

Ethical Dilemma 11.1 — Is It Really 45 Percent Off?[43]

For the truly fashionable—or at least those who consider themselves as members of that group—the trade-off between luxury and affordability can be a tricky one. You want the newest, hottest fashion, but trying to keep up can be tough on your wallet. What's a maven to do?

Private sale online sites such as Gilt, RueLaLa, and HauteLook promise a solution. They host limited-time sales of products from high-end fashion brands. A sale starts at a specified time and lasts for 48 hours, or until the sale is sold out. So, if you must have the Nova Armored Baby Beaton handbag from Burberry, you can have it for 45 percent off the list price, or $877 instead of $1,595, as long as you are on Hautelook.com when the sale starts. Brick-and-mortar retailers are following suit with "flash sales," such as when Banana Republic offers 40 percent off its full-priced sweaters but only between 11:00 a.m. and 2:00 p.m. on specific days.

But is it really 40 or 45 percent off, and 45 percent off what? A reference price like $1,595 gives consumers a cue as to what that specific handbag should be worth. Research shows that the greater the difference between a suggested retail and a sale price, the greater the perceived value. When customers see Sears offering a refrigerator for $1,300 off its original price, that huge number is nearly impossible to ignore. The better the deal, the more consumers will be attracted to buy. But if the retailer inflates the suggested or original price, the percentage discount and dollars off seem much better than they actually are.

When the private sale sites have been caught inflating the suggested retail prices to show a greater percentage discount, they generally claim that the original prices they list are accurate and come from the manufacturer. Any errors, they argue, are because the manufacturer gave them the wrong price, or due to employee error. For example, if the suggested retail price of the Burberry bag was actually only $1,100 instead of $1,595, then the bag was discounted only 20 percent. A customer in the heat of the moment may buy the bag because it is reported to be 45 percent off; were it only 20 percent off, she might not have purchased.

In some cases, the complicated coupon, discount, and flash pricing offers make it nearly impossible to determine the extent of the deal without a calculator. Because consumers rarely have the time or energy to calculate exactly what kind of discount they are getting, retailers can play on their excitement when it seems like a great deal.

Should private sale sites and in-store retailers be required to substantiate their reference prices? Which price should they use as the reference price? Is it their responsibility if the manufacturer gives them the wrong pricing information? Do you think they are intentionally misleading their customers?

---

though that difference is only a penny. The main finding from research on the odd pricing approach is that odd prices signal to consumers that the price is low.[44] So if sellers want to suggest that a deal is to be had, odd prices may be appropriate.

Everyday Low Pricing (EDLP)

everyday low pricing (EDLP)
A strategy companies use to emphasize the continuity of their retail prices at a level somewhere between the regular, nonsale price and the deep-discount sale prices their competitors may offer.

With an **everyday low pricing (EDLP)** strategy, companies stress the continuity of their retail prices at a level somewhere between the regular, nonsale price and the deep-discount sale prices their competitors may offer.[45] By reducing consumers' search costs, EDLP adds value; consumers can spend less of their valuable time comparing prices, including sale prices, at different stores. For example, Walmart relies on EDLP to communicate to consumers that, for any given group of often purchased items, its prices are lower than those of any other company in that market. This claim does not necessarily mean that every item that consumers may purchase will be priced lower at Walmart than anywhere else—in fact, some competitive retailers will offer lower prices on some items. However, on average, Walmart's prices tend to be lower. Social and Mobile Marketing 11.1 reinforces the advantages of offering everyday low prices.

High/Low Pricing

high/low pricing
A pricing strategy that relies on the promotion of sales, during which prices are temporarily reduced to encourage purchases.

Alternatively, some retailers prefer a **high/low pricing** strategy, which relies on the promotion of sales, during which prices are temporarily reduced to encourage purchases. In the end, which consumers prefer which strategy depends on how those consumers evaluate prices and quality. Some prefer not to expend the time to find the lowest price and favour EDLP as an efficient way to get low prices. Alternatively,

Social and Mobile Marketing 11.1

Price-Check on Aisle ... Anywhere[46]

Most marketers assume that a Gen X guy and his mom would shop in very different ways. But the benefits offered by the latest mobile phone software are blending those shopping methods by helping consumers of all types shop smarter.

Eric Olson wanted a Blu-ray version of *Heat*, but at Best Buy, where he was shopping before Christmas, the disc cost $26, which seemed high to the 33-year-old consumer. Therefore, while still in Best Buy, he scanned the UPC barcode using his Android smartphone and went on the mobile application ShopSavvy to check the price of the disc at nearby stores. Walmart.com was charging only $19. Eric's mom Carrie Olson also regularly uses a RedLaser application to scan the bar codes of books and DVDs.

Amazon wants both Eric and Carrie to shop its site instead, for everything they need, so its price-checking application is not only free to customers, but, at times, it even offers them money to use it. In the preholiday shopping season, Amazon promised customers a $5 discount on their order if they scanned a barcode on an item in a competitor's store, then bought that same item from Amazon.[47]

It is nothing new to check prices online. It is the mobility of these checks that is really

Using a smartphone with the ShopSavvy app, consumers can find out which nearby stores carry the desired product at the lowest price, as well as which stores are closest to them.

advancing the practice—and making some sellers really nervous. Anyone with a smartphone can use ShopSavvy to find out which nearby stores carry the desired product at the lowest price, as well as which stores are closest to the consumer. Amazon's version compares prices only with the items available on its site, but as the site continues to grow, that includes a lot of items.

ShopSavvy's database instead includes tens of thousands of retailers and millions of store locations, such as Walmart, Target, American Eagle, Best Buy, The Gap, and online-only retailers. Because these technologies rely on the retailers' websites or databases for pricing information, sometimes the details provided are a little out of date, especially if the retailer decides to change the price at the last minute. But 20 million people have downloaded the application, and 10 million of them use it frequently—about 20 percent of the total population of smartphone users in the United States.

For Eric and Carrie Olson, the options are nearly endless. But for retailers, especially those that cannot compete very well on price, the options seem to be shrinking fast. If everyone can instantly perform price research, what is a higher priced seller to do?

---

other consumers may relish the challenge of getting the lowest price or be so price sensitive that they are willing to expend the time and effort to seek out the lowest price every time.

But even this categorization gets more complicated, in that it needs to include quality perceptions as well. Some consumers perceive that stores that use EDLP carry lower quality goods, whereas high/low pricing stores tend to carry better quality items. In part, this perception forms because consumers view the initial price at a high/low store as the reference price. In the end, however, the consumer's decision, once again and as always, comes down to value. In the next section, we discuss how to apply psychological factors in the pricing decisions for new products.

PRICING TACTICS

LO4

It is important to distinguish clearly between pricing strategies and pricing tactics. A *pricing strategy* is a long-term approach to setting prices broadly in an integrative effort (across all the firm's products) based on the five Cs (company objectives, customers, costs, competition, and channel members) of pricing. **Pricing tactics**, in contrast, offer short-term methods to focus on select components of the five Cs. Generally, a pricing tactic represents either a short-term response to a competitive threat (e.g., lowering price temporarily to meet a competitor's price reduction) or a broadly accepted method of calculating a final price for the customer that is short term in nature. We separate

pricing tactics
Short-term methods, in contrast to long-term pricing strategies, used to focus on company objectives, customers, costs, competition, or channel members; can be responses to competitive threats (e.g., lowering price temporarily to meet a competitor's price reduction) or broadly accepted methods of calculating a final price for the customer that is short term in nature.

EXHIBIT 11.7	Pricing Tactics Aimed at Consumers
Tactic	
Price lining	Establishing a price floor and a price ceiling for an entire line of similar products and then setting price points in between to represent distinct differences in quality.
Price bundling	Pricing of more than one product for a single, lower price.
Leader pricing	Building store traffic by aggressively pricing and advertising a regularly purchased item, often priced at or just above the store's cost.

our discussion of pricing tactics into those aimed at intermediaries in a business-to-business (B2B) setting and those directed at end consumers.

Pricing Tactics Aimed at Consumers

When firms sell their products and services directly to consumers, rather than to other businesses, the pricing tactics they use naturally differ. In this section, we analyze some tactics for products and services aimed directly at consumers: price lining, price bundling, and leader pricing (see Exhibit 11.7).

Price Lining   When marketers establish a price floor and a price ceiling for an entire line of similar products and then set a few other price points in between to represent distinct differences in quality, the tactic is called **price lining**.

Consider the specific price lines used by Moores Clothing for Men. The firm prices its sports jackets at different price points. For example, its house brand, Joseph & Feiss, sells for around $119. Move up to a middle-range price point and you can buy an Alfred Sung jacket for between $159 and $199. At the top end of the line, you can find a pure wool Pronto Uomo sports jacket for $229.

While it may be difficult to determine which is the better jacket, having options at different price points means Moores can satisfy a range of tastes and budgets.

Price Bundling   When you signed up for your high-speed Internet connection, did you also get cable TV and telephone? If so, you probably pay less than if you were to get the three services separately. This practice of selling more than one product for a single, lower price is called **price bundling**. Firms bundle products together to encourage customers to stock up so they won't purchase competing brands, to encourage trial of a new product, or to provide an incentive to purchase a less desirable product or service to obtain a more desirable one in the same bundle.

We present a price bundling example in Exhibit 11.8. Imagine we have four different offerings for sale: home phone line, long-distance, Internet, and satellite TV services. Customers use combinations of these products and services differently, and each customer has unique needs. Subscribing to each service separately is the most expensive option, as shown in the first line. However, if customers bundle together three or more services, they can take advantage of lower prices.

Let's look at how Bell uses price bundling to add value for its customers. For example, a student away at university on a tight budget may elect to subscribe to only the essentials: Internet and a cellphone. Regular price for these items would be $121.95/month. Through its bundled service offering, Bell can entice the student to also sign up for cable TV by reducing the price of the Internet service when the cable TV service is added. The company benefits from enhancing the relationship with the customer and by collecting additional revenue. While the student's monthly bill will rise slightly to $168.71, he will save $192.00/year from the unbundled service prices and should now be able to enjoy playoff hockey matches while at home!

price lining
Consumer market pricing tactic of establishing a price floor and a price ceiling for an entire line of similar products and then setting a few other price points in between to represent distinct differences in quality.

price bundling
Consumer pricing tactic of selling more than one product for a single, lower price than the items would cost sold separately; can be used to sell slow-moving items, to encourage customers to stock up so they won't purchase competing brands, to encourage trial of a new product, or to provide an incentive to purchase a less desirable product or service to obtain a more desirable one in the same bundle.

EXHIBIT 11.8	An Illustration of Price Bundling					
	Home Phone Basic	**Bell Fibe Internet 25/10**	**Bell Fibe TV Good Package**	**Bell Mobility Voice & Data Plus 60**	**Total**	**Annual Savings**
Regular price	$41.94	$61.95	$46.76	$60.00		
Bundled price	$37.94	$57.95	$38.76	$56.00		
Student example: Internet and cellphone						
Full-price services		$61.95		$60.00	$ 121.95	
Full price with added service		$61.95	$46.76	$60.00	$168.71	
Bundled services		$57.95	$38.76	$56.00	$ 152.71	$192.00
Family example: Home phone, Internet, Cable TV, and cellphone						
Full-price services	$41.94	$61.95		$60.00	$ 163.89	
Full price with added service	$41.94	$61.95	$46.76	$60.00	$ 210.65	
Bundled services	$37.94	$57.95	$38.76	$56.00	$ 190.65	$240.00

Source: Prices from "Bundle and Save," http://bundles.bell.ca/en (accessed July 29, 2013).

Similarly, a family could be currently subscribing to home phone, cellphone, and Internet service through Bell for $163.89/month, while obtaining its cable TV service from another provider. Again, by bundling the services, Bell can entice the family to switch its cable TV service to Bell by reducing the price of the other services. Adding the new service increases the monthly fee to $190.65, but the family saves $240.00/year compared to the regular-priced services and will also enjoy the convenience of receiving a single bill each month.

Leader Pricing **Leader pricing** is a tactic that attempts to build store traffic by aggressively pricing and advertising a regularly purchased item, often priced at or just above the store's cost. The rationale behind this tactic is that, while in the store to get the great deal on, say, milk, the consumer will also probably pick up other items he or she needs. The store has priced these items at higher profit margins, so their purchase will more than cover the lower markup on the milk. Imagine the marketing potential of various combinations of products; the store uses leader pricing on cocktail sauce, which gives employees the perfect opportunity to ask, "How about a pound of fresh shrimp to go with the cocktail sauce you're purchasing?"

leader pricing
Consumer pricing tactic that attempts to build store traffic by aggressively pricing and advertising a regularly purchased item, often priced at or just above the store's cost.

Consumer Price Reductions

The final price a customer pays for a product or service often has been adjusted from the original price because marketers have used various techniques designed to enhance value. Some of these techniques include markdowns, quantity discounts, coupons, and rebates.

Markdowns **Markdowns** are the reductions retailers take on the initial selling price of the product or service.[48] An integral component of the high/low pricing strategy we described previously, markdowns enable retailers to get rid of slow-moving or obsolete merchandise, sell seasonal items after the appropriate season, and match competitors'

markdowns
Reductions retailers take on the initial selling price of the product or service.

Customers get a size discount for buying larger sizes. With Cheerios, the larger the box, the less it costs per gram.

size discount
The most common implementation of a quantity discount at the consumer level; the larger the quantity bought, the less the cost per unit (e.g., per gram).

coupon
Provides a stated discount to consumers on the final selling price of a specific item; the retailer handles the discount.

rebate
A consumer discount in which a portion of the purchase price is returned to the buyer in cash; the manufacturer, not the retailer, issues the refund.

seasonal discount
Pricing tactic of offering an additional reduction as an incentive to retailers to order merchandise in advance of the normal buying season.

prices on specific merchandise. Retailers must get rid of merchandise that isn't selling because holding on to such items hurts the retailer's image and ties up money in inventory that could be used more productively elsewhere.

Retailers also use markdowns to promote merchandise and increase sales. Particularly when used in conjunction with promotions, markdowns can increase traffic into the store, which many retailers view as half the battle. Once customers are in the store, retailers always hope they will purchase other products at regular prices.

Quantity Discounts for Consumers We have already discussed how firms use quantity discounts in the B2B marketplace, but the most common implementation of a quantity discount at the consumer level is the **size discount**. For example, there are three sizes of General Mills' popular cereal Cheerios: 425 gram, 575 gram, and 1.5 kilogram boxes, priced at approximately $4.19, $4.49, and $6.89, respectively. The larger the quantity, the less the cost per gram, which means the manufacturer is providing a quantity discount. Most grocery stores now post the price per 100 grams on the shelves so consumers can easily compare value for money. The goal of this tactic is to encourage consumers to purchase larger quantities each time they buy. In turn, these consumers are less likely to switch brands and often tend to consume more of the product, depending on the product usage characteristics. Typically, buying a larger package of toilet tissue does not mean consumers will use it faster, but buying a larger box of cereal may encourage them to eat more of it or to eat it more often.[49]

Coupons and Rebates Coupons and rebates both provide discounts to consumers on the final selling price. However, for the **coupon**, the retailer handles the discount, whereas the manufacturer issues the refund in the case of the **rebate**, which is defined as a portion of the purchase price returned to the buyer in the form of cash.

The goal of coupons is to prompt consumers to try a product, reward loyal customers, or encourage repurchases. By saving the consumer money, firms add value to their products. Whereas a coupon provides instant savings when presented, a rebate promises savings, usually mailed to the consumer at some later date. The "hassle factor" for rebates is higher than for coupons; the consumer must first buy the item during a specified time period, then mail in the required documentation—which usually includes the original sales receipt—and finally wait four to six weeks (or more!) for a cheque to arrive. Although consumers may believe this process adds value when the potential rebate is $50, they might question whether a rebate for a couple of dollars is worth their time and effort. From the marketer's viewpoint, however, rebates offer greater control than coupons and provide valuable customer information. Coupons and rebates are considered to be sales promotion tools as well as pricing tactics so you'll read more about them in Chapter 15.

Business-to-Business Pricing Tactics and Discounts

The pricing tactics employed in B2B settings differ significantly from those used in consumer markets. Among the most prominent are seasonal and cash discounts, allowances, quantity discounts, and uniform delivered versus geographic pricing (see Exhibit 11.9).

Seasonal Discounts A **seasonal discount** is an additional reduction offered as an incentive to retailers to order merchandise in advance of the normal buying season. For instance, Lennox may offer its air conditioning dealers an additional seasonal discount if they place their orders and receive delivery before April 1, prior to the warm months when air conditioner sales are highest. If it can ship earlier in the season, Lennox can plan

EXHIBIT 11.9	B2B Pricing Tactics

Tactic	
Seasonal discounts	An additional reduction offered as an incentive to retailers to order merchandise in advance of the normal buying season.
Cash discounts	An additional reduction that reduces the invoice cost if the buyer pays the invoice prior to the end of the discount period.
Allowances	Advertising or listing allowances (additional price reductions) offered in return for specific behaviours. *Advertising allowances* are offered to retailers if they agree to feature the manufacturer's product in their advertising and promotional efforts. *Listing allowances* are offered to get new products into stores or to gain more or better shelf space.
Quantity discounts	Providing a reduced price according to the amount purchased.
Uniform delivered versus geographic pricing	With *uniform* delivered pricing, the shipper charges one rate, no matter where the buyer is located. With *geographic pricing*, different prices are charged depending on the geographical delivery area.

its production schedules more easily and lessen its finished goods inventory. Its dealers, however, must weigh the benefits of a larger profit because of the discount versus the extra cost of carrying the inventory for a longer period of time.

Cash Discounts   A **cash discount** reduces the invoice cost if the buyer pays the invoice prior to the end of the discount period. Typically, it is expressed in the form of a percentage, such as "3/10, n/30," or "3 percent, 10 days, net 30," all of which means the buyer can take a 3 percent discount on the total amount of the invoice if the bill is paid within 10 days of the invoice date; otherwise, the full, or net, amount is due within 30 days. Why do B2B sellers offer cash discounts to customers? By encouraging early payment, they benefit from the time value of money. Getting money earlier rather than later enables the firm to either invest the money to earn a return on it or to avoid borrowing money and paying interest on it. In both instances, the firm is better off financially.

Allowances   Another pricing tactic that lowers the final cost to channel members is allowances, such as advertising or listing allowances, offered in return for specific behaviours. An **advertising allowance** offers a price reduction to channel members if they agree to feature the manufacturer's product in their advertising and promotional efforts. **Listing allowances** are fees paid to retailers simply to get new products into stores or to gain more or better shelf space for their products. Some argue that listing allowances are unethical because they put small manufacturers that cannot readily afford allowances at a competitive disadvantage. Demanding large listing allowances could be considered a form of bribery—that is, paying off the retailer to get preferential treatment.

Quantity Discounts   A **quantity discount** provides a reduced price according to the amount purchased. The more the buyer purchases, the higher the discount and, of course, the greater the value.

A **cumulative quantity discount** uses the amount purchased over a specified time period and usually involves several transactions. This type of discount encourages resellers to maintain their current supplier because the cost to switch must include the loss of the discount. For example, automobile dealers often attempt to meet a quota or a sales goal for a specific period, such as a quarter or a year. If they meet their quotas, they earn discounts on all the cars they purchased from the manufacturer during that period in the form of a rebate cheque. For this very reason, you will often find good deals on cars at the end of a quarter or fiscal year. If the dealership can just sell a few more cars to meet

cash discount
Tactic of offering a reduction in the invoice cost if the buyer pays the invoice prior to the end of the discount period.

advertising allowance
Tactic of offering a price reduction to channel members if they agree to feature the manufacturer's product in their advertising and promotional efforts.

listing allowances
Fees paid to retailers simply to get new products into stores or to gain more or better shelf space for their products.

quantity discount
Pricing tactic of offering a reduced price according to the amount purchased; the more the buyer purchases, the higher the discount and, of course, the greater the value.

cumulative quantity discount
Pricing tactic that offers a discount based on the amount purchased over a specified period and usually involves several transactions.

its quota, the rebate earned can be substantial, so taking a few hundred dollars less on those last few cars is well worth the opportunity to receive a rebate worth many times the amount of the losses.

noncumulative quantity discount
Pricing tactic that offers a discount based on only the amount purchased in a single order.

A **noncumulative quantity discount**, though still a quantity discount, is based only on the amount purchased in a single order. Therefore, it provides the buyer with an incentive to purchase more merchandise immediately. Such larger, less frequent orders can save manufacturers order processing, sales, and transportation expenses. For example, a jeans store might get a 40 percent discount off the manufacturer's suggested retail price for placing a $500 order; a 50 percent discount for an order of $501 to $4,999, and a 60 percent discount for an order greater than $5,000.

Uniform Delivered Versus Geographic Pricing These pricing tactics are specific to shipping, which represents a major cost for many manufacturers. With a **uniform delivered pricing** tactic, the shipper charges one rate, no matter where the buyer is located, which makes things very simple for both the seller and the buyer. **Geographic pricing**, however, sets different prices depending on a geographical division of the delivery areas. For example, a manufacturer based in Montreal might divide Canada into five different zones and use different shipping rates for each zone to reflect the average shipping cost for customers located therein. This way, each customer in a zone is charged the same cost for shipping. Geographic pricing can be advantageous to the shipper because it reflects the actual shipping charges more closely than uniform delivered pricing can.

uniform delivered pricing
The shipper charges one rate, no matter where the buyer is located.

geographic pricing
The setting of different prices depending on a geographical division of the delivery areas.

With so many different pricing strategies and tactics, it is no wonder that unscrupulous firms find ample opportunity to engage in pricing practices that can hurt consumers. We now take a look at some of the legal and ethical implications of pricing.

L05 | LEGAL AND ETHICAL ASPECTS OF PRICING

Prices tend to fluctuate naturally and respond to varying market conditions. Though we rarely see firms attempting to control the market in terms of product quality or advertising, they often engage in pricing practices that can unfairly reduce competition or harm consumers directly through fraud and deception. A host of laws and regulations at both the federal, provincial, and municipal levels attempt to prevent unfair pricing practices, but some are poorly enforced, and others are difficult to prove.

Deceptive or Illegal Price Advertising

Is this a legitimate sale or is the retailer using deceptive reference prices?

Although it is always illegal and unethical to lie in advertising, a certain amount of "puffery" is typically allowed (see Chapter 15). But price advertisements should never deceive consumers to the point of causing harm. For example, a local car dealer's advertising that it had the "best deals in town" would likely be considered puffery. In contrast, advertising "the lowest prices, guaranteed" makes a very specific claim and, if not true, can be considered deceptive.

Deceptive Reference Prices Previously, we introduced reference prices, which create reference points for the buyer against which to compare the selling price. If the reference price is bona fide, the advertisement is informative. If the reference price has been inflated or is just plain fictitious, however, the advertisement is deceptive and may cause harm to consumers. The Competition

Bureau fined Suzy Shier $1 million after an investigation revealed that the company placed price tags on garments showing a "regular" price and a "sale" price when in fact the clothes had not been sold in any significant quantity for any reasonable time at the "regular" price.[50] But it is not easy to determine whether a reference price is bona fide. If an advertisement specifies a "regular price," what qualifies as regular? How many units must the store sell at this price for it to be a bona fide regular price? Finally, what if the store offers the item for sale at the regular price but customers do not buy any? Can it still be considered a regular price? In general, if a seller is going to label a price as a regular price, the Better Business Bureau suggests that at least 50 percent of the sales have occurred at that price.[51]

Loss Leader Pricing As we discussed previously, leader pricing is a legitimate attempt to build store traffic by pricing a regularly purchased item aggressively but still above the store's cost. **Loss leader pricing** takes this tactic one step further by lowering the price below the store's cost. No doubt you have seen "buy one, get one free" offers at grocery and discount stores. Unless the markup for the item is 100 percent of the cost, these sales obviously do not generate enough revenue from the sale of one unit to cover the store's cost, which means it has essentially priced the total for both items below cost.

loss leader pricing
Loss leader pricing takes the tactic of leader pricing one step further by lowering the price below the store's cost.

Bait and Switch Another form of deceptive price advertising occurs when sellers advertise items for a very low price without the intent to really sell any. This **bait and switch** tactic is a deceptive practice because the store lures customers in with a very low price on an item (the bait), only to aggressively pressure these customers into purchasing a higher-priced item (the switch) by disparaging the low-priced item, comparing it unfavourably with the higher-priced model, or professing an inadequate supply of the lower-priced item. Again, the laws against bait and switch practices are difficult to enforce because salespeople, simply as a function of their jobs, are always trying to get customers to trade up to a higher-priced model without necessarily deliberately baiting them. The key to proving deception centres on the intent of the seller, which is also difficult to prove.

bait and switch
A deceptive practice of luring customers into the store with a very low advertised price on an item (the bait), only to aggressively pressure them into purchasing a higher-priced item (the switch) by disparaging the low-priced item, comparing it unfavourably with the higher-priced model, or professing an inadequate supply of the lower-priced item.

Predatory Pricing

When a firm sets a very low price for one or more of its products with the intent to drive its competition out of business, it is using **predatory pricing**. Predatory pricing is illegal under the Competition Act because it constrains free trade and represents a form of unfair competition. It also tends to promote a concentrated market with a few dominant firms (an oligopoly).

But again, predation is difficult to prove. First, one must demonstrate intent—that is, that the firm intended to drive out its competition or prevent competitors from entering the market. Second, the complainant must prove that the firm charged prices lower than its average cost, an equally difficult task.

predatory pricing
A firm's practice of setting a very low price for one or more of its products with the intent of driving its competition out of business; illegal under the Competition Act.

Price Discrimination

There are many forms of price discrimination, but only some of them are considered illegal under the Competition Act. When firms sell the same product to different resellers (wholesalers, distributors, or retailers) at different prices, it can be considered **price discrimination**; usually, larger firms receive lower prices.

We have already discussed the use of quantity discounts, which is a legitimate method of charging different prices to different customers on the basis of the quantity they purchase. The legality of this tactic stems from the assumption that it costs less to sell and service 1,000 units to one customer than 100 units to 10 customers. But quantity discounts must be available to all customers and not be structured in such a way that they consistently and obviously favour one or a few buyers over others. Still,

price discrimination
The practice of selling the same product to different resellers (wholesalers, distributors, or retailers) or to the ultimate consumer at different prices; some, but not all, forms of price discrimination are illegal.

Is this price
discrimination illegal?

some marketers have found ways to get around these rules, for example, offering "preferred member" pricing. The Competition Act requires companies to demonstrate only that their price discounts do not restrict competition. While quantity discounts may be a grey area, it is perfectly legitimate to charge a different price to a reseller if the firm is attempting to meet a specific competitor's price. In addition, a barter agreement, in which buyers and sellers negotiate a mutually agreed upon price, is commonplace and absolutely legal in retail settings such as car sales and collectibles markets.

Price Fixing

price fixing
The practice of colluding with other firms to control prices.

Price fixing is the practice of colluding with other firms to control prices. Tate & Lyle, which makes Splenda, a low-calorie sweetener, agreed to pay $650,000 to settle a lawsuit in British Columbia that accused sugar substitute companies of conspiring to fix prices in the 1980s and 1990s.[52] More recently, the former head of Nestlé Canada and two other executives were criminally charged with price fixing after a six-year investigation by the Competition Bureau. Charges were also laid against Cadbury Adams Canada, Mars Canada, and Hershey Canada for colluding with Nestlé to raise prices of chocolate products. Penalties for price fixing include fines of up to $10 million and up to five years in prison.[53] The four companies deny the allegations yet agreed to pay $23.2 million to settle the lawsuit.[54]

horizontal price fixing
Occurs when competitors that produce and sell competing products collude, or work together, to control prices, effectively taking price out of the decision process for consumers.

This particular case of price fixing is especially interesting because it includes both horizontal and vertical price fixing. **Horizontal price fixing** occurs when competitors that produce and sell competing products collude, or work together, to control prices, effectively taking price out of the decision process for consumers. In one case, prosecutors alleged that horizontal price fixing had occurred among record companies that specified pricing terms associated with the sale and distribution of CDs. **Vertical price fixing** occurs when parties at different levels of the same marketing channel (e.g., manufacturers and retailers) collude to control the prices passed on to consumers. In the music industry case, prosecutors alleged that the music companies colluded with music retailers to maintain retail prices for CDs.

vertical price fixing
Occurs when parties at different levels of the same marketing channel (e.g., manufacturers and retailers) collude to control the prices passed on to consumers.

As these legal issues clearly demonstrate, pricing decisions involve many ethical considerations. In determining both their pricing strategies and their pricing tactics, marketers must always balance their goal of inducing customers, through price, to find value and the need to deal honestly and fairly with those same customers. Whether another business or an individual consumer, buyers can be influenced by a variety of pricing methods; it is up to marketers to determine which of these methods works best for the seller, the buyer, and the community.

LEARNING OBJECTIVES REVIEW

 Explain what price is and its importance in establishing value in marketing

Price is the only element of the marketing mix that generates revenues. It is also half the value equation. Although costs and other factors should be taken into consideration when setting prices, the most important factor is how the customer views the price in relationship to what he or she receives.

 Illustrate how the five Cs—company objectives, customers, costs, competition, and channel members—influence pricing decisions

Successful pricing strategies are built on the five Cs—company objectives, customers, costs, competition, and channel members. Company goals and objectives set the framework for pricing strategies. Companies focusing on image set high prices, while those that focus on value tend to use everyday low prices. Understanding customers' reactions to different prices helps marketers set prices that are consistent with their customers' attitudes and preferences. The demand curve and price elasticity of demand are two related tools that marketers use to gauge customers' sensitivity to prices changes. Customers' income and the availability of substitute products also influence customers' reaction to price changes. The third C, costs, is a major determinant of pricing. Cost of producing a good helps marketers determine the possible prices they can charge and the levels of profitability they can expect. Break-even analysis is a helpful tool that is used to help marketers determine the price level at which the number of units sold exactly covers the cost of producing the good. The fourth C, competition, influences pricing because a firm usually pays close attention and reacts to a competitor's moves. Intense competition may produce price wars. The level of competition is usually determined by the market structure of the industry. That is, whether the industry structure is oligopolistic, monopolistic, pure competition, or a monopoly. The final, C, channel members—manufacturers, wholesalers, retailers—influence prices because they play a key role in getting the product to the final consumer, and they are independent and usually have their own objectives and competitive situation to deal with. The company may want to set a certain price level for its products in order to reflect quality and value, but retailers may decide they want to move more volume and so reduce the price, hence the possibility for conflict. Also, manufacturers may give discounts to channel members, which may influence the price the ultimate consumer pays.

 Describe various pricing methods (e.g., cost-based pricing, competitor-based pricing, and value-based pricing) and strategies (e.g., new product pricing, and psychological pricing) used in marketing

The various methods of setting prices each have their own set of advantages and disadvantages. The fixed percentage and markup approaches are quick and easy but fail to reflect the competitive environment or consumer demand. Although it is always advisable to be aware of what competitors are doing, using competitor-based pricing should not occur in isolation without considering consumers' reactions. Taking a value-based approach to pricing, whether the improvement value or the total cost of ownership, in conjunction with these other methods provides a nicely balanced method of setting prices.

Companies tend to use different pricing strategies for different products or different markets. Pricing strategies are a long-term approach to pricing products. The various pricing strategies can be grouped into three broad categories: cost-based strategies, value-based strategies, and competitor-based strategies. Cost-based strategies are based on the firm ascertaining the cost of producing and marketing the product, and then adding some markup for profit. Competitor-based pricing is based on a firm understanding what competitors are doing and reacting accordingly. Firms may choose to set prices below, at, or above competitors' prices. Value-based pricing is based on a firm understanding consumers' perceptions of value as reflected in the price of the product (e.g., cheap, expensive, bargain). Consumers' assessments of value may be influenced by their reference prices of similar products or may use marketers' prices to infer a price–quality relationship. Marketers often use price skimming or penetration pricing when they introduce new products in the marketplace based on the nature of the product and their marketing goals; for example, whether they want to gain market share, show price leadership, or signal innovation.

LO4 **Identify pricing tactics targeted to channel members and consumers**

Pricing tactics focus more on the short-term aspects of the five Cs of pricing. Companies may use a wide variety of pricing tactics from two categories: (1) business-to-business pricing tactics and discounts, and (2) pricing tactics aimed at consumers. B2B pricing tactics and discounts usually include seasonal discounts, cash discounts, quantity discounts, allowances, and geographic pricing. Pricing tactics aimed at consumers include markdowns, quantity and seasonal discounts, and coupons and rebates.

LO5 **Summarize the legal and ethical issues involved in pricing**

There are almost as many ways to get into trouble by setting or changing a price as there are pricing strategies and tactics. Three of the most common legal issues pertain to advertising deceptive prices. Specifically, if a firm compares a reduced price with a "regular" or reference price, it must actually have sold that product or service at the regular price. Advertising the sale of products priced below the retailer's cost constitutes an unfair competitive practice, as does bait and switch advertising. Charging different prices to different customers is sometimes, but not always, illegal, whereas any collusion among firms to fix prices is always illegal.

KEY TERMS

- advertising allowance
- bait and switch
- break-even point
- cash discount
- competitive parity
- competitor orientation
- competitor-based pricing method
- complementary products
- contribution per unit
- cost of ownership method
- cost-based pricing method
- coupon
- cross-price elasticity
- cross-shopping
- cumulative quantity discount
- customer orientation
- demand curve
- elastic
- everyday low pricing (EDLP)
- experience curve effect
- fixed costs
- geographic pricing
- grey market

- high/low pricing
- horizontal price fixing
- improvement value
- income effect
- inelastic
- leader pricing
- listing allowances
- loss leader pricing
- markdowns
- market penetration pricing
- maximizing profits strategy
- monopolistic competition
- monopoly
- noncumulative quantity discount
- odd prices
- oligopolistic competition
- predatory pricing
- prestige products or services
- price bundling
- price discrimination
- price elasticity of demand
- price fixing
- price lining

- price skimming
- price war
- pricing tactics
- profit orientation
- pure competition
- quantity discount
- rebate
- reference price
- sales orientation
- seasonal discount
- showrooming
- size discount
- substitute products
- substitution effect
- target profit pricing
- target return pricing
- total cost
- uniform delivered pricing
- value-based pricing method
- variable costs
- vertical price fixing

CONCEPT REVIEW

1. Explain the importance of pricing in the marketing mix from the perspective of the firm and the consumer.

2. List the five Cs of pricing. Which one do you consider to be the most important and why?

3. Explain how companies try to determine consumers' sensitivity to price changes. What factors influence their price sensitivity?

4. Why is it important for firms to determine costs when setting prices?

5. Why does a company need to understand a product's break-even point?

6. How has the Internet changed the way some people use price to make purchasing decisions?

7. What is the major difference between pricing strategies and pricing tactics? Give three examples of each.

8. Explain how psychological factors may influence a firm's pricing strategy.

9. In what conditions should a price skimming strategy be used? When is it appropriate to use a market penetration strategy?

10. Explain the four types of illegal or unethical pricing practices.

MARKETING APPLICATIONS

1. You and your two roommates are starting a pet grooming service to help put yourself through university. There are two other well-established pet services in your area. Should you set your price higher or lower than that of the competition? Justify your answer.

2. One roommate believes the most important objective in setting prices for the new pet grooming business is to generate a large profit, while keeping an eye on your competitors' prices; the other roommate believes it is important to maximize sales and set prices according to what your customers expect to pay. Who is right and why?

3. Assume you have decided to buy an advertisement in the local newspaper to publicize your new pet grooming service. The cost of the ad is $1000. You have decided to charge $40 for a dog grooming, and you want to make $20 on each dog. How many dogs do you have to groom to break even on the cost of the ad? What is your break-even point if you charge $50 per dog?

4. On your weekly grocery shopping trip, you notice that the price of ground beef has gone up 50 cents a kilogram. How will this price increase affect the demand for ground beef, ground turkey, and hamburger buns? Explain your answer in terms of the price elasticity of demand.

5. Zinc Energy Resources Co., a new division of a major battery manufacturing company, recently patented a new battery that uses zinc-air technology. The unit costs for the zinc-air battery are as follows: battery housing, $8; materials $6; and direct labour, $6 per unit. Retooling the existing factory facilities to manufacture the zinc-air batteries amounts to an additional $1 million in equipment costs. Annual fixed costs include sales, marketing, and advertising expenses of $1 million; general and administrative expenses of $1 million; and other fixed costs totalling $2 million.

   a. What is the total per-unit variable cost associated with the new battery?

   b. What are the total fixed costs for the new battery?

   c. If the price for the new battery was set at $35, what would the break-even point be?

6. How do pricing strategies vary across markets that are characterized by monopoly, monopolistic, oligopolistic, and pure competition?

7. Though the practice is not illegal, many firms operating over the Internet have been experimenting with charging different consumers different prices for the same product or service. Since stores in different parts of the country might have different prices, some websites require postal code information before providing prices. Why would retailers charge different prices in different markets or postal codes? Is it ethical for retailers to do so? Is it a good business practice?

8. Suppose you have been hired as the pricing manager for a grocery store chain that typically adds a fixed percentage onto the cost of each product to arrive at the retail price. Evaluate this technique. What would you do differently?

9. Coupons and rebates benefit different channel members. Which would you prefer if you were a manufacturer, a retailer, and a consumer? Why?

10. Imagine that you are the newly hired brand manager for a T-shirt company whose new line is about to come out. Because of a major fashion magazine's very positive review of the line, the company wants to reposition the brand as a premium youth brand. Your boss asks what price you should charge for the new T-shirt line. The current line, considered mid-range retail, is priced at $20. What steps might you undertake to determine what the new price should be?

TOOLKIT

BREAK-EVEN ANALYSIS

A shoe manufacturer has recently opened a new manufacturing plant in Asia. The total fixed costs are $50 million. It plans to sell the shoes to retailers for $50, and its variable costs (material and labour) are $25 per pair. Calculate the break-even volume. Now see what would happen to the break-even volume if the fixed costs were increased to $60 million because of the purchase of new equipment, or the variable costs were decreased to $20 because of a new quantity discount provided by the supplier. Use the toolkit provided on Connect to experiment with changes in fixed cost, variable cost, and selling price to see what happens to break-even volume.

NET SAVVY

1. Several different pricing models can be found on the Internet. Each model appeals to different customer groups. Go to http://www.ebay.com and try to buy this book. What pricing options and prices are available? Do you believe that everyone will choose the least expensive option? Why or why not? Now go to http://www.amazon.ca. Is there more than one price available for this book? If so, what are those prices? If you had to buy another copy of this book, where would you buy it, and why would you buy it there?

2. Prices can vary depending on the market being served. Because Dell sells its computers directly to consumers all around the world, the Dell website makes it easy to compare prices for various markets. Go to http://www.dell.com. Begin on the Dell Canada site and determine the price of a Dimension 3000 desktop computer. Next go to the Dell U.K. website and another country of your choice to find the price of the same computer. (If you need to convert currency, go to http://www.xe.com.) How does the price of the desktop computer vary? What would account for these differences in price?

CHAPTER CASE STUDY

BATTLE ROYALE: APPLE VERSUS AMAZON[55]

As commentators far and wide have acknowledged, Apple radically changed the music industry when it introduced the iPod and its affiliated iTunes site. The very way musicians and media companies marketed music had to change in response, and one of the most significant changes occurred with regard to pricing.

Apple set the pricing model. Most songs on iTunes sell for around 99 cents, and album costs usually equal the single-song price multiplied by the number of songs on that album. In creating this pricing model, Apple also instituted a technology unique to digital music, namely, digital rights management (DRM). This technology ensures that songs will expire or prevents them from being shared multiple times or between multiple devices. Thus, one consumer cannot download a song, copy it innumerable times, and share it with all of her friends. Although DRM technology therefore protects copyright holders, it also seems to frustrate consumers.

Apple also dictated that its iPods, iPhones, and related devices would play only songs equipped with its own proprietary FairPlay DRM solution or those without any DRM protection at all. Producers were faced with an either–or choice: Use iTunes or go DRM free. Many music companies, including Warner Music Group, swore they would never allow their songs to be sold without DRM protection. However, Warner has since made its music catalogue available DRM-free through Amazon's MP3 store.

Apple has thus far refused to license FairPlay to any other music players. Therefore, the company has almost a stranglehold on the digital music market and limits the markets for media companies to iPod or iPhone owners who use the FairPlay DRM.

Everything changed when Amazon.com started selling music downloads of Universal and EMI songs without any DRM protection at all. The days in which music companies could tell listeners when and how they might listen to their songs essentially were over. The online retailer's offering contains about 2 million songs that sell, on average, for 40 percent less than they would cost through iTunes.

The likely result seems to be an all-out price war. In just a few years, Apple and iTunes could be forced to engage in the kind of deep discounting that Tower Records and CD Warehouse undertook in the years before digital downloads swept both aside. Such a price war could help rejuvenate the sales of songs and albums, and perhaps lower prices for consumers.

The price war also could quickly decrease the margins of music stores such as Amazon and Apple. In announcing its new music store, Amazon didn't say how the discounts would affect its margins, but the implications cannot be minor.

Yet according to one music industry insider, the industry "needs to have a lot of successful retailers or they won't have a growing market. You can't satisfy consumers if there is only one place to buy music. In every industry, you see market growth when there are lots of different places to buy the product."

The music companies that have signed up with Amazon currently are making less on each copy sold, and the copies include no protections against copying or expiration dates. The situation may be headed into a price war, which will mean smaller margins for all the players.

Questions

1. Who are the key players in this industry?

2. Why do you think different music companies, such as Warner and Universal, have taken such different stances on DRM protection?

3. What would represent an effective response by Apple to Amazon's lower prices? Should it lower download prices to match the offer? Why or why not?

4. If a price war will reduce margins, as the case suggests, why would any company embrace this strategy?

CHAPTER **12**

Distribution Channels

When a company saves a dollar by increasing the efficiency of its distribution system, the overall benefits are worth much more than that single dollar. So for example, if a retailer can get its goods to its stores quickly, in the right quantities, and when its customers want them, customers are happy, which ultimately increases sales and profits. At the same time, the retailer can reduce one of its costliest expenses, namely its distribution costs. Also, because of these distribution systems, manufacturers that sell products in their own stores have a good sense of how much they need to make and when, which reduces their inventory costs. Thus profits rise, and everyone is happy.

That claim is perhaps too simplistic, but when we consider Walmart, the largest retailer in the world, it seems about right. Most of Walmart's power—in terms of setting prices, growing rapidly, and pleasing customers—stems directly from its notable innovations in distribution channel and supply chain management. Its influence has also spread to its vendors, altering the way they manufacture and deliver merchandise.

Walmart's co-operation with the consumer goods giant Procter & Gamble (P&G) is unusual in its scope. Software links the two corporations closely, such that the moment Walmart's distribution centres run out of a certain brand or size of a P&G product, P&G initiates a shipment to replenish it. Such co-operation helps P&G plan its production, but it also enables Walmart to track arrivals at its distribution centres and co-ordinate shipments to stores more effectively.

Other innovations (many of which have been copied throughout the retail industry) by Walmart include extensive information systems, to transmit the millions of point-of-sale transactions that take place in its stores everyday; cross-docking to ensure that approximately half the goods that arrive at a distribution centre move out to stores within 24 hours; the widespread adoption of bar codes and radio frequency identification tags for keeping track of inventory; and consolidated global sourcing to purchase directly from suppliers rather than relying on third-party procurement services.[1]

Even with its remarkable supply chain successes, Walmart is hesitant to rest on its laurels, so it constantly reviews its supply chain to find new efficiencies. In recent years, the company has sought out ways to keep its delivery trucks full more often, instead of allowing them to make return trips with empty trailers.

Many of the retailer's 6,500 trucks and 55,000 trailers now pick up goods directly from manufacturers, rather than just travelling back and forth from stores to a distribution centre (though they still make these trips, of course). As a result, its travel miles have fallen by 100 million miles relative to the past year—simply by reducing the number of trips and avoiding trucks on the move with empty trailers.[2]

In all of these cases, Walmart's superior distribution channel and supply chain management has enabled it to reap the rewards of higher levels of customer service and satisfaction, lower production and transportation costs, and more productive uses of its retail space. Fundamentally, Walmart has a unique ability to link together suppliers, distribution centres, retail outlets, and, ultimately, customers, regardless of their location. As a result, the cost savings achieved by both Walmart and its suppliers benefit their bottom lines. Even more, when those cost savings are passed on, they benefit customers in the form of lower prices, which is another reason for them to shop the world's largest retailer. ▌

In this chapter, we discuss the third P, place, which includes all activities required to get the right product to the right customer when that customer wants it. Students of marketing often overlook or underestimate the importance of place in the marketing mix simply because it happens behind the scenes. Yet distribution channels, or place, add value for customers because they get products to customers efficiently: quickly and at low cost.

We begin by understanding the importance of distribution, how distribution channels are designed, how they are structured, and how they are managed. Then we move to a discussion of the supply chain and the critical role it plays in distribution strategy. We end the chapter by examining how logistics management integrates activities from the efficient flow of raw materials through to the delivery of finished goods.

LO1   THE IMPORTANCE OF DISTRIBUTION

So far in this book, we've examined how companies conduct in-depth market research, gain insights into consumer and business behaviour, carefully segment markets and select the best target markets, develop new products and services, and set prices that signal good value. However, even if they execute these activities flawlessly, if they are unable to secure appropriate distribution channels that reach prospective customers, their products and services are unlikely to ever meet their revenue targets.

Convincing intermediaries, such as wholesalers and retailers, to carry new products can prove to be more difficult than you might think. For example, a typical grocery store may carry between 30,000 and 40,000 different items. But a good number of these would have to be cleared off the shelves to make room for all the new foods, beverages, household goods, pet products, and other miscellaneous items launched each year. With dozens of new products being introduced each day, the fight for shelf space is fierce. For many companies, distribution is not only difficult, but also expensive and involves paying listing fees to get shelf space, as we discuss later in the chapter.

All goods and services organizations need a well-thought-out distribution strategy to convince retailers to carry their products. PenAgain, a small manufacturer of ergonomic pens and other writing instruments, wanted to put its offerings in Walmart stores, but first it had to convince Walmart to buy its products.[3] After tough negotiations, Walmart agreed to give PenAgain a one-month trial in 500 stores, but only if it lowered its costs. PenAgain moved production overseas to meet this requirement. Walmart provided no marketing support and since PenAgain was too small to afford traditional print or television advertising, it developed a viral marketing program and produced displays to use in the stores. To keep track of sales, it relied on Walmart's Internet-based Retail Link system, and hired a firm that sends representatives into stores to check out display placement and customer traffic. Finally, PenAgain also agreed to adhere to strict packaging, labelling, and shipping requirements. And remember, for all this effort, its entry in stores was only a test, and a very expensive gamble! But if it could succeed in Walmart stores, PenAgain would be well on its way to prosperity.

As seen in Entrepreneurial Marketing 12.1, a good distribution strategy that is integrated with other marketing mix elements is key to the successful launch of a new product.

 **Entrepreneurial Marketing 12.1**   **Chocolate with a Purpose[4]**

Reading this chapter and struggling to stay awake? The founders of AWAKE Chocolate hope that their caffeinated chocolate bar will become your new study buddy. Think KitKat meets Red Bull, or, as a cofounder Matt Schnarr says, "chocolate with a purpose." Schnarr and two friends, Dan Tzotzis and Adam Deremo, had worked together at Pepsi. With backgrounds in Consumer Packaged Goods (CPG) they followed macro trends to see what was driving sales of food products. Companies took existing products and shook them up by adding new ingredients such as probiotics in yogurt, vitamins in water, or caffeine in energy drinks. Although the energy drink category was exploding and was very profitable, the three partners noted that most drinks were expensive and didn't taste very good. A caffeinated chocolate bar could compete in the energy drink space and at a lower cost.

When Schnarr, Tzotzis, and Deremo launched AWAKE Chocolate in 2012, they knew they needed to do things right to get shelf space for their new product. Packaging and pricing quickly became two key elements in their distribution strategy. So they abandoned their first package design and hired Seattle-based ad agency Tether. Its chief creative officer, Stanley Hainsworth, who had worked with Lego, Starbucks, and Nike, was tasked with designing an eye-catching package for AWAKE. The chocolate bar category is crowded so the package had to jump off the shelf and grab the attention of consumers. The new design featuring mascot Nevill the Owl was used to introduce the product to the brand's primary target market of 18- to 25-year-olds in

AWAKE Chocolate cofounders knew their packaging had to stand out in order to get shelf space.

a back-to-school sampling campaign on university campuses.

Pricing was another element AWAKE founders knew would impact distribution. Since most energy drinks were sold through gas stations and convenience stores, these outlets became key distribution channels. A decision was made to price the caffeinated chocolate bars at a premium, still lower than energy drinks but higher than regular chocolate bars. The rationale to sell at $2.49 was to "margin up" the category, since vendors would be more likely to carry the product knowing they could make more margin on AWAKE than on a regular chocolate bar.

They pitched their concept on CBC's *Dragons' Den* only four weeks after they first started shipping products and signed a deal with David Chilton. They already had distribution in gas bars (Husky, Shell) and drug stores (Shoppers Drug Mart, Rexall.) Two days after they taped the show, they got a listing at Loblaws. This was followed with a host of other gas stations, convenience and grocery stores, and university campus stores. Not only did AWAKE get distribution in Canada, it was also able to get shelf space in the United States in similar outlets.

Less than a year later, the company had booked $1 million in total sales and increased distribution to 10,000 locations. A new, smaller format was introduced (one third the size and with half the amount of caffeine of the original product) in an effort to make consumption more of an everyday ritual. With a product that tastes like a chocolate bar but performs like coffee, and good distribution, the company will keep consumers awake.

Distribution Channels, Supply Chain, and Logistics Are Related

distribution channel
The institutions that transfer the ownership of and move goods from the point of production to the point of consumption.

supply chain management
Refers to a set of approaches and techniques firms employ to efficiently and effectively integrate their suppliers, manufacturers, warehouses, stores, and transportation intermediaries into a seamless value chain in which merchandise is produced and distributed in the right quantities, to the right locations, and at the right time.

wholesalers
Those firms engaged in buying, taking title to, often storing, and physically handling goods in large quantities, and then reselling the goods (usually in smaller quantities) to retailers or industrial or business users.

People often talk about distribution channel management, supply chain management, and logistics management as if they were the same thing. It's because these business practices are closely interrelated. A **distribution channel** is the set of institutions that transfer the ownership of and move goods from the point of production to the point of consumption; as such, it consists of all the institutions and marketing activities in the marketing process.[5] The terms *distribution channel* and *supply chain* are virtually the same and are often used interchangeably. As indicated in Exhibit 12.1, distribution channels make products available to consumers, whether they are individuals or businesses. In some cases, companies use direct market channels to deliver their goods to consumers; in other instances, distribution is accomplished indirectly through the use of intermediaries.

As we noted in Chapter 1, **supply chain management** refers to a set of approaches and techniques firms employ to efficiently and effectively integrate their suppliers, manufacturers, warehouses, stores, and transportation intermediaries into a seamless value chain in which merchandise is produced and distributed in the right quantities, to the right locations, and at the right time, as well as to minimize systemwide costs while satisfying the service levels their customers require.[6] Zara, a well-known global specialty apparel chain, has a completely integrated supply chain because the company owns or at least has considerable control over each phase. It not only owns most of its own stores, but also produces the majority of its own clothes and makes more than 40 percent of its own fabric. As a result, it is able to conceive of, design, manufacture, transport, and ultimately sell high-fashion apparel much more quickly and efficiently than any of its major competitors.

A simplified supply chain would be one in which manufacturers make products and sell them to intermediaries such as retailers or wholesalers. This chain becomes much more complicated if we include suppliers of materials to manufacturers and all of the manufacturers, wholesalers, and stores in a typical supply chain. **Wholesalers** are firms that buy products from manufacturers and resell them to

EXHIBIT 12.1 Distribution Components

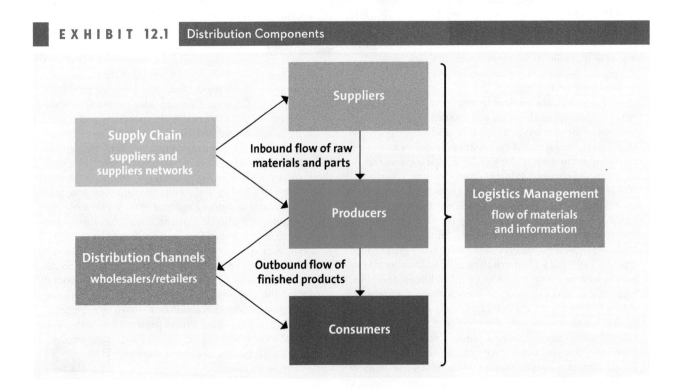

retailers, and **retailers** sell products directly to consumers. Manufacturers ship to a wholesaler, or, in the case of many multistore retailers, to the retailer's distribution centre or directly to stores. The more intermediaries that are involved in the supply chain, the greater the complexity and number of transactions involved for a company to reach consumers.

retailers
Sell products directly to consumers.

Although the above discussion reflects the typical flow of manufactured goods, many variations to this supply chain exist. Some retail chains, such as Home Depot and Costco, function as both retailers and wholesalers; they act as retailers when they sell to consumers directly and as wholesalers when they sell to other businesses, such as building contractors or restaurant owners. When manufacturers such as Dell or Avon sell directly to consumers, they are performing both production and retailing activities. When Dell sells directly to a university or business, it becomes a business-to-business (B2B) transaction, but when it sells to the students or employees individually, it is a business-to-consumer (B2C) operation.

Supply chain management focuses on the relationships among members of the supply chain and distribution channel and the need to co-ordinate efforts to provide customers with the best value.

Logistics management describes the integration of two or more activities to plan, implement, and control the efficient flow of raw materials, in-process inventory, and finished goods from the point of origin to the point of consumption. These activities may include, but are not limited to, customer service, demand forecasting, distribution communications, inventory control, materials handling, order processing, parts and service support, plant and warehouse site selection, procurement, packaging, return goods handling, salvage and scrap disposal, traffic and transportation, and warehousing and storage.[7] Supply chain management takes a systemwide approach to co-ordinating the flow of merchandise and includes both distribution management and logistics management.

logistics management
The integration of two or more activities for the purpose of planning, implementing, and controlling the efficient flow of raw materials, in-process inventory, and finished goods from the point of origin to the point of consumption.

Distribution channel management, supply chain management, and logistics management are related but have been handled differently in the past. Distribution channel management traditionally has been the responsibility of marketing departments, under the direction of a marketing vice-president. Logistics was traditionally the responsibility of operations, under a vice-president of operations. Although their goals were similar, they often saw solutions differently, and sometimes they worked at cross-purposes. For instance, the marketing department's goal might have been to make sales, whereas logistics wanted to keep costs low. Firms have come to realize there is tremendous opportunity in co-ordinating marketing and logistics activities not only within a firm, but also throughout the supply chain.

DESIGNING DISTRIBUTION CHANNELS

LO2

Channel Structure

When a firm is just starting out or entering a new market, it doesn't typically have the option of designing the "best" distribution channel structure—that is, choosing from whom it buys or to whom it sells. A new sporting goods retailer may not have the option of carrying all the manufacturer lines it wants, because other competing retailers in its market might carry the same products. Some manufacturers won't want to sell to this new retailer initially because its credit isn't established. On the other hand, a small specialty sporting goods manufacturer may not be able to get shelf space in major stores like SportChek because its line is unproven. Further, its products might duplicate lines that the retailer already carries. Every company must develop a distribution strategy for how it will sell goods to consumers. The distribution system may take the form of direct distribution, indirect distribution, and multichannel distribution, or some combination of these forms.

Direct Distribution   As shown in Exhibit 12.2, direct distribution channels allow manufacturers to deal directly with consumers. Many products and services are distributed this way. For decades, Dell's distribution strategy was based exclusively on using direct channels. This strategy has since changed, with its decision to begin selling select personal computers at Walmart and other stores. Other companies, such as TigerDirect.com, Avon, and Tupperware, continue to use a direct-only model. Social and Mobile Marketing 12.1 discusses how Clearly Contacts uses a direct model to sell glasses and contact lenses. Direct distribution also plays a significant role in B2B dealings with companies that sell directly to their largest customers in the public and private sectors. For example, IBM sells its mainframe computers directly to its largest customers in the government and in the banking and insurance industries. Nestlé, the world's largest food company, adopted a direct distribution strategy to reach customers in Brazil, sailing a supermarket barge down two Amazon River tributaries.[8] Lastly, some companies may be forced to distribute their goods directly because they are unable to secure shelf space in retail outlets or are unable to pay the high listing fees demanded by retailers for the shelf space.

Indirect Distribution   With indirect distribution channels, one or more intermediaries work with manufacturers to provide goods and services to consumers. In some cases, there may be only one intermediary involved. Many automotive manufacturers, such as Ford and Coca-Cola, use indirect distribution with dealers acting as the retailer, as shown in Exhibit 12.2. Typically only one intermediary is used in the case of large retailers such as The Bay (not shown in the exhibit). Wholesalers are often used when a company does not buy in sufficient quantity to make it cost-effective for a manufacturer to deal directly with a retailer. The use of wholesalers is quite common for low-cost or low-unit value items such as candy and chips, as shown in the last example in Exhibit 12.2.

Multichannel Distribution   Today, many companies are embracing a multichannel, or hybrid, approach to distribution. As shown in Exhibit 12.3, companies such as Sony are better able to reach both consumers and business customers by using a combination of both direct and indirect distribution channels. In very large cities, Sony may sell directly via its own branded stores, while in other areas it may sell indirectly through retailers such as Best Buy and Future Shop. Some companies engage a sales force to deliver products to customers while others pursue a direct marketing approach through the use of catalogues. Sears Canada sells directly at its retail stores as well as online and through the use of catalogues.

EXHIBIT 12.2   Direct and Indirect Distribution

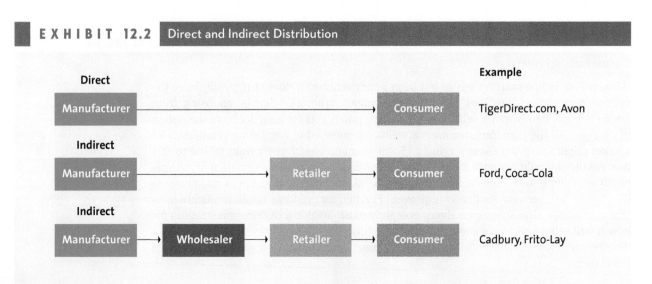

EXHIBIT 12.3 | Multichannel Distribution

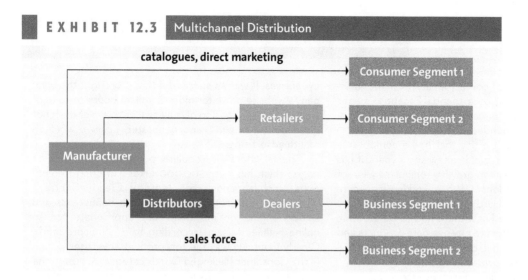

Push Versus Pull Distribution Strategies

When developing its distribution strategy, a company may choose to use a **push marketing strategy** or a **pull marketing strategy** as illustrated in Exhibit 12.4. With a push strategy, a manufacturer focuses its promotional efforts—for example, personal selling or sales promotion—on channel members to convince them to carry its product. This strategy literally pushes the product through distribution channels to end consumers. As mentioned earlier, companies often need to pay listing fees to get shelf space.

push marketing strategy
Designed to increase demand by focusing on wholesalers, distributors, or salespeople, who push the product to consumers via distribution channels.

pull marketing strategy
Designed to get consumers to pull the product into the supply chain by demanding retailers carry it.

EXHIBIT 12.4 | Push Versus Pull Marketing Strategies

Social and Mobile Marketing 12.1

Clearly a Winning Strategy

Would you buy glasses or contact lenses over the Internet or because of a post on a friend's Facebook page? You might for the right price. Roger Hardy and his sister Michaela Tokarksi founded Clearly Contacts in 2000 in a Vancouver basement office that had a computer, a phone, and a Ping-Pong table. In a few short years, it has become the world's fastest growing online retailer of eyeglasses and contact lenses. While working for a contact lens manufacturer, Hardy realized that the margins were extremely high. He knew there had to be a better, cheaper way for consumers to buy eye-care products and so he set out to change that, defining his mission as "Saving the World from Overpriced Eyeglasses."[9]

In the past, the prescription glasses market has been dominated by opticians. The Clearly Contacts business model eliminates the middleman, automates the order process, and ships direct to consumers for 50 to 70 percent less than traditional eye-care retailers. Prices range from $38 to $198, great value for designer brands such as Prada, Dior, Armani, and Fendi.[10] Still, Hardy discovered that although consumers were willing to purchase books or clothes over the Internet, they had reservations about buying eyeglasses online. Curtis Petersen, director of acquisition and retention for Clearly Contacts notes that it's a more complex purchase. You have to convince consumers to change their behaviour and do something a little different to complete the purchase.[11] A Virtual Mirror application lets customers see how some of the 500 designs would look on their faces. In fact, more than 10 percent of purchases are made after someone uses this application.[12] Free shipping and liberal payment terms help minimize the risk of the purchase.

To persuade Vancouverites to try the products, the company gave 3,000 pairs of designer glasses away for free in June 2010. Consumers signed up online to get a coupon code for the glasses. Clearly Contacts' strategy was to get the high-quality glasses in the hands of consumers to dispel concerns about buying them on the Internet. The company ran a similar promotion in Toronto the year before with a one-day offer of free prescription eyeglasses. It was so successful that it brought the company's website down for more than two hours. In spite of the crash, it managed to give away 1000 pairs of designer glasses by 1:00 p.m.[13] and generated positive word-of-mouth advertising.

Special offers are regularly posted on its Facebook page, which has over 500,000 Likes[14] offering tremendous reach at a low cost. Most of Clearly Contact's advertising budget is spent online on banner ads and search engine optimization, very appropriate for an online retailer. In fact, according to a comScore study, Clearly Contacts was the top product advertised online in the Consumer Packaged Goods category in 2012.[15] The company has found a winning formula, capturing about 10 percent of the eyeglasses market and earning a spot on Profit 100's Top Fastest Growing Companies in Canada. Today it has operations in North America, Europe, and Asia, more than 2 million customers, and cumulative revenues surpassing $1 billion.[16] The company opened its first brick-and-mortar store in Vancouver[17] to help it expand its direct to consumer distribution strategy. The strategy is working. Clearly Contacts has opened a store in Toronto and a second location in Vancouver.

Would the right price entice you to buy contacts or glasses online?"

Manufacturers can pay thousands of dollars in listing fees to have their products stocked. Many large grocery store chains charge listing fees that cover their costs in rearranging the store shelves and the warehouse, plus the administration costs associated with adding a new product. Listing fees can determine whether an item gets placed at eye level or down on a bottom shelf where it's harder to find. In Canada, listing fees can range from a few hundred dollars, to $25,000 per item per store, to $1 million per item per grocery chain.[18] The fee depends on many variables, including potential sales volume, trade allowances, product promotion offered (e.g., samples, in-store demos, promotional pricing, co-op advertising), product category, and company size. Grocery retailers know that large companies such as Kraft or Colgate-Palmolive can afford listing fees. However, some category leaders don't have to pay them because retailers know they simply must stock popular products such as Coke and Tide. To get shelf space, companies need to get retailers onside and show them how their product can help them grow a category, bring new consumers to the category, or add to their profit.

Sometimes, if channel members are reluctant to stock new products, manufacturers may use a pull strategy. In this case, promotional efforts are directed at consumers to build demand for products that, in turn, may convince retailers to carry them. Consumers who see TV commercials or print advertisements or who receive direct mail information or coupons regarding new products may approach local retailers and request that they stock these products, thus pulling them through the distribution channels.

Martin's used a sampling campaign as part of a pull strategy to launch Apple Chips to consumers.

One of Canada's leading growers and packers, Martin's Family Fruit Farm in Elmira, Ontario, produces and distributes apples and apple cider. Recently, the company decided to diversify and access new markets and suppliers. It came up with a concept that lets it use less than perfect apples to produce dried apple "chips" made from apples sliced into circles and then dehydrated. The chips are all-natural, fat free, gluten free, wheat free, dairy free, and vegan. They contain no preservatives, artificial colouring or sugar, and have only 100 calories for 25 grams. To be accepted on grocery store shelves, the company had to prove that consumer demand for healthier snacks would translate to sales of its Apple Chips. Working with Vancouver advertising agency BrandFX, the company launched a sampling campaign targeting 45,000 GoodLife Fitness members and also sent the product home with 35,000 children in Ontario daycare centres.[19] This pull strategy reached the target market of nutrition-conscious moms and helped pave the way for a distribution agreement with Loblaws, which agreed to carry Apple Chips at 37 Real Canadian Superstores.[20]

Distribution Intensity

When setting up distribution for the first time or introducing new products, firms decide the appropriate level of **distribution intensity**—the number of channel members to use at each level of the supply chain. Distribution intensity commonly is divided into three levels: intensive, exclusive, and selective (see Exhibit 12.5). Although increased sales and access to more consumers is often desirable, that's not always the case. Over the years, companies such as Walmart and Esso have asked to carry M&M Meat Shops products. These retailers would have dramatically expanded the company's distribution intensity; however, the company decided against such deals, sensing the move would ultimately hurt the brand. M&M Meat Shops prides itself on offering high quality, whereas retailers such as Walmart focus on low price.

distribution intensity
The number of channel members to use at each level of the supply chain.

EXHIBIT 12.5 Distribution Intensity

Intensive

Selective

Exclusive

Most consumer packaged-goods companies, such as PepsiCo (top), strive for intensive distribution—they want to be everywhere. But cosmetics firms such as Estée Lauder (bottom) use an exclusive distribution strategy by limiting distribution to a few select, higher-end retailers in each region.

intensive distribution
A strategy designed to get products into as many outlets as possible.

exclusive distribution
Strategy of granting exclusive rights to sell to one or very few retail customers so no other customers can sell a particular brand.

selective distribution
Lies between the intensive and exclusive distribution strategies; uses a few selected customers in a territory.

Intensive Distribution An **intensive distribution** strategy is designed to get products into as many outlets as possible. Most consumer packaged-goods companies, such as PepsiCo, P&G, Kraft, and most other nationally branded products found in grocery and discount stores, strive for and often achieve intensive distribution. PepsiCo, for instance, wants its product available everywhere: grocery stores, convenience stores, restaurants, and vending machines. Timex watches, starting at around $60, can also be found in many locations. The more exposure these products get, the more they sell. Google is hoping to achieve intensive distribution of e-books by distributing them directly to anyone with a web browser with the launch of Google Editions.

Exclusive Distribution Manufacturers also might use an **exclusive distribution** policy by granting exclusive geographic territories to one or very few retail customers so no other customers in the territory can sell a particular brand. Exclusive distribution can benefit manufacturers by assuring them that the most appropriate customers represent their products. Cosmetics firms such as Estée Lauder, for instance, limit their distribution to a few select, higher-end retailers in each region. They believe that selling their products to drugstores, discount stores, and grocery stores would weaken their image. Likewise, Rolex watches are sold only by high-end jewellers and a few retail outlets in keeping with their prestigious brand image. In some cases, limiting distribution can limit sales. Nespresso invented the single-serve capsule coffee machine and sells the pods only in a direct-to-consumer model through its own physical and online stores. In spite of competition from new entrants such as Kraft (Tassimo), Green Mountain (Keurig K-Cup), and Starbucks (Verismo), Nespresso refuses to sell in grocery stores and mass merchants. This notable absence on retail shelves has led other brands to introduce pods that fit Nespresso machines[21] thus impacting sales potential.

In cases of limited supply or when a firm is just starting out, providing an exclusive territory to one customer helps ensure enough inventory to offer the customer an adequate selection. For instance, Cervélo is a Canadian bicycle manufacturer that makes lightweight racing bikes. It selects its authorized dealers carefully. By controlling sales territories, it guarantees dealers adequate supply, which gives them a strong incentive to push Cervélo's products. Dealers know there will be no competing retailers to cut prices, so their profit margins are protected, which also gives them an incentive to carry more inventory and use extra advertising, personal selling, and sales promotions.

Selective Distribution Between the intensive and exclusive distribution strategies lies **selective distribution**, which uses a few selected customers in a territory. Similar to exclusive distribution, selective distribution helps a seller maintain a particular image and control the flow of merchandise into an area, so many shopping goods manufacturers use it. Recall that shopping goods are those products for which consumers are willing to spend time comparing alternatives, such as most apparel items; home items such as branded pots and pans, sheets, and towels; branded hardware and tools; and consumer electronics. Seiko uses a selective distribution strategy for its watches to match its more upscale image and pricing. Retailers still have a strong incentive to sell the products but not to the same extent as if they had an exclusive territory.

DISTRIBUTION CHANNELS ADD VALUE   LO3

Why would a manufacturer want to use a wholesaler or a retailer? Don't these supply chain members just cut into their profits? Wouldn't it be cheaper for consumers to buy directly from manufacturers? In a simple agrarian economy, the best supply chain may in fact follow a direct route from manufacturer to consumer: the consumer goes to the farm and buys food directly from the farmer. But how will the food get cooked? The consumer doesn't know how to make a stove, nor does she have the materials to do so. The stove maker who has the necessary knowledge must buy raw materials and components from various suppliers, make the stove, and then make it available to the consumer. If the stove maker isn't located near the consumer, the stove must be transported to where the consumer has access to it. To make matters even more complicated, the consumer may want to view a choice of stoves, hear about all their features, and have the stove delivered and installed.

How many companies are involved in making and getting a stove to your kitchen?

Each participant in the supply chain thus adds value. The components manufacturer helps the stove manufacturer by supplying parts and materials. The stove maker then turns the components into the stove. The transportation company gets the stove to the retailer. The retailer stores the stove until the customer wants it, educates the customer about product features, and delivers and installs the stove. At each step, the stove becomes more costly but also more valuable to the consumer.

Exhibits 12.6A and 12.6B show how using supply chain partners can provide value overall. Exhibit 12.6A shows three manufacturers, each of which sells directly to three consumers in a system that requires nine transactions. Each transaction costs money—for example, the manufacturer must fill the order, package it, write up the paperwork, and ship it—and each cost is passed on to the customer. Exhibit 12.6B shows the same three manufacturers and consumers; but, this time they go through a single retailer. The number of transactions falls to six, and as transactions are eliminated, the supply chain becomes more efficient, which adds value for customers by making it more convenient and less expensive to purchase merchandise.

When products are designed and manufactured, how and when the critical components reach the factory must be co-ordinated with production. The sales department must co-ordinate its delivery promises with the factory or distribution centres. A **distribution centre**, a facility for the receipt, storage, and redistribution of goods to company stores or customers, may be operated by retailers, manufacturers, or distribution specialists.[22] Furthermore, advertising and promotion must be co-ordinated with those departments

distribution centre
A facility for the receipt, storage, and redistribution of goods to company stores or customers; may be operated by retailers, manufacturers, or distribution specialists.

EXHIBIT 12.6A   Direct Supply Chain with No Retailer

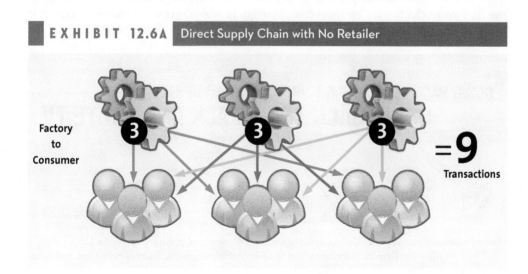

Factory to Consumer

=9 Transactions

EXHIBIT 12.6B   Indirect Supply Chain with Retailer

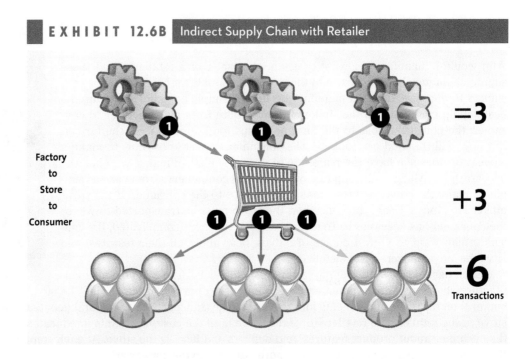

that control inventory and transportation. There is no faster way to lose credibility with customers than to promise deliveries or run a promotion and then not have the merchandise when the customer expects it.

Distribution channels are composed of various entities that are buying, such as retailers or wholesalers; selling, such as manufacturers or wholesalers; or helping facilitate the exchange, such as transportation companies. Like interactions between people, these relationships can range from close working partnerships to one-time arrangements. In almost all cases though, they occur because the parties want something from one another. For instance, Home Depot wants hammers from Stanley Tool Company; Stanley wants an opportunity to sell its tools to the public; and both companies want UPS to deliver the merchandise.

Each channel member performs a specialized role. If one member believes that another isn't doing its job correctly or efficiently, it usually can replace that member. So, if Stanley isn't getting good service from UPS, it can switch to FedEx. Likewise, if Home Depot believes its customers don't perceive Stanley tools to be a good value, it may buy from another tool company. Home Depot could even decide to make its own tools or use its own trucks to pick up tools from Stanley. However, even if a channel member is replaced, the function it performed remains, so someone needs to complete it.

Home Depot and Stanley Tool Company have a mutually beneficial partnership. Home Depot buys tools from Stanley because its customers find value in Stanley products. Stanley sells tools to Home Depot because it has established an excellent market for its products.

As the chapter end case notes, Zara gains its competitive advantage by bringing fashions to the store and its customers much faster than other clothing retailers. It holds minimal inventory, produces new fashion quickly, and rarely gets stuck with old inventory. Deliveries are made to stores once a week, and the clothes rarely remain on shelves for more than a week. But this speedy system is not limited to the retail side; Zara also takes only four to five weeks to design a new collection and then about a week to manufacture it; so it continually cycles through its inventory of fabric and materials needed to make its clothing. Its competitors, in comparison, need an average of six months to design a new collection and another three weeks to manufacture it.

Distribution channels perform a variety of transactional, logistical, and facilitating functions, as noted in Exhibit 12.7. One important role played by intermediaries is to reduce the number of marketplace contacts, resulting in more efficient systems. Intermediaries also match the requirements of individual consumers to the goods that manufacturers produce; handle physical distribution and storage of goods, making them available for customers to purchase; facilitate searches by both buyers and sellers; and standardize exchange transactions. While channel functions may shift from one intermediary or channel member to another, it's important to recognize that they cannot be eliminated. As noted in the Home Depot example above, these functions must be completed by some organization to get the right products to the right customers when they want them.

Managing Distribution Channels

Like any large complicated system, a distribution channel is difficult to manage. Whether the balance of power rests with large retailers like Walmart or with large manufacturers like Procter & Gamble, channel members benefit by working together to develop and implement their channel strategy. If a distribution channel is to run efficiently, the participating members must co-operate. Oftentimes, however, channel members have conflicting goals. For instance, Stanley wants Home Depot to carry all its tools but not those of its competitors so that Stanley can maximize its sales. But Home Depot carries a mix of tool brands so it can maximize the sales in its tool category. When channel members are not in agreement about their goals, roles, or rewards, **channel conflict** results.

Avoiding vertical channel conflicts demands open, honest communication. Buyers and vendors all must understand what drives the other party's business, their roles in

channel conflict Results when supply chain members are not in agreement about their goals, roles, or rewards.

E X H I B I T 12.7	Functions Performed by Intermediaries
Transactional Function	
Buying	Purchase goods for resale to other intermediaries or consumers
Risk Taking	Own inventory that can become outdated
Promotion	Promote products to attract consumers
Selling	Transact with potential customers
Logistical Function	
Physical Distribution	Transport goods to point of purchase
Risk Taking	Maintain inventory and protect goods
Facilitating Function	
Gather Information	Share competitive intelligence about customers or other channel members
Financing	Extend credit and other financial services to consumers

Walmart and Procter & Gamble (P&G) recognize that it is in their common interest to remain profitable business partners.

the relationship, each firm's strategies, and any problems that might arise over the course of the relationship. As we mentioned in the opening vignette for this chapter, Walmart and Procter & Gamble (P&G) recognize that it is in their common interest to remain profitable business partners. Walmart's customers demand and expect to find P&G products in stores; P&G needs the sales generated through the world's largest retailer. Walmart cannot demand prices so low that P&G cannot make money, and P&G must be flexible enough to accommodate the needs of its biggest customer. With a common goal, both firms then have the incentive to co-operate, because they know that by doing so, each will boost its sales.

Companies can manage distribution channels by developing strong relationships with supply chain partners. Or they can co-ordinate the channel by using a vertical marketing system.

Managing Channels Through Vertical Marketing Systems Although conflict is likely to occur in any distribution channel, it is generally more pronounced when the channel members are independent entities. Distribution channels that are more closely aligned, whether by contract or ownership, share common goals and therefore are less prone to conflict.

In an independent distribution channel (the left panel of Exhibit 12.8), the several independent members—a manufacturer, a wholesaler, and a retailer—each attempt to satisfy their own objectives and maximize their own profits, often at the expense of the other members. None of the participants has any control over the others.

For instance, the first time Zara purchases cotton fabric from Tessuto e Colore in Northern Italy, both parties try to extract as much profit from the deal as possible, and after the deal has been consummated, neither party feels any responsibility to the other. Over time, Zara and Tessuto might develop a relationship in which their transactions become more routine and automatic, such that Zara depends on Tessuto for fabric, and

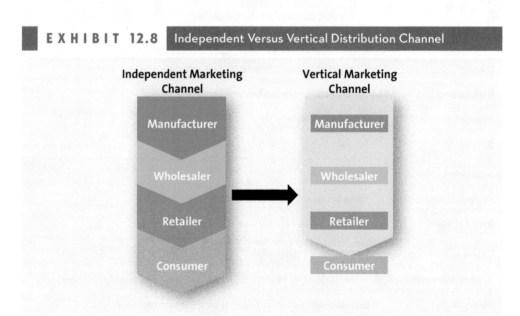

EXHIBIT 12.8 Independent Versus Vertical Distribution Channel

Tessuto depends on Zara to buy a good portion of its output. This scenario represents the first phase of a **vertical marketing system** (the right panel of Exhibit 12.8) in which the members act as a unified system because they realize that each party can maximize its individual benefits by working together to make the distribution system more efficient rather than individually or at cross-purposes. There are three types, or phases, of vertical marketing systems, each with increasing levels of formalization and control. The more formal the vertical marketing system, the less likely conflict will ensue.

Administered Vertical Marketing System   The Zara/Tessuto channel relationship offers an example of an **administered vertical marketing system**. In an administered vertical marketing system, there is no common ownership and no contractual relationships, but the dominant channel member controls the channel relationship. In our example, because of its size and relative power, Zara imposes some control over Tessuto; it dictates, for instance, what Tessuto should make and when it should be delivered. Zara also has a strong influence over the price. If either party doesn't like the way the relationship is going, however, it can simply walk away.

Contractual Vertical Marketing System.   Over time, Zara and Tessuto may formalize their relationship by entering into contracts that dictate various terms, such as how much Zara will buy each month, at what price, and the penalties for late deliveries. In **contractual vertical marketing systems** like this, independent firms at different levels of the supply chain join together through contracts to obtain economies of scale and co-ordination and to reduce conflict.[23]

Franchising is the most common type of contractual vertical marketing system; franchising companies and their franchisees account for $100 billion in Canadian retail sales—an astonishing 26 percent of all retail sales in this country—and employ more than 1 million people.[24] **Franchising** is a contractual agreement between a franchisor and a franchisee that allows the franchisee to operate a retail outlet, using a name and format developed and supported by the franchisor. Exhibit 12.9 lists some of Canada's favourite franchises.

In a franchise contract, the franchisee pays a lump sum plus a royalty on all sales in return for the right to operate a business in a specific location. The franchisee also agrees to operate the outlet in accordance with the procedures prescribed by the franchisor. The franchisor typically provides assistance in locating and building the business, developing

vertical marketing system
A supply chain in which the members act as a unified system; there are three types: administrated, contractual, and corporate.

administered vertical marketing system
A supply chain system in which there is no common ownership and no contractual relationships, but the dominant channel member controls the channel relationship.

contractual vertical marketing system
A system in which independent firms at different levels of the supply chain join together through contracts to obtain economies of scale and co-ordination and to reduce conflict.

franchising
A contractual agreement between a franchisor and a franchisee that allows the franchisee to operate a retail outlet, using a name and format developed and supported by the franchisor.

EXHIBIT 12.9	The 10 Largest Franchises in Canada		
Rank	**Franchise**	**Type**	**Number of Outlets**
1	Tim Hortons	Coffee, doughnuts, sandwiches	3,436
2	Subway	Submarine sandwiches, salads	2,563
3	McDonald's	Hamburgers, chicken, salads	1,421
4	YUM! Restaurants	Pizza Hut, Taco Bell, KFC	1,261
5	Shoppers Drug Mart	Pharmacy	1,241
6	H&R Block Canada	Tax preparation	1,100
7	A&W Food Services	Hamburgers, onion rings, root beer	750
8	Cara Operations	Harvey's, Kelseys, Montana's, Milestones, Swiss Chalet	686
9	Jan-Pro Cleaning Systems	Commercial Janitorial Services	600
10	Jani-King Canada	Commercial Janitorial Services	600

Source: Canadian Franchise Association "Franchise Facts."

American Apparel represents a corporate vertical marketing system because it manufacturers its own products and operates its own retail stores.

the products or services sold, management training, and advertising. To maintain the franchisee's reputation, the franchisor also makes sure that all outlets provide the same quality of services and products. M&M Meat Shops opened its first franchise nine months after the first store was launched. Today it has over 450 locations across Canada. Some franchisees invest their life savings (a typical store costs around $325,000) and the company wants them to be successful. So it does careful screening to ensure the right people are invited to join the team. And while entrepreneurial skills are an asset, M&M Meat Shops also needs franchisees who will adhere to the corporate formula instead of doing things their own way.

A franchise system combines the entrepreneurial advantages of owning a business with the efficiencies of vertical marketing systems that function under single ownership (a corporate system, as we discuss next). Franchisees are motivated to make their stores successful because they receive the profits, after they pay the royalty to the franchisor. The franchisor is motivated to develop new products, services, and systems and to promote the franchise because it receives royalties on all sales. Advertising, product development, and system development are all done efficiently by the franchisor, with costs shared by all franchisees. Canada has the second largest franchise industry in the world (outdone only by the United States) that generates more than $100 billion in annual sales.[25]

corporate vertical marketing system

A system in which the parent company has complete control and can dictate the priorities and objectives of the supply chain; it may own facilities such as manufacturing plants, warehouse facilities, retail outlets, and design studios.

Corporate Vertical Marketing System. Because Zara deals with "fast fashion," it is imperative that it have complete control over the most fashion-sensitive items. So Zara manufactures these items itself and contracts out its less fashionable items to other manufacturers.[26] The portion of its supply chain that Zara owns and controls is called a **corporate vertical marketing system**. Because Zara's parent company Inditex owns the manufacturing plants, warehouse facilities, retail outlets, and design studios, it can dictate the priorities and objectives of that supply chain, and thus conflict is lessened.

Five interrelated activities emerge in supply chain management: designing distribution channels (discussed earlier in this chapter), making information flow, managing the relationships among supply chain partners, making merchandise flow, and managing inventory. In the next few sections, we examine these remaining activities.

L04   LOGISTICS MANAGEMENT: MAKING INFORMATION FLOW

Information flows from the customer to stores, to and from distribution centres, possibly to and from wholesalers, to and from product manufacturers, and then on to the producers of any components and the suppliers of raw materials. To simplify our discussion and because information flows are similar in other supply chain links and B2B channels, we shorten the supply chain in this section to exclude wholesalers, as well as the link from suppliers to manufacturers. Exhibit 12.10 illustrates the flow of information that starts when a customer buys a Sony HDTV at Future Shop. The flow follows these steps:

universal product code (UPC)

The black and white bar code found on most merchandise.

● *Flow 1 (Customer to Store).* The sales associate at Future Shop scans the **universal product code (UPC)** tag (the black and white bar code found on most merchandise) on the HDTV packaging, and the customer receives a receipt. The

EXHIBIT 12.10 Information Flows

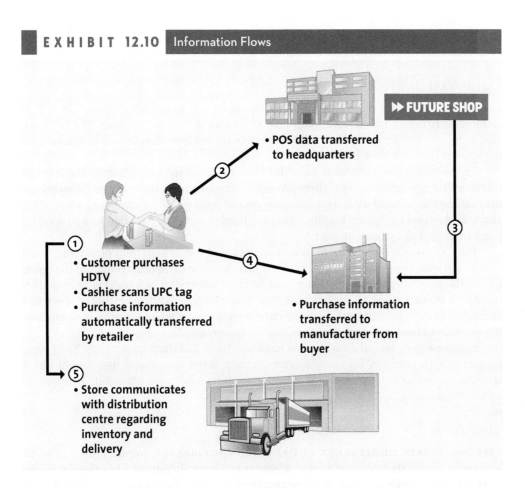

UPC tag contains a 13-digit code that includes the manufacturer of an item and information about special packaging and special promotions. In the future, RFID tags, discussed later in this chapter, may replace UPC codes.

- *Flow 2 (Store to Buyer)*. The point-of-sale (POS) terminal records the purchase information and electronically sends it to the buyer at Future Shop's corporate office. The sales information is incorporated into an inventory management system and used to monitor and analyze sales and to decide to reorder more HDTVs, change a price, or plan a promotion. Buyers also send information to stores on overall sales for the chain, how to display merchandise, upcoming promotions, and so on.

- *Flow 3 (Buyer to Manufacturer)*. The purchase information from each Future Shop store is typically aggregated by the retailer as a whole, which creates an order for new merchandise and sends it to Sony. The buyer at Future Shop may also communicate directly with Sony to get information and negotiate prices, shipping dates, promotional events, or other merchandise-related issues.

- *Flow 4 (Store to Manufacturer)*. In some situations, the sales transaction data are sent directly from the store to the manufacturer, and the manufacturer decides when to ship more merchandise to the distribution centres and the stores. However, if the merchandise is reordered frequently, the ordering process can become automatic and virtually bypass the buyer.

- *Flow 5 (Store to Distribution Centre)*. Stores also communicate with the Future Shop distribution centre to co-ordinate deliveries and check inventory status. When the store inventory drops to a specified level, more HDTVs are shipped to the store and the shipment is sent to the Future Shop computer system.

In Flow 3, the retailer and manufacturer exchange business documents through a system called electronic data interchange.

Data Warehouse

Consumers' purchase data collected at the point of sale (information flow 2 in Exhibit 12.10) goes into a huge database known as a data warehouse. The information stored in the data warehouse is accessible on various dimensions and levels, as depicted in the data cube in Exhibit 12.11.

As shown on the horizontal axis, data can be accessed according to the level of merchandise aggregation: SKU (item), vendor, category (e.g., dresses), or all merchandise. Along the vertical axis, data can be accessed by level of the company: store, divisions, or the total company. Finally, along the third dimension, data can be accessed by point in time: day, season, or year.

The CEO might be interested in how the corporation is generally doing and could look at the data aggregated by quarter for a merchandise division, a region of the country, or the total corporation. A buyer may be more interested in a particular manufacturer in a certain store on a particular day. Analysts from various levels of the retail operation extract information from the data warehouse to make a plethora of marketing decisions about developing and replenishing merchandise assortments.

In some cases, manufacturers also have access to this data warehouse. They communicate with retailers by using electronic data interchange and use supply chain systems known as vendor-managed inventory and collaborative planning, forecasting, and replenishment.

Electronic Data Interchange

Electronic data interchange (EDI) is the computer-to-computer exchange of business documents from a retailer to a vendor and back. In addition to sales data, purchase orders, invoices, and data about returned merchandise can be transmitted back and forth.

Many retailers now require vendors to provide them with notification of deliveries before they take place by using an **advanced shipping notice**, an electronic document

electronic data interchange (EDI)
The computer-to-computer exchange of business documents from a retailer to a vendor and back.

advanced shipping notice
An electronic document that the supplier sends the retailer in advance of a shipment to tell the retailer exactly what to expect in the shipment.

EXHIBIT 12.11　Retail Data Warehouse

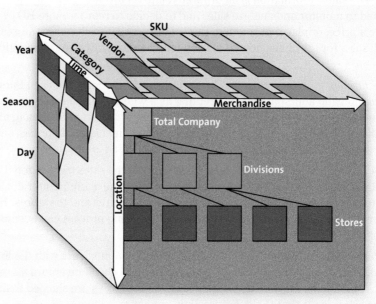

that the supplier sends the retailer in advance of a shipment to tell the retailer exactly what to expect in the shipment. If the advanced shipping notice is accurate, the retailer can dispense with opening all the received cartons and checking in merchandise. In addition, EDI enables vendors to transmit information about on-hand inventory status, vendor promotions, and cost changes to the retailer, as well as information about purchase order changes, order status, retail prices, and transportation routings.

Using EDI, suppliers can describe and show pictures of their products, and buyers can issue requests for proposals. The two parties can then electronically negotiate prices and specify how the product will be made and how it should look.

Hasbro makes toys and games such as this Trivial Pursuit Star Wars Edition. It communicates efficiently with its vendors with EDI.

The use of EDI provides three main benefits to supply chain members. First, EDI reduces the cycle time, or the time between the decision to place an order and the receipt of merchandise. When EDI is used, information flows more quickly, which means that inventory turnover is higher. Second, EDI improves the overall quality of communications through better record keeping; fewer errors in inputting and receiving an order; and less human error in the interpretation of data. Third, the data transmitted by EDI are in a computer-readable format that can be easily analyzed and used for a variety of tasks, ranging from evaluating vendor delivery performance to automating reorder processes.

Because of these benefits, many retailers are asking their suppliers to interface with them by using EDI. However, small to medium-sized suppliers and retailers face significant barriers, specifically cost and the lack of information technology (IT) expertise, to becoming EDI-enabled. However, EDI remains an important component of any vendor-managed inventory system.

Toy giant Hasbro, for example, launched an EDI initiative to improve its order processing. Before this, roughly 70 percent of all incoming orders filtered through 100 vendors in Asia. Each order was sent from the vendor to the appropriate manufacturer, and the manufacturer manually reviewed all vendor requests. When exceptions or delays occurred, the process became laborious because of the numerous faxes and phone calls needed to resolve any issue. After Hasbro implemented EDI for its manufacturers, 80 percent of the orders needed no human interaction at all. As a result, the Asian operations were able to handle a 100 percent increase in their order volume without any additional resources.[27]

Managing Supply Chains Through Strategic Relationships

There is more to managing supply chains than simply exercising power over other members in an administered system or establishing a contractual or corporate vertical marketing system. There is also a human side.

In a conventional distribution channel, relationships between members often are based on the argument over the split of the profit pie: if one party gets ahead, the other party falls behind. Sometimes this type of transactional approach is acceptable if the parties have no interest in a long-term relationship. If Harry Rosen sees a trend for very narrow white belts, it would be interested in purchasing from a vendor in which an ongoing relationship would be built. Harry Rosen would not purchase from a vendor on a one-time basis just to get a one-time good price because long-term relationship building is important to the company's business practices.

strategic relationship (partnering relationship) A supply chain relationship that the members are committed to maintaining long term, investing in opportunities that are mutually beneficial; requires mutual trust, open communication, common goals, and credible commitments.

More often than not, firms seek a **strategic relationship (partnering relationship)**, in which the supply chain members are committed to maintaining the relationship over the long term and investing in opportunities that are mutually beneficial. In a conventional or administered supply chain, there are significant incentives to establishing a strategic relationship, even without contracts or ownership relationships. Both parties benefit because the size of the profit pie has increased, so both the buyer and the seller increase their sales and profits. These strategic relationships are created explicitly to uncover and exploit joint opportunities, so members depend on and trust each other heavily; share goals and agree on how to accomplish those goals; and are willing to take risks, share confidential information, and make significant investments for the sake of the relationship. Successful strategic relationships require mutual trust, open communication, common goals, and credible commitments.[28]

Mutual Trust Mutual trust holds a strategic relationship together. When vendors and buyers trust each other, they're more willing to share relevant ideas, clarify goals and problems, and communicate efficiently. Information shared between the parties thus becomes increasingly comprehensive, accurate, and timely. With trust, there's also less need for the supply chain members to constantly monitor and check up on each other's actions, because each believes the other won't take advantage, even given the opportunity. RFID systems that enable sealed cartons to be checked into a distribution centre without being opened would be impossible without mutual trust. Although it is important in all relationships, monitoring supply chain members becomes particularly pertinent when suppliers are located in less-developed countries, where issues such as the use of child labour, poor working conditions, and below-subsistence wages have become a shared responsibility. Ethical Dilemma 12.1 highlights how Apple has both stumbled in this responsibility and changed its practices to improve its dedication to ethical choices.

Open Communication To share information, develop sales forecasts together, and co-ordinate deliveries, Harry Rosen and its suppliers maintain open and honest communication. This maintenance may sound easy in principle, but most businesses don't tend to share information with their business partners. But open, honest communication is key to developing successful relationships because supply chain members need to understand what is driving each other's business, their roles in the relationship, each firm's strategies, and any problems that arise over the course of the relationship.

Harry Rosen grew from a single 46 square metre Toronto tailor shop to a national upscale menswear chain. It works hard to develop strategic partnerships with its suppliers based on mutual trust, open communications, common goals, and credible commitments.

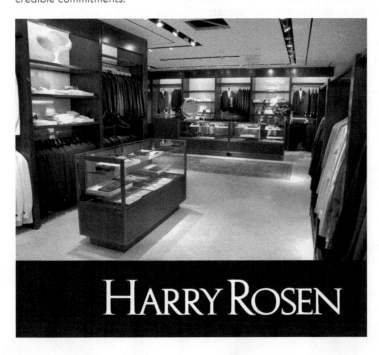

Common Goals Supply chain members must have common goals for a successful relationship to develop. Shared goals give both members of the relationship an incentive to pool their strengths and abilities and exploit potential opportunities together. For example, Harry Rosen and its local suppliers recognize that it is in their common interest to be strategic partners. Harry Rosen needs the quick response local manufacturers afford, and those manufacturers recognize that if they can keep Harry Rosen happy, they will have more than enough business for years to come. So if Harry Rosen needs a special production run to make an emergency shipment, suppliers will work to meet the challenge. If one of Harry Rosen's suppliers has difficulty getting a particular fabric or financing its inventory, it is in Harry Rosen's best interest to help it because they are committed to the same goals in the long run.

Do Customers Care More about the Newest iPhone or about Working Conditions in China?[29]

An iPad user reading an issue of *The New York Times* on their tablet might have suffered a strange sense of guilt. The newspaper published reports of labour abuses that seemingly run rampant in the Chinese factories responsible for producing Apple's most popular products. These in-depth reports catalogued a long list of failures: the presence of child workers, more than 12-hour shifts, regular work weeks of longer than 60 hours, workers housed in tiny dormitories with approximately 20 people limited to three rooms, allegations of suicides, and lax safety standards that have led to fatal explosions.

The reports focus mostly on a Foxconn factory in Chengdu, in southwestern China, that manufactures iPhones and iPads. An explosion caused by insufficient ventilation of aluminum dust (created when the cases for the gadgets get polished) killed four workers. A similar explosion followed six months later at another factory. The ensuing investigations by *The New York Times* revealed multiple other violations of the code of conduct that Apple has established for its suppliers.

With this code of conduct, as well as the frequent audits it performs, Apple asserts that it is doing the best that it can to ensure its suppliers live up to reasonable standards and fair labour practices. An anonymous former Apple executive asserts, "There is a genuine, companywide commitment to the code of conduct." Yet abuses continue, as Apple's own corporate responsibility reports reveal. Audits show that several supply companies continue to engage in labour practices that violate the code, with few punishments or changes to the supply chain.

Part of the reason stems from Apple's need for secrecy—once it finds a supply partner that can manufacturer its high-tech gadgets, it wants to maintain that relationship to avoid any leakage of innovation information. So even if a supplier violates the code again and again, Apple is unlikely to switch.

Furthermore, Apple's focus on innovation means that it must work constantly to come up with new ideas and products, which it needs to produce quickly and in sufficient quantities to keep customers happy. This demanding supply chain leaves little room for

flexibility. When Apple says it needs 1 million products, then its supplier will do whatever it takes to get those products ready in time. The code of conduct might ask that factory workers be limited to 60-hour work weeks, but in truth, Apple is asking the factories to keep running all day, every day, to make the order.

To keep its costs low, Apple also offers very slim profit margins to suppliers. In turn, these factories aim to reduce their own costs. Another Apple supplier thus began using a toxic chemical, instead of rubbing alcohol, to polish the screens of iPhones, because the chemical dries faster. But it exposes workers to the threat of paralysis and nerve damage.

The primary reason for these labour abuses may come only at the end of the supply chain—the consumer. A survey of Apple consumers showed that only 2 percent of them recognized labour issues as a concern. In a remarkably succinct summary of the challenge, another anonymous Apple executive asserted, "You can either manufacture in comfortable, worker-friendly factories, or you can reinvent the product every year, and make it better and faster and cheaper, which requires factories that seem harsh by American standards. And right now, customers care more about a new iPhone than working conditions in China."

Although Apple attempts to monitor its channel partners' behaviour with regard to labour issues, sometimes abuses fall through the cracks.

Credible Commitments Successful relationships develop because both parties make credible commitments to, or tangible investments in, the relationship. These commitments involve spending money to improve the products or services provided to the customer.[30] For example, if Harry Rosen makes a financial commitment to its suppliers to help them develop state-of-the-art manufacturing facilities and computer systems for improved communication, it is making a credible commitment—putting its money where its mouth is.

Just like many other elements of marketing, managing the supply chain can seem like an easy task at first glance: Put the merchandise in the right place at the right time. But the various elements and actors involved in a supply chain create unique and compelling complexities and require that firms work carefully to ensure they are achieving the most efficient and effective chain possible.

LOGISTICS MANAGEMENT: MAKING MERCHANDISE FLOW

To explore the different types of merchandise flows, consider the following scenario.[31] Merchandise is shipped from Sony to Future Shop's distribution centres or from Sony directly to stores. If the merchandise goes through distribution centres, it is then shipped to stores and then to the customer.

Inbound Transportation

dispatcher
The person who co-ordinates deliveries to distribution centres.

Because its distribution centres typically are quite busy, a **dispatcher**—the person who co-ordinates deliveries to Future Shop's distribution centres—assigns a time slot for each shipment of HDTVs to arrive. If the truck misses the time slot, it is fined. Although many manufacturers pay transportation expenses, some retailers negotiate with their vendors to absorb this expense. These retailers believe they can lower net merchandise cost and control their merchandise flow better if they negotiate directly with truck companies and consolidate shipments from many vendors.

Receiving and Checking

Receiving refers to the process of recording the receipt of merchandise as it arrives at a distribution centre or store. Checking is the process of going through the goods upon receipt to ensure they arrived undamaged and that the merchandise ordered was the merchandise received.

radio frequency identification (RFID) tags
Tiny computer chips that automatically transmit to a special scanner all the information about a container's contents or individual products.

Today, many distribution systems use EDI designed to minimize, if not eliminate, these processes. The advance shipping notice tells the distribution centre what should be in each box. The recipient scans the UPC label on the shipping carton or the radio frequency identification tag, which identifies the carton's contents, and those contents then are automatically counted as being received and checked. **Radio frequency identification (RFID) tags** are tiny computer chips that automatically transmit to a special scanner all the information about a container's contents or individual products. A key advantage of RFID is that it eliminates the need to handle items individually by enabling distribution centres and stores to receive whole truckloads of merchandise without having to check in each carton. Another advantage is that manufacturers and distributors are able to reduce overall inventory thanks to greater supply chain efficiency. Marks & Spencer (U.K.) is replacing bar codes with an RFID system, including tags for the millions of containers that hold food being shipped from suppliers to its stores. It takes a mere five seconds to receive data from 50 containers, an 85 percent improvement over the time it takes to scan bar codes. The savings of time, as well as reduced costs of spoiled food, are expected to make the system's $3 million price tag feasible.[32]

Storing and Cross-Docking

There are three types of distribution centres: traditional, cross-docking, and combinations. A traditional distribution centre is a warehouse in which merchandise is unloaded from trucks and placed on racks or shelves for storage. When the merchandise is needed in the stores, a worker goes to the rack, picks up the item, and places it in a bin. A

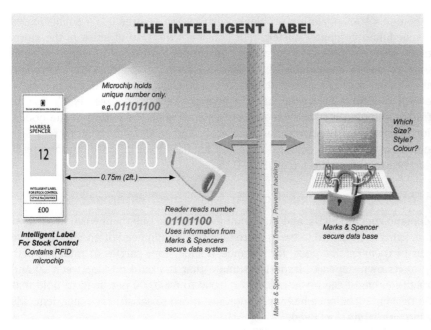

THE INTELLIGENT LABEL

Microchip holds unique number only.
e.g. *01101100*

MARKS & SPENCER

12

INTELLIGENT LABEL FOR STOCK CONTROL
STYLE No XX/XXX

£00

Intelligent Label For Stock Control
Contains RFID microchip

← 0.75m (2ft.) →

Reader reads number
01101100
Uses information from Marks & Spencers secure data system

Marks & Spencers secure firewall. Prevents hacking

Which Size? Style? Colour?

Marks & Spencer secure data base

conveyor system or other material-handling equipment transports the merchandise to a staging area, where it is consolidated and made ready for shipment to stores.

The second type, called a cross-docking distribution centre, is one to which vendors ship merchandise prepackaged in the quantity required for each store. The merchandise already contains price and theft detection tags. Because the merchandise is ready for sale, it goes straight to a staging area rather than into storage. When all the merchandise going to a particular store has arrived in the staging area, it is loaded onto a truck, and away it goes.

Most modern distribution centres combine the two previous approaches. It is difficult for a firm to operate without some storage facilities, even if merchandise is stored for only a few days. For instance, some merchandise, such as tent stakes at Mountain Equipment Co-op, has relatively slow sales but must be carried because it rounds out an assortment. These items are good candidates for storage in a distribution centre, even if the rest of the merchandise is cross-docked. Also, no matter how good a sales forecasting system may be, sometimes the merchandise arrives before it is needed in the stores. In these cases, the retailer must have a system to store the merchandise temporarily.

Marks & Spencer expects its RFID system to save time and reduce costs.

Getting Merchandise Floor-Ready

Floor-ready merchandise is merchandise that's ready to be placed on the selling floor immediately. Getting merchandise floor-ready entails ticketing, marking, and, in the case of apparel, placing garments on hangers. Ticketing and marking refers to creating price and identification labels and placing them on the merchandise. It is more efficient for a retailer to perform these activities at a distribution centre than in its stores because the work is time consuming and messy. Some retailers require their suppliers to ship merchandise floor-ready, thus totally eliminating this expensive, time-consuming process for themselves.

In a cross-docking distribution centre, merchandise moves from vendors' trucks to the retailer's delivery trucks in a matter of hours.

Shipping Merchandise to Stores

Shipping merchandise to stores is quite complex for multistore chains. A Future Shop distribution centre will run approximately 100 trucks to its stores per day. To handle such complex transportation problems, distribution centres use a sophisticated routing and scheduling computer system that considers the rate of sales in the store, road conditions, and transportation operating constraints to develop the most efficient routes possible. (Refer to Sustainable Marketing 12.1 for an example of how Frito-Lay Canada deals with optimizing routes and its fleet of vehicles.) As a result, stores receive an accurate estimated time of arrival, and the supply chain maximizes vehicle use. In Canada, different shipping methods are chosen depending on the nature of the goods, costs, location of customers relative to manufacturers, and needs of the customers. These methods include air (e.g., Air Canada), rail (e.g., Canadian Pacific Railway), land (e.g., Challenger Motor Freight), and sea (e.g., SEA-CAN.)

Inventory Management Through Just-in-Time Systems

Customers demand specific SKUs, and they want to be able to buy them when needed. At the same time, firms can't afford to carry more than they really need of an SKU, because to do so is very expensive. Suppose, for instance, a shoe store carries $1 million worth of inventory at its own expense. Experts estimate that it would cost between 20 and 40 percent of the value of the inventory, or $200,000 to $400,000 per year, to hold that inventory! So firms must balance having enough inventory to satisfy customer demands with not having more than they need.

To help reconcile these seemingly conflicting goals, many firms have adopted just-in-time inventory systems. **Just-in-time (JIT) inventory systems**, also known as **quick-response (QR)** systems in retailing, are inventory management systems designed to

just-in-time (JIT) inventory systems
Inventory management systems designed to deliver less merchandise on a more frequent basis than traditional inventory systems; the firm gets the merchandise "just in time" for it to be used in the manufacture of another product; also known as *quick response (QR)* systems in retailing.

quick response (QR)
An inventory management system used in retailing; merchandise is received just in time for sale when the customer wants it.

Sustainable Marketing 12.1   Driving the Bottom Line

If you like Frito-Lay SunChips, you may remember its 100 percent compostable bag. Made primarily of the plant-based material polylactic acid, the bag will completely break down in 14 weeks. It was all part of Frito-Lay Canada's "Leave No Trace" sustainability vision. The company set clear goals to use less water, electricity, and fuel and to reduce waste for everything it makes, moves, and sells.[33] At Frito-Lay, financial achievement is gauged by social and environmental performance.

With one of the largest private delivery fleets in Canada, Frito-Lay is keenly aware of the profound effect efficient vehicles can have on its carbon footprint. It has taken measures to enhance fleet performance, including the use of custom-designed vehicles that weigh less than comparable models, new low-emission engine technology, and even low-drag mud flaps and belly fairings. Optimization of delivery routes has allowed Frito-Lay to reduce the number of trucks it uses for distribution, an amazing feat given it is one of the fastest-growing consumer packaged-goods companies in Canada. Strategic sequencing of vendors on routes also resulted in reducing the number of kilometres travelled by 3 percent and diesel consumption by 7 percent.[34]

Frito-Lay Canada was the first food manufacturer to make zero-emission electric vehicles part of its delivery fleet.[35] The initial six trucks introduced had a range of 60 kilometres per day, which met the daily needs of

the majority of routes from its distribution centres in Brampton, Ottawa, Surrey, and Laval. The electricity the vehicles used was offset by renewable energy credits, and even the batteries could be recycled at the end of their lives. Due to the impact of cold Canadian winters on overall battery life, the trucks have since been relocated to the United States, where the fleet is enjoying a dramatic expansion.

The company's sustainability initiatives go far beyond fleet management. Frito-Lay Canada's efforts have resulted in saving 5.4 billion litres of water since 1999. It has been able to divert over 95 percent of manufacturing waste for reuse. Steam stack heat recovery systems are in place at all its plants to capture waste heat from the exhaust manufacturing line and divert it to warm its buildings, to dry starch, and to heat water and oil.[36] Since 1999, it has also reused 40 million cardboard shipping cartons, the equivalent of saving more than 300,000 trees annually. The focus on sustainability by Frito-Lay and its parent company, PepsiCo Canada, has not gone unnoticed, as PepsiCo was named as one of Canada's top 50 socially responsible companies by *Maclean's*.[37]

Commitment to sustainable growth is a core Frito-Lay Canada value, one that helps the company keep pace with an ever-changing market. It views sustainability as a journey and thus has many more initiatives planned for the future.

REAL MARKETER PROFILE | David Chilton

Armed with a degree in economics and an award for achieving the highest mark in the country on the Canadian Securities Course, David Chilton started his career as a stockbroker. Working with clients led him to the realization that while there were a lot of books about personal finances, there weren't many that made the topic easy to understand. He soon changed that, publishing *The Wealthy Barber* when he was only 27 years old. The book introduced Canadians to Roy, a barber who imparted sound financial advice while cutting his customers' hair. Based on common sense and an uncommon sense of humour, the book quickly became a bestseller with over 3 million copies sold. It is still the best-selling book of all-time in Canada.

The success of the book led to a career on the speaking circuit. His talks include topics such as "Success Strategies from the Wealthy Barber" and revolve around lessons from his business and personal experience. He claims his recipe for success is "a clear vision, hard work, and some clever marketing."[38] In truth, Chilton has experienced both success and failure, and says that "if you're not failing a lot, you're probably not trying enough."[39]

His publishing success brought sisters Janet and Greta Podleski to his door with a plea to help them get distribution for their *LooneySpoons* cookbook. Chilton famously says he can't cook. Fortunately his mother does. She tested the recipes and was so impressed she told him he had to back the venture. It was sound advice. The book spent 85 consecutive weeks on the bestseller list. He joined the Podleski sisters in Granet Publishing to produce two more best-selling cookbooks: *Crazy Plates* and *Eat, Shrink & Be Merry!*

Chilton also worked with the sisters to bring a frozen entrée, Crazy Plates, to Loblaws grocery stores. While normally very difficult to secure distribution, Chilton said that "having a great brand and sales of over 1.3 million cookbooks"[40] helped open doors. However, initial sales of the frozen food line did not meet expectations. While consumers loved the concept, the packaging and large size didn't work. The trio revitalized their marketing efforts with new package designs and a smaller size. While the product sold well after these changes, it has since been withdrawn from the market.

Although he swore he'd never write another book, 22 years later Chilton published *The Wealthy Barber Returns*. Unlike the first book, which focuses on saving more, the second book offers advice on spending less. It advises readers to track their spending and to live within their means. For anyone who knows Chilton, this is not surprising. He has a very modest lifestyle and isn't much of a shopper, in stark contrast to many people whose lives revolve around buying "stuff."

More recently, Chilton became the newest Dragon on popular CBC's *Dragons' Den*. It's gruelling work with long days spent listening to business pitches while taping shows. The "aw shucks, down-to-earth" personality you see on the show reflects Chilton's true character: a genuinely nice guy who often stays in touch with companies even when deals collapse after taping a show. With a sincere interest in people and their businesses, he likes to help if he can.

---

deliver less merchandise on a more frequent basis than traditional inventory systems. The firm gets the merchandise "just-in-time" for it to be used in the manufacture of another product, in the case of parts or components, or for sale when the customer wants it, in the case of consumer goods. The benefits of a JIT system include reduced **lead time** (by eliminating the need for paper transactions by mail and overnight deliveries), increased product availability, and lower inventory investment. JIT systems lower inventory investments, but product availability actually increases.

To illustrate a JIT system, consider P&G's five-step process: Managers start with demand data, which they obtain directly from their retailers. They work closely with these retailers to develop sales forecasts and shipping schedules that better align P&G's production with demand at the retail store. This effort reduces both excess inventory and out-of-stock situations. Most importantly, P&G produces just enough to meet demand. To achieve this balance, the company has moved from producing every product once a month to a system in which it produces every item every day, which it then delivers to the customer the following day.[41]

lead time
The amount of time between the recognition that an order needs to be placed and the arrival of the needed merchandise at the seller's store, ready for sale.

LEARNING OBJECTIVES REVIEW

 LO1 **Explain the importance of distribution and the interrelationships among distribution channels, supply chain management, and logistics management**

Companies cannot take the distribution of products for granted. Appropriate distribution channels must be identified and channel members need to be convinced to carry these new products, both of which are integral to a successful distribution strategy. A distribution channel is the set of institutions and marketing activities that transfer the ownership of and move goods from the manufacturer or producer to the consumer. Supply chain management refers to the effort to co-ordinate suppliers, manufacturers, warehouses, stores, and transportation intermediaries so that the merchandise the customer wants is produced in the right quantities and sent to the right locations at the time the customer wants it. In this sense, the supply chain is considered to be longer and covers more aspects of the distribution strategy since it extends backward to include suppliers. Logistics concentrates on the physical movement and control of the products, whereas supply chain management includes the managerial aspects of the process as well.

LO2 **Describe distribution channel design and management decisions and strategies**

Sometimes, particularly when firms are starting out, companies cannot choose their ideal partners but instead take any partners they can get to obtain the materials or customers they need. In general, the larger and more sophisticated the company, the more likely it will perform some supply chain activities itself rather than use third-party intermediaries. When deciding on the distribution channel structure, firms can choose from direct, indirect, and multichannel distribution. Firms that want as much market exposure as possible use intensive distribution, whereas firms that either want to maintain an exclusive image or are not large enough to sell to everyone tend to use an exclusive distribution strategy. Somewhere in the middle lies a selective distribution strategy.

LO3 **Identify how distribution channels add value to businesses and consumers**

Without distribution channels, consumers would be forced to find raw materials, manufacture products, and somehow get them to where they could be used, all on their own. Each channel member adds value to the product by performing one of these functions. Supply chain management creates value for each firm in the chain and helps bind together many company functions, including manufacturing, inventory management, transportation, advertising, and marketing.

LO4 **Explain how logistics management affects distribution strategy**

For a supply chain to operate properly, the flow of information and merchandise must be co-ordinated, and supply chain members must work together to their mutual benefit. In more sophisticated supply chains, information flows seamlessly between supply chain members through EDI. Many of the best supply chains use a JIT or QR inventory management system, which provides the right amount of inventory just when it is needed. The JIT systems thus improve product availability and reduce inventory investments. The increasing use of RFID technology is expected to have a revolutionary impact on distribution channels, supply chain management, and logistics management in the future. The expectation is that the overall system of producing and delivering will become much more sophisticated and efficient.

The more closely aligned the supply chain members are with each other, the less likely there will be significant conflict. An administered supply chain occurs when a dominant and powerful supply chain member has control over the other members. In a contractual supply chain (e.g., franchising), co-ordination and control are dictated by contractual relationships between members. Corporate supply chains can operate relatively smoothly because one firm owns the various levels of the chains. Supply chains also can be effectively managed through strong relationships developed with supply chain partners. To create such relationships, the partners must trust each other, communicate openly, have compatible goals, and be willing to invest in each other's success.

KEY TERMS

- administered vertical marketing system
- advanced shipping notice
- channel conflict
- contractual vertical marketing system
- corporate vertical marketing system
- dispatcher
- distribution centre
- distribution channel

- distribution intensity
- electronic data interchange (EDI)
- exclusive distribution
- franchising
- intensive distribution
- just-in-time (JIT) inventory systems
- lead time
- logistics management
- pull marketing strategy
- push marketing strategy

- quick response (QR)
- radio frequency identification (RFID) tags
- retailers
- selective distribution
- strategic relationship (partnering relationship)
- supply chain management
- universal product code (UPC)
- vertical marketing system
- wholesalers

CONCEPT REVIEW

1. Explain why having a well thought out distribution strategy is important to a company's success.

2. Explain the factors that must be considered when designing a distribution strategy.

3. Explain the differences between direct, indirect, and multichannel distribution systems. What role do technologies and consumer behaviour play in the rise of multichannel distribution?

4. Describe the functions performed by intermediaries. Why would companies choose to have intermediaries fulfill these functions rather than perform them themselves?

5. Explain how customer expectations and channel member characteristics impact a company's distribution strategy.

6. Explain intensive, selective, and exclusive distribution intensity. Under what circumstances would it be best to use each of these strategies?

7. Describe how companies manage distribution channels by using vertical marketing systems.

8. Explain how supply chain management and logistics management add value to a company's consumer offerings.

9. Explain how supply chain management improves marketing activities.

10. What are the major elements of a logistics management system? Explain the benefits of a well-run just-in-time inventory management system.

MARKETING APPLICATIONS

1. Explain distribution strategy and identify the major activities that distribution channels, supply chain, and logistics management involve. Identify several ways that supply chain management adds value to a company's offerings, with regard to both consumers and business partners.

2. You are hired by a small bakery that is interested in distributing its product through supermarkets. The market for the bakery's products has been steadily growing and it is time to expand distribution now that the bakery has expanded its production capacity. You have an appointment with the manager of a local grocery chain. The manager is familiar with the bakery's products and is excited about the possibility of having them in the store. He presents the contract and you notice a $10,000 fee for stocking the product. When you ask about the fee, you are told it is simply the cost of doing business and that the bigger bakeries are not in favour of adding your product line to the chain. You know that the bakery cannot afford to pay the fee. What should you do now?

3. Discuss the advantages and disadvantages of Dell's decision to change from using a direct distribution strategy to a multichannel approach to distribution.

4. Research the "100-mile diet" trend and discuss how growing consumer awareness of shipping costs and environmental concerns has led to a push for more locally produced foods.

5. Give an example of a retailer that participates in an independent (conventional) supply chain and one involved in a vertical marketing system. Discuss the advantages and disadvantages of each.

6. In what ways can the flow of information be managed in the supply chain? How can the ready flow of information increase a firm's operating efficiencies?

7. Describe how B2B transactions might employ EDI to process purchase information. Considering the information discussed in Chapter 5 about B2B buying situations, determine which buying situation (new task, modified rebuy, or straight rebuy) would most likely align with the use of EDI technology. Justify your answer.

8. Discuss the advantages to a retailer such as SportChek of expending the time and effort to get merchandise floor-ready at either the point of manufacture or in the distribution centre rather than having retail store staff members do it in the stores. Provide the logic behind your answer.

9. Why would a large company such as Nike want to develop strategic partnerships with locally owned running stores? Describe what Nike would have to do to maintain such relationships.

10. You are hired as an assistant brand manager for a popular consumer product. One day in an emergency meeting, the brand manager informs the group that there is a problem with one of the suppliers and that he has decided to send you over to the manufacturing facilities to investigate the problem. When you arrive at the plant, you learn that a key supplier has become increasingly unreliable in terms of quality and delivery. You ask the plant manager why he doesn't switch suppliers since this is becoming a major problem for your brand. He informs you that the troubled supplier is his cousin, whose wife has been very ill, and he just can't switch right now. What course of action should you take?

NET SAVVY

1. Dell is considered exemplary in its ability to manage its supply chain efficiently. Go to the company's website (http://www.dell.com) and go through the process of configuring a computer to purchase. Print a copy of the computer system you have designed, making note of the delivery date and price. Describe how Dell has revolutionized computer sales and delivery. Is there any indication that Dell has partnered with other companies to sell periph-eral equipment such as printers or scanners? How would this partnership add value to customers?

2. The chapter case study examines how Zara, a division of Inditex, successfully manages its supply chain. Visit Inditex's website (http://www.inditex.com) and review the company's commitment to social responsibility, particularly the section that pertains to its code of conduct. Considering the discussion in this chapter about strategic relationships, how does Inditex address the factors necessary for mutually beneficial partnerships according to its code of conduct?

CHAPTER CASE STUDY

ZARA DELIVERS FAST FASHION[42]

In the fast fashion retail business strategy, supply chain management processes serve to introduce fashionable merchandise rapidly, such that stores can respond immediately to customer demand for merchandise. This was pioneered by Zara, a global specialty apparel chain located in La Coruna, Spain. It has also been adopted by other retailers, including American Apparel, H&M (headquartered in Sweden), TopShop (U.K.) and Forever 21 (U.S.).

The approach is particularly effective for specialty apparel retailers that target fashion-conscious consumers who simply must have the latest looks—but they want to do so on a very limited budget. These shoppers load up on new fast fashions every few weeks, instead of purchasing a few higher-priced basics every few months.

To fit with such short cycles and meet customers' demands, the fast fashion process starts with the receipt of timely information from store managers. At Zara, store managers always have their reporting devices literally in hand. These handheld devices, which are linked directly to the company's corporate office in Spain, enable daily reports on what customers are buying (or not) and what they are asking for but not finding.

For example, customers might want a purple version of a pink shirt that they see on the shop floor. Managers immediately pass the information on to the designers in Spain. Those designers then communicate electronically with the factory that produces fabric for shirts. This factory starts up its automated equipment, which is run by assemblers who live in close proximity to the factory. (The undyed fabric comes from Asia, where Zara finds inexpensive sources, and then bulk ships fabric to Spain and Portugal to be manufactured into apparel.) The robots in the company's 23 highly automated factories start cutting out shirts and mixing purple dye. For final construction, a network of 300 or so small assemblers, located near the factories in Galicia, Spain, and northern Portugal, take responsibility for making the final product. Finally, to ensure timely delivery, the shirts get shipped by truck to stores in Europe and by air express to stores in the rest of the world.

> Zara's competitive advantage in specialty apparel retailing is based on its efficient supply chain that delivers fashionable merchandise to its stores frequently.

The Benefits of Fast Fashion for Zara

Zara's main advantage over its competitors, such as The Gap and H&M, has resulted from its highly responsive and tightly organized supply chain. Unlike these competitors, Zara selects factory locations that are in close geographic proximity to the company's headquarters in Spain. Although this approach increases labour costs, compared with outsourced production in lower-cost countries in Asia, it also improves communication, reduces shipping costs and time, and reduces the time before new fashions appear in stores. It also gives Zara the flexibility to modify its operations in one supply chain function to expedite processes in another, such as pricing or tagging. It might hang merchandise on racks in the warehouse so that store employees can move apparel directly from delivery to the sales floor. And it can do all this because it maintains complete control over the entire process.

Furthermore, instead of shipping new products a few times a season, as many of its competitors do, Zara makes deliveries to every one of its stores every few days. The purple shirts would be in stores in two weeks—compared with the several months it would take most department stores and other specialty apparel stores to accomplish the same feat. Because its fast fashion system also ensures shorter lead times, it's less likely that any Zara store will be out of stock before the next sweater shipment arrives. Limiting the stock in stores even can create a sense of scarcity among its customers. If they don't buy now, the item might not be available next time they visit the store. By producing and shipping in these small quantities, Zara can quickly recover from its (rare) fashion faux pas.

Finally, the efficiency of its supply chain means Zara rarely has to discount merchandise that is not selling. At Zara, the number of items that end up marked down is about half the industry average. Even with these results, Zara still manages to introduce around 10,000 new designs and 40,000 new SKUs each year.

Moving Too Fast? The Negative Effects of Fast Fashion

Despite some strong signals of success—including annual growth rates of approximately 20 percent in terms of sales and number of stores—Zara started to outgrow its own strategy. By their very nature, fashion trends change rapidly and constantly, and so must the merchandise on Zara's shop floors. Faced with disappointed customers, some sales managers ordered extra quantities of hot items, to avoid stockouts. Even with this attempt to circumvent the replenishment system, some stores still suffered from stockouts, because they received fewer units than they had ordered when overall demand exceeded inventory levels. For some items, Zara even confronted perhaps the most frustrating scenario in a supply chain: inventory sat unused, eating up storage costs, at one location, even as another store desperately pleaded for the same inventory to meet its customers' demand.

As noted above, the company launches as many as 10,000 new styles annually, with a range of colours and sizes, resulting in hundreds of thousands of SKUs in the system. Counting replenishment orders, which are received twice weekly, Zara's average shipping total reached nearly 2.5 million items per week, all coming from the company's distribution centre. Its legendary supply chain efficiency thus was in danger of a clogged artery.

In response, Zara has adopted some new mathematical processes that turn human experience and mountains of data into actionable information. These models factor in store managers' unique requests for merchandise replenishments, together with historical trends in the sales of the same item. Merchandise display practices have been altered, such as removing all sizes of a garment from the sales floor if a popular size is not available. This practice helps reduce customer frustration, in that they never see an item that might not be available in their size. It also diminishes shipping; if the medium size is unavailable, the small and large sizes do not get shipped either. Instead, these remaining sizes head toward the stores that still have all sizes in stock, so they can be available to customers there.

Growth, costs, market demand, and technology advances all can push retail executives to rethink their business processes. But truly savvy managers search for ways to optimize operations, even when business is running smoothly. As Zara learned, current approaches will not necessarily work tomorrow. As the founder of Zara's corporate owner Inditex told the company's first deputy chair and CEO, "Once a month, come here thinking that we are near bankruptcy. You will find a lot of things to change."[43]

Questions

1. How does an individual firm like Zara manage a supply chain? How does it get new products from design to store so quickly?

2. What are some of the ways that Zara's supply chain management system has helped create value for its customers? Provide specific examples.

3. What challenges did Zara's focus on supply chain efficiency create? Are all such systems destined to suffer such "growing pains"?

CHAPTER **13**

Retailing and Multichannel Marketing

As fast as the dry cleaners, as friendly as the concierge at a hotel—can Apple stores leap tall buildings too?[1] Apple retail stores, crucial for the company's success and accounting for 20 percent of the company's revenue, have led to its recognition as one of *Fortune*'s Most Admired Companies. Before it opened its own retail stores, Apple allowed product sales through large retailers, which meant the company depended on these electronics retailers. The retailers had no special incentive to market Apple products, nor did they have the training necessary to sell the technologically advanced items. Apple therefore realized that the only way it could ensure its unique products really stood out was by taking the responsibility for selling into its own hands.

In the course of this decision, Apple spent significant time and effort designing its stores. The company leased warehouse space to create a prototype store that it could then replicate throughout North America. After a few iterations, the ultimate Apple Store emerged that changed the retail game. The store was bright and modern, a complete reverse from past electronics stores. It was based on a design that considered how customers shop for products, not just the product categories themselves. Apple's largest flagship store in Boston looks like a glass cube with a glowing Apple logo. Even some of the smaller stores carry this theme, with ceilings that make the stores appear as if they are lit by the sun. In Canada, most of Apple's 28 retail locations[2] are housed in malls; yet, all are designed to be bright, open, and inviting. Computers are connected to the Internet, and customers are free to surf the Internet and chat online. If you are in need of an Internet café, Apple Stores provide the service for free!

The Apple Store has become more than just a retailer to sell its iPods, iPhones, iPads, and so forth. The store offers an array of free services and is designed to allow customers to try out the different products before buying them. This benefit is especially important for early adopters who want to try new technologies as soon as they are available. For customers who need more assistance with products or who are pressed for time, the store offers personal shopping. A customer can make an appointment with a "Specialist" at a store to learn about the products of interest without being obligated to make a purchase. For

LEARNING OBJECTIVES

After studying this chapter you should be able to

LO1 Outline the considerations associated with choosing retail partners

LO2 Identify what types of retailers are available to distribute products

LO3 Describe the components of a retail strategy building on the four Ps to create value for consumers

LO4 Identify the benefits and challenges of multichannel retailing

free technical services, the store offers a Genius Bar, with "Geniuses" who have been trained at the corporate headquarters on Apple products.

The stores also offer free workshops, focusing on everything from the basics of using Apple products to using Adobe Photoshop to create business presentations. For professional photographers, musicians, and filmmakers, workshops teach the detailed applications that they can use to optimize their finished products. The Apple stores also offer camps for children, workshops for families, and more.

When customers enter the store, a person wearing an orange shirt, the "Concierge," directs them where they need to go. The store avoids checkout counters; instead, salespeople use EasyPay: mobile wireless credit card readers to check out customers right on the sales floor.

Apple also can brag about achieving the best-per-square-foot sales in the country—$5,791 per square foot in 2012[3], far more than Best Buy at $857,[4] Tiffany & Co. at $3,453, and Lululemon at $2,464.[5] However, this apple got bruised as sales per square foot fell to $4,542 the following year.[6] Some analysts feel that Apple's store experience is getting stale and that the company needs to apply its famous powers of innovation to reinvent it. To stay on top of its game, Apple must demonstrate retail leadership and vision while still producing the best technology and the best customer service in the industry. ▌

Retailing sits at the end of the supply chain, where marketing meets the consumer. As Apple realized before it started to open its retail stores, regardless of how strong a firm's strategy is or how great the product or service is, if it isn't available when the customer wants it, where he or she wants it, at the right price, and in the right size, colour, and style, it simply won't sell. It is primarily the retailer's responsibility to make sure that these customers' expectations are fulfilled.

In this chapter, we explain how manufacturers choose retailers to carry their products and we discuss the types of retailers currently operating in Canada. Then we examine how retailers create value by implementing marketing mix strategies. We follow this with a discussion of how multichannel options are changing the face of retailing and the ongoing evolution toward multichannel marketing.

Retailing is defined as the set of business activities that add value to products and services sold to consumers for their personal or family use. Our definition of retailing includes products bought at stores, through catalogues, and over the Internet, as well as services such as fast-food restaurants, airlines, and hotels. Some retailers claim they sell at "wholesale" prices, but if they sell to customers for their personal use, they are still retailers, regardless of how low their prices may be. Wholesalers, in contrast, are those firms engaged in buying, taking title to, often storing, and physically handling goods in large quantities, and then reselling the goods (usually in smaller quantities) to retailers or industrial or business users (as defined in Chapter 12).

Retailing today is changing, both in Canada and around the world. No longer do manufacturers rule many marketing channels, as they once did. Retailers such as Walmart, Carrefour (a French hypermarket), Home Depot, Loblaws, and Metro (a German retail conglomerate)[7]—the largest retailers in the world—dictate to their suppliers

retailing
The set of business activities that add value to products and services sold to consumers for their personal or family use; includes products bought at stores, through catalogues, and over the Internet, as well as services such as fast-food restaurants, airlines, and hotels.

what should be made, how it should be config-
ured, when it should be delivered, and, to some
extent, what it should cost. These retailers are
clearly in the driver's seat.

Retailing in the aggregate is a big business.
Virtually every penny you personally spend,
except for taxes, goes to retailers. Food, rent,
clothing, tuition, insurance, and haircuts are
all either retail services or goods provided by
retailers. Even nonprofit organizations such
as the Salvation Army, Goodwill Industries,
and the Ontario Science Centre have retail
operations. Canadian retail sales in 2012 were
$469.9 billion,[8] representing more than 227,000
retail establishments. Retailing is Canada's third
largest industry by size, employing approximately 2 million people.[9]

Even nonprofit
organizations such as
Goodwill Industries have
retail operations.

This chapter examines how and why manufacturers use retailers. The manufacturer's
strategy depends on its overall market power and on how consistent a new product or
product line is with its current offerings.

Exhibit 13.1 illustrates four factors manufacturers consider when developing strategies for working with retailers.[10] In choosing retail partners, the first factor, manufacturers assess how likely it is for certain retailers to carry their products. Manufacturers
also consider where their target customers expect to find the products, because those
are exactly the stores in which they want to place their products. The overall size and
level of sophistication of the manufacturer will determine how many of the supply
chain functions it performs and how many it will hand off to other channel members.
Finally, the type and availability of the product and the image the manufacturer wishes
to portray will determine how many retailers within a geographic region will carry
the products.

For the second factor, manufacturers identify the types of retailers that would
be appropriate to carry its products. Although the choice is often obvious—such as a
supermarket for fresh produce—manufacturers may have a choice of retailer types for
some products.

As we discussed in Chapter 12, a hallmark of a strong distribution channel is that
manufacturers and retailers co-ordinate their efforts in it. In the third factor, manufacturers and retailers therefore develop their strategy by implementing the four Ps.

Finally, many retailers and some manufacturers are exploring a **multichannel
strategy** in which they sell in more than one channel (e.g., store, catalogue, kiosk,
and Internet). The fourth factor therefore consists of examining the circumstances
in which sellers may prefer to adopt a particular strategy. Although these factors
are listed consecutively, manufacturers may consider them all simultaneously or in a
different order.

multichannel strategy
Selling in more than one
channel (e.g., store, catalogue, kiosk, and Internet).

EXHIBIT 13.1 Factors for Establishing a Relationship with Retailers

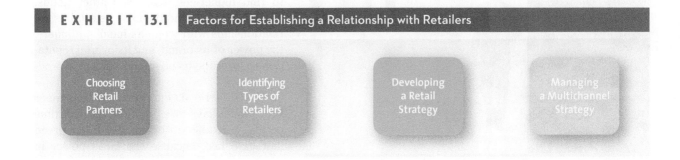

Choosing Retail Partners | Identifying Types of Retailers | Developing a Retail Strategy | Managing a Multichannel Strategy

LO1 CHOOSING RETAIL PARTNERS

Imagine trying to buy a suit for a job interview without being able to visit a retailer. You would have to figure out exactly what size, colour, and style of suit you wanted. Then you'd have to contact various manufacturers, whether in person, by phone, or over the Internet, and order the suit. Assuming it fit you reasonably well, you might still need to take it to a tailor to have the sleeves shortened. Then you'd have to go through the same process for a shirt or blouse, accessories, and shoes. It would not be very convenient.

Retailers such as Moores Clothing for Men create value by pulling it all together for you. The store offers a broad selection of suits, shirts, ties, and other accessories that it has carefully chosen in advance. You can see, touch, feel, and try on each item while in the store. You can buy one suit or shirt at a time or buy several shirts to go with your new suit. Finally, the store provides a salesperson to help you co-ordinate your outfit and a tailor to make the whole thing fit perfectly.

When choosing retail partners, manufacturers must look at the basic channel structure, where their target customers expect to find the products, and channel member characteristics. As discussed in Chapter 12, distribution intensity is also a factor to be considered. Consider the following scenarios:

- **Scenario 1**: Cosmetics conglomerate Estée Lauder's subsidiary brand MAC is introducing a new line of mascara.

- **Scenario 2**: Coach, well-known for its women's handbags, is introducing a line of men's leather goods, apparel, shoes, and accessories—products not previously in its assortment.

- **Scenario 3**: Britt, a young entrepreneur, is launching a new line of environmentally friendly (green) hair care products.

Each of these scenarios is different and requires the manufacturer to consider different alternatives for reaching its target markets through retailers.

Channel Structure

The level of difficulty a manufacturer has in getting retailers to purchase its products is determined by the degree to which the channel is vertically integrated, as described in Chapter 12; the degree to which the manufacturer has a strong brand or is otherwise desirable in the market; and the relative power of the manufacturer and retailer.

Scenario 1 represents a corporate vertical marketing system. Because MAC is made by Estée Lauder and operates its own stores, when the new mascara line is introduced, the stores will simply receive the new line automatically. They have no choice.

However, when an established firm such as Coach enters a new market with men's leather goods, apparel, shoes, and accessories, as is the case in Scenario 2, it cannot just place the products with any retailer. It must determine where its customers would expect to find higher-end scarves, leather goods, and accessories, and then use its established relationships with women's handbag buyers, the power of its brand, and its overall reputation to leverage its position in this new product area.

In Scenario 3, our young entrepreneur Britt would have an even more difficult time getting a retailer to buy and sell her green hair care line, because she lacks power in the marketplace—she is small, and her brand

Moores Clothing for Men creates value by helping men put it all together. Its wardrobe consultants provide fashion advice, and their tailors make sure everything fits properly.

is unknown. It would be difficult to get buyers to see her, let alone consider her line. She might face relatively high listing fees (see Chapter 12) just to get space on retailers' shelves. But like Coach in Scenario 2, when choosing retailers to which to sell, Britt should consider where the end customer expects to find her products, as well as some important retailer characteristics.

Customer Expectations

From a retailer's perspective, it is important to know from which manufacturers its customers want to buy. Manufacturers, in contrast, need to know where their target market customers expect to find their products and those of their competitors. Customers generally expect to find certain products at some stores but not at others. For example, Estée Lauder and Coach would not choose to sell to Target or Giant Tiger because their customers would not expect to shop at those stores for high-end cosmetics or leather goods. Instead, Target might carry less expensive cosmetic brands, such as Revlon and Maybelline, and discontinued lines probably appear at Giant Tiger. But Coach customers would definitely expect to find the brand's clothing offerings at major department stores and at Coach stores.

Companies need to stay abreast of changes in where customers buy products and what products they request, and then change their distribution strategies accordingly. As an example, when country singer Garth Brooks realized that the majority of his CDs were purchased at Walmart, he signed an exclusive distribution deal with the retailer that eliminated his record label. Similarly, 1970s Rock and Roll Hall of Fame band The Eagles released *Long Road out of Eden* exclusively at Walmart. Other bands, such as Journey and Foreigner, have since taken the same path. Although decisions such as these limit distribution to just one retailer, artists benefit from increased promotion and an increased share of the profits.

Channel Member Characteristics

Several factors pertaining to the channel members themselves will help determine the channel structure. Generally, the larger and more sophisticated the channel member, the less likely that it will use supply chain intermediaries. Britt will probably use a group of independent salespeople to help sell her green hair care line, whereas a large manufacturer such as Estée Lauder will use its own sales force that already has existing relationships in the industry. In the same way, an independent grocery store might buy merchandise from a wholesaler; but Walmart, the world's largest grocer, buys only directly from the manufacturer. Larger firms often find that by performing the channel functions themselves, they can gain more control, be more efficient, and save money.

As we noted in Chapter 12, like any large complicated system, a distribution channel is difficult to manage. Whether the balance of power rests with large retailers like Walmart or with large manufacturers like P&G, channel members benefit by working together to develop and implement their channel strategy. In the next section, we explore the different types of retailers with an eye toward which would be most appropriate for each of our scenarios: MAC Cosmetics, Coach's products for men, and Britt's new line of environmentally friendly hair care products.

IDENTIFYING TYPES OF RETAILERS

LO2

Although it may seem clear which type of retailer Coach and Britt may wish to pursue when attempting to place their new lines, the choice is not always straightforward. Manufacturers need to understand the general characteristics of different types of retailers so they can determine the best channels for their product. For instance, the characteristics of a retailer that are important to a food manufacturer may be quite different than those of a cosmetics manufacturer. In the next few sections, we examine the various types of retailers, identify some major players, and discuss some of the issues facing each type.

Food Retailers

The food retailing landscape is changing dramatically. Not too long ago, people shopped for food primarily at traditional grocery stores. Today, however, you can buy food at drugstores, discount stores, warehouse clubs, and convenience stores. Pharmacy chains such as Shoppers Drug Mart offer milk, bread, and even fresh fruit in some locations. Walmart and the Real Canadian Superstore both provide supercentres whose product mix contains 30 to 40 percent food items. Even Amazon is getting into the grocery business. To stay competitive, Loblaw is testing e-commerce sales.

Food sales represent about 50 percent of the total sales in warehouse clubs such as Costco. Convenience stores now offer more than a slushie and gasoline; for example, Petro-Canada Neighbours stores provide upscale sandwiches and salads. And retailers such as Walmart and IKEA have in-store restaurants, making it easy for customers to shop longer. And, of course, restaurants also compete for consumers' food dollars. The characteristics of the three major categories of food retailers—**conventional supermarkets**, **big-box food retailers**, and convenience stores—are summarized in Exhibit 13.2.

All this competition can mean trouble for traditional grocery stores. Yet some continue to thrive because they offer their target customers great value—they are conveniently located, make shopping easy, have fair prices, and find special products and services that are important to their customers. Pete's Frootique, a Halifax-based grocery store, effectively competes on selection and service. Knowledgeable staff members offer information about the selection of produce, storage, and cooking tips, and an in-house registered dietitian helps shoppers understand which foods can re-energize their health.[11] Entrepreneurial Marketing 13.1 shows how one company is trying to stand out in grocery stores.

General Merchandise Retailers

The main types of **general merchandise retailers** are discount stores, specialty stores, category specialists, department stores, drugstores, off-price retailers, and extreme-value retailers. Many of these general merchandise retailers sell through multiple channels, such as the Internet and catalogues, as discussed later in this chapter.

conventional supermarket
Offers groceries, meat, and produce with limited sales of nonfood items, such as health and beauty aids and general merchandise, in a self-service format.

big-box food retailers
Come in three types: supercentre, hypermarket, and warehouse club; larger than a conventional supermarket; carries both food and nonfood items.

general merchandise retailers
May be discount stores, specialty stores, category specialists, department stores, drugstores, off-price retailers, or extreme-value retailers; may sell through multiple channels, such as the Internet and catalogues.

EXHIBIT 13.2	Food Retailer Characteristics	
Category	**Description**	**Examples**
Conventional supermarket	Offers groceries, meat, and produce with limited sales of nonfood items, such as health and beauty aids and general merchandise, in a self-service format.	Safeway is a popular supermarket in Western Canada; Sobeys is common on the East Coast.
Big-box food retailer	Comes in three types: supercentres, hypermarkets, and warehouse clubs. Larger than conventional supermarkets, they carry both food and nonfood items.	Supercentres and warehouse clubs are popular in Canada, whereas hypermarkets tend to flourish in Europe and South America. Hypermarkets (Carrefour) and warehouse clubs (Costco) generally carry a greater percentage of food.
Convenience store	Provides a limited number of items at convenient locations in small stores with speedy checkout.	Stores such as 7-Eleven generally charge higher prices than most other types of food stores. Most convenience stores also sell gasoline, which accounts for more than 55 percent of their annual sales.

| Entrepreneurial Marketing 13.1 | Our Ice Is Cooler[12] |

For years ice has been considered a commodity product. After all, how do you differentiate it? Enter Danielle Nesbit and Jennifer Trayler, Vancouver-based entrepreneurs with a crystal clear vision of how to make ice cool. They launched On the Rocks to provide ice for special events. With a 5 centimetre sphere, their ice cubes melt slowly and don't dilute drinks as fast as regular ice cubes.

After supplying events in the Vancouver area for two years, the partners wanted to expand to retail channels, specifically, bagged ice in grocery stores. Bright blue packaging was designed to make their product stand out in store freezers while still allowing consumers to see the ice cubes through opaque sections of the bag. The challenge was how to get retailers on side. They pitched their concept on CBC's *Dragons' Den* to help them in their quest to become "Ice Princesses."

The Dragons weren't keen to invest. Nevertheless, Nesbit and Trayler have convinced retailers to get on board. Chains such as Whole Foods, Urban Fare, and T&T Supermarket now carry this cool product. These high-end

Bright blue packaging makes this ice stand out in the freezer section of grocery stores.

stores align perfectly with On the Rocks' upscale positioning. Shipping frozen products presents a distribution challenge so sales are focused on the Vancouver lower mainland area until they can break the ice to sell in other provinces.

Discount Stores   A **discount store** offers a broad variety of merchandise, limited service, and low prices. Walmart and Target dominate the discount store industry in Canada and vie for similar target markets. But because their competencies are slightly distinct, they both can survive. Walmart pioneered the everyday low-price concept, and its efficient operations have allowed it to offer the lowest-priced basket of merchandise in every market in which it competes—which doesn't necessarily mean that Walmart has the lowest price on every item in every market. But it does try to be the lowest across a wide variety. Target, which first opened stores in Canada in 2013, offers fashionable merchandise at low prices in a pleasant shopping environment. It has delivered an image of "cheap chic" by offering limited-edition exclusive apparel and cosmetic lines.

discount store
Offers a broad variety of merchandise, limited service, and low prices.

Specialty Stores   **Specialty stores** concentrate on a limited number of complementary merchandise categories in relatively small stores. These stores tailor their retail strategy toward very specific market segments by offering deep but narrow assortments and sales associate expertise. For example, Payless ShoeSource is the largest specialty family footwear retailer in the Western hemisphere. Payless stores feature fashionable, quality footwear and accessories for women, men, and children at affordable prices in a self-selection format. Some specialty stores are expanding their online specialty profile as well, as Social and Mobile Marketing 13.1 describes.

Estée Lauder's MAC line of cosmetics sells in the company's own retail specialty stores, as well as in some department stores. Specialty stores would be excellent outlets for the new lines by Estée Lauder and Britt. Customers likely expect to find Coach's line of men's leather goods and accessories in men's apparel, gift, or leather stores. Britt's line of green hair care products would fit nicely in a specialty store such as Sephora.

Sephora, France's leading perfume and cosmetic chain—a division of the luxury goods conglomerate LVMH (Louis Vuitton–Moët Hennessy)—is an example of an innovative specialty store concept. In Canada, prestigious cosmetics are typically sold in

specialty stores
Concentrate on a limited number of complementary merchandise categories in a relatively small store.

Social and Mobile Marketing 13.1

Buy, Play, and Sell, Wherever You Choose

To become the one-stop shop for video gamers, GameStop not only provides unique in-store experiences but also encourages online interactions by its customers, both among themselves and with its representatives. Gaming enthusiasts thus can hang out at the stores to compete in the latest version of the hottest game, or they can interact online.[13] In these social settings, video game players chat with other gamers, discover codes and tricks in the game, and find passwords that help them achieve higher levels of play.

In this entertainment category—the fastest growing overall—GameStop has continually achieved strong sales increases, including double-digit increases in same-store sales, through its GameStop, EB Games, Electronics Boutique, EBgames.com, and GameStop.com brands. Although the typical video gamer is a 31-year-old man, 58 percent of Canadians actively participate in gaming, and 46 percent of gamers are women.[14]

A typical video game is used for approximately 80 hours, making it a great value on a cost per hour basis, especially compared with other forms of entertainment. Yet despite this value, new video games are relatively expensive, costing around $60. So GameStop sells used games and equipment and grants customers credit for used games they trade in to the store. In addition, it has developed the GameStop Network online, which includes four sectors: Kongregate, Jolt, Impulse Driven, and GameStop.

On Kongregate, for example, players can access more than 50,000 free games that they play with others. There are varied ways to connect: chat rooms and forums, competitions in the games, and through the mobile app, Kongregate Arcade. By playing, users also can earn PowerUp Rewards points, which they can redeem on the other GameStop sites for access to paying games and other in-game benefits.[15] On Jolt, they can participate in a social gaming soccer league by joining the *Championship Manager: Rivals* series and providing the decisions for their chosen team.[16] Most of these options also have Facebook links, enabling friends to play through their pages.

Such tactics have made GameStop the largest multichannel video game retailer in the world and led to new innovations as well, such as Spawn Labs, its new streaming technology platform.[17] To get to the gamers, GameStop is ready to go anywhere they are.

---

category specialist
Offers a narrow variety but a deep assortment of merchandise.

Sephora is an innovative specialty store that sells cosmetics.

department stores. Each brand has a separate counter and a commissioned salesperson is stationed behind the counter to help customers. Sephora is a cosmetic and perfume specialty store offering a deep assortment in a self-service, 550 to 840 square metre format. Its stores provide more than 15 000 SKUs and more than 200 brands, including its own, private-label brand. Merchandise is grouped by product category, with the brands displayed alphabetically so customers can locate them easily. Customers are free to shop and experiment on their own. Product testing is encouraged. The knowledgeable salespeople, always available to assist customers, are paid a salary by Sephora, unlike department store cosmetic salespeople, who are compensated in part by incentives provided by the vendors. The low-key, open-sell environment results in customers spending more time shopping.

Category Specialists A **category specialist** offers a narrow variety but a deep assortment of merchandise. Some are like large specialty stores, such as Paderno (home and kitchen tools) or Chapters Indigo (books); others resemble discount stores in appearance and have similar low prices but offer a more concentrated assortment of goods, such as Future Shop (consumer electronics) or RONA (home improvement). Most category specialists use a self-service approach, but some, such as Home Depot, provide extensive customer service. Because category specialists offer such an extensive assortment in a particular category, they can so overwhelm the category that other retailers have difficulty competing; in these cases, the specialists are frequently called **category killers**.

Department Stores   Department stores refer to those retailers that carry many different types of merchandise (broad variety) and lots of items within each type (deep assortment), offer some customer services, and are organized into separate departments to display their merchandise. Department stores often resemble a collection of specialty shops, including women's, men's, and children's clothing and accessories; home furnishings and furniture; and kitchenwares and small appliances.

With the demise of Eaton's, the largest remaining department store chains in Canada are Sears and Hudson's Bay. Other store chains are very diverse. Some, such as Sears, carry less expensive products and compete more closely with discount stores, whereas others, such as Holt Renfrew, sell expensive, exclusive merchandise and compete with high-end specialty store chains.

Department stores have lost market share to specialty stores, discount stores, and category specialists in recent years. They seem to have gotten stuck in the middle, between those retailers that provide a better value at lower prices and those that offer more complete and fashionable assortments and better customer service, according to consumer perceptions. But they are fighting back with a vengeance. Hudson's Bay has begun placing a greater emphasis on high-fashion, private-label merchandise than it did in the past. Facing a flood of American rivals, including Nordstrom, Nordstrom Rack, Bloomingdales, and J. Crew, that plan to open Canadian locations, both Holt Renfrew and Hudson's Bay have leapt into the discount category. Holt's launched hr2 stores in Brossard, Quebec, and Vaughan, Ontario, offering leading brands at discount prices.[18] Hudson's Bay unveiled its first outlet store outside Toronto featuring "mid-tier" brands such as Calvin Klein, Guess, and DKNY.[19]

Stores such as Home Depot are known as category specialists because they offer a narrow variety but a deep assortment of merchandise.

Drugstores   **Drugstores** are specialty stores that concentrate on health and personal grooming merchandise, though pharmaceuticals often represent more than 60 percent of their sales. The largest drugstore chains in Canada—Shoppers Drug Mart (Pharmaprix in Quebec), Jean Coutu, PharmaSave, and London Drugs[20]—face a major challenge because of the low margins they earn on prescription drugs; health insurance companies and government programs pay most of the cost of many prescriptions, and the health insurance companies negotiate substantially lower prices with drugstores. These drugstores therefore are attempting to make up for their lost profits on prescriptions by concentrating their efforts on nonpharmaceutical products. General merchandise has long been a staple in drugstores, but food, and particularly fresh food such as milk and fruit, is a relatively new addition to their assortment.[21]

Off-Price Retailers   **Off-price retailers**, such as Winners, Designer Depot, and HomeSense, offer an inconsistent assortment of merchandise at relatively low prices. They typically buy from manufacturers or other retailers with excess inventory or at the end of a season for one-quarter to one-fifth the original wholesale price. Because of the way these retailers buy, customers can never be confident that the same type of merchandise will be in stock each time they visit the store. Different bargains also will be available on each visit. To improve their offerings' consistency, some off-price retailers

category killer
Offers an extensive assortment in a particular category, so overwhelming the category that other retailers have difficulty competing.

drugstore
A specialty store that concentrates on health and personal grooming merchandise, though pharmaceuticals may represent more than 60 percent of its sales.

off-price retailer
A type of retailer that offers an inconsistent assortment of merchandise at relatively low prices.

extreme-value retailer
A general merchandise
discount store found in
lower-income urban or
rural areas.

complement their opportunistically bought merchandise with merchandise purchased at regular wholesale prices. In addition to their low prices, the key to off-price retailers' success is the treasure hunt environment they create.

Extreme-value retailers are a subset of off-price retailers and one of the fastest growing retailing segments. **Extreme-value retailers**, such as Dollarama, are general merchandise discount stores found in lower-income urban or rural areas. They are much smaller than traditional discount stores, usually less than 840 square metres.

services retailers
Firms that primarily
sell services rather
than merchandise.

Services Retailers   The retail firms discussed in the previous sections sell products to consumers. However, **services retailers**, or firms that primarily sell services rather than merchandise, are a large and growing part of the retail industry. Consider a typical Saturday: After a bagel and cup of coffee at a nearby Great Canadian Bagel, you go to the laundromat to wash and dry your clothes, drop a suit off at a dry cleaner, have a prescription filled at a Rexall drugstore, and make your way to Jiffy Lube to have your car's oil changed. In a hurry, you drive through a Burger King so you can eat lunch quickly and be on time for your haircut at Supercuts. By mid-afternoon, you're ready for a workout at the YMCA. After stopping at home for a change of clothes, you're off to dinner, a movie, and dancing with a friend. Finally, to end your day, you buy a caffè latte at Starbucks, having interacted with 10 different services retailers during the day.

There are a wide variety of services retailers, along with some national companies, that provide these services. These companies are retailers because they sell goods and services to consumers. However, some are not just retailers. For example, airlines, banks, hotels, and insurance and express mail companies sell their services to businesses as well as consumers.

Organizations such as banks, hospitals, health spas, legal clinics, entertainment firms, and universities that offer services to consumers traditionally have not considered themselves retailers. Yet due to increased competition, these organizations are adopting retailing principles to attract customers and satisfy their needs.

Several trends suggest considerable future growth in services retailing. For example, the aging population will increase demand for health care services. Younger people are also spending more time and money on health and fitness. Busy parents in two-income families are willing to pay to have their homes cleaned, lawns maintained, clothes washed and pressed, and meals prepared so they can spend more time with their families.

L03 DEVELOPING A RETAIL STRATEGY

In a time when more and more Canadian consumers are value conscious, retailers need strategies that deliver. Today's consumers shop at any retailer or through any retailing channel they feel provides the best value for their money. And the lines between the different types of retailers are increasingly becoming blurred as retailers expand the range of their merchandise and services. For example, Walmart, and to a lesser extent Shoppers Drug Mart, have moved into the grocery business. Thus, it is extremely important for retailers to develop effective retailing strategies and market positioning in order to differentiate themselves in the increasingly competitive landscape and give customers a compelling reason to shop at their stores.

retail mix
Product (merchandise
assortment), pricing,
promotion, place, person-
nel, and presentation
(store design and display)
strategies to reach and
serve consumers.

In developing an effective retailing strategy, many of the principles we discussed in Chapter 6 on segmentation, targeting, and positioning can be very helpful. Retailers must first obtain a deep understanding of the consumers in their markets—their attitudes, behaviours, and preferences. Then they must use this knowledge of their consumers to develop market segments and select those segments they want to serve. Retailers that try to be all things to all people often end up not being able to serve any particular segment appropriately and soon find themselves in serious trouble. Once the target market is selected, retailers must develop the **retail mix**: product (merchandise assortment), pricing, promotion, place, personnel, and presentation (store design and display) strategies to reach and serve these consumers. These elements must be closely co-ordinated so that they portray a consistent and clear positioning so consumers know what type of customers the retailer is targeting and how it wants to serve them. For example, a retailer such as Harry Rosen, which wants to be perceived as a high-end clothing retailer, carries high-quality clothing, offers personalized services, and charges premium prices for its merchandise. Harry Rosen's store image and atmospherics (presentation) also portray an image of affluence and professionalism—an image that is consistent with its customers' perceptions of themselves.

Like other marketers, retailers perform important functions that increase the value of products and services they sell to consumers. We now examine in more detail how retailers develop the retail mix.

Product (Merchandise Assortment)

A typical grocery store carries 30,000 to 40,000 different items; a regional department store might carry as many as 200,000. Providing the right mix of merchandise and services that satisfies the needs of the target market is one of retailers' most fundamental activities. Offering assortments gives customers choice and helps attract new and existing customers: Loblaw has created many different store formats for different target customers. For example, Loblaw's Real Canadian Superstores are for customers who want high-quality products, a wide range of product assortments, and high levels of service, and are willing to pay a premium but Loblaw's No Frills stores are for customers who want to pay much lower prices and don't mind narrower product assortments and less service.

Hudson's Bay added designer shoe lines to its mix when its analysis showed that footwear sales trends were rising, while clothing and accessory sales were falling.[22] It is now the top seller of women's shoes in Canada. To further boost sales, it will focus on shoes and other key areas including clothing, handbags, jewellery, and cosmetics.[23] HMV Canada shook up music retailing with the addition of headphones, books, gadgets, and clothing designed to attract teens and 20-somethings looking to make a fashion statement into its stores.[24] And Staples added more upscale headphones, such as Beats by Dre and Monster, which resulted in double-digit sales increases.[25]

Manufacturers don't like to store inventory because their factories and warehouses are typically not available to customers. Consumers don't want to store more than they need because it takes up too much space. Neither group likes to store inventory that isn't being used because doing so ties up money that could be used for something else. Retailers thus provide value to both manufacturers and customers by performing the storage function, though many retailers are beginning to push their suppliers to hold the inventory until they need it. (Recall our discussion of just-in-time inventory systems in Chapter 12.)

It is difficult for retailers to distinguish themselves from their competitors through the merchandise they carry because competitors can purchase and sell many of the same popular brands. So many retailers have developed private-label brands (also called store brands), which are products developed and marketed by a retailer and available only from that retailer. For example, if you want House & Home bedding, you have to go to Hudson's Bay.

Price

Price helps define the value of both the merchandise and the service, and the general price range of a particular store helps define

You can get House & Home private-label bedding only at Hudson's Bay.

its image. Although both Banana Republic and Old Navy are owned by The Gap, their images could not be more different. Banana Republic prices its merchandise to attract young professionals, whereas Old Navy aims to satisfy trendy, price-sensitive consumers. Thus, when a manufacturer considers which of these stores is most appropriate for its new line of scarves and accessories, it must keep customers' perceived images of these retailers' price–quality relationship in mind.

As we showed in Chapter 11, there is much more to pricing than simply adding a markup onto a product's cost. Manufacturers must consider at what price they will sell the product to retailers so that both the manufacturer and the retailer can make a reasonable profit. At the same time, both the manufacturer and the retailer are concerned about what the customer is willing to pay. Canadian Tire has addressed this in part by launching a mobile app for iPhone, BlackBerry, and Android smartphones. The app allows in-store shoppers to scan product bar codes to get price, availability, and product information, as well as ratings and reviews by other customers. Shoppers can also access the Canadian Tire weekly flyer to check out current sales and special pricing.[26] This information can shape customer expectations of price by enabling them to quickly and easily get the most current prices.

Retailers that provide great value, such as Costco, were once known largely as a destination for monthly stock-up trips. But today, they have penetrated the weekly shopping routine. Consumers of all ages, nearly all income groups, and practically all segments have undertaken the "shift to value." Consumers have fundamentally changed their reference points for both price and quality, such that they have been trained to expect significantly lower prices from many retailers.

Price must always be aligned with the other elements of the retail mix: product, promotion, place, personnel, and presentation. For instance, you would not expect to pay $20 for a chocolate bar sold in your local grocery store, but a limited-edition bar, made of fine Belgian dark chocolate, packaged in a gold-plated keepsake box, sold at Holt Renfrew, might be a real steal at $20. Entrepreneurial Marketing 13.2 describes a man with incredible vision and a concept based on very inexpensive merchandise.

Costco attracts people of all ages and income brackets as consumers shift to value retailers.

Entrepreneurial Marketing 13.2

Giant Tiger Stakes Its Territory

On May 13, 1961, Gordon Reid opened his first Giant Tiger store in Ottawa. The business concept was simple: keep the cost of operation low and sell a large volume of merchandise at everyday low prices. The large general merchandise store aimed to offer everything a customer could need, all under one roof. This all-Canadian company has now grown to 200 stores, employing more than 7,000 people, who all work in support of that same original idea.[27]

The main thrusts of Giant Tiger's roaring success are maintaining low rent, using efficient transportation, and keeping the cost of store operations low. Tiger Trucking is the private fleet that transports merchandise for the chain to the majority of stores, which are in Ontario and Quebec. In store, employees work directly with customers on the store floor. Many stores don't even advertise a phone number, because having an employee answer the phone would increase costs and take him or her away from helping customers![28] The company's refund policy is clear: if you present a receipt, you get your money back, no matter how many days have passed.[29]

Each store offers a large assortment of casual clothing and footwear, and everyday needs in groceries, cleaning supplies, housewares, stationary, toys, and health and beauty products. The identical quality and fashion items offered by major chain stores are sold at Giant Tiger at lower prices. Discontinued items and one-offs are available frequently for special deals on a store-by-store basis. Beyond the Giant Tiger brand, the GT Boutique (http://www.gtboutique.com) has been developed to showcase new fashions and trends. A deep-rooted commitment to the community shows that Giant Tiger truly cares about its customers. Along with contributing funds to local charities and supporting fundraising events, many storefronts feature murals that not only beautify, but also bring attention to political issues.[30]

People love to shop at Giant Tiger stores because their merchandise is inexpensive, the stores are conveniently located and easy to shop in, and treasures are found every day among the basics.

The success shows no signs of slowing. A franchise agreement with Northwest Company in 2002 to open 72 new stores made a big impact, with the first 20 stores in cities such as Regina, Winnipeg, Edmonton, and Calgary bringing a flood of success for Giant Tiger.[31] Also, 2005 brought expansion stores in and around the Greater Toronto Area. The 2006 federal government announcement to lower the goods and services tax to 6 percent was even made from an Ottawa-area Giant Tiger store! Press coverage of events like this and returning loyal customers have helped keep Giant Tiger's bottom line strong. Despite tough competitors such as Walmart and Target, Giant Tiger is a homegrown retailer that Canadians continue to loyally support.

Promotion

Retailers and manufacturers know that good promotion, both within their retail environments and in the media, can mean the difference between flat sales and a growing consumer base. Advertising in traditional media such as newspapers, magazines, and television continues to be important to get customers into the stores. New media vehicles that communicate with consumers electronically are becoming increasingly important. Once in the store, however, retailers use displays and signs, placed at the point of purchase or in strategic areas such as the end of aisles, known as end caps, to inform customers and stimulate purchases of the featured products.

A co-ordinated effort between the manufacturer and retailer helps guarantee that the customer receives a cohesive message. The extent to which manufacturers work with their retailers to co-ordinate promotional activities can ensure that both the manufacturer and the retailer can maintain their consistent images. For example, Coach for Men might work with its most important retailers to develop advertising and point-of-sale signs. It may

co-operative (co-op) advertising
An agreement between a manufacturer and retailer in which the manufacturer agrees to defray some advertising costs.

even help defray the costs of advertising by paying all or a portion of the advertising's production and media costs, an agreement called **co-operative (co-op) advertising**.

Store credit cards and gift cards are more subtle forms of promotion that also facilitate shopping. Retailers also might offer pricing promotions—such as coupons, rebates, in-store or online discounts, or perhaps buy-one-get-one-free offers—to attract consumers and stimulate sales. These promotions play a very important role in driving traffic to retail locations, increasing the average purchase size, and creating opportunities for repeat purchases. But retail promotions also are valuable to customers; they inform customers about what is new and available and how much it costs. Another type of promotion occurs inside the store, where retailers use displays and signs, placed at the point of purchase (POP) or in strategic areas such as the end of aisles, to inform customers and stimulate purchases of the featured products.

Augmented reality is starting to show up as retailers test the technology in their stores. For example, Walmart, Sony, and Marvel Entertainment teamed up to promote The *Amazing Spiderman* movie. Children could watch the movie hero come to life after scanning in-store signage. Lowes Canada used augmented reality technology to allow customers using an iPhone to see 3D renderings of Maytag appliances. From the comfort of their homes, users were able to not only view refrigerators, washers and dryers, but also open and close doors and get a feel for how the appliances worked.[32]

Presentation (Store Design and Display)

In addition to more traditional forms of promotion, many retailers are devoting more resources to their overall retail environment as a means to promote and showcase what the store has to offer. Their displays of merchandise, both in the store and in windows, have become an important form of promotion. For example, Shoppers Drug Mart has redesigned its cosmetics counters as Beauty Boutiques. Since many shopping activities can be rather mundane, those retailers that can distinguish themselves with unusual and exciting store atmospherics add value to the shopping experience. G.A.P. Adventures™, founded by Calgarian Bruce Poon Tip, has opened concept stores in Vancouver, Toronto, Calgary, Melbourne, and New York City where visitors can watch G.A.P. Adventures™ documentaries featuring travellers on expeditions around the world.[33] And Mark's (formerly Mark's Work Wearhouse) installed a custom walk-in freezer in stores to allow customers to test out the warmth of clothing before buying. It's all part of the company's new merchandising strategy. In addition to walk-in freezers, Mark's also lets customers try out anti-slip work boots on ramps in the store that are covered with roof shingles, tiles, rocks, or stainless steel to mimic conditions found on construction sites. These features enhance customers' visual and sensory experiences, provide them with educational information, and increase the store's sales potential by enabling customers to "try before they buy."

A walk-in freezer at Mark's in Edmonton lets customers test out how warm clothing really is before they buy it.

Sears Canada has also found new ways to better connect with shoppers, especially younger ones. It now offers Skype access in 10 of its trendy fashion stores. Based on its research, Sears found that many young women shop with friends, with one of them serving as the style expert.[34] Skype allows shoppers to have instant access to a friend's virtual opinion by connecting them to a style expert who isn't physically at the store.

Retailers continue to improve their "shopability," providing more convenient store layouts and shopping experiences that make the task faster, easier, or more interesting. The Body Shop has embraced a concept known as "entertailing" to provide stories behind products and a more interactive experience that encourages customers to stay in stores longer.[35]

Apple Stores have used experiential retailing by giving customers something to touch, read, or play with, at their Genius Bars. At SportChek, technology is transforming the in-store experience with the launch of digital walls that allow browsers to learn more about its products. For example, by picking up two Nike shoes that are connected to a gaming controller, customers can compare features and get in-depth product information, sizes and colours available, and even learn about the performance of athletes who wear the shoes.[36] The digital signage is intended to inspire and enhance the customer service experience. So far, the strategy has been translating to sales that are running 150 percent higher than expected.[37]

Shoppers Drug Mart redesigned its cosmetic counters as Beauty Boutiques to better display and promote merchandise.

Various theories have been developed to explain the structure and evolution of the retail industry.[38] The Wheel of Retailing (shown in Exhibit 13.3) offers one view of how new forms of retail outlets compete in the market. Generally, retailers enter with low prices, low margins, and low status. Over time, they add more and more service and other improvements and thus are able to raise prices, earn higher margins, and achieve higher status with consumers. For example, the first menu at McDonald's offered only hamburgers, french fries, and milkshakes for takeout. Today, McDonald's has a wide and varied menu, upscale coffee, indoor seating, WiFi access, and play areas for children.

In the Wheel of Retailing concept, as stores add services and improvements expand the mix of merchandise carried and upgrade their facilities, costs are generally added to the day-to-day operations, which results in higher prices. This change opens up opportunities for new lean, mean entrants at the beginning of the wheel.

EXHIBIT 13.3 The Wheel of Retailing

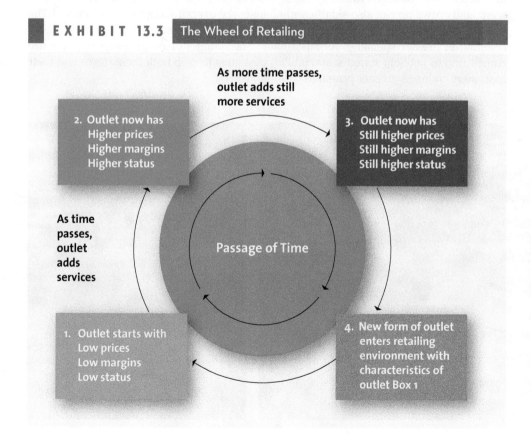

In some Canadian McDonald's outlets, tasteless plastic is being replaced by appealing colours and natural materials, fireplaces, flat-screen TVs, leather chairs, and modern lighting fixtures. Stores are being redesigned, featuring up to four different zones geared to the needs of different target markets; for example, a high-traffic zone for people on the go, a comfortable seating area where customers can linger, and an area specifically for families and large groups.[39] The retrofit is linked to McDonald's strategy to gain a large part of the specialty beverage market, which is dominated by retailers such as Starbucks and Second Cup. By introducing upscale coffee and comfortable seating, McDonald's can earn higher margins and gain higher status. These innovations have enabled McDonald's to continue to serve its existing loyal customers and reach out to new target segments while charging competitive prices—key factors for successful retailing. Thus, it is hardly surprising that McDonald's continues to dominate its industry and stave off competition from new entrants.

Even beer stores across Canada are sprucing up their outlets in attempt to improve the customer experience. In British Columbia, signature stores now offer broader selection and better presentation of products. To refresh the store experience in Manitoba, the government has opened new express and mini-stores. You can browse product selection on wall-mounted tablets in Ontario stores that feature upbeat music and trained staff who suggest food pairings for your beer. Whenever a lease comes up for renewal, the Société des alcohols du Québec invests heavily in improving the look of the stores. Although most store fronts in Nova Scotia were renovated years ago, the focus is now on the back area, in pursuit of a browsing experience that doesn't feel like being in a warehouse. And in Prince Edward Island, a rebranding effort has taken place to provide a new name, new colours, and new store layout and design.[40]

A variety of factors influence whether customers will actually buy once they are in the store; some of these are quite subtle. Consumers' perceptions of value and their subsequent patronage are heavily influenced by their perceptions of the store's "look and feel." Consider the difference between having coffee at Tim Hortons versus Second Cup. In which outlet would you rather spend time socializing with your friends? Music, colour, scent, and crowding can also significantly impact the overall shopping experience.[41] The extent to which stores offer a more pleasant shopping experience fosters a good mood, resulting in greater spending. As Sustainable Marketing 13.1 notes, some retailers are committing to publicly stated sustainability measures to help both their stores and their customers embrace greener practices.

McDonald's redesigned restaurant in Scarborough, Ontario (right) is considerably more upscale compared to early restaurants (left).

Personnel

Personal selling and customer service representatives are also part of the overall promotional package. Retailers must provide services that make it easier to buy and use products. As a part of the Dairy Farmers of Canada's Cooking with Cheese campaign, brand ambassadors were sent to stores armed with handheld scanners. In the stores, the ambassadors could scan items in shoppers' carts on the spot and then print out cheese-based recipes and dinner suggestions based on the ingredients.[42] Retail associates, whether in the store, on the phone, or over the Internet, provide customers with information about product characteristics and availability. They can also facilitate the sale of products or services that consumers perceive as complicated, risky, or expensive, such as an air conditioning unit or a diamond ring. Manufacturers can play an important role in getting retail sales and service associates prepared to sell their products. Estée Lauder, for example, could conduct seminars about how to use and sell a new line of cosmetics. In some retail firms, these salesperson and customer service functions are being

Sustainable Marketing 13.1 — IKEA's Never-ending List

For most companies, sustainability means taking small steps in the hopes of making a positive long-term impact. However, IKEA initiatives are taking a giant leap. As the world's largest furniture retailer, any sustainability efforts by IKEA will make a noticeable difference. With more than 10 million customers in Canada, changes in IKEA's 12 Canadian stores make a huge difference.

Since its beginning in 1943 as a household goods catalogue by young entrepreneur Ingvar Kamprad, IKEA has built on a simple concept: "Offer quality furniture at the lowest possible price to contribute to helping more people live a better life at home." Since then, IKEA has evolved from a household-goods catalogue to a global furniture giant, while still working to help people live a better life.

The company embraces sustainability in many ways, from partnerships with other organizations, to its physical stores and its relationships with customers. With the introduction of its Never Ending List in 2010, IKEA publicly demonstrates its commitment to sustainability by outlining its accomplishments and setting goals to expand its sustainability initiatives.[43] The company has international initiatives with UNICEF, Save the Children, and the WWF. It also has a long-standing partnership with Tree Canada. At its retail locations, IKEA has in-store recycling bins and has created green parking spaces to reward customers who drive hybrid or fuel-efficient vehicles. Additionally, it is the first Canadian retailer to begin phasing out incandescent light bulbs. IKEA not only integrates changes

IKEA has designated preferred parking spaces to reward customers who drive hybrid or fuel-efficient vehicles.

inside its stores, but also takes its initiative outside; it installed solar panels in 150 stores and distribution centres for electricity production.

Along with its in-store efforts, IKEA is making an effort to help customers consume in a more environmentally friendly manner. IKEA has launched a free shuttle bus service in Toronto so that customers can use a more sustainable method of transport and leave their cars at home. In addition, IKEA offers free delivery for customers who use the bus.[44] Its Bag the Bag program encouraged customers to be more environmentally conscious by charging 5 cents for plastic bags. The program raised $280,000, which was donated to Tree Canada.[45] Since 2009, IKEA no longer provides plastic bags. Instead, customers are encouraged to purchase the recyclable blue bag for 59 cents, to cut down on plastic bag waste.

Its sustainability efforts have not gone unnoticed. For five consecutive years, IKEA has been the only retailer to be honoured by Mediacorp as one of Canada's Greenest Employers.[46] With $1.4 billion in annual sales, Canada has become one of IKEA's strongest markets.[47] It takes its commitment to sustainability very seriously; it releases annual Global Sustainability Reports that highlight IKEA's global development and tracks its progress toward achieving its sustainability goals. IKEA is incorporating environmental, economic, and social responsibility across the organization, taking a huge leap forward.

To offer more convenience, some Shoppers Drug Mart stores are open 24 hours a day so customers can pick up prescriptions or other items at any time.

share of wallet
The percentage of the customer's purchases made from a particular retailer.

augmented, or even replaced, by technology used through in-store kiosks, the Internet, or self-checkout lanes.

Traditionally, retailers treated all their customers the same. Today, the most successful retailers concentrate on providing more value to their best customers. The knowledge retailers gain from their store personnel, the Internet browsing and buying activities of customers, and the data they collect on customer shopping habits can be used in customer relationship management (CRM). Using this information, retailers may modify product, price, and/or promotion attempt to increase their **share of wallet**—the percentage of the customer's purchases made from that particular retailer. For instance, multichannel retailers use consumer information collected from the customers' Internet browsing and buying behaviour to send personalized emails promoting specific products or services. Retailers may also offer special discounts to good customers to make them even more loyal.

Place

Retailers already have realized that convenience is a key ingredient to success, and an important aspect of this success is convenient locations.[48] As the old cliché claims, the three most important things in retailing are "location, location, location." Many customers choose stores on the basis of where they are located, which makes great locations a competitive advantage that few rivals can duplicate. Although fashion retailer Zara spends almost nothing on advertising, it invests heavily in locating its shops in venues that offer beauty and historical appeal.[49] And once Starbucks saturates a market by opening in the best locations, it will be difficult for a new competitor to break into that same market—where would it put its stores?

In pursuit of better and better locations, retailers are experimenting with different options to reach their target markets. Canada's largest drugstore retailer, Shoppers Drug Mart, now has some stores that are open 24 hours a day so customers can pick up prescriptions and other items at any time. P&G took the store to consumers when it opened a virtual store in Toronto's Union Station. Partnering with Well.ca, the month-long initiative presented consumers with photos of products with QR codes that could be scanned, allowing them to order 120 different items and have them delivered to their homes at no cost.[50] It followed with another mobile exercise that launched mobile stores in 50 Toronto bus shelters offering P&G personal care, baby, and beauty items from Walmart. The shopping experience let consumers turn idle time waiting for the bus productively, ordering products on the go.[51]

LO4   MANAGING MULTICHANNEL OPTIONS

So far in this chapter, we have explored the most traditional method for a manufacturer to get merchandise to the ultimate consumer, namely, through retailers. There are, however, other options. For example, Canadian fast-food chain Pizza Pizza gives customers the choice of ordering in store, by phone, on the company's website, and now through a free app for the iPhone, iPod Touch, and iPad. The app lets customers order and pay for their pizza and then track the guaranteed delivery time.[52] For instance, a manufacturer can sell directly to consumers by using its own stores, kiosks, catalogues, or the Internet. In this section, we explore the relative advantages of each of these options from both a manufacturer's and a retailer's perspective. We also consider the synergies inherent to providing products through multiple channels.

As more consumers embrace a variety of channels available for browsing and purchasing, retailers must develop an **omnichannel** strategy to create a consistent experience across all channels. James Connell, Vice President of Marketing and E-Commerce for Roots says that they "focus on providing a seamless multi-channel experience. We know a customer will interact five or six times [with us] before they make a purchase."[53]

omnichannel
An omnichannel strategy creates a consistent experience for consumers across all distribution channels.

Benefit of Stores for Consumers

In this section, we explore the relative advantages of the most traditional retail channels, the brick-and-mortar store, from consumers' perspective. In the following section, we examine how kiosks, catalogues and the Internet channel add value to retailers' ability to satisfy their customers' needs. Each channel—stores, kiosks, catalogues, and the Internet—offers its own unique benefits for selling to consumers (see Exhibit 13.4).

Store Channel   Traditional stores, or brick-and-mortar retailers as they often are called, offer several benefits to customers that they cannot get when they shop through catalogues or on the Internet.

Browsing.   Shoppers often have only a general sense of what they want (e.g., a sweater, something for dinner, a gift) but don't know the specific item they want. They go to a store to see what is available before they decide what to buy. Although some consumers surf the Web and look through catalogues for ideas, many still prefer browsing in stores. Some use both approaches, getting a sense of what's available through catalogues or the Internet, and then going to the store to try on apparel or view the actual product.

Touching and Feeling Products.   Perhaps the greatest benefit offered by stores is the opportunity for customers to use all five of their senses—touching, smelling, tasting, seeing, and hearing—when examining products.

Personal Service.   Sales associates have the capability to provide meaningful, personalized information. Sales people can be particularly helpful when purchasing a complicated product, such as consumer electronics, or something the customer doesn't know much about, such as a diamond ring.

Cash and Credit Payment.   Stores are nearly the only channel that accepts cash payments. Some customers prefer to pay with cash because it is easy, resolves the transaction immediately, and does not result in potential interest payments. Some customers prefer to use their credit or debit card in person rather than send payment information electronically.

Entertainment and Social Interaction.   In-store shopping can be a stimulating experience for some people, providing a break in their daily routine and enabling them to interact with friends.

Instant Gratification.   Stores have the advantage of allowing customers to get the merchandise immediately after they buy it.

■ **E X H I B I T 13.4**	**Benefits Provided by Different Channels**		
Stores	**Kiosks**	**Catalogues**	**Internet**
• Browsing • Touching and feeling merchandise • Personal service • Cash and credit payment • Entertainment and social interaction • Instant gratification • Risk reduction	• Broader selection than stores • Access to items online that are out of stock in stores • Access to wish lists and gift registries • Access to loyalty program information	• Convenience • Information • Safety	• Deeper and broader selection • More information • Personalization • Expanded market presence

Risk Reduction.   When customers purchase merchandise in physical stores, it reduces their perceived risk of buying and increases their confidence that any problems with the merchandise will be corrected.

Benefits of Internet and Multichannel Retailing

In the previous section, we detailed the relative benefits of stores from the consumers' perspective. In this section, we examine how the Internet has improved retailers' ability to serve their customers and build a competitive advantage. In 2012, online retail sales in Canada reached $18.9 billion, up 24 percent from 2010,[54] demonstrating that Canadians are embracing ecommerce.

Internet Channel

First, the addition of an Internet channel has the potential to offer a greater selection of products. Second, an Internet channel enables retailers to provide customers with more personalized information about products and services. Third, it offers sellers the unique opportunity to collect information about consumer shopping behaviour—information that they can use to improve the shopping experience across all channels. Finally, the Internet channel allows sellers to enter new markets economically.

Deeper and Broader Selection.   One benefit of the Internet channel is the vast number of alternatives available to consumers without stores having to grow their aisles or increase their square footage. By shopping on the Internet, consumers can easily "visit" and select merchandise from a broader array of retailers. People living in London, Ontario, can shop electronically at Harrod's in London, England, in less time than it takes them to visit their local supermarket. Websites typically offer deeper assortments of merchandise (more colours, brands, and sizes) than are available in stores or catalogues. This expanded offering enables them to satisfy consumer demand for less popular styles, colours, or sizes and still keep their overall inventory costs low.[55] Many retailers also offer a broader assortment (more categories) on their websites. Staples.com, for instance, offers soft drinks and cleaning supplies, which are not available in stores, so that its business customers will view it as a one-stop shop.

More Information to Evaluate Merchandise.   Using an Internet channel, firms can provide as much information as each customer wants and more information than he or she could get through store or catalogue channels. Customers can drill down through web pages until they have enough information to make a purchase decision. Unlike in catalogues, the information on an electronic channel database can be frequently updated and will always be available—24-7, 365 days per year. Furthermore, the cost of adding information to an Internet channel is likely to be far less than the cost of continually training sales associates.

The depth of information available on a website even can provide solutions to customer problems. Home Depot walks its online customers through the steps of installation and repair projects, thereby giving do-it-yourselfers confidence prior to tackling home improvement tasks. The directions include the level of difficulty and a list of the tools and materials needed to complete the project successfully.

Personalization.   The most significant potential benefit of the Internet channel is its ability to personalize promotions and services for each customer economically. Canadian consumers are increasingly embracing personalized offers received on their smartphones with 82 percent saying they like to get detailed product information while they are in stores shopping.[56] Refer to Exhibit 13.5 for more details on personalizing the mobile experience for shoppers.

Personalized Customer Service.   Traditional Internet channel approaches for responding to customer questions—such as frequently asked questions (FAQ) pages and offering a toll-free number or email address to ask questions—often do not provide the timely information customers are seeking. To improve customer service from an electronic channel, many firms offer live, online chats. The online chat feature provides customers with the opportunity to click a button at any time and have an instant messaging email or voice conversation with a customer service representative. This technology also enables firms

EXHIBIT 13.5 Keeping It Personal: Marketing Success in a Mobile World

Keeping It Personal: Marketing Success in a Mobile World

Research report finds that retailers and marketers have an excellent opportunity to increase customer loyalty and satisfaction with real-time mobile marketing and location-based offers.

PERSONALIZATION MATTERS

Interested in receiving personalized promotions on their smartphones.

6/10

CUSTOMER LOYALTY

47% Would be more likely to return to a store that offers personalized promotions on smartphones.

ELECTRONIC PERSONAL SHOPPER
Most Canadian consumers want a tailored shopping experience on their mobile devices.

Find it helpful to get product or service information on their mobile devices while browsing in a store. 82%

Have purchased an item via their mobile phone using the browser or an app. 67%

Would be interested in getting promotions when they are out shopping. 58%

50% OFF YOUR ENTIRE PURCHASE

71% Would make some sort of purchase if presented with a promotion on their smartphones for a complementary product.

38% Would buy more (they would buy both) if they received promotions for complementary products while they shopped.

A PROFILE OF WOMEN SHOPPERS
Tailored promotions provide greater up-sell opportunities with female consumers.

51% Will return to the store.

44% Will purchase the intended item as well as the promotional one.

* Sources: Research sponsored by SAS and conducted by Leger, The Research Intelligence Group, May 6–11, 2013. | 1,506 Canadians with a smartphone were surveyed.

§sas THE POWER TO KNOW.

---

to send a proactive chat invitation automatically to customers on the site. The timing of these invitations can be based on the time the visitor has spent on the site, the specific page the customer is viewing, or a product on which the customer has clicked. At Bluefly. com, for example, if a visitor searches for more than three items in five minutes, thereby demonstrating more than a passing interest, Bluefly will display a pop-up window with a friendly face offering help.[57]

Personalized Offering. The interactive nature of the Internet also provides an opportunity for retailers to personalize their offerings for each of their customers. Using a cookie that provides identifying information, Amazon.ca enhances the shopping experience by serving up personalized homepages with information about books and other products of interest based on visitors' past purchases. Amazon.ca will also send interested customers customized email messages that notify them that their favourite author or recording artist has published a new book or released a new CD. Another personalized offering that online retailers are able to present to customers is recommendations of complementary merchandise. Just as a well-trained salesperson would make recommendations to customers prior to checkout, an

At Bluefly.com, customers can have an instant messaging, email, or voice conversation with a customer service representative.

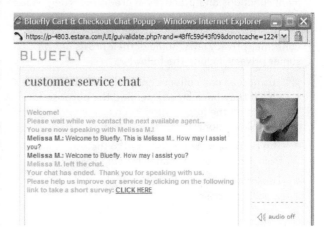

interactive web page can make suggestions to the shopper about items that he or she might like to see, such as what other customers who bought the same item also purchased.

Some multichannel retailers are able to personalize promotions and Internet homepages on the basis of several attributes tied to the shopper's current or previous web sessions, such as the time of day, time zone as determined by a computer's Internet address, and assumed gender.[58] However, some consumers worry about this ability to collect information about purchase histories, personal information, and search behaviour on the Internet. How will this information be used in the future? Will it be sold to other firms, or will the consumer receive unwanted promotional materials online or in the mail? To answer these questions, consider Ethical Dilemma 13.1.

Expanded Market Presence. With the Internet's low entry costs and constantly improving search engines and shopping bots, smaller niche sources for hard-to-find products, collectibles, and hobbies can expand their trade area—the geographical area that contains the potential customers of a particular retailer or shopping centre—from a few city blocks to the world. The Internet has facilitated market expansions by traditional retailers as well. Not only can a customer in Zurich shop online at Sears.ca or Lee Valley Tools Ltd. (leevalley.com), but a Staples customer can buy a computer online and pick it up at the store. In addition to increasing sales by expanding the current customer base and attracting new customers, multichannel retailers can achieve economies of scale by co-ordinating their buying and logistics activities across channels and consolidating their marketing information and activities. Generally, consumers who shop at multichannel retailers typically buy more than those who shop in only one retail channel.

Ethical Dilemma 13.1   Protecting Customer Privacy

The definition of personal privacy depends on which country you're in and with which person you're speaking. Some people define personal information as all information that is not publicly available. Others tend to include both public information (e.g., driver's license, mortgage data) and private details (hobbies, income). Internet retailers need to take the necessary precautions to protect consumer privacy by incorporating privacy safety software such as firewalls and data encryption every time any data is transferred to prevent it from being intercepted.[59]

Canadians rely on government legislation to protect their privacy. The situation in the United States is different: existing legislation for consumer privacy is restricted to the protection of information in government functions and practices in credit reporting, video rentals, banking, and health care. Canada, the European Union, Australia, and New Zealand have more stringent consumer privacy laws. Some of their provisions on consumer privacy include the following:

- Businesses can collect consumer information only if they have clearly defined the purpose for collecting the information, such as completing the transaction.

- The purpose must be disclosed to the consumer from whom the information is being collected.

- The information can be used only for that specific purpose.

- The business can keep the information only for the stated purpose. If the business wants to use the information for another purpose, it must initiate a new collection process.

In Canada, consumers own their personal information so retailers must get consumers to agree explicitly to share this personal information through an opt-in agreement. In contrast, personal information in the United States is generally viewed as being in the public domain and retailers can use it in any way they desire. American consumers must explicitly tell retailers not to use their personal information—they must opt out,[60] something for Canadian consumers to consider when purchasing from U.S. retailers.

There is growing consensus that personal information must be fairly collected, that the collection must be purposeful, and that the data should be relevant, maintained as accurate, essential to the business, subject to the rights of the owning individual, kept reasonably secure, and transferred only with the permission of the consumer. To address these concerns, many Internet sellers that collect customer information now have lengthy privacy policies that state what information is collected and how it will be used, give consumers a choice as to whether they give information, and allow them to view and correct any personal information held by an online retail site. Internet sellers need to assure their customers that information about them is held securely and not passed on to other companies without the customer's permission.

Kiosk Channel One of the greatest constraints facing store-based retailers is the size of their stores. The amount of merchandise that can be displayed and offered for sale in stores is limited. By blending stores with Internet-enabled kiosks, retailers can dramatically expand the assortment offered to their customers. Retailers using a kiosk channel may simply provide store associates with access to the company website so that they can more easily help customers find product information or place orders. Other retailers, such as Chapters, offer self-service kiosks that allow customers to check product selection and availability at their stores. Self-serve movie rental kiosks in grocery stores allow consumers to select, pay for, and take movies home. Of course, today many consumers arrive in store armed with a mobile kiosk in the form of a smartphone capable of accessing product information and even comparing prices at other retailers via the Internet.

Another limitation that store-based retailers face is inconsistent execution. The availability and knowledge of sales associates can vary considerably across stores or even within a store at different times during the day. This inconsistency is most problematic for retailers selling new, complex merchandise. For example, consumer electronics retailers such as Best Buy find it difficult to communicate the features and benefits of the newest products to all of their sales associates. To address this problem, Best Buy installed kiosks designed to be used by sales associates and customers to obtain product information.

Broader Selection. Customers with the ability to shop in a store and look up products at a kiosk generally get access to an expanded assortment of products than are in stock in the store. For example, Staples carries roughly five times as many items online as in stores.

Access to Items Online That Are Out of Stock in Store. Retailers using in-store kiosks can often save a sale if an item is out of stock or if their location does not carry a broad product assortment.

Access to Wish Lists and Gift Registries. Customers buying gifts can check gift registries for wedding or baby shower gifts as well as wish lists for themselves or the gift recipient.

Access to Loyalty Program Information. Being able to check the status of a loyalty program and determine whether points are available to be used is a benefit to consumers. It also allows retailers to overcome resource constraints by freeing up staff to provide sales assistance to other customers.

Catalogue Channel The catalogue channel provides some benefits to customers that are not available from the store or Internet channels. However, once a catalogue is printed, it cannot be updated with price changes and new merchandise. Therefore, retailers such as Lands' End use Internet sites to provide customers with real-time information about stock availability and price reductions on clearance merchandise. Like all nonstore formats, catalogues offer the convenience of looking at merchandise and placing an order 24-7. Catalogues have other advantages over other nonstore formats as follows.

Convenience. The information in a catalogue is easily accessible for a long period of time. Consumers can refer to the information in a catalogue anytime by simply picking it up from the coffee table. The development of magalogs—catalogues with magazine-type editorial content—enhances consumers' desire to keep catalogues readily available. Williams-Sonoma produces a magalog featuring its gourmet cooking tools and foods for sale, along with kitchen tips and recipes.

Information. Catalogues have information about the products and how they can be used. For example, the IKEA catalogue shows consumers how its products can be put together in a kitchen, office, or child's room.

Safety. Security in malls and shopping areas is becoming an important concern for many shoppers, particularly the elderly. Nonstore retail formats offer the advantage of enabling customers to view merchandise and place orders from a safe environment—their homes.

Effective Multichannel Retailing

Consumers want a seamless omnichannel experience when interacting with multichannel retailers. They want to be recognized by a retailer, whether they interact with a sales associate, the retailer's website, or the retailer's call centre by telephone. Customers want to buy a product through the retailer's Internet or catalogue channels and pick it up or return it to a local store; find out if a product offered on the Internet channel is available at a local store; and, when unable to find a product in a store, determine if it is available for home delivery through the retailer's Internet channel.

Adding an electronic channel is particularly attractive to firms with strong brand names but limited locations and distribution. For example, retailers such as Harrod's, IKEA, and Harry Rosen are widely known for offering unique, high-quality merchandise, but they require customers to travel to England or major cities to buy many of the items they carry. Interestingly, most of these store-based retailers currently are multichannel retailers through their successful catalogue and Internet offerings. Harry Rosen has annual sales of around $300 million. While its e-commerce sales make up only a small portion of overall revenues, they increased 90 percent the first six months of 2013.[61]

There are challenges and advantages in selling merchandise via the Internet. When you buy products from brick-and-mortar stores, some critical information might include "touch-and-feel" attributes, such as how a shirt fits, the ice cream flavour tastes, or the perfume smells. This information cannot be experienced via the Internet. As a result, e-tailers strive for "look-and-see" attributes, such as colour, style, and things like grams of carbohydrates. Fit can be predicted if the apparel has consistent sizing and the consumer has learned over time which size to buy from a particular brand. Because of the problems of providing touch-and-feel information, apparel retailers experience return rates of more than 20 percent on purchases made through an electronic channel but only 10 percent for purchases made in stores. Whereas some products, such as apparel, can be difficult for customers to purchase over the Internet because of their need to touch, feel, and try on these products, Amazon's offerings do well in the worldwide Internet marketplace.

Role of Brands Brands provide a consistent experience for customers that helps overcome the difficulty of not being able to touch and feel merchandise prior to purchase online. Because consumers trust familiar brands, products with important touch-and-feel attributes, such as clothing, perfume, flowers, and food, with well-known name brands sell successfully through nonstore channels, including the Internet, catalogues, and TV home shopping. Consider branded merchandise such as Tommy Hilfiger perfume. Even if you can't smell a sample of the perfume before buying it online, you know that it will smell like your last bottle because the manufacturer of Tommy Hilfiger makes sure each bottle smells the same.

Retailers need to provide a consistent brand image across all channels. For example, Mountain Equipment Co-op (MEC) reinforces its image of selling high-quality, environmentally friendly sports equipment in its stores, catalogues, and website. Each of these channels emphasizes function, not fashion, in the descriptions of MEC's products. Its position about taking care of the environment is communicated by carefully lighting its stores and using recycled polyester and organic, rather than pesticide-intensive cotton, in many of its clothes. A positive omnichannel experience yields results. According to Sandy Treagus, chief financial officer for Mountain Equipment Co-op, "Our e-commerce presence has had a profound impact on our retail stores, and vice versa."[62]

Using Technology Firms with electronic channels are using technology to convert touch-and-feel information into look-and-see information that can be communicated through the Internet. Websites are going beyond offering the basic image to giving customers the opportunity to view merchandise from different angles and perspectives by using 3-D imaging and/or zoom technology.

To overcome the limitations associated with trying on clothing, apparel retailers have started to use virtual models on their websites. These virtual models enable consumers to see how selected merchandise looks on an image with similar proportions to their own and then rotate the model so the "fit" can be evaluated from all angles. The virtual models are either selected from a set of "prebuilt" models or, constructed on the basis of the shopper's response to questions about his or her height, weight, facial, leg, and other body dimensions. At Timberland.com, customers can design custom boots in a variety of colours, monograms, sole colours, and stitching.

Increasing Share of Wallet[63] Although offering an electronic channel may draw away some sales from other channels, using it with other channels can result in consumers making more total purchases from the seller. Traditional single-channel retailers can use one channel to promote the services offered by other channels. For example, the URL of a store's website can be advertised on in-store signs, shopping bags, credit card billing statements, POS receipts, and the print or broadcast advertising used to promote the stores. The retailer's electronic channel can be used to stimulate store visits by announcing special store events and promotions. Store-based retailers can leverage their stores to lower the cost of fulfilling orders and processing returned merchandise if they use the stores as "warehouses" for gathering merchandise for delivery to customers. Customers also can be offered the opportunity to pick up and return merchandise at the retailer's stores rather than pay shipping charges. Many retailers will waive shipping charges when orders are placed online or through the catalogue if the customer physically comes to the store. Research has shown that multichannel consumers spend substantially more than those who shop at a single channel—between 25 to 100 percent more![64]

My Virtual Model overcomes the limitations associated with trying on clothing.

Consumers who shop at multichannel retailers—retailers that sell merchandise in more than one retail channel (such as a Sears Canada store (right), catalogue (middle), and Internet (left)—typically buy more than those who shop in only one retail channel.

Gaining Insights into Customers' Shopping Behaviours It is difficult to observe customers' behaviour in stores or when they shop catalogues, because most people prefer not to have sales clerks constantly monitoring them in stores or visiting their homes, pestering them with questions about each action they've taken. Therefore, online retailing provides key insights into the choices consumers make since the data can be collected unobtrusively. However, people often shop differently in the different channels; for example, they might browse extensively online but dash into and out of stores to get what they need. If a retailer gathers data about a customer's actions in all of its channels, it should be able to put together a clearer, more detailed picture of how and why customers patronize—or don't patronize—its channels and offerings.

LEARNING OBJECTIVES REVIEW

  Outline the considerations associated with choosing retail partners

Because manufacturers want their offerings available where, when, and in the form that customers prefer, they must consider whether customers expect to find their products at specific retailers. For example, customers probably do not expect, or want, to find a value-priced product at a luxury retailer. The manufacturer also must consider the basic channel structure in which it functions, along with the characteristics of the members of that channel. Finally, manufacturers need to determine the distribution intensity they prefer.

LO2 **Identify what types of retailers are available to distribute products**

Retailers generally fall into one of two categories: food retailers and general merchandise retailers. Each of the categories consists of various formats, including supermarkets, supercentres, warehouse clubs, convenience stores, department stores, discount stores, specialty retailers, drugstores, category specialists, extreme-value retailers, and off-price stores.

LO3 **Describe the components of a retail strategy building on the four Ps to create value for consumers**

To develop a co-ordinated strategy—which represents a key goal for an effective channel partnership between retailers

and manufacturers—these functions need to consider the four Ps. Retailers provide customers with a choice of merchandise in the quantities they want to buy and services that facilitate the sale and use of those products. They offer convenient locations to shop and an atmosphere and presentation that enhance the shopping experience. Promotions, both in the store and outside, provide customers with information. Finally, price provides signals to the customer about the image of the store, its merchandise, and its services.

LO4 **Identify the benefits and challenges of multichannel retailing**

The various types of retail channels—stores, kiosks, catalogues, and the Internet—each offer their own benefits and limitations, including those related to availability, convenience, and safety, among others. If a retailer adopts a multichannel strategy, it can exploit the benefits and mitigate the limitations of each channel and expand its overall market presence. Furthermore, a multichannel strategy offers the chance to gain a greater share of customers' wallets and more insight into their buying behaviour. Of course, there are challenges as well. To function in multiple channels, retailers must organize their operations carefully to ensure an integrated customer experience. In particular, they have to have an integrated CRM system, and determine how to maintain a consistent brand image across the various channels, whether to charge the same or different prices, and how best to deliver merchandise to multiple channels.

KEY TERMS

- big-box food retailers
- category killer
- category specialist
- conventional supermarket
- co-operative (co-op) advertising
- discount store

- drugstore
- extreme-value retailer
- general merchandise retailers
- multichannel strategy
- off-price retailer
- omnichannel

- retail mix
- retailing
- services retailers
- share of wallet
- specialty stores

CONCEPT REVIEW

1. Describe the factors that manufacturers must consider when choosing retail partners.

2. How would a manufacturer's strategy for choosing a retailer change depending on its overall market power and the consistency of the new product with existing offerings?

3. Discuss the types of retailers that operate in Canada and identify some of the issues facing each type.

4. Generally merchandise retailers are classified into several different groups such as discount stores, specialty stores, category killers, and so on. However, it seems that increasingly many of these retailers are looking quite similar. Why is this so and what factors may explain this trend?

5. How do marketers use the four Ps to create value in retailing?

6. Assume that adidas, the shoe manufacturer, has decided to sell expensive wristwatches for men and women. What factors should it consider when developing its strategy for choosing retail partners?

7. In this chapter, we discuss the fact that researchers have found that store image and atmospherics exert a huge impact on customers' shopping behaviour. What are the key elements of a store's atmospherics and image and why do you think that they affect consumers so strongly?

8. Explain how the Internet has helped reshape retail marketing strategies. What are some of the unique advantages of physical store retailing, website selling, and kiosks?

9. Discuss the advantages of multichannel retailing from the perspectives of both retailers and consumers.

10. Explain why it is important for retailers to develop effective retailing strategy and positioning. How do retailers develop such a strategy? *Hint:* Look at the various store formats of Loblaw or any national grocery chain.

MARKETING APPLICATIONS

1. Assume you have been given some money to invest in a retailer's stock. What type of retailer would you choose? Provide a rationale for your answer.

2. Why don't traditional department stores have the same strong appeal to Canadian consumers that they once enjoyed during their height in the last half of the 20th century? Discuss which types of retailers are now competing with department stores.

3. What do retailers do to increase the value of products and services for consumers? Discuss the extent to which brick-and-mortar retailers are threatened by Internet-only retailers with regard to these factors.

4. Some argue that retailers can be eliminated from the distribution channel because they add only costs to the final product without creating any value-added services in the process. Do you agree with this perspective? Is it likely that consumers will make most purchases directly from manufacturers in the near future? Provide justification for your answers.

5. Many years ago, the corporations that sold gasoline made the strategic move to include a substantial offering of food items. Today, it is rare to find a gas station that does not sell food items. Into which category of food retailer did these service stations fall? Do you think this was a prudent strategic direction for these corporations? Explain your logic.

6. Identify three categories of products especially suited for sale on the Internet. Identify three categories that are not currently suitable for sale on the Internet. Justify your choices.

7. How does Staples.com or Officedepot.com provide value to their customers beyond the physical products that they sell? Identify some of the ways that the companies have overcome the inhibitors to successful Internet retailing.

8. What options do you have for purchasing food in your community? Under what circumstances would you shop at each option? What would a family with two young children consider while making this choice?

9. You can purchase apparel at a discount store, specialty store, category specialist, off-price retailer, department store, or Internet-only store. From which of these types of stores do you shop? Explain why you prefer one type over another.

10. Suppose you are the confectionary buyer for a regional chain of grocery stores. The store policy is to charge a "substantial" listing fee for the placement of new items. Listing fees were originally designed to cover the costs of placing new products on the shelves, such as adjustments to computer systems and realignment of warehouse and store space. Over the years, these fees have become larger, and they are now a significant source of revenue for the chain. A local manufacturer of a popular brand of specialty candy would like to sell to your chain, but claims that the listing fee is too high and does not reflect the real cost of adding the candy. Discuss the ethical implications of such a policy. What should the chain do?

NET SAVVY

1. Companies such as Lee Valley Tools have expanded their offerings beyond their original channels to sell through multiple channels. Visit the company's website (http://www.leevalley.com) and determine in which channels it operates (Internet, stores, and/or catalogue). Discuss the advantages of using a multichannel strategy over a single channel strategy.

2. Select a familiar multichannel retailer. Evaluate its website in terms of how well it provides value to its customers. Do you believe that offering multiple selling channels to customers enhances their shopping experience? How does it help the retailer? Explain your answer.

CHAPTER CASE STUDY

TARGET AND ITS NEW GENERATION OF PARTNERSHIPS

Target has been an innovator in structuring retail partnerships that offer customers something special: fashion-forward housewares and apparel at prices they can afford. In addition to its Target.com website, the company operates nearly 1,800 stores in 49 states, along with 37 distribution centres nationally, as well as 127 stores in Canada, and a separate headquartered location in India.[65] Apparel and accessories account for approximately 20 percent of Target's annual sales.

Similar to its more standardized rival Walmart, Target offers the vast breadth of a full-line discount store, featuring everything from cosmetics to baby clothes, housewares to electronics. But Target also has uniquely positioned itself through a series of exclusive partnerships with top designers, such as Michael Graves and Isaac Mizrahi, who have collaborated with the retailer to offer limited-edition, distinctive products. Although other retailers also have developed relationships with designers to create exclusive brands—such as Kohl's Simply Vera line from designer Vera Wang, which accounted for 51 percent of its apparel sales in 2010—these competitors have struggled to maintain their lower prices.[66]

Though it is not alone in partnering with designers, Target appears to be the best practitioner of this strategy. The company launched its first retail partnership in 1999 with renowned architect Michael Graves, whose tea kettles and toasters were hailed for having brought the word "design" back to the housewares category.[67] Since then, the company has worked with more than 80 design partners who have generally welcomed the chance to reach a mass market with their exclusive labels.[68]

Most of the partnerships have been limited to a specific time, which also has built a sense of urgency and exclusivity around the offers. Target's holiday offerings have featured a number of designer labels: Harajuku Mini kids' clothing from designer Gwen Stefani; hats from Albertuse Swanepoel; and a jewelry line featuring designs by Dana Kellin. Whether time-limited or longer term, such partnerships have consistently offered high-profile labels at moderate prices, helping the retailer boost its bottom line.

Target's collaboration with Missoni made the biggest splash though. The fashion world was stunned when the Italian fashion house agreed to create a collection for Target. The big American retail store is the diametric opposite of the high-end shops that have typically carried Missoni's expensive knitwear and apparel. Target's announcement through Facebook, other social media sites, and a Manhattan pop-up shop for fashion editors, celebrities, and other Missoni clientele helped stoke public excitement. Of course, such excitement can cause problems as well. Target's website crashed just moments after the Missoni launch, as customers clicked in droves to buy up the designer duds.[69]

So when Target announced plans to expand to Canada, other retailers were justifiably concerned about losing customers. Even before Target opened a single store, brand awareness was high—70 percent of Canadians were aware of the store and 30,000 of them already had a Target U.S. credit card.[70] The retailer's entry in Canada was made easier through the acquisition of Zellers' stores. However, significant renovations were needed since many of the sites varied in age and size. Part of that renovation effort was concentrated on store design, which featured wider aisles than Zellers's stores and no pallets of merchandise, all part of Target's clean floor approach to ensure an easier shopping flow and better browsing experience.[71]

Target shoppers have come to expect a steady stream of exclusive new designer brands, along with the constant possibility of finding something unique, even unpredictable, in the next aisle over. Some of the brands available in Target Canada locations include collections from Nate Berkus, Sonia Kashuk, Giada De Laurentiis for Target, Shaun White for Target, as well as a limited-time-only Roots collection.[72] The Roots line featured T-shirts, sweatshirts, and sweatpants, and coincided with the company's 40th anniversary. In the future, Target will need to generate a high level of excitement with ongoing collections and partnerships to keep customers coming back.

Consumers looking to pay the same low prices for Target merchandise at Canadian stores as in American stores were disappointed. Retail prices are higher in Canada for a number of reasons including economies of scale, taxes and higher labour costs. To ensure its prices are competitive with the lowest-cost Canadian retailers, Target plans to implement weekly price checks.[73] And price-conscious consumers can sign up for Target's REDcard loyalty program to get a flat five percent discount.

Other retailers were quick to respond to this new competitor. For example, Hudson's Bay added new designers, opened an outlet store, and increased its focus on customer service. So far it seems to be paying off. A survey by Forum Research indicated that customer satisfaction at Hudson's Bay went up after Target opened its Canadian stores—40 percent of Hudson's Bay shoppers said they were "very satisfied" compared to only 27 percent of those who rated their experience at Target as "very satisfied."[74]

To date, Target's entry into the Canadian retail space has missed the bull's-eye with a disappointing loss of $941 million at the end of 2013 and a projected loss of $314 million for 2014.[75] The question going forward will be whether Target—the store loyal customers have dubbed "Tarzhay" for its supply of "cheap chic"—can keep existing customers, while attracting more shoppers with new rounds of boutique surprises.

Questions

1. Assess the role of consumer expectations in Target's success as a major discount retailer.

2. What differentiates Target's new retail partnership model from its longstanding partnerships with top designers? What are the relative strengths of each?

3. What explains Target's ability to attract top designers and high-end specialty shops as retail partners?

4. Using the factors for choosing retail partners outlined in the chapter, do you believe that Eva's line of green cosmetics should attempt to get placement in Target?

5. Develop a strategy for Target to promote Eva's line of green cosmetics as part of its new specialty shop partnership program.

For more information on the resources available from McGraw-Hill Ryerson, go to www.mheducation.ca/he/solutions.

CHAPTER **14**

Integrated Marketing Communications

Launched in 2003, the McDonald's "I'm Lovin' It" tagline has become the platform for the company's worldwide integrated marketing communications. As the company's most successful and longest-running campaign, "I'm Lovin' It" has outperformed the iconic "You Deserve a Break Today," and "Food, Folks and Fun," in both longevity and sales increases.[1] After only two years, the campaign was credited for bringing some 50 million customers to McDonald's daily, a gain of more than 2 million per day.[2]

When the tagline first launched, ads featured U.S. pop star Justin Timberlake, whose single was used as the theme. The goal was to make "I'm Lovin' It" a full campaign, not just a tagline. As such, the campaign made use of traditional media such as TV, radio, and print ads, and also incorporates billboards, signage, and sponsorship, ranging from Little League sports to the Olympic Games.

According to the company's chief marketing officer, Mary Dillon, the campaign lifted the relevance of McDonald's and revitalized its image, framing it as a modern and contemporary lifestyle brand.[3] It's not surprising that the company is sticking with the campaign and has asked its myriad of advertising agencies to kick it up a notch to make "I'm Lovin' It" even better. New marketing communication initiatives will see the tagline take prominence over the Golden Arches by having the tagline appear independently and having the Arches introduced later in TV ads. The tagline is being integrated into the action to help celebrate what the company calls "uniquely McDonald's moments."

Given the cost of launching global campaigns, being able to build on one platform helps McDonald's deliver a consistent global message and achieve cost savings. While most countries elected to work with the English version of the tagline, others chose to translate or localize it to adapt it to local culture. For example, in Spanish the tagline is *me encanta*, which translates loosely to "I really like it."[4] The unique musical sound bite featured in ads needs no translation and helps to tie the campaign together around the world.

Having a solid platform facilitates the introduction of unique components. In its efforts to be completely transparent about the ingredients used and how its

LEARNING OBJECTIVES

After studying this chapter you should be able to

LO1 Outline the process that firms use to communicate with consumers

LO2 List the steps in planning an integrated marketing communications campaign

LO3 Describe what appeals advertisers use to get customers' attention

LO4 Identify how firms determine which media to use

LO5 Summarize how firms measure integrated marketing communications success

LO6 Explain the six tools of integrated marketing communications campaigns

food is made, McDonald's Canada launched an integrated campaign called "Our Food. Your Questions." The campaign included a website, television ad, video projections on buildings, and transit ads. Consumers asked questions related to calorie counts, why food looked different in ads than when they bought it in store, and why some McDonald's foods don't rot even after being left out for long periods of time.[5] The campaign answered 18,462 questions and generated over 13 million views of the video, plus 132 million media impressions and 2.3 billion social media impressions. It also won four gold trophies and top honours for the Best of Show at the Marketing Awards in 2013.[6]

Although new advertising campaigns will always be introduced, they are built on the same solid foundation. For now, McDonald's plans to use "I'm Lovin' It," with its distinctive "Ba-da-ba-ba-ba" sound bite, to build brand equity and drive sales in the future. ▮

Throughout the last six chapters, we focused our attention on how firms create value by developing products and services and delivering them to consumers when and where they want to buy them. However, consumers are not likely to come flocking to new products and services unless they are aware of them. Marketers must consider how to communicate the value of a new product and/or service—or more specifically, the value proposition—to the target market. The chapter vignette about McDonald's illustrates how a firm can develop a communication strategy to increase the relevance and value of its product. Let's begin by examining what integrated marketing communications is, how it has developed, and how it contributes to value creation.

Integrated marketing communications (IMC) represents promotion, the last of the four Ps. It encompasses a variety of communication disciplines—advertising, personal selling, sales promotion, public relations, direct marketing, and digital media—in combination to provide clarity, consistency, and maximum communicative impact.[7] Rather than consisting of separate marketing communication elements with no unified control, IMC programs regard each of the firm's marketing communications elements as part of a whole, each of which offers a different means to connect with the target audience. This integration of elements provides the firm with the best means to reach the target audience with the desired message, and it enhances the value story by offering a clear and consistent message.

There are three components in any IMC strategy: the consumer or target market, the channels or vehicles through which the message is communicated, and the evaluation of the results of the communication. In the first section of this chapter, we focus on *consumers*, examining the communication process: how consumers receive communications, whether via media or other methods, and how the delivery of that communication affects a message's form and content. The second section identifies the steps involved in planning successful campaigns, from identifying a target audience to creating an actual ad and assessing its performance. Although we apply these steps specifically to advertising, the same process can be used when planning sales promotions, direct marketing, public relations, and digital media. We also consider how the level of complexity in IMC strategies leads marketers to design new ways to measure the *results* of IMC campaigns. Our last section examines the six distinct *tools* of IMC—advertising, personal selling, sales promotion, direct marketing, public relations, and digital media—and how each is used in an overall IMC strategy.

integrated marketing communications (IMC) Represents the promotion dimension of the four Ps; encompasses a variety of communication disciplines—general advertising, personal selling, sales promotion, public relations, direct marketing, and digital media—in combination to provide clarity, consistency, and maximum communicative impact.

COMMUNICATING WITH CONSUMERS

As the number of communication media has increased, the task of understanding how best to reach target consumers has become far more complex. In this section, we examine a model that describes how communications go from the firm to the consumer, and the factors that affect the way the consumer perceives the message. Then we look at how marketing communications influence consumers—from making them aware that a product or service exists to moving them to buy.

The Communication Process

Exhibit 14.1 illustrates the communication process. Let's first define each component and then discuss how they interact.

The Sender   The message originates from the **sender**, who must be clearly identified to the intended audience. For instance, an organization such as Home Depot working with one of its vendors, Stanley Tools Company, can send a message that it is having a special "Father's Day sale."

In the quest for innovative ways to reach consumers, some marketers have been accused of **deceptive advertising**, which is a representation, omission, act, or practice in an advertisement that is likely to mislead consumers acting reasonably under the circumstances. For example, to promote its film *Godsend*, Lion's Gate Films created a website (http://www.godsendinstitute.org) to look like a legitimate fertility clinic, disguising the true sender of the message, and deliberately misleading or confusing visitors to the site.

The Transmitter   The sender works with the creative department, whether in-house or from a marketing (or advertising) agency, to develop marketing communications. Stanley likely develops advertising materials with its ad agency and provides the materials to Home Depot. Such an agent or intermediary is the **transmitter**.

Encoding   **Encoding** means converting the sender's ideas into a message, which could be verbal, visual, or both. Home Depot may take out full-page ads in every major

sender
The firm from which an IMC message originates; the sender must be clearly identified to the intended audience.

deceptive advertising
A representation, omission, act, or practice in an advertisement that is likely to mislead consumers acting reasonably under the circumstances.

transmitter
An agent or intermediary with which the sender works to develop the marketing communications; for example, a firm's creative department or an advertising agency.

encoding
The process of converting the sender's ideas into a message, which could be verbal, visual, or both.

EXHIBIT 14.1   The Communication Process

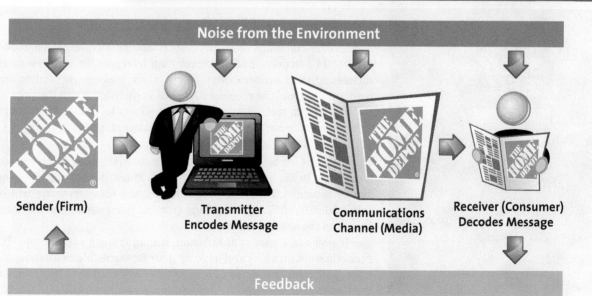

Noise from the Environment

Sender (Firm) — Transmitter Encodes Message — Communications Channel (Media) — Receiver (Consumer) Decodes Message

Feedback

communication channel
The medium—print, broadcast, the Internet—that carries the message.

receiver
The person who reads, hears, or sees and processes the information contained in the message or advertisement.

decoding
The process by which the receiver interprets the sender's message.

noise
Any interference that stems from competing messages, a lack of clarity in the message, or a flaw in the medium; a problem for all communication channels.

feedback loop
Allows the receiver to communicate with the sender and thereby informs the sender whether the message was received and decoded properly.

Receivers decode messages differently. What does the Taco Bell sign mean to you?

newspaper proclaiming, "Amazing Father's Day Deals at 25 Percent Off!" A TV commercial showing men examining and testing tools at Home Depot is another way to encode the message that "there are great deals to be had." As the old saying goes, a picture is worth a thousand words. But the most important facet of encoding is not what is sent but rather what is received. Home Depot shoppers must believe that the sale is substantial enough to warrant a trip to a store.

The Communication Channel   The **communication channel** is the medium—print, broadcast, the Internet—that carries the message. Home Depot could transmit through TV, radio, and various print ads, and it realizes that the media chosen must be appropriate to connect itself (the sender) with its desired recipient. So Home Depot might advertise on channels such as HGTV and in magazines such as *Canadian Homes & Cottages*.

The Receiver   The **receiver** is the person who reads, hears, or sees and processes the information contained in the message or advertisement. The sender, of course, hopes that the person receiving it will be the one for whom it was originally intended. For example, Home Depot wants its message received and decoded properly by people who are likely to shop in its stores. **Decoding** refers to the process by which the receiver interprets the sender's message.

Noise   **Noise** is any interference that stems from competing messages, a lack of clarity in the message, or a flaw in the medium, and it poses a problem for all communication channels. Home Depot may choose to advertise in newspapers that its target market doesn't read, which means the rate at which the message is received by those to whom it has relevance has been slowed considerably. As we have already defined, encoding is what the sender intends to say, and decoding is what the receiver hears. If there is a difference between them, it is probably due to noise.

Feedback Loop   The **feedback loop** allows the receiver to communicate with the sender and thereby informs the sender whether the message was received and decoded properly. Feedback can take many forms: a customer's purchase of the item, a complaint or compliment, the redemption of a coupon or rebate, and so forth. If Home Depot observes an increase in store traffic and sales, its managers know that their intended audience received the message and understood that there were great Father's Day bargains to be found in the store.

How Consumers Perceive Communication

The actual communication process is not as simple as the model in Exhibit 14.1 implies. Each receiver may interpret the sender's message differently, and senders often adjust their message according to the medium used and the receivers' level of knowledge about the product or service. And in spite of marketers' best efforts to create clear messages, consumers may not always respond as expected.

Receivers Decode Messages Differently   Each receiver decodes a message in his or her own way, which is not necessarily the way the sender intended. Different people shown the same message will often take radically different meanings from it. For example, what does the image on the left convey to you?

If you are a user of this brand, it may convey satisfaction. If you recently went on a diet and gave up your favourite Mexican food, it may convey dismay or a sense of loss. If you have chosen to be a nonuser, it may convey some disgust. If you are a recently terminated employee,

Senders must adjust messages according to the receivers' traits. LG, for instance, uses the ad on the left to target consumers for its Super Blue high-definition players. The ad on the right targets a B2B audience.

it may convey anger. The sender has little, if any, control over what meaning any individual receiver will take from the message.[8]

Senders Adjust Messages According to the Medium and Receivers' Traits

Different media communicate in very different ways. So marketers make adjustments to their messages and media depending on whether they want to communicate with suppliers, shareholders, customers, or the general public.[9] Kellogg's would not, for instance, send the same message to its shareholders in a targeted email as it would to its consumers on Saturday morning TV.

Now that we've examined various aspects of the communication process, let's look at the steps in planning an IMC campaign that achieves the organization's strategic objectives.

STEPS IN PLANNING AN IMC CAMPAIGN

LO2

Designing a successful IMC campaign requires a great deal of planning. Exhibit 14.2 shows some of the key steps in the planning process, each of which helps ensure that the intended message reaches the right audience and has the desired effect. As mentioned earlier, these steps can be used for all IMC tools. Let's examine each of these steps as they pertain to developing a campaign.

EXHIBIT 14.2 Steps in Planning an IMC Campaign

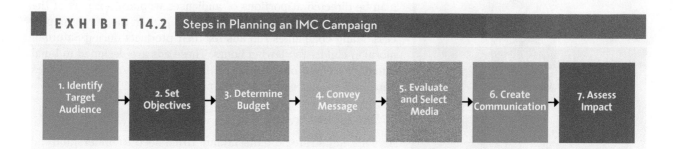

1. Identify Target Audience → 2. Set Objectives → 3. Determine Budget → 4. Convey Message → 5. Evaluate and Select Media → 6. Create Communication → 7. Assess Impact

Who is the target audience for this ad, men or women?

2010 Toyota RAV4 4x2	2010 Chevy Equinox FWD
MPG: 28 ~ EPA est hwy	MPG: 32 ~ EPA est hwy
Hwy Driving Range: 445 miles	Hwy Driving Range: 600 miles
Five-Star Crash Safety Rating: no*	Five-Star Crash Safety Rating: yes*
Powertrain Warranty: 5 years/60,000 miles**	Powertrain Warranty: 5 years/100,000 miles**
A Consumers Digest Best Buy: no	A Consumers Digest Best Buy: yes
Automatic Crash Response: not available	Automatic Crash Response: OnStar*/1 year standard†
Link to Emergency Services: not available	Link to Emergency Services: OnStar/1 year standard

MAY THE BEST CAR WIN.
visit chevy.com

1. Identify Target Audience

The success of any campaign depends on how well the advertiser can identify its target audience. Firms conduct research to identify their target audience, and then use the information they gain to set the tone for the advertising program and help them select the media they will use to deliver the message to that audience.

During this research, firms must keep in mind that their target audience may or may not be the same as current users of the product. Think about jewellery. Research shows that in a typical year, some 43 percent of the North American adult population—more than 95 million people—purchase jewellery. Although women have a significantly higher purchase incidence (48 percent) and purchase more often than men (36 percent), men spend significantly more money on their jewellery purchases than do women. Perhaps it is no surprise that the majority of men's jewellery purchases are gifts.[10]

Columbia Sportswear Company's "Greater Outdoors" campaign's goal is to showcase the company's technical innovation and overcome perceptions of inferior products.

Another example is adidas. It knows that NBA fans likely are familiar with its offerings, even if they do not currently purchase sports gear from adidas. Some advertisements feature Chicago Bulls guard Derrick Rose to encourage them to buy more of the brand's products. But teenaged pop music fans might be less likely to pay attention to sporting goods. So in its marketing, adidas also features Katy Perry. Another example of marketing and advertising toward different segments (e.g., consumer vs. business users) is illustrated by Visa and MasterCard, which have different ads and offerings aimed at these segments. Some advertising messages also may be directed at portions of audiences who are not part of the marketer's target market but who participate in the purchase process. Many companies run ads for their products during Saturday morning children's viewing hours. These ads are designed to build brand awareness on the part of the children who, the companies hope, will influence their parents' purchases.

2. Set Objectives

As with any strategic undertaking, firms need to understand the outcome they hope to achieve before they begin. Objectives, or goals, are crucial since they will later serve as the yardstick against which success or failure is measured. These objectives can be short term, such as generating inquiries, increasing awareness, and prompting trial. Or they can be long term in nature, such as increasing sales, market share, and customer loyalty. Driving traffic and sales was the primary and long-term goal of the McDonald's "I'm Lovin' It" campaign but, in the short term, McDonald's needed to establish heightened brand awareness. Thus, the campaign was designed to get consumers' attention through TV, print, and billboard advertisements. Both short- and long-term goals should be explicitly defined and measured. We discuss how firms measure IMC success later in this chapter.

Exhibit 14.3 outlines some campaign goals for a variety of companies as well as the target markets, media used, and outcomes.

All marketing communications aim to achieve certain objectives: to inform, persuade, and remind customers. These objectives are examined in more depth in Chapter 15. Communication objectives also need to consider focus—for example, does the company hope to stimulate demand for a new product or service or to increase awareness for the company in general?

This ad informs consumers about Winners' accessories selection.

In Chapter 12, you learned about using push or pull marketing in determining distribution channel strategy. When setting objectives, the overarching strategy used is one of push versus pull. However, marketers also have to consider other factors, such as the nature of the market (consumer versus business), the nature of the product (simple versus technologically complex), and the stage in the product life cycle (PLC). Generally, when advertising to consumers, the objective is a pull strategy in which the goal is to get consumers to pull the product into the supply chain by demanding retailers carry it. Push strategies also exist and are designed to increase demand by focusing on wholesalers,

---

EXHIBIT 14.3 Sample Marketing Goals and Related Campaigns

Company and Campaign	Goals	Target Market	Media Used	Outcome
ASICS Sound Mind, Sound Body	Branch out beyond serious runner market segment and target casual runners.	Even split males and females, age 30–49	Television and print ads, online advertising	12% increase in market share
Columbia Sportswear Company Greater Outdoors	Showcase Columbia's technical innovation ability and overcome perceptions of inferior products.	60% males, age 20–59	Print ads, mobile media, social media, videos, online advertising	1% increase in sales, and +2 point brand awareness increase compared with previous year
GAP Ready for Holiday Cheer	Capture consumers' attention and get them to shop in the store during the holiday season.	Even split males and females, age 20–39	Print inserts, television ads, special website, social media, customizable videos	Kelly Awards Best Inset Winner; sales turned from a 12% decline in the previous year to a 1% increase
BMW Diesel Reinvented	Overcome the negative image of diesel that most consumers have.	Three segments: idea class, enthusiasts, and environmentally conscious	Print ads, videos	+1,463% year-to-year sales increase

Source: http://www.magazine.org/advertising/case_studies/

objective-and-task method
An IMC budgeting method that determines the cost required to undertake specific tasks to accomplish communication objectives; process entails setting objectives, choosing media, and determining costs.

competitive parity method
A method of determining a communications budget in which the firm's share of the communication expenses is in line with its market share.

percentage-of-sales method
A method of determining a communications budget that is based on a fixed percentage of forecasted sales.

affordable method
A method of determining a communications budget based on what is left over after other operating costs have been covered.

distributors, or salespeople, who push the product to consumers via distribution channels. These campaigns attempt to motivate the seller to highlight the product, rather than the products of competitors, and thereby push the product onto consumers.

Once the campaign's objectives are defined, the firm sets the advertising budget.

3. Determine Budget

Firms use a variety of methods to plan their IMC budgets (see Exhibit 14.4). Because all the methods of setting a promotional budget have both advantages and disadvantages, no one method should be used in isolation.[11] Budgeting is not a simple process. It may take several rounds of negotiations among the company's managers, who are each competing for resources for their own areas of responsibility.

The **objective-and-task method** determines the budget required to undertake specific tasks to accomplish communication objectives. To use this method, marketers first establish a set of communication objectives, and then determine which media best reach the target market and how much it will cost to run the number and types of communications necessary to achieve the objectives. This process—set objectives, choose media, and determine costs—must be repeated for each product or service. The sum of all the individual communication plan budgets becomes the firm's total marketing communications budget.

In addition to the objective-and-task method, three rule-of-thumb methods: **competitive parity method**, **percentage-of-sales method**, and **affordable method** of budgeting can be used to set budgets.

These rule-of-thumb methods use prior sales and communication activities to determine the present communication budget. Although they are easy to implement, they obviously have various limitations, as noted in Exhibit 14.4. While small companies often use the affordable budgeting method, it generally results in underspending

EXHIBIT 14.4 Budgeting Methods

Method	Definition	Limitations
Objective and Task	The communication budget is set based on the cost of specific tasks required to achieve stated communication objectives.	• It can be difficult to identify the specific tasks that will achieve the objectives and, as a result, it is the most difficult method to use.
Competitive Parity	A method of determining a communications budget in which the firm's share of the communication expenses is in line with its market share.	• Prevents firms from exploiting the unique opportunities or problems they confront in a market. • If all competitors use this method to set communication budgets, their market shares will stay approximately the same over time.
Percentage of Sales	A method of determining a communications budget that is based on a fixed percentage of forecasted sales. For example, a company with $2.5 million in projected sales that allocates 3.5% to advertising would have a budget of $87,500.	• Assumes the percentage used in the past, or by competitors, is still appropriate for the firm. • Does not take into account new plans (e.g., to introduce a new line of products in the current year).
Affordable Budgeting	A method of determining a communications budget based on what is left over after other operating costs have been covered. That is, marketers forecast their sales and expenses, excluding communication, during the budgeting period. The difference between the forecast sales, minus expenses plus desired profit is applied to the communication budget (i.e., the budget is the money available after operating costs and profits).	• Assumes communication expenses do not stimulate sales and profit.

and thus may not accomplish the company's sales objectives. Large companies such as Coca-Cola and PepsiCo may use the competitive parity method. However, this method is setting a budget based on market share, which may result in PepsiCo being outspent. The percentage-of-sales method is popular as well, and standard percentages are sometimes used in some product categories, as shown in Exhibit 14.5. Since everyone needs to eat, the grocery industry needs to spend only a small percentage—around 1 percent—of its revenues on advertising, whereas the toy and game industry must spend about 11 percent.

When selecting the various budgeting methods for marketing communications, firms must first consider the role that advertising plays in their attempt to meet their overall promotional objectives. Second, advertising expenditures vary over the course of the PLC, with considerably higher levels of spending during the introduction stage. Third, the nature of the market and the product influence the size of advertising budgets. For example, advertising for the Scion was less than 14 percent of the total promotional budget because Toyota used so many kinds of nontraditional media to get the attention of its young target customers. For other products or services, the advertising portion of the total promotional budget may be as high as 95 percent. Amway Canada recently shifted its entire advertising budget to online media.[12] It all depends on the objectives of the overall IMC campaign.

EXHIBIT 14.5 Advertising Spending as a Percentage of Sales for Illustrative Product Categories

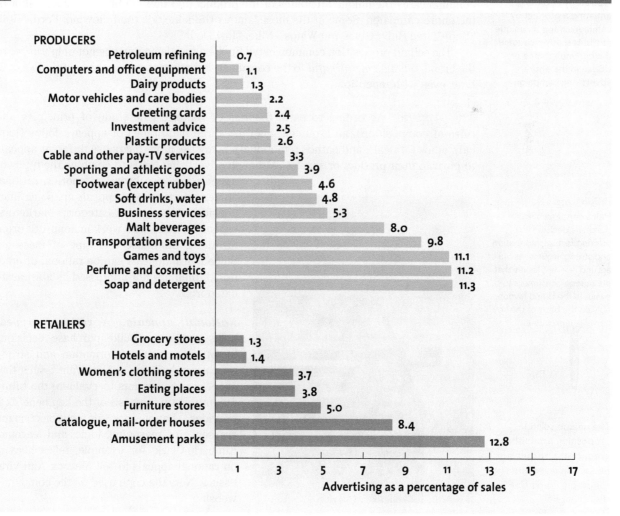

PRODUCERS

Category	%
Petroleum refining	0.7
Computers and office equipment	1.1
Dairy products	1.3
Motor vehicles and care bodies	2.2
Greeting cards	2.4
Investment advice	2.5
Plastic products	2.6
Cable and other pay-TV services	3.3
Sporting and athletic goods	3.9
Footwear (except rubber)	4.6
Soft drinks, water	4.8
Business services	5.3
Malt beverages	8.0
Transportation services	9.8
Games and toys	11.1
Perfume and cosmetics	11.2
Soap and detergent	11.3

RETAILERS

Category	%
Grocery stores	1.3
Hotels and motels	1.4
Women's clothing stores	3.7
Eating places	3.8
Furniture stores	5.0
Catalogue, mail-order houses	8.4
Amusement parks	12.8

Advertising as a percentage of sales

The nature of the market also determines the amount of money spent on advertising. For instance, less money is spent on advertising in B2B marketing contexts than in B2C markets. Personal selling, as we discuss in Chapter 15, likely is more important in B2B markets.

LO3

4. Convey Message

In this step, marketers determine what they want to convey about the product or service. First, the firm determines the key message it wants to communicate to the target audience. Second, the firm decides what appeal would most effectively convey the message. We present these decisions sequentially but, in reality, they must be considered simultaneously.

The Message   The message provides the target audience with reasons to respond in the desired way. A logical starting point for deciding on the advertising message is to tout the key benefits of the product or service. The message should communicate the product's problem-solving ability clearly and in a compelling fashion. In this context, advertisers must remember that products and services solve problems, whether real or perceived. That is, people are not looking for 1/4-inch drill bits; they are looking for 1/4-inch holes.[13] Because there are many ways to make a 1/4-inch hole, a firm such as Black and Decker must convey to consumers that its drill bit is the best way to get that hole.

Another common strategy differentiates a product by establishing its unique benefits. This distinction forms the basis for the **unique selling proposition (USP)**, which is often the common theme or slogan in an advertising campaign. Briefly, a good USP communicates the unique attributes of the product and thereby becomes a snapshot of the entire campaign. Some of the most famous USPs include the following: Ford, "Built Tough"; Red Bull, "Gives You Wings"; Nike, "Just Do It."

The selling proposition communicated by the advertising must be not only *unique* to the brand, but also *meaningful* to the consumer; it furthermore must be *sustainable* over time, even with repetition.

The Appeal   According to early theories of rhetoric (the study of principles and rules of composition), an argument may use three main types of appeals: logos (logical), ethos (ethical), and pathos (emotional). Likewise, advertisers use different appeals to portray their product or service. Although advertising tends to combine the types of appeals into two broad categories, rational and emotional; moral appeals are sometimes considered as a third category. Marketers, especially those who work in nonprofit organizations, often use this type of message. Since moral appeals can be rational or emotional, they are not addressed as a separate category.

Rational appeals. A **rational appeal** helps consumers make purchase decisions by offering factual information and strong arguments built around relevant issues that encourage consumers to evaluate the brand favourably on the basis of the key benefits it provides.[14] Rational appeals focus on consumers' sense of reasoning, logic, and learning. Kimberly-Clark, for example, relies heavily on rational appeals to sell Kleenex Anti-Viral tissues. Note the copy used on the company's website:

---

unique selling proposition (USP)
A strategy of differentiating a product by communicating its unique attributes; often becomes the common theme or slogan in the entire advertising campaign.

rational appeal
Helps consumers make purchase decisions by offering factual information and strong arguments built around relevant issues that encourage consumers to evaluate the brand favourably on the basis of the key benefits it provides.

The unique selling proposition establishes a product or firm's unique benefits in an advertising campaign. Ford's USP is "Built Tough.".

No hesitation.

Our success is measured by what we do, not what we say.

So we're going to let our cars and trucks do the talking.

Get ready for incredible power and a strong, daunting presence.

We're on the move.

fordvehicles.com

BUILT TOUGH

BOLD MOVES

Coca-Cola uses emotional appeals with its polar bears to create a bond between the consumer and the brand.

The emotional appeal of Halle Berry's perfume is sex.

Only KLEENEX® Anti-Viral Tissue has a moisture-activated middle layer that is scientifically proven to kill cold and flu viruses. When moisture from a runny nose, cough or sneeze comes in contact with KLEENEX® Anti-Viral Tissue's special middle layer, cold and flu viruses are trapped and killed.[15]

This appeal is perfectly suited to this type of product. The source of its competitive advantage is a tangible feature of the product. By stressing the superior benefits of this product over regular facial tissue, the advertising copy directly delivers a rational persuasive message.[16]

Emotional appeals. An **emotional appeal** aims to satisfy consumers' emotional desires rather than their utilitarian needs. The key to a successful emotional appeal is the use of emotion to create a bond between the consumer and the brand. For example, think about Coca-Cola's use of polar bears in its ads. The emotions most often invoked in advertising include fear appeal and humour appeal, but also safety, happiness, love (or sex), comfort, and nostalgia. Companies must pay attention to cultural influences because humour is not perceived the same way across different cultural groups and sexual appeals are taboo in some cultures.

Although the term *emotion* often conveys the image of tears, many other effective emotional appeals are used in advertising, ranging from sex appeal (e.g., Axe Body Spray), need for affiliation, need for guidance (e.g., Betty Crocker), and attention (e.g., cosmetics). People need a sense of self-esteem, so advertisements for Bowflex and Jenny Craig tend to feature celebrities or regular people talking about how much better they feel about themselves after they've joined the program and lost weight. Weight-loss ads also tend to play a bit on consumers' fears, showing "before and after" pictures as if the heavier version were a horror to behold.

5. Evaluate and Select Media

L04

The content of an advertisement is tied closely to the characteristics of the media that firms select to carry the message, and vice versa. **Media planning** refers to the process of evaluating and selecting the **media mix**—the combination of the media used and the frequency of advertising in each medium—that will deliver a clear, consistent, compelling

emotional appeal
Aims to satisfy consumers' emotional desires rather than their utilitarian needs.

media planning
The process of evaluating and selecting the media mix that will deliver a clear, consistent, compelling message to the intended audience.

media mix
The combination of the media used and the frequency of advertising in each medium.

message to the intended audience.[17] For example, Target may determine that a heavy dose of television, radio, print, and billboards is appropriate for the back-to-school selling season between August and September each year.

Because the **media buy**, the purchase of airtime or print pages, is generally the largest expense in the advertising budget, marketers must make their decisions carefully. TV advertising is by far the most expensive. Total ad spending in Canada is $14.4 billion per year. With the exception of online advertising, which has grown dramatically, advertising expenditures per medium have remained relatively constant over time: TV, 30 percent; direct mail, 9 percent; newspapers, 16.5 percent; radio, 13.2 percent; Yellow Pages, 5 percent; magazines, 5 percent; and online, 21.7 percent. Other media, such as out-of-home advertising (e.g., billboards, bus wraps, posters) account for the remainder.[18] To characterize these various types of media, we again use a dichotomy: mass and niche media.

Mass and Niche Media
Mass media channels include national newspapers, magazines, radio, and television, and are ideal for reaching large numbers of anonymous audience members. **Niche media** channels are more focused and are generally used to reach narrower segments, often with unique demographic characteristics or interests. Cable TV, direct mail, and specialty magazines such as *Skateboarder* or *CosmoGirl* all provide examples of niche media. In some cases, niche media offer advertisers the opportunity to change and even personalize their messages, which is generally not an option with mass media. For example, magazine advertisers can print response cards with the name of the subscriber already on the card or change advertisements to reflect local differences, such as climate or preferences.

Choosing the Right Medium
For each class of media, each alternative has specific characteristics that make it suitable for meeting specific objectives (see Exhibit 14.6). For example, consumers use different media for different purposes, to which advertisers should match their messages. Television is used primarily for escapism and entertainment, so most TV advertising relies on a mix of visual and auditory techniques. Out-of-home advertising can also be effectively used to deliver a message. MINI Cooper developed an innovative method of advertising to its current customers in select cities through an interactive billboard. Owners received an RFID chip–embedded key fob. Every time they passed by the billboard, they received a customized message that displayed their name on the billboard.

Communication media also vary in their ability to reach the desired audience. For instance, radio is a good medium for products such as grocery purchases or fast food

media buy
The purchase of airtime or print pages.

mass media
Channels, such as national newspapers, magazines, radio, and television, that are ideal for reaching large numbers of anonymous audience members.

niche media
Channels that are focused and generally used to reach narrow segments, often with unique demographic characteristics or interests.

Mini Cooper uses out-of-home advertising and humour to effectively deliver messages to prospective customers.

EXHIBIT 14.6 Types of Media Available for Advertising

Medium	Advantages	Disadvantages
Television	• Wide reach • Creativity • Impact	• High absolute cost • Clutter • Lack of involvement
Radio	• Relatively inexpensive • Target audience selectivity • Wide reach • Frequency	• Not limited by constraints of visuals • Unlikely to get consumers' focused attention • Short, selective exposure
Magazines	• Very targeted • Reach wider audience if subscribers pass them along to others • Attention	• Scheduling inflexibility • Long lead times • Clutter
Newspapers	• Scheduling flexibility • Timely • Can localize	• Expensive in some markets • Short lifespan • Clutter
Digital	• Can be linked to detailed content • Highly flexible and interactive • Allows for specific targeting	• Difficult to compare costs to other media • Clutter • Can be blocked by software prohibiting delivery
Out-of-Home	• Relatively inexpensive • Frequency • Scheduling flexibility	• Placement problems in some markets • Low involvement • Clutter
Direct Mail	• Highly targeted • Allows for personalization	• Relatively expensive • Often considered "junk mail"

because many consumers decide what to purchase either on the way to the store or while in the store. Because many people listen to the radio in their cars, it becomes a highly effective means to reach consumers at a crucial point in their decision process. Each medium also varies in its reach and frequency. Advertisers can determine how effective their media mix has been in reaching their target audience by calculating the total gross rating points (GRP) (reach × frequency) of the advertising schedule, which we discuss later in this chapter.

The cost of each medium differs as well, with television being the most expensive. Many marketers are shifting their budgets to more digital media as a result. For example, Mondelez, which owns the Oreo brand, has been steadily shifting its budget toward digital media based on research that indicates the ROI is higher. According to the Television Bureau of Canada, advertising expenditures in 2012 reached almost $13 billion. The breakdown in billions of dollars is as follows: TV $3.58; Newspapers, $3.55; Digital $3.06; Radio $1.59; Magazines, $.57; and Out-of-Home $.49.[19]

Determining the Advertising Schedule Another important decision for the media planner is the **advertising schedule**, which specifies the timing and duration of advertising. There are three types of schedules:[20]

- A **continuous advertising schedule** runs steadily throughout the year and therefore is suited to products and services that are consumed continually at relatively steady rates and that require a steady level of persuasive or reminder advertising. For example, P&G advertises its Tide brand of laundry detergent continuously.

- A **flighting advertising schedule** refers to one implemented in spurts, with periods of heavy advertising followed by periods of no advertising. This pattern

advertising schedule
Specifies the timing and duration of advertising.

continuous advertising schedule
Runs steadily throughout the year and therefore is suited to products and services that are consumed continually at relatively steady rates and that require a steady level of persuasive or reminder advertising.

flighting advertising schedule
Implemented in spurts, with periods of heavy advertising followed by periods of no advertising.

generally functions for products whose demand fluctuates, such as tennis racquets, which manufacturers may advertise heavily in the months leading up to and during the summer.

- A **pulsing advertising schedule** combines the continuous and flighting schedules by maintaining a base level of advertising but increasing advertising intensity during certain periods. For example, furniture retailer IKEA advertises throughout the year but boosts its advertising expenditures to promote school supplies in August.

pulsing advertising schedule
Combines the continuous and flighting schedules by maintaining a base level of advertising but increasing advertising intensity during certain periods.

6. Create Communication

After the marketer has decided on the message, type of ad, and appeal, its attention must shift to the actual creation of the advertisement. During this step, the message and appeal are translated creatively into words, pictures, colours, and/or music. Often, the execution style for the ad will dictate the type of medium used to deliver the message. For example, crash tests demonstrating the safety of cars often rely on the visual impact of the crash. This style of execution works only on television. Therefore, it is common for advertisers to make decisions about their message and appeal, the appropriate medium, and the best execution concurrently.

Automobile manufacturers and their dealers advertise by using many media vehicles, taking care that the media fits the message. To demonstrate an image, they may use television and magazines. To promote price, they can use newspapers and radio. To appeal to specific target markets, they can use some of the digital media vehicles described earlier. When using multiple media to deliver the same message, however, advertisers must maintain consistency across the execution styles—that is, integrated marketing—so the different executions deliver a consistent and compelling message to the target audience.

Although creativity plays a major role in the execution stage, advertisers must be careful not to let their creativity overshadow the message. Whatever the execution style, the advertisement must be able to attract the audience's attention, provide a reason for the audience to spend its time viewing the advertisement, and accomplish what it set out to do. In the end, the execution style must match the medium and objectives. An additional complication in Canada is the necessity to design some advertising messages in two official languages. And, as mentioned earlier, Canada's multicultural population means that companies must carefully consider cultural influences so as not to alienate groups through inappropriate messages.

Print advertising can be especially difficult because it is a static medium: no sound, no motion, and only one dimension. Instead, print relies on several key components that appear in most ads: the *headline*, or large type designed to draw attention and be read first; the *body copy*, which represents the main text portion of the ad; the *background* for the ad, usually a single colour; the *foreground*, which refers to everything that appears on top of the background, and the *branding*, which identifies the sponsor of the ad. The advertiser must convey its message by using compelling visuals and limited text. To create an ad, go to Connect and access the Interactive Toolkits.

IKEA uses a pulsing strategy when it sets its advertising schedule. It advertises throughout the year but has more advertising directed at the back-to-school market in August.

One particularly effective ad in the Stupid.ca print and online campaign won two Gold awards at the Cassies, the Canadian Advertising Success Stories. The campaign was based on insights that kids think parents are lame, teachers are pathetic, and the government is worse. The campaign needed a single, blunt message that kids would relate to. This message, developed in part by an advisory panel of kids, boiled down to a single defining thought: smoking is just about the stupidest thing you can do. It was delivered in a tone that was honest and funny, not preachy. The results were positive, with 91 percent of kids saying that the ads would help prevent their peers from smoking. Better yet, a Statistics Canada study showed that smoking rates declined by 2 percent among 12- to 17- year-olds, and there was a 9 percent increase in the number of kids who never started to smoke at all.[21]

7. Assess Impact Using Marketing Metrics

LO5

The effectiveness of an advertising campaign must be assessed before, during, and after the campaign has run. Each step in the IMC process can be measured to determine how effective it has been at motivating consumers to move to the next step in the buying process. **Pretesting** refers to assessments performed before an ad campaign is implemented to ensure that the various elements are working in an integrated fashion and doing what they are intended to do.[22] **Tracking** includes monitoring key indicators, such as daily or weekly sales volume, while the advertisement is running to shed light on any problems with the message or the medium. **Post-testing** is the evaluation of the campaign's impact after it has been implemented. At this last stage, advertisers assess the sales and/or communication impact of the advertisement or campaign.

Measuring sales impact can be especially challenging because of the many influences other than advertising on consumers' choices, purchase behaviour, and attitudes. These influences include the level of competitors' advertising, economic conditions in the target market, sociocultural changes, and even the weather, all of which can influence consumer purchasing behaviour. Advertisers must try to identify these influences and isolate those of the particular advertising campaign.

For frequently purchased consumer goods in the maturity stage of the PLC, such as cola, sales volume offers a good indicator of advertising effectiveness. Because their sales are relatively stable, and if we assume that the other elements of the marketing mix and the environment have not changed, we can attribute changes in sales volume to changes in advertising.

For other types of goods in other stages of the PLC, sales data offer but one of the many indicators that marketers need to examine to determine advertising effectiveness. For instance, in high-growth markets, sales growth alone can be misleading because the market as a whole is growing. In such a situation, marketers measure sales relative to those of competitors to determine their relative market share. Firms find creative ways to identify advertising effectiveness; for example, digital cable allows them to present a specific advertisement to certain neighbourhoods and then track sales by local or regional retailers. Some product categories experience so many influences that it is almost impossible to identify advertising's contribution to any individual consumer's choice to purchase a particular product. This is especially true for products such as cigarettes and alcohol or those with potentially negative health consequences, such as fast food or high-sugar breakfast cereals.

Because of the cumulative effect of marketing communications, it may take several exposures before consumers are moved to buy, so firms cannot expect too much too soon. They must invest in the marketing communications campaign with the idea that it may not reach its full potential for some time. One internal campaign to increase an advertising agency's environmental scorecard wasn't measured by conventional methods. Instead, as presented in Sustainable Marketing 14.1, success was measured by how good it made employees feel about the company.

pretesting
Assessments performed before an ad campaign is implemented to ensure that the various elements are working in an integrated fashion and doing what they are intended to do.

tracking
Includes monitoring key indicators, such as daily or weekly sales volume, while the advertisement is running to shed light on any problems with the message or the medium.

post-testing
The evaluation of an IMC campaign's impact after it has been implemented.

Sustainable Marketing 14.1   Ideas That Build Sustainability

Advertising agency Quarry Integrated Communications (http://www.quarry.com) helps its clients build their brands through innovative research, advertising, branding, PR, sales, online, and digital media. Although the company's roots go back to an agricultural base, it has successfully expanded to a wide variety of industries and has worked with companies such as Bell, BlackBerry, Sprint, Budget, Wyndham Hotels and Resorts, and FedEx.

Quarry's long-time tagline has been "Ideas That Build." When the company moved its head office from Waterloo, Ontario, to nearby St. Jacobs, sustainable ideas built its new work environment. "If you're going to be a business in a community, it's your responsibility to help that community sustain itself," says chairman and CEO Alan Quarry. That idea is not only his personal philosophy but also written into the company's core values.

The company joined Sustainable Waterloo, a not-for-profit group that guides organizations in Waterloo Region toward a more environmentally sustainable future, as a way to focus its efforts and achieve meaningful and measurable results related to its sustainability strategy.[23] However, the company's commitment to sustainability began many years earlier. While recruiting new talent, the company found that prospective employees were becoming more environmentally enlightened about the type of organization they wanted to join. Quarry realized it needed to make changes and started with small efforts. It gave compact fluorescent light bulbs to employees and eliminated bottled water and polystyrene cups in the office. A "cardigan contest" helped employees generate enthusiasm and warmth when the heat was turned down in the office. To mark the company's 35th anniversary, employees planted 100 trees in a nearby conservation area. Transit passes were given to employees to encourage them to leave their cars at home.

Sustainable thinking naturally flowed through to the design of the company's new headquarters, where the guiding principle was R4: Rethink, Reduce, Reuse, and Recycle. Wherever possible, materials from the existing site were reused. Movable walls were used throughout the building. All new finishes have recycled content or are sustainable in their longevity and maintenance, including carpets, porcelain tile, acrylic panels, and solid-surface countertops. Additional windows were added to the north side of the building to increase access to daylight. A secure bike room was built and showers were installed for employees who wanted to cycle to work. Air-cleaning snake plants were placed throughout the office, and environmentally friendly soaps are used in the kitchens and washrooms. Even new seating was sourced from a company that manufactures with 100 percent Forest Stewardship Council–certified wood products, in support of responsible forest management.

Alan Quarry says these initiatives make employees feel good about the company and were the right thing to do. Although he hasn't calculated the payback, he views the company's sustainability efforts as generating positive ROI or, as he likes to say, return on involvement.

Quarry's new office was designed to be both sustainable and functional.

Traditional Media When measuring IMC success, the firm should examine when and how often consumers have been exposed to various marketing communications. Specifically, firms use measures of *frequency* and *reach* to gauge consumers' *exposure* to marketing communications. For most products and situations, a single exposure to a communication is not enough to generate the desired response. Therefore, marketers measure the **frequency** of exposure—how often the target audience is exposed to a communication within a specified period of time. The other measure used to determine consumers' exposure to marketing communications is **reach**, which describes the percentage of the target population exposed to a specific marketing communication, such as an advertisement, at least once.[24] Marketing communications managers usually state their media objectives in terms of **gross rating points (GRP)**, which represents reach multiplied by frequency (GRP = reach × frequency). This measure can be used for various media advertising—print, radio, or television.

GRP can be measured for print, radio, or television but, when comparing the calculations, they must refer to the same medium. Suppose that Unilever, the maker of Sunsilk, places five advertisements in *Flare* magazine, which reaches 50 percent of the "fashion forward" target segment. The total GRP generated by these five magazine ads is 50 reach × 5 advertisements = 250 GRP. Now suppose that Sunsilk includes 15 TV ads as part of the same campaign, run during the program *Lost*, which has a rating of 9.2. The total GRP generated by these 15 advertisements is 138 (9.2 reach × 15 ads = 138 GRP). However, ads typically appear during more than one TV program, so the total GRP equals the sum of the GRP generated by each program.

Digital Media   Firms in Canada spend over $2.8 billion annually on online advertising, which includes paid search, display ads, email, and sponsorships.[25] Although GRP is an adequate measure for TV and radio ads, assessing the effectiveness of any digital communications efforts in an IMC campaign generally requires web tracking software to indicate how much time viewers spend on particular web pages and the number of pages they view. **Click-through tracking** measures how many times users click on banner advertising on websites. All these performance metrics can be easily measured and assessed by using tools such as Google Analytics. Facebook also helps companies see who has been visiting their fan pages, what these people are doing on the fan pages, and who is clicking on their ads. By keeping track of who is visiting their fan pages, marketers can get to know these visitors and better customize the material on these pages for them.

Planning, Implementing, and Evaluating IMC Programs—An Illustration of Google Advertising

Imagine a hypothetical upscale sneaker store in New York City, called Transit, that is modelled after vintage New York City subway trains. Transit's target market is young, well-educated, hip men and women aged 17–34 years. The owner's experience indicates the importance of personal selling for this market because they (1) make large purchases, and (2) seek considerable information before making a decision. Jay Oliver, the owner, spends part of his communication budget on training his sales associates. Oliver has realized his communication budget is considerably less than that of other sneaker stores in the area. He has therefore decided to concentrate his limited budget on a specific segment and use digital media exclusively in his IMC program.

The IMC program Oliver has developed emphasizes his store's distinctive image and uses his website, social shopping, and some interesting community-building techniques. For instance, he has an extensive customer database as part of his CRM system from which he draws information for matching new merchandise with his customers' past purchase behaviours and little personal nuggets of information that he or other sales associates have collected on the customers. He then emails specific customers information about new products that he believes they will be interested in. He also encourages customers to use blogs hosted on his website. Customers chat about the "hot" new sneakers, club events, and races. He does everything with a strong sense of style.

To reach new customers he uses **search engine marketing (SEM)**. In particular, he uses Google AdWords, a search engine marketing tool that allows advertisers to show up in the Sponsored Links section of the search results page based on the keywords

---

frequency
Measure of how often the target audience is exposed to a communication within a specified period of time.

reach
Measure of consumers' exposure to marketing communications; the percentage of the target population exposed to a specific marketing communication, such as an advertisement, at least once.

gross rating points (GRP)
Measure used for various media advertising—print, radio, or television; *GRP = reach × frequency*.

click-through tracking
Measures how many times users click on banner advertising on websites.

search engine marketing (SEM)
Uses tools such as Google AdWords to increase the visibility of websites in search engine results.

Advertisers pay Google to show up in the Sponsored Link section in the right-hand column of this screen grab.

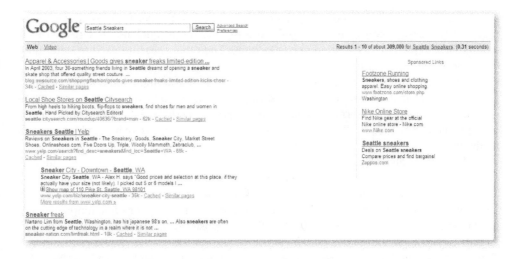

potential customers use (see the sponsored link section in the right-hand column of the Google screen grab above).

Oliver must determine the best keywords to use for his sponsored link advertising program. Some potential customers might search using the key words, "sneakers," "sneakers in New York City," "athletic shoes," or other such versions. Using Google AdWords, Oliver can assess the effectiveness of his advertising expenditures by measuring the reach, relevance, and return on investment for each of the keywords that potential customers used during their Internet searches.

impressions
The number of times an ad appears to a user.

To estimate reach, Oliver uses the number of **impressions** (the number of times the ad appears in front of the user) and the **click-through rate (CTR)**. To calculate CTR, he takes the number of times a user clicks on an ad and divides it by the number of impressions. For example, if a sponsored link was delivered 100 times and 10 people clicked on it, then the number of impressions is 100, the number of clicks is 10, and the CTR would be 10 percent.

click-through rate (CTR)
The number of times a user clicks on an ad divided by the number of impressions.

The relevance of the ad describes how useful an ad message is to the consumer doing the search. Google provides a measure of relevance through its AdWords system using a quality score. The quality score looks at a variety of factors to measure how relevant a keyword is to an ad's text and to a user's search query. In general, a high quality score means that a keyword will trigger ads in a higher position and at a lower cost per click.[26] In a search for "sneaker store," the Transit ad showed up fourth, suggesting high relevance.

return on investment (ROI)
Used to measure the benefit of an investment, ROI is calculated by dividing the gain of an investment by its cost.

Using the following formula, Oliver also can determine an ad's **return on investment (ROI)**:

$$ROI = \frac{Sales\ revenue - Advertising\ cost}{Advertising\ Cost}$$

For the two keyword searches in Exhibit 14.7, Oliver finds how much the advertising cost him (Column 3), the sales produced as a result (Column 4), and the ROI (Column 6). For "sneaker store," the Transit website had a lot more clicks (110) than the clicks received from "New York City sneakers" (40) (Column 2). Even though the sales were lower for the keywords "sneaker store" at $35/day, versus $40/day for the keywords "New York City sneakers," the ROI was much greater for the "sneaker store" keyword combination. In the future, Oliver should continue this keyword combination, in addition to producing others that are similar to it, in the hope that he will attain an even greater return on investment.

To evaluate his IMC program, Oliver compares the results of the program with his objectives (Exhibit 14.8). To measure his program's effectiveness, he conducted an

EXHIBIT 14.7 ROI Assessment

(1) Keyword	(2) Clicks	(3) Cost	(4) Sales	(5) Sales Revenue (Col. 4) − Cost (Col. 3)	(6) ROI = (Col. 5/Col. 3) × 100
Sneaker store	110	$10/day	$35/day	$25	250%
New York City sneakers	40	$25/day	$40/day	$15	60%

inexpensive online survey using the questions in Exhibit 14.8, which shows the survey results for one year. The results show a steady increase in awareness, knowledge of the store, and choice of the store as a primary source of sneakers. This research provides evidence that the IMC program was conveying the intended message to the target audience.

As IMC programs become more sophisticated, measurement is not the only concern. Marketers need to worry about a host of legal and ethical issues, which we will examine in the next chapter. Now that we've examined the steps in planning integrated marketing communications, let's look at the specific tools used in creating IMC campaigns.

INTEGRATED MARKETING COMMUNICATIONS TOOLS

L06

For any communications campaign to succeed, the firm must deliver the right message to the right audience through the right media. Reaching the right audience is becoming more difficult, however, as the media environment grows more complicated and fragmented. No single communication channel is better than another. The goal of IMC tools is to use them in a way so that the sum exceeds the total of the parts.

Advances in technology have led to a variety of new media options, such as satellite radio, wireless technology, pop-up and banner ads on websites, brand-sponsored websites, and text messaging, all of which vie for consumers' attention. Not so long ago, advertisers could reach the masses with media buys on three TV networks. Today, they have to buy on 74 stations to reach the same number of people. Print media have also grown and become more specialized. In Canada, there are currently 121 daily newspapers,

EXHIBIT 14.8 Program Effectiveness Results

Communication Objective	Questions	Before Campaign	6 months After	One Year After
Awareness (% mentioning store)	What stores sell sneakers?	38%	46%	52%
Knowledge (% giving outstanding rating for sales assistance)	Which stores would you rate outstanding on the following characteristics?	9	17	24
Attitude (% first choice)	On your next shopping trip for sneakers, which store would you visit first?	13	15	19
Visit (% visited store)	Which of the following stores have you been to?	8	15	19

1,100 plus community newspapers, well over 1,300 consumer magazines, and 759 business publications.[27]

This proliferation of media has led many firms to shift their promotional dollars from advertising to direct marketing, website development, product placements, and other forms of promotion in search of the best way to deliver messages to their target audiences. Media fragmentation has also occurred on television. Networks are dedicated to certain types of sports (Outdoor Life Network, Golf Channel), to children (YTV), to ethnic minorities (APTN—Aboriginal Peoples Television Network), and to religions (CTS). Each of these channels allows IMC planners to target their desired audience narrowly.

We now examine the individual tools of IMC and the way each contributes to a successful IMC campaign (see Exhibit 14.9). Most of these tools work along a continuum from passive to interactive and can be used either offline or online. Some tools—advertising, personal selling, and sales promotion—appear in detail in the next chapter, and so we discuss them only briefly here.

Advertising

advertising

A paid form of communication from an identifiable source, delivered through a communication channel, and designed to persuade the receiver to take some action, now or in the future.

Perhaps the most visible of the IMC components, **advertising** is a paid form of communication from an identifiable source, delivered through a communication channel, and designed to persuade the receiver to take some action, now or in the future.[28] Traditionally, advertising has been passive and offline; however, these days advertising is increasingly placed online and is interactive. For instance, print ads in newspapers and magazines are offline, with customers simply viewing them (passive). In contrast, banner ads, web-based contests, or online coupons are all offered online and require customers to provide some information or take some action (interactive). Basically, advertising can be either offline or online and either passive or interactive.

In Chapter 15, we discuss the purpose of advertising and its various types, but for now, we note that advertising is extremely effective for creating awareness of a product

EXHIBIT 14.9 Integrated Marketing Communications Tools

or service and generating interest. However, advertising can also be used to remind consumers of existing brands. As mentioned in the chapter vignette, the McDonald's "I'm Lovin' It" ads helped revitalize interest in the company's products, driving both traffic and sales.

Advertising can entice consumers into a conversation with marketers. However, advertising must break through the clutter of other messages to reach its intended audience. To do so, many advertisers rely on certain images. Ethical Dilemma 14.1 notes the conflict when advertisers use underweight, skinny models in ads they aim at teenage consumers. In the past decade, advertising's share of total promotional dollars has fallen as the budgets for other forms of sales promotion, especially direct marketing and public

Ethical Dilemma 14.1 Too Skinny

The objective of an integrated marketing communications (IMC) campaign is to build profits by encouraging consumers to purchase more products. But what happens if the campaign leads to harmful behaviours? Companies could claim that shoppers have a choice about the goods they purchase, or assert that marketing influences only brand decisions. But sometimes marketing directed at younger consumers complicates that reasoning, because few children or teens can separate unhealthy body images from the popular fashion looks that surround them.

Advertising models have always tended to be thin. But they have become increasingly so in the past decade or so. The tragic deaths of Ana Carolina Reston and Isabelle Caro—two very thin models suffering from anorexia—led some fashion industry leaders to call for a change. That was nearly a decade ago, and still underage and dangerously thin young girls continue to find work as fashion advertising models.

Promoting products using ultra-thin models sends dangerously inappropriate style signals to teenage girls.

The designers and clothing companies continue to hire girls as young as 14 years of age to walk the runway—a clear child-labour law violation according to critics.[29] Even worse, it continues to reinforce the notion that to be beautiful, women and girls need to starve themselves.

These concerns apply not only to the teenage girls targeted by such ads but also to the models themselves—young girls who are working long hours, subjected to harsh criticisms and widespread rejection. Most child development research suggests that children younger than 16 years are ill prepared to deal with such scenarios.

In the United Kingdom, the Advertising Standards Authority (ASA) thus has banned some ads outright for being "socially irresponsible." An ad run by Drop Dead, a British clothing line, prompted the watchdog agency to condemn the brand's image: a shockingly thin model who sends dangerously inappropriate style signals to teenage girls. In its statement, the ASA complained that the young model's "hip, rib and collar bones were highly visible" and noted that she had visible (and unnatural) "hollows in her thighs."[30] Under such pressures, some U.K. companies have begun to respond. The fashion brand Topshop removed an ad from its website after advocates complained that the featured model was dangerously gaunt and thus a negative influence on young shoppers.[31]

The Council of Fashion Designers of America (CFDA) also has denounced the hiring of underage models, yet violations continue. Recently, it called on designers and modelling agencies to require identification from models, showing that they were at least 16 years old. It also began educating industry members to recognize early signs of eating disorders, called for the provision of healthy snacks backstage, and banned the use of models under 18 years at fittings or photo shows held after midnight. Despite widespread skepticism that the industry can regulate itself, the National Eating Disorders Association has applauded the CFDA guidelines.

Change thus appears to be coming, but slowly. Designers such as Tommy Hilfiger and Tory Burch complain that the models who apply with them continue to appear young and thin. "I still see some girls coming in who are really emaciated," Burch said. "It's still a problem." Those concerned about the ultra-thin style promoted by fashion advertising for young girls will be watching, but changing the tone of this communication is more challenging than just checking IDs and offering a snack.

relations, have increased, resulting in a more balanced approach to the use of marketing communications elements.

Personal Selling

Personal selling is the two-way flow of communication between a buyer and a seller that is designed to influence the buyer's purchase decision. Personal selling can take place in various settings: face to face, video teleconferencing, on the telephone, or over the Internet. Although consumers don't often interact with professional sales people, personal selling represents an important component of many IMC programs, especially in business-to-business (B2B) settings.

The cost of communicating directly with a potential customer is quite high compared with other forms of promotion, but it is simply the best and most efficient way to sell certain products and services. Customers can buy many products and services without the help of a salesperson, but salespeople simplify the buying process by providing information and services that save customers time and effort. In many cases, sales representatives add significant value, which makes the added expense of employing them worthwhile. Chapter 15 devotes more attention to personal selling.

Sales Promotions

Sales promotions are special incentives or excitement-building programs that encourage the purchase of a product or service, such as coupons, rebates, contests, free samples, and point-of-purchase displays. While some sales promotions are offline (e.g., printed coupons or contest entries), others are online (e.g., e-coupons downloaded to a smartphone.) Marketers typically design these incentives for use in conjunction with other advertising or personal selling programs. Many sales promotions, such as free samples or point-of-purchase displays, are designed to build short-term sales; though others, such as contests and sweepstakes, have become integral components of firms' CRM programs as means to build customer loyalty. We discuss such sales promotions in more detail in Chapter 15.

Direct Marketing

The component of IMC that has received the greatest increase in aggregate spending recently is **direct marketing**, or marketing that communicates directly with target customers to generate a response or transaction.[32] Unlike mass media, which communicate to a wide audience, direct marketing allows for personalization of the message, a key

Direct marketers now use mobile devices to reach potential customers.

advantage. Direct marketing contains a variety of traditional and new forms of marketing communication initiatives, including offline forms such as direct mail, direct response TV commercials (infomercials), catalogues, and kiosks, as well as online technologies such as email, mobile, and podcasts. Digital technologies have had a profound effect on direct marketing initiatives. Email, for instance, can be directed to specific consumers to inform them about new merchandise and special promotions, confirm receipt of an order, and indicate when an order has been shipped. Currently available technologies also mean handheld devices can function as a payment medium: Just tap your smartphone, and the transaction occurs in much the same way it occurs with a credit card.[33]

Direct marketing has four defining characteristics: it is targeted, motivates an action, is measurable, and can provide information for the development of a marketing database.[34] It is an information-driven process that enables marketers to narrowly target the appropriate audiences. For example, a company selling a health supplement can use direct marketing to reach only people who subscribe to health-related magazines in an effort to motivate them to take action, such as calling a toll-free number, visiting a website, or placing a mail order. The company can easily measure the response for each magazine by using uniquely assigned coded coupons, toll-free numbers, or Internet microsites. The use of response-generating direct marketing forms, such as direct mail, direct response television, or telemarketing can provide meaningful results and allow the evaluation of a marketing campaign in a timely manner.[35]

Direct marketing offers benefits to both buyers and sellers. Companies that use direct marketing campaigns appreciate the ability to sell to a much wider target audience than could be reached with traditional marketing channels. In comparison to personal selling or mass media advertising, the cost of reaching consumers is much lower with direct marketing. As mentioned earlier, one of the defining characteristics of direct marketing is its measurability—campaigns can be closely monitored to track results. Measurability means marketers know who responds to their campaigns, allowing them to build rich databases that can be used to cross-sell, tailor offers, and create specific promotions geared to individual customers in future campaigns.

The increased use of customer databases has enabled marketers to identify and track consumers over time and across purchase situations, which has contributed to the rapid growth of direct marketing. Marketers have been able to build these databases thanks to consumers' increased use of credit and debit cards, store-specific credit and loyalty cards, and online shopping, all of which require the buyer to give the seller personal information that becomes part of its database. Because firms understand customers' purchases better when they possess such information, they can more easily focus their direct marketing efforts appropriately.

As shown in Exhibit 14.10, direct marketing can take a number of forms, including direct mail/email, catalogues, direct response TV, kiosks, and personal selling. We focus on the first four forms here. Personal selling is addressed in Chapter 15.

Direct Mail/Email

We consider **direct mail/email** primarily as targeted forms of communication distributed to a prospective consumer's mailbox or inbox. Mailing lists are a critical component of direct mail. Choose the wrong list and your promotion will be perceived as "junk mail" since the information and offer will not be targeted to the appropriate audience. Canada Post research shows that Canadian households receive an average of 27 pieces of direct mail per week. In spite of such high volumes, addressed mail continues to be welcomed by Canadians—83 percent spend time with addressed direct mail every day and 63 percent are likely to read it as soon as it is received.[36] Studies consistently report that consumers are more receptive to direct mail than email. Most of us receive far more email marketing messages, not all of which are welcome. And today, 45 percent of marketing emails are received and opened on mobile devices, making it critical for marketers to ensure their messages are optimized for mobile platforms.[37]

direct mail/email
A targeted form of communication distributed to a prospective customer's mailbox or inbox.

E X H I B I T   14.10   Forms of Direct Retailing

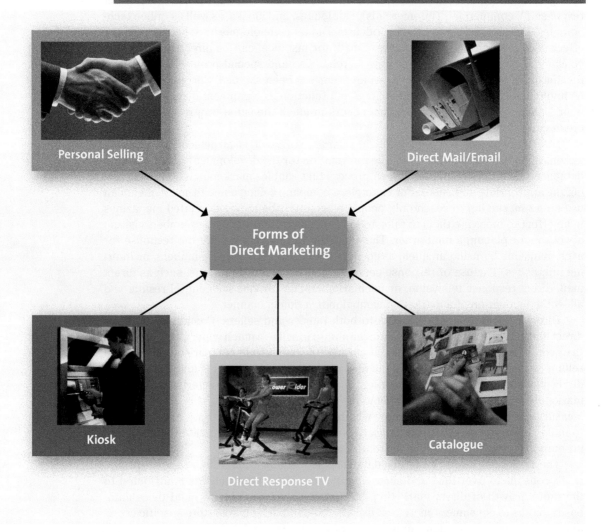

According to the Direct Marketing Association, direct mail generates $12 of revenue for every dollar invested. For direct mail to be effective, a good contact list is a must and a good offer is also needed to compel consumers to take immediate action. Good offers must be relevant to both consumers and to the product, and are important whether a company is promoting products to consumers or businesses. But offers don't always involve selling a product. Registered charities rely on direct mail in their fundraising efforts. For example, the Heart and Stroke Foundation of Canada, which receives no operational funding from government sources, uses direct mail extensively to promote its cause. The Foundation's efforts have resulted in the recruitment of more than 140,000 volunteers and 13 million donors[38] and have raised more than $125 million in donations.[39]

Catalogues   Many companies use catalogues to strategically build their business. They represent a medium that Canadians accept, with 80 percent welcoming retail catalogues into their homes. More than half of Canadians have ordered items from catalogues in the past year.[40] Typically, catalogues have been mailed, which can become an issue as a company grows. Although Mountain Equipment Co-op has 2.6 million customers, it mails catalogues to only about 200,000 of them because of the cost and environmental impact.

However, it makes catalogues available for download from its website. Today, most companies with physical catalogues, such as IKEA and Business Depot, also offer online catalogues. Canadian Tire discontinued its physical catalogue several years ago and replaced it with an online interactive version called The Canadian Way. Despite the ease of online shopping, the vast majority of Canadians still prefer hard-copy catalogues. The Sears *Wish Book* holds fond memories for many adults who remember leafing through its pages as children in anticipation of gifts they might receive.

Catalogues are particularly important for companies with no bricks-and-mortar locations. Toronto-based educational toy company Grand River Toys has never had a physical store. It started out as a mail order business selling only from its catalogue. As the company grew, it took its catalogue online and added e-commerce capabilities, extending its reach and its sales.

Catalogues are an important communication vehicle that help Sears build its business, allowing consumers to purchase a wide variety of merchandise.

Direct Response TV **Direct response TV (DRTV)** refers to TV commercials or infomercials with a strong call to action, usually via toll-free number, return mail address, or website. Although many people may question the effectiveness of this form of direct marketing, DRTV and the Shopping Channel are the two most welcome forms of direct marketing among Canadians.[41] DRTV now accounts for 25 percent of all TV commercials, with the top purchases being exercise products, diet/health/weight merchandise, videos, and beauty products/cosmetics.[42]

direct response TV (DRTV)
TV commercials or infomercials with a strong call to action.

Most DRTV ads have short 60- and 120-second formats or are much longer 30-minute infomercials. For many people, the term *infomercial* conjures up images of a late-night TV pitchman telling them how his product slices and dices better than anything on the market. Most infomercials appear to be selling products that seem too good to be true: fitness routines that promise to melt the pounds away, a miracle knife so sharp you'll never have to buy another, or rejuvenating face creams that magically erase wrinkles. Almost everyone has heard of the George Foreman Grill but not nearly as many people recognize Foreman as a heavyweight boxing champion.

DRTV is used for its power to drive results not only through infomercials, but also in shorter-format ads. When Canadian Blood Services launched its "Save a Life" campaign, it exceeded targets by more than 50 percent,[43] which was to bring in 2,000 new blood donors. More than 3,000 new and lapsed donors made appointments to give blood. The new donor drive DRTV campaign took home the Gold award in the DRTV category at the Canadian Marketing Association Awards.[44]

The George Foreman Grill is promoted and sold using DRTV infomercials.

Dell's mall kiosks allow shoppers to find a computer that's just right for them.

Kiosks   As discussed in Chapter 10, digital kiosks can be used to facilitate the way services companies deliver their services to customers; for example, allowing passengers at airports to quickly print prebooked tickets. However, kiosks can also be used to sell both services and products to end consumers. For example, after you print your ticket at an airport kiosk, you can get a 10-minute manicure at another kiosk while you wait for your flight. Some kiosks are temporary, such as the kiosks that are set up in malls primarily to sell gift items in the weeks leading up to Christmas. Others kiosks are permanent. For example, Dell's mall kiosks allow shoppers to talk to a Dell representative face-to-face and find the computer that's just right for them. Consumers can customize their PC, order it, and have it shipped directly to their homes. In Ontario, Virgin Mobile unveiled a network of mall kiosks, which it may use to sell other Virgin products and services in the future.[45] Real estate companies such as Century 21 use kiosks in malls where thousands of potential buyers can connect with property listings. Kiosks from Hallmark allow customers to create their own personalized cards. Disposable cameras and batteries are available at kiosks throughout the Rogers Centre in Toronto.[46] Business marketers use kiosks as well, particularly at trade shows to collect sales leads and to provide information on their products.

Public Relations

public relations (PR)
The organizational function that manages the firm's communications to achieve a variety of objectives, including building and maintaining a positive image, handling or heading off unfavourable stories or events, and maintaining positive relationships with the media.

Public relations (PR) is the organizational function that manages the firm's communications to achieve a variety of objectives, including building and maintaining a positive image, handling or heading off unfavourable stories or events, and maintaining positive relationships with the media. Like advertising, this tactic is relatively passive in that customers do not have to take any action to receive it. However, PR efforts span both offline and online media. PR activities support the other promotional efforts by the firm by generating "free" media attention and general goodwill. For example, McDonald's "I'm Lovin' It" campaign was frequently in the news and discussed in numerous newspaper and magazine articles. While it can be very difficult to convince the media to write about a company or its products and services, this media attention can be crucial to a company's success.

In essence, PR is the free placement of a company's message in the media. In the past, many companies used PR primarily to communicate with the news media, hoping their messages would be picked up. Today, PR is more about connecting with consumers and interacting in the hopes of having a conversation.[47] Electric car maker Tesla spends minimally on advertising because it benefits from PR resulting from media coverage, bloggers, and word-of-mouth. Unilever's Dove Campaign for Real Beauty demonstrates the viral power of digital media to quickly spread a message and generate a wealth of valuable publicity. Its "Evolution" film is credited with generating over $150 million in unpaid media impressions. Its "Real Beauty Sketches" video was the most watched online ad ever, generating more than 163 million YouTube views.[48]

Car Heaven's support of MADD Canada illustrates how using a combination of promotional and PR campaigns can enhance a firm's image while supporting a worthwhile cause.[49] The Car Heaven program gives car owners a way to conveniently dispose of old vehicles by towing them at no charge to a recycling facility. The proceeds from the scrap metal are donated to MADD Canada and donors receive charitable tax receipts.[50] The program creates a positive association between the brand and a social cause, in this case, drunk driving. This form of promotional campaign, called **cause-related marketing**, refers to commercial activity in which businesses and charities form a partnership to market an image, product, or service for their mutual benefit.[51]

Designers vie to have celebrities, especially those nominated for awards, wear their fashions on the red carpet. These sightings can create both positive and negative publicity. When Fergie wore an Emilio Rucci dress to the Grammy's, paired with a Judith Lieber clutch, both brands sent out press releases to make sure everyone knew.[52] The dress got so much press that the designer's cachet increased significantly. Chanel, Valentino, Zac Posen, and Christian Dior are all red carpet veterans that commonly provide dresses or tuxedos to celebrities, whose images will be broadcast around the world.[53] The placement of designer apparel at media events benefits both the designer and the celebrity. And neither happens by accident. PR people on both sides help orchestrate the events to get the maximum benefit for both parties.

Good PR has always been an important success factor. Yet in recent years, the importance of PR has grown, as the cost of other forms of marketing communications has increased. At the same time, the influence of PR has become more powerful, as consumers have become increasingly skeptical of marketing claims made in other media.[54] In many instances, consumers view media coverage generated through PR as more credible and objective than any other aspects of an IMC program, because the firm does not "buy" the space in print media or time on radio or television.

For example, TOMS Shoes, a company founded by Blake Mycoskie, illustrates how a well-orchestrated IMC effort, using a combination of promotional and PR campaigns, can enhance a firm's image while supporting a worthwhile cause.[55] Mycoskie took traditional Argentinean shoes, known as *alpargatas*, and began selling and marketing them to consumers outside the generally impoverished nation in which they originated. The company's website proclaims that Mycoskie's inspiration was simple. Noting the comfort of the shoes and the extreme poverty of Argentina, he promises that "With every pair you purchase, TOMS will give a pair of new shoes to a child in need." This message is found on his website and other press vehicles, including a mention as the "Good Guy of the Month" in *O, The Oprah Winfrey Magazine*. TOMS Shoes embraces cause-related marketing. The company is not just about making and selling shoes, but also partners with groups

cause-related marketing
Commercial activity in which businesses and charities form a partnership to market an image, product, or service for their mutual benefit; a type of promotional campaign.

TOMS Shoes embraces cause-related marketing. For every pair of shoes consumers buy, the company gives a pair of new shoes to a child in need.

The annual Subaru Ironman Triathlon in Penticton, British Columbia, lets Subaru link the performance and durability of its vehicles to the grueling race.

event sponsorship
A popular PR tool; occurs when corporations support various activities (financially or otherwise), usually in the cultural or sports and entertainment sectors.

digital media
Tools ranging from simple website content to far more interactive features such as corporate blogs, online games, text messaging, social media, and mobile apps.

such as Insight Argentina, an organization offering volunteer activities in Argentina to help that area address its most pressing social issues.[56]

Another very popular PR tool is event sponsorship. **Event sponsorship** occurs when corporations support various activities (financially or otherwise), usually in the cultural or sports and entertainment sectors. For example, Subaru sponsors the Subaru Ironman Canada Triathlon, regarded as one of the best Ironman events in the world. The race helps Subaru promote its vehicles, which, like athletes, must possess both the versatility to excel in a variety of environments and the durability to outlast the competition. And sponsoring the 2012 Summer Olympics helped Procter & Gamble boost sales by about $500 million.[57]

Firms often distribute a PR toolkit to communicate with various audiences. Some toolkit elements are designed to inform specific groups directly, whereas others are created to generate media attention and disseminate information. We depict the various elements of a PR toolkit in Exhibit 14.11.

Digital Media

The Internet has had a dramatic impact on how marketers communicate with their customers. **Digital media** tools range from simple website content to far more interactive features such as corporate blogs, online games, text messaging, social media, and mobile apps. (Chapter 16 explores social and mobile media in much more detail.) Unlike the other IMC tools discussed previously, these forms of digital media were designed only for the online world. Marketers are using them more and more often for the following reasons, among others: they can be targeted to specific customer segments, their impact can be easily and quickly measured in real time, modifications can be quickly made to increase their effectiveness, and customers can be engaged to forward the message to their social networks. Entrepreneurial Marketing 14.1 examines a digital marketing agency that understands the power of digital media to create extraordinary experiences for consumers.

Websites Firms have increased their emphasis on communicating with customers through their websites. They use them to build their brand image and educate customers about their products or services and where they can be purchased. Retailers and some manufacturers sell merchandise directly to consumers online. For example, in addition to selling merchandise, Office Depot's website has a Business Resource Centre that provides advice and product knowledge, as well as a source of networks to other businesses. It includes forms that businesses would use to comply with Occupational Safety and Health Act (OSHA) requirements, to check job applicant records, to estimate cash flow, and to develop a sexual harassment policy; workshops for running a business; and local and national business news. By providing this information on its website, Office Depot reinforces its image as the essential source of products, services, and information for small businesses. Many firms, especially retailers, encourage customers to post reviews of products they have bought or used and even have visitors to their websites rate the quality of the reviews. Research has shown that these online product reviews increase customer loyalty and provide a competitive advantage for sites that offer them.[58]

EXHIBIT 14.11	Elements of a PR Toolkit

PR Element	**Function**
Publications: brochures, special-purpose single-issue publications such as books	Inform various constituencies about the activities of the organization and highlight specific areas of expertise
Video and audio: programs, public service announcements	Highlight the organization or support cause-related marketing efforts
Annual reports	Give required financial performance data and inform investors and others about the unique activities of the organization
Media relations: press kits, news releases, speeches, event sponsorships	Generate news coverage of the organization's activities or products/services
Digital media: websites, email campaigns	Websites can contain all the previously mentioned toolbox elements, while email directs PR efforts to specific target groups

Blogs A **blog (weblog)** contains periodic posts on a common web page. A well-received blog can communicate trends, promote special events, create positive word-of-mouth, connect customers by forming a community, increase sales, improve customer satisfaction because the company can respond directly to customers' comments, and develop a long-term relationship with the company. By its very nature, a

blog (weblog or web log)
A web page that contains periodic posts; corporate blogs are a new form of marketing communications.

Entrepreneurial Marketing 14.1   **From Driving Range to Digital Agency**

When you think about the background needed to head up a digital marketing agency, a career as an LPGA golf pro probably isn't the first thing that comes to mind. Yet those are the skills Critical Mass CEO Dianne Wilkins brought to the job. Golf paid her way through university and, after doing her MBA, she taught professional golf management. And it was a golf pro friend who introduced her to company founder Ted Hellard, who hired her in 1998 to go to Sweden and work on a Saab campaign. She served as CEO of the Critical Mass spinoff she established in Stockholm, growing it to 65 employees in only six months.

After two years, Wilkins moved to the firm's Calgary head office where she was later promoted to Canadian CEO. Today, Critical Mass has offices in Calgary, Toronto, Chicago, New York, Nashville, London, and Costa Rica. The company has grown to more than 600 employees, who work with global clients such as AT&T, Budweiser, Infiniti, Las Vegas Convention and Visitors Authority, Moen, and Nissan to bring together creative thinking, smart ideas, and emerging technologies. Wilkins says one of her favourite campaigns is a microsite created for NIKEiD, which allows consumers to interactively design their own shoes, upload the patterns, add the sole of their choice, include their name on the shoe, and have the shoes custom manufactured and delivered to their door.

Although the company focus revolves around all things digital, Wilkins sees "a world where customers no longer consider experiences as online or offline, but focus on the quality of interactions they have with brands."[59] Today, online behaviour has fragmented with dozens of touchpoints. Critical Mass knows each one is important to the total customer experience. Its research division, Curious, helps the company gather consumer insights and mine information from online communities.

Getting and keeping the right people with the right attitude is critical to the company's success. A focus on professional development and office "hives," equipped with Nintendo Wiis, helps employees relax and stay in touch with new technology.[60] Wilkins notes that, in a digital agency, it's important to be focused and stick to a course rather than trying to be all things to all people. That doesn't mean that Wilkins is averse to change; in fact, once the decision to implement change has been made, she says it's critical to drive that change relentlessly.[61]

Wilkins says it's been a fun ride. While her golf handicap may have suffered, Critical Mass has benefited from her leadership. *Marketing Magazine* has named it the number one interactive agency in Canada and one of the top interactive agencies in the world.[62]

blog is supposed to be transparent and contain authors' honest observations, which can help customers determine their trust and loyalty levels. Nowadays, blogs are becoming more interactive as the communication between bloggers and customers has increased.

Social Media Social media is media content distributed through social interactions. Although there is a broad spectrum of online communities and social networking sites, the three most popular are YouTube, Facebook, and Twitter. In these online sites, consumers review, communicate about, and aggregate information about products, prices, and promotions. These social media also allow users to interact among themselves (e.g., form a community), as well as provide other like-minded consumers (i.e., members of their community) and marketers their thoughts and evaluations about a firm's products or services. Social media help facilitate the consumer decision process (Chapter 4) by encouraging need recognition, information search, alternative evaluation, purchase, and postpurchase reviews.

Marketers can use social media to engage their customers in a proactive dialogue, as seen in many of the Social and Mobile Marketing boxes throughout this book. When it comes to social media, there is considerably more transparency and honesty than in most other forms of marketing communication. And, because members share so much personal information, marketers can tailor messages and applications to very specific and desirable target markets. For example, New Brunswick's Mount Allison University is using Facebook groups and student-made videos on YouTube (commissioned and paid for by the university) to recruit future students.[63] And as seen in Social and Mobile Marketing 14.1, Visa used social media to promote small purchases to consumers.

Like him or not, Justin Bieber's vast social media platform reaches millions of followers worldwide, including around 40 million fans on his Facebook site, and more than 21,000 new members join every day. His music on MySpace has registered more than 108 million plays.[64] In 2011, Bieber broke YouTube records by reaching 2 billion views.[65] Twitter helped build so much buzz that one New York concert had to be cancelled after 5,000 fans suddenly swarmed the venue in a flash mob.[66] In 2011 with 14 million followers, Bieber's account represented 3 percent of the total traffic on Twitter.[67] Today he has over 43 million Twitter followers.[68]

Mobile Apps Mobile marketing is marketing through wireless handheld devices, such as cellular telephones. Smartphones have become far more than tools to place calls; they offer a kind of mobile computer with the ability to obtain sports scores, weather, music, videos, and text messages, as well as purchase merchandise. Marketing success rests on integrating marketing communications with fun, useful apps that are consistent with these consumer attitudes toward mobile devices. In response, firms are steadily improving customers' potential experience with their mobile interface. Apps (applications) have become very popular. Apps are used for a variety of purposes, from games and advertising to business applications, or even to order a pizza and then track its delivery. Apple's App Store boasts the world's largest collection of mobile apps, with more than 900,000 applications, including a wide range of categories such as music, cooking, travelling, the great outdoors, learning tools for students, and business. CIBC was the first Canadian bank to introduce an iPhone banking app that allows customers to access their bank accounts. The Android Marketplace has experienced huge growth, making it one of the fastest-growing mobile application stores on the market today.

Technology will continue to improve, and other new means of communicating with consumers will undoubtedly be added to the IMC media mix.

Social and Mobile Marketing 14.1

Do You #smallenfreuden?

When orange billboards popped up in Toronto asking "DO YOU #smallenfreuden?," consumers were confused. No identifying information was included—no tagline, no logo, no hints as to what company was behind the teaser campaign. And what the heck did *smallenfreuden* mean?

One week later, Visa Canada stepped forward claiming the #smallenfreuden campaign stood for the joy of small; in this case, making small purchases using your Visa card. Because smallenfreuden was an unusual word, the creative team at Visa's ad agency, BBDO, felt it made sense to introduce consumers to the term and link it to the brand later.[69] The billboards were followed by a TV ad featuring a couple at a hockey game who pay for drinks with their Visa card via a mobile debit machine. As an official NHL sponsor, the ad was aired during playoff games. Social media saw heavy use throughout the campaign with promoted trends and promoted tweets on Twitter. Consumers could win a trip to NHL final games through "The Visa Ultimate NHL Experience Contest" which was run on Facebook.

The objectives of the campaign were to spark intrigue, create awareness, and drive engagement. It certainly created a buzz, generating more than 20,000 social media mentions for @VisaCA (five times higher than the usual daily average), and 50 million views on Twitter.[70] A YouTube video attracted 400,000 views.[71]

Twitter Canada chose #smallenfreuden as one of the most talked about campaigns in 2013. Consumer engagement significantly exceeded existing social media benchmarks. More importantly, there was a 30 percent increase[72] in credit card usage during the campaign.

Mysterious billboards launched Visa Canada's teaser campaign to convince consumers to use their credit cards for small purchases.

REAL MARKETER PROFILE   Ami Shah

My undergraduate degree, a Bachelor of Business Administration, gave me both thorough theoretical and practical exposure to the business world through the academic and co-op programs. Through the program, I decided to focus my career in marketing.

I landed my first job at Procter & Gamble while still at university. After meeting with individuals at the company, I felt like I fit in with the company; we had similar values. I joined the P&G family and looking back, I am really happy I took the job, as I loved my experience there.

My career in marketing began as an assistant business manager. I undertook the challenge to turn around two marginally performing hair colour brands: Natural Instincts and L'Image. Collaborating with my multifunctional team, I evaluated the marketing mix and then developed and implemented unique strategies to increase market share for each brand. This effort resulted in the Natural Instincts brand growing by 15 percent during my first year versus nearly flat sales growth in the previous three years, and the L'Image business delivering sales 12 percent higher than forecasted.

When promoted to business manager at P&G, I was given the opportunity to lead the launch of Perfect 10, a new brand that would revolutionize hair colour technology for the first time in over 50 years. This project was a significant accomplishment for me because it was extremely high profile and was the most demanding project I've led to date. Specifically, I faced a number of challenges: condensed timelines, budget constraints, supply chain issues, and a downsized launch team. However, after six months of dedicated work, I was able to overcome these obstacles and successfully execute the launch plans.

While still at P&G, I took a leave of absence for six months to volunteer and work abroad in Vietnam and India. During that time, I ended up finding innovative social enterprises and traded my expertise in marketing for the opportunity to learn about their experiences as social entrepreneurs in developing markets.

After a number of years of work experience, I decided to return to school to obtain my MBA at INSEAD, an international program that has campuses in France and Singapore. This was a great experience, as it put all my work experience into perspective and helped guide me toward my interest in leveraging my experience in a more entrepreneurial and socially conscious organization.

After my master's degree, I also got the chance to work with my own family businesses, one in the retail industry and the other in the wholesale business. This was a neat experience because when you're working with your own money, you quickly learn to be very pragmatic. At the same time, I learned I also had the flexibility to test and learn new tools really quickly. For example, our retail store (http://www.shalimardesigns.com) quickly grew over the last couple of years, now contributing 25 percent of overall gross revenue after establishing a stronger presence on Google and through social media tools.

After INSEAD, I took the role as brand manager and later as the director of retail marketing for a Profit Hot 50, consumer goods startup, Planet People. I learned to work more hands on and with smaller budgets to launch a number of eco-friendly cleaning solutions across North America. This involved leadership over all retail marketing, social media, PR and in-store programs, and also close collaboration with the VP of Sales to help secure +1,300 new retail/online distribution points. I also initiated and led a new product development process involving the senior executive team to build a pipeline of innovation over the next two to five years. Lastly, I developed a corporate community outreach program with 10 nonprofits to provide mould training workshops and over $10,000 worth of donations to assist with Hurricane Sandy relief.

Most recently, I started my own company. Peekapak is a monthly subscription of storytelling adventure packs that brings play and inquiry-based learning into the home, to inspire creativity and imagination in children ages 3 to 7. Every month families receive a storybook designed with educators to guide the learning experience and all the needed materials to create two or three hands-on craft projects that extend the adventure into real life. To start our company and quickly validate there was interest, we launched a campaign on Kickstarter, which successfully crowdfunded over $10k. Furthermore, the campaign generated over 900 shares on Facebook, received coverage on Huffington Post and allowed our team to deliver our first batch of Peekapaks. Since the Kickstarter campaign, we have gathered feedback from our first customers and have launched our ecommerce website, which has already secured coverage on CTV News and CH Morning Live, in the Toronto Star, and on a number of notable parenting blogs. To keep costs low as a startup, we are focusing our marketing efforts on social media and online marketing tools such as Facebook ads, affiliate marketing, and referral marketing. Starting my own business has been an amazing learning experience and has truly made marketing more and more hands-on for me.

There's so much about marketing I love. Beyond it being such a dynamic, interactive, and fun field to work in, I love that as a marketer you really need to understand who your consumer is. My best marketing plans are rooted in deep consumer understanding and ensuring my plans consider the key insights and consumer trial barriers. The fun part of acquiring this understanding is actually meeting and talking to consumers. From conducting formal focus groups or shop-alongs for P&G to doing ad hoc in-store demos for Planet People, by interacting with consumers, asking them questions, and getting to know them, I feel I've been able to make decisions for my brands that will best meet the consumer's needs and drive results for my business.

LEARNING OBJECTIVES REVIEW

LO1 Outline the process that firms use to communicate with consumers

On the surface, marketing communications look simple: People become aware of a product or service, then grow interested, then desire it, and finally take an action such as purchasing it. But it isn't quite that simple. First, there is the cumulative effect of marketing communications, or messages a company has sent to consumers. Even ads from the past help influence consumers' actions in the future. Second, messages are encoded, and everyone interprets commercial messages differently, thus making it difficult for a marketer to be assured that a particular, clear signal is getting through. Third, to be effective, marketers must adjust their messages to fit the media, or communications channel, and the receiver's knowledge level. Lastly, consumers receive and decode the messages.

LO2 List the steps in planning an integrated marketing communications campaign

Firms (1) identify their target market; (2) set objectives; (3) determine the budget; (4) convey the message; (5) evaluate and select the media; (6) create the communication; and (7) assess the impact of the ad.

LO3 Describe what appeals advertisers use to get customers' attention

Advertising appeals are either rational or emotional. Rational appeals influence purchase decisions with factual information and strong arguments built on relevant key benefits that encourage consumers to evaluate the brand favourably. Emotional appeals indicate how the product satisfies emotional desires rather than utilitarian needs.

LO4 Identify how firms determine which media to use

Firms can use mass media channels such as newspapers or television to reach large numbers of anonymous audience members. Niche media, such as cable TV, direct mail, and specialty magazines, are generally used to reach narrower segments with unique demographic characteristics or interests. When choosing the media, firms must match their objectives to the media. Also, certain media are better at reaching a particular target audience than others.

LO5 Summarize how firms measure integrated marketing communications success

Planning an IMC budget should encompass a combination of factors. The process could start by setting the overall IMC budget as a percentage of sales. Then, the firm might examine what other firms are spending on similar product categories. When it gets down to planning the budget for individual product categories or items, the firm should set its objectives for the campaign and allocate enough money to meet those objectives.

Marketers rely on a mix of traditional and nontraditional measures to determine IMC success. Because potential customers generally need to be exposed to IMC messages several times before they will buy, firms estimate the degree to which customers are exposed to a message by multiplying frequency (the number of times an audience is exposed to a message) by reach (the percentage of the target population exposed to a specific marketing communication). Measuring Internet IMC effectiveness requires different measures, such as click-through tracking, which measures how many times users click on banner advertising on websites.

LO6 Explain the six tools of integrated marketing communications campaigns

The six tools of IMC campaigns are advertising, personal selling, sales promotions, direct marketing, public relations, and digital media. In the past, most of a firm's promotional budget was spent on advertising. Although advertising still demands a sizable portion, other media channels have taken up a substantial chunk of the total budget. While the cost of personal selling to reach potential customers directly is quite high, it remains the best and most efficient way to sell certain products and services. Sales promotions are incentives or programs that promote immediate purchase. Many drive sales in the short run, while others exist as part of a company's customer loyalty programs. Direct marketing expenditures are growing because the number of direct marketing media options has increased in recent years; direct mail, infomercials, alternative media such as catalogues, and other new communication technologies such as PDAs and cellphones are all expanding. Public relations also has become increasingly important as other media forms become more expensive and as consumers grow more skeptical of commercial messages. Finally, digital media have spawned innovative new ways to promote products and services.

KEY TERMS

- advertising
- advertising schedule
- affordable method
- blog (weblog or Web log)
- cause-related marketing
- click-through rate
- click-through tracking
- communication channel
- competitive parity method
- continuous advertising schedule
- deceptive advertising
- decoding
- direct mail/email
- direct marketing
- direct response TV (DRTV)
- digital media
- emotional appeal

- encoding
- event sponsorship
- feedback loop
- flighting advertising schedule
- frequency
- gross rating points (GRP)
- impressions
- integrated marketing communications (IMC)
- mass media
- media buy
- media mix
- media planning
- niche media
- noise
- objective-and-task method
- percentage-of-sales method
- personal selling

- post-testing
- pretesting
- public relations (PR)
- pulsing advertising schedule
- rational appeal
- reach
- receiver
- return on investment (ROI)
- sales promotions
- search engine marketing (SEM)
- sender
- tracking
- transmitter
- unique selling proposition (USP)

CONCEPT REVIEW

1. Briefly describe the marketing communication process and identify the possible sources of noise at each stage of the process.

2. What is meant by integrated marketing communications?

3. Describe the IMC tools marketers use in campaigns.

4. Explain the differences between advertising and sales promotion.

5. Describe some of the elements in a PR toolkit. Why would a company include PR in its IMC mix?

6. Identify some of the key digital media that marketers use to communicate with their customers. How are these media changing the nature of the communication between the firm and its customers?

7. What are the steps involved in developing an IMC campaign? Briefly explain each step.

8. Describe why a company would use a pull strategy versus a push strategy in its marketing communications.

9. Briefly describe the two main appeals of advertising.

10. Explain the three different ways marketers measure the success of their marketing communications. What types of information does each method provide?

MARKETING APPLICATIONS

1. The designer jean company Juicy Couture has embarked on a new IMC strategy. It has chosen to advertise on the NBC *Nightly News* and in *Time* magazine. The message is designed to announce new styles for the season and uses a 17-year-old woman as the model. Evaluate this strategy.

2. It's holiday time, and you've decided to purchase a jewellery item for a friend at Birks. Evaluate how the company's advertising, personal selling, public relations, and digital media might influence your purchase decision. How might the relative importance of each of these IMC tools be different if your parents were making the purchase?

3. Choose one of the ads featured in this book and explain whether it uses a rational or emotional appeal.

4. Bernard's, a local furniture company, targets its marketing at college and university students with apartments and households of young people purchasing their first furniture items. If you worked for Bernard's, what type of media would you use for your advertising campaign? Justify your answer.

5. Should Bernard's use continuous, pulsing, or flighting for its advertising schedule? Why?

6. Suppose you saw your instructor for this course being interviewed on TV about the impact of gift certificates on upcoming holiday's sales. Is this interview part of your university's IMC program? If so, do you believe it benefits the university? How?

7. A retail store places an ad for yoga pants in the local newspaper. The sales of the featured pants increase significantly for the next two weeks; sales in the rest of the sportswear department go up as well. What do you think are the short- and long-term objectives of the ad? Justify your answer.

8. As an intern for Michelin tires, you have been asked to develop an IMC budget. The objective of the IMC strategy is to raise Michelin's market share by 5 percent in Canada in the next 18 months. Your manager explains,

"It's real simple; just increase the budget 5 percent over last year's." Evaluate your manager's strategy.

9. McDonald's spends millions of dollars on advertising. Discuss how it can assess the impact of its advertising by using marketing metrics.

10. You heard a friend talking about GNC's healthy drinks and decided to visit its website. Assume that GNC used the services of behavioural advertising firm Tacoda to track how consumers move through its website and to create more targeted advertising. Would you view these efforts as an invasion of privacy? Do you believe this action constitutes an ethical IMC strategy? How will it affect your attitude toward GNC and the likelihood that you will purchase its products?

TOOLKIT

RETURN ON MARKETING EXPENDITURES

Suppose Jay Oliver (marketing manager of Transit sneaker store) is considering two search engine marketing options to reach out to new customers to market Transit. In particular, he is using Google AdWords, a search engine marketing tool that allows firms to show up in searches based on the keywords potential customers use. Transit is targeting young adults ages 17 to 28. The sneaker market accounts for about $500,000,000 of sales annually, and the target

market is about 35 percent of that. Transit's gross margins are 20 percent. Oliver estimates that Transit will capture a 2 percent market share of the target market with a $500,000 advertising and keyword budget (option 1) and a 3 percent market share with a $1,000,000 advertising and keyword budget (option 2). Which marketing plan produces the higher ROI for the year? Use the toolkit provided on Connect to assess the ROI of the two options.

NET SAVVY

1. View the website of Taxi (http://www.taxi.ca), a well-known IMC consulting firm. The site contains a lot of information about what IMC is and how it can be used effectively by a wide variety of companies. Of particular interest is the case studies section. Locate the case studies link, read a case, and discuss the following: What were the goals of the IMC campaign? Which IMC components were used in that particular campaign? How do those components contribute to the success of the IMC campaign in achieving its stated goals?

2. The Canadian Marketing Association (CMA) is the primary source of information about direct marketing activities for both academics and practitioners. The website for the CMA (http://www.the-cma.org) contains information about direct marketing practices and self-regulation. How many different target markets does the CMA address on its home page? Click on the Consumer Information tab. What services does the CMA provide for consumers? Why do you think it offers those services? Now return to the home page and click on the Marketing Resources tab and check out some of the articles, case studies, or white papers and reports.

CHAPTER CASE STUDY

JAY-Z AND BING: THE CAMPAIGN TO CONVERT JAY-Z DECODERS INTO BING USERS

When Microsoft needed a strategy to boost people's use of its Bing search engine, it found an oddly perfect vehicle in an integrated marketing campaign—one that also has been called a "transmedia event."[73] The ad agency that Microsoft hired proposed that the Bing campaign could work in conjunction with the new campaign for another of its clients: Jay-Z, the rap star and dominating producer, who wanted a global marketing strategy for the publication of his memoir, *Decoded*.

The creative process that led to this innovative marketing campaign—integrated in more ways than one—started with the ad agency, Droga5. It had these two separate mega-clients: Microsoft wanted to drive more users to its search engine, and Jay-Z wanted a way to promote his memoir. Proposing a new kind of synergy, the agency developed a plan to transform each client into the other's promotional vehicle.

Using outdoor advertising, search engines, a broad media strategy, and open source publishing,[74] Droga5 staged a month-long "transmedia" scavenger hunt, before the book was actually released. Jay-Z sent out clues through Facebook, Twitter, and a Bing page that told fans where to look for enormous versions of the individual pages from his book, pasted onto public locations. A facsimile of each of the 320 pages in the book would appear in a real-world location (e.g., New York, Los Angeles, New Orleans, Miami, Detroit, London) that reflected the story being told on that page. For example, a bronze plaque bolted to the wall of the Marcy Avenue apartment building where Jay-Z spent his childhood displayed pages 2 and 3 of *Decoded*, where Jay-Z wrote about the summer of 1978, "when I was nine years old."

Fans plugged the clues that Jay-Z had released into the Bing search engine, to search for the specific locations where they would find pages. The clues could be decoded only through Bing's search and street-mapping interface. Every public posting of a *Decoded* page also featured the URL for Bing.com/Jay-Z, along with the Bing logo.[75] The plan also created a public art project; if a relevant location could not be found, it was conjured up and created.

In turn, the campaign engaged consumers in at least a dozen cities worldwide. The majority of the wall-sized mock-ups of *Decoded* pages appeared on building walls in New York's Bedford-Stuyvesant neighbourhood, where Jay-Z grew up. There were installations at subway stops, on a boardwalk in front of a Brooklyn beach, and on the backboard of a basketball hoop in Bedford-Stuyvesant where Jay-Z hung with friends, all in reference to events or moments discussed in the book. Secured through a partnership with the outdoor advertising firm Clear Channel, enormous billboards appeared overnight, often atop dingy, store-fronted buildings, apartment towers, and other cityscapes.[76] Accordingly, fans could "walk through Jay-Z's life"[77]—both virtually through Bing and on the streets he once walked.

In New Orleans, a huge replica of pages 220–21 spread across the Orpheum Theater's roof, depicting Jay-Z's reaction to Hurricane Katrina's devastation. In a guitar shop in the Chelsea neighborhood of New York, an electric guitar was imprinted with pages 100–101, which recalled Kurt Cobain and how he "OD'd on fame." In Gleason's Gym in New York City, the pages were imprinted on two punching bags. Imprints also appeared on the stage curtains of the Apollo Theater in Harlem; on plates in The Spotted Pig, one of Jay-Z's favorite restaurants; and on a billboard at a subway stop in Abbey Road in London. Then *Decoded* pages showed up in the lining of custom-made Gucci leather jackets; on the sky-blue, painted bottom of the concrete pool at Miami's Delano Hotel, with an excerpt talking about the rapper's hit, "Big Pimpin"; and on the green felt surface of the pool table at the 40/40 Club, an upscale sports bar he owns.[78]

Over the course of a month, fans tracked down all 320 pages of the book, relying solely on the clues Jay-Z released through social media and their searches for the location on Bing. Bing's street-maps function helped those likely to get lost easily; it also enabled people who lived far from any of the sites to get a virtual visual tour of any neighbourhood. Fans posted their photos of the found pages on the dedicated website. Through this collaboration, they assembled the entire memoir, even before any books were available on shelves. The first users to discover each page also became eligible to win a signed copy of the book and enter into a drawing for the grand prize: a trip to Las Vegas to see Jay-Z and Coldplay in concert on New Year's Eve.[79]

In addition to putting up the pages, Clear Channel helped build more buzz by running promotional spots, interviews on its radio stations, and exclusive videos of the performer on its websites. The campaign thus drew coverage in mainstream media as well, including *The New York Times* and *New York Observer*, which headlined its description, "Jay-Z's Book to Be Utterly Inescapable Thanks to Bing, Clear Channel."[80] The campaign was financed by Bing, not by the publisher of *Decoded*.[81]

The Jay-Z–Bing collaboration was clearly innovative. It drew rave reviews for its stunning creativity and novel approaches. But even more important, it was also effective. It converted millions of offline Jay-Z fans and prospective book buyers into online Bing users, and vice versa. In addition to winning two international awards at the Cannes International Festival of Creativity,[82] the campaign pushed Bing onto the global list of the top 10 visited sites for the first time. In numerical terms, it increased visits to the search engine by nearly 12 percent, many of them by new users.[83] Meanwhile, *Decoded* became a national bestseller and sat on that list for 19 consecutive weeks. The performer also picked up around a million new Facebook followers.

The prepublication event thus became a major cultural event. Celebrities like Ryan Seacrest and Snoop Dogg used their own Twitter accounts to get in on the conversation too. Snoop Dogg sent this tweet: "My big homie Jay-Z is hidin' pages of his book all over the world and fans gotta find it on Bing."[84]

The advertising agency's massive, cross-platform campaign to herald the publication of Jay-Z's memoir using the Bing search engine succeeded in reaching and engaging Jay-Z fans globally. Droga5's creative, transmedia campaign to increase the reach and name recognition of the Bing search engine using a connection with a popular musician succeeded in reaching and engaging search engine users worldwide. Thus, this masterfully integrated marketing campaign managed to push two mega-brands forward mainly by bringing them together. There are several postings on YouTube (e.g., http://www.youtube.com/watch?v5XNic4wf8AYg&feature5player_embedded) where you can learn more about the campaign and view some of the pages posted at unusual sites.

Questions

1. What different IMC components did the Jay-Z–Bing campaign use? Were these marketing elements integrated, in the sense defined in this chapter?

2. How might the various interested parties (e.g., Jay-Z, his publisher, Droga5, Clear Channel, Bing) measure the effectiveness of the campaign?

For more information on the resources available from McGraw-Hill Ryerson, go to www.mheducation.ca/he/solutions.

TRADER.ca
The most cars in one place.

Advertising, Sales Promotions, and Personal Selling

Ask your parents what comes to mind when you say auto-TRADER and chances are they will mention newsprint magazines displayed in convenience store racks. Looking for a used car via a print publication sounds like something an older generation might embrace. But it does not reflect a youthful tone or today's digital realities, so autoTRADER set out to change consumer perceptions of its brand.[1] The company's redesigned website lets people search for cars by make, model, price, location, and set up email alerts for desired vehicles. It also provides tips on selling or trading cars, finding a dealer, and even getting a loan.

Now the company needed to increase awareness and drive traffic to that website. An advertising campaign was launched to highlight the ease of using the new digital platform to buy or sell used cars. The campaign used research insights from ad agency DDB Canada that showed consumers viewed auto-TRADER as having the largest inventory of cars in Canada.[2] This qualitative research became the backbone of the informative campaign and was incorporated in the tagline, "The Most Cars in One Place." Consumers who used the autoTRADER.ca site could be confident they had conducted the most comprehensive search to find the perfect car.

To drive traffic to the website, the integrated campaign featured television, radio and online ads, social media, and public relations. The television ads used humour to show how easy it was to list and sell a car that was no longer "cool." A Facebook app called the autoLYZER allowed Canadians to explore cars for sale on the autoTRADER.ca website that matched their personalities, lifestyles, and interests. The app used real-time data from Facebook, including opinions from friends' posts, to narrow down recommendations for suitable cars.[3] The campaign increased traffic to autoTRADER.ca by 18 percent, grew unique visitors to the site by 27 percent, and won the Grand Prize at the 2013 Cassies Awards for advertising effectiveness.[4]

LEARNING OBJECTIVES

After studying this chapter you should be able to

LO1 Describe advertising and three objectives of advertising

LO2 Summarize the regulatory and ethical issues of concern to advertisers

LO3 Explain how sales promotions supplement a firm's IMC strategy

LO4 Describe personal selling and how it adds value for customers

LO5 Identify the steps in the personal selling process

The site now attracts more than 3.5 million visitors each month.[5] Having successfully increased awareness and website traffic, a new campaign was launched to showcase tools available on autoTRADER.ca.[6] For example, an Owner Reviews section rates cars on elements such as comfort, performance, fuel economy, reliability, design of the interior and exterior styling.[7] The tool provides prospective buyers with insights and feedback directly from existing car owners. Other tools help facilitate buying or selling cars, a process that intimidates most consumers. Tools for dealers help them convert online traffic to sales, drive traffic to dealerships, optimize their investment in marketing, and maximize the profitability of their used inventory.[8]

Advertising objectives seem to have progressed from informative to persuasive. Now autoTRADER needs to ensure it stays top-of-mind with reminder-oriented advertising. ▌

In the previous chapter, we discussed the tools of integrated marketing communications (IMC) and the steps involved in planning a campaign. While we briefly touched on all of these tools in Chapter 14, we now focus more attention on three elements in particular: advertising, sales promotions, and personal selling. We begin by introducing the AIDA model, which is the process, or mental stages, marketers try to move consumers through as they are making purchase decisions. As a consumer, you are exposed only to the end product—for example, a finished advertisement—yet many decisions must take place before you actually get to see an ad. We discuss some of these decisions, starting with determining the advertising objectives and the focus of advertisements. We consider some of the regulatory and ethical issues in advertising and those arising from the use of new forms of marketing communications. Then we move on to examine sales promotions and how they add value both as consumer promotions and in the trade channel. The chapter concludes with an examination of how companies use personal selling to influence the buyer's purchase.

ADVERTISING

As we saw in Chapter 14, marketing communication is not a straightforward process. After being exposed to an advertisement, consumers go through several steps before actually buying or taking some other action. There is not always a direct link between a particular marketing communication and a consumer's purchase.

The AIDA Model

AIDA model
A common model of the series of mental stages through which consumers move as a result of marketing communications: **A**ttention leads to **I**nterest, which leads to **D**esire, which leads to **A**ction.

To create effective advertising, marketers must understand how marketing communications work. Generally, marketing communications move consumers step-wise through a series of mental stages, for which there are several models. The most common is the **AIDA model** (Exhibit 15.1),[9] which suggests that **A**ttention leads to **I**nterest, which leads to **D**esire, which leads to **A**ction. At each stage, the consumer makes judgments about whether to take the next step in the process. Customers actually have three types of responses, so the AIDA model is also known as the "think, feel, do" model. In making a purchase decision, consumers go through each of the AIDA steps to some degree, but the

EXHIBIT 15.1 The AIDA Model

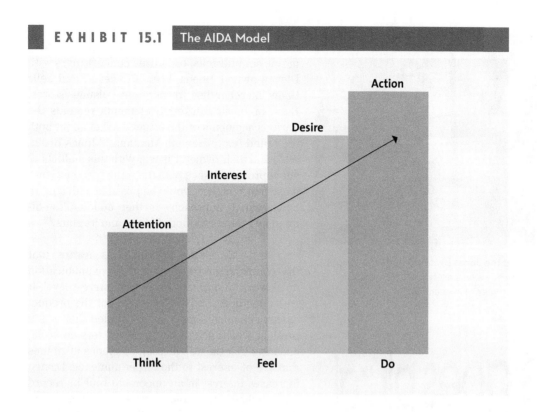

steps may not always follow the AIDA order. For instance, during an impulse purchase, consumers may "feel" and "do" before they "think."

Attention   Even the best marketing communication can be wasted if the sender doesn't gain the attention of the consumer first. Brand awareness refers to a potential customer's ability to recognize or recall that the brand name is a particular type of retailer or product/service. As such, brand awareness is the strength of the link between the brand name and the type of merchandise or service in the minds of customers. Coca-Cola already has excellent brand awareness and might not have to focus as much effort on this step when it wants to introduce a new flavour. In contrast, when Jay-Z wanted to promote his memoir, he needed to exert more effort to get consumers to think of him as an author, rather than a musician, as the case study in the previous chapter described.

There are a number of awareness metrics, from aided recall to top-of-mind awareness. **Aided recall** occurs when consumers recognize the brand when its name is presented to them. **Top-of-mind awareness**, the highest level of awareness, occurs when a brand has a prominent place in people's memories that triggers a response without them having to put any thought into it. For example, Harley-Davidson has top-of-mind awareness if a consumer responds "Harley" when asked about motorcycles. High top-of-mind awareness means that a particular brand will probably be carefully considered when customers decide to shop for that product or service. Manufacturers, retailers, and service providers build top-of-mind awareness by having memorable names; repeatedly exposing their name to customers through advertising, locations, and sponsorships; and using memorable symbols.

As an example of memorable symbols, imagine two smaller circles, sitting on opposite sides atop a larger circle. Did you think of Mickey Mouse ears and Disney? The company uses images to ensure that its name comes easily to the front of young consumers' minds. Whether they are individual acts like Miley Cyrus, Selena Gomez, or Demi Lovato or groups such as the KSM, Lemonade Mouth, and Allstar Weekend, Disney starts off its stars with Disney Channel shows, records them on the Disney-owned

aided recall
Occurs when consumers recognize the brand when its name is presented to them.

top-of-mind awareness
A prominent place in people's memories that triggers a response without them having to put any thought into it.

When young consumers read the Jonas Brothers' blog, they might have begged their parents to buy a concert ticket. The marketing communication drives the customer to take action.

Toyota's "Prius Goes Plural" campaign promoted a new family-sized (Prius v) and urban version (Prius c) of its popular hybrid car.

Hollywood Record label, plays the songs in heavy rotation on Radio Disney and Disney movie soundtracks, organizes concert tours with Disney-owned Buena Vista Concerts, and sells tie-in merchandise throughout Disney stores. Each of these marketing elements reminds the various segments of the target market about both the brand (e.g., "Hannah Montana," "Jonas Brothers") and their owner, Disney. With this multichannel approach, Disney gets the same "product" into more markets than would be possible with a more conservative approach—further building top-of-mind awareness for both Disney and its stars.[10]

Interest Once the consumer is aware that the company or product exists, communication must work to increase his or her interest level. It isn't enough to let people know that the product exists; consumers must be persuaded that it is a product worth investigating. Marketers do so by ensuring that the ad's message includes attributes that are of interest to the target audience. Disney increases interest in an upcoming tour or record by including a mention, whether casual or not, in the stars' television shows. Because the primary target market for the tour is also probably watching the show, the message gets received by the correct recipient.

Desire After the firm has piqued the interest of its target market, the goal of subsequent messages should move the consumer from "I like it" to "I want it." If Allstar Weekend appears on *Good Morning America* and talks about their upcoming activity and how great it is going to be, the viewing audience is all the more likely to demand access—in this case, probably parents who hope to score points with their adolescent children by buying the latest album or reserving seats to an upcoming tour.

Action The ultimate goal of any marketing communication is to drive the receiver to action. If the message has caught consumers' attention and made them interested enough to consider the product as a means to satisfy a specific desire of theirs, they likely will act on that interest by making a purchase. If young consumers follow Selena Gomez on Twitter, they might in turn beg their parents to purchase a concert ticket or album related to this favourite former Disney Channel star.

lagged effect
A delayed response to a marketing communication campaign.

The Lagged Effect Sometimes consumers don't act immediately after receiving a marketing communication because of the **lagged effect**—a delayed response to a marketing communication campaign. It generally takes several exposures to an ad before a consumer fully processes its message.[11] In turn, measuring the effect of a current campaign becomes more difficult because of the possible lagged response to a previous one.[12] For example, Toyota's "Prius Goes Plural" campaign promoted the addition of a family-sized (Prius v) and urban version (Prius c) of its popular hybrid car model. The campaign demanded consumer participation, by challenging the viewing public to come up with a plural form of the word "Prius" (e.g., Prii, Prien, Priuses), as touted in online banner and television ads, virtual polling booths, and videos. But the Prius v was not slated for release until six months after the campaign started, and the lag time for the Prius c was even longer. Toyota may never know for sure whether exposure to this campaign led consumers to check out or purchase the new vehicles.[13]

Advertising Objectives

As noted in Chapter 14, advertising is a paid form of communication from an identifiable source, delivered through a communication channel, and designed to persuade the receiver to take some action, now or in the future.[14] This definition provides some important distinctions between advertising and other forms of promotion, which we discussed in the previous chapter. First, unlike public relations, advertising is not free; someone has paid, with money, trade, or other means, to get the message shown. Second, advertising must be carried by some medium: television, radio, print, the Internet, T-shirts, sidewalks, and so on. Third, legally, the source of the message must be known or knowable. Fourth, advertising represents a persuasive form of communication, designed to get the consumer to take some action. That desired action can range from "Don't drink and drive" to "Buy a new Mercedes."

Some activities that are called advertising really are not, such as word-of-mouth advertising. Even political advertising technically is not advertising because it is not for commercial purposes and thus is not regulated in the same manner as true advertising.

Advertising encompasses an enormous industry and clearly is the most visible form of marketing communications—so much so that many people think of *marketing* and *advertising* as synonymous. Global advertising expenditures are projected to exceed $500 billion. It is not just a perception that advertising is everywhere; it *is* everywhere.[15]

Yet how many of the advertisements that you were exposed to yesterday do you remember today? Probably not more than three or four. As you learned in Chapter 4, perception is a highly selective process. Consumers simply screen out messages that are not relevant to them. When you notice an advertisement, you may not react to it; or, even if you react to it, you may not remember it later. Say you remember seeing it—you still may not remember the brand or sponsor of the advertisement, or, worse yet (from the advertiser's point of view), you may remember it as an advertisement for another product.[16]

To get you to remember their ad and the brand, advertisers must first get your attention. As we discussed in Chapter 14, the increasing number of communication channels and changes in consumers' media usage have made the job of advertisers far more difficult.[17] As the chapter vignette demonstrated, advertisers attempt to use creativity and a mix of promotional elements that offer better opportunities to reach their target markets. As a consumer, you are exposed only to the end product: the finished advertisement. But many actions must take place before you actually get to see an ad, as the Toolkit at the end of this chapter will show you.

As mentioned in Chapter 14, all advertising campaigns aim to achieve certain objectives: to inform, persuade, and remind customers. Another way of looking at advertising objectives is to examine an ad's focus. Is the ad designed to stimulate demand for a particular product or service, or is its focus, more broadly, the institution in general? Marketers use ads to stimulate demand for a product category or an entire industry, or for a specific brand, firm, or item. Let's look at the broad overall objectives of informing, persuading, and reminding.

Informative advertising was used to change the brand perception for autoTRADER.

The Most Cars in One Place.

autoTRADER.ca

The Canadian National Institute for the Blind uses informative advertising to warn consumers of the damage the sun's UV rays could do to their eyes.

Kobo's "The Gift of Reading" hopes to persuade consumers to give an e-reader to someone who inspired them to read.

informative advertising
Communication used to create and build brand awareness, with the ultimate goal of moving the consumer through the buying cycle to a purchase.

persuasive advertising
Communication used to motivate consumers to take action.

Informative Advertising **Informative advertising** communicates to create and build brand awareness, with the ultimate goal of moving the consumer through the buying cycle to a purchase. Such advertising helps determine some important early stages of a product's life cycle (PLC; see Chapter 8), particularly when consumers have little information about the specific product or type of product. Retailers often use informative advertising to tell their customers about an upcoming sales event or the arrival of new merchandise. autoTRADER used informative advertising to change its brand perception, as discussed in the chapter vignette.

The Canadian National Institute for the Blind (CNIB) works with people who are blind or visually impaired to get rehabilitation support and help them lead more independent lives. Part of the registered charity's mandate includes public education efforts with the goal of eliminating avoidable sight loss. To help achieve this objective, it launched a campaign to inform consumers that the sun's UV rays are the leading cause of vision loss in Canada.[18] While many people love the sun, its rays are dangerous, increasing the risk of developing cataracts, macular degeneration, and other serious eye problems. The ad cites stats to inform Canadians that one in two of them did not realize the need to wear sunglasses even in the shade and urges them to wear UV protective sunglasses even on cloudy days. The campaign is also promoted on social media including a Facebook page (cnib.ca/wearapair) that reflects a daily weather forecast for the city of your choice.

Persuasive Advertising When a product has gained a certain level of brand awareness, firms use **persuasive advertising** to motivate consumers to take action. Persuasive advertising generally occurs in the growth and early maturity stages of the PLC, when competition is most intense, and attempts to accelerate the market's acceptance of the product. In later stages of the PLC, persuasive advertising may be used to reposition an established brand by persuading consumers to change their existing perceptions of the advertised product. Firms often use persuasive advertising to convince consumers to take action: switch brands,[19] try a new product, or even continue to buy the advertised product.

Kobo has grown from a Toronto startup to a global company that sells in over 190 countries.[20] To recognize people who are book lovers and to inspire others to embrace the joy of reading, Kobo launched two persuasive campaigns. The first, "Reader's Passion," focused on people who read on a daily basis as a way to stimulate their imaginations and grey cells. The second campaign, "The Gift of Reading," used an emotional appeal, tapping images of mothers reading to young children. The second campaign, which was introduced just before Mother's Day, encouraged people to give an e-reader to whomever sparked their passion for reading. Until this point, Kobo had done very little advertising. However, research showed that the number of people who did not use an e-reader was two to three times higher than those who did.[21] While partnerships with booksellers and publishers helped attract early adopters, to reach and persuade other consumers, a mass advertising push was needed. The multimillion dollar campaign represents a tripling of the previous advertising budget, which coincidentally, mirrors Kobo's sales increases year over year.[22]

Reminder Advertising Finally, **reminder advertising** is communication used to remind consumers of a product or to prompt repurchases, especially for products that have gained market acceptance and are in the maturity stage of their life cycle. For instance, have you ever gone to a restaurant with a group of friends and ordered a Coke when you really wanted iced tea? In this case, the product has achieved top-of-mind awareness. Just the sight of a reminder ad, like a Coca-Cola logo on an umbrella, may be enough to stimulate the desired response. Entrepreneurial Marketing 15.1 discusses a unique form of reminder advertising on hangers, exposing consumers to product ads each time they hang up their clothes.

Although most children grow up drinking milk, consumption drops during the teen years and into adulthood. In the past, many campaigns have focused on winning back these consumers. However, a new initiative by the Strategic Milk Alliance (members include the BC Dairy Association, Alberta Milk, SaskMilk, Dairy Farmers of Manitoba, and Dairy Farmers of Canada) hopes to attract new parents. Research provided two key insights. First, since milk is always located at the back corner of stores, it's easy to miss or forget. Second, focus groups conducted by DDB Canada found that consumers believe that some foods simply taste better when paired with milk.[23] To capitalize on these insights, point of sale signs were placed strategically in stores—for example, in the cookie aisle—to evoke childhood memories of eating milk and cookies. The message was literally, if it tasted great then, it will still taste great now. Nostalgia was further developed in television, radio, print and billboard ads. A contest, called "Milk Your Moments," encouraged consumers to share photos of themselves or of other family members depicting memorable childhood moments.[24]

Focus of Advertisements To help determine the focus for advertisements, many companies consider the stages in the AIDA model discussed earlier. Some companies will focus their efforts on attracting awareness, for example, in the case of a new product introduction. If consumers are already aware of a product or service, the company will need to build interest and then desire. Lastly, they need to ensure that consumers will be motivated to take action as a result of the company's advertising efforts.

The ad campaign's objectives determine the specific ad's focus. **Product-focused advertisements** are used to inform, persuade, or remind consumers about a specific product or service. The Pepsi Max ad shown here is designed to generate sales for PepsiCo. The focus of **institutional advertisements** is to inform, persuade, and

reminder advertising
Communication used to remind consumers of a product or to prompt repurchases, especially for products that have gained market acceptance and are in the maturity stage of their life cycle.

product-focused advertisements
Used to inform, persuade, or remind consumers about a specific product or service.

institutional advertisements
Used to inform, persuade, and remind consumers about issues related to places, politics, an industry, or a particular corporation.

In-store signage and billboards were all part of a campaign to remind consumers to buy milk.

Entrepreneurial Marketing 15.1 | Responsible Advertising Hangs on the Smart Hanger

Leigh Meadows has an unusual piece of advice for entrepreneurs: listen to your children. Her six-year-old son, Jacob, got upset when she threw old metal hangers in the garbage. When she explained that they couldn't be recycled, he asked why someone didn't make hangers out of paper.[25] His question was her inspiration for a new product, the smart hanger (http://www.thesmart hanger.com). The hanger is made from 100 percent Forest Stewardship Council–approved recycled paper, including 90 percent postconsumer content: in other words, the paper has had a previous life as another product. Meadows says that's a pretty big deal, as some "green" coffee cups are made up of only 10 percent postconsumer content.

Only 10 percent of the population reuses wire hangers. Metal, plastic, and other paperboard hangers don't meet recycling standards, resulting in about 350 million hangers going to landfill each year. Before designing her hanger, Meadows approached the City of Toronto to learn about what materials are recyclable to ensure that her product would be environmentally friendly not only from the cradle to the grave, but also from "cradle to cradle."

To understand the shape and strength requirements of the hangers, Meadows spent time working in a dry cleaning plant. In late 2009, after two years of research and planning, her Toronto-based company, Media Hook, launched the smart hanger. Having a Brampton-based manufacturer produce the hanger was a big plus for Meadows, whose mission is to manufacture Canadian-made, practical, and sustainable alternatives to environmentally damaging products.[26]

Meadows began her career as an entrepreneur in her native London, England, where she bought an insurance brokerage when she was only 21 years old. She now describes herself as a serial entrepreneur who starts the new venture process by making a list of what she wants to achieve. Then she looks for businesses that are ailing or are very small but have the potential to be a lot bigger. In the case of the smart hanger, her list focused on the environment and leaving a legacy, something her son would be proud of.

Even though Meadows felt the smart hanger had the potential to be a success, to make it financially viable, she needed it to do double duty. The obvious answer was to advertise on the hangers, a great way to directly reach consumers in their homes and ensure they will be exposed to the message. Consumers see the message multiple times: when they bring their dry cleaning home, and every time they get dressed and hang the clothing up again. A media engagement study showed that hanger advertising places well above brand recall for TV ads, free-standing inserts, and online ads.[27]

Since her slogan is "Responsible Advertising Hangs on It," Meadows targeted companies and retailers that

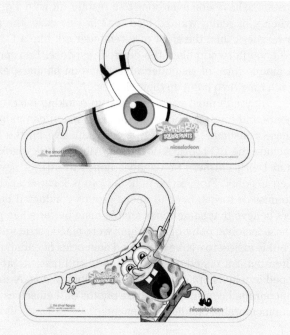

Leigh Meadows's six-year-old son Jacob was the inspiration for The Smart Hanger.

wanted to make an environmental difference.[28] The space is an ideal vehicle for socially responsible messages. Media Hook signed a contract with the Ontario Fabricare Association, formerly The Dry Cleaners and Launderers Institute of Ontario, to distribute smart hangers.[29]

The company's big break came when Meadows was named runner up in a special "Greenvention" episode of the hit TV show *Dragons' Den* in June 2010. The win opened previously closed doors and led to a contract with Global Edge Brands, which is now the exclusive North American distributor of the hangers. The company is a national leader in the licensed apparel industry and gives Media Hook access to retailers. Although people associate dry cleaners with hangers, Meadows says the retail market contributes more hangers to landfills since many clothes get shipped to stores prehung.

Other deals include a contract with Adidas to provide hangers to locker rooms of fitness clubs. In addition, after listening to her son, who suggested that SpongeBob SquarePants should be on hangers, Meadows now has a licensing deal with Nickelodeon. Under Armour will use the smart hanger for the launch of a new environmentally friendly clothing line, and deals are in the works with Sears and other retailers. Media Hook is also looking to develop sales promotion initiatives, such as coupons to drive traffic to advertiser's websites.

The smart hanger is not only a functional product but also an effective advertising platform and an environmental solution that makes Meadows's son proud of her.

remind consumers about issues related to places, politics, an industry, or a particular corporation. Some advertisements are designed to generate demand for the product category (e.g., the ironic "Stop Cooking with Cheese!" campaign) or an entire industry (e.g., the Strategic Milk Alliance), while others are designed to generate demand for a specific brand (e.g., Cracker Barrel cheese), firm (e.g., Kraft), or item.

product placement
Inclusion of a product in nontraditional situations, such as in a scene in a movie or TV program.

Perhaps the best-known campaign to build demand for a product category is the long-running institutional campaign "Got Milk?" which encouraged milk consumption by appealing to consumers' needs to affiliate with the milk-mustached celebrities shown in the ads.[30] One campaign, as exemplified in the ad with Rebecca Romijn and her babies, promised that drinking milk will help families stay together. Most ads highlight the beneficial properties of milk for building strong bones, which reflects an informative appeal, combined with a mild emotional fear appeal in its assertion that failing to drink milk can lead to medical problems.

Product Placement When marketers use **product placement**, they include their product in nontraditional situations, such as in a scene in a movie or TV program. The first visible movie product placement was Hershey's Reese's Pieces in the film *ET*. The product actually became part of the storyline, offered the candy high levels of visibility, and resulted in a large increase in sales.[31] Although Hershey's did not pay to place Reese's Pieces in *ET*, other firms have been more than willing to shell out for product placements. Companies spend approximately $4.38 billion on product placements in television and movies annually (e.g., Sony laptops in the James Bond film *Casino Royale*). Coca-Cola and Ford paid approximately $30 million each to gain product placements and advertising space on *American Idol*.[32]

A new Bollywood film is taking product placement further. In the popular roadtrip film *Zindagi Na Milegi Dobara* (*You Only Live Once*), the lead characters are inspired by a Spanish flamenco dancer and proceed through a series of adventures in Seville, Costa Brava, Pamplona, and other locations in Spain. The selection of these locales was made not by the film's writers or its director, but by Turespana, Spain's tourism agency, which helped turn the film into a kind of feature-length tourism guide. The agency also helped promote the film, spending more than $660,000 on television ads. And its investment worked: Indian tourism to Spain increased 65 percent after the film's release.[33] Although other countries have worked with Bollywood too, offering tax breaks or subsidies, no other site has gained so much influence over the production, plot, and promotion of a major Indian film.

The hard part is determining which movies will be successes. For Apple, the challenge is a little less stringent, because U.S. film directors seem to love its sleek white laptops, ear-budded iPods, and ubiquitous iPhones. More than one-third of all top-grossing films at the box office—129 of 374 movies—have included Apple-branded products in the past decade. Recent appearances include both hits and Oscar-nominated offerings, such as *Green Lantern*, *Transformers: Dark of the Moon*, *Rise of the Planet of the Apes*, *Bridesmaids*, *The Girl with the Dragon Tattoo*, and *Diary of a Wimpy Kid*.[34] Matt Damon's *We Bought a Zoo* even featured an extended scene showing how to use the iPhoto app. An analytics firm that estimates the dollar value of product placements

This product-focused advertisement is designed to inform, persuade, or remind consumers about Pepsi Max.

The "Got Milk?" institutional advertising campaign is used to encourage milk consumption, appealing to consumers by associating it with milk-mustached celebrities like Rebecca Romijn.

The Bollywood film *Zindagi Na Milegi Dobara* was partially sponsored by Spain's tourism agency. After the film's release, Indian tourism to Spain increased 65 percent.

public service announcement (PSA)
Advertising that focuses on public welfare and generally is sponsored by nonprofit institutions, civic groups, religious organizations, trade associations, or political groups; a form of social marketing.

social marketing
The application of marketing principles to a social issue to bring about attitudinal and behavioural change among the general public or a specific population segment.

has reported that Apple's five-minute screen time in *Mission Impossible* alone was worth more than $23 million.[35] Apple is also unique in that it claims it does not pay for product placement.

Other companies have also been lucky enough not to pay for product placement. The day after her wedding, Kate Middleton, Duchess of Cambridge, was spotted wearing a Zara blue, pleated polyester dress.[36] Zara was the lucky recipient of the ensuing publicity. However, there are far more examples of paid placement, especially in music videos where product placement revenues exceed $20 million annually.[37] Lady Gaga, Jennifer Lopez, Britney Spears, Eminem, Avril Lavigne, and numerous other artists have all promoted products through their videos.

Public Service Announcements A special class of demand advertising is the **public service announcement (PSA)**, which focuses on public welfare and generally is sponsored by nonprofit institutions, civic groups, religious organizations, trade associations, or political groups.[38] PSAs represent a form of **social marketing**, which is the application of marketing principles to a social issue to bring about attitudinal and behavioural change among the general public or a specific population segment.[39] Because PSAs are a special class of advertising, under the Canadian Radio-television and Telecommunications Commission rules, broadcasters must devote a specific amount of free airtime to them. Some of the most successful PSA campaigns include wildfire prevention (Smokey the Bear), smoking cessation (Stupid.ca), Internet safety (BeWebAware.ca), and breast cancer screening (Breast Cancer Society of Canada).

Because they often are designed by top advertising agencies for nonprofit clients, PSAs usually are quite creative and stylistically appealing. For example, what is your reaction to the Internet safety campaign BeWebAware.ca from the Media Awareness Network? The Ottawa-based nonprofit organization is designed to educate parents about the risks and benefits of letting their kids surf in cyberspace. Supported by Microsoft Canada and Bell Canada, ads highlight eye-opening statistics—such as the

Public service advertising, for causes such as breast cancer awareness, focus on public welfare and generally are sponsored by nonprofit institutions.

fact that 25 percent of kids have been asked to meet someone they've only met online—and encourage people to check out BeWebAware.ca, a website created to help parents get involved in monitoring their children's online activity. One print ad shows a middle-aged man at a computer, typing away in a kids' chat room. The accompanying copy reads, "To 12 year old Lisa, he was simply 11 year old Jenny."

Regardless of whether the advertising campaign's objective is to inform, persuade, or remind, or to focus on a particular product or the institution in general, each campaign's objectives must be specific and measurable. For a brand awareness campaign, for example, the objective might be to increase brand awareness among the target market by 50 percent within six months. Another campaign's goal may be to persuade 10 percent of a competitor's customers to switch to the advertised brand.

REGULATORY AND ETHICAL ISSUES IN ADVERTISING

LO2

IMC brings together many diverse forms of communication under one umbrella. But, in Canada, each form of communication media traditionally has been regulated separately. For example, rather than ban cigarette advertising completely, the federal 1997 Tobacco Act imposed numerous restrictions, including a phased-in ban on tobacco sponsorship of events.[40] However, in 2007, the Supreme Court of Canada struck down the tobacco industry's appeal to remove the advertising ban and also opened the door to new advertising. Companies are allowed to advertise in places where only people over the age of 18 are permitted and in magazines where adults account for more than 85 percent of their readership.[41] We begin this section by detailing the various agencies that regulate the different forms and media for advertising. Then we discuss some controversies surrounding new forms of potential deception.

In Canada, the regulation of advertising involves a complex mix of formal laws and informal restrictions designed to protect consumers from deceptive practices. Many federal and provincial laws, as well as a wide range of self-regulatory agencies and agreements, affect advertising (see Exhibit 15.2). The primary federal agencies that regulate advertising activities are the Competition Bureau, the Canadian Radio-television and Telecommunications Commission (CRTC), the Food and Drug Act, and Advertising Standards Canada.

EXHIBIT 15.2	**Agencies that Regulate Advertising**	
Agency/Legislation	**General Purpose**	**Specific Jurisdiction**
Competition Bureau Canada The Competition Act (1986)	Enforces federal laws that ensure businesses in Canada operate in a fair and equitable manner.	Enforces laws relating to misleading advertising and deceptive marketing practices.
Canadian Radio-television and Telecommunications Commission (CRTC; 1968)	Regulates and supervises all aspects of the Canadian broadcasting system, and regulates telecommunications common carriers and service providers that fall under federal jurisdiction.	Enforces restrictions on broadcasting material. Also administers codes that have an impact on specific categories of advertising; for example, the Code for Broadcast Advertising of Alcoholic Beverages.
Health Canada Food and Drug Act (1954)	Regulates food, drugs, cosmetics, and medical devices.	Establishes standards and requirements for the safety and sanitation of products. Regulates the labelling of food products pertaining to nutrition labelling, nutrient content, and health claims.
Advertising Standards Canada (ASC; 1957)	Monitors voluntary advertising industry codes.	Administers the Canadian Code of Advertising Standards, the Gender Portrayal Guidelines, and the Broadcast Code for Advertising to Children.

In addition to these agencies, marketers must adhere to other pieces of legislation such as the Consumer Packaging and Labelling Act and the Tobacco Act.

The Competition Bureau enforces the Competition Act, the most comprehensive legislation affecting the marketing activities of companies in Canada. The Competition Act maintains and encourages competition while protecting consumers from misleading and deceptive advertising practices. Rogers Communications promised "fewer dropped calls" when it launched its discount cellphone service, Chatr. The Competition Bureau charged Rogers with false advertising when the company failed to back up its claims and will impose a $10 million fine.[42] More recently the Competition Bureau accused furniture retailers The Brick and Leon's of deceptive marketing over their "buy now, pay later" promotions. Although ads promise consumers they need no down payment and will pay "absolutely nothing," the watchdog claims consumers are required to pay hundreds of dollars of upfront fees.[43]

The CRTC controls the advertising industry and governs broadcast media and licensing. The CRTC must approve all TV and radio advertisements before they can be broadcast. The Food and Drug Act prohibits the advertising or selling of unsafe or misbranded foods, cosmetics, and drugs. It also requires companies to adhere to regulations regarding health claims. Although used for many years in the United States, diet-related health claims for food products, related to risk reduction of heart disease, cancer, osteoporosis, and high blood pressure, have only recently been allowed in Canada. The Consumer Packaging and Labelling Act requires manufacturers, packers, and distributors to disclose full information about their products. All prepackaged products must be labelled in both French and English and bear the quantity in metric and imperial for weight, volume, or measures.

Many product categories fall under self-regulatory restrictions or guidelines. For example, Advertising Standards Canada (ASC) is a self-regulating body that monitors voluntary industry codes. Advertising to children is regulated primarily through self-regulatory mechanisms designed by ASC and its Broadcast Code for Advertising to Children. The exception is the province of Quebec, where all advertising to children under the age of 13 is prohibited under the Quebec Consumer Protection Act. Messages with no promotional or selling intent are protected by the Charter of Rights and Freedoms. As seen in Ethical Dilemma 15.1, even airbrushing photos in ads is considered wrong in the United Kingdom.

Recently, to make matters even more complicated for advertisers whose products sell in the United States, state Attorneys General's offices have begun to assert their authority to regulate advertising in their states. The European Union also has increased its regulation of advertising for EU member nations. Many of these state and European regulations are more restrictive than existing federal or self-regulatory requirements.

Another difference between advertising regulations in Canada and the European Union pertains to **puffery**, the legal exaggeration of praise, stopping just short of deception, lavished on a product.[44] In Canada, consumers are viewed as rational and capable of evaluating advertising claims. Does a certain sneaker brand really make you run faster and jump higher? Does Papa John's pizza really have "better ingredients" that make "better pizza"? In the European Union, however, puffery is considered deception. For instance, Kraft had no problem advertising its orange-flavoured drink Tang surrounded by oranges in North America. But in Germany, the ad was declared deceptive because there are no oranges in Tang. Advertisers must understand these differences to keep from violating EU advertising laws.

puffery
The legal exaggeration of praise, stopping just short of deception, lavished on a product.

Is this billboard ad an example of puffery or deception?

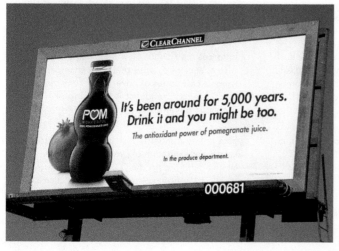

Ethical Dilemma 15.1

When Makeup Companies Really Do Make Up Models' Faces

Is Julia Roberts really that good looking? Of course, she's beautiful, but the portrayal of her face in advertising has, more likely than not, been given a "Photoshop fix." Airbrushing may be as old as advertising, but improved technology makes the changes nearly imperceptible—can you tell the difference between the normal thickness of an eyelash and the version that Taylor Swift sported in a CoverGirl NatureLeuxe Mousse Mascara ad? Ultimately, the National Advertising Division of the Council of Better Business Bureaus ruled the ad was misleading,[45] prompting the brand to pull the ad.

But in other cases, cosmetics and fashion companies claim that "fixing" elements of appearance is both ubiquitous and expected by consumers. They assert they are not misleading anyone but rather creating a perfect image for their brand. So is it wrong for cosmetic companies to retouch ads,

When selling cosmetics, is it ethical to touch up photos of models and celebrities like Julia Roberts to make them more beautiful?

brushing away wrinkles and skin imperfections digitally?[46]

The U.K. Advertising Standards Agency considers touching up photos in ads to be wrong. That oversight agency banned two separate ads by L'Oreal recently, charging that they were misleading. One ad featured Julia Roberts promoting Teint Miracle, a new Lancome skin product that, according to the company, provides "luminosity to the skin." The other featured the model Christy Turlington, promoting a cosmetic concealer called Eraser that promises to hide wrinkles and skin discoloration. Although the company protested that the ads did not exaggerate their product effectiveness, the U.K. Advertising Standards Agency was not convinced.[47]

Do consumers want realistic images and measured promises, or do they accept and even prefer exaggerated claims and unrealistic images of beauty?

SALES PROMOTION

L03

Advertising rarely provides the only means to communicate with target customers. As we discussed in Chapter 14, a natural link appears between advertising and sales promotion. Sales promotions are special incentives or excitement-building programs that encourage consumers to purchase a particular product or service, typically used in conjunction with other advertising or personal selling programs. In the context of IMC campaigns, advertising generally creates attention, interest, and desire, while the value in sales promotions is in closing the deal. Many sales promotions, such as free samples or point-of-purchase (POP) displays, attempt to build short-term sales, whereas others, such as loyalty programs, contests, and sweepstakes, have become integral components of firms' long-term customer relationship management (CRM) programs, which they use to build customer loyalty. In this section, we examine the various tools firms use for their sales promotions and how those tools complement the advertiser's efforts to achieve its strategic objectives.

The tools of any sales promotion can be focused on either channel members, such as wholesalers or retailers, or end-user consumers. Just as we delineated for advertising, when sales promotions are targeted at channel members, the marketer is employing a push strategy; when it targets consumers themselves, it is using a pull strategy. Some sales promotion tools can be used with either a push or pull strategy. We now consider each of the tools and how they are used.

Consumer Sales Promotions

Exhibit 15.3 displays the many different types of tools used in consumer sales promotions, along with their advantages and disadvantages. We will discuss how marketers

| | **EXHIBIT 15.3** | **Types of Consumer Sales Promotions** | |

Promotion	Objective	Advantages	Disadvantages
Coupons	Stimulate demand.	• Encourage retailer support. • Allow for direct tracing of sales.	• Have low redemption rates. • Have high cost.
Deals	Encourage trial.	• Reduce consumer risk. • Retaliate against competitive action.	• May reduce perception of value.
Premiums	Build goodwill.	• Increase perception of value.	• Results in consumers who buy for premium not the product. • Have to be carefully managed.
Contests	Increase consumer involvement.	• Generate excitement.	• Requires creativity. • Must be monitored.
Sweepstakes	Encourage higher consumption.	• Minimize brand switching among existing consumers.	• Sales often decline after.
Samples	Encourage trial.	• Offer direct involvement.	• Have high cost to the firm.
Loyalty Programs	Encourage repurchase.	• Create loyalty.	• Have high cost to the firm.
POP Displays	Increase brand trial.	• Provide high visibility. • Provide in-store support.	• Is difficult to get a good location in the store. • Can be costly to the firm.
Rebates	Stimulate demand.	• Increase value perception.	• Is easily copied by competitors. • May just advance future sales.

choose which tool to use based on their specific marketing objectives. Then, we examine some ways in which IMC programs make use of sales promotions.

Coupons   A coupon offers a discount on the price of specific items when they're purchased. Coupons are issued by manufacturers and retailers in newspapers, magazines, and free-standing inserts, on products, on shelves, at the cash register, over the Internet, and by mail. They are commonly used in supermarkets, but other retailers, such as department stores and restaurants, also use coupons to pull customers away from the competition. Some retailers even accept coupons from competitors. More than 300 billion coupons are distributed every year in North America, yet only about 2 percent of them are ever redeemed.[48] However, these redemption rates vary dramatically depending on how consumers obtain the coupon. A segment of the market, the diehard "coupon clippers," devote a great deal of time and effort to searching for, clipping, and redeeming coupons. Many coupon clippers have streamlined this process by using the Internet, which offers entire forums dedicated to coupon sharing and management (e.g., http://www.couponforum.com). Coupons carried in newspapers, magazines, in-store displays, and direct mail have very low redemption rates of only 1 to 2 percent, whereas those downloaded from the Internet experience a 56 percent redemption rate. The reason for this dramatic difference is that consumers seek out online coupons for specific items or stores, whereas many people who have no interest in purchasing the product receive traditional coupons.

Some coupons, whether printed from the Internet or sent to mobile phones, also contain information about the customer who uses them.[49] The bar code may identify the customer, his or her Internet address, Facebook page information, and even the search terms the customer used to find the coupon in the first place. These new breeds of coupons may look standard, but they offer up a startling amount of data, which promises benefits for advertisers who want to target their marketing more closely. A Clorox promotion benefited from Facebook's ability to narrowly target, as Social and Mobile Marketing 15.1 recognizes.

Traditionally, coupons had low redemption rates and were therefore a relatively inexpensive sales promotion tool, but firms like Groupon have resulted in higher redemption rates, increasing their expense. Still, online coupon sites and daily deal sites, such as Groupon, WagJag, and Living Social, have changed the way some businesses offer promotions. The Cellar Bar and Grill in Bedford, Nova Scotia, sold 200 half-price vouchers worth $20 for only $10 through Kijiji's Daily Deals site.[50] While the coupon offer drew in new customers, the challenge for the bar's owner, Cathy Levangie, will be to entice the bargain seekers to return and pay full price. Facebook Deals also offers online coupons to Canadians through retail partners such as Chapters Indigo, H&M, Wind Mobile, and Town Shoes.[51] Consumers simply post their location to their Facebook page while they are out and about to access special deals from retailers in the area.

Deals A **deal** refers generally to a type of short-term price reduction that can take several forms, such as a "featured price," a price lower than the regular price; a "buy one, get one free" offer; or a percentage "more free" offer contained in larger packaging. Another form of a deal involves a special financing arrangement, such as reduced percentage interest rates or extended repayment terms. Deals encourage trial because they lower

deal
A type of short-term price reduction that can take several forms, such as a "featured price," a price lower than the regular price; a "buy one, get one free" offer; or a certain percentage "more free" offer contained in larger packaging.

Social and Mobile Marketing 15.1 | Effective Friending

The use of social networking in marketing is so new that inexperienced marketers have launched poorly conceived Facebook campaigns with the hope that any strategy that includes social media is "good enough." But good enough is rarely sufficient in a competitive marketplace, and some brands have hurt their images by launching campaigns that are out of step with social media culture.

When a group of industry professionals discussed the ingredients necessary to attract positive attention from Facebook's 1 billion users,[52] they agreed that a successful campaign must tell a story. Ideally, the story should involve and engage users in the plotline. Equally important, these creative heavyweights highlighted the need to connect the campaign to the real world, as Heinz did with its campaign that allowed users to send personalized cans of soup to sick friends.

Making good use of consumer data available on Facebook can also improve campaign success by giving marketers the ability to hone in on target audiences and track consumer response. After months of flat reactions to a Facebook promotion of its environmentally friendly cleaners, Clorox launched new initiatives designed to educate people about and increase sales of its Green Works products. The campaign targeted

only those women whose Facebook profiles featured the words "clean" or "green."[53] At the same time, Clorox aimed to enhance the experience of other potential users by inviting consumers to nominate green heroes in their community to receive a $15,000 grant. In yet another effort, Clorox offered a $3-off coupon to people who connected to the Green Works web page. The result was a record-breaking engagement rate for the company, demonstrating that social media, when used properly, can be a valuable marketing tool.

Clorox's Facebook promotion is designed to educate people about and increase sales of its Green Works products.

This sales promotion deal for Payless ShoeSource is a short-term price promotion that encourages consumers to buy a second pair of shoes at one-half off.

the risk for consumers by reducing the cost of the good, but they can also alter perceptions of value.

But deals can also alter perceptions of value—a short-term price reduction may signal a different price/quality relationship than would be ideal from the manufacturer's perspective. As Old Spice learned, offering too many deals can offset likely gains. Its popular "Old Spice Guy" campaign attracted consumer attention through funny television commercials and interactive online campaigns, and sales of Old Spice jumped. But the company offered so many buy one, get one free deals at the same time that the potential profit impact of the great ads was essentially eliminated by the costs of the deals.[54]

Premiums   A **premium** offers an item for free or at a bargain price to reward some type of behaviour, such as buying, sampling, or testing. These rewards build goodwill among consumers, who often perceive high value in them. Premiums can be distributed in a variety of ways. They can be included in the product packaging, such as the toys inside cereal boxes; placed visibly on the package, such as a coupon for free milk on a box of Cheerios; handed out in the store; or delivered in the mail, such as the free perfume offers Victoria's Secret mails to customers.

Furthermore, premiums can be very effective if they are consistent with the brand's message and image and highly desirable to the target market. Finding a premium that meets these criteria at a reasonable cost can be a serious challenge. At fast-food restaurants such as McDonald's and Burger King, for instance, the average order cost is around $5, while the average premium distributed costs less than 50 cents.

premium
An item offered for free or at a bargain price to reward some type of behaviour, such as buying, sampling, or testing.

contest
A brand-sponsored competition that requires some form of skill or effort.

Contests   A **contest** refers to a brand-sponsored competition that requires some form of skill or effort. In Canada, you cannot give a prize away by chance alone. There must also be a skill component, which is why skill-testing questions are used, making the game one of mixed chance and skill. The effort required by these contests often keeps participation lower than that for other forms of promotion. When Jason Priestley joked about a donut called "The Priestley" (strawberry-vanilla donut stuffed with a chocolate Timbit) in a cameo appearance on *How I Met Your Mother*, Tim Hortons kept the publicity going strong by launching a contest. The winning entry in the Duelling Donuts contest was the Tortoise Torte, a concoction of chocolate, caramel and pecans. It beat out 63,000 other entries and earned contestant Andrew Shepherd $10,000.[55]

Contests are often used to drive sales, draw attention to a company's initiatives and even promote environmental causes. Sustainable Marketing 15.1 discusses how Nabob's "Green Bean Initiative" promotional contest helped to showcase its commitment to making positive change in the world of coffee growers worldwide. To be effective, contests must be advertised and enjoy high levels of retailer or dealer support. SportChek ran an online contest to drive up its membership database and increase store traffic. Shoppers received unique contest-entry PIN codes on their receipts. They got a discount coupon when they registered at GetIntoGear.ca. In the first week, 3,000 people registered for the contest and sent information about it to friends 1,000 times.[56]

sweepstakes
A form of sales promotion that offers prizes based on a chance drawing of entrants' names.

Sweepstakes   A form of sales promotion that offers prizes based on a chance drawing of entrants' names, **sweepstakes** do not require the entrant to complete a task other than

Sustainable Marketing 15.1

Nabob: Blending Quality with Sustainability[57]

When it comes to our planet, even the smallest changes can make a positive difference to sustainability in the long run. This is the Nabob Coffee Company's new stance. But Nabob is not just making small changes; it is also making huge companywide changes at all levels to align its brand with its new sustainability philosophy. Nabob has come a long way since it was established in 1896 by two determined grocers who started blending premium imported beans. In 1994, Kraft acquired Nabob, which is now the largest premium roast and ground coffee brand in Canada.

Nabob has had a long journey of success and is now embarking on a new endeavour of supporting environmental, social, and economic sustainability. The company is committed to recognizing the role it plays in safeguarding coffee-growing environments and improving the lives of coffee growers worldwide; it knows it must balance the needs of producers and consumers with the long-term health of the environment. Its slogan "Better Beans. Better Coffee. Better Planet" demonstrates the recent focus on sustainability and making a positive impact on the world by changing coffee production for the better. One of the company's small changes is the creation of a new canister made from recyclable materials. In addition, Nabob now sources Rainforest Alliance Certified coffee beans. The Rainforest Alliance is an organization that invests in the conservation of biodiversity and the quality of life of local people in their environment. It has developed a socioeconomic certification program for agriculture, which is based on more than 200 criteria. These criteria are focused on creating respect for people and the environment, along with considering rural traditions and local culture.

To encourage consumers to become involved in sustainability efforts, the company ran the "Nabob Green Bean Initiative" contest, generating excitement and awareness about Nabob's increased commitment to sustainability. The cross-Canada contest required entrants

Nabob is committed to safeguarding coffee-growing environments and the lives of coffee growers.

to write a 1,200-word essay creatively describing the actions their community could take and explaining how the Nabob Green Bean Initiative would have a positive impact on their community. Initiatives included things such as investing in solar panels or adding more recycling bin containers to a community facility. The winning community received $10,000 to bring its Nabob Green Bean Initiative to fruition.

This contest took Nabob's commitment to supporting sustainability one step further by encouraging consumer involvement. And it put Nabob on the path of integrating sustainability in all aspects of its organization, including its marketing communications strategy.

buying a ticket or completing a form. Often the key benefit of sweepstakes is that they encourage current consumers to consume more if the sweepstakes form appears inside the packaging or with the product. Unlike contests, sweepstakes winners are determined by a random draw. Reader's Digest Canada runs an annual national sweepstakes for which it invites both subscribers and others to enter.

Samples   **Sampling** offers potential customers the opportunity to try a product or service before they make a buying decision. Distributing samples is one of the most costly sales promotion tools but also one of the most effective. Quick-service restaurants and grocery stores frequently use sampling. For instance, McDonalds offers free coffee a couple of times a year to attract customers to its outlets. Costco uses so many samples that customers can eat an entire meal. Sometimes trial-size samples come in the mail or

sampling
Offers potential customers the opportunity to try a product or service before they make a buying decision.

The Look Fab Studio temporarily offered free beauty tips, makeovers, and workshops from industry experts such as celebrity makeup artist Paul Venoit. Pop-up retail stores are set in temporary locations to generate excitement about a brand or product.

POP displays are merchandise displays located at the point of purchase, such as at the checkout counter in a grocery store.

loyalty program
Specifically designed to retain customers by offering premiums or other incentives to customers who make multiple purchases over time.

point-of-purchase (POP) display
A merchandise display located at the point of purchase, such as at the checkout counter in a grocery store.

are distributed in stores. P&G set up a pop-up retail outlet, Look Fab Studio, in the upscale Yonge and Bloor area of Toronto for a single month. The temporary beauty boutique allowed visitors to benefit from free samples, beauty tips, makeovers, and workshops from industry experts, such as celebrity makeup artist Paul Venoit.[58] One of the key purposes of the Look Fab Studio was to help establish P&G as an authority on beauty and to position its beauty brands.

Loyalty Programs   As part of a sales promotion program, a **loyalty program** is specifically designed to retain customers by offering premiums or other incentives to customers who make multiple purchases over time. Such sales promotions are growing increasingly popular and are often tied to long-term CRM systems. In Canada, some of the most popular loyalty programs include Canadian Tire "Money," Aeroplan, Air Miles, and the Shoppers Drug Mart Optimum program.

Point-of-Purchase Displays   A **point-of-purchase (POP) display** is a merchandise display located at the point of purchase, such as at the checkout counter in a grocery store. Marketers spend almost as much on POP materials as they do on consumer magazine advertising, but the key to a successful POP is to make the display "pop out" in a crowded store. In addition, manufacturers must encourage retailers to feature and use the POP displays to maximize their investments. The use of shelf displays along with other promotional tactics led to the successful launch of XOXO, a new brand of wine. Shying away from traditional wine drinkers, the brand was targeted to women looking to complement a "Girl's Night In." Eye-catching on-shelf displays coupled with simple but recognizable packaging were an instant hit, selling 36,000 bottles in just four weeks. In-store sampling produced a conversion rate of 35 to 50 percent, much higher than the 15 to 20 percent expected from such trials.[59]

Rebates   Rebates refer to a particular type of price reduction in which a portion of the purchase price is returned by the seller to the buyer. Many products, such as consumer electronics, now offer significant mail-in rebates that may lower the price of the item significantly. Firms offer such generous rebates because the likelihood that consumers will actually apply for the rebate is low, even though consumers indicate that rebate offers are a factor in their purchase decisions. The firms thus garner considerable value from rebates because they attract consumers with a minimal risk that the firm will have to pay off all the rebates offered.

Recently, heavy rebate users, such as Best Buy, have begun scaling back their programs.[60] Like any promotional tool, too much of a good thing can be a problem. Best Buy found that consumers were becoming increasingly annoyed by having to mail in the rebate forms and wait to receive their money. Many were requesting that the rebate be given at the time of purchase and wondering why this immediate reduction was not possible. In addition, a growing number of lawsuits claim rebate cheques were never sent to consumers and that rebate offers contain overly detailed clauses that cause consumers to have to submit and resubmit their claims.[61]

Trade Channel Sales Promotions

Although sales promotions are often associated with coupons, contests, and other consumer tactics, far more money is spent on trade channel sales promotions than on consumer sales promotions. Trade channel promotions help convince retailers and wholesalers to stock a new brand, give it eye-level shelf space, and promote it in their flyers and other advertisements. Many types of consumer sales promotions can be used for channel members, including discounts and allowances, co-operative advertising, and sales force training.

Discounts and Allowances Discounts and allowances are effective incentives used to maintain or increase inventory levels in the distribution channel. Manufacturers sometimes offer a case allowance, for example, a discount or dollar amount taken off each case ordered during a specific time period. Alternatively, retailers may receive a set quantity of products free, for example, one case at no charge with an order of 10 cases. A merchandise allowance may be offered in return for extra in-store support or for featuring the product in some way by the retailer. For instance, if a store agreed to run an ad with a coupon promoting a specific product, the merchandise allowance may provide a discounted case price for orders received during the promotional period.

Co-operative Advertising One of the important functions retailers perform is promoting products to consumers. Co-operative (co-op) advertising helps to compensate trade channel members for money they spend promoting products and encourages them to feature products more often. Generally, manufacturers will pay 50 percent of the cost of advertising up to an agreed-upon limit. This limit is usually determined based on the amount of business a retailer does with a manufacturer. To ensure high-quality advertisements are placed at the local level, some companies will provide a selection of final ads to choose from, ready to place in a variety of media or adapt as necessary.

Sales Force Training Because retailers have contact with end consumers and are ultimately responsible for selling the products they carry, manufacturers may offer to train the retailer's sales staff. This training gives a company's sales force more in-depth product knowledge, which enhances their confidence in the product and increases the likelihood of future sales. When VitalScience Corp. launched its Dermaglow skin care line, it trained cosmeticians at Shoppers Drug Mart, since they were the staff members who would most likely field questions about the new product. Other training activities might include providing manuals or brochures, sales meetings, or field visits. Manufacturers sometimes run contests to help motivate trade channel members to sell their products.

Using Sales Promotion Tools

Marketers must be careful in their use of promotions, especially those that focus on lowering prices. Depending on the item, consumers may stock up when items are offered at a lower price, which simply shifts sales from the future to now and thereby leads to short-run benefits at the expense of long-term sales stability. For instance, using sales promotions such as coupons to stimulate sales of household cleaning supplies may cause consumers to stockpile the products and decrease demand for those products in the future. But a similar promotion used with a perishable product such as Danone yogurt should increase its demand at the expense of competitors like Yoplait.

The tools connected to sales promotions are as varied as the imaginations of the marketers who devise them, and new forms are constantly popping up. For example, **pop-up stores**—such as P&G's Look Fab Studio in Toronto discussed earlier or the Diet Coke Lounges that popped up in Canadian malls—exist only for a limited time and generally focus on a new product or a limited group of products offered by a retailer, manufacturer, or service provider. These temporary storefronts give consumers a chance to interact with the brand and build brand awareness, but they are not designed primarily to sell the

pop-up stores
Temporary storefronts that exist for only a limited time and generally focus on a new product or a limited group of products offered by a retailer, manufacturer, or service provider; they give consumers a chance to interact with the brand and build brand awareness.

product. Instead, companies hope that consumers who have visited the pop-up will follow up with a visit to a retailer that carries the products or the company's website.[62]

Retailers tend not to mind manufacturers' pop-up stores because most are designed to drive traffic to the retailers through give-aways of coupons and samples. Because pop-ups are short lived, they don't pose any long-term competition to retailers or cause channel conflict.

Many firms are also realizing the value of **cross-promoting**, when two or more firms join together to reach a specific target market. To achieve a successful cross-promotion, the two products must appeal to the same target market and together create value for consumers. J. Crew has teamed up with several famous brands, including Belstaff, Levi's, Barbour, Timex, and Sperry Top-Sider, to offer exclusive products in J. Crew stores and its website.

The goal of any sales promotion is to create value for both the consumers and the firm. By understanding the needs of its customers, as well as how best to entice them to purchase or consume a particular product or service, a firm can develop promotional messages and events that are of interest to and achieve the desired response from those customers. Traditionally, the role of sales promotion has been to generate short-term results, whereas the goal of advertising was to generate long-term results. As this chapter demonstrates, though, both sales promotion and advertising can generate both long- and short-term effects. The effective combination of both types of activities leads to impressive results for the firm and the consumers.

Evaluating Sales Promotions by Using Marketing Metrics

Many sales promotion opportunities undertaken by retailers are initiated by manufacturers. For example, Sharp might offer the following special promotion to Costco: during a one-week period, Costco can order 37-inch Sharp Aquos LCD HDTVs at $300 below the standard wholesale price. However, if Costco elects to buy these HDTVs at the discounted price, then it must feature them prominently on its web page for $1099.00 ($325 below the suggested retail price). In addition, Costco must agree to purchase enough of this particular model to have front-of-store displays in each of its stores.

Before Costco decides whether to accept such a trade promotion and promote the Sharp HDTV to its customers, it needs to assess the promotion's impact on its own profitability. Such a promotion may be effective for Sharp but not for Costco.

To evaluate a trade promotion, retailers consider

- the realized margin from the promotion
- the cost of the additional inventory carried because of buying more than the normal amount of the product
- the potential increase in sales from the promoted merchandise
- the long-term impact on sales of the promotion
- the potential loss suffered when customers switch to the promoted merchandise from more profitable TVs
- the additional sales made to customers attracted to the store by the promotion

When the HDTV's price is reduced to $1099.00, Costco will sell more Sharp HDTVs than it normally does. But Costco's margin on the HDTVs will be less because the required retail discount of $325 isn't offset by the normal wholesale discount of $300. In addition, Costco might suffer losses because the promotion encourages customers to buy these special HDTVs, which have a lower margin than Costco makes on its other HDTVs. In contrast, the promotion may attract customers who don't normally purchase electronics at Costco but who will visit to buy the Sharp HDTV at the discounted price. These customers might buy additional merchandise, providing a sales gain to the store that it wouldn't have realized if it hadn't promoted this item.

cross-promoting Efforts of two or more firms joining together to reach a specific target market.

PERSONAL SELLING

Almost everyone is engaged in some form of selling. On a personal level, you sell your ideas or opinions to your friends, family, employers, and professors. Even if you have no interest in personal selling as a career, a strong grounding in the topic will help you in numerous career choices. Consider, for instance, Tony D'Souza, a very successful labour attorney. He worked his way through university selling alpaca sweaters to fraternities across the country. Although he loved his part-time job, D'Souza decided to become an attorney. When asked whether he misses selling, he said, "I use my selling skills every day. I have to sell new clients on the idea that I'm the best attorney for the job. I have to sell my partners on my legal point of view. I even use selling skills when I'm talking to a judge or jury." In this chapter though, we take a straightforward business perspective on selling.

The Scope and Nature of Personal Selling

Personal selling is the two-way flow of communication between a buyer (or buyers) and a seller that is designed to influence the buyer's purchase decision. Personal selling can take place in various situations: face to face, via video teleconferencing, on the telephone, or over the Internet. More than 1 million people are employed in sales positions in Canada,[63] including those involved in B2B transactions—such as manufacturers' representatives selling to retailers or other businesses—and those completing B2C transactions—such as retail salespeople, real estate agents, and insurance agents. Salespeople are referred to in many ways: as sales representatives or reps; account executives; or agents. And, as Tony D'Souza found, most professions rely on personal selling to some degree.

Salespeople don't always get the best coverage in popular media. In Arthur Miller's play *Death of a Salesman*, the main character, Willy Loman, leads a pathetic existence and suffers from the loneliness inherent in being a travelling salesman.[64] Unfortunately, this powerful Pulitzer Prize–winning piece of literature weighs heavily on our collective consciousness and often overshadows the millions of hard-working professional salespeople who have fulfilling and rewarding careers and who add value to their firm and provide value for their customers.

Professional selling can be a satisfying career for several reasons. First, many people love the lifestyle. Salespeople are typically out on their own. Although they occasionally work with their managers and other colleagues, salespeople are usually responsible for planning their own day. This flexibility translates into an easier balance between work and family than many office-bound jobs can offer. Many salespeople now rely on virtual offices, which enable them to communicate via the Internet with colleagues and customers. Because salespeople are evaluated primarily on the results they produce, as long as they meet and exceed their goals, they experience little day-to-day supervision.

Second, the variety of the job often attracts people to sales. Every day is different, bringing different clients and customers, often in a variety of places. Their issues and problems and the solutions to those problems all differ and require creativity.

Third, professional selling and sales management can be a very lucrative career. Sales is among the highest-paying careers for college and university graduates, and compensation often includes perks, such as the use of a company car and bonuses for high performance.

Many salespeople now rely on virtual offices, which enable them to communicate via the Internet with colleagues and customers.

Professional selling can be a very lucrative career and is very visible to management.

A good CRM system provides salespeople with the information they need to suggest specific items and services to individual customers.

A top performer can have a total compensation package of more than $150,000; even lower-level salespeople can make well over $50,000. Although the monetary compensation can be significant, the satisfaction of being involved in interesting, challenging, and creative work is rewarding in and of itself.

Fourth, because salespeople are the front-line emissaries for their firm, they are very visible to management. Because it is fairly straightforward for management to identify top performers, those high-performing salespeople who aspire to management positions are in a good position to be promoted.

Although personal selling is an essential part of many firms' IMC strategy, it offers its own unique contribution to the four Ps. Because of the one-to-one nature of sales, a salesperson is in a unique position to customize a message for a specific buyer—a preplanned sales presentation or demonstration can be altered at any time as the need arises. In a personal selling situation, the salesperson can probe the buyer for his or her potential reservations about a product or service, educate the buyer when appropriate, and ask for the order at the appropriate time. Unlike other types of promotion, the sales presentation can be directed toward those customers with the highest potential. This highly directed approach to promotion is important because experts estimate that the average cost of a single B2B sales call is about $400.[65]

The Value Added by Personal Selling

Why have salespeople in the supply chain? They are expensive and can be a challenge to manage. Some firms, such as retailers, have made the decision not to use a sales force and become, for the most part, almost completely self-service. Other firms have turned to the Internet and technology to lower the costs of personal selling. Those that use personal selling as part of their IMC program do so because it adds value to their product or service mix—that is, personal selling is worth more than it costs. Personal selling adds value by building relationships, educating and providing advice, and saving customers time and simplifying things for them.[66]

Sales People Build Relationships. As we discussed in Chapter 12, building strong distribution channel relationships is a critical success factor. Who in the organization is better equipped to manage this relationship than the salesperson, the firm's front-line representative? The most successful salespeople are those who build strong relationships with their customers. They don't view themselves as being successful if they make a particular sale or one transaction at a time. Instead, they take a long-term perspective. Thus, building on the strategic relationship concept introduced in Chapter 12, **relationship selling** is a sales philosophy and process that emphasizes a commitment to maintaining the relationship over the long term and investing in opportunities that are beneficial to all parties. Relationship salespeople work with their customers to find mutually beneficial solutions to their wants and needs.

Research has shown that a positive customer–salesperson relationship contributes to trust, increased customer loyalty, and the intent to continue the relationship with the salesperson.[67] To help build strong relationships, many firms undertake active CRM programs that identify and focus on building loyalty with the firm's most valued customers.

relationship selling
A sales philosophy and process that emphasizes a commitment to maintaining the relationship over the long term and investing in opportunities that are mutually beneficial to all parties.

Because the sales force interacts directly with customers, its members are in the best position to help a firm accomplish its CRM objectives.

CRM programs have several components. There is a customer database or data warehouse. Whether the salesperson is working for a retail store or managing a selling team for an aerospace contractor, he or she can record transaction information, customer contact information, customer preferences, and market segment information about the customer. Once the data has been analyzed and CRM programs developed, salespeople can help implement the programs. For instance, bankers use a "high-touch approach" in which they frequently call on their best customers or contact them by phone. A salesperson can contact customers when there are new products or changes to existing product lines. He or she can probe customers about what they liked or disliked about their recent transactions with the firm. Or the purpose of the call can be purely social. If done properly, customers will feel special and important when a salesperson calls just to see how things are going.

Salespeople Educate and Provide Advice. Imagine how difficult it would be to buy a new suit, a diamond engagement ring, or a plasma TV without the help of a salesperson. Similarly, UPS wouldn't dream of investing in a new fleet of airplanes without the benefit of Boeing's selling team. Sure, it could be done, but customers see the value in and are willing to pay indirectly for the education and advice salespeople provide. Retail salespeople can provide valuable information about how a garment fits, new fashions, or directions for operating products. Boeing's sales team can provide UPS with the technical aspects of the aircraft, as well as the economic justification for the purchase.

Internet travel services such as Expedia are great for booking relatively simple trips. But when multiple people and multiple destinations are involved, a good travel agent can be worth his or her weight in gold.

Five years ago, many observers thought that travel agents and other service providers would be replaced by more efficient Internet services, and the Internet has certainly changed the way many consumers make travel decisions. Thousands use sites such as Expedia.ca and Travelocity.ca or visit airlines, rail, hotels, and car rental firms online to make reservations directly. But when planning to visit an exotic locale or booking a complicated trip or cruise, or for those who don't feel comfortable buying online, travel agents add significant value. They can help with itineraries, give helpful tips, and even save the customer money.

Salespeople Save Time and Simplify Buying. Time is money! Customers perceive value in time and labour savings. In many grocery and drugstore chains, salespeople employed by the vendor supplying merchandise straighten stock, set up displays, assess inventory levels, and write orders. In some cases, such as with baked goods or soft drinks, salespeople and truck drivers even bring in the merchandise and stock the shelves. These are all tasks that retail employees would otherwise have to do.

Sometimes, however, turning over too many tasks to suppliers' salespeople can cause problems. If they take over the inventory management function, for instance, they may buy a suboptimal quantity of competitors' products. They might also place competitor products in disadvantageous shelf positions. Salespeople can help facilitate a buying situation, but they shouldn't take it over.

THE PERSONAL SELLING PROCESS   LO5

Although selling may appear a rather straightforward process, successful salespeople follow several steps. Depending on the sales situation and the buyer's readiness to purchase, the salesperson may not use every step, and the time required for each step will vary depending on the situation. For instance, if a customer goes into The Bay already prepared to purchase some khaki pants, the selling process will be fairly quick. But if

Dell is attempting to sell personal computers for the first time to a university, the process may take several months. With this in mind, let's examine each step of the selling process (see Exhibit 15.4).

Step 1: Generate and Qualify Leads

leads
A list of potential customers.

qualify
The process of assessing the potential of sales leads.

trade shows
Major events attended by buyers who choose to be exposed to products and services offered by potential suppliers in an industry.

cold calls
A method of prospecting in which salespeople telephone or go to see potential customers without appointments.

telemarketing
A method of prospecting in which salespeople telephone potential customers.

The first step in the selling process is to generate a list of potential customers (**leads**) and assess their potential (**qualify**). Salespeople who already have an established relationship with a customer will skip this step, and it is not used extensively in retail settings. In B2B situations, however, it is important to work continually to find new and potentially profitable customers.

Salespeople generate leads in a variety of ways.[68] They can discover potential leads by talking to their current customers, doing research on the Internet, and networking at events such as industry conferences or chamber of commerce meetings. The Internet has been a boon for generating leads. For instance, salespeople can gather information collected on the firm's website or Google a few keywords and instantly generate enough potential leads to keep them busy for weeks. Another excellent forum for finding leads is **trade shows**, which are major events attended by buyers who choose to be exposed to products and services offered by potential suppliers in an industry. For instance, Meetings + Incentive Travel hosts the IncentiveWorks Show at the Metro Toronto Convention Centre every August. More than 400 exhibit booths, representing more than 700 companies, from a variety of domestic and international destinations; hotels; resorts; meeting/incentive travel services; and business gifts, premium, and reward merchandise exhibit at the show.[69]

Cold calls are a method of prospecting in which salespeople telephone or go to see potential customers without appointments. **Telemarketing** is similar to a cold call, but it always occurs over the telephone. Sometimes professional telemarketing firms, rather than the firm's salespeople, make such calls. However, cold calls and telemarketing have become less popular than they were in the past. First, the success rate is

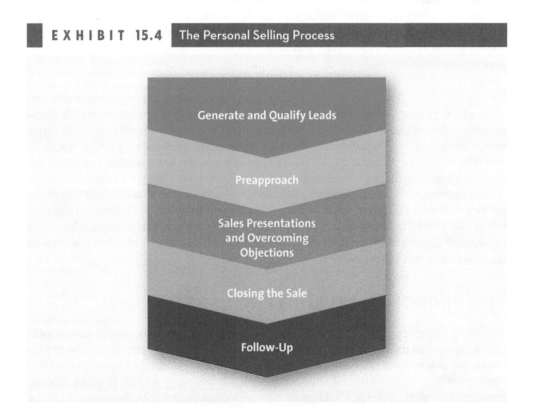

EXHIBIT 15.4   The Personal Selling Process

Generate and Qualify Leads

Preapproach

Sales Presentations and Overcoming Objections

Closing the Sale

Follow-Up

fairly low because the potential customer's need has not been established ahead of time. As a result, these methods can be very expensive. Second, both federal and provincial governments have begun to regulate the activities of telemarketers. Federal rules prohibit telemarketing to consumers whose names appear on the national Do-Not-Call list, which is maintained by the Canadian Marketing Association. The CRTC has levied more than $3.6 million in fines since 2008. Weed Man lawn care franchises were fined $200,000 for calling people whose names were on the list.[70] Even for those consumers whose names are not on the list, the rules prohibit calling before 8:00 a.m. or after 9:00 p.m. (in the consumer's time zone) or after the consumer has told the telemarketer not to call. Federal rules also prohibit unsolicited fax messages and unsolicited telephone calls, as well as email messages to cellphones.

A great place to generate leads is at a trade show.

After salespeople generate leads, they must qualify those leads by determining whether it is worthwhile to pursue them and attempt to turn the leads into customers. In a retail setting, qualifying potential can be a very dangerous and potentially illegal practice. Retail salespeople should never "judge a book by its cover" and assume that a person in the store doesn't fit the store's image or cannot afford to purchase there. Imagine going to an upscale jewellery store to purchase an engagement ring, only to be snubbed because you are dressed in your everyday, casual school clothes. But in B2B settings, where the costs of preparing and making a presentation can be substantial, the seller must assess a lead's potential. Salespeople should consider, for instance, whether the potential customer's needs pertain to a product or a service. They should also assess whether the lead has the financial resources to pay for the product or service.

Retail salespeople should never "judge a book by its cover" and assume that a person in the store doesn't fit the store's image or cannot afford to purchase there.

Step 2: Preapproach

The **preapproach** occurs prior to meeting the customer for the first time and extends the qualification of leads procedure described in Step 1. Although the salesperson has learned about the customer during the qualification stage, in this step, he or she must conduct additional research and develop plans for meeting with the customer. Suppose, for example, a management consulting firm wants to sell a bank a new system for finding chequing account errors. The consulting firm's salesperson should first find out everything possible about the bank: How many cheques does it process? What system is the bank using now? What are the benefits of the consultant's proposed system compared with the competition? The answers to these questions provide the basis for establishing value for the customer.

Having done the additional research, the salesperson establishes goals for meeting with the customer; it is important that he or she know ahead of time exactly what should be accomplished. For instance, the consulting firm's salesperson can't expect to get a commitment from the bank that it will buy on the first visit. But a demonstration of the system and a short presentation about how the system would benefit the customer would be appropriate.

preapproach
In the personal selling process, occurs prior to meeting the customer for the first time and extends the qualification of leads procedure; in this step, the salesperson conducts additional research and develops plans for meeting with the customer.

Step 3: Sales Presentation and Overcoming Objections

The Presentation.   Once all the background information has been obtained and the objectives for the meeting are set, the salesperson is ready for a person-to-person meeting. Let's continue with our bank example. During the first part of the meeting, the salesperson needs to get to know the customer, get his or her attention, and create interest in the presentation to follow. The beginning of the presentation may be the most important part of the entire selling process, because this is when the salesperson establishes exactly where the customer is in his or her buying process (see Exhibit 15.5). (For a refresher on the B2B buying process, see Chapter 5.) Suppose, for instance, the bank is in the first stage of the buying process, need recognition. It would not be prudent for the salesperson to discuss the pros and cons of different potential suppliers because doing so would assume that the customer already had reached Stage 4, proposal analysis and supplier selection. By asking a series of questions, however, the salesperson can assess the bank's need for the product or service and adapt or customize the presentation to match the customer's need and stage in the decision process.[71]

Asking questions is only half the battle; carefully listening to the answers is equally important. Some salespeople, particularly inexperienced ones, believe that to be in control, they must do all the talking. Yet it is impossible to really understand where the customer stands without listening carefully. What if the COO says, "It seems kind of expensive"? If the salesperson isn't listening carefully, he or she won't pick up on the subtle nuances of what the customer is really thinking. In this case, it probably means that the COO doesn't see the value in the offering.

EXHIBIT 15.5   Aligning the Personal Selling Process with the B2B Buying Process

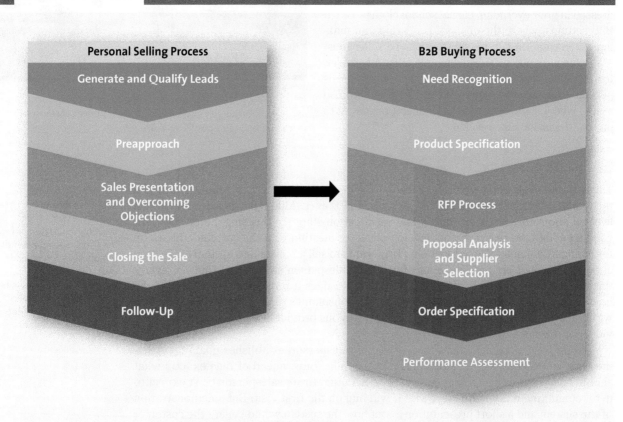

When the salesperson has a good feel for where the customer stands, he or she can apply that knowledge to help the customer solve its problem or satisfy its need. The salesperson might begin by explaining the features or characteristics of the system that will reduce chequing account errors. It may not be obvious, based solely on these features, however, that the system adds value beyond the bank's current practices. Using the answers to some of the questions the customer posed earlier in the meeting, the salesperson can clarify the product's advantages over current or past practices, as well as the overall benefits of adopting the new system. The salesperson might explain, for instance, that the bank can expect a 20 percent decrease in chequing account errors and that, based on the size of the bank and the number of cheques it processes per year, this improvement would represent $2 million in annual savings. Because the system costs $150,000 per year and will take only three weeks to integrate into the current system, it will add significant and almost immediate value.

Handling Objections.

An integral part of the sales presentation is handling objections that the buyer might have about the product or service. Although objections can arise during each stage of the selling process, they are very likely to occur during the sales presentation. Customers may raise objections pertaining to a variety of issues, but they usually relate in some way to value, such as that the price is too high for the level of quality or service.

Good salespeople know the types of objections buyers are likely to raise. They may know, for instance, that their service is slower than competitors' or that their selection is limited. Although not all objections can be forestalled, effective salespeople can anticipate and handle some of them. For example, when the bank COO said the cheque service seemed expensive, the salesperson was ready with information about how quickly the investment would be recouped.

Similar to other aspects of the selling process, the best way to handle objections is to relax and listen, and then to ask questions to clarify any reservations. For example, the salesperson could respond to the COO's objection by asking, "How much do you think the bank is losing through chequing account errors?" Her answer might open up a conversation about the positive trends in a cost/benefit analysis. Such questions are usually more effective than trying to prove the customer's objection is not valid because the latter approach implies the salesperson isn't really listening and could lead to an argument. In an attempt to handle objections and start the process of closing the sale, a salesperson may offer creative deals or incentives that may be unethical.

closing the sale
Obtaining a commitment from the customer to make a purchase.

Step 4: Closing the Sale

Closing the sale means obtaining a commitment from the customer to make a purchase. Without a successful close, the salesperson goes away empty-handed, so many salespeople find this part of the sales process very stressful. Although losing a sale is never pleasant, salespeople who are involved in a relationship with their customers must view any particular sales presentation as part of the progression toward ultimately making the sale. An unsuccessful close on one day may just be a means of laying the groundwork for a successful close the next meeting.

Although we have presented the selling process in a series of steps, closing the sale rarely follows the other steps so neatly. However, good salespeople listen carefully to what potential customers say and pay attention to their body language. Reading these signals carefully can help salespeople achieve an early close. Suppose that our hypothetical bank, rather than being in the first step of the

Good salespeople, particularly in difficult selling situations such as door-to-door sales, don't easily take no for an answer. They keep coming back until they get a yes.

buying process, was in the final step of negotiation and selection. An astute salesperson will pick up on these signals and ask for the sale.

Step 5: Follow-Up

With relationship selling, the sale is never really over, even after it has been made. The attitudes customers develop after the sale become the basis for how they will purchase in the future. The follow-up therefore offers a prime opportunity for a salesperson to solidify the customer relationship through great service quality. Let's apply the five service quality dimensions we discussed in Chapter 10 to the follow-up:[72]

- *Reliability.* The salesperson and the supporting organization must deliver the right product or service on time.

- *Responsiveness.* The salesperson and support group must be ready to deal quickly with any issue, question, or problem that may arise.

- *Assurance.* Customers must be assured through adequate guarantees that their purchase will perform as expected.

REAL MARKETER PROFILE   Arlene Dickinson

Advertising and sales promotion is all about persuasion. According to Arlene Dickinson, CEO of Venture Communications and author of *Persuasion*, in business and in life it's important to be honest and authentic and to understand that *"persuasion doesn't involve tricks, coercion, or shading the truth."*[73]

Born in South Africa, Dickinson emigrated to Canada when she was only three years old. She did well academically and finished high school early at age 16. Although her father wanted her to attend university, having grown up in a strict Mormon household Arlene's goal was to get married and have children. She married at 19 and had four children in quick succession. When the marriage fell apart, she worked at almost every job imaginable. Her sales experience led to an offer to join Venture Communications in 1988, working without pay for two years. Ten years later, she bought the company.

Since then, she has grown the business from a small local firm based in Calgary to one of the largest independent marketing firms in Canada.[74] Clients include organizations such as Cenovus and Toyota. An out of home campaign for Travel Alberta aimed to make the province the number-one choice for Ontario skiers. Tactics included station domination at Toronto's Union Station and resulted in traffic to the Travel Alberta website increasing by over 150 percent.[75]

Dickinson is also the CEO of Arlene Dickinson Enterprises (ADE) and YouInc.com, companies she launched in late 2012 that work to invest in, serve, and support entrepreneurs. She is working on a second book based on interviews with successful Canadian entrepreneurs as well.[76]

From single mom living in poverty to self-made millionaire, Dickinson is a Canadian success story. Although she has won numerous awards and been ranked as one of PROFIT Magazine's Top 100 Women Entrepreneurs many years in a row, Dickinson is quick to admit that she's made mistakes. "Go out there and try. Don't be afraid to make mistakes. You never know what's around the corner if you just put yourself out there."[77] Looking back, she says one of her marketing blunders was passing up on the opportunity to work with a snowboard company. She thought snowboards were just a fad and wouldn't last. The experience taught her to pay attention to trends and to bear in mind that just because she didn't like something didn't mean others would feel the same.[78]

Today Dickinson is perhaps best known for her role as one of the venture capitalists on CBC television series *Dragons' Den* and *The Big Decision*. Companies that pitch on the shows are often looking for just the kind of marketing expertise Arlene Dickinson brings to deals.

- *Empathy.* The salesperson and support group must have a good understanding of the problems and issues faced by their customers. Otherwise, they cannot give them what they want.

- *Tangibles.* Because tangibles reflect the physical characteristics of the seller's business, such as its website, marketing communications, and delivery materials, their influence is more subtle than that of the other four service quality dimensions. That doesn't mean it is any less important. Retail customers are generally more pleased with a purchase if it is carefully wrapped in nice paper instead of being haphazardly thrown into a crumpled plastic bag. The tangibles offer a signal that the product is of high quality, even though the packaging has nothing to do with the product's actual performance.

When customers' expectations are not met, they often complain—about deliveries, the billing amount or process, the product's performance, or after-sale services such as installation or training. Effectively handling complaints is critical to the future of the relationship. As we noted in Chapter 10, the best way to handle complaints is to listen to the customer, provide a fair solution to the problem, and resolve the problem quickly.

The best way to nip a postsale problem in the bud is to check with the customer right after he or she takes possession of the product or immediately after the service has been completed. This speed demonstrates responsiveness and empathy; it also shows the customer that the salesperson and the firm care about customer satisfaction. Finally, a postsale follow-up call, email, or letter takes the salesperson back to the first step in the sales process for initiating a new order and sustaining the relationship.

Personal selling is an integral component of some firms' IMC strategy. Although it doesn't make sense for all firms, it is widely used in B2B markets, as well as in B2C markets in which the price of the merchandise is relatively high and customers need some one-to-one assistance before they can buy. Because of the relatively high expense of maintaining a personal selling force, it is important that salespeople be adequately trained, motivated, and compensated.

LEARNING OBJECTIVES REVIEW

  Describe advertising and three objectives of advertising

Advertising is a paid form of communication from an identifiable source, delivered through a communication channel, that is designed to persuade consumers to take action. All advertising campaigns are designed to either inform, persuade, or remind customers. Ads can also be used to stimulate demand for a particular category or industry, or for a specific brand, firm, or item.

  Summarize the regulatory and ethical issues of concern to advertisers

Advertising is regulated by a plethora of federal and provincial agencies. The most important agencies are the Competition Bureau, which protects consumers against general deceptive advertising; the Canadian Radio-television and Telecommunications Commission, which has jurisdiction over radio, television, wire, satellite, and cable, and covers issues regarding the use of tobacco products; and Health Canada, whose Food and Drug Act regulates food, drugs, cosmetics, and medical devices. Advertising Standards Canada maintains a strict broadcast code regarding advertising to children.

If a message is designed to promote or sell a product or service, it is generally considered to have an economic motivation, but if the message has no promotional or selling intent, it is fully protected by the Charter of Rights and Freedoms. The line becomes blurred, however, when normally noncommercial venues are used to sell something. Another practice that is causing a stir emerges when the sender of a commercial message is not clearly identified. Activities such as bogus websites or certain stealth marketing programs, in which the identity of the sponsor of an activity or event is intentionally kept from prospective customers, can be considered deceptive promotional practices.

L03 **Explain how sales promotions supplement a firm's IMC strategy**

Sales promotions are special incentives or excitement-building programs that encourage purchase and include coupons, rebates, contests, free samples, and POP displays. They either push sales through the channel, as is the case with contests directed toward retail salespeople, or pull sales through the channel, as coupons and rebates do. Sales promotions usually occur in conjunction with other elements of a firm's IMC strategy, such as price promotions or loyalty programs. Trade channel sales promotions include discounts and allowances, co-op advertising, and sales force training.

L04 **Describe personal selling and how it adds value for customers**

Personal selling is the two-way flow of communication between a buyer and a seller and can take place in a variety of situations. Although the cost of an average B2B sales call is considerable (about $400), many firms believe they couldn't do business without their sales force. Customers can buy many products and services without the help of a salesperson, but in many other cases, it is worth the extra cost built into the price of a product to be educated about the product or to get valuable advice. Salespeople can also simplify the buying process and therefore save the customer time and hassle.

L05 **Identify the steps in the personal selling process**

Although we discuss selling in terms of steps, it truly represents a process, and the time spent in each step varies according to the situation. In the first step, the salesperson generates a list of viable customers. During the second step, the preapproach, the salesperson gathers information about the customer and prepares for the presentation. The third step, the sales presentation, consists of a personal meeting between the salesperson and the customer. Through discussion and by asking questions, the salesperson learns where the customer is in the buying process and tailors the discussion around what the firm's product or service can do to meet that customer's needs. During the fourth step, closing the sale, the salesperson asks for the order. Finally, during the follow-up, the salesperson and support staff solidify a long-term relationship by making sure the customer is satisfied with the purchase and by addressing any complaints. The follow-up therefore sets the stage for the next purchase.

KEY TERMS

- AIDA model
- aided recall
- closing the sale
- cold calls
- contest
- cross-promoting
- deal
- informative advertising
- institutional advertisements
- lagged effect

- leads
- loyalty program
- persuasive advertising
- point-of-purchase (POP) display
- pop-up stores
- preapproach
- premium
- product placement
- product-focused advertisements
- public service announcement (PSA)

- puffery
- qualify
- relationship selling
- reminder advertising
- sampling
- social marketing
- sweepstakes
- telemarketing
- top-of-mind awareness
- trade shows

CONCEPT REVIEW

1. What is advertising?

2. What is the AIDA model? How does the AIDA model facilitate the planning and execution of marketing communications?

3. What are the three primary objectives of advertising?

4. List and explain some of the potential regulatory and ethical issues firms should consider when developing their marketing communications strategy.

5. What is sales promotion? What are the main objectives of sales promotion?

6. List six different kinds of consumer sales promotion tactics and discuss the advantages and disadvantages of each.

7. Describe the different kinds of sales promotions targeted to distribution channel members. Why are these trade channel promotions necessary? Are they ethical?

8. What is personal selling? Describe the steps in the personal selling process. Which stage do you consider to be the most important and why?

9. What is sales management? Why is sales management considered a complicated task?

10. What are the main considerations involved in recruiting, training, and compensating salespeople?

MARKETING APPLICATIONS

1. Choose one of the ads featured in this book and note its page number. What are the objectives of this ad? Does the ad have more than one objective? Explain your answer.

2. Using the steps in the AIDA model, explain why a potential consumer who views advertising by designer jean company Parasuco may not be ready to go out and purchase a new pair of jeans.

3. Suppose Lexus is introducing a new line of light trucks and has already created the advertising campaign. How would you assess the effectiveness of the campaign?

4. Suppose now Lexus is planning a sales promotion campaign to augment its advertising campaign for the new line of light trucks. Which sales promotion tools do you believe would be the most effective? Why?

5. How would the Lexus sales promotion differ if it was geared to a business organization with a fleet of company-owned trucks?

6. Choose an ad that you believe unreasonably overstates what the product or service can do. (If you can't think of a real ad, make up one.) Explain whether the ad is actually deceptive or just puffery. How would your answer change if you lived in France?

7. You are invited to your six-year-old niece's birthday party and bring her the new superhero doll being advertised on TV. She's thrilled when she unwraps the gift but is in tears a short time later because her new doll is broken. She explains that, on TV, the doll flies and does karate kicks, but when she tried to play with the doll this way, it broke. You decide to call the manufacturer, and a representative tells you he is sorry your niece is so upset but that the ad clearly states the doll does not fly. The next time you see the televised ad, you notice very small print at the bottom of the screen that states the doll does not fly. You decide to write a letter to Advertising Standards Canada about this practice. What information should you include in your letter?

8. "Salespeople just make products cost more." Agree or disagree with this statement and discuss why you've taken that position.

9. Choose an industry or a specific company that you would like to work for as a salesperson. How would you generate and qualify leads?

10. You have taken a summer job in the windows and doors department of a large home improvement store. During sales training, you learn about the products, how to best address customers' needs, why the lifetime value of the customer concept is so important to a store like this, and how to sell customers the best product to fit their needs regardless of price point. One day your manager informs you that you are to recommend Smith Windows to every window customer. Smith Windows are more expensive than other brands and don't really provide superior benefit except in limited circumstances. The manager is insistent that you recommend Smith Windows. Not knowing what else to do, you recommend Smith Windows to customers who would have been better served by lower-cost windows. The manager rewards you with a sales award. Later, the manager tells you that he received an all-expenses-paid cruise for his family from Smith Windows. What, if anything, should you do with this information?

TOOLKIT

MAKE AN ADVERTISEMENT

Suppose you have been hired to develop a new ad for a product or service to help target the college and university student market. These ads will appear in student newspapers around the world. Use the toolkit provided on Connect to develop the ad.

NET SAVVY

1. Go to the website for Companies Committed to Kids (http://cck-eee.ca), an agency that produces and delivers social messaging campaigns on issues of challenge in children's lives. Click on the About tab and examine the history and activities of the organization. How does the role it plays in responsible advertising complement the formal regulation of other agencies? Now look under the Public Service Announcements tab. Choose one of the PSAs and discuss how these ads are used to deliver CCK's message.

2. Go to https://www.smartsource.ca and identify five of the products featured. How effective are coupons for selling these products? Why? What are the benefits to the seller of using SmartSource.ca over other IMC options? How do you think SmartSource.ca makes money?

CHAPTER CASE STUDY

MAKING MASTERCARD PRICELESS

How do you pay for books, clothing, groceries, or travel? For many consumers, the answer is MasterCard, which has 203 million cards in circulation.[79] Yet despite the credit card's popularity, it lags behind its major competitor, Visa, by nearly 100 million cards. It is also outstripped by American Express for both monthly and annual purchases and spending volume. Because MasterCard's primary function is to process transactions between each customer's bank and each merchant's bank, the company must appeal to two customer bases to build market share: the merchants who accept MasterCard for payment and the purchasers who use the card. These audiences are closely related, which implies that a single campaign can target both, likely even for an extended period.

In 1997, MasterCard International and the advertising agency McCann Erickson Worldwide launched the emotion-based "Priceless" campaign, which celebrated life's most precious moments with the tagline, "There are some things money can't buy. For everything else, there's MasterCard."[80] The campaign was hugely successful, saving MasterCard from disaster, even in direct competition with the more widely accepted Visa card. Let's look at how MasterCard evolved to where it is today.

Expanding Services to Meet Market Demand

In 1966, a group of California banks created a member-owned association called the Interbank Card Association. This association grew its services, changing its name to MasterCard in 1979 to reflect a commitment to international growth.[81] As it reached new markets across the globe, MasterCard also focused on technology innovation to help make economic transactions faster, more convenient, and more secure. The company acquired interest in the international credit card EuroCard (known today as Europay International), as well as Cirrus, a worldwide interbank network that links MasterCard, Maestro, and Diner's Club credit, debit, and prepaid cards to an international network of ATMs. The company also added fraud/risk management providers to its network of services.

Today MasterCard's technology platform can handle more than 160 million transactions every hour with a 99.9 percent reliability rate,[82] and the company has issued a contactless, or smart, card that communicates with terminals via radio waves. This payment method does not require a signature and can be a card or key fob that is tapped rather than swiped; it also appears as a smartphone app. To provide even more value to customers, the company has added sophisticated consulting and information services that help merchants gain insight into consumer spending, according to their transaction data and in-depth analyses.[83] These efforts have dovetailed with changes in consumer behaviour as shoppers have begun relying more on electronic payment options and less on paper-based currency. In 2006, the company transitioned to a new corporate governance and ownership structure and began trading on the New York Stock Exchange.

Priceless Revisited

MasterCard began its Priceless campaign by identifying its target audience, which in this case focused on consumers. Hoping to persuade shoppers to keep their MasterCard at the top of their wallets, the campaign stressed the relationship between the card and experiences, as opposed to possessions. In early television ads, the narration linked the price of beauty parlor visits and new outfits to the "priceless" expression on an ex-boyfriend's face at a reunion, to create positive self-assessment feelings.[84] In another, the cost of tickets, refreshments, and souvenirs at a game were tied to the "priceless" opportunity for meaningful conversation between father and son, to invoke both happiness and love.[85] The Priceless campaign included various promotions and competitions, in addition to these television spots.

In 2004, Priceless print ads took a new tack, weaving well-known retailers into the ads, together with MasterCard's theme. These retailers—which represented another of MasterCard's target audiences—received value from the prominent placement of their names and product images in the ads. Messaging moved from the general to the specific; an ad showing a teenage rock band playing in a garage that might once have said, "extra-long extension cord, $11; moving them out of the living room: priceless," was modified to indicate that the extension cord was from Radio Shack. The result was a form of symbiotic marketing in which well-known brand names helped attract consumer attention to MasterCard ads, and each brand appeared to be endorsing the other.[86]

Magic Moments, Priceless Cities

However, even the most successful campaigns can grow stale. As consumer values and needs changed and the marketplace evolved, MasterCard faced a new challenge: how to retain customer loyalty and brand identification while reinvigorating its advertising. The solution was the "Priceless Cities" campaign, an expanded campaign launched in July 2011. The campaign kicked off initially in New York, offering cardholders special experiences in major cities that can be shared with family and friends.[87] A few months later, the campaign made its debut in Toronto, where MasterCard piqued the interest of consumers by placing a huge vault in Maple Leaf Square. Messaging invited Torontonians to discover what was inside the vault and their city, and tweet about it using #unlockTO.[88] Designed to provide busy consumers with memorable opportunities in the realms of sports, music, entertainment, shopping, travel, arts, culture, and dining out, the campaign offers exclusive discounts and experiences for MasterCard holders. Current promotions include $10 off the CN Tower EdgeWalk, $50 off Porter Airlines flights, and 20 percent off Ontario Science Centre admission.[89] The idea, says MasterCard's chief marketing officer, is to transform consumers' perception of the card from simply part of a priceless moment to being the force that enables such experiences. In a shaky economy, when most competitors focus on deals and discounts, the MasterCard campaign attracts attention by appealing to emotions rather than wallets and stressing unforgettable experiences rather than cost savings. The campaign forges an additional bond with card users, because it places MasterCard at the centre of these memorable social activities.

The ads run in more than 100 countries and air in more than 50 languages and the overall campaign uses print, radio, transit, outdoor advertising, and television. It also includes digital platforms to drive home its message, including a new section of the MasterCard website created specifically for the campaign, as well as social media channels such as Facebook and Twitter. Cardholders register at the site to access special offers; World Elite MasterCard holders get preferred access to the events, as well as special offers.

Marketers must continuously evaluate their campaigns and update them to ensure they are effectively communicating with their customers. New channels like social marketing can change shopping behaviours, creating opportunities that must be considered as part of any marketing strategy. As MasterCard has shown, even the best ideas need new infusions and innovations to keep appealing to their targets.

Questions

1. Why was the original Priceless campaign such a success?

2. Why has MasterCard started to use "Priceless" more actively in its messaging?

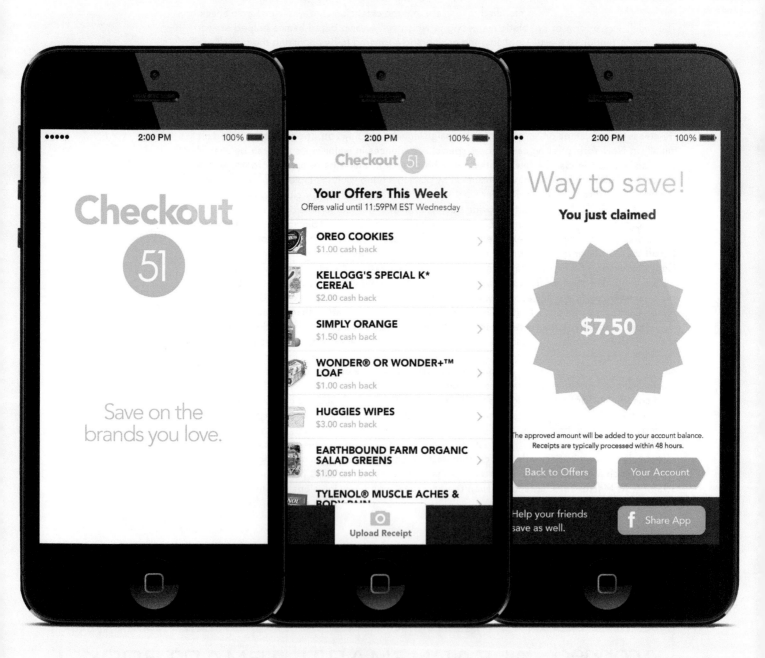

CHAPTER 16

Social and Mobile Marketing

Have you ever stopped to consider the power of a grocery store receipt? It contains a list of products purchased, how much was spent, the prices paid for each item, and more—data critical to marketers for understanding shopping behaviour. The founders of Checkout 51 (CO51) came to this realization while brainstorming their next big venture in a Toronto-area café in 2011.

Using CO51 is simple: download the mobile app that showcases new coupon offers each week. When you make a qualifying purchase at any Canadian retailer, simply use your mobile phone to snap a picture of your receipt and upload it. Each time you redeem a coupon offered, your account balance grows until you request payout. You not only get real dollars refunded, but also don't have to fumble with clippings at the register or deal with the stares of impatient customers behind you. And having CO51 on your smartphone allows you to have the coupons in-store with you while you shop.

It's appealing for marketers too, because the app's digital nature gives them complete control. They can design a coupon offer for a budget of any level, and instantly end the offer as soon as the budget is spent. The app can also target groups of consumers based on demographics or previous purchasing behaviour. The summary report at the end of the offer can show marketers who was redeeming the offers, when, and where. This data is then used to gain insights about shopping behaviour or to target different users the next time. The app also virtually eliminates coupon fraud since the CO51 team can limit redemption by receipt submitted by mobile phone.

Coming up with the idea behind the CO51 app was easy. To prove it would work, the team recruited a dozen couponing mothers and asked them to test the concept. After showing great promise with a basic model, they expanded to 1,000 locals to continue the testing. With encouraging results and savings over $10,000 for the participants,[1] the Checkout 51 team knew they were on to something.

Once they built the receipt-reading technology and back-end database that recognized every product at every store in Canada, the team established the

LEARNING OBJECTIVES

After studying this chapter you should be able to

LO1 Describe the 4E framework of social media marketing.

LO2 Understand the types of social media.

LO3 Understand the types of mobile applications.

LO4 Recognize and understand the three components of a social media strategy.

LO5 Understand the methods for marketing yourself using social media.

first coupon offers and created the user interface that consumers would see. CO51 was formally launched in December 2012. The crew leveraged strong PR to encourage app downloads. Just two weeks after launch it was the number one lifestyle app in Canada. The team continued to drive the value proposition through extremely targeted Facebook and Google advertising and in-game ads. Less than one year later, over 500,000 Canadians were using it, making CO51 the leading mobile coupon app.

Enrollment numbers like this made it possible to attract major corporate interest from Kraft, Unilever, Kellogg's, VISA and others, without a single outbound sales call. Creating true value for marketers and combining that with media agency partnerships and word-of-mouth promotion resulted in calls from nearly all major packaged-goods companies, which wanted to work with CO51.

Such rapid success caught the attention of investors, too. In 2013, the company raised over $9 million in capital, allowing an expansion into a desktop version of the tool to attract users beyond mobile, and also enable a platform launch into the United States, expanding the company's potential target audience. By early 2014, CO51 had grown much faster than expected with 700,000 Canadian and 1.25 million US subscribers.[2]

In the end, everyone is happy: consumers have a new and convenient way to save money, manufacturers can build a direct relationship with their shoppers and access valuable consumer data, and retailers can expedite register times and watch basket sizes grow.[3] ∎

LO1   # THE 4E FRAMEWORK FOR SOCIAL MEDIA

As we have seen throughout the book, social media has become an integral component of any integrated marketing communications strategy. The term *social media* refers to content distributed through online and mobile technologies to facilitate interpersonal interactions. These media utilize various firms that offer services or tools to help consumers and firms build connections. Through these connections, marketers and customers share information of all forms—from their thoughts about products or images to uploaded pictures, music, and videos.

The diffusion of technology used to bring us social media has been accelerating since the Internet came on the scene in the mid- to late-1990s, as depicted in Exhibit 16.1. The ideas were exciting, but ultimately, there was little to engage people. After the turn of the 20th century, social media got more serious and professional. Sites recognized that they had to offer surfers something exciting, educational, or experiential if they were to keep them coming back. Today, we have entered the entrepreneurial era, in which companies work to find ways to earn profits from the ways that consumers use and enjoy social media.

The changes and advances in social, mobile, and online technologies have created a perfect storm, forcing firms to change how they communicate with their customers. Traditional ways to market their products, using brick-and-mortar stores, traditional mass media (e.g., print, television, radio), and other sales promotional vehicles (e.g., mail,

EXHIBIT 16.1 Technology Evolution over the Life of the Social Web

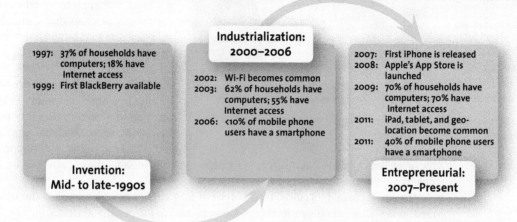

Source: Adapted from: Coca-Cola Retailing Research Council and the Integer Group, "Assessing the Social Networking Landscape," in *Untangling the Social Web: Insights for Users, Brands, and Retailers,* January 2012.

telemarketing) are insufficient for many firms. The presence of social, mobile, and online marketing is steadily expanding relative to these more traditional forms of integrated marketing communication (IMC).

The changing role of traditional media, sales promotions, and retail, coupled with the new media of social, mobile, and online, has led to a different way of thinking about the objectives of marketing communications using the 4E framework (see Exhibit 16.2):

- Excite customers with relevant offers.
- Educate them about the offering.
- Help them Experience products, whether directly or indirectly.
- Give them an opportunity to Engage with their social network.

Excite the Customer

Marketers use many kinds of social media–related offers to excite customers, including mobile applications and games to get customers excited about an idea, product, brand, or company. Firms actively use social networks like Facebook and Google+ to communicate

EXHIBIT 16.2 The 4E Framework for Social Media

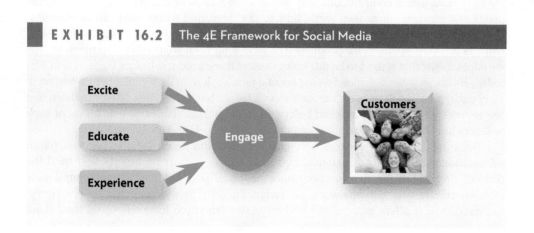

Staples excites its customers by giving them instant rewards through their mobile phones while they are in the store.

deals that are likely to excite consumers, such as a Groupon price promotion that is communicated through the social networks of already interested consumers.

To excite customers, an offer must be relevant to its targeted customer. Relevancy can be achieved by providing personalized offers, which are determined through insights and information obtained from customer relationship management and/or loyalty programs. To obtain these insights and information, the firm might use online analytic tools such as Google analytics or a listening system such as those provided by Radian6, described later in this chapter.

In some cases location-based software and applications help bring the offer to the customers when they are in the process of making a purchase decision. For instance, Staples may provide a loyal customer a relevant coupon based on previous purchases through his or her mobile phone, while he or she is in the store—a very relevant and, it is hoped, exciting experience.

Educate the Customer

An imperative of well-designed social media marketing offers is that they have a clear call to action: To draw customers through their computers, tablets, and mobile devices into online websites or traditional retail stores. When potential customers arrive at the websites or stores, the marketer has a golden opportunity to educate them about its value proposition and communicate the offered benefits. Some of this information may be new, but in some cases, education is all about reminding people about what they already know. Therefore, by engaging in appropriate education, marketers are expanding the overlap of the benefits that they provide with the benefits that customers require. In this sense, the second E of the 4E framework constitutes a method to develop a sustainable competitive advantage.

Several social media tools are critical in helping marketers educate their potential customers, such as blogs and blogging tools (e.g., WordPress and Twitter), HubSpot (all-in-one marketing software), YouTube and Google+, as well as some lesser-known options, such as Roost or Schedulicity.

Experience the Product or Service

Although most of the top videos on YouTube are funny, silly, or otherwise entertaining, the site's most useful contributions may be the vivid information it provides about a firm's goods and services—how they work, how to use them, and where they can be obtained. YouTube and similar sites can come relatively close to simulating real experiences. Such benefits are very common for products that have long been sold online—so much so that we might forget that it used to be difficult to assess these products before buying them. But today, consumers can download a chapter of a new book onto their tablet before buying it. They can try out a software option for a month before buying it. They often can listen to a few seconds or even an entire song before purchasing from iTunes. The diffusion of such products has expanded to feature a wealth of new channels and media options.

For other offerings, such as services, social media again offer experience-based information that was not previously available unless consumers bought and tried the product or service. Need help choosing a new nail polish colour or applying a new makeup trend? Check blogs such as Temptalia (http://www.temptalia.com/category/tutorials), which offers both advice and tutorials. Relied too long on clip-on ties? Head over to Tie-a-Tie (http://www.tie-a-tie.net) to find pictures, videos, and step-by-step instructions on how to manage a Windsor, Pratt, or bowtie knot, as well as advice on what to wear to an interview.

Home Depot has long been a source for do-it-yourselfers (DIYers). But if eager customers forget what the salesclerk said about installing a newly purchased water heater, they can check the retailer's website (http://www6.homedepot.com/how-to/index.html) to get detailed, in-depth instructions. They also will find a section that enables them to chat with other users who might have run into similar problems in their own installation projects.

Nikon's Digital Learning Centre (see http://www.flickr.com/groups/nikondigital learningcenter; http://www.flickr.com/Nikon) provides Flickr members with "tutorials, practical photography tips and advice from Nikon photo professionals to assist them in taking the photos they've always dreamed of capturing."[4] Beyond just providing static photography tips that could be found in a book, Nikon created a two-way dialogue with customers, inviting professional photographers to provide instruction and host question-and-answer sessions, and encouraging users to post their own photos. The more than 64,000 members of the learning centre thus learn from others' experiences, even as they create their own.

Engage the Customer

In a sense, the first three Es set the stage for the last one: engaging the customer. With engagement comes action, the potential for a relationship, and possibly even loyalty and commitment. Through social media tools such as blogging and microblogging, customers actively engage with firms and their own social networks. Such engagement can be negative or positive. Positively engaged consumers tend to be more profitable consumers, purchasing 20 to 40 percent more than less engaged customers.[5]

On the other hand, Dave Carroll, a travelling musician whose guitar was roughly handled by United baggage handlers, was also closely engaged (in a negative manner) with the company and other users. He spent considerable time and effort to release three songs and their videos, just to convince others that they should not fly United.

But that story also offers an example of positive engagement. Carroll's music, face, and story gained international recognition as an example of how just one social media user could have a huge negative influence on a giant company. To leverage this fame, Carroll established a website and blog, where he talks about his experiences. His book offers automatic links to copies of his famous United songs with every purchase. In this sense, Carroll is trying to move beyond the excitement and education he initially elicited from other consumers. Now he wants to engage those same people as consumers—of his book.

Next let's look at the role of various social media tools in shaping the 4E framework for social media.

CATEGORIES OF SOCIAL MEDIA   **L02**

Consider your own Facebook account. Are all your real-life friends your online friends too? Do you actually know all your Facebook friends? In all likelihood, you have online friends you've never met, and your circle of virtual friends may be larger than the number of people you see regularly or talk to personally. Accordingly, the audience for marketers is bigger on social media sites than through other, more traditional forms of media. Such a huge potential audience has captured the attention of marketers. Spending on social media continues to rise. Canadian marketers spent $257 million on paid social advertising in 2013, an increase of 35 percent over the previous year.[6]

Marketers rely on the three types of social media: social network sites, media-sharing sites, and thought-sharing sites (or blogs) (see Exhibit 16.3) to achieve three objectives.

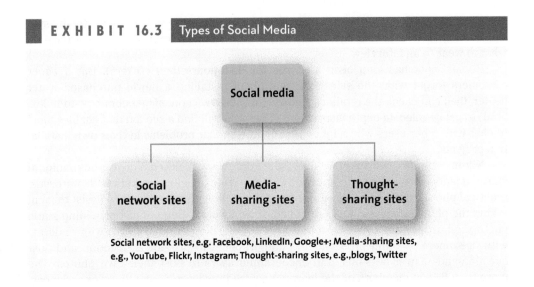

EXHIBIT 16.3 Types of Social Media

Social network sites, e.g. Facebook, LinkedIn, Google+; Media-sharing sites, e.g., YouTube, Flickr, Instagram; Thought-sharing sites, e.g.,blogs, Twitter

First, members promote themselves to gain more friends. Second, the sites promote to get more members. Third, outside companies promote their products and services to appeal to the potential consumers that are active on the sites.

Social Network Sites

Social network sites are an excellent way for marketers to create excitement, the first of the 4 Es. People can interact with friends (e.g., Facebook) or business acquaintances (e.g., LinkedIn). Although the amount of time people spend on such sites varies, research indicates that they are widely used.[7] Specifically, Exhibit 16.4 shows how much social networks are used by different types of consumers based on their motivations and habits. Note that the vast majority of people in this study use social network sites between one and four hours every day!

- Creators, those hip, cool contributors, sit at the cutting edge and plan to stay there. Social media give them new ways to post and share their creative, clever ideas.

- Bonders are social butterflies who use social media to enhance and expand their relationships, which they consider all-important in their lives.

- Professionals, who are constantly on the go and busy, want to appear efficient, with everything together, so they use social media to demonstrate just how smart they are.

- Sharers really want to help others, and the best way to do so is by being constantly well informed so that they can provide genuine insights to others.

All four segments use various types of social networking, as the following sections detail.

Facebook On this well-known social network platform, more than 1.1 billion active users give companies a forum for interacting with their fans. In Canada, over 19 million people log on to Facebook at least once a month and 14 million people check their account daily. Of these users, 9.4 million use a phone or tablet to access their accounts.[8] In fact, Canadians have higher daily Facebook usage at 74 percent than the global daily average of 61 percent. This fact not only lets individual users connect with others but also gives marketers the ability to carefully target their audience.

Companies have access to the same features that regular users do, including a "wall" where they can post company updates, photos, and videos or participate in a discussion board. Through this form of free exposure, the company can post content and information regarding products, events, news, or promotions that might be exciting to

EXHIBIT 16.4 Length of Time Using Social Networking Sites Daily

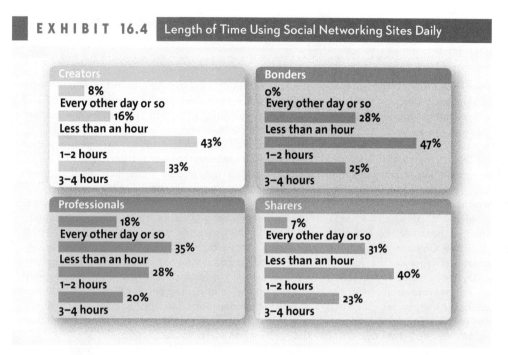

Creators
- 8% — Every other day or so
- 16% — Less than an hour
- 43% — 1–2 hours
- 33% — 3–4 hours

Bonders
- 0% — Every other day or so
- 28% — Less than an hour
- 47% — 1–2 hours
- 25% — 3–4 hours

Professionals
- 18% — Every other day or so
- 35% — Less than an hour
- 28% — 1–2 hours
- 20% — 3–4 hours

Sharers
- 7% — Every other day or so
- 31% — Less than an hour
- 40% — 1–2 hours
- 23% — 3–4 hours

Source: Coca-Cola Retailing Research Council and the Integer Group, "Social Networking Personas: A Look at Consumer and Shopper Mind Sets," in *Untangling the Social Web: Insights for Users, Brands, and Retailers,* March 2012

their customers. Only the fans of their page generally have access to such information, so the company can specifically target its fans. Successful companies on Facebook attempt to excite their customers regularly. FedEx used its fan page to promote its status as official transporter of Chinese pandas as seen in Social and Mobile Marketing 16.1. When a fan indicates that he or she "likes" a certain post, for example on the fan page for the discount clothing retailer Forever 21,[9] the message gets relayed to a news feed. Then every friend of that user sees what he or she likes, creating an exciting and huge multiplier effect.[10] Imagine the multiplier effect for Coca-Cola with over 71 million followers on its fan page!

More than 71 million people like Coca-Cola on Facebook.

Social and Mobile Marketing 16.1

Toronto Zoo and FedEx Cause "Pandamonium"

Facebook and Twitter are very powerful tools. In addition to being ideal for sharing updates, news, and opinions, their ability to measure, count, and categorize Likes and tweets help to monitor popular news stories and track growing trends. Adding a hash tag to words in a tweet enables searching and tracking. In the past, this feature helped the Toronto Zoo spread important messages about the environment using polar bears to help educate consumers about global warming.

Following the success of the polar bear campaign, social media was used again to promote the arrival of two giant pandas loaned by the Chinese government. The loan is part of a program that will allow the Toronto Zoo to contribute to research efforts aimed at protecting this endangered species.[11] To generate excitement, the zoo created a Twitter account for the pandas, @Toronto ZooPanda, and tweeted out regular updates. Some messages were educational, informing consumers that there

are fewer than 250 captive pandas in the world.[12] Others included a countdown until the exhibit opened and humorous messages supposedly written by the pandas, Er Shun and Da Mao.

As the official transportation services provider responsible for moving the pandas from China to Toronto, FedEx tweeted out photos from its @FedExCanada account that showed Er Shun and Da Mao receiving VIP treatment and eating fresh bamboo en route to Toronto. The company changed its Facebook page to capitalize on the publicity generated by this very special delivery. It also ran a contest on Facebook offering 5 pairs of tickets to the Toronto Zoo or one of 10 FedEx plush pandas.[13]

Social media efforts by the zoo continue to keep the exhibit top of mind for consumers. And when FedEx moves the pandas to the Calgary Zoo after their five-year stay in Toronto, fans will undoubtedly continue to follow their journey on social media platforms.

FedEx changed its Facebook page to reflect the fact that the company was the official transportation services provider of the giant pandas.

In an attempt to extend the viral reach of posts, Facebook added the use of hashtags in late 2013. However, early studies show that hashtags actually reduce reach and engagement.[14] Trending topics were added in 2014 in an attempt to turn Facebook into more of a news discovery platform. Facebook is testing video ads as well.

A controversy occurred when Burger King launched a Facebook campaign in which customers could earn a free Whopper if they defriended 10 friends. The so-called "Whopper Sacrifice" was intended to show what someone would give up for a Whopper, and the campaign attracted the participation of more than 200,000 active users. After a "Whopper Sacrifice," the ex-friends received notification, which was also published on the Facebook "mini-feed" and thus helped spread the word even more quickly. As the campaign caught on though, Facebook disabled it. The Facebook page for Burger King read: "Facebook has disabled Whopper Sacrifice after your love for the Whopper sandwich proved to be stronger than 233,906 friendships." Burger King created a notable form of excitement—despite being shut down quickly.[15]

Display advertising with Facebook ads targets specific groups of people, according to their profile information, browsing histories, and other preferences. If online users reveal an interest in ski equipment or Burton snowboards, marketers can target both groups. Thus, Facebook offers a variation on more traditional forms of promotion, with the promise of more accurate targeting and segmentation. But being effective and relevant on Facebook is not simply a matter of shifting an offline ad into social network sites.

LinkedIn   A professional, instead of casual or friendship-based site, LinkedIn allows users to share their professional lives. With more than 300 million users, it is a place where users can post their résumés, network with other professionals, and search for jobs.[16] It is not the place where you will see games such as Mafia Wars or FarmVille; instead, users post to question-and-answer forums, do job searches, and post personal intellectual property, such as presentations they have given.

The professional networking benefits of LinkedIn are particularly beneficial for small business owners. More than 12 million of LinkedIn's users are small business owners, making it an excellent resource for entrepreneurs to network with like-minded firms, identify the best vendors, or build brand reputation by participating in LinkedIn's professional association groups. With more than 150,000 company profiles on LinkedIn, it also offers a great place to prospect for new business customers, and keep an eye on and get key information about competitors.[17]

Google+   The launch of Google+ represents an attempt to compete with the excitement of Facebook. Its effect on social media and gaming communities was nearly immediate. Within six weeks of its launch, Google+ had added 16 games to its lineup, including Angry Birds and Zynga Poker. The goal was to excite users who love to play, especially games that let them interact with one another—the people who made such a massive success out of Facebook's FarmVille game.[18] If Google+ can attract players effectively, it hopes they never go back to Facebook. With this tactic, Google+ attracted more than 20 million unique visitors within weeks of its launch. But advertisers, users, and gaming companies continue to watch closely to discover how the Google+ network will fare. Are users going to be loyal to Google+, or are they just signing on to check out the newest thing from an Internet giant?[19]

Media-sharing Sites

The Internet has the ability to connect people more easily and in more ways than have ever been possible before. Media-sharing sites explicitly rely on this capability to enable users to share content they have generated, from videos on YouTube, Vimeo, and Vine to pictures on Flickr, Picasa, and Instagram. In terms of the 4E framework, companies use such sites to highlight how consumers can experience their goods or services, as well as encourage consumers to engage with the firm, its other social media outlets, and other consumers.

Marketers are increasingly investing in online video. According to eMarketer research, in 2014 Canadian advertisers will spend $255.1 million on online video, up 51.8 percent over 2013.[20] Taulia uses video to increase qualified leads for its cloud invoicing and supplier financing offerings. Working with the world's leading video marketing platform, Vidyard in Kitchener, Ontario, Taulia discovered that "it's easier to get people to press play and watch a minute long video" then it is to convince them to download a white paper.[21]. Knowing it would be difficult to make one video suited for everyone, Taulia creates separate videos to appeal to each audience it serves. By narrowcasting humourous videos that target the company's audience types and buying personas, they get better sales results. Testing shows that 79 percent of their viewers watched one video in its entirety. That's a key point. According to Unruly, viewer enjoyment increases purchase intent by 97 percent.[22] Video helps leverage social capital to build brand identity and relationships.[23] And, according to a study done by Twitter, adding video boosts retweet rates by 28 percent.[24]

Because video and social media are a perfect match, Vidyard has a solution that meshes them. Most companies don't know what to do with all their videos ,which can get lost in a black hole when hosted on YouTube or Vimeo.[25] Through a Vidyard app, users can put their entire video library on the HootSuite dashboard and add video to any social post directly from HootSuite. Measurement of video performance can track metrics such as number of views, click-through rates, attention spans, and shares on social media sites. Being able to see how much of the video was watched and when/if it was stopped helps to determine what content is striking a chord with viewers. And the inherent trackability shows marketers whether a video posted to Facebook is engaging consumers more effectively than on Twitter or other social media platforms.

While video is a natural fit for social media, companies can use it to enhance customer service, too. By monitoring social media, companies may see tweets from customers who can't figure out how to use a product. Companies could respond and include a video that helps customers better understand how the product functions.

YouTube   On this video-sharing social media platform, users upload, share, and view videos. This medium gives companies a chance to express themselves in a different way than they have in the past. YouTube videos also show up in Google searches, making YouTube an appealing vehicle for retailers.[26] The site's demographics indicate visitors are affluent, of the age range most appealing to retailers, and racially reflective of the wider population.[27]

YouTube also provides an effective medium for hosting contests and posting instructional videos. The Home Depot attracts more than 4,400 viewers with an array of videos detailing new products available in stores, as well as instructional do-it-yourself videos, like "How-to Tips for Mowing Your Lawn" or "How to Repair a Toilet."[28] These videos maintain the core identity of the Home Depot brand while also adding value for consumers, who learn useful ways to improve their homes. As a good example of IMC, Home Depot reinforces its brand image and makes itself more relevant to the consumer's life.

Companies can broadcast from their own channel, that is, a YouTube site that contains content relevant only to the company's own products.[29] For example, Home Shopping Network (HSN) offers consumers an interesting vehicle to utilize the 4E framework—excite, educate, experience, and engage—using a multichannel strategy with its television channel as its central focus. As competition in this field has increased, HSN has added to its communication arsenal an e-commerce site, and Facebook and MySpace pages. But perhaps the most powerful tool it has added is its dedicated YouTube channel, which it exploits to reach target shoppers in an exciting way that maximizes the value of its media content. Products promoted on HSN, such as Tori Spelling's jewellery line,[30] are available on YouTube almost immediately after they appear on television. Then HSN marketers can use the information gathered from YouTube to target its direct mail campaigns. For example, it could send jewellery promotions to households that viewed the YouTube video clip for a necklace from the Tori Spelling Collection. Consumer responses are monitored 24/7 and measured against hourly sales goals.

Photo Sites   Whereas YouTube allows users to share videos, Flickr, Picasa, TwitPic, Photobucket, and Instagram allow them to share photos. They tend to be less popular as marketing tools, yet some innovative companies have found ways to engage with customers, such as by hosting picture posting competitions or using photos to communicate core tenets and values.[31]

The U.K. brand Innocent, known for selling pure 100 percent fruit smoothies, uses Flickr to communicate its quirky brand image. Its photo posting competitions, such as the Funny Shaped Fruit Competition (http://www.flickr.com/groups/funnyshapedfruit/), provide significant entertainment value. But it also uses Flickr for more serious purposes, such as to post photos related to its Big Knit charity promotion, which provides knitted hats and funding to help keep older residents in the U.K. warm during cold winter months.[32]

Thought-sharing Sites

Thought-sharing sites consist of different types of blogs: corporate, professional, personal, and micro. In terms of the 4E framework, blogs are particularly effective at educating and engaging users, and in many cases enhance their experience with the products and services being discussed.

Blogs Once confined to a journal or diary in a person's room, the blog (from "web log") on the Internet has allowed us to air our thoughts to the world through thought-sharing websites. For corporations, the comment section allows marketing managers to create a two-way dialogue directly with the end users. The wide availability of free blogging tools such as WordPress, Blogger, and TypePad, which enable non–technically oriented people to create their own blogs, has made blogging a very popular pastime. In 2009 Technorati estimated that 200 million English language blogs existed, and in only three years, that number had grown to 450 million.[33]

Innocent uses Flickr to post photos for its Big Knit charity promotion.

Companies have responded to this interest and now have several ways to include blogging in their social media marketing strategy. Blogs provide firms the opportunity to educate their customers about their offerings, and to engage them by responding to their communications, both positive and negative. The reach that marketers have to their customers from blogs can be categorized by the level of control they offer. Corporate blogs, which are created by the companies themselves, have the highest level of control, because to a large degree, they can control the content posted on them. Of course, blogs also allow customers to respond to posts, so the content can never be completely controlled, but marketing managers have a good opportunity to pepper their blogs with the messages they wish their customers to see. The best corporate blogs illustrate the importance of engaging customers around the core brand tenets without being overly concerned with a hard sell.

Starbucks (http://mystarbucksidea.force.com) uses its blog for new product development by generating new product and *experience* ideas from its customers. General Electric (http://www.gereports.com) *educates* customers through its blog by telling entertaining stories geared at getting customers to realize it sells more than just light bulbs.[34]

From a marketing perspective, professional blogs are those written by people who review and give recommendations on products and services. Marketers often offer free products or provide modest remuneration to top-rated professional bloggers, in the hopes of getting a good product review. Marketers have less control over professional bloggers than they do their own corporate blogs. But consumers seem to trust professional bloggers' reviews much more than corporate blogs and other more traditional media, like advertising. Such trust may be fleeting, however, as more consumers realize that professional bloggers are often compensated for positive reviews. "Mommy Blogs," a particularly popular type of professional blog, feature advice and product recommendations from one mother to many others. Dooce, written by Heather Armstrong, has more than 1.5 million followers.[35]

Finally, personal blogs are written by people who receive no products or remuneration for their efforts. Thus, of the various types of blogs, marketers have the lowest level of control over this type. However, personal blogs are useful for monitoring what is going on in the marketplace and for responding to customer complaints or compliments.

Microblogs   As the name implies, a microblog differs from a traditional blog in size—short sentences, short videos, or individual images. On the most popular microblogging site, Twitter, users are limited to 140-character messages. Twitter provides another option for companies to educate their customers by providing corporate and product information, and to engage them by providing a platform for two-way communications. Even companies that may have once resisted social media are now realizing that Twitter offers an important communications channel.

As much as Twitter can help build a firm's brand image though, it can also tarnish it instantly. Firms have to watch out for hacked Twitter accounts or ill-considered tweets. And Twitter can also act as an international, rapidly spread complaint forum.[36] Companies also need to consider the frequency of their tweets since over-communication can have negative effects on a brand. A study by Brandwatch showed that at 32 times per week, American brands out-tweeted those in the United Kingdom with only 23 tweets per week. The average for the research sample of 253 top global brands, was 30 times a week.[37]

A central problem for companies is ownership of relevant Twitter handles and responsibility for outgoing Twitter communication. If Twitter control is shared by a lot of people, the message usually gets muddled. But if only one or two people are in charge, the need to respond to the vast number of incoming tweets might become overwhelming. Different companies thus manage their Twitter strategies in various ways.

Whole Foods tries to develop a broader engagement with customers by interacting with its 3.5 million Twitter followers. It instituted a weekly Twitter chat, for an hour every Thursday, during which Whole Foods representatives discuss topics such as holiday menu planning and healthy eating. Many Whole Foods stores also have their own Twitter accounts to answer questions directly related to their stores.

In contrast, Best Buy hires an army of specialists to manage its Twitter accounts: not just the main account @Best Buy, but also @BestBuy_Deals, @GeekSquad, and @BestBuyNews. The specialists who work Best Buy's help desk also will answer questions through Twitter, at @Twelpforce. Users who tweet the help desk receive an almost instant response from one of Best Buy's 3,000 employees who have signed up to participate on the task force, which further helps showcase the broad spectrum of expertise available through Best Buy.[38]

For small companies with limited marketing budgets, the use of tweeted promotional messages is particularly appealing. A local bakery tweeted, "Two new scones: Lemon Blueberry and Chorizo Cheddar!" and received responses from 400 Twitter followers—a huge captive audience for a local entity.

Of course, some of the most famous Twitter users are celebrities, who have their own brands to manage and marketing goals to reach. Teen idol Justin Bieber and his management team have relied

Justin Bieber has relied on social media to reach his target audience.

The use of social media by astronaut Chris Hadfield made him a celebrity in space.

on Twitter and other social media to reach his target audience. Social media turned astronaut Chris Hadfield into a celebrity. Many Canadians got to know him through his regular Twitter posts and the photos he took from space while on a space exploration mission. He shared videos of creating meals in space, doing experiments with water, and even singing the David Bowie hit song, *Space Oddity* while playing his guitar. Hadfield also hosted a live Google+ Hangout from space and took part in an "Ask Me Anything" on Reddit.[39]

Paid, Owned, Earned Media

Marketers know that they must use a combination of media when implementing their IMC plans. As shown in Exhibit 16.5, they use **paid media**, such as TV, print, radio, or display ads to reach mass markets. Paid media is created and controlled by the advertiser. **Owned media**, such as a website, is also controlled by the advertiser. Other forms of owned media include a company's blog, YouTube channel, or Facebook fan page. While there are costs associated with these media, they are less expensive than paid media. Lastly, **earned media** comes as a result of word-of-mouth, buzz, or publicity. Customers, the public, or the press become the media channel. Brand mentions are given voluntarily by customers, the public, or the press, and so the company "earns" the visibility.

paid media
Media such as TV, print, radio, or display ads used to reach mass markets.

owned media
Media controlled by the advertiser, such as its website, Facebook fan page, or YouTube channel.

earned media
Media that results from word-of-mouth, buzz, or publicity.

UNDERSTANDING MOBILE APPLICATIONS

L03

Although 97 percent of consumers access social media through their computers, 37 percent access these media via their mobile phones, 3 percent through iPads, and 2 percent through e-readers.[40] Of the more than 100 million people who have smartphones in North America, approximately half make purchases on them. In this huge market, consumers generally are younger and wealthier than others who own older-model mobile phones (or none at all). For example, more than 50 percent of mobile retail consumers earn at least $75,000 annually. Not surprisingly, mobile ad spending is growing fast. It is expected that by 2018, mobile spending will reach more than $2 billion, representing one out of every four digital advertising dollars spent.[41]

In terms of the 4E framework, mobile marketing is particularly useful for creating excitement with consumers at the time of sale. Several applications have been developed

EXHIBIT 16.5   Paid, Owned, Earned Media

PAID	**OWNED**	**EARNED**
Definition: Use of paid advertising channels to deliver a brand's message and/or drive traffic to owned or controlled properties.	**Definition:** Media, content, assets and community platforms partially or wholly owned and controlled by the brand.	**Definition:** Unique brand presence on established channels gained through editorial influence other than advertising.
Role: Create awareness, drive traffic and jumpstart owned, earned, and shared and efforts.	**Role:** Platform to house robust brand content and create long-term relationships /engagement with customers.	**Role:** Expand reach and credibility of the brand's message in trusted channels.
Tactics: Engagement ads, display, ads, email, TV, print, radio, OOH experiential, paid influencer outreach.	**Tactics:** Pre-existing social properties, social links on website, email database.	**Tactics:** Word-of-mouth, influencer outreach, blogs, social engagement.

to better market goods and services to these attractive consumers, as seen in Entrepreneurial Marketing 16.1. We briefly discuss a few other types: price check apps, fashion apps, and location apps.

Price Check Apps   When out shopping, smartphone users no longer have to go from store to store or stop home to go online and compare prices. Using a price checking app, such as at Amazon, or Stylish Girl, customers can scan a product in a store and instantly compare the prices online to see whether a better deal is available. Although price checking can encourage competition, as we discuss in Ethical Dilemma 16.1, companies can stray into ethical grey areas depending on how they promote their apps.

Realizing that online price checking could be damaging to business, retailers are responding in kind. Lowe's arms its employees with smartphones to help them instantly search the in-store and nearby inventories and place orders online if products are out of stock, to ensure that no customer ever leaves empty handed.[42] Target is working with vendors to create exclusive in-store items, to match online retailer pricing, and to develop a subscription-based online pricing strategy that gives regular buyers special discounts.[43]

Fashion Apps   The consumers who are most likely to use mobile media also are likely to buy from technology and fashion-oriented firms, whether they are fashion or technology retailers, or sell fashion magazine content or brand information. Style.com offers a mobile application for people to access the same content available on the *Style* magazine website, including blogs, reviews, couture shows, and video feeds.[44] Other apps provide a more in-depth look at a particular brand. Louis Vuitton's NOWNESS app combines magazine content with brand promotion. Pose is not brand-specific; instead, this photo-sharing app shares various style and fashion views and tips. Pinterest allows people to "pin"

Entrepreneurial Marketing 16.1 | **PumpedUp on Social Media**[45]

A personal trainer in your pocket is how PumpUp wants consumers to see its mobile fitness app. Based out of the Velocity garage in the Communitech Hub in Kitchener, Ontario, PumpUp was founded in May 2012 by Garrett Gottlieb and Phil Jacobson.

Garrett noticed he was plateauing in his fitness workouts and decided to build an algorithm that emulated the brain of a personal trainer, creating high-quality, personalized workout routines. He designed *PumpUp: Workout Coach* for his own use and also for coaching friends who were just starting to work out. His background in computer science at the University of Waterloo and co-op work terms with RIM, TribeHR, and other start-ups were key to getting started. But he lacked business and marketing skills, precisely what Phil Jacobson brought to the partnership. Phil graduated with a business degree from Wilfrid Laurier University and did co-op work terms with Unilever, PepsiCo, and ConAgra Foods.

PumpUp's app solves a problem most people have with fitness—incorporating it into your life is hard. Additionally, many people don't really know what they're doing when it comes to working out and lack the motivation to stay active. A whopping 80 percent of gym memberships go unused. *PumpUp: Workout Coach* lets people create personalized workout routines. Users enter basic information (age, weight, sex, and workout goals) as well as the amount of time they want to spend working out. The app removes the guesswork from working out, provides a low-cost, personal training experience, and isn't tied to an expensive gym or trainer.

Officially launched on the iTunes App Store in January 2013, the app uses a "freemium" business model with a free and a pro (paid) version. Although there are over 13,000 health and fitness apps on iTunes, *PumpUp: Workout Coach* quickly ranked among the top three free apps.[46] Looking for investors, Gottlieb and Jacobson pitched on CBC's *Dragons' Den*. They didn't end up taking any of the offers made, however, the exposure resulted in more than 8,000 app downloads.

As a start-up, the marketing budget is small so the company used social media to spread the word. Its primary social media channels are on Facebook, Twitter, and a Tumblr Blog but it also has a presence on YouTube,

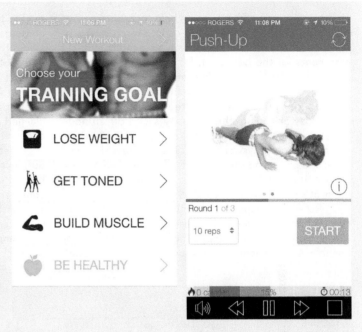

After users enter basic information, the PumpUp app coaches users through a fitness workout.

Instagram, Pinterest, and Vine. Over 125,000 followers on Instagram and 36,000 on Twitter share information about the app with their networks. The company's website regularly highlights success stories from PumpUp users. These stories are shared on Facebook, Twitter, and the blog.

Social Media Sites
- **Website:** pumpup.co
- **App Page:** itunes.apple.com/app/id573070442
- **Blog:** blog.pumpup.co
- **Facebook:** facebook.com/pumpupfitness
- **Twitter:** twitter.com/pumpup

Social media promotion is credited for generating over 1 million downloads of *PumpUp: Workout Coach*. Designed to fit busy lives, the app makes it easy for beginners and intermediates to get a personalized workout routine for home, the gym, or on the go.

merchandise, services, recipes, or ideas onto a virtual bulletin board. For instance, Pinterest users can "pin" clothing and accessories that match their personal taste; while others can browse their pinboards to discover new things and make comments. Marketers therefore can receive unlimited exposure to their products and services as like-minded people share pinned items and services.

Ethical Dilemma 16.1 — Internet vs. Brick-and-Mortar Stores

Smartphone price check apps help consumers save money by using a scanned bar code, search query, or photo and spoken product name to search multiple merchants for the best price for a particular item. The results tend to favour online merchants, which don't have to bear the cost of brick-and-mortar stores. But Amazon took price checking a step further: Just in time for holiday shopping, the company sliced off an additional 5 percent for shoppers using Amazon's Price Check app in a physical store.[47] The app revealed only Amazon's price, and the discount, which applied to toys, electronics, and DVDs, could be used for up to three items at a maximum savings of $5 per item.

Retailers complained that the app rewarded consumers for using brick-and-mortar stores as showrooms where shoppers could experience an item in a comfortable environment, learn about it from sales staff, decide to buy it, and then receive a discount for purchasing it online—oftentimes while the customer was still in the store. Although the discount didn't apply to books, it triggered outrage and a call for an Amazon boycott from bookstores already hurt by the Internet retailer's low prices and ability to avoid collecting state sales tax.[48] Critics called the promotion predatory and claimed Amazon was compromising the personality and economic stability of communities.

Retailers compete for customers, particularly during the holiday season, and Amazon's promotion helped shoppers save money. But should Amazon have considered the "showroom" effect on brick-and-mortar stores? On a broader scale, how aggressive can a marketer be before triggering backlash that can harm the company's reputation?

---

gamification
The process of using games or gamelike elements to encourage participation.

Location-based "Gamified" Apps Smartphone owners are increasingly using location-based apps. Customers can download several free apps that use the GPS function of their phone to share what they are doing, where they are, and when they're doing it. Companies use these apps to build loyalty by making patronage a game, a process known as **gamification**.

Users of FourSquare can check in at their favourite restaurants and stores, sharing their location on Facebook. They can compete with other users for the title of "Mayor" by achieving the most number of check-ins at a retail location in a 60-day period. Another spin on location-based gamification is SCVNGR. This app takes location-based gaming and direct sales to the next level. Users logging onto the app will be provided with a list of stores near them participating in SCVNGR. By completing challenges at these stores, ranging from simply checking in to "bumping phones" with other SCVNGR users at the establishment to making a portrait of the person sitting across from them out of food and taking a picture of it, users accrue points that unlock in-app badges and real-world coupons such as free coffee. Another interesting app is Snapette, which focuses on shoes and bags, and aims to help customers find the merchandise they want according to their immediate location.

In the past two decades, marketers have developed websites and other methods to communicate information about and to sell their goods and services. Their quest for new ways to improve, integrate, and enhance these outcomes has resulted in a confluence of social, mobile, and online marketing. Exhibit 16.6 is a brief summary of how these forces and their manifestations align with our 4E framework. It highlights how social network and mobile applications and the associated relevant offers are ideal for stimulating excitement in the offers. In particular, mobile location-based apps are exciting because they provide customers with highly relevant offers when they are in close proximity to the retailer or

Users of FourSquare can check in at their favourite restaurants and stores, sharing their location on Facebook.

EXHIBIT 16.6 Firms' Use of Social and Mobile Tools from the 4E Lens

	Excite	Educate	Experience	Engage
Social networks	✓ ✓			
Media-sharing sites			✓ ✓	✓ ✓
Thought-sharing sites		✓ ✓	✓	✓ ✓
Mobile applications	✓ ✓			✓

service provider or they can even be used to provide competitive offers. Media-sharing sites (e.g., YouTube and Flickr) are excellent social media tools that provide customers visual experiences of other customers or professionals who are using these goods and services. They also provide customers an opportunity to engage with the firms as well as their own social network by posting their own experiences (i.e., uploading videos), as well as sharing their thoughts (blogs and Twitter posts). Finally, thought-sharing sites, like blogs, are excellent for providing customer education.

ENGAGING CUSTOMERS USING SOCIAL MEDIA

L04

Now that we have an understanding of the various social and mobile media that are at the firm's disposal, it is important to determine how firms should go about engaging customers through social and mobile media. The three-stage process is to listen to what customers have to say, analyze the information available through various touch points, and finally implement social media tactics to excite customers.

Listen

From a market research point of view, companies can learn a lot about their customers by listening (and monitoring) what they say on their social networks, blogs, review sites, etc. Customers appear willing to provide their opinions about just about anything including their interests and purchases—both their own and those of their friends. Writing blogs and providing opinions via polls about such diverse topics as Botox treatments, ASICS running sneakers, or a particular play of an NFL team during the playoffs all constitute new ways that customers communicate with one another—and with marketers who are paying attention.

Marketers can analyze the content found on sites like Facebook, Twitter, online blogs, and reviews to assess the favourableness or unfavourableness of the sentiments, using a technique known as **sentiment analysis**. Sentiment analysis allows marketers to analyze data from these sources to collect consumer comments about companies and their products. The data are then analyzed to distill customer attitudes and preferences, including reactions to specific products and IMC campaigns. Scouring millions of sites

sentiment analysis
An analysis of online content to determine favourability or unfavourability.

with sentiment analysis techniques provides new insights into what consumers really think. Companies plugged into such real-time information and insights can become more nimble, allowing for numerous quick changes, such as in a product roll-out, a new advertising campaign, or a reaction to customer complaints.

There are several companies that specialize in monitoring social media.[49] For example, Radian6 offers social media listening and engagement tools to help its clients such as Dell, GE, Kodak, Microsoft, and PepsiCo connect with its customers.[50] Using sentiment analysis techniques, it processes a constant stream of online consumer opinion from blogs, Facebook, and other networking sites, including 400 million tweets a day. The Radian6 tools for managing consumer sentiment data allow companies to identify opinion trends that might warrant an online corporate response. For instance, Radian6 may identify negative consumer sentiment and then provide services to help its client respond. Reacting to attitudes uncovered in sentiment analysis allows companies to counteract negative opinions, maybe influence those perceptions, and perhaps win customer loyalty.[51]

As an example of how a firm like Radian6 can help its clients engage its customers, consider the New York–based nonprofit Let's Get Ready that helps low-income high school students get into college.[52] When it decided to compete for Chase American Giving Awards funding, Let's Get Ready needed broader support. Radian6 helped the organization find Web-based conversations among individuals and groups who might share its educational mission. It further helped Let's Get Ready reach out to potential supporters, share information about its work, and ask for votes. The campaign worked: Let's Get Ready placed second, winning $500,000 for free SAT preparation and college admission counselling to motivated students. Sentiment analysis thus is fundamentally transforming how companies interact with and engage their customers.

Analyze

Fortunately, the companies that help facilitate listening also provide analytic tools to assess what customers are saying about the firm and its competitors. There are three main categories of analysis used for understanding data collected from social media.[53]

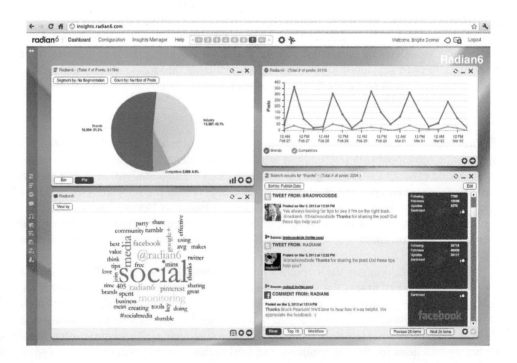

Radian6 analyzes customer sentiment for its customers, which enables them to identify opinion trends that might warrant an online corporate response.

First, it is important to determine the amount of traffic using their sites, visiting their blogs, or tweeting about them. Measures used for this purpose include **hits** (i.e., total requests for a page), visits to a particular site or page, unique visitors to the site, and **page views** (i.e., the number of times any page gets viewed by any visitor).

Second, while knowing how many people are using a firm's social media is important, it is even more critical to learn who those visitors are, what they are doing, and what engages and excites them. To analyze these factors, social media marketers uses such metrics as the **bounce rate**, which refers to the percentage of times a visitor leaves the site almost immediately, such as after viewing only one page. Analyzing which pages are the most frequent entry and exit locations provides direction on how to make a website more effective. In addition, following visitors' **click paths** shows how users proceed through the information—not unlike how grocery stores try to track the way shoppers move through their aisles. A firm can use this information to provide users with an easier navigation experience through the site so they can more quickly find what they are looking for. The data analysis can also reveal **conversion rates**, a measure that indicates what percentage of visitors or potential customers act as the marketer hopes, whether by clicking, buying, or donating. Click paths and conversion rates can also reveal what users might have wanted, but not found, on the site.

Third, some companies want to analyze data that comes from other sites, such as measuring where people have come from to get to the company's site. Did they search through Google or Amazon? Did they receive a referral from a friend? Which keywords did they use to find the firm? Firms can use **keyword analysis** to determine what keywords people use to search on the Internet for their products and services. With this information, they can refine their websites by using keywords to use on their site that their customers use. Then they can assess the ROI of the investment made by improving the site. This would be done by calculating the incremental profit increase divided by the investment on the site improvement. For social media, it is more challenging to determine ROI than for more traditional IMC applications, because the revenue generated by social media is often not directly related to the expenditure. So, instead of traditional ROI measures, firms often examine questions like: Does having more Twitter followers correlate with having higher sales? Do Facebook fans of the company buy more than nonfans? [54]

These analyses require well-trained marketing managers, marketing analytic software, and perhaps some help from consulting specialists (e.g., IBM, SAS, PricewaterhouseCoopers). But almost everyone seems to be turning to Google Analytics these days, because it offers a sophisticated, in-depth form of analysis, all for free. Google Analytics not only tracks the elements that are shown in Exhibit 16.7, but also is highly customizable.[55]

Do

Even the greatest analysis has little use if firms fail to implement what they have learned from analyzing their social and mobile media activity. That is, social media may be all about relationships, but ultimately, firms need to use their connections to increase their business.[56] They might launch a new Facebook campaign, actively blog, or provide mobile offers.

When Facebook first introduced its new Page format, many users balked, complaining about having to reformat all their posts. But some companies jumped on the chance to refresh their image among Facebook followers, tell a better story, and develop a testing lab for new promotions and offers. If one user notes her dream of a beach vacation, the company might contact her with an offer for bathing suits—even in the dead of winter.

Deciding which tactics to employ and when is key. The social media marketer needs to act like an orchestra conductor, waving a wand to make sure that hundreds of "musicians," playing a variety of instruments, come together to create some beautiful music. A well-developed marketing strategy involves a host of social and mobile tools, working in

hits
The total number of requests for a web page.

page views
The number of times any web pages are viewed by visitors.

bounce rate
The percentage of times a visitor leaves a site almost immediately.

click paths
Shows how users navigate through a site.

conversion rates
The percentage of visitors to a site who click, buy, or donate.

keyword analysis
Determines which keywords visitors to a site use to find it.

EXHIBIT 16.7	Analytics	
Type of Analytic	**How It's Used**	**Competitors Offering Similar Analytics**
Content	Understand what's popular and what's not on a firm's website, including page load times and site navigation.	Adobe SiteCatlyst, Clickstream, Coremetrics, IBM SurfAid, Mtracking, VisiStat
Social	Track effectiveness of social media programs, including information on social media referred conversion rates, and engagement metrics.	Facebook Insights, Twitter Web Analytics, Webtrends
Mobile	Track website access from mobile devices, track which ads direct people to a firm's app, understand what mobile platform performs best.	AppClix, Bango, Flurry, Localytics, Medialets, Webtrends
Conversion	Moving beyond page views and visitor counts, conversion analytics measures sales, downloads, video plays, or any other action important to a firm.	Clicktale, KeyMetric, Latitude
Advertising	Track the effectiveness of social, mobile, search and display ads, divide ad effectiveness by device, platform, or type.	AdTech, MediaMelon MediaCloud, Metronome, Snoobi, YieldMetrics,

Source: http://www.google.com/analytics/features/index.html.

conjunction with the firm's traditional IMC tactics, to move the consumer up the purchase decision hierarchy from awareness to purchase to loyalty.

To illustrate how firms might go about undertaking such campaigns, consider the steps involved in developing and implementing a Facebook marketing campaign.[57] These steps are not unlike the steps used in any integrated marketing communications (IMC) program. (See Chapters 14 and 15 for more details.) Assume a marketer was developing a Facebook marketing campaign for a new product.

1. *Identify strategy and goals.* The firm has to determine exactly what it hopes to promote and achieve through its campaign. Does it want to increase awareness of the product? Is it hoping more potential customers might visit and like its Facebook page? Is its focus mainly on increasing sales of the product? Depending on what the company aims to achieve, it might focus on developing a Facebook page, creating a Facebook app, or hosting a Facebook event.

2. *Identify target audience.* The next step is to determine whom the company is targeting. Facebook enables the firm to perform targeting that is based on location, language, education, gender, profession, age, relationship status, likes/dislikes, and friends or connections. The marketer's aim is to find a big enough audience to reach those who might adopt the product without being so big that the company ends up trying to appeal to someone way outside its target audience.

3. *Develop the campaign: experiment and engage.* Now that the firm knows whom it is targeting, the next step is to develop the communication, including the copy and images. Here again, the process is not very different from any other IMC campaign. There should be a call to action that is clear and compelling. Strong, eye-catching images and designs are important. And the campaign must appeal to the right customers. However, an aspect that is more critical with social media than other forms of IMC is that the images and messages need to be updated almost constantly. Because people expect changing content online, it would be inappropriate to run the same campaign for several months, as the firm might if it were advertising on television, for example.

4. *Develop the budget.* Budgeting is key. Facebook allows advertisers to set a daily budget: Once their costs (usually per click) reach a certain level, the ad disappears for the rest of the day. Of course, this option can be risky if the firm is getting great feedback and, suddenly, a compelling ad disappears. Therefore, similar to the campaign content, budgets demand nearly constant review. For example, if a competitor lowers its price significantly, it might be necessary to follow suit to avoid being excluded from customers' consideration sets.

5. *Monitor and change.* The final step is to review the success of the campaign and make changes as necessary. Facebook's Ad Manager offers various metrics and reports, such as number of clicks on ads, audience demographics, and ad performance for specific time periods.

MANAGING YOUR PERSONAL BRAND IN A SOCIAL MEDIA WORLD

L05

The branding concepts examined in Chapter 9 apply in unique ways in the social media world, in which people engage in self-branding in new and exciting ways. Recall that brands attempt to build awareness, aim to develop loyalty, and exert an impact. If one applies these concepts to individual brand equity, one might think of individual brand management in some of the following ways.

Measures of individual social media effectiveness or equity use metrics such as **social reach**, which refers to how many people a person influences (e.g., number of individuals in the person's social networks such as Facebook and LinkedIn); **influence**, which is the extent to which the person influences others (e.g., how much do the people in a person's network read that person's content); and **extended network**, or the influence of the person's extended network, that is, the cumulative number of members (10,000) = 100 members each having 100 members of their own.

Several firms have developed metrics to assess a person's social impact (e.g., Klout, PeerIndex, Twitalyzer, and Kred). For example, Klout combines these three elements—social reach, influence, and extended network—to define a Klout score that can range from 0 to 100. The average score earned by regular people who aren't celebrities nor heavily involved in social media, such as bloggers, is around 20. Justin Bieber is the only person ever to earn a perfect 100. But a person does not have to be a star to earn a high Klout score.

Although Klout offers a good general view of social influence, various other options exist for more specific or detailed analyses, such as PeerIndex (http://www.peerindex.net), Tweetlevel (http://tweetlevel.edelman.com), Twitalyzer (http://twitalyzer.com), How Sociable (http://www.howsociable.com), Postrank (http://www.postrank.com), or TwitterGrader (https://mokumax.com/).[58] Links shared through Twitter or Facebook also affect search rankings on search engines such as Google or Bing, such that greater influence increases the chances that people can find a more influential source of information or fashion.[59]

In a sense, social media are like high school:[60] In both places, people self-select into groups or cliques. Many people define their self-worth based on how many "friends" they can count. People's expressions and actions determine their reputation—whether negatively or positively. The environment can be either inclusive or exclusive—and sometimes both. Users seek out others, both as individuals and as groups. Wallflowers get ignored; fun, active, exciting contributors attract attention.

But remember, "No matter how brilliant and talented you are, you won't be sufficiently appreciated ... until the broader public recognizes you."[61] Thus, beyond creating an online presence, people with true influence also make use of networks of contacts they make in various realms, give presentations and speeches, publish books and articles as well as blogs, submit themselves for prestigious awards, and try to get on television or other national news outlets.

social reach
The number of people a person influences.

influence
The extent to which a person influences others.

extended network
The influence of a person's extended network.

Even if a person's goal is not necessarily to become the premier expert on a particular topic, social influence can have significant effects on other elements of his or her life, such as hiring success.[62] Employers can check these social presence scores or impact factors, along with other sources of information, to assess how well connected, creative, and active a potential hire is. This source is particularly critical for the rapidly expanding field of social media jobs for marketers.

A student who graduates with a marketing degree likely has a good foundation for one of the following social media jobs:[63]

1. Social media strategist. In this quite high paying social media job, people create social media marketing campaigns, then measure the results, using an effective strategic plan.

2. Community manager. These positions are responsible for handling corporate forums and blogs, increasing traffic to the site, and broadening their company's community.

3. Blogger. These highly sought jobs provide great flexibility and freedom. By posting articles on relevant websites, bloggers can earn $35–$75 hourly.

4. Social media marketing specialist. These well-paid professionals distribute promotional channels using a range of social media channels, which requires strong online marketing skills.

5. Search engine marketing associate. Focusing on search engines, these online marketers rely on their knowledge of optimization techniques to increase the organic search rankings for a website.

6. Online customer service representative. Customers like to provide feedback, often online, and the best service companies make sure that someone is on hand to respond.

Regardless of the exact job title, social media jobs are increasing. On the Monster.com job search site for example, the number of social media–related jobs recently jumped by approximately 75 percent.[64] They also offer good salaries and the promise of continued growth.

Getting such jobs implies that candidates truly have influence, and these social media impact scores offer some idea about what personal branding really means.[65] First, influence by itself has little impact. Rather, a person needs to leverage his or her personal brand to induce some action, whether that entails convincing friends to support a cause the person likes or convincing a company to hire that person for an internship. Second, just as it does for a product or service brand, building a personal brand takes time, as well as consistent effort. It would be impossible to become really influential by exhibiting a flurry of activity for a couple of days, and then taking a month-long break. Third, there is a big difference between being active and being influential. Simply retweeting comments from other creators is insufficient to achieve true influence. To be influential, a personal brand must follow the 4Es: You need to excite, educate, give experience, and engage your followers.

Moreover, just like any other marketing tactic, personal branding needs to take ethical considerations under advisement. For example, we might think carefully about the spread of metrics especially amid reports about the ways they are being used, perhaps without people's knowledge. For example, at the Palms Casino Resort Hotel, clerks check the Klout scores of guests as they check in and then offer upgrades to those with the highest scores.[66] Is that great marketing, or an ethically questionable exploitation?

The importance of such scores also implies the potential for abuse. What if firms "game" the system, such that the only search engine results you see are those that have developed influence because the companies have paid legions of followers to tweet about their offering?[67] Are you really getting the best choices then?

On a more personal note, it has been pretty well established that embarrassing pictures on Facebook can be detrimental to your future career. But what about just basic posts and influence efforts? Despite the benefits of building your social influence, the more information available about you online, the more information potential employers and others have. One study even suggests that human resource managers should assess social media sources to determine if a potential hire is agreeable (pleasant in interactions, or caustic in humour?), emotionally stable (did an interpersonal fight go viral?), or conscientious.[68] Such information also is available for use in legal cases.[69] You thus may be liable for everything you do to enhance your social influence. So think before you post, tweet, or blog: Is this something you want to answer for in court, or even just in the court of public opinion?

LEARNING OBJECTIVES REVIEW

LO1 **Describe the 4E framework of social media marketing.**

The 4E framework recognizes that marketers must excite customers with relevant offers; educate them about the offering; help them experience products, whether directly or indirectly; and give them an opportunity to engage.

LO2 **Understand the types of social media.**

Users of social media employ them to promote themselves or their products and services. They do so through three main categories: social networking sites (e.g., Facebook, LinkedIn), media-sharing sites (e.g., YouTube), and thought-sharing sites (e.g., blogs, Twitter).

LO3 **Understand the types of mobile applications.**

As mobile users increase in number and diversity, the applications developed to appeal to them are spreading as well. For now, most of these apps constitute three broad categories: price checking apps, location-based apps, and fashion apps. However, many applications span more than one category.

LO4 **Recognize and understand the three components of a social media strategy.**

Firms engage with customers through social and mobile media using a three-step process. First, they listen to the customer using techniques like sentiment analysis. Second, they analyze the data collected in the first step using metrics like bounce rates, click paths, and conversion rates. Finally, they use this information to develop tactics to engage their customers.

LO5 **Understand the methods for marketing yourself using social media.**

To market themselves, people need to ensure they reach a large number of people, that they influence those people, and that the network of people that they influence is also influential. Several firms, such as Klout, have devised metrics to assess one's social network impact. Having a social network presence is becoming increasingly important in finding certain types of marketing jobs. But, on a cautionary note, it is important for people to carefully choose how they are portrayed in social media because once something is posted, it is there for all to see, including potential employers.

KEY TERMS

- bounce rate
- click paths
- conversion rates
- earned media
- extended network
- gamification
- hits
- influence
- keyword analysis
- owned media
- paid media
- page views
- sentiment analysis
- social reach

CONCEPT REVIEW

1. What are the 4Es?

2. What social media elements work best for each of the 4Es?

3. What is an example of a social network, a media-sharing site, a thought-sharing site, and a mobile application?

4. On which of the 4E dimensions do social networks, media-sharing sites, thought-sharing sites, and mobile applications excel?

5. What are the three steps in developing social media engagement strategies?

6. How do firms examine customer sentiments?

7. What are the steps in developing a social media campaign?

8. Why might it be important to develop a personal social media presence?

MARKETING APPLICATIONS

1. Evaluate Dell's social media strategy using the 4E framework.

2. Using the components of the 4E framework, outline how an entrepreneur marketing T-shirts can augment or enhance his or her marketing mix efforts.

3. Suppose David's Tea introduced a new product called mint-enhanced tea—mint and lemon herbal tea. How should it go about creating excitement using various social and mobile media tools?

4. If you were marketing a new sneaker, what sort of mobile applications might enhance your marketing efforts?

5. Assume you work for a large consumer packaged goods firm that has discovered that its latest line of snack foods is moving very slowly off store shelves. Recommend a strategy for listening to what consumers are saying on

blogs, review sites, and the firm's website. Describe how your strategy might provide insights into consumers' sentiments about the new product line.

6. If you were assessing the effectiveness of your social media marketing campaign, would sentiment analysis be helpful?

7. As an intern for Tim Hortons, you have been asked to develop a social media campaign for a new glazed muffin. The objective of the campaign is to increase awareness and trial of the new line of muffins. How would you go about putting such a campaign together?

8. What is your Klout score? Do you believe it is "high enough" for what you are planning to do after graduation? How would you go about increasing your score?

NET SAVVY

1. Go to http://www.facebook.com/business and learn about how to build pages, ads, sponsored stories, and take advantage of mobile applications. What are some of the steps that Facebook suggests a person consider when marketing using ads?

2. Go to http://www.radian6.com/about-us and check out its top case studies. How do these case studies provide insights into how listening and analytic systems can help firms improve their social media marketing?

CHAPTER CASE STUDY

SOCIAL MEDIA GIVE DELL A DIRECT CONNECTION TO ITS CUSTOMERS

Michael Dell was 19 years old when he launched his company in 1984, with $1,000 and a vision of how technology should be designed, manufactured, and sold.[70] That vision put customer relationships at the forefront of Dell's core business model, under a simple mantra: "Be direct."[71] The company rolled out its first computers with a risk-free return policy.[72] Taking its products directly to the consumer, with the launch of its Dell.com website in March 1996, Dell was generating $1 million a day in sales within six months of going online. The site linked customers to technical assistance through online chat, telephone, and email access points. Bolstered by its comprehensive online support service, Dell.com was generating $40 million a day in revenue in 2000, making it one of the highest-volume e-commerce sites in the world.[73]

A few years later, Dell fundamentally changed its interaction with customers by making a major commitment to social media. Today, by fully exploiting the potential of Facebook, Twitter, and other social media channels, the company has developed the capacity to engage customers even more directly. One of the first corporate social media adopters, Dell is now a leader in the use of social media to transform company performance.[74]

Dell.com is still a customer support workhorse, with all the traditional online marketing strengths. Customers have access to an exhaustive online sales catalogue, which complements Dell's worldwide presence through retailers.[75] The website offers product support, technical assistance with downloads, Windows operating systems, and a multitude of other issues.[76] Online user forums help strengthen the customer relationship, offering Q&A discussions about disk drives, mobile devices, and other topics, as well as more specialized discussions for distinct groups, like new buyers trying to select the right product, small business owners, or those with a special interest, like digital entertainment.[77]

But Dell's social media channels offer the customer a radically different experience. And they provide the company with invaluable customer reactions—both positive and negative—to new products, proposed ad campaigns, service problems, and other aspects of its technology business.

On Facebook, Dell speaks to a variety of market segments, with separate pages for home and business users, small and medium businesses, and large corporate users, along with separate entry points for Dell in Malaysia, Australia, and other countries. A Facebook search in the United States brings the user to Dell's Marketplace, a trendy-looking page that opens to ads and a display of the products currently being promoted.

Links offer users a variety of options. Dell Support plugs users into Dell's online forums, while also showing a scrolling series of live posts offering conversation entry points on questions like how to burn a CD.[78] The Dell Wall feels familiar to any Facebook user. It promotes Dell events and new service offerings. The Buzz Room provides a selection of breaking news from the major media, on topics like Entrepreneurship, Product News, and Mobility, with each page also streaming a relevant Twitter feed.[79]

Other links move in a hipper direction. The Lounge is an edgy Facebook wall, with news of Dell's XPS13 Ultrabook event in Brooklyn, New York, and an online "social media salary guide."[80] The Social Shop offers "the scoop on how real people use and rate their computers," with links to topics like gaming, music, and cloud computing.[81] The Ask Rev link serves up weekly YouTube-like video updates from Dell staffers under a banner that reads "You've got questions. I know stuff."[82]

Twitter gives Dell an entirely different stream of conversations with users. Its main Twitter page[83] links to Dell's multiple Twitter accounts. DellHome announces product launches and gives consumers other product news.[84] Other accounts serve IT professionals at large corporations worldwide (DellEnterprise);[85] customers needing product support (DellCares), with separate Twitter feeds in multiple languages;[86] users who want the headlines from Direct2Dell, Dell's official corporate blog (Direct2Dell);[87] and those who want to tweet directly with Michael Dell (MichaelDell).[88] To boost sales, the company's Dell Outlet site offers flash promotions through Twitter.[89]

Dell.com's blogs facilitate active dialogue between user-subscribers and company leaders. These include Direct2Dell, the company's flagship blog;[90] DellShares, providing investor updates;[91] and DellSoftwareNews, which discusses software products, pricing, and licensing.[92] Working professionals who access Dell through LinkedIn find product updates, recent blog posts, and direct links to Dell managers.[93] Through Google+, Dell offers product news and updates but also invites users to join the group conversations, or "circles," that interest them.[94] Dell has also come up with the ultimate digital suggestion box: IdeaStorm.com, which facilitates crowd-sourced suggestions, inviting customers to collaborate and prioritize product and service improvements.[95]

These multiple channels give Dell an unprecedented ability to build a positive sense of its brand while also gathering insight from thousands of users who personally text, post, and tweet their comments daily, in real time. The corporate learning that Dell derives from that enormous information flow is made possible through the powerful social media infrastructure it has built.

By some estimates, the company has invested tens of millions of dollars in the development of its robust social media platform, considered by many to be a national model.[96] Through its partnership with Radian6, the social media monitoring company, Dell catalogues and analyzes 25,000 user conversations daily.[97] That analysis is critical, notes Karen Quintos, Dell's chief marketing officer: "It's only when you step back from individual problems that patterns emerge that help a company understand the root causes of problems."[98] The nerve centre for Dell's operations is the company's new Social Media Listening Command Centre, which provides almost instantaneous support in 11 languages to Dell customers around the world.[99] Members of Dell's trained social media staff conduct the listening operation behind a panel of sliding blue glass doors, as they face a bank of digital flat screens alive with data.

"Listening works, even if you can't resolve every issue," says Maribel Sierra, Dell's director of global social media and communities, "because customers appreciate that you listen to their ideas and concerns." That social media connection—the unfiltered conversation between a Dell employee and the customer—has a powerful impact on customer loyalty, brand, and more.[100] Annual training updates and Dell's global social media policy guide all listening conducted by members of Dell's social media staff. They must protect Dell confidential information and personal customer information. Disclosing that they work for Dell is required during every social media contact with someone online. They must adhere to all legal and Dell conduct code requirements. Responding to customer needs is the bottom line.[101]

But Manish Mehta, Dell's VP of social media and community, has stressed that the command centre is not intended to simply listen or even just triage, but to remain vigilant, identifying key discussions early, so that employees worldwide can be given the tools to respond.[102] According to a Forrester report, that approach has enabled Dell customer support to reach 46 percent more users, and has produced additional tangible results, including quicker response times; improved issue recognition, mitigation, and management; enhanced coordination and response consistency; and an early warning system to avoid faulty product launches.[103]

Dell also reaches offline to deepen the impact of its social media listening, inviting brand supporters and detractors encountered online to attend its annual consumer advisory meetings. While some companies shun social media critics, fearing that unhappy customers will spread their wrath, Dell seeks to engage with them, reporting that its customer service teams can convert a detractor to a promoter about 30 percent of the time. The company also nurtures influential brand loyalists through special online recognition and invitations to test new products or host online chats.[104]

From its earliest days, Dell has been driven by the potential to engage with its customers. With a corporate culture that has fully embraced social media connectivity,[105] today's Dell is leveraging more powerful interactions with consumers to improve products and services, retain loyal customers, and increase revenues.[106]

Questions

1. What social and mobile media tools are Dell's people using?

2. Evaluate Dell's social media marketing strategy using the 4E framework.

3. Assess their listening capabilities and how they respond to insights gained by their social media command centre.

For more information on the resources available from McGraw-Hill Ryerson, go to www.mheducation.ca/he/solutions.

Global Marketing

Known best for its toothpaste, the Colgate-Palmolive Company provides oral, personal, and home care products and pet nutrition products to consumers around the globe.[1] Colgate's strategic plan includes international growth, and the company has built brand loyalty and market share in emerging markets, as well as a global leadership position for the sales of toothpaste and toothbrushes. It is a $17.1 billion company[2], ranked as one of the world's most powerful brands, selling its products in over 200 countries.[3] The roots of this success lie in Colgate's commitment to understanding local tastes, educating consumers about the importance of better oral hygiene, developing relationships with dental professionals, and supporting communities.

In India, for example, Colgate researchers spent two days in a rural village studying the habits and values of inhabitants. The main insight: Mothers hoped desperately for better lives for their children. The resulting campaign stressed the health implications of good oral care habits and offered opportunities for scholarships. In other countries, similar interactions with locals have spawned ideas for new products, including a highly energy efficient toothbrush manufacturing plant in China that adheres to the highest standards of environmental protection. Visits with storeowners in rural Russia led to new packaging options for use in small, crowded shops.

A new tapered bristle toothbrush, Colgate Slim Soft, was created for Asian consumers who wanted soft, flexible bristles that still reached those hard-to-get spots. The product, which drove Colgate's share in the manual toothbrush category to a record high, is now being rolled out globally.[4] Continually innovating, the company entered the billion-dollar rechargeable toothbrush category in Europe, and is set to expand sales of its breakthrough whitening brand, Colgate Optic, to international markets.[5]

In addition to consumers and store owners, Colgate builds bonds with dental professionals, who are in a position to endorse the brand and provide product samples. These relationships have prompted significant numbers of dentists and hygienists in Brazil, India, and China to recommend Colgate over any other brand to patients. In the United States, Colgate is creating new ties with hygienists by providing oral health education tools and inviting their participation in the company's oral health advisory board.

LEARNING OBJECTIVES

After studying this chapter you should be able to

LO1 Explain the components of global market assessments

LO2 Understand the marketing opportunities in BRIC countries

LO3 Describe the various global market entry strategies

LO4 List the similarities of and differences between a domestic marketing strategy and a global marketing strategy

LO5 Explain how ethical issues affect global marketing practices

Colgate's commitment to community support stems from its global values of caring, continuous improvement, and global teamwork. Its initiatives have resulted in Colgate being ranked among the World's Most Ethical Companies.[6] In Canada, it launched *Colgate Bright Smiles, Bright Futures**, an oral health program for use by kindergarten and Grade One teachers.[7] It teamed with the international retailer Tesco in the United Kingdom in a customizable "Share a Smile" program that benefits local communities. A partnership in the African country of Malawi promoted healthy oral care habits.

By paying close attention to the unique sociocultural characteristics of consumers in each country and tailoring its product strategies, Colgate brightens smiles as it successfully competes in global and emerging markets. ▌

The increasing globalization of markets affects all companies—large, small, medium, and entrepreneurial—in Canada, and around the world. Many Canadian companies find themselves becoming part of the global supply chain. Competition is no longer local, provincial, or even national; it is global. Canadian companies have to compete with other global companies not only for raw materials, labour, knowledge, and other inputs, but also for markets for their products. Most people don't think about how globalization impacts their daily lives, but just take a minute and read the labels on the clothing you are wearing right now. Chances are that most of the items, even if they carry Canadian or U.S. brand names, were manufactured in another part of the world, such as China, India, Thailand, Mexico, Brazil, and dozens of other developing countries.

In Canada, the market has evolved from a system of local and provincial marketplaces, to national markets, to geographically regional markets (e.g., Canada and the United States together), to international markets, and finally to global markets. According to the Government of Canada and the Business Development Bank of Canada, **globalization** refers to the increased flow of goods, services, people, technology, capital, information, and ideas around the world. Its impacts are economic, political, social, cultural, and environmental.[8] Global markets are the result of several fundamental changes, such as reductions or eliminations of trade barriers by country governments, the decreasing concerns of distance and time with regard to moving products and ideas across countries, the standardization of laws across borders, and globally integrated production processes.[9] For instance, consider the lululemon pants that you perhaps own. It is possible that lululemon athletica buys its raw materials from a supplier in one country and its sewing machines and washers from a supplier in another country, while its workers come from a third country, and its marketers are placed in several countries around the world where its pants are sold (i.e., customers are spread across the globe).

Globalization has not only created economies of scale because of the global scale in which research, production, and marketing are performed, but also made it possible for many market niches that are not profitable at the provincial or national level to become profitable at the global level. For instance, Gennum of Burlington, Ontario, which makes specialized parts for the hearing instrument industry, found that the Canadian market is too small for its products; however, on a global scale, it can profitably serve this market niche. To exploit global market niches, it has design, R&D, and sales offices in Japan, Taiwan, Korea, and the United Kingdom. Indeed, many Canadian

globalization
Refers to the increased flow of goods, services, people, technology, capital, information, and ideas around the world; has economic, political, social, cultural, and environmental impacts.

companies are part of the global supply chain, supplying inputs and raw materials rather than marketing finished products.

These fundamental changes have paved the way for marketing to flourish in other countries. The elimination of trade barriers and other governmental actions, for instance, allows goods and ideas to move quickly and efficiently around the world, which in turn facilitates the quick delivery of goods to better meet the needs of global consumers. As a consequence, consumers have easy access to global products and services. When we walk into a toy store, we expect to find Lego from Denmark. In the local sporting goods store, we anticipate finding running shoes made in China by the German firm adidas. In the grocery store, we demand out-of-season produce like blueberries from Chile in January. Or consider how a $12 digital camera for your keychain, made in Taiwan, could be produced, transported halfway around the world, and sold for so little money at your local Target. These are the questions we will be examining in this chapter.

We begin by looking at how firms assess the potential of a given market, with particular attention to the BRIC countries (Brazil, Russia, India, and China.) We'll see how firms assess the potential of a given market, make decisions to go global, and choose markets in which to sell globally. Then we explore how to build the marketing mix for global products and consider some of the ethical issues of globalization.

ASSESSING GLOBAL MARKETS   LO1

Because different countries, at their various stages of globalization, offer marketers a variety of opportunities, firms must assess the viability of a variety of international markets. This assessment is done through an environmental analysis similar to what is described in Chapter 3. As illustrated in Exhibit 17.1, four sets of factors are often used to assess a country's market: **P**olitical/Legal, **E**conomic, **S**ociocultural, and **T**echnology and infrastructure factors. The acronym *PEST* is used as shorthand to refer to these factors. Analysis of these four factors offers marketers a more complete picture of a country's potential as a market for products and services. Although we describe each factor separately, it is important to note that marketers consider them together in order to obtain a complete picture of a country's marketing potential. In fact, marketers often have to

EXHIBIT 17.1   Components of a Country Market Assessment

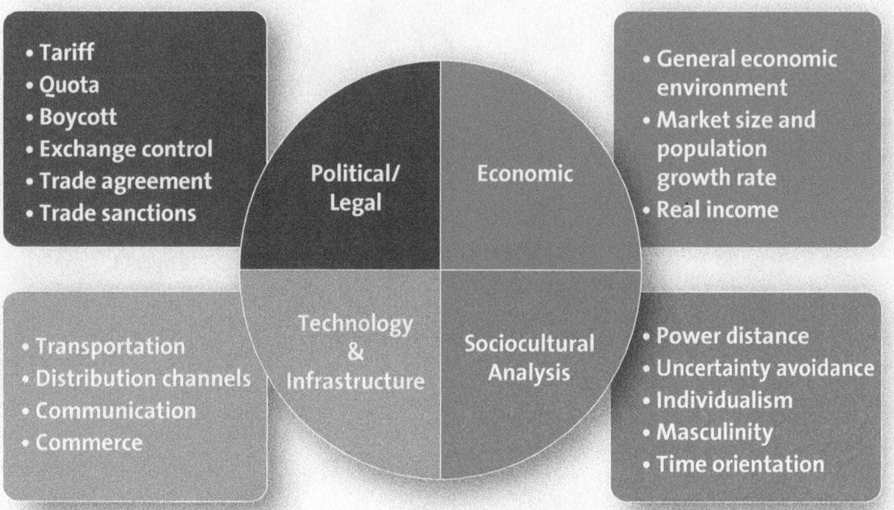

Political/Legal
- Tariff
- Quota
- Boycott
- Exchange control
- Trade agreement
- Trade sanctions

Economic
- General economic environment
- Market size and population growth rate
- Real income

Technology & Infrastructure
- Transportation
- Distribution channels
- Communication
- Commerce

Sociocultural Analysis
- Power distance
- Uncertainty avoidance
- Individualism
- Masculinity
- Time orientation

make trade-offs between these factors when entering or doing business in a foreign market. For instance, Canadian oil and mining companies may enter markets where the economic opportunity is great but the political risks are higher.

Analyzing the Political and Legal Environment

Governmental actions, as well as the actions of nongovernmental political groups, can significantly influence firms' ability to sell goods and services, because they often result in laws or other regulations that either promote the growth of the global market or close off the country and inhibit growth. Policies aimed at restricting trade and global marketing are called protectionist policies, and those that encourage global trade and marketing are referred to as trade liberalization policies. The White Spot restaurant chain, based in Vancouver, opened its first Asian location in Hong Kong. CEO Warren Earhart says the company evaluates new markets on a country-by-country basis since countries have different rules that need to be considered. For example, Thailand and South Korea have protectionist policies regarding the import of beef products.[10] In this section, we discuss various forms of protectionist and liberalization policies. These issues include trade sanctions such as tariffs, quotas, boycotts, exchange controls, and trade agreements (see Exhibit 17.2).

trade sanctions
Penalties or restrictions imposed by one country over another country for importing and exporting of goods, services, and investments.

Trade Sanctions   **Trade sanctions** are penalties or restrictions imposed by one country over another country for importing and exporting goods, services, and investments. In 2011, Canada imposed sweeping trade sanctions on Libya because of escalating human rights abuses by the Libyan government on its citizens. Some of the measures announced include a ban on all goods exported from Canada to Libya and a ban on all goods imported from Libya into Canada.[11] An embargo is a form of trade sanction that prohibits trading with a certain country or trading in specific goods (e.g., oil embargo) by other signatory countries.

tariff (or duty)
A tax levied on a good imported into a country.

Tariffs   A **tariff** (or **duty**) is a tax levied on a good imported into a country. In most cases, tariffs are intended to make imported goods more expensive and thus less competitive with domestic products,[12] which in turn protects domestic industries from foreign

---

EXHIBIT 17.2   Government Actions

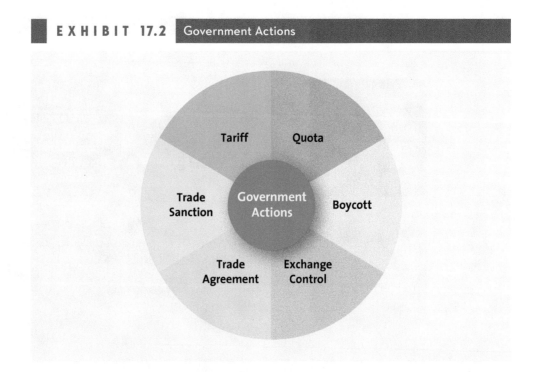

competition. In other cases, tariffs might be imposed to penalize another country for trade practices that the home country views as unfair. For example, companies wishing to export dairy products to Canada face a whopping 240 percent tariff put in place to protect Canadian dairy farmers. In 2002, the United States imposed a 9.31 percent duty on Canadian softwood lumber exported to the United States because the U.S. softwood industry claimed that Canada was subsidizing Canadian softwood lumber and Canadian lumber producers were **dumping**—the practice of selling a good in a foreign market at a price that is lower than its domestic price or below its cost—low-cost softwood lumber on the U.S. market. The duty increased the prices of Canadian lumber sold in the United States by 27 percent, making it difficult for Canadian companies to compete with U.S. lumber producers.[13] In 2010, the Government of Canada basically made Canada a tariff-free zone for industrial manufacturers by eliminating all tariffs on machinery, equipment, and goods imported into Canada for further manufacturing. When fully implemented, this change will provide $300 million in annual duty savings for Canadian business to support investment and growth and create jobs.[14]

dumping
The practice of selling a good in a foreign market at a price that is lower than its domestic price or below its cost.

Quotas   A **quota** designates the maximum quantity of a product that may be brought into a country during a specified time period. Many Canadian quotas on foreign-made textiles were eliminated in 2005, which reduced the cost of imported apparel products sold in Canada. It opened the floodgates for garments made in Bangladesh. Some firms have chosen to pass on the bulk of these savings to consumers—in Walmart's case, 75 percent of them—whereas others, such as bebe, planned to share only 25 percent and keep the rest as profit.[15]

quota
Designates the maximum quantity of a product that may be brought into a country during a specified time period.

Tariffs and quotas can impose a potentially devastating blow on a firm's ability to sell products in another country. Tariffs artificially raise prices and therefore lower demand, and quotas reduce the availability of imported merchandise. Conversely, tariffs and quotas benefit domestically made products because they reduce foreign competition. In the case of softwood lumber, tariffs and quotas benefit U.S. lumber producers and reduce competition from Canadian lumber producers. Unfortunately, U.S. consumers end up paying higher prices for U.S. softwood lumber rather than benefiting from cheaper Canadian lumber, and Canadian lumber producers lost huge market share.

Boycott   A **boycott** pertains to a group's refusal to deal commercially with some organization to protest against its policies. Boycotts might be called by governments or

boycott
A group's refusal to deal commercially with some organization to protest against its policies.

Many quotas on foreign-made textiles have been eliminated. Some firms chose to pass on the bulk of these savings to consumers—in Walmart's case (left), 75 percent of the savings; whereas other firms, such as bebe (right), planned to share only 25 percent of the savings and keep the rest as profit.

The increase in value of the Canadian dollar against the U.S. dollar has made Canadian exports to the United States more expensive, and imports from the United States less expensive.

exchange control
Refers to the regulation of a country's currency exchange rate.

exchange rate
The measure of how much one currency is worth in relation to another.

trade agreement
Intergovernmental agreement designed to manage and promote trade activities for specific regions.

trading bloc
Consists of those countries that have signed a particular trade agreement.

nongovernmental organizations, such as trade unions, or human rights or environmental groups. For example, the United States continues to impose economic sanctions against Cuba and Iran, and in 2010 Canada imposed its own sanctions on Iran.

Exchange Control   **Exchange control** refers to the regulation of a country's currency **exchange rate**, the measure of how much one currency is worth in relation to another.[16] A designated agency in each country, often the central bank, sets the rules for currency exchange. In Canada, the Bank of Canada sets the rules for the currency exchange rates. The value of the Canadian dollar against the U.S. dollar increased significantly, from around CAD$0.60 for US$1.00 in 2001, to CAD$1.10 in November 2007. The exchange rate held steady at par until 2014 when it slipped back to $0.90. The fluctuating Canadian dollar has a twofold effect on the ability of Canadian firms to conduct global business. For Canadian firms that depend on U.S. imports of finished products, raw materials, or services, the cost of doing business has gone up dramatically. However, U.S. buyers find the costs of Canadian goods and services less expensive than they were before. This tends to have a positive impact on Canadian manufacturing exports to the United States, as Americans will find that their dollar can buy them more in Canada while Canadians find that they can buy less in the United States with their Canadian dollars.

Trade Agreements   Marketers must consider the trade agreements to which a particular country is a signatory or the trading bloc to which it belongs. A **trade agreement** is an intergovernmental agreement designed to manage and promote trade activities for a specific region, and a **trading bloc** consists of those countries that have signed the particular trade agreement.[17]

Some major trade agreements cover two-thirds of the world's international trade: the European Union (EU), the North American Free Trade Agreement (NAFTA), the Central America Free Trade Agreement (CAFTA), Mercosur, and the Association of Southeast Asian Nations (ASEAN).[18] These trade agreements are summarized in Exhibit 17.3. The European Union represents the highest level of integration across individual nations, whereas the other agreements vary in their integration levels.

EXHIBIT 17.3   Trade Agreements

Name	Countries
European Union	Austria, Belgium, Bulgaria, Cyprus, Czech Republic, Denmark, Estonia, Finland, France, Germany, Greece, Hungary, Ireland, Italy, Latvia, Lithuania, Luxembourg, Malta, the Netherlands, Poland, Portugal, Romania, Slovakia, Slovenia, Spain, Sweden, United Kingdom of Great Britain. There are five official candidate countries to join the EU: Croatia, Macedonia, Turkey, Iceland, and Montenegro.
NAFTA	Canada, Mexico, the United States
CAFTA	Costa Rica, the Dominican Republic, El Salvador, Guatemala, Honduras, Nicaragua, the United States
Mercosur	Full members: Argentina, Brazil, Paraguay, Uruguay, Venezuela
ASEAN	Brunei, Darussalam, Cambodia, Indonesia, Laos, Malaysia, Myanmar, Philippines, Singapore, Thailand, Vietnam

The European Union has resulted in lowering trade barriers and strengthening global relationships among member nations.

These trading blocs affect how Canadian firms can conduct business in the member countries. Some critics contend that such blocs confer an unfair advantage on their member nations because they offer favourable terms for trade, whereas others believe they stimulate economies by lowering trade barriers and allowing higher levels of foreign investment.

Political Risk Analysis   Before a company decides to engage in global marketing, it must conduct a political risk analysis—assessing the level of political, socioeconomic, and security risks of doing business with a country. Such analysis usually involves weighing the likelihood of certain events, such as change in government, violence, and the imposition of restrictive trade policies, taking place over a specific period of time. This type of analysis requires sophisticated expertise, which most companies do not possess. Thus, they rely on government agencies (e.g., Export Development Canada, Foreign Affairs, Trade, and Development) and private companies that specialize in political risk analysis to provide information and guidance. Political risk analysis helps to reduce the risk of a company losing its investment or goods and the possibility of harm to its employees.

Analyzing the Economic Environment Using Metrics

The greater the wealth of people in a country, generally, the better the opportunity a firm will have in that particular country. A firm conducting an economic analysis of a country's market must look at three major economic factors: general economic environment, market size and population growth, and real income (see Exhibit 17.4).

Evaluating the General Economic Environment   Generally, healthy economies provide better opportunities for global marketing expansions. A firm can measure the relative health of a particular country's economy in several ways. Each way offers a slightly different view, and some may be more useful for some products and services than for others.

To determine the market potential for its particular product or service, a firm should use as many measures as it can obtain. One measure is the relative level of imports and exports. Canada, for example, enjoys a trade surplus, while the United States suffers a

EXHIBIT 17.4 Economic Analysis

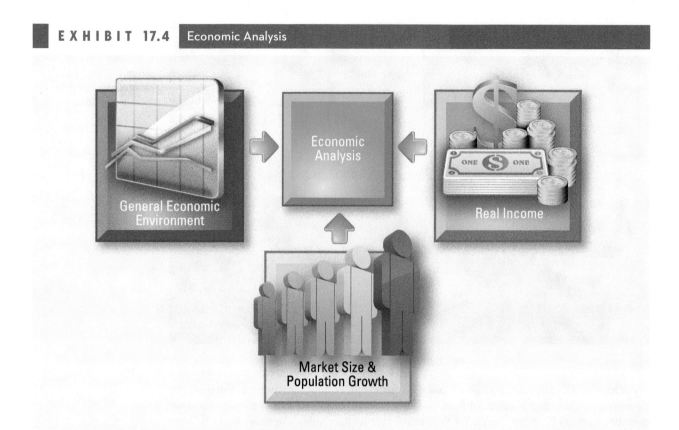

trade deficit. A **trade deficit** means that the country imports more goods than it exports. Firms would prefer to manufacture in a country, such as Canada, that has a **trade surplus**, or a higher level of exports than imports, because it signals a greater opportunity to export products to more markets.

The most common way to gauge the size and market potential of an economy, and therefore the potential the country has for global marketing, is to use standardized measures of output. One of the most widely used measures is **gross domestic product (GDP)**, which is defined as the market value of the goods and services produced by a country in a year. So what does the size of a country's GDP have to do with global marketing? GDP growth means that production and consumption in the country is expanding, therefore, there are greater marketing opportunities for most goods and services. When GDP growth is slowing, it means that the economy is contracting, or that production and consumption are falling, and marketing opportunities for certain goods and services will decline.

Another frequently used measure of an overall economy is the **purchasing power parity (PPP)**, a theory that states that if the exchange rates of two countries are in equilibrium, a product purchased in one will cost the same in the other, expressed in the same currency.[19] A novel measure that employs PPP to assess the relative economic buying power among nations is *The Economist's* Big Mac Index, which suggests that exchange rates should adjust to equalize the cost of a basket of goods and services, wherever it is bought around the world. Using McDonald's Big Mac as the market basket, Exhibit 17.5 shows that the cheapest burger is in India, where it costs $1.89, compared with an average Canadian price of $5. This difference implies that the Indian rupee is undervalued by 62 percent: that is, the rupee is priced too low relative to the Canadian dollar. In this case, the undervalued rupee makes India's exports to Canada cheaper than they would otherwise be, thereby providing an unfair trade advantage to India. It also makes Canadian exports to India more expensive.

EXHIBIT 17.5   Big Mac Index

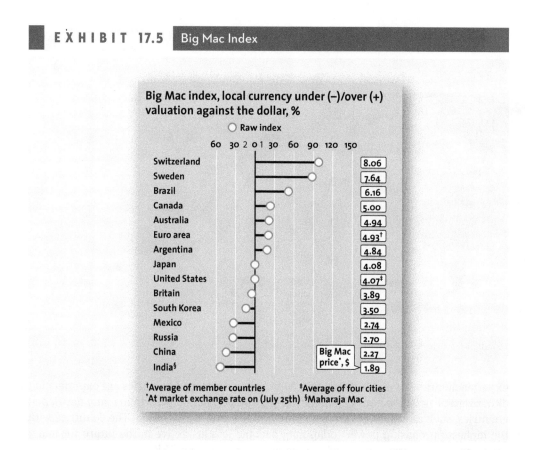

Big Mac index, local currency under (–)/over (+) valuation against the dollar, %

○ Raw index

		Big Mac price*, $
60 30 2 0 1 30 60 90 120 150		
Switzerland		8.06
Sweden		7.64
Brazil		6.16
Canada		5.00
Australia		4.94
Euro area		4.93†
Argentina		4.84
Japan		4.08
United States		4.07‡
Britain		3.89
South Korea		3.50
Mexico		2.74
Russia		2.70
China		2.27
India§		1.89

†Average of member countries   ‡Average of four cities
*At market exchange rate on (July 25th)   §Maharaja Mac

These various metrics help marketers understand the relative wealth of a particular country; however, as scholars have argued, they may not give a full picture of the economic health of a country because they are based solely on material output.[20] As a corollary measure to those described previously, the United Nations has developed the **human development index (HDI)**, a composite measure of three indicators of the quality of life in different countries: life expectancy at birth; educational attainment; and whether the average incomes, according to PPP estimates, are sufficient to meet the basic needs of life in that country. For marketers, these measures determine the lifestyle elements that ultimately drive consumption (recall that Chapter 4 discussed the influence of consumer lifestyle on consumption). The HDI is scaled from 0 to 1: those countries that score lower than 0.5 are classified as nations with low human development, those that score 0.5 to 0.8 have medium development, and those that score above 0.8 are classified as having high human development. Exhibit 17.6 shows a map of the world with the various HDI scores. Higher HDI means greater consumption levels, especially of discretionary goods and services.

These macroeconomic measures provide a snapshot of a particular country at any one point in time. Because they are standardized measures, it is possible to compare countries across time and to identify those that are experiencing economic growth and increased globalization.

Although an understanding of the macroeconomic environment is crucial for managers facing a market entry decision, of equal importance is the understanding of economic metrics of individual income and household size.

Evaluating Market Size and Population Growth Rate   Global population has been growing dramatically since the turn of the 20th century. It is estimated that by 2050, the world population will reach 9.6 billion people.[21] From a marketing perspective, however, growth has not been equally dispersed. Less-developed nations, by and large, are

human development index (HDI)
A composite measure of three indicators of the quality of life in different countries: life expectancy at birth, educational attainment, and whether the average incomes are sufficient to meet the basic needs of life in that country.

EXHIBIT 17.6 Global Human Development Index Scores

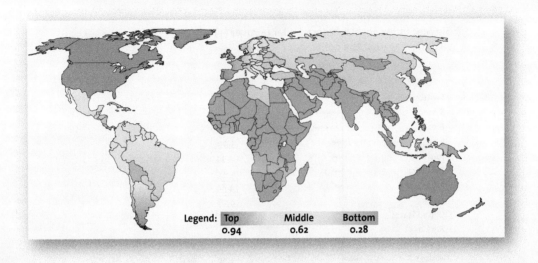

Legend: **Top** 0.94   **Middle** 0.62   **Bottom** 0.28

Source: http://www.nationmaster.com/red/graph/eco_hum_dev_ind-economy-human-development-index&int=1&b_map=1#.

experiencing rapid population growth, while many developed countries are experiencing either zero or negative natural population growth. Population growth in many developed countries, such as Canada, is attributed to high levels of immigration. The countries with the highest purchasing power today may become less attractive in the future for many products and services because of stagnated growth. And the BRIC countries are likely to be the source of most market growth.

In response, consumer goods companies are paying close attention to the strong demand in BRIC nations. Procter & Gamble, which enjoys a strong advantage in the Chinese market, is expanding aggressively into India and Brazil (as well as sub-Saharan Africa).[22] With 1.33 billion people, China offers such promise that international companies such as PepsiCo and Coca-Cola cannot afford not to focus their efforts there. Each company plans to invest more than $2.5 billion immediately in China, with the goal of achieving at least double-digit annual growth. Pepsi also plans to build a research and development centre for its Asian products to ensure that it correctly targets this new consumer market. In some cases, the companies will sell the same products in China and in North America; in other situations, they are creating new products to meet Chinese consumers' tastes. The "Minute Maid Pulpy Super Milky" combines fruit juice, milk powder, whey protein, and coconut bits. Pepsi offers cucumber-flavoured and crispy prawn–flavoured potato chips.[23]

Another aspect related to population and growth pertains to the distribution of the population within a particular region; namely, is the population located primarily in rural or urban areas? This distinction determines where and how products and services can be delivered. Long supply chains, in which goods pass through many hands, are necessary to reach rural populations and therefore add costs to products. India's 1.1 billion people live overwhelmingly in rural areas, though the population is moving toward urban areas to meet the demands of the growing industrial and service centres located in major cities such as Bangalore and New Delhi. This population shift, perhaps not surprisingly, is accompanied by rapid growth in the middle class.[24] Another major trend in India involves the age of the population; more than half of

"Minute Maid Pulpy Super Milky" combines fruit juice, milk powder, whey protein, and coconut bits for the Chinese market.

India's citizens are younger than 25 years.[25] In Canada, in contrast, the median age is 39.7 years.[26] Furthermore, relatively careful banking policies and minimal dependence on exports have helped protect India from the global financial crisis. The business impacts of these combined trends of increasing urbanization, a growing middle class, a degree of protectionism by the central government, and a youthful populace make India an absolutely enormous market for consumer goods.

Developed for the Indian market, the Nano is the world's cheapest car—about $2,000.

In the capital of India, New Delhi, crowded streets traditionally were filled with horse-drawn carts, bicycles, scooters, and taxis. Yet the growing Indian middle class is demanding more products previously available only to the wealthy. Therefore, the Nano, the world's cheapest car, has begun to appear, jockeying for position with the multitude of other vehicles. The Nano costs only about 100,000 rupees ($2,000). It weighs half as much as a Honda Accord, and it gets 56 miles per gallon. It can even achieve a top speed of 60 miles per hour, though it needs 23 seconds to reach that speed from a standstill. During the 16-day prebooking period, the manufacturer received orders for 203,000 tiny cars.[27]

Similarly, the prevalence of cellphones has grown with the emerging Indian middle class. Fifteen years ago, the country hosted only 5 million total telecom connections, and that number included ground lines. Today, there are more than 752 million.[28] The rapid growth rates of industries create significant opportunities for global companies to sell products. In the telecommunications industry, for example, sellers of accessories such as ringtones and new batteries are enjoying a greatly expanded market. In general, India's economy is expected to continue to outpace world growth.

Evaluating Real Income   Real income—income adjusted for inflation—affects consumers' buying power, and thus will influence the marketing mixes companies develop for their overseas markets. Firms can make adjustments to an existing product or change the price to meet the unique needs of a particular country market. Such shifts are particularly common for low-priced consumer goods. For instance, Procter & Gamble developed a single-use shampoo packet for consumers in less developed nations who cannot afford an entire bottle at one time. To increase consumption of Coca-Cola in rural India, the company lowered its price to the equivalent of about 10 cents per bottle; Cadbury International introduced the Dairy Milk Shots for the equivalent of about 4 cents.[29] Textbook publishers sell paperback versions of Canadian books for a fraction of the Canadian price to countries where students would not be able to otherwise afford a text. But pricing adjustments aren't only for inexpensive products. Fashion and jewellery manufacturers also make downward adjustments to their prices in countries where the incomes of their target markets cannot support higher prices.

To adjust for India's lower income, Cadbury International sells its Dairy Milk Shots for the equivalent of about four cents.

Speaking of affordability, who would believe that Africa is the fastest-growing market for cellphones, given the stereotypes of poverty in Africa? Today, one in 10 Africans is a cellphone user. The main reason for this explosive growth is a combination of government policy—many African governments privatized their telephone monopolies—and fierce competition among cellphone operators, which led to dramatic price decreases for airtime and handsets.[30]

Even as multinationals battle for dominance in emerging economies, local marketers also are becoming increasingly price competitive in selling their wares, as the example of India's Tata Motors and its Nano shows. Local marketers already have strong familiarity with their markets, existing distribution channels, and good name recognition. These smaller firms can often exhibit greater flexibility in their pricing to hold on to market share. The best outcome for everyone involved is not just a higher share of an existing market but rather the ongoing development of the market for everyone.[31]

Analyzing Sociocultural Factors

Understanding another country's culture is crucial to the success of any global marketing initiative. Culture, or the set of values, guiding beliefs, understandings, and ways of doing things shared by members of a society, exists on two levels: visible artifacts (e.g., behaviour, dress, symbols, physical settings, ceremonies) and underlying values (thought processes, beliefs, and assumptions). Visible artifacts are easy to recognize, but businesses often find it more difficult to understand the underlying values of a culture and appropriately adapt their marketing strategies to them.[32]

For example, IKEA stores around the world are open seven days a week—except in France. French law prevents retailers from selling on Sundays, and when IKEA tried to challenge the law by keeping one of its stores open, it provoked a lawsuit from a French workers' union. Although IKEA would love to sell over the whole weekend, when it earns approximately one-quarter of its weekly revenues, neither the workers' unions nor French consumers are likely to change their ways any time soon; leaving Sunday as a day of relaxation constitutes a fundamental foundation of French culture.[33] For the Swiss, a similar prohibition against Sunday retailing may soon fall to the wayside though. If stores remain closed, Switzerland will continue to lose tourism revenues, because most foreign visitors, who tend to visit on the weekend, are accustomed to shopping on Sundays. Opening retail stores on Sundays could mean increased consumption and wages for workers who work more hours, as well as employment for more people. But the loss of a day traditionally designated for family time and relaxation might be something the country cannot abide.[34] There may be no completely right answer to this dilemma, but global marketers clearly must be aware of the regulations and cultural norms of the countries they enter.

Even global companies with many years of experience operating in a country occasionally end up offending their customers, which causes the companies huge embarrassment, lost sales, and financial losses. Several examples of these cultural gaffes are presented in this section for illustrative purposes.

One important cultural classification scheme that firms can use is Geert Hofstede's cultural dimensions concept, which sheds more light on these underlying values. Hofstede believes cultures differ on five dimensions:[35]

1. *Power distance.* Willingness to accept social inequality as natural.
2. *Uncertainty avoidance.* The extent to which the society relies on orderliness, consistency, structure, and formalized procedures to address situations that arise in daily life.
3. *Individualism.* Perceived obligation to and dependence on groups.
4. *Masculinity.* The extent to which dominant values are male oriented. A lower masculinity ranking indicates that men and women are treated equally in all aspects of society; a higher masculinity ranking suggests that men dominate in positions of power.[36]
5. *Time orientation.* Short- versus long-term orientation. A country that tends to have a long-term orientation values long-term commitments and is willing to accept a longer time horizon for, say, the success of a new product introduction.

To illustrate two of the five dimensions, consider the data and graph in Exhibit 17.7. Power distance is on the vertical axis and individualism is on the horizontal axis. Several Latin American countries cluster high on power distance but low on individualism; Canada, the United States, Australia, and the United Kingdom, in contrast, cluster high on individualism but low on power distance. Using this information, firms should expect that if they design a marketing campaign that stresses equality and individualism, it will be well accepted in the English-speaking countries, all other factors being equal. The same campaign, however, might not be as well received in Latin American countries.

China scores very high on its time orientation but low in individualism; India has medium to high levels on all five dimensions; and Russia posts notably high uncertainty avoidance and power distance scores. Hofstede is careful to warn that these scores are informative only in a comparative sense, but marketers clearly can use them to design strategies for the varied, promising, BRIC growth markets.[37]

Another means of classifying cultures distinguishes them according to the importance of verbal communication.[38] In Canada, the United States, and most European countries, business relationships are governed by what is said and written down, often through formal contracts. In countries such as China and South Korea, however, most relationships rely on nonverbal cues, so that the situation or context means much more than mere words. For instance, business relationships in China often are formalized by just a handshake, and trust and honour are often more important than legal arrangements.

Overall, culture affects every aspect of consumer behaviour: why people buy; who is in charge of buying decisions; and how, when, and where people shop. Essentially, understanding consumer behaviour is about understanding consumers' culture, particularly in global marketing. For example, in India, McDonald's sells its Maharajah Mac made from lamb instead of beef because the cow is sacred in Hindu culture. In Israel, McDonald's

Business relationships in China often are formalized by just a handshake, and trust and honour are often more important than legal arrangements.

EXHIBIT 17.7   Country Clusters

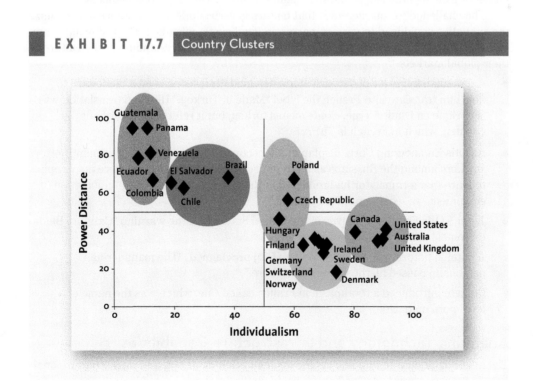

Source: Based on data available at http://www.geert-hofstede.com. Data from: Geert Hofstede, *Culture's Consequences,* 2nd edition (Thousand Oaks: Sage, 2001). Copyright © Geert Hofstede, reproduced with permission.

In Israel, McDonald's Kosher restaurants use the blue and white colours of Israel's flag.

Kosher restaurants use the blue and white colours of Israel's flag instead of the yellow and red of its Golden Arches.[39] Similarly, Coca-Cola developed a new drink, Vitango, to be sold in Africa, and P&G developed its Nutristar for Venezuelan consumers.[40] Both companies claim that their soft drinks have special health benefits for their customers in these markets. In North America, people often use their BlackBerrys almost everywhere—in subways, lobbies, restaurants, ballparks, and hockey arenas, as well as while driving. However, in Japan, sending a message on your BlackBerry when in company—say during a sit-down dinner or a child's little league baseball game—could be viewed as bad manners.[41]

The challenge for marketers is that culture is very subtle, and a failure to recognize the subtleties could lead to very embarrassing and costly mistakes. The following examples illustrate what happens when marketers have a poor understanding of the culture of their global markets.[42]

- A Canadian importer of Turkish shirts destined for Quebec used a dictionary to help him translate into French the label "Made in Turkey." His final translation was "Fabrique en Dinde." True, *dinde* means turkey, but it refers to the bird not the country, which in French is *Turquie*.

- An Otis Engineering Corp. display at a Moscow exhibition produced as many snickers among the Russians as it did praise. Company executives were not happy to learn that a translator had rendered in Russian a sign identifying "completion equipment" as "equipment for orgasms."

- Japan's Olfa Corp. sold knives in the United States with the warning "Caution: Blade extremely sharp. Keep out of children."

- A hotel in notoriously polluted Mexico City proclaimed, "The manager has personally passed all the water served here."

- Colgate introduced a toothpaste in France called Cue, which was the name of a local porn magazine.

Analyzing Technology and Infrastructure Capabilities

infrastructure
The basic facilities, services, and installations needed for a community or society to function, such as transportation and communications systems, water and power lines, and public institutions such as schools, post offices, and prisons.

The next component of any market assessment is a technology and infrastructure analysis. **Infrastructure** is defined as the basic facilities, services, and installations needed for a community or society to function, such as transportation and communications systems, water and power lines, and public institutions such as schools, post offices, and prisons. In Pakistan, companies struggled with an electricity crisis and daily blackouts for over a year. The energy shortage has fuelled demand for solar power from companies such as Canadian Solar[43] in Guelph, Ontario.

Marketers are especially concerned with four key elements of a country's infrastructure: transportation, distribution channels, communications, and commerce. First, there must be a system to transport goods throughout the various markets and to consumers in geographically dispersed marketplaces. Second, distribution channels must exist to deliver products in a timely manner and at a reasonable cost. Third, communications systems, particularly media access, must be sufficiently developed to allow consumers to find information about the products and services available in the marketplace. Fourth, the commercial infrastructure consists of the legal, banking, and regulatory systems that allow markets to function. Marketers, especially those that are interested in offshoring research, production, and marketing will be particularly interested in the technical sophistication of the workforce of the country. Generally, a more sophisticated workforce means that a higher proportion of product design, development, and marketing activities can be decentralized to the foreign country.

Sustainable Marketing 17.1 highlights how Canada's Bombardier, a world leader in the transportation industry, is implementing sustainable business practices across its global operations with great success.

For a country to be a viable option for a new market entry, firms must assess its transportation, distribution channels, communications, and commerce.

Sustainable Marketing 17.1

Bombardier: Moving Forward Responsibly[44]

Canada's Bombardier is a global transportation company that operates in more than 60 countries on five continents. It is a world-leading manufacturer of innovative transportation solutions, from commercial aircraft and business jets to rail transportation equipment, systems, and services. Its revenues for the fiscal year 2013 were US$18.2 billion. Bombardier's 76,400 employees around the globe do everything from R&D to the design, manufacture, sales, and support stages for a broad range of world-class products in aerospace and rail transportation. Some high-profile projects include a fully automated people mover in the Beijing airport and high-altitude railcars for a railway to Lhasa, Tibet.

Bombardier has made sustainability an integral part of its global business strategy, implementing a wide range of initiatives across the entire global organization. According to Pierre Beaudoin, president and CEO of Bombardier, "Our ongoing investments attest to our belief that excellence in corporate social responsibility makes business sense in all economic cycles. That is why we made corporate social responsibility a key element of our new business strategy." The company also actively promotes the UN Global Compact's principles of social responsibility and has embedded these principles in its Code of Ethics and Business Conduct. To demonstrate its commitment and to measure and communicate its progress, Bombardier has undertaken to produce an annual report card, Moving Forward Responsibly, detailing its many initiatives and accomplishments.

On the product innovation side, for example, Bombardier has developed the all-new *CSeries* commercial aircraft. When the *CSeries* takes flight in 2013, it will burn up to 20 percent less fuel and generate up to 20 percent less carbon dioxide emissions than other aircraft in its class. Similarly, the *ZEFIRO* portfolio features the world's most economical and eco-friendly high-speed trains. It includes *ECO4* technologies, which can yield overall energy savings of up to 50 percent.

Between 2009 and 2013, Bombardier successfully achieved its goal of reducing its water consumption by 12.6 percent, energy consumption by 15 percent, and greenhouse gas emissions by 24.4 percent.[45] The progress made by Bombardier in the area of sustainability has earned it a spot on two prestigious Dow Jones Sustainability Indexes and, for the second time, on the Carbon Disclosure Project (CDP), the world standard for carbon disclosure methodology and process. The CDP named Bombardier one of the 10 Canadian Climate Disclosure Leaders.

In keeping with its theme of Moving Forward Responsibly, Bombardier has identified four areas in which it will make additional investments over the next few years: community investment, stakeholder engagement, employee volunteering, and corporate social responsibility reporting and communication.

L02

The Appeal of the BRIC Countries

Changes in technology, especially communications, have been a driving force for growth in global markets for decades. The telegraph, radio, television, computer, and Internet have increasingly connected distant parts of the world. Today, communication is instantaneous. Sounds and images from across the globe are delivered to TV sets, radios, and computers in real time, which enables receivers in all parts of the world to observe how others live, work, and play. Perhaps the greatest change facing the global community in recent years has been the growth and expansion of four countries that together have come to be known as the BRIC countries: Brazil, Russia, India, and China. Let's examine each in turn.

Brazil[46]   Long a regional powerhouse, Brazil's ability to weather and even thrive during the most recent economic storm has transformed it into a global contender. Currently, Brazil is the world's seventh largest economy, but predicted growth rates indicate it will move into the fifth spot within a few years. This growth has been aided by a large, literate population and the impositions of social programs that have allowed more than half of the 190 million Brazilians to enter the middle class. This large South American democracy welcomes foreign investors.

Russia[47]   Relations with Russia are a little more complicated than for Brazil. Since the fall of the former Soviet Union, Russia has undergone multiple up- and downturns in its economy. However, its overall growth prospects appear promising, especially as a consumer market. Long denied access to consumer goods, the well-educated population exhibits strong demand for North American products and brands. In particular, the 60 million Russian Internet users are growing at a rate of approximately 15 percent annually. Russia is likely to become Europe's largest online market in the next few years. The country also is negotiating to enter the World Trade Organization (WTO) to improve trade relations with other countries. Russia still faces an aging population and low birth rates. If these trends persist, Russia's population could decline by one-third in the next half-century. At the same time, corruption is widespread, creating ethical dilemmas for firms trying to market their goods and services.

India[48]   With more than 1.1 billion people, or approximately 15 percent of the world's population, together with expanding middle and upper classes, India is one of the world's fastest-growing markets. With a median age of 25 years, India has one of the youngest populations in the world. Its young inhabitants increasingly are adopting global attitudes while living in growing urban centres and shopping at large malls. The well-educated modern generation is largely fluent in English, and the highly skilled workforce holds great attraction for firms that hope to expand using local talent, especially in technical fields.

India's retail environment is still dominated by millions of small stores, and lacks modern supply chain management facilities and systems.[49] Recent changes by the Indian government, however, have the potential to significantly modernize the retail landscape. Foreign retailers that carry multiple brands, like Walmart, are now allowed to own up to 51 percent of joint ventures in India, whereas previously these retailers were permitted only to enter into wholesale joint ventures. Also, retailers that carry only their own brand, like Nike, can now own 100 percent of their Indian businesses, whereas in the past they were allowed to own up to only 51 percent of a partnership with an Indian company.

China[50]   For most of the 20th century, China experienced foreign occupation, civil unrest, major famine, and a strict one-party communist regime. However, since 1978, China's leadership, while maintaining communist political ideals, has embraced market-oriented economic development, which has led to startlingly rapid gains. For many

Chinese, recent developments have dramatically improved their living standards and their levels of personal freedom. Increasing liberalization in the economy has prompted a large increase in China's gross domestic product (GDP); it is now the second-largest economy and the third-largest market for U.S. exports. It makes an excellent target for consumer goods, assuming they can be produced at the right price.

Yet the country continues to suffer from drastically unequal economic distribution, which has led to a significant migrant workforce who subsist on part-time, low-paying jobs. These workers were hit hard by the global financial crisis, which reduced demand for Chinese exports for the first time in years. Furthermore, actual growth of the 1.3 billion-strong Chinese population slowed as a result of government population controls that limit each family to one child. Although China's median age is slightly younger than that in North America currently, at 34.1 years, the application of the one-child policy means that China is one of the most rapidly aging countries in the world.

Even as vast numbers of North American companies actively target the massive Chinese market or explore options for entering it, Ethical Dilemma 17.1 highlights some challenges that one famous potential entrant faces before it makes this choice.

Ethical Dilemma 17.1   Can Social Networking and Censorship Coexist?

By Facebook CEO Mark Zuckerberg's own admission, Facebook grew exponentially for years without a strategic plan for international growth.[51] As the company has matured, however, Facebook has refocused its attention on developing a strategy for China. But attempting to combine the inherent openness of social networking with China's censorship rules presents significant challenges. Add in local competitors and human rights advocacy groups concerned with government backlash against users, and Facebook may be looking at the same fate that has befallen other Western technology companies trying to expand to the East—including such marketing geniuses as Google, eBay, and Twitter.[52]

Successful entry into the Chinese market requires a particular blend of timing, skill, cultural understanding, and political savvy, and these factors may not be quite in alignment for Facebook yet. The timing may be wrong, because China's autocratic leaders have enforced greater controls on social networking and blogging in response to the Arab Spring uprisings. Nor do Facebook executives appear to have a full grasp of the political and cultural nuances of business in China, despite a good track record of respecting local cultural values, such as when it agreed to block content about Nazism in Germany or drawings of Muhammad in Pakistan. And even if Facebook were to navigate these challenges safely, China has a strong, enduring preference for companies owned and run by its own people.

Zuckerberg can (and does) claim that his company will employ diplomacy in China, but censorship issues are highly complex. For instance, how would Facebook respond to retaliation against users who criticize the government?[53] For Google, whose mission statement

CEO Mark Zuckerberg (centre) claims that Facebook will employ diplomacy in China, but censorship issues are highly complex.

simply advises, "Don't Be Evil," such questions became all too pertinent when hackers in China gained access to the email accounts of prominent human rights activists. When Western companies have cooperated with the Chinese government, some operations have led to the imprisonment of online activists.

Censorship has global repercussions too. Blocking a comment generated by someone outside China, so that readers within China cannot see it, affects access globally. But the question is about more than whether users can enjoy all the fun of Facebook. When a post on Facebook can lead to jail time, it becomes a question of basic human rights.

L03   CHOOSING A GLOBAL MARKET ENTRY STRATEGY

When a firm has concluded its assessment analysis of the most viable markets for its products and services, it must then conduct an internal assessment of its capabilities. As we discussed in Chapter 2, this analysis includes an assessment of the firm's access to capital, the current markets it serves, its manufacturing capacity, its proprietary assets, and the commitment of its management to the proposed strategy. These factors ultimately contribute to the success or failure of a market expansion strategy, whether at home or in a foreign market. After these internal market assessments, it is time for the firm to choose its entry strategy.

A firm can choose from many approaches when it decides to enter a new market. These approaches vary according to the level of risk the firm is willing to take. Many firms actually follow a progression in which they begin with less risky strategies to enter their first foreign markets and move to increasingly risky strategies as they gain confidence in their abilities, as illustrated in Exhibit 17.8. Generally, profit potential increases with higher levels of risks. We examine these different approaches that marketers take when entering global markets, beginning with the least risky.

Exporting

exporting
Producing goods in one country and selling them in another.

Exporting means producing goods in one country (exporting country) and selling them in another (host country). This entry strategy requires the least financial risk but also allows for only a limited return to the exporting firm. Global expansion often begins when a firm receives an order for its product or service from another country, in which case it faces little risk because it can demand payment before it ships the merchandise. By the same token, it is difficult to achieve economies of scale when everything has to be shipped internationally. The Swiss watchmaker Rolex sells relatively small numbers of expensive watches all over the world. Because its transportation costs are relatively small compared with the cost of the watches, the best way for it to service any market is to export from Switzerland. Exporting generally provides less employment for

EXHIBIT 17.8   Entry Strategies

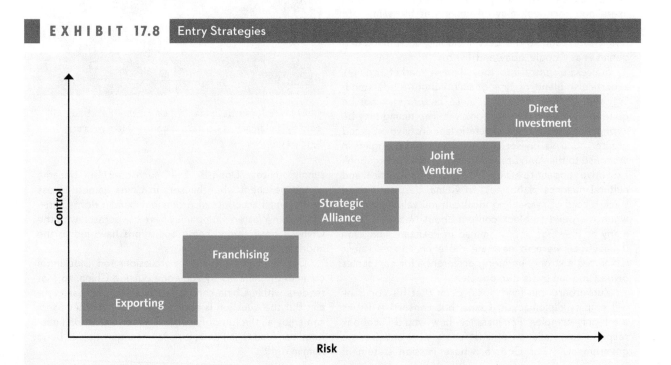

citizens of the host country than either joint venture or direct investment.

Exporting may take two forms: indirect or direct. Indirect exporting occurs when the exporting firm sells its goods in the host country through an intermediary; for example, BlackBerry products are sold in Japan through NTT DOCOMO, Japan's largest cellphone operator.[54] Ossetra Wondrous Earth in Newfoundland produces an organic skincare line that uses water from local icebergs. It has distributors in the United States, Greece, Hong Kong, and South Korea, ensuring the company is in compliance with international regulations.[55] This approach carries the least risk but probably returns the least profit for the exporting company. This approach is likely to be used when the company has limited contacts in the foreign country but wants to market to that country. Direct exporting is when the exporting company sells its products in the host country directly without the intermediaries. This approach carries more risk and offers greater returns to the exporting firm than indirect exporting. For example, Christie Digital, a firm based in Kitchener, Ontario, manufacturers a variety of display technologies and solutions for cinemas, large audience environments, control rooms, business presentations, training facilities, 3-D and virtual reality, simulation, education, media, and government. Christie has installed more than 75,000 projection solutions in the United States, the United Kingdom, Japan, China, and many other countries around the world.[56] Similarly, Cognos, an Ottawa-based company of business intelligence tools and applications, sells its solutions to businesses around the world by using its own sales force. Entrepreneurial Marketing 17.1 describes how Steeped Tea successfully entered the U.S. market using a direct sales model.

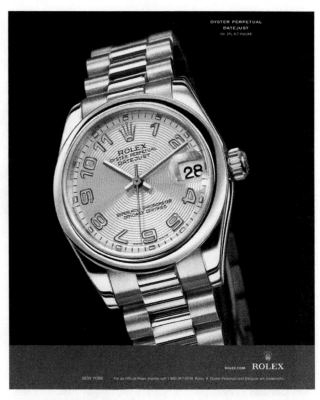

Rolex exports its watches to countries all over the world from its factory in Switzerland.

In Canada, the top five Canadian exporters account for 25 percent of Canada's export and the top 50 Canadian exporters account for 50 percent of Canada's exports. The remaining 45 210 exporters are responsible for the remaining 50 percent. Almost three-quarters (72.6 percent) of Canadian exporters had exports of less than $1 million. More than two-thirds of Canada's exports come from two sectors: manufacturing and wholesale trade.[57]

Franchising

Franchising is a contractual agreement between a firm, the franchisor, and another firm or individual, the franchisee. A franchising contract allows the franchisee to operate a business—a retail product or service firm or a B2B provider—using a name and format developed and supported by the franchisor. Many of the best-known retailers in Canada are also successful global franchisers, including McDonald's, Pizza Hut, Starbucks, Domino's Pizza, KFC, and Holiday Inn, all of which have found that global franchising entails lower risks and requires less investment than does opening units owned wholly by the firm. However, when it engages in franchising, the firm has limited control over the market operations in the foreign country, its potential profit is reduced because it must be split with the franchisee, and, once the franchise is established, there is always the threat that the franchisee will break away and operate as a competitor under a different name. White Spot, one of Canada's oldest restaurant chains, successfully used franchising to expand its operations into Asia. To protect its brand reputation, it provides experienced

Entrepreneurial Marketing 17.1   Get Ready to ParTea[58]

After water, tea is the most consumed beverage in the world. Tonia Jashan fell in love with tea while on vacation with her husband. She shared her love of tea with friends at a party in her home, serving them a variety of loose-leaf blends and talking about tea's amazing health benefits. When people started asking her to hold parties in their homes, Steeped Tea was born. It didn't take long for her Hamilton, Ontario, business to become a veritable tempest in a teapot. Only 15 months after hosting her first event, she was doing 15 parties a month.

Steeped Tea's consultants work on a direct sales model in Canada and in the United States.

To help manage the rapid growth, Tonia got her husband, Hatem, involved in her business. With a chemistry degree, a chemical engineering degree, and an MBA, you might question the fit for the tea business. However, he had also owned three Subway franchises. Based on this experience, Hatem felt that franchising wasn't the best approach to expansion. Instead, they opted for a direct sales model based on commission. Six years later Tonia had 500 consultants in Canada selling the company's loose-leaf teas and tea accessories.

Consultants present Steeped Tea's products at parties and facilitate sales to consumers. Creativity is encouraged with some consultants using themes, such as MarTEAni, to drive sales beyond the $500 party average. There are strict guidelines about what consultants can and cannot say. For example, they are not allowed to comment on health issues and must refer consumers to their doctors. All consultants have the option to upgrade the services they receive from Steeped Tea to set up their own personal site with an online shopping cart and the ability to send newsletters. A party management system lets consultants set up a website for hostess to do evites and collect orders from people who can't attend the party.

Ranked number 27 on the PROFIT 500 of Canada's fastest-growing companies, Tonia was ready to expand to the U.S. market. Knowing she would need help, she pitched her story on CBC's *Dragons' Den*. With

impressive annual sales of $1.3 million, she earned financial backing from David Chilton and Jim Treliving. David Chilton even got his daughter to sign up as a consultant to test the business model.[59] In the first month and a half, Steeped Tea signed up 60 U.S. consultants, most of them in northeast Michigan, Ohio, and New York State, but also from Florida, California, and Hawaii.

Hatem Jahshan says the beauty of direct sales is that it builds from word-of-mouth. He expects to have 3,000 consultants in the United States in two years. Growth can take off quickly and he says they need to be prepared. As orders grew, they needed to find new suppliers—they were completely buying out the supply of small companies. Today they source tea from all around the world, buying it in lots, six months in advance of when they need it. Even with such long lead times, it can be difficult to forecast demand or know if suppliers will run out.

Although they have just scratched the surface with U.S. sales, they have received calls to expand to the United Kingdom and Australia. One of the biggest challenges entering the U.S. market was getting FDA approval because tea is a food product. Since the United Kingdom has a whole different set of standards, Steeped Tea is not actively pursuing this option yet. For now, the company's focus is on steeping strong TEAms in North America.

supervisors and "off the shelf" marketing programs to ensure consistency.[60] In Canada, more than 78 000 franchise operations employ over 1 million people and generate in excess of $100 billion in annual sales.[61]

Strategic Alliance

strategic alliance
A collaborative relationship between independent firms, though the partnering firms do not create an equity partnership; that is, they do not invest in one another.

Strategic alliances refer to collaborative relationships between independent firms, though the partnering firms do not create an equity partnership; that is, they do not invest in one another. For example, Star Alliance constitutes one of the most complex strategic alliances in the world, with 27 airline members representing different

KFC and Pizza Hut are successful global franchisors.

countries: Adria Airways (Slovenia), Aegean Airlines (Greece), Air Canada, Air China, Air New Zealand, All Nippon Airways (Japan), Asiana Airlines (South Korea), Austrian Airlines, Blue1 (Finland), BMI (United Kingdom), Brussels Airlines (Belgium), Continental Airlines (USA), Croatia Airlines, EgyptAir, LOT (Poland), Lufthansa (Germany), Scandinavian Airlines (Denmark, Norway, and Sweden), Singapore Airlines, South African Airways, Spanair (Spain), Swiss International Air Lines, TAM Airlines (Brazil), TAP Portugal, Thai Airways International, Turkish Airlines, United Airlines (United States), and US Airways.[62]

What began as a series of bilateral agreements among five airlines grew over time into Star Alliance, which now acts as a separate legal entity in which each member is a stakeholder but no member is an equity owner in the others. Star Alliance coordinates the members on projects of mutual interest, such as helping members in their individual brand-building efforts by creating value through their membership in the Alliance. This plan offers passengers benefits from individual airlines when they purchase from alliance

The Star Alliance is a strategic alliance with 27 airline members, including Air Canada.

partners. For instance, an Air Canada frequent-flier member could earn Aeroplan miles by flying Spanair. This coalition also allows seamless booking and other transactions across the Alliance membership.

Joint Venture

joint venture
Formed when a firm entering a new market pools its resources with those of a local firm to form a new company in which ownership, control, and profits are shared.

A **joint venture** is formed when a firm entering a new market pools its resources with those of a local firm to form a new company in which ownership, control, and profits are shared. In addition to sharing the financial burden, the local partner offers the foreign entrant greater understanding of the market and access to resources such as vendors and real estate. Tesco, the U.K. supermarket, finance, telecom, and insurance superstar, entered China through a joint venture in which it has purchased a 50-percent share in Ting Hsin—which owns and operates the 25-store hypermarket chain Hymall—for $250 million.[63] China usually requires joint ownership from entering firms, as do many other countries, though these restrictions are loosened as a result of WTO negotiations. Bombardier signed a $3.4 billion contract with Russia for the sale of 100 Q400 NextGen airplanes. Until 2013, all of its airplanes had been assembled in Canada; however, the Q400s will be assembled in Russia as part of the joint venture agreement.[64] Problems with this entry approach can arise when the partners disagree or if the government places restrictions on the firm's ability to move its profits out of the foreign country and back to its home country or if the objectives, responsibilities, and benefits of the venture are not clearly defined from the outset. Conflicts could also arise if larger partners benefit more than smaller partners, which could threaten the venture. Differences in organizational cultures, management styles, and leadership, as well as disagreements about marketing and investment policies, could seriously affect the performance of the venture.

Two variants of joint ventures are contract manufacturing and management contracting. Contract manufacturing is when a foreign firm contracts with a local firm in the host market to manufacture the product. For example, NutraLab Canada is a contract manufacturer that has provided original equipment manufacture (OEM) and private label service for vitamin, natural health, and dietary supplement products for more than 10 years.[65] NutraLab Canada produces many of the pharmaceutical softgels, capsules, liquid, and tablets that we consume.

Tesco, the U.K. supermarket chain, has a joint venture in China in which it has purchased a 50 percent share in Ting Hsin—which owns and operates the 25-store hypermarket chain Hymall.

Management contracting occurs when the domestic firm provides management consulting and advice to a foreign firm. For example, many Canadian technology companies will supply their technology to firms and governments in developing countries with a specific agreement that only the Canadian supplier can maintain the technology or provide know-how regarding technology use and repair. Management contracting is a low-risk method of entering a country's market without setting up operations in the country. It also generates returns immediately upon execution of the agreement. Management contracting tends to be long term since it extends over the life of the technology.

Direct Investment

Direct investment requires a firm to maintain 100 percent ownership of its plants, operation facilities, and offices in a foreign country, often through the formation of wholly owned subsidiaries. This entry strategy requires the highest level of investment and exposes the firm to significant risks, including the loss of its operating and/or initial investments. For example, a dramatic economic downturn caused by a natural disaster or war, political instability, or changes in the country's laws can increase a foreign entrant's risk considerably. Many firms believe that in certain markets these potential risks are outweighed by the high potential returns; with this strategy, none of the potential profits must be shared with other firms. In addition to the high potential returns, direct investment offers the firm complete control over its operations in the foreign country.

direct investment
When a firm maintains 100 percent ownership of its plants, operation facilities, and offices in a foreign country, often through the formation of wholly owned subsidiaries.

Hundreds of Canadian mining, manufacturing, and technology companies have direct investments in several countries around the world. For example, Barrick Gold is the world's largest gold producer, with a portfolio of 25 operating mines, and advanced exploration and development projects in South America, North America, Africa, and Australia. Similarly, Bombardier has direct investments in Japan, the United States, Denmark, and Ireland.[66]

As we noted, each of these entry strategies entails different levels of risk and rewards for the foreign entrant. But even after a firm has determined how much risk it is willing to take, and therefore how it will enter a new global market, it still must establish its marketing strategy, as we discuss in the next section.

CHOOSING A GLOBAL MARKETING STRATEGY

L04

Just like any other marketing strategy, a global marketing strategy includes two components: determining the target market(s) to pursue and developing a marketing mix that will sustain a competitive advantage over time. In this section, we examine marketing strategy as it relates specifically to global markets.

Target Market: Segmentation, Targeting, and Positioning

Global segmentation, targeting, and positioning (STP) is more complicated than domestic STP for several reasons. First, firms considering a global expansion have much more difficulty understanding the cultural nuances of other countries. Second, subcultures within each country also must be considered. Third, consumers often view products and their role as consumers differently in different countries.[67]

Clearly Contacts in Vancouver originally set up online operations to sell contact lenses to Canadian consumers. A decade later, it diversified by adding eyeglasses, a category with rapid growth that now accounts for 25 percent of its revenues. Based on data showing that the number of American consumers over 50 years old would increase by 19 percent in the next 10 years, it set up a new division, Coastal.com, to meet demand from boomers needing glasses. After only three years, sales to the United States made up 16 percent of the company's revenues.[68]

A product or service often must be positioned differently in different markets. For example, Tang, the fruit-flavoured drink produced by Kraft, is positioned as a low-priced

Tropicana uses a global positioning strategy that stresses around the world that Tropicana is fresh-squeezed Florida orange juice.

drink in the United States but such a positioning strategy would not work in Brazil, where fresh orange juice already is a low-priced drink. Consequently, Kraft promotes a pineapple-flavoured Tang and positions it as a drink for special occasions. In a similar fashion, McDonald's generally competes on convenience and low price but, in countries such as China and India, where consumers already have lower-priced and more convenient alternatives, McDonald's positions itself as an "American" restaurant.[69]

The most efficient route is to develop and maintain a global positioning strategy; one position means only one message to get out. For instance, Tropicana is the best-selling orange juice brand in the United States and owns 6 percent of the global juice market. Tropicana's parent company, PepsiCo, therefore takes a global positioning strategy that stresses around the world that Tropicana is fresh-squeezed Florida orange juice.[70]

Segments and target markets can and should be defined by more than just geography. For example, when Yahoo determines its segmentation and positioning strategies, it relies on research into a segment familiar throughout the world: moms. By working with a global market research firm, Yahoo investigates how moms in Russia, Colombia, China, the United States, Mexico, India, the United Kingdom, Argentina, and France understand and use social media and other modern technologies. This study of "global moms" also aims to determine how digital technology affects family interactions, such as mealtimes, special occasions, and scheduling.[71]

When it identifies its positioning within the market, the firm then must decide how to implement its marketing strategies by using the marketing mix. Just as firms adjust their products and services to meet the needs of national target market(s), they must alter their marketing mix to serve the needs of global markets.

The Global Marketing Mix

The PEST factors described earlier in this chapter, as well as consumers' psychological, social, and situational factors, influence how marketers configure the marketing mix and implement their marketing strategy. In this section, we explore the four Ps (product, place, promotion, price) from a global perspective.

Global Product or Service Strategies
There are three potential global product strategies:

- Sell the same product or service in both the home country market and the host country.

- Sell a product or service similar to that sold in the home country but include minor adaptations.

- Sell totally new products or services.

The strategy a firm chooses depends on the needs of the target market. The level of economic development and differences in product and technical standards help determine the need for product adaptation. Cultural differences such as food preferences, language, and religion also play a role in product strategy planning. In varied cultural settings, bringing even the simplest consumer goods to new markets can be challenging. For example, Campbell discovered that though Russia and China are two of the largest markets for soup in the world, cooks in those countries have unique demands. Chinese consumers drink 320 billion bowls of soup each year, and Russian buyers consume 32 billion servings. However, Chinese cooks generally refuse to resort to canned soup; though the average Chinese consumer eats soup five times each week, he or she also takes great pride in preparing it personally with fresh ingredients. In contrast, Russian consumers, though they demand very high quality in their soups, had grown tired of spending hours preparing their homemade broths. To identify opportunities in these markets, Campbell sent teams of social anthropologists to study how Chinese and Russian cooks prepare and consume soup. When it faced further hurdles, it entered into a joint venture with the Swire soup company in China. Its efforts in Russia never panned out, forcing Campbell to withdraw after around four years. Even with extensive, devoted efforts by an industry giant, global marketing remains a challenge.[72]

Nestlé created 20 unique flavours of KIT KAT for Japanese consumers; in Japan, KIT KAT is one of the top confectionary brands. By creating flavours that reflect the local produce and tastes of different regions of Japan, Nestlé aims to promote its unique KIT KAT as regional souvenirs. KIT KAT varieties now range from yubari melon from Hokkaido Island, to green beans and cherries from Tohoku in northeastern Japan, to yuzu fruit and red potatoes from Kyushu/Okinawa region at the southernmost tip of the country. The Kanto region, including Tokyo, contributed the sweet potato, blueberry, and soy sauce flavours. Wasabi-flavoured white chocolate KIT KAT is also quite popular with Japanese consumers.[73]

Campbell's research found that Russians eat a lot of soup and want time-saving preparation help. It developed broths so cooks could make soup adding their own flair.

The level of economic development also affects the global product strategy because it relates directly to consumer buying behaviour. Consumers in developed countries tend to demand more attributes in their products than do consumers in less-developed countries. In Canada, Honda does not offer its line of "urban" motorcycles, available in Mexico, China, and India, because the product line resembles a motor scooter more than a motorcycle, which does not tend to appeal to consumers. Motorcycles sold in North America have more horsepower and bigger frames and come with an array of options that are not offered in other countries.

Referred to as **glocalization**, some firms also standardize their products globally but use different promotional campaigns to sell them. The original Pringles potato chip product remains the same globally, as do the images and themes of the promotional campaign, with limited language adaptations for local markets. However, the company does change Pringles' flavours in different countries, including paprika-flavoured chips, which are sold in Italy and Germany.[74] McCain Foods, which markets frozen potato specialties

glocalization
When firms offer standardized products globally and change promotional campaigns geared to local markets.

The level of economic development affects the global product strategy. Consumers in North America prefer larger motorcycles with more amenities, like the Honda Goldwing on the left with the air bag deploying. Motorcycles in India are generally smaller.

in 100 countries, localizes its product by, for instance, calling french fries *chips* in the United Kingdom and developing local advertising for markets by region.[75]

Manufacturers are not the only ones that must adapt their offering. On the retail side, for example, Whole Foods is making shopping an experience in the United Kingdom to compete with the local organic supermarket chains.

Despite persistent differences across borders, marketers have found a growing convergence in tastes and preferences in many product categories. Starbucks is a good example of a company that has both influenced and exploited this global convergence in tastes. Even in China and Great Britain, traditional strongholds for tea marketers, coffee is quickly gaining as the beverage of choice. Increasingly, because of the Internet and other information technologies, there seems to be not only a convergence of taste among youths but also the emergence of global homogenous segments. That is, groups of consumers from around the world now share similar buying characteristics. One study identified the "global teen segment," which they describe as teenagers from around the world—from Japan to Vancouver, London, Beijing, and San Francisco—who generally buy the same brand-name clothing, electronics, and accessories; listen to the same music; and eat the same food. Such trends make it easier for marketers to target these consumers with standardized products.[76]

Global Pricing Strategies

Determining the selling price in the global marketplace is an extremely difficult task.[77] Many countries still have rules governing the competitive marketplace, including those that affect pricing. For example, in parts of Europe, including Belgium, Italy, Spain, Greece, and France, promotional sales are allowed only twice a year, in January and in June or July. In most European countries, retailers can't sell below cost, and they can't advertise reduced prices in advance of sales or discount items until they have been on shelves for more than a month. For firms such as Walmart and other discounters, these restrictions threaten their core competitive positioning as the lowest-cost provider in the market. Other issues, such as tariffs, quotas, antidumping laws, and currency exchange policies, can also affect pricing decisions.[78]

Competitive factors influence global pricing in the same way they do home country pricing, but because a firm's products or services may not have the same positioning in the global marketplace as they do in their home country, market prices must be adjusted to reflect the local pricing structure. Spain's fashion retailer Zara, for instance, is relatively inexpensive in the European Union but is priced about 40 percent higher in North America, putting it right in the middle of its moderately priced competition.[79] Since it is important for Zara to get its fashions to the consumers in a timely manner, it incurs additional transportation expenses, which it passes on to its North American customers. Finally, as we discussed earlier in this chapter, currency fluctuations impact global pricing strategies.

Global Distribution Strategies

Global distribution networks form complex value chains that involve intermediaries, exporters, importers, and different transportation systems. These additional intermediaries typically add cost and ultimately increase the final selling price of a product. As a result of these cost factors, constant pressure exists to shorten distribution channels wherever possible.

The number of firms with which the seller needs to deal to get its merchandise to the consumer determines the complexity of a channel. In most developing countries, manufacturers must go through many different types of distribution channels to get their products to end users, who often lack adequate transportation to shop at central shopping areas or large malls. Therefore, these consumers shop near their homes at small, family-owned retail outlets. To reach these small retail outlets, most of which are located far from major rail stations or roads, marketers have devised a variety of creative solutions. In the Amazon jungle in Brazil, for instance, Avon products are sometimes delivered by canoe. Alternatively, Unilever's strategy in India is a prime example of how a global company can adopt its distribution network to fit local conditions. Unilever trained 25,000 Indian women to serve as distributors, who in turn extended Unilever's reach to 80,000 villages across India. The program generates $250 million each year in villages that otherwise would be too costly to serve.[80]

Global Communication Strategies The major challenge in developing a global communication strategy is identifying the elements that need to be adapted to be effective in the global marketplace. For instance, literacy levels vary dramatically across the globe. Consider again the BRIC nations: In India, approximately 37 percent of the adult population is illiterate (and for Indian women, the illiteracy rate surpasses 50 percent), compared with 9.6 percent in Brazil, 4.9 percent in China, and less than half a percent in Russia.[81] And even though Japan has one of the world's most sophisticated digital-media markets, Nestlé took a low-tech route to promote its unique 20 flavours of KIT KAT, which are sold as souvenirs in railway stations, airports, and expressway service shop areas. Nestlé was struck by the discovery that KIT KAT sounds similar to the Japanese phrase *Kitto Katsu*, which means "surely win." The company realized the chocolate bar could be paired with the tradition of sending students good-luck wishes before they take tough higher-education entrance exams. So it partnered with Japan's postal service to create Kit Mail, a postcard-like product sold only at the post office that could be mailed to students as an edible good-luck charm. Nestlé decorates post offices with a cherry blossom theme that coincides with Japan's annual exam period. It also stocks a sales point in each post office, a move that became possible when Japan's postal service was privatized in 2007. Nestlé noted that, if post offices were still government-owned, the company probably could not have done this: "The post office is a great distribution channel for KIT KAT, because there is no competition, unlike in convenience stores or supermarkets," said Mr. Kageyama, CEO of JWT Japan, Nestlé Japan's advertising agency.[82]

Media availability also varies widely; some countries offer only state-controlled media. Advertising regulations differ too. In an attempt at standardization, the European Union recently recommended common guidelines for its member countries regarding advertising to children, and it is currently reviewing a possible ban on "junk food" advertising.[83]

Differences in language, customs, and culture also complicate marketers' ability to communicate with customers in various countries. Language can be particularly vexing for advertisers. For example, in the United Kingdom and Australia, a thong is a sandal; whereas in Canada, it can also be an undergarment. To avoid the potential embarrassment that language confusion can cause, firms spend millions of dollars to develop brand names that have no pre-existing meaning in any known language, such as Accenture (a management consulting firm) or Avaya (a subsidiary of Lucent Technologies, formerly Bell Labs).

Within many countries, there are multiple variants on a language. Some firms choose names that sound similar to their English-language names, such as Nike, whose Chinese brand name is pronounced *nai ke*. Others focus on the meanings of the characters, such that Citibank is known as *hui qi yinhang*, which means "star-spangled banner bank." Still other firms, such as Mercedes-Benz, have adapted their names for

Distribution can be challenging in some countries if the transportation infrastructure is inadequate. In the Amazon jungle in Brazil, for instance, Avon products are sometimes delivered by canoe.

Nestlé's Kit Mail could be mailed to students as an edible good-luck charm.

each language: *peng zee* in Cantonese for Hong Kong, *peng chi* in Mandarin for Taiwan, and *ben chi* in Mandarin for mainland China. Naming is a constant challenge in China, especially to avoid the threat that a brand name evokes unwanted connotations, such as when Microsoft realized that the sound of its search engine name, Bing, meant "virus" in China—not the best image for an online company![84]

Even with all these differences, many products and services serve the same needs and wants globally with little or no adaptation in their form or message. Firms whose products have global appeal can run global advertising campaigns, an advantage that results in significant savings. According to Coca-Cola's advertising firm, McCann-Erickson, over a 20-year period, it saved Coca-Cola $90 million by reusing advertisements it had already created and by changing only a few elements for different local markets.[85] Furthermore, as Social and Mobile Marketing 17.1 highlights, social networks grant brands, including Lady Gaga, access to a global market.

Other products require a more localized approach because of cultural and religious differences. In a classic advertisement for Longines watches, a woman's bare arm and hand appear, with a watch on her wrist. The advertisement was considered too risqué for predominantly Muslim countries, where women's bare arms are never displayed in public. The company changed the advertisement to show a gloved arm and hand wearing the same watch.

Social and Mobile Marketing 17.1   Lady Gaga Is More Popular than Barack Obama

Lady Gaga's nearly unsurpassed status in modern pop culture has arrived as the result of her shock tactics, carefully orchestrated media blitz, and expert use of varied social media channels—not to mention some serious musical talent.

Granted, wearing a dress made of meat and creating music videos that veer close to pornography will get anyone's attention, even through traditional media settings. And indeed, nearly 12,000 traditional media stories mentioned her only two years after she first arrived on the scene.[86] But Lady Gaga's worldwide domination involves far more.

Since 2008, Gaga has been available to her fans nearly all the time, in a vast array of forums. In the early days, she was constantly available for interviews, and she made content, including videos and photos, available for music bloggers to post. Her iPhone application, Haus of Gaga, acts as a portal for her fans, widely known as "Little Monsters," to stay easily connected through exclusive content, videos, news, and chats. She personally manages her daily posts, even when she is backstage at a concert. Gaga keeps her fans interested by speaking to them directly via social media. Her Facebook page is managed by her with the help of others, and she handles her Twitter account on her own. This authentic one-to-one contact has strengthened her personal connection with her fans.[87]

Through these efforts, she has become the most popular living thing on Facebook, with more than 58 million Facebook fans[88]; has more Twitter followers than anyone else, at almost 40 million,[89] even more than

Lady Gaga can mix fashion with her music and get away with it.

Barack Obama; and has prompted more than 1 billion views on her YouTube channel. She is strategic in her decisions on what she wears and what she does, knowing that people will be talking about it later. Gaga makes sure that she feeds her fans the content she wants them to talk about—namely, just what unexpected thing she has done most recently.

Regulatory actions in the host country can also affect communication strategies. For example, the WTO has become involved in several cases that involve firms' rights to use certain names and affiliations for their products and promotions. Several products in the European Union have established worldwide brand recognition on the basis of where they are made. For instance, the European Union currently allows only ham made in Parma, Italy, to be called Parma ham and sparkling wine made in the Champagne region of France to be called Champagne. However, the European Union has also refused to grant requests from non-EU countries for similar protection, notably Florida orange juice.[90] The WTO is expected to ask the European Union to either remove all such protections or grant them to non-EU countries as well. In one case, similar arguments have even led to a global beer brawl, in which the American beer giant Budweiser must contend with claims by the tiny, 700-year-old Czech brewery Budvar that the U.S. company stole its name. The two companies coexisted in an uneasy truce before the fall of the Berlin Wall, because Budweiser could not access Budvar's Eastern European market, and Budvar could not easily get its products out of that area. But since then, the competition between the two has heated up, leading some countries to provide exclusive registrations to one of the two and other countries to place them both on shelves. Most indications suggest the WTO will deny both companies' claims to the exclusive use of the Budweiser/Budvar names, meaning that someday soon; consumers may have to clarify what they mean when they say, "I'll have a Bud."[91]

ETHICAL ISSUES IN GLOBAL MARKETING

L05

Although ethical issues abound domestically, an extra layer of complexity arises for global marketing. Firms that market globally must recognize that they are, in essence, visitors in another country and, as such, must be aware of the ethical concerns of their potential customers, both at home and abroad. In this section, we examine three areas of particular concern: environmental concerns, labour issues, and impact on host country culture.

Environmental Concerns

People throughout the world are worried about the amount of waste being generated, especially in developed countries. Current **environmental concerns** include, but are not limited to, the excessive use of natural resources and energy, refuse from manufacturing processes, excess trash created by consumer goods packages, and hard-to-dispose-of products such as tires, cellphones, and computer monitors.

　　Many developed countries produce almost two tonnes of household and industrial waste per person per year![92] Although developing countries do not produce nearly the same level of waste, much of the waste in these areas is not properly disposed of.

Global Labour Issues

Global labour issues, especially concerns about working conditions and wages paid to factory workers in developing countries, have become increasingly prominent.[93] Many large U.S. firms, such as Nike, PepsiCo, and Walmart, have been questioned by various groups, including nongovernmental organizations and human rights activists, about the degree to which workers the companies employ are paid less than a living wage or forced to work long hours in poor working conditions.[94]

environmental concerns Include, but are not limited to, the excessive use of natural resources and energy, refuse from manufacturing processes, excess trash created by consumer goods packages, and hard-to-dispose-of products such as tires, cellphones, and computer monitors.

global labour issues Includes concerns about working conditions and wages paid to factory workers in developing countries.

Many developed countries produce almost two tonnes of household and industrial waste per person per year that requires proper disposal.

In this context, high prices offer no guarantee of a supply chain free of sweatshops. Recently, Apple has been repeatedly questioned about the working conditions in the manufacturing plants that produce iPods and iPhones. Even though iPod boxes proudly state that the music player was designed in California, the entire manufacturing process has been subcontracted to Taiwanese and Chinese manufacturers.[95] Because Apple does not own the plants in which its goods are produced, it must negotiate with factory owners to improve or ensure adequate working conditions and wages, while at the same time attempting to get the cheapest prices. Because Apple negotiates very hard on price, suppliers sometimes try to make money by paying labourers less, making them work long hours, or providing unsafe working conditions. Labour conditions for Chinese workers in "iPod city" recently became so deplorable that several high-profile strikes protested their working conditions, and many Chinese workers resorted to committing suicide.

Impact on Host Country Culture

cultural imperialism
The belief that one's own culture is superior to that of other nations; can take the form of an active, formal policy or a more subtle general attitude.

The final ethical issue involves **cultural imperialism**, or the belief that one's own culture is superior to that of other nations. Cultural imperialism can take the form of an active, formal policy or a more subtle general attitude.[96] Critics of U.S. firms entering foreign markets claim that U.S. products and services overwhelm the local culture, often replacing its foods, music, movies, and traditions with those of the West.

In Iran, for example, the ruling clerics have forbidden the celebration of Valentine's Day.[97] Despite strict Iranian laws regarding the interactions of men and women, especially unmarried men and women, Valentine's Day has become a popular holiday among the youth market. These Iranians were exposed to Valentine's Day through the Internet and satellite television, two information sources the government cannot control. Holiday-themed products arrive through underground distribution channels and are displayed in local shops. Risking legal action, florists, gift shops, and restaurants make special accommodations for the holiday. Many parents sponsor Valentine parties with both men and women in attendance. Apparently, there is no stopping love. Half the Iranian population is younger than 25 years of age, and this youth market has embraced the holiday and continues to celebrate it in traditional Western ways.

For other Iranians though, this type of celebration represents a threat to Iran's culture. Many U.S. firms find themselves squarely in the middle of this cultural conflict.[98] Various countries around the world encompass competing desires: the desire to modernize and participate in the global marketplace versus the desire to hold on to traditional cultural values and ways of life. There is no simple way to resolve these dilemmas. Firms that enter new markets simply must tread lightly to ensure that their business practices, products, and services do not create any unnecessary friction or offence in the host country.

When Western firms enter foreign markets, they must be cognizant of the host country's culture.

LEARNING OBJECTIVES REVIEW

 Explain the components of global market assessments

First, firms must determine whether a proposed country has a political and legal environment that favours business. Second, firms must assess the general economic environment. For instance, countries with a trade surplus, strong domestic and national products, population growth, and income growth tend to be favourable prospects. Third, firms should be cognizant of the sociocultural differences between their home and host countries and adapt to those differences to ensure successful business relationships. Fourth, firms should assess a country's technology and infrastructure capabilities. To be successful in a particular country, the firm must have access to adequate transportation, distribution channels, and communications.

 Understand the marketing opportunities in BRIC countries

Technology, particularly in the communication field, has facilitated the growth of global markets. Firms can communicate with their suppliers and customers instantaneously, easily take advantage of production efficiencies in other countries, and bring together parts and finished goods from all over the globe. Four countries that provide tremendous marketing opportunities are the BRIC nations—Brazil, Russia, India and China. These countries have large populations that are increasingly interested in the latest goods and services.

Describe the various global market entry strategies

Firms have several options for entering a new country, each with a different level of risk and control. Direct investment is the most risky but also has the potential to be the most lucrative. Firms that engage in a joint venture with other firms already operating in the host country share the risk and obtain knowledge about the market and how to do business there. A strategic alliance is similar to a joint venture, but the relationship is not as formal. A less risky method of entering a new market is franchising, in which, similar to domestic franchise agreements, the franchisor allows the franchisee to operate a business using its name and strategy in return for a fee. The least risky method of entering another country is exporting.

 List the similarities of and differences between a domestic marketing strategy and a global marketing strategy

The essence of a global marketing strategy is no different than that of a domestic strategy. The firm starts by identifying its target markets, chooses specific markets to pursue, and crafts a strategy to meet the needs of those markets. However, additional issues make global expansion more difficult. For instance, the company needs to ask the following questions: Should the product or service be altered to fit the new market better? Does the firm need to change the way it prices its products in different countries? What is the best way to get the product or service to the new customers? How should the firm communicate its product or service offering in other countries?

 Explain how ethical issues affect global marketing practices

In particular, firms must be cognizant of the impact their businesses have on the environment. When producing merchandise or employing service personnel in another country, companies must be certain that the working conditions and wages are fair and adequate, even if the workers are employed by a third party. Finally, marketers must be sensitive to the impact their business has on the culture of the host country.

KEY TERMS

- boycott
- cultural imperialism
- direct investment
- dumping
- environmental concerns
- exchange control
- exchange rate
- exporting
- global labour issues
- globalization
- glocalization
- gross domestic product (GDP)
- human development index (HDI)
- infrastructure
- joint venture
- purchasing power parity (PPP)
- quota
- strategic alliance
- tariff (or duty)
- trade agreement
- trade deficit
- trade sanctions
- trade surplus
- trading bloc

CONCEPT REVIEW

1. What is globalization? What are the factors that facilitate globalization? Explain how globalization has influenced marketing in Canada.

2. List and describe the four components of market assessments firms must conduct to evaluate the viability of different global markets.

3. Which of the four components of market assessment do you think are often most difficult to assess? Why?

4. List the five types of strategies companies can use to enter global markets. Compare these strategies in terms of level of risk, expected return, and control.

5. Discuss the advantages and disadvantages of using a global product strategy (i.e., offering the same product both at home and in overseas markets).

6. What are the primary considerations marketers should use in deciding whether to customize its four Ps to specific markets?

7. What is political risk? Why is it important to assess political risks? How is political risk assessed? List two or three organizations in Canada that provide marketers with political risk assessments.

8. Protectionist policies restrict trade and global marketing while trade agreements facilitate global marketing. Explain the reasons a country may want to impose protectionist policies in some industries and liberalize other industries.

9. Explain how measures such as GDP, PPP (i.e., the Big Mac Index), and HDI help marketers decide whether to enter a global market. What are the weaknesses of these measures?

10. Explain how useful Hofstede's five dimensions of culture are to our understanding of different cultures around the world. Where and how can marketers learn about the culture of a country to which they are interested in marketing?

MARKETING APPLICATIONS

1. Of the four BRIC markets, explain why you think one country might be more welcoming to lululemon than others.

2. Cervélo is a high-end Canadian bicycle manufacturer. Assume the company is considering entering the United Kingdom and Chinese markets. When doing its market assessment, what economic factors should Cervélo consider when making its decision? Which market do you expect will be more lucrative for Cervélo? Why?

3. Now consider the political, economic, and legal systems of China versus the United Kingdom. Explain why you think one country might be more hospitable to Cervélo than the other.

4. Volkswagen sells cars in many countries throughout the world, including Mexico and Latin America. How would you expect its market position to differ in those countries compared with that in Canada?

5. Global brands that gain status on a local level have the best of both worlds: local loyalty with all the advantages of global connections. How do huge global companies such as McCain Foods and McDonald's achieve multi-local status?

6. What is cultural imperialism? Why would a recording company such as Def Jam Recordings need to be aware of and sensitive to this issue?

7. Provide an example of a potentially ethically troubling practice by a foreign firm doing business in Canada.

8. Many Canadian and U.S.–based firms are relocating their production facilities and services overseas (outsourcing or offshoring). Why do you believe they are doing so? Do the benefits outweigh the potential losses of Canadian and U.S. jobs? Why or why not?

9. Assume you work for a Canadian-based financial services firm that positions itself as having experts that personally manage the clients' accounts. The clients are unaware that most of the tax preparation work, the bookkeeping, and other record keeping are done by a company in India. The local office simply reviews the file and signs the cover letters. Yet as your manager pointed out, there is still only one person who *manages* each account. After recent news stories about the practice of offshoring sensitive transactions such as tax preparation, clients have been commenting about how grateful they are to have a local firm. What, if anything, should you tell your clients about the firm's practice of offshoring?

10. Canadian companies such as Tim Hortons and lululemon have expanded their global presence through company-owned stores. In what instances might these companies consider using joint ventures as their global market entry strategy into new markets?

NET SAVVY

1. For many small businesses, the idea of entering a foreign market is frightening. The Government of Canada, as well as most provincial and territorial governments, now offers assistance designed specifically for small business owners. Two such government departments are Foreign Affairs and International Trade Canada (DFAIT) and Industry Canada. Visit Industry Canada's Canada Business website at http://www.canadabusiness.ca and examine the types of services it provides for Canadian businesses wishing to do business in a foreign country. Evaluate the usefulness of the information provided.

2. McCain Foods is a global brand but it alters its products and promotions to accommodate local tastes in each country. Go to http://www.mccain.ca and visit the Canadian site. Then click on "Worldwide Sites" at the bottom of the page and check out the South American site, the U.S. site, and the site for France. How are these three websites different from the Canadian site? What products are different? What promotional elements are different?

CHAPTER CASE STUDY

RACING TO CAPTURE CHINA'S LUXURY CAR MARKET

China's car market dates back just three decades, yet the Asian giant is well on its way to surpassing the United States as the world's most lucrative and strategically important auto market. Government investment in infrastructure, including the development of roads and bridges, has helped the nascent car industry, and sales growth in the overall market has soared by 30 percent annually for several years. Last year, Chinese consumers bought 25.6 million vehicles more than United States drivers purchased,[99] and more than 60 percent of them were foreign-origin brands, produced in China through joint ventures.[100]

Perhaps the fiercest arena of competition is China's luxury car market, projected to become the world's largest within five to seven years.[101] The dominant players include Audi and BMW holding 29.6 percent and 23.6 percent of the market share respectively,[102] as well as Mercedes-Benz and Buick. Audi has reported 61 percent increases in Chinese sales; BMW sales in China, Hong Kong, and Taiwan were projected to rise by 85.3 percent over their previous rates.[103]

Yet these figures are not the whole story: China is a challenging market to penetrate, especially because of its continent-sized geographic area, complex cultural diversity, and growing gaps (both economic and social) between poorer rural regions and the booming cities on the coastline. Furthermore, prevailing stereotypes and images of particular car brands are rooted in history, and no foreign carmaker can safely ignore these strong opinions and ideas.[104] Some foreign companies, such as Audi, have eased the path by entering into joint ventures.

Audi was the earliest entrant into the Chinese prestige car market, when its German owner, Volkswagen, struck a joint venture agreement with the Chinese carmaker Yiqi in 1988. By the time BMW opened a plant in China in 2003, Audi had secured a place on the central government's authorized purchase list, and its A6 line had become the de facto car of choice for Chinese bureaucrats. The company captured so much of China's government-car market that it has given rise to the stereotype that the sleek looking A6—invariably with dark, tinted windows—must be carrying a party technocrat whenever it appears on city streets.

Audi has done well with this market segment. A basic Audi A6 costs 383,000 renminbi, or $62,576.[105] Its key competitor, the BMW 5, is more expensive, at 428,600 renminbi, or $70,026.[106] Audi's sales to the government accounts, for approximately 20 percent of its Chinese revenues, and it sold 405,838 cars in China in 2012,[107] more than twice the number that it sold in the United States.[108]

Not to be outdone, U.S. carmakers have worked to establish effective brand perceptions and reputations, largely based on improving stereotyping about the car's "face." The American-made Buick seemed "damaged" at the start of the 21st century because of the car's longstanding popularity and association with older retirees, but in China, it played on unique historical connections to help ignite demand by reminding car buyers that China's last emperor and its one-time premier Zhou Enlai both drove Buicks. Thus the brand gained a strong position as a top-tier luxury carmaker. Its 2010 Chinese sales were more than triple the firm's revenue in

Dominated by BMW, Audi, Mercedes-Benz and Buick, the Chinese luxury car market is projected to become the world's largest.

the United States.[109] But for Mercedes-Benz, such stereotyping has persisted. Whereas most U.S. consumers view both these automobiles as cars for people with established wealth, the Mercedes in China may be for the wealthy, but it is still associated with older, retired drivers.[110]

The most dynamic market niche for luxury cars reflects a rising class of young, affluent entrepreneurs with flashy buying habits. BMW, the world's top-selling luxury car brand,[111] has vigorously targeted these brash new drivers with exotic marketing campaigns. The Munich-based automaker began offering test drives and cross-country expeditions with its high-end X5 SUV in the deserts of Inner Mongolia and along the Silk Road, enticing thrill-bound luxury-car customers.[112] Their campaign showcases new technology, and it has helped build brand loyalty: China is BMW's third-largest market.[113]

Yet its targeting strategy has also left behind some negative Chinese attitudes that link BMW to careless, nouveau riche drivers. That stereotype grew after two young BMW drivers, in separate incidents, were charged in fatal accidents. When a young woman intentionally ran over an indigent man after he dented her BMW X5, then settled out of court for $11,000, the story helped fan the tensions between China's rich and poor. In the cross-fire, BMW was tagged with a reputation for catering to the arrogant and the reckless. That tag now extends to other BMW drivers; government officials who show up in a BMW, rather than the typical, less expensive Audi, run the risk of being accused of corruption.[114]

In a push to innovate and perhaps revive a broader appeal, BMW has launched a strategic alliance with Toyota, focused on sustainable technologies. The companies will collaborate on diesel engines, which dominate Europe's fuel-efficient car market. They also have agreed to develop a next-generation lithium battery, a key component of laptops and electric cars.[115]

Other examples of market expansion by luxury carmakers include ventures into some of China's less-developed cities. These second- and third-tier locations provide access to a new class of potential buyers, that is, affluent consumers who live farther from the major metropolitan centres. Major cities such as Beijing and Shanghai are limiting car purchases, because their streets cannot handle more traffic, but smaller cities in outlying provinces offer promising alternative markets.

Its early entrance into the market, through a joint venture with a Chinese carmaker, allowed Audi to become deeply entrenched in the government's purchasing system. But with BMW courting wealthier young drivers, the competition between these two foreign automakers is heating up. Strategic partnerships will continue to play a key role in shaping new opportunities, though limits on car registration in some major cities may shift those opportunities to other geographic segments. Amid all these dynamics, Chinese brand attitudes will continue to determine the buying decisions of drivers in the world's largest car market.

Questions

1. Assess China as a potential market for luxury cars. If you worked for a luxury car manufacturer, such as Volvo, would you enter or attempt to increase your presence in China? What entry strategy would you use? Why?

2. Drivers in China approach the luxury car market with a set of strong associations that influence their perceptions of the foreign brands currently available in the marketplace. Multiple factors affect those consumer attitudes, including history, class, and social status. Why are these attitudes so entrenched in China, and why do they play such a critical role in shaping car customer preferences?

3. Both Audi and BMW have allied with other companies to target particular market segments. Assess the relative strength of these two very different positioning strategies.

4. BMW has successfully targeted China's affluent, young car drivers, but the brand's success in that market has also provoked public backlash. What drives such public hostility to the brand, and how serious a problem is it? What marketing approach, if any, should the company undertake in response?

For more information on the resources available from McGraw-Hill Ryerson, go to www.mheducation.ca/he/solutions.

CHAPTER 18

Ethics and Socially Responsible Marketing

In an effort to entice consumers with an appetite for bargains to their stores, retailers often struggle to make the trade-off between keeping costs as low as possible and ensuring acceptable working conditions. Unfortunately, lower costs are often achieved at the price of poor labour safety and below-average labour costs.[1] Bangladesh is the world's second-largest apparel exporter, just behind China. The Canadian government opened the floodgates when it eliminated the 18 percent duty on clothing made in Bangladesh.[2] Today the country's garment industry is worth $20 billion a year, employing 3.6 million people, some with incomes as low as $38 a month.[3]

The collapse of Rana Plaza, an eight-story commercial building in Savar, Bangladesh, resulted in 1,129 casualties and injuries to over 2,500 textile employees. It was the worst disaster in the industry's history. The plaza housed a number of stores, a bank, and a garment factory. Following the detection of cracks in the building on April 23, 2013, the shops and bank were promptly closed due to the warnings issued. However, garment factory workers were ordered to return and were working the next day when the collapse occurred.[4]

The tragedy raised questions about the ethical implications of outsourcing manufacturing to developing countries with substandard wages and poorly implemented safety measures. It also shifted scrutiny to retailers, including Loblaw, since some of its Joe Fresh clothing line was manufactured in the factory. At a time when corporate social responsibility and ethical practices are increasingly important to consumers, the factory collapse is a threat to the family-friendly brand. Compounding the issue is the growing belief that purchasing a company's products translates into supporting said company's actions.

While there was deafening silence and even denial from many companies whose products were produced in the factory,[5] Loblaw took immediate action. It called a press conference, publicly expressed its condolences, offered compensation to the victims' families, and put a plan in place to prevent future tragedies. Disney, whose products were also produced in the factory, decided to suspend operations in Bangladesh.[6] Loblaw pledged to remain in the country and work

LEARNING OBJECTIVES

After studying this chapter you should be able to

LO1 Identify why marketers should be concerned about ethics

LO2 Distinguish between ethics and social responsibility

LO3 Describe consumerism and explain how it fosters ethical and socially responsible business practices

LO4 Identify the four steps in ethical decision making

LO5 Outline how ethics and social responsibility can be integrated into a firm's marketing strategy

to improve safety regulations and working conditions. It committed to sign an Accord on Fire and Building Safety, a legally binding contract aimed at improving worker safety within garment factories in Bangladesh. Independent inspections will be conducted and the findings disclosed to the public. Loblaw will pay $500,000 annually to ensure that all workers are granted a voice through a union. It will not conduct business with any factory refusing to make the necessary safety upgrades.[7] And it will send high-level executives to Bangladesh to manage these initiatives.

As a result of the tragedy in Bangladesh, Loblaw issued a call for the entire garment industry to make changes to ensure worker safety. Several retailers including Bennetton, H&M, C&A, Tesco, Primark, and Inditex, have since agreed to sign the Accord. Through its actions, Loblaw has demonstrated that a disastrous event, if handled in a responsible manner, can strengthen the brand by demonstrating to stakeholders that it can always be trusted to do the right thing. ▌

Which is the more important corporate objective: making a profit or obtaining and keeping customers?[8] Although firms cannot stay in business without earning a profit, using profit as the sole guiding light for corporate action can lead to short-term decisions that may in fact cause the firm to lose customers in the long run. The balancing act may turn out to be the quest to place the company on the firmest footing possible. This question leads into the primary ethical dilemma facing managers; that is, how to balance shareholder interests with the needs of society. In the Loblaw example, managers resolved their balancing act by choosing to focus on the long-term welfare of garment workers in Bangladesh, potentially at the cost of short-term profits.

New regulations enforced by the European Union places the responsibility for content and safety on toy producers, importers, and distributors.[9] They are responsible for documenting that the products in any toys imported into the EU contain no dangerous materials, avoid potential allergens, and are not choking risks.

Or maybe that's the wrong place to look. In North America, new regulations similarly have been designed to prevent the sort of massive toy recalls that Mattel had to undertake when hundreds of millions of its most popular toys, including Barbie dolls, Matchbox cars, and Laughing Elmo, turned out to be safety risks.[10] In the process, manufacturers, regulators, retailers, parents, and various other groups have been battling over the definition of "children's products."[11] Is a stuffed bear with a Valentine's Day theme a product for children or one for adults?

As these examples show, sometimes the ethical dilemma has as much to do with defining our terms as with what the products contain. But even if the question seems to be one of terminology, if customers believe that they can no longer trust a company or that the company is not acting responsibly, they will no longer support it by purchasing its products or services or investing in its stock. For marketers, the firm's ability to build and maintain consumer trust by conducting ethical transactions must be of paramount importance.

In this chapter, we start by examining what marketing ethics is and why behaving ethically is so important to successful marketing. We then discuss how firms can create an ethical climate among employees and how individual behaviour can affect the ability of the firm to act ethically. Next, we discuss how consumers contribute to the corporate social responsibility (CSR) decisions that businesses make. To help you make ethical marketing decisions, we also provide a framework for ethical decision making and then examine some ethical issues within the context of the strategic marketing planning process (from Chapter 2). Finally, we then present some scenarios that highlight typical ethical challenges marketing managers often must face.

THE SCOPE OF MARKETING ETHICS

Business ethics refers to a branch of ethical study that examines ethical rules and principles within a commercial context, the various moral or ethical problems that might arise in a business setting, and any special duties or obligations that apply to persons engaged in commerce.[12] The cartoon below illustrates the importance of making good ethical decisions. **Marketing ethics**, in contrast, refers to those ethical problems that are specific to the domain of marketing. Because the marketing profession often is singled out among business disciplines as the root cause of a host of ethical concerns (e.g., unethical advertising or the promotion of shoddy products), anyone involved in marketing activities must recognize the ethical implications of their actions. These can include societal issues, such as the sale of products or services that may damage the environment; global issues, such as the use of sweatshops and child labour; and individual consumer issues, such as deceptive advertising and the marketing of dangerous products.[13]

ETHICAL ISSUES ASSOCIATED WITH MARKETING DECISIONS

Unlike other business functions, such as accounting or finance, people in marketing interact directly with the public. Because they are so much in the public eye, it should not be surprising that marketing and sales professionals sometimes rank poorly in ratings of the most trusted professions. In a recent Gallup survey, most professions were rated much higher than marketing (see Exhibit 18.1): advertising practitioners fared only slightly better than telemarketers who came in last, faring worse than lawyers![14] For marketers, who depend on the long-term trust of their customers, this low ranking is very disappointing.

Yet there is some good news. In a recent survey, it was found that more than two-thirds of Canadians pay attention to issues related to corporate ethics and social responsibility and that three-quarters of Canadian firms are actively engaged in key corporate social responsibility activities.[15] Many consumers remain highly skeptical of business,

business ethics
Refers to a branch of ethical study that examines ethical rules and principles within a commercial context, the various moral or ethical problems that might arise in a business setting, and any special duties or obligations that apply to persons engaged in commerce.

marketing ethics
Refers to those ethical problems that are specific to the domain of marketing.

LO1

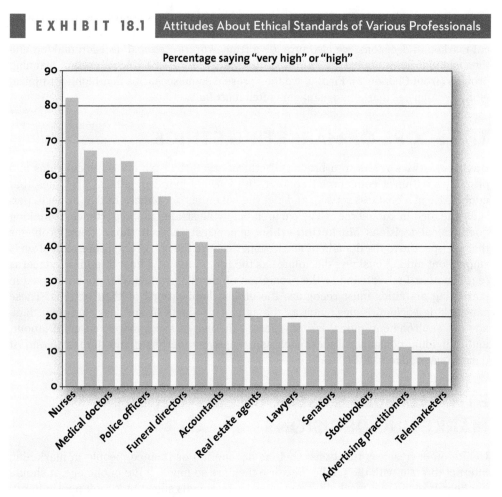

EXHIBIT 18.1   Attitudes About Ethical Standards of Various Professionals

Source: Gallup Poll, "Attitudes about the Ethical Standards of Various Professions." Used by permission.

however, and especially of marketing. But because the marketing function interacts with so many entities outside the firm on a regular basis, it has a tremendous opportunity to build the public's trust. As many marketing executives correctly believe, creating an ethical climate that establishes the health and well-being of consumers as the firm's number-one priority just makes good business sense.

Creating an Ethical Climate in the Workplace

ethical climate
The set of values within a marketing firm, or in the marketing division of any firm, that guides decision making and behaviour.

The process of creating a strong **ethical climate** within a marketing firm (or in the marketing division of any firm) includes having a set of values that guides decision making and behaviour. General Robert Wood Johnson wrote and published the first "Credo" for Johnson & Johnson (J&J) in 1943[16]—a one-page document outlining the firm's commitments and responsibilities to its various stakeholders. The J&J Credo can be summarized as follows:

> We believe our first responsibility is to doctors, nurses, patients, mothers, fathers, and all others who use our products and services. We are responsible to our employees. We must respect their dignity and recognize their merit. Compensation must be fair and adequate and working conditions clean, orderly, and safe. We are responsible to the communities in which we live and work and to the world community as well. Our final responsibility is to our stockholders. When we operate according to these principles, the stockholders should realize a fair return.

Today, J&J continues to follow this credo in its daily business practices, as was evidenced by the infamous Tylenol recall. In the 1980s, seven people taking Tylenol died of cyanide poisoning. Without worrying initially about whether the poison got into the products during production or on the shelf, J&J immediately and voluntarily withdrew all Tylenol from the market until it could ensure its products' safety.

Even more recently, J&J responded to new limits on acetaminophen dosages (the active ingredient in Tylenol) by reassuring consumers that they were safe—as long as they followed the dosage instructions on the packaging.[17] In advertising communications that touted Tylenol as "the safest brand of pain reliever you can choose," J&J also was careful to remind people that taking more than the recommended dosage could cause serious liver damage.

Johnson & Johnson, makers of Tylenol, continues to act in accordance with its 1943 "credo."

Everyone within the firm must share the same understanding of these values and how they translate into the business activities of the firm, and they must share a consistent language to discuss them. Once the values are understood, the firm must develop a set of explicit rules and implicit understandings that govern all the firm's transactions. Top management must commit to establishing an ethical climate, but employees throughout the firm also must be dedicated because the roots of ethical conflict often are the competing values of individuals. Each individual holds his or her own set of values, and sometimes those values result in conflicts between employees or even within them. For instance, a salesperson may feel pressure to make a sale because her family depends on her for support; but, at the same time, she may feel that the product she is selling is not appropriate for a particular customer. Once the rules are in place, there must be a system of controls that rewards appropriate behaviour—that is, behaviour consistent with the firm's values—and punishes inappropriate behaviour.

Many professions, including marketing, have their own codes of ethics that firms and individuals in the profession agree to abide by. The generally accepted code in marketing, developed by the Canadian Marketing Association (CMA; see Exhibit 18.2), flows from general norms of conduct to specific values to which marketers should aspire. Each subarea within marketing, such as marketing research, advertising, pricing, and so forth, has its own code of ethics that deals with the specific issues that arise when conducting business in those areas.

Now we examine the role of the individuals within the firm and how they contribute to the firm's ethical climate.

The Influence of Personal Ethics

Every firm is made up of individuals, each with his or her own needs and desires. Let's look at why people may make unethical decisions and how firms can establish a process for decision making that ensures individuals choose ethical alternatives instead.

Why People Act Unethically Every individual is a product of his or her culture, upbringing, genes, and various other influences. In spite of these factors, however, people do continue to grow emotionally in their understanding of what is and is not ethical behaviour. For example, a six-year-old child might think nothing of bonking a brother on the head with a toy but adults are expected to recognize that violence is an unethical means to interact with others. All of us vary in the way we view various situations, depending on our own level of understanding about ethical dilemmas.

Corporate scandals at companies such as Enron, WorldCom, Bre-X, Nortel Networks, and Hollinger Corp. have many people asking two simple questions: What makes people take actions that create so much harm? Are all the individuals who engaged in that behaviour just plain immoral or unethical? These questions have very complex answers.

| EXHIBIT 18.2 | Canadian Marketing Association's Code of Ethics |

ETHICAL NORMS AND VALUES FOR MARKETERS

B. Purpose of CMA Code of Ethics and Standards of Practice

The CMA Code of Ethics and Standards of Practice (the "Code") is designed to establish and maintain standards for the conduct of marketing in Canada.

Marketers acknowledge that the establishment and maintenance of high standards of practice are a fundamental responsibility to the public, essential to winning and holding consumer confidence, and the foundation of a successful and independent marketing industry in Canada.

Members of the Canadian Marketing Association recognize an obligation—to the consumers and the businesses they serve, to the integrity of the discipline in which they operate and to each other—to practice to the highest standards of honesty, truth, accuracy, fairness and professionalism.

E. Responsibility for Marketing Communications

Marketers are responsible for the content of their marketing communications and the practices of their suppliers and advertising agencies when in the course of executing marketing communications on their behalf. This responsibility extends to suppliers which are not CMA members.

H. Overarching Ethical Principles

H2 Truthfulness: Marketing communications must be clear and truthful. Marketers must not knowingly make a representation to a consumer or business that is false or misleading.

I. Universal Marketing Practices

These practices apply regardless of industry sector, sub-discipline or marketing medium employed.

I1 Accuracy of Representation

I1.1 Marketers must not misrepresent a product, service or marketing program and must not mislead by statement or manner of demonstration or comparison.

I2 Clarity

Marketing communications must be executed in a manner that is simple and easy to understand.

I5 Disguise

I5.1 Marketers must not engage in marketing communications in the guise of one purpose when the intent is a different purpose.

J. Protection of Personal Privacy

All consumer marketers must abide by the *Personal Information Protection and Electronics Documents Act* (PIPEDA), and/or applicable provincial privacy laws and the following ten Privacy Principles from the National Standard of Canada and five additional requirements as outlined in this section.

J5 Source of Personal Information

Marketers must provide consumers with the source of their personal information, upon request.

L. Special Considerations in Marketing to Teenagers

L2 Responsibility

Marketing to teenagers imposes special responsibilities on marketers. Marketers will use discretion and sensitivity in marketing to teenagers, to address the age, knowledge, sophistication and maturity of teenagers. Marketers should exercise caution that they do not take advantage of or exploit teenagers.

P. Protection of the Environment

Marketers recognize and acknowledge a continuing responsibility to manage their businesses to minimize environmental impact.

Q. Enforcement Procedures for the CMA Code of Ethics and Standards of Practice

Q1 Upon receipt of a consumer complaint regarding violation of this Code, whether regarding a member or a non-member, the Canadian Marketing Association will contact the organization and use the Association's internal mediation procedures to attempt to resolve the consumer complaint.

Source: http://www.the-cma.org.

In many cases, people must choose between conflicting outcomes. For example, a brand manager for a car company discovers, from conversations with a member of the development team, that a potentially dangerous design flaw resides in the hot new energy-efficient hybrid model that is set to go into full production shortly. The brand manager can (1) delay production and remedy the design flaw, which pushes production off schedule, delays revenue, and may result in layoffs and loss of a bonus, or (2) stay on schedule, put the flawed design into production, and hope it does not result in injuries to consumers and loss of revenue for the firm. This type of dilemma, and its competing outcomes, occurs nearly every day in thousands of different business environments.

What is the "real" price? Did the manager bring the T-shirts in at an artificially high level and then immediately mark them down?

When asked in a survey whether they had seen any unethical behaviour among their colleagues, chief marketing officers responded that they had observed employees participating in high-pressure, misleading, or deceptive sales tactics (45 percent); misrepresenting company earnings, sales, and/or revenues (35 percent); withholding or destroying information that could hurt company sales or image (32 percent); and conducting false or misleading advertising (31 percent).[18] Did all the marketers in these situations view their actions as unethical? In making marketing decisions, managers are often faced with the dilemma between doing what is beneficial for them and possibly the firm in the short run, and doing what is right and beneficial for the firm and society in the long run.

For instance, a manager might feel confident that earnings will increase in the next few months and therefore believe it benefits himself, his branch, and his employees to exaggerate current earnings just a little. Another manager might feel considerable pressure to increase sales in a retail store, so she brings in some new merchandise, marks it at an artificially high price, and then immediately puts it on sale. Consumers are deceived into thinking they are getting a good deal because they view the initial price as the "real" price. Each decision may have been justifiable at the time for the individual, but each decision would have potentially serious ethical and legal consequences for the company.

To avoid these ethical consequences, the long-term goals of the firm must be aligned with the short-term goals of each individual within the firm. In our hybrid car example, the brand manager's short-term drive to receive a bonus conflicted with the firm's long-term aim of providing consumers with safe, reliable cars. As discussed in the previous section, to align personal and corporate goals, firms need to have a strong ethical climate; explicit rules for governing a firm's transactions, including a code of ethics; and a system for rewarding and punishing behaviour. In the next section, we discuss this link between ethics and social responsibility by businesses.

Corporate Social Responsibility

LO2

Although no single, established definition of the concept exists,[19] **corporate social responsibility (CSR)** describes the voluntary actions taken by a company to address the ethical, social, and environmental impacts of its business operations and the concerns of its stakeholders.[20] For a company to act in a socially responsible manner, the employees within the company must also maintain high ethical standards and recognize how their individual decisions lead to the collective actions of the firm. Firms with strong ethical climates tend to be more socially responsible.

Today, companies are undertaking a wide range of corporate social responsibility initiatives, such as establishing corporate charitable foundations, supporting and associating with existing nonprofit groups, supporting minority activities, and following responsible marketing, sales, and production practices. Social responsibility is even one

corporate social responsibility (CSR) Refers to the voluntary actions taken by a company to address the ethical, social, and environmental impacts of its business operations and the concerns of its stakeholders.

of the key measures that *Fortune* magazine uses to create its list of the most admired companies. One of those companies is McDonald's as noted in Sustainable Marketing 18.1.

Some economists and social commentators suggest that CSR is unnecessary, that the goal of any corporation in a capitalist economy is single and simple: Make money.[21] How does it benefit the company or its shareholders if a company worries about such unquantifiable issues as being a good citizen? But the fallout from the most recent global economic crisis seems to have pushed economists to repudiate this school of thought.

Sustainable Marketing 18.1 | McDonald's Global Sustainability Scorecard

One of *Fortune*'s most admired companies, McDonald's, concentrates its sustainability efforts in several areas.[22] Some specific highlights include:

- *Nutrition and well-being.* It promotes awareness of fruit, vegetable, and low-fat or fat-free dairy options for children through advertising and promotions. For example, McDonald's France and Italy introduced "free fruit" campaigns, during which fruit bags were given free with every Happy Meal on selected days.

- *Sustainable supply chain.* It is committed to sourcing all of its food and packaging from sustainable sources,

with an initial focus on beef, poultry, coffee, palm oil, fish, and fibre.

- *Environmental responsibility.* It has developed better, more reliable energy-related metrics that are used to measure energy savings. It is implementing energy-efficient lighting, occupancy sensors, and energy-efficient equipment.

- *Community.* It supports the Ronald McDonald House charities by, for instance, having raised $170 million during McHappy Day/Give a Hand events since 2002.[23]

McDonald's measures its progress on sustainability initiatives against a scorecard as shown above.

However, it is important to distinguish between ethical business practices and corporate social responsibility programs. Ideally, firms should implement programs that are socially responsible, *and* employees should act in an ethically responsible manner (see Exhibit 18.3, upper left quadrant). Dannon yogurt, for example, has long supported internal research into healthy eating, which supports its ethical commitment to bring "health food to as many people as possible."[24] It is also socially responsible since it donates food and money to the hunger-relief charity Feeding America, encourages employees to volunteer in their communities, holds annual "Children's Day" outreach programs, and tries to reduce its environmental footprint.

But being socially responsible is generally considered beyond the norms of corporate ethical behaviour. For example, a firm's employees may conduct their activities in an ethically acceptable manner but still not be considered socially responsible because their activities have little or no impact on anyone other than their closest stakeholders: their customers, employees, and shareholders (Exhibit 18.3, upper right quadrant). In this case, employees would not, for instance, be involved in volunteer activities to clean up a local park, coach the community's youth baseball league, or take part in any other socially responsible activities that improve the communities in which the company operates.

Likewise, some firms that are perceived as socially responsible can still take actions that are viewed as unethical (Exhibit 18.3, lower left quadrant). For instance, a firm might be considered socially responsible because it makes generous donations to charities but is simultaneously involved in questionable sales practices. After the 2010 oil spill in

DANACOL contains 1g of plant sterols.

PLANT STEROLS HELP REDUCE CHOLESTEROL.
80ml of Danacol® provides 50% of the daily amount of plant sterols shown to help reduce cholesterol in adults. As part of a balanced diet and a healthy lifestyle.

DAILY CONSUMPTION CAN MAKE A REAL DIFFERENCE.

danacol.ca

Dannon is both ethical and socially responsible. It has an ethical commitment to make healthful food. It is socially responsible since it is involved in many activities and charities that help people.

EXHIBIT 18.3 | Ethics Versus Social Responsibility

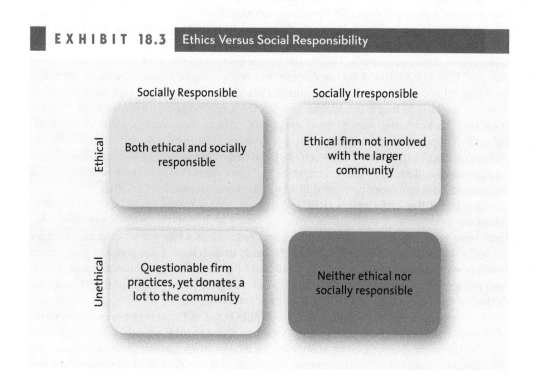

Oil spills are a major catastrophe for all parties.

the Gulf of Mexico, BP committed to donating millions of dollars to help economically impacted states promote tourism.[25] Ethically, how do we characterize a firm that obtains its profits through illicit actions but then donates a percentage of those profits to charity?

The worst situation, of course, is when firms behave both unethically *and* in a socially irresponsible manner (Exhibit 18.3, lower right quadrant). For example, Premier Fitness Club was fined $30,000 for four violations of the Employment Standards Act (ESA 2000) in connection with wages owed to former employees and paid a $200,000 settlement to the Competition Bureau for misleading advertising.[26] Both of these situations go against the norms of socially acceptable business practices.

Consumers and investors increasingly appear to want to purchase products and services from and invest in companies that act in socially responsible ways. According to the Conference Board of Canada, CSR is the business issue of the 21st century. The importance of CSR is underlined by the finding that a majority of Canadians have rewarded or punished companies for their corporate citizenship. About 55 percent said they consciously decided to buy a product or service from one company over another because they felt the company was a good corporate citizen. Fifty-two percent consciously refused to support companies they felt were not socially responsible.[27] Nielsen's Global Survey on Corporate Social Responsibility indicated that consumers were more willing to buy products and services from companies with programs that give back to society. This willingness to spend more increased in 43 of 58 countries from 2011 to 2013.[28]

The Royal Bank of Canada (RBC) recognizes that it makes good business sense to adopt the principles of sustainable development, which could provide short- and long-term returns for its shareholders, clients, and employees while preserving the environment for future generations. RBC's beliefs led it to purchase 1,000 megawatt hours of green power, mitigating 640 tonnes or 7 percent of greenhouse gas emissions annually. It also reduces its paper consumption by approximately 20 tonnes by providing clients the option of receiving electronic rather than paper statements.[29]

Companies earn both tangible and intangible benefits for acting in a socially desirable manner because it just makes good business sense to take actions that benefit society. Consider, for example, companies such as Tim Hortons and HP Canada, which have established strong programs to support Canadian children. The Tim Hortons Children's

Our pledges and priorities

		Our pledges	Our priorities
Corporate integrity	Financial services companies depend on a foundation of trust and on effective risk management for their long-term success. We maintain trust by acting with integrity in everything we do.	We will conduct ourselves with integrity in everything we do, guided by our comprehensive Code of Conduct.	■ Govern responsibly ■ Manage risk effectively ■ Uphold principles, policies and procedures that promote integrity and ensure compliance with applicable regulatory requirements
Economic impact	Like all businesses, RBC strives to generate profits. Our goal is to have a positive impact on the economies of the communities and countries in which we do business.	We will have a positive impact on the economy by delivering shareholder returns, creating good jobs, paying our fair share of taxes and purchasing goods and services responsibly from suppliers of all sizes. We will provide credit to households and businesses responsibly so they can prosper.	■ Deliver top-quartile Total Shareholder Returns (TSR¹) over the medium term ■ Create employment ■ Support small business ■ Promote community economic development ■ Foster economic growth by supporting infrastructure development projects ■ Foster innovation and entrepreneurship ■ Purchase goods and services responsibly
Marketplace	Our vision is to "always earn the right to be our clients' first choice." Our practices and performance in the marketplace, including our products, services and the expertise and manner in which we provide them, are essential to helping us meet this goal.	We will "earn the right to be our clients' first choice" by serving them responsibly. We will strive to provide our clients with the right products, services and advice so that they can make the best financial decisions possible.	■ Promote financial literacy among clients and the general public ■ Provide access to basic banking through a range of channels ■ Develop and provide financial products responsibly, including those that have a positive social or environmental impact ■ Respect clients' privacy, safeguard their information and help to protect them from fraud ■ Listen and respond to clients

An abbreviated look at some of RBC's pledges and priorities.

Foundation was established in 1975 to honour Tim Horton's love for children and his desire to help those less fortunate. To support this initiative, Tim Hortons storeowners hold an annual Camp Day, donating coffee sales and collecting public donations. In 2013, the foundation raised more than $11.8 million, enabling the company to send 16,000 children from economically disadvantaged homes to camp.[30]

Corporations such as RBC, Tim Hortons, Sleep Country Canada, and many others increasingly include socially responsible programs when planning and defining their strategic initiatives. Unfortunately, being a socially responsible corporation does not ensure that all members of the firm or all subunits within it will act ethically; rather, it means only that the firm is committing time and resources to projects in the community that may not directly relate to generating profit.

CONSUMERISM, ETHICS, AND SOCIALLY RESPONSIBLE PRACTICES

L03

Companies that do not pay sufficient attention to ethical conduct and strong corporate responsibility are often targeted by consumer groups and other advocacy groups, which generate negative publicity and sometimes even boycott their products. *Consumer Reports* and *Lemon Aid* are two key publications that are dedicated to inform and protect consumers from harmful products and poor business practices by marketers. *Consumer Reports* states its mission as "We test, inform, and protect." **Consumerism**—a social movement aimed at protecting consumers from business practices that infringe upon their rights—and enhanced environmental awareness and activism are two key factors that have been driving the trend toward greater CSR in Canada. Today, more than 75 percent of Canadian companies have CSR policies and projects that support their communities.[31]

consumerism
A social movement aimed at protecting consumers from business practices that infringe upon their rights.

Many companies have established CSR programs that enable consumers to safely dispose of the products they buy in order to minimize the harmful effects on the environment. For example, Mountain Equipment Co-op offers a recycling program where customers can bring their worn-out polyester garments back to a store to be recycled into new items,[32] and Loblaw introduced reusable shopping bags made from 100 percent recycled material.[33] Similarly, personal computer vendors such as Dell and Hewlett-Packard collect used equipment for recycling. All HP laser cartridges come with instructions for returning the old cartridges. Cellphone manufacturers are also starting to promote recycling of old phones and batteries, encouraging consumers to drop them off at collection depots across the country. Even governments have gotten into the action. For example, the government of Prince Edward Island has established its Lead Acid Take Back Program[34] and imposed regulations that require retailers to charge $5 on new battery purchases unless an old battery is returned within 30 days. The program focuses on lead acid batteries, which includes all vehicle batteries (for cars, trucks, snowmobiles, motorcycles, off-road vehicles, and ride-on lawnmowers). Similarly, the Ontario government introduced its wine and liquor bottle recycling program: consumers are given a refund when they take their empty bottles to the Beer Store for recycling rather than throwing them in their blue box or garbage bins.

Consumers increasingly want to purchase products and services from companies that act in socially responsible ways. Most large companies understand this and actively promote their efforts. Guelph-based The Co-operators, a co-operatively owned insurance company, has built a reputation for caring about its members' needs and the quality of life in their communities. Safety-related events such as car-seat inspection clinics and bike safety rodeos, anti–drinking and driving initiatives, and sponsorship of the Block Parent Program of Canada are funded by its Community Economic Development program. Like many other companies with CSR response programs, The Co-operators focuses on what's known as the triple bottom line, meaning the economic, social, and environmental sustainability of a company.[35] Some companies have social responsibility woven into the very fabric of their business as Entrepreneurial Marketing 18.1 demonstrates.

When companies embrace CSR, they appeal not only to their shareholders but also to their key stakeholders, including their own employees, consumers, the marketplace, and society at large. Let's consider each of these stakeholder categories to understand the meaning and effects of corporate social responsibility in the modern marketing arena, as well as how CSR ultimately can benefit the firm that undertakes it.

Employees   Perhaps the most basic corporate social responsibility to employees is to ensure a safe working environment, free of threats to their physical safety, health, or well-being. In some cases though, this basic level of safety seems insufficient to achieve responsibility to workers. Insurance provider Aflac regards its pay-for-performance structure a key element of its responsibility to its employees, with the notion that everyone, from call centre operators to the CEO, faces the same compensation standards. In this sense, it ensures equality of treatment and fairness in compensation. In doing so, Aflac earns a reputation as a good place to work and increases the number of people who apply for jobs there. These happy employees also should provide better service to customers, which in turn ensures better outcomes for the firm.

In addition to focusing on employees, more and more firms realize that happy employee families make happy and productive employees. Consequently, firms are focusing their efforts on outreach programs aimed at their employees' families.

Customers   Especially as changes in the marketing environment emerge, firms must consider the effects on the customers who currently patronize them and future customers whom they are targeting. Corporate social responsibility programs must take such shifts and trends into account and react to them quickly. A few of the trends that are receiving the most attention include respecting and protecting privacy in an electronic

 **Entrepreneurial Marketing 18.1** | **Money Does Grow on Trees**[36]

When Saskatchewan brothers Kalen and Derrick Elmsley and their friend David Luba realized that there was no option for consumers to buy clothing and give back to society, they decided to do something about it. Social responsibility and concern for the environment were foremost in their minds when they started Ten Tree Apparel, which makes T-shirts, tank tops, hats, and hoodies.

They came up with a unique approach to demonstrate that their company was socially responsible in a way that also gives customers the opportunity to contribute to sustainability. For every item it sells, the company plants 10 trees. It produces clothing in a responsible fashion manner in Oregon, not offshore or in a developing country with low labour costs and a poor safety record. It was important for Ten Tree to source a manufacturer close to home to avoid environmental issues related to shipping and oil consumption. Of course, local production increases the costs of the clothing. And it costs about $3 to plant 10 trees. As a result, the company's clothing sells for up to $6 more at retailers than comparable clothing.

In spite of this, Kalen Elmsley says it not been an issue—there has been no pushback from consumers on price. It helps that Ten Tree's products are tagged with the message "ten trees are planted for every item purchased," which helps to attract an audience of socially and/or environmentally enlightened consumers. In Canada, trees are planted near Edenwold, about 30 minutes outside Regina. Through a partnership with WeForest, Ten Tree can plant trees in 14 countries, including Ethiopia, Burkina Faso, India, Madagascar, Senegal, Tanzania, the Philippines, and Haiti. In the future, the WeForest arrangement will allow Ten Tree's customers to visit its website to indicate the country in which they wish to have trees planted.

Although the trio had been operational for only three months when they appeared on CBC's *Dragons' Den*, they had already earned revenues of $120,000. While some of the Dragons were skeptical, Bruce Croxon and Arlene Dickinson were sold. Since Ten Tree made the pitch, it has secured distribution at 300 retailers across Canada and is looking to expand in the United States, having successfully tested the waters for online sales.

Ten Tree was formally recognized when it won the Saskatchewan Young Professional and Entrepreneurs Volta award. It was also showcased during Saskatchewan Fashion Week as a hot new design company.[37] More importantly, says Elmsley, its sustainability efforts resulted in planting over 400,000 trees in the company's first year of operation, contributing to the financial, social, and environmental bottom line.

ten trees
are planted for
every item purchased

tentree.org

For every T-shirt sold, Ten Tree Apparel plants 10 trees.

world and ensuring the healthfulness of products, especially those aimed at children. Moreover, CSR often increases consumer awareness of the firm, which can lead to better brand equity and sales in the long run.

ParticipACTION Canada has helped launch a variety of initiatives to help develop a healthier way of life through an active lifestyle, offering tools and programs for teenagers and corporations.[38] The goal of such programs is to increase consumer awareness of the need to make healthier, more active choices. These efforts ultimately benefit consumers too, who not only gain additional consumption choices but also suffer less risk of the dangers associated with inactivity.

Marketplace   When one firm in the industry leads the way toward CSR, its partners and competitors often have no choice but to follow—or run the risk of being left behind. To address issues such as global warming, water scarcity, and energy, GE uses a program it calls ecomagination, which encompasses a business strategy comprising four commitments: to double investments in clean R&D, increase revenues from ecomagination products, reduce greenhouse gas emissions, and inform the public about these issues.[39] When confronted with such initiatives, other energy companies are forced to make a decision: continue as they have been doing, or adopt more responsible practices themselves. In either case, the initiating firm enjoys an advantage by gaining a reputation for being on the cutting edge of CSR efforts.

Society   Firms expend considerable time and energy engaging in activities aimed at improving the overall community and the physical environment. According to a McKinsey & Co. survey, 95 percent of CEOs believe that society increasingly expects companies to take on public responsibilities.[40] That is, in a broad sense, companies cannot ignore societal demands that they act responsibly. A firm that fails to do so causes damage to all the preceding stakeholders, as well as itself. Perhaps the most famous recent example is BP, which failed to offer adequate protections to the workers on the Deep Horizon deep

GE is the industry leader in CSR with its ecoimagination program.

ecomagination℠

JUST CALLED SHOTGUN.

While the world's been waiting for the electric car, maybe the whole time, the electric car has been waiting for this. The WattStation™ from GE enables charging for electric vehicles, and is going to change the way we all get to where we want to go. Ecomagination, it's technology that makes the world work.

GE imagination at work

sea oil rig, ensure that consumers could enjoy waters free of oil contamination, or live up to marketplace standards for safety. As a result, society as a whole suffered, as did BP's corporate reputation, profits, and outlook for the future.

Are consumers doing their part to promote and support various CSR programs aimed at protecting the environment? When you buy a new digital camera or cellphone, do you first consider what will happen to your old one? When you buy a popular Harry Potter book, do you care that author J.K. Rowling has expressed a desire for her books to be printed on forest-friendly paper?[41] What do you think? Should marketers take more responsibility for educating consumers on the downside of consumption or is it up to consumers to take a proactive role?

A Framework for Ethical Decision Making

LO4

We cannot expect every member of a firm to always act ethically. However, a framework for ethical decision making can help move people to work toward common ethical goals. Exhibit 18.4 outlines a simple framework for ethical decision making. Let's consider each of the steps.

Step 1: Identify Issues.   The first step is to identify the issue. For illustrative purposes, we'll investigate the use (or misuse) of data collected from consumers by a marketing research firm. One of the issues that might arise is the way the data are collected. For instance, are the respondents told about the real purpose of the study? Another issue questions whether the results are going to be used in a way that might mislead or even harm the public.

Step 2: Gather Information and Identify Stakeholders.   In this step, the firm focuses on gathering facts that are important to the ethical issue, including all relevant legal information. To get a complete picture, the firm must also identify and have discussions with the individuals and groups that have a stake in how the issue is resolved.

Stakeholders typically include the firm's current and retired employees, suppliers, the government, customer groups, shareholders, environmentalists, and members of the community in which the firm operates. Beyond these, many firms now also analyze the needs of the industry and the global community, as well as one-off stakeholders, such as future generations, and the natural environment itself.

Step 3: Brainstorm and Evaluate Alternatives.   After the marketing firm has identified the stakeholders and their issues and gathered the available data, all parties relevant to the decision should come together to brainstorm any alternative courses of action. In our example, these might include halting the market research project, making responses anonymous, instituting training on the CMA's Code of Ethics for all researchers, and so forth. Management then reviews and refines these alternatives, leading to the final step.

EXHIBIT 18.4 Ethical Decision-Making Framework

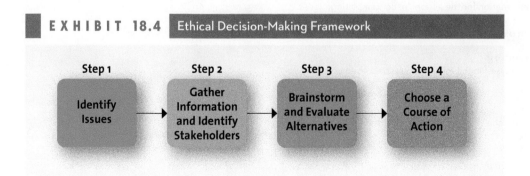

Step 1 — Identify Issues → Step 2 — Gather Information and Identify Stakeholders → Step 3 — Brainstorm and Evaluate Alternatives → Step 4 — Choose a Course of Action

Step 4: Choose a Course of Action. The objective of this last step is to weigh the various alternatives and choose a course of action that generates the best solution for the stakeholders by using ethical practices. Management will rank the alternatives in order of preference, clearly establishing the advantages and disadvantages of each. It is also crucial to investigate any potential legal issues associated with each alternative. Of course, any illegal activity should immediately be rejected.

To choose the appropriate course of action, marketing managers will evaluate each alternative by using a process something like the sample ethical decision-making metric in Exhibit 18.5. The marketer's task here is to ensure that he or she has applied all relevant decision-making criteria and to assess his or her level of confidence that the decision being made meets those stated criteria. If the marketer isn't confident about the decision, he or she should re-examine the other alternatives.

Using Exhibit 18.5, you can gauge your own ethical response. If your scores tend to be in the low numbers (1 and 2), then the situation is not an ethically troubling situation for you. If, in contrast, your scores tend to be in the high numbers (6 and 7), it is ethically troubling and you know it. If your scores are scattered or in the middle numbers, you need to step back and reflect on how you wish to proceed. At the end of the chapter you will find a series of ethical scenarios designed to assist you in developing your skills at identifying ethical issues. Use Exhibit 18.5 to help you evaluate these scenarios.

In using such an ethical metric or framework, decision makers must consider the relevant ethical issues, evaluate the alternatives, and then choose a course of action that will help them avoid serious ethical lapses.

Next, let's illustrate how the ethical decision-making metric in Exhibit 18.5 can be used to make ethical business decisions.

EXHIBIT 18.5 | Ethical Decision-making Metric

Test	Decision						
	Yes		**Maybe**				**No**
	1	**2**	**3**	**4**	**5**	**6**	**7**
1. The Publicity Test Would I want to see this action that I'm about to take described on the front page of the local paper or in a national magazine?							
2. The Moral Mentor Test Would the person I admire the most engage in this activity?							
3. The Admired Observer Test Would I want the person I admire most to see me doing this?							
4. The Transparency Test Could I give a clear explanation for the action I'm contemplating, including an honest and transparent account of all my motives, that would satisfy a fair and dispassionate moral judge?							
5. The Person in the Mirror Test Will I be able to look at myself in the mirror and respect the person I see there?							
6. The Golden Rule Test Would I like to be on the receiving end of this action and all its potential consequences?							

Source: Adapted from Tom Morris, *The Art of Achievement: Mastering the 7 Cs of Success in Business and in Life* (Kansas City, MO: Andrew McMeel Publishing, 2002); http://edbrenegar.typepad.com/leading_questions/2005/05/real_life_leade.html (accessed December 29, 2007).

Myra Jansen, the head cook at Confederation High School in Anytown, Canada, has had enough. Reports showing that children rarely eat enough vegetables have combined with studies that indicate school kids have a limited amount of time to eat their lunches. The combination has led to increasing obesity rates and troublesome reports about the long-term effects. Jansen has therefore decided that the tater-tots and hotdogs are out. Vegetables and healthy proteins are in.

The problem, of course, is getting the kids to eat raw vegetables, plant proteins, and lean meat. For many teenagers, recommending that they eat healthy food at lunch is akin to calling detention a play date. But Myra has a plan: She's going to reformulate various menu items using different ingredients, and just never tell the students. Thus the regular hot dogs will be replaced with turkey or soy dogs. The hash browns will contain more nutrient-dense sweet potatoes instead of the vitamin-deficient regular spuds they used to be made out of. She is convinced she can make such switches for most of the menu items, and none of the children need to know.

Most of the kitchen staff is onboard with the idea and even have suggested other possible menu switches that would benefit the students by ensuring that they received a well-balanced meal at school. When apprised of the idea, school board members got very excited and praised Myra for her innovative thinking. But the community liaison for the school, whose job it is to communicate with parents and other members of the community, is not so sure. Salim Gibran is nervous about how students will react when they learn that they have been deceived. He also has two small children of his own, one of whom has a severe wheat allergy. Thus the Gibrans are extremely cautious about eating out, always asking for a detailed, specific list of ingredients for anything they order.

Using his training in ethical decision making, Salim sits down to evaluate his alternatives, beginning with identifying possible options available to the school district, as well as the various stakeholders that might be impacted by the decision. He comes up with the following list:

1. Switch out the food without telling students.

2. Leave menus as they are.

3. Switch out the food ingredients but also tell students exactly what is in each item in the cafeteria.

To make a clear recommendation to the board about what would be the best ethical choice, Salim decides to evaluate each alternative using a series of questions similar to those in Exhibit 18.5.

Question 1: Would I want to see this action described on the front page of the local paper? The school board's reaction caused Salim to think that the larger community would appreciate the effort to improve students' health. Thus, option 1 appears best for these stakeholders, and possibly for society, which may reduce the prevalence of obesity among these students. However, he shudders to think about how angry students might be if they learned they had been tricked. They also likely are accustomed to their menu as it is and, therefore, they would prefer option 2.

Question 2: Would the person I admire most engage in this activity, and would I want him or her seeing me engage in this activity? For most of his life, Salim has held up Mahatma Gandhi as his ideal for how to act in the world. For Mahatma Gandhi, truth was an absolute concept, not something that could be changed depending on the situation. Therefore, Salim believes Mahatma Gandhi would strongly disapprove of option 1. However, Mahatma Gandhi also worried about the ethics of eating and took care to avoid food choices that had negative effects on society, so he might reject option 2 as well.

Question 3: Can I give a clear explanation for my action, including an honest account of my motives? In thinking about his children, Salim realizes that he is prioritizing their needs, more so than the needs of other children, such as those who struggle with weight issues. That is, he worries that his daughter might unknowingly be exposed to wheat in a school cafeteria, so he prefers option 3.

Question 4: Will I be able to look at myself in the mirror and respect what I see? By bringing up the ethics of this decision, even when it seems as if everyone else has agreed with it, Salim feels confident that he has taken the right first step. The option chosen is still important, but it is a group decision, and Salim thinks he is doing his part.

Question 5: Would I want to be on the receiving end of this action and its consequences? Salim struggles most with this question. He remembers the kind of junk foods he chose when he was in college, and the 10 kilograms he put on as a result. He wishes now that his parents had given him rules to follow about what to eat at school. But he also remembers how rebellious he was and knows that he probably would not have followed those rules. And at the same time, he hates the idea that someone could give him food to eat with falsified ingredients.

On the basis of this exercise, Salim decides that he wants to recommend option 3 to the school board. When he does so, Myra Jansen protests loudly: "This is ridiculous! I know better what kids should be eating, and I know too that some community liaison has no idea what they are willing to eat. You've got to trick them to get them to eat right." Another school board member agrees, noting, "They're just kids. They don't necessarily have the same rights as adults, so we are allowed to decide what's best for them. And hiding the healthy ingredients to get the kids to eat healthy foods is what's best."

So what does the school board decide?

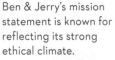

INTEGRATING ETHICS INTO MARKETING STRATEGY

Ethical decision making is not a simple process, though it can get easier as decision makers within the firm become accustomed to thinking about the ethical implications of their actions from a strategic perspective. In this section, we examine how ethical decision making can be integrated into the strategic marketing planning process introduced in Chapter 2.

The questions vary at each stage of the strategic marketing planning process. For instance, in the planning stage the firm will decide what level of commitment to its ethical policies and standards it is willing to declare publicly. In the implementation stage, the tone of the questions switches from "*Can we* serve the market with the firm's products or services in an ethically responsible manner?" to "*Should we* be engaging in particular marketing practices?" The key task in the control phase is to ensure that all potential ethical issues raised during the planning process have been addressed and that all employees of the firm have acted ethically. Let's take a closer look at how ethics can be integrated at each stage of the strategic marketing planning process.

Ben & Jerry's mission statement is known for reflecting its strong ethical climate.

Planning Phase

Marketers can introduce ethics at the beginning of the planning process simply by including ethical statements in the firm's mission statement. Many Canadian firms such as RBC, Sleep Country, and others have clearly articulated ethical and corporate social responsibility policies and programs, recognizing that profits and social responsibility go hand in hand. Some firms use mission statements that include ethical precepts for shaping the organization. The mission statements from organizations such as The Body Shop and Ben & Jerry's are known for reflecting strong ethical climates. Even large firms such as General Mills provide a statement of values that defines the priorities of the organization and its commitment to promoting those values in all that the firm does. Every year, General Mills issues a report discussing how the firm has performed against its own standards of ethical conduct.[42]

For example, General Mills recently announced it would be switching to whole grains in all its breakfast cereal lines—making it the first of the mass-marketed cereal manufacturers to do so. This switch has been applauded by nutritionists who claim it dramatically improves the dietary benefits of the cereals. General Mills made the switch not necessarily to increase consumer demand, but, in keeping with its stated values, to improve the health of its consumers.[43]

Implementation Phase

In the implementation phase of the marketing strategy, when firms are identifying potential markets and ways to deliver the 4Ps to them, firms must consider several ethical issues. Sometimes a firm's choice of target market and how it pursues it can lead to charges of unethical behaviour. For instance, Molson Brewery launched a Facebook campaign targeted towards university and college students in which it asked them to post party pictures, which it would use to identify the "top party school." This effort not only encouraged underage drinking but also deeply irritated universities across both Canada and the United States, which had little interest in being thus identified. Although these student groups might have been responsive to the firm's efforts, they did not represent an appropriate target market. Marketing through social media has some particular ethical concerns associated with it, as Social and Mobile Marketing 18.1 shows.

General Mills is switching to whole grains in all its breakfast cereal lines, which should improve their dietary benefits.

The question of resource allocation in the implementation phase can be an ethical minefield, and perhaps no business is more susceptible to charges of unethical resource allocation than the pharmaceutical industry. For example, AIDS activists claim that pharmaceutical companies are not doing enough to develop affordable drugs for underdeveloped countries to treat AIDS among their poor citizens. Some public health officials also have sounded alarm bells about the lack of research into the next generation of antibiotics, at a time when bacteria continue to become increasingly resistant to existing drugs. Critics of the pharmaceutical industry can also point to the increasing number of "lifestyle" drugs, such as those for erectile dysfunction, obesity, male-pattern baldness, nail fungus, and such, as possible causes for the lack of new treatments for serious diseases, even though the pharmaceutical companies vehemently deny that they have been transferring assets from research on treatments for life-threatening illnesses to fund lifestyle drugs.

Sourcing decisions are another problem area for some firms as discussed in the chapter opener with companies choosing to do business with factories in Bangladesh. Charges that they use sweatshop labour to produce their goods have been made against many well-known companies. Locating production in an underdeveloped country can make economic sense, because it allows the company to take advantage of the lower production costs offered in poorer nations but it also opens a Pandora's Box of ethical issues, the most prominent of which deals with responsibility. Who is responsible for ensuring that the workers in the factories that produce the goods are treated fairly and paid a living wage? Even the public faces of firms, such as Kathy Lee Gifford, have been faulted for failing to take responsibility for the conditions in factories that produce products bearing their names. Environmental organizations have also joined the attack recently, noting that many overseas factories do not maintain the highest environmental standards.

Once the strategy is implemented, controls must be in place to be certain that the firm has actually done what it has set out to do. These activities take place in the next phase of the strategic marketing planning process.

Social and Mobile Marketing 18.1

Who Tweeted Me to Buy a Ford Fiesta?[44]

Auto manufacturers have long paid celebrities to be spokespeople for their lines of vehicles. But maybe customers really want to hear from people like themselves, rather than a celebrity paid millions of dollars to promote a car. Although car companies can save a lot of money by paying normal people less than they pay celebrities, they do not want just anyone to promote their products. They want social media gurus or popular Twitter and blog figures with legions of followers.

Marketing campaigns by Lexus, Ford, and LandRover all promote their products socially on the web. Ford recruited 100 people with strong online followings to test drive the Ford Focus and then talk about their experiences online. Ford previously had been successful with its Ford Fiesta campaign, in which anyone who test drove the newly introduced car posted YouTube videos, Flickr photos, and Twitter tweets—adding up to more than 7 million views on YouTube and 4 million mentions on Twitter. As a result, over 130,000 people visited the Ford Fiesta website, 83 percent of whom had never owned a Ford before. The campaign certainly received a lot of attention, though the actual sales conversion has not been disclosed.

Influential online informants also can have negative influences though. Even if a firm pays a blogger or tweeter, no rule can force them to write positive reviews. But the likelihood is that a paid blogger will be more positive than an unpaid, disinterested reviewer. In the United States, the Federal Trade Commission (FTC) has created guidelines for blogging and tweeting, saying that those who post messages must disclose any compensation they may have received for talking about the product. They also must disclose if there is a connection, such as an employee/employer relationship, between the endorser and the marketer of the product that might affect how people evaluate the endorsement.

Ford Fiesta's social media campaign draws attention to its traditional media ads.

Are these guidelines strong enough to let potential customers know that the message being received through social media is a paid form of promotion, not unlike an ad on TV? Should Canada implement similar guidelines?

Control Phase

During the control phase of the strategic marketing planning process, managers must be evaluated on their actions from an ethical perspective. Systems must be in place to check whether each ethical issue raised in the planning process was actually successfully implemented. Systems used in the control phase must also react to change. The emergence of new technologies and new markets ensures that new ethical issues continually arise. Ethical Dilemma 18.1 uncovers some of these new privacy issues.

Many firms have emergency response plans in place just in case they ever encounter a situation similar to the Tylenol tampering case or an industrial accident at a manufacturing plant. Firms that respond in the first few hours of a crisis with an organized plan and compassion for those affected suffer fewer long-term negative effects on their reputation, credibility, and level of trust among consumers.[45]

Ethics thus remains a crucial component of the strategic marketing planning process and should be incorporated into all the firm's decision making. At issue is the problem of policing potential violations of human rights and labour laws. As we saw in the

Ethical Dilemma 18.1   Check-ins and Facebook Photos Can Be Dangerous

The rise of social media has been a boon for many marketers: When consumers "like" a brand on Facebook, tweet about a consumption experience on Twitter, and check in on Foursquare, they are providing the company free marketing. But they are also giving criminals and unethical marketers an easy means to take advantage of them. Thus the vast benefits of social media combine some threats to consumers.

Consider these examples: On your commute to work each day, you might pay for your train fare with a monthly transit card that identifies you as the specific user. Say you are running a bit late one day and decide to blame the trains, instead of admitting you slept in late. Conceivably, your boss could check the data gathered when you swiped your card and confront you with the fact that you didn't even get on the train until 9:15. Or your mother could check to see that you got on at a different stop than usual and ask where exactly you spent the night.

These possibilities may seem harmful to your reputation or pride more than anything else. However, when people post their vacation plans or softball schedules on Facebook, they also inform potential burglars exactly when they will be away from their homes. Checking in on Foursquare gives criminals an immediate indication; if you check in at a restaurant, chances are you will not be home for another couple of hours. To highlight this issue, the mash-up website Please Rob Me (http://www. pleaserobme.com) randomly taps people's posts on Facebook and Twitter to identify those who have clearly broadcast that they are not at home.

Now imagine that an unscrupulous marketer fails to protect information about the items you have bought from it. With just a few clicks of a mouse and some technology savvy, criminals know not only when your house will be empty but also exactly what kinds of valuables they might steal when they break in.

Many users have grown more aware of such concerns and work to avoid such obvious releases of their information. But smartphone cameras stamp each photo taken with latitude and longitude information. Thus, even if you never mention the location of your favourite haunts, stalkers can obtain information about the places where you are likely to be based on the photos you have posted on Facebook, especially if they are uploaded in real time.

The need for a new kind of privacy is thus a critical issue for marketers and consumers alike. Ethical marketers must find a way to collect the priceless data that customers make available through social media while avoiding collecting details that violate people's right to **locational privacy**—defined as a person's ability to move normally in public spaces with the expectation that his or her location will not be recorded for subsequent use.[46]

---

chapter opener, many firms have had to publicly defend themselves against allegations of human rights, labour, or other abuses involving the factories and countries in which their goods are made.[47]

locational privacy A person's ability to move about in public spaces with the expectation the location will not be recorded for future use.

UNDERSTANDING ETHICS BY USING SCENARIOS

In this section, we present a series of ethical scenarios designed to assist you in developing your skills at identifying ethical issues. There is no one right answer to the dilemmas below, just as there will be no correct answers to many of the ethical situations you will face throughout your career. Instead, these scenarios can help you develop your sensitivity toward ethical issues, as well as your ethical reasoning skills.

Exhibit 18.5 provides simple tests to assist you in evaluating these scenarios. By asking yourself these simple questions, you can gauge your own ethical response.

Scenario 1: Retailers Lack Ethical Guidelines

Renata has been working at Peavy's Bridal for less than a year now. Her sales figures have never been competitive with those of her coworkers, and the sales manager has called her in for several meetings to discuss her inability to close the sale. Things look desperate; in the last meeting, the sales manager told her that if she did not meet her quota next month, the company would likely have to fire her.

In considering how she might improve her methods and sales, Renata turned to another salesperson, namely, the one with the most experience in the store. Marilyn

has been with Peavy's for nearly 30 years, and she virtually always gets the sale. But how?

"Let me tell you something sweetie," Marilyn tells her. "Every bride-to-be wants one thing: to look beautiful on her wedding day, so everyone gasps when they first see her. And hey, the husband is going to think she looks great. But let's be honest here—not everyone is all that beautiful. So you have to convince them that they look great in one, and only one, dress. And that dress had better be the most expensive one they try, or they won't believe you anyway! And then you have to show them how much better they look with a veil. And some shoes. And a tiara . . . you get the picture! I mean, they need all that stuff anyway, so why shouldn't we make them feel good while they're here and let them buy from us?"

Should she follow Marilyn's advice and save her job?

Scenario 2: Giving Credit Where Credit Isn't Due

A catalogue retailer that carries home and children's items, such as children's furniture, clothing, and toys, was seeking a way to reach a new audience and stop the declining sales and revenue trends it was suffering. A market research firm hired by the cataloguer identified a new but potentially risky market: lower-income single parents. The new market seems attractive because of the large number of single parents, but most of these homes are severely constrained in terms of their monetary resources.

The research firm proposed that the cataloguer offer a generous credit policy that would allow consumers to purchase up to $500 worth of merchandise on credit without a credit check, provided they sign up for direct payment of their credit account from a chequing account. Because these are high-risk consumers, the credit accounts would carry extremely high interest rates. The research firm believes that even with losses, enough accounts will be paid off to make the venture extremely profitable for the catalogue retailer.

Should the cataloguer pursue this new strategy?

Scenario 3: The Jeweller's Tarnished Image

Sparkle Gem Jewellers, a family-owned and -operated costume jewellery manufacturing business, traditionally sold its products only to wholesalers. Recently however, Sparkle Gem was approached by the charismatic Barb Stephens, who convinced the owners to begin selling through a network of distributors she had organized. The distributors recruited individuals to host "jewellery parties" in their homes. Sparkle Gem's owners, the Billing family, has been thrilled with the revenue generated by these home parties and started making plans for the expansion of the distributor network.

However, Mrs. Billing just received a letter from a jewellery party customer, who expressed sympathy for her loss. Mrs. Billing was concerned and contacted the letter writer, who told her that Barb Stephens had come to the jewellery party at her church and told the story of Sparkle Gem. According to Barb's story, Mrs. Billing was a young widow struggling to keep her business together after her husband died on a missionary trip. The writer had purchased $200 worth of jewellery at the party and told Mrs. Billing that she hoped it helped. Mrs. Billing was stunned. She and her very much alive husband had just celebrated their 50th wedding anniversary.

What should Mrs. Billing do now?

Scenario 4: No Wonder It's So Good

Enjoy Cola is a new product produced by ABC Beverage and marketed with the slogan "Relax with Enjoy." Unlike other colas on the market, Enjoy does not contain caffeine and therefore is positioned as the perfect beverage to end the day or for a slow-paced weekend, and as a means to help consumers relax and unwind. The market response has been tremendous, and sales of Enjoy have been growing rapidly, especially among women.

ABC Beverage decided not to list on the ingredient label that Enjoy contains a small amount of alcohol because the government does not require it to do so unless the alcohol content is more than 1 percent.

Mia Rodriquez, the marketing director for Enjoy, only recently learned that Enjoy contains small amounts of alcohol and is troubled about ABC's failure to disclose this information on the ingredients list. If the alcohol content is less than 1 percent, the beverage is not an alcoholic beverage. But she worries about the impact of this omission on consumers who have alcohol sensitivities or those who shouldn't be consuming alcohol, such as pregnant women, recovering alcoholics, and children.

What should Mia do? What would you do in Mia's place?

Scenario 5: Bright Baby's Bright Idea

Bartok Manufacturing produces a line of infant toys under the Bright Baby brand label. The Consumer Product Safety Commission (CPSC) recently issued a recall order for the Bright Baby car seat gym, a very popular product. According to the CPSC, the gym contains small parts that present a choking hazard. The CEO of Bartok Manufacturing, Bill Bartok, called an executive meeting to determine the firm's strategy in response to the recall.

Mike Henderson, Bartok's CFO, stated that the recall could cost as much as $1 million in lost revenue from the Bright Baby line. Noting that there had been no deaths or injuries from the product, just the *potential* for injury, Mike proposed that the remaining inventory of car seat gyms be sold in Mexico, where there are no rules such as the CPSC's. Sue Tyler, the marketing director for Bartok, recommended that the product be repackaged and sold in Mexico under a different brand name so that the Bright Baby name would not be associated with the product. Bill, though a bit leery of the plan, agreed to go along with it to avoid the monetary losses.

What would you have recommended to the CEO?

LEARNING OBJECTIVES REVIEW

Identify why marketers should be concerned about ethics

The most important reason to worry about making ethically correct decisions is that it is simply the right thing to do! Being a part of an ethically responsible firm should be important to every employee, but it is particularly important to marketers because they interact most directly with customers and suppliers, which offers them a multitude of opportunities to address ethically challenged issues. It is often challenging to make ethically correct decisions because they can conflict with other personal or corporate objectives.

LO2 **Distinguish between ethics and social responsibility**

Individuals and firms can (and should) act ethically, but the outcome of their acts may not affect anyone other than the firm's immediate stakeholders, such as its employees, customers, and suppliers. To be socially responsible, a firm also must take actions that benefit the community in a larger sense, such as helping people who have been affected by a natural disaster such as a hurricane. Socially responsible firms try to conduct their business operations in such a way as to eliminate or minimize the negative impacts on the natural environment and vulnerable groups of consumers such as children, elderly people, and people with disabilities. They also inform consumers of potential harmful effects of their products, promote their products and services in a truthful and responsible way, and are quick to take corrective actions when deficiencies in their products and services are revealed.

LO3 **Describe consumerism and explain how it fosters ethical and socially responsible business practices**

Consumers can pressure businesses to practice ethical and socially responsible behaviour in a variety of ways. They can protest poor practices, boycott companies' products or services, and publicly call for higher ethical standards. In addition, consumers encourage companies to be socially responsible by supporting those companies that have strong ethical practices. Consumerism—a social movement aimed at protecting consumers from business practices that infringe upon their rights—has been a major force driving the trends of increased ethics and CSR. Unfortunately, many consumers are not making full use of the CSR programs established by corporations and governments to foster greater environmental responsibility. Marketers must also be aware that consumers have levelled ethical and social criticisms against marketing, especially when marketers breach the trust of consumers with inappropriate business practices.

LO4 **Identify the four steps in ethical decision making**

First, firms can include ethics and social responsibility in their corporate mission. Second, they should institute policies and procedures to ensure that everyone working for the firm is acting in an ethically responsible manner. Third, firms can model their ethical policies after a well-established code of ethics such as the one provided by the Canadian Marketing Association. The ethical decision framework described in this chapter could be used as a template for developing policies and procedures. Fourth, when making ethically sensitive decisions, firms can utilize an ethical decision-making evaluation questionnaire, such as that described in Exhibit 18.5. Firms could also recognize and reward employees for making ethical decisions.

LO5 **Outline how ethics and social responsibility can be integrated into a firm's marketing strategy**

Firms can ensure that ethics and social responsibility issues are an integral part of their planning processes. These considerations even could be integrated into the firm's mission statement, as long as top management commits to supporting a strong ethical climate within the organization. When considering their marketing strategy, firms should ask not only "*can we* implement a certain policy?" but also "*should we* do it?" Firms should ensure that their marketing mix—the four Ps—are held to the highest standard of social responsibility, that is, they must develop safe products, price their products fairly at all times, promote them truthfully, and distribute without undue discrimination. Finally, in the control phase, marketers must determine whether they truly have acted in an ethical and socially responsible manner. If not, they should quickly rectify the situation.

KEY TERMS

- business ethics
- consumerism

- corporate social responsibility (CSR)
- ethical climate

- locational privacy
- marketing ethics

CONCEPT REVIEW

1. Explain the meaning of ethics and corporate social responsibility in marketing. What are the main differences between ethics and social responsibility?

2. List four factors that determine whether an individual or firm will act ethically. List the different ways firms could demonstrate their commitment to corporate social responsibility.

3. Describe how firms can integrate ethics and corporate social responsibility into their marketing strategy.

4. Explain how the use of a sustainability scorecard could add value to a company in the eyes of its consumers.

5. Is it possible for companies that have a code of ethics to behave unethically? How might this happen?

6. What is consumerism? Name two organizations that you think are at the forefront of consumerism in Canada. How has consumerism helped foster ethical behaviour and good corporate social responsibility in Canadian companies?

7. Is it ever possible to eliminate or reduce the social and ethical criticisms of marketing? What actions might help in this regard?

8. Problems can arise when businesses from one culture (the United States) operate in another culture (China) that has vastly different ethical standards. Google can be seen as trying to impose its ethical standards on China and meddling in China's domestic politics. Do you agree with this perception? Should North American firms abide by the standards of foreign countries even though they may conflict with U.S. or Canadian standards?

9. Many commentators suggest that socially responsible marketing is not only a fad but also can actually enhance the revenues and profitability of a firm. Explain how socially responsible marketing may contribute to improved revenues and profitability. Can you name one or two firms in Canada that explicitly make the claim that their corporate social responsibility efforts have resulted in increased revenues and profitability?

10. Many marketers have developed programs to help consumers dispose of their products after use in safe and environmentally responsible ways, either through recycling or by taking the used product to a retailer or depot. Yet tonnes of recyclable materials end up in landfills all across Canada. What factors do you think might explain the behaviours of consumers who do not dispose of their products in an environmentally friendly manner?

MARKETING APPLICATIONS

1. Why are marketers likely to be faced with more ethical dilemmas than members of other functional areas of the firm, such as finance, accounting, or real estate?

2. Develop an argument for why a pharmaceutical firm should build and maintain an ethical climate.

3. An insurance company gives generously to charities and sponsors cancer awareness programs. It also makes it difficult for elderly consumers to make claims on policies that they have owned for years. Evaluate this company from an ethical and social responsibility perspective.

4. A clothing company gives generously to charities and sponsors donation drives to help lower-income teen girls get reasonably priced prom dresses. It also locates its manufacturing plants in countries with few labour laws, such that it does not know if children are working in its factories, and works to prevent union activity among its employees. Evaluate this company from an ethical and social responsibility perspective.

5. Based on the evaluation you developed for Question 4, provide responses to the ethical decision-making metric from Exhibit 18.5. Provide a rationale for your score for each question.

6. A company that makes granola and other "healthful" snacks has the following mission statement: "Our goal is to profitably sell good-tasting, healthy products and to better society." Although its products are organic, they are also high in calories. The company gives a small portion of its profits to United Way. Evaluate the mission statement.

7. The granola company described in Question 6 is thinking about starting an advertising campaign directed at children that would air on Saturday morning television. Explain why you think it should or should not do so.

8. A health inspector found some rodent droppings in one batch of granola made by this same company. What should the company do?

9. A women's clothing retailer has been found guilty of misleading pricing practices. In spite of significant fines, its pricing practices remain unchanged. Explain how consumerism could force the company to act more ethically in the future.

10. Consumers who were unhappy about the Canadian seal hunt expressed their displeasure by promoting an international boycott of Canadian seafood. While this action might prompt the sealing industry to change, it could also result in job losses in the fishing industry. Are consumers taking the most ethical approach?

NET SAVVY

1. Perhaps no subdiscipline of marketing receives more scrutiny regarding ethical compliance than direct marketing, a form of nonstore retailing in which customers are exposed to and purchase merchandise or services through an impersonal medium such as telephone, mail, or the Internet.[48] Ethical issues in direct marketing cover a broad spectrum because this means of selling is conducted through all forms of communication. The Canadian Marketing Association (CMA) takes ethics very seriously and has several programs to ensure that its member organizations comply with its Code of Ethics. Go to the CMA website (http://www.the-cma.org) and type the word *ethics* in the search box. Discuss the results of your search. How many different ways did you find that the CMA was involved in assisting consumers and the industry to create a more ethical marketplace?

2. An increasing number of firms are stating their strong commitment to corporate social responsibility initiatives. The Corporate Social Responsibility Newswire service keeps track of these various initiatives and posts stories on its website about what various corporations are doing. Go to http://www.csrwire.com and choose one story. Write a description of the corporation and the initiative.

CHAPTER CASE STUDY

WHOSE SIDE ARE YOU ON?[49]

Lauren Smith was recently hired by a large architecture and engineering firm as an assistant account manager in the government contracts division. The firm specializes in building hospitals, schools, and other large-scale projects. Lauren is excited to learn that she will be part of the marketing team that presents the firm's proposals to the clients. In this case, the clients are primarily federal and provincial governmental agencies. The presentations are elaborate, often costing $50,000 or more to prepare. But the projects can be worth millions to the firm, so the investment is worth it. The firm has a solid record for building quality projects, on time, and the majority of the time within budget. The firm also has an impressive track record, being awarded government contracts an incredible 85 percent of the time. No other firm in the industry comes close to this record.

Should Lauren go to the company's ethics officer and report what she knows about the use of insider information?

The first project Lauren is assigned to is an enormous project to design a new hospital complex. The team leader, Brian Jenkins, has stressed how crucial it is for the firm to land this contract. He hints that if the team is successful the members will be well compensated. In fact, Lauren heard that the members of the winning team for the last contract this size each received a $10,000 bonus.

Not long after the project commences, Brian invites Lauren to have lunch so they can get to know each other better. During lunch, a man approaches Brian and asks if he has received the information. The man says that he knows that with this information the firm is a sure winner. He also reminds Brian that he is due a bonus for getting such crucial information. After he leaves Brian explains that the man is George Miller, who was the former head of the division awarding the hospital contract. George has been helping Brian by talking to the decision team and getting information relevant to the bid. Brian explains that the information George has gathered about the internal discussions among the buying team will be what makes their proposal a clear winner, obviously good news for the team since a winning bid means bonuses are almost assured.

After lunch Lauren looks at the firm's ethics manual that she was given just last week at a new employee orientation. Lobbying without disclosure and paying for insider information are clearly discussed as unethical practices in the manual. Yet Brian seemed perfectly comfortable discussing George's role with Lauren.

Lauren decides she should check with another team member about the use of insider information, so she asks Sue Garcia. Sue tells Lauren that this kind of thing happens all the time. She jokes that most of the people in the division have at one time or another worked for the government. They all still know people in the various agencies. As far as Sue is concerned, friends will talk and that is not illegal, so there is no problem. It's a win–win situation: the government will get its building, the firm its funding, and the employees their bonuses.

Lauren realizes that with her overdue credit card bill and her needed car repairs, the bonus money would really help out. Besides, she is the most junior member of the team. If all the others are comfortable with this practice, why should she be concerned? After all, it is just friends talking, isn't it?

Questions

1. Using the framework for ethical decision making presented in the chapter (Exhibit 18.4), analyze Lauren's dilemma. Should she go to the company's ethics officer and report what she knows about the use of insider information?

2. Do you feel that Lauren, as the most junior member of the team, has less of an ethical duty than more senior members of the team do? Why or why not?

3. If you were the ethics officer for this firm, would you address the belief among employees that it is acceptable to discuss a pending proposal with members of the decision team? If so, how? If you would not discuss this belief, why not?

glossary

administered vertical marketing system A supply chain system in which there is no common ownership and no contractual relationships, but the dominant channel member controls the channel relationship.

advanced shipping notice An electronic document that the supplier sends the retailer in advance of a shipment to tell the retailer exactly what to expect in the shipment.

advertising A paid form of communication from an identifiable source, delivered through a communication channel, and designed to persuade the receiver to take some action, now or in the future.

advertising allowance Tactic of offering a price reduction to channel members if they agree to feature the manufacturer's product in their advertising and promotional efforts.

advertising schedule Specifies the timing and duration of advertising.

affective component A component of attitude that reflects what a person feels about the issue at hand—his or her like or dislike of something.

affordable method A method of determining a communications budget based on what is left over after other operating costs have been covered.

AIDA model A common model of the series of mental stages through which consumers move as a result of marketing communications: **A**ttention leads to **I**nterest, which leads to **D**esire, which leads to **A**ction.

aided recall Occurs when consumers recognize the brand when its name is presented to them.

alpha testing An attempt by the firm to determine whether a product will perform according to its design and whether it satisfies the need for which it was intended; occurs in the firm's R&D department.

associated services (or augmented product) The nonphysical attributes of the product, including product warranties, financing, product support, and after-sale service.

attitude A person's enduring evaluation of his or her feelings about and behavioural tendencies toward an object or idea; consists of three components: cognitive, affective, and behavioural.

autocratic buying centre A buying centre in which one person makes the decision alone, though there may be multiple participants.

B2B (business-to-business) The process of selling merchandise or services from one business to another.

B2C (business-to-consumer) The process in which businesses sell to consumers.

baby boomers Generational cohort of people born after World War II until 1965.

bait and switch A deceptive practice of luring customers into the store with a very low advertised price on an item (the bait), only to aggressively pressure them into purchasing a higher-priced item (the switch) by disparaging the low-priced item, comparing it unfavourably with the higher-priced model, or professing an inadequate supply of the lower-priced item.

behavioural component A component of attitude that comprises the actions a person takes with regard to the issue at hand.

behavioural segmentation Groups consumers based on the benefits they derive from products or services, their usage rate, their loyalty, and the occasion.

benefit segmentation Groups consumers based on the benefits they derive from products or services.

beta testing Having potential consumers examine a product prototype in a real-use setting to determine its functionality, performance, potential problems, and other issues specific to its use.

big-box food retailers Come in three types: supercentre, hypermarket, and warehouse club; larger than a conventional supermarket; carry both food and nonfood items.

blog (weblog or Web log) A web page that contains periodic posts; corporate blogs are a new form of marketing communications.

bounce rate The percentage of times a visitor leaves a site almost immediately.

boycott A group's refusal to deal commercially with some organization to protest against its policies.

brand associations The mental links that consumers make between a brand and its key product attributes; can involve a logo, slogan, or famous personality.

brand awareness Measures how many consumers in a market are familiar with the brand and what it stands for; created through repeated exposures of the various brand elements (brand name, logo, symbol, character, packaging, or slogan) in the firm's communications to consumers.

brand dilution Occurs when a brand extension adversely affects consumer perceptions about the attributes the core brand is believed to hold.

brand equity The set of assets and liabilities linked to a brand that add to or subtract from the value provided by the product or service.

brand extension The use of the same brand name for new products being introduced to the same or new markets.

brand licensing A contractual arrangement between firms, whereby one firm allows another to use its brand name, logo, symbols, or characters in exchange for a negotiated fee.

brand loyalty Occurs when a consumer buys the same brand's product or service repeatedly over time rather than buying from multiple suppliers within the same category.

brand personality Refers to a set of human characteristics associated with a brand, which has symbolic or self-expressive meanings for consumers.

brand repositioning (rebranding) A strategy in which marketers change a brand's focus to target new markets or realign the brand's core emphasis with changing market preferences.

brands The names, terms, designs, symbols, or any other features that identify one seller's good or service as distinct from those of other sellers.

break-even point The point at which the number of units sold generates just enough revenue to equal the total costs; at this point, profits are zero.

business ethics Refers to a branch of ethical study that examines ethical rules and principles within a commercial context, the various moral or ethical problems that might arise in a business setting, and any special duties or obligations that apply to persons engaged in commerce.

business-to-business (B2B) marketing The process of buying and selling goods or services to be used in the production of other goods and services, for consumption by the buying organization, or for resale by wholesalers and retailers.

buyer The buying centre participant who handles the paperwork of the actual purchase.

buying centre The group of people typically responsible for the buying decisions in large organizations.

C2C (consumer-to-consumer) The process in which consumers sell to other consumers.

cash discount Tactic of offering a reduction in the invoice cost if the buyer pays the invoice prior to the end of the discount period.

category killer Offers an extensive assortment in a particular category, so overwhelming the category that other retailers have difficulty competing.

category specialist Offers a narrow variety but a deep assortment of merchandise.

cause-related marketing Commercial activity in which businesses and charities form a partnership to market an image, product, or service for their mutual benefit; a type of promotional campaign.

channel conflict Results when supply chain members are not in agreement about their goals, roles, or rewards.

click paths Show how users navigate through a site.

click-through rate (CTR) The number of times a user clicks on an ad divided by the number of impressions.

click-through tracking Measures how many times users click on banner advertising on websites.

closing the sale Obtaining a commitment from the customer to make a purchase.

cobranding The practice of marketing two or more brands together, on the same package or promotion.

cognitive component A component of attitude that reflects what a person believes to be true.

cold calls A method of prospecting in which salespeople telephone or go to see potential customers without appointments.

communication channel The medium—print, broadcast, the Internet—that carries the message.

communication gap Refers to the difference between the actual service provided to customers and the service that the firm's promotion program promises.

compensatory decision rule Is at work when the consumer is evaluating alternatives and trades off one characteristic against another, such that good characteristics compensate for bad ones.

competitive intelligence (CI) Used by firms to collect and synthesize information about their position with respect to their rivals; enables companies to anticipate changes in the marketplace rather than merely react to them.

competitive parity A firm's strategy of setting prices that are similar to those of major competitors.

competitive parity method A method of determining a communications budget in which the firm's share of the communication expenses is in line with its market share.

competitor orientation A company objective based on the premise that the firm should measure itself primarily against its competition.

competitor-based pricing method An approach that attempts to reflect how the firm wants consumers to interpret its products relative to the competitors' offerings.

complementary products Products whose demand curves are positively related, such that they rise or fall together; a percentage increase in demand for one results in a percentage increase in demand for the other.

concentrated (or niche) targeting strategy A marketing strategy of selecting a single, primary target market and focusing all energies on providing a product to fit that market's needs.

concept testing The process in which a concept statement that describes a product or a service is presented to potential buyers or users to obtain their reactions.

concepts Brief written descriptions of a product or service; its technology, working principles, and forms; and what customer needs it would satisfy.

consensus buying centre A buying centre in which all members of the team must reach a collective agreement that they can support a particular purchase.

consultative buying centre A buying centre in which one person makes the decision, but he or she solicits input from others before doing so.

consumer decision rules The set of criteria consumers use consciously or subconsciously to quickly and efficiently select from among several alternatives.

consumer products Products and services used by people for their personal use.

consumerism A social movement aimed at protecting consumers from business practices that infringe upon their rights.

contest A brand-sponsored competition that requires some form of skill or effort.

continuous advertising schedule Runs steadily throughout the year and therefore is suited to products and services that are consumed continually at relatively steady rates and that require a steady level of persuasive or reminder advertising.

contractual vertical marketing system A system in which independent firms at different levels of the supply chain join together through contracts to obtain economies of scale and co-ordination and to reduce conflict.

contribution per unit Equals the price less the variable cost per unit; variable used to determine the break-even point in units.

control phase The part of the strategic marketing planning process when managers evaluate the performance of the marketing strategy and take any necessary corrective actions.

convenience goods/services Products or services for which the consumer is not willing to spend any effort to evaluate prior to purchase.

conventional supermarket Offers groceries, meat, and produce with limited sales of nonfood items, such as health and beauty aids and general merchandise, in a self-service format.

conversion rates The percentage of visitors to a site who click, buy, or donate.

co-operative (co-op) advertising An agreement between a manufacturer and retailer in which the manufacturer agrees to defray some advertising costs.

core customer value The basic problem-solving benefits that consumers are seeking.

corporate brand The use of a firm's own corporate name to brand all of its product lines and products.

corporate social responsibility (CSR) Refers to the voluntary actions taken by a company to address the ethical, social, and environmental impacts of its business operations and the concerns of its stakeholders.

corporate vertical marketing system A system in which the parent company has complete control and can dictate the priorities and objectives of the supply chain; it may own facilities such as manufacturing plants, warehouse facilities, retail outlets, and design studios.

cost of ownership method A value-based method for setting prices that determines the total cost of owning the product over its useful life.

cost-based pricing method Determines the final price to charge by starting with the cost, without recognizing the role that consumers or competitors' prices play in the marketplace.

country's culture Easy-to-spot visible nuances that are particular to a country, such as dress, symbols, ceremonies, language, colours, and food preferences, and more subtle aspects, which are trickier to identify.

coupon Provides a stated discount to consumers on the final selling price of a specific item; the retailer handles the discount.

cross-price elasticity The percentage change in demand for Product A that occurs in response to a percentage change in price of Product B.

cross-promoting Efforts of two or more firms joining together to reach a specific target market.

cross-shopping The pattern of buying both premium and low-priced merchandise or patronizing both expensive, status-oriented retailers and price-oriented retailers.

cultural imperialism The belief that one's own culture is superior to that of other nations; can take the form of an active, formal policy or a more subtle general attitude.

culture The shared meanings, beliefs, morals, values, and customs of a group of people.

cumulative quantity discount Pricing tactic that offers a discount based on the amount purchased over a specified period and usually involves several transactions.

customer excellence Involves a focus on retaining loyal customers and excellent customer service.

customer lifetime value (CLV) The expected financial contribution from a particular customer to the firm's profits over the course of their relationship.

customer orientation Pricing orientation that explicitly invokes the concept of customer value and setting prices to match consumer expectations.

customer relationship management (CRM) A business philosophy and set of strategies, programs, and systems that focus on identifying and building loyalty among the firm's most valued customers.

customer service Specifically refers to human or mechanical activities firms undertake to help satisfy their customers' needs and wants.

data Raw numbers or other factual information of limited value.

data mining The use of statistical analysis tools to search for patterns in data or relationships among variables.

deal A type of short-term price reduction that can take several forms, such as a "featured price," a price lower than the regular price; a "buy one, get one free" offer; or a certain percentage "more free" offer contained in larger packaging.

deceptive advertising A representation, omission, act, or practice in an advertisement that is likely to mislead consumers acting reasonably under the circumstances.

decider The buying centre participant who ultimately determines any part of or the entire buying decision—whether to buy, what to buy, how to buy, or where to buy.

decision heuristics Mental shortcuts that help consumers narrow down choices; examples include price, brand, and product presentation.

decline stage Stage of the product life cycle when sales decline and the product eventually exits the market.

decoding The process by which the receiver interprets the sender's message.

delivery gap The difference between the firm's service standards and the actual service it provides to customers.

demand curve Shows how many units of a product or service consumers will demand during a specific period at different prices.

democratic buying centre A buying centre in which the majority rules in making decisions.

demographic segmentation The grouping of consumers according to easily measured, objective characteristics such as age, gender, income, and education

demographics Characteristics of human populations and segments, especially those used to identify consumer markets, such as age, gender, income, race, ethnicity, and education.

derived demand The linkage between consumers' demand for a company's output and its purchase of necessary inputs to manufacture or assemble that particular output.

differentiated targeting strategy A strategy through which a firm targets several market segments with a different offering for each.

diffusion of innovation The process by which the use of an innovation, whether a product or a service, spreads throughout a market group over time and over various categories of adopters.

digital media Tools ranging from simple website content to far more interactive features such as corporate blogs, online games, text messaging, social media, and mobile apps.

direct investment When a firm maintains 100 percent ownership of its plants, operation facilities, and offices in a foreign country, often through the formation of wholly owned subsidiaries.

direct mail/email A targeted form of communication distributed to a prospective customer's mailbox or inbox.

direct marketing Marketing that communicates directly with target customers to generate a response or transaction.

direct response TV (DRTV) TV commercials or infomercials with a strong call to action.

discount store Offers a broad variety of merchandise, limited service, and low prices.

dispatcher The person who co-ordinates deliveries to distribution centres.

distribution centre A facility for the receipt, storage, and redistribution of goods to company stores or customers; may be operated by retailers, manufacturers, or distribution specialists.

distribution channel The institutions that transfer the ownership of and move goods from the point of production to the point of consumption.

distribution intensity The number of channel members to use at each level of the supply chain.

distributive fairness Pertains to a customer's perception of the benefits he or she received compared with the costs (inconvenience or loss) that resulted from a service failure.

diversification strategy A growth strategy whereby a firm introduces a new product or service to a market segment that it does not currently serve.

downsizing Exiting markets, reducing product portfolios, or closing certain businesses or store or plant locations.

drugstore A specialty store that concentrates on health and personal grooming merchandise, though pharmaceuticals may represent more than 60 percent of its sales.

dumping The practice of selling a good in a foreign market at a price that is lower than its domestic price or below its cost.

early adopters The second group of consumers in the diffusion of innovation model, after innovators, to use a product or service innovation; generally don't like to take as much risk as innovators.

early majority A group of consumers in the diffusion of innovation model that represents approximately 34 percent of the population; members don't like to take much risk and therefore tend to wait until bugs are worked out.

earned media Media that results from word-of-mouth, buzz, or publicity.

economic situation Economic changes that affect the way consumers buy merchandise and spend money; see inflation, foreign currency fluctuations, interest rates, and recession.

elastic Refers to a market for a product or service that is price sensitive; that is, relatively small changes in price will generate fairly large changes in the quantity demanded.

electronic data interchange (EDI) The computer-to-computer exchange of business documents from a retailer to a vendor and back.

emotional appeal Aims to satisfy consumers' emotional desires rather than their utilitarian needs.

empowerment In the context of service delivery, means allowing employees to make decisions about how service is provided to customers.

encoding The process of converting the sender's ideas into a message, which could be verbal, visual, or both.

environmental concerns Include, but are not limited to, the excessive use of natural resources and energy, refuse from manufacturing processes, excess trash created by consumer goods packages, and hard-to-dispose-of products such as tires, cellphones, and computer monitors.

esteem needs Allow people to satisfy their inner desires.

ethical climate The set of values within a marketing firm, or in the marketing division of any firm, that guides decision making and behaviour.

ethnography An observational method that studies people in their daily lives and activities in their homes, work, and communities.

evaluative criteria Consist of a set of salient, or important, attributes about a particular product that are used to compare alternative products.

event sponsorship A popular PR tool; occurs when corporations support various activities (financially or otherwise), usually in the cultural or sports and entertainment sectors.

everyday low pricing (EDLP) A strategy companies use to emphasize the continuity of their retail prices at a level somewhere between the regular, nonsale price and the deep-discount sale prices their competitors may offer.

exchange The trade of things of value between the buyer and the seller so that each is better off as a result.

exchange control Refers to the regulation of a country's currency exchange rate.

exchange rate The measure of how much one currency is worth in relation to another.

exclusive distribution Strategy of granting exclusive rights to sell to one or very few retail customers so no other customers can sell a particular brand.

experience curve effect Refers to the drop in unit cost as the accumulated volume sold increases; as sales continue to grow, the costs continue to drop, allowing even further reductions in the price.

experimental research A type of quantitative research that systematically manipulates one or more variables to determine which variable has a causal effect on another variable.

exporting Producing goods in one country and selling them in another.

extended network The influence of a person's extended network.

extended problem solving A purchase decision process during which the consumer devotes considerable time and effort to analyzing alternatives; often occurs when the consumer perceives that the purchase decision entails a great deal of risk.

external locus of control Refers to when consumers believe that fate or other external factors control all outcomes.

external search for information Occurs when the buyer seeks information outside his or her personal knowledge base to help make the buying decision.

extreme-value retailer A general merchandise discount store found in lower-income urban or rural areas.

family brand The use of a combination of the company brand name and individual brand name to distinguish a firm's products.

feedback loop Allows the receiver to communicate with the sender and thereby informs the sender whether the message was received and decoded properly.

financial risk Risk associated with a monetary outlay; includes the initial cost of the purchase, as well as the costs of using the item or service.

first movers Product pioneers that are the first to create a market or product category, making them readily recognizable to consumers and thus establishing a commanding and early market share lead.

fixed costs Those costs that remain essentially at the same level, regardless of any changes in the volume of production.

flighting advertising schedule Implemented in spurts, with periods of heavy advertising followed by periods of no advertising.

focus group A research technique in which a small group of persons (usually 8 to 12) comes together for an in-depth discussion about a particular topic, with the conversation guided by a trained moderator using an unstructured method of inquiry.

foreign currency fluctuations Changes in the value of a country's currency relative to the currency of another country; can influence consumer spending.

franchising A contractual agreement between a franchisor and a franchisee that allows the franchisee to operate a retail outlet, using a name and format developed and supported by the franchisor.

frequency Measure of how often the target audience is exposed to a communication within a specified period of time.

functional needs Pertain to the performance of a product or service.

gamification The process of using games or gamelike elements to encourage participation.

gatekeeper The buying centre participant who controls information or access to decision makers and influencers.

general merchandise retailers May be discount stores, specialty stores, category specialists, department stores, drugstores, off-price retailers, or extreme-value retailers; may sell through multiple channels, such as the Internet and catalogues.

Generation X Generational cohort of people born between 1966 and 1971.

Generation Y/millennials Generational cohort of people born between 1972 and 1992; the biggest cohort since the original postwar baby boom.

generational cohort A group of people of the same generation who typically have similar purchase behaviours because they have shared experiences and are in the same stage of life.

generic A product sold without a brand name, typically in commodities markets.

geodemographic segmentation The grouping of consumers on the basis of a combination of geographic, demographic, and lifestyle characteristics.

geographic pricing The setting of different prices depending on a geographical division of the delivery areas.

geographic segmentation The grouping of consumers on the basis of where they live.

global labour issues Includes concerns about working conditions and wages paid to factory workers in developing countries.

globalization Refers to the increased flow of goods, services, people, technology, capital, information, and ideas around the world; has economic, political, social, cultural, and environmental impacts.

glocalization When firms offer standardized products globally and change promotional campaigns geared to local markets.

green marketing Involves a strategic effort by firms to supply customers with environmentally friendly merchandise.

grey market Employs irregular but not necessarily illegal methods; generally, it legally circumvents authorized channels of distribution to sell goods at prices lower than those intended by the manufacturer.

gross domestic product (GDP) The market value of the goods and services produced by a country in a year; the most widely used standardized measure of output.

gross rating points (GRP) Measure used for various media advertising—print, radio, or television; $GRP = reach \times frequency$.

growth stage Stage of the product life cycle when the product gains acceptance, demand and sales increase, and competitors emerge in the product category.

habitual decision making A purchase decision process in which consumers engage with little conscious effort.

high/low pricing A pricing strategy that relies on the promotion of sales, during which prices are temporarily reduced to encourage purchases.

hits The total number of requests for a web page.

horizontal price fixing Occurs when competitors that produce and sell competing products collude, or work together, to control prices, effectively taking price out of the decision process for consumers.

human development index (HDI) A composite measure of three indicators of the quality of life in different countries: life expectancy at birth, educational attainment, and whether the average incomes are sufficient to meet the basic needs of life in that country.

hypothesis A statement or proposition predicting a particular relationship among multiple variables that can be tested through research.

ideal point The position at which a particular market segment's ideal product would lie on a perceptual map.

ideas Thoughts, opinions, philosophies, and intellectual concepts.

implementation phase Where marketing managers identify and evaluate different opportunities by engaging in a process known as segmentation, targeting, and positioning. They then develop and implement the marketing mix by using the four Ps.

impressions The number of times an ad appears to a user.

improvement value Represents an estimate of how much more (or less) consumers are willing to pay for a product relative to other comparable products.

impulse buying A buying decision made by customers on the spot when they see the merchandise.

income effect Refers to the change in the quantity of a product demanded by consumers because of a change in their income.

inconsistent A characteristic of a service: its quality may vary because it is provided by humans.

in-depth interview A research technique in which trained researchers ask questions, listen to and record the answers, and then pose additional questions to clarify or expand on a particular issue.

individual brand The use of individual brand names for each of a firm's products.

inelastic Refers to a market for a product or service that is price insensitive; that is, relatively small changes in price will not generate large changes in the quantity demanded.

inflation Refers to the persistent increase in the prices of goods and services.

influence The extent to which a person influences others.

influencer The buying centre participant whose views influence other members of the buying centre in making the final decision.

information Data that has been organized, analyzed, interpreted, and converted into a useful form for decision makers.

informative advertising Communication used to create and build brand awareness, with the ultimate goal of moving the consumer through the buying cycle to a purchase.

infrastructure The basic facilities, services, and installations needed for a community or society to function, such as transportation and communications systems, water and power lines, and public institutions such as schools, post offices, and prisons.

initiator The buying centre participant who first suggests buying the particular product or service.

innovation The process by which ideas are transformed into new products and services that will help firms grow.

innovators Those buyers who want to be the first to have the new product or service.

inseparable A characteristic of a service: it is produced and consumed at the same time—that is, service and consumption are inseparable.

institutional advertisements Used to inform, persuade, and remind consumers about issues related to places, politics, an industry, or a particular corporation.

intangible A characteristic of a service; it cannot be touched, tasted, or seen like a pure product can.

integrated marketing communications (IMC) Represents the promotion dimension of the four Ps; encompasses a variety of communication disciplines—general advertising, personal selling, sales promotion, public relations, direct marketing, and digital media—in combination to provide clarity, consistency, and maximum communicative impact.

intensive distribution A strategy designed to get products into as many outlets as possible.

interest rates Represent the cost of borrowing money.

internal locus of control Refers to when consumers believe they have some control over the outcomes of their actions, in which case they generally engage in more search activities.

internal search for information Occurs when the buyer examines his or her own memory and knowledge about the product or service, gathered through past experiences.

introduction stage Stage of the product life cycle when innovators start buying the product.

inventory A characteristic of a service: it is perishable and cannot be stored for future use.

joint venture Formed when a firm entering a new market pools its resources with those of a local firm to form a new company in which ownership, control, and profits are shared.

just-in-time (JIT) inventory systems Inventory management systems designed to deliver less merchandise on a more frequent basis than traditional inventory systems; the firm gets the merchandise "just in time" for it to be used in the manufacture of another product; also known as quick response (QR) systems in retailing.

keyword analysis Determines which keywords visitors to a site use to find it.

knowledge gap Reflects the difference between customers' expectations and the firm's perception of those expectations.

laggards Consumers who like to avoid change and rely on traditional products until they are no longer available.

lagged effect A delayed response to a marketing communication campaign.

late majority The last group of buyers to enter a new product market.

lead time The amount of time between the recognition that an order needs to be placed and the arrival of the needed merchandise at the seller's store, ready for sale.

lead users Innovative product users who modify existing products according to their own ideas to suit their specific needs.

leader pricing Consumer pricing tactic that attempts to build store traffic by aggressively pricing and advertising a regularly purchased item, often priced at or just above the store's cost.

leads A list of potential customers.

learning Refers to a change in a person's thought process or behaviour that arises from experience and takes place throughout the consumer decision process.

lifestyle Refers to the way consumers spend their time and money.

lifestyles Lifestyles are how we live our lives to achieve goals.

limited problem solving Occurs during a purchase decision that calls for, at most, a moderate amount of effort and time.

listing allowances Fees paid to retailers simply to get new products into stores or to gain more or better shelf space for their products.

locational excellence Involves a focus on a good physical location and Internet presence.

locational privacy A person's ability to move about in public spaces with the expectation the location will not be recorded for future use.

logistics management The integration of two or more activities for the purpose of planning, implementing, and controlling the efficient flow of raw materials, in-process inventory, and finished goods from the point of origin to the point of consumption.

loss leader pricing Loss leader pricing takes the tactic of leader pricing one step further by lowering the price below the store's cost.

love (social) needs Relate to our interactions with others.

loyalty program Specifically designed to retain customers by offering premiums or other incentives to customers who make multiple purchases over time.

loyalty segmentation Strategy of investing in retention and loyalty initiatives to retain the firm's most profitable customers.

macroenvironmental factors Aspects of the external environment—culture, demographics, social trends, technological advances, economic situation, and political/legal environment (CDSTEP)—that affect companies.

manufacturer brands Brands owned and managed by the manufacturer.

markdowns Reductions retailers take on the initial selling price of the product or service.

market Refers to the groups of people who need or want a company's products or services and have the ability and willingness to buy them.

market development strategy A growth strategy that employs the existing marketing offering to reach new market segments, whether domestic or international or segments not currently served by the firm.

market growth rate The annual rate of growth of the specific market in which the product competes.

market penetration pricing A pricing strategy of setting the initial price low for the introduction of the new product or service, with the objective of building sales, market share, and profits quickly.

market penetration strategy A growth strategy that employs the existing marketing mix and focuses the firm's efforts on existing customers.

market positioning Involves the process of defining the marketing mix variables so that target customers have a clear, distinct, desirable understanding of what the product does or represents in comparison with competing products.

market segment A group of consumers who respond similarly to a firm's marketing efforts.

market segmentation The process of dividing the market into distinct groups of customers—where each individual group has similar needs, wants, or characteristics—who therefore might appreciate products or services geared especially for them in similar ways.

marketing A set of business practices designed to plan for and present an organization's products or services in ways that build effective customer relationships.

marketing ethics Refers to those ethical problems that are specific to the domain of marketing.

marketing mix (four Ps) Product, price, place, and promotion—the controllable set of activities that a firm uses to respond to the wants of its target markets.

marketing plan A written document composed of an analysis of the current marketing situation, opportunities and threats for the firm, marketing objectives and strategy specified in terms of the four Ps, action programs, and projected or pro forma income (and other financial) statements.

marketing research A set of techniques and principles for systematically collecting, recording, analyzing, and interpreting data that can aid decision makers involved in marketing goods, services, or ideas.

marketing strategy Identifies a firm's target market(s), a related marketing mix—the four Ps, and the bases upon which the firm plans to build a sustainable competitive advantage.

mass customization The practice of interacting on a one-to-one basis with many people to create custom-made products or services; providing one-to-one marketing to the masses.

mass media Channels, such as national newspapers, magazines, radio, and television, that are ideal for reaching large numbers of anonymous audience members.

maturity stage Stage of the product life cycle when industry sales reach their peak, so firms try to rejuvenate their products by adding new features or repositioning them.

maximizing profits strategy A mathematical model that captures all the factors required to explain and predict sales and profits, which should be able to identify the price at which its profits are maximized.

media buy The purchase of airtime or print pages.

media mix The combination of the media used and the frequency of advertising in each medium.

media planning The process of evaluating and selecting the media mix that will deliver a clear, consistent, compelling message to the intended audience.

micromarketing (one-to-one) marketing An extreme form of segmentation that tailors a product or service to suit an individual customer's wants or needs.

mission statement A broad description of a firm's objectives and the scope of activities it plans to undertake; attempts to answer two main questions: What type of business is it? and What does it need to do to accomplish its goals and objectives?

modified rebuy Refers to when the buyer has purchased a similar product in the past but has decided to change some specifications, such as the desired price, quality level, customer service level, and options.

monopolistic competition Occurs when many firms sell closely related but not homogeneous products; these products may be viewed as substitutes but are not perfect substitutes.

monopoly Occurs when only one firm provides the product or service in a particular industry.

motive A need or want that is strong enough to cause the person to seek satisfaction.

multichannel strategy Selling in more than one channel (e.g., store, catalogue, kiosk, and Internet).

need Basic necessities, such as food, clothing, shelter, and safety.

need recognition The beginning of the consumer decision process; occurs when consumers recognize they have an unsatisfied need and want to go from their needy state to a different, desired state.

negative word-of-mouth Occurs when consumers spread negative information about a product, service, or store to others.

new buy In a B2B setting, a purchase of a good or service for the first time; the buying decision is likely to be quite involved because the buyer or the buying organization does not have any experience with the item.

niche media Channels that are focused and generally used to reach narrow segments, often with unique demographic characteristics or interests.

noise Any interference that stems from competing messages, a lack of clarity in the message, or a flaw in the medium; a problem for all communication channels.

noncompensatory decision rule Is at work when consumers choose a product or service on the basis of a subset of its characteristics, regardless of the values of its other attributes.

noncumulative quantity discount Pricing tactic that offers a discount based on only the amount purchased in a single order.

North American Industry Classification System (NAICS) codes A classification scheme that categorizes all firms into a hierarchical set of six-digit codes.

objective-and-task method An IMC budgeting method that determines the cost required to undertake specific tasks to accomplish communication objectives; process entails setting objectives, choosing media, and determining costs.

observation A qualitative research method that entails examining purchase and consumption behaviours through personal or video camera scrutiny.

occasion segmentation Groups consumers based on when they purchase or consume a product or service.

odd prices Prices that end in odd numbers, usually 9, such as $3.99.

off-price retailer A type of retailer that offers an inconsistent assortment of merchandise at relatively low prices.

oligopolistic competition Occurs when only a few firms dominate a market.

omnichannel An omnichannel strategy creates a consistent experience for consumers across all distribution channels.

operational excellence Involves a focus on efficient operations and excellent supply chain management.

organizational culture Reflects the set of values, traditions, and customs that guides a firm's employees' behaviour.

owned media Media controlled by the advertiser, such as its website, Facebook fan page, YouTube channel.

page views The number of times any web pages are viewed by visitors.

paid media Media such as TV, print, radio, or display ads used to reach mass markets.

panel data A type of quantitative research that involves collecting information from a group of consumers (the panel) over time; data collected may be from a survey or a record of purchases.

perceived value The relationship between a product or service's benefits and its cost.

percentage-of-sales method A method of determining a communications budget that is based on a fixed percentage of forecasted sales.

perception The process by which people select, organize, and interpret information to form a meaningful picture of the world.

perceptual map Displays, in two or more dimensions, the position of products or brands in the consumer's mind.

performance risk Involves the perceived danger inherent in a poorly performing product or service.

personal selling The two-way flow of communication between a buyer and a seller that is designed to influence the buyer's purchase decision.

persuasive advertising Communication used to motivate consumers to take action.

physiological needs Relate to the basic biological necessities of life: food, drink, rest, and shelter.

physiological risk Risk associated with the fear of an actual harm should the product not perform properly.

pioneers New product introductions that establish a completely new market or radically change both the rules of competition and consumer preferences in a market; also called breakthroughs.

planning phase Where marketing executives and other top managers define the mission and objectives of the business, and evaluate the situation by assessing how various players, both inside and outside the organization, affect the firm's potential for success.

point-of-purchase (POP) display A merchandise display located at the point of purchase, such as at the checkout counter in a grocery store.

political/legal environment Comprises political parties, government organizations, and legislation and laws that promote or inhibit trade and marketing activities.

pop-up stores Temporary storefronts that exist for only a limited time and generally focus on a new product or a limited group of products offered by a retailer, manufacturer, or service provider; give consumers a chance to interact with the brand and build brand awareness.

positioning The mental picture that people have about a company and its products or services relative to competitors.

positioning statement Expresses how a company wants to be perceived by consumers.

postpurchase dissonance An internal conflict that arises from an inconsistency between two beliefs, or between beliefs and behaviour; buyer's remorse.

post-testing The evaluation of an IMC campaign's impact after it has been implemented.

preapproach In the personal selling process, occurs prior to meeting the customer for the first time and extends the qualification of leads procedure; in this step, the salesperson conducts additional research and develops plans for meeting with the customer.

predatory pricing A firm's practice of setting a very low price for one or more of its products with the intent of driving its competition out of business; illegal under the Competition Act.

premarket test Conducted before a product or service is brought to market to determine how many customers will try and then continue to use it.

premium An item offered for free or at a bargain price to reward some type of behaviour, such as buying, sampling, or testing.

prestige products or services Those that consumers purchase for status rather than functionality.

pretesting Assessments performed before an ad campaign is implemented to ensure that the various elements are working in an integrated fashion and doing what they are intended to do.

price The overall sacrifice a consumer is willing to make—money, time, energy—to acquire a specific product or service.

price bundling Consumer pricing tactic of selling more than one product for a single, lower price than the items would cost sold separately; can be used to sell slow-moving items, to encourage customers to stock up so they won't purchase competing brands, to encourage trial of a new product, or to provide an incentive to purchase a less desirable product or service to obtain a more desirable one in the same bundle.

price discrimination The practice of selling the same product to different resellers (wholesalers, distributors, or retailers) or to the ultimate consumer at different prices; some, but not all, forms of price discrimination are illegal.

price elasticity of demand Measures how changes in a price affect the quantity of the product demanded; specifically, the ratio of the percentage change in quantity demanded to the percentage change in price.

price fixing The practice of colluding with other firms to control prices.

price lining Consumer market pricing tactic of establishing a price floor and a price ceiling for an entire line of similar products and then setting a few other price points in between to represent distinct differences in quality.

price skimming A strategy of selling a new product or service at a high price that innovators and early adopters are willing to pay to obtain it; after the high-price market segment becomes saturated and sales begin to slow down, the firm generally lowers the price to capture (or skim) the next most price-sensitive segment.

price war Occurs when two or more firms compete primarily by lowering their prices.

pricing tactics Short-term methods, in contrast to long-term pricing strategies, used to focus on company objectives, customers, costs, competition, or channel members; can be responses to competitive threats (e.g., lowering price temporarily to meet a competitor's price reduction) or broadly accepted methods of calculating a final price for the customer that is short term in nature.

primary data Data collected to address the specific research needs/questions currently under investigation. Some primary data collection methods include focus groups, in-depth interviews, and surveys.

private-label brands (store brands) Brands developed and marketed by a retailer and available only from that retailer.

procedural fairness Refers to the customer's perception of the fairness of the process used to resolve complaints about service.

product category An assortment of items that the customer sees as reasonable substitutes for one another.

product development Entails a process of balancing various engineering, manufacturing, marketing, and economic considerations to develop a product.

product development strategy A growth strategy that offers a new product or service to a firm's current target market.

product excellence Involves a focus on achieving high-quality products and effective branding and positioning.

product-focused advertisements Used to inform, persuade, or remind consumers about a specific product or service.

product life cycle Defines the stages that new products move through as they enter, get established in, and ultimately leave the marketplace and thereby offers marketers a starting point for their strategy planning.

product line A group of products that consumers may use together or perceive as similar in some way.

product line depth The number of products within a product line.

product lines Groups of associated items, such as those that consumers use together or think of as part of a group of similar products.

product mix The complete set of all products offered by a firm.

product mix breadth The number of product lines, or variety, offered by the firm.

product placement Inclusion of a product in nontraditional situations, such as in a scene in a movie or TV program.

profit orientation A company objective that can be implemented by focusing on target profit pricing, maximizing profits, or target return pricing.

projective technique A type of qualitative research in which subjects are provided a scenario and asked to express their thoughts and feelings about it.

prototype The first physical form or service description of a new product, still in rough or tentative form, that has the same properties as a new product but is produced through different manufacturing processes, sometimes even crafted individually.

psychographics This segmentation base delves into how consumers describe themselves; allows people to describe themselves by using those characteristics that help them choose how they occupy their time (behaviour) and what underlying psychological reasons determine those choices.

psychological needs Pertain to the personal gratification consumers associate with a product or service.

psychological risk Associated with the way people will feel if the product or service does not convey the right image.

PSYTE clusters The grouping of all neighbourhoods in Canada into 60 different lifestyles clusters.

public relations (PR) The organizational function that manages the firm's communications to achieve a variety of objectives, including building and maintaining a positive image, handling or heading off unfavourable stories or events, and maintaining positive relationships with the media.

public service announcement (PSA) Advertising that focuses on public welfare and generally is sponsored by nonprofit institutions, civic groups, religious organizations, trade associations, or political groups; a form of social marketing.

puffery The legal exaggeration of praise, stopping just short of deception, lavished on a product.

pull marketing strategy Designed to get consumers to pull the product into the supply chain by demanding retailers carry it.

pulsing advertising schedule Combines the continuous and flighting schedules by maintaining a base level of advertising but increasing advertising intensity during certain periods.

purchasing power parity (PPP) A theory that states that if the exchange rates of two countries are in equilibrium, a product purchased in one will cost the same in the other, expressed in the same currency.

pure competition Occurs when different companies sell commodity products that consumers perceive as substitutable; price usually is set according to the laws of supply and demand.

push marketing strategy Designed to increase demand by focusing on wholesalers, distributors, or salespeople, who push the product to consumers via distribution channels.

qualify The process of assessing the potential of sales leads.

qualitative research Attempts to begin to understand the phenomenon of interest; also provides initial information when the problem lacks any clear definition.

quantitative research Provides the information needed to confirm preliminary insights, which managers can use to pursue appropriate courses of action.

quantity discount Pricing tactic of offering a reduced price according to the amount purchased; the more the buyer purchases, the higher the discount and, of course, the greater the value.

questionnaire A form that features a set of questions designed to gather information from respondents and thereby accomplish the researchers' objectives; questions can be either unstructured or structured.

quick response (QR) An inventory management system used in retailing; merchandise is received just in time for sale when the customer wants it.

quota Designates the maximum quantity of a product that may be brought into a country during a specified time period.

radio frequency identification (RFID) tags Tiny computer chips that automatically transmit to a special scanner all the information about a container's contents or individual products.

rational appeal Helps consumers make purchase decisions by offering factual information and strong arguments built around relevant issues that encourage consumers to evaluate the brand favourably on the basis of the key benefits it provides.

reach Measure of consumers' exposure to marketing communications; the percentage of the target population exposed to a specific marketing communication, such as an advertisement, at least once.

rebate A consumer discount in which a portion of the purchase price is returned to the buyer in cash; the manufacturer, not the retailer, issues the refund.

receiver The person who reads, hears, or sees and processes the information contained in the message or advertisement.

recession A period of economic downturn when the economic growth of the country is negative for at least two consecutive quarters.

reference group One or more persons an individual uses as a basis for comparison regarding beliefs, feelings, and behaviours.

reference price The price against which buyers compare the actual selling price of the product and that facilitates their evaluation process.

relational orientation A method of building a relationship with customers based on the philosophy that buyers and sellers should develop a long-term relationship.

relationship selling A sales philosophy and process that emphasizes a commitment to maintaining the relationship over the long term and investing in opportunities that are mutually beneficial to all parties.

relative market share A measure of the product's strength in a particular market, defined as the sales of the focal product divided by the sales achieved by the largest firm in the industry.

reliability The extent to which the same result is achieved when a study is repeated under identical situations.

reminder advertising Communication used to remind consumers of a product or to prompt repurchases, especially for products that have gained market acceptance and are in the maturity stage of their life cycle.

request for proposals (RFP) A process through which buying organizations invite alternative suppliers to bid on supplying their required components.

resellers Marketing intermediaries that resell manufactured products without significantly altering their form.

retail mix Product (merchandise assortment), pricing, promotion, place, personnel, and presentation (store design and display) strategies to reach and serve consumers.

retailers Sell products directly to consumers.

retailing The set of business activities that add value to products and services sold to consumers for their personal or family use; includes products bought at stores, through catalogues, and over the Internet, as well as services such as fast-food restaurants, airlines, and hotels.

return on investment (ROI) Used to measure the benefit of an investment, ROI is calculated by dividing the gain of an investment by its cost.

reverse engineering Involves taking apart a competitor's product, analyzing it, and creating an improved product that does not infringe on the competitor's patents, if any exist.

ritual consumption Refers to a pattern of behaviours tied to life events that affect what and how people consume.

safety needs Pertain to protection and physical well-being.

sales orientation A company objective based on the belief that increasing sales will help the firm more than will increasing profits.

sales promotions Special incentives or excitement-building programs that encourage the purchase of a product or service, such as coupons, rebates, contests, free samples, and point-of-purchase displays.

sample A segment or subset of the population that adequately represents the entire population of interest.

sampling Offers potential customers the opportunity to try a product or service before they make a buying decision.

sampling The process of picking a sample.

scanner data A type of quantitative research that uses data obtained from scanner readings of UPC codes at checkout counters.

search engine marketing (SEM) Uses tools such as Google AdWords to increase the visibility of websites in search engine results.

seasonal discount Pricing tactic of offering an additional reduction as an incentive to retailers to order merchandise in advance of the normal buying season.

secondary data Pieces of information that have been collected prior to the start of the focal project.

selective distribution Lies between the intensive and exclusive distribution strategies; uses a few selected customers in a territory.

self-actualization Occurs when you feel completely satisfied with your life and how you live.

self-concept The image a person has of himself or herself; a component of psychographics.

self-values Goals for life, not just the goals one wants to accomplish in a day; a component of psychographics that refers to overriding desires that drive how a person lives his or her life.

sender The firm from which an IMC message originates; the sender must be clearly identified to the intended audience.

seniors North America's fastest-growing generational cohort; people aged 65 and older.

sentiment analysis An analysis of online content to determine favourability or unfavourability.

service Any intangible offering that cannot be physically possessed.

service gap Results when a service fails to meet the expectations that customers have about how it should be delivered.

service quality Customers' perceptions of how well a service meets or exceeds their expectations.

services Intangible customer benefits that are produced by people or machines and cannot be separated from the producer.

services retailers Firms that primarily sell services rather than merchandise.

share of wallet The percentage of the customer's purchases made from a particular retailer.

shopping goods/services Products or services, such as apparel, fragrances, and appliances, for which consumers will spend time comparing alternatives.

showrooming Occurs when consumers visit a physical store to get information about a product but then buy online from another retailer that offers a lower price.

situation analysis (SWOT) The second step in a marketing plan; uses a SWOT analysis that assesses both the internal environment with regard to its **s**trengths and **w**eaknesses and the external environment in terms of its **o**pportunities and **t**hreats.

situational factors Factors affecting the consumer decision process; those that are specific to the purchase and shopping situation and temporal state that may override, or at least influence, psychological and social issues.

size discount The most common implementation of a quantity discount at the consumer level; the larger the quantity bought, the less the cost per unit (e.g., per gram).

social marketing The application of marketing principles to a social issue to bring about attitudinal and behavioural change among the general public or a specific population segment.

social media The use of digital tools to easily and quickly create and share content to foster dialogue, social relationships, and personal identities.

social reach The number of people a person influences.

social risk Involves the fears that consumers suffer when they worry others might not regard their purchases positively.

specialty goods/services Products or services toward which the customer shows a strong preference and for which he or she will expend considerable effort to search for the best suppliers.

specialty stores Concentrate on a limited number of complementary merchandise categories in a relatively small store.

standards gap Pertains to the difference between the firm's perceptions of customers' expectations and the service standards it sets.

stock keeping units (SKUs) Individual items within each product category; the smallest unit available for inventory control.

STP The processes of segmentation, targeting, and positioning that firms use to identify and evaluate opportunities for increasing sales and profits.

straight rebuy Refers to when the buyer or buying organization simply buys additional units of products that had previously been purchased.

strategic alliance A collaborative relationship between independent firms, though the partnering firms do not create an equity partnership; that is, they do not invest in one another.

strategic business unit (SBU) A division of the company that can be managed somewhat independently from other divisions since it markets a specific set of products to a clearly defined group of customers.

strategic relationship (partnering relationship) A supply chain relationship that the members are committed to maintaining long term, investing in opportunities that are mutually beneficial; requires mutual trust, open communication, common goals, and credible commitments.

structured questions Closed-ended questions for which a discrete set of response alternatives, or specific answers, is provided for respondents to evaluate.

substitute products Products for which changes in demand are negatively related—that is, a percentage increase in the quantity demanded for Product A results in a percentage decrease in the quantity demanded for Product B.

substitution effect Refers to consumers' ability to substitute other products for the focal brand, thus increasing the price elasticity of demand for the focal brand.

supply chain The group of firms and set of techniques and approaches firms use to make and deliver a given set of goods and services.

supply chain management Refers to a set of approaches and techniques firms employ to efficiently and effectively integrate their suppliers, manufacturers, warehouses, stores, and transportation intermediaries into a seamless value chain in which merchandise is produced and distributed in the right quantities, to the right locations, and at the right time.

survey A systematic means of collecting information from people using a questionnaire.

sustainable competitive advantage Something the firm can persistently do better than its competitors that is not easily copied and thus can be maintained over a long period of time.

sweepstakes A form of sales promotion that offers prizes based on a chance drawing of entrants' names.

syndicated data Data available for a fee from commercial research firms such as Symphony IRI Group, National Diary Panel, Nielsen, and Leger Marketing.

target market The customer segment or group to whom the firm is interested in selling its products and services.

target marketing/targeting The process of evaluating the attractiveness of various segments and then deciding which to pursue as a market.

target profit pricing A pricing strategy implemented by firms when they have a particular profit goal as their overriding concern; uses price to stimulate a certain level of sales at a certain profit per unit.

target return pricing A pricing strategy implemented by firms less concerned with the absolute level of profits and more interested in the rate at which their profits are generated relative to their investments; designed to produce a specific return on investment, usually expressed as a percentage of sales.

tariff (or duty) A tax levied on a good imported into a country.

technological advances Technological changes that have contributed to the improvement of the value of both products and services in the past few decades.

telemarketing A method of prospecting in which salespeople telephone potential customers.

test marketing Introduces a new product or service to a limited geographical area (usually a few cities) prior to a national launch.

top-of-mind awareness A prominent place in people's memories that triggers a response without them having to put any thought into it.

total cost The sum of the variable and fixed costs.

tracking Includes monitoring key indicators, such as daily or weekly sales volume, while the advertisement is running to shed light on any problems with the message or the medium.

trade agreement Intergovernmental agreement designed to manage and promote trade activities for specific regions.

trade deficit Results when a country imports more goods than it exports.

trade sanctions Penalties or restrictions imposed by one country over another country for importing and exporting of goods, services, and investments.

trade shows Major events attended by buyers who choose to be exposed to products and services offered by potential suppliers in an industry.

trade surplus Results when a country exports more goods than it imports.

trading bloc Consists of those countries that have signed a particular trade agreement.

transmitter An agent or intermediary with which the sender works to develop the marketing communications; for example, a firm's creative department or an advertising agency.

tweens Generational cohort of people who are not quite teenagers but are not young children either (ages 9 to 12); they're in beTWEEN.

undifferentiated targeting strategy (mass marketing) A marketing strategy a firm can use if the product or service is perceived to provide the same benefits to everyone, with no need to develop separate strategies for different groups.

uniform delivered pricing The shipper charges one rate, no matter where the buyer is located.

unique selling proposition (USP) A strategy of differentiating a product by communicating its unique attributes; often becomes the common theme or slogan in the entire advertising campaign.

universal product code (UPC) The black and white bar code found on most merchandise.

unstructured questions Open-ended questions that allow respondents to answer in their own words.

user The person who consumes or uses the product or service purchased by the buying centre.

validity The extent to which a study measures what it is supposed to measure.

VALS™ A psychographical tool developed by Strategic Business Insights, classifies consumers into eight segments: Innovators, Thinkers, Believers, Achievers, Strivers, Experiencers, Makers, or Survivors.

value Reflects the relationship of benefits to costs, or what the consumer gets for what he or she gives.

value-based pricing method Focuses on the overall value of the product offering as perceived by consumers, who determine value by comparing the benefits they expect the product to deliver with the sacrifice they will need to make to acquire the product.

variable costs Those costs, primarily labour and materials, that vary with production volume.

vertical marketing system A supply chain in which the members act as a unified system; there are three types: administrated, contractual, and corporate.

vertical price fixing Occurs when parties at different levels of the same marketing channel (e.g., manufacturers and retailers) collude to control the prices passed on to consumers.

voice-of-customer (VOC) program An ongoing marketing research system that collects customer insights and intelligence to influence and drive business decisions.

want The particular way in which a person chooses to satisfy a need, which is shaped by a person's knowledge, culture, and personality.

wholesalers Those firms engaged in buying, taking title to, often storing, and physically handling goods in large quantities, and then reselling the goods (usually in smaller quantities) to retailers or industrial or business users.

zone of tolerance The area between customers' expectations regarding their desired service and the minimum level of acceptable service—that is, the difference between what the customer really wants and what he or she will accept before going elsewhere.

endnotes

CHAPTER 1

1. Canada Newswire, "Tim Hortons Ranks Number One in the Reputation Institute's Survey of Canada's Top Brands in 2013," http://www.newswire.ca/en/story/1155265/tim-hortons-ranks-number-one-in-the-reputation-institute-s-survey-of-canada-s-top-brands-in-2013 (accessed May 17, 2013).

2. 2013 Tim Hortons Annual Report on Form 10-K, http://www.timhortons.com/ca/pdf/Tim_Hortons_2013_AR_full.pdf (accessed June 26, 2014.)

3. Canada Newswire, "Tim Hortons Celebrates Earth Day with Its First LEED Certified Restaurant," http://www.newswire.ca/en/story/1150315/tim-hortons-celebrates-earth-day-with-its-first-leed-certified-restaurant (accessed May 17, 2013).

4. Canada Newswire, "Tim Hortons Announces Electric Vehicle Charging Station Pilot in Canada," http://www.newswire.ca/en/story/1113505/tim-hortons-announces-electric-vehicle-charging-station-pilot-in-canada (accessed May 17, 2013).

5. Alicia Androich, "TimsTV Coming Soon to More Restaurants," *Marketing Magazine*, January 9, 2014, http://www.marketingmag.ca/news/marketer-news/timstv-soon-coming-to-more-restaurants-97952 (accessed April 3, 2014).

6. The Canadian Marketing Association, http://www.the-cma.org (accessed December 17, 2007). More discussion on marketing is provided by Stephen L. Vargo and Robert F. Lusch, "Evolving to a New Dominant Logic for Marketing," *Journal of Marketing* 68 (January 2004), pp. 1–17; and George S. Day, John Deighton, Das Narayandas, Evert Gummesson, Shelby D. Hunt, C.K. Prahalad, Roland T. Rust, and Steven M. Shugan, "Invited Commentaries on 'Evolving to a New Dominant Logic for Marketing,'" *Journal of Marketing* 68 (January 2004), pp. 18–27. Also see W. Stephen Brown et al., "Marketing Renaissance: Opportunities and Imperatives for Improving Marketing Thought, Practice, and Infrastructure," *Journal of Marketing*, 69, no. 4 (2005), pp. 1–25.

7. Mike Esterl, "Coke Tailors Its Soda Sizes," *The Wall Street Journal*, September 19, 2011, http://online.wsj.com/article/SB10001424053111903374004576578980270401662.html; Natalie Zmuda, "Diet Coke Blasts Past Pepsi," *Advertising Age*, March 17, 2011, http://adage.com/article/news/diet-coke-blasts-past-pepsi/149453; Natalie Zmuda, "Can Pepsi's Big Marketing Shake-Up Bring Back Fizz to Its Beverage Brands?" *Advertising Age*, June 20, 2011, http://adage.com/article/news/pepsi-s-marketing-reorg-bring-back-fizz-beverages/228292 (accessed June 16, 2014).

8. http://www.lexus.com/models/LSh/index.html (accessed June 16, 2014).

9. The idea of the four Ps was conceptualized by E. Jerome McCarthy, *Basic Marketing: A Managerial Approach* (Homewood, IL: Richard D. Irwin, 1960). Also see Walter van Watershoot and Christophe Van den Bulte, "The 4P Classification of the Marketing Mix Revisited," *Journal of Marketing* 56 (October 1992), pp. 83–93.

10. http://www.bottledwaterweb.com (accessed April 22, 2011).

11. Bottled Water Free Campus, http://www.sustainable.uottawa.ca/index.php?module=CMS&id=52 (accessed June 16, 2014).

12. Pew Internet and American Life Project, "Social Networking Sites and Our Lives," June 16, 2011, http://pewinternet.org/~/media//Files/Reports/2011/PIP%20-%20Social%20networking%20sites%20and%20our%20lives.pdf; "Statistics," http://www.facebook.com/press/info.php?statistics; Mike Elgan, "Click 'Like' If You Like 'Like,'" *BusinessWeek*, May 4, 2011; David Goldman, "Get Ready for Some Big Facebook Changes," CNNMoney.com, April 21, 2010; Venture Capital Dispatch, "Giving Credits Where Credits Are Due: Facebook to Aid Developers," *The Wall Street Journal*, April 22, 2010; Liz Gannes, "Facebook: The Entire Web Will Be Social," Gigaom.com, April 21, 2010; Jessica Vascellaro, "Facebook Wants to Know More Than Just Who Your Friends Are," *The Wall Street Journal*, April 22, 2010; Samuel Axon, "Facebook's Open Graph Personalizes the Web," Mashable.com, April 21, 2010; Harry McCracken, "Microsoft Melds Office with Facebook," Technologizer.com, April 21, 2010.

13. Craig Smith, "By the Numbers: 98 Amazing Facebook User Statistics (updated June 2014), Digital Media Ramblings, http://expandedramblings.com/index.php/by-the-numbers-17-amazing-facebook-stats/#.Uz8ZPKhdXvE (accessed June 16, 2014).

14. Jennifer Wadsworth, "Canadians Are the Most Active Facebook Users in the World," Inside Facebook, http://www.insidefacebook.com/2013/08/23/canadians-still-the-most-active-facebook-users-in-the-world (accessed June 16, 2014).

15. Websites such as http://www.whymilk.com and http://www.milkdelivers.org/campaign/index.cfm provide examples of this popular campaign.

16. "How Companies Manage Sustainability: McKinsey Global Survey Results," http://www.mckinseyquarterly.com/How_companies_manage_sustainability_McKinsey_Global_Survey_results_2558 (accessed June 16, 2014).

17. Rebecca Harris, "Greenwashing: Cleaning Up By Saving the World," http://www.marketingmag.ca/news/marketer-news/greenwashing-cleaning-up-by-saving-the-world-77259 (accessed June 16, 2014).

18. George S. Day, "Aligning the Organization with the Market," *Marketing Science Institute* 5, no. 3 (2005), pp. 3–20.

19. Dhruv Grewal, Kent B. Monroe, and R. Krishnan, "The Effects of Price Comparison Advertising on Buyers' Perceptions of Acquisition Value and Transaction Value," *Journal of Marketing* 62 (April 1998), pp. 46–60; Kent B. Monroe, *Pricing: Making Profitable Decisions*, 3rd ed. (New York: McGraw-Hill, 2004).

20. Anne L. Roggeveen, Michael Tsiros, and Dhruv Grewal, "Understanding the Co-Creation Effect: When Does Collaborating with Customers Provide a Lift to Service Recovery?" *Journal of the Academy of Marketing Science* (2011), forthcoming; Sigurd Troye and Magne Supphellen, "Consumer Participation in Coproduction: 'I Made It Myself' Effects on Consumers' Sensory Perceptions and Evaluations of Outcome and Input Product," *Journal of Marketing* (forthcoming); Neeli Bendapudi and Robert P. Leone, "Psychological Implications of Customer Participation in Co-Production," *Journal of Marketing* 67 (January 2003), pp. 14–28.

21. Shelley Emling, "Low-Cost Flying No Longer Just a U.S. Sensation," *Atlanta Journal* December 26, 2003: F1.

22. In 2005, the *Journal of Marketing* ran a special section entirely devoted to relationship marketing. The section included these articles: William Boulding et al., "A Customer Relationship Management Roadmap: What Is Known, Potential Pitfalls, and Where to Go," *Journal of Marketing* 69, no. 4 (2005), pp. 155–166; Jacquelyn S. Thomas and Ursula Y. Sullivan, "Managing Marketing Communications with Multichannel Customers," *Journal of Marketing* 69, no. 4 (2005), pp. 239–251; Lynette Ryals, "Making Customer Relationship Management Work: The Measurement and Profitable Management of Customer Relationships," *Journal of Marketing* 69, no. 4 (2005), pp. 252–261; and Martha Rogers, "Customer Strategy: Observations from the Trenches," *Journal of Marketing* 69 no. 4 (2005), pp. 262–263.

23. Rajendra K. Srivastava, Tasadduq A. Shervani, and Liam Fahey, "Marketing, Business Processes, and Shareholder Value: An Embedded View of Marketing Activities and the Discipline of Marketing," *Journal of Marketing* 63 (special issue, 1999), pp. 168–179; R. Venkatesan and V. Kumar, "A Customer Lifetime Value Framework for Customer Selections and Resource Allocation Strategy," *Journal of Marketing* 68, no. 4 (October 2004), pp. 106–125; V. Kumar, G. Ramani, and T. Bohling, "Customer Lifetime Value Approaches and Best Practice Applications," *Journal of Interactive Marketing* 18, no. 3 (Summer 2004),

pp. 60–72; and J. Thomas, W. Reinartz, and V. Kumar, "Getting the Most Out of All Your Customers," *Harvard Business Review* (July–August 2004), pp. 116–123.

24. Randy Schrum, "Social Media 2010, The Fastest Growth Ever," mycorporatemedia.com, January 30, 2011; http://www.onlinemarketing-trends.com/2011/03/50-of-us-users-will-be-facebook-in-2013.html; Jonah Berger and Katherine L Milkman, "What Makes Online Content Viral?" *Journal of Marketing Research* (forthcoming).

25. http://mobithinking.com/stats-corner/global-mobile-statistics-2011-all-quality-mobile-marketing-research-mobile-web-stats-su (accessed June 16, 2014).

26. http://thenextweb.com/socialmedia/2011/01/20/could-facebook-reach-one-billion-users-in-2011 (accessed June 16, 2014).

27. "Facebook Newsroom," https://newsroom.fb.com/company-info (accessed April 4, 2014); "Twitter Statistics," http://www.statisticbrain.com/twitter-statistics (accessed April 4, 2014); "About Us," http://press.linkedin.com/about (accessed April 4, 2014); "Press Room," https://www.youtube.com/yt/press (accessed April 4, 2014); "About Foursquare," https://foursquare.com/about (accessed April 4, 2014).

28. Julie Weed, "Hotels Turn to Social Media to Connect with Travelers," *The New York Times*, April 18, 2011.

29. Elizabeth Olson, "Restaurants Reach Out to Customers with Social Media," *The New York Times*, January 19, 2011.

30. Hennes & Mauritz AB, http://www.hm.com (accessed May 22, 2011).

31. Zara, http://www.zara.com (accessed May 22, 2011).

32. Example based on Loblaw Company Limited Supply Chain Management, http://www-acad.sheridanc.on.ca/syst35412/patenime/intro.htm (accessed March 29, 2007).

33. "HP Canada Social Investment," http://www.hp.com/canada/corporate/philanthropy/home.html (accessed April 23, 2011).

34. "Understanding the Power Behind Today's Leading Brands—2011 Harris Poll EquiTrend," http://www.harrisinteractive.com; Calvert, "Corporate Responsibility and Investor Confidence Survey," November 18, 2003: http://www.harrisinteractive.com. Also see the Trustees of Boston College, "The State of Corporate Citizenship in the United States: 2003," July 2003; Luisa Kroll and Allison Fass, "The World's Billionaires," http://www.forbes.com (accessed March 29, 2007).

35. http://dictionary.reference.com/search?q=Entrepreneurship (accessed May 16, 2005).

36. "Monumental Moments" http://www.timhortons.com/ca/en/about/index.html# (accessed May 22, 2013).

37. Tina Rosenberg, "A Scorecard for Companies with a Conscience," *The New York Times*, April 11, 2011, http://opinionator.blogs.nytimes

38. "P&G Professional's Green Guarantee," http://www.greenguarantee.com/faqs.htm.

39. "Commitment to Everyday Life," 2011 Sustainability Overview, http://www.pg.com/en_US/downloads/sustainability/reports/PG_2011_Sustainability_Overview.pdf (accessed June 16, 2014).

40. Jonathan Bardeline, "P&G Scorecard Puts Supply Chain on Notice," *Greenbiz.com*, April 7, 2011, http://www.greenbiz.com/news/2011/04/07/procter-gamble-scorecard-puts-supply-chain-notice (accessed June 16, 2014).

41. "Ron Joyce," http://www.timhortons.com/ca/en/about/bio_ronjoyce.html (accessed May 22, 2013).

42. Clare O'Connor, "Billionaire Founder Chip Wilson Out at Yoga Giant Lululemon," http://www.forbes.com/sites/clareoconnor/2012/01/09/billionaire-ceo-chip-wilson-out-at-yoga-giant-lululemon (accessed May 22, 2013).

43. "Financial Information," http://investor.lululemon.com/financials.cfm (accessed May 22, 2013).

44. "Store Finder," http://www.lululemon.com/stores/#show-location-list (accessed May 22, 2013).

45. "Canada to See Unprecedented Boom in New Businesses in the Coming Decade: CIBC," http://www.newswire.ca/en/story/1041489/canada-to-see-unprecedented-boom-in-new-businesses-in-the-coming-decade-cibc (accessed June 16, 2014).

46. This case was written by Ajax Persaud and Shirley Lichti for use in a class discussion; it was not written as an illustration of effective or ineffective marketing practices.

47. This case is based on information from lululemon's SEC 10K Filings and complemented with information from the following sources: http://www.lululemon.com (accessed April 25, 2011); http://en.wikipedia.org/wiki/lululemon (accessed May 23, 2013); http://www.mindspring.com/~wilma-munsey/uhcw/BBCNews (accessed May 23, 2007); http://sev.prnewswire.com/retail/20061003/LAMO2203102006-1.html (accessed May 23, 2007); http://www.hoovers.com/lululemon/--ID_156721--/free-cofactsheet.xhtml (accessed May 23, 2007); Laura Bogomolny, "Toned and Ready," *Canadian Business* (April 24–May 7, 2006), pp. 59–63; Martha Strauss, "As It Stretches, Lululemon Tries Not to Bend, *The Globe and Mail* October 2, 2006.

48. "lululemon athletica inc. Announces Fourth Quarter and Full Year Fiscal 2013 Results," http://investor.lululemon.com/releasedetail.cfm?ReleaseID=835961 (accessed June 16, 2014).

49. Ibid.

50. Retail Insider, "Lululemon's Top Selling Store Is at West Edmonton Mall," http://www.retail-insider.com/2013/12/lululemons-top-selling-store-is-at-west.html, December 16, 2013 (accessed June 16, 2014).

51. Competition Bureau, "Lululemon Vitasea Clothing," http://www.competitionbureau.gc.ca/eic/site/cb-bc.nsf/eng/02517.html (accessed July 16, 2010).

52. Georgie Binks, "Taking It All Off, Even If You Don't Want To," *CBC News ViewPoint*, http://www.cbc.ca/news/viewpoint/vp_binks/20051212.html (accessed August 12, 2010).

CHAPTER 2

1. "About Nike Inc.," http://nikeinc.com/pages/about-nike-inc.

2. Bob Young, "No NBA? Let the Shoe Wars Begin," *The Arizona Republic*, October 16, 2011, http://www.azcentral.com/sports/suns/articles/2011/10/16/20111016heat-index-nba-lockout-shoe-wars.html (accessed June 16, 2014).

3. Nike, 10-K report, July 20, 2010.

4. "Sneaker Wars: adidas Puts a Chainsaw to Kobe Bryant's Nikes," http://balljunkie.com/2011/05/27/sneaker-wars-adidas-puts-a-chainshaw-to-kobe-bryants-nikes (accessed June 16, 2014).

5. "Nike 1 iPod," http://www.apple.com/ipod/nike/run.html.

6. "Nike vs. Adidas," http://recomparison.com/comparisons/100305/nike-vs-adidas (accessed June 16, 2014).

7. Georgios Dogiamis and Narain Vijayshanker, "adidas: Sprinting Ahead of Nike," white paper, Winter 2009.

8. "Nike Crushes adidas on the Track in Olympic Shoe Wars," http://www.tracktownusa.com/track.item.79/Nike-Crushes-Adidas-on-the-Track-in-Olympic-Shoe-Wars.html

9. Cynthia Montgomery, "Creating Corporate Advantage," *Harvard Business Review* 76 (May–June 1998), pp. 71–80; Shelby Hunt and Robert Morgan, "The Comparative Advantage Theory of Competition," *Journal of Marketing* 59, no. 2 (1995), pp. 1–15; Kathleen Conner and C.K. Prahalad, "A Resource-based Theory of the Firm: Knowledge versus Opportunism," *Organizational Science* 7 (September–October 1996), pp. 477–501; David Collins and Cynthia Montgomery, "Competing on Resources: Strategy for the 1990s," *Harvard Business Review* 73 (July–August 1995), pp. 118–128; William Werther and Jeffrey Kerr, "The Shifting Sands of Competitive Advantage," *Business Horizons* 38 (May–June 1995), pp. 11–17; "10 Quick Wins to Turn Your Supply Chain into a Competitive Advantage,"

http://marketindustry.about.com/library/bl/bl_ksa0112.
htm?terms=competitive+advantage (January 2002); Market
Forward Inc., "Multi-Channel Integration: The New Market
Battleground," http://www.pwcris.com (March 2001).

10. Michael Treacy and Fred Wiersema, *The Disciplines of Market
Leaders* (Reading, MA: Addison Wesley, 1995).

11. "How It All Began," http://www.beautygram.com/story (accessed
May 23, 2013).

12. "How She Did It: BeautyGram Founder Taps into Gift Market in
a Fun, Unique Way," http://empowerlounge.com/how-she-did-
it-beautygram-founder-taps-into-gift-market (accessed June 16,
2014).

13. Telephone interview with Jennifer Ruparell, May 31, 2013.

14. Gerrard Macintosh and Lawrence Lockshin, "Market Relationships
and Store Loyalty: A Multi-Level Perspective," *International
Journal of Research in Marketing* 14 (1997), pp. 487–497.

15. Venkatesan and Kumar, pp. 106–125; Kumar, Ramani, and Bohling,
pp. 60–72; J. Thomas, W. Reinartz, and V. Kumar (2004), "Getting
the Most Out of All Your Customers," *Harvard Business Review*
(July–August 2004), pp. 116–23.

16. Jo Marney, "Bringing Consumers Back for More," *Marketing
Magazine* 33 (September 10, 2001); Niren Sirohi, Edward
McLaughlin, and Dick Wittink, "A Model of Consumer
Perceptions and Store Loyalty Intentions for a Supermarket
Marketer," *Journal of Marketing* 74, no. 3 (1998), pp. 223–247.

17. Rosemarky McCracken, "Rewards Have Their Own Virtues,
National Post April 26, 2007: IS1.

18. Mary Jo Bitner, "Self Service Technologies: What Do Customers
Expect?" *Marketing Management* (Spring 2001), pp. 10–34;
Mary Jo Bitner, Stephen W. Brown, and Matthew L. Meuter,
"Technology Infusion in Service Encounters," *Journal of Academy
of Marketing Science* 28, no. 1 (2000), pp. 138–49; Matthew
L. Meuter et al., "Self-Service Technologies: Understanding
Customer Satisfaction with Technology-based Service
Encounters," *Journal of Marketing* 64, no. 3 (2000), pp. 50–64;
A. Parasuraman and Dhruv Grewal, "The Impact of Technology
on the Quality-Value-Loyalty Chain: A Research Agenda,"
Journal of the Academy of Marketing Science 28, no. 1 (2000),
pp. 168–174.

19. James R. Stock, Stefanie L. Boyer, and Tracy Harmon, "Research
Opportunities in Supply Chain Management," *Journal of the
Academy of Marketing Science,* 2010, 38, no. 1, pp. 32–41. Also
see articles in special issue edited by John T. Mentzer and Greg
Gundlach, "Exploring the Relationship between Marketing and
Supply Chain Management: Introduction to the Special Issue,"
Journal of the Academy of Marketing Science, 2010, 38, no. 1,
pp. 1–4.

20. "The Top 100 Brands," *Business Week,* http://www.businessweek.
com/pdfs/2003/0331_globalbrands.pdf (accessed August 29,
2006); "Best Canadian Brands 2006," *Report on Business &
Interbrand,* http://www.ourfishbowl.com/images/surveys/
Interbrand_BCB2006.pdf (accessed July 9, 2011).

21. WestJet Airlines, http://www.westjet.com (accessed April 23,
2011); http://www.newswire.ca/en/releases/archive/April2007/23/
c8051.html (accessed June 16, 2014).

22. http://www.marketingpower.com/live/mg-dictionary.
php?SearchFor=marketing+plan&Searched=1 (accessed August 31,
2006).

23. Donald Lehman and Russell Winer, *Analysis for Marketing
Planning,* 5th ed. (Burr Ridge, IL: McGraw-Hill/Irwin, 2001); David
Aaker, *Strategic Market Management,* 6th ed. (New York: John
Wiley, 2001).

24. Andrew Campbell, "Mission Statements," *Long Range Planning*
30 (1997), pp. 931–933.

25. Alfred Rappaport, *Creating Shareholder Value: The New
Standard for Business Performance* (New York: Wiley, 1988);
Robert C. Higgins and Roger A. Kerin, "Managing the Growth-

26. Financial Policy Nexus in Marketing," *Journal of Marketing* 59,
no. 3 (1983), pp. 19–47; and Roger Kerin, Vijay Mahajan, and
P. Rajan Varadarajan, *Contemporary Perspectives on Strategic
Market Planning* (Boston: Allyn & Bacon, 1991), Chapter 6.

26. Tom Hortons, "About Us," http://www.timhortons.com/ca/en/
about/faq.html (accessed April 23, 2011).

27. Michael McCarthy, "NBA Lockout Not Good for the Shoes," *USA
Today,* November 1, 2011, http://www.usatoday.com/sports
/basketball/nba/story/2011-10-30/NBA-lockout-not-good-for-the-
shoes/51007210/1.

28. Matt Townsend, "As Nike Scoffs, Toning Shoes Gain Traction,"
Bloomberg Business Week, June 7–13, 2010, pp. 22–24.

29. Eric Siemers, "Nike Takes New Marketing Tack," *Portland
Business Journal,* September 12, 2010, http://www.bizjournals.
com/portland/stories/2010/09/13/story9.html (accessed June 16,
2014).

30. Nike 10-K report, July 20, 2010.

31. Russel Parsons, "Nike Beating Official Sponsor adidas in World
Cup Stakes," *Marketing Week,* June 24, 2010, p. 7.

32. Eric Siemans, "New Balance TV Spots Target Nike," *Portland
Business Journal,* March 7, 2011, http://www.bizjournals.com/
portland/blog/2011/03/new-balance-tv-spots-target-nike.
html?page52 (accessed June 16, 2014).

33. Nike 10-K report, July 20, 2010.

34. http://www.hertz.com/rentacar/vehicleguide/
index.jsp?targetPage5vehicleGuideHomeView.
jsp&countryCode5UScategory5Car/Sedan.

35. Lisa D'Innocenzo, "Frito Lay Canada: Potato Chips ... for Dinner?"
Strategy Magazine (January 2007), p. 11.

36. TNW, Could Facebook Reach One Billion Users in 2011?, http://
thenextweb.com/socialmedia/2011/01/20/could-facebook-reach-
one-billion-users-in-2011 (accessed June 19, 2014).

37. http://www.leevalley.com (accessed April 30, 2007);
"Conversations on Working and Well-Being: Working by the
Golden Rule: Lee Valley Tools," http://www.vifamily.ca/library/
social/lee_valley.html (accessed April 30, 2007); "Lee Valley Tools
Case Study," http://www.nerac.com/research-victories/lee-valley-
tools-case-study (accessed April 30, 2007); A Visit to Lee Valley
Tools: A Company Built on Innovation and Customer Service,
http://www.woodcentral.com/shots/shot643.shtml (accessed
June 16, 2014).

38. Interview with owner of the Country Grocer.

39. Bios from W network, http://www.wnetwork.com/Shows/
TheCupcakeGirls/CharacterBios.aspx (accessed August 5, 2010);
http://cupcakestakethecake.blogspot.com/2009/06/cupcake-
reality-show-cupcake-girls.html (accessed June 16, 2014).

40. http://www.adstandards.com (accessed December 17, 2007).

41. Based on an article by Carly Weeks, "Charities' Cash
Conundrum," *The Globe and Mail,* http://www.theglobeandmail.
com/life/charities-cash-conundrum/article1504383 (accessed
June 16, 2014).

42. Human Resources and Skills Development Canada. "Social
Participation—Charitable Donations" http://www4.hrsdc.
gc.ca/.3ndic.1t.4r@-eng.jsp?iid=69 (accessed May 22, 2011).

43. *Globe and Mail* Report on Business Special Case Studies
with Concordia University, "Can Sustainability Be Luxury's
New Gold Standard?" May 2010: http://news.concordia.ca/
pdf/GlobeMail_Feb26.pdf (accessed July 9, 2011); "Social
Responsibility," http://birkscareers.com/social-responsibility
(accessed April 7, 2014); "Sustainable Precious Metals," http://
secure.birksrecognition.com/en/static/about/about_metals.
htm (accessed June 16, 2014).

44. http://www.loblaw.ca/en/abt_corprof.html (accessed April 30,
2007). ® President's Choice, PC Financial, PC are registered
trademarks of Loblaws Inc., used with permission.

45. This discussion is adapted from Roger A. Kerin et al., *Marketing*, 7th ed. (Burr Ridge, IL: McGraw-Hill/Irwin, 2003), p. 39.

46. Farris et al., *Marketing Metrics: 50+ Metrics Every Executive Should Master* (Upper Saddle River, NJ: Prentice Hall, 2006), p. 17.

47. Relative market share = brand's market share ÷ largest competitor's market share. If, on the one hand, there are only two products in a market, A and B, and product B has 90 percent market share, then A's relative market share is 10 ÷ 90 = 11.1 percent. If, on the other hand, B has only 50 percent market share, then A's relative market share is 10 ÷ 50 = 20 percent. Farris et al., *Marketing Metrics*, p. 19.

48. "Strong Demand for Smartphones and Heated Vendor Competition Characterize the Worldwide Mobile Phone Market at the end of 2012, IDC Says," IDC January 24, 2013, https://www.idc.com/getdoc.jsp?containerId=prUS23916413 (accessed June 16, 2014).

49. Jay Yarrow, "Apple Tanks After Whiffing on iPhone Sales," *Business Insider*, January 27, 2014, http://www.businessinsider.com/apple-q1-earnings-2014-1 (accessed June 16, 2014).

50. Darcy Travlos, "The iPad will Mirror the iPod's Market Dominance. Here's Why and It Matters," Forbes, July 13, 2012, http://www.forbes.com/sites/darcytravlos/2012/07/13/the-ipad-will-mirror-the-ipods-market-dominance-heres-why-and-why-it-matters (accessed June 16, 2014).

51. James Hall, "MP3 Players Are Dead," *Business Insider*, December 26, 2012, http://www.businessinsider.com/mp3-players-are-dead-2012-12 (accessed June 16, 2014).

52. "Apple Reports Record Results," Apple January 23, 2013, http://www.apple.com/pr/library/2013/01/23Apple-Reports-Record-Results.html (accessed June 16, 2014).

53. Ibid.

54. "Apple Reports Second Quarter Results," Apple, April 23, 2013, http://www.apple.com/pr/library/2013/04/23Apple-Reports-Second-Quarter-Results.html (accessed June 16, 2014).

55. "Media Tablet Shipments Outpace Fourth Quarter Targets; Strong Demand for New iPad and Other Forthcoming Products Leads to Increase in 2012 Forecast, According to IDC," IDC March 13, 2012, http://www.idc.com/getdoc.jsp?containerId=prUS23371312 (accessed May 24, 2013).

56. "Low Cost Products Drive Forecast Increases in Tablet Market, According to IDC," IDC March 12, 2013, http://www.idc.com/getdoc.jsp?containerId=prUS24002213 (accessed May 24, 2013).

57. Kerin, Mahajan, and Varadarajan, *Contemporary Perspectives on Strategic Market Planning*; See also Susan Mudambi, "A Topology of Strategic Choice in Marketing," *International Journal of Market & Distribution Management* (1994), pp. 22–25.

58. http://www.gamestop.com/xbox-360/movies-tv/yoostar-on-mtv/91616.

59. http://www.mtv.com/shows/teen_mom/season_3/series.jhtml.

60. http://www.viacom.com/ourbrands/globalreach/Pages/default.aspx.

61. http://www.stayteen.org; http://www.mtv.com/mobile.

62. http://www.mtv.com/shows/made/series.jhtml; Tim Arango, "Make Room, Cynics; MTV Wants to Do Some Good," *The New York Times*, April 18, 2009; Robert Seidman, "MTV Continues to Diversify Slate with New Scripted Comedies "The Hard Times of RJ Berger" and "Warren the Ape,"" tvbythenumbers.com, January 15, 2010.

63. http://solutions.3m.com/wps/portal/3M/en_US/about-3M/information/about/businesses/.

64. http://www.netflix.com; "Netflix," http://en.wikipedia.org/wiki/Netflix#cite_note-QwisterBlogPost-19; Scott Stein, "Netflix on iPad, More to Follow?" *CNET Reviews*, April 1, 2010; Jessie Baker, "Netflix Introduces New Plans and Announces Price Changes," Netflix blog, July 12, 2011, http://blog.netflix.com/2011_07_01_archive.html (accessed June 16, 2014); Brian Stelter, "Netflix Stock Falls After Change," *The New York Times*, September 15, 2011, http://mediadecoder.blogs.nytimes.com/2011/09/15/price-hike-sends-netflixs-stock-downward (accessed June 16, 2014); Reed Hastings, "An Explanation and Some Reflections," Netflix blog, September 18, 2011, http://blog.netflix.com/2011_09_01_archive.html (accessed June 16, 2014); Elizabeth Harris, "Netflix to Break Business in Two," *The New York Times*, September 19, 2011, http://mediadecoder.blogs.nytimes.com/2011/09/19/netflix-c-e-o-apologizes-for-handling-of-price-increase (accessed June 16, 2014); Jenna Wortham and Brian Stelter, "Latest Move Gets Netflix More Wrath," *The New York Times*, September 19, 2011, http://mediadecoder.blogs.nytimes.com/2011/09/19/netflix-strategy-prompts-backlash (accessed June 16, 2014); Reed Hastings, "DVDs Will Be Staying at Netflix.com," Netflix blog, October 10, 2011, http://blog.netflix.com/2011_10_01_archive.html (accessed June 16, 2014), Netflix Form-10K Annual Report Feb. 2013, http://ir.netflix.com/secfiling.cfm?filingID=1065280-13-8&CIK=1065280 (accessed June 16, 2014), "Netflix Media Centre," https://signup.netflix.com/MediaCenter?id=5380, Samson Okalow, "Why Netflix Won't Conquer Canada, Part 2," February 5, 2013, http://www.canadianbusiness.com/companies-and-industries/why-netflix-wont-conquer-canada-part-2, Steve Ladurantaye, "Rogers Determined to Butt Heads with Netflix," May 7, 2013, http://www.theglobeandmail.com/report-on-business/rogers-determined-to-butt-heads-with-netflix/article11766948 (accessed June 16, 2014); Etan Vlessing, "Netflix: Q4 Growth of Canadian Subscribers Will Be 'Steady and Up,'" *Media in Canada*, October 22, 2013, http://mediaincanada.com/2013/10/22/netflix-q4-growth-of-canadian-subscribers-will-be-steady-or-up (accessed June 16, 2014)

APPENDIX 2A

1. This appendix was written by Tom Chevalier, Britt Hackmann, and Elisabeth Nevins Caswell in conjunction with the textbook authors (Dhruv Grewal and Michael Levy) for class discussion; it was not written as an illustration of effective or ineffective marketing practices.

2. "How to Write a Marketing Plan," http://www.knowthis.com/tutorials/principles-of-marketing/how-to-write-a-marketing-plan.htm (accessed June 16, 2014); also see "Marketing Plan Online," http://www.quickmba.com/marketing/plan (accessed May 16, 2008); "Marketing Plan," http://www.businessplans.org/Market.html (accessed May 18, 2008).

3. Roger Kerin, Steven Hartley, and William Rudelius, *Marketing* (New York: McGraw-Hill/Irwin, 2008), p. 53.

4. Kerin, Hartley, and Rudelius, p. 54; "How to Write a Marketing Plan."

5. This list of sources largely comes from the *Babson College Library Guide* May 12, 2008, http://www3.babson.edu/Library/research/marketingplan.cfm (accessed May 15, 2008). Special thanks to Nancy Dlott.

6. This marketing plan presents an abbreviated version of the actual plan for PeopleAhead. Some information has been changed to maintain confidentiality.

7. Publishers' and Advertising Directors' Conference, September, 21, 2005.

8. Mintel International Group, "Online Recruitment–US," January 1, 2005, http://www.marketresearch.com (accessed September 1, 2005).

9. Corzen Inc., http://www.wantedtech.com (accessed May 17, 2004).

10. Mintel International Group, "Online Recruitment–US."

CHAPTER 3

1. "Annual Report 2013," Canadian Tire Corporation, http://corp.canadiantire.ca/EN/Investors/Documents/2013%20Annual%20Report.pdf (accessed June 30, 2014).

2. Canadian Tire Outlines Strategy for Growth Focused on Core Business, http://www.newswire.ca/en/releases/archive/April2010/07/c8276.html (June 30, 2014).

3. "Canadian Tire Maintains Growth Strategy," Canwest News Service, October 3, 2007: http://www.canada.com/vancouversun/news/business/story.html?id=38979fb4-178f-4f3b-b009-435b918de558&k=18791 (accessed August 5, 2010).

4. "Canadian Tire Corporation, Limited," http://www.referenceforbusiness.com/history/Ca-Ch/Canadian-Tire-Corporation-Limited.html (accessed June 30, 2014).

5. "Canadian Tire Corporation, Limited."

6. "2010 Strategic Objectives, Strengthen the Core, Create a Great CTR with a Strong Automotive Division," http://corp.canadiantire.ca/EN/Investors/CorporateInformation/Pages/BusinessStrategy.aspx (accessed August 5, 2010).

7. Q1 2010 Canadian Tire Corporation Earnings Conference Call, May 13, 2010. http://corp.canadiantire.ca/EN/Investors/EventsPresentations/Documents/Q1%202010%20Conference%20Call%20Presentation.pdf.

8. Ibid.

9. Peter F. Drucker, *The Essential Drucker* (New York: HarperCollins, 2001).

10. http://www.crestcanada.com and http://www.colgate.com (accessed April 23, 2011).

11. Linda Doell, "In Razor vs. Razor, Neither Gillette Nor Schick Gains Edge With Ad Watchdog," March 17, 2011, http://www.dailyfinance.com/2011/03/17/in-razor-vs-razor-neither-gillette-nor-schick-gains-edge-with.

12. Matt Fish, "Silicon Belly: The Value of Competitive Intelligence," November 10, 2003, http://lexis-nexis.com (accessed September 6, 2006).

13. Steve Mossop, "Companies Not Spending Enough on Business Intelligence Activities," http://www.ipsos-na.com/news/pressrelease.cfm?id=2874 (accessed June 30, 2014).

14. Mark Rogowsky, "Without Much Fanfare, Apple Has Sold Its 500 Millionth iPhone," *Forbes*, March 25, 2014, http://www.forbes.com/sites/markrogowsky/2014/03/25/without-much-fanfare-apple-has-sold-its-500-millionth-iphone (accessed June 30, 2014).

15. Seth Fiegerman, "Apple Vs. Samsung: Everything You Need to Know About the (Patent) Trial of the Century." *Business Insider*, n.p., July 30, 2012, http://www.businessinsider.com/apple-vs-samsung-everything-you-need-to-know-about-the-patent-trial-of-the-century-2012-7?op=1 (accessed June 30, 2014).

16. Ibid.

17. Nick Wingfield, "Jury Awards $1 Billion to Apple in Samsung Patent Case," *The New York Times*, n.p., August 24, 2012, http://www.nytimes.com/2012/08/25/technology/jury-reaches-decision-in-apple-samsung-patent-trial.html?_r=0 (accessed June 30, 2014).

18. Ian Sherr, "Apple Faces Product Ban after Samsung Victory," *The Globe and Mail*, June 5, 2013, p. B8.

19. "Air Canada, WestJet Settle Spying Lawsuit," http://www.cbc.ca/canada/calgary/story/2006/05/29/ca-westjet-settlement-20060529.htm l (accessed May 15, 2007).

20. http://www.nau.com (accessed April 29, 2010); Polly Labarre, "Leap of Faith," *Fast Company* June 2007.

21. Michael Solomon, *Consumer Behavior: Buying, Having and Being* (Upper Saddle River, NJ: Prentice Hall, 2006).

22. Rob Gerlsbeck, "Research: A Distinct Shopping Society," http://www.marketingmag.ca/magazine/current/quebec_rpt/article.jsp?content=20070625_69884_69884 (accessed June 25, 2007).

23. John Feto, "Name Games," *American Demographics*, February 15, 2003.

24. "Orthodox," *American Demographics*, May 2004, p. 35.

25. Greg Smith, "Tweens R' Shoppers: A Look at the Tween Market & Shopping Behaviour," *Popai*, March, 2013, http://www.popai.com/store/downloads/POPAIWhitePaper-Tweens-R-Shoppers-2013.pdf (accessed June 30, 2014).

26. "2005 YTV Tween Report, Solutions Research Group, A Corus Entertainment Inc. Company," http://www.corusmedia.com/ytv/research/index.asp (accessed May 15, 2007); J.K. Wall, "Tweens Get Retailers into Parents' Wallets," *Knight Ridder Tribune Business News* September 12, 2003: 1. Research attributed to WonderGroup in Cincinnati.

27. The term *speeders* was coined by Cynthia Cohen, president of Strategic Mindshare.

28. Brian Braiker, "The Next Great American Consumer," *Adweek*, September 26, 2011, http://www.adweek.com/news/advertising-branding/next-great-american-consumer-135207?page51 (accessed June 30, 2014).

29. Dan Hardy, "To Balance Budgets, Schools Allow Ads," October 16, 2011, http://articles.philly.com/2011-10-16/news/30286428_1_pennsbury-ads-middle-and-high-school (accessed June 30, 2014); Tonyaa Wethersby, "Ad on School Busses a Tacky Idea," October 5, 2011, http://jacksonville.com/opinion/columnists/2011-10-06/story/ads-school-buses-tacky-idea (accessed June 30, 2014).

30. "That Facebook Friend Might Be 10 Years Old, and Other Troubling News," *Consumer Reports*, June 2011, http://www.consumerreports.org/cro/magazine-archive/2011/june/electronics-computers/state-of-the-net/facebook-concerns/index.htm (accessed June 30, 2014); Matt Richtel and Miguel Helft, "Facebook Users Who Are Underage Raise Concerns," *The New York Times*, March 12, 2011, http://www.nytimes.com/2011/03/12/technology/internet/12underage.html?_r51&ref5magazine (accessed June 30, 2014).

31. Yale Rudd Center for Food Policy and Obesity, "Sugary Drink Facts," report, October 2011.

32. http://www.statscan.ca (accessed May 15, 2007).

33. Pamela Paul, "Getting Inside Gen Y," *American Demographics* 23, no. 9.

34. Noah Rubin Brier, "Move Over Prime-Time!" *American Demographics* (July/August 2004), pp. 14–20; John Hoeffel, "The Next Baby Boom," *American Demographics* (October 1995), pp. 22–31.

35. "Generations in Canada," Statistics Canada, January 8th, 2013, http://www12.statcan.gc.ca/census-recensement/2011/as-sa/98-311-x/98-311-x2011003_2-eng.cfm (accessed June 30, 2014).

36. "Lesley Young, Portrait of the New Family," http://www.marketingmag.ca/magazine/current/feature/article.jsp?content=20040315_61585_61585 (accessed May 11, 2007).

37. David Crary, "Boomers Will Be Pumping Billions into Anti-Aging Industry," http://www.huffingtonpost.com/2011/08/20/boomers-anti-aging-industry_n_932109.html (accessed June 30, 2014)

38. http://www.statscan.ca (accessed May 15, 2007).

39. "The Canadian Population in 2011: Age and Sex," Statistics Canada, January 16, 2013, http://www12.statcan.gc.ca/census-recensement/2011/as-sa/98-311-x/98-311-x2011001-eng.cfm (accessed June 30, 2014).

40. Kristin Davis, "Oldies But Goodies; Marketers, Take Note: Baby Boomers Have Lots of Money to Spend," *U.S. News & World Report* (Washington edition), March 14, 2005: 45.

41. "Median Total Income by Family Type, By Province and Territory," Statistics Canada, October 10, 2013, http://www.statcan.gc.ca/tables-tableaux/sum-som/l01/cst01/famil108a-eng.htm (accessed June 30, 2014).

42. http://www.statscan.ca (accessed April 23, 2011).

43. "The Daily—Survey of Household Spending, 2011," Statistics Canada, January 30, 2013, http://www.statcan.gc.ca/daily-quotidien/130130/dq130130b-eng.htm (accessed June 30, 2014).

44. http://www.hammacher.com (accessed May 3, 2010).

45. http://www.statscan.ca (accessed April 23, 2011); U.S. Bureau of the Census, http://www.census.gov/population/www/socdemo/educ-attn.html.

46. "Table 7 Average Income by Highest Level of Education Attained, School/Work Status and Gender," Statistics Canada, January 30, 2013, http://www.statcan.gc.ca/pub/81-595-m/2009075/tbl/tbl7-eng.htm (accessed June 30, 2014).

47. "Median Earnings of Recent Immigrants and Canadian Born Earners, Both Sexes, Aged 25 to 54 With or Without University Degree, 2005, For Canada, Provinces and Territories—20% Sample Data," Statistics Canada, October 6, 2010, http://www12.statcan.ca/census-recensement/2006/dp-pd/hlt/97-563/T802-eng.cfm?Lang=E&T=802&GH=4&SC=13&SO=99&O=A (accessed June 30, 2014).

48. Bethany Clough, "Home-Improvement Store Empower Female Customers with Do-It-Herself Tools," *Knight Ridder Tribune Business Service* March 20, 2005: 1; Fara Warner, "Yes, Women Spend (And Saw and Sand)," *The New York Times* February 29, 2004: C1.

49. http://www.statscan.ca (accessed April 23, 2011).

50. http://www.statscan.ca (accessed April 23, 2011); *OECD Employment Outlook 2010.* Chart LMF1.5.A: Gender Gap in Median Earnings of Full-Time Employees, http://www.oecd.org/dataoecd/1/35/43199347.xls (accessed May 25, 2011).

51. http://www.theglobeandmail.com/servlet/story/RTGAM.20071205.wcensusmain1005/BNStory/census2006/home (accessed December 18, 2007).

52. http://www.statscan.ca (accessed May 15, 2007).

53. "Tapping into the Hot Chinese and South Asian Marketplace," *Ipsos Ideas,* http://www.ipsos-ideas.com/article.cfm?id=3391 (accessed June 30, 2014).

54. "Aboriginal Peoples in Canada: First Nations People, Metis and Inuit," Statistics Canada, May 7, 2013, http://www12.statcan.gc.ca/nhs-enm/2011/as-sa/99-011-x/99-011-x2011001-eng.cfm (accessed June 30, 2014).

55. "Income Statistics, in Constant (2005) Dollars, Age Groups, Aboriginal Identity, Registered Indian Status and Aboriginal Ancestry, Highest Certificate, Diploma or Degree and Sex for the Population 15 Years and Over with Income of Canada, Provinces, Territories, 2000 and 2005—20% Sample Data," Statistics Canada, April 7, 2011, http://www12.statcan.gc.ca/census-recensement/2006/dp-pd/tbt/Rp-eng.cfm?LANG=E&APATH=3&DETAIL=0&DIM=0&FL=0&FREE=0&GC=0&GID=0&K=0&GRP=1&PID=96254&PRID=0&PTYPE=88971,97154&S=0&SHOWALL=0&SUB=0&Temporal=2006&THEME=73&VID=0&VNAMEE=&VNAMEF= (accessed May 31, 2013).

56. Rebecca Harris, "Skin Deep, Canada's Big Banks Have Taken Great Strides to Reach Newcomers to the Country but, They Need to Look Beneath the Surface to Truly Connect to Multicultural Consumers," *Marketing Magazine* January 29, 2007.

57. Harris, "Skin Deep."

58. "About Us," http://www.freshco.com/About-Us.aspx (accessed May 29, 2013).

59. "How Sobey's Is Taking on Loblaws," http://www.theglobeandmail.com/report-on-business/rob-magazine/top-1000/how-sobeys-is-taking-on-loblaws/article1603663 (accessed June 30, 2014); Andy Holloway, "Getting Fresh," *Canadian Grocer* (June/July 2010), p. 23; "Sobeys Inc. Launches FreshCo. Discount Stores" (press release), http://www.sobeyscorporate.com/App_Themes/SobeysCorporate/media/en/Sobeys-Inc-Launches-FreshCo-Discount-Stores.pdf (accessed June 30, 2014).

60. "How Sobey's"; Holloway, "Getting Fresh," p.23; "Sobeys Inc. Launches FreshCo."

61. Ibid.

62. Marianne Wilson, "Growing Power of Mobile," *Chain Store Age,* December 2010; Deena M. Amato-McCoy, "Focus on: The Mobile Channel," *Chain Store Age,* March 2011.

63. "What Is Foursquare?" https://foursquare.com/about. Membership data as of April 2011.

64. Mark Didas, "Market Your Regional Product or Service with Foursquare," http://www.wavespawn.com/market-regional-product-service-foursquare (accessed June 30, 2014).

65. Craig Smith, "By the Numbers: 98 Amazing Facebook User Statistics (updated March 2014), Digital Media Ramblings, http://expandedramblings.com/index.php/by-the-numbers-17-amazing-facebook-stats/#.Uz8ZPKhdXvE (accessed June 30, 2014).

66. "About Foursquare," https://foursquare.com/about, January 2013 (accessed June 30, 2014).

67. http://www.cbc.com (accessed April 24, 2011).

68. http://www.yourdictionary.com (accessed September 5, 2006).

69. http://www.bankofcanada.ca/en (accessed May 15, 2007).

70. "Financial Conditions," Bank of Canada http://www.bankofcanada.ca/core-functions/monetary-policy/key-interest-rate (accessed July 7, 2014).

71. Heather Scoffield, "Outlook Dims as Rates Fall to Record Low," http://v1.theglobeandmail.com/servlet/story/LAC.20090121.RECONOMY21/TPStory/Business (accessed August 6, 2010).

72. This section draws heavily from Jacquelyn A. Ottman, *Green Marketing: Opportunity for Innovation* (Chicago, IL: NTC Publishing, 1997), also available online at http://www.greenmarketing.com.

73. "How Is the Environment on this Day?," *The Globe and Mail,* Wednesday June 5, 2013, P. A9.

74. "Cleanshowing," *Marketing Magazine,* April 22, 2013, p. 40.

75. *Dragons' Den* Episode 14," aired January 28, 2013. http://www.cbc.ca/dragonsden/2013/01/episode-14-3.html (accessed May 26, 2013).

76. "Our Story," http://www.growingcity.com/our-story (accessed May 26, 2013).

77. Sean Stanleigh, "Best Business Award Winners Compete for $20,000," *The Globe and Mail,* October 18, 2012, http://www.theglobeandmail.com/report-on-business/small-business/sb-tools/small-business-briefing/best-business-award-winners-compete-for-20000/article4621103 (accessed June 30, 2014).

78. Kristin Laird (2010), "BullFrog Invites Consumers to Pay More," http://www.marketingmag.ca/english/news/marketer/article.jsp?content=20100422_145930_3524 (accessed August 6, 2010).

79. Centre for Science in the Public Interest, "Guidelines for Marketing Food to Kids Proposed" (press release), January 5, 2005.

80. Ibid.

81. "Massive Epsilon E-mail Breach Hits Citi, Chase, and Many More," http://www.pcworld.com/article/224147/massive_epsilon_email_breach_hits_citi_chase_many_more.html (accessed June 30, 2014).

82. "Target Stores Hit by Data Breach Affecting 40 Million Cards," The Associated Press, December 19, 2013, http://www.cbc.ca/news/world/target-stores-hit-by-data-breach-affecting-40-million-cards-1.2469895 (accessed June 30, 2014).

83. http://www.statscan.ca (accessed April 23, 2011).

84. Martin Peers, "Buddy, Can You Spare Some Time?" *The Wall Street Journal,* January 26, 2004: B1, B3.

85. Ibid.

86. Statistics Canada, "Body Mass Index," http://www.statcan.gc.ca/tables-tableaux/sum-som/l01/cst01/health81b-eng.htm (accessed June 30, 2014).

87. "Yoga Statistics," http://www.statisticbrain.com/yoga-statistics (accessed June 30, 2014).

88. This case was written by the textbook authors (Ajax Persaud and Shirley Lichti) for use in a class discussion; it was not written as an illustration of effective or ineffective marketing practices. It is based on publicly available information.

89. This case was developed by using the following sources: Frederic Lardinois, "EReader and E-book Market Ready for Growth," http://www.readwriteweb.com/archives/report_ereader_and_ebook_market_ready_for_growth.php (accessed June 30, 2014); http://www.kobobooks.com/about_us (accessed June 16, 2013); "The 30 Benefits of E-books," http://epublishersweekly.blogspot.com/2008/02/30-benefits-of-ebooks.html (accessed June 30, 2014); Anton Shilov, "E-books Industry Set to Raise," http://www.xbitlabs.com/news/multimedia/display/20091107152810_Electronic_Book_Industry_Set_to_Explode_in_2010_Analysts.html (accessed June 30, 2014); "The Great Canadian Debate: Future of eBooks in Canadian Retail," http://knol.google.com/k/the-great-canadian-ebook-debate# (accessed April 24, 2011); "Looking into the Future: Price, Color, Video—and the End of the Chain Bookstore," http://www.readwriteweb.com/archives/report_ereader_and_ebook_market_ready_for_growth.php (accessed June 30, 2014); Paul Miller, "Kobo's $149 eReader Gets Reviewed" http://www.engadget.com/2010/04/11/kobos-149-ereader-gets-reviewed (accessed June 30, 2014); Mark Medley, "Testing the Kobo e-reader," http://network.nationalpost.com/NP/blogs/afterword/archive/2010/04/17/testing-the-kobo-ereader.aspx#ixzz0rrO1lc7T (accessed April 24, 2011); "Test Drive of Canadian Company's New e-book Hardware," cbc.ca (accessed April 24, 2011); Canadian Press, "E-book Sales Plateauing: BookNet Canada Report," The Globe and Mail, May 21, http://www.theglobeandmail.com/technology/e-book-sales-plateauing-booknet-canada-report/article12038237 (accessed June 30, 2014), Omar El Akkad, "Do E-readers Have Another Chapter?," The Globe and Mail, April 15, 2013, http://www.theglobeandmail.com/technology/tech-news/do-e-readers-have-another-chapter/article11248534 (accessed June 30, 2014), Canadian Press, "Kobo Bucks Softening e-reader Market, Adds 2.5 million Customers," The Globe and Mail, May 28, 2013, http://www.theglobeandmail.com/technology/business-technology/kobo-bucks-softening-e-reader-market-adds-25-million-customers/article12185743 (accessed June 30, 2014), Laura Hazard Owen, "PwC: The U.S. Consumer e-book Market Will Be Bigger than the Print Book Market by 2017," http://paidcontent.org/2013/06/04/pwc-the-u-s-consumer-ebook-market-will-be-bigger-than-the-print-book-market-by-2017 (accessed June 30, 2014), Jayne Atherron, "Kobo's e-Reader Book Fans Grow to 14.5 Million," http://metro.co.uk/2013/05/28/kobos-e-reader-book-fans-grow-to-14-5-million-3811369 (accessed June 30, 2014), Laura Hazard Owen, "Kobo Says the $170 Aura HD e-reader Now Accounts for "up to 27%" of Its Device Sales," http://gigaom.com/2013/05/28/kobo-says-the-170-aura-hd-e-reader-now-accounts-for-up-to-27-of-its-device-sales (accessed June 30, 2014), Top Ten Reviews, "2013 Best eBook Reader Reviews and Comparisons," http://ebook-reader-review.toptenreviews.com (accessed June 30, 2014).

90. Associated Press, "Amazon Says e-book Sales Pass Paper," http://www.marketingmag.ca/news/media-news/amazon-says-e-book-sales-pass-paper-27662 (accessed June 30, 2014).

CHAPTER 4

1. Andrea Edwards, "Dell—a Top Five Social Media Brand—Looking for Fresh Ideas," SAJE ... Communication, October 12, 2011, http://sajeideas.wordpress.com/2011/10/12/dell-a-top-five-social-media-brand-%E2%80%93-looking-for-fresh-ideas (accessed July 1, 2014).

2. Dell.com, "Introducing Dell's Social Media Command Center," http://content.dell.com/us/en/corp/d/videos~en/Documents~dell-social-media-command-center.aspx.

3. Edwards, op. cit.

4. Dell.com, "Social Media," http://content.dell.com/us/en/corp/about-dell-social-media.aspx?c5us&l5en&s5corp&~ck5mn.

5. Ed Twittel, "How Dell Really Listens to Its Customers," ReadWriteEnterprise, July 22, 2011, http://www.readwriteweb.com/enterprise/2011/07/how-dell-really-listens-to-its.php (accessed July 1, 2014).

6. Ibid.

7. Susan Payton, "Closing Comments at Dell's 2nd Annual Consumer Advisory Panel," Flickr, July 21, 2011, http://www.flickr.com/photos/dellphotos/5960769218/in/set-7215762723464190 8 (accessed July 1, 2014).

8. Dhruv Grewal et al., "The Internet and the Price-Value-Loyalty Chain," Journal of Business Research 56 (May 2003), p. 391.

9. See Henry Assael, Consumer Behaviour and Marketing Action (Boston: Kent Publishing, 1987); John A. Howard and Jadish Sheth, The Theory of Consumer Behaviour in Marketing Strategy (Upper Saddle River, NJ: Prentice Hall, 1989); Philip Kotler, Gary Armstrong, and Peggy Cunningham, Principles of Marketing, 6th Can. ed. (Toronto: Pearson, 2005), pp. 279–280.

10. Pamela Sebastian, "'Aspirational Wants' Form the Basis of a Modern Retailing Strategy," The Wall Street Journal October 15, 1998: A1; Barry Babin, William Darden, and Mitch Griffin, "Work and/or Fun: Measuring Hedonic and Utilitarian Shopping Value," Journal of Consumer Research 20 (March 1994), pp. 644–656.

11. "Christian Louboutin Styles for the Uptown Girl," http://www.newshoefashion.com (accessed April 24, 2011); Cindy Clark, "Christian Louboutin's Red-Soled Shoes Are Red-Hot," USA Today, http://www.usatoday.com/life/lifestyle/fashion/2007-12-25-louboutin-shoes_N.htm (accessed July 1, 2014).

12. http://www.bloomberg.com/news/2011-04-07/louboutin-sues-yves-saint-laurent-over-red-sole-shoes-trademark-violation.html (accessed July 1, 2014).

13. The term determinance was first coined by James Myers and Mark Alpert nearly three decades ago. http://www.sawtoothsoftware.com/productforms/ssolutions/ss12.shtml (accessed September 4, 2006).

14. 2011 U.S. Organic Industry Overview, Organic Trade Association, http://www.ota.com/pics/documents/2011OrganicIndustrySurvey.pdf (accessed July 1, 2014).

15. Ashby Jones, "Is Your Dinner 'All Natural'?," The Wall Street Journal, September 20, 2011; "Diet and Nutrition Report," Consumer Reports, February 2009, http://www.consumerreports.org/health/healthy-living/diet-nutrition/healthy-foods/grocery-aisle-gotchas/natural/grocery-aisle-gotchas-natural.htm (accessed July 1, 2014).

16. Rachel Gross, "Farmers Seek to Raise Standards for Berries," The New York Times, September 23, 2011, http://www.nytimes.com/2011/09/23/us/farmers-seek-to-raise-standards-for-berries.html?pagewanted5all (accessed July 1, 2014).

17. Stacey R. Finkelstein and Ayelet Fishbach, "When Healthy Food Makes You Hungry," Journal of Consumer Research 37, no. 3 (October 2010) pp. 357–367.

18. Tralee Pearce, "Are Shoppers Being Duped by the 'Health Halo Effect'?," The Globe and Mail, April 2, 2013, P. B4.

19. http://www.sawtoothsoftware.com/productforms/ssolutions/ss12.shtml (accessed September 4, 2006).

20. Jim Oliver, "Finding Decision Rules with Genetic Algorithms," http://www.umsanet.edu.bo/docentes/gchoque/MAT420L07.htm (accessed June 2004).

21. Emili Vesilind, "MAC Cosmetics Launches Technology That Lets You e-shop with Your Friends," LATimes.com, April 27, 2011; Tyna Werner, "MAC Shop Together—Shopping Buddies Around the World Unite!," weheartthis.com, May 4, 2011; "Shopping with Friends: The Ultimate Shopping Experience, November 8, 2011, http://www.janrain.com/blogs/shopping-friends-ultimate-shopping-experience (accessed July 1, 2014); http://www.decisionstep.com/solutions/social-shopping/shoptogether-friends; maccosmetics.com; http://www.sesh.com; http://www.wetseal.com/content.jsp?pageName5ShopWithFriends; "New Shopping App Lets Facebook Friends Help You Decide," The Realtime Report, November 15, 2011, http://therealtimereport.com/2011/11/15/new-shopping-app-lets-facebook-friends-help-you-decide (accessed July 1, 2014).

22. Paul S. Richardson, Alan S. Dick, and Arun K. Jain, "Extrinsic and Intrinsic Cue Effects on Perceptions of Store Brand Quality," *Journal of Marketing* 58 (October 1994), pp. 28–36; Rajneesh Suri and Kent B. Monroe, "The Effects of Time Constraints on Consumers' Judgments of Prices and Products," *Journal of Consumer Research* 30 (June 2003), pp. 92–104.

23. Merrie Brucks, Valerie A. Zeithaml, and Gillian Naylor, "Price and Brand Name as Indicators of Quality Dimensions for Consumer Durables," *Journal of the Academy of Marketing Science* 28, no. 3 (2000), pp. 359–374; Niraj Dawar and Philip Parker, "Marketing Universals: Consumers' Use of Brand Name, Price, Physical Appearance, and Retailer Reputation as Signals of Product Quality," *Journal of Marketing* 58 (April 1994), pp. 81–95; William B. Dodds, Kent B. Monroe, and Dhruv Grewal, "Effects of Price, Brand, and Store Information on Buyers' Product Evaluations," *Journal of Marketing Research* 28 (August 1991), pp. 307–319.

24. Mary Jo Bitner, "Servicescapes: The Impact of Physical Surroundings on Customers and Employees," *Journal of Marketing* 56 (April 1992), pp. 57–71; Dhruv Grewal and Julie Baker, "Do Retail Store Environmental Factors Affect Consumers' Price Acceptability? An Empirical Examination," *International Journal of Research in Marketing* 11 (1994), pp. 107–115; Eric R. Spangenberg, Ayn E. Crowley, and Pamela W. Henderson, "Improving the Store Environment: Do Olfactory Cues Affect Evaluations and Behaviors?" *Journal of Marketing* 60 (April 1996), pp. 67–80; Kirk L. Wakefield and Jeffrey G. Blodgett, "Customer Response to Intangible and Tangible Service Factors," *Psychology and Marketing* 16 (January 1999), pp. 51–68.

25. Ruby Roy Dholakia and Miao Zhao, "Retail Web Site Interactivity: How Does It Influence Customer Satisfaction and Behavioral Intentions? *International Journal of Retail & Distribution Management*, 37, 2009, pp. 821–838.

26. Claire Cain Miller, "Closing the Deal at the Virtual Checkout Counter," *The New York Times*, October 12, 2009 (accessed December 13, 2009).

27. Ruby Roy Dholakia and Miao Zhao, "Retail Web Site Interactivity: How Does It Influence Customer Satisfaction and Behavioral Intentions?" *International Journal of Retail & Distribution Management* 37 (2009), pp. 821–838.

28. Youngme Moon and John A. Quelch, "Starbucks: Delivering Customer Service," *Harvard Business Review* (July 31, 2003).

29. A.H. Maslow, *Motivation and Personality* (New York: Harper & Row, 1970).

30. "About Us," Cole + Parker, http://coleandparker.co/about (accessed April 10, 2014).

31. "About Us," Kiva, http://www.kiva.org/about (accessed April 10, 2014).

32. Telephone Interview with Diana House, Friday April 11, 2014.

33. Michael Levy and Barton A. Weitz, *Retailing Management*, 6th ed. (Burr Ridge IL: Irwin/McGraw-Hill, 2007), Chapter 4.

34. "2005 YTV Tween Report, Solutions Research Group, A Corus Entertainment Inc. Company," http://www.corusmedia.com/ytv/research/index.asp (accessed June 14, 2013).

35. Sandra Yin, "Kids; Hot Spots," *American Demographics* (December 1, 2003); Peter Francese, "Trend Ticker: Trouble in Store," *American Demographics* (December 1, 2003).

36. "Canada's Organic Market National Highlights 2013," Canada's Organic Trade Association, http://www.ota.com/pics/media_photos.171.img_filename.pdf (accessed April 11, 2014).

37. A. Kristallis and G. Chryssohoidis, "Consumers' Willingness to Pay for Organic Food: Factors That Affect It and Variation per Organic Product Type." *British Food Journal* 107, no. 5 (2005), pp. 320–343.

38. "Canada's Organic Market National Highlights 2013," Canada's Organic Trade Association, http://www.ota.com/pics/media_photos.171.img_filename.pdf (accessed July 1, 2014).

39. L. Zepeda and J. Li, "Characteristics of Organic Food Shoppers." *Journal of Agricultural and Applied Economics* 39, no. 1 (2007), pp. 17–28.

40. "Survey Reveals Teen Spending Habits, Retail Brand Perceptions," http://money.cnn.com/news/newsfeeds/articles/newstex/VNU-0016-16243010.htm (accessed May 20, 2007).

41. Rebecca Harris, "Skin Deep, Canada's Big Banks Have Taken Great Strides to Reach Newcomers to the Country. But, They Need to Look Beneath the Surface to Truly Connect to Multicultural Consumers," *Marketing Magazine* January 29, 2007.

42. Jonathan Paul, "Brita's First Ethnic Program Turns Red to Green," *Strategy Magazine*, March 13, 2012. http://strategyonline.ca/2012/03/13/britas-first-ethnic-program-turned-red-into-green (accessed Jun 12, 2013).

43. The concept of atmospherics was introduced by Philip Kotler, "Atmosphere as a Marketing Tool," *Journal of Retailing* 49 (Winter 1973), pp. 48–64.

44. Anna S. Mattila and Jochen Wirtz, "Congruency of Scent and Music as a Driver of In-Store Evaluations and Behavior," *Journal of Retailing* 77, no. 2 (Summer 2001), pp. 273–289; Teresa A. Summers and Paulette R. Hebert, "Shedding Some Light on Store Atmospherics; Influence of Illumination on Consumer Behavior," *Journal of Business Research* 54, no. 2 (November 2001), pp. 145–150; for a review of this research, see Joseph A. Bellizzi and Robert E. Hite, "Environmental Color, Consumer Feelings, and Purchase Likelihood," *Psychology and Marketing* 9, no. 5 (September–October 1992), pp. 347–363; J. Duncan Herrington and Louis Capella, "Effects of Music in Service Environments: A Field Study," *Journal of Services Marketing* 10, no. 2 (1996), pp. 26–41; Richard F. Yalch and Eric R. Spangenberg, "The Effects of Music in a Retail Setting on Real and Perceived Shopping Times," *Journal of Business Research* 49, no. 2 (August 2000), pp. 139–148; Michael Hui, Laurette Dube, and Jean-Charles Chebat, "The Impact of Music on Consumer's Reactions to Waiting for Services," *Journal of Retailing* 73, no. 1 (1997), pp. 87–104; and Julie Baker, Dhruv Grewal, and Michael Levy, "An Experimental Approach to Making Retail Store Environmental Decisions," *Journal of Retailing* 68 (Winter 1992), pp. 445–460; Maxine Wilkie, "Scent of a Market," *American Demographics* (August 1995), pp. 40–49; Spangenberg, Crowley, Henderson, "Improving the Store Environment"; Paula Fitzgerald Bone and Pam Scholder Ellen, "Scents in the Marketplace: Explaining a Fraction of Olfaction," *Journal of Retailing* 75, no. 2 (Summer 1999), pp. 243–263.

45. Abercrombie and Fitch, http://en.wikipedia.org/wiki/Abercrombie_&_Fitch (accessed May 20, 2007).

46. Julie Baker et al., "Wait Expectations, Store Atmosphere and Store Patronage Intentions," *Journal of Retailing* 79, no. 4 (2003), pp. 259–268.

47. Jagdish Sheth, Banwari Mittal, and Bruce I. Newman, *Customer Behavior: Consumer Behavior and Beyond* (Fort Worth, TX: The Dryden Press, 1999); J. Paul Peter and Jerry C. Olson, *Consumer Behavior and Marketing Strategy* (McGraw-Hill/Irwin, 2007); Michael R. Solomon, *Consumer Behavior: Buying, Having, and Being* (Toronto: Prentice Hall, 2009).

48. Karen M. Stilley, J. Jeffrey Inman, and Kirk L. Wakefield, "Planning to Make Unplanned Purchases? The Role of In-Store Slack in Budget Deviation," *Journal of Consumer Research*, DOI: 10.1086/651567; R. Puri, "Measuring and Modifying Consumer Impulsiveness: A Cost-Benefit Accessibility Framework," *Journal of Consumer Psychology* 5 (1996), pp. 87–113.

49. This case was written by Kate Woodworth in conjunction with Dhruv Grewal and Michael Levy for use in a class discussion; it was not written as an illustration of effective or ineffective marketing practices.

50. Statistics Canada, *Canadian Health Measures Survey 2007–2009*, http://www.statcan.gc.ca/daily-quotidien/110302/dq110302c-eng.htm (accessed July 1, 2014).

51. http://www.statcan.gc.ca (accessed April 25, 2011).

52. Vauhini Vara, "New Gadets Aim to Help Users Watch Their Weight," *The Wall Street Journal Online* May 12, 2005.

53. http://jennycraig.com/programs (accessed April 19, 2010).

54. Jennifer Fermino, "Jenny Craig Is Top Heavy Hitter," *New York Post*, May 10, 2011, http://www.nypost.com/p/news/national/craig_is_top_heavy_hitter_Le5SprctcoGlp93YLL55XJ (accessed July 1, 2014).

55. http://www.slim-fast.com/plan.

56. Maura Shenker, "Men's Slim-Fast Diet Health," Livestrong.com, July 20, 2011, http://www.livestrong.com/article/497109-mens-slim-fast-diet-health.

57. Jennifer LaRue Huget, "Weight Watchers and Jenny Craig Offer Programs for Men Who Want to Shed Pounds," *The Washington Post*, March 25, 2010.

58. http://www.bestdietforme.com/top60dietreviews/SlimFast.htm.

CHAPTER 5

1. This chapter vignette is based on http://www.rbcroyalbank.com and "RBC Procurement" http://www.rbc.com/sourcing (accessed June 17, 2013).

2. Arun Sharma, R. Krishnan, and Dhruv Grewal, "Value Creation in Markets: A Critical Area of Focus for Business-to-Business Markets," *Industrial Marketing Management* 30, no. 4 (2001), pp. 391–402; Ajay K. Kohli and Bernard J. Jaworski, "Market Orientation: The Construct, Research Propositions, and Managerial Implications," *Journal of Marketing* 54, no. 2 (1990), pp. 1–13; John C. Narver and Stanly F. Slater, "The Effect of Market Orientation on Business Profitability," *Journal of Marketing* 54, no. 4 (1990), pp. 20–33.

3. http://www.magna.com (accessed April 24, 2011).

4. Martin Hofmann, Emily-Sue Sloane, and Elena Malykhina, "VW Revs Its B2B Engine," *Optimize*, March 2004, pp. 22–26, http://www.volkswagenag.com/vwag/vwcorp/content/en/brands_and_companies/automotive_and_financial.html.

5. http://www.vwgroupsupply.com/b2bpub/zusammenarbeit/kbp/daten_fakten.html (accessed June 17, 2013).

6. Retail Council of Canada, "Canadian Retailer Media Package 2013," http://www.retailcouncil.org/training/publications/canadianretailer/canadian_retailer_media_kit_2013.pdf (accessed June 17, 2013).

7. Statistics Canada, "Retail and Wholesale Trade, http://www.statcan.gc.ca/pub/11-402-x/2012000/chap/retail-detail/retail-detail-eng.htm (accessed July 1, 2014).

8. http://www.charityvillage.com (accessed June 17, 2013).

9. Based on Naomi Carniol, "Printer Impresses Clients with Eco-changes," http://www.theglobeandmail.com/report-on-business/your-business/business-categories/sustainability/printer-impresses-clients-with-eco-changes/article1525300 (accessed July 1, 2014).

10. Personal Interviews with Hongwei Lui and Stacey Tozer between April and July 2013.

11. http://www.pwgsc.gc.ca (accessed April 24, 2011).

12. https://buyandsell.gc.ca and https://www.merx.com (accessed June 3, 2011).

13. http://www.merx.com (accessed April 24, 2011).

14. "Odyssey Identified as Buyers of 10 Bombardier CSeries Jets," *CBC News* June 17, 2013, http://www.cbc.ca/news/business/story/2013/06/17/business-bombardier-cseries.html (accessed July 1, 2014).

15. "Bombardier Bank," http://www.canadianbusiness.com/article.jsp?content=20040329_59236_59236 (accessed April 24, 2011).

16. http://www.shepherd.ca (accessed May 21, 2007); http://www.shepherd.ca; "RoyNat Capital Entrepreneurial Profile," *Financial Post* May 7, 2007: FP12.

17. www.census.gov/epcd/naics02/SICN02E.HTM#S48; http://www.census.gov/epcd/www/naics.html; http://www.census.gov/epcd/naics02/N2SIC51.HTM.

18. Michael Posner, "ROM Asks Caterers for Preferred-list Fee," *The Globe & Mail*, October 22, 2012, http://www.theglobeandmail.com/news/toronto/torontos-rom-to-ask-caterers-for-preferred-list-fee-of-10000/article4627477 (accessed July 1, 2014).

19. Tilting Pixels on the Web is based on a personal interview between Matt Inglot (CEO of Tilted Pixels) and Shirley Lichti, June 25, 2010.

20. http://www.marketingpower.com/live/mg-dictionary-view435.php. These definitions are provided by http://www.marketing-power.com (the American Marketing Association's website). We have bolded our key terms.

21. Amber Bowerman, *The Economics of Donation*, http://www.avenuecalgary.com/articles/page/item/the-economics-of-donations (accessed April 25, 2011); Value Village, http://www.valuevillage.com/downloads/SaversValueVillagePressKits.pdf (accessed April 25, 2011).

22. Kimberly Maul, "More B-to-B companies Find That Social Media Is an Essential Business Platform," PRweekus.com, June 2009; Ellis Booker, "B-to-B Marketers Apply Analytics to Social Media," *BtoB* April 12, 2010; Elisabeth A. Sullivan, "A Long Slog," *Marketing News* February 28, 2009.

23. http://www.tweetdeck.com (accessed July 20, 2010).

24. Daniel B. Honigman, "Make a Statement," *Marketing News* May 1, 2008.

25. LinkedIn Press Center, "About Us," http://press.linkedin.com/about (accessed June 17, 2013).

26. Heidi Cohen, "5 LinkedIn Business Goals," March 25, 2011, http://heidicohen.com/linkedin-business-goals (accessed July 1, 2014).

27. Maria Tabaka, "How to Launch a LinkedIn Company Page," *Inc.*, April 17, 2011, http://www.inc.com/how-to-launch-a-linkedin-company-page.html (accessed July 1, 2014).

28. Susan Kuchinskas, "Data-based Dell," *Adweek Magazine's Technology Marketing* 23, no. 6 (September 2003), p. 20.

29. Barton A. Weitz, Stephen B. Castleberry, and John F. Tanner, *Selling Building Partnerships*, 5th ed. (Burr Ridge, IL: McGraw-Hill/Irwin, 2003), p. 93.

30. Andy Macaulay, founder and former CEO of zig, a company based in Waterloo, Ontario. Presentation at Wilfrid Laurier University.

31. This case was written by Kate Woodworth in conjunction with Dhruv Grewal and Michael Levy as the basis of class discussion rather than to illustrate either effective or ineffective marketing practices.

32. UPS 2010 Sustainability Report, "Sustainability Is ...," http://www.sustainability.ups.com/Sustainability?WT.mc_id5iPros_UPS-Green_45809923&WT.srch51&gclid5CJzOrZuy16wCFQ1x5QodszUEpw.

33. http://www.ups.com/content/corp/companies/index.html#Customer1Solutions.

34. "UPS Canada Fact Sheet," http://www.ups.com/content/ca/en/about/facts/canada.html (accessed July 1, 2014).

35. Laura K. Cowan, "Brown Goes Green: UPS Purchases 100 EV Delivery Trucks for Its Next-Gen California Fleet," *inhabitat*, August 30, 2011, http://inhabitat.com/brown-goes-green-ups-purchases-100-ev-delivery-trucks-for-its-next-gen-california-fleet.

36. National Biodiesel Board, "UPS Goes Green with Biodiesel Switch," June 6, 2011, http://westernfarmpress.com/management/ups-goes-green-biodiesel-switch (accessed July 1, 2014).

37. UPS, http://www.community.ups.com/Environment/Innovative1Fleets1and1Facilities.

38. Thomas Friedman agrees with this assessment in his best-selling book *The World Is Flat* (New York: Farrar, Straus and Giroux, 2006), in which he cites UPS's supply chain as a prime example of a global "flattener."

39. The Conference Board of Canada, "The Future of Postal Service in Canada," April 2013, http://www.conferenceboard.ca/temp/f2529c05-073a-42fa-a94d-46bbffbb7ba4/13-290_postalservice.pdf (accessed June 18, 2013).

40. FedEx, "About FedEx?" http://about.van.fedex.com/fedex_corporation (accessed July 1, 2014).

41. "Is Insourcing the New In Thing?" June 9, 2008, http://www.geekpreneur.com/is-insourcing-the-new-in-thing (accessed July 1, 2014).

42. Kate O'Brien, "UPS Canada releases BlackBerry and Android app," November 29, 2010, http://mobilesyrup.com/2010/11/29/ups-canada-releases-blackberry-and-android-app (accessed July 1, 2014).

CHAPTER 6

1. "Heritage," http://www.thecocacolacompany.com/heritage/chronicle_birth_refreshing_idea.html (accessed June 5, 2010).

2. Coca-Cola Company, "FAQs," http://www.coca-colacompany.com/contact-us/faqs (accessed July 1, 2014).

3. Betsy McKay, "Zero Is Coke's New Hero," *The Wall Street Journal* April 17, 2007 (accessed January 14, 2008).

4. "The Chronicle of Coca-Cola," http://www.thecocacolacompany.com/heritage/chronicle_global_business.html (accessed June 5, 2010).

5. Kate Fitzgerald, "Coke Zero," *Advertising Age*, November 12, 2007 (accessed January 14, 2008).

6. "Brands," http://www.thecocacolacompany.com/brands/index.html (accessed June 5, 2010).

7. Kate MacArthur, "Coke Bets on Zero to Save a Cola Category." *Advertising Age*, January 1, 2007 (accessed January 14, 2008).

8. This Sustainable Marketing box was written with information gathered in a telephone interview with Joanne Secord of PaperNuts on Tuesday June 18, 2013.

9. Packaging Association of Canada, International Sustainable Packaging Executive to Lead PAC NEXT, September 23, 2012, http://sustainability-in-packaging.com/international-sustainable-packaging-executive-to-lead-pac-next.aspx (accessed July 1 2014).

10. Susan Krashinsky, "Oz Casts Its Spell on Canada's Millennials," *The Globe and Mail*, April 12, 2013, p. B5.

11. Susan Krashinsky, "Stalking the Elusive Millennial Male," *The Globe and Mail*, July 20, 2012, p. B5.

12. Melanie Shortman, "Gender Wars," *American Demographics* (April 2002), p. 22.

13. Sheth, Mittal, and Newman, *Customer Behavior*.

14. Tamara Mangleburg et al., "The Moderating Effect of Prior Experience in Consumers' Use of User-Image Based versus Utilitarian Cues in Brand Attitude," *Journal of Business & Psychology* 13 (Fall 1998), pp. 101–113; M. Joseph Sirgy et al., "Direct versus Indirect Measures of Self-Image Congruence," *Journal of the Academy of Marketing Science* 25, no. 3 (1997), pp. 229–241.

15. Sheth, Mittal, and Newman, *Customer Behavior*.

16. James M. Hagerty, "Harley, with Macho Intact, Tries to Court More Women," *The Wall Street Journal*, October 31, 2011, http://online.wsj.com/article/SB1000142405297020450530457665 5244217556816.html#articleTabs%3Darticle (accessed July 1, 2014); Harley-Davidson, "Global Customer Focus," http://investor.harley-davidson.com/phoenix.zhtml?c587981&p5irol-demographics.

17. VALS1, the original lifestyle survey, assessed general values and lifestyles. The VALS survey focuses more on values and lifestyles related to consumer behaviour and thus has more commercial applications. Another lifestyle segmentation system is Yankelovich's Monitor Mindbase (yankelovich.com).

18. http://www.strategicbusinessinsights.com/vals/applications/apps-pos.shtml (accessed June 6, 2010).

19. Michael D. Lam, "Psychographic Demonstration: Segmentation Studies Prepare to Prove Their Worth," *Pharmaceutical Executive*, January 2004.

20. Kathleen Krhialla, "CRM Case Study: The Analytics That Power CRM at Royal Bank [of Canada]," http://www.teradata.com/library/pdf/towergroup_020701.pdf (accessed June 6, 2010).

21. John Melloy, "Heinz Facebook Gaffe: 'Where's My Balsamic Ketchup?,'" *Fast Money*, November 14, 2011, http://www.cnbc.com/id/45293583/Heinz_Facebook_Gaffe_Where_s_My_Balsamic_Ketchup (accessed July 1, 2014); Andrew Adam Newman, "Ketchup Moves Upmarket, with a Balsamic Tinge," *The New York Times*, October 25, 2011, http://www.nytimes.com/2011/10/26/business/media/ketchup-moves-upmarket-with-a-balsamic-tinge.html?_r52&ref5consumerbehavior (accessed July 1, 2014); Brian Steinberg, "Recognition Factor," *Boston Globe*, March 25, 2009; Mary H.J. Farrell, "New Heinz Balsamic Ketchup Available Only on Facebook," *Consumer Reports*, November 16, 2011, http://news.consumerreports.org/home/2011/11/new-heinz-balsamic-ketchup-available-only-on-facebook.html (accessed July 1, 2014).

22. Stowe Shoemaker and Robert Lewis, "Customer Loyalty: The Future of Hospitality Marketing," *Hospitality Management* 18 (1999), p. 349.

23. V. Kumar and Denish Shah, "Building and Sustaining Profitable Customer Loyalty for the 21st Century," *Journal of Retailing* 80, no. 4 (2004), pp. 317–330.

24. Rebecca Harris, "Canadians Love Loyalty," *Marketing Daily* May 31, 2007.

25. Aricanada.com (accessed June 1, 2007).

26. Michael J. Weiss, *The Clustered World* (Boston: Little, Brown, 2000).

27. PSYTE Advantage, http://www.tetrad.com/pricing/can/psyteadvantage.html (accessed June 1, 2007).

28. http://www.tetrad.com/demographics/canada/environics/prizmce.html (accessed June 1, 2007).

29. Pete Jacques, "Aspirational Segmentation," *LIMRA's MarketFacts Quarterly* 22 (Spring 2003), p. 2[0].

30. G.R. Iyer et al., "Linking Web-based Segmentation to Pricing Tactics," *Journal of Product & Brand Management* 11, no. 5 (2002), pp. 288–302; B. Jaworski and K. Jocz, "Rediscovering the Consumer," *Marketing Management* (September/October 2002), pp. 22–27; L. Rosencrance, "Customers Balk at Variable DVD Pricing," *Computer World* September 11, 2000: 4; M. Stephanek, "None of Your Business: Customer Data Were Once Gold to E-Commerce. Now, Companies are Paying a Price for Privacy Jitters," *BusinessWeek* June 26, 2000: 78; D. Wessel, "How Technology Tailors Price Tags," *The Wall Street Journal* June 23, 2001: A1.

31. http://www.aa.com/content/AAdvantage/programDetails/eliteStatus/main.jhtml (accessed March 3, 2005).

32. http://www.microsoft.com/info/cookies.htm (accessed September 30, 2005).

33. Pete Jacques, "Aspirational Segmentation," *LIMRA's MarketFacts Quarterly* 22 (Spring 2003), p. 2.

34. http://www.lasenza.com (accessed December 18, 2007).

35. Dhruv Grewal, "Marketing Is All about Creating Value: 8 Key Rules," in *Inside the Mind of Textbook Marketing* (Boston: Aspatore Inc., 2003), 79–96.

36. James L. Heskett, W. Earl Sasser Jr., and Leonard A. Schlesinger, *The Service Profit Chain: How Leading Companies Link Profit and Growth to Loyalty, Satisfaction, and Value* (New York: Simon & Schuster Adult Publishing Group, 1997); Christopher D. Ittner and David F. Larcker, "Are Nonfinancial Measures Leading Indicators of Financial Performance? An Analysis of Customer Satisfaction," *Journal of Accounting Research* 35 (Supplement 1998), pp. 1–35; Thomas O. Jones and E. Earl Sasser Jr., "Why Satisfied Customers Defect," *Harvard Business Review* (November/December 1995), pp. 88–99; A. Parasuraman and Dhruv Grewal, "The Impact of Technology on the Quality-Value-Loyalty Chain: A Research Agenda," *Journal of the Academy of Marketing Science* 28, no. 1 (2000), pp. 168–174; Frederick F. Reichheld, "Loyalty-based Management," *Harvard Business Review* 2 (March/April 1993), pp. 64–73; Frederick F. Reichheld, "Loyalty and the Renaissance of Marketing," *Marketing Management* 2, no. 4 (1994), pp. 10–21; Frederick F. Reichheld and Phil Schefter, "E-Loyalty," *Harvard Business Review* (July/August 2000), pp. 105–113; Anthony J. Rucci, Richard T. Quinn, and Steven P. Kirn, "The Employee-Customer-Profit Chain at Sears," *Harvard Business Review* (January/February 1998), pp. 83–97; Roland T. Rust, Valarie Zeithaml, and Katherine N. Lemon, *Driving Customer Equity* (New York: The Free Press, 2000); Russell S. Winer, "A Framework for Customer Relationship Management," *California Management Review* 43, no. 4 (2001), pp. 89–105; Valarie Zeithaml, Roland T. Rust, and Katherine N. Lemon, "The Customer Pyramid: Creating and Serving Profitable Customers," *California Management Review* 43, no. 4 (2001), pp. 118–142.

37. lasenza.com (accessed December 18, 2007).

38. Marie Driscoll, "Abercrombie & Fitch: Power Shopper," *Standard & Poor's Equity Research*, October 30, 2007 (accessed January 16, 2008).

39. Nicholas Kohler, "Abercrombie & Fitch: Come Shop in Our Dungeon," *Maclean's* (November 13, 2006) (accessed June 6, 2010).

40. B. Joseph Pine, *Mass Customization: The New Frontier in Business Competition* (Cambridge, MA: Harvard Business School Publishing, 1999); James H. Gilmore and B. Joseph Pine, eds., *Markets of One: Creating Customer-Unique Value through Mass Customization* (Cambridge, MA: Harvard Business School Publishing, 2000).

41. Kristin Laird, "High Wired Retail," *Marketing Magazine*, February 25, 2013, p. 14.

42. "The Founder," http://www.chezcora.com/a/01-belle-histoire/1-3-fondatrice2.htm (accessed June 7, 2010).

43. Sabritir Ghosh, "Made to Order," *Report on [Small] Business* (September 2009), http://www.theglobeandmail.com/report-on-business/your-business/start/franchising/made-to-order/article1265158 (accessed July 1, 2014).

44. "The Founder," http://www.chezcora.com/a/01-belle-histoire/1-3-fondatrice2.htm (accessed June 7, 2010).

45. C. Page Moreau, Leff Bonney, and Kelly B Herd, "It's the Thought (and the Effort) That Counts: How Customizing for Others Differs from Customizing for Oneself," *Journal of Marketing* 75, no. 5 (September 2011), pp. 120–133.

46. Vanessa O'Connell, "Fashion Journal: Bubble Gum at Bergdorf's," *The Wall Street Journal* February 15, 2007 (accessed January 15, 2008).

47. Vanessa O'Connell, "Fashion Bullies Attack—in Middle School." *The Wall Street Journal* October 25, 2007 (accessed January 15, 2008).

48. "Frequently Asked Questions," http://www.gatorade.com/frequently_asked_questions/default.aspx (accessed July 1, 2014).

49. "7UP," http://www.drpeppersnapplegroup.com/brands/7up (accessed July 1, 2014).

50. Allen Adamson, "Pitch Your Luxury Offering as an 'Investment Brand,'" *Forbes*, May 4, 2010, http://www.forbes.com/2010/05/04/luxury-branding-platinum-brands-bmw-hermes-investment-branding-cmo-network-allen-adamson.html.

51. Jean Halliday, "Maloney Wants Volvo Viewed as Both Safe and Luxurious," *Advertising Age* 75, no. 12 (2004), p. 22.

52. "Our Story," http://www.lolewomen.com/ca/en/story; "About La Senza," http://www.lasenza.ca/about-lasenza, and "About Us," http://www.abercrombie.ca (accessed July 3, 2014).

53. "Avis: We Try Harder," http://www.buildingbrands.com/didyouknow/16_avis_we_try_harder.php (accessed December 18, 2007).

54. "McDonald's Legal Cases," http://en.wikipedia.org/wiki/McDonald's_legal_cases (accessed December 18, 2007).

55. Crane et al., *Marketing* (6th Can. ed.) (Whitby, ON: McGraw-Hill Ryerson, 2006), p. 243.

56. Carly Lewis, "The Source Continues Brand Repositioning with On the Go," *Marketing Magazine*, March 12, 2013. http://www.marketingmag.ca/news/marketer-news/the-source-continues-brand-repositioning-with-on-the-go-74015 (accessed July 1, 2014).

57. Stephen Brown, Robert V. Kozinets, and John F. Sherry Jr., "Teaching Old Brands New Tricks: Retro Branding and the Revival of Brand Meaning," *Journal of Marketing* 67, no. 2 (July 2003), p. 19.

58. Jane Levere, "Ivory Soap Refreshes Its Ads and Its Look, But Is Resolutely Simple," *The New York Times*, November 7, 2011.

59. This case was written by Shirley Lichti, the textbook co-author, for the basis of class discussion; it was not written as an illustration of effective or ineffective marketing practices.

60. Tobi Cohen, "Canada Census 2011: Immigrants and Newcomers Drive Population Growth," *The National Post*, http://news.nationalpost.com/2012/02/08/canada-census-2011-immigrants-and-newcomers-drive-population-growth (accessed July 1, 2014).

61. Matt Semansky, "M&M Goes Downtown with Uptown," http://www.marketingmag.ca/daily/20071017/topstory.html (accessed October 16, 2007).

CHAPTER 7

1. In-Store Marketing Institute, "Shaping Retail: The Use of Virtual Store Simulations in Marketing Research and Beyond," http://kelley.iu.edu/cerr/files/09ismi_virtualretailing.pdf, p. 3.

2. Alliston Ackerman, "P&G Shapes the Store," *Consumer Goods Technology*, November 16, 2011, http://consumergoods.edgl.com/case-studies/P-G-Shapes-the-Store75556.

3. Accenture, "Accenture and Procter & Gamble Partner in Delivering Virtual Solutions BPO Services." http://www.accenture.com/SiteCollectionDocuments/PDF/Accenture_CGS_PG_Virtual_Solutions.pdf.

4. Michael Letchford, "Pioneering Virtual Stores with Procter and Gamble," *Insights in Retail*, http://www.insightsinretail.com/virtual-stores/pioneering-virtual-stores-with-procter-and-gamble (accessed July 2, 2014).

5. Michael Letchford, "Virtual Shelf–Next Generation Visual Merchandising?" *Insights in Retail*, http://www.insightsinretail.com/visual-merchandising-virtual-shelf/virtual-shelf-a-new-generation-of-visual-merchandising.

6. A. Parasuraman, Dhruv Grewal, and R. Krishnan, *Marketing Research* (Boston: Houghton Mifflin, 2004), p. 9.

7. Holly Bailey, "Where the Voters Are," *Newsweek* 143, no. 13 (March 29, 2004), p. 67.

8. Erhard K. Valentin, "Commentary: Marketing Research Pitfalls in Product Development," *Journal of Product & Brand Management* 3, no. 4–6 (1994), pp. 66–69.

9. Detailed illustrations of scales are provided in two books: Gordon C. Bruner, *Marketing Scales Handbook, Volume V: A Compilation of Multi-Item Measures* (Carbondale, IL: GCBII Productions, 2009); William O. Bearden and Richard G. Netemeyer, *Handbook of Marketing Scales: Multi-Item Measures for Marketing and Consumer Behavior Research* (Thousand Oaks, CA: Sage Publications, 1999). Sources for the scales used in the exhibit are Dhruv Grewal, Gopalkrishnan Iyer, Jerry Gotlieb, and Michael Levy, "Developing a Deeper Understanding of Post-Purchase Perceived Risk and Repeat Purchase Behavioral Intentions in a Service Setting," *Journal of the Academy of Marketing Science* 35, no. 2 (2007), pp. 250–258; Anthony Miyazaki, Dhruv Grewal, and Ronald C. Goodstein, "The Effect of Multiple Extrinsic Cues on Quality Perceptions: A Matter of Consistency," *Journal of Consumer Research* 32 (June 2005), pp. 146–153.

10. This example was based on information taken from Coinstar's website (www.coinstar.com) and a case study about Coinstar, available on the SPSS Inc. website, http://www.spss.com (accessed September 18, 2006).

11. For a more thorough discussion of effective written reports, see Parasuraman, Grewal, and Krishnan, *Marketing Research*, Chapter 16.

12. Thomas Davenport, "Realizing the Potential of Retail Analytics," Babson Executive Education, August 2008; Marc-Andre Kamel, Nick Greenspan, and Rudolf Pritzl, "Standardization Is Efficient but Localization Helps Shops to Stand Out," *The Wall Street Journal*, January 21, 2009, http://online.wsj.com/news/articles/SB123257087731503397.

13. Adapted from Crane, Kerin, Hartley, Berkowitz, and Rudelius, *Marketing*, 6th Canadian ed. (Whitby ON: McGraw-Hill Ryerson, 2007).

14. http://www.legermarketing.com/eng/qui.asp (accessed April 24, 2011).

15. Edward G. Carmines and Richard A. Zeller, *Reliability and Validity Assessment (Quantitative Applications in the Social Sciences)* (London, UK: Sage University Press, 1979).

16. Carmines and Zeller, *Reliability and Validity Assessment*.

17. Virginia Galt, "Embedding Sustainability in Company Culture," http://www.theglobeandmail.com/report-on-business/your-business/business-categories/sustainability/embedding-sustainability-in-company-culture/article1548519 (accessed July 2, 2014).

18. Jennifer Reingold, "Can P&G Make Money in a Place Where People Make Earn $2 Per Day?" *CNN Money*, January 6, 2011, http://features.blogs.fortune.cnn.com/2011/01/06/can-pg-make-money-in-places-where-people-earn-2-a-day (accessed July 2, 2014).

19. Elisabeth A. Sullivan, "Be Sociable," *Marketing News*, January 15, 2008.

20. Harry McCracken, "The Best Blogs of 2011," *Time*, June 6, 2011, http://www.time.com/time/specials/packages/article/0,28804,2075431_2075447_2075479,00.html (accessed July 2, 2014); http://videogum.com.

21. http://www.thetruthaboutcars.com.

22. Andrew Adam Nieman, "Bloggers Don't Follow the Script, to ConAgra's Chagrin," *The New York Times*, September 6, 2011, http://www.nytimes.com/2011/09/07/business/media/when-bloggers-dont-follow-the-script-to-conagras-chagrin.html (accessed July 2, 2014).

23. "History: The Science of Shopping," http://www.envirosell.com/index.php?option5com_content&task5view&id540&Itemid545.

24. Michael P. Cook and Hy Mariampolski, "How Culture Helps Marketers Understand Sensory Experiences," *Quirk's Marketing Research Review*, November 2009, p. 26.

25. "Client Story: Kraft," http://www.communispace.com/assets/pdf/C_Cli_casestudy_kraft_final.pdf.

26. Sarah Needleman, "For Companies, a Tweet in Time Can Avert PR Mess," *The Wall Street Journal*, August 3, 2009.

27. Adapted from Kieran Griffiths, "Social Media in Research: Pros and Cons," May 17, 2012, http://www.intersperience.com/blog/post/05/2012/Social-Media-in-Research--Pros-and-Cons (accessed July 2, 2014), Mike Moran, "Will Social Media Listening Replace Market Research," April 4, 2011, http://www.biznology.com/2011/04/will_social_media_listening_re (accessed July 2, 2014).

28. Rachael King, "Sentiment Analysis Gives Companies Insight Into Consumer Opinion," *Bloomberg BusinessWeek*, March 1, 2011, http://www.businessweek.com/technology/content/feb2011/tc20110228_366762.htm

29. "My Starbucks Idea," https://Twitter.com/MyStarbucksIdea (accessed April 15, 2014).

30. Sheila Shayon, "My Starbucks Idea Turns 5, Sparking a Latte Innovations," April 1, 2013, http://www.brandchannel.com/home/post/2013/04/01/My-Starbucks-Idea-Turns-5-040113.aspx (accessed July 2, 2014).

31. http://mystarbucksidea.force.com/apex/ideaList?lsi=2 (accessed July 2, 2014).

32. "Campbell's Select Harvest Soups Top 2009 IRI New Product Pacesetters List: Second Time in Three Years That Campbell's Soups Top List," *MarketWatch*, March 23, 2010, http://www.marketwatch.com/story/campbells-select-harvest-soups-top-2009-iri-new-product-pacesetters-list-2010-03-23?reflink5MW_news_stmp.

33. http://www.campbellsoup.com/select.aspx.

34. http://www.e-focusgroups.com/online.html.

35. Allison Fass, "Collective Opinion," Forbes.com November 11, 2005, http://www.forbes.com/forbes/2005/1128/076.html (accessed July 9, 2011).

36. Adapted from A. Parasuraman, D. Grewal, and R. Krishnan, *Marketing Research* (Boston: Houghton Mifflin, 2004), p. 64.

37. Dan Ralph, "Canadian Families Shunning Hockey, Survey Finds," *The Globe and Mail*, August 2, 2013, p. S4.

38. Adapted from A. Parasuraman, Dhruv Grewal, and R. Krishnan, *Marketing Research*, 2nd ed. (Boston, MA: Houghton Mifflin, 2007), Ch. 10.

39. Stanley E. Griffis, Thomas J. Goldsby, and Martha Cooper, "Web-based and Mail Surveys: A Comparison of Response, Data and Cost," *Journal of Business Logistics* 24, no. 2 (2003), pp. 237–259; Chris Gautreau, "Getting the Answers," *The Greater Baton Rouge Business Report* 22, no. 29 (September 28, 2004), p. 17; Alf Nucifora, "Weaving Web Surveys That Work," *njbiz* 15, no. 46 (November 11, 2002), p. 28.

40. Chris Powell, "Shaw Establishes New Online Research Tool the Viewers Lounge," *Marketing Magazine*, February 12, 2014, http://www.marketingmag.ca/news/media-news/shaw-establishes-new-online-research-tool-the-viewers-lounge-100742 (accessed July 2, 2014).

41. https://pulse.asda.com (accessed April 15, 2010); Joel Warady, "Asda Takes the 'Pulse of the Nation,'" *Retail Wire* (July 16, 2009).

42. "Canadian Privacy Legislation," http://www.media-awareness.ca/english/issues/privacy/canadian_legislation_privacy.cfm (accessed June 1, 2007).

43. Natasha Singer, "Face Recognition Makes the Leap from Sci-Fi," *The New York Times*, November 12, 2011.

44. Adam Penenberg, "NeuroFocus Uses Neuromarketing to Hack Your Brain," *Fast Company*, August 8, 2011, http://www.fastcompany.com/magazine/158/neuromarketing-intel-paypal.

45. This case was written by Priya Persaud in conjunction with the textbook authors (Ajax Persaud and Shirley Lichti) for use in a class discussion; it was not written as an illustration of effective or

ineffective marketing practices. Priya Persaud is a student research assistant on this book. This case was prepared on April 20, 2011.

46. http://www.shoelessjoes.com (accessed August 6, 2010).

47. ibid.

48. "Shoeless Joe's Gains Access to Real-time Customer Data," *Direct Marketing* (September 2009), http://www.dmn.ca (accessed August 6, 2010).

49. "Shoeless Joe's Gains Access."

APPENDIX 7A

1. V. Kumar, A. Petersen, and R.P. Leone, "How Valuable Is the Word of Mouth?" *Harvard Business Review* (October 2007), pp. 139–146; V. Kumar and Morris George, "Measuring and Maximizing Customer Equity: A Critical Analysis," *Journal of the Academy of Marketing Science* 35, no. 2 (June 2007), pp. 157–171; V. Kumar, Denish Shah, and Rajkumar Venkatesan, "Managing Retailer Profitability: One Customer at a Time!" *Journal of Retailing* 82, no. 4 (October 2006), pp. 277–294; V. Kumar, "Profitable Relationships," *Marketing Research: A Magazine of Management and Applications* 18, no. 3 (Fall 2006), pp. 41–46; V. Kumar, "Customer Lifetime Value: A Databased Approach," *Journal of Relationship Marketing* 5, no. 2/3 (2006), pp. 7–35; Sunil Gupta et al., "Modeling Customer Lifetime Value," *Journal of Service Research* 9 (November 2006), pp. 139–155; V. Kumar, R. Venkatesan, and Werner Reinartz, "Knowing What to Sell, When and to Whom," *Harvard Business Review* (March 2006), pp. 131–137; Werner Reinartz, J. Thomas, and V. Kumar, "Balancing Acquisition and Retention Resources to Maximize Profitability," *Journal of Marketing* 69 (January 2005), pp. 63–79; R. Venkatesan and V. Kumar, "A Customer Lifetime Value Framework for Customer Selection and Resource Allocation Strategy," *Journal of Marketing* 68 (October 2004), pp. 106–125; V. Kumar and J. Andrew Petersen, "Maximizing ROI or Profitability: Is One Better Than the Other," *Marketing Research: A Magazine of Management and Applications* 16, no. 3 (Fall 2004), pp. 28–34; V. Kumar, G. Ramani, and T. Bohling, "Customer Lifetime Value Approaches and Best Practice Applications," *Journal of Interactive Marketing* 18, no. 3 (Summer 2004), pp. 60–72; J. Thomas, Werner Reinartz, and V. Kumar, "Getting the Most out of All Your Customers," *Harvard Business Review* (July–August 2004), pp. 116–123; Werner Reinartz and V. Kumar, "The Impact of Customer Relationship Characteristics on Profitable Lifetime Duration," *Journal of Marketing* 67 (January 2003), pp. 77–99; Werner Reinartz and V. Kumar, "The Mismanagement of Customer Loyalty," *Harvard Business Review* (July 2002), pp. 86–97; W. Reinartz and V. Kumar, "On the Profitability of Long Lifetime Customers: An Empirical Investigation and Implications for Marketing," *Journal of Marketing* 64 (October 2000), pp. 17–32.

2. We have made some minor adjustments to the formula suggested by Gupta et al., "Modeling Customer Lifetime Value."

3. Sunil Gupta and Donald R. Lehmann, *Managing Customers as Investments* (Philadelphia, PA: Wharton School Publishing, 2005); Gupta et al., "Modeling Customer Lifetime Value."

CHAPTER 8

1. "LEGO History Timeline," http://aboutus.lego.com/en-us/lego-group/the_lego_history (accessed July 2, 2013).

2. "MyLegoNetwork," http://mln.lego.com/en-us/network/status.aspx?icmp5COUSCreateShareSL100MLN (accessed July 2, 2013).

3. Brad Wieners, "Lego Is for Girls," *BusinessWeek*, December 14, 2011.

4. Shari Roan, "A New Lego Line for Girls Is Offensive, Critics Say," *Los Angeles Times*, January 23, 2012, http://www.latimes.com/health/boostershots/la-heb-lego-girls-toy-protest-20120123,0,141471.story (accessed July 2, 2014).

5. "Lego Friends," http://friends.lego.com/en-us/Products/Default.aspx (accessed July 2, 2014).

6. Carrie Goldman, "Legos for Girls: Let's Focus the Discussion on the Right Issues," *Portrait of an Adoption*, January 30, 2012, http://www.chicagonow.com/portrait-of-an-adoption/2012/01/legos-for-girls-lets-focus-the-discussion-on-the-right-issues Ruth Davis Konigsberg, "Lego Friends for Girls: Have They Stooped to Stereotype?" *Time Magazine*, January 2, 2012, http://ideas.time.com/2012/01/02/lego-friends-for-girls-have-they-stooped-to-stereotype; "Whether Pink Legos Are Just Building Stereotypes," *NPR*, January 24, 2012, http://www.npr.org/templates/story/story.php?storyId5145705192.

7. Scott Stinson and Hollie Shaw, "Gender Games," *National Post*, January 21, 2012, http://www.nationalpost.com/arts/books/Gender1games/6030953/story.html.

8. "Thinking outside the Cardboard Box," http://metronews.ca/news/165605/thinking-outside-the-cardboard-box (accessed July 4, 2014).

9. "Doing the Right Thing," http://www.frogbox.com/therightthing.php (accessed June 10, 2010).

10. http://www.dove.com.

11. Koen Pauwels et al., "New Products, Sales Promotions, and Firm Value: The Case of the Automobile Industry," *Journal of Marketing* 68, no. 4 (October 2004), p. 142.

12. Keith O'Brien, "Should We All Go Gluten-Free?" *The New York Times*, November 25, 2011, http://www.nytimes.com/2011/11/27/magazine/Should-We-All-Go-Gluten-Free.html?pagewanted5all (accessed July 2, 2014).

13. Kalpesh Kaushik Desai and Kevin Lane Keller, "The Effects of Ingredient Branding Strategies on Host Brand Extendibility," *Journal of Marketing* 66, no. 1 (January 2002), pp. 73–93.

14. Don Reisinger, "Madden Sales Up 10 Percent Over Last Year," *cnet.com*, September 8, 2011, http://news.cnet.com/8301-13506_3-20103229-17/madden-sales-up-10-percent-over-last-year.

15. IDEO, "Safeway Supply Chain Innovation for Kraft Foods," http://www.ideo.com/work/safeway-supply-chain-innovation-for-kraft (accessed July 2, 2014).

16. Rajesh K. Chandy, Jaideep C. Prabhu, and Kersi D. Antia, "What Will the Future Bring? Dominance, Technology Expectations, and Radical Innovation," *Journal of Marketing* 67, no. 3 (July 2003), pp. 1–18; Harald J. van Heerde, Carl F. Mela, and Puneet Manchanda, "The Dynamic Effect of Innovation on Market Structure," *Journal of Marketing Research* 41, no. 2 (May 2004), pp. 166–183.

17. http://www.apple.com; Clayton M. Christensen and Michael E. Raynor, *The Innovator's Solution* (Boston: Harvard Business School Press, 2003).

18. Philip Kotler, *Marketing Management*, 11th ed. (Upper Saddle River, NJ: Prentice-Hall, 2003), pp. 330–331. Kotler's work was based on the following research: William T. Robinson and Claes Fornell, "Sources of Market Pioneer Advantages in Consumer Goods Industries," *Journal of Marketing Research* 22, no. 3 (August 1985), pp. 305–317; Glen L. Urban et al., "Market Share Rewards to Pioneering Brands: An Empirical Analysis and Strategic Implications," *Management Science* 32 (June 1986), pp. 645–659; and G.S. Carpenter and Kent Nakamoto, "Consumer Preference Formation and Pioneering Advantage," *Journal of Marketing Research* 26, no. 3 (August 1989), pp. 285–298.

19. Raji Srinivasan, Gary L. Lilien, and Arvind Rangaswamy, "First in, First out? The Effects of Network Externalities on Pioneer Survival," *Journal of Marketing* 68, no. 1 (January 2004), p. 41.

20. Cyndee Miller, "Little Relief Seen for New Product Failure Rate," *Marketing News* June 21, 1993: 1, 10; "Flops," *BusinessWeek* (August 16, 1993), p. 76ff; Lori Dahm, "Secrets of Success: The Strategies Driving New Product Development at Kraft," *Stagnito's New Products Magazine* 2 (January 2002), p. 18ff.

21. http://www.marketingpower.com (accessed September 18, 2006).

22. www.appleinsider.com/articles/04/11/29/ipod_adoption_rate_faster_than_sony_walkman.html (accessed July 2, 2014).

23. Eliot Van Buskirk, "Apple iPad Reaches '1 Million Sold' Twice as Fast as iPhone," http://www.wired.com/epicenter/2010/05/apple-ipad-reaches-one-million-sold-twice-as-fast-as-iphone (accessed July 2, 2014).

24. http://www.quickmba.com (accessed September 16, 2006).

25. Erica Ogg, "ZOMG: Amazon.com Drops Kindle Price 10 Percent," *CNET News*, May 27, 2008.

26. Dylan F. Tweney, "Large-Screen Kindle Won't Mean Squat If Apple Tablet Arrives," *Wired*, May 4, 2009.

27. David Streitfeld, "Will the Kindle Fire Kill E-Readers," *The New York Times*, January 10, 2012, http://bits.blogs.nytimes.com/2012/01/10/will-the-kindle-fire-kill-e-readers; Julie Bosman, "Table and E-Reader Sales Soar," *The New York Times*, January 22, 2012, http://mediadecoder.blogs.nytimes.com/2012/01/22/tablet-and-e-reader-sales-soar/# (accessed July 2, 2014).

28. Jeffrey A. Trachtenberg, "E-Book Readers Face Sticker Shock," *The Wall Street Journal*, December 15, 2011.

29. "Kindle vs the iPad," Go4Expert.com, November 3, 2010, http://www.go4expert.com/forums/showthread.php?t523749.

30. Subin Im and John P. Workman Jr., "Market Orientation, Creativity, and New Product Performance in High-Technology Firms," *Journal of Marketing* 68, no. 2 (April 2004), p. 114.

31. Dana Mattioli, Kris Maher, "At 3M, Innovation Comes in Tweaks and Snips," *The Wall Street Journal*, March 2, 2010.

32. Chuck Salter, "The 9 Passions of 3M's Mauro Porcini," *Fast Company*, October 2011, pp. 128–134.

33. Natalie Zmuda, "P&G, Levi's, GE Innovate by Thinking in Reverse," *Ad Age*, June 13, 2011, http://adage.com/article/global-news/p-g-levi-s-ge-innovate-thinking-reverse/228146 (accessed July 2, 2014); "Minute Maid Pulpy Joins Growing List of Billion Dollar Brands for the Coca-Cola Company," press release, February 1, 2011, http://www.thecoca-colacompany.com/dynamic/press_center/2011/02/pulpy-joins-roster-of-billion-dollar-brands.html.

34. Standard & Poor's Industry Surveys, Healthcare: Pharmaceuticals, June 24, 2004.

35. This Entrepreneurial Marketing box was written with information gathered in an in-person interview with Lee Renshaw, May 30, 2013.

36. Geoffrey York and Simon Avery, "China's Got RedBerry," www.theglobeandmail.com/servlet/story/RTGAM.20060411.wredberry11/BNStory/Business/home (accessed June 11, 2007).

37. Glen L. Urban and John R. Hauser, "'Listening In' to Find and Explore New Combinations of Customer Needs," *Journal of Marketing* 68, no. 2 (April 2004), p. 72; Steve Hoeffler, "Measuring Preferences for Really New Products," *Journal of Marketing Research* 40, no. 4 (November 2003), pp. 406–420.

38. Glen L. Urban and John R. Hauser, *Design and Marketing of New Products*, 2nd ed. (Upper Saddle River, NJ: Prentice Hall, 1993), pp. 120–121.

39. Associated Press, "Wal-Mart Adds Products as Store Brands Boom," *Boston Globe*, March 17, 2009; Matthew Boyle, "Wal-Mart Gives Its Store Brand a Makeover," *BusinessWeek*, March 16, 2009.

40. Interview with Jevin Eagle (executive vice-president of merchandising and marketing at Staples), June 18, 2009.

41. http://www.betterproductdesign.net/tools/user/leaduser.htm (accessed November 12, 2004); Eric von Hippel, "Successful Industrial Products from Consumers' Ideas," *Journal of Marketing* 42, no. 1 (January 1978), pp. 39–49; Eric von Hippel, "Lead Users: A Source of Novel Product Concepts," *Management Science* 32 (1986), pp. 791–805; Eric von Hippel, *The Sources of Innovation* (New York: Oxford University Press, 1988); Glen L. Urban and Eric von Hippel, "Lead User Analysis for the Development of Industrial Products," *Management Science* 34 (May 1988), pp. 569–582.

42. Karl T. Ulrich and Steven D. Eppinger, *Product Design and Development*, 2nd ed. (Boston: Irwin-McGraw-Hill, 2000).

43. http://www.marketingpower.com (accessed September 18, 2006).

44. Ulrich and Eppinger, *Product Design and Development*, p. 166.

45. Ely Dahan and V. Srinivasan, "The Predictive Power of Internet-Based Product Concept Testing Using Visual Depiction and Animation," *Journal of Product Innovation Management* 17 (2000), pp. 99–109.

46. http://www.marketingpower.com (accessed September 18, 2006).

47. Ulrich and Eppinger, *Product Design and Development*.

48. Ellen Byron, "A Virtual View of the Store Aisle," *The Wall Street Journal* October 3, 2007.

49. http://www2.acnielsen.com/products/crs_bases2.shtml (accessed September 20, 2006).

50. Kotler, *Marketing Management*.

51. Tonya Vinas, "P&G Seeks Alternatives to Animal Tests," *Industry Week* 253, no. 7 (July 2004), p. 60; "EU to Ban Animal Tested Cosmetics," http://www.cnn.com (accessed March 31, 2006); http://www.leapingbunny.org; Gary Anthes, "P&G Uses Data Mining to Cut Animal Testing," http://www.computerworld.com (accessed December 6, 1999).

52. Noriko Suzuki, "The Truth about the Body Shop," http://www.tsujiru.net/compass/compass_1996/reg/suzuki_noriko.htm (accessed June 12, 2007).

53. Emily Wexler, "McDonald's Plans to Win," http://www.strategyonline.ca/articles/magazine/20090901/bizmcdonalds.html (accessed July 2, 2014).

54. Patricia Sellers, "P&G: Teaching an Old Dog New Tricks," *Fortune* (May 31, 2004), pp. 166–180.

55. "Tim Hortons Tests Its First New Coffee Blend in 49 Years," *The Globe and Mail*, October 28, 2013, http://www.theglobeandmail.com/report-on-business/tim-hortons-targets-rivals-tests-new-dark-roast-coffee/article15114207 (accessed July 2, 2014).

56. Hollie Shaw, "Loblaw to Test New Health Store Concept, Take on Whole Foods as Grocery Battle Heats Up," July 11, 2013, http://business.financialpost.com/2013/07/11/loblaw-nutshell-live-life-well (accessed July 2, 2014).

57. Associated Press, "KFC Looks Upmarket with New Restaurant Format," http://www.marketingmag.ca/news/marketer-news/kfc-looks-upmarket-with-new-restaurant-format-83832 (accessed July 2, 2014).

58. http://www.infores.com/public/us/analytics/productportfolio/bscannewprodtest.htm (accessed April 2, 2006).

59. J. Daniel Sherman and William E. Souder, "Managing New Technology Development," http://books.google.com/books?id=6p3hdSUXOlsC&pg=PA104&lpg=PA104&dq=kellogg+%22toast+ems%22&source=web&ots=xP30aQrfMe&sig=YAxE8134Djzngytp3DcC_H8g_FA (accessed June 12, 2007).

60. Product of the Year is the world's largest consumer-voted award for product innovation and publishes a list of best new products launched each year (http://productoftheyear.ca) The products listed were winners in the 2013Product of the Year Awards, a competition judged by thousands of Canadian consumers coast to coast.

61. Product Development Management Association, *The PDMA Handbook of New Product Development*, 2nd ed., Kenneth K. Kahn, ed. (New York: John Wiley & Sons, 2004).

62. Ashwin W. Joshi and Sanjay Sharma, "Customer Knowledge Development: Antecedents and Impact on New Product Success," *Journal of Marketing* 68, no. 4 (October 2004), p. 47.

63. Katherine Bourzac, "Colorful Quantum Dot Displays Coming to Market," *Technology Review*, http://www.technologyreview.com/computing/25460/?a5f (accessed July 2, 2014).

64. Bell Mobility "BlackBerry Q10," http://www.bell.ca/Mobility/Products/BlackBerry-Q10?EXT=MOB_PDL_Google_TXT_DEF_ACQ_030613_CS_Gname=BlackBerry_Q10_AG=BlackBerry_Q10_General_Kw=blackberry_q10&gclid=CNiQqZP8ubgCFaY-MgodojUAnw (accessed July 2, 2014).

65. Yuhong Wu, Sridhar Balasubramanian, and Vijay Mahajan, "When Is a Preannounced New Product Likely to Be Delayed?" *Journal of Marketing* 68, no. 2 (April 2004), p. 101.

66. "Ten of the Biggest Product Flops of All Time," *The Calgary Herald*, March 22, 2103, http://www.calgaryherald.com/business/biggest+product+flops+time/8148934/story.html (accessed July 2, 2014).

67. http://www.pdma.org (accessed September 15, 2006).

68. Amberly McAteer, "Will McDonald's Ditch the Salad," *The Globe and Mail*, May 30, 2013, http://www.theglobeandmail.com/life/the-hot-button/will-mcdonalds-ditch-the-salad/article12279474 (accessed July 2, 2014).

69. "Coca-Cola Freestyle, Best Global Brands 2011," *Interbrand,* 2011.

70. Natalie Zmuda, "Coca-Cola's Futuristic Soda Fountain to get 2012 Ad Push," Advertising Age, August 8, 2011, http://adage.com/article/news/coca-cola-s-futuristic-soda-fountain-2012-ad-push/229154 (accessed on July 2, 2014).

71. "Coca-Cola Freestyle," http://www.coca-colafreestyle.com/#!/mobile-app (accessed July 2, 2014).

72. Theodore Levitt, *Marketing Imagination* (New York: The Free Press, 1986).

73. Donald R. Lehmann and Russell S. Winer, *Analysis for Marketing Planning,* 6th ed. (Boston: McGraw-Hill/Irwin, 2004).

74. Urban and Hauser, *Design and Marketing.*

75. http://www.organicearthday.org/DelMonteFoods.htm (accessed June 10, 2010); http://www.delmonte.com/Products (accessed June 10, 2010).

76. Miriam Jordan and Jonathan Karp, "Machines for the Masses; Whirlpool Aims Cheap Washer at Brazil, India and China; Making Due with Slower Spin," *The Wall Street Journal* December 9, 2003: A19.

77. Om Malik, "The New Land of Opportunity," *Business 2.0*, July 2004, pp. 72–79.

78. Ellen Byron, "Purex Tackles Tough Market, Using New Spin," *The Wall Street Journal,* April 28, 2009.

79. Claire Briney, "Wiping Up the Market," *Global Cosmetic Industry* 172, no. 4 (April 2004), pp. 40–43.

80. Kara Swisher, "Home Economics: The Hypoallergenic Car; Wave of Cleaning Products Caters to Finicky Drivers; Premoistened Auto Wipes," *The Wall Street Journal* (Eastern Edition; May 6, 2004): D1.

81. http://www.toiletwand.com (accessed September 20, 2006).

82. http://www40.statcan.ca/l01/cst01/arts28.htm (accessed June 12, 2007).

83. "Vinyl Lovers Spur New Boom for Old Medium," http://www.cbc.ca/consumer/story/2007/01/03/vinyl-boom.html (accessed June 12, 2007).

84. "Vinyl Lovers Spur New Boom."

85. Kevin J. Clancy and Peter C. Krieg, "Product Life Cycle: A Dangerous Idea," *Brandweek*, March 1, 2004, p. 26; Nariman K. Dhalla and Sonia Yuseph, "Forget the Product Life-Cycle Concept," *Harvard Business Review* (January–February 1976), p. 102ff.

86. David Pogue, "Appeal of iPad 2 Is a Matter of Emotions," *The New York Times*, March 9, 2011, http://www.nytimes.com/2011/03/10/technology/personaltech/10pogue.html (accessed July 2, 2014).

87. Ibid.; Nick Bilton, "The iPad 2, 5.1 Seconds and Smart Covers," *The New York Times*, March 11, 2011, http://bits.blogs.nytimes.com/2011/03/11/the-ipad-2-5-seconds-and-smart-covers (accessed July 2, 2014).

88. Ibid.

89. Jenna Wortham, "So Far Rivals Can't Beat iPad's Price," *The New York Times*, March 6, 2011, http://www.nytimes.com/2011/03/07/technology/07tablet.html (accessed July 2, 2014).

90. Ibid.

91. IDC, "IDC Forecasts Worldwide Tablet Shipments to Surpass Portable PC Shipments in 2013, Total PC Shipments in 2015," May 28, 2013. http://www.idc.com/getdoc.jsp?containerId=prUS24129713 (accessed July 2, 2014).

92. Dana Mattioli, "Tablets Ultimate Buying Machines," *The Wall Street Journal*, September 22, 2011, http://online.wsj.com/article/SB10001424052970204010604576597151983657300.html (accessed July 2, 2014).

93. Charles Arthur, "iPad to Dominate Tablet Sales Until 2015 As Growth Explodes, says Gartner," *The Guardian*, September 22, 2011, http://www.guardian.co.uk/technology/2011/sep/22/tablet-forecast-gartner-ipad.

94. Pogue, op. cit.

95. "iPad 3 News," January 24, 2012, http://www.ipad-3-news.com/.

96. D.C. Denison, "Textbook Publishers Sign On with Apple to Take Advantage of iPad," *The Boston Globe*, January 26, 2012.

97. "iPad 3 News," op. cit.

98. Don Reisenger, "IDC: Apple iPad Secures 87 Percent Market Share," CNET, January 18, 2011 http://news.cnet.com/8301-13506_3-20028801-17.html (accessed July 2, 2014).

99. "Apple (appl) iPad Mini, 4th Generation iPad Sales Break Record," iStockAnalyst, November 5, 2012, http://www.istockanalyst.com/finance/story/6124084/apple-aapl-ipad-mini-4th-generation-ipad-sales-break-record (accessed July 2, 2014).

100. Barrie McKenna, "The New Tech King: Consumers Help Apple Steal Microsoft's Crown," *The Globe and Mail*, May 27, 2010: A1.

101. Bianca Bosker, "How Apple's Losing Its Monopoly on Magic," The Huffington Post, March 6, 2013, http://www.huffingtonpost.com/2013/03/06/apple-future-monopoly-on-magic_n_2814015.html (accessed July 2, 2014).

102. Nick Kolakowski "One Year After Jobs' Death, Apple Still Has Momentum," Slashdot, October 5, 2012. http://slashdot.org/topic/cloud/one-year-after-jobs-death-apple-still-has-momentum/ (accessed on June 18, 2013).

CHAPTER 9

1. Josh O'Kane, "Canada Goose CEO's 'Aha' Moment: 'I realized the brand was real,'" *The Globe and Mail*, April 11, 2013, http://www.theglobeandmail.com/report-on-business/small-business/sb-growth/day-to-day/canada-goose-ceos-aha-moment-i-realized-the-brand-was-real/article10982951 (accessed July 18, 2014).

2. Greig Dyomd, "Guiding the Flock," The Grid, March 6, 2013, http://www.thegridto.com/life/fashion/guiding-the-flock (accessed July 18, 2014).

3. "Frequently Asked Questions," http://www.canada-goose.com/faq (accessed July 22, 2013).

4. Josh O'Kane, "Canada Goose CEO's 'Aha' Moment: 'I realized the brand was real,'" *The Globe and Mail*, April 11, 2013, http://www.theglobeandmail.com/report-on-business/small-business/sb-growth/day-to-day/canada-goose-ceos-aha-moment-i-realized-the-brand-was-real/article10982951 (accessed July 18, 2014).

5. Jesse Silvertown, "Canada Goose: The South Korean Opportunity," Richard Ivey School of Business, February 6, 2012, http://www.asiapacific.ca/sites/default/files/canada_goose_9b11a036.pdf (accessed July 18, 2014).

6. American Marketing Association, *Dictionary of Marketing Terms* (Chicago, IL: American Marketing Association, 2004), http://www.marketingpower.com/live/mg-dictionary-view329.php?.

7. "All Colgate Toothpastes," http://www.colgate.com (accessed September 16, 2006).

8. John A. Quelch and David Kenny, "Extend Profits, Not Product Lines," *Harvard Business Review* (September–October 1994), pp. 153–160.

9. Simon Pittman, "Revlon Switches CEO as Pressure Mounts over Performance," *Cosmeticsdesign.com*, September 19, 2006.

10. Naoko Fujimura and Mike Firn, "Starbucks Says Via Sales May Pass $1 Billion Globally," http://www.businessweek.com/news/2010-04-13/starbucks-says-via-sales-may-pass-1-billion-globally-correct-.html (accessed May 30, 2010).

11. "Starbucks Introduces Starbucks®Natural Fusions Naturally Flavored Coffee in Grocery Stores Nationwide," http://news.starbucks.com/article_display.cfm?article_id=388 (accessed May 30, 2010).

12. "J&J to Buy Skin Care Business," *The Wall Street Journal*, December 18, 1998: 1.

13. http://scjohnson.com/products (accessed September 20, 2006).

14. Louis Lee, "Jean Therapy, $23 a Pop," *BusinessWeek*, June 28, 2004, pp. 91, 93.

15. Andrew Adam Newman, "Axe Adds Fragrance for Women to Its Lineup," *The New York Times*, January 8, 2012, http://www.nytimes.com/2012/01/09/business/media/axe-adds-fragrance-for-women-to-its-lineup.html?_r51&scp54&sq5brandi.ng&st5cse (accessed July 18, 2014).

16. Dianna Dilworth, "Axe Campaign Has Fans Collaboratively Write Graphic Novel Online," *Direct Marketing News*, January 10, 2012, http://www.dmnews.com/axe-campaign-has-fans-collaboratively-write-graphic-novel-online/article/222581 (accessed July 18, 2014).

17. Todd Wasserman, "Axe Launches Fragrance with a Graphic Novel on YouTube," *Mashable Business*, January 10, 2012, http://mashable.com/2012/01/10/axe-graphic-novel (accessed July 18, 2014).

18. Ernest Beck, "Unilever to Cut 25,000 Jobs, Close Factories—Consumer-Goods Company to Focus on Core Brands in Restructuring Asian," *The Wall Street Journal* February 23, 2000: 2.

19. http://www.rbc.com/aboutus/index.html (accessed June 6, 2007).

20. http://www.rbcroyalbank.com/RBC:RmcqJo71A8UAAWzg3w8/products/deposits/view-all-bank-accounts.html (accessed June 6, 2007).

21. Kevin Lane Keller, *Strategic Brand Management: Building, Measuring, and Managing Brand Equity*, 2nd ed. (Upper Saddle River, NJ: Prentice Hall, 2003).

22. This discussion on the advantages of strong brands is adapted from Keller, *Strategic Brand Management*, pp. 104–112; Elizabeth S. Moore, William L. Wilkie, and Richard J. Lutz, "Passing the Torch: Intergenerational Influences as a Source of Brand Equity," *Journal of Marketing* 66, no. 2 (April 2002), p. 17.

23. Angela Y. Lee and Aparna A. Labroo, "The Effect of Conceptual and Perceptual Fluency on Brand Evaluation," *Journal of Marketing Research* 41, no. 2 (May 2004), pp. 151–165.

24. Grant Robertson, "Year of the Goose," *The Globe and Mail*, February 25, 2010, http://www.theglobeandmail.com/report-on-business/rob-magazine/year-of-the-goose/article4307839/?page=all (accessed July 18, 2014).

25. Hollie Shaw, "Canada Goose's Made-in-Canada Marketing Strategy Translates Into Success," Financial Post, May 18, 2012. http://business.financialpost.com/2012/05/18/canada-gooses-made-in-canada-marketing-strategy-translates-into-success (accessed July 18, 2014).

26. http://www.interbrand.com/best_brands_2004.asp (accessed September 14, 2006). The net present value of the earnings over the next 12 months is used to calculate the value.

27. Jennifer Hough, "Brand Finance Canada Names Country's Most Valuable Brands, *Marketing Magazine*, February 27, 2014, http://www.marketingmag.ca/news/marketer-news/brand-finance-canada-names-countrys-most-valuable-brands-102230 (accessed July 18, 2014).

28. David A. Aaker, *Managing Brand Equity* (New York: Free Press, 1991).

29. "Best Global Brands 2013," http://www.interbrand.com/en/best-global-brands/2013/Best-Global-Brands-2013-Brand-View.aspx (accessed July 18, 2014).

30. Jennifer Van Grove, "Barbie Joins Foursquare," *Mashable Business*, July 15, 2010, http://mashable.com/2010/07/15/barbie-joins-foursquare (accessed July 18, 2014).

31. "Video Girl Scavenger Hunt: Lights! Barbie! Action!" http://alldolldup.typepad.com/all_dolld_up/2010/07/video-girl-scavenger-hunt-lights-barbie-action.html (accessed July 18, 2014).

32. Campaign for a Commercial-Free Childhood, "The Commercialization of Childhood," http://www.commercialfreechildhood.org/issues/overview.html.

33. T.L. Stanley, "Mattel, Hasbro Transform Themselves," *BrandWeek*, June 2010, http://login.vnuemedia.com/bw/superbrands/article_toys.html (accessed July 18, 2014).

34. Claude Brodesser-Akner, "Thanks to a Big Mattel Move, Toys and Movies Come One Step Closer to Being the Exact Same Thing," *New York Magazine*, March 24, 2010, http://nymag.com/daily/entertainment/2010/03/mattel_hollywood_new_movie_syn.html (accessed July 18, 2014).

35. Claude Brodesser-Akner, "Disney to Hollywood: If It Can't Sell Toys, It Had Better Be Cheap," February 17, 2010, http://nymag.com/daily/entertainment/2010/02/the_middle_is_toast_at_disney.html (accessed July 18, 2014).

36. David A. Aaker, "Measuring Brand Equity Across Products and Markets," *California Management Review* 38 (Spring 1996), pp. 102–120.

37. http://en.wikipedia.org/wiki/List_of_generic_and_genericized_trademarks (accessed December 22, 2007).

38. Keller, *Strategic Brand Management*.

39. Jennifer L. Aaker, "Dimensions of Brand Personality," *Journal of Marketing Research* 34, no. 3 (August 1997), pp. 347–356.

40. Kevin Lane Keller, "Conceptualizing, Measuring, and Managing Customer-based Brand Equity," *Journal of Marketing* 57, no. 1 (January 1993), pp. 1–22.

41. Dave Larson, "Building a Brand's Personality from the Customer Up," *Direct Marketing*, October 2002, pp. 17–21.

42. http://www.marketingpower.com/live/mg-dictionary.php?SearchFor=brand+loyalty&Searched=1 (accessed September 17, 2006).

43. James H. McAlexander, John W. Schouten, and Harold F. Koenig, "Building Brand Community," *Journal of Marketing* 66, no. 1 (January 2002), pp. 38–54.

44. Christine Bittar, "Big Brands: Stronger than Dirt," *BrandWeek*, June 23, 2003, pp. S52–S53.

45. "President's Choice Continues Brisk Pace," *Frozen Food Age*, March 1998, pp. 17–18.

46. Laura Liebeck, "Private Label Goes Premium," *Discount Store News* (November 4, 1996): F38; "New Private-Label Alternatives Bring Changes to Supercenters, Clubs," *DSN Retailing Today*, February 5, 2001, p. 66.

47. http://www.marketinghalloflegends.ca/visionaries_david_nichol.php (accessed June 7, 2007).

48. http://www.pg.com.

49. Harvey Schacter, "What's in a Name? Plenty," *The Globe and Mail* May 5, 2004: C4.

50. Eve Lazarus, "New Beer Goes with Flies and a Croak," http://www.marketingmag.ca/magazine/marketingdaily/article.jsp?content=20060914_102950_5424 (accessed June 7, 2007).

51. For recent research on brand extensions, see Subramanian Balachander and Sanjoy Ghose, "Reciprocal Spillover Effects: A Strategic Benefit of Brand Extensions," *Journal of Marketing* 67, no. 1 (January 2003), pp. 4–13; Kalpesh Kaushik Desai and Kevin Lane Keller, "The Effects of Ingredient Branding Strategies on Host Brand Extendibility," *Journal of Marketing* 66, no. 1 (January 2002), pp. 73–93; Tom Meyvis and Chris Janiszewski, "When Are Broader Brands Stronger Brands? An Accessibility Perspective on the Success of Brand Extensions," *Journal of Consumer Research* 31, no. 2 (September 2004), pp. 346–357.

52. David Aaker, "Brand Extensions: The Good, the Bad, and the Ugly," *Sloan Management Review* 31 (Summer 1990), pp. 47–56.

53. http://www.braun.com (accessed June 10, 2011).

54. http://www.neutrogena.com; Vanitha Swaminathan, Richard J. Fox, and Srinivas K. Reddy, "The Impact of Brand Extension Introduction on Choice," *Journal of Marketing* 65, no. 3 (2001), pp. 1–15.

55. http://www.fritolay.com/consumer.html (accessed June 10, 2011).

56. Jennifer Aaker, Susan Fournier, and S. Adam Brasel, "When Good Brands Do Bad," *Journal of Consumer Research* 31, no. 1 (June 2004), pp. 1–16.

57. Barbara Loken and Deborah Roedder John, "Diluting Brand Beliefs: When Do Brand Extensions Have a Negative Impact?" *Journal of Marketing* 57, no. 3 (July 1993), pp. 71–84.

58. Aaker, "Brand Extensions," pp. 47–56.

59. David A. Aaker and Kevin Lane Keller, "Consumer Evaluations of Brand Extensions," *Journal of Marketing* 54, no. 1 (January 1990), pp. 27–41.

60. Susan M. Broniarczyk and Joseph W. Alba, "The Importance of the Brand in Brand Extension," *Journal of Marketing Research* 31, no. 2 (May 1994), pp. 214–228.

61. "Marriott Hotel Brands," http://www.marriott.com/corporateinfo/glance.mi (accessed July 18, 2014).

62. This section is based on Akshay R. Rao and Robert W. Ruekert, "Brand Alliances as Signals of Product Quality," *Sloan Management Review* 36 (Fall 1994), pp. 87–97.

63. Cathy Enz, "Multibranding Strategy: The Case of Yum! Brands," *Cornell Hotel & Restaurant Administration Quarterly*, February 2005.

64. Kristen Laird, "Joe Fresh Begins Relationship with Barbie," http://www.marketingmag.ca/english/news/marketer/article.jsp?content=20101103_164846_9592 (accessed April 27, 2011).

65. "Sprinkles on Your Doughnut ... or Your Ice Cream?," *The Globe and Mail* June 12, 2009, B7.

66. T. Kippenberger, "Co-Branding as a Competitive Weapon," *Strategic Direction* 18 (October), pp. 31–33.

67. Tom Blacket and Bob Boad, eds., *Branding: The Science of Alliance* (London: Macmillan Press, 1999).

68. Keller, *Strategic Brand Management*.

69. "NASCAR Launches New Stock Car Racing Series in Canada and National Title Sponsorship Agreement with Canadian Tire," http://www.newswire.ca/en/releases/archive/September2006/12/c5003.html (accessed June 7, 2007).

70. Keller, *Strategic Brand Management*.

71. William Makely, "Being the Beauty, Being the Brand," *Global Cosmetic Industry* (January 2004), pp. 28–30.

72. This Entrepreneurial Marketing box was written with information gathered in a telephone interview with Elysia Vanenkurk Secord of Three Farmers on Tuesday July 23, 2013.

73. "Packages: Tracing an Evolution," *Packaging Digest* (December 2003), pp. 37–42.

74. http://www.packagingdigest.com/articles/200605/6.php (accessed June 8, 2007).

75. Annette Bourdeau, "A Green Future: Three Eco-Friendly Trends You Should Be Keeping an Eye On," http://www.strategymag.com/articles/magazine/20070501/what.html?word=biodegradable&word=palm&word=fibre-based&word=packaging (accessed July 18, 2014).

76. Annette Bourdeau, "P&G Rallies Allies (and Foes)," http://www.strategymag.com/articles/magazine/20071001/upfronttide.html (accessed July 18, 2014).

77. Sustainable Agriculture, http://www.thecoca-colacompany.com/citizenship/sustainable_agriculture.html (accessed May 30, 2010).

78. David Ebener. "Green Message in a Bottle," *The Globe and Mail* November 17, 2009, B3.

79. Rebecca Harris, "Nice Package: Look Better, Greener on the Shelves," *Marketing Magazine*, March 26, 2012, http://www.marketingmag.ca/news/marketer-news/nice-package-look-better-greener-on-the-shelves-49220 (accessed July 18, 2014).

80. "Sourcing," http://www.thecoca-colacompany.com/citizenship/plantbottle_sourcing.html (accessed May 30, 2010).

81. "The Coca-Cola Company PlantBottle™ Packaging Receives Prestigious Global Award," http://www.thecoca-colacompany.com/presscenter/nr_20100525_plantbottle_award.html (accessed May 30, 2010).

82. "Frequently Asked Questions," http://www.thecoca-colacompany.com/citizenship/plantbottle_faq.html (accessed May 30, 2010).

83. "Danone Expands Goodies Low-Fat Line of Desserts," *Marketing*, February 12, 2004, p. 4; http://www.landwriter.co.uk/landwriter/premium/TemplateParser.asp?aId=3778&page=FreeTemplate (accessed August 30, 2005).

84. This case was written by Jeanne L. Munger and Julie Rusch in conjunction with the U.S. textbook authors (Dhruv Grewal and Michael Levy) for use in a class discussion; it was not written as an illustration of effective or ineffective marketing practices. Jeanne Munger is an associate professor at the University of Southern Maine.

85. http://www.bandaid.com/brand_story.shtml; http://www.bandaid.com/new_products.shtml; Christine Bittar, "J&J Stuck on Expanding BAND-AID® Franchise," *Brandweek*, March 3, 2003, p. 4; Richard Gutwillig, "Billion-Dollar Bandages," *Supermarket Business*, August 15, 2000, p. 58; "United States Top 10 First Aid Tape/Bandages/Gauze Brands Ranked by Dollar Sales and Unit Volume for 2003," *Chain Drug Review*, June 21, 2004, p. 238; Andrea M. Grossman, "Personal and Beauty Care: News Bites," *Drug Store News*, January 11, 1999, p. 61; "O-T-C Health Care: United States Over-the-Counter Heath Care Product Sales in Dollars and Percent Change for 2003," *Chain Drug Review*, May 24, 2004, p. 32.

86. Christine Bittar, "J&J Stuck on Expanding Band-Aid Franchise," *Brandweek* 44, no. 9 (March 3, 2003), p. 4.

87. Megan Hynes, "Mobile: Who's Doing It Best, *Strategy Magazine*, January 28, 2013, http://strategyonline.ca/2013/01/28/mobile-whos-doing-it-best (accessed July 18, 2014).

CHAPTER 10

1. This opening vignette was written with information gathered in a telephone interview with Heather Murphy, Co-Founder, GoTire, on Friday June 21, 2013.

2. "Why GoTire? http://www.gotirefranchise.com (accessed July 29, 2013).

3. Leonard L. Berry and A. Parasuraman, *Marketing Services: Competing through Quality* (New York: The Free Press, 1991), p. 5.

4. Valarie A. Zeithaml, A. Parasuraman, and Leonard L. Berry, *Delivering Quality Service: Balancing Customer Perceptions and Expectations* (New York: The Free Press, 1990).

5. "MyFinanceTracker from RBC a First for Canada," http://www.clickweekly.com/articles/June 1_2010/RBC.htm (accessed July 18, 2014).

6. Konrad Yakabuski, "The Greatest Canadian Company on Earth," *Report on Business Magazine* (September 2007), p. 57.

7. M. Levy, Jerry Gotlieb, and Gopal Iyer, *Developing a Deeper Understanding of Post-Purchase Perceived Risk and Repeat Purchase Behavioral Intentions in a Service Setting* (unpublished working paper), Babson College, 2006; Mary Jo Bitner, Stephen W. Brown, and Matthew L. Mueter, "Technology Infusion in Service Encounters," *Journal of the Academy of Marketing Science* 28, no. 1 (2000), pp. 138–149; Jerry Gotlieb, Dhruv Grewal, Michael Levy, and Joan Lindsey-Mullikin, "An Examination of Moderators of the Effects of Customers' Evaluation of Employee Courtesy on Attitude Toward the Service Firm," *Journal of Applied Social Psychology* 34 (April 2004), pp. 825–847.

8. Choice Hotels, "Special Guest Policies," 2004, http://www7.choice-hotels.com/ires/en-US/html/GuestPolicies?sid=hPTj.2R60elpGw.7 (accessed September 10, 2006).

9. http://www.clubmed.com (accessed June 13, 2011).

10. Rebecca Harris, "Confident Customers," http://www.marketingmag.ca/magazine/current/in_context/article.jsp?content=20060410_76174_76174 (accessed June 17, 2007).

11. Michelle DiPardo, "Hailo Launches Its First Paid Campaign," *Marketing Magazine*, May 10, 2013, http://www.marketingmag.ca/news/marketer-news/hailo-launches-first-paid-campaign-78523 (accessed July 18, 2014).

12. "Hailo," iTunes App Store (accessed July 29, 2013).

13. "Problem in the Bagging Area?— Why Self-Service Tills are a Turn Off for Consumers," Ipsos Retail Performance, http://www.ipsos-retailperformance.com/blog/2013/11/08/problem-in-the-bagging-area-why-self-service-tills-are-a-turn-off-for-consumers (accessed July 18, 2014).

14. Cineplex Galaxy Annual Report 2012, http://cineplexgalaxy.disclosureplus.com/cmsAssets/docs/pdf/Reports_Filings/2012%20Annual%20Report_FINAL.pdf (accessed July 29, 2013).

15. Greg Michetti, "Webify Your Workout," http://www.backbone-mag.com/Magazine/Hot_Tech_12310602.asp (accessed June 17, 2007).

16. Andrew Willis, "Sports Fan Munchies Fatten Cineplex's Bottom Line," http://www.theglobeandmail.com/servlet/story/LAC.20070104.RCINEPLEX04/TPStory/Entertainment (accessed June 17, 2007).

17. Steve Ladurantaye, "Introducing the Biggest Outdoor Water Park in Canada," http://www.theglobeandmail.com/report-on-business/your-business/start/location/introducing-the-biggest-outdoor-water-park-in-canada/article1598930 (accessed July 18, 2014).

18. "Waterpark Industry General & Fun Facts," http://www.waterparks.org/otherArticles/Waterpark Industry General & Fun Facts.pdf (accessed June 13, 2010).

19. Ladurantaye, "Introducing."

20. Ibid.

21. "Canada's Largest Theme Waterpark Gearing up for Big Splash Grand Opening," http://www.calypsopark.com/_files/press_release_042010.pdf (accessed June 13, 2010).

22. The discussion of the Service Gap Model and its implications draws heavily from Michael Levy and Barton A. Weitz, *Retailing Management*, 6th ed. (Burr Ridge, IL: Irwin/McGraw-Hill, 2007) and also is based on Deon Nel and Leyland Pitt, "Service Quality in a Retail Environment: Closing the Gaps," *Journal of General Management* 18 (Spring 1993), pp. 37–57; Zeithaml, Parasuraman, and Berry, *Delivering Quality Customer Service*; Valerie Zeithaml, Leonard Berry, and A. Parasuraman, "Communication and Control Processes in the Delivery of Service Quality," *Journal of Marketing* 52, no. 2 (April 1988), pp. 35–48.

23. Kenneth Clow, David Kurtz, John Ozment, and Beng Soo Ong, "The Antecedents of Consumer Expectations of Services: An Empirical Study across Four Industries," *The Journal of Services Marketing* 11 (May–June 1997), pp. 230–248; Ann Marie Thompson and Peter Kaminski, "Psychographic and Lifestyle Antecedents of Service Quality Expectations," *Journal of Services Marketing* 7 (1993), pp. 53–61.

24. Zeithaml, Parasuraman, and Berry, *Delivering Quality Customer Service.*

25. Rebecca Harris, "Marketing 2.0," http://www.marketingmag.ca/magazine/current/feature/article.jsp?content=20070430_69539_69539 (accessed June 17, 2007).

26. Harris, "Marketing 2.0."

27. Harris, "Marketing 2.0."

28. Leonard Berry and A. Parasuraman, "Listening to the Customer—The Concept of a Service-Quality Information System," *Sloan Management Review* 38, no. 3 (1997), pp. 65–77; A. Parasuraman and Dhruv Grewal, "Serving Customers and Consumers Effectively in the 21st Century" (working paper), University of Miami, Coral Gables, Florida, 1998.

29. Teena Lyons, "Complain to Me—If You Can," *Knight Ridder Tribune News* December 4, 2005: 1.

30. http://www.enermodal.com/Canadian/company_profile.html (accessed June 14, 2010).

31. http://www.enermodal.com/Canadian/news/EEL-Newsroom-Fifth.pdf (accessed June 14, 2010).

32. "Sustainable Waterloo," *The Record* (special advertising feature), March 20, 2010: D4.

33. http://www.enermodal.com/Canadian/company_building.html (accessed June 14, 2010).

34. http://www.enermodal.com/Canadian/company_green_policies.html (accessed June 14, 2010).

35. Joanna LaFleur, "Business Motivations for Sustainability," http://www.enermodal.com/Canadian/news/EEL-Newsroom-Sustainability.pdf (accessed June 14, 2010).

36. Diane Jermyn, "The Top 50 Greenest Employers," http://www.theglobeandmail.com/report-on-business/the-top-50-greenest-employers/article1543083 (accessed July 18, 2014).

37. http://www.nwa.com/plan/index.html (accessed September 20, 2006).

38. "2013 Annual Report," http://www.westjet.com/guest/en/media-investors/2013-annual-report/financial-results/financial-highlights.shtml (accessed July 18, 2014).

39. Joe Castaldo, "Just Be Nice: Providing Good Customer Service," http://www.canadianbusiness.com/managing/strategy/article.jsp?content=20061009_81513_81513 (accessed June 17, 2007).

40. http://www.westjet.com/guest/en/business-travel/on-time-performance.shtml (accessed July 18, 2014).

41. Jim Poisant, *Creating and Sustaining a Superior Customer Service Organization: A Book about Taking Care of the People Who Take Care of the Customers* (Westport, CT: Quorum Books, 2002); "People-focused HR Policies Seen as Vital to Customer Service Improvement," *Store* (January 2001), p. 60; Michael Brady and J. Joseph Cronin, "Customer Orientation: Effects on Customer Service Perceptions and Outcome Behaviors," *Journal of Service Research* (February 2001), pp. 241–251; Michael Hartline, James Maxham III, and Daryl McKee, "Corridors of Influence in the Dissemination of Customer-Oriented Strategy to Customer Contact Service Employees," *Journal of Marketing* 64, no. 2 (April 2000), pp. 25–41.

42. Conrad Lashley, *Empowerment: HR Strategies for Service Excellence* (Boston: Butterworth/Heinemann, 2001).

43. "Future Success Powered by Employees," *DSN Retailing Today* 44 (January 2006), pp. 22–24.

44. "Canada's 50 Best Employers," *Maclean's*, November 7, 2013, http://www.macleans.ca/economy/business/canadas-best-employers (accessed July 18, 2014).

45. Alicia Grandey and Analea Brauburger, "The Emotion Regulation Behind the Customer Service Smile," in *Emotions in the Workplace: Understanding the Structure and Role of Emotions in Organizational Behavior*, eds. R. Lord, R. Klimoski, and R. Kanfer (San Francisco: Jossey-Bass, 2002); Mara Adelman and Aaron Ahuvia, "Social Support in the Service Sector: The Antecedents, Processes, and Consequences of Social Support in an Introductory Service," *Journal of Business Research* 32 (March 1995), pp. 273–282.

46. Colin Armistead and Julia Kiely, "Creating Strategies for Managing Evolving Customer Service," *Managing Service Quality* 13, no. 2 (2003), pp. 64–171; http://www.robertspector.com/NordWay_extract.html (accessed September 20, 2006).

47. Wency Leung, "Why Remote Workouts Are the Next Big Thing," *The Globe and Mail*, April 8, 2013, http://www.theglobeandmail.com/life/health-and-fitness/why-remote-workouts-are-the-next-big-thing/article10823458 (accessed July 18, 2014).

48. Rhett H. Walker et al., "Technology-Enabled Service Delivery: An Investigation of Reasons Affecting Customer Adoption and Rejection," *International Journal of Service Industry Management* 13, no. 1 (2002), pp. 91–107; Mary Jo Bitner, Steven W. Brown, and Matthew L. Meuter, "Technology Infusion in Service Encounters," *Journal of the Academy of Marketing Science* 28, no. 1 (2000), pp. 138–149; Stephen W. Brown, "Service Recovery through IT," *Marketing Management* 6 (Fall 1997), pp. 25–27; P.A. Dabholkar, "Technology-based Service Delivery: A Classification Scheme for Developing Marketing Strategies," in *Advances in Services Marketing and Management*, Vol. 3, eds. T.A. Swartz, Deborah E. Bowen, and Stephen W. Brown (Greenwich, CT: JAI Press, 1994), pp. 241–271.

49. Anne Eisenberg, "Thinking of Going Blond? Consult the Kiosk First," *The New York Times*, March 29, 2009; Marianne Wilson, "Digital Dining," *Chain Store Age*, September 2008.

50. Subimal Chatterjee, Susan A. Slotnick, and Matthew J. Sobel, "Delivery Guarantees and the Interdependence of Marketing and Operations," *Production and Operations Management* 11, no. 3 (Fall 2002), pp. 393–411; Piyush Kumar, Manohar Kalawani, and Makbool Dada, "The Impact of Waiting Time Guarantees on Customers' Waiting Experiences," *Marketing Science* 16, no. 4 (1999), pp. 676–785.

51. David Streitfeld, "For $2 a Star, an Online Retailer Gets 5-Star Product Reviews," *The New York Times*, January 26, 2012, http://www.nytimes.com/2012/01/27/technology/for-2-a-star-a-retailer-gets-5-star-reviews.html?_r52&src5me&ref5general (accessed July 18, 2014); David Streitfeld, "Faking It to Make It: A Beautiful Try," *The New York Times*, January 27, 2012, http://bits.blogs.nytimes.com/2012/01/27/faking-it-to-make-it-a-beautiful-try/?scp520&sq5customer%20service&st5cse (accessed July 18, 2014).

52. HubSpot company website, http://www.hubspot.com/internet-marketing-company; Canadian Mountain Holidays website, http://www.canadiananmountainholidays.com/heli-skiing/trips; http://www.hubspot.com/customer-case-studies/bid/31288/Travel-and-Leisure-Industry-Sucess-Story-CMH-Heli-Skiing-Summer-Adventures.

53. K. Douglas Hoffman, Scott W. Kelley, and H.M. Rotalsky, "Tracking Service Failures and Employee Recovery Efforts," *Journal of Services Marketing* 9, no. 2 (1995), pp. 49–61; Scott W. Kelley and Mark A. Davis, "Antecedents to Customer Expectations for Service Recovery," *Journal of the Academy of Marketing Science* 22 (Winter 1994), pp. 52–61; Terrence J. Levesque and Gordon H.G. McDougall, "Service Problems and Recovery Strategies: An Experiment," *Canadian Journal of Administrative Sciences* 17, no. 1 (2000), pp. 20–37; James G. Maxham III and Richard G. Netemeyer, "A Longitudinal Study of Complaining Customers' Evaluations of Multiple Service Failures and Recovery Efforts," *Journal of Marketing* 66, no.

3 (October 2002), pp. 57–71; Amy K. Smith, Ruth N. Bolton, and Janet Wagner, "A Model of Customer Satisfaction with Service Encounters Involving Failure and Recovery," *Journal of Marketing Research* 36, no. 3 (August 1999), pp. 356–372; Scott R. Swanson and Scott W. Kelley, "Attributions and Outcomes of the Service Recovery Process," *Journal of Marketing Theory and Practice* 9 (Fall 2001), pp. 50–65; Stephen S. Tax and Stephen W. Brown, "Recovering and Learning from Service Failure," *Sloan Management Review* 40, no. 1 (1998), pp. 75–88; Stephen S. Tax, Stephen W. Brown, and Murali Chandrashekaran, "Consumer Evaluations of Service Complaint Experiences: Implications for Relationship Marketing," *Journal of Marketing* 62, no. 2 (April 1998), pp. 60–76; Scott Widmier and Donald W. Jackson Jr., "Examining the Effects of Service Failure, Customer Compensation, and Fault on Customer Satisfaction with Salespeople," *Journal of Marketing Theory and Practice* 10 (Winter 2002), pp. 63–74; Valarie A. Zeithaml and Mary Jo Bitner, *Services Marketing: Integrating Customer Focus across the Firm* (New York: McGraw-Hill, 2003).

54. James Maxham III, "Service Recovery's Influence on Consumer Satisfaction, Positive Word-of-Mouth, and Purchase Intentions," *Journal of Business Research* (October 2001), pp. 11–24; Michael McCollough, Leonard Berry, and Manjit Yadav, "An Empirical Investigation of Customer Satisfaction after Service Failure and Recovery," *Journal of Service Research* (November 2000), pp. 121–137.

55. "Correcting Store Blunders Seen as Key Customer Service Opportunity," *Stores* (January 2001), pp. 60–64; Stephen W. Brown, "Practicing Best-in-Class Service Recovery: Forward-thinking Firms Leverage Service Recovery to Increase Loyalty and Profits," *Marketing Management* (Summer 2000), pp. 8–10; Tax, Brown, and Chandrashekaran, "Customer Evaluations"; Amy Smith and Ruth Bolton, "An Experimental Investigation of Customer Reactions to Service Failures and Recovery Encounters: Paradox or Peril?" *Journal of Service Research* 1 (August 1998), pp. 23–36; Cynthia Webster and D.S. Sundaram, "Service Consumption Criticality in Failure Recovery," *Journal of Business Research* 41 (February 1998), pp. 153–159.

56. Ko de Ruyter and Martin Wetsel, "The Impact of Perceived Listening Behavior in Voice-to-Voice Service Encounters," *Journal of Service Research* (February 2000), pp. 276–284.

57. Hooman Estelami, "Competitive and Procedural Determinants of Delight and Disappointment in Consumer Complaint Outcomes," *Journal of Service Research* (February 2000), pp. 285–300.

58. Michael Tsiros, Anne Roggeveen, and Dhruv Grewal, *Compensation as a Service Recovery Strategy: When Does It Work?* (unpublished working paper), Babson College, 2006. Amy K. Smith, Ruth N. Bolton, and Janet Wagner, "A Model of Customer Satisfaction with Service Encounters Involving Failure and Recovery," *Journal of Marketing Research* 36 (August 1999), pp. 356–372. Scott R. Swanson and Scott W. Kelley, "Attributions and Outcomes of the Service Recovery Process," *Journal of Marketing: Theory and Practice* 9 (Fall 2001), pp. 50–65.

59. "About Us," http://www.zipcar.com (accessed July 26, 2013).

60. "Zipcar Media Kit Backgrounder," http://zipcar.mediaroom.com/media-kit (accessed July 29, 2013).

61. April Kilcrease, "A Conversation with Zipcar's CEO Scott Griffith," GigaOM, December 5, 2011, http://gigaom.com/cleantech/a-conversation-with-zipcars-ceo-scott-griffith (accessed July 18, 2014)

62. "Zipcar Media Kit Backgrounder," http://zipcar.mediaroom.com/media-kit (accessed July 29, 2013).

63. United States Securities and Exchange Commission, "Zipcar S-1 Filing," June 1, 2010, http://sec.gov/Archives/edgar/data/1131457/000095013010001923/ds1.htm (accessed July 18, 2014).

64. Kilcrease, op. cit.

65. "Rates and Plans," http://www.zipcar.ca/toronto/check-rates (accessed July 30, 2013).

66. United States Securities and Exchange Commission, op. cit.; JP Morgan SMid Cap Conference, December 11, 2011.

67. United States Securities and Exchange Commission, op. cit.

68. "Zipcar Canada Inc." Livegreen Toronto, http://www.livegreencard.ca/business/96 (accessed July 18, 2014).

69. United States Securities and Exchange Commission, Kilcrease, op. cit.

70. "Zipcar Invests in Barcelona-based Avancar," PR Newswire, December 18, 2011, http://www.prnewswire.com/news-releases/zipcar-invests-in-barcelona-based-avancar-79609022.html (accessed July 30, 2013).

71. http://www.zipcar.com.

72. United States Securities and Exchange Commission, op. cit.

73. Courtney Rubin, "How Will the IPO Market Treat Zipcar?" Inc.com, June 2, 2010, http://www.inc.com/news/articles/2010/06/zipcar-files-for-ipo.html (accessed July 18, 2014).

74. Guy Dixon, "Avis Overcomes Reservations with Purchase of Zipcar," *The Globe and Mail*, January 2, 2013, http://www.theglobeandmail.com/globe-investor/avis-overcomes-reservations-with-purchase-of-zipcar/article6841893 (accessed July 18, 2014)

75. Greg Keenan, "Zipcar Coming to Toronto's Pearson Airport," *The Globe and Mail*, May 2, 2013, http://www.theglobeandmail.com/report-on-business/zipcar-coming-to-torontos-pearson-airport/article11684468 (accessed July 18, 2014).

CHAPTER 11

1. Groupon, "The Wizard of Oz"— Ed Mirvish Theatre, http://www.groupon.com/deals/gl-wizard-of-oz-ed-mirvish-theatre (accessed July 18, 2014).

2. http://www.bespokecuisine.com/cooking-parties/index.php.

3. Groupon, "Q1 2013 Fact Sheet," http://files.shareholder.com/downloads/AMDA-E2NTR/2619414771x0x671255/9D236C11-780C-4CE9-8FC5-66816521BD82/Groupon_Q1_2013_Public_Fact_Sheet.pdf (accessed August 4, 2013).

4. Ibid.

5. Groupon Q1 2014 Public Fact Summary, http://files.shareholder.com/downloads/AMDA-E2NTR/0x0x755979/14157104-D916-4D45-9468-E5104B66F7E1/2014_Q1_Public_Fact_Sheet.pdf (accessed July 18, 2014).

6. Ibid.

7. Kent B. Monroe, *Pricing: Making Profitable Decisions*, 3rd ed. (New York: McGraw-Hill, 2003); Dhruv Grewal, Kent B. Monroe, and R. Krishnan, "The Effects of Price Comparison Advertising on Buyers' Perceptions of Acquisition Value and Transaction Value," *Journal of Marketing* 62 (April 1998), pp. 46–60.

8. "American Shoppers Economize, Show Greater Interest in Nutrition and Awareness of Food Safety Issues, According to Trends in the United States: Consumer Attitudes and the Supermarket 2003," http://www.fmi.org/media/mediatext.cfm?id=534 (accessed December 10, 2005). A key finding was that low price was the third most important feature in selecting a supermarket; it was viewed as important by 83 percent of respondents; see also "The New Value Equation," *Supermarket News* 50 (June 10, 2002), p. 12.

9. Anthony Miyazaki, Dhruv Grewal, and Ronnie Goodstein, "The Effects of Multiple Extrinsic Cues on Quality Perceptions: A Matter of Consistency," *Journal of Consumer Research* 32 (June 2005), pp. 146–153; William B. Dodds, Kent B. Monroe, and Dhruv Grewal, "The Effects of Price, Brand, and Store Information on Buyers' Product Evaluations," *Journal of Marketing Research* 28 (August 1991), pp. 307–319.

10. Robert J. Dolan, "Note on Marketing Strategy," *Harvard Business School* (November 2000), pp. 1–17; Dhruv Grewal and Larry D. Compeau, "Pricing and Public Policy: An Overview and a Research Agenda," *Journal of Public Policy & Marketing* 18 (Spring 1999), pp. 3–11.

11. Ethan Smith and Yukari Iwatani Kane, "Apple Changes Tune on Music Pricing," *The Wall Street Journal*, January 7, 2009, http://online.wsj.com/news/articles/SB123126062001057765 (accessed July 21, 2014).

12. "We Did It Again! Paradigm Wins Inside Track's Best Price/Value Award," May 14, 2012, http://paradigmspeakers.blogspot.ca/2012/05/we-did-it-again-paradigm-wins-inside.html (accessed July 18, 2014).

13. Monroe, *Pricing: Making Profitable Decisions*.

14. http://www.corporate.canada.travel/en/ca/research_statistics/trends_outlook/tib/tib.html (accessed June 23, 2010).

15. http://www.marketingpower.com/mg-dictionary-view669.php? (accessed September 19, 2006).

16. Ruth N. Bolton and Venkatesh Shankar, "An Empirically Derived Taxonomy of Retailer Pricing and Promotion Strategies," *Journal of Retailing* 79, no. 4 (2003), pp. 213–224; Rajiv Lal and Ram Rao, "Supermarket Competition: The Case of Every Day Low Pricing," *Marketing Science* 16, no. 1 (1997), pp. 60–80.

17. A.R. Rao, M.E. Bergen, and S. Davis, "How to Fight a Price War," *Harvard Business Review* 78 (March–April 2000), pp. 107–116.

18. Rao, Bergen, and S. Davis, "How to Fight a Price War."

19. *Merriam-Webster's Dictionary of Law*, 1996.

20. "Fujitsu Institutes New Warranty Policy For Plasmavision® Monitors," May 15, 2002, http://www.plasmavision.com/buying_online.htm (accessed January 25, 2005).

21. Joseph P. Bailey, "Electronic Commerce: Prices and Consumer Issues for Three Products: Books, Compact Discs, and Software," *Organization for Economic Cooperation and Development, OECD, GD* 98 (1998), p. 4; J. Yannis Bakos, "Reducing Buyer Search Costs: Implications for Electronic Marketplaces," *Management Science* 43, no. 12 (1997), pp. 1676–1692; Erik Brynjolfsson and Michael D. Smith, "Frictionless Commerce? A Comparison of Internet and Conventional Retailers," *Management Science* 46, no. 4 (2000), pp. 563–585; Rajiv Lal and Miklos Sarvary, "When and How Is the Internet Likely to Decrease Price Competition?" *Marketing Science* 18, no. 4 (1999), pp. 485–503; Xing Pan, Brian T. Ratchford, and Venkatesh Shankar, "Can Price Dispersion in Online Markets Be Explained by Differences in E-Tailer Service Quality?" *Journal of the Academy of Marketing Science* 30, no. 4 (2002), pp. 433–445; Michael D. Smith, "The Impact of Shopbots on Electronic Markets," *Journal of the Academy of Marketing Sciences* 30, no. 4 (2002), pp. 446–454; Michael D. Smith and Erik Brynjolfsson, "Consumer Decision-making at an Internet Shopbot: Brand Still Matters," *The Journal of Industrial Economics* 49 (December 2001), pp. 541–558; Fang-Fang Tang and Xiaolin Xing, "Will the Growth of Multi-Channel Retailing Diminish the Pricing Efficiency of the Web?" *Journal of Retailing* 77, no. 3 (2001), pp. 319–333; Florian Zettlemeyer, "Expanding to the Internet: Pricing and Communications Strategies When Firms Compete on Multiple Channels," *Journal of Marketing Research* 37 (August 2000), pp. 292–308; Dhruv Grewal et al., "The Internet and the Price-Value-Loyalty Chain," *Journal of Business Research* 56 (May 2003), pp. 391–398; Gopalkrishnan R. Iyer et al., "Linking Web-based Segmentation to Pricing Tactics," *Journal of Product & Brand Management* 11, no. 4/5 (2002), pp. 288–302.

22. "The Internet Is Saving You Almost $9,000 per Year," *Backbone Magazine*, March/April 2013, p. 8.

23. Uptal Dholakia, Barbara Kahn, Randy Reeves, Aric Rindfleish, David Stewart, and Earl Taylor (2010), "Consumer Behavior in a Multichannel, Multimedia Retailing Environment, *Journal of Interactive Marketing*, forthcoming; P.K. Kannan, Barbara K. Pope, and Sanjay Jain (2009), "Pricing Digital Content Product Lines: A Model and Application for the National Academies

Press," *Marketing Science*, Brian Ratchford (2009), "Online Pricing: Review and Directions for Research," *Journal of Interactive Marketing*, 23 (1), 82–90; Koen Pauwels and Allen Weiss (2008), "Moving from Free to Fee: How Online Firms Market to Successfully Change their Business Model," *Journal of Marketing Perspectives*, 19 (2), 139–158; Dhruv Grewal, Gopalkrishnan R. Iyer, R. Krishnan, and Arun Sharma, "The Internet and the Price-Value-Loyalty Chain," *Journal of Business Research*, 56 (May 2003), pp. 391–398.

24. Tim Kildaze, "Ninety-Nine Bucks for $400 Worth of Organic Meat. Seriously?," *The Globe and Mail* April 16, 2011: M1.

25. Ayaz Nanji, "Consumer Price Sensitivity and Deal Seeking Up in 2013," MarketingProfs.com, May 24, 2013, http://www.marketingprofs.com/charts/2013/10833/consumer-price-sensitivity-and-deal-seeking-up-in-2013?adref=nl052413 (accessed July 18, 2014)

26. Mason Wright, "Online Sources Gain, but CD Still Reigns," *The Globe and Mail*, August 6, 2012: R3.

27. Simon Houpt and Steve Ladurantaye, "Kids: Not Coming Soon to a Theatre Near You," *The Globe and Mail*, October 16, 2012, Page B1.

28. Thomas T. Nagle and Reed K. Holden, *The Strategy and Tactics of Pricing*, 3rd ed. (Upper Saddle River, NJ: Pearson, 2002).

29. Walmart Launches Major Initiative to Make Food Healthier and Healthier Food More Affordable; http://walmartstores.com/pressroom/news/10514.aspx; Stephanie Rosenbloom, "At Walmart, Labeling to Reflect Green Intent," *The New York Times*, July 16, 2009; Stephanie Rosenbloom, "Wal-Mart to Toughen Standards," *The New York Times*, October 22, 2008; Adam Aston, "Walmart: Making Its Suppliers Go Green," *BusinessWeek*, May 18, 2009.

30. Sustainable Plant Staff, "Walmart's 2012 Sustainability Report Talks Softly about Suppliers," Sustainable Plant, April 19, 2012, http://www.sustainableplant.com/2012/04/walmart-s-2012-sustainability-report-talks-softly-about-suppliers (accessed July 18, 2014).

31. Wal-Mart to Toughen Standards" http://www.nytimes.com/2008/10/22/business/22walmart.html?_r=0

32. Lisa E. Bolton, Luk Warlop, and Joseph W. Alba, "Consumer Perceptions of Price (Un)Fairness," *Journal of Consumer Research* 29 (March 2003), pp. 474–491; Margaret C. Campbell, "Perceptions of Price Unfairness: Antecedents and Consequences," *Journal of Marketing Research* 36 (May 1999), pp. 187–199; Peter R. Darke and Darren W. Dahl, "Fairness and Discounts: The Subjective Value of a Bargain," *Journal of Consumer Psychology* 13, no. 3 (2003), pp. 328–338; Sarah Maxwell, "What Makes a Price Increase Seem 'Fair'?" *Pricing Strategy & Practice* 3, no. 4 (1995), pp. 21–27.

33. Dhruv Grewal, Kent B. Monroe, and R. Krishnan, "The Effects of Price Comparison Advertising on Buyers' Perceptions of Acquisition Value and Transaction Value," *Journal of Marketing* 62 (April 1998), pp. 46–60.

34. Noreen M. Klein and Janet E. Oglethorpe, "Reference Points in Consumer Decision Making," in *Advances in Consumer Research*, Vol. 14, eds. Melanie Wallendorf and Paul Anderson (Provo, UT: Association for Consumer Research, 1987), pp. 183–187.

35. Sonia Verma, "Can Canadian Perfume Help Afghanistan Break Its Poppy Habit?" *The Globe and Mail* March 19, 2010: A1.

36. Trisse Laxley, "A Fragrance with a Political Scent," *The Globe and Mail* March 19, 2010: A18.

37. Verma, "Can Canadian Perfume Help?"

38. Andrea Nemetz, "Opportunity Blossoms," http://www.the7virtues.com/AnyNewsM/1177760.html (accessed June 24, 2010).

39. Nemetz, "Opportunity Blossoms."

40. "Vetiver of Haiti," http://www.the7virtues.com/vetiver_of_haiti.php (accessed July 18, 2014).

41. "Middle East Peace," http://www.the7virtues.com/middle_east_peace.php (accessed July 18, 2014).

42. "The 7 Virtues CEO Barb Stegemann named Top Game Changer in the history of CBC's Dragons' Den," http://www.the7virtues.com/pdfs/Halifax_CEO_Named_Top_Game_Changer_in_History_of_CBCs_Dragons_Den.pdf (accessed July 18, 2014).

43. Carl Bialik, Elizabeth Holmes, Ray A. Smith, "Many Discounts, Few Deals," *The Wall Street Journal*, December 15, 2010, http://online.wsj.com/article/SB10001424052748704694004576019771942029048.html (accessed July 18, 2014); Vanessa O'Connell, "It's 50% Off ... Well, Maybe 35%. How Good Are Deals on Members'-Only Web Sites?" *The Wall Street Journal*, January 16, 2010; http://www.hautelook.com; http://www.gilt.com.

44. Robert Schindler, "The 99 Price Ending as a Signal of a Low-Price Appeal," *Journal of Retailing* 82, no. 1 (2006).

45. Michael Levy and Barton A. Weitz, *Retailing Management*, 6th ed. (Burr Ridge, IL: Irwin/McGraw-Hill, 2007).

46. Geoffrey A. Fowler and Yukari Iwatani Kane, "New Mobile Applications Use Bar-Code Scanners," *The Wall Street Journal*, December 16, 2009; http://shopsavvy.mobi/.

47. Brad Tuttle, "Use Amazon's Price Check App and Save $15," *Time*, December 8, 2011, http://moneyland.time.com/2011/12/08/use-amazons-price-check-app-and-save-15-this-saturday (accessed July 18, 2014); Susan Payton, "Amazon Price Check App: Small Business Threat or Sign of the Times?" *Small Business Trends*, December 15, 2011, http://smallbiztrends.com/2011/12/amazon-price-check-app-small-business-threat-or-sign-of-the-times.html (accessed July 18, 2014).

48. This section draws from Levy and Weitz, *Retailing Management*.

49. Sha Yang and Priya Raghubir, "Can Bottles Speak Volumes? The Effect of Package Shape on How Much to Buy," *Journal of Retailing* 81, no. 4 (2005), pp. 269–281.

50. "Competition Bureau Investigation Leads to $1-Million Settlement with Suzy Shier Inc.," http://www.competitionbureau.gc.ca/internet/index.cfm?itemID=305&lg=e (accessed June 24, 2007).

51. Compeau and Grewal, "Comparative Price Advertising"; Larry D. Compeau, Dhruv Grewal, and Diana S. Grewal, "Adjudicating Claims of Deceptive Advertised Reference Prices: The Use of Empirical Evidence," *Journal of Public Policy & Marketing* 14 (Fall 1994), pp. 52–62; Dhruv Grewal and Larry D. Compeau, "Comparative Price Advertising: Informative or Deceptive?" *Journal of Public Policy & Marketing* 11 (Spring 1992), pp. 52–62; Larry Compeau, Joan Lindsey-Mullikin, Dhruv Grewal, and Ross Petty, "An Analysis of Consumers' Interpretations of the Semantic Phrases Found in Comparative Price Advertisements," *Journal of Consumer Affairs* 38 (Summer 2004), pp. 178–187.

52. Joe Schneider, "Victory Is Sweet in BC Price-Fixing Case," *The Globe and Mail* April 13, 2010: B13.

53. Jeff Gray, "Chocolate Fix: Three Charged in Alleged Pricing Scheme," *The Globe and Mail*, June 6, 2013, http://m.theglobeandmail.com/report-on-business/industry-news/the-law-page/chocolate-bar-executives-accused-of-price-fixing-in-canada/article12380660 (accessed July 18, 2014).

54. "Chocolate Companies to Pay $23.2M in Price-fixing Class Action," Canadian Press, September 16, 2013, http://www.ctvnews.ca/business/chocolate-companies-to-pay-23-2m-in-price-fixing-class-action-1.1457685 (accessed July 18, 2014).

55. This case was written by Elisabeth Nevins Caswell in conjunction with the textbook authors (Dhruv Grewal and Michael Levy) for use in a class discussion; it was not written as an illustration of effective or ineffective marketing practices; David Kravets, "Like Amazon's DRM-Free Music Downloads? Thanks Apple," Wired.com, September 25, 2007 (accessed January 20, 2008); Kevin Kelleher, "Let the MP3 Price Wars Begin," TheStreet.com September 28, 2007: http://www.thestreet.com/newsanalysis/technet/10381387.html (accessed July 18, 2014).

CHAPTER 12

1. William B. Cassidy, "Wal-Mart Tightens the Chain," *Journal of Commerce*, January 18, 2010, http://www.joc.com/economy-watch/wal-mart-tightens-chain_20100118.html (accessed July 21, 2014).

2. Chris Burritt, Carol Wolf, and Matthew Boyle, "Wal-Mart Asks Suppliers to Cede Control of Deliveries" *Bloomberg Businessweek*, June 1, 2010, http://www.bloomberg.com/apps/news?pid=newsarchive&sid=aiL3Mymd_y_g&pos=12 (accessed July 21, 2014).

3. Based on Barton A. Weitz, "PenAgain Sells to Walmart," in Michael Levy and Barton A. Weitz, *Retailing Management*, 8th ed. (Burr Ridge, IL: McGraw-Hill/Irwin, 2012), pp. 564–565; http://www. Penagain.com; Gwendolyn Bounds, "The Long Road to Walmart," *The Wall Street Journal*, September 19, 2005, p. R1: Gwendolyn Bounds, "One Mount to Make it," *The Wall Street Journal*, May 30, 2006, p. B1.

4. This Entrepreneurial Marketing box was written with information gathered in a telephone interview with AWAKE Chocolate co-founder Matt Schnarr on Thursday June 20, 2013.

5. http://www.marketingpower.com/live/mg-dictionary.

6. Based on David Simchi-Levi, Philip Kaminsky, and Edith Simchi-Levi, *Designing and Managing the Supply Chain: Concepts, Strategies and Case Studies*, 2nd ed. (New York: McGraw-Hill/Irwin, 2003); Michael Levy and Barton A. Weitz, *Retailing Management*, 5th ed. (New York: McGraw-Hill/Irwin, 2004).

7. http://www.marketingpower.com/live/mg-dictionary. Definition from the Council of Logistics Management.

8. Bloomberg, "Nestle to Sail Amazon Rivers to Reach Consumers," *The Globe and Mail* June 18, 2010: B8.

9. Independent Equity Research Corp., "Coastal Contacts Inc. Update Report" (eResearch coastal contacts.pdf), http://eresearch.ca/profile.asp?companyID=437 (accessed June 24, 2010).

10. Mary Biti, "Clearly a Winning Strategy," http://investors.coastalcontacts.com/mediacoverage.asp?ticker=T.COA&report=show&id=6151&lang=EN&title=null (accessed June 24, 2010).

11. Eve Lazarus, "Trevor Linden Plays with Clearly Contacts," http://www.marketingmag.ca/english/news/marketer/article.jsp?content=20100528_164119_13472 (accessed June 24, 2010).

12. Jennifer Horn, "ClearlyContacts Opens First Brick-and-Mortar Store," *Strategy Magazine*, February 14, 2013, http://strategyonline.ca/2013/02/14/clearlycontacts-ca-opens-first-brick-and-mortar-store/#ixzz2b0dipjvJ (accessed July 18, 2014).

13. Biti, "Clearly a Winning Strategy."

14. Clearly Contacts Facebook page, https://www.facebook.com/ClearlyContacts.ca (accessed August 8, 2013).

15. comScore, "2012 Digital Advertising Highlights," http://iabcanada.com/files/comScore_Various-Categories-Canada-IAB-Report_Feb-26-20131.pdf (accessed July 18, 2014).

16. "The Timeline," http://investors.coastalcontacts.com/custommessage.asp?ticker=t.coa&message=fifth&title=null (accessed August 8, 2013).

17. Jennifer Horn, "ClearlyContacts."

18. Shirley Lichti, "Listing Fees Can Decide a Food Product's Fate," http://www.marketingmagic.ca/articles/ListingFees.htm (accessed July 18, 2014).

19. Eve Lazarus, "Martin's Puts New Apple Snack on Ontario Shelves," *Marketing Magazine*, July 2, 2013, http://www.marketingmag.ca/news/marketer-news/martins-puts-new-apple-snack-on-ontario-shelves-82737 (accessed July 18, 2014).

20. Frances Barrick, "Fruit Farm Bites into New Market with Apple Chips," *The Record*, August 1, 2013, http://www.therecord.com/news-story/3915759-fruit-farm-bites-into-new-market-with-apple-chips (accessed August 7, 2013).

21. Dale Buss, "Nespresso Sticks with Distribution Model Despite Increased Competition," Brand Channel, May 22, 2013, http://www.brandchannel.com/home/post/2013/05/22/Nespresso-Growth-052213.aspx (accessed July 18, 2014).

22. http://www.marketingpower.com/live/mg-dictionary.

23. Ibid.

24. Canadian Franchise Directory, http://www.franchisedirectory.ca (accessed July 18, 2014).

25. "Franchise Guide Fast Facts," http://www.canadianfranchisedirectory.ca/franchiseguide.aspx (accessed July 18, 2014).

26. Ghemawat and Nueno, "ZARA: Fast Fashion."

27. Sharyn Leaver, Joshua Walker, and Tamara Mendelsohn, "Hasbro Drives Supply Chain Efficiency with BPM," *Forester Research*, July 22, 2003.

28. Erin Anderson and Anne Coughlan, "Structure, Governance, and Relationship Management," in *Handbook of Marketing*, eds. B. Weitz and R. Wensley (London, UK: Sage, 2002).

29. Charles Duhigg and David Barbosa, "In China, Human Costs Are Built into an iPad," *The New York Times*, January 25, 2012, http://www.nytimes.com/2012/01/26/business/ieconomy-apples-ipad-and-the-human-costs-for-workers-in-china.html?pagewanted51&_r53&ref5business&src5me&adxnnlx51331046030-59qBpuAMRNH8OEl6dxh/7g (accessed July 18, 2014).; Melissa J. Anderson, "The Supply Chain Enters the Spotlight," *Evolved Employer*, February 14, 2012, http://www.evolvedemployer.com/2012/02/14/the-supply-chain-enters-the-spotlight (accessed July 18, 2014).

30. Erin Anderson and Barton Weitz, "The Use of Pledges to Build and Sustain Commitment in Distribution Channels," *Journal of Marketing Research* 29 (February 1992), pp. 18–34.

31. This section draws from Levy and Weitz, *Retailing Management*, Chapter 10.

32. "RFID Technology Transforming Food Retailers Like Wal-Mart," http://seekingalpha.com/article/194466-rfid-technology-transforming-food-retailers-like-wal-mart (accessed July 18, 2014).

33. "PepsiCo Foods Canada," http://www.pepsico.ca/en/Purpose/EnvironmentalSustainability/ES_ENG_PFC.html (accessed July 18, 2014).

34. "High-Efficiency Fleet at Frito Lay Canada" (pdf provided by Frito Lay Canada June 28, 2010).

35. "Frito Lay Canada is Canada's First Food Manufacturer to Introduce Zero-Emission Electric Vehicles into Delivery Fleet," http://smr.newswire.ca/en/frito-lay-canada/frito-lay-canada-is-canadas-first-food-manufacturer (accessed June 29, 2010).

36. "Performance with a Purpose," http://www.pepsico.ca/en/downloads/PEPC_PwP_Environment_EN_FINAL%202013.pdf (accessed July 18, 2014).

37. Jantzi-Sustainalytics, "Top 50 Socially Responsible Corporations," *Maclean's*, June 9, 2011, http://www2.macleans.ca/2011/06/09/better-business (accessed July 18, 2014).

38. "David Chilton," Speakers' Spotlight, http://www.speakers.ca/speakers/david-chilton (accessed July 18, 2014).

39. "David Chilton," The Lavin Daily, http://www.thelavinagency.com/blog-finance-speaker-david-chilton-on-failure.html (accessed July 18, 2014).

40. Shirley Lichti, "Listing Fees Can Decide a Food Product's Fate," *The Record*, December 17, 2003, http://www.marketingmagic.ca/articles/ListingFees.htm (accessed July 18, 2014).

41. Larry Kellam, "P&G Rethinks Supply Chain," *Optimize* (October 2003), p. 35.

42. Vertica Bhardwaj and Ann Fairhurst, "Fast Fashion: Response to Changes in the Fashion Industry," *International Review of Retail, Distribution and Consumer Research* 20 (February 2010), pp. 165–73; Felipe Caro, Jérémie Gallien, Miguel Díaz Miranda, Javier García Torralbo, Jose Manuel Corrediora Corras, Marcos

Montes Vazques, José Antonio Ramos Calamonte, and Juan Correa, "Zara Uses Operations Research to Reengineer Its Global Distribution Process," *Interfaces* 40 (2010), pp. 71–84; Carmen Lopez and Ying Fan, "Case Study: Internationalisation of the Spanish Fashion Brand Zara," *Journal of Fashion Marketing and Management* 13, no. 2 (2009), pp. 279–96; Mark Mulligan, "Spanish Professor Who Uncovers the Detail in Retail; Constant Contact with Corporate Life Is a Valuable Teaching Tool," *Financial Times*, August 18, 2008, p. 12; "Combining Art with Science, Zara Competes with 'Fast Fashion'," *SupplyChainBrain*, February 7, 2008.

43. Zeynep Ton, Elena Corsi, and Vincent Dessain, "Zara: Managing Stores for Fast Fashion," Harvard Business School, March 2011.

CHAPTER 13

1. Stephen Fenech, "Apple's Theme Park," *Herald Sun* May 28, 2008; http://www.apple.com (accessed May 28, 2008); Jerry Useem, "Apple: America's Best Retailer," *Fortune* March 8, 2007.

2. "Apple Store Locations," http://www.apple.com/ca/retail/storelist (accessed August 13, 2013).

3. Ian Sheer and Joann S. Lublin, "Apple Stores Lose Their Lustre," *The Globe and Mail*, August 2, 2013: B8.

4. Best Buy Financial News Release, "Best Buy Reports Fiscal Second Quarter 2013 Results," http://phx.corporate-ir.net/phoenix.zhtml?c=83192&p=irol-newsArticle&ID=1727161 (accessed July 18, 2014).

5. Ian Sheer and Joann S. Lublin, "Apple Stores.".

6. Ibid.

7. Deloitte and Stores Media, "Top 250 Global Retailers 2008," http://www.stores.org/global-powers-retailing-top-250 (accessed July 4, 2011).

8. Statistics Canada, "Retail Trade May 2013," http://www.statcan.gc.ca/daily-quotidien/130723/dq130723a-eng.htm (accessed July 18, 2014).

9. http://www.retailcouncil.org/news/media/profile/print/default.asp (accessed January 4, 2008).

10. This chapter draws heavily from Michael Levy and Barton A. Weitz, *Retailing Management*, 7th ed. (Burr Ridge, IL: McGraw-Hill/Irwin, 2009), Chapters 2 and 3.

11. "Nutrition Center," http://www.petesfrootique.com/LorieMcNeil.asp (accessed June 23, 2007).

12. This Entrepreneurial Marketing box was written with information gathered in a telephone interview with Danielle Nesbitt of On The Rocks May 6, 2014.

13. Craig Guillot, "Masters of the Game," *Stores*, July 2009; http://www.gamestop.com/gs/tournaments/h3o/default.aspx.

14. "Essential Facts About the Canadian Computer and Video Game Industry (2012)," The Entertainment Software Association, http://theesa.ca/?page_id=22 (accessed August 14, 2013).

15. "About Kongregate," http://www.kongregate.com/pages/about.

16. GameStop, "Jolt Online Gaming Brings Long-Time Soccer Management Franchise to Facebook with Championship Manager: Rivals," http://news.gamestop.com/press-release/jolt-online-gaming/jolt-online-gaming-brings-long-time-soccer-management-franchise-fac (accessed July 18, 2014).

17. "Corporate Profile," http://phx.corporate-ir.net/phoenix.zhtml?c5130125&p5irol-irhome.

18. Holt Renfrew, "About hr2," http://www.holtrenfrew.com/en/holt/twocolumn/footer/hr2/about-hr2 (accessed August 14, 2103).

19. Jermony Lloyd, "Hudson's Bay Opens First Outlet Store Near Toronto," *Marketing Magazine*, August 1, 2013, http://www.marketingmag.ca/news/marketer-news/hudsons-bay-opens-first-outlet-store-near-toronto-85013 (accessed July 18, 2014).

20. "Shoppers Drug Mart Opens its 1,000th Drug Store in Canada," http://www.shoppersdrugmart.ca/english/corporate_information/investor_relations/press_releases/articles/april_26_2007.html (accessed June 25, 2007).

21. "An Industry That's Regaining Its Fighting Trim," *Chain Drug Review* June 7, 2004: 20.

22. Marina Strauss, "The Bay Steps up Its Game with a Focus on Shoes," *The Globe and Mail* June 5, 2010: B3.

23. Marina Strauss, "New-Look Hudson's Bay Pushes Retail Growth Plan," *The Globe and Mail*, April 8, 2013, http://www.theglobeandmail.com/report-on-business/new-look-hudsons-bay-pushes-retail-growth-plan/article10836382(accessed July 18, 2014).

24. Marina Strauss, "HMV Moves Beyond Music," *The Globe and Mail* June 14, 2010: B1.

25. Marina Strauss, "In Store Aisles, Dr. Dre Meets Big Data," *The Globe and Mail*, March 5, 2013, http://www.theglobeandmail.com/technology/business-technology/in-store-aisles-dr-dre-meets-big-data/article9302024 (accessed July 18, 2014).

26. "Canadian Tire Introduces New Barcode App," *Click! Weekly* November 30, 2010.

27. "About Giant Tiger," http://www.gianttiger.com/about (accessed May 6, 2014).

28. "Facts and Questions," http://www.gianttiger.com/en/faq.php (accessed June 20, 2007).

29. Ibid.

30. "Community/Murals," http://www.gianttiger.com/en/community/murals (accessed June 20, 2007).

31. "The North West Company: Alberta," http://www.northwest.ca/BackOffice/DesktopDefault.aspx?tabindex=0&tabid=10080 (accessed June 20, 2007).

32. Megan Hynes, "Augmenting the Shopping Experience Reality," *Strategy Magazine*, July 16, 2012, http://strategyonline.ca/2012/07/16/augmenting-the-shopping-experience-reality (accessed July 18, 2014).

33. Wes Lafortune, "Concept Retailing Trend Costly But Growing," http://www.businessedge.ca/article.cfm/newsID/11401.cfm (accessed June 24, 2007).

34. Marina Straus, "Does This Blouse Make Sears Look Plugged-In?," *The Globe and Mail* April 22, 2011: B4.

35. Leane Delap, "At the Body Shop, It's an Experience with the World," *The Globe and Mail*, May 28, 2012, http://www.theglobeandmail.com/report-on-business/industry-news/property-report/at-the-body-shop-its-an-experience-with-the-world/article4217870 (accessed July 18, 2014).

36. Marjo Johne, "Sport Chek Sprints into Digital," *The Globe and Mail*, May 24, 2013, http://www.theglobeandmail.com/technology/tech-news/sport-chek-sprints-into-digital/article12098883 (accessed August 15, 2013).

37. Ibid.

38. For descriptions of the Wheel of Retailing theory, see Stanley Hollander, "The Wheel of Retailing: What Makes Skilled Managers Succumb to the 'Prosper, Mature, and Decay' Pattern?" *Marketing Management* (Summer 1996), pp. 63–65; Stephen Brown, "Postmodernism, the Wheel of Retailing, and Will to Power," *The International Review of Retail, Distribution, and Consumer Research* (July 1995), pp. 387–412; Arieh Goldman, "Institutional Change in Retailing: An Updated Wheel of Retailing," in *Foundations of Marketing Channels*, eds. A. Woodside et al. (Austin, TX: Lone Star, 1978), pp. 193–201. For a description of the Accordion theory, see Stanley C. Hollander, "Notes on the Retail Accordion," *Journal of Retailing* 42 (Summer 1966), pp. 20–40, 54. For a description of the Dialectic Process theory, see Thomas J. Maronick and Bruce J. Walker, "The Dialectic Evolution of Retailing," in *Proceedings: Southern Marketing Association*, ed. Barnett Greenberg (Atlanta: Georgia State University, 1974), p. 147. For descriptions of Natural Selection theory, see A.C.R. Dreesmann, "Patterns of Evolution in Retailing," *Journal of Retailing* (Spring 1968),

pp. 81–96; Murray Forester, "Darwinian Theory of Retailing," *Chain Store Age* (August 1995), p. 8. A summary of these theories can be found in Michael Levy and Barton A. Weitz, *Retailing Management*, 6th ed. (Burr Ridge, IL: Irwin/McGraw-Hill, 2007).

39. Paul Brent, "McLatte Anyone?" *Marketing Magazine* December 10, 2007: 10.

40. Susan Krashinsky, "Beer Spruces up in Battle for Market Share," *The Globe and Mail*, May 18, 2013, http://www.theglobeandmail.com/report-on-business/industry-news/marketing/beer-spruces-up-in-battle-for-market-share/article12000094 (accessed July 18, 2014).

41. Julie Baker et al., "The Influence of Multiple Store Environment Cues on Perceived Merchandise Value and Patronage Intentions," *Journal of Marketing* 66 (April 2001), pp. 120–141; Eric R. Spangenberg, Ayn E. Crowley, and Pamela W. Henderson, "Improving the Store Environment: Do Olfactory Cues Affect Evaluations and Behaviors?" *Journal of Marketing* 60 (April 1996), pp. 67–80; Michael K. Hui and John E.G. Bateson, "Perceived Control and the Effects of Crowding and Consumer Choice on the Service Experience," *Journal of Consumer Research* 18 (September 1991), pp. 174–184.

42. "Shelf Help: A Guide to Shopper Marketing," *Strategy Magazine* (July 2010), p. S56.

43. "IKEA Canada Launches New Sustainability Program—The Never Ending List," http://www.newswire.ca/en/releases/archive/February2010/02/c6012.html (accessed July 18, 2014).

44. "Greener Ways to Get Here," http://theneverendinglist.ikea.ca/en/Greener-Ways-to-Get-Here.html (accessed July 28, 2010).

45. "Blue Bag Program," http://theneverendinglist.ikea.ca/en/Blue-Bag-Program.html (accessed July 28, 2010).

46. "IKEA Canada Gets a 'High Five' for its Sustainability Initiatives," April 22, 2013, http://www.ikea.com/ca/en/about_ikea/newsitem/greenest_employer (accessed July 18, 2014).

47. Marina Strauss, "An IKEA Special, with a Side of Modest Pie." *The Globe and Mail*, June 1, 2013: B3.

48. Leonard Berry, Kathleen Seiders, and Dhruv Grewal, "Understanding Service Convenience," *Journal of Marketing* 66 (July 2002), pp. 1–17.

49. Rupal Parekh, "How Zara Ballooned Into a Multi-Billion Dollar Brand Without Advertising," *Advertising Age*, August 19, 2013, http://adage.com/article/cmo-strategy/zara-grew-a-multi-billion-dollar-brand-sans-ads/243730 (accessed August 20, 2013).

50. Matt Semansky, "Well.ca Opens Virtual Store in Toronto," *Marketing Magazine*, April 12, 2012, http://www.marketingmag.ca/news/marketer-news/well-ca-opens-virtual-store-in-toronto-49725 (accessed July 18, 2014).

51. Alicia Androich, "Walmart Canada and P&G Launch Bus Shelter Mobile Store," *Marketing Magazine*, June 5, 2013. http://www.marketingmag.ca/news/marketer-news/walmart-canada-and-pg-launch-bus-shelter-mobile-store-80530 (accessed July 18, 2014).

52. Amit Shilton, "Convenience Is Key for Pizza Pizza's New App," *The Globe and Mail* April 5, 2011: B9.

53. "Demystifying the Online Shopper, 10 Myths of Multi-Channel Retailing," PricewaterhouseCoopers, http://www.pwc.com/ca/multichannelshopping (accessed July 18, 2014).

54. "Canadian Online Shopping Rises 25% in Two Years," Canadian Press, October 28, 2013, http://www.marketingmag.ca/news/marketer-news/canadian-online-shopping-rises-24-in-two-years-92065 (accessed July 18, 2014).

55. "Can't Find That Dress on the Rack? Retailers Are Pushing More Shoppers to the Net," *Knowledge@Wharton*, November 1, 2006.

56. Jeff Fraser, "Infographic: Canadians Want In-Store Mobile Offers, But Only If They're Relevant," *Marketing Magazine*, July 19, 2013, http://www.marketingmag.ca/news/marketer-news/infographic-canadians-want-in-store-mobile-offers-but-only-if-theyre-relevant-84006 (accessed July 18, 2014).

57. Kenneth Hein, "Study: Web Research Nets In-Store Sales," *Brandweek*, May 7, 2007 (accessed December 24, 2007).

58. "Sponsored Supplement: Expanding the Reach of Personalization," *Internet Retailer*, March 2010.

59. Forsythe et al., "Development of a Scale."

60. Brodkin, "TJX Breach."

61. Marina Strauss. "New Boxes on the Block," *The Globe and Mail*, August 3, 2013: B7.

62. "Demystifying the online shopper."

63. For more information on approaches for increasing share of wallet, see Tom Osten, *Customer Share Marketing* (Upper Saddle River, NJ: Prentice Hall, 2002).

64. Barry Berman and Shawn Thelen, "A Guide to Developing and Managing a Well-integrated Multi-Channel Retail Strategy," *International Journal of Retail & Distribution Management* 32, no. 3 (2004), p. 4.

65. Target.com, "Corporate Fact Sheet," http://pressroom.target.com/corporate (accessed May 6, 2014).

66. Jessica Wohl, "Target Hopes Exclusive Designer Deals Boost Sales," *Reuters*, August 2, 2011.

67. Mary Catherine O'Connor, "Target Shoppers: Say Goodbye to Michael Graves' Budget-Friendly Design," *smartplanet*, February 16, 2012, http://www.smartplanet.com/blog/design-architecture/target-shoppers-say-goodbye-to-michael-graves-budget-friendly-design/4215 (accessed July 18, 2014).

68. Target.com, "Target Unveils New Design Partnership Program," January 13, 2012, http://pressroom.target.com/pr/news/target-unveils-new-design-partnership-221743.aspx (accessed July 18, 2014).

69. Emanualla Grinberg, "'Missoni for Target' Line Crashes Site," CNN.com, September 13, 2011, http://articles.cnn.com/2011-09-13/living/living_missoni-for-target-line-creates-black-friday-like-demand_1_missoni-isaac-mizrahi-target-com?_s5PM:LIVING (accessed July 18, 2014).

70. Hollie Shaw, "Target Unveils Canadian Stores," *The Financial Post*, May 26, 2011, http://business.financialpost.com/2011/05/26/target-unveils-canadian-stores (accessed July 18, 2014).

71. Ibid.

72. Kristin Laird, "Video: Target Finds Canadian Roots with New Partnership," *Marketing Magazine*, January 25, 2013, http://www.marketingmag.ca/news/marketer-news/target-finds-canadian-roots-with-new-partnership-70572 (accessed July 18, 2014).

73. Marina Strauss and Susan Krashinsky, "The Target Invasion: How Pricing Will Be Key to Canadian Success," *The Globe and Mail*, January 19, 2013, http://www.theglobeandmail.com/globe-investor/the-target-invasion-how-pricing-will-be-key-to-canadian-success/article7550145 (accessed August 20, 2013).

74. Canadian Press, "HBC Beats Target in Customer Satisfaction Survey, Costco Ahead of Both," *Marketing Magazine*, August 20, 2013, http://www.marketingmag.ca/news/marketer-news/hbc-beats-target-in-customer-satisfaction-survey-costco-ahead-of-both-86163 (accessed July 18, 2014).

75. Marina Strauss, "Target Shuffle Puts Canadian Retreat on Table," *The Globe and Mail*, May 6, 2014: B1.

CHAPTER 14

1. Emily Bryson York, "McDonald's Unveils 'I'm Lovin' It' 2.0," http://adage.com/article?article_id=143453 (accessed August 14, 2014).

2. Kate MacArthur, "McD's to Shops: Make 'Lovin' It' More Than Tag," http://adage.com/article?article_id=107083 (accessed August 14, 2014).

3. Ibid.

4. Randall Frost, "Lost in Translation," http://www.brandchannel.com/features_effect.asp?pf_id=340 (accessed August 14, 2014).

5. Rebecca Harris, "McDonald's Canada Launches Integrated Ad Campaign Around Our Food. Your Questions," *Marketing Magazine*, September 26, 2012, http://www.marketingmag.ca/news/marketer-news/mcdonalds-canada-launches-integrated-ad-campaign-around-our-food-your-questions-62657 (accessed August 14, 2014).

6. Marketing Staff, "*Our Food. Your Questions* Wins Big at 2013 Marketing Awards," *Marketing Magazine*, May 31. 2013, http://www.marketingmag.ca/news/agency-news/our-food-your-questions-wins-big-at-2013-marketing-awards-80094 (accessed August 14, 2014).

7. T. Duncan and C. Caywood, "The Concept, Process, and Evolution of Integrated Marketing Communication," in *Integrated Communication: Synergy of Persuasive Voices*, eds. E. Thorson and J. Moore (Mahwah, NJ: Lawrence Erlbaum Associates, 1996); http://jimc.medill.northwestern.edu/2000/pettegrew.htm.

8. Deborah J. MacInnis and Bernard J. Jaworski, "Information Processing from Advertisements: Toward an Integrative Framework," *Journal of Marketing* 53, no. 4 (October 1989), pp. 1–23.

9. Deborah J. MacInnis, Christine Moorman, and Bernard J. Jaworski, "Enhancing and Measuring Consumers' Motivation, Opportunity," *Journal of Marketing* 55, no. 4 (October 1991), pp. 32–554. Joan Meyers-Levy, "Elaborating on Elaboration: The Distinction between Relational and Item-Specific Elaboration," *Journal of Consumer Research* 18 (December 1991), pp. 358–367.

10. http://retailindustry.about.com/library/bl/q2/bl_um041701.htm (accessed September 26, 2006).

11. This section draws from Michael Levy and Barton A. Weitz, *Retailing Management*, 6th ed. (Burr Ridge, IL: McGraw-Hill/Irwin, 2007).

12. Michelle DiPardo, "Amway Canada Moves 100% of Its Ad Spend Online," *Marketing Magazine*, April 4, 2013, http://www.marketingmag.ca/news/marketer-news/amway-canada-moves-100-of-its-ad-spend-online-75654 (accessed August 14, 2014).

13. Theodore Leavitt, *The Marketing Imagination* (New York: The Free Press, 1986).

14. George E. Belch and Michael A. Belch, *Advertising and Promotion: An Integrated Marketing Communications Perspective*, 7th ed. (New York: McGraw-Hill/Irwin, 2007).

15. http://www.kleenex.com/us/av/index.asp (accessed September 26, 2006).

16. Martin, Lang, and Wong, "Conclusion, Explicitness in Advertising."

17. http://wps.prenhall.com/ca_ph_ebert_busess_3/0,6518,224378-,00.html.

18. The Television Bureau of Canada, "Canadian Net Advertising Volume (NAV)," http://www.tvb.ca/pages/nav2_htm (accessed August 23, 2013).

19. "Net Advertising Volume, 2012," *The Globe and Mail*, October 4, 2013, page B4.

20. William F. Arens, *Contemporary Advertising*, 8th ed. (New York: McGraw-Hill, 2003).

21. "Cassies Canadian Advertising Success Stories 2006," http://cassies.ca/winners/2006Winners/winners_04.html (accessed July 4, 2007).

22. Dean M. Krugman et al., *Advertising: Its Role in Modern Marketing* (New York: The Dryden Press, 1994), pp. 221–226.

23. "Celebrating Carbon Commitments," *Sustainable Waterloo's 2009 Report*, http://www.sustainablewaterloo.org/index.php?p=2009report (accessed July 28, 2010).

24. http://www.riger.com/know_base/media/understanding.html (accessed November 15, 2004).

25. IAB Canada, "2011 Actual and 2012 Estimated Canadian Online Advertising Revenue Survey Detailed Report," http://iabcanada.com/files/Canadian_Online_Advertising_Revenue_Survey_English.pdf (accessed August 14, 2014).

26. Publishing 2.0, "Google AdWords: A Brief History of Online Advertising Innovation," http://publishing2.com/2008/05/27/google-adwords-a-brief-history-of-online-advertising-innovation (accessed August 14, 2014).

27. Canadian Media Directors' Council, "Media Digest," 2012, http://www.yellowhouseevents.com/img/CMDC_images/CMDC_Digital_Ed_2012.pdf (accessed August 21, 2013).

28. American Marketing Association, *Dictionary of Marketing Terms* (Chicago, IL: American Marketing Association, 2008).

29. Eric Wilson, "Checking Models' IDs at the Door," *The New York Times*, February 8, 2012, http://www.nytimes.com/2012/02/09/fashion/efforts-to-stop-use-of-underage-models-during-new-york-fashion-week.html?pagewanted5all (accessed August 14, 2014).

30. Ellie Krupnick, "Drop Dead Ads Banned by ASA for Too-Skinny Model," *The Huffington Post*, November 10, 2011, http://www.huffingtonpost.com/2011/11/10/drop-dead-ads-banned-asa_n_1085903.html (accessed August 14, 2014).

31. David Gianastasio, "Fashion Site Nixes Photo of Freakishly Thin-Looking Model," *AdWeek*, July 13, 2011, http://www.adweek.com/adfreak/fashion-site-nixes-photo-freakishly-thin-looking-model-133367 (accessed August 14, 2014).

32. http://online.wsj.com/article/SB10001424052748703481004574646904234860412.html; George E. Belch and Michael A. Belch, *Advertising and Promotion: An Integrated Marketing Communications Perspective* (New York: McGraw-Hill, 2007).

33. Rebecca Lieb, "Q&A: Cindy Krum Cuts Through the Mobile Marketing Alphabet Soup of NFC and RFID," March 16, 2010, http://econsultancy.com/blog/5608-q-a-cindy-krum-cuts-through-the-mobile-marketing-alphabet-soup-of-nfc-and-rfid (accessed August 14, 2014).

34. Ruth Stevens, "Crash Course in Direct Marketing," http://www.marketingprofs.com/premium/seminar_detail.asp?adref=semsrch&semid=104 (accessed August 14, 2014).

35. Canadian Media Directors' Council, "Media Digest."

36. *Marketing Research Group Fact Sheet: Canadian Consumer Attitudes to Direct Mail (Part II)*, http://www.canadapost.ca/business/prodserv/mdm/market-e.asp (accessed June 26, 2007).

37. Russ Martin, "5 Tips for Mobile E-Mail Marketing," *Marketing Magazine*, June 30, 2013, http://www.marketingmag.ca/news/media-news/5-tips-for-mobile-e-mail-marketing-84815 (accessed August 14, 2014).

38. Heart & Stroke Foundation of Canada, "About Us," ww2.heartandstroke.ca/Page.asp?PageID=88&CategoryID=10&Src=about (accessed June 26, 2007).

39. Heart & Stroke Foundation of Canada, "Annual Report 2006," ww2.heartandstroke.ca/Images/HSFC_AR_2006_eng.pdf (accessed June 26, 2007).

40. "Marketing and Selling Solutions: Catalogues," http://www.canadapost.ca/tools/pdf/getpdf.asp?pdf=/offerings/catalogue_mail/pdf/cat-e.pdf&lang=e (accessed June 26, 2007).

41. "Marketing Research Group Fact Sheet: Canadian Consumer Attitudes to Direct Mail (Part II)," http://www.canadapost.ca/business/prodserv/mdm/market-e.asp (accessed June 26, 2007).

42. "Direct Response Television," http://www.direct-response-television.com (accessed June 26, 2007).

43. "Canadian Blood Services & Northern Lights to Present at Interactive Marketing Conference," http://www.nldrtv.com/news/CBS_CaseStudy_PressRelease.htm (accessed June 26, 2007).

44. "Northern Lights and Canadian Blood Services Capture Gold at CMA Awards," http://www.nldrtv.com/news/CMA_PressRelease. htm (accessed June 26, 2007).

45. Paul-Mark Rendon, "Virgin Builds on Buzz," http://www. marketingmag.ca/magazine/current/feature/article. jsp?content=20051212_73030_73030 (accessed June 26, 2007).

46. "About Rogers Centre," http://www.rogerscentre.com/inaround/ visitors/policies/index.html (accessed June 26, 2007).

47. Emily Wexler, "Marketer Survey 2012," *Strategy Magazine*, December 7, 2012, http://strategyonline.ca/2012/12/07/2012-marketer-survey (accessed August 14, 2014).

48. "Real Beauty Shines Through: Dove Wins Titanium Grand Prix 163 Million Views on YouTube," Google Think Insights, http://www. thinkwithgoogle.com/case-studies/dove-real-beauty-sketches. html (accessed August 14, 2014).

49. http://www.yoplait.com/breastcancer_lids.aspx (accessed September 22, 2006).

50. Madd Canada, "Cause Related Marketing," http://www.madd.ca/ madd2/en/giving/giving_cause_related_programs.html (accessed August 14, 2014).

51. Jackie Huba, "A Just Cause Creating Emotional Connections with Customers," 2003, http://www.inc.com/ articles/2003/05/25537.html.

52. Christina Binkley, "Which Stars Sell Fashion?" *The Wall Street Journal*, February 4, 2010.

53. Katherine Rosman, "And the Loser Is ... Fashion," *The Wall Street Journal* January 9, 2008.

54. Carl Obermiller and Eric R. Spangenberg, "On the Origin and Distinctness of Skepticism toward Advertising," *Marketing Letters* 11, no. 4 (2000), p. 311.

55. http://www.tomsshoes.com/ourcause.aspx (accessed July 31, 2010).

56. http://www.insightargentina.org (accessed July 31, 2010).

57. "P&Gs Olympic Strategy: Stick with What Works," *The Globe and Mail*, January 10, 2014, B6.

58. Yubo Chen, Scott Fay, and Qi Wang, "The Role of Marketing in Social Media: How Online Consumer Reviews Evolve," *Journal of Interactive Marketing* 25, no. 2 (May 2011), pp. 85–94; Bonnie Rochman, "Sweet Spot," *Time*, November 2009.

59. "Critical Mass," http://www.dmnews.com/critical-mass/ article/136612 (accessed August 14, 2014).

60. Annette Bourdeau, "Critical Mass: The Unagency," http://www. strategyonline.ca/articles/magazine/20070601/bizcritical.html (accessed August 14, 2014).

61. http://www.criticalmass.com/about/news/profile-dianne-wilkins-ceo-critical-mass.htm (accessed July 31, 2010).

62. Christina Reynolds, "Q & A with Ted Hellard Founder and Chairman of Critical Mass Inc," excerpted from the *Calgary Herald*, http://www.criticalmass.com/about/news/259.htm (accessed July 31, 2010).

63. Elizabeth Church, "Newsfeed Update: Universities Sign onto Facebook," *The Globe and Mail*, December 26, 2007, A14.

64. Famecount, "Justin Bieber Facebook Statistics," http://www. famebook.com/facebook/justin-bieber.

65. Ibid.

66. Goldstein, op. cit.

67. Babu, op. cit.

68. "Justin Bieber," https://twitter.com/justinbieber (accessed August 18, 2013).

69. Russ Martin, "Visa Canada and BBDO Talk "smallenfreuden" Phase Two," *Marketing Magazine*, May 14, 2013, http://www. marketingmag.ca/uncategorized/visa-canada-and-bbdo-talk-smallenfreuden-phase-two-78634 (accessed August 14, 2014).

70. Twitter Canada, "Visa Canada: How Can a Payments Technology Company Spark Enough Buzz to Shift Consumer Spending Habits?," https://business.twitter.com/success-stories/visa-canada (accessed May 12, 2014).

71. Russ Martin, "Visa Canada and BBDO Talk "smallenfreuden" Phase Two," *Marketing Magazine*, May 14, 2013, http://www. marketingmag.ca/uncategorized/visa-canada-and-bbdo-talk-smallenfreuden-phase-two-78634 (accessed August 14, 2014).

72. Russ Martin, "Twitter Canada Publishes Visa as Its First Case Study," *Marketing Magazine*, March 19, 2014, http://www. marketingmag.ca/news/marketer-news/twitter-canada-publishes-visa-as-its-first-case-study-104372 (accessed August 14, 2014).

73. Drew Davis, "Jay-Z's Offline Campaign Leads to Online Action," *Tipping Point Labs*, August 25, 2011, http://tippingpointlabs. com/2011/08/25/jay-zs-offline-campaign-leads-to-online-action (accessed August 14, 2014).

74. Teressa Iezzi, "Jay-Zs 'Decoded' Campaign Wins Integrated Grand Prix and Titanium at Cannes," *Fast Company*, June 25, 2011, http://www.fastcocreate.com/1679205/jay-z-decoded-wins-integrated-grand-prix-and-titanium-at-cannes (accessed August 14, 2014).

75. Ibid; Andrew Adam Newman, "Find Jay-Z's Memoir at a Bookstore, or on Billboard," *The New York Times*, October 18, 2010, http://www.nytimes.com/2010/10/18/business/ media/18adco.html (accessed August 14, 2014).

76. Newman, op. cit.

77. Droga5, "Bing/Decode Jay-Z Case Study," YouTube, http://www. youtube.com/watch?v5XNic4wf8AYg&feature5player_embedded (accessed August 14, 2014).

78. http://bing.decodejay-z.com/?fbid5Xbh8cDvdLDY&wom5false.

79. Newman, op. cit.

80. Dan Duray, "Jay-Z's Book to Be Utterly Inescapable, Thanks to Bing, Clear Channel," *New York Observer*, October 18, 2010, http://www.observer.com/2010/10/jayzs-book-to-be-utterly-inescapable-thanks-to-bing-clear-channel/?utm_medium5partial-text&utm_campaign5home (accessed August 14, 2014).

81. Newman, op. cit.

82. Iezzi, op. cit.

83. Droga5, op. cit.

84. Ibid.

CHAPTER 15

1. Jennifer Horn, "Autotrader.ca Launches a Refreshing Campaign," March 12, 2012, http://mediaincanada.com/2012/03/12/autotrader-ca-launches-a-refreshing-campaign (accessed August 25, 2014).

2. Cassies 2103, "autoTRADER.ca: The Most Cars in One Place," http://cassies.ca/News/Winners_Grand_Prix (accessed August 25, 2014).

3. Ibid.

4. Ibid.

5. Autotrader.ca, "Consumer Products," http://www. tradercorporation.com/en/consumer-products (accessed August 25, 2014).

6. Autotrader.ca, "Buying or Selling a Car? There's a Better Way," March 4, 2103, http://www.tradercorporation.com/en/buying-or-selling-a-car-theres-a-better-way (accessed August 25, 2014).

7. Autotrader.ca, "Guesswork Be Gone—Owner Reviews on autoTRADER.ca Make Their Debut," April 9, 2013, http://www. tradercorporation.com/en/guesswork-be-gone-owner-reviews-on-autotrader-ca-make-their-debut (accessed August 25, 2014).

8. Autotrader.ca, "Dealer Solutions," http://www.tradercorporation. com/en/dealer-solutions (accessed August 25, 2014).

9. E.K. Strong, *The Psychology of Selling* (New York: McGraw-Hill, 1925).

10. Disney, "Music Stars," http://disney.go.com/characters/#/characters/musicstars; Belinda Luscombe, "How Disney Builds Stars," *Time*, November 2, 2009.

11. John Philip Jones, "What Makes Advertising Work?" *The Economic Times* July 24, 2002.

12. http://www.legamedia.net/lx/result/match/0591dfc9787c111b1b24dde6d61e43c5/index.php.

13. http://popsop.com/wp-content/uploads/toyota_prius_plural_02.jpg; http://www.youtube.com/watch?v5nUor4gdFoyg&feature5player_embedded#!; http://www.saatchi.com/news/archive/prius_goes_plural_through_new_integrated_campaign.

14. Jef I. Richards and Catherine M. Curran, "Oracles on 'Advertising': Searching for a Definition," *Journal of Advertising* 31, no. 2 (Summer 2002), pp. 63–77.

15. Noreen O'Leary, "GroupM Revises 2013 Global Ad Spending Downward," August 14, 2103, http://www.adweek.com/news/advertising-branding/groupm-revises-2013-global-ad-spending-downward-151844 (accessed August 25, 2014).

16. Raymond R. Burke and Thomas K. Srull, "Competitive Interference and Consumer Memory for Advertising," *Journal of Consumer Research* 15 (June 1988), pp. 55–68; Kevin Lane Keller, "Memory Factors in Advertising: The Effect of Advertising Retrieval Cues on Brand Evaluation," *Journal of Consumer Research* 14 (December 1987), pp. 316–333; Kevin Lane Keller, "Memory and Evaluation Effects in Competitive Advertising Environments," *Journal of Consumer Research* 17 (March 1991), pp. 463–477; Robert J. Kent and Chris T. Allen, "Competitive Interference Effects in Consumer Memory for Advertising: The Role of Brand Familiarity," *Journal of Marketing* 58, no. 3 (July 1994), pp. 97–106.

17. Anthony Bianco, "The Vanishing Mass Market," *BusinessWeek*, July 12, 2004, pp. 61–68.

18. CNIB, "Protect Your Eyes. Wear a Pair," https://cni053.3he.ca/pdfs/CNI053_Plaintext_IG_Eng.pdf (accessed August 27, 2013).

19. Matthew Shum, "Does Advertising Overcome Brand Loyalty? Evidence from the Breakfast Cereal Market," *Journal of Economics and Management Strategy* 13, no. 2 (2004), pp. 77–85.

20. Susan Krashinsky, "Kobo Targets Mother in Biggest Ad Campaign Ever," *The Globe and Mail*, May 1, 2013, http://www.theglobeandmail.com/report-on-business/industry-news/marketing/kobo-targets-mothers-in-biggest-ad-campaign-to-date/article11669886 (accessed August 25, 2014).

21. Ibid.

22. Ibid.

23. Megan Haynes, "The Strategic Milk Alliance Milks Every Store Moment," *Strategy Magazine*, July 15, 2013, http://strategyonline.ca/2013/07/15/the-strategic-milk-alliance-milks-every-store-moment (accessed August 25, 2014).

24. "Canadians Reminded to 'Milk Every Moment' in Strategic Milk Alliance Campaign via DDB Canada," June 13, 2013, http://www.campaignbrief.us/2013/06/canadians-reminded-to-milk-eve.html (accessed August 25, 2014).

25. Kelly Gadzala, "Entrepreneur Credits Her Son, 6, for Eco-savvy Idea," http://www.mytowncrier.ca/entrepreneur-credits-her-son-6-for-eco-savvy-idea.html (accessed August 3, 2010).

26. "Media Hook," http://www.thesmarthanger.com/media_hook.html (accessed August 2, 2010).

27. Mike Friskney, "E-Hanger in Home Media wears green well," *Direct Marketing* (June 2010), p. 6.

28. Diane Jermyn, "No More (Environmentally Insensitive) Wire Hangers," http://www.theglobeandmail.com/report-on-business/your-business/business-categories/sustainability/no-more-environmentally-insensitive-wire-hangers/article1654921 (accessed August 2, 2010).

29. "Toronto Firm Launches Recyclable Clothes Hanger," http://www.cbc.ca/consumer/story/2009/09/16/smart-hanger.html (accessed August 2, 2010).

30. http://www.gotmilk.com/fun/decade/year_1993.html (accessed September 26, 2006).

31. http://www.itvx.com/SpecialReport.asp (accessed September 26, 2006).

32. Bill Shepard, "Jumping on the Brand Wagon: The Allure of Product Placement," *Wisconsin Business Alumni Update* 25, no. 1 (June 2007).

33. Neil Munshi, "Spain's Starring Role in Bollywood Movie a Boon to Tourism," *AdAge*, February 6, 2012, http://adage.com/article/global-news/spain-s-starring-role-bollywood-movie-a-boon-tourism/232511.

34. Abe Sauer, "Announcing the 2012 Brandcameo Product Placement Award Winners," *brandchannel.com*, February 13, 2012, http://www.brandchannel.com/home/post/2012-Brandcameo-Product-Placement-Awards-021312.aspx#one (accessed August 25, 2014).

35. Ibid.

36. Rupal Parekh," How Zara Ballooned into a Multi-Billion Dollar Brand Without Advertising," *Advertising Age*, August 19, 2013, http://adage.com/article/cmo-strategy/zara-grew-a-multi-billion-dollar-brand-sans-ads/243730/ (accessed August 27, 2013).

37. Abe Sauer, "Avril Lavigne May Have Just Pulled Off the Greatest (and Worst) Product Placement of All Time, Brand Channel, August 20, 2013, http://www.brandchannel.com/home/post/2013/08/20/Avril-Lavigne-Product-Placement-Rock-N-Roll-082013.aspx (accessed August 15, 2014).

38. http://advertising.utexas.edu/research/terms/index.asp#P (accessed November 15, 2004).

39. http://www.grantstream.com/glossary.htm (accessed September 26, 2006).

40. "The Battle to Ban Advertising," http://www.idrc.ca/en/ev-28820-201-1-DO_TOPIC.html (accessed July 2, 2007).

41. Grant Robertson, "Tobacco Ban Stays, But Expect Ad Blitz Anyway," http://www.theglobeandmail.com/servlet/ArticleNews/freeheadlines/LAC/20070629/TOBACCO29/national/National (accessed July 2, 2007).

42. Jeff Gray, "Chatr Ads Misleading, Court Told," *The Globe and Mail*, May 14, 2013, p. B3.

43. Jeff Gray, "Watchdog Clamps Down on Leon's, Brick," *The Globe and Mail*, July 10, 2013, p. B1.

44. http://advertising.utexas.edu/research/terms/index.asp#O (accessed September 26, 2006).

45. David Kiefaber, "Taylor Swift's CoverGirl Ad Is Pulled Over Bogus Eyelashes," *Adweek*, December 23, 2011, http://www.adweek.com/adfreak/taylor-swifts-covergirl-ad-pulled-over-bogus-eyelashes-137269 (accessed August 15, 2014).

46. David Gianastasio, "Turlington Ads: So Photoshopped They're Misleading?" *Adweek*, July 28, 2011, http://www.adweek.com/adfreak/julia-roberts-christy-turlington-ads-so-photoshopped-theyre-misleading-133731 (accessed August 15, 2014).

47. Tanzina Vega, "British Authority Bans Two Ads by L'Oreal," *The New York Times*, July 27, 2011, http://mediadecoder.blogs.nytimes.com/2011/07/27/british-authority-bans-two-ads-by-loreal (accessed August 15, 2014).

48. This section draws from Tom Duncan, *Principles of Advertising and IMC*, 2nd ed. (Burr Ridge, IL: Irwin/McGraw-Hill, 2005).

49. Stephanie Clifford, "Web Coupons Know Lots About You, and They Tell," *The New York Times*, April 16, 2010.

50. Wency Leung, "Online Coupon Sites Turn up the Heat on Restaurants," *The Globe and Mail* May 4, 2011, p. L1.

51. Simon Houpt, "There Could Be a Deal Right Where You Are Standing," *The Globe and Mail* February 1, 2011, p. B9.

52. Ann-Christine Diaz, "Facebook 101: Is Your Brand Worth a Like?" *Ad Age Digital*, January 30, 2012.

53. Pam Dyer, "Facebook Advertising Case Study: Clorox Green Works," http://www.pamorama.net/2011/02/26/facebook-advertising-case-study-clorox-green-works.

54. Jack Neff, "Old Spice Is Killing It on YouTube Again, But Sales Are Down Double-Digits," *AdAge*, August 4, 2011, http://adage.com/article/the-viral-video-chart/spice-killing-youtube-sales/229080.

55. The Canadian Press, "Tortoise Torte Finishes the Race First," *The Guelph Mercury*, August 20, 2013, http://www.guelphmercury.com/whatson-story/4038979-tortoise-torte-finishes-the-race-first (accessed August 15, 2014).

56. Annette Bourdeau, "Sport Chek, Contiki and Subaru Rally for Data," http://www.strategymag.com/articles/magazine/20070601/sportchek.html (accessed July 5, 2007).

57. "Nabob Over the Years," http://www.nabob.ca/en/history.html (accessed July 27, 2010).

58. "Pop-up Branding," http://www.strategymag.com/articles/magazine/20070601/escapism.html (accessed July 3, 2007).

59. Paul-Mark Rendon, "Agency of the Year," *Capital C Blog*, http://capitalc.typepad.com/my_weblog/agency_of_the_year/index.html (accessed June 25, 2007).

60. http://www.msnbc.msn.com/id/7357071 (accessed September 26, 2006).

61. http://www.engadget.com/entry/1234000103038638 (accessed September 26, 2006).

62. Betsy Spethmann, "For a Limited Time Only," *Promo: Ideas, Connections and Brand*, 2004, http://promomagazine.com/mag/marketing_limited_time.

63. Statistics Canada, *Canada Year Book*, (Ottawa, 2005).

64. This section draws from Mark W. Johnston and Greg W. Marshall, *Relationship Selling and Sales Management* (Burr Ridge, IL: Irwin/McGraw-Hill, 2004).

65. John Fox, "What Is the Real Cost of a B2B Sales Call?" http://www.marketing-playbook.com/sales-marketing-strategy/what-is-the-real-cost-of-a-b2b-sales-call.

66. Bill Stinnett, *Think Like Your Customer*, 1st ed. (Burr Ridge, IL: McGraw-Hill, 2004).

67. Michael Beverland, "Contextual Influences and the Adoption and Practice of Relationship Selling in a Business-to-Business Setting: An Exploratory Study," *Journal of Personal Selling and Sales Management* (Summer 2001), p. 207.

68. Johnston and Marshall, *Relationship Selling and Sales Management*.

69. Meetings + Incentive Travel, "IncentiveWorks 2013 Media Kit," http://www.incentiveworksshow.com/wp-content/uploads/2012/11/MK2013-IW.pdf (accessed August 15, 2014).).

70. Chris Powell, "Weed Man Operator Pays $200,000 in Fines for Do-Not-Call List Violations," *Marketing Magazine*, January 15, 2014, http://www.marketingmag.ca/media/weed-man-operator-pays-200000-in-fines-for-do-not-call-list-violations-98318 (accessed August 15, 2014).

71. Barton A. Weitz, Harish Sujan, and Mita Sujan, "Knowledge, Motivation, and Adaptive Behavior: A Framework for Improving Selling Effectiveness," *Journal of Marketing* (October 1986), pp. 174–191.

72. Al Jury, "The Golden Ratio of Virtual Meetings to Face-to-Face," June 19, 2011, http://virtualteamsblog.com/2011/the-golden-ratio-of-virtual-meetings-to-face-to-face.

73. Arlene Dickinson, *Persuasion* (Harper Collins Publishers, 2011), p. 12.

74. Sarah Hamspon, "Arlene Dickinson Proves 'Emotion' Doesn't Have to Be a Dirty Word," *The Globe and Mail*, Sept. 26, 2011, http://www.theglobeandmail.com/life/relationships/arlene-dickinson-proves-emotion-doesnt-have-to-be-a-dirty-word/article1361388 (accessed August 15, 2014).).

75. "We'll Move Mountains for You," Venture Communications, http://www.openminds.ca (accessed August 1, 2013).

76. Charlotte Herrold, "Lessons from a Dragon: A Profile of Arlene Dickinson," http://www.postcity.com/Eat-Shop-Do/Do/May-2013/Lessons-from-a-Dragon (accessed August 15, 2014).).

77. "*Persuasion* Book Launch for Arlene Dickinson (Sept. 2011)," http://youinc.com/video/persuasion-book-launch-for-arlene-dickinson-sept-2011 (accessed August 6, 2013).

78. "Arlene Dickinson: What Was Your Worst Marketing Blunder and What Did You Learn from It?" *Financial Post*, July 29, 2013, http://business.financialpost.com/2013/07/29/arlene-dickinson-what-was-your-worst-marketing-blunder-and-what-did-you-learn-from-it (accessed August 15, 2014).).

79. Card Hub, "Market Share by Credit Card Network," http://www.cardhub.com/edu/market-share-by-credit-card-network (accessed August 15, 2014).).

80. YouTube.com, "1998—Commercial—Mastercard—Class Reunion—Priceless," http://www.youtube.com/watch?v=3dcxQ2dvqmc (accessed August 15, 2014).).

81. MasterCard, "About Us," http://www.mastercard.com/corporate/ourcompany/about-us.html (accessed August 26, 2013).

82. MasterCard 2012 Annual Report, p. 8, http://investorrelations.mastercardintl.com/phoenix.zhtml?c=148835&p=irol-reportsannual (accessed August 26, 2013).

83. MasterCard Advisors, "Information Services," http://www.mastercardadvisors.com/information-services.html (accessed August 26, 2013).

84. YouTube.com, "1998—Commercial."

85. YouTube.com, "MasterCard Priceless Baseball (Commercial, 1997)," http://www.youtube.com/watch?v=Q_6stXKGuHo (accessed August 15, 2014).).

86. Stuart Elliott, "MasterCard Revamps Print Ads," *The New York Times*, August 11, 2004.

87. Stuart Elliott, "MasterCard Brings 'Priceless' to a Pricey Place," *The New York Times*, July 7, 2011; http://www.creditcardeducation.com/news/mastercard-offers-priceless-city-experiences.html.

88. MasterCard, "Torontonians Know Their City is Unique, But Now It's Priceless!," November 7, 2011, http://newsroom.mastercard.com/canada/press-releases/torontonians-know-their-city-is-unique-but-now-its-priceless (accessed August 15, 2014).).

89. MasterCard, "Priceless Toronto" https://www.priceless.com/toronto/Home (accessed August 15, 2014).

CHAPTER 16

1. Erin Bury, "Checkout 51 Makes Coupon Clipping Easy," Financial Post, December 24, 2102, http://business.financialpost.com/2012/12/24/checkout-51-makes-coupon-clipping-easy (accessed August 15, 2014).

2. Jennifer Horn, "Checkout51 Grows Staff, User Base," Strategy Online, http://strategyonline.ca/2014/04/16/checkout51-grows-staff-user-base (accessed August 15, 2014).

3. Based on information taken from personal telephone interview by Stacey Biggar with Pema Hegan, September 21, 2013.

4. Nikon, press release, August 22, 2007, http://press.nikonusa.com/post/2007/08/22/nikons-new-digital-learning-center-on-flickr-provides-a-first-of-its-kind-interactive-experience-that-assists-everyday-people-in-taking-better-photos.

5. Chris Barry, Rob Markey, Eric Almquist and Chris Brahm (2011), "Putting Social Media to Work," Bain & Co.

6. Russ Martin, "Canadian Social Ad Spend Rises to $267 million," *Marketing Magazine*, October 7, 2013, http://www.marketingmag.ca/news/media-news/canadian-social-ad-spend-rises-to-267-million-90500 (accessed August 15, 2014).

7. Coca-Cola Retailing Research Council and the Integer Group, "Social Networking Personas: A Look at Consumer and Shopper Mind Sets," in *Untangling the Social Web: Insights for Users, Brands, and Retailers*, March 2012, http://www.cokesolutions.

8. Canadian Press, "Facebook Releases Canadian User Statistics," *Marketing Magazine*, August 14, 2013, http://www.marketingmag.ca/news/media-news/facebook-releases-canadian-user-statistics-85727 (accessed August 15, 2014).

9. Forever 21 Facebook Fan Page, http://www.facebook.com/#!/Forever21?ref5ts.

10. Ibid.

11. Ken Yeung, "Study: Hashtags Are a Turn-off on Facebook, Reducing the Viral Reach of Posts," Sept, 3, 2013, http://thenextweb.com/facebook/2013/09/03/study-hashtags-are-a-turn-off-on-facebook-reducing-the-viral-reach-of-posts (accessed August 15, 2014

12. Federal Express, "FedEx Canada to Deliver Giant Pandas to Toronto Zoo," February 27, 2013, http://www.marketwire.com/press-release/fedex-express-canada-to-deliver-giant-pandas-to-toronto-zoo-1762517.htm (accessed August 15, 2014).

13. "Toronto's Pandas," https://twitter.com/TorontoPandas (accessed August 18, 2013).

14. FedEx Express Canada Facebook page, "Zoo Passes Contest," https://www.facebook.com/FedExCanada/app_134425496630143 (accessed August 15, 2014).

15. Andrew LaVallee, "Burger King Cancels Facebook Ad Campaign," *The Wall Street Journal*, January 15, 2009.

16. Russ Martin, "Social Scanner: The State of Community Management," *Marketing Magazine*, April 23, 2014, http://www.marketingmag.ca/news/media-news/social-scanner-the-state-of-community-management-108361 (accessed August 15, 2014).

17. Guy Kawaski, "Ten Ways for Small Businesses to Use LinkedIn," *LinkedIn Blog*, April 12, 2010, http://blog.linkedin.com/2010/04/12/linkedin-small-business-tips.

18. Catherine Smith, "Google 1 Adds Games: Angry Birds, Zynga Poker, and Bejeweled," Huffington Post, August 11, 2011.

19. Ibid.

20. Chris Powell, "Online Video to Grow More Than 51% in 2014: eMarketer," *Marketing Magazine*, May 14, 2014, http://www.marketingmag.ca/news/media-news/online-video-to-grow-more-than-51-in-2014-emarketer-111017 (accessed August 15, 2014).

21. "Vidyard Customer Case Study: Taulia, How Taulia Uses Video to be the Most Remarkable Supplier Financing Provider," http://www.vidyard.com/resources (accessed August 15, 2014).

22. Ibid.

23. Jennifer Pepper, "Jill Rowley: Leveraging Video for Social Selling," Thought Leadership, http://www.vidyard.com/blog/jill-rowley-video-for-social-selling (accessed August 15, 2014).

24. Jessica Lee, "Twitter Reveals Which Tweets Get the Most Engagement," http://searchenginewatch.com/article/2335279/Twitter-Reveals-Which-Tweets-Get-the-Most-Engagement-Study (accessed August 15, 2014).

25. Candace So, "Vidyard Adds HootSuite Hookup to Its Video Marketing Integration Powers," August 15, 2013, http://www.itbusiness.ca/news/vidyard-adds-hootsuite-hookup-to-its-video-marketing-integration-powers/41928 (accessed August 15, 2014).

26. M.P. Mueller, "Small Businesses That Understand Social Media," *The New York Times*, July 11, 2011, http://boss.blogs.nytimes.com/2011/07/11/small-businesses-that-understand-social-media.

27. Ibid.

28. David H. Freedman, "Debating the Merits of Facebook and Google+," *The New York Times*, February 7, 2012, http://boss.blogs.nytimes.com/2012/02/07/debating-the-merits-of-facebook-and-google.

29. Ross Blum, "Where Have All the Customers Gone?" p. 8.

30. Leah Shafer, "Re-Branding the Dynasty: Tori Spelling's HSN Clips on YouTube," March 25, 2010, http://mediacommons.futureofthebook.org/imr/2010/03/24/re-branding-dynasty-tori-spellings-hsn-clips-youtube.

31. "Brands on Flickr," *Supercollider*, July 12, 2008. http://geoffnorthcott.com/blog/2008/07/brands-on-flickr.

32. "What's the Big Knit?,"http://thebigknit.co.uk/about (accessed August 16, 2014)."

33. "So How Many Blogs Are There Anyways?" *Hat Trick Associates*, February 1, 2012. http://www.hattrickassociates.com/tag/how-many-blogs-exist.

34. Mark W. Schaefer, "The 10 Best Corporate Blogs in the World," *BusinessGrow.com*, January 1, 2011, http://www.businessesgrow.com/2011/01/05/the-10-best-corporate-blogs-in-the-world.

35. "Top 10 Most Influential Mommy Blogs," *Cision Navigator*, May 5, 2011, http://navigator.cision.com/Top-10-Most-Influential-Mommy-Bloggers.aspx.

36. Elizabeth Holmes, "Tweeting Without Fear," *The Wall Street Journal*, December 9, 2011.

37. Marketing Charts staff, "Majority of Top Brands Tweeting At Least 30 Times Per Week," August 19, 2013, http://www.marketingcharts.com/wp/interactive/majority-of-top-brands-tweeting-at-least-30-times-per-week-35991 (accessed August 15, 2014).

38. Ibid.

39. Allan Woods, "Chris Hadfield: The Superstar Astronaut Taking Social Media by Storm," theguardian, February 22, 2013, http://www.theguardian.com/science/2013/feb/22/chris-hadfield-canada-superstar-astronaut (accessed August 15, 2014).

40. Coca-Cola Retailing Research Council and the Integer Group, "Assessing the Social Networking Landscape," in *Untangling the Social Web: Insights for Users, Brands, and Retailers*, January 2012.

41. Mira Shenker, "Mobile Ad Spending Outpacing Digital: Report," *Marketing Magazine*, March 24, 2014, http://www.marketingmag.ca/news/marketer-news/mobile-ad-spending-outpacing-digital-report-105047 (accessed August 15, 2014).

42. This Entrepreneurial Marketing box was written with information gathered in personal interviews with Phil Jacobson of PumpUp between April and July 2013.

43. "PumpUp: Workout Coach," https://itunes.apple.com/app/id573070442 (accessed August 15, 2014).

44. Brad Tuttle, "Use Amazon's Price Check App and Save $15 This Saturday," http://moneyland.time.com/2011/12/08/use-amazons-price-check-app-and-save-15-this-saturday (accessed August 15, 2014).

45. "Local Bookstores Ask Customers to Boycott Amazon Over New Price Check App Offer," http://www.commondreams.org/headline/2011/12/12-3 (accessed August 15, 2014).

46. Brad Tuttle, "Use Amazon's Price Check App and Save $15 This Saturday."

47. Tom Ryan, "Target Looks to Battle Pricing App," *Retail Wire*, January 24, 2012.

48. Marguerite Darlington, "The History and Future of Mobile's Role in Fashion," FashionablyMarketing.me, November 22, 2011.

49. Katie Van Domelin, "Social Media Monitoring Tools–How to Pick the Right One," July 7, 2010, http://www.convinceandconvert.

50. "New Radian6 Features Help to Scale 'Social' Across the Enterprise," Radian6 website, November 12, 2011, http://www.radian6.com/wp-content/uploads/2010/12/NovemberRelease.pdf.

51. Radian6 website, http://www.radian6.com/2011.

52. Let's Get Ready website, http://www.letsgetready.org/About/MissionAndVision.

53. Laura S. Quinn and Kyle Andrei, "A Few Good Web Analytics Tools," May 19, 2011, http://www.techsoup.org/learningcenter/internet/page6760.cfm.

54. Christina Warren, "How to Measure Social Media ROI," October 27, 2009, http://mashable.com/2009/10/27/social-media-roi/.

55. "iNoobs: What Is Google Analytics?" http://inspiredm.com/what-is-google-analytics/. http://www.google.com/analytics/features/index.html; http://www.advanced-web-metrics.com/docs/web-data-sources.pdf; http://mobile.tutsplus.com/articles/marketing/7-solutions-for-tracking-mobile-analytics; http://www.practicalecommerce.com/articles/3062-10-Web-Analytics-Solutions-for-Ecommerce-Merchants.

56. Amy Porterfield, "3 Steps to an Effective Social Media Strategy," *Social Media Examiner*, March 1, 2012, http://www.socialmediaexaminer.com/3-steps-to-an-effective-social-media-strategy.

57. Andy Shaw, "How to Create a Facebook Ad Campaign," *Social Media Tips*, September 23, 2011, http://exploringsocialmedia.com/how-to-create-a-facebook-ad-campaign.

58. "What Is the Best Alternative to Klout?" http://www.quora.com/What-is-the-best-alternative-to-Klout.

59. Mark W. Schaefer, "Google and Bing Reveal that Social Influence Bumps Search Engine Results," December 2, 2010, http://www.businessesgrow.com/2010/12/02/google-and-bing-reveal-that-social-influence-bumpdrives-search-engine-results.

60. Erin Griffith, "Getting Your Klout Out," *AdWeek*, May 17, 2011, http://www.adweek.com/news/advertising-branding/getting-your-klout-out-131629.

61. Landman, "Are You a V.I.P.? Check Your Klout Score," *The New York Times*, November 18, 2011.

62. "Social Media Career Advice from Leading Marketers," http://www.onwardsearch.com/Social-Media-Career-Advice; Griffith, op. cit.

63. James Tomerson, "Looking for Job Opportunities in Social Media?" http://www.jobdiagnosis.com/myblog/social-media-jobs.htm.

64. Shan Li, "Employers Are Liking—and Hiring—Social Media Workers," *Los Angeles Times*, September 28, 2011, http://articles.latimes.

65. "The Klout Score," http://klout.com/understand/score.

66. Seth Stevenson, "What Your Klout Score Really Means," *Wired*, April 24, 2012, http://www.wired.com/epicenter/2012/04/ff_klout.

67. Schaefer, op. cit.

68. Kashmir Hill, "Facebook Can Tell You If a Person Is Worth Hiring," *Forbes*, March 5, 2012, http://www.forbes.com/sites/kashmirhill/2012/03/05/facebook-can-tell-you-if-a-person-is-worth-hiring/?partner5yahoo.

69. Barry Murphy, "The Next Governance Frontier: Social Media," *Forbes*, http://www.forbes.com/sites/barrymurphy/2012/02/28/the-next-governance-frontier-social-media.

70. Dell.com, "The History of Dell," http://content.dell.com/us/en/corp/our-story-company-timeline.aspx.

71. Sean McDonald, "Dell—A Leader in Social Media Innovation," Ant'sEyeView.com, February 7, 2011, http://www.antseyeview.com/blog/dell-still-the-leader-in-social-media-innovation.

72. Dell.com, "History."

73. Ibid.

74. Chris Barry, Rob Markey, Eric Almquist, and Chris Brahm, "Putting Social Media to Work," Bain Brief, September 12, 2011, http://www.bain.com/publications/articles/putting-social-media-to-work.aspx.

75. Dell.com, "Shop for Home and Office," http://www.dell.com/us/p.

76. Dell.com, http://support.dell.com/support/index.aspx?c5us&l5en&s5dhs&~ck5mn.

77. Dell.com, "Welcome to Home User Support," http://en.community.dell.com/support-forums/default.aspx.

78. Dell, "Dell Support," http://www.facebook.com/dell?ref5ts#!/dell?sk5app_155719871129476.

79. Dell, "Dell Buzz Room," http://apps.facebook.com/dellbuzzroom/?cat5product_news.

80. Dell, "Dell Lounge," http://www.facebook.com/dell?ref5ts#!/DellUniversity.

81. Dell, "Social Shop," http://www.facebook.com/dell?ref5ts#!/dell?sk5app_131112203596270.

82. Dell, "Ask Rev," http://www.facebook.com/dell?ref5ts#!/dell?sk5app_236634689716925.

83. Dell, "Dell," https://twitter.com/#!/search/Dell.

84. Dell, "DellHomeUS," https://twitter.com/#!/DellHomeUS.

85. Dell, "DellEnterprise," https://twitter.com/#!/DellEnterprise.

86. Dell, DellCares," https://twitter.com/#!/DellCares.

87. Dell,"Direct2Dell," https://twitter.com/#!/Direct2Dell.

88. Dell, "Michael Dell," https://twitter.com/#!/MichaelDell.

89. Barry et al., op. cit.

90. Dell.com, "Direct2dell," http://en.community.dell.com/dell-blogs/direct2dell/b/direct2dell/default.aspx.

91. Dell.com, "DellShares," http://en.community.dell.com/dell-blogs/dell-shares/b/dell-shares/default.aspx.

92. Dell.com, "DellSoftwareNews," http://en.community.dell.com/dell-blogs/software/b/software/default.aspx.

93. Dell, http://www.linkedin.com/company/1093?goback5%2Efcs_MDYS_Dell_false_*2_*2_*2_*2_*2_*2_*2_*2_*2_*2_*2&trk5ncsrch_hits.

94. Dell, https://plus.google.com/117161668189080869053/posts#117161668189080869053/postsGoogle+.

95. Chris Barry, Rob Markey, Eric Almquist, and Chris Brahm, "Putting Social Media to Work," Bain Brief, September 12, 2011, http://www.bain.com/publications/articles/putting-social-media-to-work.aspx.

96. Ibid.

97. Ed Twittel, "How Dell Really Listens to Its Customers," *ReadWriteEnterprise*, July 22, 2011, http://www.readwriteweb.com/enterprise/2011/07/how-dell-really-listens-to-its.php.

98. Cory Edwards and Dell, "When It Comes to Social Media, How Big Are Your Company's Ears?" *Forbes*, December 6, 2011, http://www.forbes.com/sites/dell/2011/12/06/when-it-comes-to-social-media-how-big-are-your-companys-ears/.

99. Zocalo Group, "Forrester Groundswell Awards: The Dell Listening & Command Center," Empowered, http://groundswelldiscussion.com/groundswell/awards2011/detail.php?id5699.

100. Ginger Conlon, "Dell Takes Command of Social Media Listening," Think Customers: The 1to1 Blog, September 9, 2011, http://www.1to1media.com/weblog/2011/09/dell_takes_command_of_social_m.html.

101. Dell.com, "Global Social Media Policy," http://content.dell.com/us/en/corp/d/corp-comm/social-media-policy.aspx.

102. Sean McDonald, "Dell—A Leader in Social Media Innovation," Ant'sEyeView.com, February 7, 2011, http://www.antseyeview.com/blog/dell-still-the-leader-in-social-media-innovation.

103. Zocalo Group, "Forrester Groundswell Awards: The Dell Listening & Command Center," Empowered, http://groundswelldiscussion.com/groundswell/awards2011/detail.php?id5699.

104. Chris Barry, Rob Markey, Eric Almquist, and Chris Brahm, "Putting Social Media to Work," Bain Brief, September 12, 2011, http://www.bain.com/publications/articles/putting-social-media-to-work.aspx.

105. Cory Edwards and Dell, "When It Comes to Social Media, How Big Are Your Company's Ears?" *Forbes*, December 6, 2011, http://www.forbes.com/sites/dell/2011/12/06/when-it-comes-to-social-media-how-big-are-your-companys-ears/.

106. Chris Barry, Rob Markey, Eric Almquist, and Chris Brahm, "Putting Social Media to Work," Bain Brief, September 12, 2011, http://www.bain.com/publications/articles/putting-social-media-to-work.aspx.

CHAPTER 17

1. Colgate, "World of Care," http://www.colgate.ca/app/Colgate/CA/EN/CompanyHomePage.cvsp (accessed August 15, 2014).

2. Colgate, "About Colgate," http://www.colgate.com/us/en/annual-reports/2012/about-colgate.html (accessed August 15, 2014).

3. Forbes, "Colgate Palmolive," May 2013, http://www.forbes.com/companies/colgate-palmolive (accessed August 30, 2013).

4. Colgate, "Developing Products Based on Local Insights" http://www.colgate.com/us/en/annual-reports/2012/brands-consumers.html (accessed August 15, 2014).

5. Colgate, "Message from the CEO," http://www.colgate.com/us/en/annual-reports/2012/message-from-the-ceo.html (accessed August 15, 2014).

6. Colgate, "Sustainability Commitment," http://www.colgate.com/us/en/annual-reports/2012/sustainability-commitment.html (accessed August 15, 2014).

7. Colgate World of Care, "Colgate Bright Smiles, Bright Futures®," http://www.colgate.ca/app/Colgate/CA/EN/Corp/CommunityPrograms/Bsbf.cvsp (accessed August 15, 2014).

8. Business Development Bank of Canada, http://www.bdc.ca (accessed April 24, 2011).

9. Pierre-Richard Agenor, *Does Globalization Hurt the Poor?* (Washington, DC: World Bank, 2002); "Globalization: Threat or Opportunity," International Monetary Fund, http://www.imf.org/external/np/exr/ib/2000/041200.htm#II (accessed September 18, 2006).

10. http://www.whitespot.com (accessed April 25, 2011); Patrick Brethour, "Burgers Go from Burnaby to Bangkok" (interview with Warren Erhart, president of White Spot Restaurants), www.theglobeandmail.com/report-on-business/your-business/start/franchising/burgers-go-from-burnaby-to-bangkok/article1336289 (accessed August 15, 2014).

11. "Canada Imposes Wide Range of Sanctions against Libya," www.theglobeandmail.com/news/politics/canada-imposes-wide-range-of-sanctions-against-libya/article1922800 (accessed August 15, 2014).

12. David L. Scott, *Wall Street Words: An A to Z Guide to Investment Terms for Today's Investor* (Boston: Houghton Mifflin, 2003).

13. http://www.international.gc.ca/eicb/softwood/menu-en.asp (accessed May 26, 2007).

14. "Budget 2010: Leading the Way on Jobs and Growth," http://www.budget.gc.ca/2010/home-accueil-eng.html (accessed August 6, 2010).

15. http://www.bloomberg.com/apps/news?pid=10000103&sid=ajtpC2UYVKwk&refer=us.

16. http://en.wikipedia.org/wiki/Exchange_rate.

17. http://ucatlas.ucsc.edu/trade/subtheme_trade_blocs.php (accessed March 5, 2005).

18. http://www.unescap.org/tid/mtg/postcancun_rterta.pps#1.

19. http://en.wikipedia.org/wiki/Purchasing_power_parity (accessed September 19, 2005); O'Sullivan-Sheffrin, *Macroeconomics: Principles and Tools activeBook*, 3rd ed. (Upper Saddle River, NJ: Prentice Hall, 2002).

20. http://hdr.undp.org/reports/global/2001/en/.NobelPrize–winning economist. Amartya Sen has proposed that developing countries should also be measured according to the capabilities and opportunities that people within that particular country possess.

21. PRB, "United Nations Raises Projected World Population," June 2013, http://www.prb.org/Publications/Articles/2013/un-world-projections.aspx (accessed August 15, 2014).

22. Jack Neff, "Emerging-Market Growth War Pits Global Brand Giants Against Scrappy Local Rivals," *Ad Age*, June 13, 2011, http://adage.com/article/global-news/global-brand-giants-battle-scrappy-local-rivals/228142 (accessed August 15, 2014).

23. Jeremiah McWilliams, "Pepsi, Coke in Race to Conquer China," *Atlanta Journal-Constitution*, May 28, 2010.

24. T.N. Ninan, "Six Mega-Trends That Define India's Future," Rediff.com, January 6, 2007 (accessed January 7, 2007).

25. "India," *The CIA World Factbook*, December 13, 2007 (accessed January 8, 2008).

26. "Canadians in Context—Aging Population," http://www4.hrsdc.gc.ca/.3ndic.1t.4r@-eng.jsp?iid=33 (accessed April 25, 2011).

27. Chris Gaylord, "World's Cheapest Car, Tata Nano, Revs Toward US," *The Christian Science Monitor*, January 15, 2011, http://www.csmonitor.com/Innovation/Horizons/2010/0115/World-s-cheapest-car-Tata-Nano-revs-toward-US; Nandini Lakshman, "Indian Car Buyers Snap Up the Nano," May 6, 2009, http://www.time.com/time/world/article/0,8599,1896414,00.html?iid5sphere-inline-sidebar. Jyoti Thottam and Niljanjana Bhowmick, "Nano Power," *Time*, April 13, 2009.

28. "India," *The CIA World Factbook*, https://www.cia.gov/library/publications/the-world-factbook/geos/in.html.

29. Sonya Misquitta, "Cadbury Redefines Cheap Luxury—Marketing to India's Poor, Candy Maker Sells Small Bites for Pennies," *The Wall Street Journal*, p. B4, June 8, 2009, http://online.wsj.com/article/SB124440401582092071.html (accessed August 15, 2014).

30. "Cellphones Catapult Rural Africa to 21st Century," http://www.nytimes.com/2005/08/25/international/africa/25africa.html (accessed December 18, 2007).

31. Jack Neff, "Emerging-Market Growth War Pits Global Brand Giants Against Scrappy Local Rivals," *Ad Age*, June 13, 2011, http://adage.com/article/global-news/global-brand-giants-battle-scrappy-local-rivals/228142.

32. Training Management Corporation (TMC), *Doing Business Internationally: The Cross Cultural Challenges, Seminar and Coursebook* (Princeton, NJ: Trade Management Corporation, 1992).

33. Devorah Lauter, "IKEA Fined for Sunday Opening in France," *Forbes*, April 6, 2008.

34. Stefania Summermatter, "Can Sunday Shopping Help Beat the Crisis," *Swissinfo.ch*, August 1, 2009.

35. Geert Hofstede, "Management Scientists Are Human," *Management Science* 40 (January 1994), pp. 4–13; Geert Hofstede and Michael H. Bond, "The Confucius Connection from Cultural Roots to Economic Growth," *Organizational Dynamics* 16 (Spring 1988), pp. 4–21; Masaaki Kotabe and Kristiaan Helsen, *Global Marketing Management* (Hoboken, NJ: John Wiley & Sons, 2004).

36. http://www.geert-hofstede.com (accessed September 10, 2006).

37. The Hofstede Centre, http://geert-hofstede.com/countries.html (accessed August 30, 2013).

38. Donghoon Kim, Yigang Pan, and Heung Soo Park, "High versus Low Context Culture: A Comparison of Chinese, Korean and American Cultures," *Psychology and Marketing* 15, no. 6 (1998), pp. 507–521.

39. http://www.brandchannel.com/features_effect.asp?pf_id=261.

40. Betsy Mckay, Procter & Gamble, "Coca-Cola Formulate Vitamin Drinks for Developing Countries," *The Wall Street Journal*, cited at http://www.chelationtherapyonline.com/articles/p9.htm (accessed May 26, 2007).

41. Amy Chozick, "Japan Finally Opens," *The Globe and Mail* September 26, 2006.

42. Laurel Delaney, "Global Marketing Gaffes," March 19, 2002, http://www.marketingpofs.com (accessed December 18, 2007).

43. Affan Chowdhry, "Pakistanis Turn to Canadian Solar Power," *The Globe and Mail*, July 15, 2013, http://www.theglobeandmail.com/news/world/pakistanis-turn-to-canadian-solar-power/article13239061 (accessed August 15, 2014).

44. About Us,http://www.bombardier.com/en/about-us.html (accessed May 17, 2014).

45. Bombardier, "Shaping the Future of Mobility, Responsibly," http://csr.bombardier.com/pdf/en/EDL_Bombardier_ENGLISH-mapL.pdf (accessed August 15, 2014).

46. "Brazil," U.S. Department of State, November 30, 2011, http://www.state.gov/r/pa/ei/bgn/35640.htm.

47. "Russia," U.S. Department of State, November 2, 2011, http://www.state.gov/r/pa/ei/bgn/3183.htm.

48. "India," U.S. Department of State, November 8, 2011, http://www.state.gov/p/sca/ci/in.

49. Megha Bahree, "India Unlocks Door for Global Retailers, *The Wall Street Journal*, November 25, 2011.

50. "China," U.S. Department of State, September 6, 2011, http://www.state.gov/r/pa/ei/bgn/18902.htm.

51. Jacon Kincaid, "Mark Zuckerberg on Facebook's Strategy for China (And His Wardrobe)," *Tech Crunch*, October 16, 2010, http://techcrunch.com/2010/10/16/mark-zuckerberg-on-facebooks-strategy-for-china-and-his-wardrobe.

52. Normandy Madden, "What Will Facebook Find If It Ventures Into China?" *Ad Age Global*, June 13, 2011, http://adage.com/article/global-news/facebook-find-ventures-china/228068.

53. Chloe Albanesius, "Human Rights Group Slams Facebook over China Strategy," *PCMag.com*, June 3, 2011, http://www.pcmag.com/article2/0,2817,2386380,00.asp.

54. Amy Chozick, "Japan Finally Opens."

55. Lisa Evans, "Skin-Care Company Finds Canada Is Just the Tip of the Iceberg," *The Globe and Mail*, October 25, 2012, http://www.theglobeandmail.com/report-on-business/economy/canada-competes/skin-care-company-finds-canada-is-just-the-tip-of-the-iceberg/article4638073 (accessed August 15, 2014).

56. http://www.christiedigital.com (accessed December 18, 2007).

57. Foreign Affairs, Trade and Development Canada, "Canada's State of Trade: Trade and Investment Update—— 2013," http://www.international.gc.ca/economist-economiste/performance/state-point/state_2013_point/index.aspx?lang=eng (accessed August 17, 2014).

58 This Entrepreneurial Marketing box was written with information gathered in a telephone interview with Hatem Jahshan, CEO, Steeped Tea, June 21, 2013.

59. Telephone interview with David Chilton, July 16, 2013.

60. http://www.whitespot.com (accessed April 25, 2011); Patrick Brethour, "Burgers Go from Burnaby to Bangkok" (interview with Warren Erhart, president of White Spot Restaurants), http://www.theglobeandmail.com/report-on-business/your-business/start/franchising/burgers-go-from-burnaby-to-bangkok/article1336289 (accessed August 15, 2014).

61. Canadian Franchise Association, "Fast Franchise Facts," http://www.cfa.ca/Publications_Research/FastFacts.aspx (accessed August 15, 2014).

62. Angela Andal-Ancion and George Yip, "Smarter Ways to Do Business with the Competition," *European Business Forum* (Spring 2005), pp. 32–37.

63. "Joint Venture with Ting Hsin Brings Tesco to China," *MMR* 11, no. 11 (July 26, 2004), p. 13.

64. Bertrand Marcotte, "Bombardier's $3.4-billion Russian Gambit," *The Globe and Mail*, August 28, 2013, http://www.theglobeandmail.com/report-on-business/international-business/bombardier-deals-with-russia-could-total-34-billion/article13994479 (accessed August 15, 2014).

65. http://www.nutralab.ca (accessed April 25, 2011).

66. Bruce D. Keillor, Michael D'Amico, and Veronica Horton, "Global Consumer Tendencies," *Psychology and Marketing* 18, no. 1 (2001), pp. 1–20.

67. http://www.consumerpsychologist.com/food_marketing.htm.

68. Brent Jang, "Setting Their Sights on U.S. Boomers," *The Globe and Mail*, February 14, 2013, https://secure.globeadvisor.com/servlet/ArticleNews/story/gam/20130214/RBCOASTALEYEGLASSESJANGATL (accessed August 15, 2014).

69. http://r0.unctad.org/infocomm/anglais/orange/market.htm; http://www.tropicana.com/index.asp?ID=27.

70. Glenn Collins, "Going Global Involves More Than Many US Companies Think," *The New York Times* January 2, 1997: C10.

71. Jack Neff, "Yahoo Ramps Up Global Study of Moms and Technology," *Ad Age*, November 17, 2011, http://adage.com/article/digital/yahoo-ramps-global-study-moms-tech-starcom/231060.

72. Julie Jargon, "Campbell Soup to Exit Russia," *The Wall Street Journal*, June 29, 2011, http://online.wsj.com/article/SB10001424052702304447804576414202460491210.html (accessed August 20, 2014).

73. Normandy Madden, "Soy-Sauce-Flavored Kit Kats? In Japan, They're No. 1," http://adage.com/globalnews/article?article_id=142461 (accessed August 6, 2010).

74. http://www.pringles.it.

75. "Local Success on a Global Scale," http://www.brandchannel.com/features_effect.asp?pf_id=261 (accessed December 18, 2007).

76. H.M. Hayes, P.V. Jenster, and N.-E. Aaby, *Business Marketing: A Global Perspective* (Boston: Irwin/McGraw-Hill, 1996).

77. Mary Anne Raymond, John F. Tanner Jr., and Jonghoon Kim, "Cost Complexity of Pricing Decisions for Exporters in Developing and Emerging Markets," *Journal of International Marketing* 9, no. 3 (2001), pp. 19–40.

78. Terry Clark, Masaaki Kotabe, and Dan Rajaratnam, "Exchange Rate Pass-through and International Pricing Strategy: A Conceptual Framework and Research Propositions," *Journal of International Business Studies* 30, no. 2 (1999), pp. 249–268.

79. "Fashion Conquistador," *BusinessWeek*, September 4, 2006 (accessed January 31, 2008).

80. Satish Shankar et al., "How to Win in Emerging Markets," *Bain Briefs* November 29, 2007 (accessed January 9, 2008).

81. Central Intelligence Agency, *The World Factbook*, https://www.cia.gov/library/publications/the-world-factbook/fields/2103.html (accessed August 31, 2013).

82. Madden, "Soy-Sauce-Flavored Kit Kats?"

83. http://www.aeforum.org/latest.nsf.

84. Michael Wines, "Picking Brand Names in Asia Is a Business Itself," *Ad Age*, November 11, 2011, http://www.nytimes.com/interactive/2011/11/12/world/asia/12brands-english-chinese-pdf.html?ref5asia; *Brand Channel*, http://www.brandchannel.com/features_effect.asp?pf_id5274.

85. Charles W.L. Hill, *Global Business Today*, 3rd ed. (New York: Irwin McGraw-Hill, 2004).

86. Simon Owens, "The Secrets of Lady Gaga's Social Media Success," *TNW Media*, March 15, 2011; "Undressing Lady Gaga's Social Strategy," http://www.houseblogger.com/houseblogger/2011/02/undressing-lady-gagas-social-strategy.html.

87. Caitlin Burns, "Lady Gaga and Social Media," http://thesocialrobot.com/2010/03/lady-gaga-and-social-media.

88. Lady Gaga Facebook fanpage, https://www.facebook.com/ladygaga (accessed August 28, 2013).

89. Twitter, "Lady Gaga," https://twitter.com/ladygaga (accessed August 28, 2013).

90. Paul Meller, "The W.T.O. Said to Weigh In on Product Names," *The New York Times* November 18, 2004: 1; Mark Jarvis, "Which Bud's for You?" *BrandChannel* January 5, 2004: http://www. brandchannel.com/start1.asp?fa_id=191 (accessed September 5, 2005); Paul Byrne, "Austrian Court Rules in Favor of Anheuser Busch," *PR Newswire* December 31, 2004.

91. Meller, "The W.T.O. Said."

92. "Disposable Planet," *BBC News*, http://news.bbc.co.uk/hi/ english/static/in_depth/world/2002/disposable_planet/waste/ statsbank.stm (accessed September 5, 2005).

93. Alladi Venkatesh, "Postmodernism Perspective for Macromarketing: An Inquiry into the Global Information and Sign Economy," *Journal of Macromarketing* 19, no. 12 (1999), pp. 15–169.

94. Michael R. Czinkota and Ilkka A. Ronkainen, "An International Marketing Manifesto," *Journal of International Marketing* 11, no. 1 (2003), pp. 13–27.

95. Bruce Einhorn, "Apple's Chinese Supply Lines," *BusinessWeek*, January 8, 2008 (accessed electronically January 9, 2008); "Responsible Supplier Management," http://www.apple.com/ supplierresponsibility (accessed January 9, 2008).

96. http://users.aber.ac.uk/pjm04/linguisticimperialism. html#culturalimperialism.

97. Farnaz Fassihi, "As Authorities Frown, Valentine's Day Finds Place in Iran's Heart; Young and in Love Embrace Forbidden Holiday; A Rush on Red Roses," *The Wall Street Journal* February 12, 2004: p. A1.

98. Fassihi, "As Authorities Frown."

99. "2012 Global Car Sales Statistics," http://visual.ly/2012-global-car-sales-statistics (accessed August 15, 2014).

100. Andrew Jacobs and Adam Century, "In China, Car Brands Evoke an Unexpected Set of Stereotypes," *The New York Times*, November 14, 2011, http://www.nytimes.com/2011/11/15/ business/global/in-china-car-brands-evoke-an-unexpected-set-of-stereotypes.html?pagewanted5all.

101. "Rich Chinese Fueling Luxury Car Market Growth," *People's Daily Online*, April 29, 2010, http://english.peopledaily.com. cn/90001/90778/90860/6967022.html.

102. Bloomberg News, "Audi Sales in China Exceed BMW, Mercedes on Demand for SUVs," May 14, 2103, http://www.bloomberg.com/ news/2013-05-13/audi-sales-in-china-exceed-bmw-mercedes-on-demand-for-suvs.html (accessed August 15, 2014).

103. "Audi AG: Strong Sales Figures in China, United Kingdom and United States," *Volkswagen News*, November 7, 2011, http://www. volkswagenag.com/content/vwcorp/info_center/en/news/2011/11/ AUDI_AG_Strong_sales_figures_in_China_United_Kingdom_and_ United_States.html; "BMW in Record Profits Helped by Strong Sales in China," *BBC News*, March 10, 2011, http://www.bbc.co.uk/ news/business-12701854.

104. Jacobs and Century, op. cit.

105. "Audi Sitemap," http://www.audi.com/cn/brand/en/models/a6/ a6l/features_and_speicfications/price.htm (accessed August 29, 2013).

106. BMW Series 5 Price List" http://www.bmw.com.cn/cn/en/ newvehicles/5series/lwb/2010/showroom/promotion/pricelist. html (accessed August 29, 2013).

107. Drew Johnson, "Audi Sets New China Sales Record for 2012," January 9, 2013, http://www.leftlanenews.com/audi-set-new-china-sales-record-in-2012.html (accessed August 15, 2014).

108. Jacobs and Century, op. cit.

109. Ibid.

110. Derek Kreindler, "Audi, Buick Still Hot in China, While Consumers Avoid Mercedes-Benz, BMW," *AutoGuide.com*, November 17, 2011, http://www.autoguide.com/auto-news/2011/11/audi-buick-still-hot-in-china-while-consumers-avoid-mercedes-benz-bmw.html.

111. Horatiu Boeriu, "July 2011: BMW Maintains Global-Sales Lead Over Rivals Audi, Mercedes," *BMW Blog*, August 9, 2011, http:// www.bmwblog.com/2011/08/09/july-2011-bmw-maintains-global-sales-lead-over-rivals-audi-mercedes.

112. Bloomberg News, "BMW Catching Audi in China by Driving X5 SUV Across Mongolian Desert," July 28, 2011, http://www. bloomberg.com/news/2011-07-27/bmw-catching-audi-in-china-by-driving-x5-suv-across-mongolian-desert-cars.htm.

113. Boeriu, op. cit.

114. Jacobs and Century, op. cit.

115. Hiroko Tabuchi, "An Alliance for BMW and Toyota," *The New York Times*, December 1, 2011, http://www.nytimes.com/2011/12/02/ business/global/toyota-and-bmw-in-technology-alliance.html.

CHAPTER 18

1. Marina Strauss, "A Retailer's Dilemma: The Line between Cost and Safety," *The Globe and Mail*, May 4, 2013, http://penny2. theglobeandmail.com/servlet/ArticleNews/story/gam/20130504/ RBBANGLADESHLOBLAWSTRAUSSATL (accessed August 15, 2014).

2. Marina Strauss, "Lower Tariffs, Fewer Quotas Make Bangladesh the Go-to Apparel Producer," *The Globe and Mail*, April 27, 2013, http://www.theglobeandmail.com/news/world/lower-tariffs-fewer-quotas-make-bangladesh-the-go-to-apparel-producer/ article11589221 (accessed August 15, 2014).

3. Amber Hildebrandt, "Can Loblaw Live up to Its Promises in Bangladesh?," May 4, 2013, http://www.cbc.ca/news/world/ story/2013/05/02/f-bangladesh-factory-loblaw-building-conditions.html (accessed August 15, 2014).

4. "Bangladesh Disasters Timeline," World Top Stories Timeline, http://www.mapreport.com/subtopics/d/countries/bangladesh. html (accessed August 15, 2014).

5. Marina Strauss, "Loblaw Calls on Industry to End 'Unacceptable Risk' in Bangladesh," *The Globe and Mail*, May 3, 2013, http:// www.theglobeandmail.com/report-on-business/loblaw-calls-on-industry-to-end-unacceptable-risk-in-bangladesh/article11676189 (accessed August 15, 2014).

6. Canadian Press, "Loblaw to Sign Building Safety Accord in Bangladesh," *The Globe and Mail*, May 15, 2013, http://www. theglobeandmail.com/report-on-business/loblaw-to-sign-building-safety-accord-in-bangladesh/article11918474 (accessed August 15, 2014).

7. Canadian Press, "Loblaw to Sign Building Safety Accord in Bangladesh," *The Globe and Mail*, May 14, 2013, http://www. theglobeandmail.com/report-on-business/loblaw-to-sign-building-safety-accord-in-bangladesh/article11918474 (accessed August 15, 2014).

8. Theodore Levitt, *Marketing Imagination* (Detroit, MI: The Free Press, 1983).

9. Kevin Peachy, "EU Toy Safety Rules to Be Stricter," *BBC News*, July 7, 2011, http://www.bbc.co.uk/news/business-14012541.

10. "Mattel Apologizes to China for Recall," *The New York Times* September 21, 2007, http://www.nytimes.com/2007/09/21/ business/worldbusiness/21iht-mattel.3.7597386.html (accessed April 21, 2010); "Plenty of Blame to Go Around," *The Economist* September 29, 2007.

11. Andrew Martin, "Toy Makers Fight for Exemption from Rules," *The New York Times*, September 28, 2010, http://www.nytimes. com/2010/09/29/business/29toys.html.

12. http://en.wikipedia.org/wiki/Business_ethics (accessed August 30, 2006).

13. William L. Wilkie and Elizabeth S. Moore, "Marketing's Contributions to Society," *Journal of Marketing* 63 (special issue, 1999), pp. 198–219.

14. http://www.gallup.com (accessed September 1, 2006).

15. http://www.cmomagazine.com/info/release/090104_ethics.html (accessed September 1, 2006).

16. Johnson & Johnson, "Our Credo Values," http://www.jnj.com/about-jnj/jnj-credo (accessed August 29, 2013).

17. Vanessa O'Connell and Shirley Wang, "J&J Acts Fast on Tylenol," *The Wall Street Journal,* July 9, 2009.

18. http://www.bsr.org (accessed September 1, 2006).

19. Alexander Dahlsrud lists 37 different definitions! See "How Corporate Social Responsibility Is Defined," *Corporate Social Responsibility and Environmental Management* 15, no. 1 (January/February 2008), pp. 1–13.

20. News Centre, http://www.ipsos-na.com/news/pressrelease.cfm?id=3054 (accessed April 26, 2007).

21. The most famous proponent of this view was Milton Friedman. See, for example, *Capitalism and Freedom* (Chicago: University of Chicago Press, 2002) or *Free to Choose: A Personal Statement* (Orlando, FL: Harcourt, 1990).

22. "McDonald's 2012 Global Sustainability Highlights," http://www.aboutmcdonalds.com/mcd/sustainability/sustainability_highlights.html (accessed August 15, 2014).

23. "McDonald's Global Sustainability Scorecard 2011," http://www.aboutmcdonalds.com/content/dam/AboutMcDonalds/Sustainability/Sustainability%20Library/2011-Sustainability-Scorecard.pdf (accessed August 15, 2014).

24. Christopher Marquis et al., "The Dannon Company: Marketing and Corporate Social Responsibility," *Harvard Business School Case 9-410-121,* April 1, 2010.

25. "Restoring the Economy," BP, http://www.bp.com/sectiongenericarticle800.do?categoryId59036578&contentId57067597.

26. http://www.competitionbureau.gc.ca/epic/site/cb-bc.nsf/en/02518e.html (accessed December 18, 2007).

27. Ipsos News Centre, "Corporate Social Responsibility (CSR) In Canada," http://www.ipsos-na.com/news/pressrelease.cfm?id=3054 (accessed April 26, 2007).

28. Nielsen, "How to Engage with Socially Conscious Consumers," August 26, 2013, http://www.nielsen.com/us/en/newswire/2013/how-to-engage-with-socially-conscious-consumers.html (accessed August 15, 2014).

29. "RBC Corporate Responsibility Report, 2006," p. 19, http://www.rbc.com/responsibility/reports/index.html (accessed April 26, 2007).

30. Tim Hortons, "Camp Day," http://www.timhortons.com/ca/en/difference/camp_day.html (accessed August 15, 2014).

31. Ipsos News Centre, http://www.ipsos-na.com/news/pressrelease.cfm?id=3054 (accessed April 26, 2007).

32. "Sustainability," Mountain Equipment Co-op, http://www.mec.ca/Main/explore.jsp?FOLDER%3C%3Efolder_id=2534374302883315&bmUID=1177625954162 (accessed April 26, 2007).

33. *The Globe and Mail,* April 23, 2007, B2.

34. http://www.ec.gc.ca/epr/inventory/en/DetailView.cfm?intInitiative=72 (accessed May14, 2007).

35. http://www.cooperators.ca/en/homepage/homepageEnglish.html (accessed December 17, 2007).

36. This Entrepreneurial Marketing box was written with information gathered in a telephone interview with Kalen Elmsley of Ten Tree Apparel on June 26, 2013.

37. Raquel Fletcher, "Ten Tree Sees the Forest and the Trees," *Degrees,* Fall/Winter 2012, http://www.uregina.ca/business/assets/about-us/news/2012/Degrees-Ten-Tree-Winter2012.pdf (accessed August 15, 2014).

38. ParticipACTION Canada, "Our Strategic Goals," http://www.participaction.com/about/our-vision (accessed August 15, 2014).

39. http://www.ge.com/news/our_viewpoints/energy_and_climate.html; "GE Launches New Ecomagination Healthcare Products, Opens Renewable Energy HQ," February 2, 2010, http://www.greenbiz.com/news/2010/02/02/ge-launches-new-ecomagination-healthcare-products-opens-renewable-energy-hq#ixzz0lsaVqopP.

40. D.B. Bielak, S. Bonini, and J.M. Oppenheim, "CEOs on Strategy and Social Issues," *McKinsey Quarterly,* 2007, http://www.mckinseyquarterly.com.

41. http://environment.about.com/od/recycling/a/harry_potter.htm (accessed May 9, 2007).

42. http://www.generalmills.com/corporate/index.aspx (accessed August 29, 2006).

43. http://www.newstarget.com/007572.html (accessed August 29, 2006).

44. Suzanne Vranica, "Tweeting to Sell Cars," *The Wall Street Journal,* November 14, 2010; http://business.ftc.gov/documents/bus71-ftcs-revised-endorsement-guideswhat-people-are-asking; Gary Hoffman, "Selling Cars on Twitter," AOL Autos, August 10, 2010.

45. http://www.drj.com/bookstore/drj502a.htm (accessed August 30, 2006).

46. Andrew J. Blumberg and Peter Eckerdsly, "On Locational Privacy, and How to Avoid Losing It Forever," Electronic Frontier Foundation White Paper, August 2009, http://www.eff.org/wp/locational-privacy.

47. This problem is based on the theory of rule utilitarianism, which requires that a person act in such a way that the rule on which his or her action is based produces more benefit than harm. For example, the rule "I will do whatever it takes to get ahead" may not always produce the most benefit if getting ahead requires that the person ignore the consequences of his or her actions to others; in this case, the rule is immoral. See Kate McKone-Sweet, Danna Greenberg, and Lydia Moland, "Approaches to Ethical Decision Making," Babson College Case Development Center, 2003.

48. Carolyn Hotchkiss, "Business Ethics: One Slide Cases," Babson College, Wellesley, Massachusetts, 2004; http://www.usatoday.com/news/nation/2004-03-23-tshirts_x.htm (accessed August 25, 2006); http://www.marketingpower.com/live/mg-dictionary.php?SearchFor=direct+marketing&Searched=1 (accessed August 5, 2005).

49. This case was written by Catharine Curran-Kelly (University of Massachusetts at Dartmouth) in conjunction with two of the textbook authors (Dhruv Grewal and Michael Levy) as the basis of class discussion rather than to illustrate either effective or ineffective marketing practice

credits

CHAPTER 1

Photos/Ads: p. 2: Tim Hortons, the Tim Hortons logo, Timbits, and Camp Day are trademarks of Tim Hortons. Used with permission; p. 6 (top left): Rex Features via AP Images; p. 6 (top right): PRNewsFoto/PepsiCo, AP Photo; p. 6 (bottom): © Stefan Gosatti/Stringer/Getty Images; p. 8 (top): Used by permission of Nestlé Waters Canada; p. 8 (bottom): Photo by Julian Finney/Getty Images; p. 9: Courtesy of Parasuco Jeans Ltd.; p. 11 (left): Courtesy National Fluid Milk Processor Promotion Board; Agency: Lowe Worldwide, Inc.; p. 11 (right): Used by permission of Deutsch Inc. as Agent for National Fluid Milk Processor Promotion Board; p. 14: © Steve White; p. 15: © PAF/Alamy; p. 16: Copyright © Intelity, LLC Inc. A Self-Service Software Solutions Company—IntegrityCorp.com; p. 17: © Levi's; p. 18: McGraw-Hill Companies, Inc./Gary He, photographer; p. 19 (top): © Andrew Stawicki/GetStock.com; p. 19 (bottom): Ian Lindsay/Vancouver Sun; p. 25: The Canadian Press/Richard Lam.

Exhibits: Exhibit 1.4 (a): H Armstrong Roberts/Retrofile/Getty Images; (b): Jamie Grill/Iconica/Getty Images; (c): Ted Dayton Photography/Beateworks/CORBIS; (d): Ciaran Griffin/Stockbyte/Getty Images; (e): Courtesy of Apple; Exhibit 1.5: Jason Reed/Getty Images; © Digital Vision/PunchStock; © Edward Rozzo/CORBIS; Andrew Ward/Life File/Getty Images; © Roy McMahon/CORBIS; © Brand X Pictures/PunchStock; BananaStock/JupiterImages; Digital Vision/Getty Images.

Case Study: This case was written by Priya Persaud In conjunction with the textbook authors (Ajax Persaud and Shirley Lichti) as the basis of class discussion rather than to illustrate either effective or ineffective marketing practice. This case was prepared on April 20, 2011.

CHAPTER 2

Photos/Ads: p. 26: Photographer: Robert Wilson; p. 28: Photo by Jun Sato/WireImage/Getty Images; p. 30: Used by permission of Beauty Gram Inc.; p. 32: Courtesy Netflix Inc.; p. 33: The Canadian Press/Richard Lam; p. 37: Photo by Getty Images for Nike; p. 39 (both): Courtesy The Hertz Corporation; p. 40 (top): Courtesy of PepsiCo.; p. 40 (bottom): Courtesy Dyson, Inc.; p. 41: Courtesy Pizza Hut; p. 42 (top): Courtesy of Lee Valley Tools Ltd.; p. 40 (bottom): The Canadian Press/Mark Abraham; p. 46: Getty Images; p. 48: Courtesy Apple; p. 51: Photo courtesy of Kelli Wood.

CHAPTER 3

Photos/Ads: p. 76: Used by permission of Canadian Tire Corporation; p. 81: © M. Hruby; p. 82: © mackney/Alamy; p. 83: Courtesy Nau & Ben Moon; p. 85 (both): Courtesy MINI USA; p. 86 (top): Jack Hollingsworth/Getty Images; p. 86 (bottom): © JuanSilva 2010/Getty Images; p. 87 (top): © The McGraw-Hill Companies, Inc./John Flournoy, photographer; p. 87 (bottom): © Chuck Savage/CORBIS; p. 88: Photo by Brian Bahr/Getty Images; p. 90: Courtesy of Hammacher Schlemmer, www.hammacher.com; p. 91 (top): The Canadian Press/Don Denton; p. 91 (bottom): Jochen Sand/Digital Vision/Getty Images; p. 92: © Tracy Leonard; p. 95: Caz Shiba/Digital Vision/Getty Images; p. 98: Used by permission of Growing City; p. 99: Courtesy of Ford Motor Company; p. 100: © Monkeybusinessimages/Dreamstime.com/GetStock.com; p. 101: AP Photo/Ric Feld.

CHAPTER 4

Photos/Ads: p. 108: © 2012 Dell; p. 112 (top): Photo by Timothy A. Clary/AFPGetty Images; p. 112 (bottom): Courtesy BMW of North America; p. 114: © M. Hruby; p. 115 (top): © Patti McConville/Alamy; p. 115 (bottom): RaminTalaie/Bloomberg via Getty Images; p. 117: Courtesy The Wet Seal, Inc.; p. 118: Bloomberg via Getty Images; p. 120: Getty Images; p. 121: Courtesy Whirlpool Corporation; p. 123 (left): Courtesy Taco Bell; p. 123 (right): UPI Photo/John Anderson/Landov; p. 124: The McGraw-Hill Companies, Inc./Andrew Resek, photographer; p. 125: Copyright © Ron Kimball/Ron Kimball Stock—All rights reserved; p. 126 (both): Photo courtesy of Cole + Parker; p. 127: ThinkStock/JupiterImages; p. 129: LEGO and the LEGO logo are trademarks of the LEGO Group of Companies, used here by permission. © 2013 The LEGO Group; p. 130: AP Photo/Rick Bowmer/The Canadian Press; p. 131: © Richard Cummins/CORBIS; p. 133 (top): © Digital Vision; p. 133 (bottom): © The McGraw-Hill Companies, Inc./Andrew Resek, photographer; p. 133 (right): © The McGraw-Hill Companies, Inc./Emily & David Tietz, photographers; p. 138: PRNewsFoto/Jenny Craig/AP Photo.

CHAPTER 5

Photos/Ads: p. 140: Used by permission of Royal Bank of Canada; p. 140: © Palex66/Dreamstime.com/GetStock.com; p. 143: Car Culture/Getty Images; p. 145 (both): Used by permission of MappedIn; p. 146: Reprinted with permission from MERX; p. 149: © Marmaduke St. John/Alamy; p. 150: Courtesy of Apple; p. 154: GRANTLAND ®. Copyright Grantland Enterprises, www.grantland.net; p. 157: AP Photo/Paul Sakuma; p. 159: Courtesy of Ryan Burgio and The Stryve Group; p. 164: Press Association via AP Images.

CHAPTER 6

Photos/Ads: p. 166: © M. Hruby; p. 171 (both): Courtesy of Paper Nuts; p. 172 (both): Courtesy The Gillette Company; p. 173: © Benetton Group SPA, photo by: Oliviero Toscani; p. 174: Jeffry Phelps/AP Images for Harley-Davidson; p. 175 (both): Ryan McVay/Getty Images; p. 177: Courtesy H.J. Heinz Corporation; p. 180: Ed Taylor/Taxi/Getty Images; p. 181 (bottom): La Senza Girl Spring 2008 website homepage; p. 182 (top): © Jerry Arcieri/CORBIS; p. 182 (bottom): The McGraw-Hill Companies, Inc./Andrew Resek, photographer; p. 183 (left): Courtesy Carhartt, Inc.; p. 183 (right): Courtesy of Canadian Tire Corporation; p. 186: Photo by Michael Loccisano/FilmMagic for Paul Wilmot Communications/Getty Images; p. 187: Used with permission of Cora; p. 188 (bottom): Photo by Oli Scarff/Getty Images; p. 191: Courtesy of Volvo of North America; p. 192: Courtesy © 2008 The Goodyear Tire & Rubber Company. All rights reserved. Agency: McCann Erickson/New York, NY. Creative Director: Craig Markus. Art Director: Tim Dillingham. Copywriter: Mark Ronquillo. Photographer: © 2007 Graam Westmoreland/Friend and Johnson; p. 194 (left): Photo by Doug Benc/Getty Images; p. 194 (right): Photo by Ezra Shaw/Getty Images; p. 195: © The Procter & Gamble Company. Used by permission; p. 199: Courtesy of M&M Meat Shops; p. 200 (top): Used with permission from M&M Meat Shops; p. 200 (bottom): The Canadian Press/Paul Chiasson.

Exhibits: Exhibit 6.5 (a): Stockbyte/PunchStock Images; (b): Getty Images; (c): Ryan McVay/Getty Images; Exhibit 6.8 (top left): © Digital Vision; (top right): © BananaStock/PunchStock; (bottom left): Royalty-free/CORBIS; (bottom right): © Digital Vision.

CHAPTER 7

Photos/Ads: p. 202: Courtesy Accenture; p. 204: © Bill Aron/PhotoEdit; p. 206: © M. Hruby; p. 210: Courtesy Coinstar, Inc.; p. 212: The McGraw-Hill Companies, Inc./John Flournoy, photographer; p. 215 (left): Sozaijiten/Datacraft/Getty Images; p. 215 (right): Courtesy The Neilsen Co.; p. 220: Photo by Benjamin Lowy/Getty Images; p. 221: Norbert Michalke Image Broker/Newscom; p. 223: © Tracy Leonard; p. 224 (top): The McGraw-Hill Companies, Inc./John Flournoy, photographer; p. 224 (bottom): Courtesy Campbell Soup Company; p. 225: LEGO and the LEGO logo are trademarks of the LEGO Group of Companies, used here by permission. © 2013 The LEGO Group; p. 227: The McGraw-Hill Companies, Inc./John Flournoy, photographer; p. 228: AP Photo/Mary Altaffer; p. 231: Photo courtesy of Tim Penner; p. 235: © Steve White.

CHAPTER 15

Photos/Ads: p. 468: Used by permission of autoTRADER; p. 472 (top): Photo by Ida Mae Astute/ABC via Getty Images; p. 472 (bottom): Jeff Kowalsky/Bloomberg via Getty Images; p. 473: Used by permission of autoTRADER; p. 474 (top): Used by permission of CNIB; p. 474 (bottom): © Pixellover RM 2/Alamy; p. 474: Strategic Milk Alliance; p. 476: Used with permission of Leigh Meadows; p. 477 (top): Courtesy Pepsi-Cola Company; p. 477 (bottom): Used by permission of Deutsch Inc. as Agent for National Fluid Milk Processor Promotion Board; p. 478 (bottom, both): Used by permission of Rethink Breast Cancer; p. 480: © Bill Aron/PhotoEdit, Inc.; p. 481: Photo by Gregg DeGuire/FilmMagic/Getty Images; p. 483: © M. Hruby; p. 484: Courtesy Payless Shoe Source, Inc.; p. 485: National Geographic/Getty Images; p. 486 (top): Photo by John M. Heller/Getty Images; p. 486 (bottom): © Michael Newman/PhotoEdit; p. 489 (both): © Royalty-Free/CORBIS; p. 490: © Photographerlondon/Dreamstime.com/GetStock.com; p. 491: © Ian Dagnall/Alamy; p. 493 (top): © Royalty-Free/CORBIS; p. 493 (bottom): Photo by Evan Agostini/Getty Images; p. 495: © Royalty-Free/CORBIS; p. 496: Photo courtesy of Arlene Dickinson.

CHAPTER 16

Photos/Ads: p. 502: Used with permission from Checkout 51 Inc.; p. 506: Courtesy Staples, Inc.; p. 509: © incamerastock/Alamy; p. 510: © Photo by CDSB/ChinaFotoPress/The Canadian Press; p. 513: © John Boud/Alamy; p. 514: © Action Press [2004] all rights reserved/The Canadian Press; p. 515: © Rex Features [2005] all rights reserved/The Canadian Press; p. 517 (both): Used by permission of PumpUp; p. 518: Courtesy foursquare © 2012; p. 520: Courtesy Salesforce Radian6.

Exhibits: Exhibit 16.2: © Royalty-Free/CORBIS; Exhibit 16.5: Used by permission of IAB Canada.

CHAPTER 17

Photos/Ads: p. 530: STRDEL/AFP/Getty Images; p. 535 (left): Photo by Tim Boyle/Getty Images; p. 535 (right): © YellowMoon/Alamy; p. 536: Bank note image used with the permission of the Bank of Canada/Images de billet de banque utilisées avec la permission de la Banque du Canada; p. 537: © Digital Vision/Getty Images; p. 540: Imaginechina via AP Images; p. 541 (top): Hand-out/EEPC INDIA/Newscom; p. 541 (bottom): © M. Hruby; p. 543: Polka Dot/JupiterImages; p. 544: © Ronen Zvulun/Reuters/CORBIS; p. 545: AP Photo/Greg Baker; p. 547: © Lao Chen/Zuma Press; p. 549: Courtesy of Rolex USA; p. 550: Used by permission of Steeped Tea; p. 551 (top, both): Imaginechina via AP Images; p. 551 (bottom): © Larry MacDougal/The Canadian Press; p. 552: Bloomberg via Getty Images; p. 554: The McGraw-Hill Companies, Inc./Andrew Resek, photographer; p. 555 (top): Courtesy Campbell Soup Company; p. 555 (bottom left): AP Photo/Jay LaPrete; p. 555 (bottom right): AP Photo/Gurinder Osan; p. 557 (top): H. John Maier Jr./Contributor; p. 557 (bottom): Used with permission from Nestlé Japan; p. 558: Photo by Jeff Kravitz/FilmMagic/Getty Images; p. 559: © Digital Vision; p. 560: AFP/Getty Images; p. 564: Courtesy of Leo Burnett Beijing.

Exhibits: Exhibit 17.5: © The Economist Newspaper Limited, London.

CHAPTER 18

Photos/Ads: p. 566 (top): © AP Photo/Wong Maye-E/The Canadian Press; p. 566 (bottom): © Lars Hagberg/The Canadian Press; p. 569: GRANTLAND ®. Copyright Grantland Enterprises, www.grantland.net; p. 571: Dynamic Graphics/JupiterImages; p. 573: © Dennis MacDonald/PhotoEdit; p. 574: http://www.aboutmcdonalds.com/mcd/sustainability/2011_sustainability_scorecard.html; p. 575: Courtesy of Danone Canada; p. 576: AP Photo/US Coast Guard; p. 577: Used by permission of Royal Bank of Canada; p. 579: Courtesy of Ten Tree Apparel; p. 580: Courtesy General Electric Company; p. 585: © M. Hruby; p. 586: Courtesy Ford Motor Company; p. 588: GRANTLAND ®. Copyright Grantland Enterprises, www.grantland.net; p. 589: GRANTLAND ®. Copyright Grantland Enterprises, www.grantland.net; p. 592: Dynamic Graphics/JupiterImages.

company index